OUR FASCINATING PLANET

The power of wind and water erosion shaped the beautiful landscapes of the Colorado Plateau – including the sandstone arches in Arches National Park.

FAMILY WORLD ATLAS

"I wish to be a citizen of the world, at home everywhere...and everywhere a traveller."

This thoroughly modern idea was actually expressed in the early 16th century by humanist, thinker and theologian Erasmus of Rotterdam, in an age when the world was "opening up": an age of discoveries and conquests, of truly great adventures.

In recent centuries, scientists and explorers have discovered every "terra incognita" and now use satellites to survey and photograph the Earth with incredible accuracy. Our planet, however, still offers countless surprises, adventures and exotic wonders: the vastness of Asia, the isolated islands of the Pacific, the dense rain forests of Africa, Alaska's wilderness, ancient villages in Europe and the summits of the Andes. Presenting all of these, and the many other fascinating places on our planet, is a difficult but rewarding task.

"A journey of a thousand miles begins with the very first step" – Lao-tzu (Chinese philosopher, 4th century BC).

And now we can begin our journey with the new Family World Atlas. The ground-breaking concept of this atlas serves several functions: the first is to offer basic geographical knowledge of our planet with detailed and clear cartography. It also functions as a comprehensive travel guide in which more than 17,000 fascinating attractions are highlighted – including landscapes, national parks, cities, cultural attractions, monuments, holiday destinations and travel routes. These sites are presented through a new system of pictograms, developed specifically for this book. The atlas cartography is complemented by an extensive and richly illustrated country encyclopedia which provides key geographical, political and economic facts and figures.

It is our hope that the Family World Atlas will inspire in our readers the feeling that they are "citizens of the world" and serve as a "first step" on a fascinating journey of discovery to the countless wonders of the planet we call home. This atlas should deepen our understanding of our Earth and its multifaceted splendour, and awaken our curiosity, tolerance and feelings of responsibility towards one another as inhabitants of this planet.

In the words of the famed Indian poet Rabindranath Tagore: "We live in this world as long as we love it".

The Publisher

Table of Contents

Islamic heritage in southern Spain: La Mezquita cathedral, once the Great Mosque of Córdoba, is a beautiful example of Moorish architecture with large chambers and splendid facades.

Beautiful landscapes on the Li River: The green, craggy mountains around the city of Guilin are located in one of China's most scenic regions.

Table of Contents

Marrakech (Morocco): Djemâa el-Fna square, located near the Koutoubia mosque, is a lively meeting place for vendors, street artists, traditional storytellers, and tourists.

Wet Tropics National Park in northeastern Australia features fascinating flora and fauna as well as beautiful landscapes such as Milla Falls.

Africa   120 – 157

North and Central America   158 – 187

South America   188 – 210

Nations of the world   211 – 274

Map locator

The Loire River valley in France, with its many historic towns and palaces – including Chateau Chamborg (photo) – is a UNESCO World Heritage Site.

Japan's former imperial capital, Kyoto, has been an important cultural center for more than 1,000 years. Kyoto's historic attractions include numerous shrines and temples.

Europe

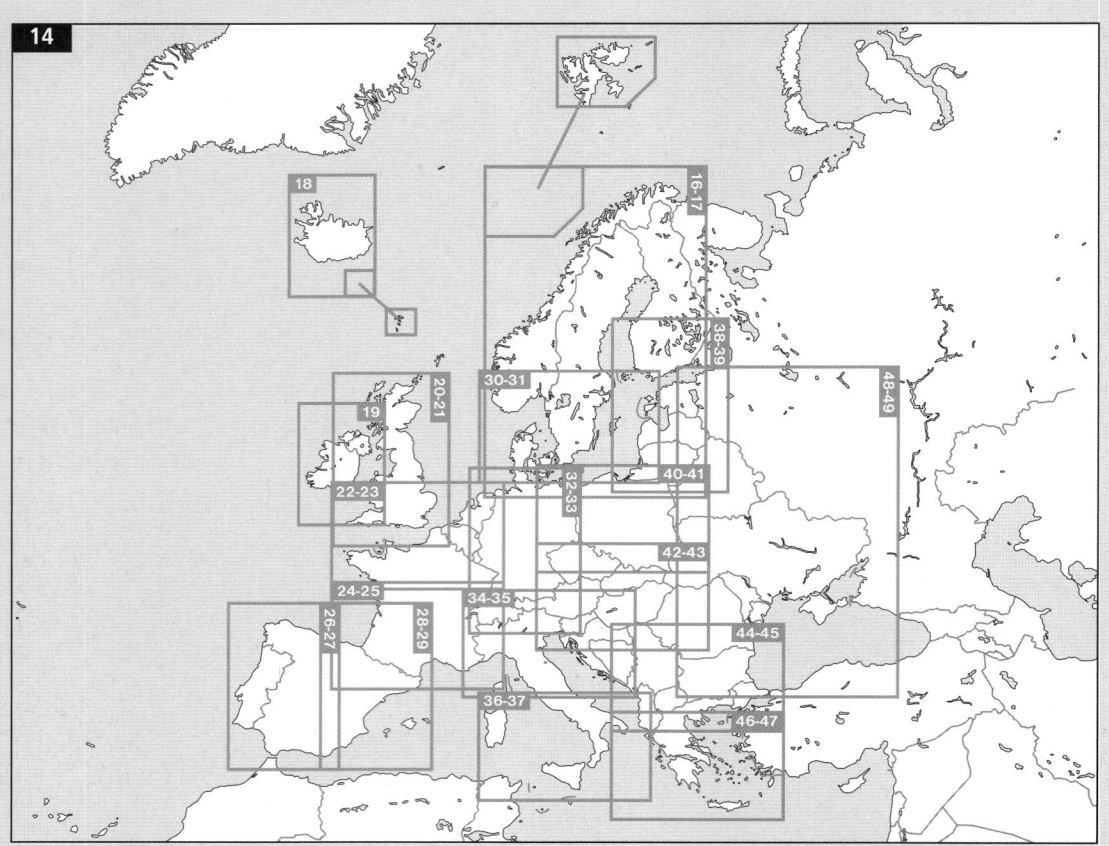

Southeastern Asia, Australia/Oceania

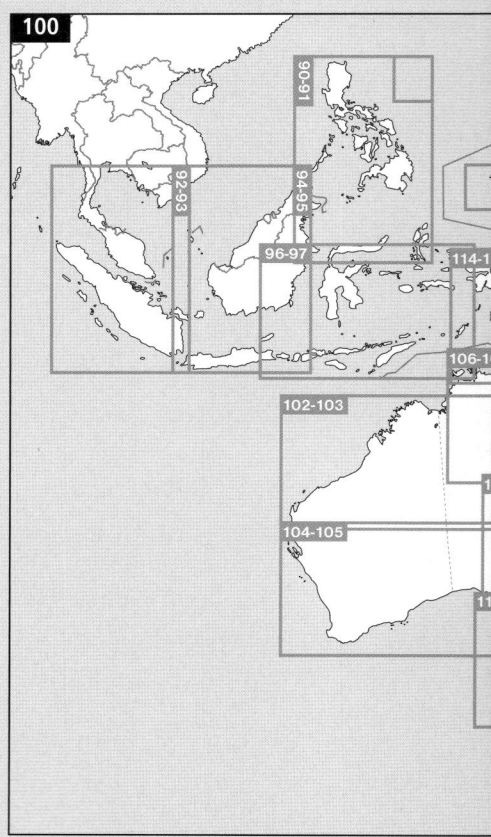

Near and Middle East, Northern Asia, Central Asia, Southern Asia

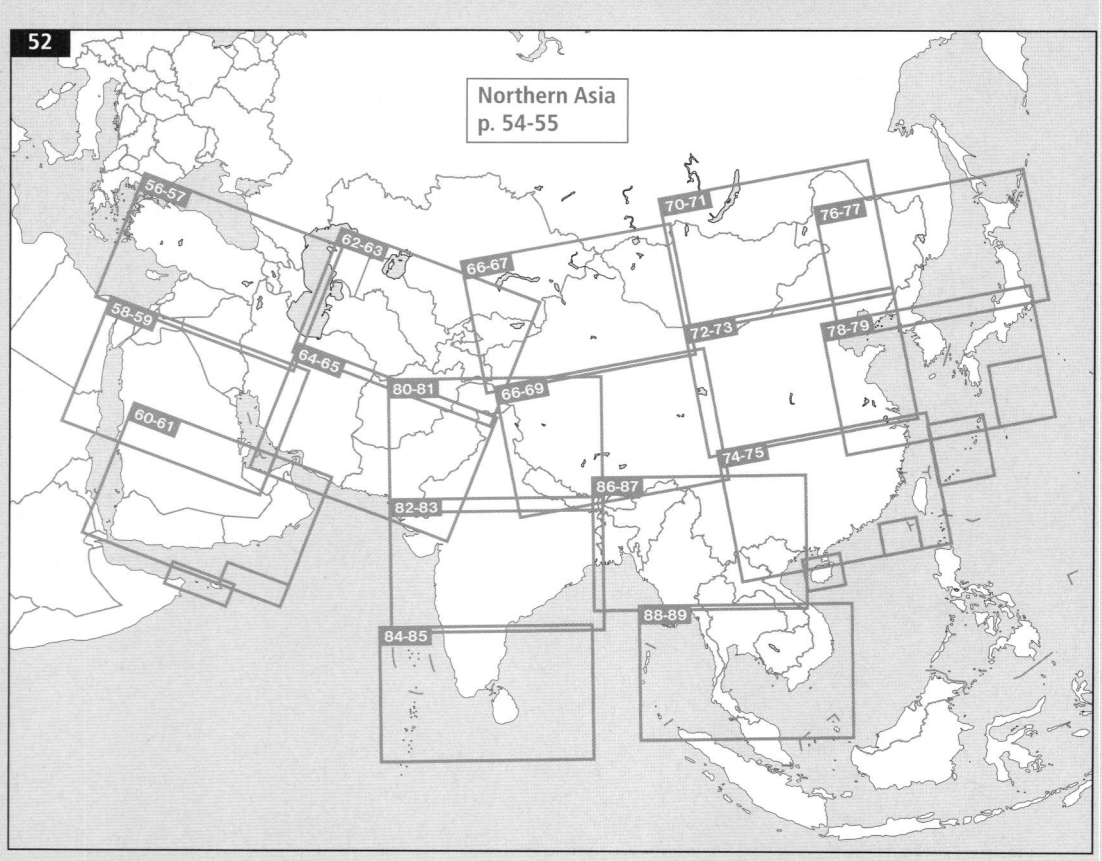

Africa

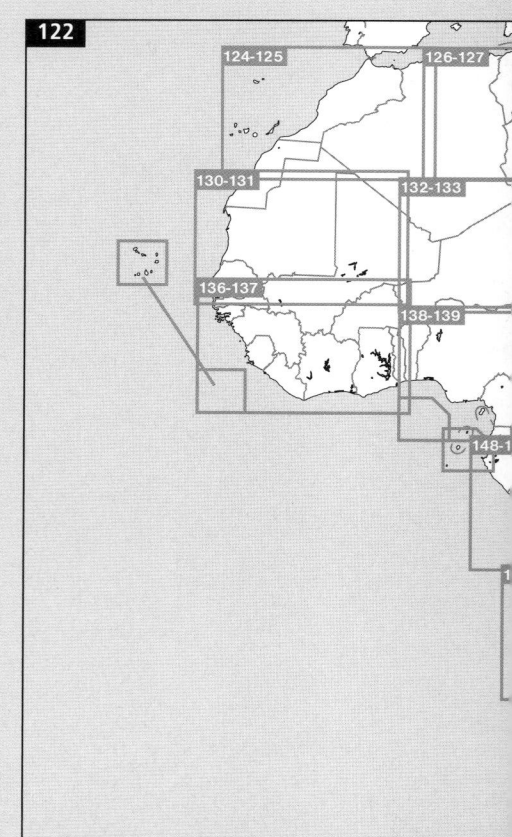

Map locator

The impressive modern skyline of Chicago, along the shores of Lake Michigan. The city is a leading commercial and financial center.

Easter Island was once home to an advanced civilization. The more than 300 stone sculptures (moai) scattered around the island are the most important remnants of this culture.

North and Central America

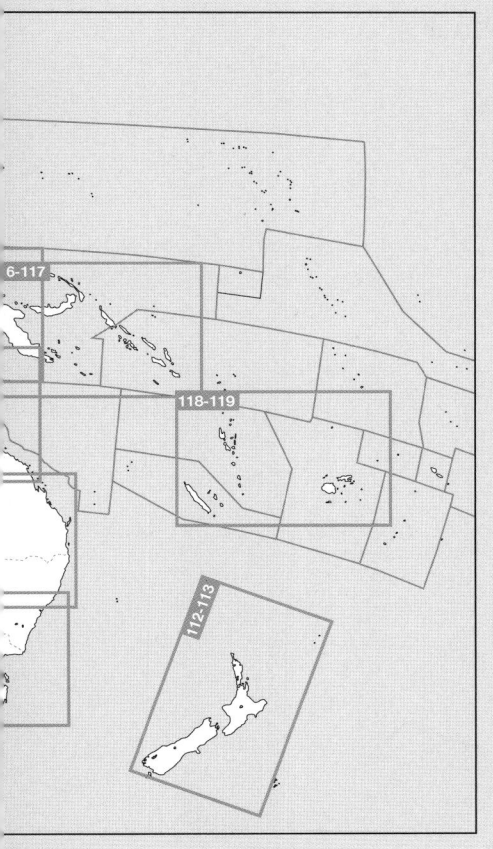

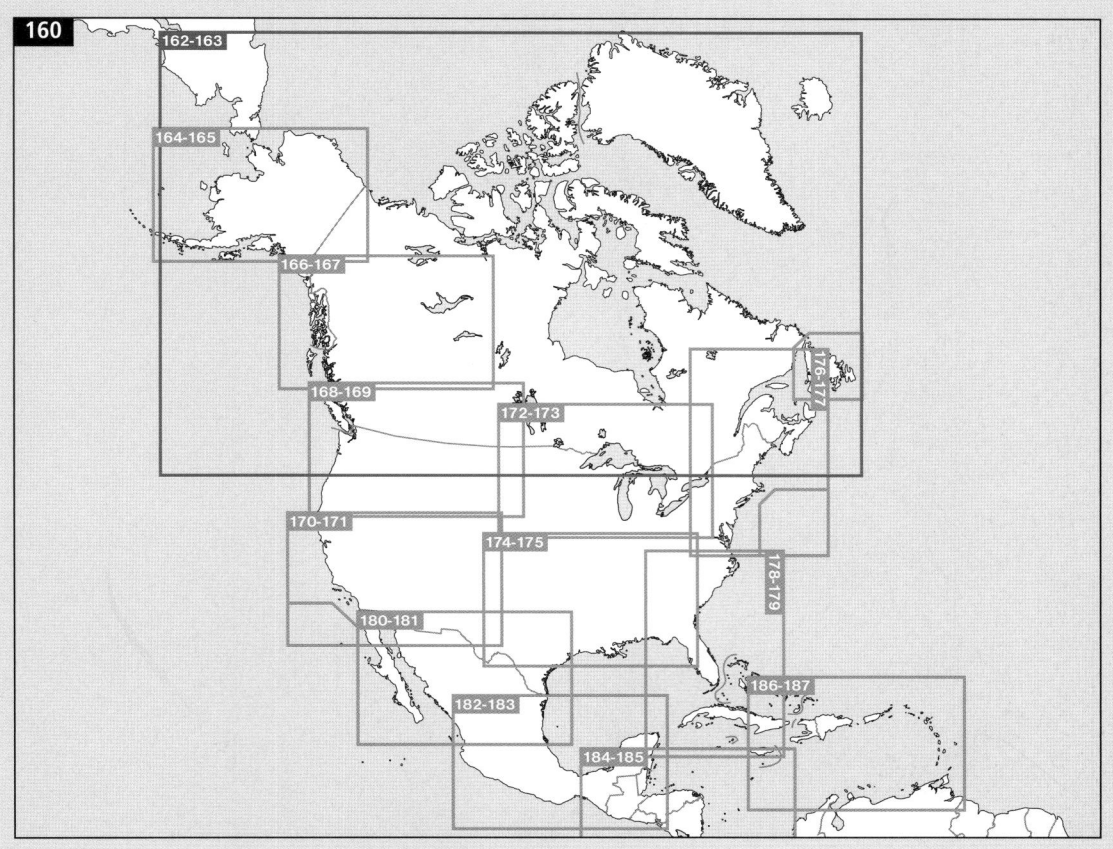

160

162-163
164-165
166-167
168-169
172-173
176-177
170-171
174-175
178-179
180-181
182-183
186-187
184-185

6-117
118-119
112-113

South America

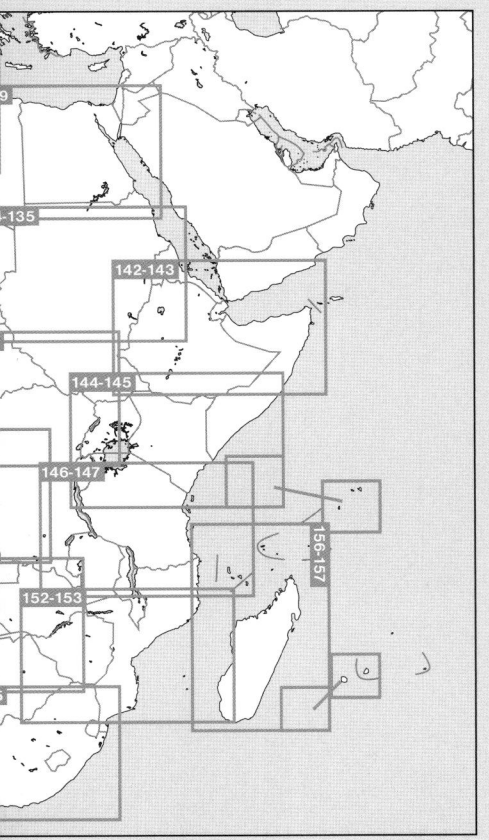

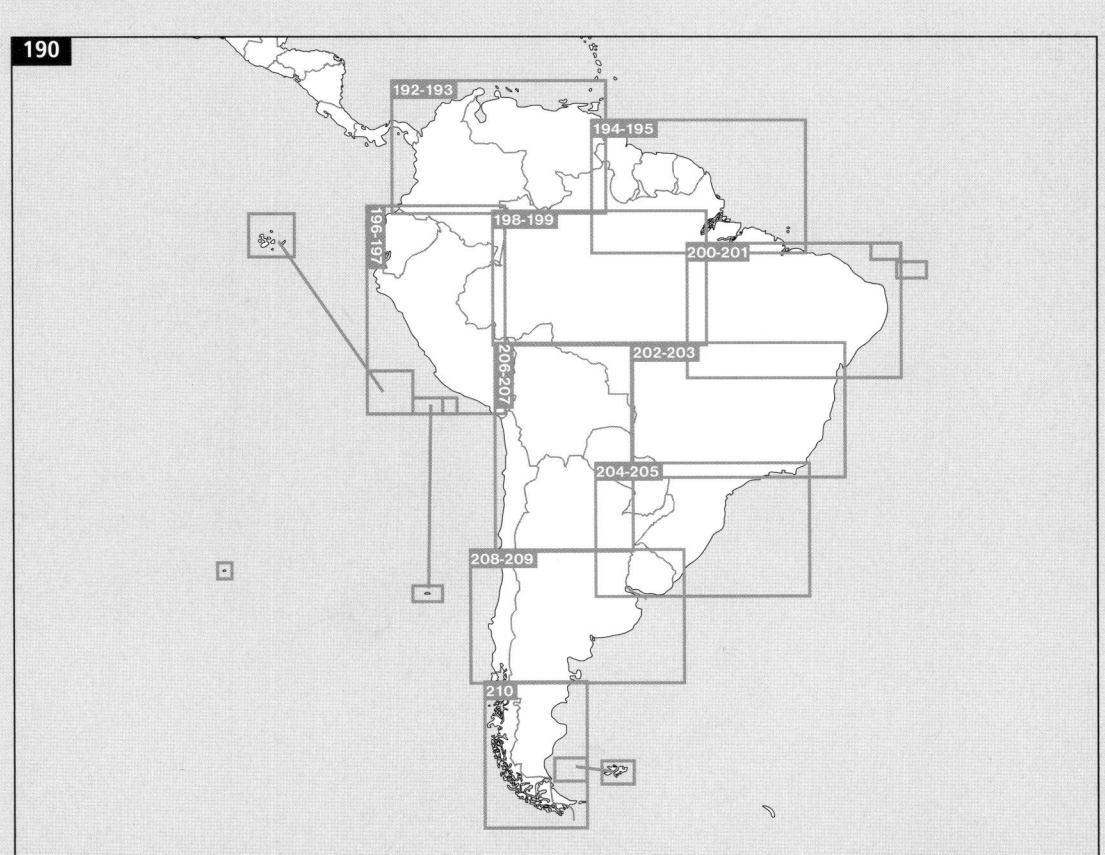

190

192-193
194-195
196-197
198-199
200-201
202-203
206-207
204-205
208-209
210

9
135
142-143
144-145
146-147
156-157
152-153

Legend • Natural geographical features

The Polynesian island of Moorea is the remnant of a massive volcano. The island, like so many in the Pacific Ocean, is surrounded by coral reefs.

The Scottish Highlands in the United Kingdom feature a variety of romantic and beautiful landscapes, including craggy mountains, pristine lakes, and rugged valleys.

Bodies of Water

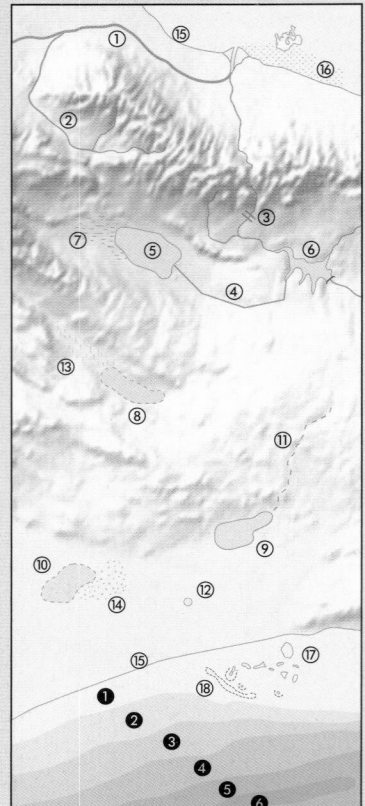

① Stream, river
② Tributary with headstreams
③ Waterfall, rapids
④ Canal
⑤ Lake
⑥ Reservoir with dam
⑦ Marsh, moor
⑧ Intermittent lake
⑨ Salt lake
⑩ Intermittent salt lake
⑪ Intermittent river (wadi)
⑫ Well, spring
⑬ Salt swamp
⑭ Salt pan
⑮ Shoreline
⑯ Mud flats
⑰ Island, archipelago
⑱ Coral reef

Depth tints

❶ 0 — 200 meters
❷ 200 — 2000 meters
❸ 2000 — 4000 meters
❹ 4000 — 6000 meters
❺ 6000 — 8000 meters
❻ below 8000 meters

Topography

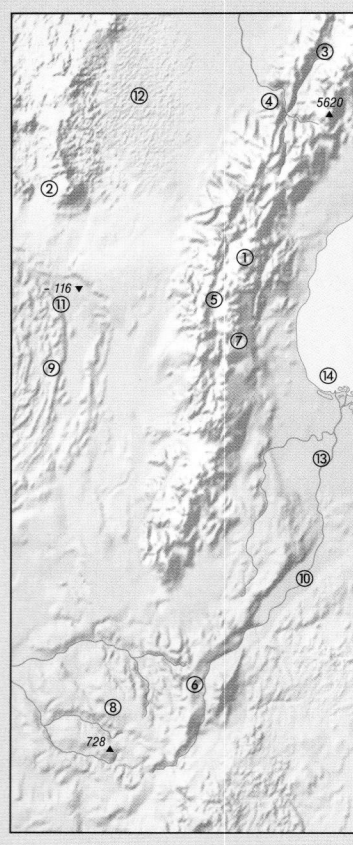

① High mountain region
② Volcano
③ V-shaped valley
④ Gorge
⑤ U-shaped valley
⑥ Canyon
⑦ Glacier
⑧ Highland with valleys
⑨ Escarpment
⑩ Rift Valley
⑪ Depression
⑫ High dunes in arid areas
⑬ Lowland
⑭ Delta

Color tints of climate and vegetation zones

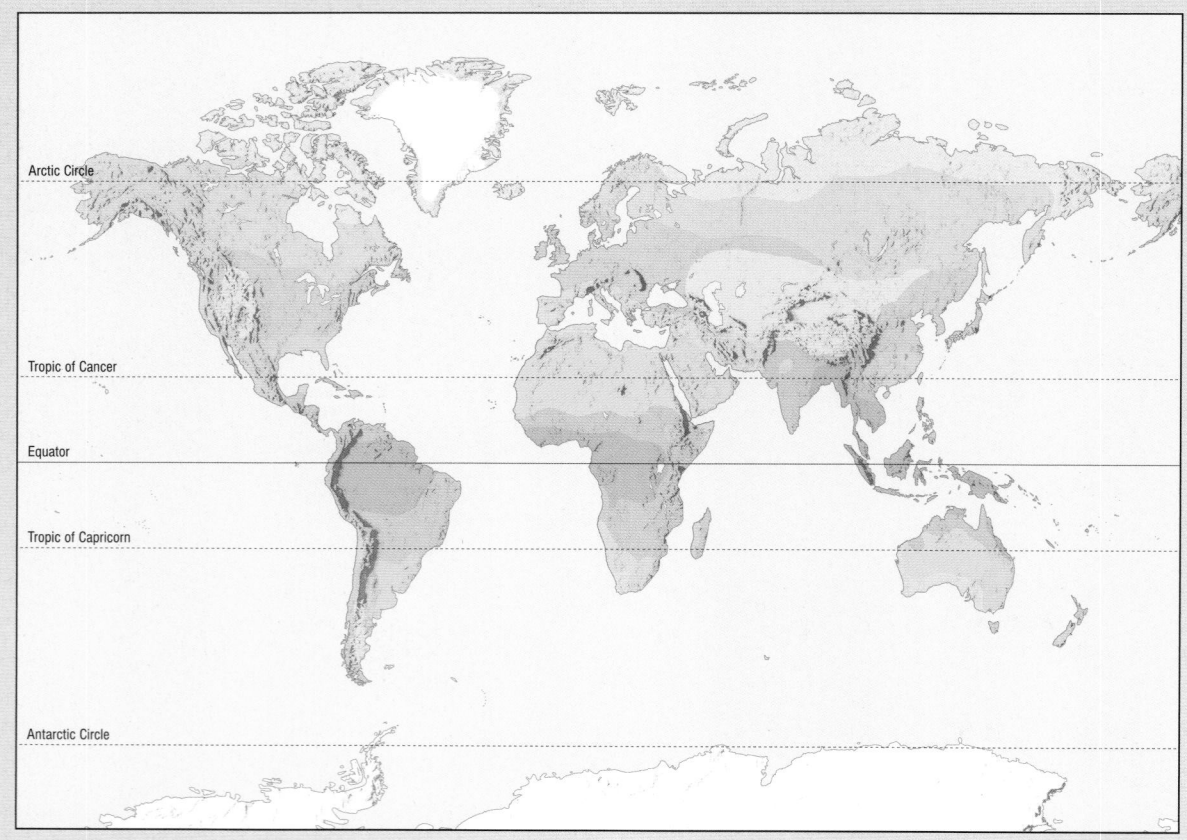

Polar and subpolar zone

Perpetual frost, all months below 0° C (32° F)

Arctic flora and Tundra (lichens, mosses, grasses, dwarf shrubs)

Boreal zone

Taiga, northern coniferous trees; pines, firs, larches, spruces

Temperate zones

Rainy climates with mild winters; deciduous broadleaf forests, mixed forests

Winter-cold desert and semidesert climates; steppe, prairie, grasslands, semideserts

Subtropics

Mediterranean climate with dry summers and moist winters; broadleaved evergreen forests

Warm, summer-humid moist climate; subtropical forests

Desert and semidesert climates; open shrub lands

Tropics

Humid and dry savannahs with dry seasons; woody savannahs

Tropical rainforest, rainy climate with no winter; high temperatures

Beijing's historic Forbidden City was the main residence of China's monarchs and the great imperial court for many centuries.

A full moon above the skyline of San Francisco in northern California. The city's beautiful Golden Gate Bridge is one of the world's longest suspension bridges.

Settlements and transportation routes

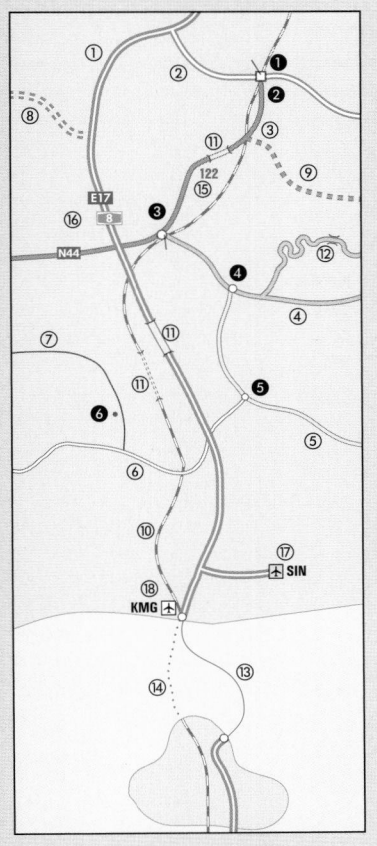

Transportation routes
① Interstate highway/motorway
② Multilane divided highway
③ Primary highway
④ Secondary highway
⑤ Main road
⑥ Secondary road
⑦ Unimproved road
⑧ Interstate highway/motorway under construction
⑨ Primary highway under construction
⑩ Railroad
⑪ Tunnel
⑫ Pass with elevation in meters
⑬ Ferry, shipping route
⑭ Railroad ferry
⑮ Distances in kilometers (in miles within USA and UK)
⑯ Road numbers
⑰ International Airport with IATA-code
⑱ Airport with IATA-code

Settlements
❶ Urban area
❷ City, over 1 million inhabitants
❸ City, 100,000 – 1 million inhabitants
❹ Town, 10,000 – 100,000 inhabitants
❺ Town, under 10,000 inhabitants
❻ Hamlet, research station

Typefaces of cities and towns

① □ **NEW YORK**
② ○ **Stuttgart**
③ ○ **Narvik**
④ ○ Porta Westfalica
⑤ ○ Storuman
⑥ ○ White Owl
⑦ • Glenayle
⑧ □ **BEIJING (PEKING)**
⑨ ○ **Firenze (Florence)**
⑩ Tikal
⑪ Grand Canyon du Verdon

① City, over 1 million inhabitants
② City, 100,000 – 1 million inhabitants
③ Significant city, 10,000 – 100,000 inhabitants
④ City, 10,000 – 100,000 inhabitants
⑤ Significant town, under 10,000 inhabitants
⑥ Town, under 10,000 inhabitants
⑦ Hamlet, research station
⑧ City, over 1 million inhabitants with translation
⑨ Town 100,000 – 1 million inhabitants with translation
⑩ Point of cultural interest
⑪ Point of natural interest

Political and other boundaries

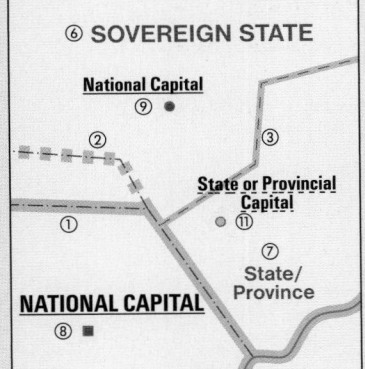

① International boundary
② Disputed international boundary
③ Administrative boundary
④ Boundary on rivers
⑤ Boundary in lake or sea
⑥ Country name
⑦ Administrative name
⑧ Capital with more than 1 million inhabitants
⑨ Capital below 1 million inhabitants
⑩ Administrative capital with more than 1 million inhabitants
⑪ Administrative capital with less than 1 million inhabitants
⑫ Dependent territory with administering country
⑬ National parks and biosphere reserves
⑭ Nature parks and other protected areas
⑮ Reservation
⑯ Walls (Great Wall of China, Hadrian's Wall)

Typefaces of topographic features

① *PACIFIC OCEAN*
② *GULF OF MEXICO*
② *Gulf of Thailand*
③ *Antalya Körfezi*
④ *Elbe Rio Grande Murray*
⑤ *White Nile Suez Canal*
⑥ *HIMALAYA*
⑦ *Great Plains*
⑧ Mt. Olympus ▲ 2424
⑨ – 116 ▼ Danakil Depression
⑩ *Tahiti*
⑪ Cape of Good Hope
⑫ <u>325</u>
⑬ 5425
⑭ *Mexican Basin*
⑮ Mariana Trench

① Ocean
② Gulf, bay
③ Small bay, strait
④ River, lake, canal
⑤ River, lake, canal (translated)
⑥ Mountain name
⑦ Area name, landscape name
⑧ Mountain name with elevation above sea level in meters
⑨ Depression with depth below sea level in meters
⑩ Island name
⑪ Cape name
⑫ Elevation of lake above sea level
⑬ Depth in oceans and lakes
⑭ Undersea landscapes, mountains and trenches
⑮ Deepsea trench

Explanation of symbols

The passenger train services that pass through South Africa's Garden Route offer spectacular views of the Indian Ocean and the Karoo Mountains.

The landscapes of Los Glaciares National Park, including large glaciers and mountains, are among the most spectacular in the region of Patagonia. Photo: Fitz Roy Massif (3,128 m).

Principal travel routes

Remarkable landscapes and natural monuments

Beautiful natural landscapes, fascinating wildlife, historic architecture, and vibrant cities – our world is rich in wonders. The modern cartography and layout of the Family World Travel Atlas highlight many of the world's attractions – unspoiled wilderness areas, the most famous and significant historic sites, culturally diverse urban areas, holiday resorts, and sporting venues. The system of pictograms developed specifically for this atlas gives the reader a clear impression of the diverse attractions in the world's regions. All of the pictograms featured on each map are listed and labeled in a legend at the bottom of the respective page.

The following pages offer brief characterizations of the various pictograms used in the atlas. The pictograms are divided by color into two groups: green and blue pictograms represent natural attractions, while yellow pictograms represent cultural attractions and other manmade sites. The names of significant towns and cities are highlighted in yellow throughout the atlas. Blue pictograms represent sporting and recreational facilities. Important and well-known transportation routes, including highways and shipping routes, are also featured in the atlas. These routes are not only highlighted by pictograms but also by distinctly colored lines that identify each type of route.

Auto route
The maps display many of the world's most famous and historically significant roads and routes, such as the ancient Silk Road in Asia and historic Route 66 in the United States, The maps also feature important modern highways, including the Pan-American Highway that stretches through the Americas from Alaska to Tierra del Fuego, the highway stretching between Bangkok in Thailand and Singapore, and the Stuart Highway, which traverses the fascinating landscapes in Australia's sparsely populated interior.

Railroad
The age of the railroads started in 1804 when the world's first steam locomotive began operation in Wales. By the end of the 19th century it was possible to travel through most regions of Europe and North America and much of Asia and South America by train. The Orient Express, Europe's first long-distance luxury passenger line, began operation in 1883 and traveled between Paris, Bucharest, and Istanbul. The Trans-Siberian line was constructed between 1891 and 1916 with the goal of connecting Siberia to European Russia. The Trans-Siberian still runs between Moscow and Vladivostok on the Pacific Ocean almost 100 years after construction ended.

High speed train
The Eurostar trains travel at speeds up to 300 kilometers an hour and transport passengers between London and Brussels or Paris in less than three hours. Japan's Shinkansen line, also known as the "bullet train", connects several of the country's major cities. In Europe, France and Germany maintain the most extensive networks of high speed trains.

Shipping route
Millions of passengers travel on cruise ships every year and experience one of the most leisurely and comfortable forms of long-distance travel. Thousands of cruise ships traverse the oceans, seas, and rivers of the world. The Caribbean Sea, Mediterranean Sea, Scandinavia, and Alaska are among the most popular locations for cruises on the open seas. Modern cruise ships offer an astounding variety of attractions including casinos, entertainment, fine restaurants, and shops.

UNESCO World (Natural) Heritage
Since 1972, UNESCO, a body of the United Nations, has compiled a growing list of specially designated natural attractions and wonders that are deemed to be of outstanding importance and "universal" significance.

Mountain landscape
Mountain ranges are among the most scenic areas in the world. Many of the world's ancient low-mountain ranges, including the Appalachians and the Central Massif, feature heavily eroded and rounded peaks. Other, younger mountain ranges feature jagged and high peaks that are often covered by snow and glaciers.

Rock landscape
Many of the world's most interesting stone formations were shaped by wind and water erosion, including the natural attractions of Monument Valley National Park in the USA.

Ravine/canyon
Canyons and gorges are narrow and often deep valleys created by river and wind erosion. The Grand Canyon, in the American state of Arizona, is the most famous and one of the most spectacular canyons on the planet.

Extinct volcano
Volcanoes are formed when solid, liquid, or gas-like materials from the Earth's interior rise to the planet's surface. Magma passes through the structure of a volcano and leaves its crater as lava, often accompanied by plumes of hot ash. An extinct volcanoe is a volcano that has not experienced an eruption in the last 10,000 years.

Active volcano
Geologists consider any volcano that has erupted in the last 10,000 years to be an active volcano. Most of the world's active volcanoes are concentrated in geologically active regions, such as areas near the boundaries of the world's tectonic plates or mid-ocean ridges. The Pacific Ring of Fire is an area of relatively frequent volcanic activity.

Geyser
Active geysers are hot springs that occasionally release plumes of water into the air. Geysers are located in volcanically active regions.

Cave
Caves are formed during the creation of stone formations (mountains, underground layers of stone, etc.) or emerge later due to the eroding effects of water that seeps into stone and often carves out entire networks of large caves containing lakes and rivers.

Glacier
Glaciers are large fields or rivers of ice that often migrate through mountain valleys. Glaciers are formed above the snow line in mountainous areas such as the Alps or in regions with cold climates such as Alaska, northern Canada, and Greenland.

River landscape
The eroding power of flowing water formed many of the world's valleys and canyons. Many of the world's early civilizations emerged in fertile river valleys such as Mesopotamia or the Indus Valley. Many rivers in lowland areas have large branching deltas containing delicate ecosystems.

Waterfall/rapids
Waterfalls are formed when rivers flow over an area with a sudden drop in elevation. They come in a variety of heights and lengths. Waterfalls are among the most stunning natural attractions on the planet.

Lake country
Most of the world's major lakes were created by glaciers during the ice ages. Several regions have a large number of lakes, often interconnected and located near one another. In addition to glacial lakes, many lakes were created as a result of tectonic and geological activity.

Desert
Vast landscapes covered by sand dunes, sand fields, or stone with sparse rainfall, deserts are the most arid regions on the earth and only a few types of plants and animals can survive in these harsh environments. Most deserts have major differences between night and daytime temperatures. Most of the world's deserts remain sparsely populated.

Oasis
Oases are fertile islands surrounded by barren, arid deserts or steppes. They are supplied with water by rivers, springs or subterranean ground-water repositories.

Depression
Depressions are small basins located on land but at significant depths below sea level. Many depressions – including the Dead Sea – were created through tectonic activity.

Explanation of symbols

Thick clouds above Mount Taranaki (2,158 m) on New Zealand's North Island, one of many active volcanoes in the Pacific Ring of Fire.

Dresden, the capital of the German state of Saxony, became a major cultural center in the 18th century. The city's waterfront along the Elbe River features many historic landmarks.

Remarkable cities and cultural monuments

Fossil site
Fossils are the ancient remnants and traces of animals and plants that have inhabited our planet during its long history.

Nature park
Conservation areas have been created to protect local flora and fauna. Most designated nature parks tend to be relatively small in size.

National park (landscape)
These large conservation areas protect areas of natural beauty and significant national or international importance. Development and industry are forbidden or heavily restricted in such area. Yellowstone National Park, in the US-State of Wyoming, is the world's oldest national park.

National park (flora)
This symbol designates national parks with interesting local flora.

National park (fauna)
This symbol designates national parks with unique local wildlife.

National park (culture)
National park with cultural attractions such as Native American historic sites.

Biosphere reserve
This symbol points out undeveloped conservation areas with pristine examples of distinct climate or vegetation zones. Many biosphere reserves exhibit high levels of biodiversity.

Wildlife reserve
These conservation areas have been created for the protection of endangered animals. Selous Game Reserve in Tanzania is home to herds of African elephants.

Whale watching
Boat tours providing the chance to observe whales or dolphins in their natural habitats.

Turtle conservation area
Several countries in the world have specially designated coastal areas where endangered sea turtle species live or lay their eggs.

Protected area for sea lions/seals
Some countries have coastal areas that have designated conservation sites to preserve the natural habitats of endangered seals and sea lions.

Protected area for penguins
These protected areas were created to preserve threatened penguin colonies and to observe these creatures in their habitats.

Zoo/safari park
Zoos are park-like areas that feature collections of animals, mostly from a variety of regions. Safari parks are large properties open to tourists that feature wildlife in open wilderness.

Crocodile farm
Most crocodile farms are commercial operations where the animals are bred. Many are open to the public.

Coastal landscape
Coastal areas often feature diverse landscapes including beaches, cliffs, tidal flats, and marshlands. Some coastal areas are flat with sand dunes, while others are lined by rock formations, stony beaches, and high cliffs. The beautiful fjords of Scandinavia are among the most stunning coastal areas in the world.

Beach
Beaches often offer diverse recreational activities. Sand beaches are common in flat areas. Many of the world's beaches are now heavily developed.

Coral reef
Coral reefs are formed by small animals called coral in warm saltwater. Many of the world's large coral reefs exhibit astonishing biodiversity and are accessible to divers. The world's largest coral reef is the Great Barrier Reef off the coast of Australia.

Island
Islands are land masses surrounded by water. Most islands are part of island groups. The islands on our planet have a combined land area of 10.5 million km². Many of the world's islands have become popular tourist destinations.

Underwater reserve
Underwater conservation areas have been created to protect local marine flora and fauna.

UNESCO World (Cultural) Heritage
Since 1972, UNESCO has compiled a list of specially designated cultural sites that are deemed to be of outstanding importance. The list now includes hundreds of cultural and historic sites around the world.

Remarkable city
Large and small cities of global importance or with an abundance of tourist attractions are highlighted in yellow on our maps.

Pre- and early history
Sites related to ancient human cultures and their ways of life during times before the emergence of written records. The most grandiose pre-historic sites include large megaliths created by different cultures, such as the circle of stone pillars at Stonehenge in the United Kingdom.

Prehistoric rockscape
Prehistoric paintings, carvings and reliefs created by nomadic peoples during ancient times. Such sites have been found on all of the world's inhabited continents and often provide scientists with valuable information about life in the times before the first civilizations emerged on our planet.

The Ancient Orient
Sites related to the ancient cultures that developed in the region comprising modern Anatolia (Asia Minor), Syria, Iraq, Israel, Lebanon, Iran, and in some cases Egypt, during the period between 7000 BC and the time of Alexander the Great (400 BC). The Sumerians developed one of the first urban civilizations on the planet. They also developed one of the first number systems. After 2000 BC, the first large empires emerged in the region including the kingdoms of the Babylonians, Assyrians, and Hittites. The region features temples, ziggurats, and palaces from ancient times.

Ancient Egypt
One of the greatest ancient civilizations developed on the banks of the Nile River in Egypt. Around 3000 BC, Egypt was unified under the reign of one ruler for the first time. Between this time and the period of Alexander the Great's conquests, Egypt was ruled by more than 31 dynasties. The all-powerful pharaohs were considered living gods in Ancient Egypt. The ancient Egyptians developed a writing system, a calendar, and eventually advanced building techniques. The greatest legacy of this fascinating culture is the spectacular pyramids. The arts of the ancient Egyptians were devoted primarily to religion and mythology.

Ancient Egyptian pyramids
The monumental pyramid tombs of Egyptian pharaohs were constructed during the Old Kingdom. The largest and most impressive pyramid is the 137-meter-high Great (Cheops) Pyramid at Giza.

Minoan culture
The advanced Bronze-Age culture of the Minoans flourished on the island Crete during ancient times. Minoan civilization first emerged during the 3rd millennium BC, after which the Minoans rapidly became the dominant power in the eastern Mediterranean. Modern Crete features the remnants of Minoan villas with impressive frescoes and interior design.

Phoenician culture
During ancient times the area encompassing modern Israel, Lebanon, and Palestine was once the center of Phoenician culture. The Phoenicians were the dominant trading power in the Mediterranean for several centuries and founded many colonies.

Early African culture
Ancient African civilizations include the cultures of the Kingdom of Ghana, Axum (Ethiopia), the Great Zimbabwe culture, and Kush, a complex and advanced society that developed south of Egypt.

Etruscan culture
The Etruscans probably originated in central Italy. During the 10th century BC, they conquered large sections of the Italian Peninsula before they were conquered by the Romans. Italy has numerous archeological and historic sites related to the culture of the ancient Etruscans.

Greek antiquity
No other civilization has had a greater influence on European culture than that of Ancient Greece. The city-state of Athens was one of the first basic democracies in history. The art, philosophy and architecture of Ancient Greece continue to inspire and shape our modern world. Ancient Greece was divided into city-states, many of which founded distant colonies in Southern Europe, the Middle East, and North Africa. Ancient Greek art dealt mostly with subjects related to Greek mythology. The Greek city-states constructed many great structures including impressive temples and amphitheaters. During the Hellenistic period – after the death of Alexander the Great – Greek-speaking cities outside the mainland, including Alexandria in Egypt, replaced the city-states as the centers of Greek civilization.

Explanation of symbols

Remarkable cities and cultural monuments

Roman antiquity
Over a period of centuries the once small city of Rome emerged as the center of a powerful empire. The Roman Empire was at its largest under the reign of the Emperor Trajan (98–117 BC); during this period its borders extended from North Africa to Scotland and from Iberia to Mesopotamia. The Roman state that existed between 509 and 27 BC is referred to as the Roman Republic. The Roman state that was created after the reforms of Caesar Augustus is known as the Roman Empire. Roman art and culture was greatly influenced by Ancient Greek and other Mediterranean cultures. The Romans constructed impressive structures including amphitheaters, temples, and aqueducts.

Nabatean culture
The ancient city of Petra (in modern Jordan) was first settled by the Nabateans in the fifth century BC. By the 1st century BC, the Nabateans ruled a powerful trading empire. The monumental ruins of Petra are the greatest remnant of this ancient culture.

Vikings
Between the 9th and 11th centuries, Scandinavian Vikings conquered territories throughout Europe. During their centuries of conquest, the Vikings founded numerous settlements and trading posts in Russia, Western Europe, and in the British Isles.

Ancient India
India has a wealth of cultural and historic attractions. The Indus Valley civilization (2600–1400 BC) was one of the first urbanized civilizations to emerge on the planet. Indian culture reached one of its high points during the period between the 7th and 13th centuries. Many of India's greatest Buddhist and Hindu architectural masterpieces, as well as artworks, were created during these centuries. During the Mogul era (16th and 17th century), many impressive works of Islamic architecture were created throughout the country, including modern India's most famous structure, the Taj Mahal.

Ancient China
The oldest remnants of early Chinese culture date from the era between 5000–2000 BC. The Shang dynasty (1600–1000 BC) was the most influential and advanced bronze-age culture in China. Daoism and Confucian philosophy were both developed in China during the 5th century BC. The first great unified Chinese Empire was forged around 220 BC by Ying Zheng, the king of Qin. After the emergence of the first Chinese Empire, China was ruled by various dynasties and experienced many periods of cultural and technological advancement. The country's most impressive historic sites include the Great Wall of China, the tomb of Emperor Qin with its army of terracotta warriors in Xi'an, and the Forbidden City in the capital city Beijing.

Ancient Japan
The Yamato period of Japanese history began around AD 400. During this period, the country was ruled by an imperial court in Nara. During the 5th century the Japanese adopted the Chinese writing system and in the 6th century Buddhism arrived in Japan. The Fujiwara clan dominated the country for more than 500 years starting in the 7th century. During this period the country's imperial capital was moved from Nara to Kyoto. Between 1192 and 1868, Japan was ruled by a series of shoguns (military rulers). The Meiji Era (1868–1912) saw the restoration of imperial power and the emergence of modern Japan.

Mayan culture
The Maya are an Amerindian people in southern Mexico and Central America. During pre-Colombian times, the Maya developed an advanced and powerful civilization that ruled over a vast territory. Mayan civilization reached its cultural and technological peak around AD 300 and was eventually devastated by the arrival of the Spanish in the 16th century. Central America and Mexico have many impressive Mayan ruins.

Inca culture
The Inca culture emerged around Cusco during the 12th century. By the 15th century, the Inca ruled a vast empire that encompassed parts of modern Peru, Bolivia, Ecuador, Chile, and Argentina. Although their empire was shortlived, the Inca left behind impressive stone monuments and structures throughout western South America. The Inca city of Machu Picchu in Peru is one of the most impressive historic sites in South America.

Aztec culture
At some point during the second millennium BC, the Aztec people migrated into Mexico, where they eventually established a powerful empire. The Aztec capital, Tenochtitlan (modern Mexico City), was founded in 1325 and was once one of the world's largest cities. The Aztecs constructed many grand temples and pyramids throughout their empire and made important cultural advances, including the creation of a writing system and calendar. Central Mexico has numerous Aztec cultural sites.

Other ancient American cultures
Advanced Amerindian cultures appeared in both North America and the Andean regions of South America. Countless Amerindian historic sites, including the remnants of ancient settlements, can be found throughout the Americas.

Places of Jewish cultural interest
Judaism is the oldest of the world's major monotheist religions. The Jerusalem temple was a great achievement of early Jewish culture – now only a section of its walls remain (the Western Wall). Historic synagogues can be found throughout the world, a legacy of the Jewish Diaspora.

Places of Christian cultural interest
Christianity is the world's most practiced and widespread religion. Christianity is based on the teachings in the old and new testaments of the Bible, and emerged in western Asia during the first century AD. Christian religious sites, including churches, cathedrals, and monasteries, can be found in most regions of the world.

Places of Islamic cultural interest
Islam, one of the world's major religions, was founded by Mohammed (AD 570–632). The teachings of the Quran (Koran) are its basis. Muslims around the world pray in the direction of Mecca in Saudi Arabia, Islam's holiest city.

Places of Buddhist cultural interest
Buddhism is based on the teachings of Siddhartha Gautama (around 560–480 BC), also known as the Buddha. Most of the world's Buddhists live in East Asia. Important Buddhist sites include temples, pagodas, stupas, and monasteries.

Places of Hindu cultural interest
Most of the at least one billion followers of Hinduism, one of the world's most practiced religions, live on the Indian subcontinent. Hinduism encompasses a variety of beliefs and practices, many of which are thousands of years old.

Places of Jainist cultural interest
Most followers of Jainism live in India. It is based on the teachings of Mahavira, who lived in the 5th century BC. Jainist sites include temples and monasteries.

Places of Sikh cultural interest
The Sikh religious philosophy emerged in 16th-century northern India, as an attempt to merge the teachings of Islam and Hinduism. The "Golden Temple" in Amritsar is the most important Sikh religious center.

Places of Shinto cultural interest
Shinto, the indigenous religion of Japan, is based on the reverence of kami (nature spirits) and ancestral spirits. Historic Shinto shrines can be seen throughout Japan.

Sites of interest to other religions
Sites related to other religious and spiritual communities.

Places of cultural interest to indigenous peoples (native peoples)
Sites related to the culture or history of indigenous peoples around the world.

Aborigine land reserves
The almost 500,000 Aborigines form only a small portion of Australia's population. Many Aborigine communities administer large land reserves.

Places of Aboriginal cultural interest
Cultural sites of the Aborigines, including rock paintings, are among the interesting attractions in Australia.

Native American reservation
Most of the Native American reservations in North America were founded during the 19th century. Despite the history of low living standards on some reservations, many Native American communities have successfully protected their traditions.

Pueblo Indian culture
The Pueblo Indians are a group of Native American communities who have lived in the southwestern United States for centuries. Their traditional settlements – known as pueblos – consist of adobe buildings.

Places of Amerindian cultural interest
The different regions of North America feature hundreds of sites related to the history and cultures of Native Americans.

Amazonian Amerindians/ protected area
Land reserves have been created to protect the Amerindian cultures in the Amazon basin in South America.

Explanation of symbols

Spanish settlers built Nuestra Senora church in Cholula, Mexico atop a series of ancient Amerindian pyramids. The historic church lies close to the snow-capped volcano Popocatepetl.

Las Vegas, the largest city in the American state of Nevada, is a popular tourist destination with numerous casinos, theme hotels, and amusement parks.

Sport and leisure destinations

Cultural landscape
Areas with landscapes that have been shaped by human settlement or cultivation.

Historical cities and towns
Historic cities and towns with well-preserved architectural attractions.

Impressive skyline
Cities featuring modern skylines, such as New York City, Chicago, and Hong Kong.

Castle/fortress/fort
Europe features the greatest concentration of these structures.

Caravansary
Historic inns along the ancient caravan routes of the Middle East, Central Asia, and North Africa.

Palace
Grand castles and palaces that once housed nobility and royalty can be found in many different regions.

Technical/industrial monument
Man-made attractions related to the achievements of industrialization and modern times.

Dam
The largest and most important dams and retaining walls on the planet.

Remarkable lighthouse
Many coastal areas feature beautiful or historic lighthouses.

Remarkable bridge
Many of the world's great bridges are considered engineering marvels.

Tomb/grave
Mausoleums, monuments, burial mounds, and other grave sites.

Theater of war/battlefield
Site where important battles occurred, including Waterloo in Belgium.

Monument
Sites dedicated to historic figures and important historical events.

Memorial
Site dedicated to the victims of wars and genocides.

Space mission launch site
Landing and launch sites of manned and unmanned space missions.

Space telescope
Radio, X-ray, and gamma-ray telescopes are important tools of modern astronomy.

Market
Important markets where people gather to trade and purchase goods.

Festivals
Large celebrations of music and culture including Rio de Janeiro's Carnaval.

Museum
Important collections of man-made works (art, technology, anthropology) and natural relics.

Theater
Famous theaters presenting opera, musicals, and other productions.

World exhibition
Cities that have hosted world expositions, including London in the United Kingdom.

Olympics
Cities and towns that have hosted the modern summer or winter Olympic Games.

Arena/stadium
The largest and most famous sporting venues in the world – including stadiums for football (soccer), baseball, rugby, hockey, and other popular sports.

Race track
Auto and motorbike racing are popular sports in many of the world's regions. The atlas highlights many of the most famous autoracing venues, including Formula 1 and NASCAR race tracks in Indianapolis, Melbourne, and numerous other cities.

Golf
Golf has become an increasingly popular sport around the world in recent years. The atlas highlights several of the most famous and beautiful golf courses as well as areas that host important golf tournaments.

Horse racing
Horse racing has a long history in many regions. Several well-known race tracks and events are highlighted in the book, including the Ascot racecourse in England, a major event for Britain's high society. The Kentucky Derby remains one of the most popular annual sporting events in the United States, while Hong Kong's Happy Valley draws thousands of visitors every week.

Skiing
The maps in the atlas point out the most important ski areas in the world, including Chamonix in the French Alps, St. Moritz in Switzerland, Aspen in the Rocky Mountains of Colorado, and Whistler in Canada. Many of these areas also offer facilities for other winter sports, including snowboarding.

Sailing
Once a sport for the wealthy, sailing is now enjoyed by millions of people. The atlas highlights areas with good conditions for recreational sailing.

Diving
Beautiful, colorful coral reefs, fascinating shipwrecks, and close encounters with wonderful marine life – this atlas presents popular and famous dive sites around the world.

Wind surfing
A mix of surfing and sailing, windsurfing is a popular aquatic sport. The atlas points out coastal areas well suited to the sport.

Surfing
Popular coastal areas with adequate waves for surfing are highlighted – including well-known beaches in Australia, California, Europe, and in Hawaii, the birthplace of surfing.

Canoeing/rafting
Travelers can enjoy both adventurous and relaxing journeys along many of the world's rivers and lakes in canoes or rafts.

Seaport
The largest and busiest harbors in the world are highlighted.

Deep-sea fishing
The atlas highlights several of the best and most well known locations on the world's seas and oceans for recreational fishing.

Waterskiing
Popular beaches, coastal areas, and lakes with ideal conditions for waterskiing.

Beach resort
Many of the world's beachside communities feature a laid-back atmosphere and excellent tourist facilities. The atlas highlights popular beaches and resorts.

Mineral/thermal spa
The atlas locates several historic and beautiful towns with spas that have attracted visitors for centuries.

Amusement/theme park
Modern amusement parks offer diverse attractions. The parks highlighted in the atlas include Walt Disney World in Orlando, Sea World in California, Disneyland Paris, and Tivoli in Copenhagen.

Casino
Well known casinos, including the historic casino of Monte Carlo and the resort-hotels of Las Vegas.

Hill resort
Exclusive resorts located in temperate highland areas. Mostly in Asia, hill resorts were once very popular destinations, especially for European colonial officials.

Lodge
Comfortable and luxurious camps or inns in pristine wilderness areas, mostly in Africa and North America.

Light and water are the sources of all life on Earth.

The crater of Mount St. Helens, an active vulcano that last erupted in 1980

THE WORLD

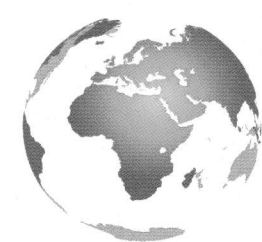

THE BLUE PLANET

The total surface area of the Earth covers 510 million km², 71 % of which is covered by water and 29 % by land. Most of the world's water is contained in the four vast oceans: Pacific, Atlantic, Indian, and the relatively small Arctic Ocean. The world's land area is divided between the seven continents: North America, South America, Europe, Asia, Africa, Australia, and Antarctica. While the surface of the planet's southern hemisphere is dominated by the oceans, the northern hemisphere is almost equally covered by land and water. The shape of the Earth's surface and the creation of the continents are the result of tectonic plate movements, a process that began billions of years ago.

Catastrophic volcanic eruptions and powerful earthquakes are not uncommon along the edges of the various tectonic plates. Compared to the total diameter of the Earth (12,700 km) the height variations on our planet's surface are small. Mount Everest, the world's tallest mountain, rises 8,850 meters, while the deepest point in the ocean, the Mariana Trench in the Pacific, extends 11,034 meters beneath the planet's surface. Including Mount Everest there are 14 mountains rising above 8,000 meters; all of them are located in Asia.

Most of the world's highest mountains are part of massive mountain chains, several of which cover large sections of the continents. The Pyrenees in Europe are the westernmost chain in an almost continuous belt of mountain systems stretching to Southeast Asia. The world's largest body of water, the Pacific Ocean, is surrounded by the circumglobal mountain belt and East Africa has a long mountain belt. Mountain chains are the source of many rivers. The longest rivers on Earth are the Nile (6,671 km) in Africa, the Amazon (6,400 km) in South America, and the Yangtze (Chang Jiang) in East Asia (6,300 km).

The vast Sahara Desert covers most of North Africa.

The location of the world's various climate and vegetation zones depends on the Earth's rotation, the tilt of its axis, and ocean currents, among other factors. In equatorial regions constant heavy rainfall leads to the growth of thick vegetation coverage. Many tropical and subtropical regions border large arid regions; the Sahara in Africa is the world's largest desert (9 million km²).

The world - physical map

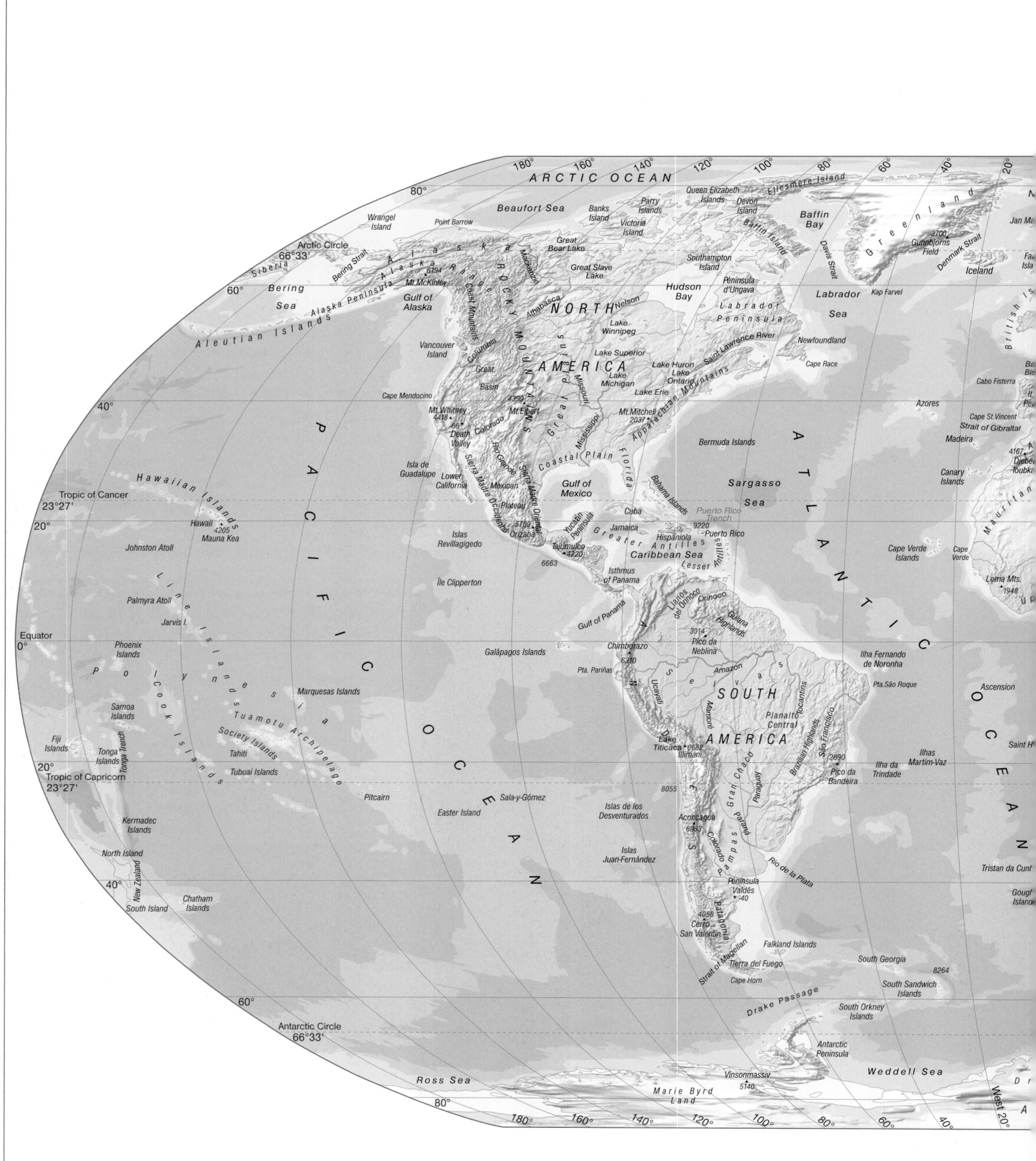

Scale 1:80,000,000

0   1000   2000   3000 Kilometers

0   1000   2000 Miles

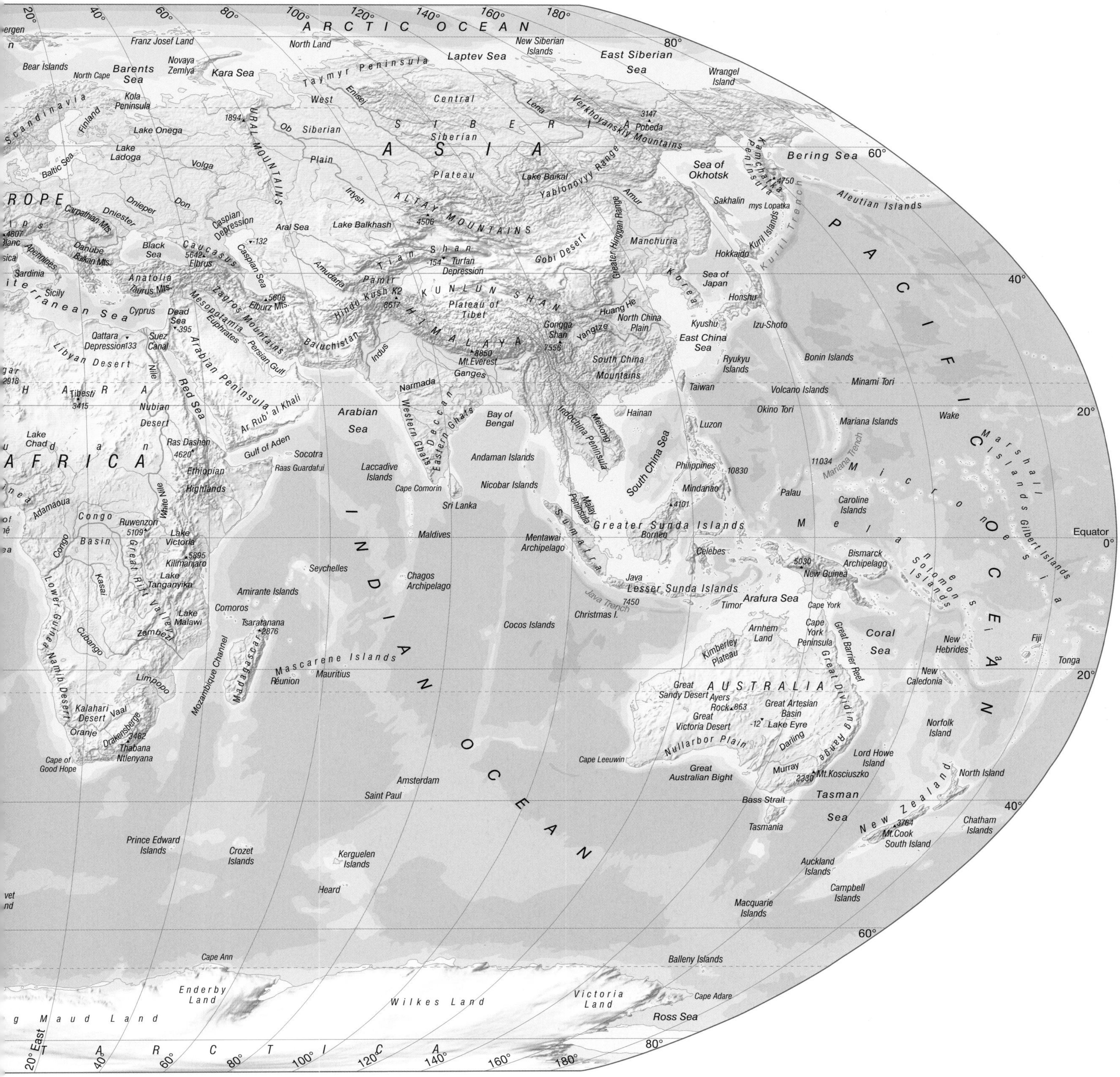

Arctic Region

Scale 1:15,000,000

0 250 500 750 Kilometers
0 250 500 Miles

175° **Tc** 170° **Tb** 165° **Ta** 160° **Sd** 155° **Sc** 150° **Sb** 145° **Sa** 55 140° **Rd** 135° **Rc** 130° **Rb**

Ra 120°
Qd 115°
Qc 110°
Qb 105°
Qa 100°
Pd 95°
Pc
Pb
Pa 85°
Od 80°
Oc 75°
Ob 70°
Oa 65°
Nd 60°

Longa Island

East Siberian Sea

o.Ajon Medvežka

Kolymskaja nizmennost'

Alazejskoe ploskogor'e

Honuu

Handyga
Amga
Amga
Čul'man
Skovorodino
Tynda
Nerjungri

o.Bol'ševik

Logaškino

Indigirka

Čekurdah

Deputatskij

2243

Janskoe ploskogor'e

Cherskiy Range

Verhojansk

2120

Ulu

Jakutsk

Aldanskoe nagor'e

Aldan
Aldan

Olëkma

g.Skalistyj Golec
2467

Stanovoy khrebet

Jano-Indigirskaja nizmennost'

Ust'-Kujga

2081
Ečijskij massiv
Džargelah

Asyma

Sangar

Olëkminsk

Taksimo

Bodajbo

hrebet Kular

Hajyr

Vana

Menkerja

Žigansk

Njurba

Lensk

Kirensk

New Siberian Islands

o.Novaja Sibir'

o.Bol. Ljahovskij

pr.Dmitrija Lapteva

m.Buor-Haja
guba Buor-Haja

Tiksi

Siktjah

Lena

Central'nojakutskaja ravnina

Vijujsk

Mimyj

Viljujskoe vdhr.

Central'no-Tungusskoe plato

ostrova Anžu

o.Kotel'nyj

Lena Delta

krjaž Čekanovskogo

plato Kystyk

Olenëk

Nakanno

Vanavara

o.Arga-Muora-Sise

Sagastyr

Saskylah

Oleněk

Surinda

Laptev Sea

Oleněkskij zaliv

Anabar

Severo-Sibirskaja

Essej

Tura

gory Byrranga nizmennost'

o.Bol.Begičev

Anabarskoe plato

1701

Putončany

Severo-Enisejsk

m.Dika

Novorybnaja

Hatanga

plato Putorana

Central Siberian Plateau

Taymyr Peninsula

oz.Tajmyr

Kotuj

Hatanga

North Land

o.Bol'ševik

m.Neupokoeva

o.Oktjabr'skoj Revoljucii

o.Komsomolec

ostrova Sedova

ostrova Sergeja Kirova

Voločanka

RUSSIA

Talnah
Noril'sk
Dudinka Enisej

Kurejskoe vdhr.

Turuhansk

Igarka

Verhneimbatsk

Bor

Enisel

Ketsko-Tymskaja ravnina

OCEAN

Abyssal Plain

01 85° 02 80° 03 75° 04 70° 05 65° 06 60° 07 54

Pjasinskij zaliv

Voroncovo

Dikson

Gydanskij p-ov

Tazovskij

West

o.Greèm-Bell

620
m.Želanija

g.Blednaja
1052

Antipajuta
Tazovskaja guba

Tazovskij p-ov

Antipajuta

Obskaya guba

Novyj Urengoj

Raduznyj

Kargasok

o.Rudol'fa

Zemlja Georga

Franz Josef Land (RUS)

360

68

170

o.Belyj

p-ov Jamal

Novyj Port

Nadym

Nojabr'sk

Nižnevartovsk

Siberian

Zemlja Aleksandry

5449

450

380

48
1547

Kara Sea

Baidarackaja guba

Salehard

Surgut

Neftejugansk

125

Ob

Kvitøya (N)

Mean Pack Ice Limit in Summer

Novaya Zemlya

pik Sedova
1115

Jugorskij p-ov

Ob

Hanty-Mansijsk

Ob

Plain

Nordaustlandet

63

Amderma

gora Pajer
1499

Belojarskij

Oc

Erik Eriksenstretet

Kong Karls Land

m.Men'šikova

o.Vajgač

URAL

Irgim

Njagan'

Irtys

Olgastretet

Spitsbergen
Barentsøya

Longyearbyen
Edgeøya

105

proliv Karskie Vorota

Vorkuta

gora Narodnaja
1894

Njagan'

Tobol'sk

Oc 70°

Kong Karls Land

Beluš'ja Guba

Pečorskoe more

Inta

MOUNTAINS

gora Tel'posiz
1617

Sovetskij

Uraj

Tavda

Zavodoukovsk

Tjumen'

Ob 65°

Svalbard (N)

Isfjorden
Storfjorden

Hopen

410

105

72

Nar'jan-Mar

Bor'šezemel'skaja tundra

Pečora

Komi

Serov

Irbit

Sadrinsk

Kamensk-Ural'skij

Kopejsk

Oa 60°

2059

Bear Islands (N)

Barents Sea

144

m.Kanin Nos

p-ov Kanin

Cëšskaja guba

Ust'-Cil'ma

Sosnogorsk

Uhta

gora Konžakovskij Kamen'
1569

Krasnotur'insk

Nižnij Tagil

YEKATERINBURG
ČELJABINSK

Pervoural'sk

Zlatoust

Miass

gian Sea

910

Murmanskoye Rise

225

260

Mean Pack Ice Limit in Winter

o.Kolgujev

White Sea

Arctic Circle

Mezen'

Mezen'

Pinega

Solikamsk
Berezniki

Syktyvkar

Krasnokamsk

PERM'

Kamskoe vdhr.

Kungur

N

T

A

I

N

S

g.Jamantau
1640

UFA

North Cape

Hammerfest

Vadsø

Kirkenes

Gremiha

Severomorsk

Murmansk

Severomorsk

Ponoj

Kola Peninsula

Arhangel'sk

Ust'-Varga

Kotlas

Glazov

Votkinsk

Neftekamsk

Udmurtia Izevsk

Bashkortostan

3214

Alta

Inari

Monćegorsk
Apatity

Ponoj

Kandalakša

Severodvinsk

Lapland

Lofoten Basin

NORWAY

Tromsø

Kandalakša

FINLAND

Lapland

Kapelauksaja guba

5° **Lb** 10° **Lc** 15° **Ld** 20° **Ma** 25° **Mb** 30° **Mc** 35° **Md** 14 40° **Na** 45° **Nb** 50° **Nc** 55° **Nd**

5

Antarctica

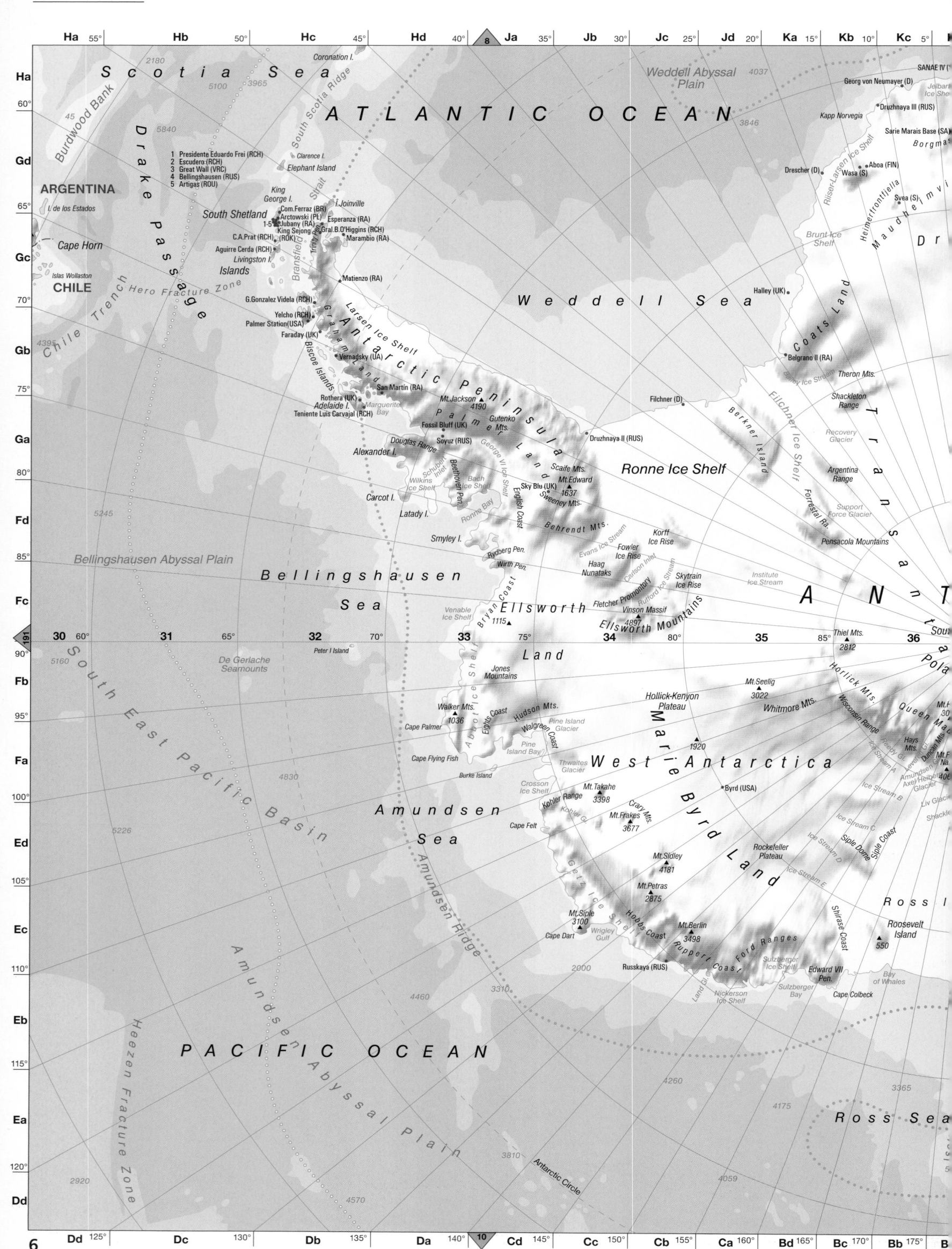

Scotia Sea

2180

Coronation I.

Weddell Abyssal Plain

4037

SANAE IV (

Georg von Neumayer (D)

5100

3965

Burdwood Bank

45

ATLANTIC OCEAN

Jelbart Ice Shel

Druzhnaya III (RUS)

5840

South Scotia Ridge

Kapp Norvegia

3846

Sarie Marais Base (SA

Clarence I.

Borgmas

1 Presidente Eduardo Frei (RCH)
2 Escudero (RCH)
3 Great Wall (VRC)
4 Bellingshausen (RUS)
5 Artigas (ROU)

Elephant Island

Drescher (D)

Wasa (S)

Aboa (FIN)

Riiser-Larsen Ice Shelf

Heimefrontfjella

Maudheimvi

ARGENTINA

King George I.

I.Joinville

Svea (S)

Dr

I. de los Estados

South Shetland

Com.Ferraz (BR)

Esperanza (RA)

Brunt Ice Shelf

Coats Land

Arctowski (PL)

Gral.B.O'Higgins (RCH)

Jubany (RA)

Drake passage

King Sejong (ROK)

Cape Horn

C.A.Prat (RCH)

Marambio (RA)

Islas Wollaston

Aguirre Cerda (RCH)

CHILE

Livingston I.

Matienzo (RA)

Halley (UK)

Weddell Sea

Belgrano II (RA)

Islands

Hero Fracture Zone

G.Gonzalez Videla (RCH)

Larsen Ice Shelf

Theron Mts.

Chile Trench

Yelcho (RCH)

Bransfield Strait

Palmer Station(USA)

Shackleton Range

Faraday (UK)

Antarctic Peninsula

4395

Vernadsky (UA)

Graham Land

Filchner (D)

Berkner Island

Recovery Glacier

Biscoe Islands

San Martin (RA)

Mt.Jackson

Druzhnaya II (RUS)

Filchner Ice Shelf

Transa

Rothera (UK)

4190

Argentina Range

Adelaide I.

Palmer Land

Gutenko Mts.

Ronne Ice Shelf

Teniente Luis Carvajal (RCH)

Fossil Bluff (UK)

Support Force Glacier

Marguerite Bay

Soyuz (RUS)

Scaife Mts.

Forrestal Ra.

Douglas Range

Mt.Edward

Pensacola Mountains

Alexander I.

George VI Ice Shelf

Sky Blu (UK)

Sweeney Mts.

English Coast

1637

5245

Schuber Inlet

Bach Ice Shelf

Beethoven Pen.

Behrendt Mts.

Korff Ice Rise

A

N

T

Bellingshausen Abyssal Plain

Wilkins Ice Shelf

Ronne Bay

Smyley I.

Evans Ice Stream

Fowler Ice Rise

Carcot I.

Latady I.

Rydberg Pen.

Haag Nunataks

Carlson Inlet

Skytrain Ice Rise

Institute Ice Stream

Bellingshausen

Wirth Pen.

Bryan Coast

Fletcher Promontory

Gutford Ice Stream

Sea

Venable Ice Shelf

Ellsworth

Vinson Massif

Ellsworth Mountains

A

N

T

1115

4897

5160

Peter I Island

Land

Thiel Mts.

2812

Pola

191

De Gerlache Seamounts

Abbot Ice Shelf

Jones Mountains

Horlick Mts.

Queen Ma

South East Pacific Basin

Walker Mts.

Eights Coast

Hudson Mts.

Hollick-Kenyon Plateau

Mt.Seelig

Mt.H

3022

30

1036

Cape Palmer

Pine Island Glacier

Whitmore Mts.

Wisconsin Range

Walgreen Coast

Hays Mts.

Cape Flying Fish

Pine Island Bay

4830

Burke Island

1920

N

5226

Thwaites Glacier

West Antarctica

Marie Byrd Land

Amundsen Ridge

Amundsen

Crosson Ice Shelf

Mt.Takahe

Byrd (USA)

Axel Heiberg Glacier

406

Kohler Range

3398

Ice Stream B

Sea

Kohler Gl.

Mt.Frakes

Liv Glacie

Cape Felt

3677

Mt.Sidley

Rockefeller Plateau

Ice Stream C

Siple Dome

Shackle

4181

Mt.Petras

Siple Coast

Ross I

2875

Ice Stream D

Amundsen Abyssal Plain

Mt.Siple

Hobbs Coast

Ice Stream E

Shirase Coast

Roosevelt Island

3100

Mt.Berlin

Ford Ranges

550

Cape Dart

Wrigley Gulf

3498

Ruppert Coast

Sulzberger Ice Shelf

Edward VII Pen.

Russkaya (RUS)

2000

Getz Ice Shelf

Heezen Fracture Zone

Land Gl.

Nickerson Ice Shelf

Sulzberger Bay

Cape Colbeck

Bay of Whales

4460

3310

PACIFIC OCEAN

4260

3365

Ross Sea

4175

Antarctic Circle

2920

3810

4570

4059

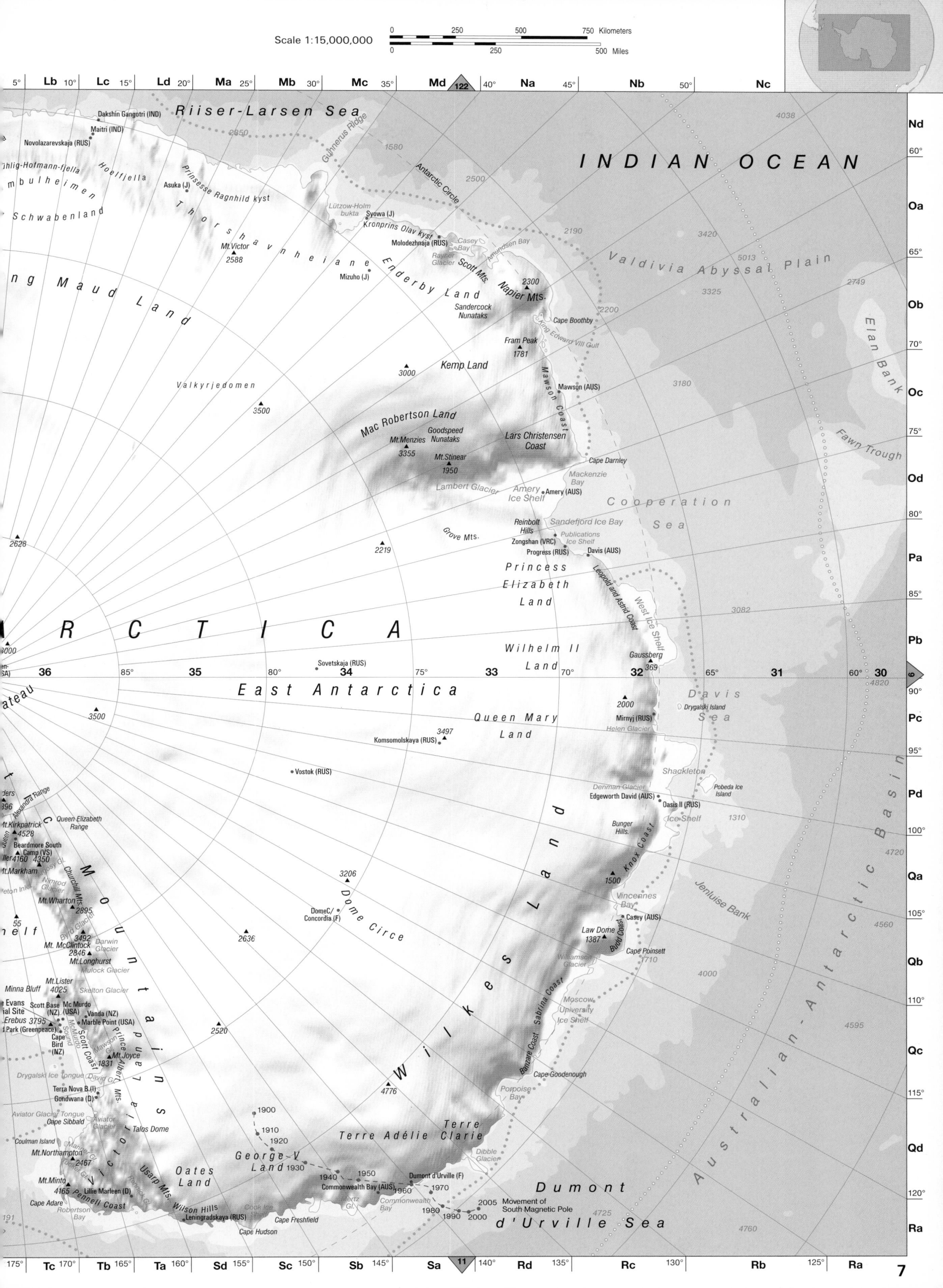

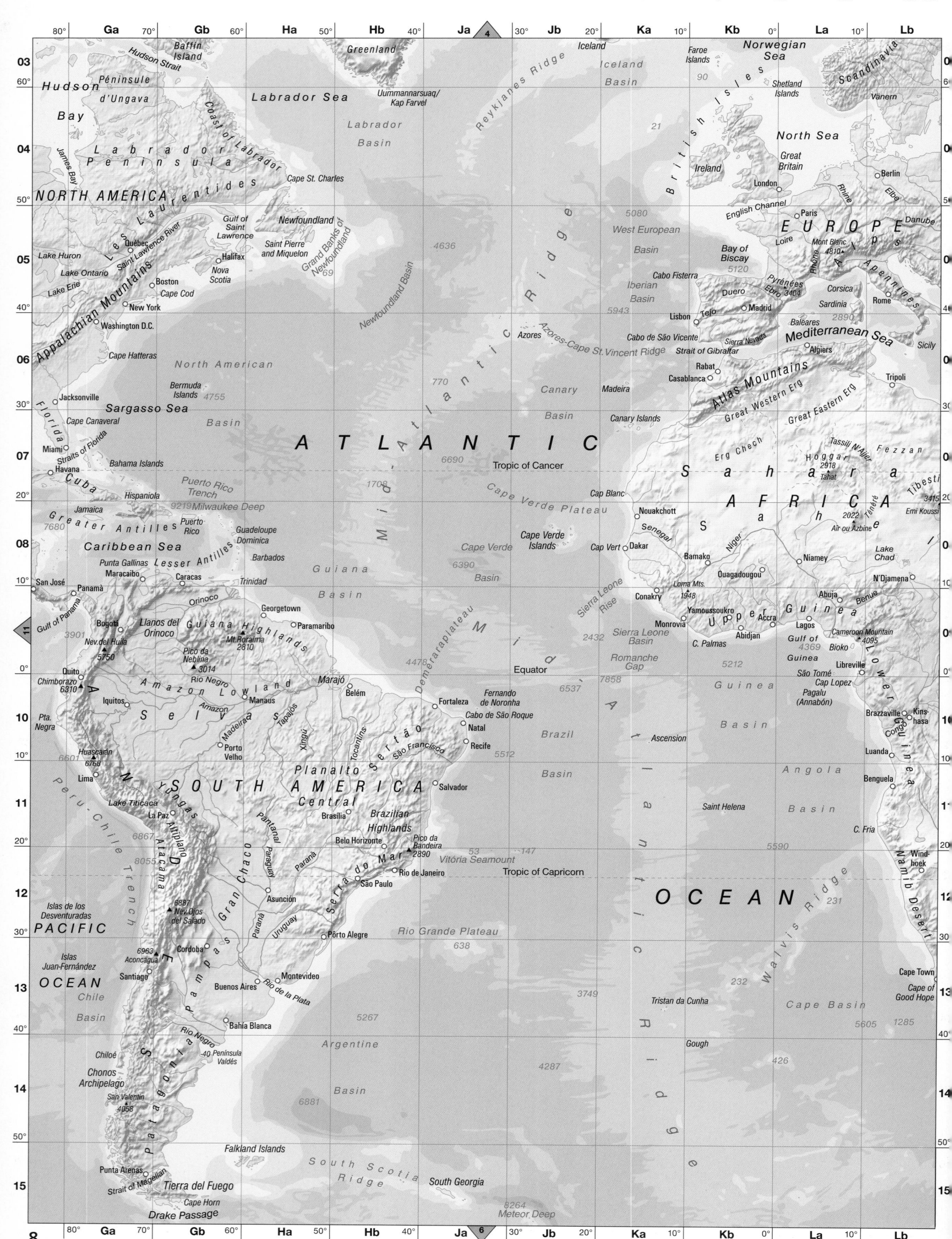

Atlantic Ocean

Scale 1:50,000,000

0 500 1000 1500 2000 Kilometers
0 500 1000 1500 Miles

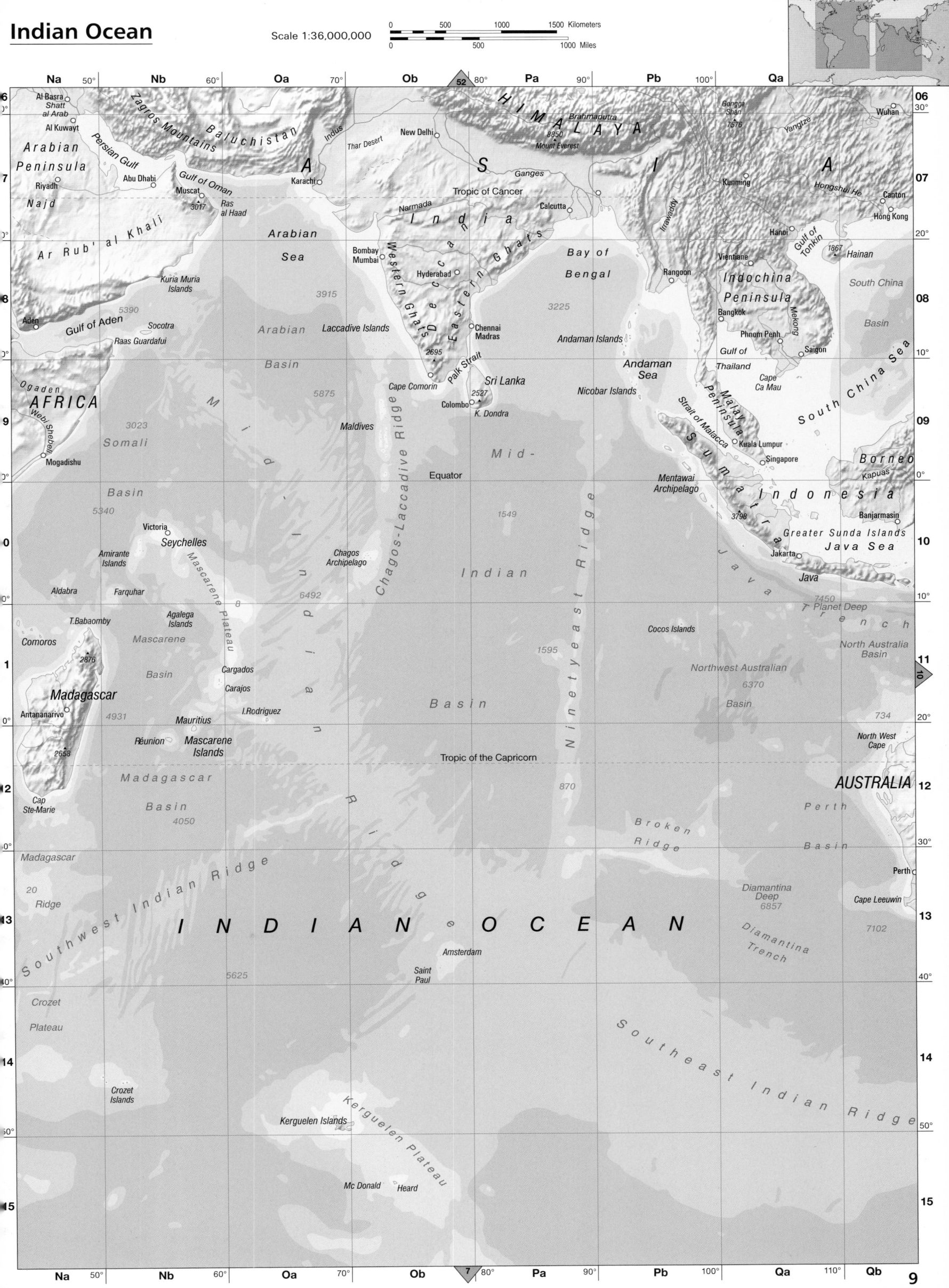

Indian Ocean

Scale 1:36,000,000

0   500   1000   1500 Kilometers

0   500   1000 Miles

Pacific Ocean

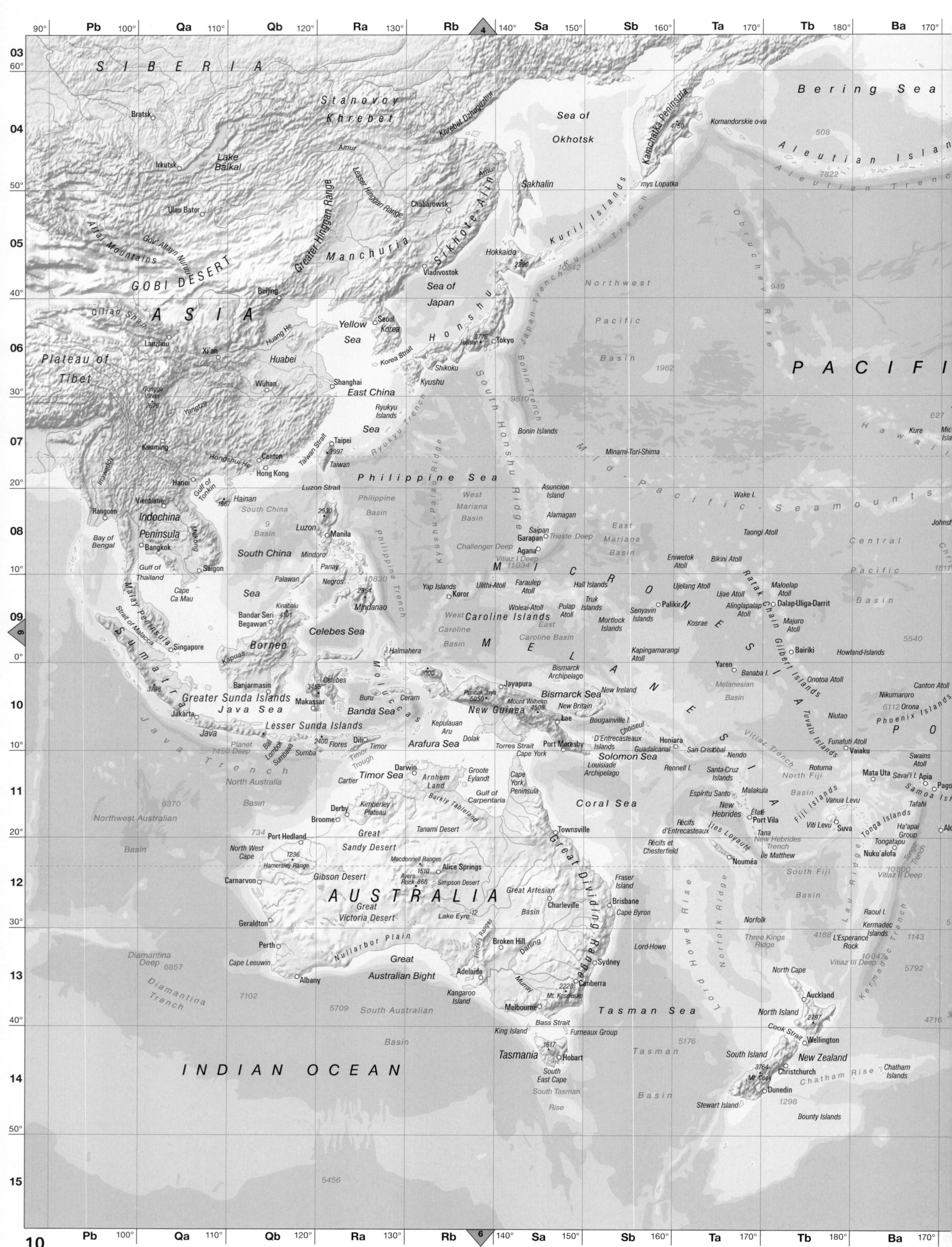

S I B E R I A

Bratsk

Stanovoy
Khrebet

Sea of
Okhotsk

Bering Sea

Kamchatka Peninsula

Komandorskie o-va

4750

508

Aleutian Islan

Irkutsk

Lake
Baikal

Amur

Khrebet Dzhugdzhur

Aleutian Trench

7822

Ulan Bator

Lesser Hingan Range

Chabarowsk

Amur

Sakhalin

mys Lopatka

Obruchev Rise

949

Greater Hingan Range

Sikhote Alin

Manchuria

Kuril Islands

Kuril Trench

10542

Northwest

Gov' Atayn Nuruu

Hokkaido

2290

Altai Mountains

Vladivostok

Sea of
Japan

Pacific

PACIFI

GOBI DESERT

A S I A

Beijing

Seoul
Korea

Honshu

Basin

1962

Qilian Shan

Lanzhou

Huang He

Xi'an

Yellow
Sea

Fujisan 3776
Tokyo

Japan Trench

627

Plateau of
Tibet

Gongga
Shan
7676

Huabei

Korea Strait

Shikoku

Bonin Trench

Ha

Kure
Isla

Wuhan

Shanghai

Kyushu

9810

w

Mid

Yangtze

East China

Ryukyu
Islands

ai

Pacific

Kunming

Taipei
3997

Taiwan Strait

Sea

Ryukyu Trench

Bonin Islands

Minami-Tori-Shima

Seamounts

Canton

Hong Kong

Hongshui He

South Honshu Ridge

Wake I.

Johnst

Irrawaddy

Hanoi

Gulf of
Tonkin

Hainan

Taiwan

Philippine Sea

Asuncion
Island

Kyushu-Palau Ridge

West
Mariana
Basin

Alamagan

East
Mariana
Basin

Taongi Atoll

Central

Vientiane

1667

Philippine
Basin

Saipan
Garapan

Trieste Deep

Agana

Pacific

Rangoon

Indochina
Peninsula

South China

2930

Luzon

Manila

Challenger Deep

Vitiaz I Deep

M

11034

Eniwetok
Atoll

Bikini Atoll

Basin

Bay of
Bengal

Bangkok

Mekong

9

Basin

Mindoro

I

C

Yap Islands

Faraulep
Atoll

Hall Islands

Ujelang Atoll

Maloelap
Atoll

Johnst

Gulf of
Thailand

Saigon

Palawan

Panay

Negros

10830

2954

Koror

Ulithi-Atoll

Pulap
Atoll

Truk
Islands

Palikir

Ujae Atoll

Ratak

Dalap-Uliga-Darrit

Cape
Ca Mau

Sea

Kinabalu
4101

Mindanao

O

Woleai-Atoll

Caroline Islands

N

Alinglapalap
Atoll

Majuro
Atoll

5540

Bandar Seri
Begawan

West
Caroline
Basin

East
Caroline

Mortlock
Islands

Senyavin
Islands

Kosrae

Chain

Bairiki

Singapore

Celebes Sea

M

Caroline Basin

E

L

Kapingamarangi
Atoll

Yaren

Banaba I.

Gilbert Islands

Howland-Islands

Malay Peninsula

Kapuas

Borneo

Halmahera

Melanesian

A

Banjarmasin

3000

Bismarck
Archipelago

New Ireland

Basin

Onotoa Atoll

Canton Island

3798

Sumatra

Greater Sunda Islands

Celebes

3455

Buru

Ceram

Moluccas

Pinzak Jaya
5050

Mount Wilhelm
4506

New Britain

Bismarck Sea

Bougainville I.

N

Tuvalu Islands

Niutao

Nikumaroro

6112 Orona

Phoenix Islands

PO

Java Sea

Makassar

Banda Sea

New Guinea

Lae

Choiseul

San Cristobal

Funafuti Atoll

Jakarta

Lesser Sunda Islands

Kepulauan
Aru

Dolak

Port Moresby

Solomon Sea

Guadalcanal

Honiara

North Fiji

Rotuma

Vaiaku

Swains
Atoll

Java

Bali

Flores

Dili

Timor

Arafura Sea

Torres Strait

Cape York

Louisiade
Archipelago

Rennell I.

Santa-Cruz
Islands

Nendo

Basin

Mata Uta

Savai'i I. Apia

Planet
Deep
7450

Lombok

Sumbawa

2400

Sumba

Timor
Trough

Darwin

Groote
Eylandt

Arnhem
Land

Gulf of
Carpentaria

Coral Sea

D'Entrecasteaux
Islands

Espíritu Santo

Malakula

Vanua Levu

Samoa Isl

Tafahi

Java
Trench

North Australia

Cartier

Barkly Tableland

Cape
York
Peninsula

New
Hebrides

Efaté
Port Vila

Viti Levu

Suva

Tonga Islands

Pago

6370

Basin

Kimberley
Plateau

Townsville

Récifs
d'Entrecasteaux

Îles Loyauté

Ha'apai
Group

Derby

Tanami Desert

Récifs et
Chesterfield

Île Matthew

Tongatapu

Broome

Great

New Hebrides
Trench

Nouméa

Nuku'alofa

Northwest Australian

734

Port Hedland

Sandy Desert

Macdonnell Ranges

1510

Alice Springs

South Fiji

10800

Vitiaz II Deep

Basin

North West
Cape

1236

Ayers
Rock 868

Simpson Desert

Basin

Hamersley Range

Gibson Desert

AUSTRALIA

Great Artesian

Fraser
Island

Brisbane

Norfolk

Lau Ridge

Carnarvon

Great
Victoria Desert

Lake Eyre

-12

Basin

Cape Byron

Lord-Howe

Three Kings
Ridge

4188

L'Esperance
Rock

1143

Geraldton

Perth

Nullarbor plain

Flinders Ranges

Broken Hill

Charleville

Darling

Sydney

Lord Howe Rise

Norfolk Ridge

North Cape

10047 m

Vitiaz III Deep

5792

Diamantina
Deep 6857

Cape Leeuwin

Great
Australian Bight

Adelaide

2281
Canberra

Murray

Mt. Kosciusko

Auckland

Diamantina
Trench

7102

Albany

5709

Kangaroo
Island

Melbourne

Tasman Sea

North Island
2797

Chatham Rise

4716

South Australian

Bass Strait

King Island

Furneaux Group

Tasman

5176

South Island

Cook Strait

Wellington

Chatham
Islands

Basin

1617

Tasmania

Hobart

Basin

3764
Mt. Cook

Christchurch

INDIAN OCEAN

South
East Cape

South Tasman
Rise

Stewart Island

Dunedin

1298

New Zealand

Bounty Islands

Scale 1:50,000,000

0 500 1000 1500 2000 Kilometers
0 500 1000 1500 Miles

03
60°
04
50°
05
40°
06
30°
07
20°
08
10°
09
8
0°
10
10°
11
20°
12
30°
13
40°
14
50°
15

Hudson
Bay

Labrador
Peninsula

Coast of Labrador

ROCKY MOUNTAINS
Coast Mountains
Mt. Waddington
4016
Vancouver
Island
Vancouver
Mt. Rainier
4392
Coast Mountains

Peace

Edmonton
Calgary

Churchill

Nelson

Lake
Winnipeg

Winnipeg

James Bay

Laurentides

Duluth
Lake
Superior

Lake
Michigan

Lake Huron

Ottawa
Québec
St.Lawrence River

Halifax
Nova
Scotia

NORTH AMERICA

Great
Salt Lake

Grand Teton
4498

Great
Basin

Denver

4399
Mt. Elbort

4343

Northeast

Mendocino Fracture Zone

San Francisco

Mt. Whitney
4418
-86
Mojave
Desert

Baldy Peak
3476

Los Angeles
San Diego

Phoenix

Colorado

Rio Grande

El Paso

Ciudad Juárez

Missouri

Chicago

Lake Ontario
Lake Erie

Ohio

St. Louis

Arkansas

Mississippi

Dallas

Mississippi

New York

Washington D.C.

Norfolk
Cape Hatteras

Cape Cod

Appalachian Mountains

Tennessee River

2037

ATLANTIC

North American

Murray Fracture Zone

OCEAN

Pacific

Isla de
Guadalupe

Lower California

Gulf of California

Tropic of Cancer

4465

La Paz

Cabo San Lucas

Mexican Plateau

Monterrey

Rio Bravo del Norte

Houston

New Orleans

Gulf of
Mexico

Florida

Jacksonville

Cape Canaveral

Miami

Straits of Florida

Havana

Bahama
Islands

Cuba

Cape Hatteras

OCEAN

North American
Basin

Guadalajara

Islas Revillagigedo

Clarion Fracture Zone

4425
Basin

Île Clipperton

Popocatepetl
5464

Mexico City

Yucatán
Peninsula

Mérida

Hispaniola

Cayman Trench

Greater Antilles

Jamaica

Puerto Rico Trench
9219 Milwaukee Deep

Puerto
Rico

Guadeloupe

Tajumulco
4220

Guatemala
San Salvador

Middle America Trench

6663
Guatemala
Basin

Managua
Lago de Nicaragua

San José
Chirripó
3820

Panamá
5775

Caribbean Sea

Punta Gallinas
P.Colón Maracaibo

Lesser Antilles

Caracas

Trinidad

Cocos Island

Cocos Ridge

Gulf of Panama

Isla de Malpelo

Bogotá

Llanos de
Orinoco

Orinoco

Nev. del Huila
5750

Guiana
Highlands

Mt.Roraima
2810

myra Atoll
4371

Teraina
Tabuaeran
Kiritimati
Atoll

226

Jarvis I.

Malden Island
Starbuck I.

5065

POLYNESIA

Manihiki
Atoll

451

Pernhyn
Atoll

Equator

4114

Galápagos Fracture Zone

Clipperton Fracture Zone

4060

Galápagos Islands

Quito

Chimborazo
6310

Pico da
Neblina
3014 Rio Negro

Selvas

Manaus

Amazon

Amazon Lowland

Iquitos

Punta Aguja

4146

6768
Huascarán

Rio Branco

Madeira

Marquesas
Islands

Hiva Oa

Caroline Atoll

Flint Atoll

4755

Tuamotu Archipelago

Rangiroa Atoll
Îles du
Désappointement

Fakarava Atoll

Makemo Atoll

3694

Lima

SOUTH AMERICA

6601

Peru
Basin

La Paz

ANDES

6520
Sajama

Motu One
Atoll
Île Raiatea
Society Islands
Aitutaki-
Atoll
Manuae-
Atoll

Papeete
Tahiti

Hao Atoll

4572

Reao Atoll

4385

Maria
Atoll

Avarua
Rarotonga 4845
Atoll

Tematangi
Atoll

Tubuai Islands

Raevavae

Rapa

Bass

Mururoa

Gambier

4645

Tuamotu Ridge

Tureia Atoll

3429

Oeno

Pitcairn
Island

Ducie

Adamstown

Tropic of Capricorn

Sala-y-Gómez

Easter Island

Sala-y-Gomez-Fracture Zone

4124

Nazca Ridge

8055

Islas de los
Desventuradas

6887
Nev.Ojos
del Salado

Aconcagua
6965

Chile Trench

Gran Chaco

Córdoba

Pampas

PACIFIC OCEAN

Southwest

5121

Pacific

Basin

2836

4248

East Pacific Rise

Pacific

3884

Islas Juan-Fernández

Chile
Basin

Chile Rise

Santiago

Puerto Montt

Chiloé

Patagonia

ANDES

4058
Co.S.Valentin

I. Wellington

Comodoro
Rivadavia

Falkland Islands

Punta Arenas
Strait of Magellan

Tierra del Fuego

Cape Horn
Drake Passage

Alaska
Peninsula

Gulf of Alaska

OCEAN

Nihoa
Kauai
Oahu
Maui
Mauna Kea
4205
Hawaii

Hawaii

Italy: The beautiful rolling hills of Tuscany.

Budapest: The Parliament on the bank of the Danube River.

EUROPE

THE OLD CONTINENT

With an area of 10.5 million km², Europe is the second smallest continent in size. Separated in the east from Asia by the Ural Mountains, Europe extends more than 5,000 kilometers to the western coast of Ireland and more than 4,000 kilometers from the North Cape to Crete in the Mediterranean north to south. The Atlantic Ocean marks the western borders of Europe, the Mediterranean and Black Sea border the continent in the south and the Arctic Ocean lies to the north.

The topography of Southern and Central Europe is dominated by a bow-shaped series of mountain chains. The mountain system extends from the Sierra Nevada, to the Pyrenees, the Alps, and the Carpathian Mountains. North of this mountain belt lies a series of medium elevation ranges – including the French Massif Central, the Harz Mountains, and the Tatras – that gives way to the plains of northern and Central Europe. One of the most striking features of Europe's geography is the large number of peninsulas (Scandinavia, Iberia, Greece, etc.) on the continent. The European mainland is also surrounded by many islands, including Great Britain and Iceland.

With a population of 740 million, Europe is the third most populous continent. Several European states have populations exceeding 50 million – including Italy, France, the United Kingdom, Russia, and Germany. Immigrants from outside Europe have changed the faces of many once homogenous European nations since the second half of the 20th century.

With the relatively recent political development in Eastern Europe – the collapse of the Soviet Union for example – many new states have emerged on the continent. The migration of people from eastern to western Europe and between southern and northern Europe continues to bring the continent's diverse cultures and nations closer together.

The Alps: Matterhorn (4,478 m).

Europe

Greenland

Kong Christian X Land

Kong Frederik VIII Land

Kong Christian IX Land

Greenland Sea

Nordaustlandet

1717 ▲

Svalbard

Edgøya

Bear Islands

Novaya Zemlya

1547 ▲

Kara Sea

Gydanskiy P-ov

Yamal P-ov

West

Siberian

Plain

380

Barents Sea

Pečorskoe more

1894 ▲

Ob

03

Arctic Circle

Denmark Strait

Jan Mayen

Greenland Basin

3069

Greenland Basin

North Cape

3188

Norwegian Sea

Lofoten Basin

Lofoten

Murmansk

Kola Peninsula

White Sea

Timanskiy Kryazh

U · R · A · L

Iceland

Reykjavik

Grímsvötn 1719 ▲

832

Iceland Basin

465

Norwegian Basin

Faroe Islands

2111 ▲ Kebnekaise

Scandinavia

Lapland

Karelia

Syktyvkar

1569 ▲

YEKATERINBURG

PERM'

M · T · S

60°

ATLANTIC

Rockall Plateau

Shetland Islands

Rockall Trough

Hébrides

Orkney Islands

Ben Nevis 1343 ▲

Jotunheimen 2472 ▲

Bergen

Oslo

Oulu

Umeå

Gulf of Bothnia

Helsinki Helsingfors

ST.PETERSBURG

Lake Onega

Lake Ladoga

Stednerusskaja vozvyšennost'

Volga Upland

UFA

KAZAN'

SAMARA

Oral

04

Ireland

OCEAN

Dublin

Cork

BIRMINGHAM

Edinburgh

Pennines

North Sea

Great Britain

240

Jutland

Stockholm

Vänern

Göteborg

459

Gotland

Riga

Lake Peipus

NIŽNIJ NOVGOROD

MOSCOW

Orel

E

P

50°

Celtic Sea

LONDON

Land's End

Amsterdam

English Channel

BRUSSELS

COLOGNE

Copenhagen

HAMBURG

BERLIN

Bornholm

Baltic Sea

Gdańsk

MINSK

WARSAW

Vistula

Elbe

KIEV

Dnieper

O

R

Don

VOLGOGRAD

ROSTOV-NA-DONU

Manych Depression

Caspian Depression

Caspian Sea

8

05

5465

Brittany

Normandie

PARIS

E

Bay of Biscay

Burgundy

Loire

Rhône

Bérne

Massif 1885 ▲ Central

Lyon

Mt.Blanc 4807 ▲

A

Rhône

Provence

Sudetes

PRAGUE

Cracow

Beskid Mts

L'viv

Dniester

DNIPROPETROVS'K

ODESSA

Crimea

g.Elbrus 5642 ▲

CAUCASUS

TBILISI

MUNICH

VIENNA

BUDAPEST

2100 ▲

L

P

S

3797 ▲

MILAN

Po

Zagreb

Alföld

Carpathian Mts

Transylvanian Alps

2544 ▲

BUCHAREST

Danube

Varna

2180

Black Sea

Trabzon

Pontic Mountains

YEREVAN

Ararat 5137 ▲

04

La Coruña

Cabo Fisterra

Gijón

Bordeaux

Cantabria Mountains

Pyrénées

3404 ▲ Pico d'Aneto

Marseille

E

Apennines

Adriatic Sea

Dinaric Alps

Dalmatia

BELGRADE

SOFIA

Balkan Mts.

Rhodope Mts.

Tiranë

İSTANBUL

ANKARA

Anatolia

A

Van Gölü

Vani

AL-MAWSIL

40°

Porto

LISBON

Cordillera Central

Sistema Ibérico

Ebro

MADRID

València

Palma d.M.

Sierra Morena

Sevilla

Cordillera Bética

Granada

3481 ▲

Corsica 2622 ▲

ROME

Sardinia

Balearic Islands

2784

1834 ▲

2914 ▲

NAPLES

Vesúvio 1281 ▲

Tyrrhenian Sea

Olymp 2917 ▲

Pindus Mts

Aegean Sea

ATHENS

İZMİR

Taurus Mts.

3524 ▲

ADANA

ALEPPO

Euphrate

A

S

06

Tangier

RABAT

CASABLANCA

MARRAKECH

AR-RIF

Haut Atlas

Fès

Oran

ALGIERS

2305 ▲

Constantine

TUNIS

Sicily

Palermo

Etna 3323 ▲

1955 ▲

Ionian Sea

Peloponnesus

5054

Rhodes

Crete

2456 ▲

2427

Cyprus

Levantine Basin

BEIRUT

DAMASCUS

JerusalemN

AMMAN

Al Widyan

An Nafud

Hejaz

30°

MARRAKECH

Hamada du Drâa

Béchar

Atlas Tellien

Atlas Saharien

Great Western Erg

Île de Jerba

Sfax

MEDITERRANEAN SEA

TRIPOLI

Tripolitania

Gulf of Sirte

Sahra Surt

Benghazi

882 ▲

Cyrenaica

Tubruq

ALEXANDRIA

Qattara Depression

734 ▼

1207

CAIRO

Port Said

Sinai

2285 ▲

El Aqaba

Eastern Desert

Red Sea

07

Erg Iguidi

Erg Chech

A

Tropic of Cancer

Taoudenni

S

Djebel Timétrine

Tanezrouft

Asedirad

Adrar

Tahat 2918 ▲

A Hoggar

Plateau du Tademaït

Hamada de Tinrhert

Tassili n'Ajjer

2158 ▲

F

Ténéré du Tafassasset

Tassili du Hoggar

Awbari Sahra

Fezzan

R

Al Jufra Oasis

Sarir Tibesti

Pic Touside 3376 ▲

Tarso Emissi 3315 ▲

Tibesti

Ramlat Rabyanah

El Kufrah Oasis

C

Libyan Desert

Great Sand Sea

1893 ▲ Djebel Al Awaynat

Erdi

A

Western Desert

Nile

Luxor

Aswân

Lake Nasser

Nubian Desert

Nubia

Ràs Banas

2300 ▲

Djebel Musbih 1445 ▲

Port Sudan

Nile

08

Scale 1:22,000,000

| 0 | 250 | 500 | 750 | Kilometers |

| 0 | 250 | 500 | Miles |

Hb 50° Ja 40° Jb 30° Ka 20° Kb 10° La 0° Lb 10° 20° 5 30° Mb 40° Na 50° Nb 60° Oa 70° Ob

50° 40° 30° 20° 10° 0° 10° 20° 5 30° 40° 50° 60° 70°

Greenland
Kalaallit Nunaat
(DK)

Greenland
Sea

Svalbard (N)

Novaya Zemlya

B a r e n t s   S e a

Nojabr'sk

03

Vorkuta

Jan Mayen (N)

Denmark Strait

N o r w e g i a n

S e a

Tromsø

Murmansk

Komi

60°

Akureyri

Reykjavik

ICELAND   Seyðisfjörður

Kiruna

Uhta

Serov

NORWAY

Arhangel'sk

Syktyvkár

Oulu

FINLAND

RUSSIA

YEKATERINBURG

04

Faroe Islands (DK)
Tórshavn

Trondheim

Umeå

Karelia

Petrozavodsk

Kostroma

PERM'

Kirov

Bergen

SWEDEN

Vaasa

Udmurtia

UFA

ATLANTIC

Stavanger

Oslo

Turku
Åbo

Uppsala

Helsinki
Helsingfors

ST.PETERSBURG

Novgorod

Rybinsk

Mari-El

KAZAN'

Bashkortostan

Tatarstan

Aberdeen

North Sea

Stockholm

Tallinn

ESTONIA

Pskov

NIŽNIJ
NOVGOROD

Chuvashia

Orenburg

Glasgow   Edinburgh

Norrköping

MOSCOW

Mordvinia

Simbirsk

SAMARA

Oral

50°

Belfast   UNITED KINGDOM

Aalborg

Göteborg

LATVIA

Riga

Smolensk

KAZAKHSTAN

Dublin   Liverpool   Leeds

Newcastle

Århus

Copenhagen   Malmö

Klaipėda

Baltic Sea

LITHUANIA

Vilnius

MINSK

Orel

Voronež

Saratov

Èngel's

IRELAND

Cork

BIRMINGHAM

DENMARK

Odense

Gdańsk

RUSSIA

BELARUS

Homel'

Astrahan'

NETHERLANDS

Amsterdam

HAMBURG

Szczecin

Poznań

WARSAW

Brèst

VOLGOGRAD

OCEAN

Plymouth

LONDON

The Hague

Hannover

BERLIN

POLAND

Łódź

Lublin

Rivne

UKRAINE

KIEV

CHARKIV

DONEC'K

ROSTOV-
NA-DONU

Kalmykia

53

Brest

BRUSSELS   COLOGNE
BELGIUM

Dortmund

Frankfurt

Dresden

Wrocław

Cracow

L'viv

DNIPROPETROVS'K

Dagestan

Mahackala

PARIS   LUXEMBOURG

Nürnberg

PRAGUE

Brno

CZECH REPUBLIC

SLOVAKIA

Bratislava

BUDAPEST

MOLDOVA

Chisinău

ODESSA

Krasnodar   Adygea

Karachay-
Cherkessia

Stavropol'

Kab.
Balk.

Chechenja

TIBILISI

Nantes

FRANCE

Strasbourg

Stuttgart

MUNICH

Zürich

Berne   SWITZERL

VIENNA

AUSTRIA

Graz

HUNGARY

Cluj-Napoca

ROMANIA

Sevastopol'

Soči

GEORGIA

Limoges

LIECHTEN-
STEIN

SLOVENIA

Ljubljana

Zagreb

BUCHAREST

Batumi

ARMENIA

40°

La Coruña

Gijón

Bilbao

Bordeaux

Lyon

MILAN

Turin

Venice

Genoa

CROATIA

BOSNIA AND
HERZEGOVINA

BELGRADE

SERBIA

Black Sea

Varna

Samsun

Trabzon

Erzurum

YEREVAN

IRAN

Van

Porto

Toulouse

Nice

MONACO

SAN MARINO

Florence

Sarajevo

Podgorica

BULGARIA

SOFIA

İSTANBUL

PORTUGAL

Zaragoza

ANDORRA

Marseille

ITALY

MONTENEGRO

Tiranë

Skopje

MACEDONIEN

İZMIR

Bursa

ANKARA

TURKEY

Şanlıurfa

AL-MAWSIL

LISBON

MADRID

BARCELONA

Corsica

ROME

Bari

ALBANIA

Salonica

Konya

ADANA

ALEPPO

IRAQ

SPAIN

València

Palma d.M.

NAPLES

GREECE

Pátra

ATHENS

Antalya

SYRIA

Homs

Tripoli

Sevilla

Sardinia

Cágliari

Palermo

Messina

Catánia

MALTA

Iráklio

Nicosia

DAMASCUS

Cádiz

Granada

Alicante

Sicily

CYPRUS

BEIRUT

LEBANON

06

Tangier

Gibraltar(UK)

Ceuta(E)

Melilla(E)

Oran

ALGIERS

Annaba

TUNIS

Haifa

ISRAEL

Jerusalem

AMMAN

RABAT

Fès

Constantine

TUNISIA

Gafsa

Sfax

MEDITERRANEAN SEA

Port Said

Gaza

JORDAN

Al Jawf

CASABLANCA

MARRAKECH

El Oued

30°

MOROCCO

Bèchar

TRIPOLI

Al Khums

Misratah

Benghazi

Tubruq

ALEXANDRIA

Tanta

Suez

GIZA   CAIRO

El Aqaba

Tabuk

SAUDI
ARABIA

El Ménia

Gulf of Sirte

Ajdabiya

Siwa

El Minia

Hurghada

Duba

ALGERIA

Ghadamis

Awjilah

Sohâg

Luxor

Marsa
Alam

07

Reggane

LIBYA

EGYPT

El Kharga

Aswân

Taoudenni

20°

Tamanrasset

Al Jawf

Port Sudan

MALI

Zouar

CHAD

SUDAN

'Atbara

08

NIGER

Kb 0° La 10° Lb 20° 123 Ma 30° Mb

15

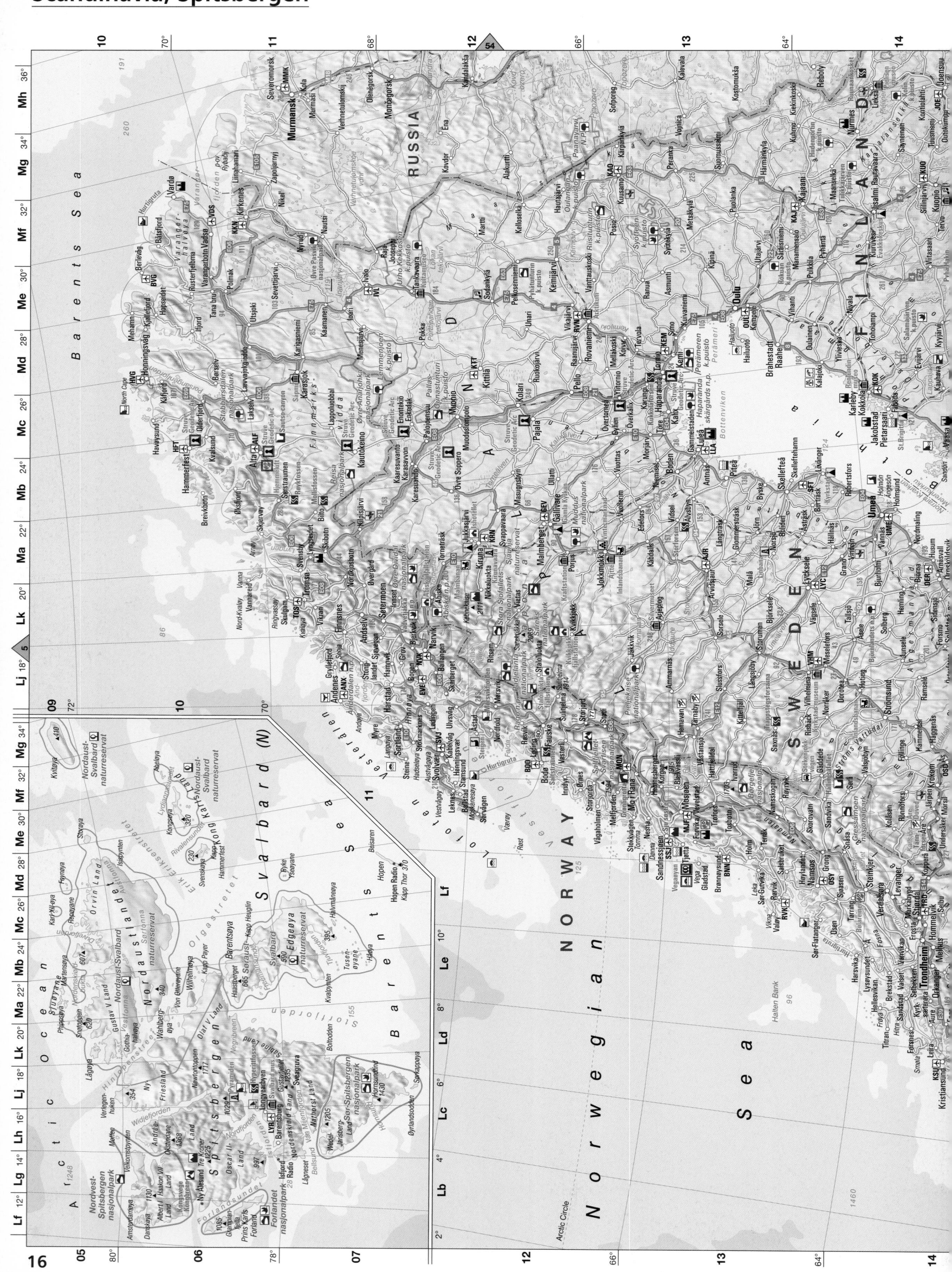

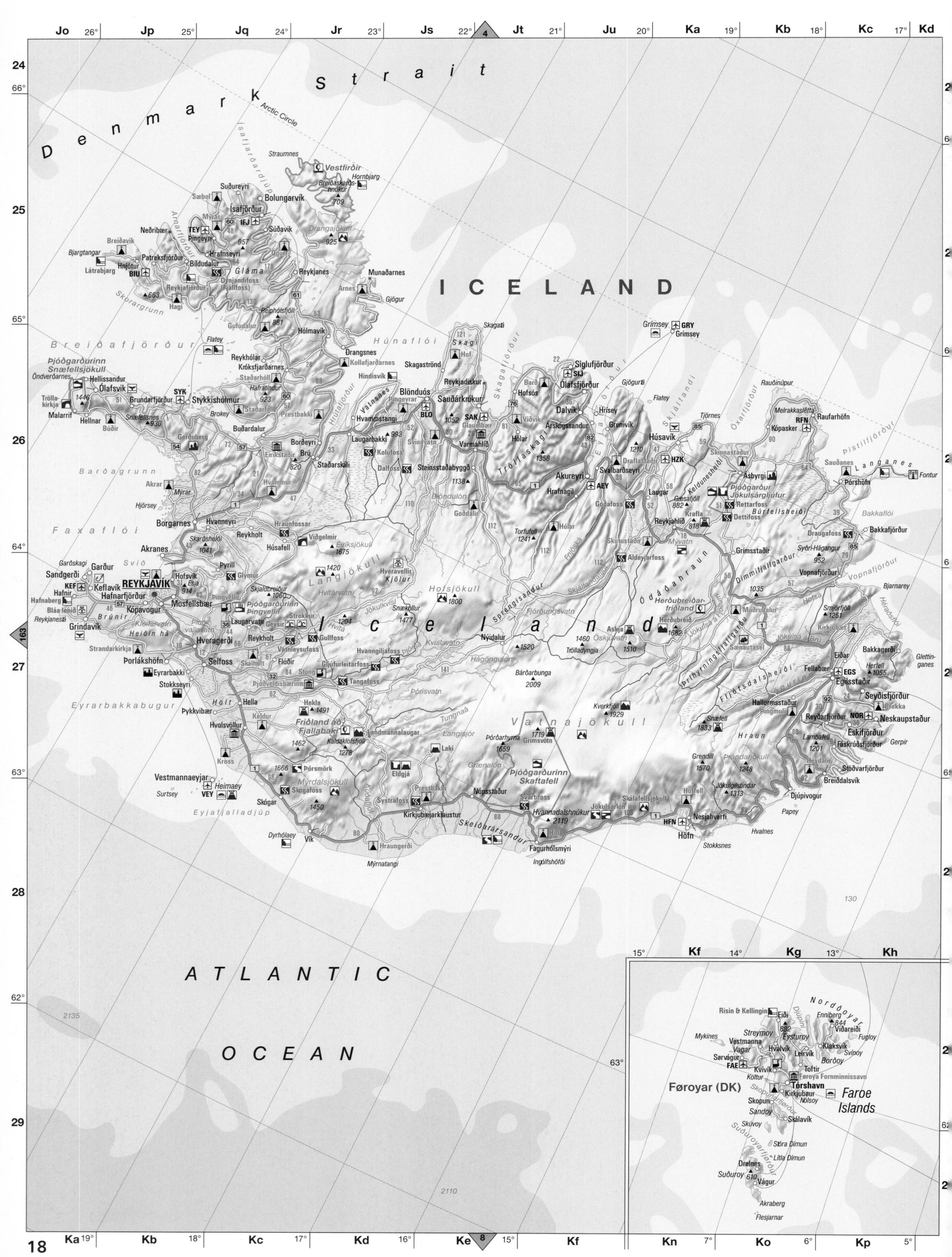

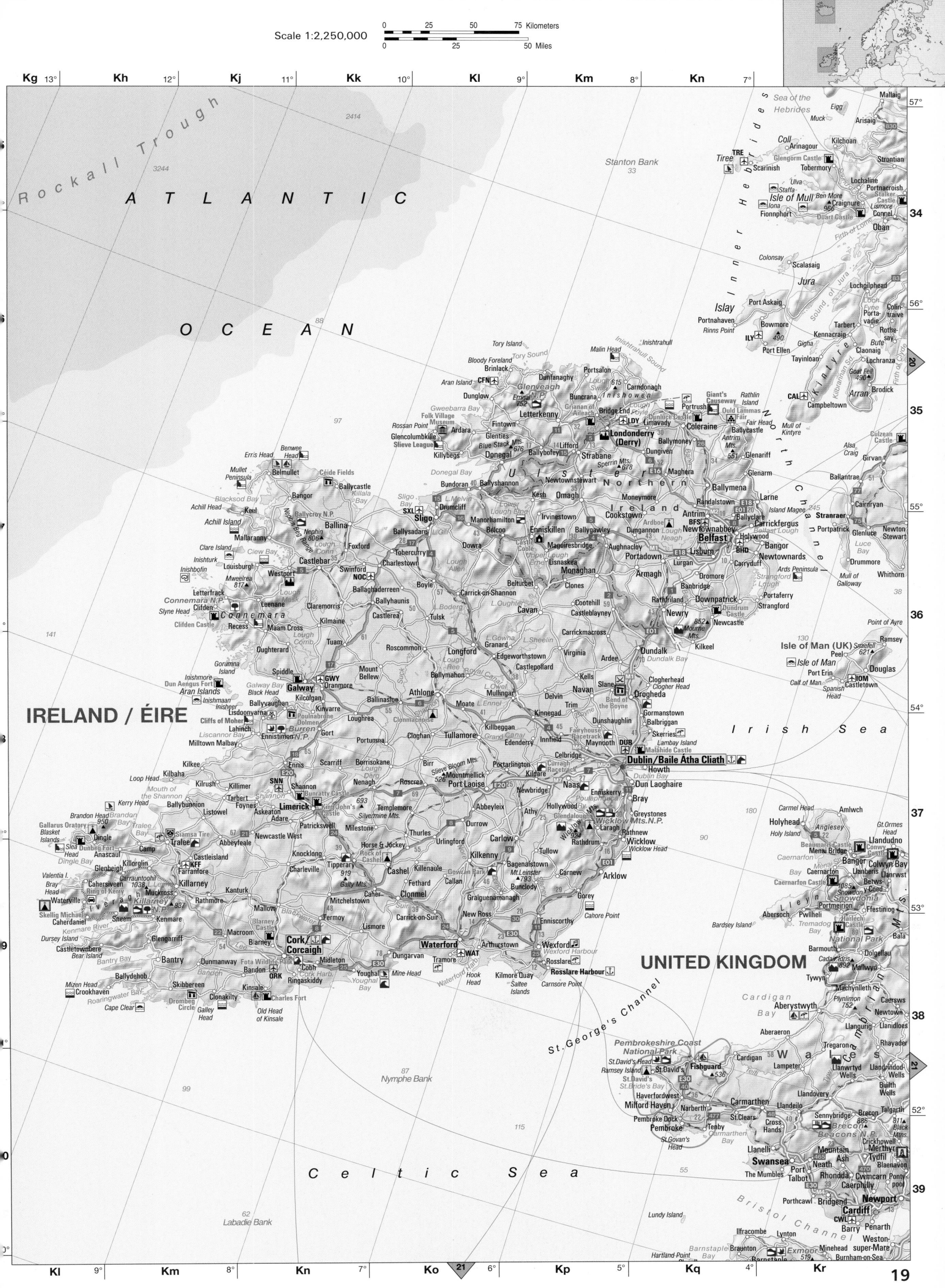

British Isles

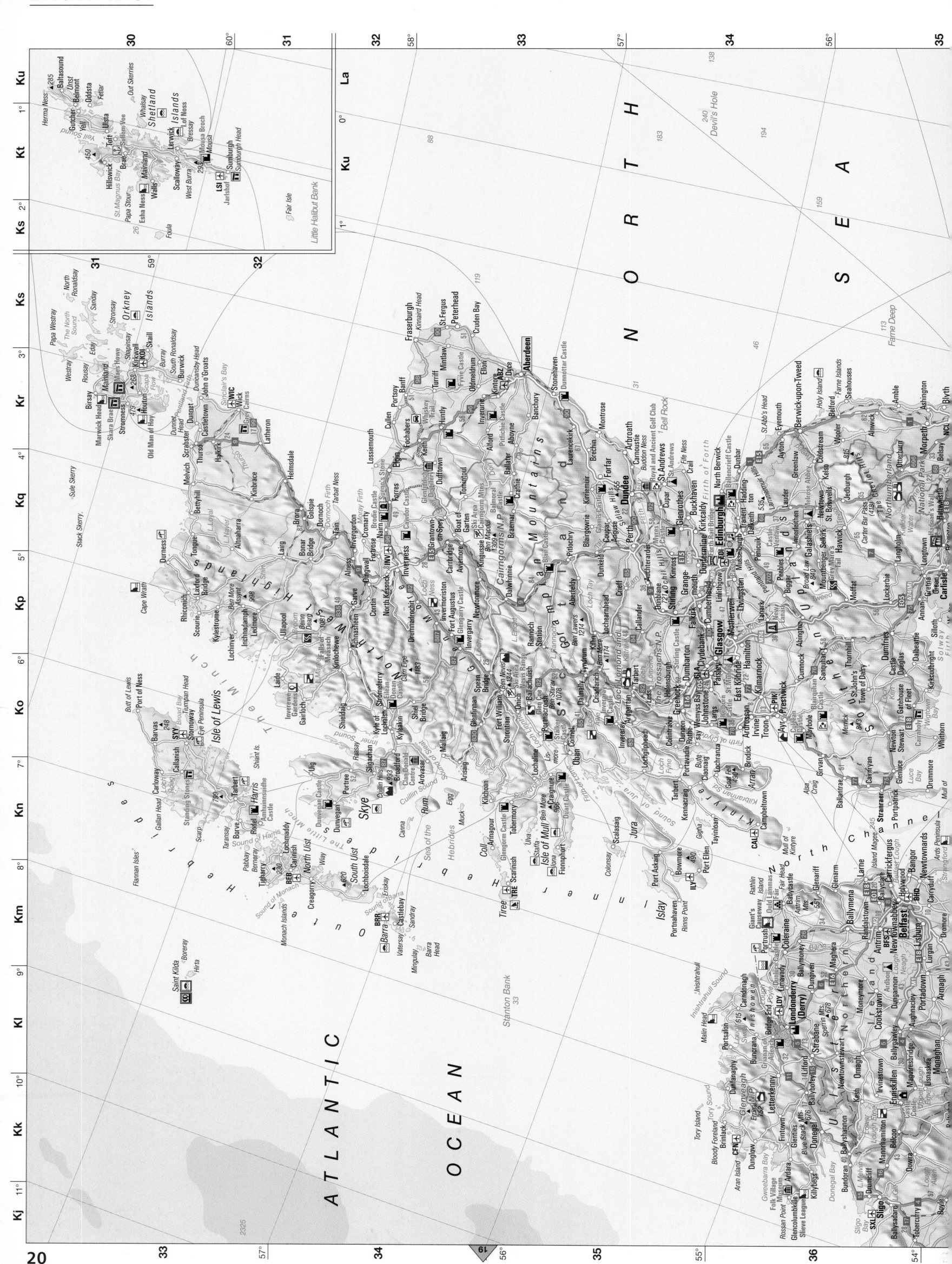

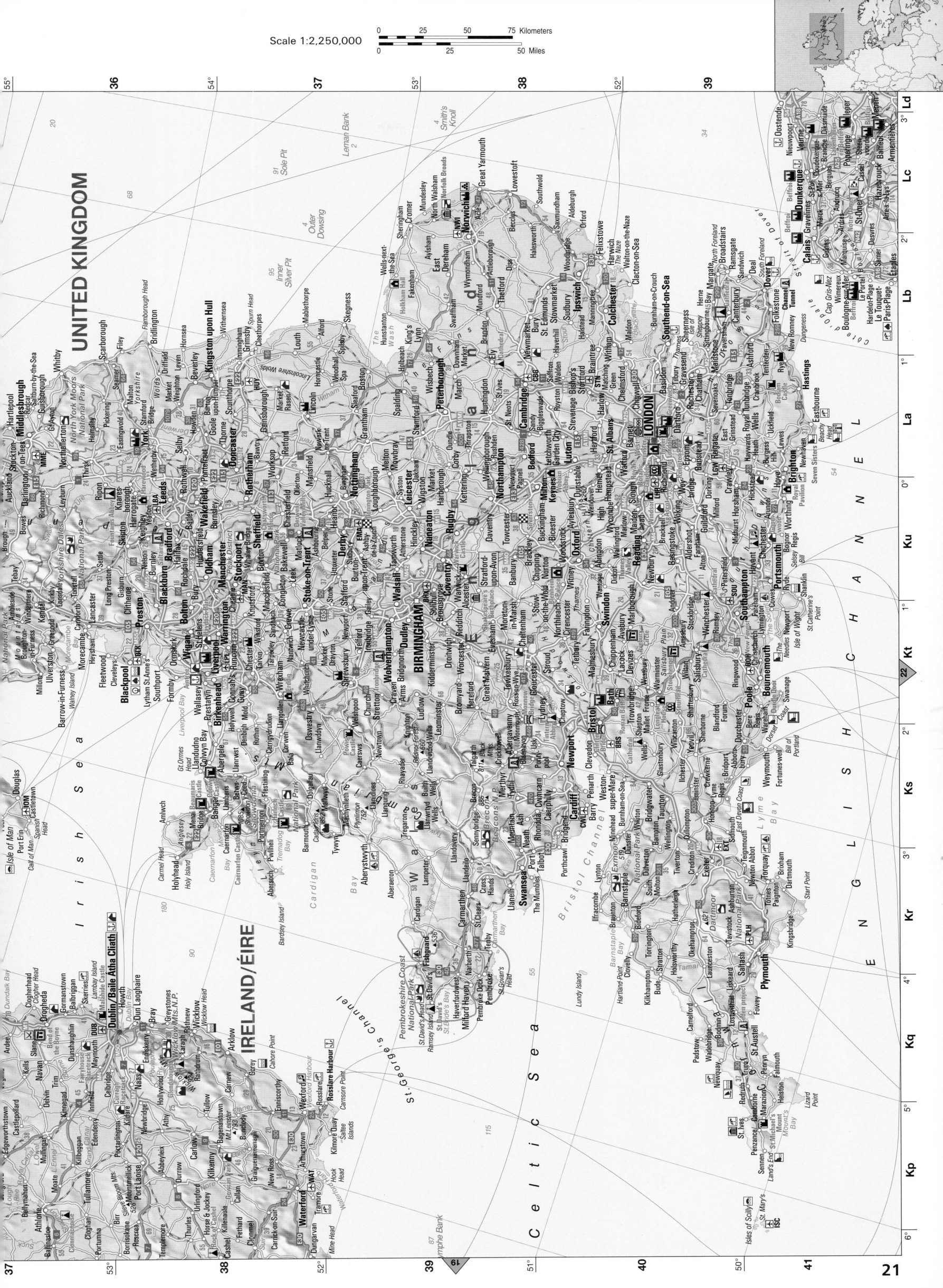

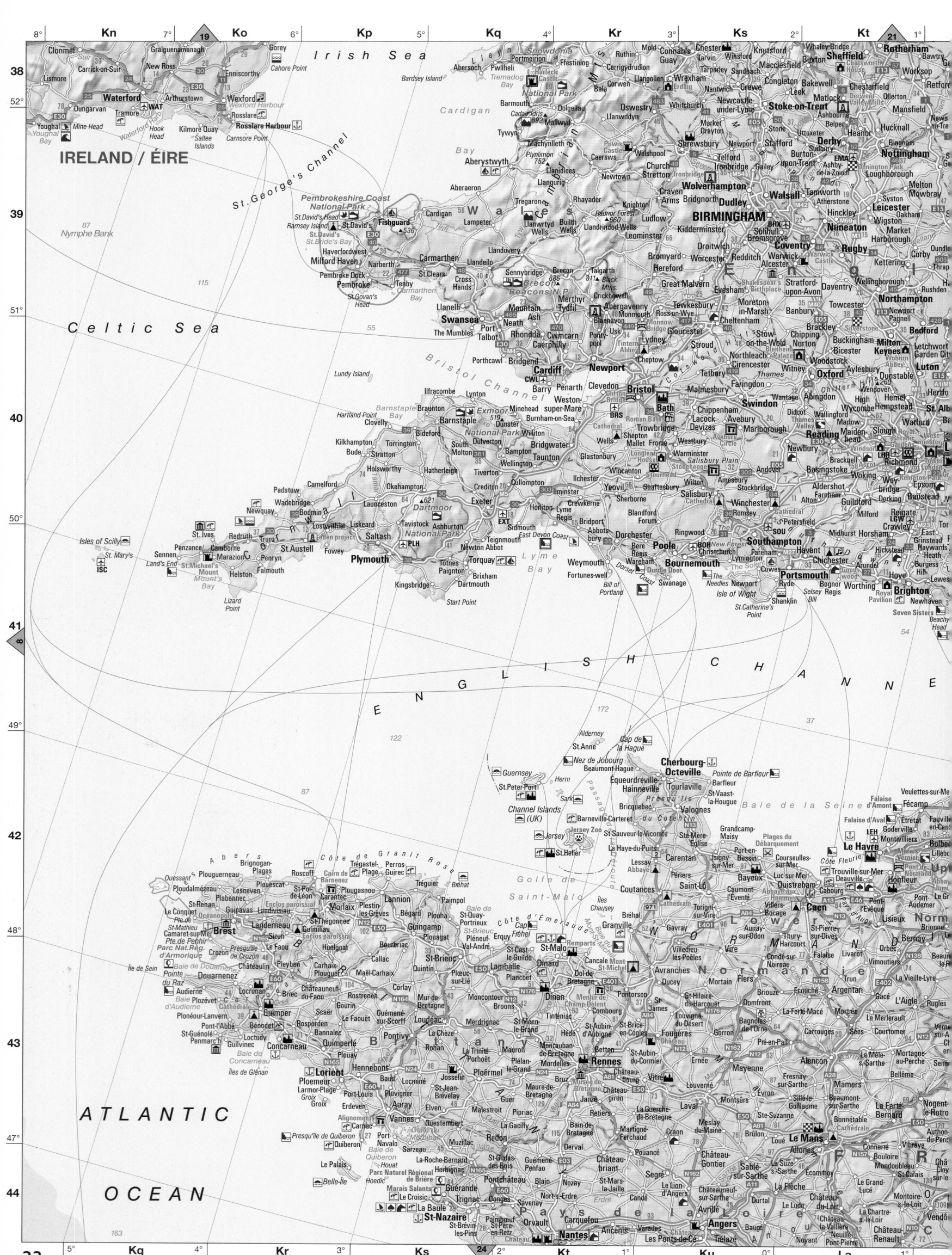

Scale 1:2,250,000

0 25 50 75 Kilometers
0   25   50 Miles

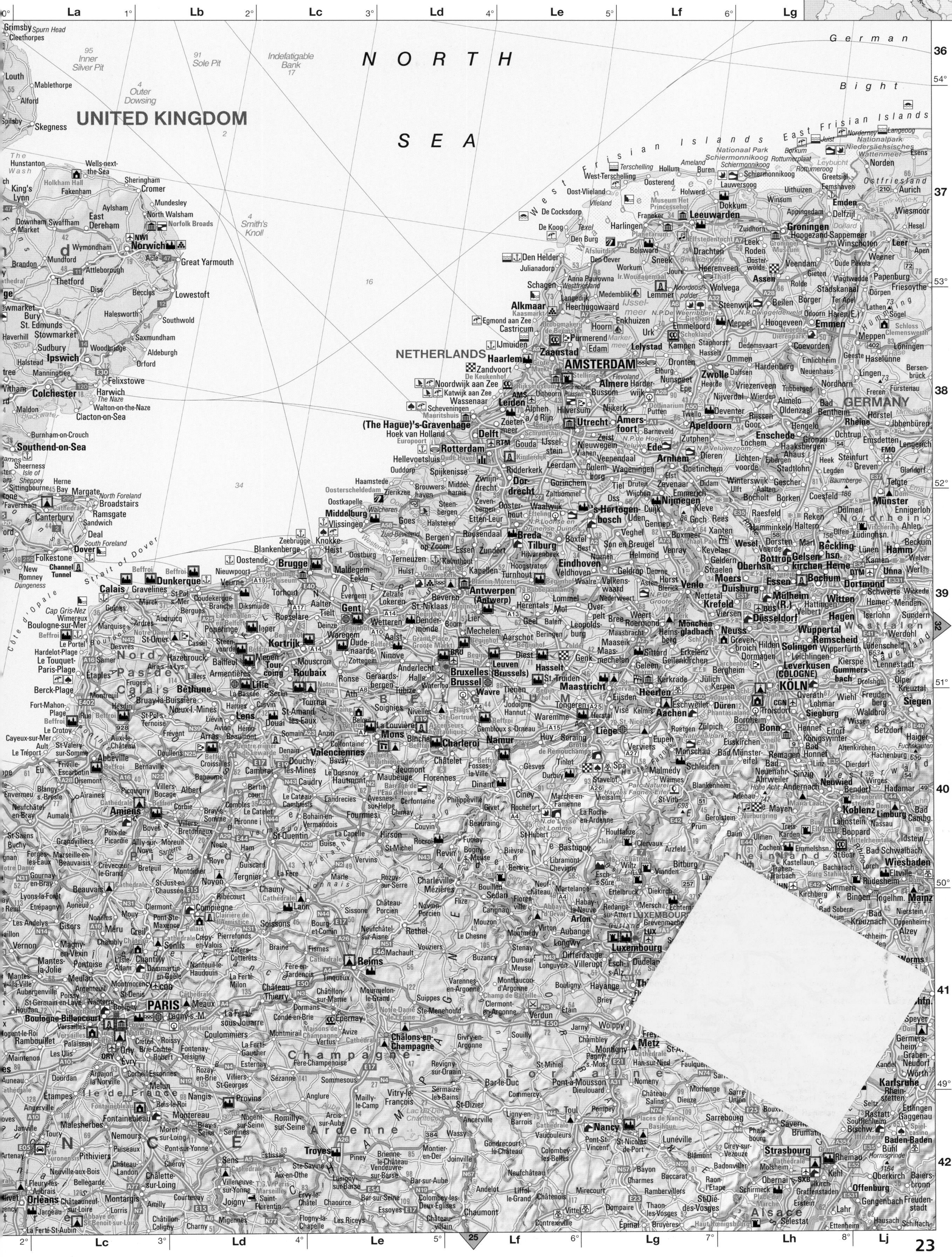

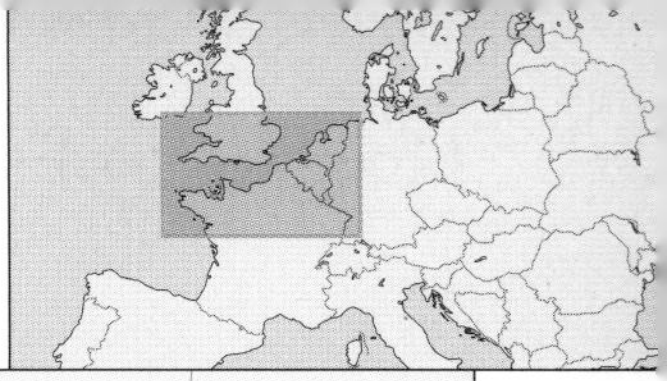

NORTH SEA

UNITED KINGDOM

NETHERLANDS

GERMANY

AMSTERDAM

BRUXELLES (Brussel)
Brussels

PARIS

LUXEMBOURG

Champagne

Lorraine

Alsace

Île-de-France

Strasbourg

23

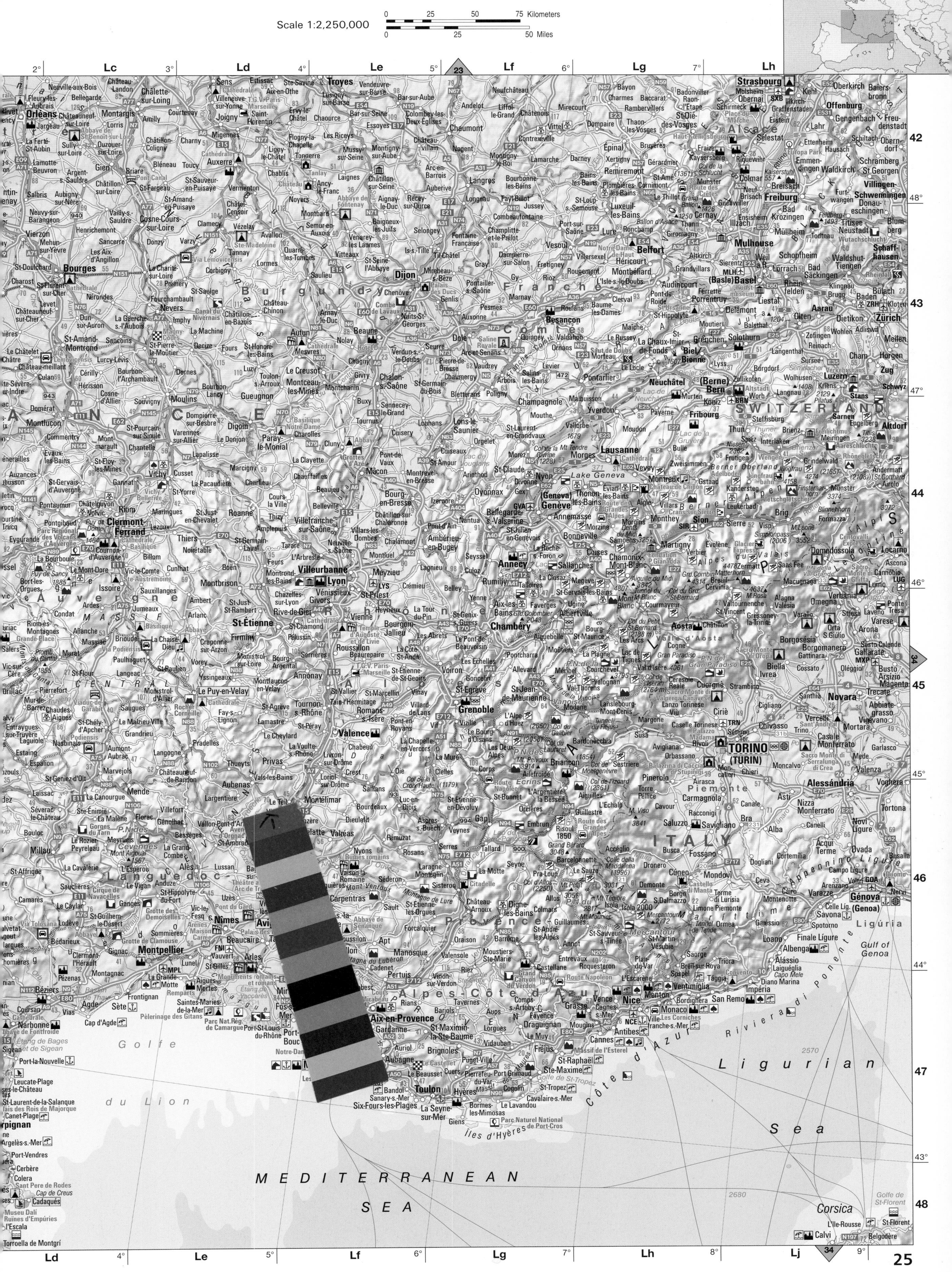

Scale 1:2,250,000

0 25 50 75 Kilometers
0 25 50 Miles

23

FRANCE / SWITZERLAND / ITALY region map

Major labels:
- Orléans, Bourges, Dijon, Troyes, Strasbourg
- Burgundy, Franche-Comté, Alsace
- Clermont-Ferrand, Lyon, Villeurbanne, St-Étienne
- Besançon, Belfort, Mulhouse, Basel, Zürich
- Neuchâtel, Bern (Berne), Fribourg, Lausanne, Geneva (Genève)
- SWITZERLAND, Berner Oberland, Interlaken
- Grenoble, Valence, Chambéry, Annecy
- Chamonix-Mont-Blanc, Aosta, Val d'Aosta
- TORINO (TURIN), Novara, Alessándria
- ITALY, Piemonte, Liguria
- Nîmes, Avignon, Montpellier, Aix-en-Provence, Arles
- Toulon, Nice, Monaco, Cannes, Antibes
- Alpes, Côte d'Azur, Provence, Languedoc
- Auvergne, Massif Central
- Narbonne, Perpignan, Béziers, Sète, Agde
- Riviera di Ponente, Génova (Genoa), San Remo, Ventimiglia
- Gulf of Genoa

Golfe du Lion

LIGURIAN Sea

MEDITERRANEAN SEA

Corsica — L'Ile-Rousse, Calvi, St-Florent

34

25

Portugal, Western Spain

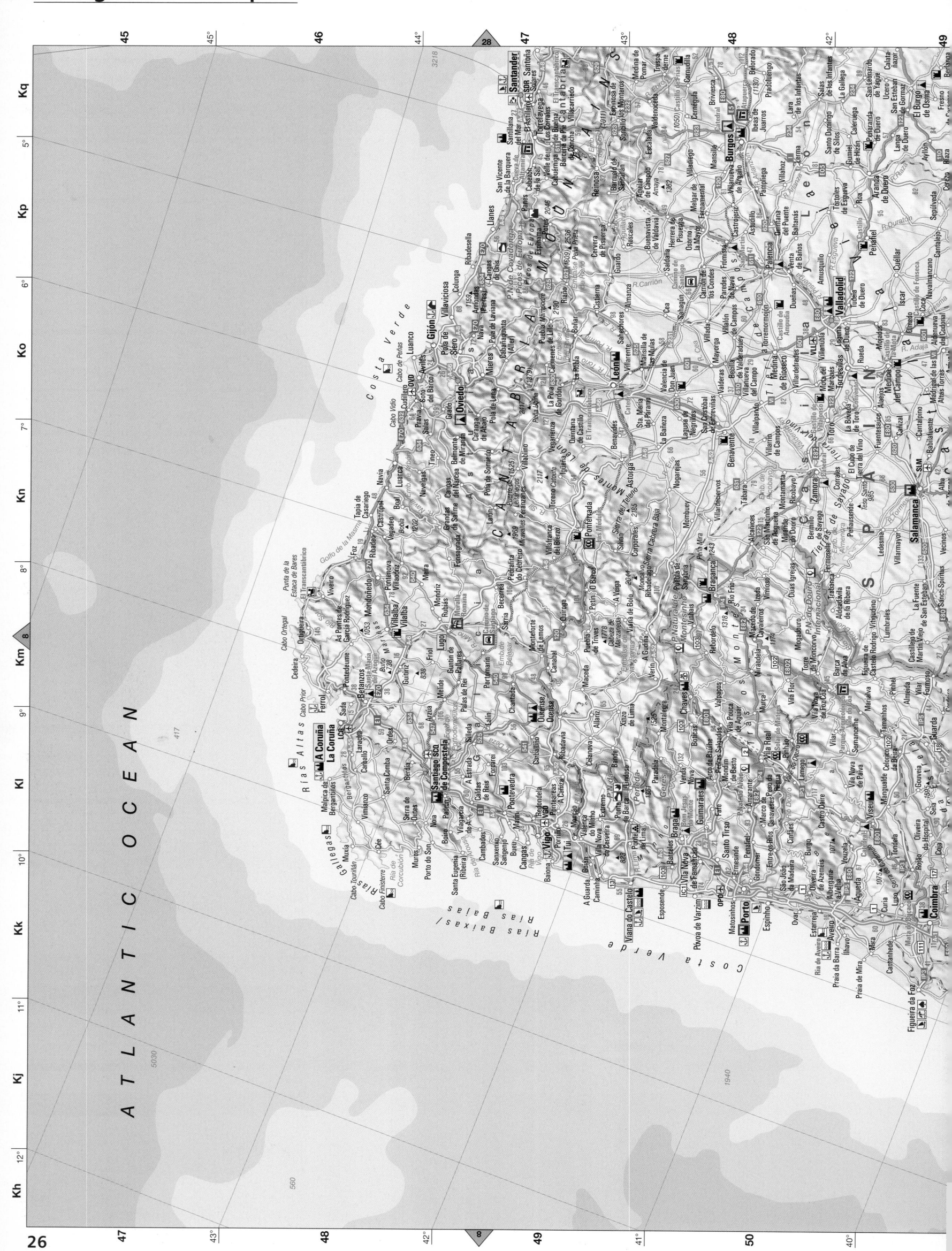

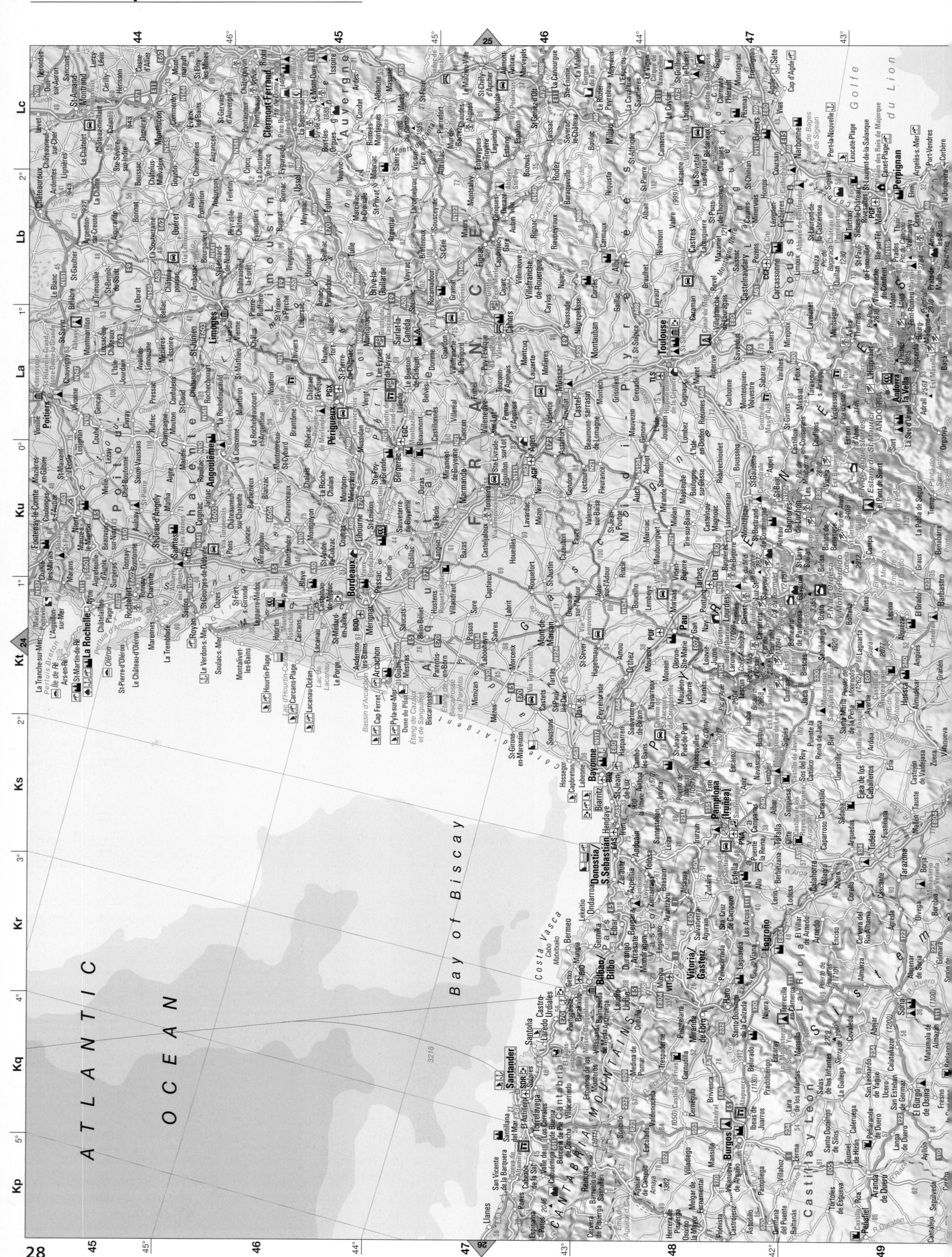

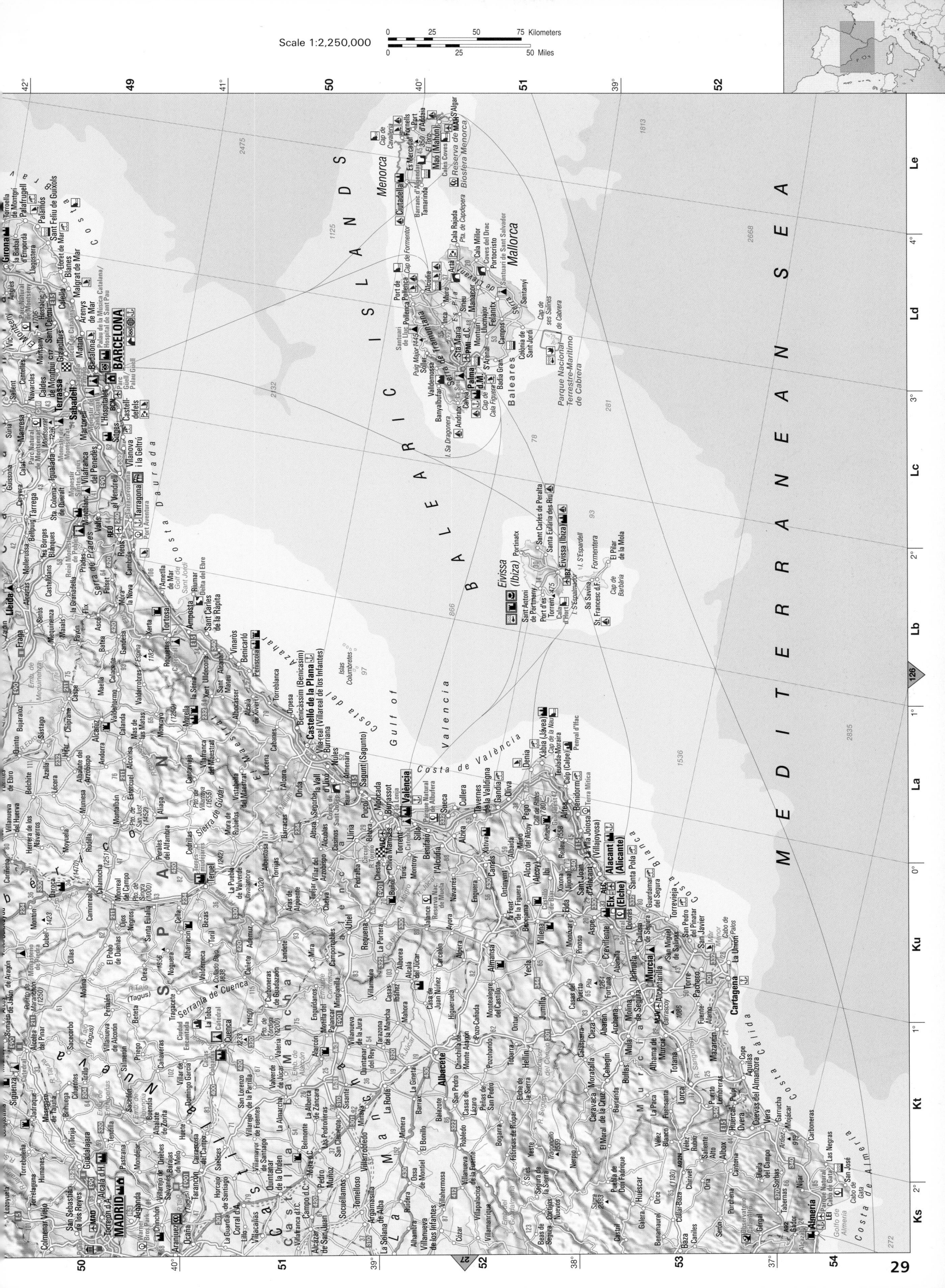

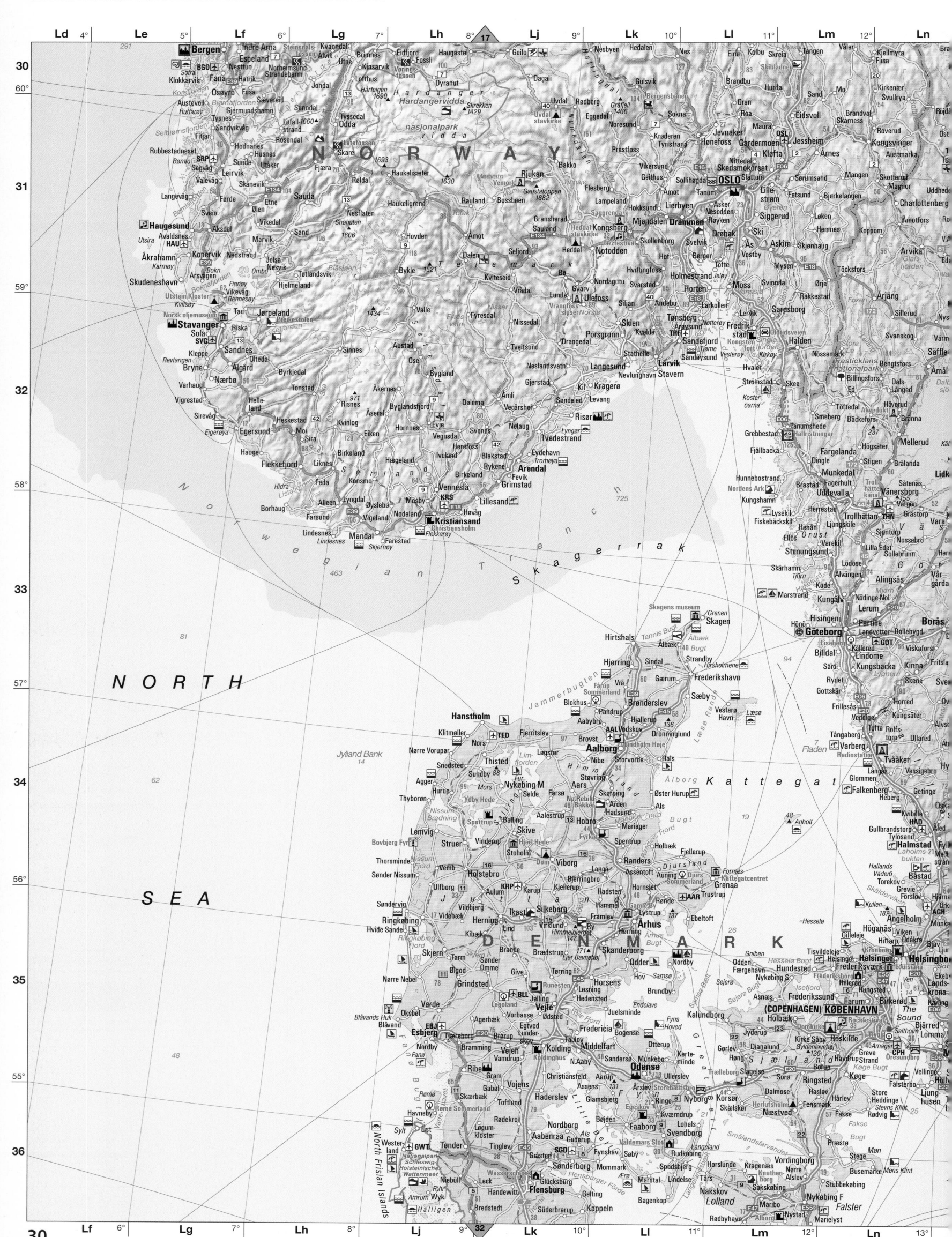

FINLAND

SWEDEN

ESTONIA

LATVIA

LITHUANIA

POLAND

RUSSIA

BALTIC SEA

Gotland

Öland

Bornholm (DK)

Åland/Ahvenanmaa

Saaremaa

Hiiumaa

STOCKHOLM

Uppsala

Turku / Åbo

Naantali

Mariehamn / Maarianhamina

Gävle

Falun

Borlänge

Västerås

Eskilstuna

Södertälje

Örebro

Karlstad

Karlskoga

Norrköping

Linköping

Jönköping

Växjö

Kalmar

Visby

Oskarshamn

Västervik

Karlskrona

Karlshamn

Ronneby

Ystad

Kristianstad

Klaipėda

Kaliningrad

Liepāja

Ventspils

Palanga

Gulf of Gdansk

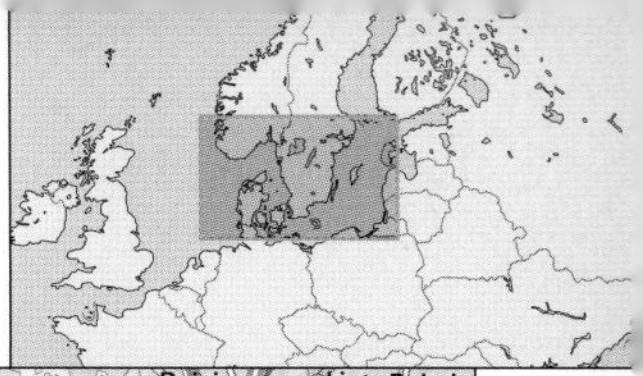

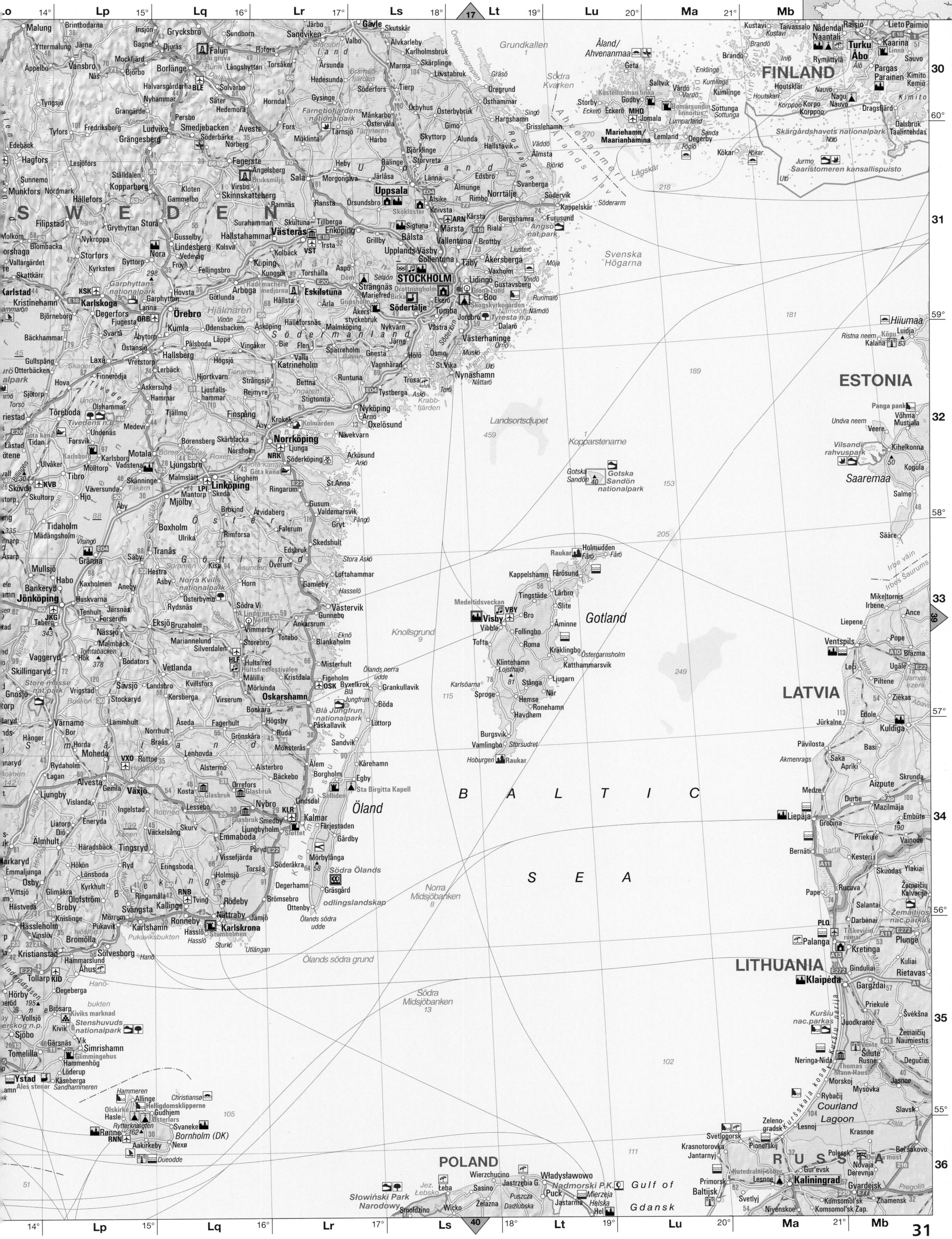

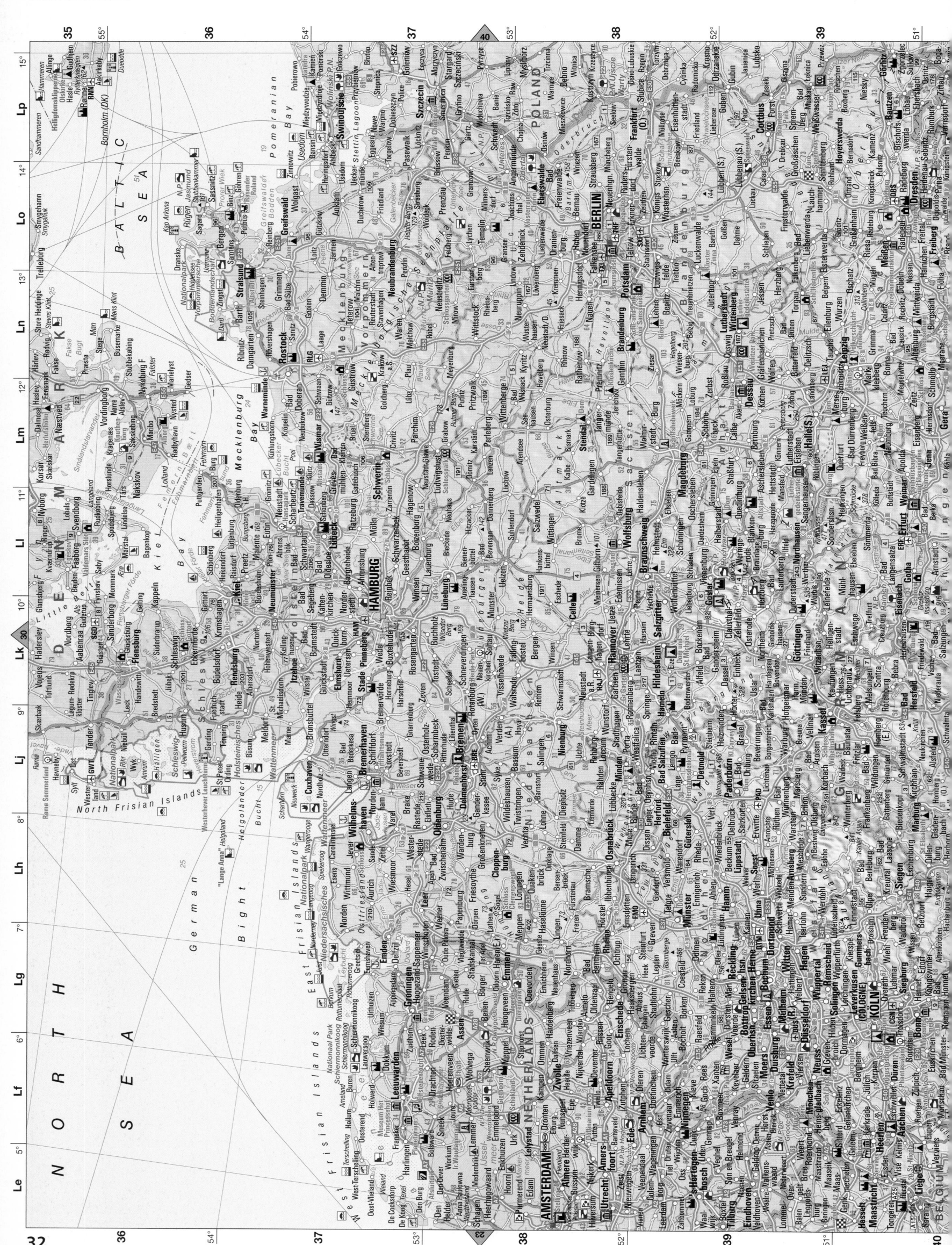

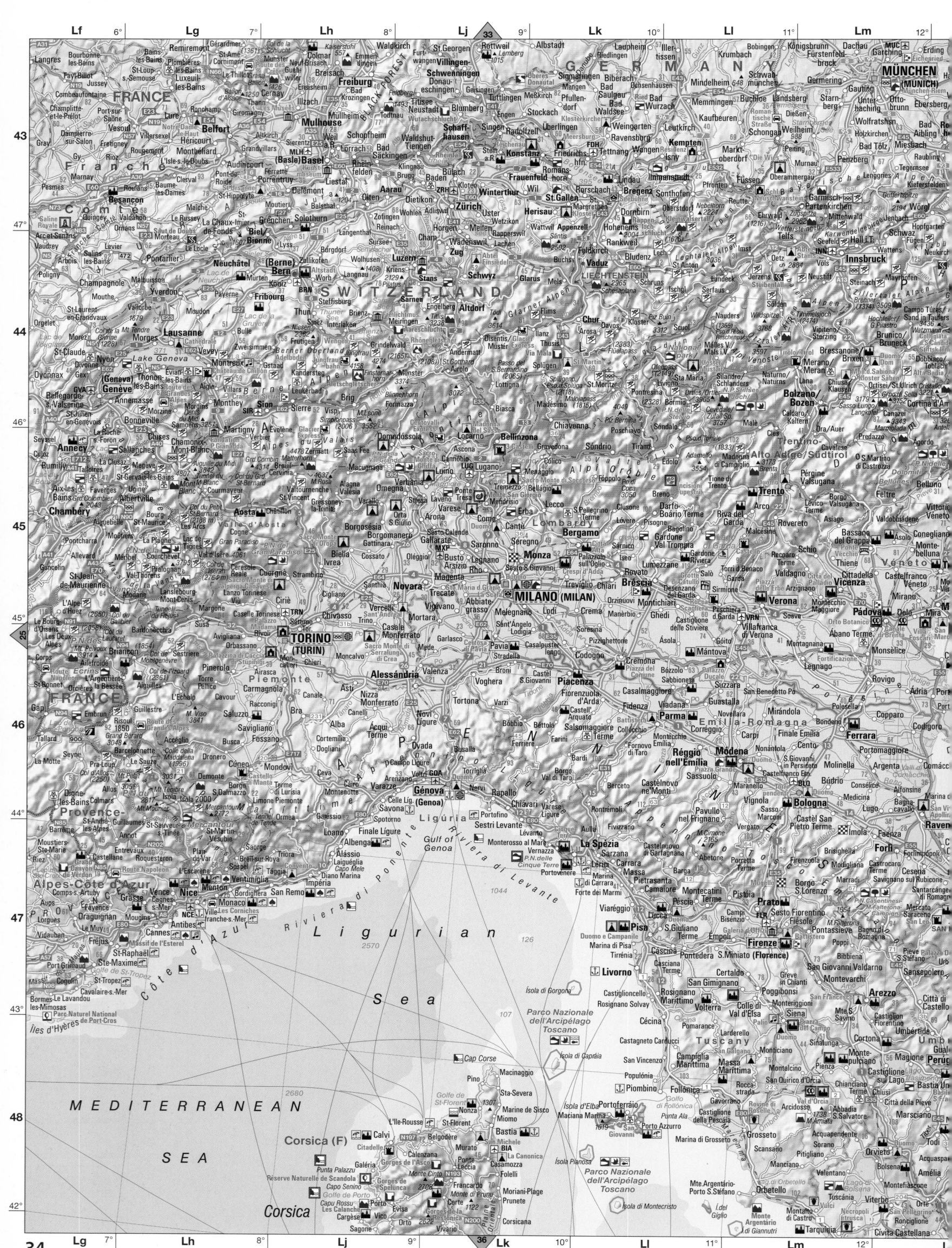

0 25 50 75 Kilometers
0 25 50 Miles

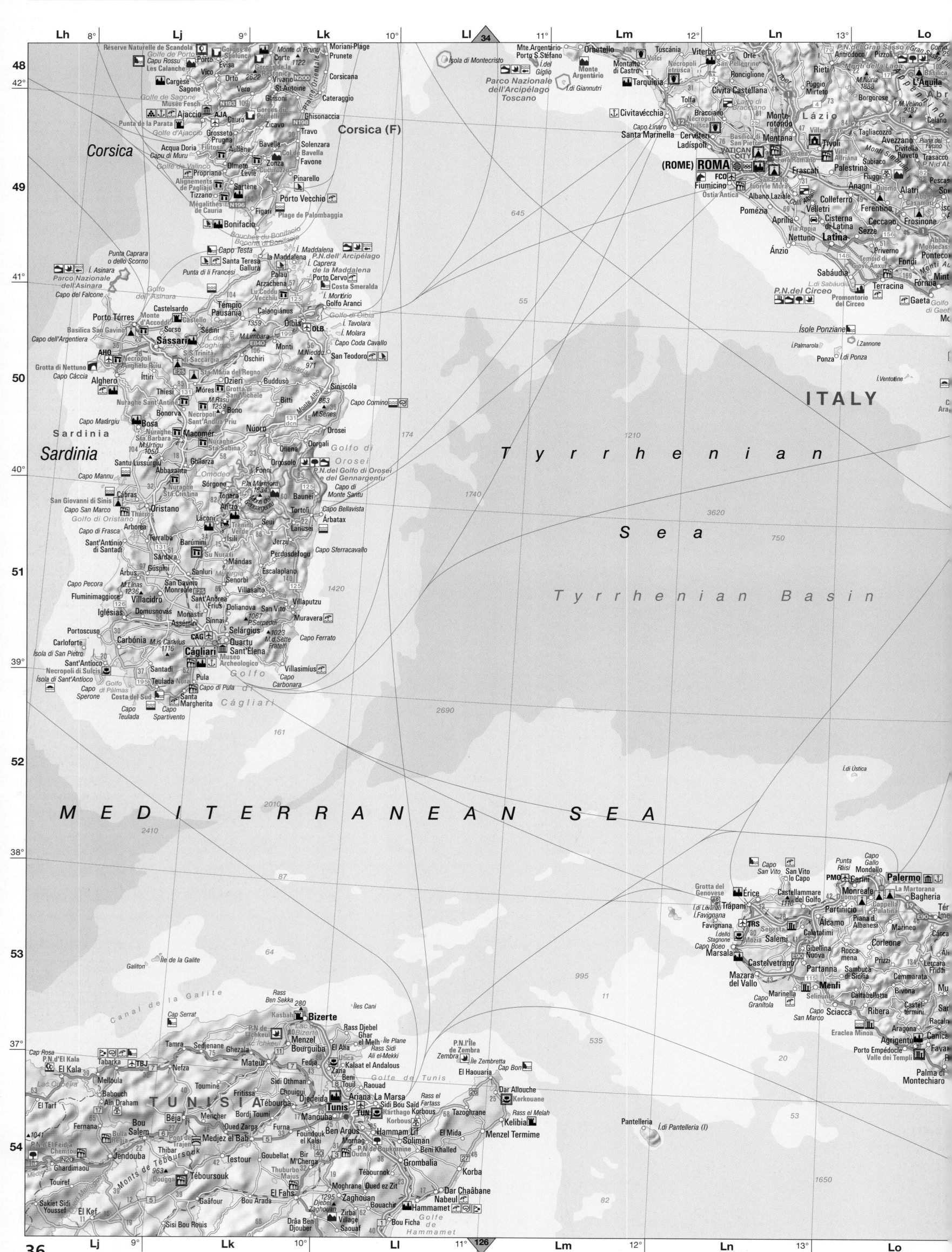

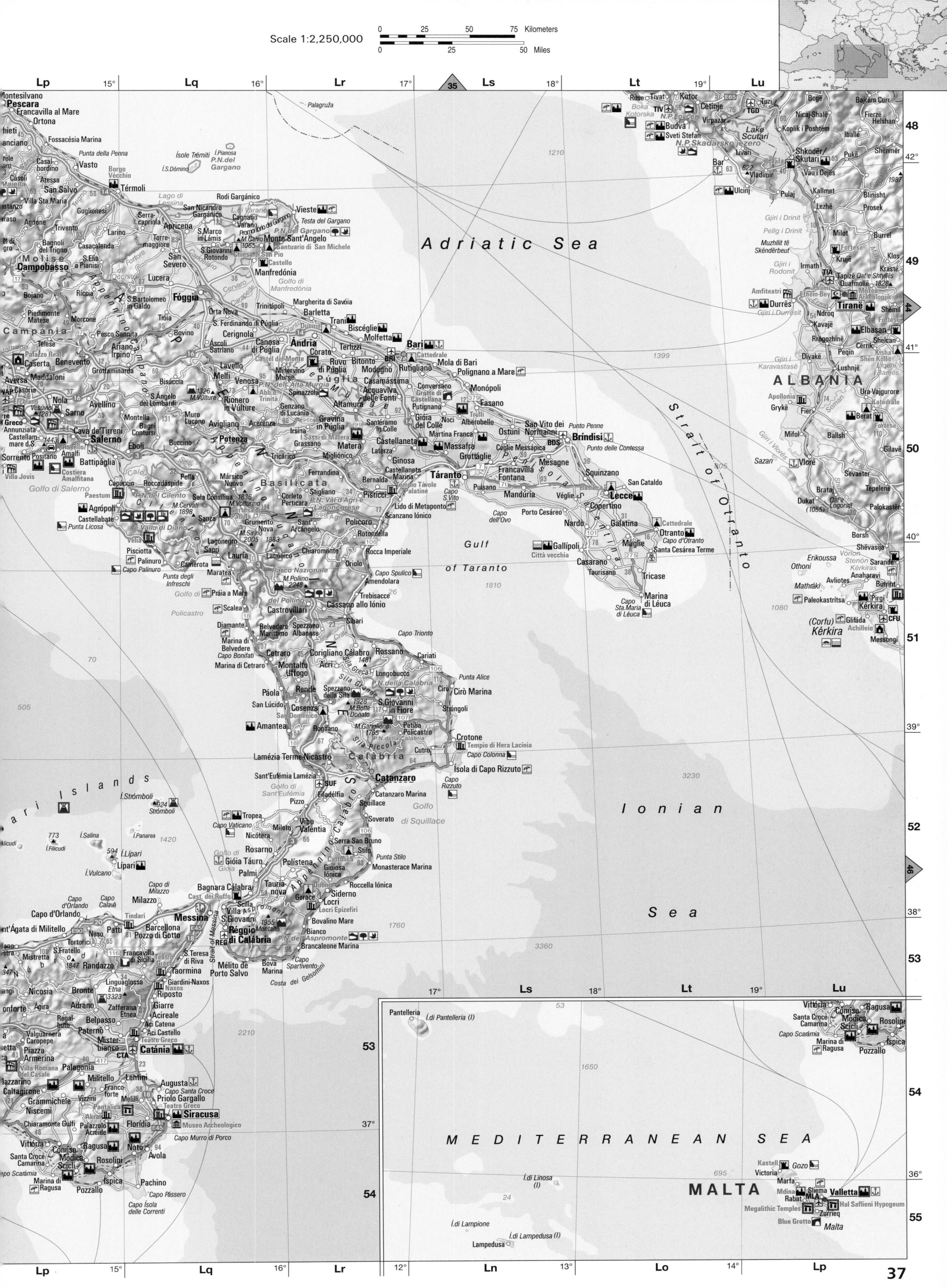

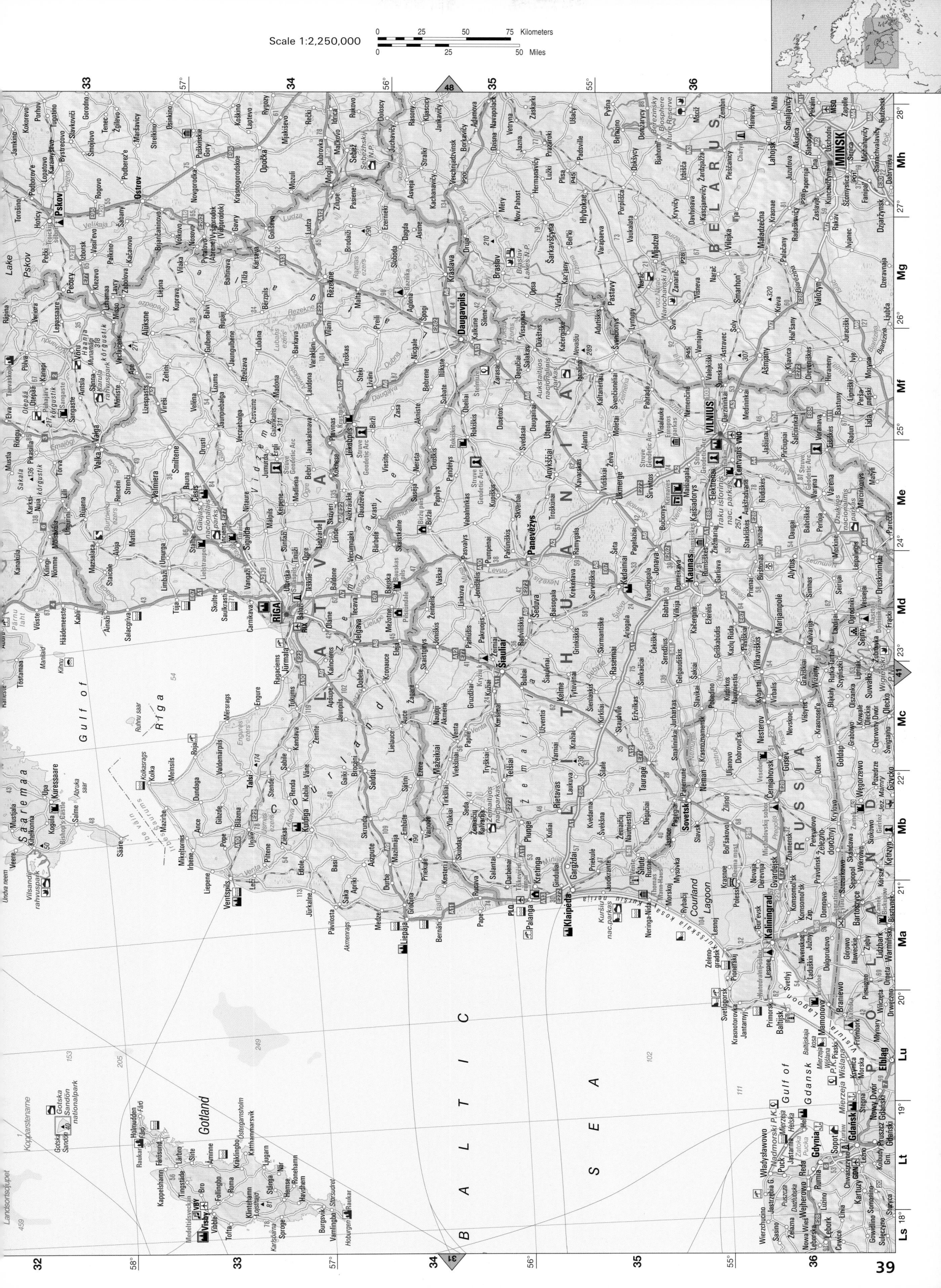

Poland

Scale 1:2,250,000

0 25 50 75 Kilometers

0 25 50 Miles

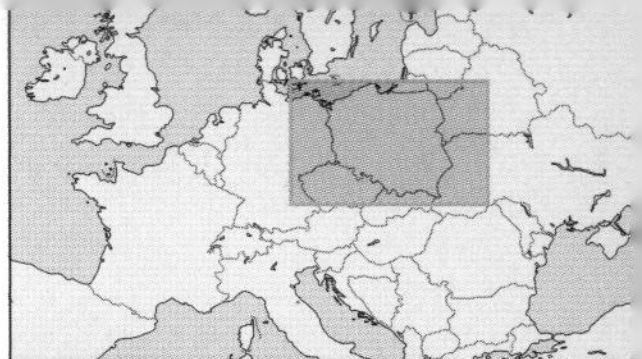

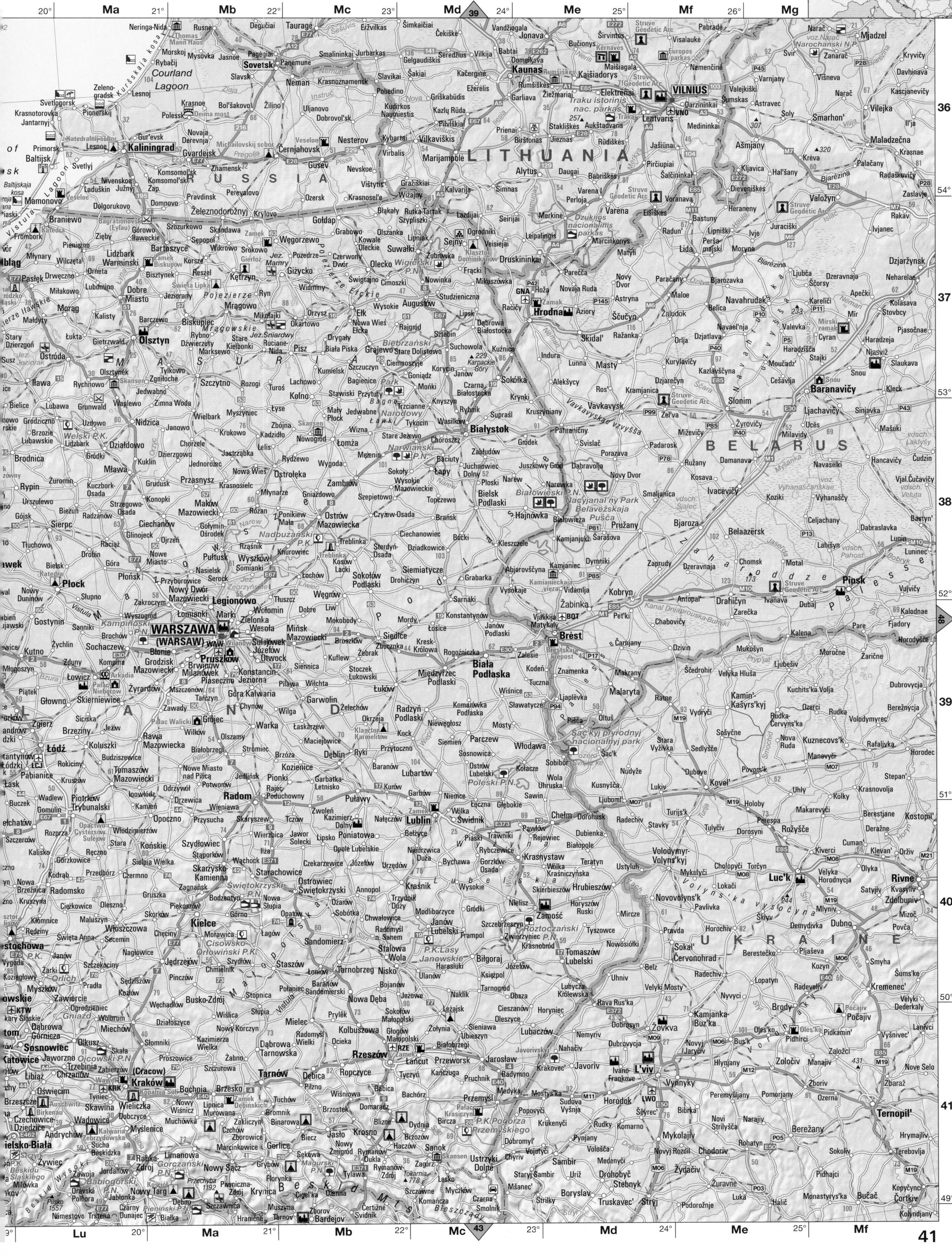

Ma 20° 21° **Mb** 22° **Mc** 23° **Md** 39 24° **Me** 25° **Mf** 26° **Mg**

RUSSIA

LITHUANIA

Kaliningrad

Kaunas

VILNIUS

Hrodna

BELARUS

Olsztyn

Białystok

Baranavičy

Słonim

WARSZAWA (WARSAW)

Płock

Łódź

Pinsk

Brèst

Biała Podlaska

Radom

Lublin

Kielce

Kraków (Cracow)

Tarnów

Rzeszów

UKRAINE

Luc'k

Rivne

L'viv

Ternopil'

36
54°
37
53°
38
52°
48
39
51°
40
50°
41
49°

Lu 3° 20° **Ma** 21° **Mb** 22° **Mc** 43 23° **Md** 24° **Me** 25° **Mf**

41

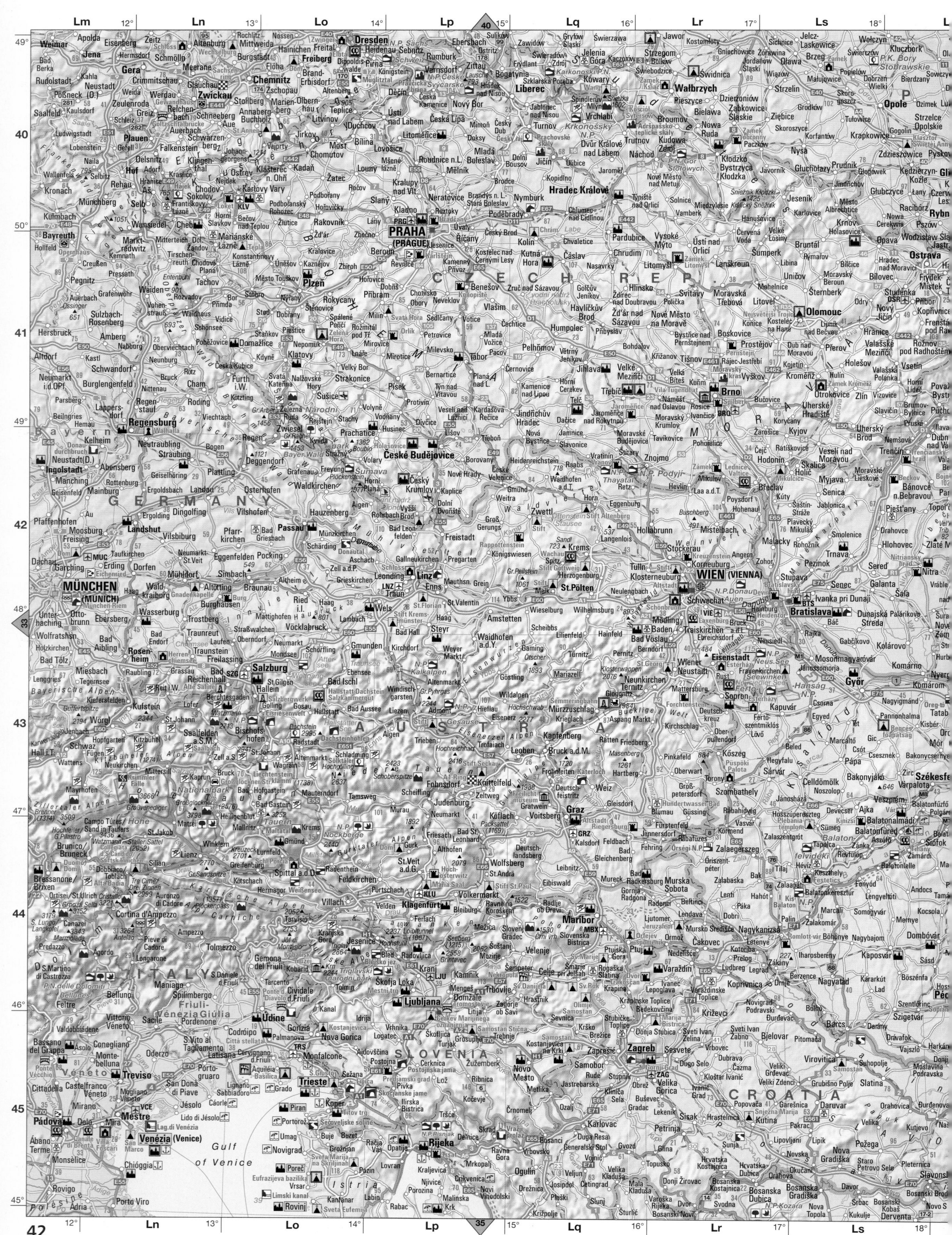

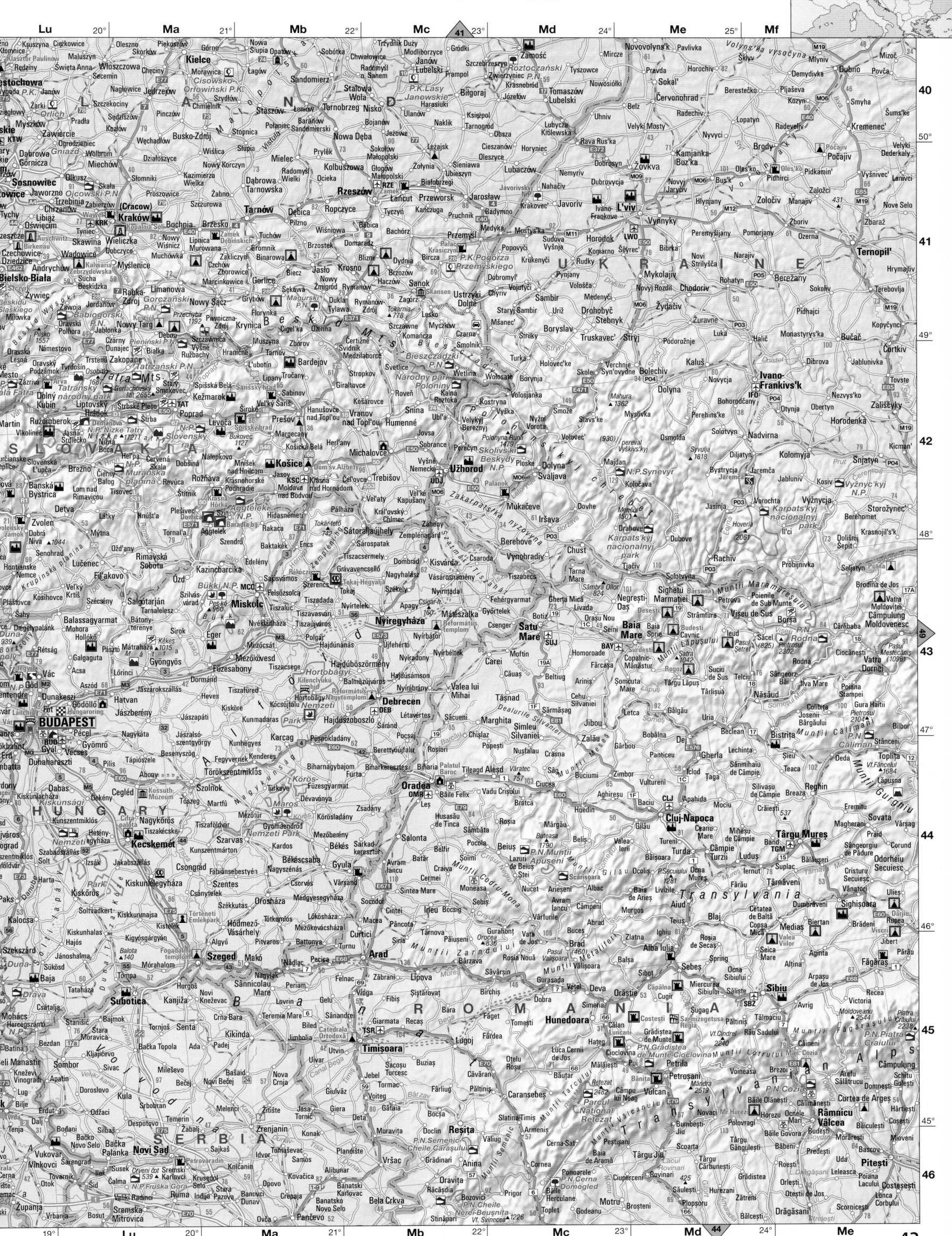

Scale 1:2,250,000

0 25 50 75 Kilometers
0 25 50 Miles

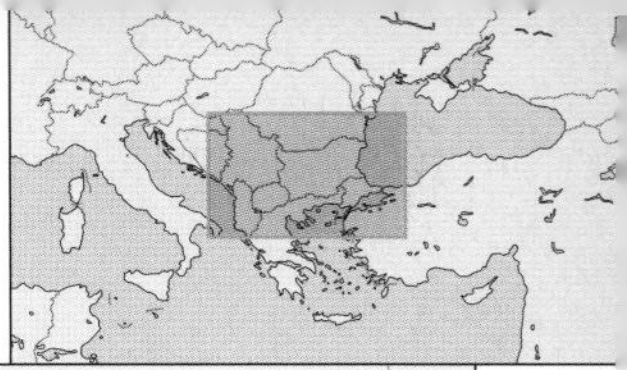

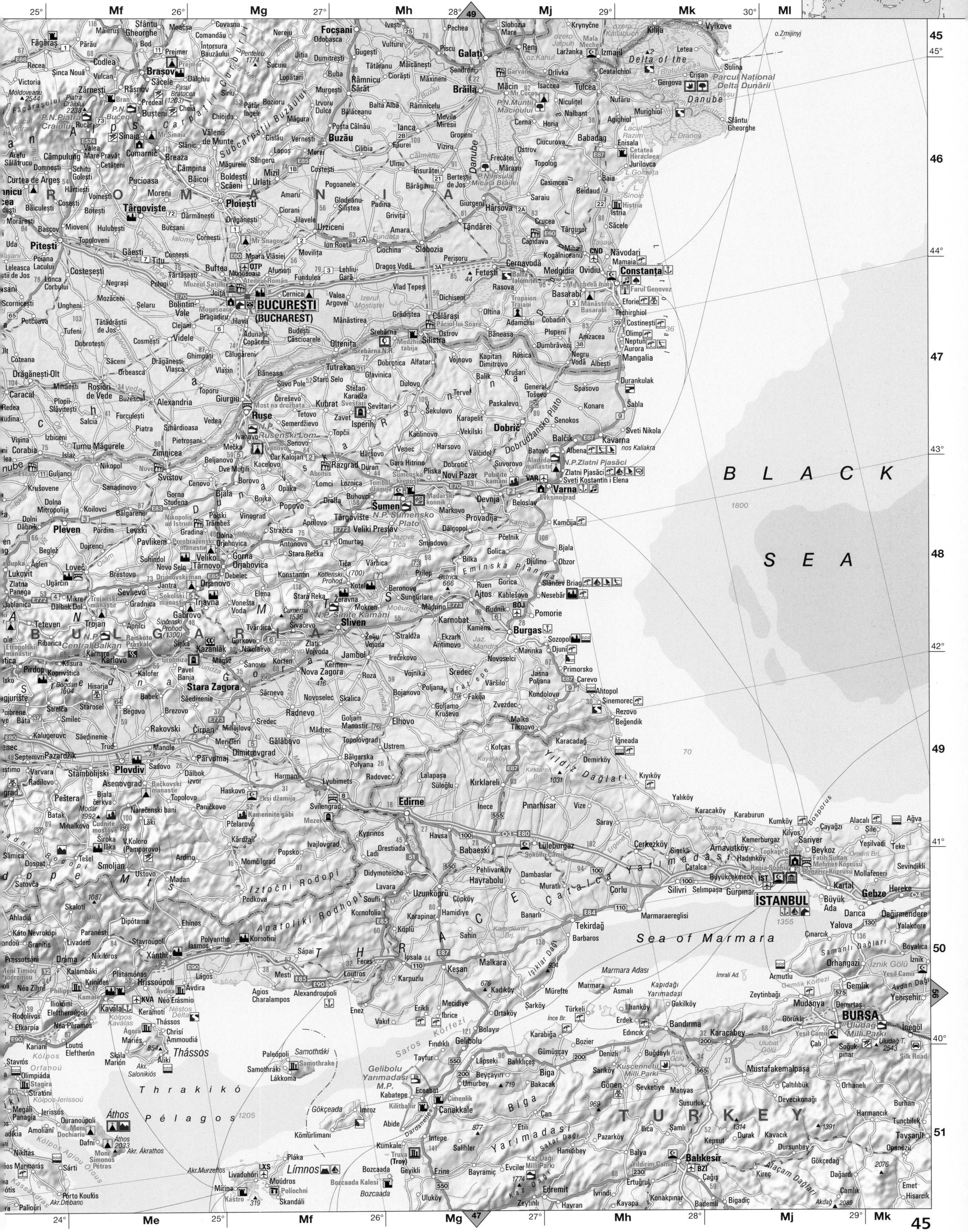

ROMANIA

Braşov · Sinaia · Câmpulung · Târgovişte · Ploieşti · Piteşti · Focşani · Galaţi · Brăila · Buzău

BUCUREŞTI (BUCHAREST)

Giurgiu · Ruse · Silistra · Călăraşi · Cernavodă · Medgidia · **Constanţa** · Mamaia · Năvodari · Eforie · Mangalia

BULGARIA

Pleven · Lovec · Gabrovo · Veliko Tărnovo · Trjavna · Sliven · Stara Zagora · Plovdiv · Pazardžik · Smoljan · Kărdžali · Haskovo · Dimitrovgrad · Čirpan

Razgrad · Šumen · Târgovište · Novi Pazar · Dobrič · Balčik · Kavarna · **Varna** · Nesebăr · Pomorie · **Burgas** · Sozopol · Primorsko · Carevo · Ahtopol

BLACK SEA

1800

Delta of the Danube · Parcul National Delta Dunării · Sulina · Sfântu Gheorghe · Tulcea · Măcin · Babadag

Edirne · Kırklareli · Lüleburgaz · Çorlu · Tekirdağ · Pınarhisar · Vize · Saray · **İSTANBUL** · Gebze · Büyükçekmece · Silivri · Çatalca

Bosporus · Sea of Marmara

THRACE · **THRÁCI**

Xánthi · Komotini · Alexandroúpoli · Kavála · Drama · Soufli · Didimóteicho

Thássos · Samothráki · Límnos · Áthos · Thrakikó Pélagos

Çanakkale · Troy · Gelibolu · Gelibolu Yarımadası M.P. · Biga · Bandırma · Gönen · Balıkesir · Mustafakemalpaşa · **BURSA** · İnegöl · Yenişehir · Mudanya · Gemlik · İznik Gölü · Yalova

TURKEY

Uludağ Milli Parkı · Uludağ T. 2543

Me Mf 45 Mg Mh Mj

24° 25° 26° 27° 28°

BURSA

Thrakikó Pélagos

Thássos

A e g e a n

S e a

S O U T H E R N   S P O R A D E S

Northern Sporades

İZMİR

Manisa

Balıkesir

Ödemiş

Aydın

Denizli

T U R K E Y

Évia

ATHÍNA
(ATHENS)

Pireás
(Piraeus)

Mirtóon Sea

Lésvos

Híos

Sámos

Ikaría

Ándros

Tínos

Míkonos

Náxos

Páros

Síros

Kéa

Kíthnos

Sérifos

Sífnos

Mílos

Amorgós

Íos

Thíra

Anáfi

D o d e c a n e s e   S p o r a d e s

Kálimnos

Kós

Léros

Pátmos

Bodrum

Ródos
(Rhodes)

Rhodes

Kárpathos

S e a   o f   C r e t e

Crete

Iráklio

Haniá
(Khania)

Réthimno

Livikó Pélagos

L e v a n t i n e   B a s i n

Md Me Mf 128 Mg Mh

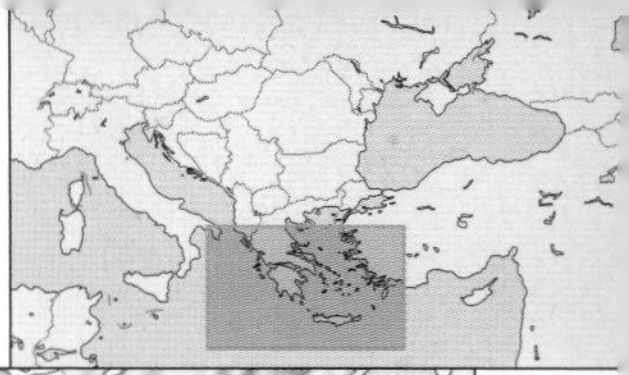

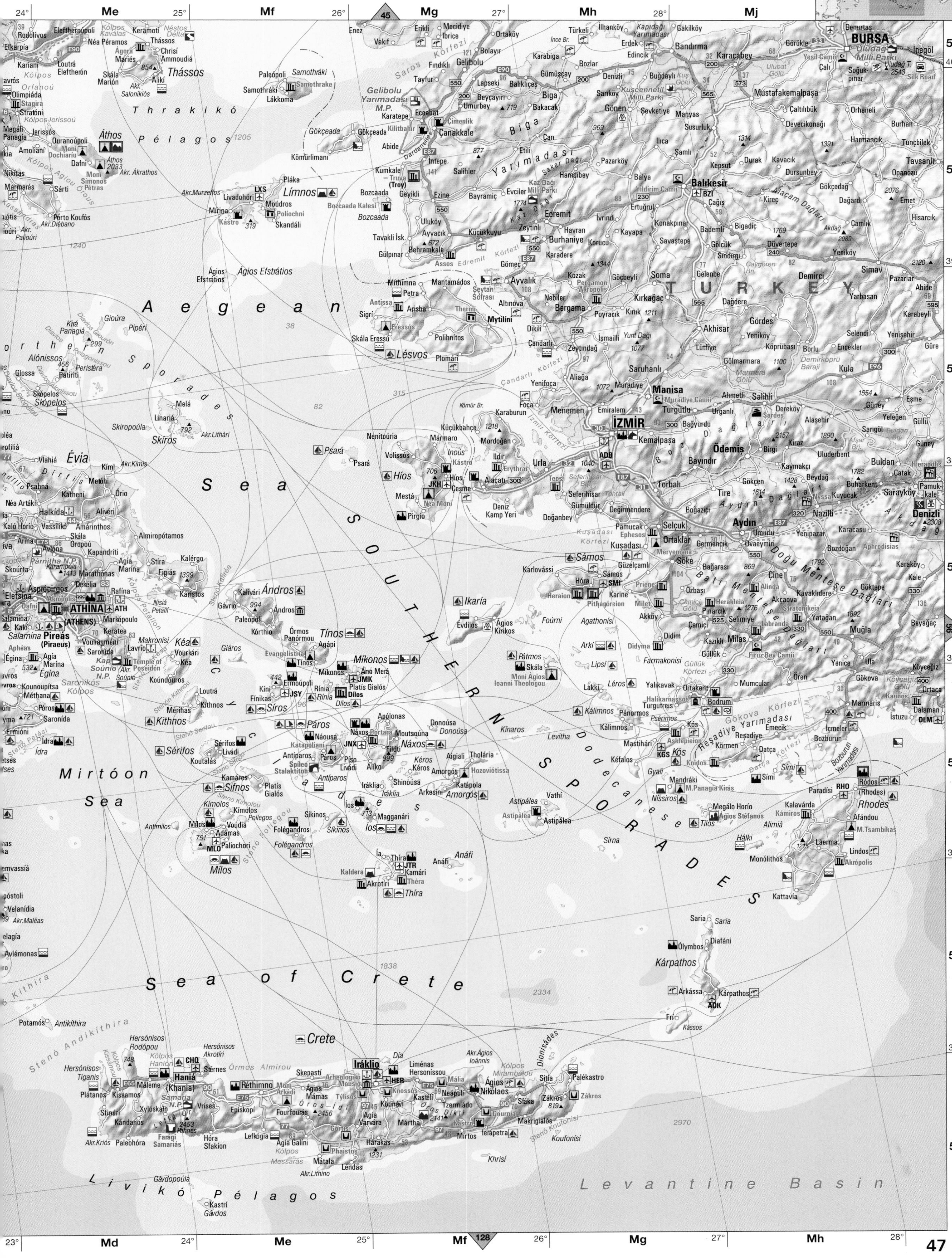

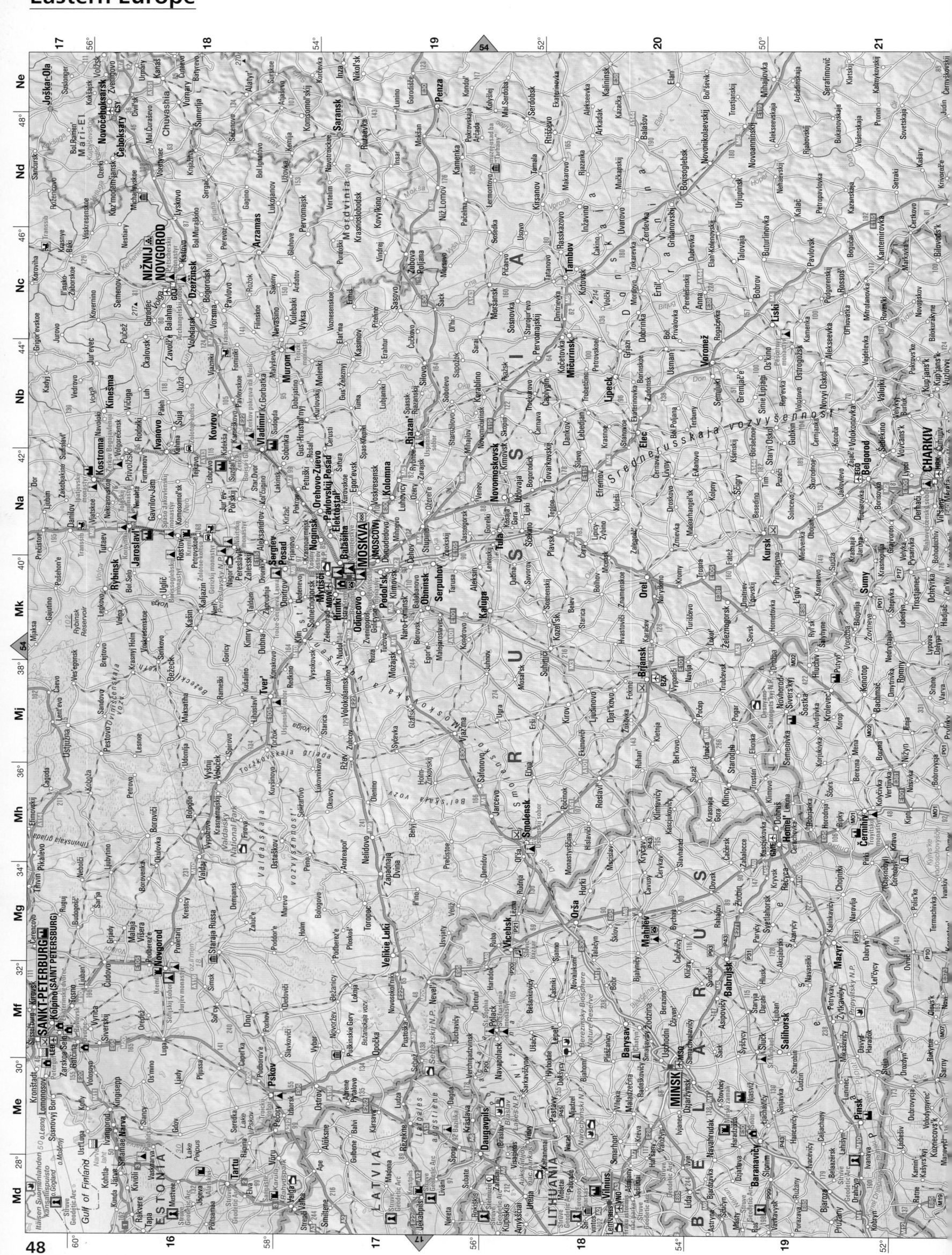

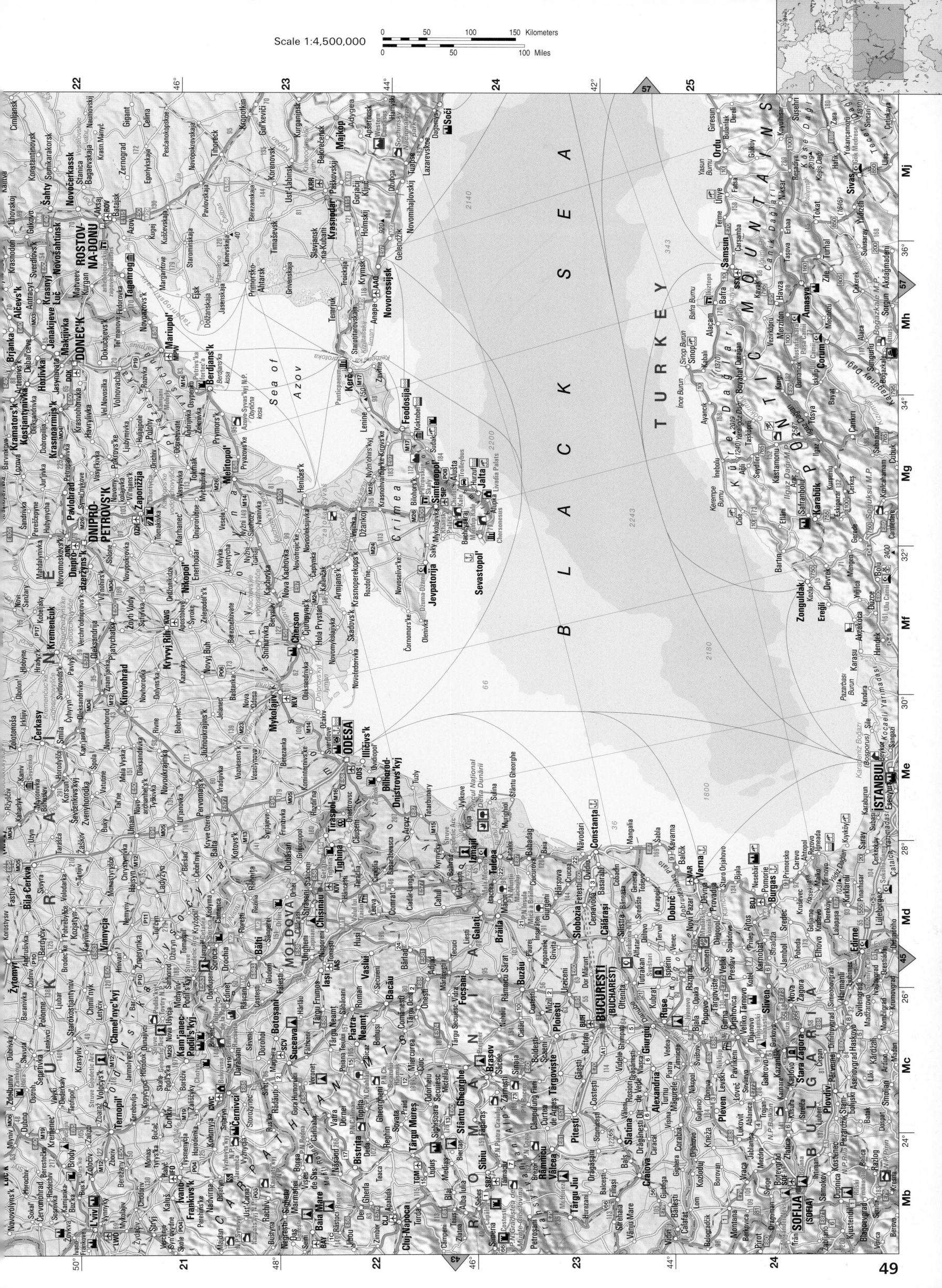

Caravans were once vital for travel through the Syrian desert.

Mount Everest (8,850 m), the world's tallest mountain.

ASIA

THE CRADLE OF CIVILIZATION

Asia has a total area of 44.4 million km² and encompasses around one-third of the world's land. The continent has a maximum length of 11,000 kilometers from east to west and a maximum of 8,500 kilometers from north to south. The vast majority of Asia's land area is above the equator in the northern hemisphere. Only a few areas in Southeast Asia and the Indian subcontinent are south of the equator. The continent borders the Arctic Ocean in the north, the Pacific Ocean in the east, and the Indian Ocean in the south. In the west, Asia borders Europe, the Mediterranean Sea, North Africa and the Red Sea. The Bering Sea, a section of the Pacific, separates Siberia in northern Asia from North America. The Arabian Peninsula, India, the Malay Peninsula, Korea, and Kamchatka are the largest and most significant of the many peninsulas on the continent. The Japanese Islands are located off the northeastern coast of mainland Asia. A large belt of mountain systems extends from the Caucasus (maximum height, 5,642 m) and the Pontic Mountains (3,937 m) in western Asia to the Himalayas and farther east into Southeast Asia.

Asia is by far the most populated of the world's seven continents and its more than 3.4 billion inhabitants are unequally distributed. Sparsely populated Mongolia has a population density of just two inhabitants per square kilometer. Bangladesh, one of the world's most crowded nations, has a population density in excess of 900 inhabitants per square kilometer. China and India, the world's most populous nations, are both home to more than one billion people.

Most of the world's major religions were founded in Asia many centuries ago. Judaism, Islam, and Christianity all originated in western Asia. India was the birthplace of Hinduism and Buddhism, while Taoism and Confucianism both originated in China.

Tokyo: Modern skyscrapers in Japan's capital and largest city (10 million inhabitants.).

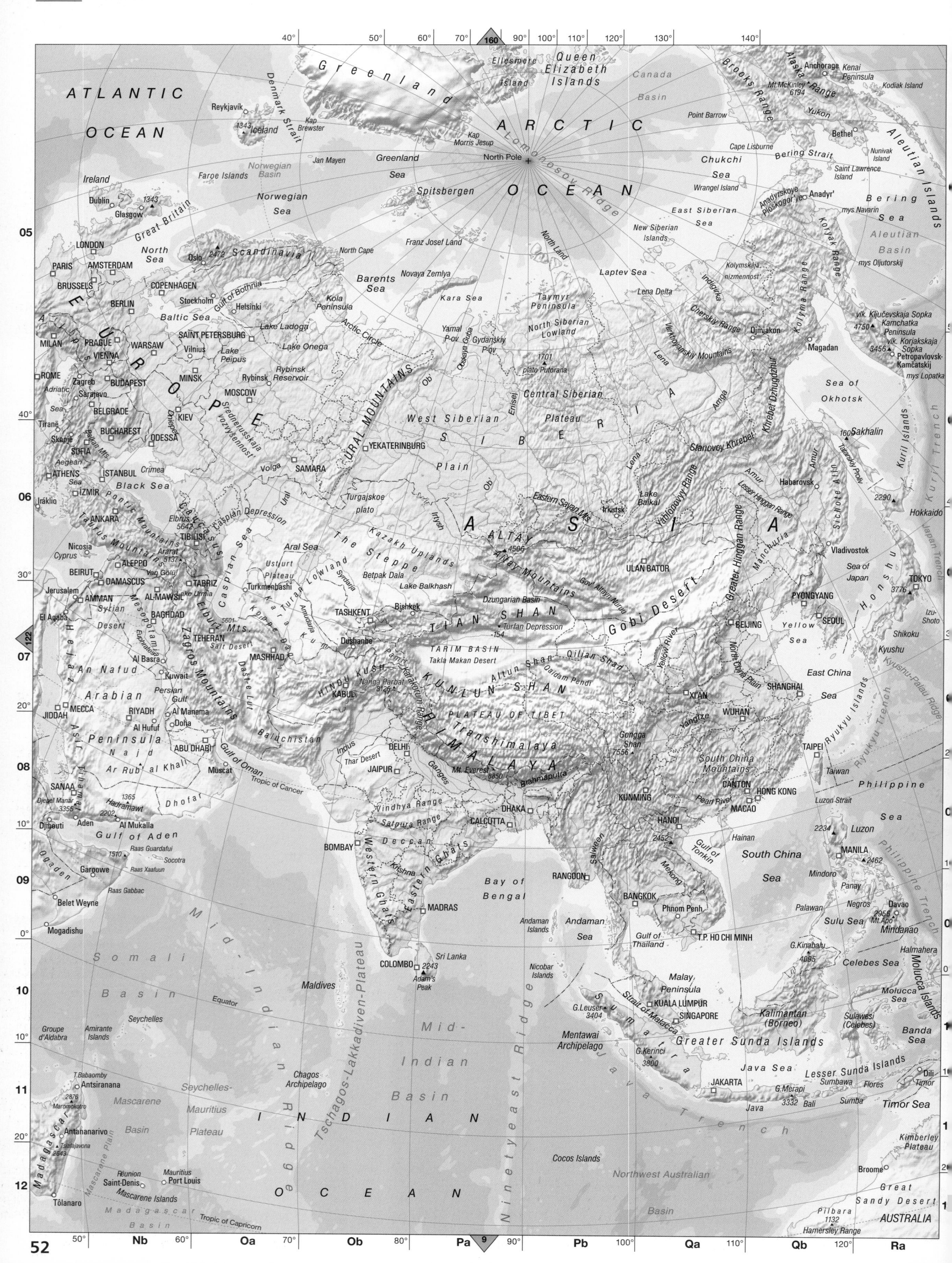

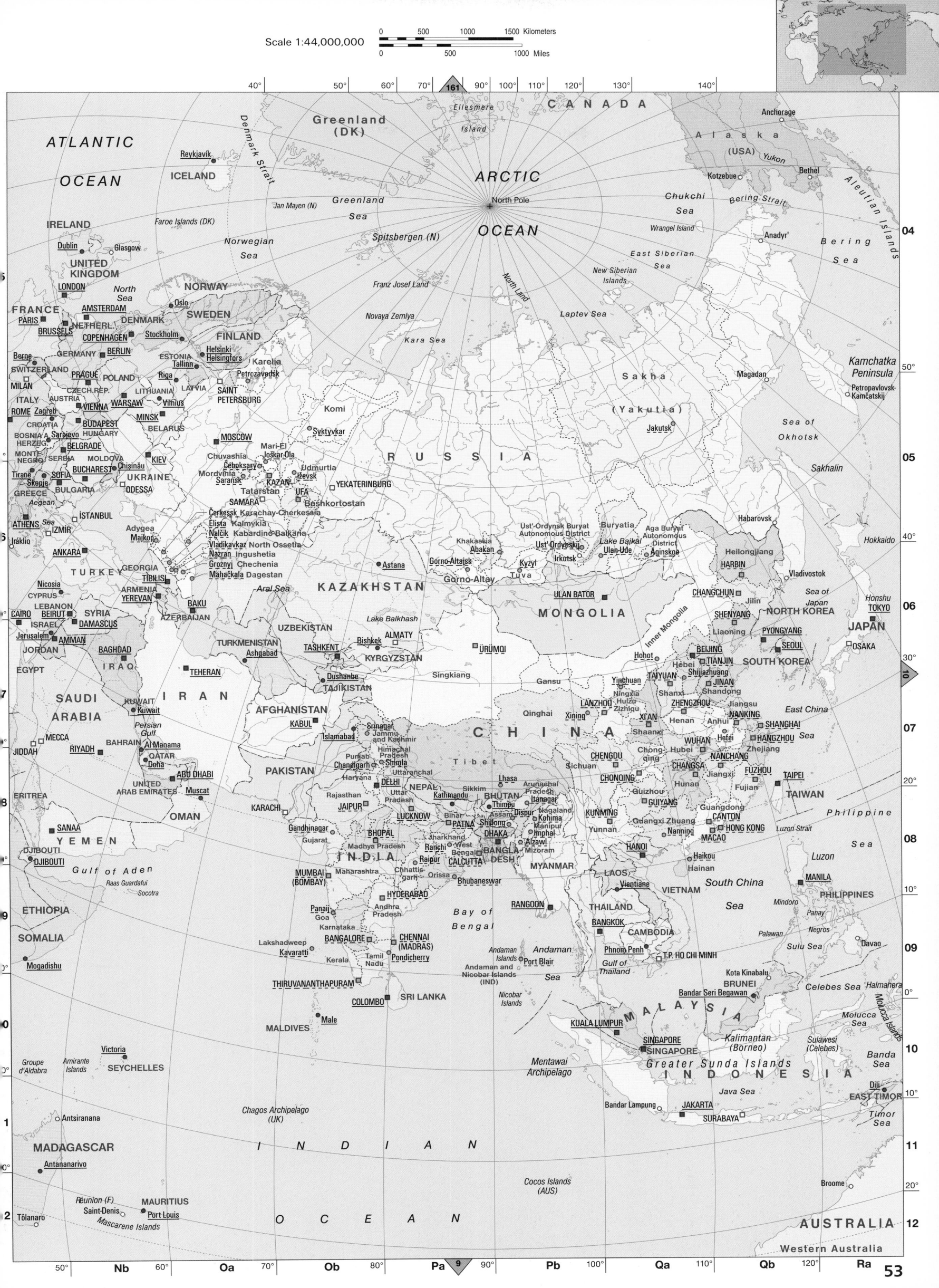

Scale 1:44,000,000

0 500 1000 1500 Kilometers
0 500 1000 Miles

40° 50° 60° 70° 161 90° 100° 110° 120° 130° 140°

ATLANTIC

OCEAN

Greenland (DK)

Ellesmere
Island

C A N A D A

Anchorage

Reykjavík

ICELAND

Jan Mayen (N)

Greenland
Sea

ARCTIC

North Pole

OCEAN

A l a s k a
(USA) Yukon

Bethel

Kotzebue

Chukchi
Sea

Bering Strait

Aleutian Islands

04

IRELAND

Dublin Glasgow

**UNITED
KINGDOM**

LONDON

FRANCE

PARIS

AMSTERDAM

BRUSSELS NETHERL.

Berne

SWITZERLAND

MILAN

ITALY Zagreb

ROME

CROATIA

BOSNIA A.

Sarajevo

MONTE-

NEGRO SERBA

Tirane

SOFIA

GREECE

Aegean
Sea

ATHENS

IZMIR

Iráklio

GERMANY BERLIN

DENMARK

COPENHAGEN

PRAGUE POLAND

CZECH.REP.

AUSTRIA

VIENNA

BUDAPEST

HUNGARY

BELGRADE

MOLDOVA Chişinău

BUCHAREST

BULGARIA

Skopje

North
Sea

Faroe Islands (DK)

NORWAY

Oslo

SWEDEN

Stockholm

ESTONIA

Tallinn

Riga

LITHUANIA

LATVIA

Vilnius

WARSAW

MINSK

BELARUS

KIEV

UKRAINE

ODESSA

Norwegian
Sea

Spitsbergen (N)

Franz Josef Land

Novaya Zemlya

Kara Sea

Helsinki
Helsingfors

FINLAND

Karelia

SAINT
PETERSBURG

Petrozavodsk

Komi

Syktyvkar

MOSCOW

Chuvashia

Čeboksary

Joskar-Ola

Mari-El

Mordvinie

Saransk

Izevsk

Udmurtia

KAZAN

UFA

Tatarstan

Bashkortostan

SAMARA

Čerkessk Karachay-Cherkeseia

Elista Kalmykiä

Nalčik Kabardino-Balkana

Vladikavkaz North Ossetia

Nazran Ingushetia

Groznyj Chechenia

Mahačkala Dagestan

North Land

East Siberian
Sea

New Siberian
Islands

Laptev Sea

R U S S I A

Sakha

(Yakutia)

Jakutsk

Wrangel Island

Anadyr'

Magadan

Sea of
Okhotsk

Sakhalin

Petropavlovsk-
Kamčatskij

Kamchatka
Peninsula

Bering
Sea

Bering Strait

04

50°

05

Adygea

Majkop

GEORGIA

TBILISI

Nicosia

CYPRUS

LEBANON

BEIRUT

Jerusalem

ISRAEL

AMMAN

JORDAN

EGYPT

SAUDI

ARABIA

MECCA

JIDDAH

RIYADH

ARMENIA

YEREVAN

AZERBAIJAN

BAKU

SYRIA

DAMASCUS

BAGHDAD

I R A Q

Aral Sea

KAZAKHSTAN

Lake Balkhash

Astana

Gorno-Altajsk

Gorno-Altay

UZBEKISTAN

TURKMENISTAN

Ashgabad

TASHKENT

Bishkek

ALMATY

KYRGYZSTAN

Dushanbe

TADJIKISTAN

Singkiang

Khakassia

Abakan

Ust'-Ordynsk Buryat
Autonomous District

Ust'-Ordynskij

Irkutsk

Kyzyl

Tuva

Lake Baikal

Ulan-Ude

Buryatia

Aga Buryat
Autonomous
District

Aginskoe

ULAN BATOR

MONGOLIA

ÜRÜMQI

Hohot

Inner Mongolia

Habarovsk

Heilongjiang

HARBIN

Vladivostok

CHANGCHUN

Jilin

SHENYANG

Liaoning

Hokkaido

Sea of
Japan

Honshu

TOKYO

JAPAN

OSAKA

06

40°

TURKEY

ANKARA

I R A N

TEHERAN

KUWAIT

Kuwait

BAHRAIN

Al Manama

QATAR

Doha

UNITED
ARAB EMIRATES

ABU DHABI

Muscat

OMAN

Persian
Gulf

KUBAL

AFGHANISTAN

KABUL

Islamabad

Srinagar

Jammu
and Kashmir

Himachal
Pradesh

Shimla

Chandigarh

Punjab

Haryana

Uttaranchal

NORTH KOREA

PYONGYANG

SEOUL

SOUTH KOREA

BEIJING

Hebei TIANJIN

TAIYUAN Shijiazhuang

Shanxi JINAN

Shandong

Yinchuan

Ningxia Huizu

Zizhigu

LANZHOU

ZHENGZHOU

Henan Anhui

XI'AN

Shaanxi

Gansu

Qinghai

Xining

Tibet

Lhasa

30°

10

07

PAKISTAN

KARACHI

Rajasthan

JAIPUR

Gandhinagar

Gujarat

DELHI

Uttar
Pradesh

NEPAL

Kathmandu

LUCKNOW

BHOPAL

Madhya Pradesh

Chong-
qing

CHENGDU

Sichuan

CHONQING

WUHAN

Hubei

Hefei

CHANGSA

Hunan

NANKING

Jiangsu

SHANGHAI

Zhejiang

HANGZHOU

NANCHANG

Jiangxi

FUZHOU

Fujian

East China
Sea

TAIPEI

TAIWAN

20°

Sikkim

BHUTAN

Thimpu

Arunachal
Pradesh

Itanagar

Assam

Nagaland

Dispur Kohima

Shillong Imphal

Manipur

Mizoram

Aizawl

Guizhou

GUIYANG

KUNMING

Yunnan

Nanning

Guangxi Zhuang

CANTON

HONG KONG

MACAO

Guangdong

Luzon Strait

Philippine

Sea

08

I N D I A

MUMBAI
(BOMBAY)

Maharashtra

HYDERABAD

Andhra
Pradesh

Panaji

Goa

Karnataka

BANGALORE

Kavaratti

Lakshadweep

Kerala

THIRUVANANTHAPURAM

Bihar

PATNA

Jharkhand

Ranchi

Chhattis-
garh

Raipur

Orissa

Bhubaneswar

West
Bengal

CALCUTTA

DHAKA

BANGLA-
DESH

RANGOON

MYANMAR

Bay of
Bengal

Andaman
Islands

Port Blair

Andaman and
Nicobar Islands
(IND)

Nicobar
Islands

Andaman
Sea

HANOI

Haikou

Hainan

LAOS

Vientiane

VIETNAM

THAILAND

BANGKOK

CAMBODIA

Phnom Penh

T.P. HO CHI MINH

Gulf of
Thailand

Mindoro

Luzon

MANILA

PHILIPPINES

Panay

Negros

Palawan

Sulu Sea

Davao

South China
Sea

10°

09

ETHIOPIA

SOMALIA

Mogadishu

Gulf of Aden

Raas Guardafui

Socotra

YEMEN

SANAA

DJIBOUTI

DJIBOUTI

ERITREA

CHENNAI
(MADRAS)

Tamil
Nadu

Pondicherry

COLOMBO

SRI LANKA

Male

MALDIVES

Kota Kinabalu

BRUNEI

Bandar Seri Begawan

Celebes Sea

Halmahera

Molucca Islands

Molucca
Sea

Sulawesi
(Celebes)

0°

Groupe
d'Aldabra

Amirante
Islands

Victoria

SEYCHELLES

Antsiranana

MADAGASCAR

Antananarivo

Réunion (F)

Saint-Denis

MAURITIUS

Port Louis

Mascarene Islands

Tôlanaro

Chagos Archipelago
(UK)

I N D I A N

O C E A N

Cocos Islands
(AUS)

KUALA LUMPUR

SINGAPORE

SINGAPORE

Mentawai
Archipelago

Greater Sunda Islands

I N D O N E S I A

Kalimantan
(Borneo)

Bandar Lampung

JAKARTA

SURABAYA

Java Sea

Banda
Sea

Dili

EAST TIMOR

Timor
Sea

Broome

10°

AUSTRALIA

Western Australia

10

11

20°

12

50° Nb 60° Oa 70° Ob 80° 9 Pa 90° Pb 100° Qa 110° Qb 120° Ra

53

Scale 1:15,000,000

0   250   500   750 Kilometers
0   250   500 Miles

85°   02   80°   03   75° ◆5   04   70°   05   65°   160°

OCEAN

Chukchi Sea   Wevek   **Alaska**
Cape Lisburne   Kotzebue   Seward   (USA)   Ud
Sound   Peninsula   Bethel

Bering Strait   165°
Wrangel   Wales   Nome   Alakanuk
Island   Ušakovskoje   Uc
proliv Longa   Uèlen   Northeast   170°
Cape
East Siberian   Mys Šmidta   Koljučinskaja guba   Lavrentija   Ub
Providenija
Sea   Pevek   **Chukotskiy**   St.Matthew   175°
New Siberian   Poluostrov   Island
ostrov Ajon   Ugol'nye   (USA)
Islands   Čaunskaja guba   Kopi   *Anadyr'*   Nagornyj   Ua

▲1775 Bilibino   **Chukchi**   *hrebet Pekul'nej*   m. Navarin   180°
o.Novaja   Čerskij   Anjujskij hrebet   Anadyr'   1651▲
Sibir'   **Autonomous District**   3795
Laptev Sea   *o.Kotel'nyj*   *Kolymskaja*   ▲1797   Td
pr.Sannikova   **nizmennost'**   Olojskij hrebet   175°
o.Bol.   Omolon   **Koryak**   Apuka   m. Oljutorskij
Ljahovskij   ▲1503   Kamenskoe   **Range**
1125▲   *pr.Dmitrija Lapteva*   ▲1613   Koryak   Tc
insula   Sagastyr   *Jano-Indigirskaja*   *Jukagirskoe*   **Autonomous District**   170°
Olenëkskij   Lena Delta   **nizmennost'**   *ploskogor'e*   ▲1411   ▲1814   *Karaginskij*   Ossora
zaliv   *Arga-*   Čekurdah   1483▲   o.Karaginskij
Muora-Sise   Žyrjanka   ▲1962   Selihova   zaliv
Saskylah   Hajyr   Ust'-Kujga   Kolyma   m. Tajgonos   Tb
krjaž Čekanovskogo   Deputatskij   *Alazejskoe*   m. Ozernoj
Janskij   *ploskogor'e*   Sejmčan   *zaliv*   Ust'-Kamčatsk
zaliv   ▲2243   *Momskij hrebet*   Koman-
Siktjah   2533▲   Honuu   Susuman   m. Tolstoj   *Sredinnyj*   dorskie o-va
Sakha   Bataga   ▲2690   Jagodnoe   m. Kamčatskij
2247▲   Lazo   Ojmjakon   Ust'-Omčug   m. Južnyj   4750▲   Tb
Olenëk   Menkerja   **Mountains**   Tomtor   **Magadan**   *hrebet*   m. Kamčatskij
Žigansk   2081▲   ▲2959   *hrebet Suntar-Hajata*   m. Alevina   3607▲   m.Kronockij   165°
Udačnyj **(Yakutia)**   *Lena*   2120▲   Handyga   Okhotsk   **Kamchatka**   vlk. Ključevskaja Sopka
Viljujskoe   Sangar   ▲2184   **Peninsula**   3456▲   vlk. Korjakskaja   Ta
plato   *Central'nojakutskaja*   *Viljuj*   **Jakutsk**   Ust'-Maja   Sopka   160°
Njurba   Viljujsk   Kerdem   Amga   2460▲
ravnina   *Linde*   Ulu   **Sea of**   Petropavlovsk-
Viljujskoe vdhr.   Amga   Čagda   *Khrebet*   Kamčatskij
Nakanno   Mirnyj   *Prilenskoe plato*   *Aldan*   1906▲   **Okhotsk**   m. Lopatka   Sd
krjaž   Lensk   *Aldanskoe*   ▲2243   ▲1890   *Dzhugdzhur*   o. Paramušir
Olëkminsk   *nagor'e*   m. Elizavety
Patomskoe nagor'e   Aldan   **Shantarskiye**   o. Onekotan
1702▲   Dlekma   Čul'man   Nerjungri   *Khrebet*   **Ostrova**   o. Šiaškotan   155°
Nerjungri   Verhnezejskaja   Čumikan   Nikolaevsk-   o. Rasšua
g. Skalistyj Golec   *ravnina*   ▲2067   na-Amure
Stanovoy   2467▲   *Zejskoe vdhr.*   2384▲   o. Simušir
2193▲   ▲3067   **Stanovoy Khrebet**   *Sakhalin*
Nagor'ye   *hr. Tukuringra*   1609▲   o. Urup
Batomskij hr.   2630▲   **Range**   Skovorodino   *Tatarskiy*   Sc
Lake Baikal   *Olëkma*   Amur   *Zeja*   *Selemdža*   Komsomol'sk-   Poronajsk m.Terpenija
Buryatia   Mohe   Šimanovsk   na-Amure   Uglegorsk
Olëkminskij Stanovik   *Zejsko-*   *hrebet Turana*   *Selendže*   Vanino
Yimube   *Bureinskaja*   *proliv*
Yablonovyy Range   Mangui   *ravnina*   *Bureinskij hrebet*   Holmsk   150°
Ulan-Ude   Čita   Jagdaqi   Blagoveščensk   Habarovsk   Južno-Sahalinsk
Petrovsk   Karymskoe   Ergun Zuoqi   Birobidžan   o. Iturup
Zabajkal'skij   Aginskoe   Ergun Youqi   Blagoveščensk   **Jewish**   *Sikhote-Alin'*   La Perouse Strait   Sb
Aga Buryat   Borzja   **Autonomous**   o. Kunašir
Autonomous District   Yakeshi   **Region**   Wakkanai
Ulan-Ude   Manzhouli   Zhalantun   Yichun   Abashiri
Kherlen Gol   Hailar   Bei'an   Hegang   Bikin   Asahikawa   ▲2290
Chojbalsan   *Hulun Nur*   **CHINA**   Jiamusi   Dal'nerečensk   Asahi dake
ULAN BATOR   Qiqihar   **Heilongjiang**   Jixi   Dal'negorsk   **HOKKAIDO**
Öndörkhaan   Mingshui   Suihua   Tonghe   Rudnaja   SAPPORO   Obihiro   **JAPAN**
OLIA   Baruun Urt   Tailai   Anda   Pristan'   Tomakomai
Baruun-   HARBIN   *Lake*   Spassk-   Kushiro
kharaa   Ulanhot   Shangzhi   *Khanka*   Dal'nij   Hakodate
Sühbaatar   Baicheng   Sanchahe   Mudanjiang   Ussurijsk

Qb   110°   Qc   115°   Qd   120°   Ra   125°   ◆76   Rb   130°   Rc   135°   Rd   140°   Sa   145°   Sb

55

Scale 1:4,500,000

0 50 100 150 Kilometers
0 50 100 Miles

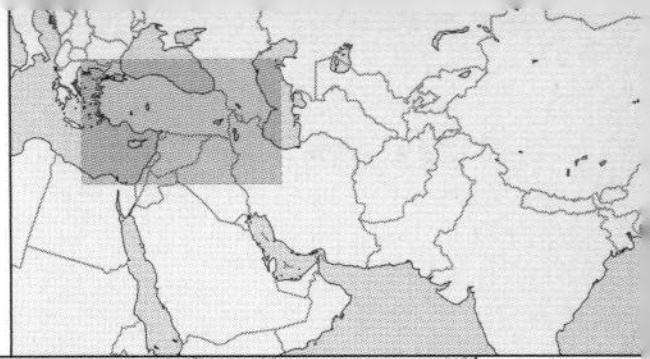

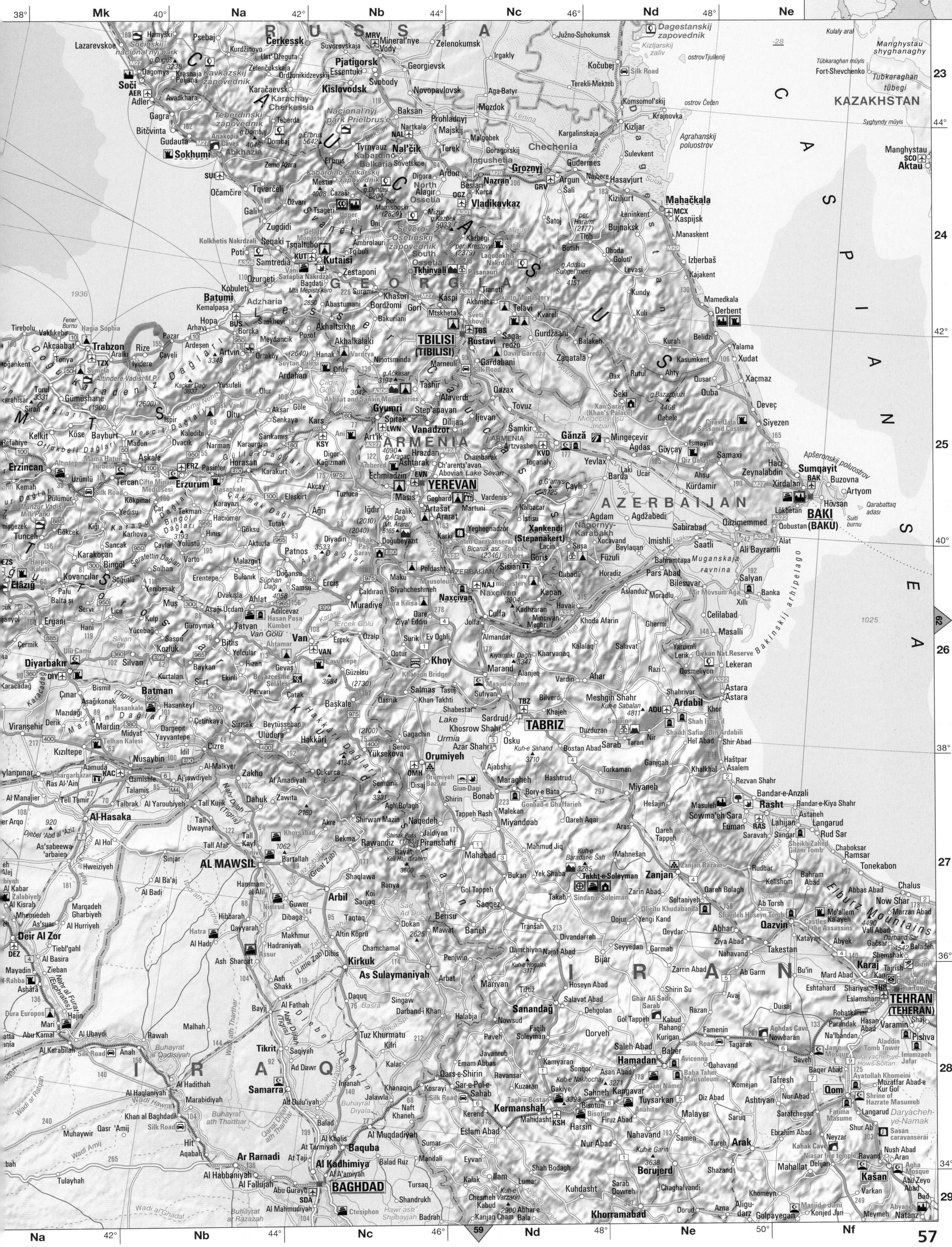

RUSSIA

CAUCASUS

GEORGIA

TBILISI (TIBILISI)

ARMENIA

YEREVAN

AZERBAIJAN

BAKI (BAKU)

KAZAKHSTAN

CASPIAN SEA

TURKEY

Sokhumi
Soči
Adler
Gagra
Batumi
Poti
Kutaisi
Rustavi
Gyumri
Vanadzor
Gänzä
Sumqayit
Trabzon
Erzurum
Erzincan
Elâzığ
Diyarbakır
Van
Batman
Al Mawsil
Arbil
Kirkuk
As Sulaymaniyah
Deir Al Zor
BAGHDAD
Samarra
Tikrit

Pjatigorsk
Kislovodsk
Essentuki
Nal'čik
Groznyj
Vladikavkaz
Nazran
Mahačkala
Kaspijsk
Derbent

IRAN
IRAQ
SYRIA

TABRIZ
Ardabil
Orumiyeh
Khoy
Naxçıvan
Naxcivan
Xankändi (Stepanakert)
Rasht
Qazvin
Zanjan
TEHRAN (TEHERAN)
Qom
Karaj
Hamadan
Sanandağ
Kermanshah
Khorramabad
Arak
Kašan

Elburz Mountains

Lake Urmia

57

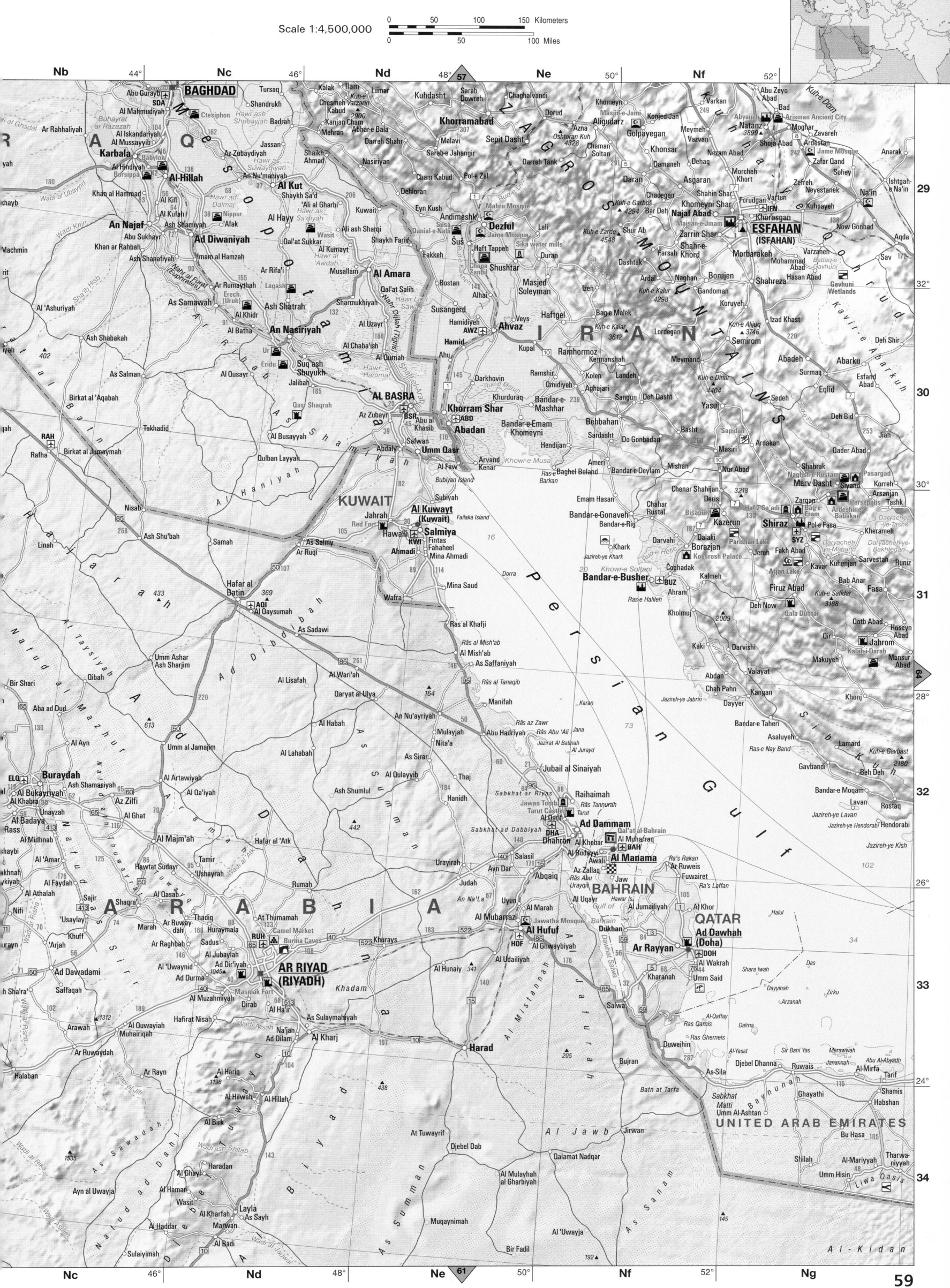

Scale 1:4,500,000

0 50 100 150 Kilometers
0 50 100 Miles

| Nb | 44° | Nc | 46° | Nd | 48° | 57 | Ne | 50° | Nf | 52° |

IRAQ

Abu Ghurayb
Al Mahmudiyah
BAGHDAD
SDA
Al Iskandariyah
Al Mussayib
Ctesiphon
Hawr ash Shubayjah
Tursaq
Kalak
Ilam
Lumar
Kuhdasht
Sarab Dowreh
Chaghalvandi
Kabud
Chesmeh Varzani
Kuh-e Ilam 2900
Konjed Jan
Abu Zeyd Abad
Bad
Varkan
Arisman Ancient City
Natanz

Karbala
Al Hindiyah
Borsippa
Babylon
Al-Hillah
Az Zubaydiyah
Hawr as Suwayqiyah
An Nu'maniyah
Shaikh Ahmad
Khorramabad
307
Malavi
Sepit Dasht
Dorud
Aligudarz 4294
Masjid-e Jami
Golpayegan
Khonsar
Asgaran
Dehaqan
Nezam Abad
Zefreh
Neyestanek
Na'in
Ishtgah-e Na'in

Khan al Hammad
Al Kifl
Al Kufah
Nippur
Afak
Jassan
Mehran
Darreh Shahr
Nasiriyan
Cham Kabud
Pol-e Zal
Darreh Tank
Chaman Soltan
Daran
291
Damaneh
Morcheh Khort
Vazvan
Forudgan
Vartun
Kuhpayeh
Khomeyni Shar
IFN
Now Gonbad

An Najaf
Ash Shamiya
Ad Diwaniyah
Imam al Hamzah
Al Hayy
Wasit
Ali ash Sharqi
'Ali al Gharbi
Kuwait
Sa'diyah
Dehloran
Eyn Kush
Andimeshk
Mahru Mosque
Rud-e
Chadegan
Shahin Shar
Khomeyni Shar
Morbarakeh
Varzneh
ESFAHAN
(ISFAHAN)
Khorasgan
Aqda

Abu Sukhayr
Khan ar Rahbah
Ash Shanafiyah
Al Qusayr
Qal'at Sukkar
Ar Rifa'i
Ar Rumaythah
Musallam
Dezful
Šuš
Danial-e Nabi
Susa
Haft Tappeh
Shushtar
Jame Mosque
Lali
Sika water mills
Zarrin Shar
Farsah
Shahr-e Khord
Mohammad Abad
Hasan Abad
Naghan
Gavhuni Wetlands
Sav

Machmin
Al 'Ashuriyah
As Samawah
Al Khidr
Ash Shatrah
Erech (Uruk)
Al Uzayr
Sharmukhiyah
Hawr al 'Awdah
Bostan
Masjed Soleyman
Alhai
Izeh
Kuh-e Zarde 4548
Duran
Shur Ab
Ardal
Borujen
Gandoman
Koruyeh
Shahreza
Abadeh
Abarku
Esfand Abad

Ash Shabakah
As Salman
Al Batha
Suq ash Shuyukh
Eridu
Jalibah
An Nasiriyah
Ur
Al Qurnah
Hawr al Hammar
Ahu
Hamidiyeh
Hamid
Susangerd
Veys
Ahvaz
AWZ
Haftgel
Kuh-e Kalar 4298
Semirom
Surmaq
Eqlid
Deh Shir
Deh Bid
Qader Abad
Jian

Birkat al 'Aqabah
RAH
Rafha
Birkat al Jumaymah
Takhadid
Qasr Shaqrah
Al Basra
BSR
Abu al Khasib
Khorram Shar
ABD
Abadan
Darkhovin
Ramhormoz
Kolen
Landeh
Ramshir
Omidiyeh
Aghajari
Sangun
Deh Dasht
Basht
Do Gonbadan
Sardasht
Sapidan
Masiri
Ardakan
Kuh-e Dinar 4404
Yasuj
Sedeh

Nisab
Ash Shu'bah
Linah
Samah
Ar Ruqi
As Salmy
Jahrah
Red Fort
Al Kuwayt
(Kuwait)
Salmiya
Hawalli
KUWAIT
Subiyah
Failaka Island
Umm Qasr
Al Faw
Abdaly
Arvand Kenar
Bubiyan Island
Khowr-e Musa
Ras-e Baghel Boland
Barkan
Bandar-e Deylam
Emam Hasan
Chahar Rustal
Bandar-e Gonaveh
Bandar-e Rig
Kharg
Jazireh-ye Khark
Deris
Zargan
Bishapur
Kazerun
Dalaki
Borazjan
Shiraz
SYZ
Pol-e Fasa
Kherameh
Sarvestan
Kavar
Kuhenjan
Runiz
Fasa

Hafar al Batin
AQI
Al Qaysumah
As Sadawi
Wafra
Mina Saud
Ras al Khafji
Khark
Ahram
Coghadak
Kalmeh
Khowr-e Soltani
Bandar-e Busher
BUZ
Ras-e Halileh
Kaki
Firuz Abad
Kuh-e Safidar 3188
Jahrom
Kalah-Darab
Darvishi
Deh Now
Qala Dohtar
Makuyeh
Qotb Abad
Hoseyn Abad
Mansur Abad

Bir Shari
Oibah
Umm Ashar
Ash Sharjim
Al Lisafah
Al Wari'ah
Al Mish'ab
Ras al Mish'ab
As Saffaniyah
Ras al Tanaqib
Manifah
Jazireh-ye Jabrin
Khonj
Bandar-e Taheri
Asaluyeh
Lamard
Kuh-e Gavbast 2180
Beh Deh
Gavbandi
Bandar-e Moqam
Lavan
Jazireh-ye Lavan
Hendorabi
Jazireh-ye Kish

Aba ad Dud
Al Ayn
Qaryat al Ulya
An Nu'ayriyah
Ras az Zawr
Ras Abu 'Ali
Jana
Jazirat al Batmah
Abu Hadriyah
Nita'a
Al Jurayd
As Sirar
Jubail al Sinaiyah

Buraydah
ELQ
Al Bukayriyah
Ash Shamasiyah
Az Zilfi
Al Ghat
Al Habah
Al Lahabah
Al Qulayyib
Thaj
Hanidh
Sabkhat ar Riyas
Raihaimah
Jawan Tomb
Tarut Castle
Tarut
Ad Dammam
DHA
Qal'at al Bahrain
Dhahran
Al Khobar
Al Muharraq
BAH
Al Manama
Al Budayyi
Awali
BAHRAIN
Ra's Rakan
Abu Ruweis
Fuwairet
Jazireh-ye Hendorabi
Rostaq

Unayzah
Al Badaya
Rass
Al Midhnab
Al Qasab
Shaqra
Al Artawiyah
Az Zilfi
Hafar al 'Atk
Umm al Jamajim
Tamir
Ushayrah
Urayrah
Ayn Dar
Abqaiq
Salasil
An Na'La
Uyun
Al Marah
Al Uqayr
Hawar Is.
Gulf of Bahrain
Al Jumailiyah
Al Khor
Halul
QATAR
DOH
Ad Dawhah
(Doha)
Ar Rayyan
Al Wakrah
Umm Said
Das

Al 'Amar
Al Faydah
Sajir
Al Athalah
Nifi
'Usaylay
Khuff
'Arjah
Ar Raghbah
Ar Ruway'at
Marah
Thadiq
Huraymila
Sadus
Al Jubaylah
RUH
Burma Caves
Al 'Uwaynid
Ad Dir'iyah
Masmak Fort
AR RIYAD
(RIYADH)
Khurays
Al Mubarraz
Jawatha Mosque
Al Hufuf
HOF
Al Ghwaybiyah
Ras Abu Urayqit
Jaw
Ras's Laffan
Dukhan
Salwa
Kharanah

Ad Dawadami
Saffaqah
Arawah
Ar Ruwaydah
Ar Rayn
Halaban
Al Hariq
Dirab
Al Ha'ir
As Sulaymaniyah
Ad Durma
Al Muzahmiyah
Hafirat Nisah
Na'jan
Ad Dilam
Al Kharj
Al Udailiyah
Al Hunaiy
Khadam
15
Harad
205
Bujran
Salwa
Djebel Dhanna
Ruwais
As-Sila
Shamis
Habshan

Al Hariq
1196
Al Hilwah
Al Hillah
Al Birk
Al Ghayl
Al Hariq
Haradan
Ayn al Uwaya
Al Hamar
Al Kharfah
Na'jan
Wadi ash Shitan
At Tuwayrif
Djebel Dab
Qalamat Nadqar
Jirwan
Batn at Tarfa
Al Jawb
UNITED ARAB EMIRATES
Bu Hasa
Shilah
Al-Mariyyah
Tharwa-niyyah
Umm Hisin
Liwa Oasis

Sulaiyimah
As Sayh
Layla
Marwan
Al Haddar
Al Badi
Muqaynimah
Al 'Uwayja
Bir Fadil
Al-Kidan

Mesopotamia
IRAN
ZAGROS MOUNTAINS
Persian Gulf
ARABIA

| Nc | 46° | Nd | 48° | Ne | 61 | 50° | Nf | 52° | Ng |

29 30 31 32 33 34

59

Southern Arabian Peninsula

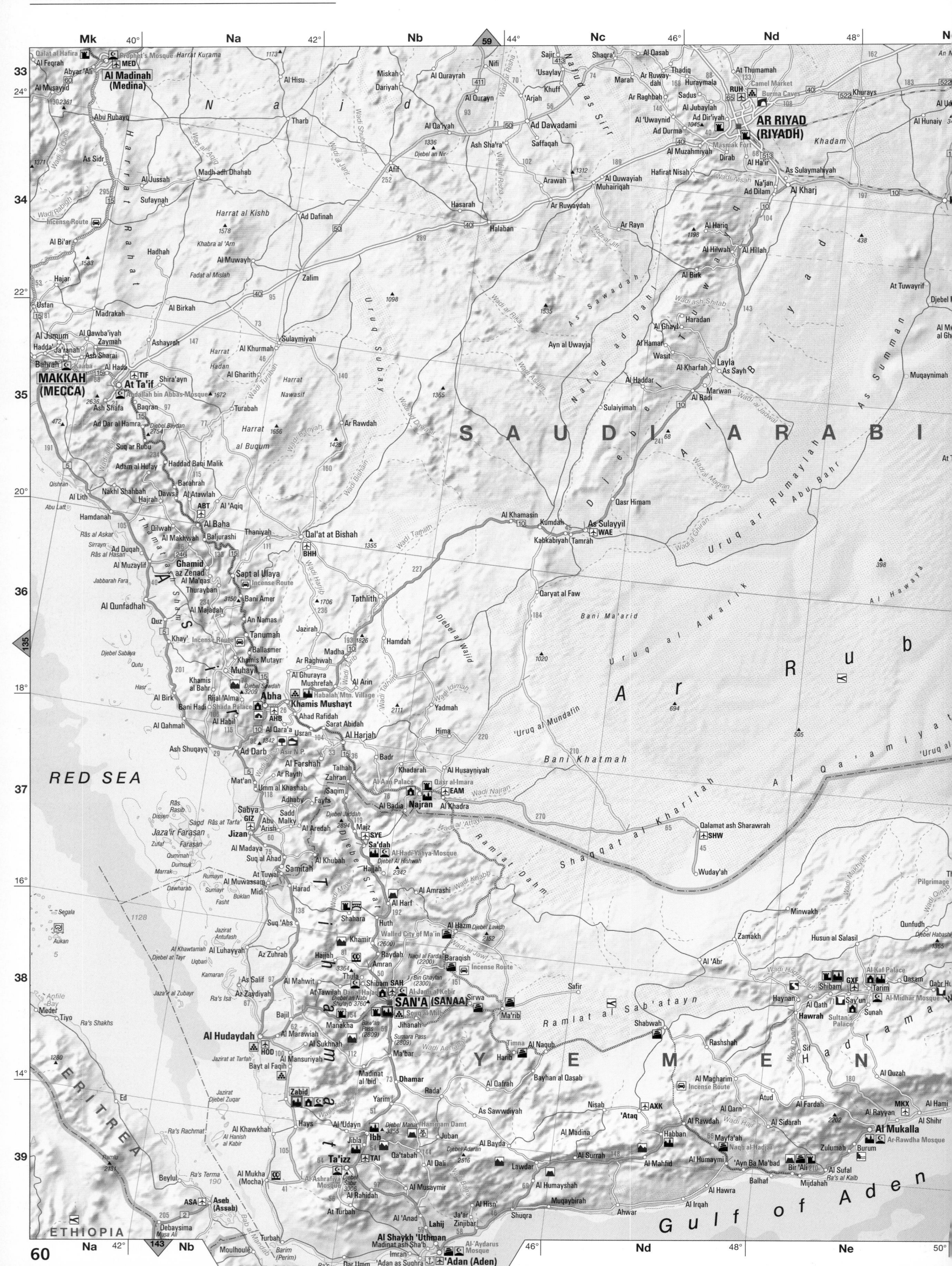

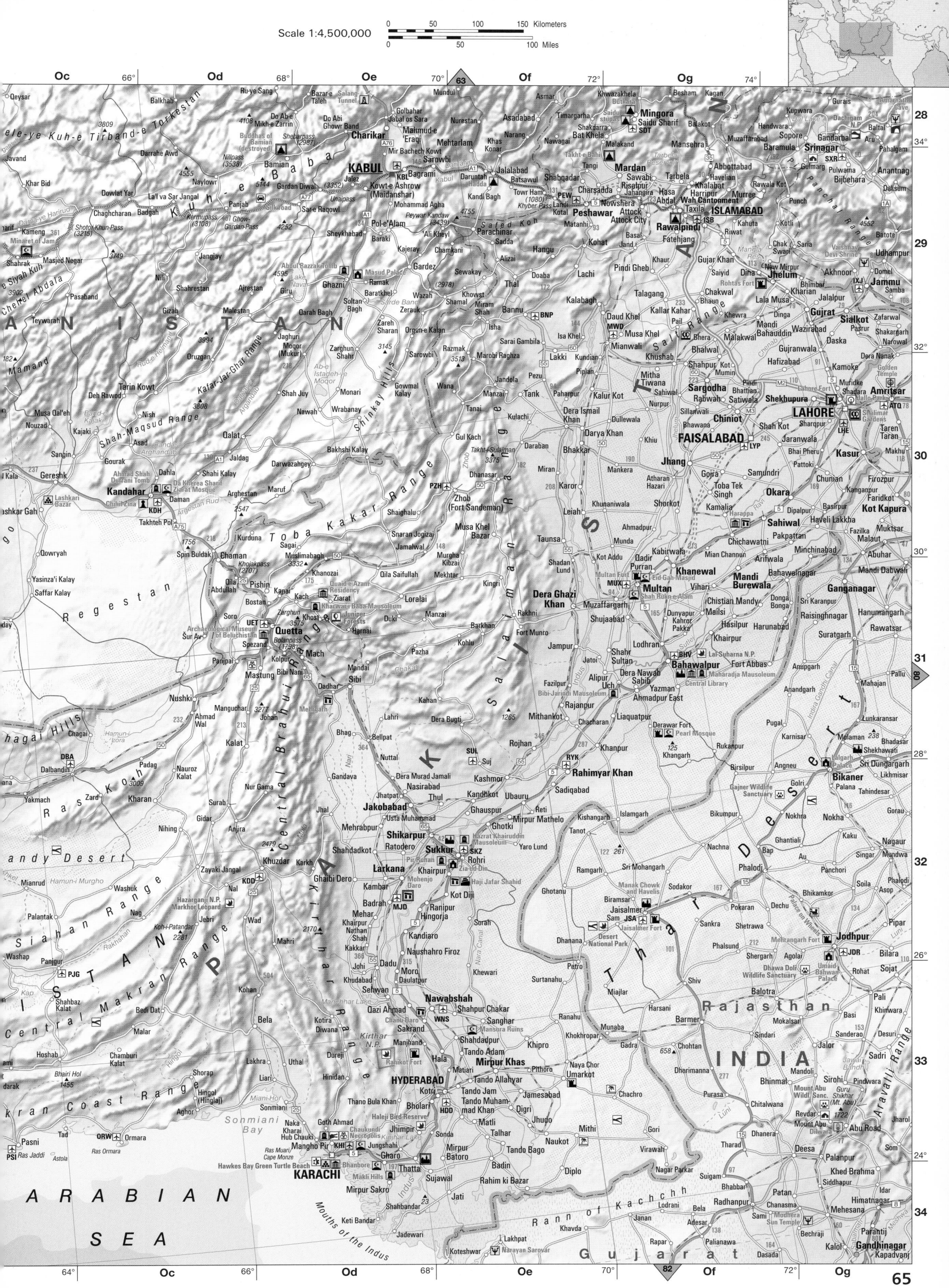

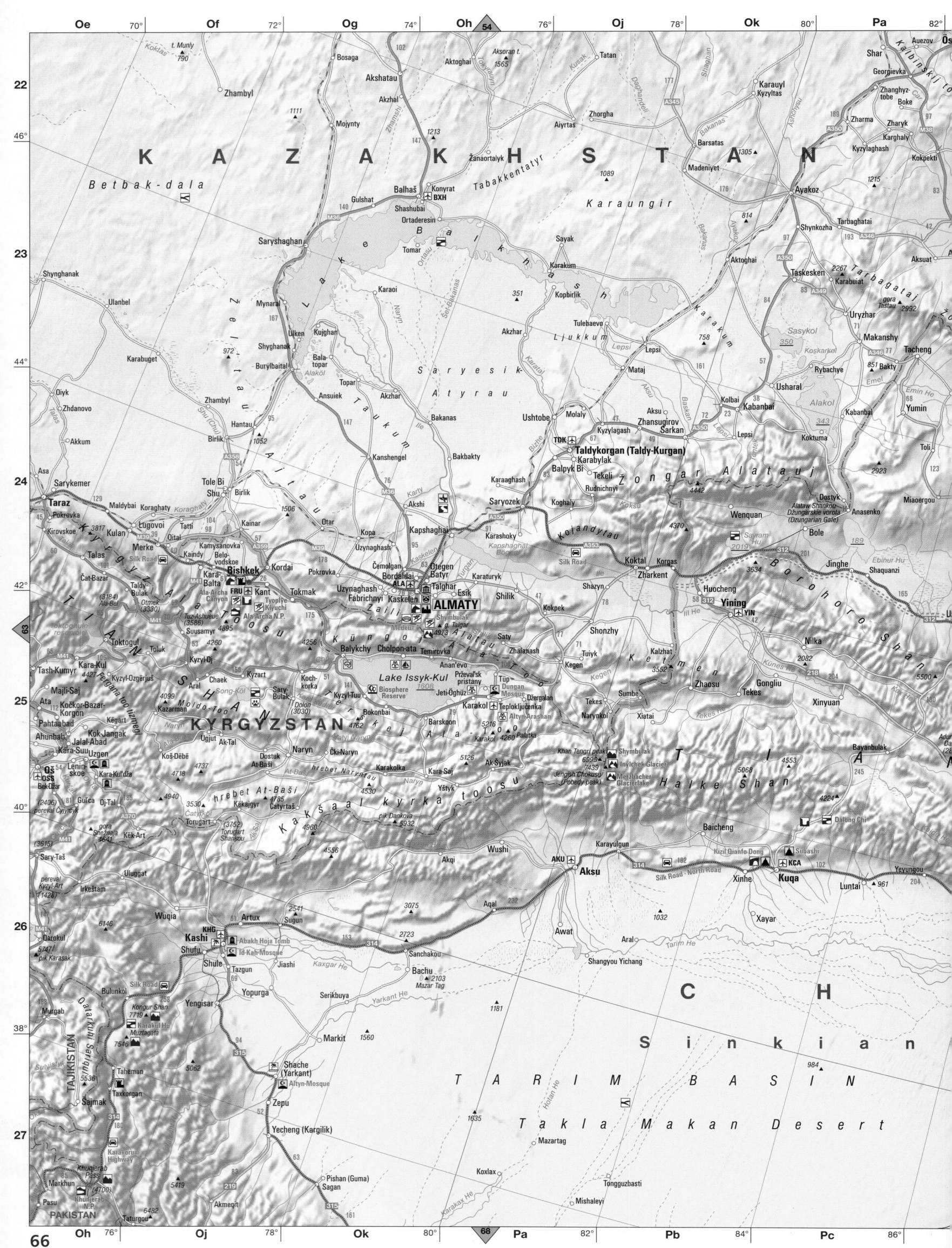

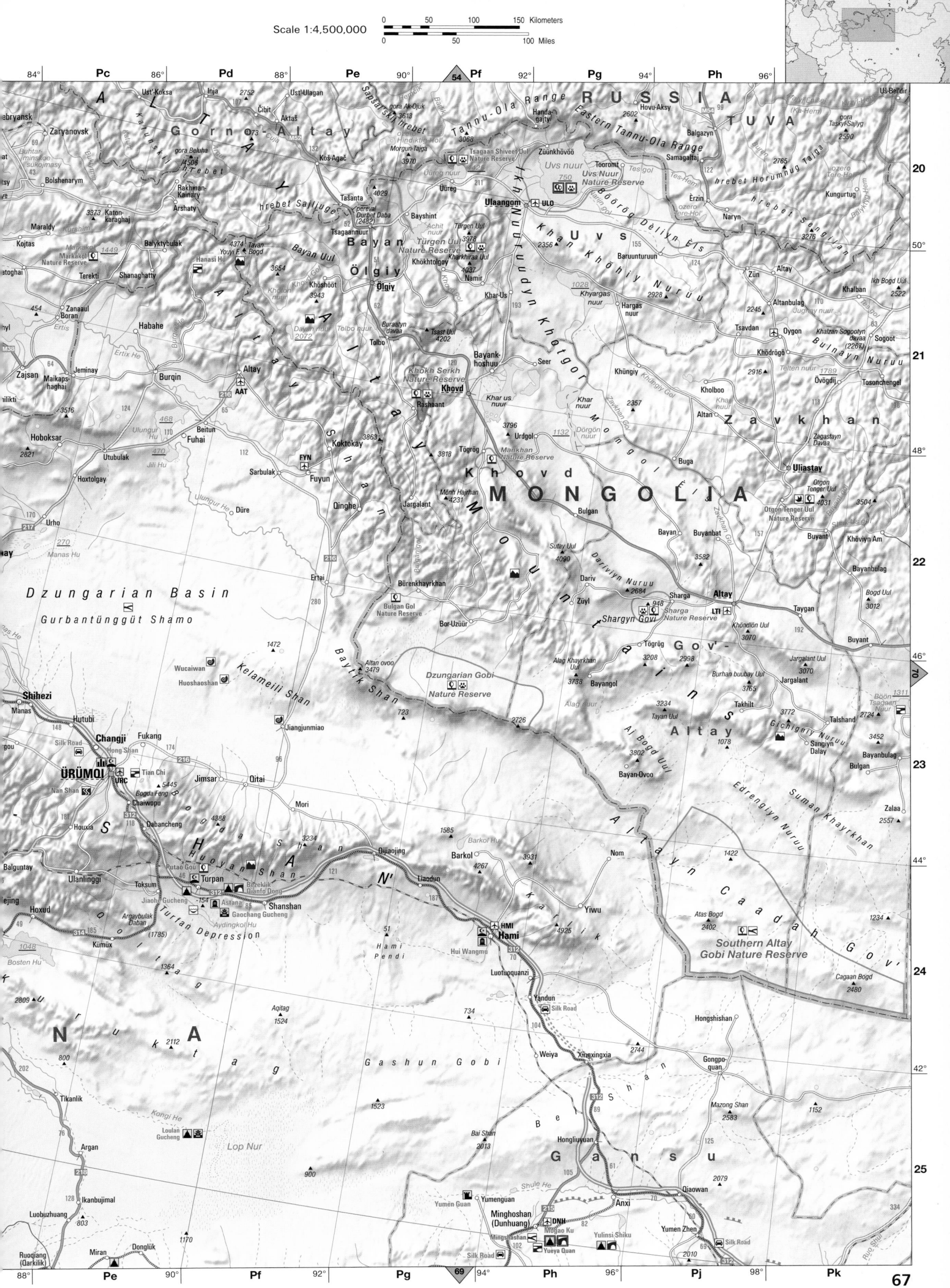

Tibet

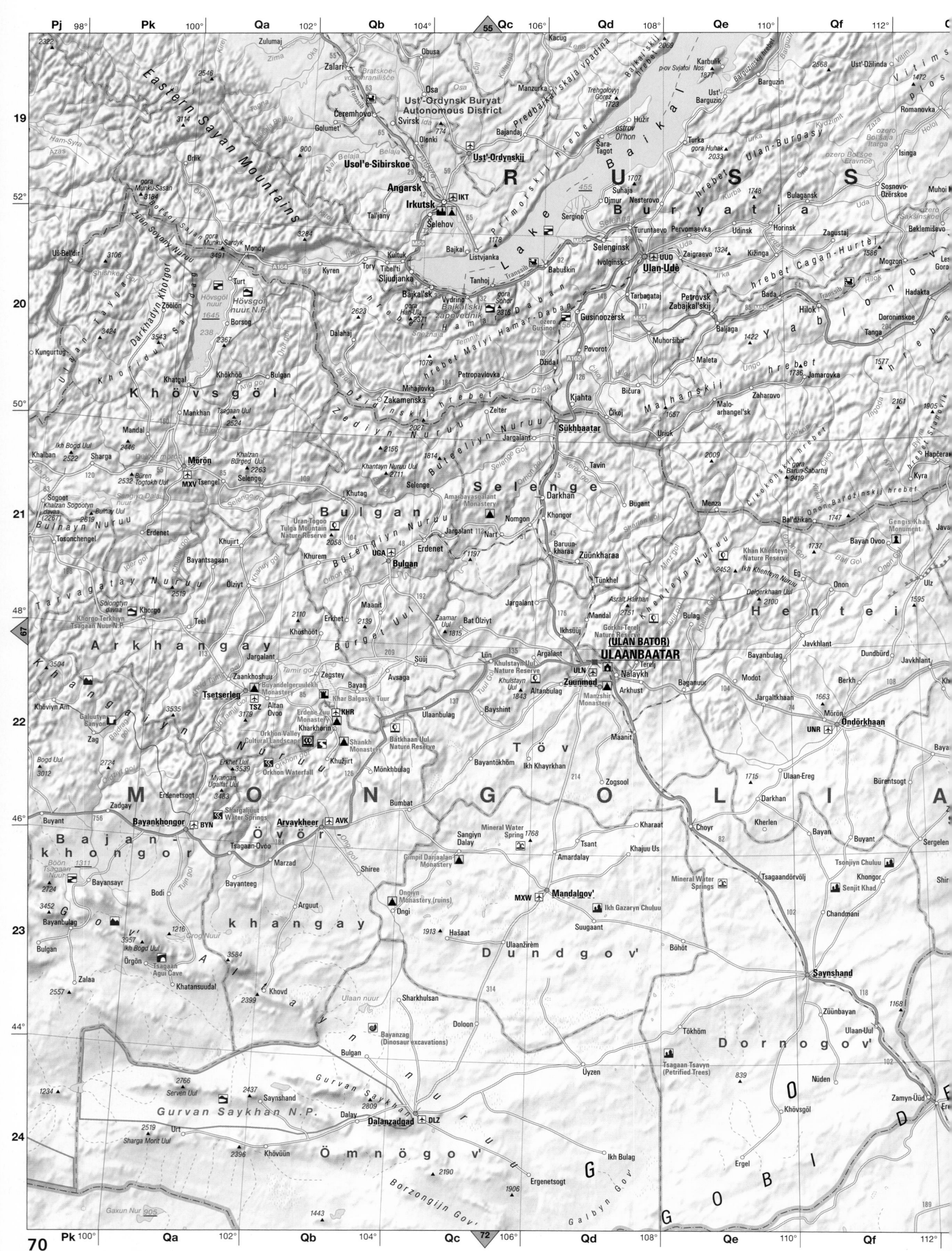

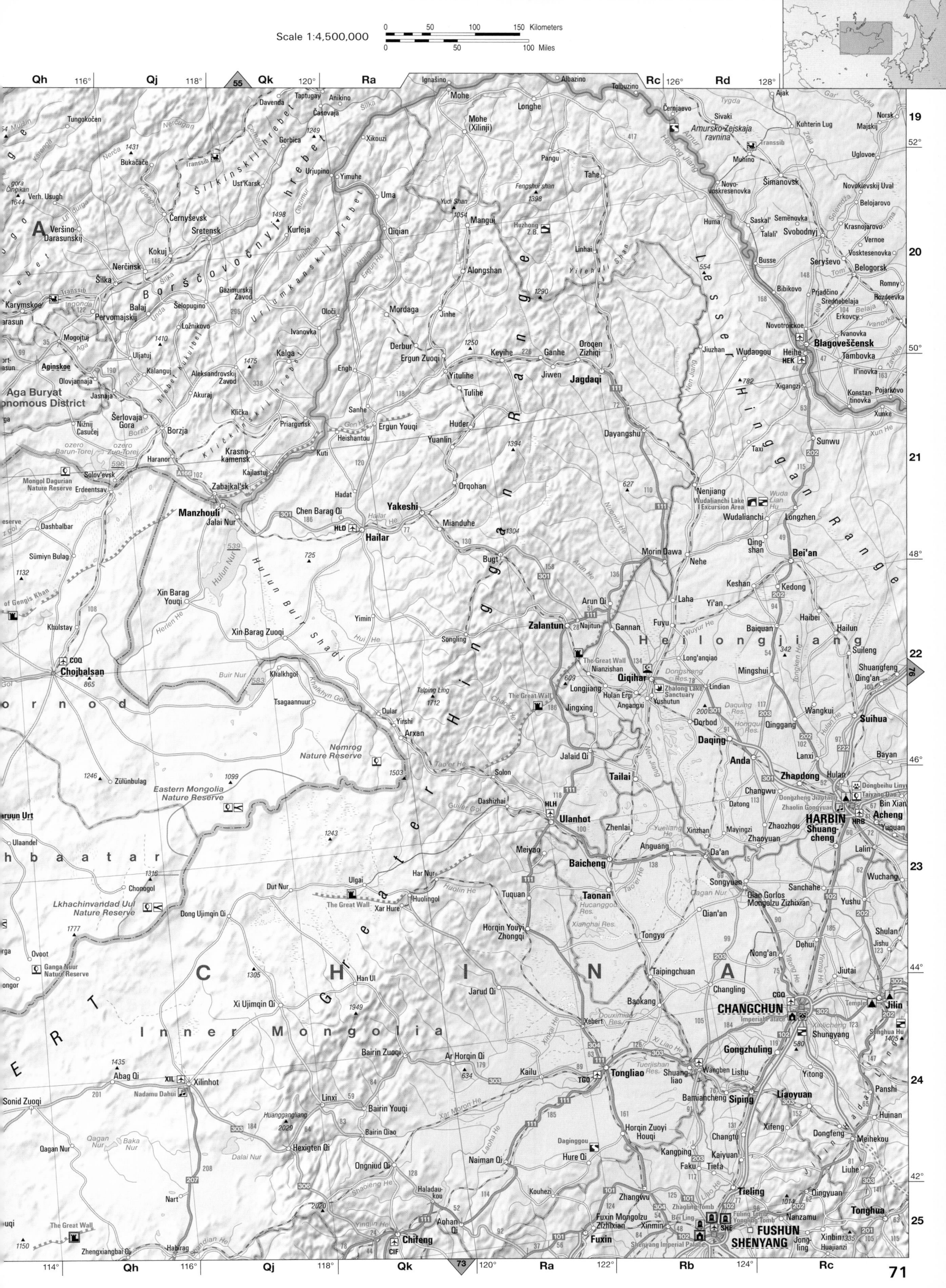

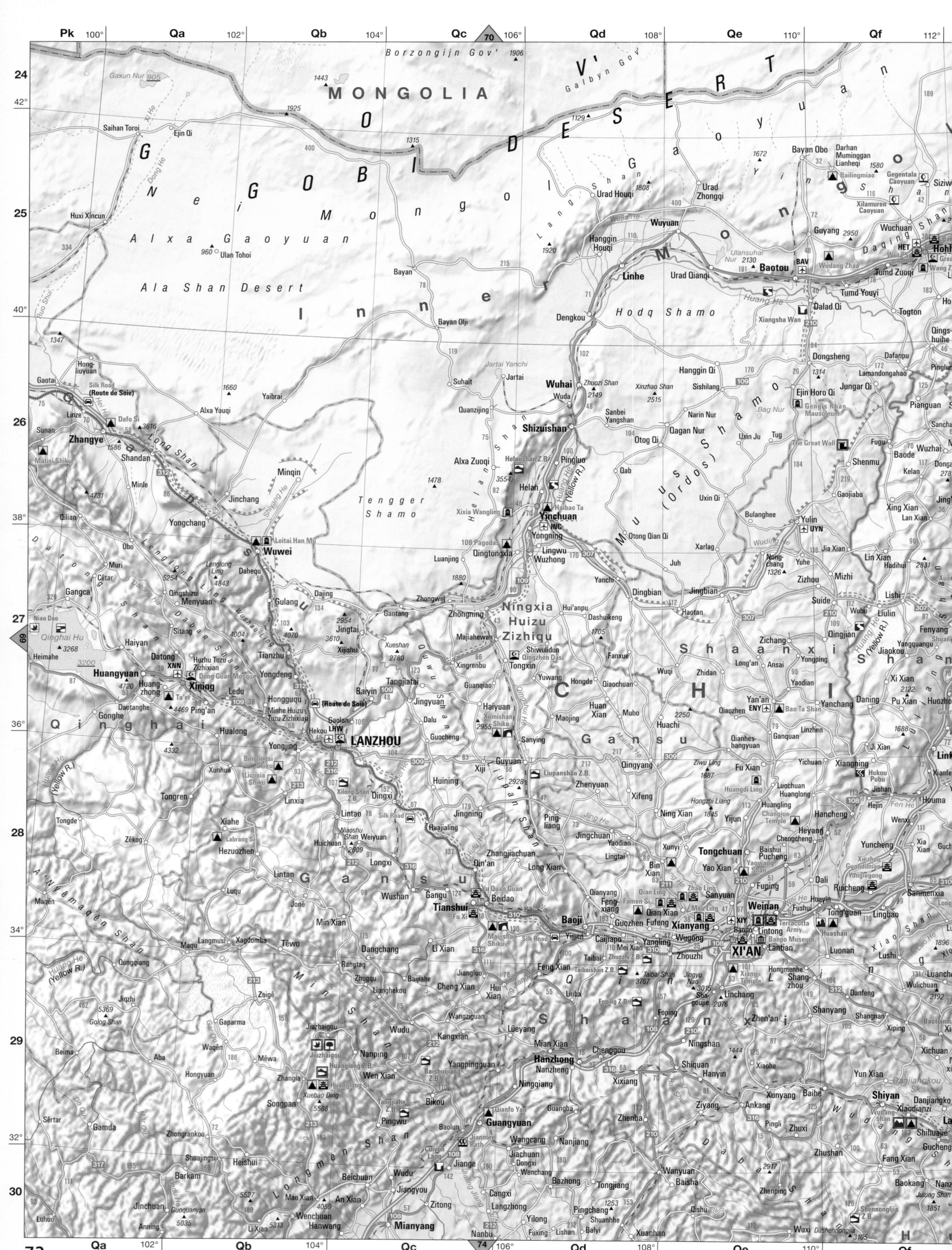

Southern China, Taiwan

WUHAN

HANGZHOU

Shanghai Shi

NANCHANG

FUZHOU

Zhejiang

Jiangxi

Fujian

Guangdong

TAIPEI

TAIWAN

KAOHSIUNG

EAST CHINA SEA

SOUTH CHINA SEA

Taiwan Strait

Luzon Strait

Gulf of Tonkin

HAINAN DAO

Hainan

Haikou

Sanya

Leizhou Peninsula

GUANGZHOU (CANTON)

HONG KONG

Hong Kong/Xianggang

Macao (Aomen)

MACAO

Tropic of Cancer

PHILIPPINES

Batan Islands

Babuyan Islands

MOUNTAINS

Penghu Islands (Pescadores)

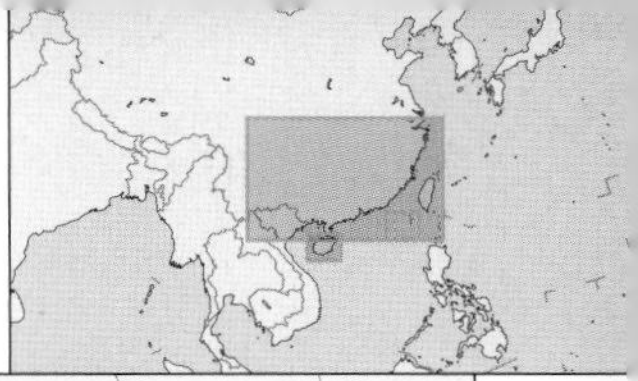

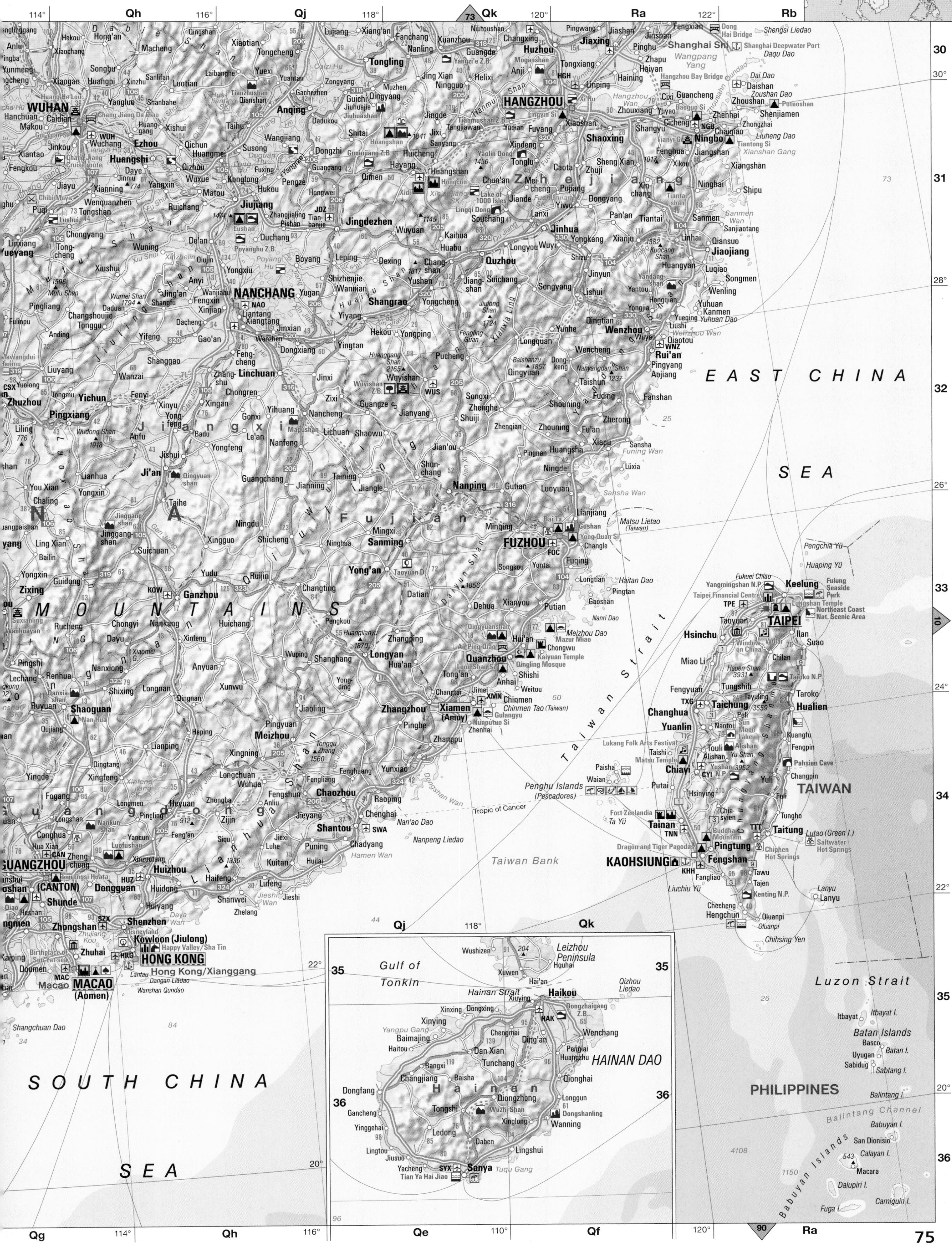

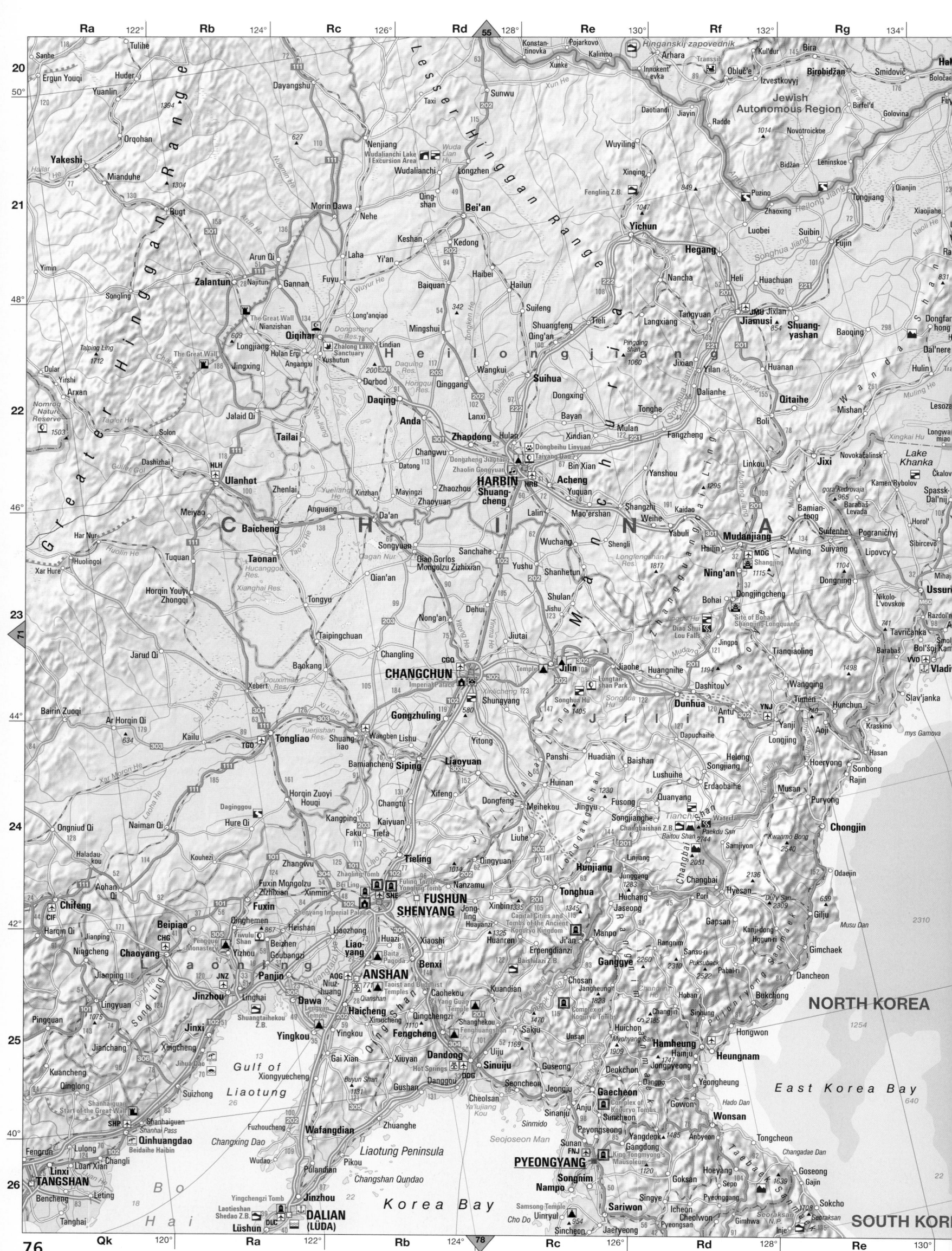

Rj 138° Rk 140° Sa 142° 55 Sb 144° Sc 146° Sd

RUSSIA

Sihote Alin'

gora Kamuj
1322
Slavnoe
zaliv
Prostor

Kuril'sk
Pioner
Rejdovo
o. Iturup
Burevestnik

gora Stokan
1634

Lesozavodskij
mys Rikorda

Sakhalin

Južno-Sahalinsk
UUS

Mordvinova
Holmsk
Ghotskoe
505
Ozerski

Korsakow
Novikovo
zaliv
Aniva
670
mys Aniva

Kuril Islands

vlk. Tjatja
1819
Tjatino
ozero Kunaśir
Južno-Kuril'sk
Sernovodsk
Golovnino

Malaja Kuril'skaja grjada
412
ozero Śikotan
880

La Perouse Strait
87
113

HOKKAIDO

Wakkanai
Soya-misaki
Sarufutsu
Hama-Tombetsu
Naku-Tombetsu

RBJ WKJ

Esashi

Omu
93

RIS

Shiretoko-misaki
Shiretoko-hanto
Shiretoko N.P.
1661
Rausu

SAPPORO

SPK/CTS

PACIFIC

OCEAN

Erimo-misaki
Erimo
Seamount
3735

Hakodate

HKD

Tsugaru Strait

Aomori

AOJ
MSJ

Hachinohe

Hirosaki

Morioka

Rikuchu-Kaigan N.P.

S e a o f J a p a n

Akita

AXT

Yamato Rise

Sakata

Tsuruoka

Ishinomaki

Izumi

Sendai

SDJ
Sendai-wan

JAPAN

Yamagata

Shiroishi
Soma

Fukushima

Haramachi
Namie

KIJ

SDO Ryotsu

Niigata

Koriyama

**Aizu
Wakamatsu**

Iwaki

Sado-jima

Nagaoka

Kashiwazaki

Hitachi

Joetsu

Nikko

Utsunomiya

Katsuta

Noto-hanto

Mito

Moka
Shimodate

Takaoka

Toyama

TOY

Maebashi

Kiryu
Ashikaga

Oyama

Nagano

Takasaki

Tsuchiura

Kanazawa

Matsumoto

MMJ

Kumagaya

Kawagoe

TYO/NRT

TOKYO

Chiba

Kashiwa

77

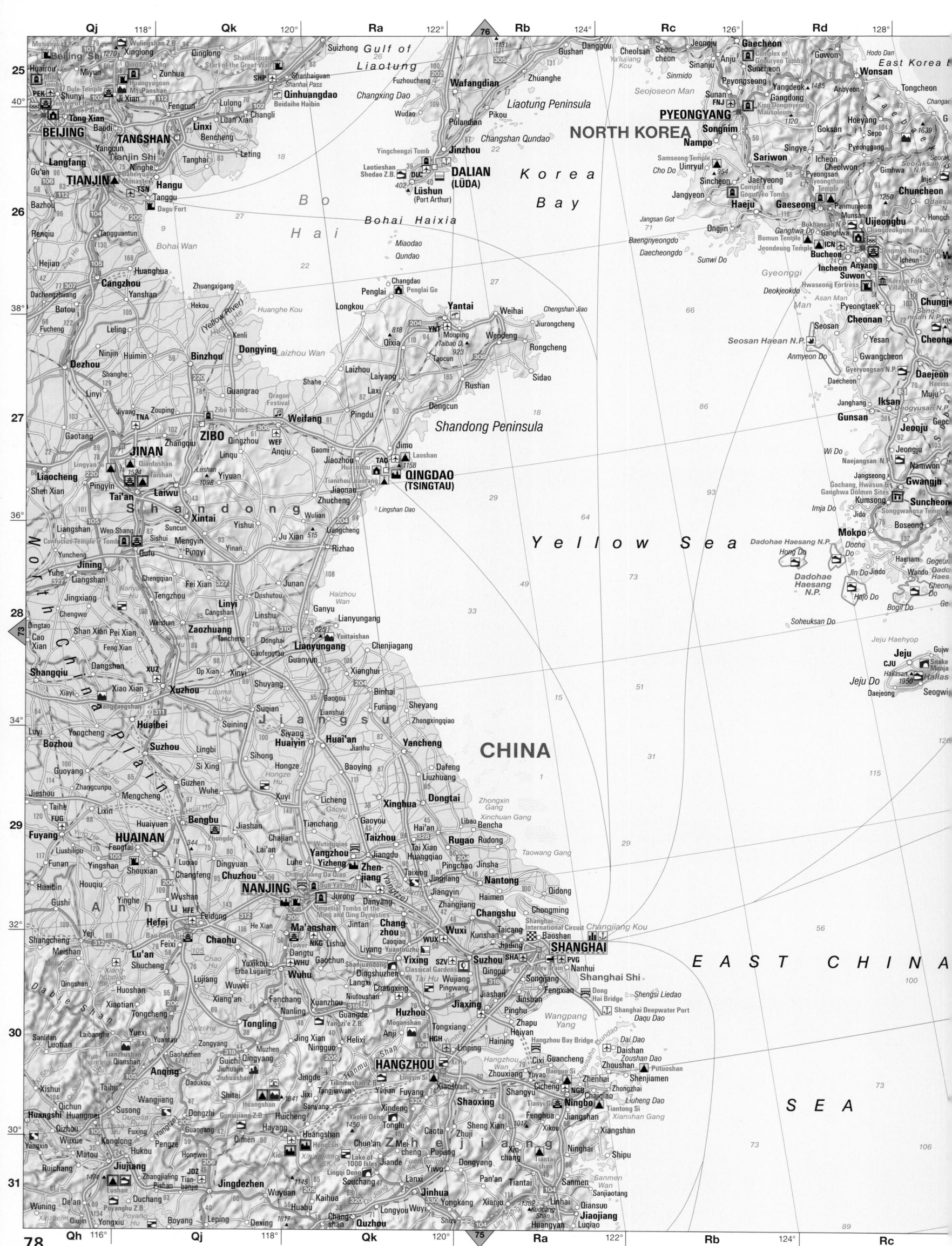

Eastern Sea

Sea of Japan

HONSHU

JAPAN

SOUTH KOREA

Taebaek
Uljin
Ullung
Ullung Do
Tok Do
Take Jima

Daisen-Oki
National Park
Oki-shoto
Nishino-jima
Nakano-jima
OKI
Dogo

Samcheok
Yeongdeok
Juwangsan N.P.

Pohang
Gyeongju
Seokguram Grotto &
Bulguksa Temple
Gyeongju Historic Areas

DAEGU
Ulsan

BUSAN
PUS

Noto-hanto
Suzu-misaki
Kashiwazaki
Ojiya
Tokamachi
Echigo-Sanzan
Tadami Q.N.P.
Yamatsun
Kitaibaraki
Kuroiso
Hitachi
Katsuta

Joetsu
Nikko N.P.
Nikko
Imaichi
Utsu-nomiya
Moka
Mito

Toyama
Takaoka
Kanazawa
Komatsu
Fukui
Takefu

Matsumoto
Nagano
Ueda
Takasaki
Kumagaya
Oyama
Tsuchiura
Narita
Choshi

Gifu
Ichinomiya
NAGOYA
Komaki
Toyota
Okazaki
Kariya
Anjo
Toyohashi
Hamamatsu

KYOTO
OSAKA
KOBE
Nara
Uji
Otsu
Suzuka
Yokkaichi
Tsu
Matsuzaka
Ise
Shrines of Ise
Ise-shima N.P.

TOKYO
YOKOHAMA
KAWASAKI
Kamakura
Yokosuka
Odawara
Hakone
Izu-hanto
Atami
Ito
Shimoda

Shizuoka
Fujieda
Fuji
Numazu
Mishima

HIROSHIMA
Yamaguchi
Tokuyama
Hofu
Ube
Shimonoseki
KITAKYUSHU
FUKUOKA

Kure
Iwakuni
Matsuyama
Imabari
Niihama
Takamatsu
Tokushima
Kochi

Okayama
Kurashiki
Fukuyama
Onomichi
Takehashi
Soja

SHIKOKU

PACIFIC
OCEAN

Saga
Kurume
Oita
Beppu
Nakatsu
Kumamoto
Yatsushiro
Nobeoka
Hyuga
Miyazaki
Miyakonojo
Kagoshima

Nagasaki
Sasebo
Omuta
Isahaya
Shimabara

KYUSHU

Amakusa N.P.
Kirishima-Yaku N.P.

Satsuma-hanto
Ibusuki
Sata misaki

EAST CHINA

SEA

JAPAN

Tanega-shima
Yakushima N.P.
Yaku-jima

Tokara Strait
Kuchino-jima
Nakano-jima
Suwanose-jima
Akuseki-jima

Tokara Islands

Ryukyu Islands
(Nansei Islands)

Satsunan Islands

Takara-jima

Yokoate-jima

Kasari
Naze
O-jima
Setouchi
Kakeroma-jima
Kikai-jima

TKN
Tokuno-shima
Tokunoshima

Amami Islands

Ryukyu Islands (Nansei Islands)

Amami Islands

Kasari
OIM
O-jima
Setouchi
Kakeroma-jima

Tori-jima
TKN
Tokuno-shima
Tokunoshima

OKE
Okinoerabu-jima
Wadomari

Yoron
Yoron-jima

Iheya-jima
Iheya
Izena-jima
Ie-jima
Motobu
Nago
Okinawa-jima

Okinawa
OKA
Naha
Nakagusuku Castle
Gyokusendo
(Cave)
Kume-jima
Kerama-retto

Okinawa Islands

Sekibisho Jima

Uotsuri
Jima
Shenkaku Islands

Sakishima Islands

Miyako Jima
Hirara
Tarama
Jima
Hirano
Ishigaki Jima
Iriomote
Jima

Ryukyu (Nansei) Islands

PACIFIC

OCEAN

Ryukyu Trench

Okinawa Trench

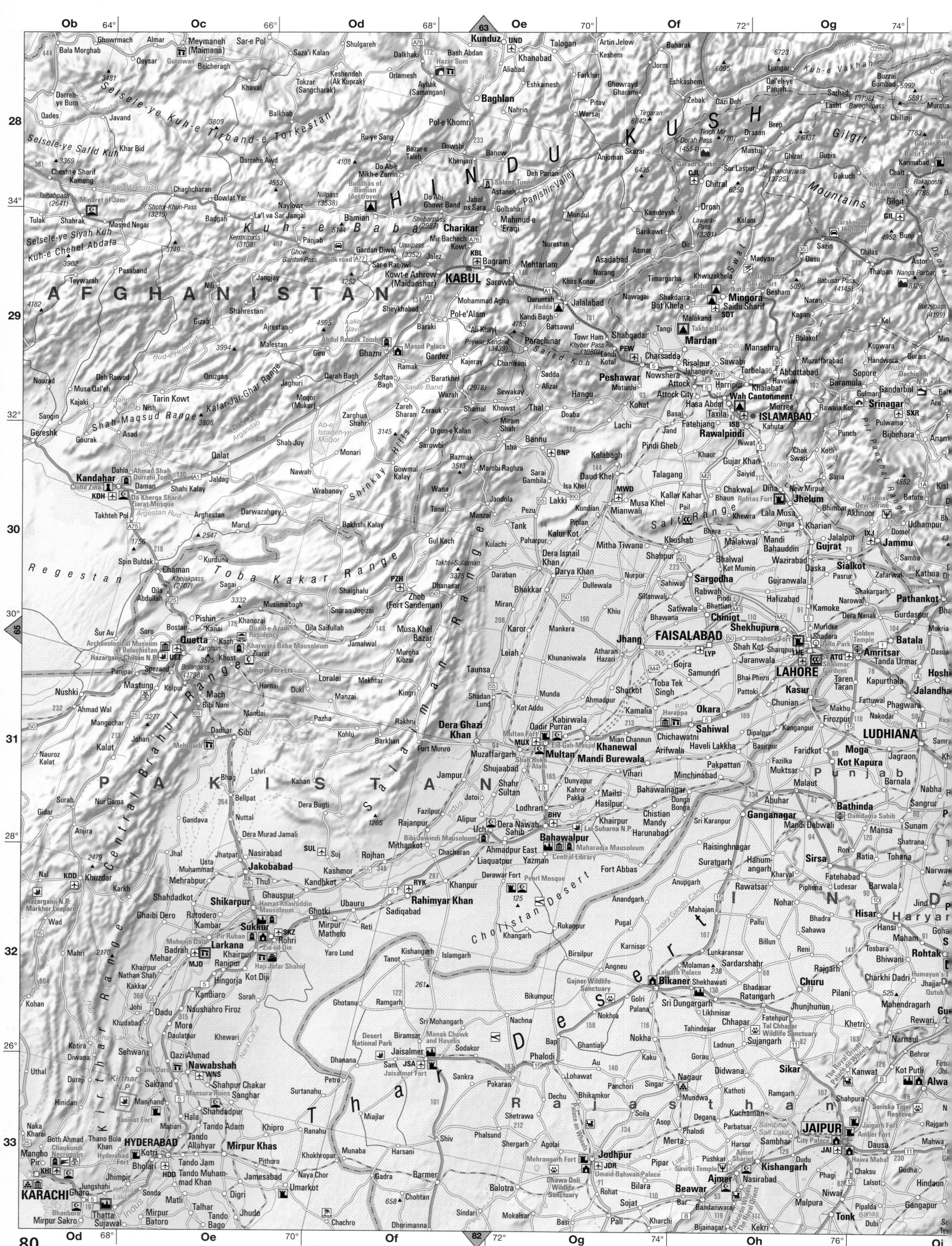

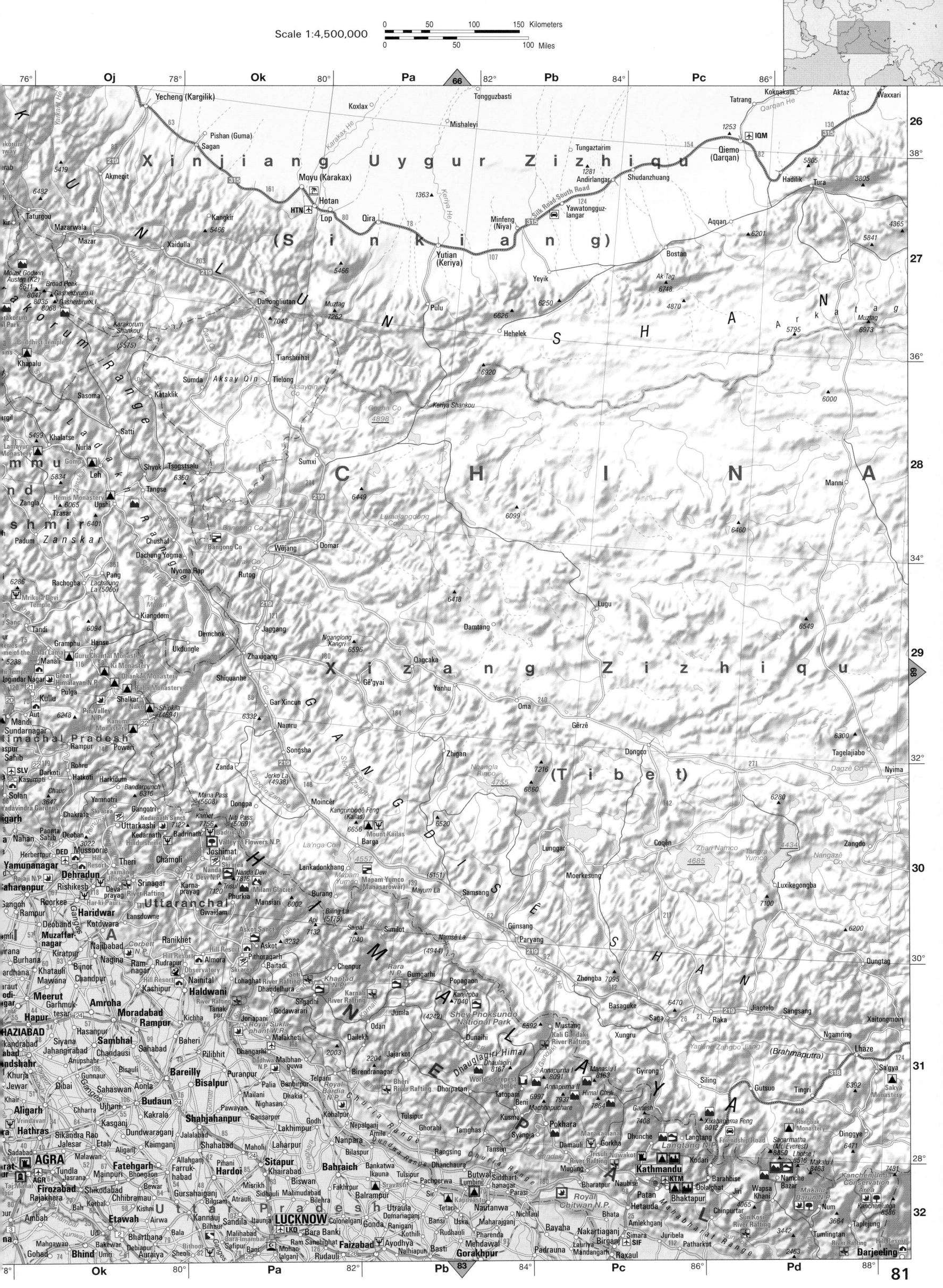

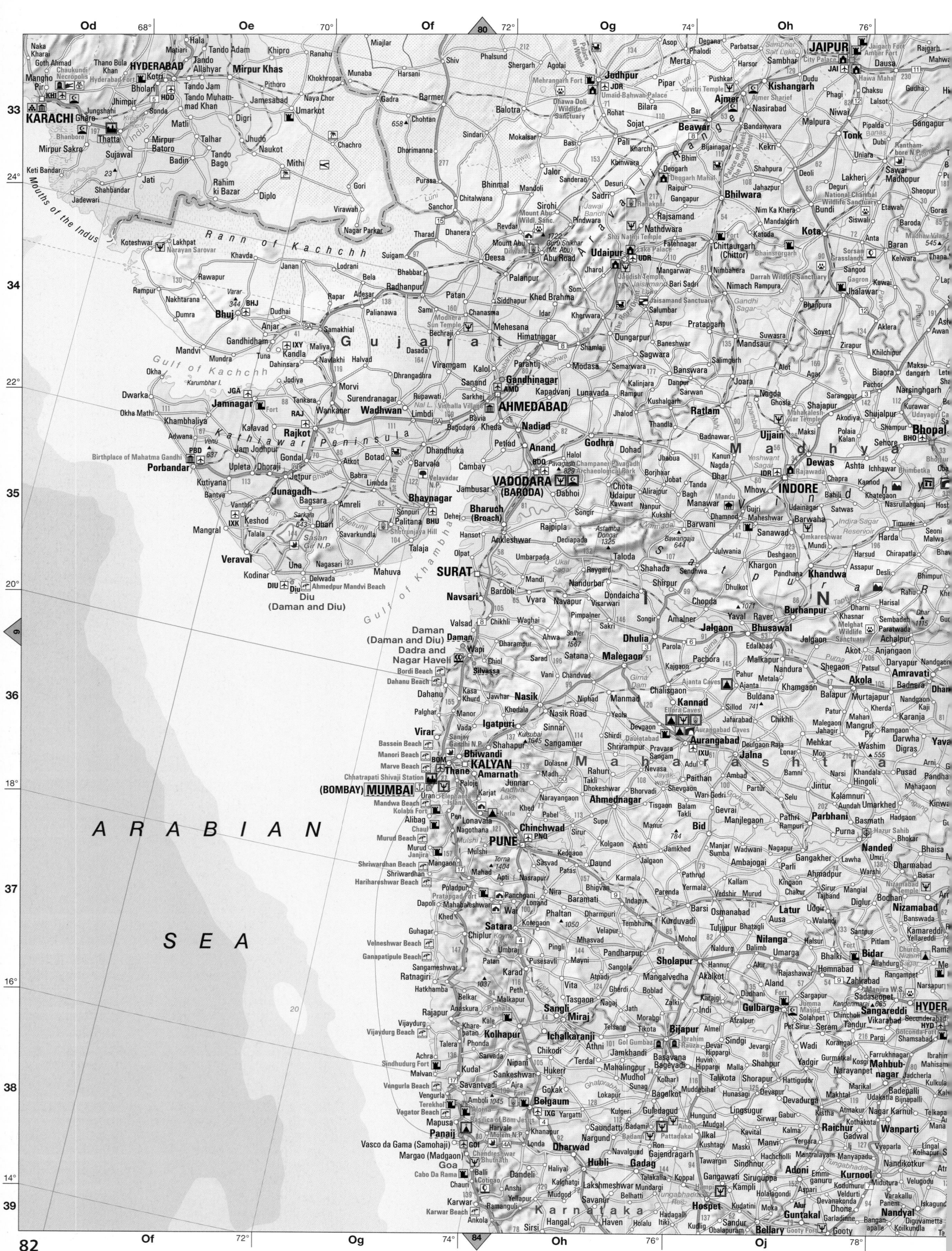

Scale 1:4,500,000

0 50 100 150 Kilometers

0 50 100 Miles

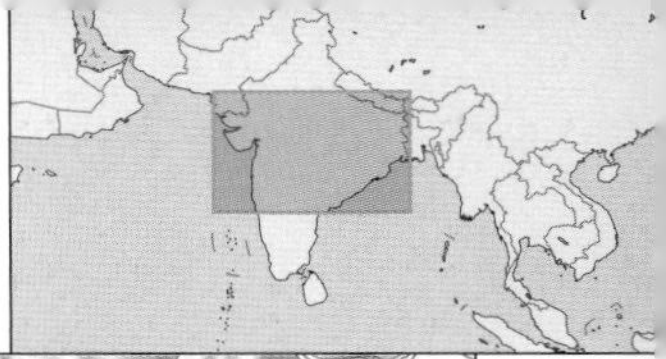

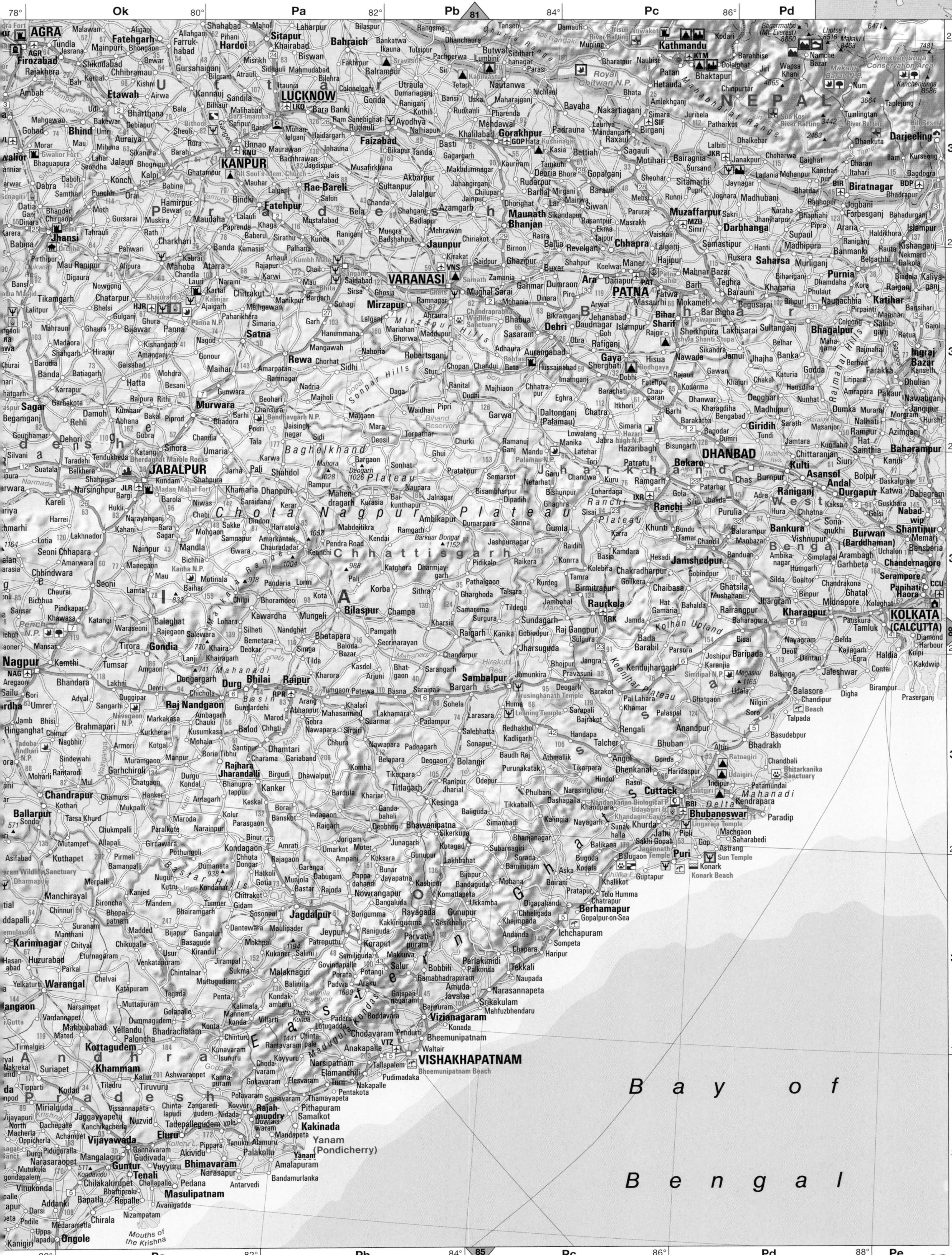

Southern India, Maldives, Sri Lanka

A R A B I A N

S E A

Laccadive Islands

Bitra I.

Chetlat I.

Amindivi Islands   Kilttan I.

Perulmar   Kadmath I.
Par I.

Bangaram I.   Amini I.
AGX   Agatti I.

Kavaratti   Andrott I.
Kavaratti I.

Suhell I.

Cannanore Islands   Kalpeni I.

Lakshadweep

Nine Degree Channel

Minicoy I.

Eight Degree Channel   Lakshadweep

Sea

Haa-Alifu Atoll
(North Thiladhunmathee Atoll)

Dhidhdhoo
Haa-Dhaalu Atoll
Makunudu Atoll   (South Thiladhunmathee Atoll)
Nolhivaranfaru

Shaviyani Atoll
(North Miladhunmadulu Atoll)
Farukolhu

Raa Atoll
(Maalhosmadulu North)   Noonu Atoll
Ugoofaaru   (South Miladhunmadulu Atoll)
Manadhoo

Pearl Island   Neifaru
Moresby Channel   Lhaviyani Atoll
Baa Atoll
(Maalhosmadulu
South)   MALDIVES
Eydhafushi   Kaashidhoo
Kardiva Channel   Gaafaru Channel
Tohddoo Atoll   North Male Atoll
Rasdhoo Atoll

Arie Atoll   Male   MLE
(Alifu Atoll)
Mahibadhoo   South Male Atoll

Beaches   Scuba diving
Felidhoo Channel
Ariadhoo Channel
Faafu Atoll   Felidhoo Atoll
(North Nilandhoo Atoll)   (Vaavu Atoll)
Magoodhoo   Vattaru Channel

Dhaalu Atoll   Meemu Atoll
(South Nilandhoo Atoll)   Muli   (Mulaku Atoll)
Kudahuvadhoo

Kudahuvadhoo Channel

Thaa Atoll
(Kolhumadulu Atoll)

Veymandhoo

Veymandhoo Channel

Laamu Atoll
Hithadhoo   (Hadhdhunmathee Atoll)

Southern India (east side)

Karwar
Karwar Beach
Ankola   Karnataka
Kumta   Siddapur   Hospet
Honavar   Sagar   Shimoga   Bellary
Bhatkal   Chitradurga
Marvanthe Beach   Chikmagalur
Malpe Beach   Udupi   Tumkur
Mangalore   Hassan   BANGALORE
Ullal Beach   Mandya
Kasaragod   Mysore
Bekal Beach   Madikeri
Hosdrug   Kannur (Cannanore)
Thalasseri (Tellicherry)
Mahé Mahe (Pondicherry)
Kozhikode (Calicut)
Beypore   Coonoor
Manjeri   Erode
Ponnani   COIMBATORE   Karur
Kerala   Palakkad (Palghat)   Pollachi
Thrissur (Trichur)
Valparai   Dindigul
Kodungallur (Cranganore)
Ernakulam   Munnar
Fort Kochi   MADURAI
Jew Town
KOCHI (COCHIN)   COK
Alappuzha (Alleppey)
Changanassery (Changanacherry)
Harippad   Rajapalaiyam   Sivakasi
Kayankulam
Kollam (Quilon)   Tirunelveli
Varkala   Palayankottai
Nedumangad   Tuticorin
THIRUVANANTHAPURAM
(TRIVANDRUM)   TRV
Kovalam Beach
Padmanabhapuram
Nagercoil
Kumari   Cape Comorin
Amman
Temple

Gu
of
Mann

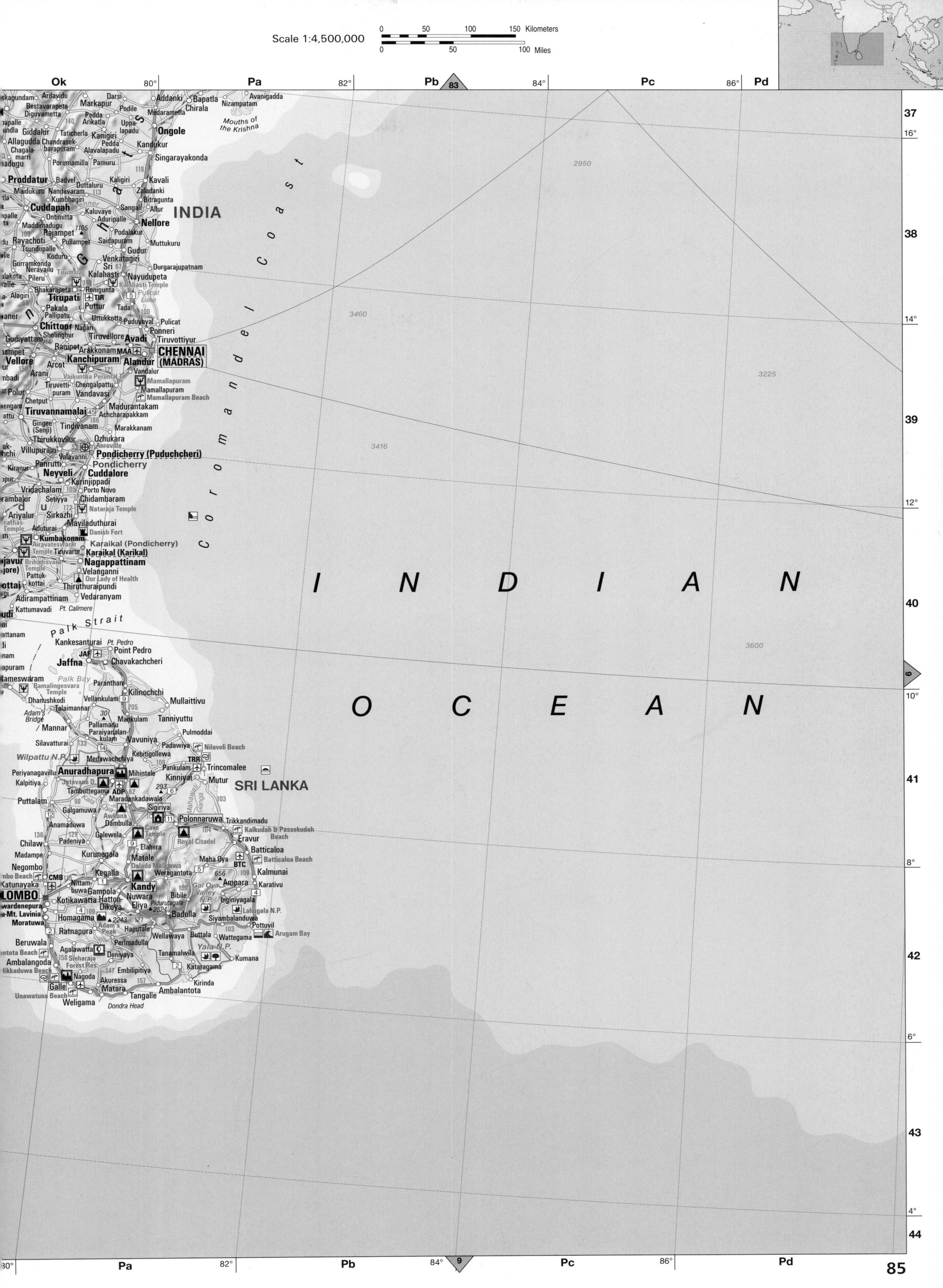

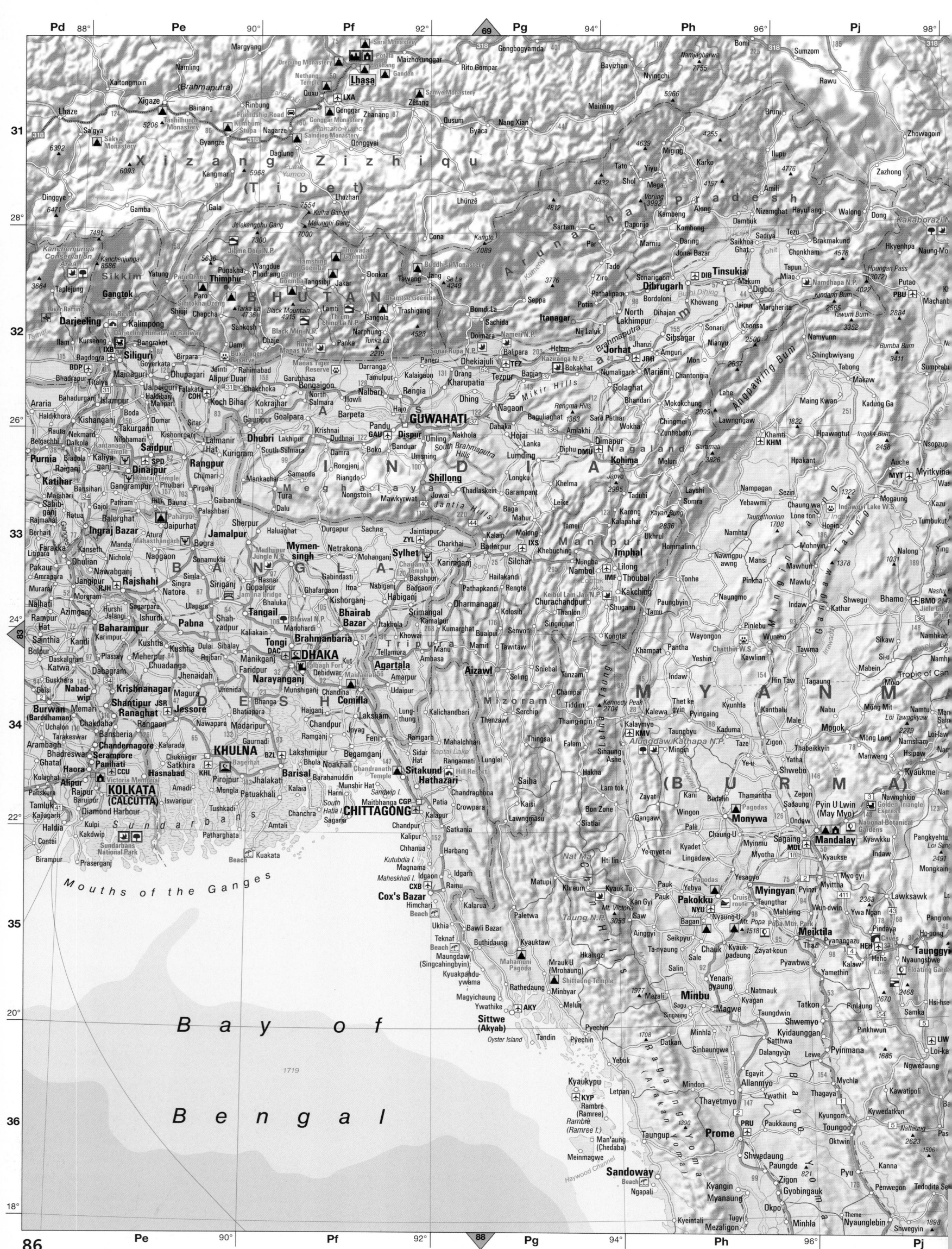

Qa   Qb   74   Qc   Qd   Qe

100°   102°   104°   106°   108°

31

28°

CHINA

Sichuan

Luzhou
Yibin
Zunyi
Bijie   **GUIYANG**
Kaili
Duyun

Zhaotong

Panzhihua (Jinjiang)
Xuanwei
Anshun
Liupanshui

32

26°

Xiaguan (Dali)
Chuxiong
KUNMING
Qujing
Guangnan

Guizhou

33

24°

Guangxi Zhuangzu Zizhiqu

Lincang
Yuxi
Kaiyuan
Geju   Mengzi   Wenshan
Bose

Nanning   NNG

34

Simao

22°

Lao Cai
Sapa
Lang Son

Jinghong

L A O S

Dien Bien Phu

Viet Tri   **HANOI**
Son Tay
Haiphong
Halong City (Hong Gai)

35

Luang Prabang

Chiang Rai

Muang Xai
Nam Tha

Thai Nguyen
Bac Ninh
Hai Duong

20°

Thanh Hóa

Gulf of Tonkin

36

THAILAND

Viangchan (Vientiane)
Nong Khai

VIETNAM

Vinh

18°

Chiang Mai
Lamphun
Lampang

Udon Thani   UTH
Nakhon Phanom   KOP
Sakhon Nakhon

Dong Hoi

37

Pk   Qa   89   Qb   Qc   Qd

100°   102°   104°   106°

87

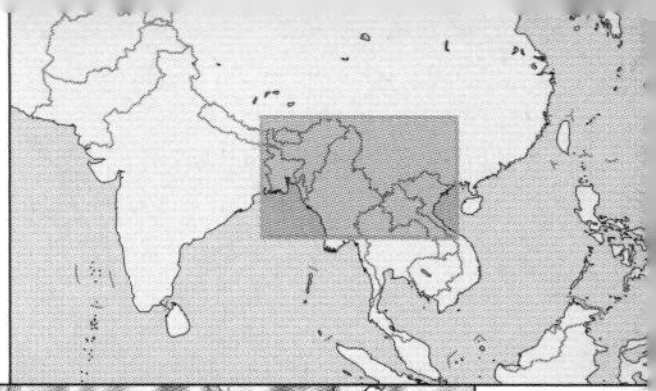

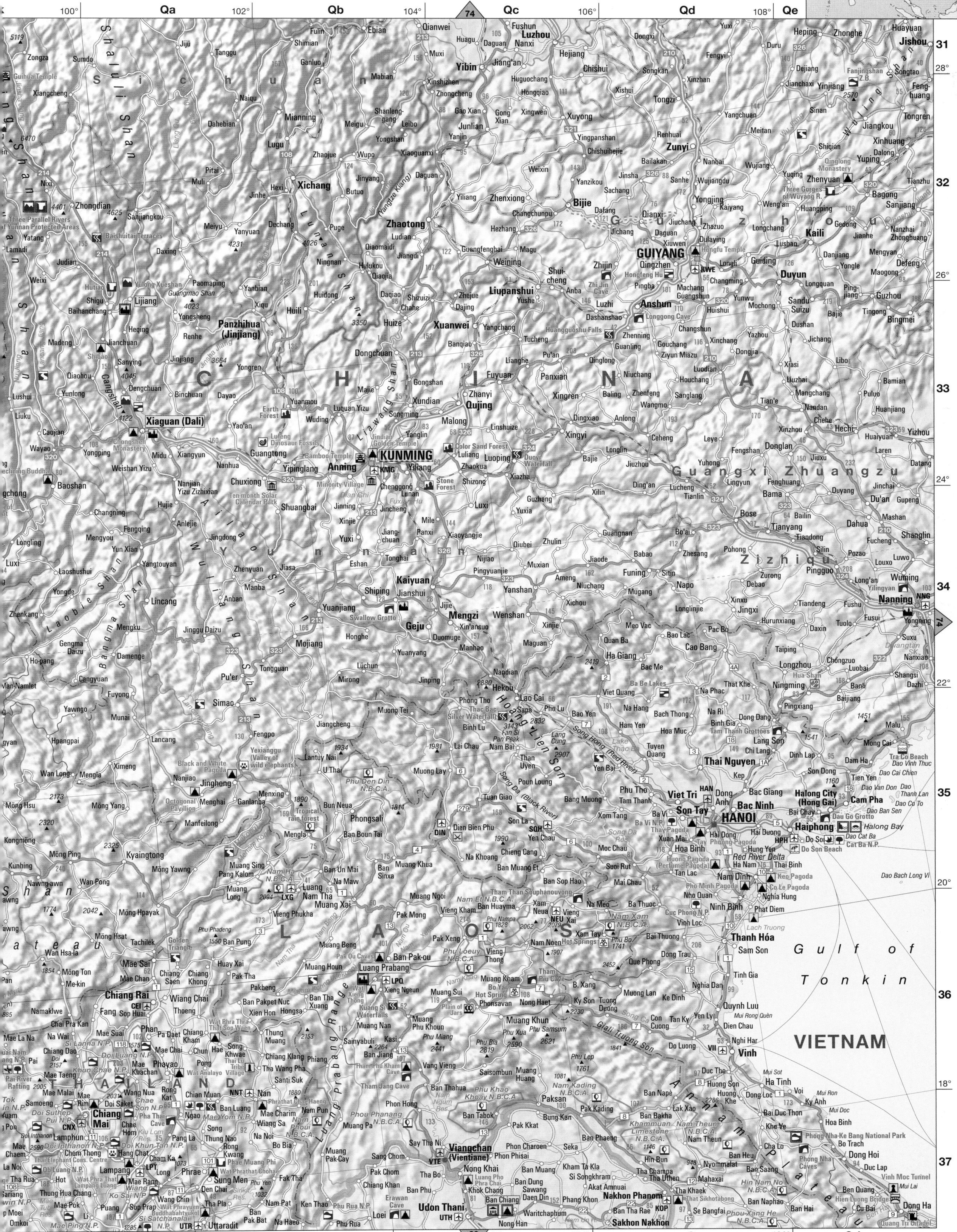

Philippines

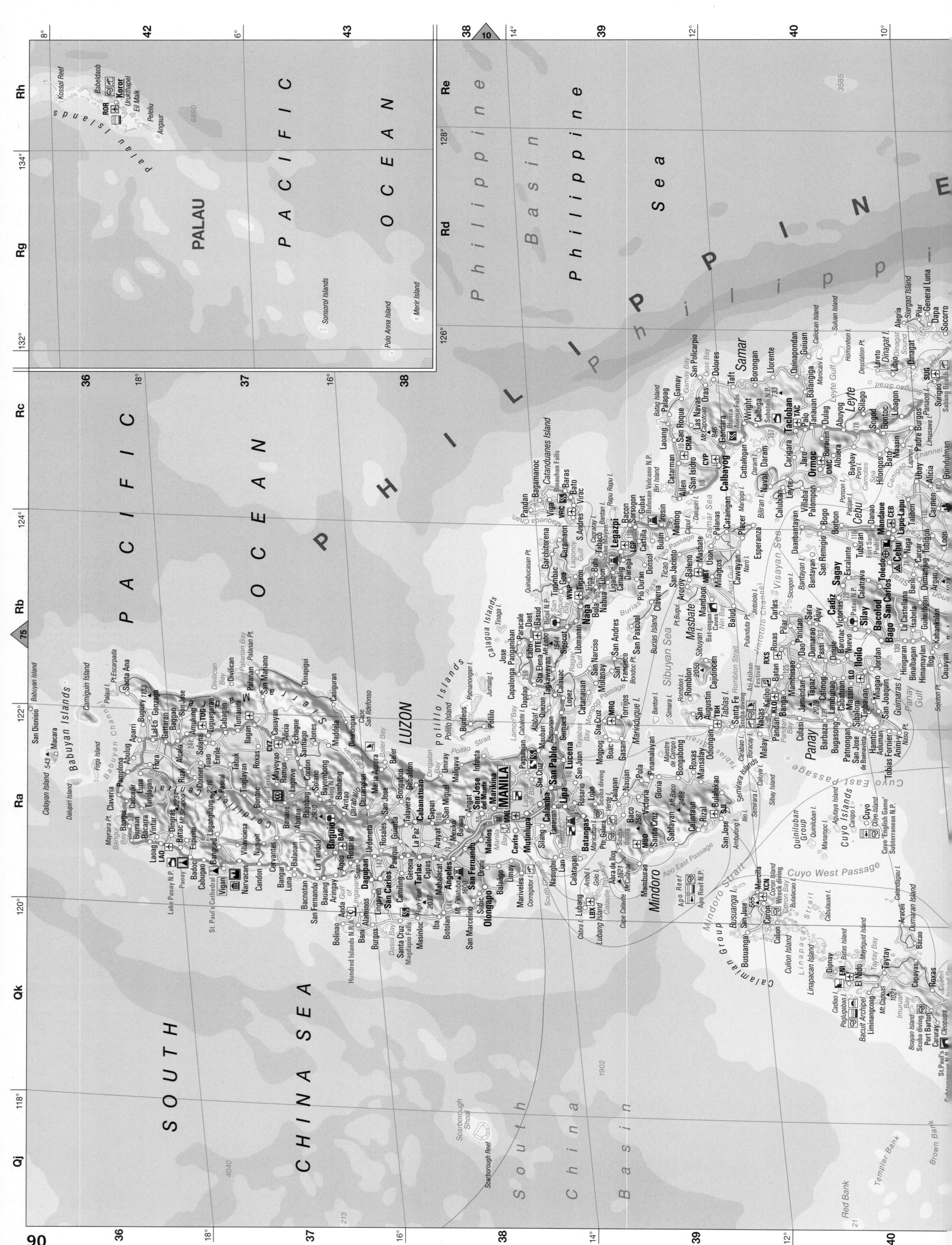

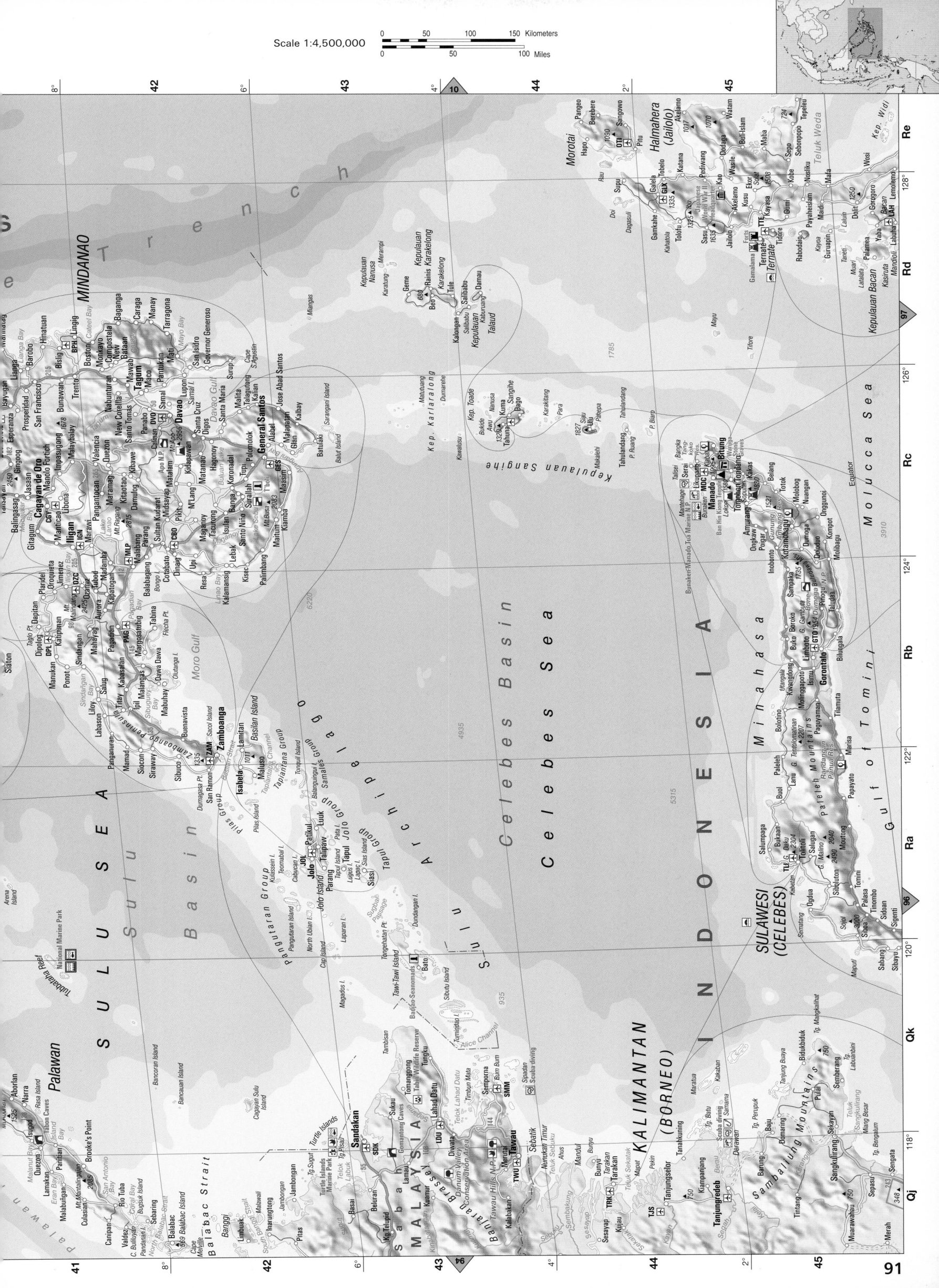

Sumatra, Malay Peninsula

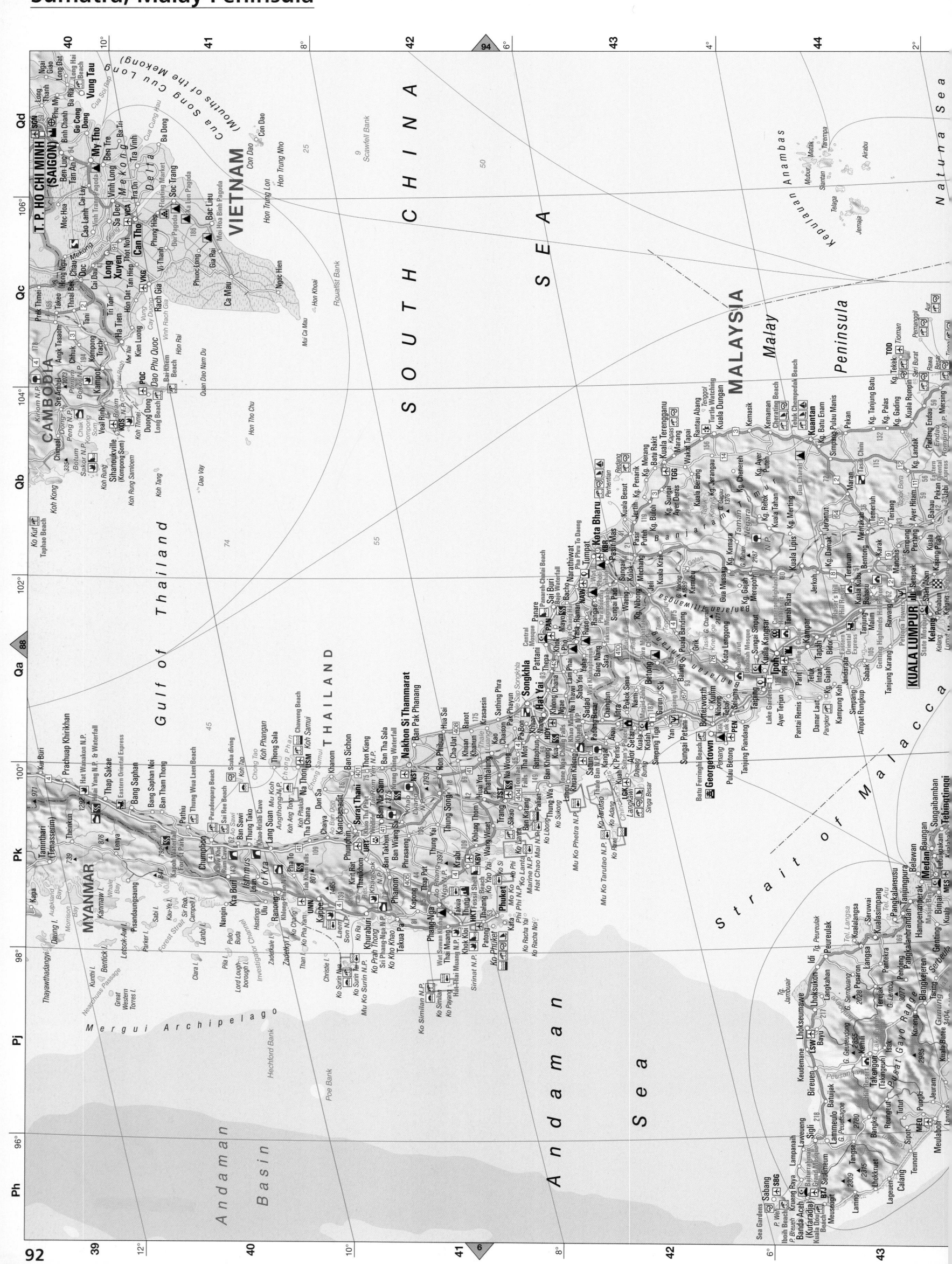

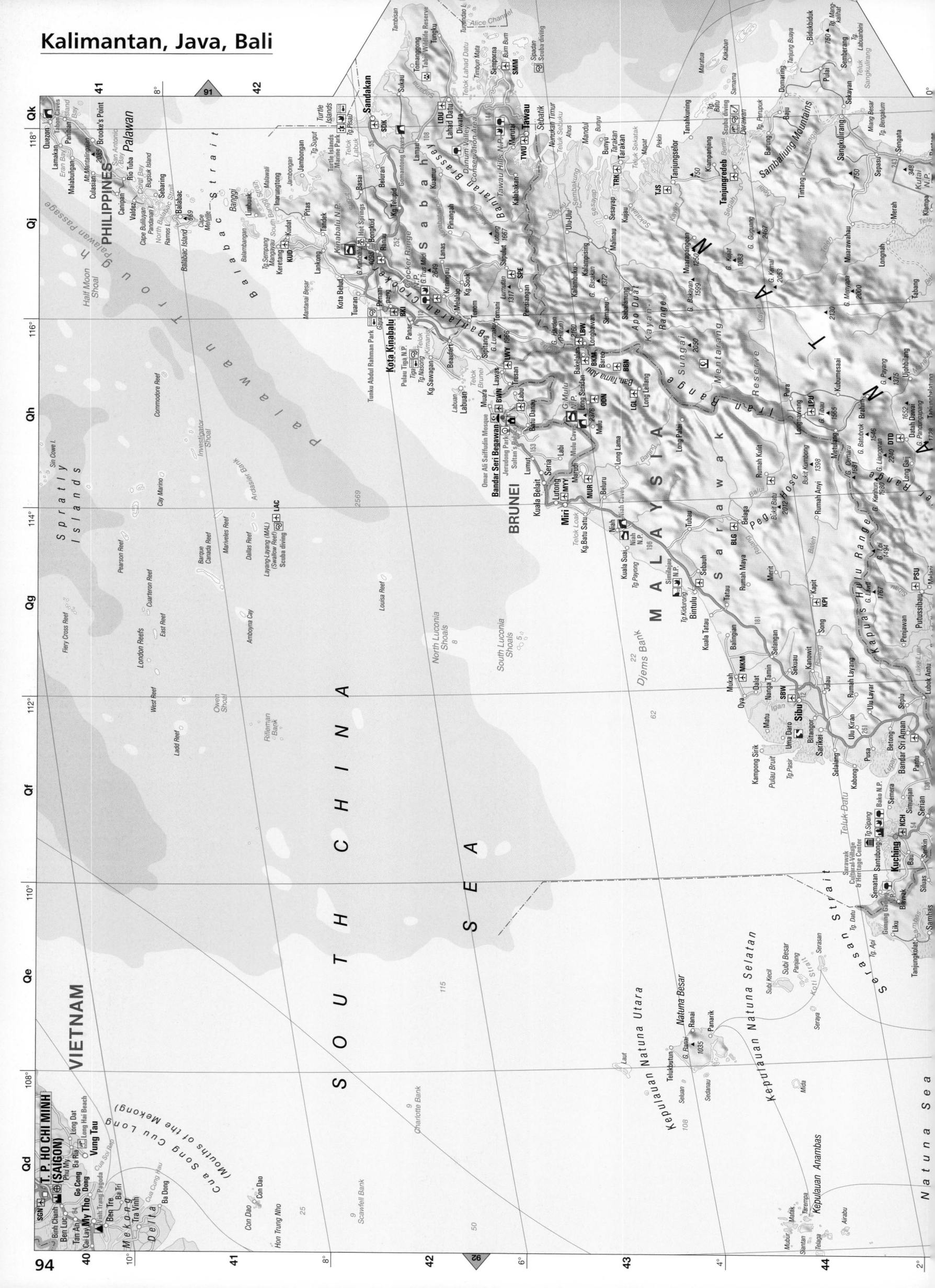

Kalimantan, Java, Bali

PHILIPPINES

Palawan

Palawan Passage

Balabac Strait

SOUTH CHINA SEA

Spratly Islands

VIETNAM

T. P. HO CHI MINH (SAIGON)

Mekong Delta

Cua Song Cuu Long (Mouths of the Mekong)

Natuna Besar

Kepulauan Natuna Utara

Natuna Sea

Kepulauan Anambas

Kepulauan Natuna Selatan

Serasan Strait

Sabah

Kota Kinabalu

Kinabalu N.P.

Crocker Range

Banjaran Crocker

Sandakan

Lahad Datu

Tawau

Darvel Bay

MALAYSIA

Sarawak

Banjaran Hulu

BRUNEI

Bandar Seri Begawan

Miri

Sibu

Kuching

Kapuas Hulu Range

Hose Range

Mentarang

Tarakan

Sambaliung Mountains

KALIMANTAN

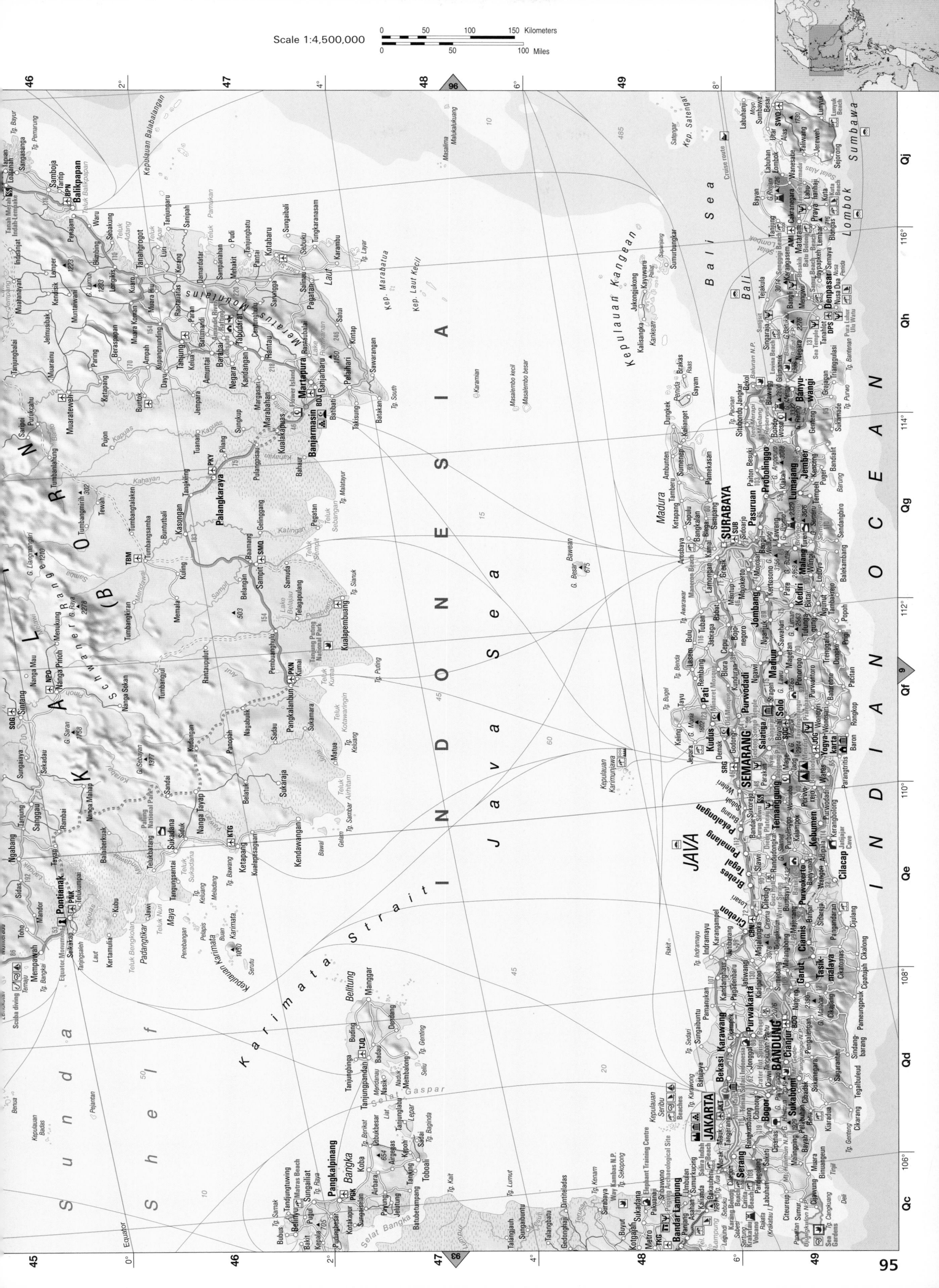

Scale 1:4,500,000

0   50   100   150 Kilometers
0   50   100 Miles

124°   126°   128°   130°

MOLUCCA SEA

Amurang   Kakas   Soputan
Ongkaw   Poigar   1830
Inobonto   Gunung   Belang
Sampaka   1735   Buludawa Mts   Totok
me-   Kotamobagu   Molobog   Nuangan
noga Buluddawa   Dumoga   Onggunei
N.P.   Doloduo   Kompot
Molibagu

Tifore   Kusu
Gamalama   Ekor   Solat   Buli-Islam
Forts   1508
Ternate   TTE   Kayasa   Maba   Yiew
Ternate   Tidore   Gumi   Kobe   Sepo
            Rabodaio   Sebonpopo   724   Tepeleu
            Payaheislam   Noskiu
            Maidi   Teluk Weda
        Kayoa   Mafa

Halmahera (Jailolo)

Sayang   Wayam   Ayu   Kep. Ayu
        Waigeo
Wawei   Kabolaa
Kawe   Selpel   Waisai   Lamlam
Kablebet   Gam   Besir

0°   Equator

Molucca Sea   3910

45

46

Equator   0°

Kepulauan Bacan

Taneti
Muari   Laluin
Latalata   Kasiruta   Dolit   1250   Wosi
Palamea   Yaba   Gorogoro
        Bacan
        Labuha   Lemolemo   Kep. Widi   **Halmahera Sea**
Mandioli   LAH   Songa
Garunggarung   2111   Gani

Wonto Koto
Tapat   Bisa
Laiwui   1318   **Obi**
Obilatu   Tawa
Kawasi   1611   Wai
    Fluk   Tobalai

GEB   Yu   Umera
Gebe   Kawe
        Batanta   Jodlo
Klaarbeck   Kep. Boo   Torobi   Hebera
Damar   Kofiau   Kofiau   Kep. Nusela
Hasii   Pisang   Weeim

Mega   G. Kwoka   2450
Bawe   Megamo
Samate   SOQ   **Sorong**
    Klamono   Rawas
Salawati   Mala   Amaru
Sailolof   Seget   Germakolo
    Wakamoek   Gasim   Teminabuan   Sekak
Tg. Wamonket   Konda
        Baru
        Saga

Doberai Peninsula (Vogelkop)

Melalih
Lokata

Tel. Kabuis
Tel. Waromge

2°

Kanari   Lenmalu
    Waigama   Fagita
        Tamulol
Erwang
Misool   Kep. Pisang   Koagas
    Polee   Daram   Sabuda   Tanisapata   Kokus
        Daram   Tg. Fatagar-   FKQ
                Tuting   Faktak

Onin (Fakfak) Pen.

47

Seram Sea   4665

Boano   Taniwel   Tg. Hewal   Opin
Putia   1354   Manusela N.P.
Kelang   Piru   1245   Bengoi   Hoti
    1006   Liang   3027   Manusela   Bula   Bolifar
Serikambelo   Kairutu   AHI   1071   Parang
Manipa   Amahai   Sepa   Tehoru   Werinama   Waru   Tg. Marsimang
        Haruku   Saparua   Kisalaut   Kiandarat
Asilulu   Tulehu   Hulaku   Seram
    AMQ   Haruku   Saparua   Laut   Kwamor-
Ambon   Namalatu   Panjang   besar
    Ambon   Beach
    Siwa Lima Museum

Seram (Ceram)

Wahai

Gorong
Ilur   Kep. Gorong
Nama   Wirmaf
Manawoka

Seram Laut

721

3°

4°

North Banda Basin

Bara   Wapotih   Waeplau
Kaplamada   Kohol   Namlea
    2736   Walu Besa
Wakatin   1174   Kayeli
Bobo   Tifu   Oki
    Namrole   Watawa
    Buru   Elara   Ambelau

5215

Kep. Banda
        656   Benteng Belgica
    NDA   G. Api   Bandaneira
    Ai   Lontar
    Run   Lontar   Rozengain

Kasiui   Gulir
Kep. Watubela
Tioor   Wirmaf

1720

48

SIA   4500

Runduma   Kepulauan Penyu   Kadola
        Selatan

Banda Sea

Manuk   Kaimer   Kur   Kep.   Tayandu   114
        Waru   Tayandu   Walir
                    Taam

2021

South Banda Basin   Weber Basin   7440   1050

6°

Wetar
Wangiwangi
Komponaone
Kaledupa   Wakatobi Marine N.P.
Tomea   Moromaho
Binongko

Gunungapi   280   Tg. Laru Mat   Molu
    Serua   Nurkaat   Maru
        Teun   Bebar   Leling-   Fordate
Damar   Bebar   luang   Larat
        Wotap   **Yamdena**   Lamdesar
            Wuliaru   Welutu   Watmuri
    Romang   Maopora   Seira   Sanglia Dol   Meyanodas
Laliki   Uwakeka   Dawera   (trad. Village)
        Dai   Daweloor   Bukrane   Amdassa
        Babar   Wasletan   SXK

Wetar   Saumlakki
Lioppa   Adaut   Saumlakki
Limar   Naumatang   Masapun   Werwaru   Namtabung   Kandar
Airpanas   Uwaki   Lebelau   Mehelata   Eliase   Selaru
Hatpass   Kisar   Serwaru   Siota   Moa   Sermata   Tg.Aro Usu

Kep. Tanimbar

49

7°

8°

Komba
Alor   1839
Waipu-   Balauring   Kabir   Cimbur   Atauro
kang   Kalabahi   Kolana   Makadede   Baukau   Tutuala
Adonara   Pantar   DIL   Manatuto   Lautem   Lospatos
KA   Lomblen   Delaki   **Dili**   G.Mata bia   Lore
Waiwe-   Likisia   Vikeke   2315   Aliambata
rang   Lamanuna   Maubisse
    Selat Ombai   Atapupu   Mt. Ramelau
    3475   Balibo   2963
Naikliu   **EAST TIMOR**
    G.Mutis   Atambua
    2427   Oekusi   Halilulik   Suai
Kupang   Camplong   Ketamenanu   **Timor**
Lasiana Beach   Soe   Besikama
Haingsisi   KOE   Toineke   Lelogama
Semau   Timor Museum   Nikiniki
Roti   2050
Papela
Baa   430

50

9°

10°

AUSTRALIA

Gurig N.P. & Cobourg Marine Park

Cape van Diemen   Lingi Pt.   Cobourg Pen.
Tiwi
Melville Island   Milikapiti   Aboriginal
    Pulumpi   Reserve
Bathurst Island   BRT   Pt. Jahleel   Dundas Strait
            Greenhill I.
            Tg. C. Keith

Timor Sea   16   55   11   3310

51

Sydney: The economic, industrial and cultural center of Australia.

The Pinnacles: a group of limestone formations in the desert near Perth.

AUSTRALIA/ OCEANIA

THE FIFTH CONTINENT AND THE ISLANDS OF THE PACIFIC

This region of the world is comprised of two unequal parts: the massive landmass of Australia and the countless scattered islands of the South Pacific. The region's islands range from the very smallest of islets to large islands such as New Guinea and New Zealand.

Australia is a continent of vast distances. Most of Central and Western Australia consist of deserts. Australia's largest desert, the Great Sandy Desert, covers 520,000 km². Ayers Rock, also known by its Aboriginal name Uluru, is located near the geographic center of Australia. Australia's highest mountains are in the Australian Alps, a section of the Great Dividing Range that stretches along the eastern coast. Mount Kosciuszko (2,228 m) is the highest mountain on the continent.

The Great Barrier Reef off the northeastern coast of Australia is the world's largest coral reef. It has a total length of more than 2,000 kilometers from north to south. The islands of Oceania are usually divided into three regions: Micronesia, Melanesia, and Polynesia. The thousands of islands in Oceania, scattered over 70 million km² in the Pacific Ocean, have a total land area around 1.3 million km².

Around 90 % of Australia's 19.7 million inhabitants occupy just 3 % of the continent's land concentrated in the Southeast with the majority of people living in a few large coastal cities. Aborigines, the continent's indigenous people, represent just 2.2 % of the population. Most Australians are the descendants of European immigrants. After the arrival of the first Europeans at the end of the 18th century, the Aboriginal population began to decline. Like the Aborigines, the Maori of New Zealand and the Papua of New Guinea were dramatically affected by the European colonization of their countries. These ethnic groups still struggle to preserve the most important aspects of their cultures, including their languages and traditional arts.

Sepik River: The region along New Guinea's longest river is home to many different tribes.

Australia/Oceania

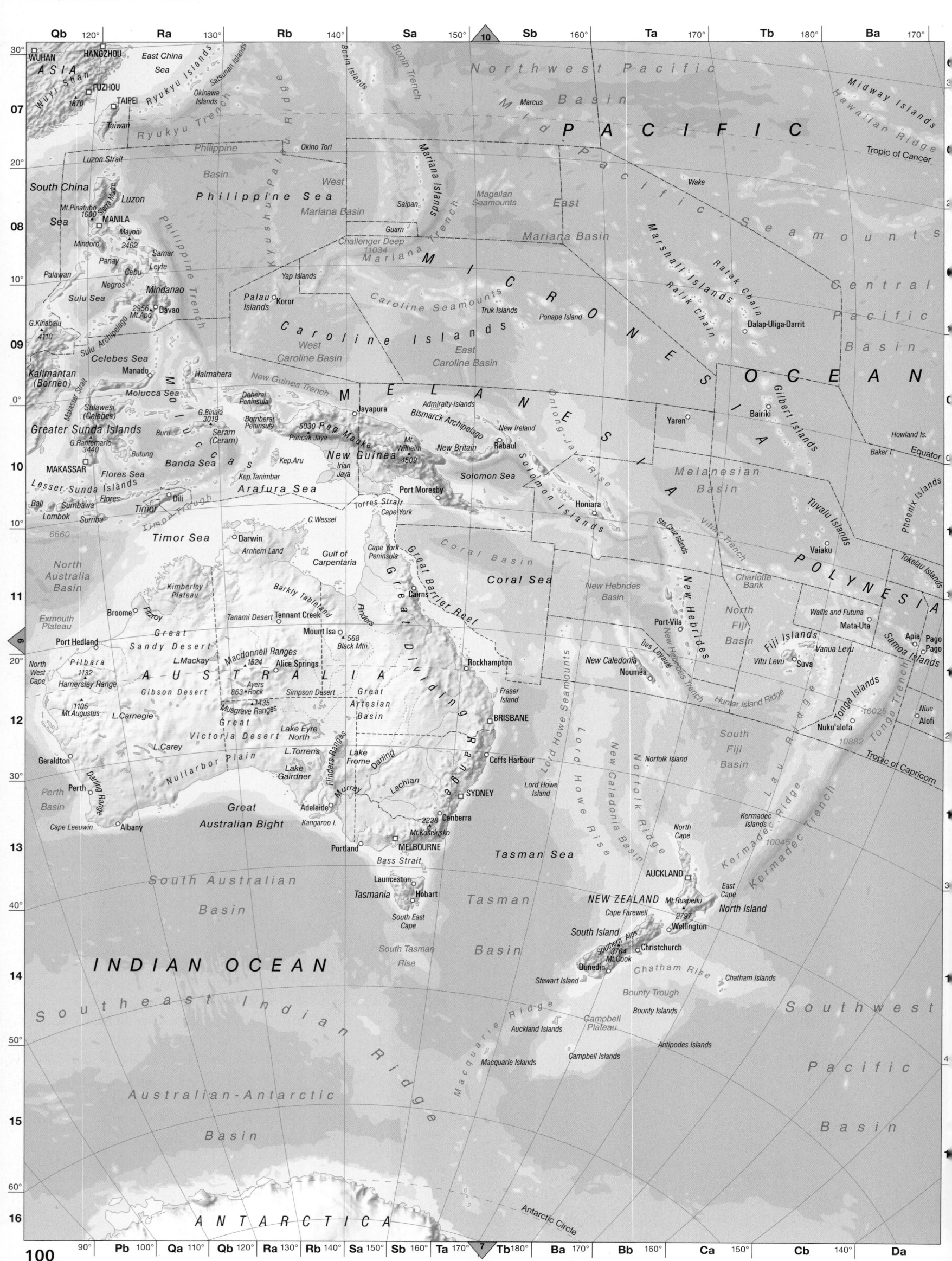

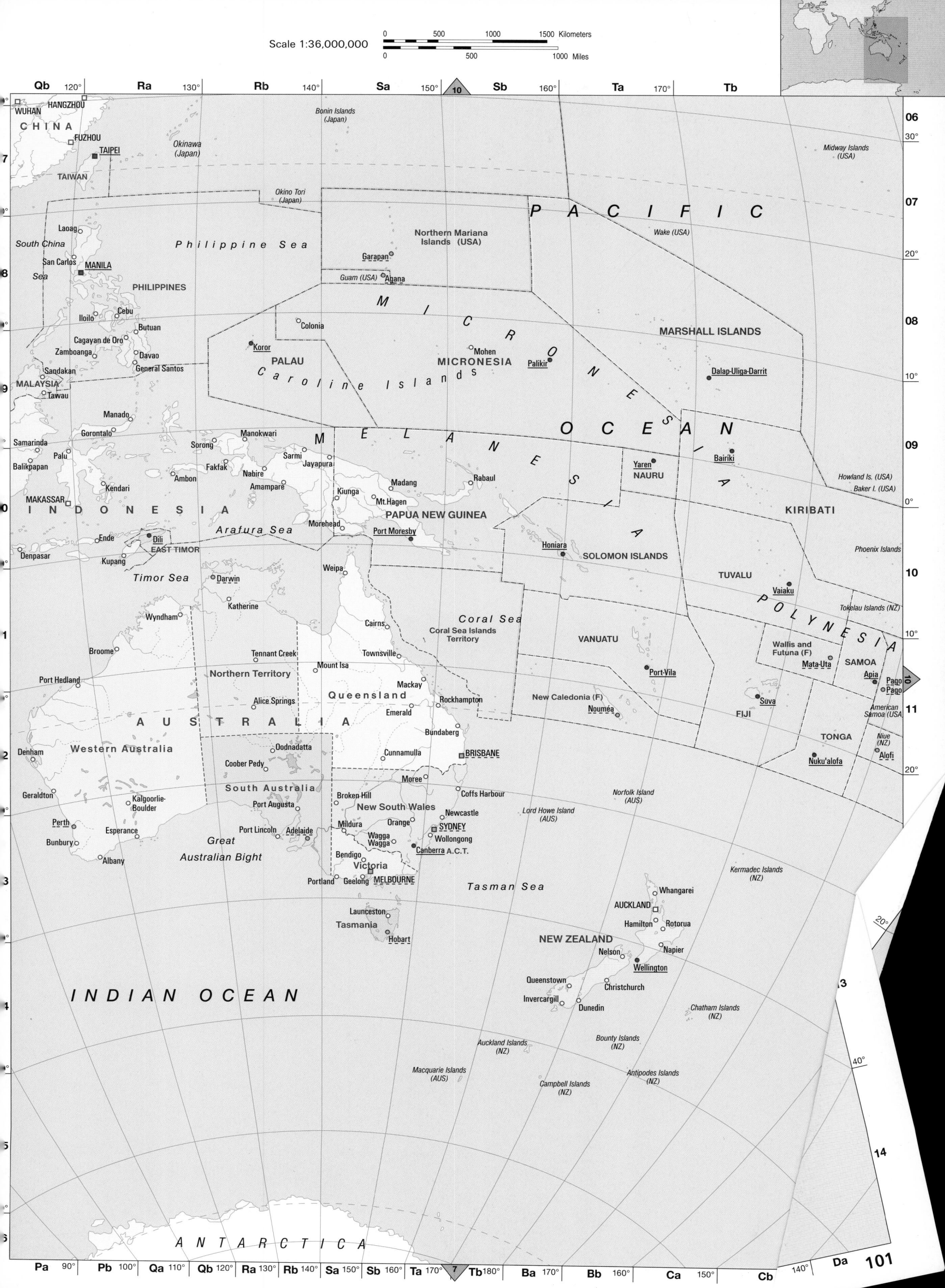

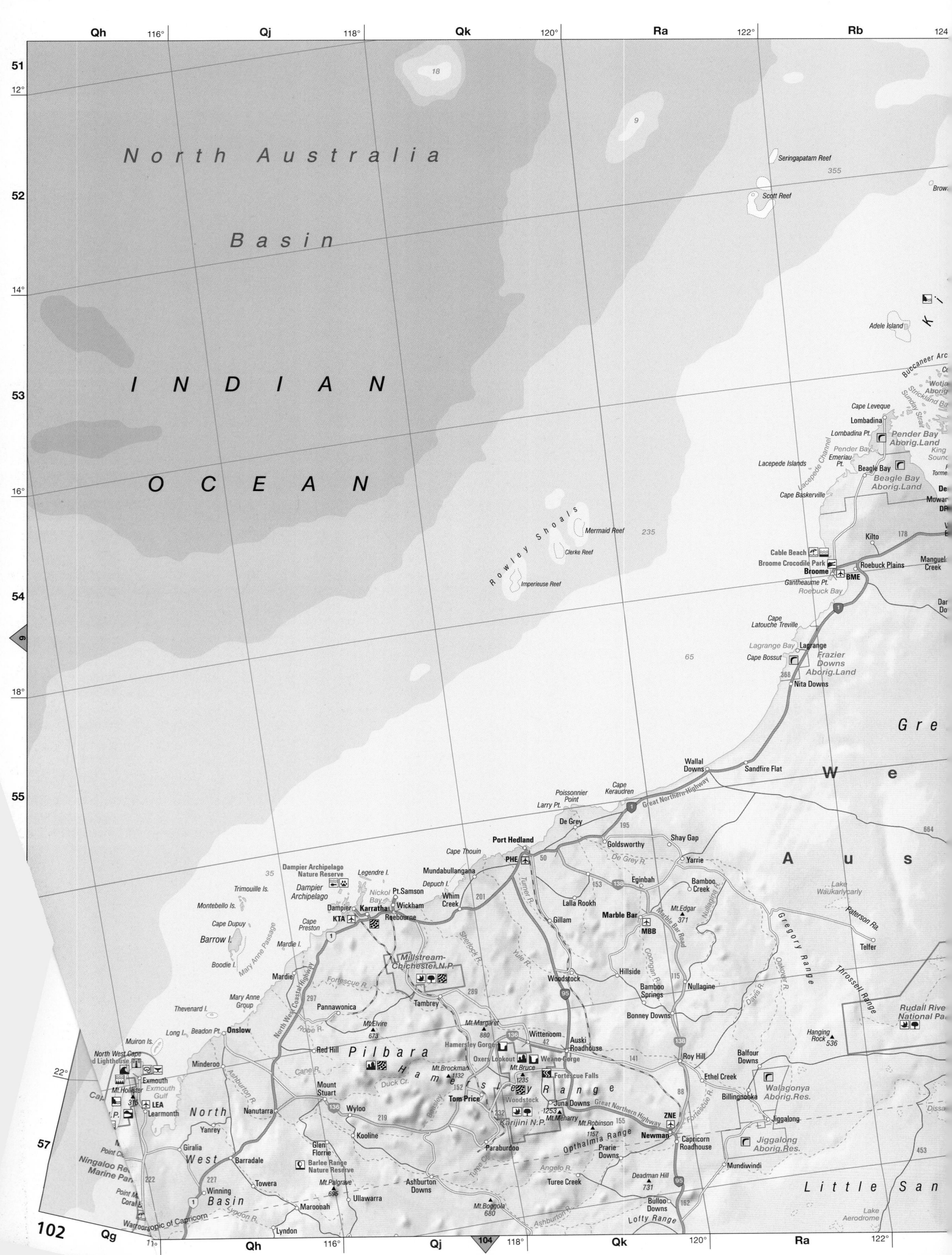

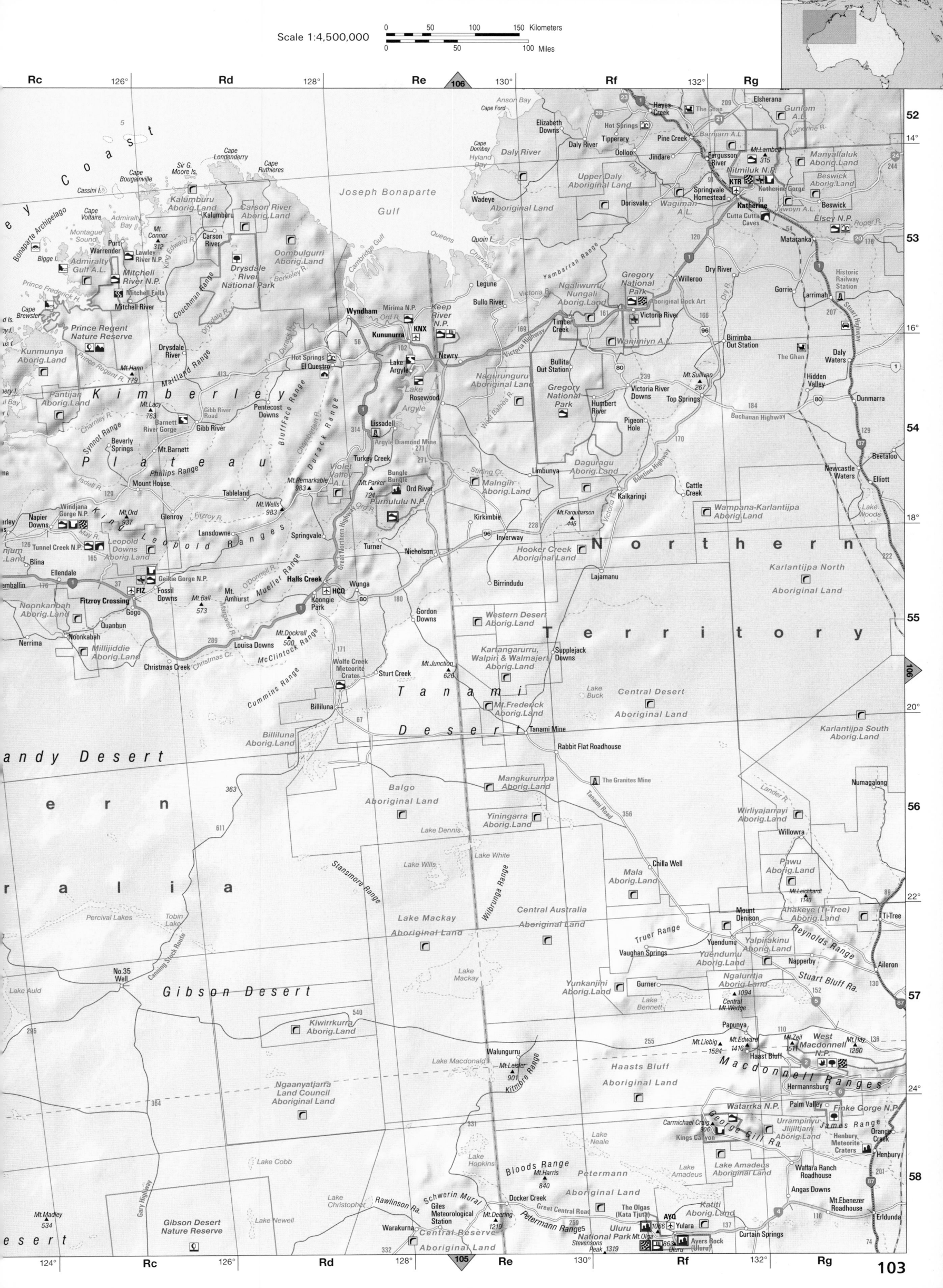

Scale 1:4,500,000

0   50   100   150 Kilometers
0   50   100 Miles

126°   128°   130°   132°
Rc   Rd   Re   Rf   Rg

Anson Bay
Cape Ford
Hayes Creek
Elsherana
Gunlom A.L.
52
14°
Elizabeth Downs
Hot Springs
Pine Creek
The Ghan
Katherine Gorge
Daly River
Tipperary
Barnjarn A.L.
Manyallaluk Aborig.Land
Cape Dombey
Daly River
Oolloo
Jindare
Fergusson River
Mt.Lambert 315
Nitmiluk N.P.
Beswick Aborig.Land
Hyland Bay
Upper Daly Aboriginal Land
Springvale Homestead
KTR
Katherine Gorge
Jawoyn A.L.
Wadeye
Dorisvale
Wagiman A.L.
Cutta Cutta Caves
Beswick
Queens Channel
Quoin I.
Elsey N.P.
53
Aboriginal Land
Willeroo
Dry River
Gorrie
Roper R.
Matanaka
Bullo River
Aboriginal Rock Art
The Ghan
Legune
Victoria R.
Gregory National Park
Historic Railway Station
Joseph Bonaparte Gulf
Ngaliwurru Nungali Aborig.Land
Larrimah
16°
Wyndham
Mirima N.P.
Keep River N.P.
Timber Creek
Victoria River
Stuart Highway
KNX
Kununurra
Newry
Victoria Highway
Bullita Out Station
Birrimba Out Station
The Ghan
Hot Springs
Lake Argyle
Nagurungguru Aboriginal Land
Gregory National Park
Humbert River
Daly Waters
El Questro
Rosewood
Victoria River Downs
Top Springs
Hidden Valley
Lake Argyle
Mt.Sullivan 267
Dunmarra
Gibb River Road
Lissadell
Argyle Diamond Mine
Stirling Cr.
Pigeon Hole
Buchanan Highway
54
Pentecost Downs
Turkey Creek
Limbunya
Daguragu Aborig.Land
Beetaloo
Drysdale River
Barnett River Gorge
Gibb River
Violet Valley A.L.
Bungle Bungle
Stirling Cr.
Newcastle Waters
Elliott
Phillips Range
Mt.Parker 724
Ord River
Malngin Aborig.Land
Cattle Creek
Lake Woods
Mount House
Tableland
Mt.Wells 983
Purnululu N.P.
Kalkaringi
Wampana-Karlantijpa Aborig.Land
18°
Windjana Gorge N.P.
Springvale
Kirkimbie
Mt.Farquharson 446
Napier Downs
Glenroy
Lansdowne
Turner
Nicholson
Inverway
Hooker Creek Aboriginal Land
Northern
Tunnel Creek N.P.
Leopold Downs Aborig.Land
Birrindudu
Lajamanu
Karlantijpa North Aboriginal Land
Ellendale
Geikie Gorge N.P.
Halls Creek
Wunga
55
Fitzroy Crossing
Fossil Downs
HCQ
Koongie Park
Gordon Downs
Western Desert Aborig.Land
Territory
Noonkanbah Aborig.Land
Gogo
Mt.Ball 573
Noonkabah
Louisa Downs
McClintock Range
Kartangarurru, Walpiri & Walmajeri Aborig.Land
Supplejack Downs
Nerrima
Millijiddie Aborig.Land
Christmas Creek
Wolfe Creek Meteorite Crater
Sturt Creek
Mt.Junction 626
Central Desert Aboriginal Land
Karlantijpa South Aborig.Land
Tanami
Cummins Range
Billiluna
Mt.Frederick Aborig.Land
Lake Buck
Tanami Mine
Desert
Rabbit Flat Roadhouse
20°
Numagalong
andy Desert
Balgo Aboriginal Land
Mangkururrpa Aborig.Land
The Granites Mine
Lander R.
Wirliyajarrayi Aborig.Land
ern
Yiningarra Aborig.Land
Tanami Road
56
ralia
Lake Dennis
Willowra
Pawu Aborig.Land
Percival Lakes
Lake Wills
Lake White
Chilla Well
Mala Aborig.Land
Mt.Leichhardt 1140
Tobin Lake
Wilurunga Range
89
22°
No.35 Well
Central Australia
Mount Denison
Ahakeye (Ti-Tree) Aborig.Land
Ti-Tree
Lake Auld
Lake Mackay
Aboriginal Land
Truer Range
Yuendumu
Yalpirakinu Aborig.Land
Reynolds Range
Gibson Desert
Aboriginal Land
Vaughan Springs
Yuendumu Aborig.Land
Napperby
Aileron
Lake Mackay
Yunkanjini Aborig.Land
Gurner
Ngalurntja Aborig.Land
Stuart Bluff Ra.
57
Kiwirrkurra Aborig.Land
Lake Bennett
Central Mt.Wedge 1094
Papunya
Mt.Liebig 1524
Mt.Edward 1416
Mt.Zeil 1531
West Macdonnell N.P.
Mt.Hay 1250
Walungurru
Haasts Bluff
Mt.Leisler 901
Kintore Range
Haast Bluff
Macdonnell Ranges
Ngaanyatjarra Land Council Aboriginal Land
Haasts Bluff Aboriginal Land
Watarrka N.P.
Palm Valley
Finke Gorge N.P.
Hermannsburg
24°
Urrampinyu Jilijiltjarri Aborig.Land
Lake Neale
Kings Canyon
George Gill Ra.
James Range
Henbury Meteorite Craters
Carmichael Crag
Lake Hopkins
Bloods Range
Petermann
Lake Amadeus
Wallara Ranch Roadhouse
Orange Creek
Mt.Harris 840
Aboriginal Land
Lake Amadeus Aborig.Land
Henbury
Gibson Desert Nature Reserve
Lake Christopher
Rawlinson Ra.
Schwerin Mural Giles Meteorological Station
Docker River
Petermann Ranges
Katiti Aborig.Land
Angas Downs
58
Mt.Madley 534
Lake Newell
Mt.Deering 1219
Great Central Road
The Olgas (Kata Tjuta)
AYQ
Mt.Ebenezer Roadhouse
Warakurna
Central Reserve Aboriginal Land
Uluru National Park
Mt.Olga 1066
Yulara
Curtin Springs
esert
Stevensons Peak 1319
Mt.Olga 863
Ayers Rock (Uluru)
Erldunda

124°   126°   128°   130°   132°
Rc   Rd   Re   Rf   Rg

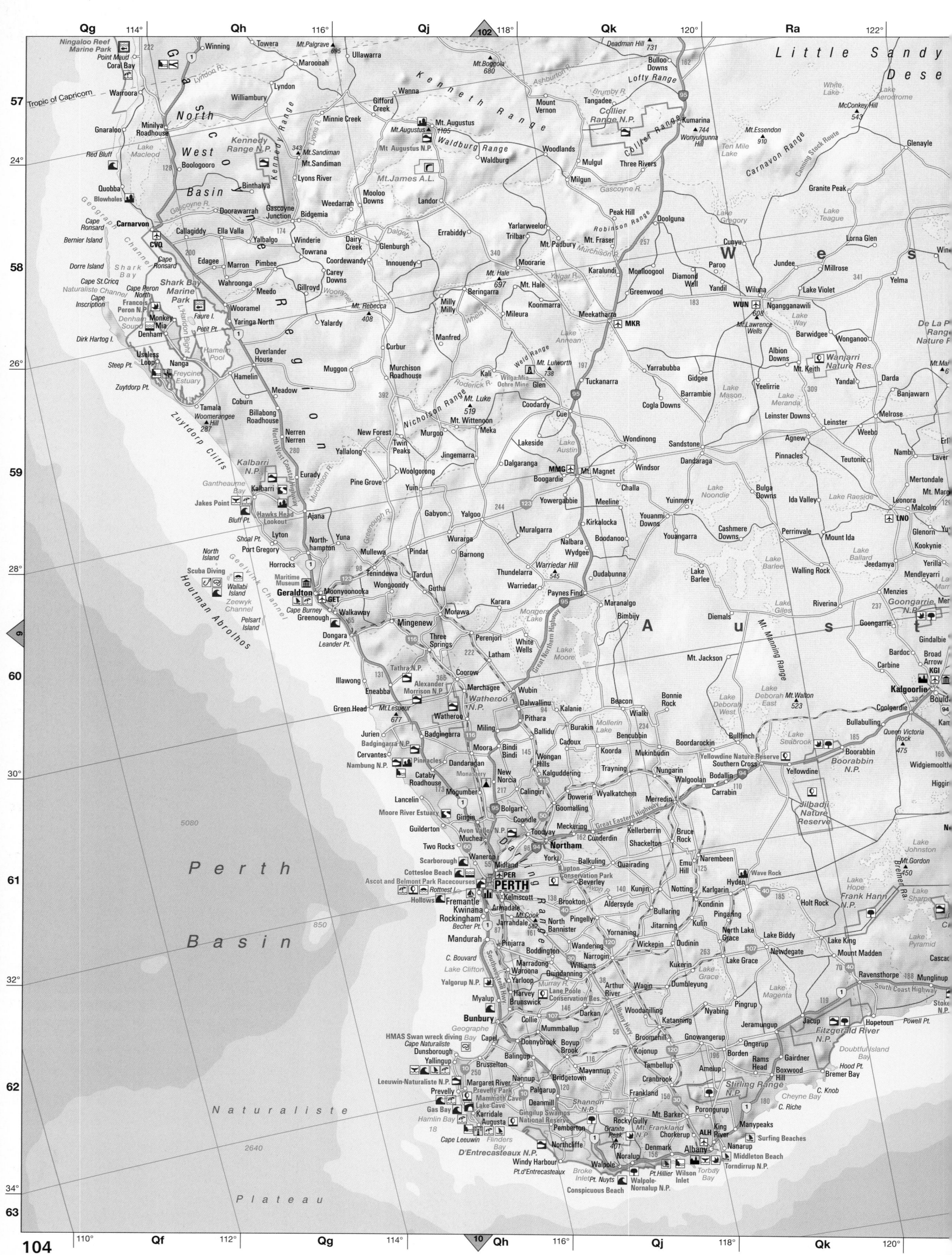

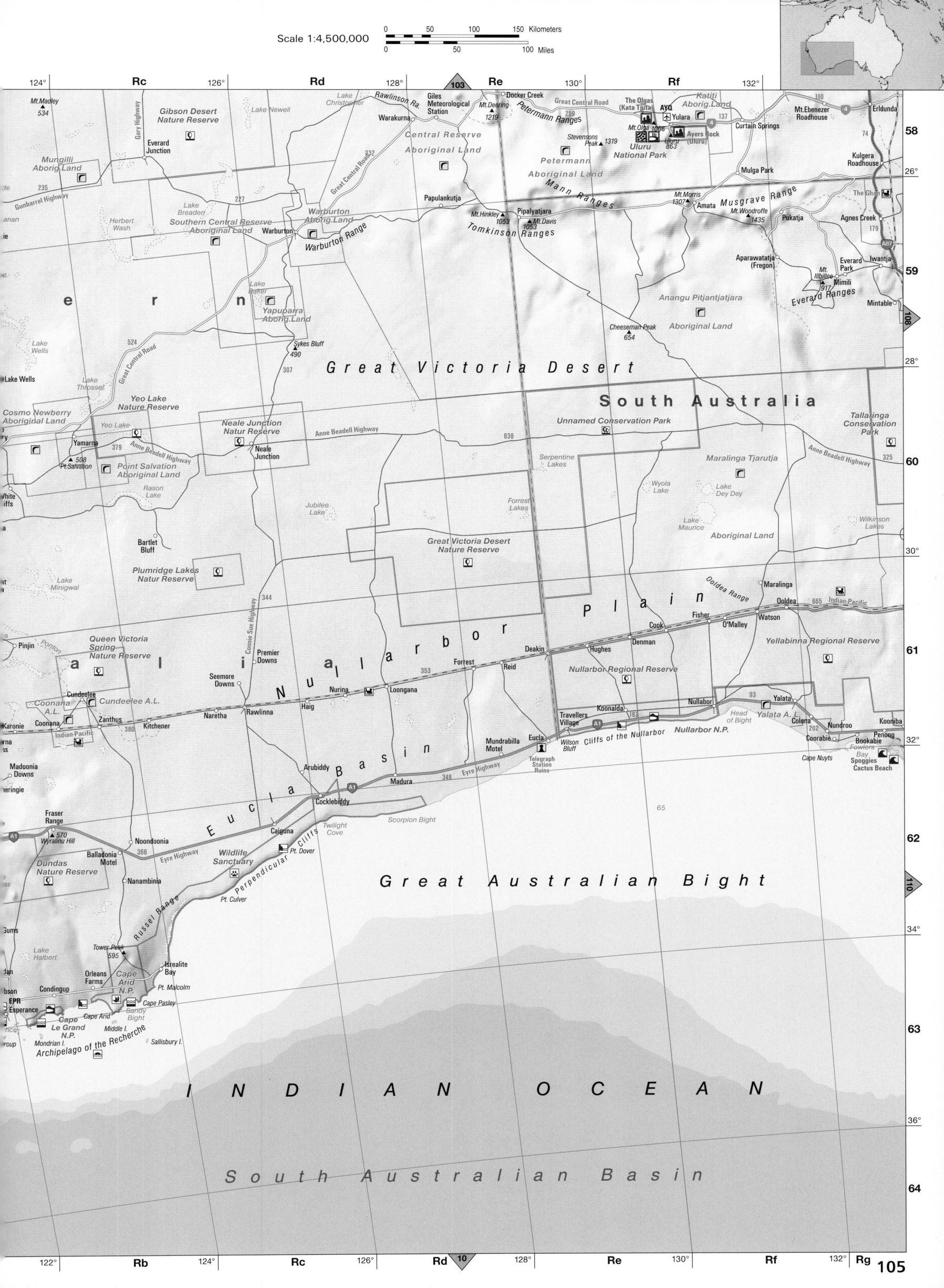

Rc   Rd   103   Re   130°   Rf   132°

124°   126°   128°   Re   130°   Rf   132°

Mt.Madley
534

Gibson Desert
Nature Reserve

Gary Highway

Lake Newell

Lake Christopher

Rawlinson Ra

Giles
Meteorological
Station

Docker Creek

Great Central Road

The Olgas
(Kata Tjuta)

AYQ
Yulara

Katiti
Aborig.Land

Mt.Ebenezer
Roadhouse   110   Erldunda   4

Warakurna

Mt.Deering
1219

Petermann Ranges

Central Reserve

Stevensons
Peak ▲ 1319

259

Uluru
National Park

Ayers Rock
863 (Uluru)   137

Curtain Springs

74

58

Everard
Junction

Mungilli
Aborig.Land

235

Gunbarrel Highway

anan

Great Central Road

232

227

Herbert
Wash

Lake
Breaden

Southern Central Reserve
Aboriginal Land

Warburton

Warburton
Aborig.Land

Aboriginal Land

Papulankutja

Mt.Hinkley
1053

Pipalyatjara

Mt.Davis
1053

Tomkinson Ranges

Petermann

Aboriginal Land

Mann Ranges

Musgrave Range

Mt.Morris
1307

Amata   Mt.Woodroffe
1435

Pukatja

Mulga Park

Kulgera
Roadhouse

The Ghan

Agnes Creek   179

26°

Lake
Wells

524

Great Central Road

Lake
Throssel

Yapuparra
Aborig.Land

Warburton Range

Aparawatatja
(Fregon)

Anangu Pitjantjatjara

Everard
Park   Iwantja

Mt.
Illbillee
917

Mimili

Everard Ranges   A87

59

Warburton Range

e   r   n

Lake
Laker

Sykes Bluff
490

Aboriginal Land

Cheeseman Peak
654

Mintable   108

Lake
Wells

307

Great Victoria Desert

South Australia

28°

Cosmo Newberry
Aboriginal Land

White
liffs

Lake
Wells

Yeo Lake
Nature Reserve

Yeo Lake

Neale Junction
Natur Reserve

Anne Beadell Highway

Neale
Junction

Anne Beadell Highway

638

Unnamed Conservation Park

Tallaringa
Conservation
Park

Yamarna

379

Pt.Salvation
508

Point Salvation
Aboriginal Land

Rason
Lake

Serpentine
Lakes

Maralinga Tjarutja

Anne Beadell Highway   325

60

Lake
Minigwal

Plumridge Lakes
Natur Reserve

Jubilee
Lake

Great Victoria Desert
Nature Reserve

Forrest
Lakes

Wyola
Lake

Lake
Dey Dey

Lake
Maurice

Aboriginal Land

Wilkinson
Lakes

30°

Bartlet
Bluff

Queen Victoria
Spring
Nature Reserve

Connie Sue Highway

344

a   l   i

Nullarbor   Plain

Ooldea Range

Maralinga

Ooldea   665   Indian-Pacific

Pinjin

Ponton

Premier
Downs

Seemore
Downs

Fisher

Cook

Watson

O'Malley

Yellabinna Regional Reserve

61

Cundeelee   Cundeelee A.L.

Nurina

Loongana

353

Forrest

Reid

Deakin

Hughes

Denman

Nullarbor Regional Reserve

Koonalda

Nullabor   93

Yalata

Coonana
A.L.

Zanthus

Kitchener

Naretha

Rawlinna

Haig

Travellers
Village   184   Yalata A.L.

Colona   202   Nundroo

Koonba

Karonie

Coonana

380

Indian-Pacific

Eucla Basin

Mundrabilla
Motel

Eucla

Wilson
Bluff

Cliffs of the Nullarbor

Nullarbor N.P.

Head
of Bight

Coorabie

Fowlers
Bay   Penong

Bookabie

Spoggies
Cactus Beach

32°

Madoonia
Downs

eringie

Arubiddy

Madura

348

Eyre Highway

Telegraph
Station
Ruins

Cape Nuyts

Fraser
Range

Wyralinu Hill
570   A1

Noondoonia

Cocklebiddy

Caiguna

Twilight
Cove

Scorpion Bight

65

62

Dundas
Nature Reserve

Balladonia
Motel

366

Eyre Highway

Perpendicular Cliffs

Pt.Dover

Wildlife
Sanctuary

Nanambinia

Pt. Culver

Russel Range

Great   Australian   Bight   110

34°

Gums

Lake
Halbert

Tower Peak
595

Isrealite
Bay

Orleans
Farms

Cape
Arid
N.P.

Condingup

EPR

Esperance

Cape Arid

Pt. Malcolm

Cape Pasley

Sandy
Bight

bson

Cape
Le Grand
N.P.

Mondrian I.   Middle I.

Sallisbury I.

Archipelago of the Recherche

63

ance

oup

I N D I A N   O C E A N

36°

S o u t h   A u s t r a l i a n   B a s i n

64

122°   Rb   124°   Rc   126°   Rd   10   128°   Re   130°   Rf   132°   Rg

105

Northern Australia

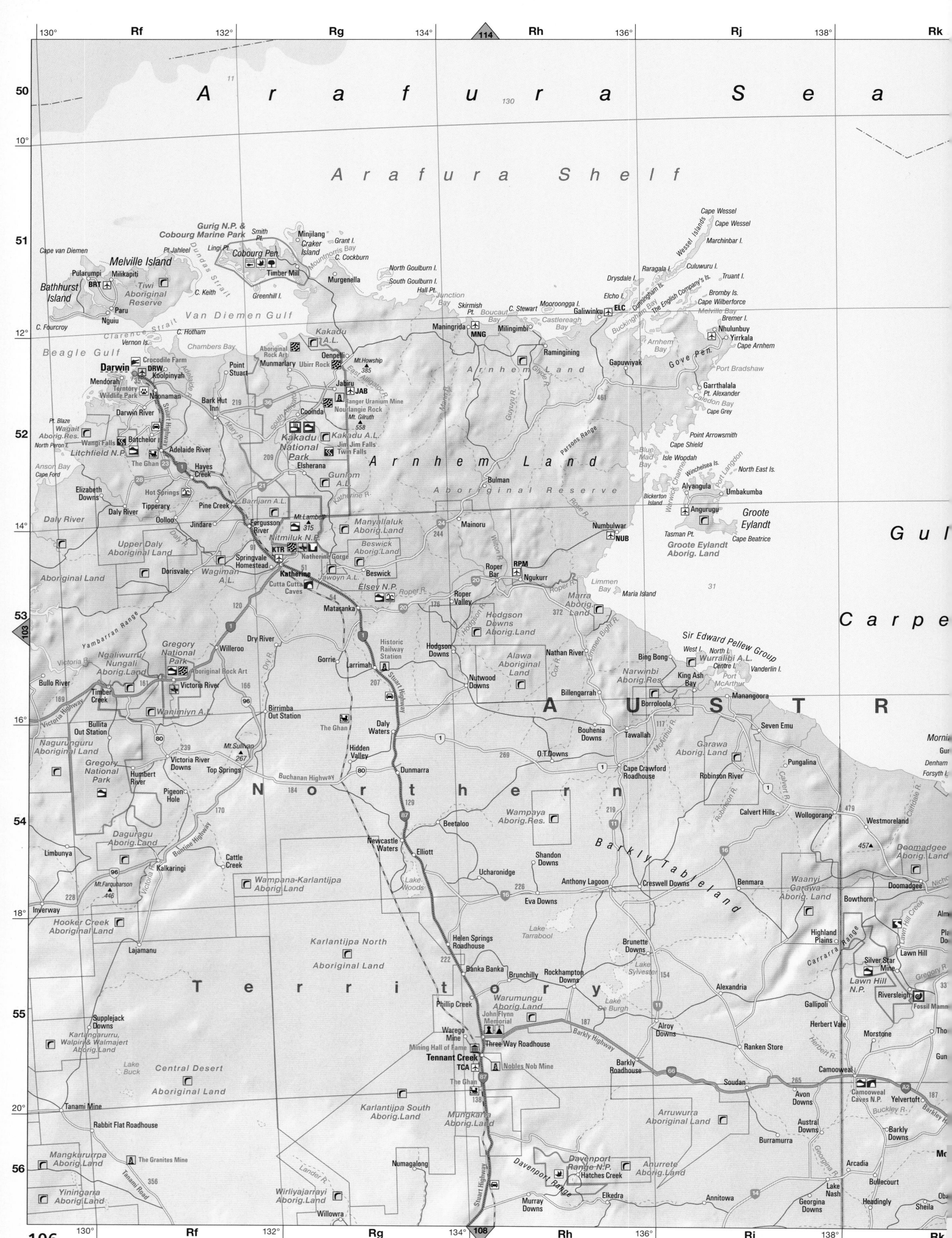

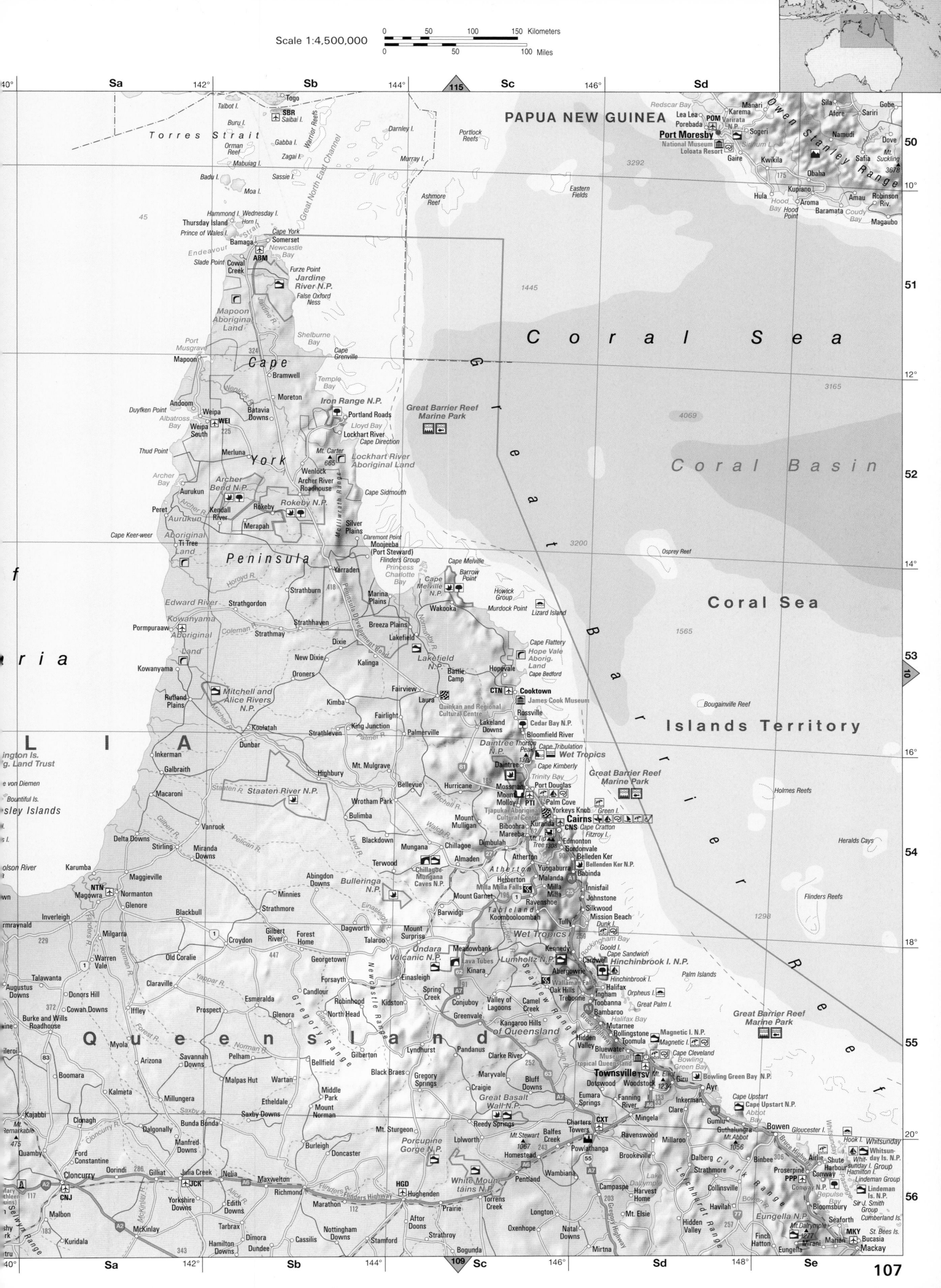

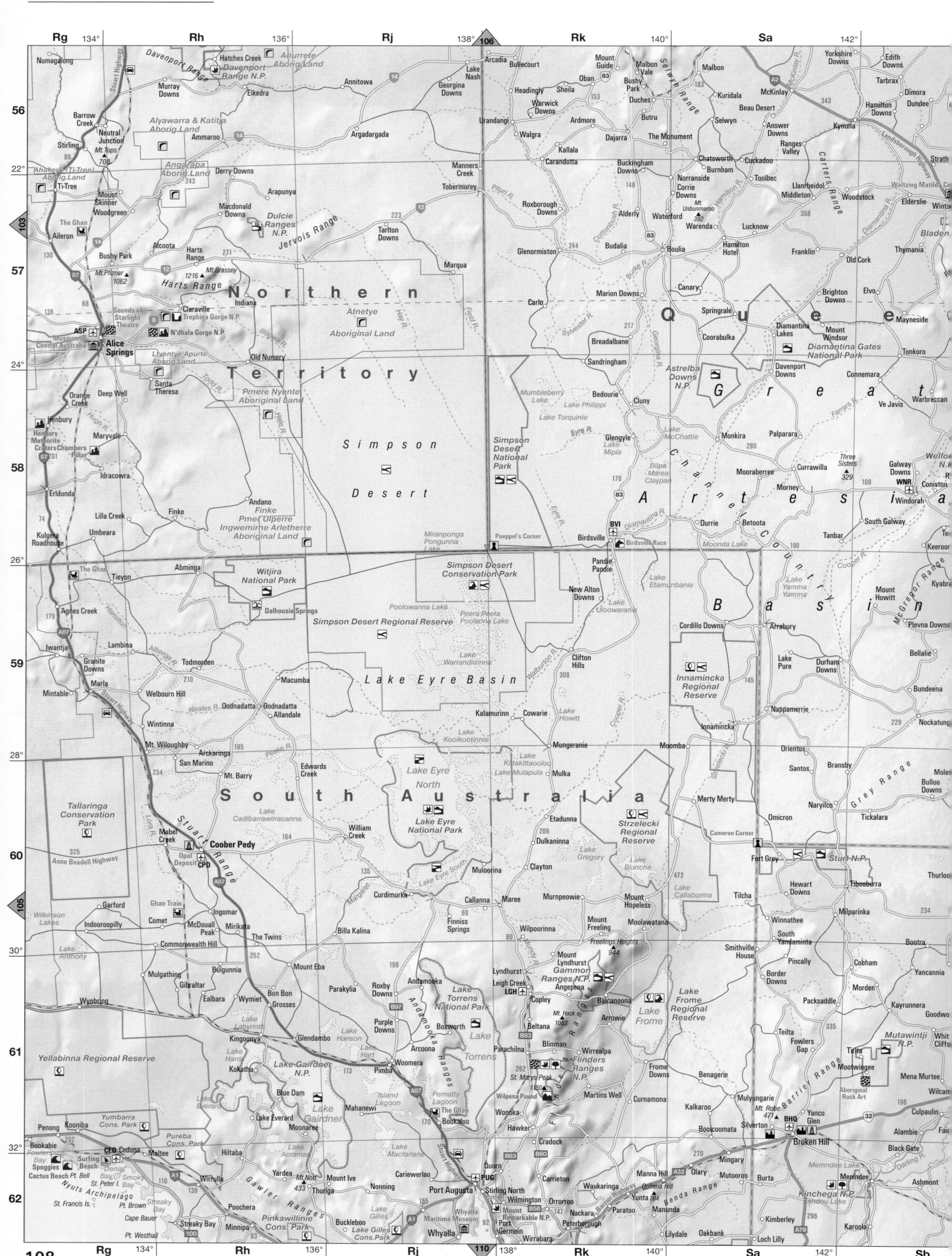

Southern Australia, Tasmania

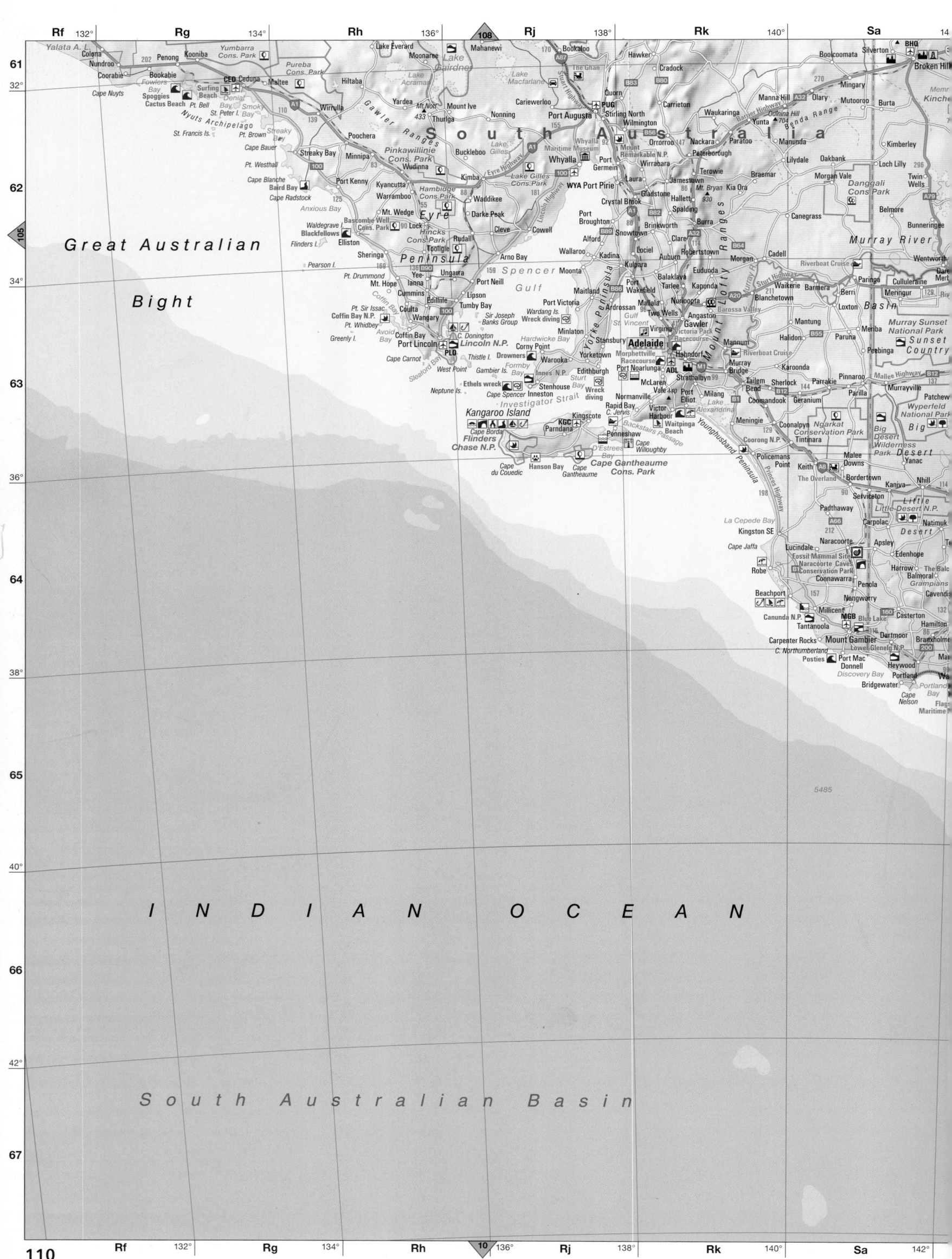

INDIAN OCEAN

Great Australian

Bight

South Australian Basin

Scale 1:4,500,000

0 50 100 150 Kilometers
0 50 100 Miles

New South Wales

Victoria

Tasmania

Great Dividing Range

Liverpool Range

Blue Mountains N.P.

Snowy Mountains

Kosciuszko N.P.

Australian Capital Territory

SYDNEY
Canberra
Newcastle
Wollongong
MELBOURNE
Geelong
Hobart
Launceston

Moama, Lerida, Mount Lewis, Warren, Coollie, Binnaway, Premer, Spring Ridge, Quirindi, Yarrowitch, Telegraph Point, Nowendoc, Port Macquarie, Wauchope, Kendall, Bonnie Hills, Crowdy Bay N.P., Wingham, Taree, Harrington

Fairmont, Baden Park, Paddington, Killala, Mount Lewis, Buddabuddah, Nevertire, Trangie, Gilgandra, Blackville, Willow Tree, Murrurundi, Moonan Flat, Mt. Barrington, Gloucester, Barrington Tops N.P., Gresford, Stroud, Singleton, Maitland, Cessnock, Kurri Kurri, Newcastle

Ashmont, Burtundy, Darnick, Ivanhoe, Yalock, Gysum Palace, Gilgunnia, Bobadah, Narromine, Dubbo, Goolma, Gulgong, Mudgee, Kandos, Wollemi N.P., Putty, Yengo N.P., Wisemans Ferry, Gosford, Budgewoi, The Entrance

Mungo N.P., Willandra Lakes World Heritage, Hillston, Lake Cargelligo, Condobolin, Parkes, Forbes, Orange, Bathurst, Lithgow, Katoomba, Richmond, Windsor, Royal Gardens, Port Jackson, SYDNEY, Royal Randwick

Griffith, Darlington Point, Narrandera, Wagga Wagga, Junee, Cootamundra, Young, Boorowa, Goulburn, Marulan, Nowra, Berry, Kiama

Hay, Deniliquin, Echuca, Shepparton, Benalla, Wangaratta, Albury, Wodonga, Corryong, Tumbarumba, Adaminaby, Cooma, Bombala, Eden, Merimbula, Bega, Narooma, Batemans Bay, Ulladulla

Swan Hill, Kerang, Bendigo, Castlemaine, Seymour, Kilmore, Bright, Mt. Buller, Mansfield, Alpine National Park, Omeo, Bairnsdale, Lakes Entrance, Orbost, Mallacoota, Croajingolong N.P., Cape Howe

Ballarat, Sunbury, Melton, MELBOURNE, Geelong, Dandenong, Warragul, Moe, Morwell, Traralgon, Sale, Maffra, Ninety Mile Beach

Colac, Torquay, Anglesea, Lorne, Apollo Bay, Cape Otway, Great Ocean Road, Wilsons Promontory N.P., Wilsons Promontory

Bass Strait

King I., Currie, Grassy, Stokes Point, Cape Wickham, Egg Lagoon, Cowper Point, Curtis I., Deal I., Hogan I.

Flinders I., Furneaux Group, Whitemark, Lady Baron, Strzelecki N.P., Cape Barren I., Clarke I., Banks Strait

Stanley, Smithton, Marrawah, Burnie, Wynyard, Penguin, Ulverstone, Devonport, Deloraine, Launceston, Perth, Longford, Scottsdale, St. Helens, St. Marys, Fingal, Avoca, Campbell Town, Swansea, Bicheno, Coles Bay, Freycinet Pen.

Queenstown, Strahan, Zeehan, Rosebery, Cradle Mt. Lake St. Clair N.P., Mt. Ossa, Miena, Bothwell, Oatlands, Triabunna, Maria Island N.P.

Franklin-Gordon Wild Rivers N.P., Southwest N.P., World Heritage Area, Strathgordon, Maydena, New Norfolk, Bridgewater, Sorell, **Hobart**, Huonville, Kingston, Dover, Southport, Bruny I., South Bruny N.P., Tasman Pen., Port Arthur, South East Cape

Tasman Sea

New Zealand

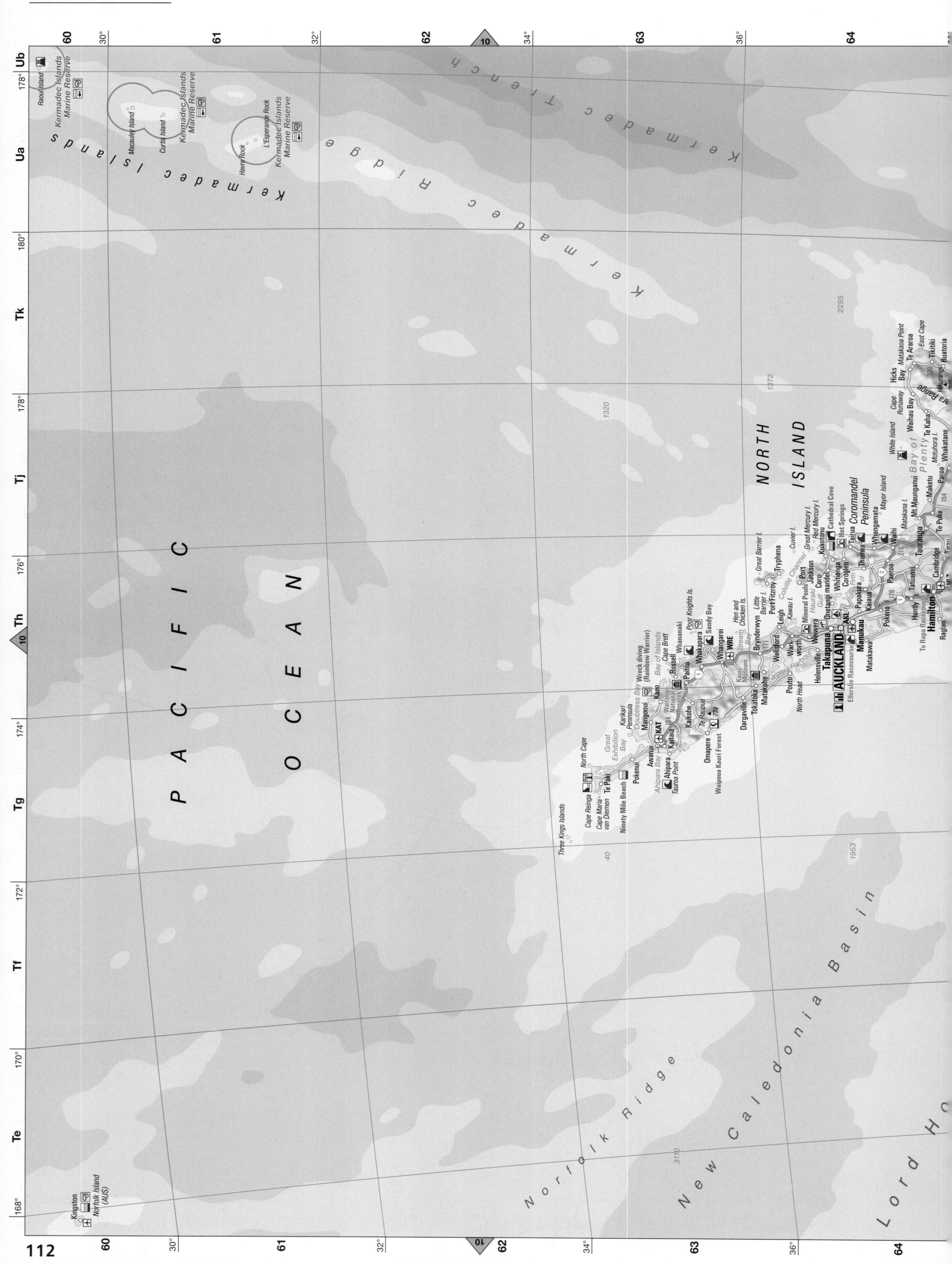

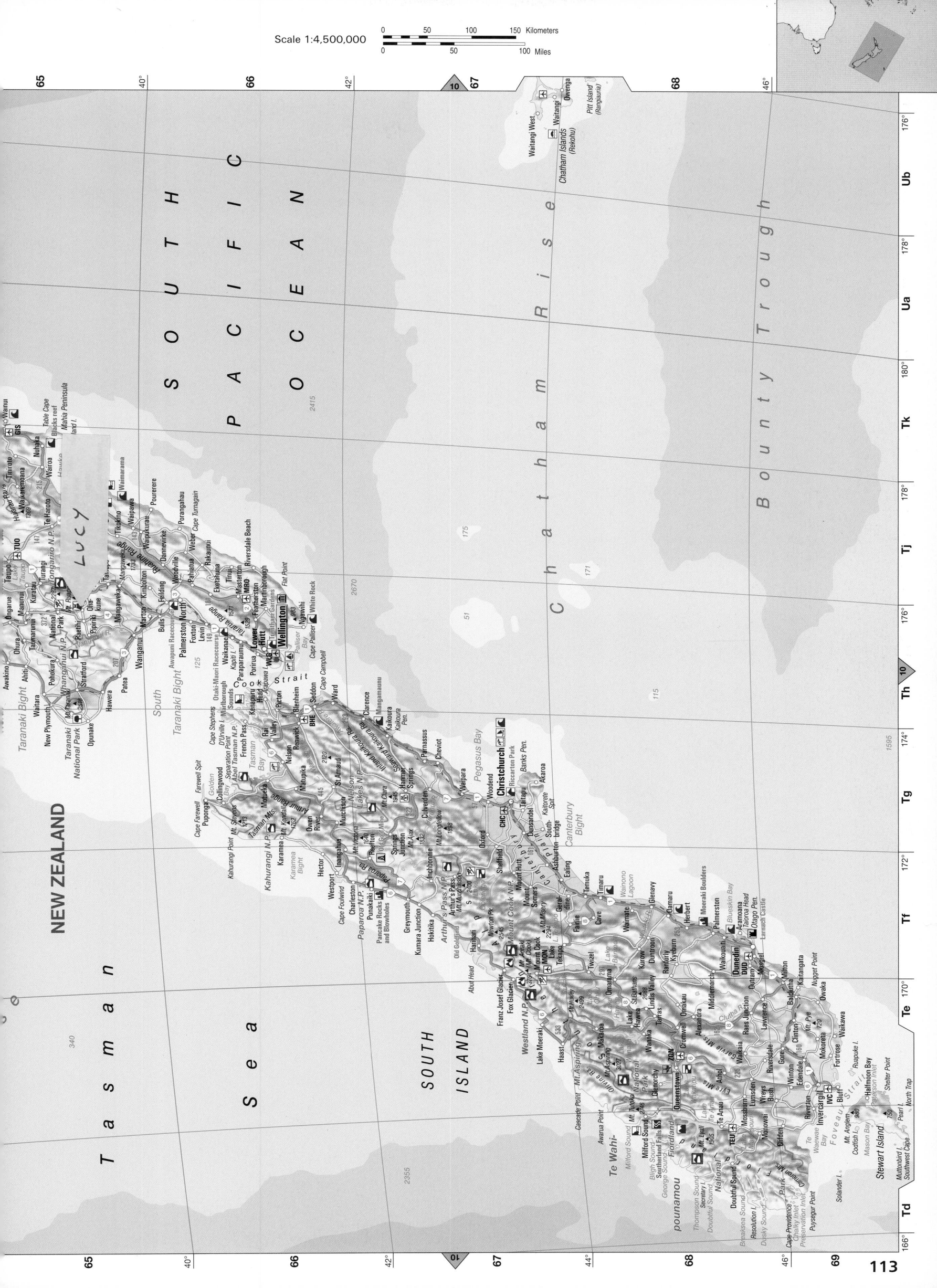

Scale 1:4,500,000

0   50   100   150 Kilometers
0   50   100 Miles

NEW ZEALAND

SOUTH PACIFIC OCEAN

Tasman Sea

SOUTH ISLAND

Chatham Rise

Bounty Trough

Chatham Islands (Rekohu)

LUCY

Wellington

Christchurch

Dunedin

Queenstown

Invercargill

Stewart Island

Fiordland

Mount Cook N.P.

Westland N.P.

Mt. Aspiring National Park

New Guinea

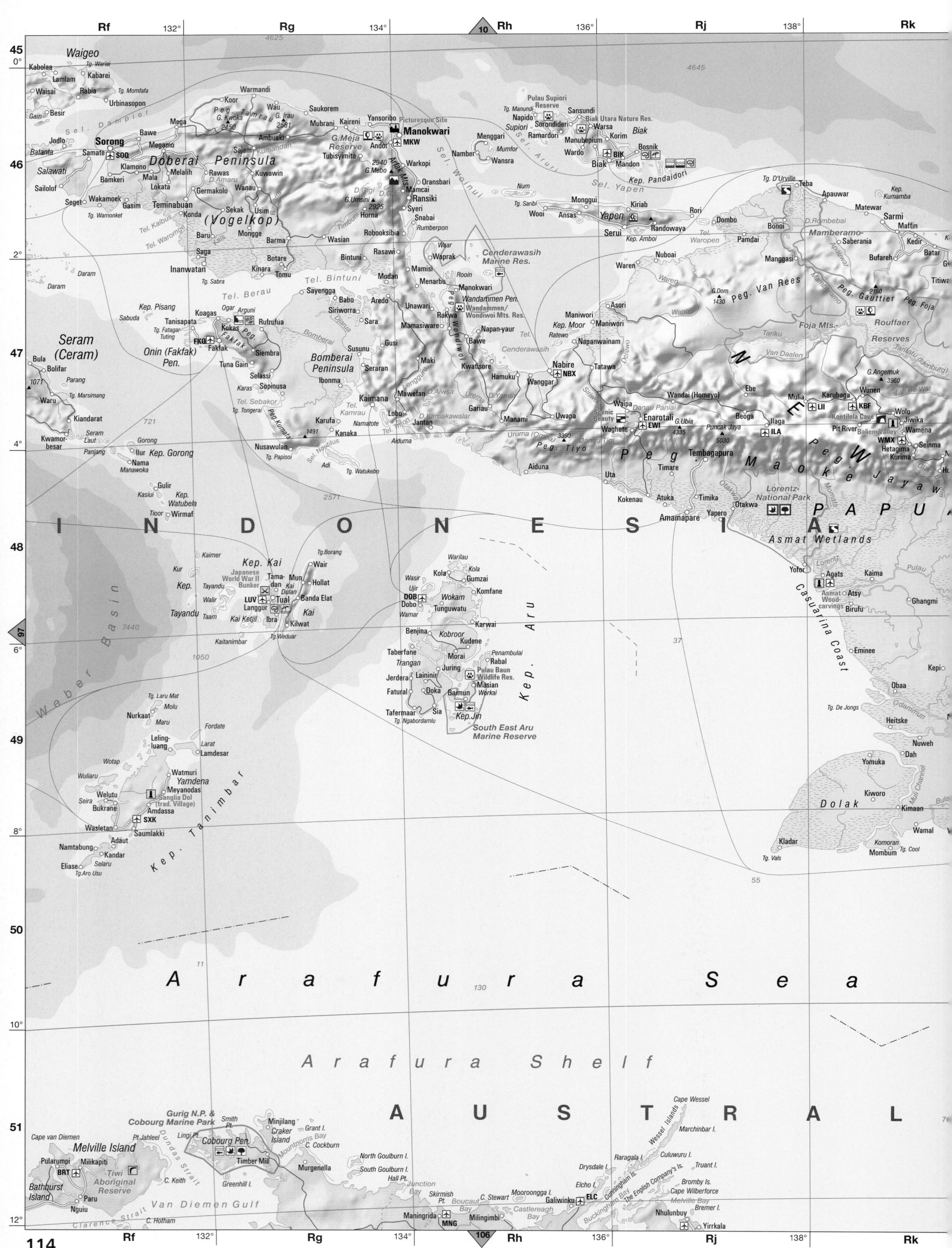

Scale 1:4,500,000

0 50 100 150 Kilometers
0 50 100 Miles

Equator 0°

P A C I F I C   O C E A N

4485

5478

46

Heina Is.

Allison I.

Samasuma I. Marl I. Hermit Is.

Aua I. Ninigo Group

Wuvulu I.

Tulu Manus Island 2°
Lessau Lorengau Momote
Mt.Dremsel
Likum Loi 702 Chalalou MAS
Demta Yafase
Depapre Netaar
Jayapura Wutung Ningera Leitre Western I. Loi Lou I. Horno Is.
enyem DJJ Entrop Skosai Vanimo Sissano Lenkau Rambutyo Is.
Pue Sentani Arso Baluan I.
Anthropological Arso Purdy Is. Admiralty Islands

P A P U A   N E W   G U I N E A

Bewani Schouten Is. 47
Imonda Kilifas Aitape Paup Suain Walis I. Vokeo I.
Serra Hills Karaitem Drome Vanimo But Kairiru I. Mushu I. Koil I.
Punda Hamlets Torricelli 1651 Boiken Vai I.
Ananab Lumi Mt.Sulen Mts. 1240 Mt. Blup Blup I. Circular Reef Sherburne Reef
Kambeta Kwieftim Yemnu Prince Alexander Mts. Ulbanep Bam I.
toro Green Nuku Hayfield 225 Wewak
River Yilui Akasame Nungwaia WWK Kadovar I. Bismarck Sea
1525 Kapaimari Nagum Kaup Mendam Cape Girgir 2165
Ama Ambunti Terebo Broken Water
May River Kubkain Pagwi Timbunke Angoram Gavien Watam Bay Manam I.
St.Albert Chambri L. Sepik River Cruises Awar Manam I.
Yosua Dome Kanduanam Giri Bogia 4°
@ Antares 3065 Biwat Kwanga Hatzfeldhafen 85
Oksibil 4168 Mt.Kusiwugasi Eram Adelbert Josephstaal Malala
3840 Mianmin Annaberg Katiati Range Karkar Karkar I.
St.Albert Central Range Mt.Morbampari Aiome Mt.Mengam 1533 Matukar
Waropko Tabubil 3725 Labalama Simbai 125 Malolo Plantation Lodge 48
Tarakbits Oksapmin Kopiago Ruti Oronga Jais Aben Resort Bagabag I.
Mt.Aiome Kau Rainforest Museum
Telefomin Porgera 2843 Mawan Alexishafen Crown I. Unea I.
Ningerum Kandep Wabag Baiyer Tabibug Kol MAG Madang
Namas Atkamba Mission Koroba River Karap 4510 Male Madang Resort Long I. Malala
Mindiptana Tari Laiagam HGU Angalimp 175 Mt.Wilhelm Usino Astrolabe Bay Wisdom Tolokiwa I.
Kiunga Margarima 165 Kundiawa Gembogl Ming Ming Umboi I. 1655 Goucester
Tanahmerah Nipa Tambul Asaro 4175 Saidor Siassi Lab Lab Garimari
Angamarut Komo Mt.Hagen Show 111 Mount Goroka Tauta Malalamai 1496 Aumo
Ungerem Mendi Hagen GKA Goroka Show Wantoat Saruwaged Kelanoa Sauren 6°
Debepare Poroma Kaupena 4105 Gumine Henganofi Kaiapit Worin Range Mt.Bangeta Sialum Arawe I. Wako
Mabaduam Lake Kutubu N.P. Lalibu Chuave Watarais Boana 4120 Mindik Huon
Murray Inuo Kagua Pangia Nomane Kainantu Nadzab Kwapsanek Findiu Peninsula
Great Erave Pangia Mt.Michael Agotu To'Okona Bonga Finschhafen
Muting Lake Papuan Kaiam Mt.Karimui 3645 Okapa Kratke Wagan Mange
Murray L. Murray Mt.Bosavi Wasi Falls 2570 Haia Waisa 3558 Range Bukaua
Abemarre Pangoa Plateau 2505 Kikori-River-Region Tua R. Wabo LAE Lae Huon
Tetehui Purari R. Marawaka Piu Wagau Markham Gulf
Bupul Hivaro Komaio Pawaia 145 Mumeng Salamaua 7020
Turama R. Kaiam Iori Komako Menyamya Bulolo Lasanga I.
Bian Omati Baimuru Ebala Aseki McAdam Wau 49
Wewei R. Misiki Veiru Karauwi 3280 N.P. Kui Maiama
Muru Kamina Mt.Amungwiwa Ilaura Morobe
Sarore Goari Akoma Kakoro Garaina Hercules Bay
Daub Yangga Deception Ihu Kerema Mt.Strong Wuwu
MKD Suki Bay KMA Malalaua 3590 Guari Manau
National Bamio Bora Terapo Tapini Mt. 8°
Tamarike Park Balimo Kenawa Wapumba I. Mirapo Albert Edward Auro Holnicote Bay
Sakiramke Morehead Goe Kiriwa Iamara Kubuna 3990 Woitape Garara
Weam Buk Sewerimabu Samari Bereina Popondetta
Wando Dimissi Oriomo Sui Oroi Kokoda Ilimo 1680 PNP Eroro Waiwa
Bula Wipim Kubuna Mt.Lamington Sila Gobe
Mari Tonda Togo Daru Redscar Bay Manari Hisui 140 210 Dyke Ackland 50
Arufi Sibidiri Hula Lea Lea Karema PDM Varirata Sogeri Bay
SBR Saibai I. Porebada Vanirata N.P. Afore Mt.Victory
Talbot I. Buru I. Darnley I. Portlock Port Moresby Sariri 1891
Torres Strait Orman Reef Gabba I. Reefs National Museum Gaire Kwikila Owen
Mabuiag I. Zagai I. Loloata Resort Hula Baramata Mt.Suckling
Sassie I. Murray I. 3292 Kupiano 3678
Badu I. Moa I. Eastern Hood Aroma Amau Robinson 10°
Hammond I. Wednesday I. Ashmore Fields Bay Hood Riv.
Thursday Island Reef Point Magaubo
Prince of Wales I. Horn I. Cape York Magarida
A Endeavour Bamaga Somerset C o r a l
Slade Point Newcastle
Cowal Creek ABM Furze Point Jardine
River N.P. 51
Mapoon Cape York False Oxford S e a
Aboriginal Ness
Land 324 1445
Port
Musgrave Cape 107 Sc Sd Se
Mapoon Bramwell Temple Bay 12°
York 2165

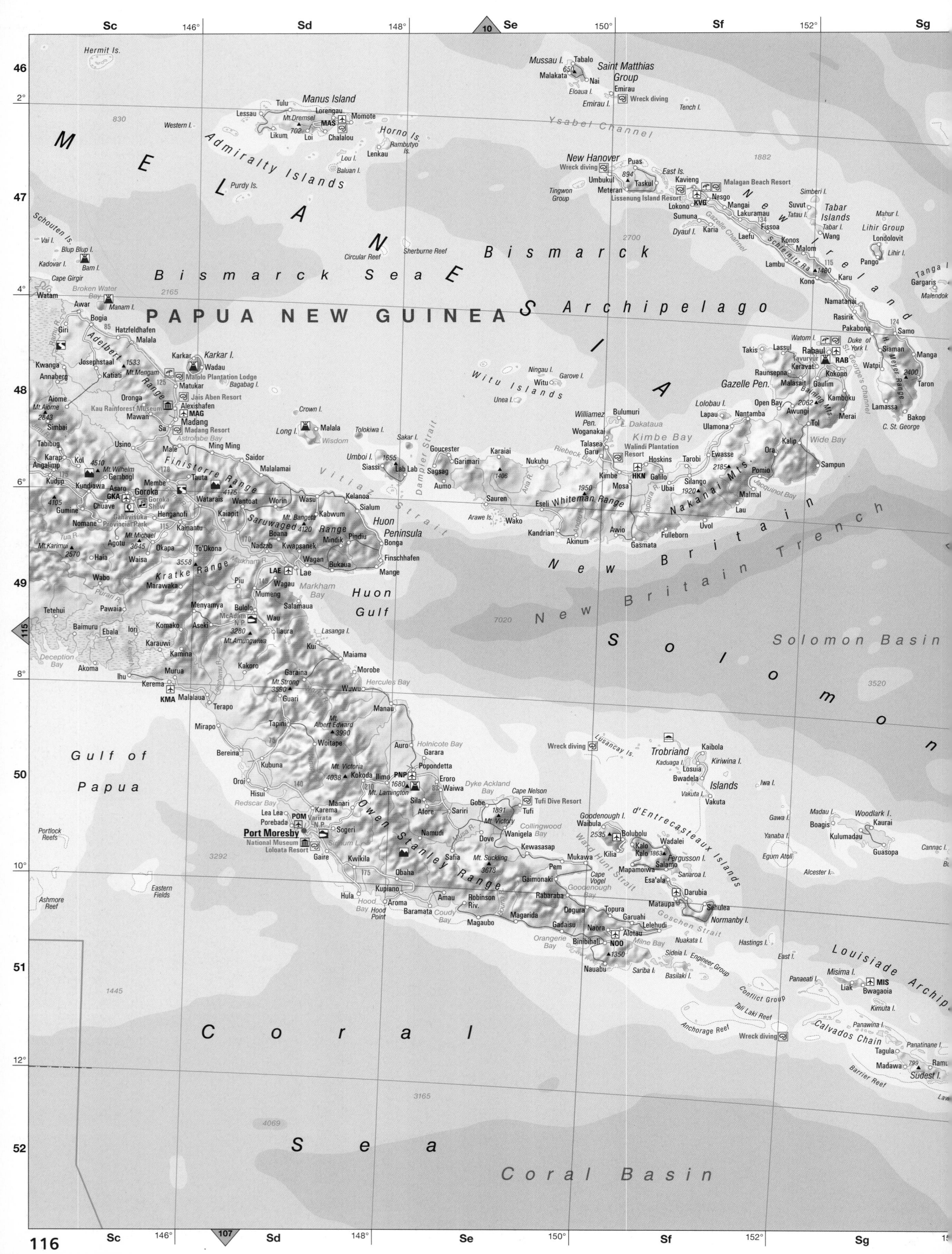

P A C I F I C

3640

3950

O C E A N

1590

2°

Malum Is.

Nuguria Islands *Nuguria I.*
Paopao I.

Tauu (Mortlock) Islands

Tasman Islands (Nukumanu Atoll)

Pinepel I.
Nissan I.
■ *Tanamalit*

Tulun Is.
Iagain I. *Han I.*

Frindsburg Reef
1745

C. Hanpan
Hanahan
Gagan *Buka Island*
Buka *Hutjena*
Siara
Taiof I. *Tinputz*
Kekesu
Sipai ▲ *Mt. Balbi* *Wakunai*
2714
Koripobi ▲ *Tarara*

Bougainville Island

Pélau I.
Ontong Java Atoll
Keila I.
Leuaniua I.

Roncador Reef

Arawa
Torokina ⊞ *Kieta*
Orami ▲ *Aropa*
Empress Augusta Bay ▲ *Mt.Taknan*
2220
Motupena Pt. **Boku** ● *Buin*

Ovau I. *Liuliu* ⊞ *C. Alexander*
Moila Pt. ⊞ **CHY** *Choiseul*
Fauro I. *Susuka*
Western Entrance *Korovou* *Kumbanikesa*
Shortland Is. *Panggoe*
Treasury Is. ▲ *Mt. Maitabi* *Luti*
■ *Maloaini* 1065 *Korasa*

Bradley Reef

4610

Taora *Vaghena*
Ghaghe I.

SOLOMON ISLANDS

4021

Kia
Barora I.
Barora Ite I.
Baolo
Filuo ▲ 760

Vella Lavella ▲ 915 *Sosolo*
Sielezavanga *Kolombangara*
Ranongga *Barakoma* ▲ *Tuki*
Kundu *Gizo* ▲ 1770
Ringgi **MUA** ⊞
Vanovano *Munda* ▲ *Hovoro*
Agnes Lodge *Hapai*
Egholo *New Georgia*

Santa Isabel
Ghoveo
Jejevo ▲ *Mt. Sasari*
1220 *Buala*
Kaevanga
Tatamba
Vulavu

Dai I.

New Georgia Group
Rendova *Seghe* ▲ *Mt.* *Uepi Island Resort*
Vangunu *Marvo Lagoon*
Tavara *Tetepare* *Mbatuna*
1123 *Vangunu*
Nggatokae

San Jorge I.
Vikenara Pt.

Maluu

Stewart Is.

Gounatolo
Dala
Auki ⊞ *Atori*
AKS

Russell Is.
Pavuvu I. ⊞ **XYA**
Yandina
Yandina Plantation Resort
Mbanika I.

Buena Vista I.
Mbokonimbeti I.
Savo I. *Nggela*
Chapuru *Sule*
Tambea *Wreck diving*
Lambi *Nggela Pile*
Honiara *Ndondo*
HIR *Mataniko*
Falls
Mbambanakira ▲ *Mt. Popomanaseu*
2449 **AVU** *Mt. Kaichui*
Avu Avu 1920
Guadalcanal

Siota

Malaita
Olomburi
Hauhui ▲ *Mt. Kalourat*
1435

Maru'ura
Aola

Maramasike (Small Malaita)
Apio ● 515
Sa'a
Makina ● *Siodjuru*
Nialaha'u Pt. *Ulawa I.*

4966

5234

Pocklington Reef

Rennell Rise

Uki Ni Masi I.
Tadahadi *Three Sisters Is. (Olu Malua)*
Tetere
IRA ⊞ *Kirakira*
Makira ▲ 1250 *Watee*
Arite *Nasuraghena*
Hauraha *Santa Ana I.*

Wreck diving

South Solomon Trench

1755

Bellona I.
Rennell I.
Manggautu
Lavanggu
155
Lake Tungano

North Reef

8308

New Caledonia, Vanuatu, Fiji Islands

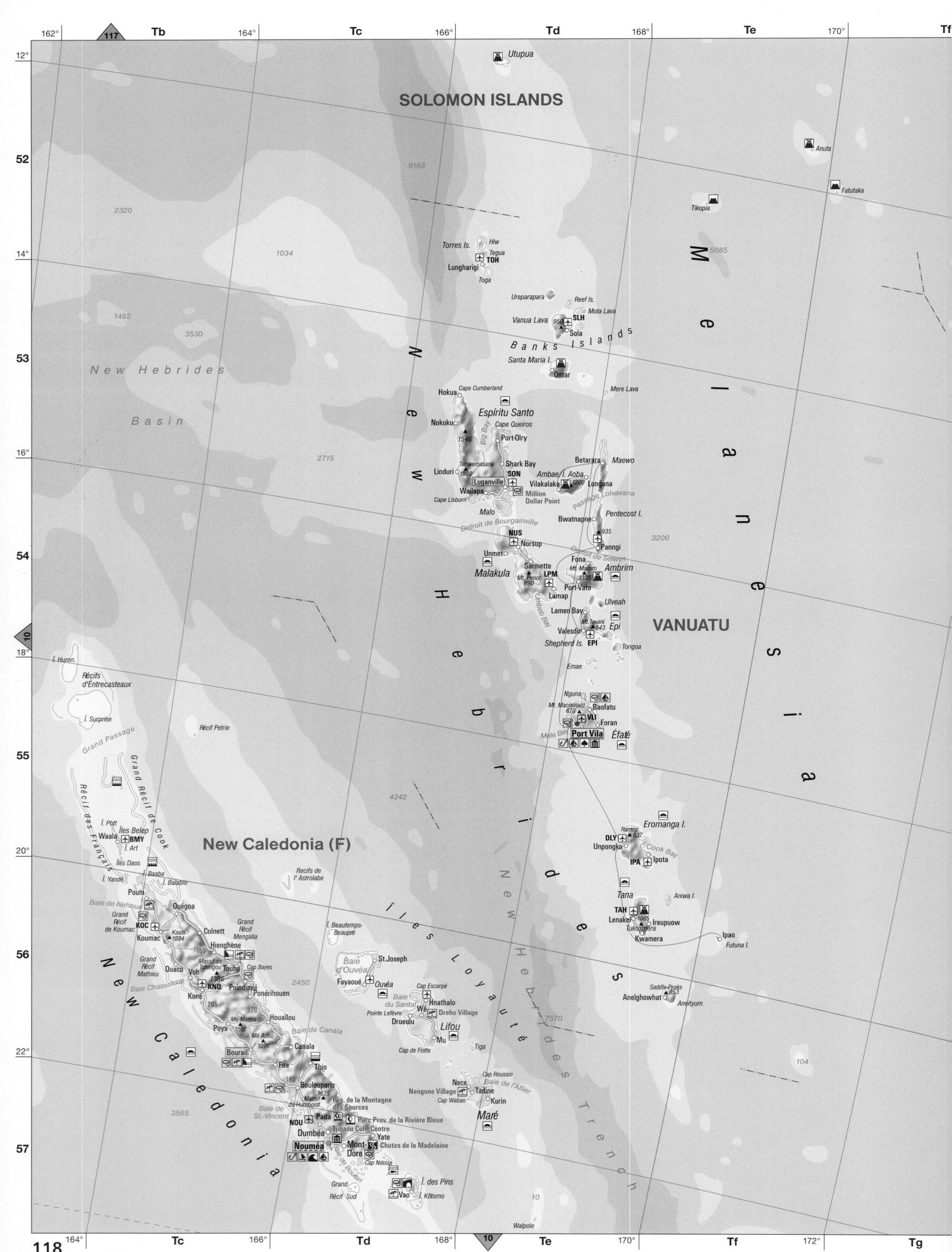

SOLOMON ISLANDS

Utupua

Anuta

Fatutaka

Tikopia

Torres Is.
Hiw
Tegua
TOH
Lungharigi
Toga

Ureparapara
Reef Is.
Mota Lava
Vanua Lava
950 **SLH**
Sola

Banks Islands

Santa Maria I.
Ontar

Mere Lava

M e l a n e s i a

New Hebrides Basin

Hokua
Cape Cumberland
Espíritu Santo
Nokuku
Cape Queiros
1546
Port-Olry

Betarara
Maewo

Tabwemasana
Shark Bay
1880
Linduri
SON
Ambae/I. Aoba
Longana
1200
Luganville
Vilakalaka
Wailapa
Million Dollar Point
Cape Lisburn
Pentecost I.
Malo
Bwatnapne
935

Detroit de Bourgainville

NUS
Norsup
3200
Unmet
Panngi
Sarmette
Fona
Detroit de Selwyn
Malakula
Mt. Penot
LPM
Mt. Marum
1335
Ambrim
890
Port-Vato
Lamap
Ulveah

Lamen Bay
Mt. Tavani
843
Epi
Valesdir
EPI
Shepherd Is.
Tongoa

Emae

N e w   H e b r i d e s

Nguna
Mt. Macdonald
610
Baofatu
VLI
Foran
Port Vila
Éfaté
Mele Bay

VANUATU

4242

Eromanga I.
Rantop
837
DLY
Unpongko
Cook Bay
IPA
Ipota

Tana
Aniwa I.

TAH
1085
Lenakel
Ireupuow
Tukosmera
Kwamera
Ipao
Futuna I.

Saddle Peaks
853
Anelghowhat
Aneityum

I. Huron
Récifs d'Entrecasteaux
I. Surprise

Grand Passage
Récif Petrie

Grand Récif de Cook
Récif des Français

I. Pott
Îles Belep
Waala
BMY
I. Art
Îles Daos
I. Yandé
I. Baaba
Poum
Balabio

New Caledonia (F)

Baie de Nehoué
Ouégoa
Grand Récif de Koumac
KOC
Koumac
Kaala
1034
Colnett
Grand Récif Mengalia
Hienghène
Quaco
Massif de Panié
Voh
1386
Touho
Cap Bayes
Grand Récif Mathieu
KNQ
Poindimié
Koné
205
Ponérihouen
170
Mé Maoya
Houaïlou
1507
Poya
Mé Adéo
1096

Baie d'Ouvéa
St.Joseph
Fayaoué
Ouvéa
Cap Escarpé
I. Beautemps-Beaupré
Baie du Santal
Hnathalo
Pointe Lefèvre
Wé
Drueulu
Drehu Village
Lifou
Mu
Tiga

Îles Loyauté

7570

Baie Chasseloup
2450
Baie de Canala
Canala
Thio
Bourail
Foa
160
Bouloupari
1633
Massif du Humboldt
Rés. de la Montagne des Sources
Baie de St-Vincent
Nece
Nengone Village
Tadine
Cap Wabao
Kurin
Maré
Cap Roussin
Baie de l'Allier
104

3565
Païta
Parc Prov. de la Rivière Bleue
NOU
Dumbéa
Tjibaou Culf Centre
Mont-Dore
Yate
Nouméa
Chutes de la Madelaine
Cap Ndoua

New Caledonia

New Hebrides Trench

Grand Récif Sud
Vao
I. des Pins
I. Kôtomo
10
Walpole

9168
2320
1034
1482
3530
2715
5085

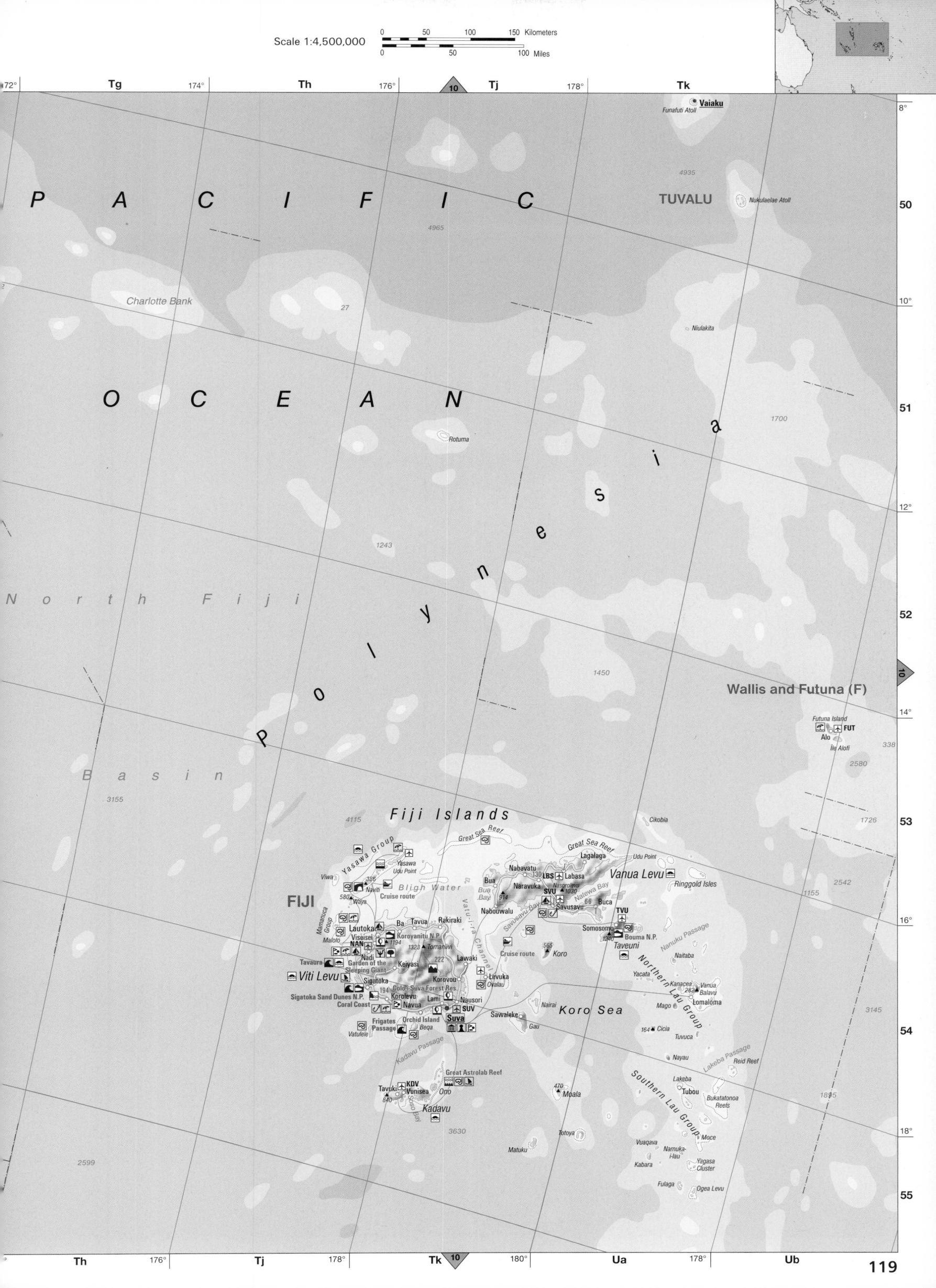

0	50	100	150 Kilometers		
0		50		100 Miles	

Vaiaku
Funafuti Atoll

Tg 174° Th 176° 10 Tj 178° Tk

8°

P A C I F I C

4935

TUVALU

Nukulaelae Atoll

50

4965

Charlotte Bank

10°

27

Niulakita

O C E A N

Rotuma

51

1700

a

s

i

1243

e

n

North Fiji

52

y

1450

10

Wallis and Futuna (F)

l

o

14°

P

Futuna Island
Alo FUT
Île Alofi 338

Basin

2580

3155

Fiji Islands

4115

Cikobia 1726 53

Great Sea Reef

Yasawa Group

Great Sea Reef

Udu Point

Lagalaga

Yasawa
Udu Point Nabavatu 130 LBS Labasa Vanua Levu

Viwa 386 Bua Naravuka SVU Nasorolevu Ringgold Isles

FIJI Naviti Bligh Water Bua 1030 Natewa Bay 2542

580 Waya Bay 974 66 Buca 1155

Mamanuca Group Lautoka Ba Tavua Rakiraki Nabouwalu Savusavu TVU

Malolo Koroyanitu N.P. Somosomo

Viseisei 1194 Vatu-i-Ra Channel 565 Bouma N.P. 16°

NAN 1323 Tomaniivi Koro Taveuni 1240

Tavarua Nadi 222 Lawaki Naitaba

Garden of the Keiyasi Cruise route Yacata

Sleeping Giant Levuka Kanacea Vanua

Viti Levu Sigatoka Korovou Ovalau Balavu

194 Colo-i-Suva Forest Res Lami Nairai Mago Lomalóma

Sigatoka Sand Dunes N.P. Korolevu Navua SUV Sawaleke

Coral Coast Nausori Koro Sea Tuvuca 3145

Frigates Orchid Island Suva Gau 164 Cicia

Passage Beqa Nayau

Vatulele Southern Lau Group Lakeba Reid Reef

Tubou

Great Astrolab Reef 470 Moala Bukatatonoa Reefs

Tavuki KDV Ono Moce 1895

Vunisea 840 Matuku Vuaqava Namuka-i-Lau Yagasa Cluster

Kadavu Kabara

3630 Totoya Fulaga Ogea Levu 55

2599

Ethiopia: Traditional two-story dwellings with thatched roofs in Lalibela.

The Sahara Desert encompasses a variety of contrasting landscapes.

AFRICA

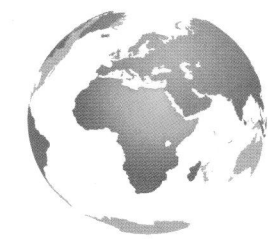

THE DEVELOPING CONTINENT

Africa has an area of approximately 30.4 million km^2. The world's second largest continent encompasses around 20% of the Earth's total land area. From north to south, Africa stretches more than 8,000 kilometers. Africa is separated from Europe by the Mediterranean Sea, but at the Strait of Gibraltar the two continents are less than 14 kilometers apart. The Red Sea is located between northeastern Africa and the Arabian Peninsula. In the west, Africa is bordered by the Atlantic Ocean, while the Indian Ocean borders the continent to the east and southeast. The coasts of Africa are remarkably smooth, with few peninsulas and large natural harbors. Madagascar is situated near a series of smaller island groups including the Comoros and the Seychelles. Several small island groups – including the Cape Verde Islands – are located near Africa's western coast. The terrain of Africa is dominated by a series of basins, including the immense Sahara basin, the Niger-Chad-White Nile basin, and the Congo basin. The Great Rift Valley, an ancient fracture on the Earth's surface, stretches through East Africa. Many of Africa's tallest mountains – including Kilimanjaro and Mount Kenya – are located in or near the Great Rift Valley.

Africa is home to more than 700 million people. North Africa is inhabited by a variety of ethnicities, including Arabs, Berbers, and the Tuareg. The areas south of the Sahara are populated mostly by dark-skinned black African ethnicities. Most black Africans are categorized into one of two distinct groups: Bantu speaking and Sudanic ethnicities. Other major ethnic groups in Africa include the Somalis, Ethiopians, and the San.

Maasai: The semi-nomadic Maasai tribe lives in northeastern Tanzania and southern Kenya.

Africa has the highest birthrates of any continent. The rapid population growth is seen by many as a major obstacle to the continent's economic and social development. Despite widespread social problems, several African states have experienced positive economic and political developments in recent years.

Africa

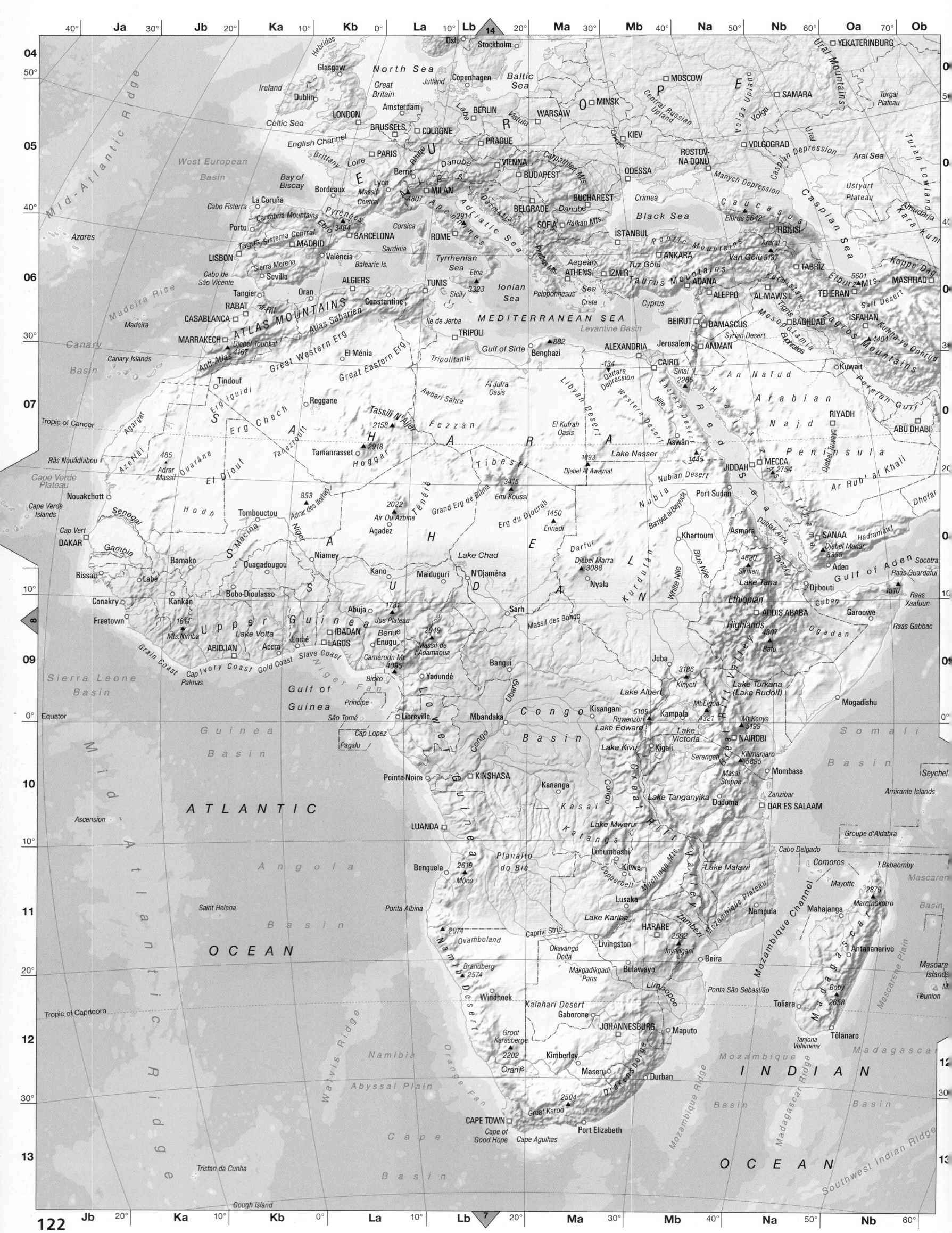

04
50°

YEKATERINBURG

Ural Mountains

Hebrides
North Sea
Glasgow
Ireland
Dublin
Great Britain

MOSCOW
SAMARA
Turgai
Plateau

Mid-Atlantic Ridge

Jutland
Copenhagen
Baltic Sea
MINSK
Central Russian Upland
VOLGOGRAD
Aral Sea

LONDON
Amsterdam
BERLIN
WARSAW
KIEV
ROSTOV-NA-DONU

West European Basin

English Channel
BRUSSELS
COLOGNE
PRAGUE
Vistula
O R
ODESSA
Caspian Depression
Turan Lowland
Ustyurt Plateau

Brittany
PARIS
Loire
Rhine
Danube
VIENNA
BUDAPEST
Carpathian Mts.
BUCHAREST
Crimea
Black Sea
Caucasus
Elbrus 5642
TIBILISI

05

Bay of Biscay
Bordeaux
Lyon
Berne
MILAN
BELGRADE
Danube
SOFIA
Balkan Mts.
Ararat
Van Gölü 5137
Koppe Dag

Azores
Cabo Fisterra
La Coruña
Cantabria Mountains
Pyrénées
3404
Corsica
ROME
ATHENS
İSTANBUL
ANKARA
TABRİZ
Elbruz 5601 Mts.
MASHHAD

Porto
LISBON
MADRID
BARCELONA
Sardinia
Tyrrhenian Sea
IZMIR
Taurus Mountains
ADANA
ALEPPO
AL-MAWSIL
TEHERAN
Zagros Mountains
4404

06
40°

ATLANTIC

Madeira Rise

Canary Basin

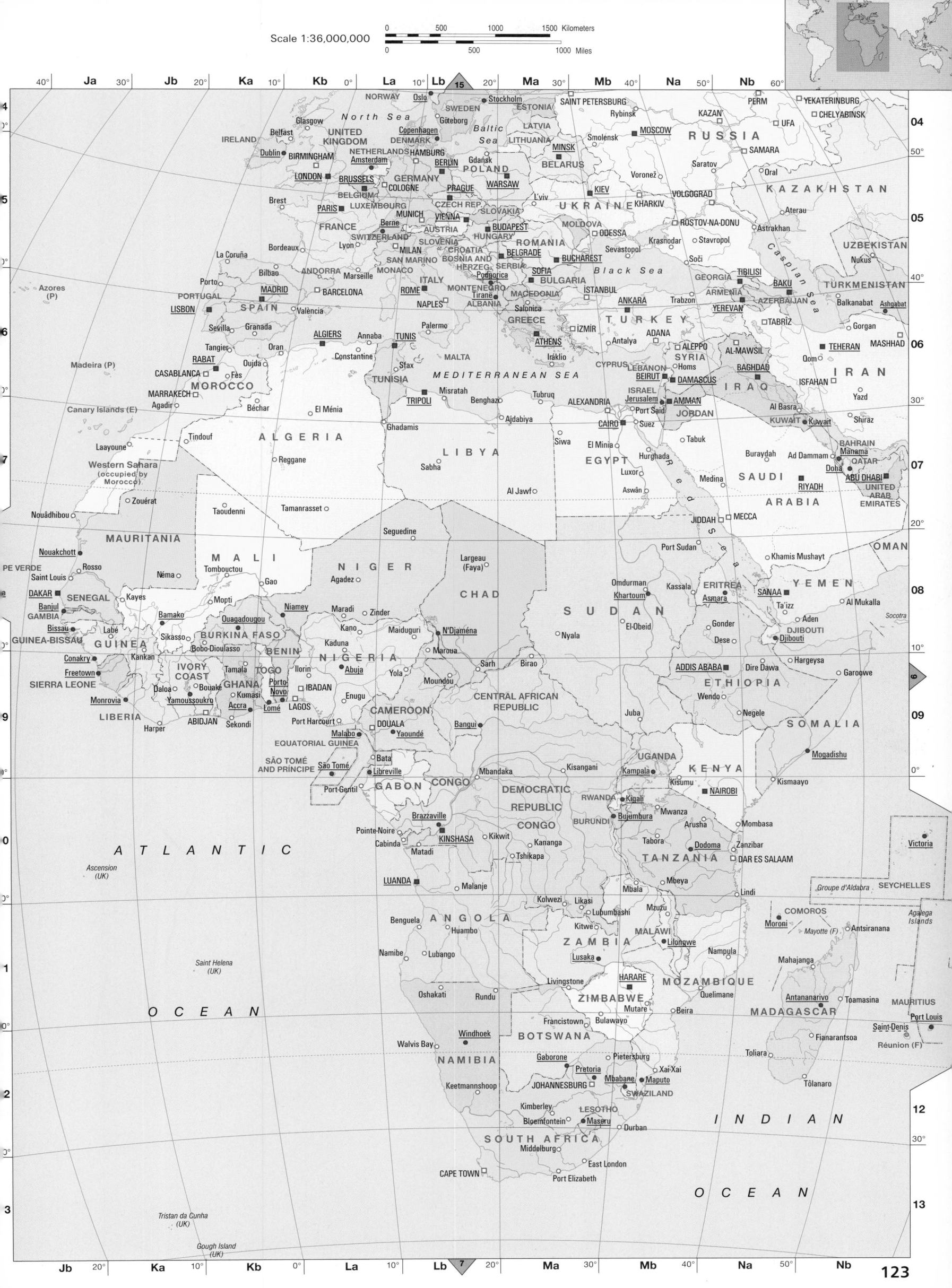

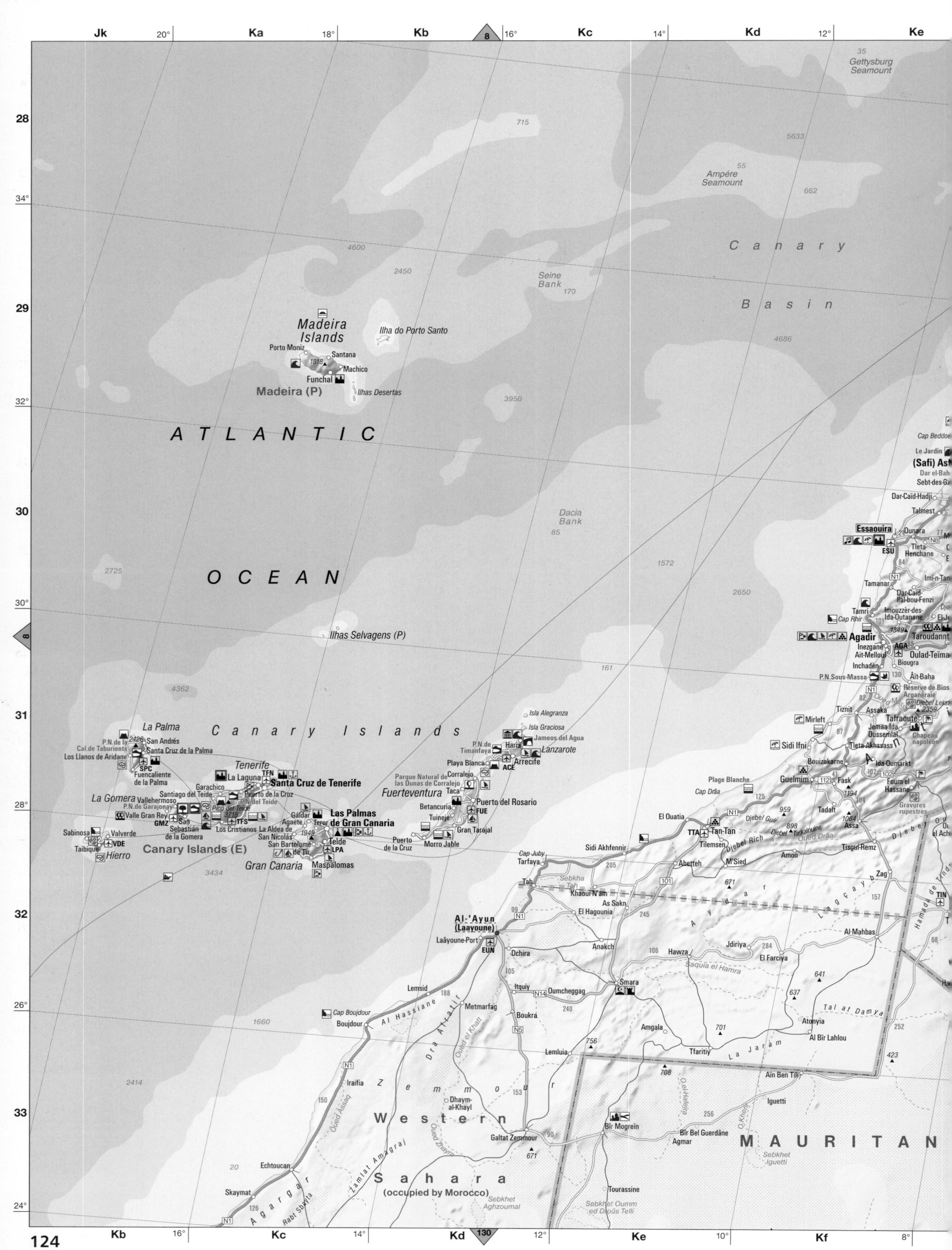

Jk 20° Ka 18° Kb 8 16° Kc 14° Kd 12° Ke

35
Gettysburg
Seamount

28

5633

55
Ampère
Seamount

34°

662

C a n a r y

4600

2450

Seine
Bank

170

29

4686

Madeira
Islands

Ilha do Porto Santo

B a s i n

Porto Moniz
Santana
1818
Machico
Funchal
Ilhas Desertas

32°

Madeira (P)

3950

A T L A N T I C

Cap Beddou
Le Jardin
(Safi) As
Dar el-Bah
Sebt-des-Ga

Dar-Caïd-Hadji
Talmest

30

Dacia
Bank

85

Essaouira
Ounara
Tleta-
Henchane
ESU

O C E A N

2725

1572

Imi-n-Tan
Tamanar
Dar-Caïd-
Ifal-bou-Fenzi
Tamri
Imouzzèr-des-
Ida-Outanane
El Je
Cap Rhir

30°

Ilhas Selvagens (P)

2650

161

Taroudannt
Agadir
AGA
Inezgane
Aït-Melloul
Biougra
Oulad-Teïma
Inchadèn
P.N.Sous-Massa
Aït-Baha

4362

Isla Alegranza
Isla Graciosa

Réserve de Bios
Arganeraie
Djebel Lek
2359

31

C a n a r y   I s l a n d s

Jameos del Agua
P.N.de
Timanfaya
Lanzarote
Playa Blanca
Corralejo
ACE
Arrecife

La Palma
P.N.de la
2426
San Andrés
Cal.de Taburiente
Santa Cruz de la Palma
Los Llanos de Aridane
SPC
Fuencaliente
de la Palma

Tiznit
Tafraoute
Jemaa Ida
Oussenlal
Mirleft
Tleta-Akhsass
Sidi Ifni
Bouizakarne
Ida-Oumarkt

Tenerife
TFN
La Laguna
Garachico
Santa Cruz de Tenerife
Parque Natural de
las Dunas de Corralejo
Fuerteventura
Taca

Guelmim
112
Fask
Foum el
Hassane

La Gomera
Pico del Teide
3718
Puerto de la Cruz
Santiago del Teide
1949
Vallehermoso
P.N.de Garajonay
Valle Gran Rey
GMZ
San
Sebastián
de la Gomera
Los Cristianos
TFS
La Aldea de
San Nicolás
Agaete
Gáldar
Teror
Las Palmas
de Gran Canaria
Betancuria
Tuineje
Puerto del Rosario
FUE
Gran Tarajal

Plage Blanche
Cap Drâa
Djebel Guir
959
898
1064
Tadaft
Assa
Djebel
Inskalouine
Gravures
rupestres

28°

Sabinosa
Valverde
VDE
Taibique
Hierro
3434
Canary Islands (E)
Telde
LPA
San Bartolomé
de Tir
Maspalomas
Gran Canaria
Puerto
de la Cruz
Morro Jable

El Ouatia
TTA
Tan-Tan
Tilemsin
Djebel Rich
Amon
Tisgul-Remz

31

El Achi

Cap Juby
Tarfaya
Sidi Akhfennir
Khaoul N'am
As Sakn
Tah
El Hagounia
L a g â y e b
157
Zag
TIN

32

Al-'Ayun
(Laâyoune)
Laâyoune-Port
EUN
Dchira
Anakch
Jdiriya
El Farciya
Al Mahbas

671
245

205
101

Al Bïr Lahlou
Atonyia
Hawza
Smara
106
El Farciya
641
Oumcheggag
N14
Itquiy
Lemsid
188
Metmarfag
Boukra
240
637

26°

Cap Boujdour
Boujdour
1660
Al Hassiane
N5
Amgala
701
Tfaritiy
Lemluia
756
Al Bïr Lahlou
252
423

33

2414
Iraifiya
Echtoucan
150
Dhaym-
al-Khayl
153
Bïr Mogreïn
Bïr Bel Guerdâne
Agmar
708
Iguetti

W e s t e r n
M A U R I T A N

Skaymat
126
20
S a h a r a
(occupied by Morocco)
Galtat Zemmour
90
671
Tourassine
Sebkhet
Aghzoumal
Sebkhet Ounm
ed Dioûs Telli
Sebkhet
Iguetti

24°

0 50 100 150 Kilometers
0 50 100 Miles

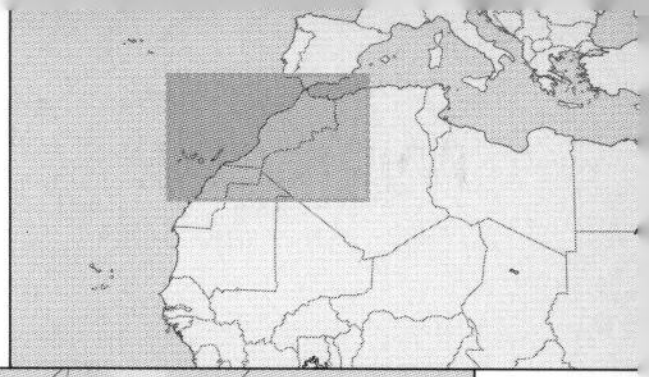

Kf 8° Kg 6° Kh 4° Kj 2° Kk

MEDITERRANEAN SEA

SPAIN

Golfo de Cádiz
Chipiona
El Puerto de Santa María
Cádiz
San Fernando
Barbate
Algeciras
Tarifa
Punta Marroquí de Tarifa
Strait of Gibraltar
Gibraltar (UK)
GIB
La Línea de la Concepción
Punta Almina
Ceuta (E) (Sebta)
(Tangier) Tanjah
TNG
Asilah
(Larache) El-Araïche
Lixus
Ksar-el-Kebir
Moulay-Bousselham
Arbaoua
Souk-el-Arba-du-Rharb
Sidi-Allal-Tazi
(Kénitra) Al-Q'nitra
Mahdija-Plage
Salé
(RABAT) AR-RIBAT
RBA
Mohammedia
CASABLANCA DD-DAR-AL-BAYDA
CMN
CAS
Azemmour
Jerez d.l. Frontera
Arcos
Olvera
Villamartín
Lebrija
Antequera
Álora AGP
Coín
Ronda
Estepona
Medina Sidonia
Marbella
Fuengirola
Torremolinos
Vélez-Málaga
Málaga
Almuñécar
Motril
Nerja
Cueva de Nerja
Berja
Adra
Sierra Nevada
P.N. de Sierra Nevada
Almería
Roquetas de Mar
Cabo de Gata
San José
Costa del Sol
Costa de Almería
El Marsa
Ténès
Bouzghaia
Achaacha
Sidi Ali
Mostaganem
Cap Carbon
Aïn-el-Türck
Wahran (Oran)
Arzew
Les Andalouses
Bou Sfer
Chlef
Bou Kadir
Oued Rhiou
Zemmora
Relizane
Massif de l'Ouarsenis
Tiaret
TID

MOROCCO

(Tétouan) Titwan
TTU
Et-Tleta-de-Oued-Laou
Bou-Ahmed
Chefchaouen
Torres-de-Alcalá
Al Hoceima
Ajdir
Beni-Boufrah
Targuist
Segangane
Melilla (E)
Nador MLN
Ras Kebdana
Marsa-Ben-Mehidi
Berkane
Saïdia
Zaïo
Aïn-el-Türck
Aïn Témouchent
Sidi Bel Abbès
Maghnia
Tlemcen TLM
Oujda
OUD
Sebdou
Ras-el-Ma

Atlas Saharien

ALGERIA

Hauts Plateaux
Chott Ech Chergui
Mécheria
Naama
Aïn Sefra
Monts des Ksours
Figuig
Béni-Ounif
Béchar
CBH
Kenadsa
Djorf Torba
Barrage Djorf-Torba
Abadla
Taghit
Hassi Hadhour
Hamadet Bet Touadjine

Great Western Erg

Beni-Abbès
El Ouata
Ougarta
Kerzaz
Timimoun
TMX
Hassi Moussa
Charouïne
Ksabi
Timoudi
Tabelbala
Hassi-Mahzez
Erg er Raoui
Erg Iguidi
Hamada de la Daoura
Kahal Tabelbala
Djebel Ben Tadjine
Hamada Tounassine
Tinfouchy
Oum el Assel
Rhemilès

Adrar
AZR
El Mannsour
Tsabit
Sbaa
El Guérara
Reggane
Aoulef
In Salah
INZ
Foggâret el Arab
Bois pétrifié
In Ghar
Tit
Tidikelt
Akabli
Plateau du Tademaït
Plaine du Tidikelt
Erg Chech
Bordj Flye Sante Marie
Oglat el Faci
Bou Ali
Erg el Krebs
Sali
Chenachane
El Mzereb
Chegga

131

125

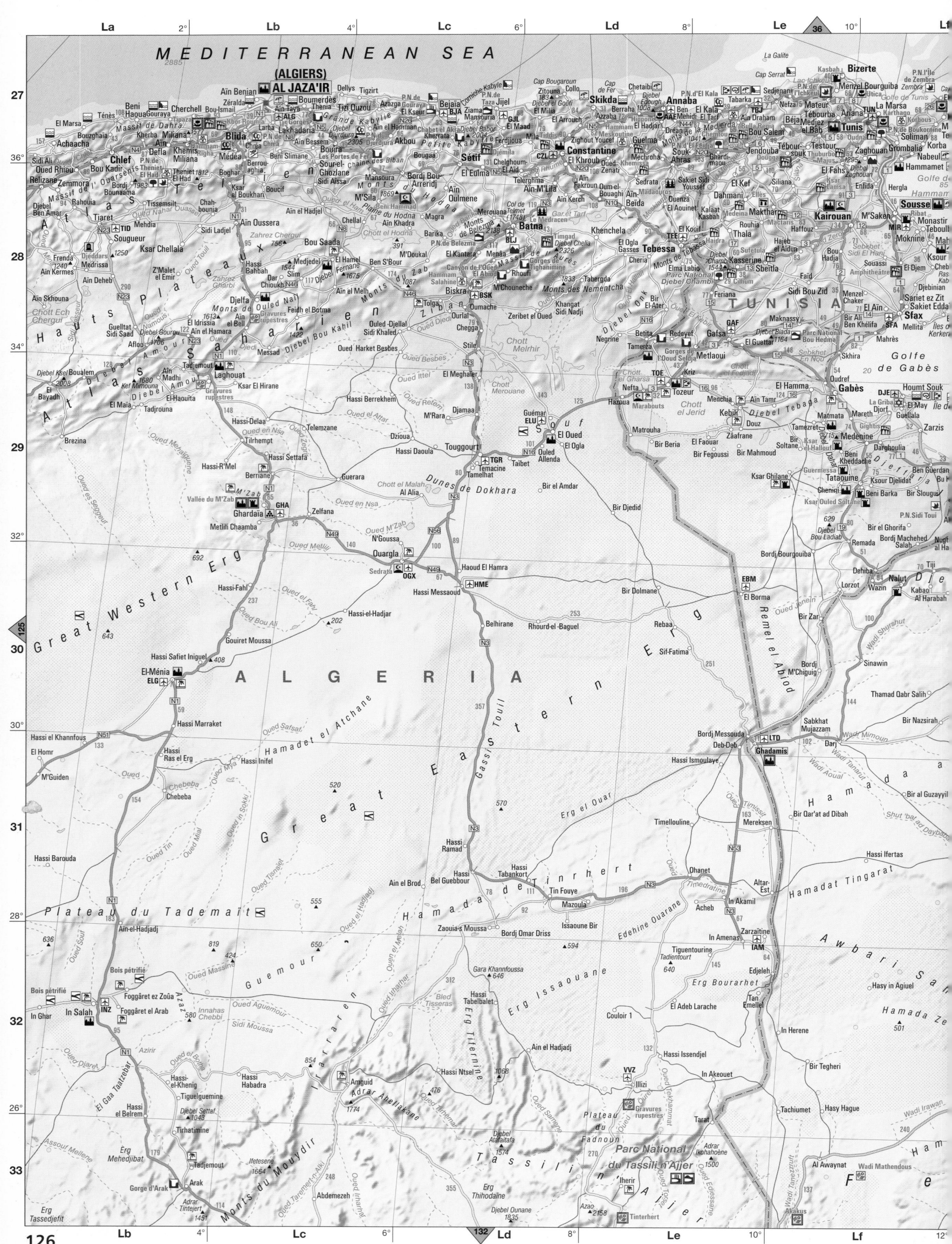

0 50 100 150 Kilometers
0   50   100 Miles

37

ITALY

Sicily

Mazara del Vallo · Castelvetrano · Menfi · Lercara Friddi 1576 · Nicosia · Adrano · Etna 3323 · Teatro Greco
Selinunte · Sciacca · Castel términi · Canicattì · Caltanissetta · Enna · Paternò · Piazza Armerina · Acireale · Naxos · Golfo de Catania
Agrigento · Valle dei Templi · Licata · Gela · Caltagirone · Villa Romana del Casale · Lentini · Augusta · CTA · Catania
Pantelleria · Ìsola di Pantelleria (I) · VL · Vittoria · Módica · Noto · Ìspica · Avola · Siracusa · Teatro Greco · Ragusa
1250 · 1650 · 13 · Capo Ìsola delle Correnti

Ìsola di Linosa (I) · Gozo · Victoria · Megalithic Temples and Hal Saflieni Hypogeum
Ìsola di Lampedusa (I) · Marfa · Rabat · Valletta · MLA
Lampedusa · Malta · MALTA · 91

GREECE
Zákinthos · Zákinthos · Keri · ZTH · Gastoúni · Amaliáda · Dáfni · Mykónes · Argos · Tripoli
Olympia · Pírgos · Megalópoli · Bassae · Kiparissía · Mistrás · Spárti
Nísio Strofádhes · Píos · Kalamáta · KLX · Dhírak · Geráki
Sapiénza · Shiza · Koróni · Messiniakós Kólpos · Máni · Lakonikós Kólpos · Álika · Akrotírio Ténaro · Areópoli
27

Ionian Sea

Ionian Basin
4116 · 4300 · 3410 · 5121 · 5015 · 5016

28

M E D I T E R R A N E A N   S E A
420 · 4300 · 187 · 3400 · 3110 · 34°

(TRIPOLI) TARABULUS · Tajura' · Al Garabull
Surman · Az Zawiyah · Bin Ghashir · Al Qasabat
Al'Aziziyah · TIP · Sug al Khamis · Al Khums (Leptis Magna) · Labdah
Bi'r al Ghanam · Mudakim · Sidi as Sayd · Tarhunah · Zlitan · Misratah · MRA
Yafran · Abu Zayyan · Bi'r Dhu'fan · Al Faid Majir · Al Kararim · Fanar Qasr Ahmad
Wamis · Bani Walid · Qaryat Shumaykh · Al Qala'a · Sabkhat Tawurgha · Tawurgha
Mizdah · Nasmah · Ras Attabil · Bu'ayrat al Hasun · Sabkhat Umm al 'Izam · Sabkhat al Hayshah
Abyar ash Shuwayrit · Qaryat Abu Qurays · Bi'r al 'Utaylah · SRX · Surt (Sidra)
Al Qaryah ash Sharqiyah · Assdadah · Bi'r Bin 'Isa · Madrasat Qasr Abu Hadi
Al Qaryah al Gharbiyah · Bi'r al Khawr · Bi'r ar Rijl · Qaryat Abu Nujaym · Annofliyah · Bin Jawwad
Bi'r al Fatiyah · Bi'r al 'Alaqah · Bi'r al Kammuniyan · Bi'r Qaryas · As Sidr · Ras Lanuf
Uwaynat Wannin · Hun · Waddan · Mabruk · Dahra Oil Field · Thimad al Fata'im
Thamad al Qattar · Bi'r al Washkah · Sawkanah · Wahat al Jufra · HUQ · Oil Gathering Station · Thamad Bu Maras
Djebel al Hasawinah · Bi'r al Qaf · Tarzah · Zillah · Bi'r al Muwaylih · Abu Na'im
Qarat al Harah · As Sawdayah · Zaltan · Maradah · Ar Raqubah
Jadid · Barqin · Agar · Birak · Dabdab · Al Fuqaha' · Qarat al Hayyirah · Al Haruj al Aswad
Adiri · Al Mahruqah · Samnu · Tamanhint · Qarat as Sab'ah · Al Hamudiyah
Bi'r Khalaf Allah · SEB · Sabha · Al Khanabah · Qarat Khalaf Allah
Germa · Qasr Khulayf · Mandara · Bab al Maknusah · Ghadduwah · Zawilah · Es Sabah · Tmassah
Al Ghrayfah · Qasr Larocu · Umm al Aranib · Al Hufrah · Khashm al Jubayl
Marzuq · Taraghin · Al Haruj al Aswad · Thamad Bu Hashishah
Bi'r al Mastutah · Waw al Kabir · Wadi al Hadh · Ad-Dhawah · Tazirbu · Zighan

I B Y A · LIBYA · Tripolitania · Sirte · Cyrenaica
Gulf of Sirte

Ajdabiya · Bi'r al Ghararah · Marsga al Burayqah · Bishr · LMQ · Al 'Uqaylah · Bargah al Bayda · Sabkhat Shunayn
Hamamah · Susah · Apollonia · Ra's al Hilal · Ptolemais · Qasr Al Bayda · Al Libya · Suluntah · Qaryat al Fa'idiyah · Darnah
Teuchira (Tocra) · Tukrah · Al Marj · Marawah · Al Djebel al Akhdar · Bi'r Tuhah · At Taban
Tansulukh · Daryanah · Madinat al Abyar · Qasr al Kharrubah · Zawiyat al Izziyat
Banghazi (Benghazi) · BEN · Taykah · Jardinah · Qaryat Jarrufah · Qaminis · Suluq · Al Maqrun · Zawiyat Masus · Bi'r al Banakish
Sultan · Bi'r Umar · Bi'r Ben Ghimah · Bi'r Tanjder
Qaryat az Zuwaytinah · Sawinnu · Hisn as Sahabi
Bu Athlah · Jalu · Jakharrah · Jalu Oasis · Awjilah
Sarir Kalanshiyú · Tazirbu · Tazirbu Oasis

128 · 27 · 28 · 29 · 30 · 30° · 31 · 28° · 32 · 33

127

Egypt

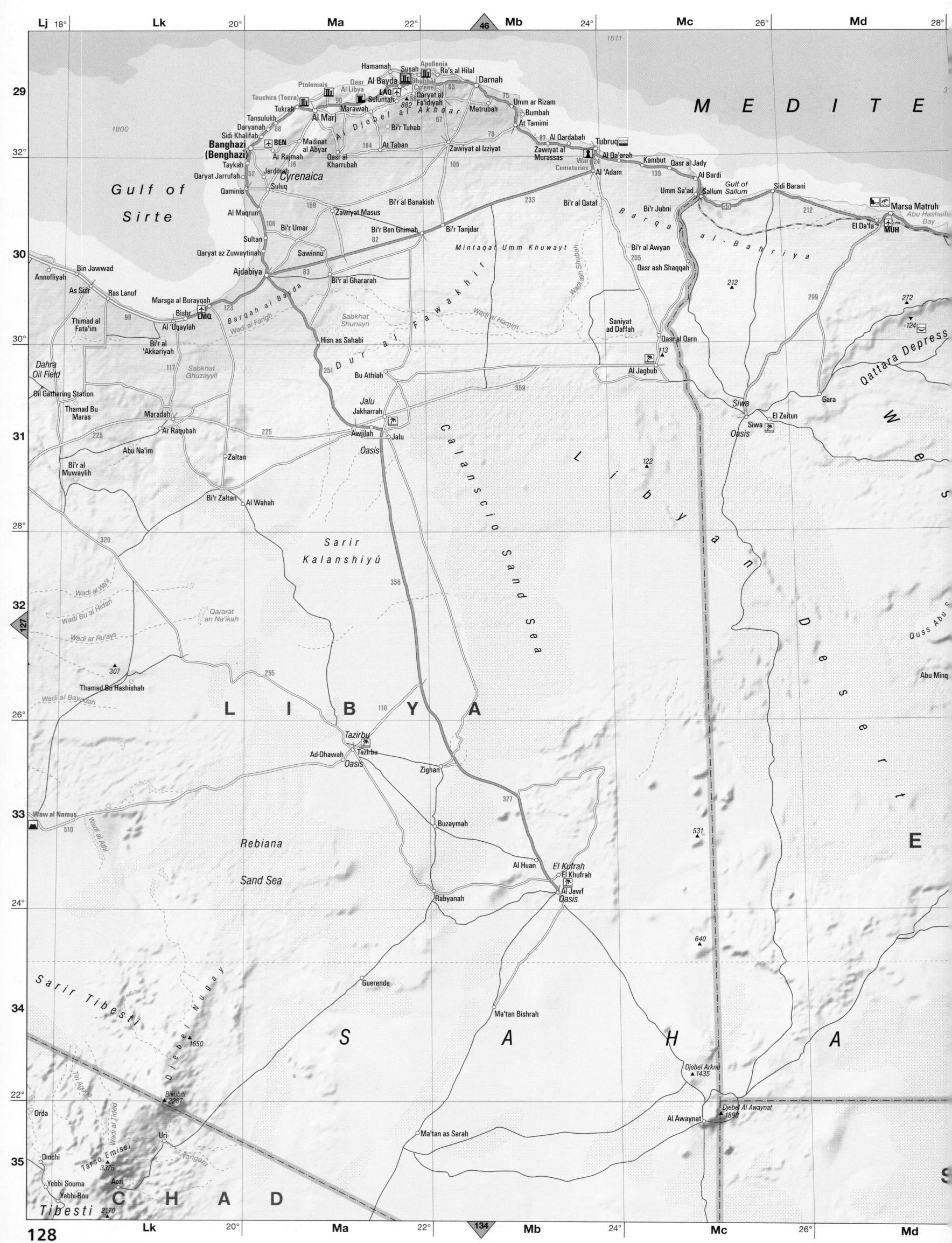

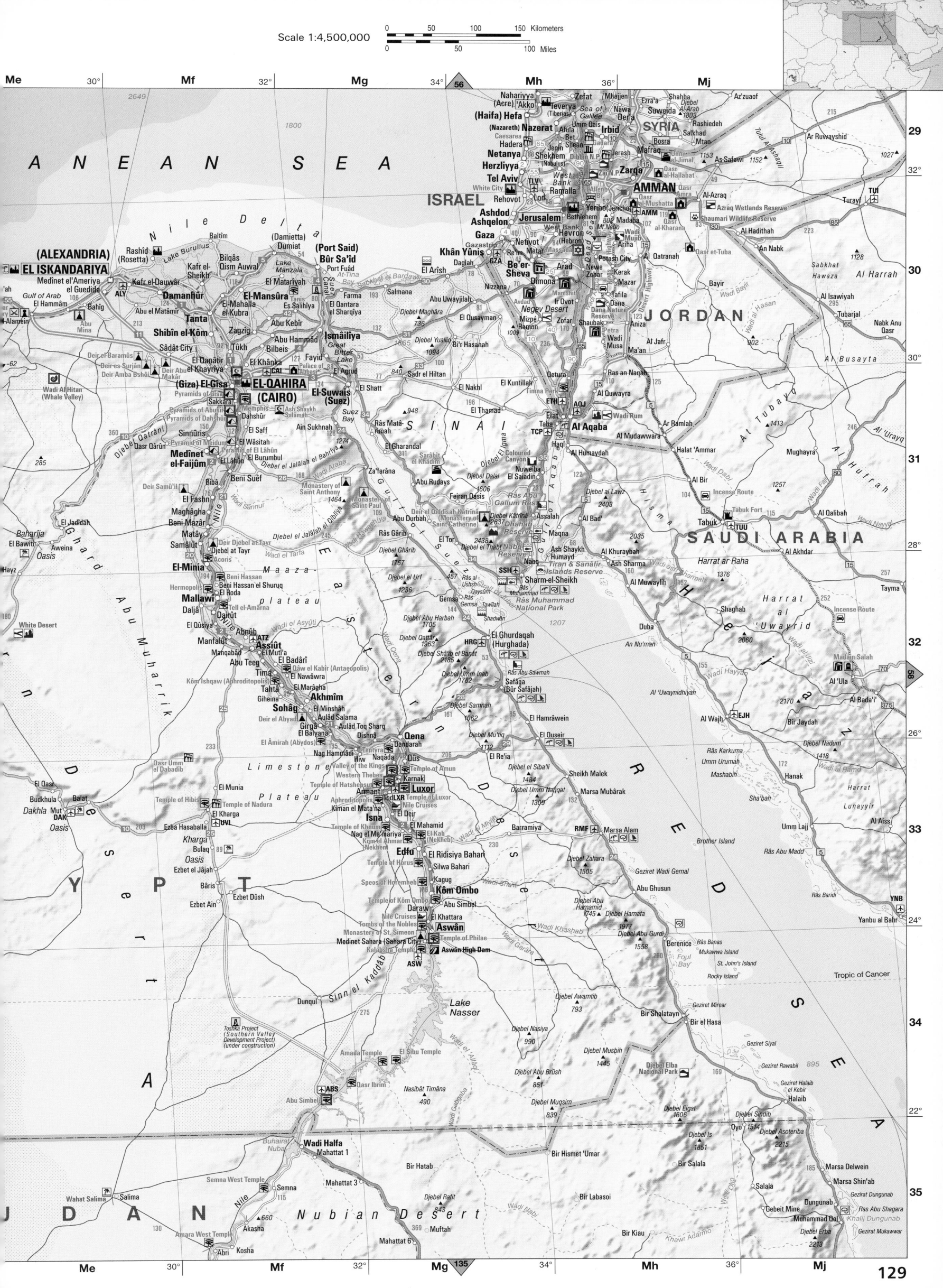

Scale 1:4,500,000

0   50   100   150 Kilometers
0   50   100 Miles

MEDITERRANEAN SEA

Nahariyya
(Acre) 'Akko   Zefat   Mhejjen   Ezra'a   Djebel   Az'zuaof
(Nazareth) Nazerat   Teverya (Tiberias)   Nawa   Der'a   Suweida   Al-'Arab   1803
(Haifa) Hefa   Umm Qais   Irbid   SYRIA   Salkhad   Ar Ruwayshid
Caesarea   Afula   Bet Shean   Jenin   Jerash   Mafraq   1153   Umm   As-Safawi   1152
Hadera   Shekhem (Nablus)   Dibbin N.P.   90   el-Jimal   Qasr   10   1027
Netanya   West   Zarga   al-Hallabat   49   215
Herzliyya   Bank   AMMAN   85
Tel Aviv   TLV   65   Qasr   Azraq Wetlands Reserve
White City   Ramalla   Allenb   AMM   118   Amra   Turayf   TUI
Rehovot   Lod   Yeriho (Jericho)   Qasr   al-Kharana
ISRAEL   Jerusalem   Madaba   Shaumari Wildlife Reserve   Al-Azraq
Ashdod   Bethlehem   Hevron (Hebron)   Mt. Nebo   Wadi   Al Hadithah
Ashqelon   Gaza   West Bank   Madaba   Qasr et-Tuba   An Nabk
Gazastrip   GZA   Netivot   Arad   Kerak   Al Qatranah   1128
Khan Yunis   40   Be'er-Sheva   Dimona   Potash City   Bayir   Sabkhat
El 'Arish   Daglah   Nizzana   Mamshit   Zohar   Mazar   Hawaza   Al Harrah
At-Tina Bay   Sabkhat el Bardawil   Abu Uwayjilah   Negev Desert   Zafar   Tafila   Al Isawiyah   295
Salmana   78   El Qusayman   Mizpe Ramon   1009   Dana Nature Reserve   Aniza   Al Bayil   Tubarjal   902
Farma   193   Djebel Maghara   736   Shaubak   Petra   Ma'an   Al Jafr   Nabk Anu Qasr
Es Salihiya   Bi'r Hasanah   Wadi Musa   Al Busayta

JORDAN

SINAI   SAUDI ARABIA

RED SEA

Tropic of Cancer

EGYPT

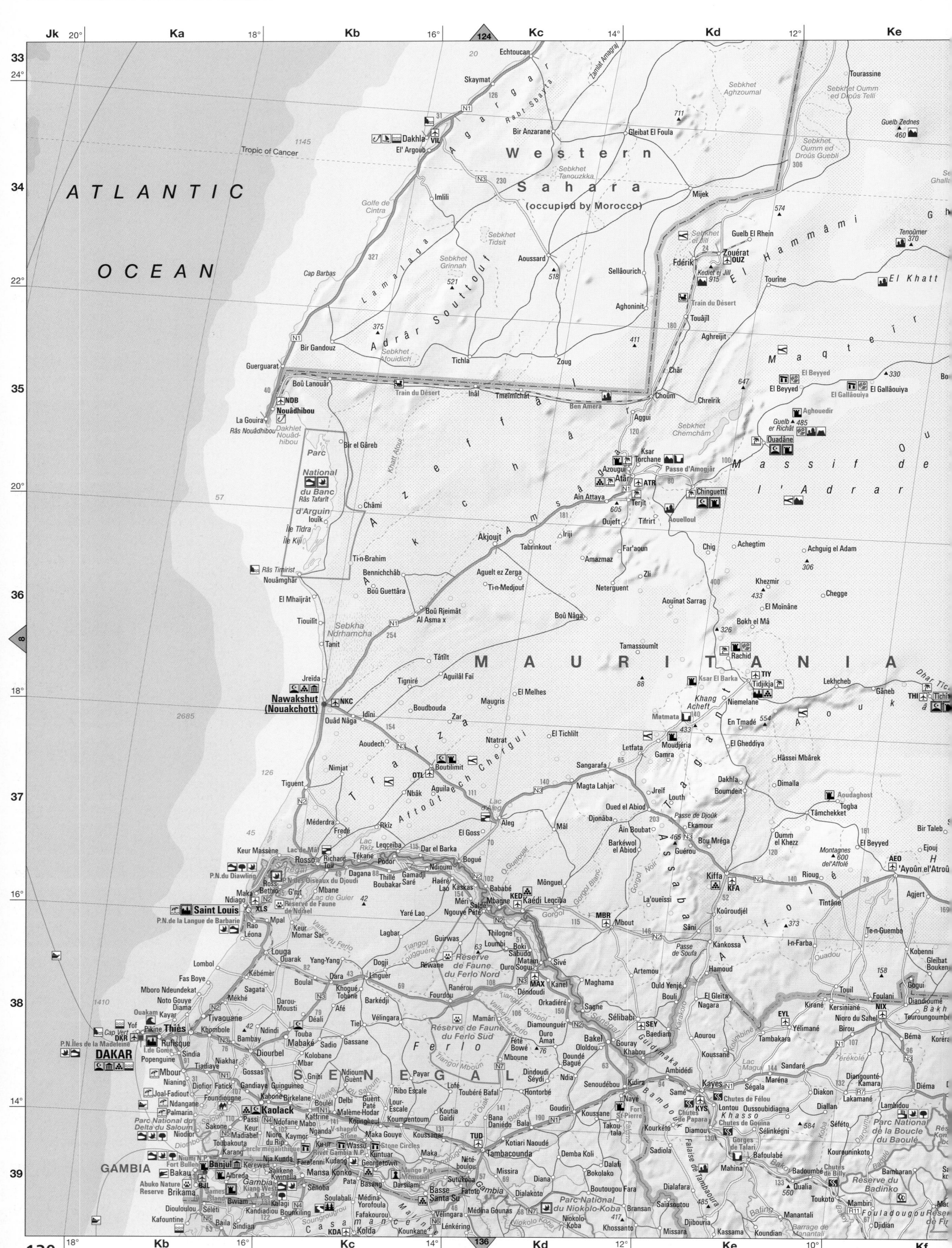

Scale 1:4,500,000

0   50   100   150 Kilometers
0   50   100 Miles

ALGERIA

Gřizim

Oued el Ma   370
333
El Mzereb

El Hank

Oued el Ma   250
Oued Khârroûb
El Mreiti
Ti-n-Bessaïs
Bîr 'Amrâne   250

Agâraktem

Aoukâr

Hamada el Harich

Erg Chech

Taoudenni

El Guettara

Oglat el Khnâchich   El Khnâchîch

Bir Ounâne

El Khnâchîch

Erg Atouilla

Foum el 'Alba   282

Douaouir

Erg l-n-Sâkâne

I-n-Techerène

Erg Azennezal

Erg Aït el Khâoua

343

324

Ancien

I-n-Akli

Tessounfat

Kreb Bekaï el Bâss   160

Tessalit

Djebel

I-n-Échaï   273   367
I-n-Akhmed

Tamandouririt

Abanko   100

Timétrine
(Ti-n-Kâr)

Mabroûk   Tichet

Aguelhok

Adrar
Tachdaït

Erîgât

Oued el Hajâr

El Mraïti

Aslegh (Asselar)

Vallée du Tilemsi

Boû Nâga

Araouane   Guîr   El Mamouel   El Mâmoûn   Timétrine   Abelbod

Sidi el Mokhtâr   Boû Djébéha   Aghezzaf   Ammouk   Anéfis

Awâna   Dahr Oualâta

Tadânet Keyna   El Ma'mour-
Ighichârene

Touérât   271

Douaya   I-n-Aleï

I-n-Milach   Tabankort

Ouélâta

I-n-Abaléha   Almoustarat

Hâssi Fouîni   Oualâta   Irîgui   Tigoumatene   Agounni Jefal   Ti-n-Aguelhaj   I-n-Ouchef   Agamor   Kerchouél   195

Latik   Ourei   Zoûgh   Nkhaïlé   El Nbeïket
el Ahouâch   El Basriyé   Ti-n-Tijot'   I-n-Amazzagh   (Tangoutranat)   Hâssi
Karkabane   Taouârdei

Agoueïnît   Nbeïket Dîm   Outeïd Arkâs   265 Bamba   Téméra Bisane   Bourem

Néma   Houeïriye   El Arhlaf   Lerneb   Râs el Mâ   Goundam   Koriome   Kahara   Gourma-Rharous   Ouani
Tondibi   Karkarichinkat   Teiskot

EMN   El Bouz   Lac
Faguibine   Bintagoungou   Mbouna   Farache   Aglal   Danga   Bambou   440   Ouïnerdene   Karouassa   Amakouladji   Sîné

Dendâra   Lac Oro   Chet Korkora   Télé   Tonka   Diré   Haïbongo   Fintrou   Tombeau
des Askia   Gao

Amourj   Nioût   Hâssi Touil   Tondidarou   Banikane   Saréyâmou   Lac
Haribomo   Haribomo   Adiora   Doro   164   Bilali Koyra   GAQ   Déhbok   Iménas

Boû Gâdoûm   Bassikounou   Lac Kabara   Koumaira   Sa   Lac
Garou   Réserve
de Gourma   Gossi   Ti-n-Azabo   Haoussa-Foulane   Gargouna

Koumbî Saleh   Lac Tanda   Saráféré   Kanioume   Bambara-
Maoundé   I-n-Adiattafene   Dorey   Tagarane Gabout   210

Mobdoua   Adel Bagrou   Léré   Ambîn   Lac Aou
Igoundou   Gourma   Lac Do   I-n-Tillit   Léléhoy   Ansongo

Balal   Koronga   Fatiba   Medd Allah   Méma   Ngorkou   Ngouma   Tanal   Réserve
de Douentza   Hombori   Ndaki   Tessit   Tassiga   Bentia
(Koukia)   140

Dali   Dilli   NRM   Goumbou   Fassâla Néré   Méma   Farimaké   Lac Débo   Korientzé   Monts du Hombori   91   Fafa

Nara   267   Boundjiguire   Oura-Ndia   Dogo   Diallloubé   Nyiminiama   Garmi Tondo   1080   (Main de Fatma)   1155   Hombori Tondo   Boumboum   Labbezanga

Falou   Sokolo   Dogofri
Diabali   Boulel   Toguéré-Koumbé   Konza   Boré   N16   Dala   Boni   Ouatagouna

Ouagadou   Mourdiah   Diondiori   Kendié   Ningari   Pays   777   Douentza   142   Kobou   Forage Christine   Ti-n-Akof   Ouanzerbé   Ayorou   Toumkou

Doubabougou   Danfa   Ndébougou   Diondiori   Kani-Bogouna   Dogon   Diankabou   Mondoro   Douna   Dunes de Sable   Oursi   Markoy   Salmossi   Dolbel   Bankilaré   Méhana

Warde   Séguéla   Niono   Dia   Sévaré   Sossobé   Sanga   Dinangourou   268   Réserve de Faune
du Sahel   Sélba   Timé   Gorom-Gorom   Gaïgou   Fonéko   NIGER

Boron   Molodo   Duro-Modi   Moptí   Bandiagara   Madougou   Yoro   So   Tongo-
mayel   Aribinda   Sikire   Falagountou   Méhana

Doura   Togou   Massina   Diafarabé   Mopti   Bandiagara   Koperokenité   Na   Ban   Tibo   Djibo   Gorel   Béléhédé   Yataka   N1   Téra

Madina-Sako   Sagala   Pogo   Kolongotomo   Kouakourou   Taga   Sofara   Bankass   Koro   Tangay   Aribinda   Bélédougou   Bourzanga   Pensa   Bani   Sebba   Dargol

Toukoroba   Markala   Banamba   Say   Sarro   Mougna   Bay   Sokoura   Tori   Kourbri   Namissiguima   Gorgadji   Dori   Kongoussi   Bani   Sampelga   Bangaré

Massantola   Ségou   Dioro   Fatimé   Ténébé   Ségué   Diallassagou   Louta   Gomboro   Ouahigouya   Kagaré   Rollo   Yalgo   Gouayá   Solna

Banamba   Séguéla   Konio   San   Tominian   Tori   Bangas-
soko   Toèni   Bangas   Zogoré   Séguénéga   Kongoussi   Lac de Bam   Barsalogo   Koala   Bossey Bangou

Sarikorola   Niamina   Goan   Somo   Koula   Tikaré   Réserve
de Bay   Tougouri   Gothèye

BURKINA FASO

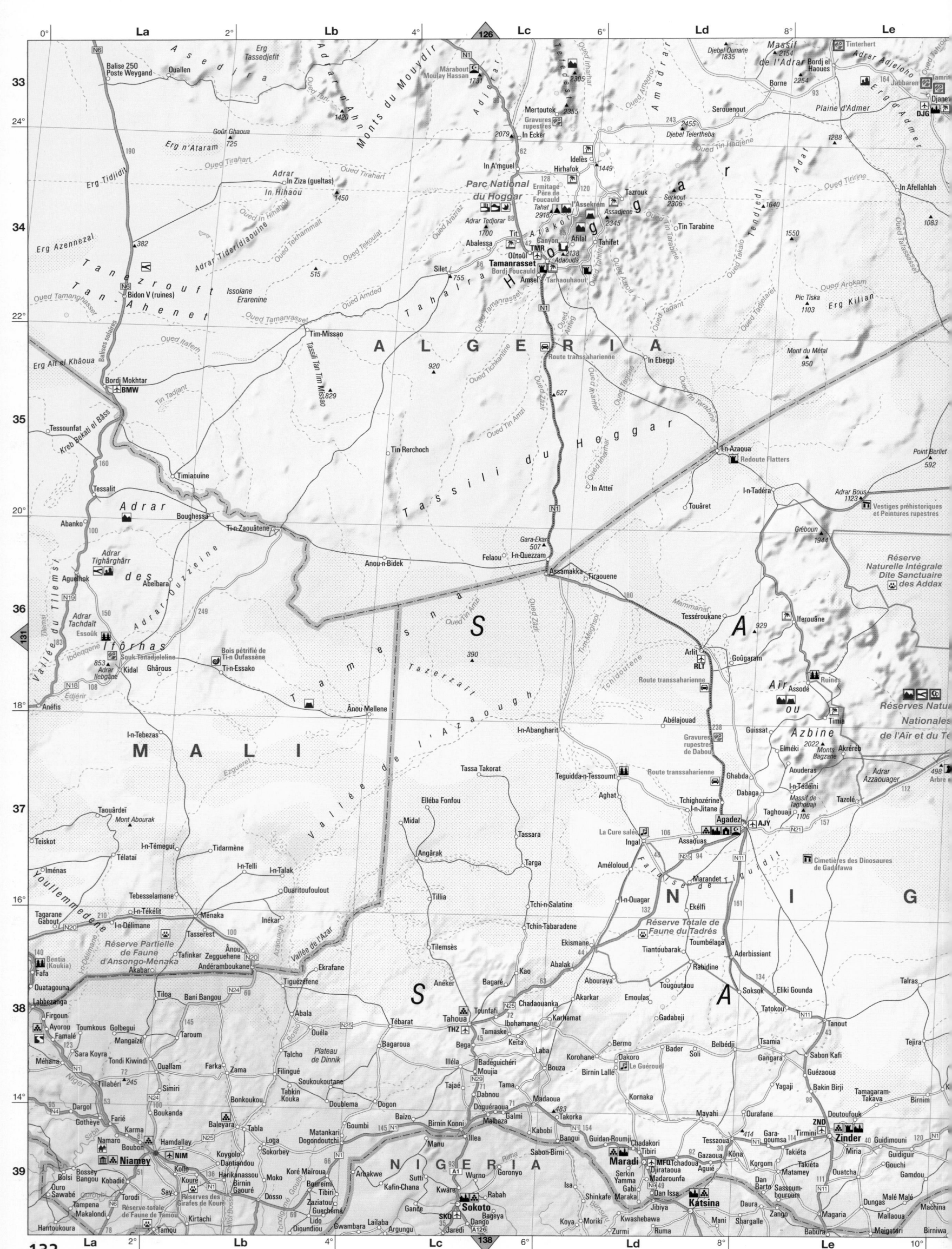

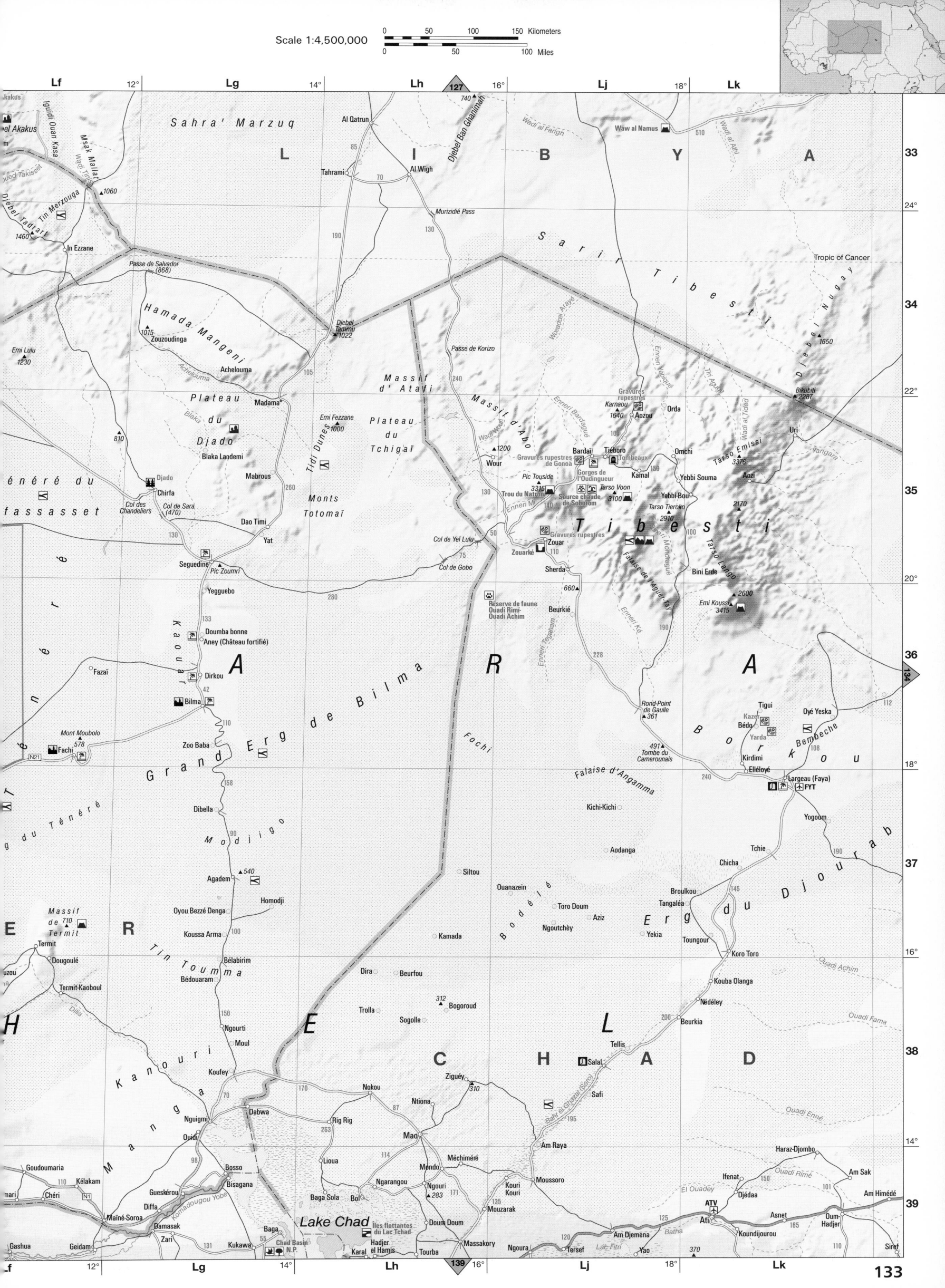

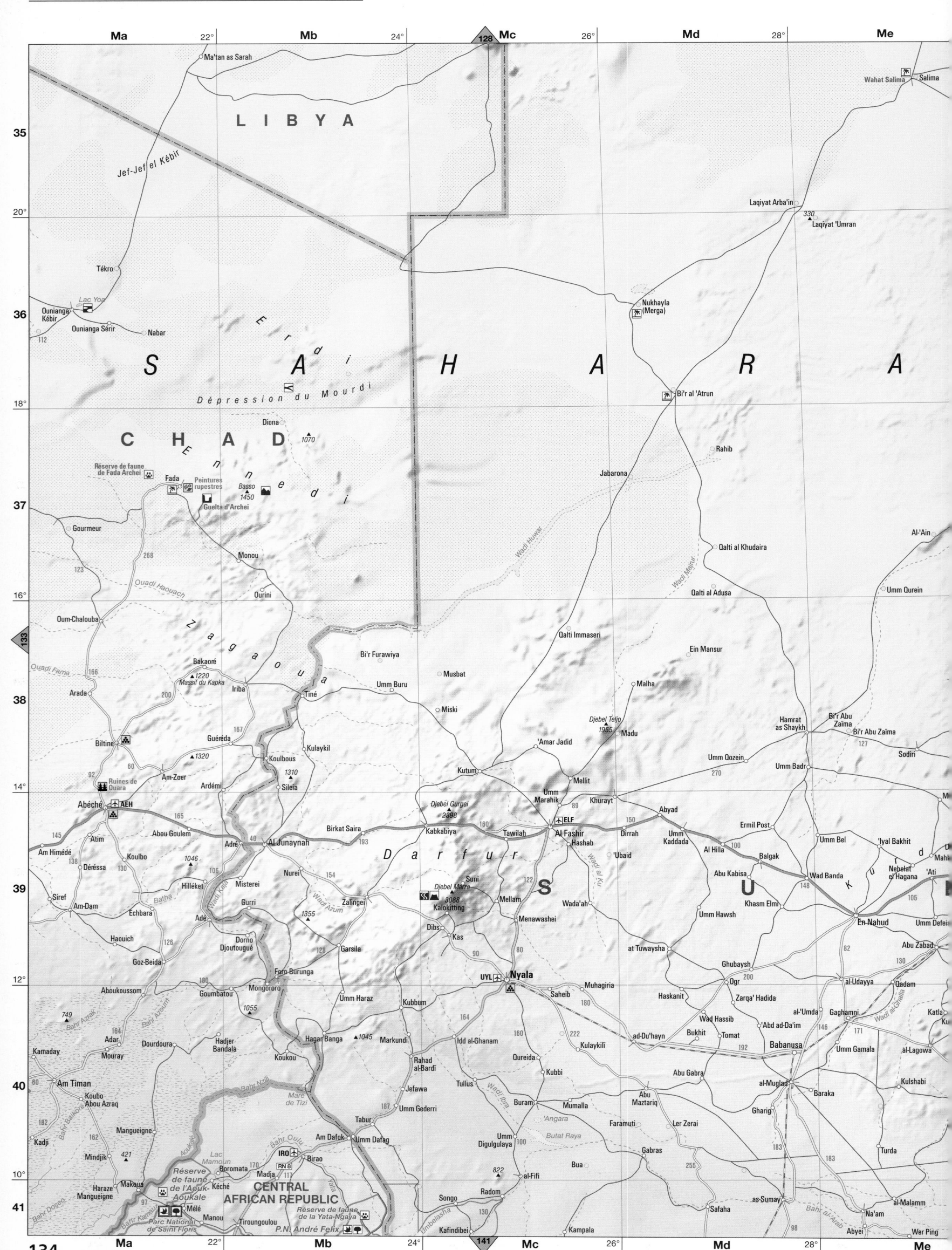

Ma 22° Mb 24° Mc 26° Md 28° Me

LIBYA

Ma'tan as Sarah

Wahat Salima
Salima

Jef-Jef el Kébir

35

Laqiyat Arba'in
330
Laqiyat 'Umran

20°

Tékro

Nukhayla
(Merga)

36
Ouanga
Kébir
Lac Yoa
Ouanga Sérir
Nabar
112

E r d i

S A H A R A

Bi'r al 'Atrun

Dépression du Mourdi

18°

Diona
1070

Rahib

CHAD

Réserve de faune
de Fada Archei
Fada
Basso
1450
Peintures rupestres
Guelta d'Archei

Jabarona

Wadi Huwar

Al-'Ain

37
Gourmeur

Qalti al Khudaira

Monou

Umm Qurein

123
268
Ouadi Haouach

Wadi Magrur

Ourini

Qalti al Adusa

16°

Oum-Chalouba

Qalti Immaseri

Ein Mansur

133

Quadi Fama
166

Bi'r Furawiya

Z a g a o u a

Bakaoré
1220
Massif du Kapka
Iriba

Musbat

Malha

Umm Buru

Umm Qurein

Arada
200

Tiné

Miski

Djebel Teljo
1955
Madu

Hamrat
as Shaykh
Bi'r Abu
Zaïma
Bi'r Abu Zaïma
127

38

Biltine

Guéréda
167

Kulaykil

'Amar Jadid

Umm Qozein
270

Umm Badr

Sodiri

60
1320
Am-Zoer
Koulbous
1310
Sileia

Kutum
Mellit

14°

Ruines de
Ouara
Ardémi

Djebel Gurgei
2098
Kabkabiya
160
Tawilah
Al Fashir
Dirrah
Umm
Kaddada
Ermil Post

Abéché
AEH

Abou Goulem
165
Adré
40
Al Junaynah
193
Birkat Saira

Hashab
'Ubaid
Al Hilla
100
Balgak
Umm Bel
'Iyal Bakhit

145
Atim
Am Himédé
138
Déressa
Koulbo
1046
Hilléket
106
Misterei
Nurei
154

D a r f u r
Suni
122
Mellam

Abu Kabisa
148
Wad Banda
105
Nebelat
el Hagana
'Ati
Mahk

39
Siref
Am-Dam
Echbara
130
Adé
Gurri
Zalingei
1355

Djebel Marra
3088
Kalokitting
Mellam

S U D
Wada'ah

Khasm Elm

En Nahud
Umm Defeis

Haouich
126
Dorno
Djoutougué
128
Garsila

Dibs
Kas

Menawashei

at Tuwaysha
Umm Hawsh

Ghubaysh
82
Abu Zabad

Goz-Beida
Foro Burunga

90
80

Muhagiria
180

Haskanit
Wad Hassib

Ogr
200
Zarqa' Hadida
130

12°

Aboukoussom
180
Goumbatou
Mongororo
1055

Umm Haraz
Kubbum

UYL
Nyala
Saheib

164
Kulaykilí
222
ad-Du'hayn
Bukhit
Tomat
192
Babanusa

al-'Umda
Gaghamni
146
171
Katla
Ku

749
Bahr Azoum
Adar
Mouray
Hadjer
Bandala
Koukou

Hagar Banga
1045
Markundi
Idd al-Ghanam
160
Qureida
Abu Gabra

Umm Gamala
al-Lagowa

Kamaday
164

Dourdoura

Rahad
al-Bardí
Kubbi

Abu
Maztariq
Gharig
al-Muglad
Baraka
Kulshabi

40
Am Timan
60
Koubo
Abou Azraq
162
Manguéigne

Jefawa
Tullus

Buram
Mumalla

Faramuti
Ler Zerai
Gabras
183
Turda

182

Kadji
Mindjik
421
Mangueigne

Maré
de Tizi
Tabur
Am Dafok
Umm Gederri
187

Umm
Digulgulaya
100
'Angara
Butat Raya

Bua
Gharig
255
as-Sumay
Na'am

Wer Ping

Makaoua
Haraze
Mangueigne
97

Réserve de
faune de
l'Aouk-
Aoukale
Mélé
Manou
Boromata
Kéché
Madja
117
Birao
RN 8
IRO

CENTRAL
AFRICAN REPUBLIC

Réserve de faune
de la Yata-Ngaya
P.N. André Felix

822
Radom
al-Fifi

Songo
130
Kafindibei

Kampala
Safaha
98
Abyei
Bahr al-'Arab

10°

41

Lac
Mamoun
Tiroungoulou
Parc National
de Saint Floris

Ma 22° Mb 24° Mc 26° Md 28° Me

134

Scale 1:4,500,000

0 50 100 150 Kilometers

0 50 100 Miles

SAUDI ARABIA

(JIDDAH) JEDDAH
MAKKAH (MECCA)
Bahrah
Hadda
Kaaba
Khumrah
Ar Rás al Aswad
Damrur
Mastabah
Qishran

R E D   S E A

Bir Hatab
Bir Salala
Marsa Delwein
Marsa Shin'ab
Salala
Bir Labasoi
Dungunab
Geziret Dungunab
Ras Abu Shagara
Gebeit Mine
Muhammad Qol
Khalij Dungunab
Gezirat Mukawwar
Djebel Erba 2213
Marsa Salak
Djebel Oda 2259
Arous
Sanganeb Atoll Marine National Park
Marsa Darur
Bur Sudan (Port Sudan)
PZU
Sallom
Kamob Sanha
Old Suakin coral stone houses
Suakin
Suakin Archipelago
Ras Asis
Ras Kasar
Aqiq

N u b i a n   D e s e r t

Semna
Mahattat 3
Djebel Rafit 843
Akasha
Kosha
Muftah
Mahattat 6
Mahattat 8
Abu Sari
Delgo
Kadruka
Kudayn
ash-Shallal ath-Thalith (3rd Cataract)
Necropolis Deffufa
Arqu
Gharb Binna
al-Koin
Temple of Kawa
Sahaba
Umm Rahaw
Birti
4th Cataract
Kehellil
El Kab
Shemkhiya
Abu Ghirban
Dagash
Kabna
Abu Hashim
Shereiq
Nadi
El Aiadia
El Begeir
Napata and Djebel Barkal Temples
Nuri Necropolis
Karima
El Karabi
Marawi
Ghazali
az-Zuma
al-Kurru
Sanam
Hannik
Abu Dom
Kanisa
Old Dongola
258
ad-Dabba
Abu Dom
Kurti
Fagrinkotti
Barriyat
5th Cataract
Gananita
Artoli
El Bauga
Berber
Abu Saffar
Atbara
ATB
Dugwaya
al-Bayyuda
Ed Damer
Saiyala
Gemmeiza
Mahmiya
Dawab
Meroe Temple and pyramids
Guwayr
Kabushiya
Taragma
Umm Rumeila
Sandi
Wad Ban Naqa
Palace
Temples of Musawwarat
al-Huqna
Temples of Naqa
al-Basabir
Abu Dawn
6th Cataract
Qerri
Bir el Fakama
Daru
Sabaluka Game Reserve
al-Gayli
Rugheiwa
Abu Deleiq

(Omdurman) Umm Durman
Camel Market
Mahdi's Tomb
(Khartoum North) al-Hartum Bahri
KRT
AL-HARTUM (KHARTOUM)
Fattasha
Djebel Auliya
Umm Inderaba
Shaykh Sadin
al-Kamilin
Abd al-Magid
al-Qutayna
Shatawi
Qurrasa
al-'Uqda
al-Husay
al-Mussallamiya
'Uraq
El Mesellemiya
Wad Madani
ad-Dubasi
al-Managil
Ma'tuq
al-'Amara
Barakat
Rudayba
Shabasha
ad-Duwayn
al-Kawa
Hag Abdullah
Wad el Haddad
Sagadi
Maya
Inderaba
Sennar
Maiurno
Es Suki
Dindar
El Hasira
Dararisa
Kabur
Kusti
Rabak
Singa
Tandalti
Tamaso
Fariq at-Fil
Abu Higar
al-Gabalayn
Keri Kera
ar-Ru'at
Djebel Bozi
Djebel Mazmun
Wad en Nail
al-'Abbasiya
Tingal 1460
Mushayfat
Dalami
Rashad
Kukur
Bobuk
Bau
Bikori
Bambudi
Amiri
Guba
Talawdi
Niaro
Djebel al-Liri 1095
Tungaru
Tekeim
Kaka
Tingya
Paloich
Malut
Ulu
Kurmuk
Belfodiyo
Gaysan
Keili
Cula Sancai 2438
Chidu
Kodok
Dawir
Fama
Belgo
Aboni
Wuntau
Kungila
Shali al-Fil
Mortesoro
Asosa
ASO
Mendi
Gelila
Mount Nasi 2975
NDM
Bambesi
Jarso
Nejo

S U D A N

Bir en Nugeim
Bir Nawari
To Awai
Bir Kiau
Bir Fanoidig
Djebel Eigrim 1257
Wadi Amur
Djebel Homor Tohadar 1754
Gebeit
Sinkat
Aqaba Pass
Erkowit
Barameiya
Trinkitat
Rawai
Djebel Abadab 1596
Er Rogel
Mismar
Togni
Djebel Mismar 958
Imasa
Haya
Tohamiyam
Herbagat
Gammams
Wadi Habob
Talguharai
Erheib
Tokar
Djebel Sabidana 1906
Djebel Hamoyet 2780
Karora
Mersa Teklay
Algena
Reserve Hagar Nish Plateau
Baden
Djebel Hamoyet 2780
Nakfa
Mersa Gulbub
Djebel Asoteriba 765
Eriba
Duredeb
Kerkebet
Anaghit
Kela Met
Nakfa Wildlife Reserve
'Amm Adam
Mitatib
Afabet
Suara 2603
Harat
Goz Regeb
Aroma
Akala
Said Abu Bakr al-Mirgani
Keren
(Massawa) Mitsiwa
Amara Abu Sin
As Sharma
Kassala
KSL
Sebderat
Bisha
Akordat
Himbirti
ASM
ASMARA
Cathedral
Nefasit
Zula
Malawiya
Djebel Takka 1390
Aderuba 1484
Haykota
Abu Gamel
Teseny
Barentu
Dukambiya
Areza
Adi Keyih
Adi Ugri
Obelisks of Cascase
Senafe
New Halfa
Sitona
Badme
Matara
Husheib
Khashm el Girba
Moqatta
Om Hajer
Himora
HUE
Chire Wildlife Reserve
Adi Da'iro
Inda Silase
Yeha
AXU
Adigrat
Udayd
Khashm el Girba Reservoir
Thowak
Adi Ark'ay
Ruins of Aksum
Adwa
Hawzen
Wad Rawa
al-Kamilin
Rufa'a
Uhaymir
Migre
(Gedaref) Al-Qadarif
Matna
Tunaydiba
Rasid
Doka 152
Ayayei
Mesfinto
Debre Damo Temple of Medhane
Idaga Hamus
Sagadi
Fargha
Qala'en Nahl
Shamman
Mek'ele
MQX
Wad el Haddad
Dindar
Shuheir
Basunda
Gallabat
Keftya
Adi Ramets
Aiy Adi
Amba Alage 3941
Abergele
Adi Gudom
Rumeila
Galegu
Metema
Wehni
Fasil Ghebbi
Gonder
GDQ
Amba Giyorgis
Amba Farit 3975
Sek'ot'a
Dinder National Park
Aykel
Azezo
Debre Sina
Gorgora 114
Safad
Debark 3150
Wolkefit Pass
Angereb
Sheikh Hasan
Dangur
T'ana Hayk (Lake Tana)
Yifag
Daga Istephanos Monastery
Zaten
Wetora
Debre Tabor
DBT
Nefas Mewch'a
Lalibela
LLI
Rock churches
Al-Garef
Er Roseires
Ed Damazin
ar-Rank
ar-Barun
RSS
Roseires Reservoir
Abu Mendi
Almahel
Belaya Terara 3131
Dangur 2488
Dangla
Dangla
Bahir Dar
BJR
Tis Isat Falls (Blue Nile Falls)
Adet
Bete Hor
Mekdela
Abu Gubayba
Hayban
Girban
Koko
Kachisi
Guba 1849
Chagne
Injibara
Amedamit 3296
Mot'a
Nedrata
Mertule Maryan
Mekane Selam
Tosi
Qurayd
Umm Barbit
Shaykh Gok
Debre Work
Bichena
Finote Selam
Bure
Dembecha
Birhan 4154
Debre Markos
DBM
Dejen
Alem Ketema
Blue Nile Canyon
Debre Libanos
Gedam
Kembolcha
Fiche
Muger Falls
Muke Turi
Shambu
Gorach'an 3276

E R I T R E A

E T H I O P I A

E T H I O P I A N   H I G H L A N D S

Simien Mountains National Park
Ras Dashen 4620
Simien Mts.
Guna Terare 4231

135

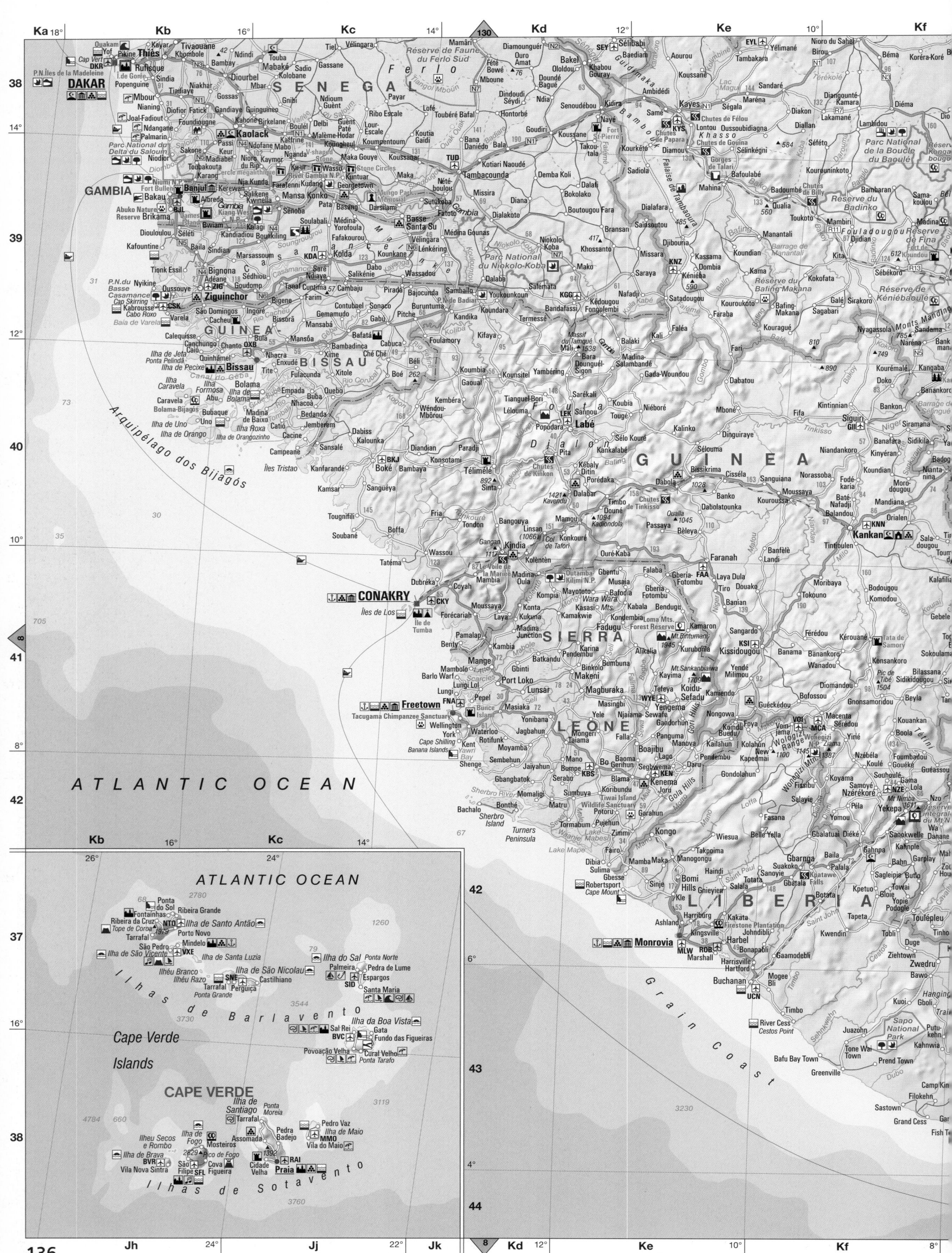

Western Africa, Cape Verde Islands

Ka 18° | Kb 16° | Kc 14° | 130 | Kd 12° | Ke 10° | Kf

ATLANTIC OCEAN

SENEGAL

GAMBIA

GUINEA-BISSAU

GUINEA

SIERRA LEONE

LIBERIA

DAKAR

Banjul

Bissau

CONAKRY

Freetown

Monrovia

Arquipélago dos Bijagós

Cape Verde Islands

CAPE VERDE

Ilhas de Barlavento

Ilhas de Sotavento

Jh 24° | Jj 22° | Jk | 8 Kd 12° | Ke 10° | Kf

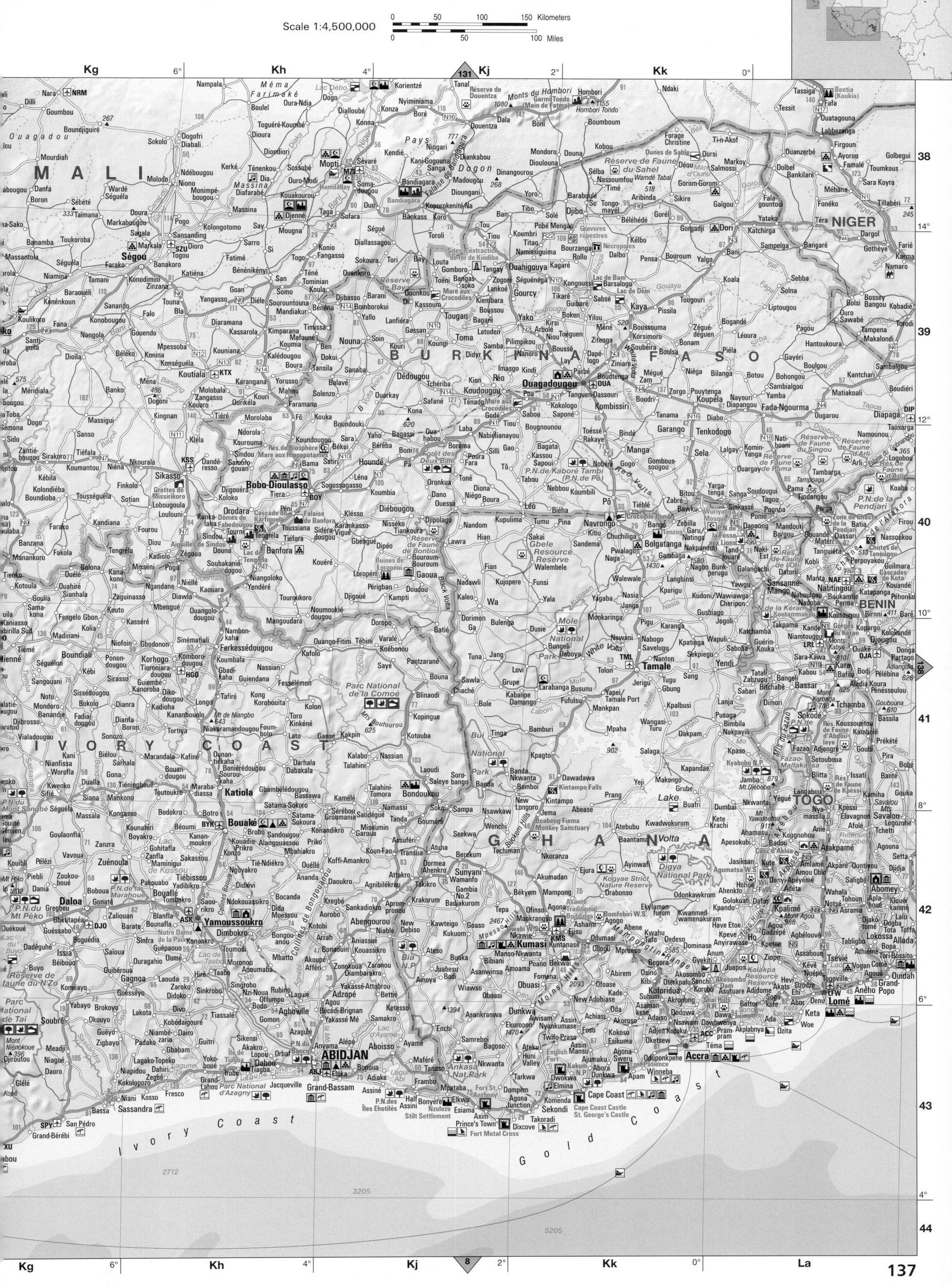

Nigeria, Cameroon

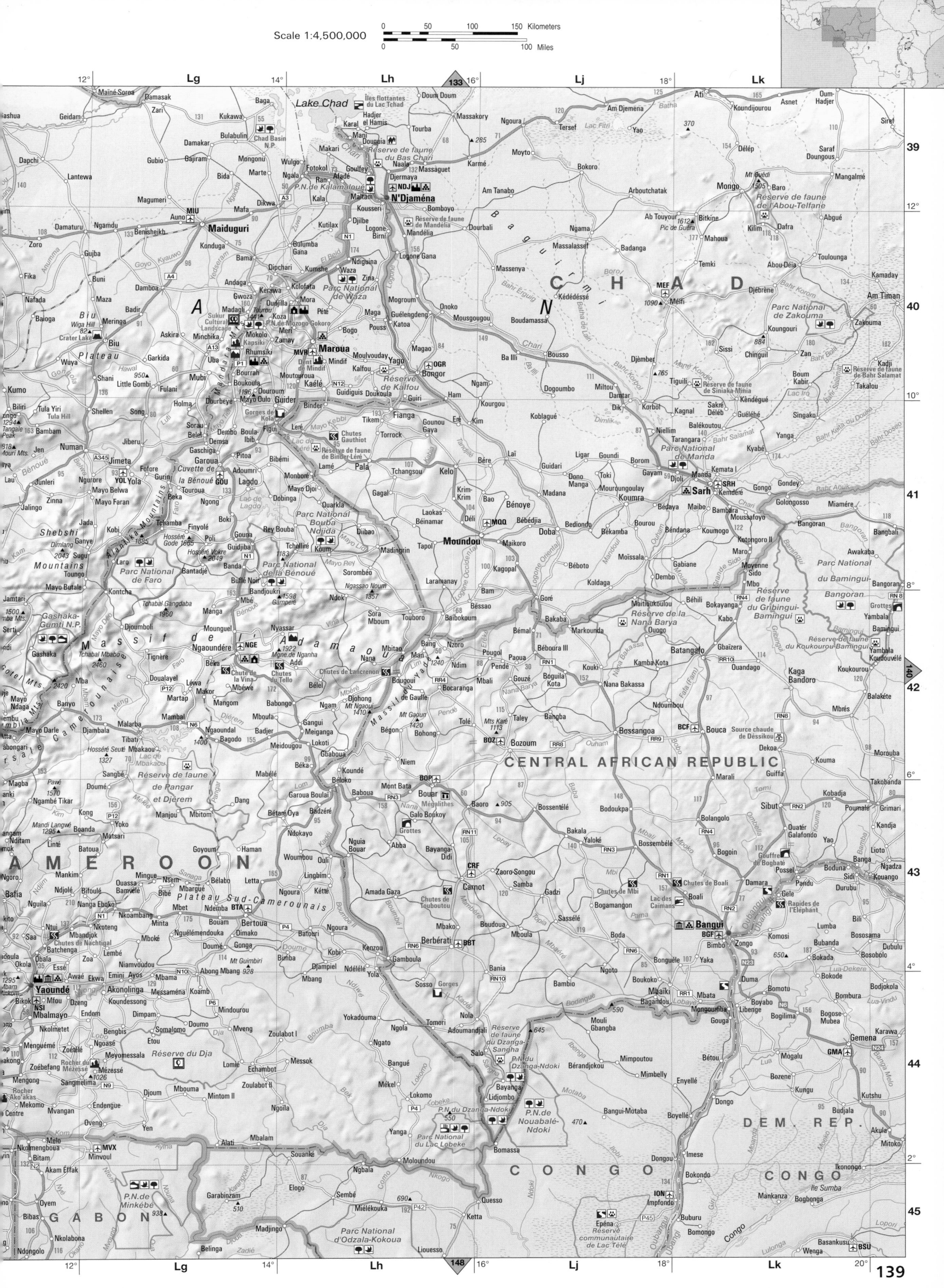

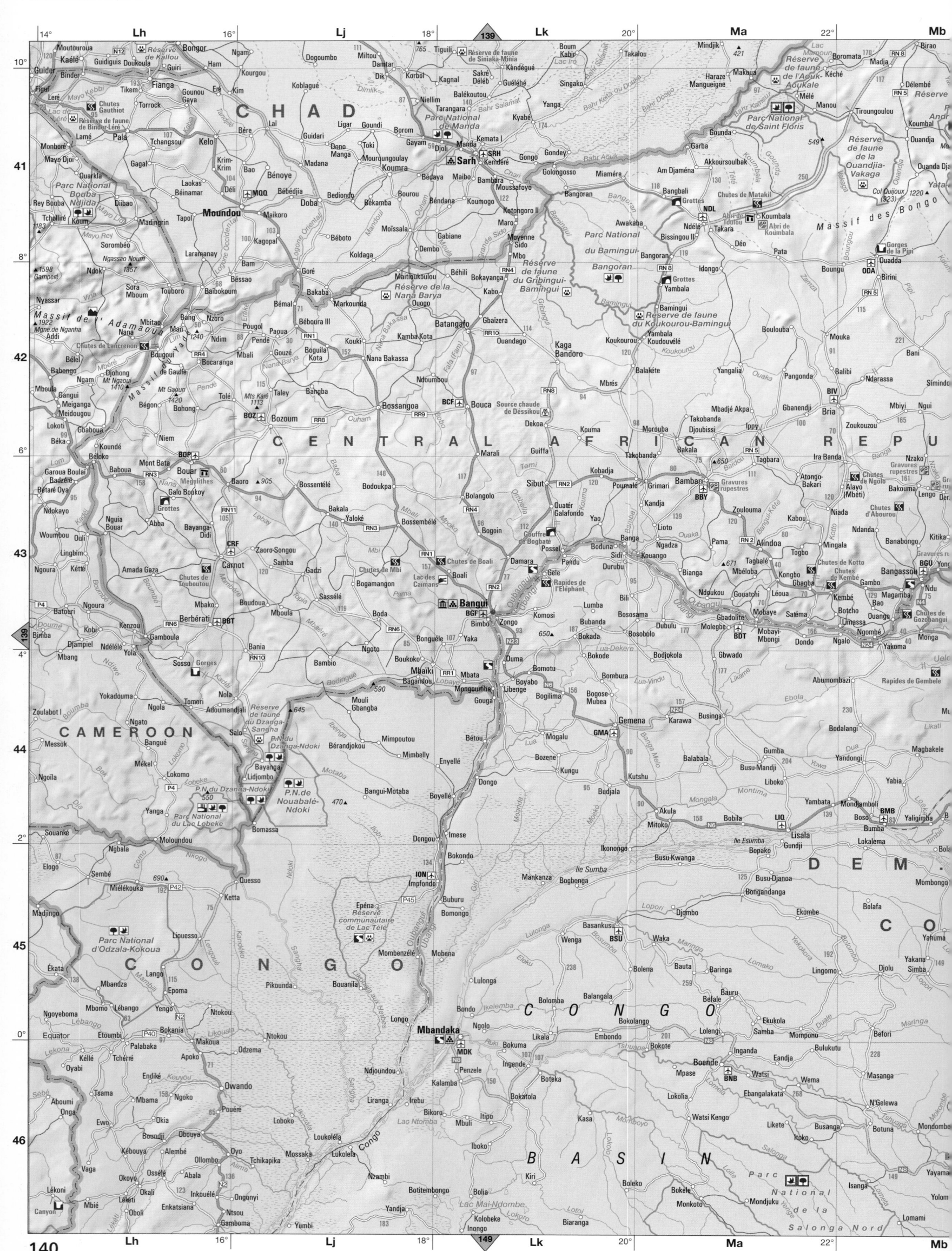

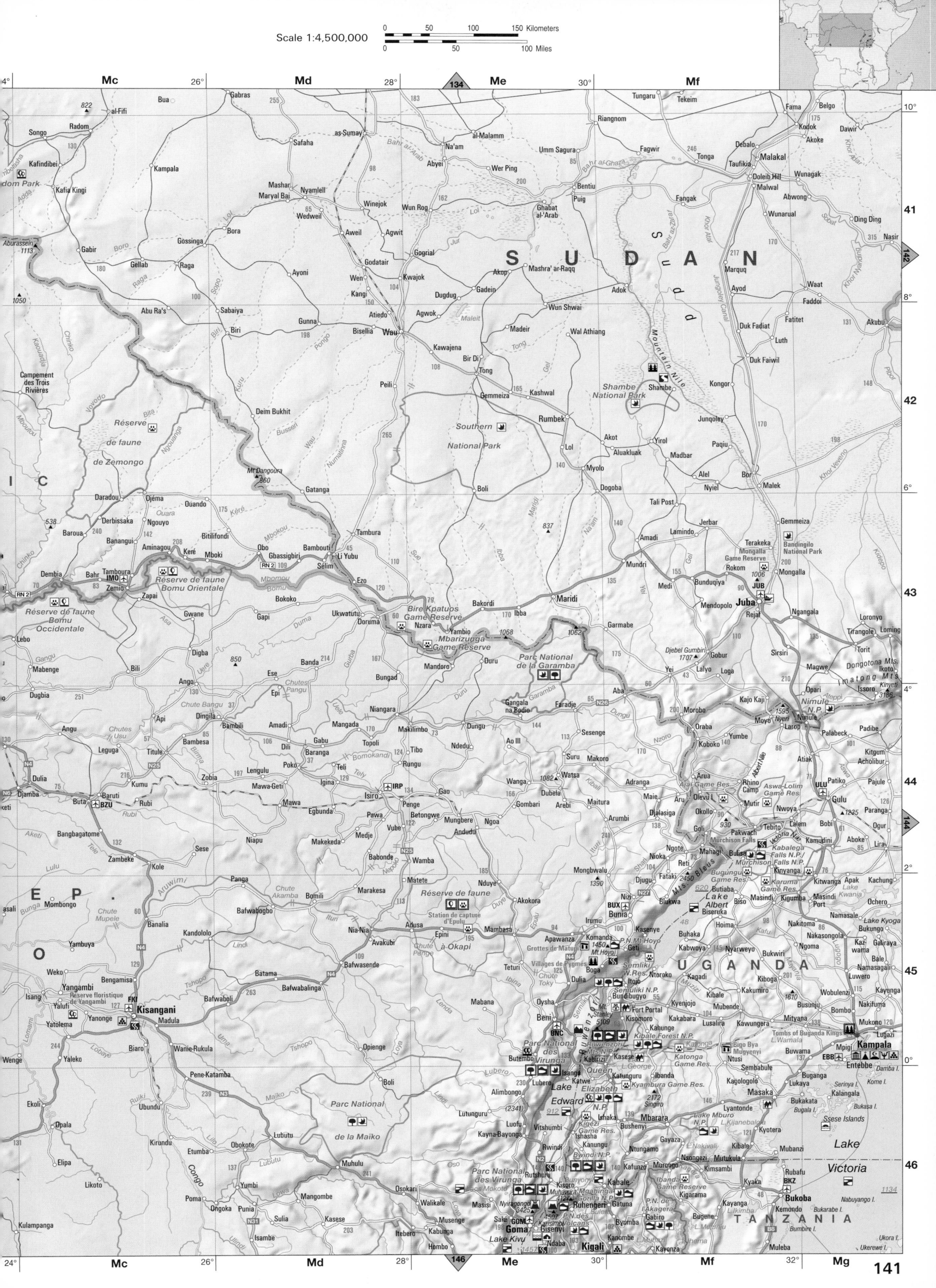

Scale 1:4,500,000

0   50   100   150 Kilometers
0   50   100 Miles

134

Mc   26°   Md   28°   Me   30°   Mf

4°

822 ▲ al-Fifi   Gabras   Tungaru   Tekeim   Fama   Belgo   10°
Songo   Radom   255   183   Riangnom   Kodok   Dawir
         Kampala   Bua   Debalo
Kafindibei   Nyamell   as-Sumay   Na'am   al-Malamm   Umm Sagura   Tonga   246   Taufikia   Malakal   41
Kafia Kingi   Mashar'   Safaha   Abyei   Wer Ping   Bentiu   Doleib Hill
                    Maryal Bai   85   Bahr al-Ghaza   Puig   Malwal
Aburassein ▲   Wedweil   200   Fangak   Abwong
1113   Bora   Winejok   Wun Rog   162   Ghabat al-'Arab   Wunarual   Ding Ding
         Gabir   Gossinga   Aweil   Agwit   Lol   Nasir   8°
1050 ▲   Gellab   Raga   Godatair   Gogrial   Akop   Mashra' ar-Raqq   Adok   Marquq   Ayod   Waat   315
         Abu Ra's   Ayoni   Wen   Jut   217   Faddoi   Fatitet   Akubu
                    Sabaiya   Kangi   Kwajok   104   Dugdug   Gadein   Adok   Ayod   170   Duk Fadiat   Luth   131   42
Campement   Daradou   Biri   Atiedo   150   Agwok   Wun Shwai   Madeir   Wal Athiang   Kongor   Duk Faiwil   148
des Trois   198   Wau   Maleit   Shambe
Rivières   Réserve   Deim Bukhit   Bir Di   108   Kawajena   Shambe
                    de faune   Gatanga   Tong   Madir   Rumbek   National Park
                    de Zemongo   Mt Dangoura ▲   165   Kashwal   Southern   Yirol   6°
538 ▲   860   Ouara   Gemmeiza   National Park   Akot   Aluakluak   Madbar   198
         Derbissaka   Ngouyo   Kéré   Mbokou   Peili   Boli   265   Lol   Myolo   Alel   Malek
Baroua   240   208   Tambura   Dogoba   Nyiel   Bor
                    Bitilifondi   145   837 ▲   Tali Post   Jerbar   Gemmeiza
Dembia   Bahr   Aminagou   Keré   Mboki   Obo   Gbassigbiri   Bambouti   Li Yubu   Amadi   Lamindo   Terakeka   Bandingilo   43
         Tamboura   IMO   Zemio   110   Sélim   1068   Mundri   155   Mongalla   National Park
RN 2   Zapai   Ezo   120   Bokoko   Bakordi   Ibba   1062   Garmabe   Medi   Bunduqiya   Rokom   Mongalla
Réserve de faune   Gwane   Doruma   Nzara   Yambio   175   Yei   1006   JUB   Juba
Bomu Occidentale   Gapi   Ukwatutu   60   Bire Kpatups   Mandoro   Duru   Parc National   Djebel Gumbiri   Mendopolo   Rejat
Lebo   Digba   Banda   214   Game Reserve   Mbarizunga   de la Garamba   1707 ▲   Gobur   Ngangala   Loronyo
Mabenge   Bili   Ese   167   Bungad   Game Reserve   Sirsiri   Tirangole   Loming   4°
Dugbia   251   Ango   Chutes   Niangara   Makilimbo   Dungu   144   Gangala   Faradje   N26   Aba   Lalyo   Loga   43   Magwe   Dongotona Mts   Ikoto
Angu   130   Api   Dingila   Bambili   Amadi   Mangada   Topoli   Tibo   Ndedu   Ao III   Sesenge   60   Moyo   210   Issoro   Kinyeti ▲ 3186
         Leguga   Titule   N25   Gabu   Baranga   Teli   Rungu   124   Suru   Makoro   170   Oraba   Yumbe   Opari   Nimule   N.P.
Dulia   75   Kumu   216   Dili   Poko   37   Igina   129   Gao   Wanga   1082 ▲   Watsa   Kibali   Adranga   Arua   Rhino   Atiak   Acholibur
Djamba   Baruti   Rubi   BZU   Zobia   197   Mawa-Geti   Isiro   IRP   134   Penge   Dubela   Gombari   Arebi   Maie   Aru   Camp   Gulu   ULU   Paranga   44
                    Bangbagatome   132   Sese   Niapu   Mawa   Egbunda   Betongwe   Mungbere   Ngoa   Maitura   Arumbi   Olevu   Okollo   Mutir   Nwoya   1235 ▲
Aketi   Buta   Rubi   Makekeda   Medje   Vube   122   Andudu   138   Goli   930   Pakwach   Tebito   Lalem   Bobi   Ogur   Lira
EP.   Panga   Babonde   N25   Wamba   Nduye   165   Mongbwalu   Nioka   Reti   Murchison Falls   Kabalega   Aboke
Mombongo   Bafwabogbo   Marakesa   Akokora   Duye   1390   Djugu   Fataki   Mahagi   Falls N.P.   Kinyanga   76   Kitwanga   Apak
O.   Chute   Bafwabinga   Bomili   Nia-Nia   Réserve de faune   Adusa   Epini   195   Mambasa   94   Irumu   Biso   Lake   Masindi   Kigumba   Masindi Port   Lake   Kwania
Mupele   Kandololo   Réserve de faune   Avakubi   Chute   Station de capture   à Okapi   Apawanza   Komanda   P.N.Mt Hoyo   Kasenye   Buhaka   Nakitoma   Ngoma   Kwania   Ochero   2°
Weko   Bengamisa   N4   Batama   Bafwasende   Pange   Toky   Teturi   125   Boga   Ntoroko   Kabwoya   Nyarweyo   Bukwiri   Namasale
Yangambi   129   Bafwabalinga   263   Mabana   Oysha   Semliki   Kagadi   Kakumiro   Ngoma   Namasagali
Isang   Yalufi   Réserve floristique   FKI   Kisangani   Madula   Opienge   Loya   Dulia   Bundibugyo   55   Kibale   Kikongo   Mukono   120
de Yangambi   127   Yanonge   Beni   Mt   Semliki N.P.   Kyenjojo   Mubende   Mityana   Luzira
Yatolema   Biaro   Wanie-Rukula   Pene-Katamba   Stanley   BNC   Ruwenzori   Fort Portal   Kisomoro   Lusalira   Kawungera   Mpigi   Kampala   46
Wenge   244   Ekoli   Ubundu   Boli   Butembo   Mts   Kasese   Kibale Forest N.P.   Tombs of Buganda Kings   Buwama   EBB   Entebbe
         Opala   Lobutu   Parc National   Isange   Queen   Katwe   Bigo Bya   Mugyenyi   Masaka   Lukaya   Damba I.
Elipa   Kirundu   des   Lubero   Lake   George   Katonga Game Res.   Ntusi   Sembabule   Buganga   Ssese Islands
Likoto   Obokote   de la Maiko   Virunga   Alimbongo   Elizabeth   Kyambura Game Res.   Kagologolo   Kalangala   Bukasa I.
Kulampanga   Etumba   Yumbi   Lutunguru   2300   Ishaka   2172   Lyantonde   Bugala I.
                    Poma   Osokari   Kayna-Bayonga   N.P.   Mbarara   Lake Mburo   Bukakata
Pene-Katamba   239   912   Kigezi   Bushenyi   N.P.   L.Kijanebalola   Kyotera   Lake
Muhulu   241   Vitshumbi   Game Res.   Ntungamo   Gayaza   Mutukula   46
         Walikale   Rwindi   Ishasha   Kanungu   Nsongezi   Rubafu   Victoria   1134
Sulia   Kasese   203   Parc National   Bwindi N.P.   Kabale   Kikimba   Kayanga   BKZ   Bukoba   Nabuyongo I.
Ongoka   Punia   Itebero   des Virunga   Rutshuru   Muhavura   Ibanda Game Reserve   Kigarama   48
Mangombe   Musenge   Masisi   Volcanoes   Kigali   Kemondo   Kubarabe I.
Isambe   Kabunga   Ndaba   Goma   Nyiragongo 3425   Ruhengeri   Gatuna   Byumba   Gabiro   L.Ikimba   Bugene   TANZANIA
         Hombo   GOM   Gisenyi   Volcans   Ndaba   Byumba   Kanombe   Kayonza   Muleba
         Lake Kivu   Kigali   Kayonza   Nyema   Ukora I.   Ukerewe I.

24°   Mc   26°   Md   28°   Me   30°   Mf   32°   Mg

146   141

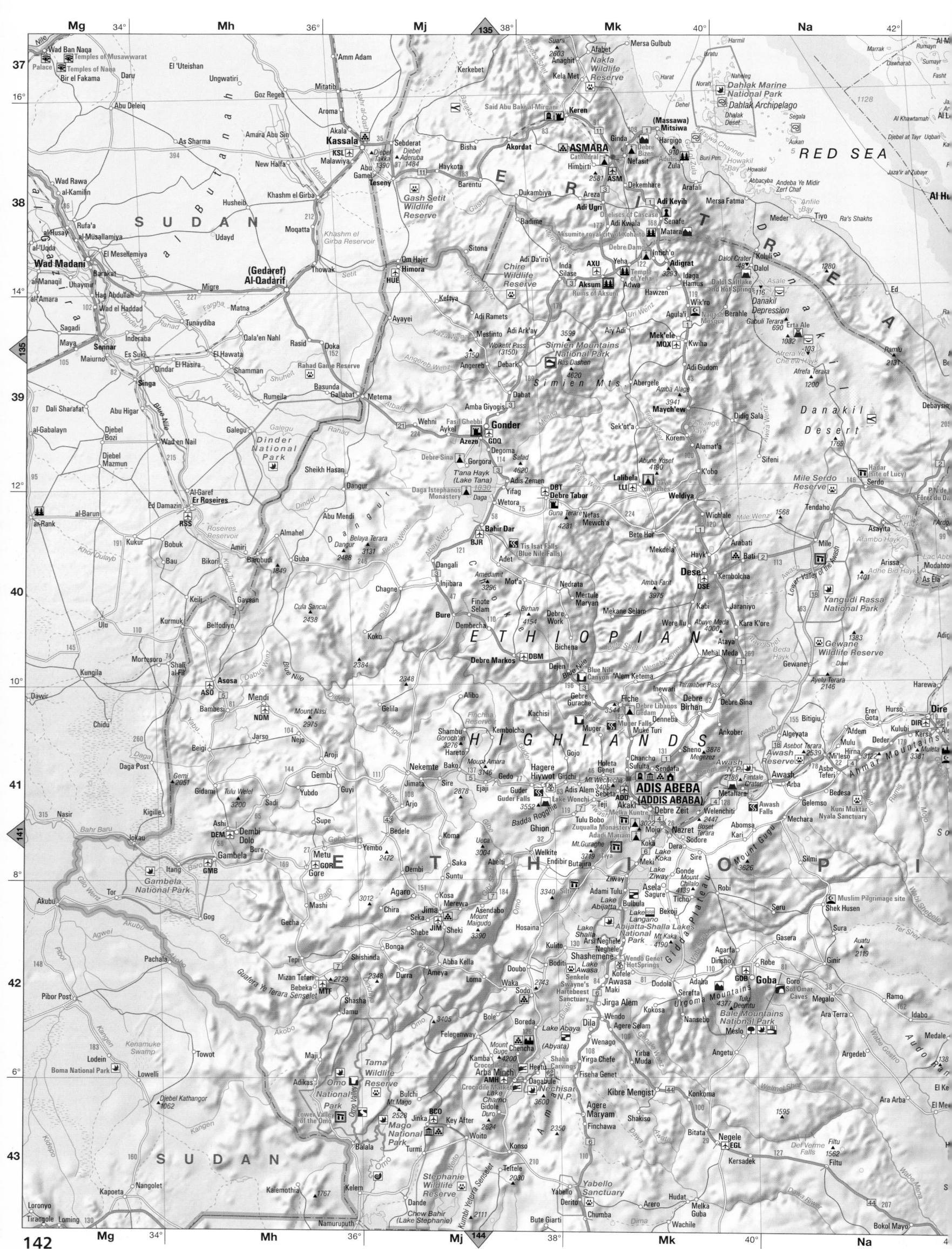

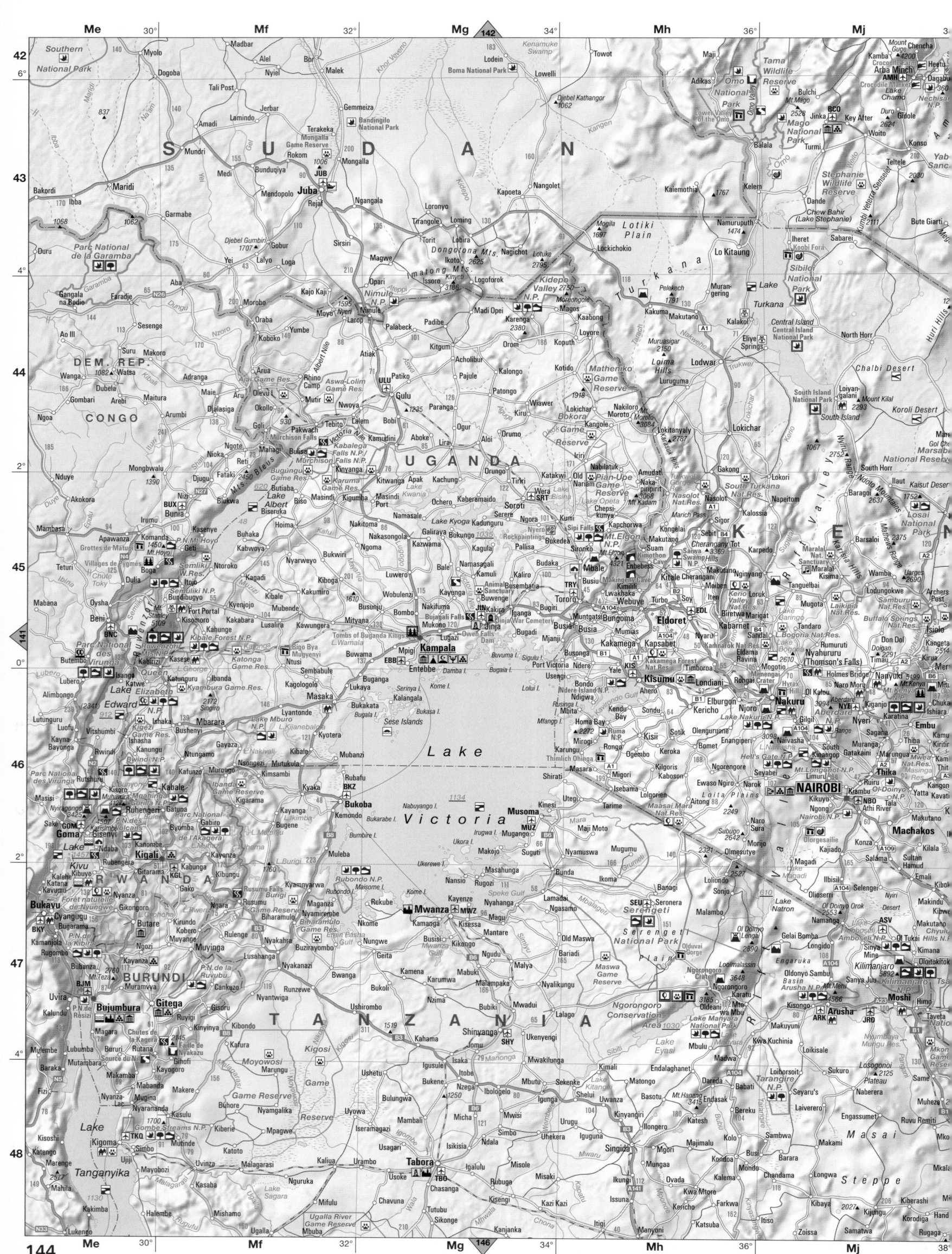

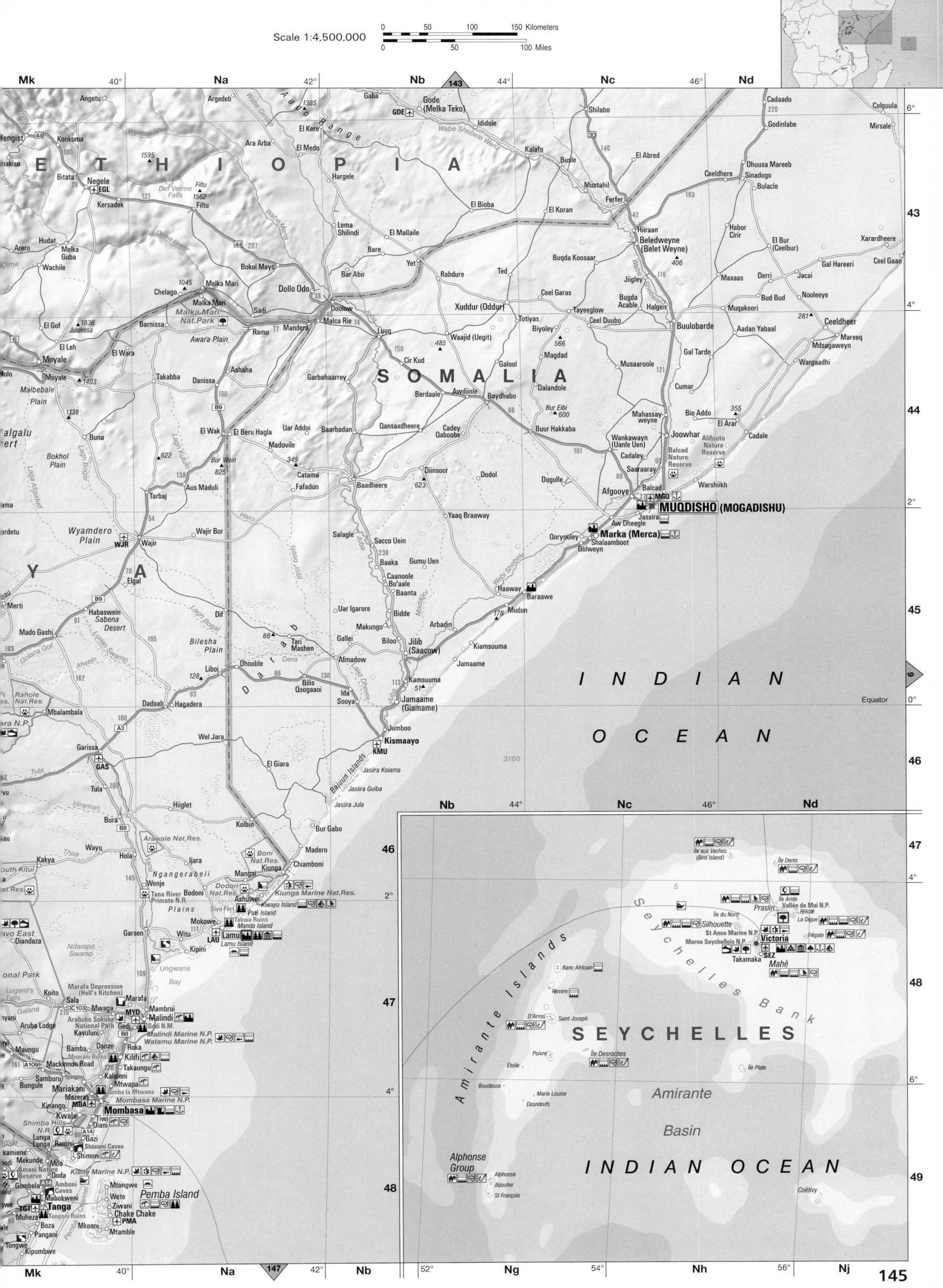

Scale 1:4,500,000

0   50   100   150 Kilometers
0   50   100 Miles

ETHIOPIA

SOMALIA

KENYA

MUQDISHO (MOGADISHU)

Marka (Merca)

Kismaayo

INDIAN OCEAN

Equator

SEYCHELLES

Amirante Islands

Seychelles Bank

Amirante Basin

INDIAN OCEAN

Alphonse Group

Victoria

Mahé

Praslin

La Digue

Mombasa

Pemba Island

Tanga

145

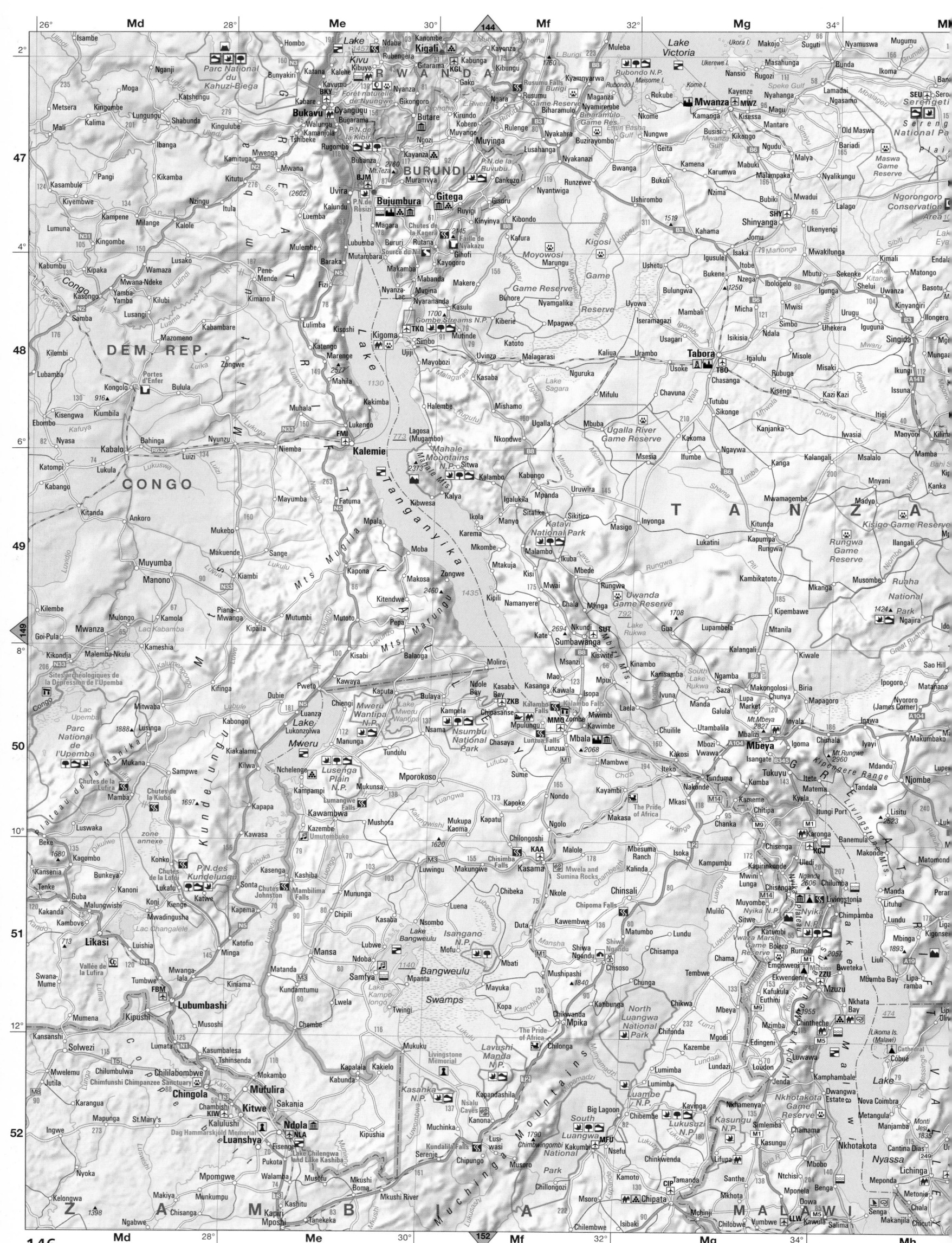

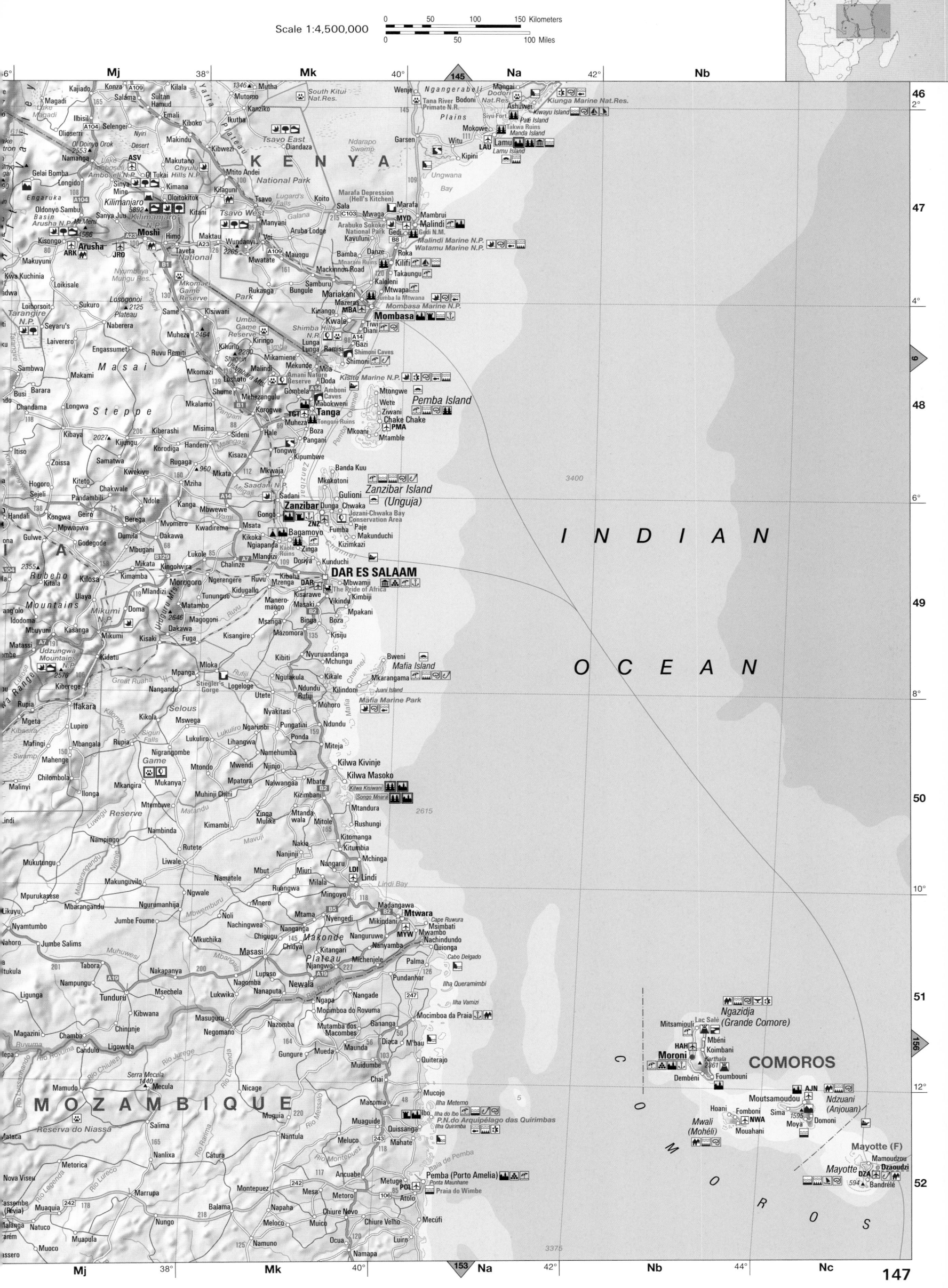

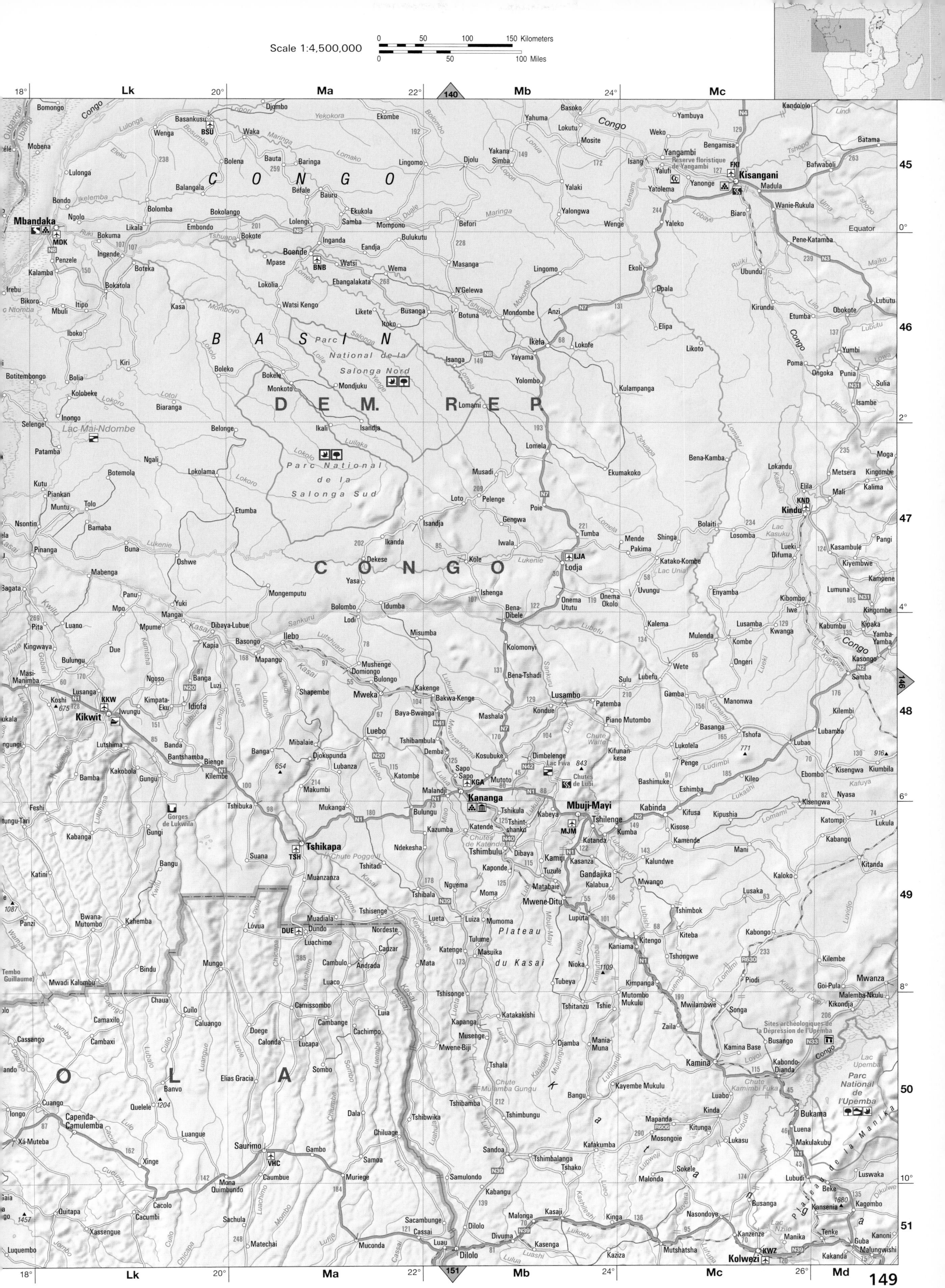
Scale 1:4,500,000
0 50 100 150 Kilometers
0 50 100 Miles
18° Lk 20° Ma 22° 140 Mb 24° Mc
45 0° 46 2° 47 4° 48 6° 49 8° 50 10° 51
18° Lk 20° Ma 22° 151 Mb 24° Mc 26° Md
146
C O N G O
B A S I N
DEM. REP.
C O N G O
O L A
Equator
Congo
Lulonga
Lomami
Tshuapa
Lokoro
Lukenie
Sankuru
Kasai
Kwilu
Lulua
Lualaba
Lubudi
Lubilash
Bushimaie
Lac Mai-Ndombe
Lac Kasuku
Lac Unia
Lac Upemba
Plateau du Kasai
Parc National de la Salonga Nord
Parc National de la Salonga Sud
Parc National de l'Upemba
Réserve floristique de Yangambi
Sites archéologiques de la Dépression de l'Upemba
Gorges de Lukwila
Chute Pogge
Chutes de Katende
Chute Mulamba Gungu
Chute Walfe
Chutes de Lubi
Lac Fwa
K a t a n g a
Plateau de la Manika
Mbandaka
MDK
Bomongo
Mobena
Lulonga
Bondo
Ngolo
Bokuma
Ingende
Penzele
Kalamba
Irebu
Bikoro
Itipo
Mbuli
Iboko
Kiri
Botitembongo
Bolia
Kolobeke
Inongo
Selenge
Patamba
Kutu
Piankan
Muntu
Nsontin
Tolo
Bamaba
Pinanga
Bagata
Pita
Luano
Kingwaya
Bulungu
Masi-Manimba
Koshi
Kikwit
KKW
Iwungu
Lutshima
Kakobola
Bamba
Gungu
Feshi
Kabanga
Gungi
Katini
Bangu
Panzi
Bwana-Mutombo
Kahemba
Bindu
Mwadi Kalumbu
Basankusu
BSU
Djombo
Wenga
Waka
Bolena
Bauta
Baringa
Balangala
Befale
Bauru
Bolomba
Bokolango
Likala
Embondo
Bokote
Boteka
Bokatola
Kasa
Boleko
Biaranga
Belonge
Ngali
Botemola
Lokolama
Etumba
Buna
Oshwe
Mabenga
Panu
Mpo
Mangai
Yuki
Mpume
Dibaya-Lubue
Kapia
Due
Basongo
Ngoso
Banga
Luzi
Kimpata-Eku
Idiofa
Banda
Bantshamba
Bienge
Kilembe
Tshibuka
Ekombe
Lingomo
Ekukola
Samba
Mompono
Lolengi
Inganda
Boende
BNB
Eandja
Mpase
Watsi
Wema
Lokolia
Ebangalakata
Watsi Kengo
Likete
Itoko
Busanga
Bulukutu
Masanga
N'Gelewa
Botuna
Bokele
Monkoto
Mondjuku
Ikali
Isandja
Isanga
Lomami
Djolu
Befori
Yakana
Simba
Yahuma
Basoko
Lokutu
Mosite
Yalaki
Yalongwa
Wenge
Lingomo
Mondombe
Anzi
Ikela
Lokofe
Yayama
Yolombo
Lomela
Musadi
Loto
Pelenge
Poie
Gengwa
Isandja
Ikanda
Iwala
Dekese
Kole
Yasa
Ishenga
Mongemputu
Bolombo
Idumba
Lodi
Bena-Dibele
Ilebo
Mapangu
Misumba
Mushenge
Domiongo
Bulongo
Shapembe
Mweka
Kakenge
Bakwa-Kenge
Baya-Bwanga
Luebo
Mibalaie
Banga
Djokupunda
Lubanza
Tshibambula
Demba
Katombe
Makumbi
Mukanga
Tshikapa
TSH
Suana
Muanzanza
Tshitadi
Ndekesha
Bulungu
Malandji
Kananga
KGA
Sapo
Mutoto
Kosubuke
Mashala
Kolomonyi
Bena-Tshadi
Lusambo
Kondue
Dimbelenge
Tshikula
Tshintshanko
Katende
Kazumba
Tshimbulu
Dibaya
Kaponde
Nguema
Moma
Tshibala
Tshisenge
Muadiala
Dundo
DUE
Lóvua
Luachimo
Nordeste
Canzar
Cambulo
Andrada
Luaco
Mata
Katenge
Lueta
Luiza
Mumoma
Tulume
Masuika
Tshisonge
Katakakishi
Kapanga
Musenge
Mwene-Biji
Tshala
Tshibamba
Tshimbungu
Sandoa
Samulondo
Kabangu
Malonga
Kasaji
Dilolo
Divuma
Kasenga
Luau
Kandolo
Yambuya
Weko
Yangambi
Bengamisa
Isangi
Yalufi
Yatolema
Yanonge
Kisangani
FKI
Madula
Batama
Bafwaboli
Wanie-Rukula
Biaro
Yaleko
Pene-Katamba
Ubundu
Ekoli
Opala
Lubutu
Kirundu
Etumba
Obokote
Elipa
Likoto
Yumbi
Poma
Ongoka
Punia
Sulia
Kulampanga
Isambe
Bena-Kamba
Ekumakoko
Moga
Lokandu
Metsera
Kingombe
Elila
Kalima
Mali
Kindu
KND
Tumba
Lodja
LJA
Mende
Pakima
Shinga
Bolaiti
Losomba
Lueki
Difuma
Pangi
Kasambule
Kiyembwe
Katako-Kombe
Onema Ututu
Onema Okolo
Uvungu
Enyamba
Kibombo
Lumuna
Iwe
Kingombe
Kalema
Lusamba
Kwanga
Kabumbu
Kipaka
Yamba-Yamba
Mulenda
Kombe
Ongeri
Kasongo
Wete
Sulu
Lubefu
Samba
Patemba
Gamba
Manonwa
Kilembi
Piano Mutombo
Basanga
Tshofa
Lubamba
Lubao
Kifunan-kese
Lukolela
Penge
Kileo
Ebombo
Kisengwa
Kiumbila
Bashimuke
Eshimba
Nyasa
Kabinda
Kisengwa
Katompi
Lukula
Mbuji-Mayi
MJM
Tshilenge
Kabeya
Kumba
Kifusa
Kipushia
Kisose
Kamende
Kabango
Katanda
Kasanza
Kamiji
Gandajika
Kalabua
Tuzule
Matabaie
Kalundwe
Mani
Kitanda
Mwango
Kaloko
Mwene-Ditu
Lusaka
Tshimbok
Luputa
Kitengo
Kiteba
Kabongo
Kaniama
Tshongwe
Nioka
Tubeya
Kimpanga
Piodi
Kilembe
Mwanza
Goi-Pula
Malemba-Nkulu
Kikondja
Mutombo Mukulu
Tshitanzu
Tshie
Mwilambwe
Songa
Zaila
Busango
Kamina Base
Kamina
Djamba
Mania-Muna
Kabondo-Dianda
Kayembe Mukulu
Luabo
Bangu
Kinda
Bukama
Mapanda
Kitunga
Mosongoie
Lukasu
Luena
Makulakubu
Kafakumba
Tshimbalanga
Tshako
Sokele
Malonda
Lubudi
Luswaka
Beke
Kansenia
Kagombo
Busanga
Nasondoye
Kinga
Mutshatsha
Kaziza
Kanzenze
Manika
Tenke
Guba
Kanoni
Malungwishi
Kakanda
Kolwezi
KWZ
Chaua
Cuilo
Caluango
Camaxilo
Cambaxi
Cassango
Camissombo
Cambange
Cachimpo
Luia
Doege
Calonda
Lucapa
Sombo
Elias Gracia
Banvo
Quelele
Cuango
Capenda-Camulemba
Xá-Muteba
Luangue
Xinge
Saurimo
VHC
Gambo
Samoa
Caumbue
Mona Quimbundo
Muriege
Cacolo
Quitapa
Cacumbi
Sachula
Xassengue
Matechai
Muconda
Sacambunge
Cassai
Luquembo
Chiluage
Dala
Tshibwika
1087
675
654
843
771
916
1109
1204
1680
1457
N1
N2
N7
N8
N20
N31
N33
N39
N40
N41
N42
R606
R630

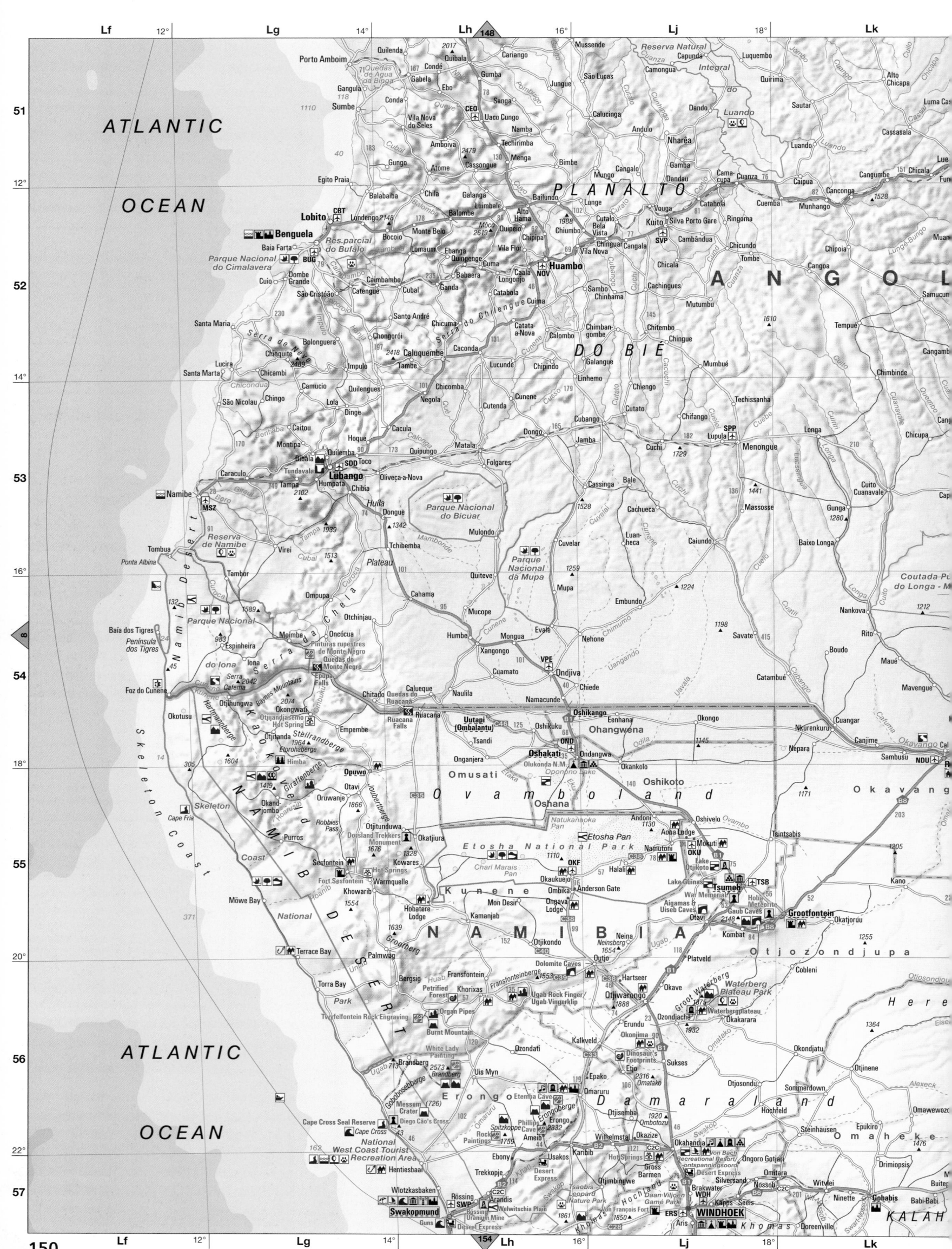

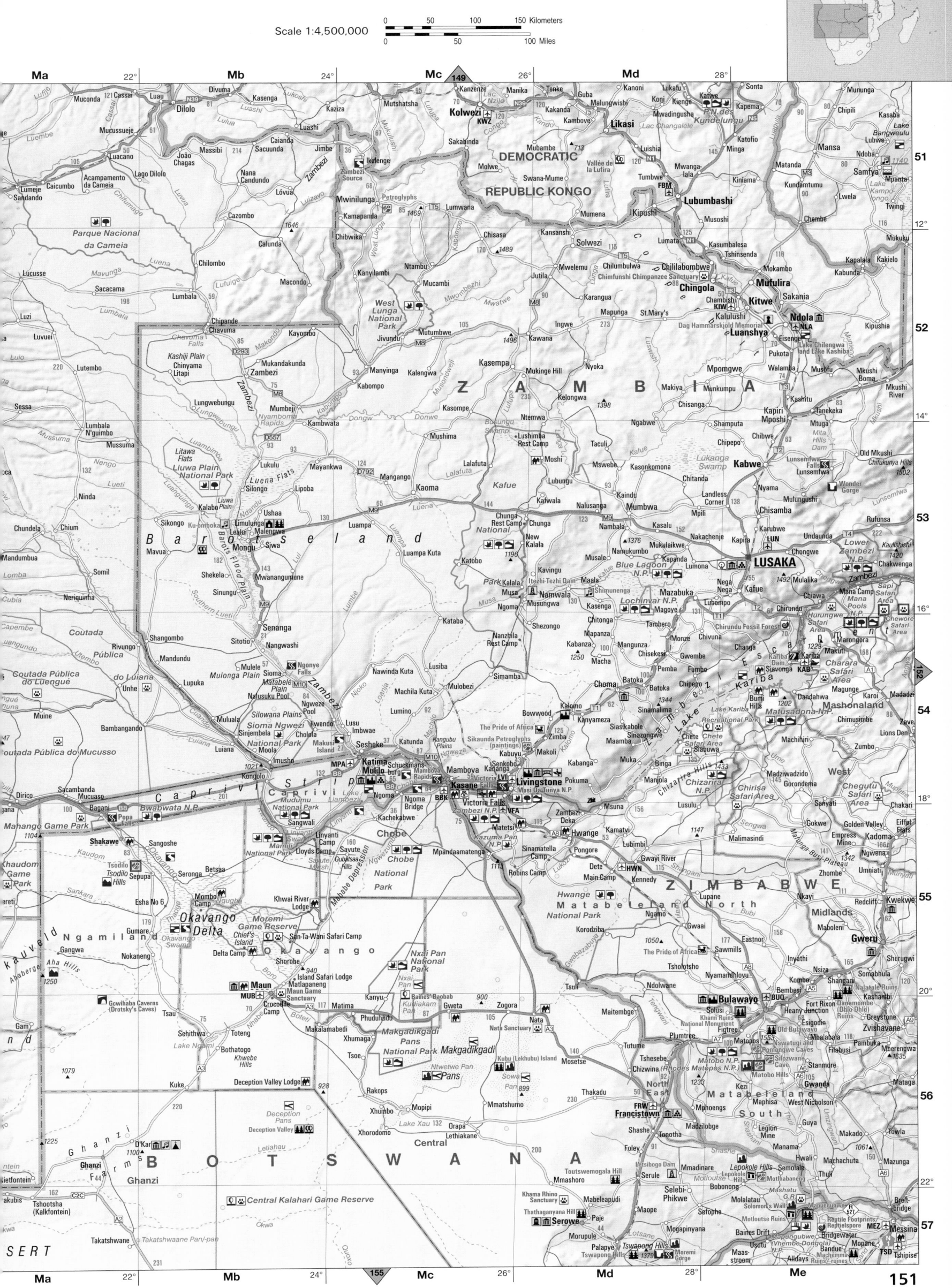

Scale 1:4,500,000

0   50   100   150 Kilometers

0   50   100 Miles

51

52

53

152

54

55

56

57

DEMOCRATIC

REPUBLIC KONGO

Z A M B I A

LUSAKA

Barotseland

Caprivi Strip

Z I M B A B W E

Mashonaland

Matabeleland North

Matabeleland South

Midlands

B O T S W A N A

Okavango Delta

Ngamiland

Ghanzi

Central

Central Kalahari Game Reserve

Makgadikgadi Pans

Kolwezi
Likasi
Lubumbashi
Mufulira
Kitwe
Chingola
Ndola
Luanshya
Kabwe
Livingstone
Victoria Falls
Kasane
Katima Mulilo
Maun
Bulawayo
Gweru
Gwanda
Francistown
Serowe
Shakawe
Ghanzi

12°

14°

16°

18°

20°

22°

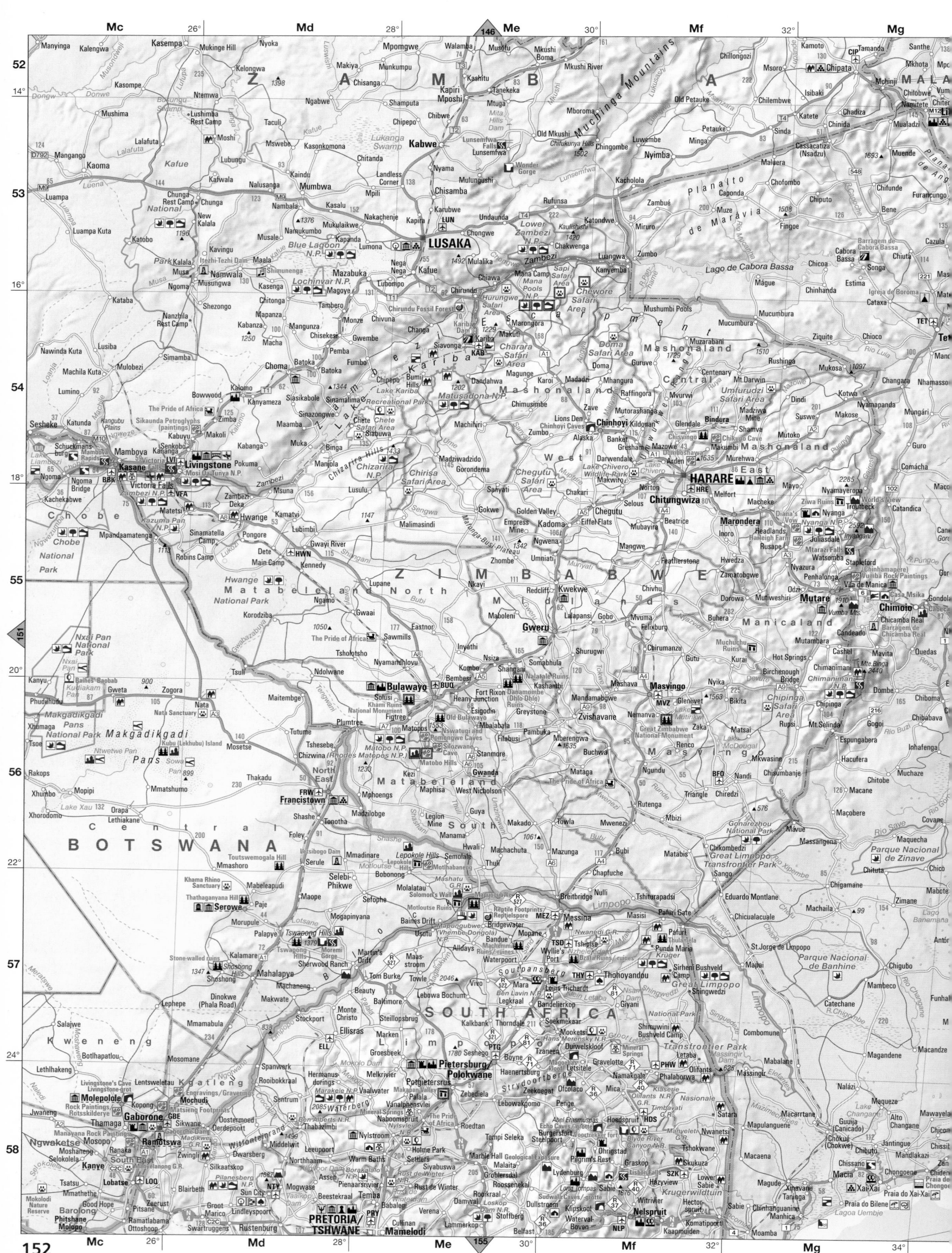

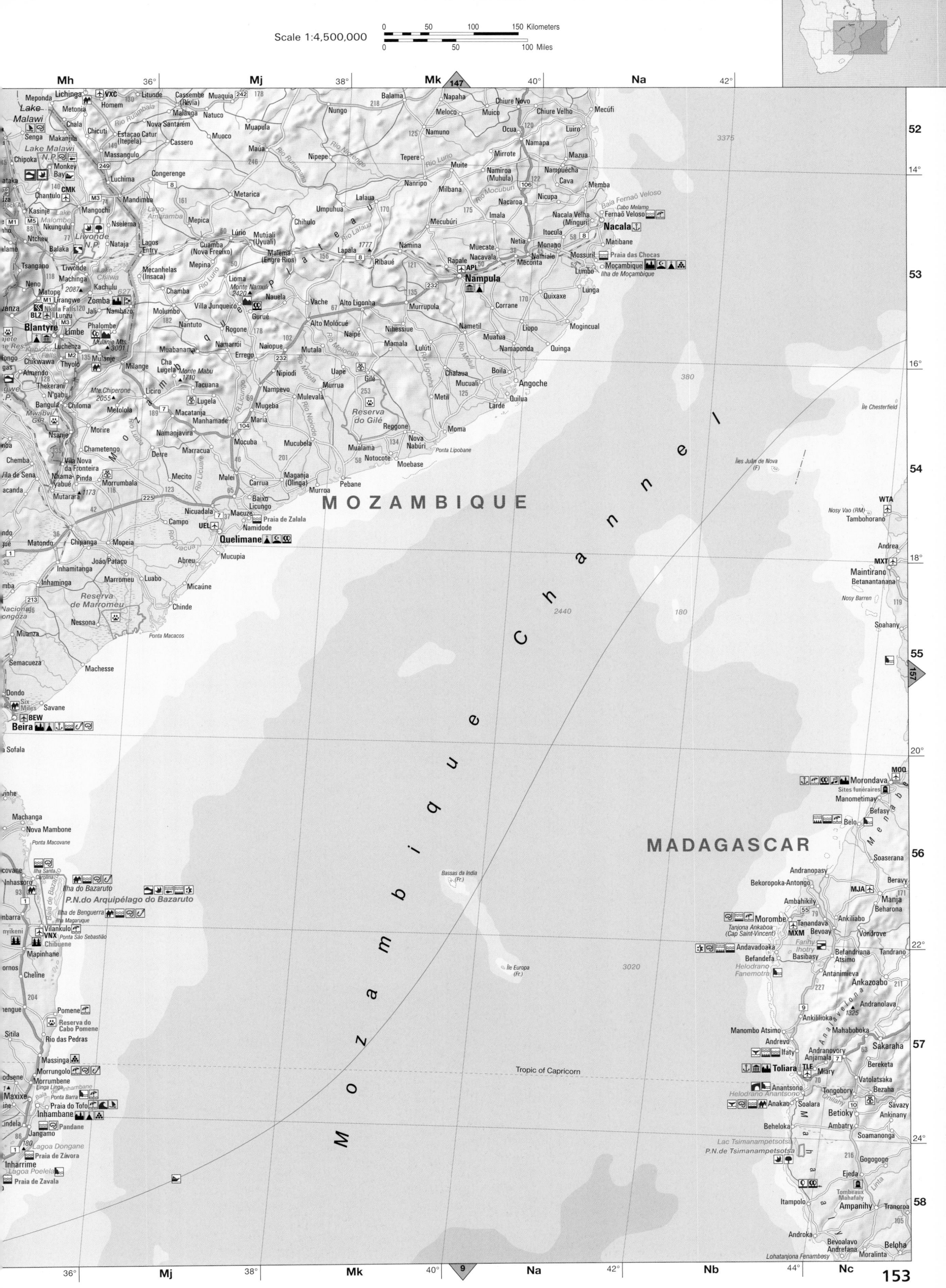

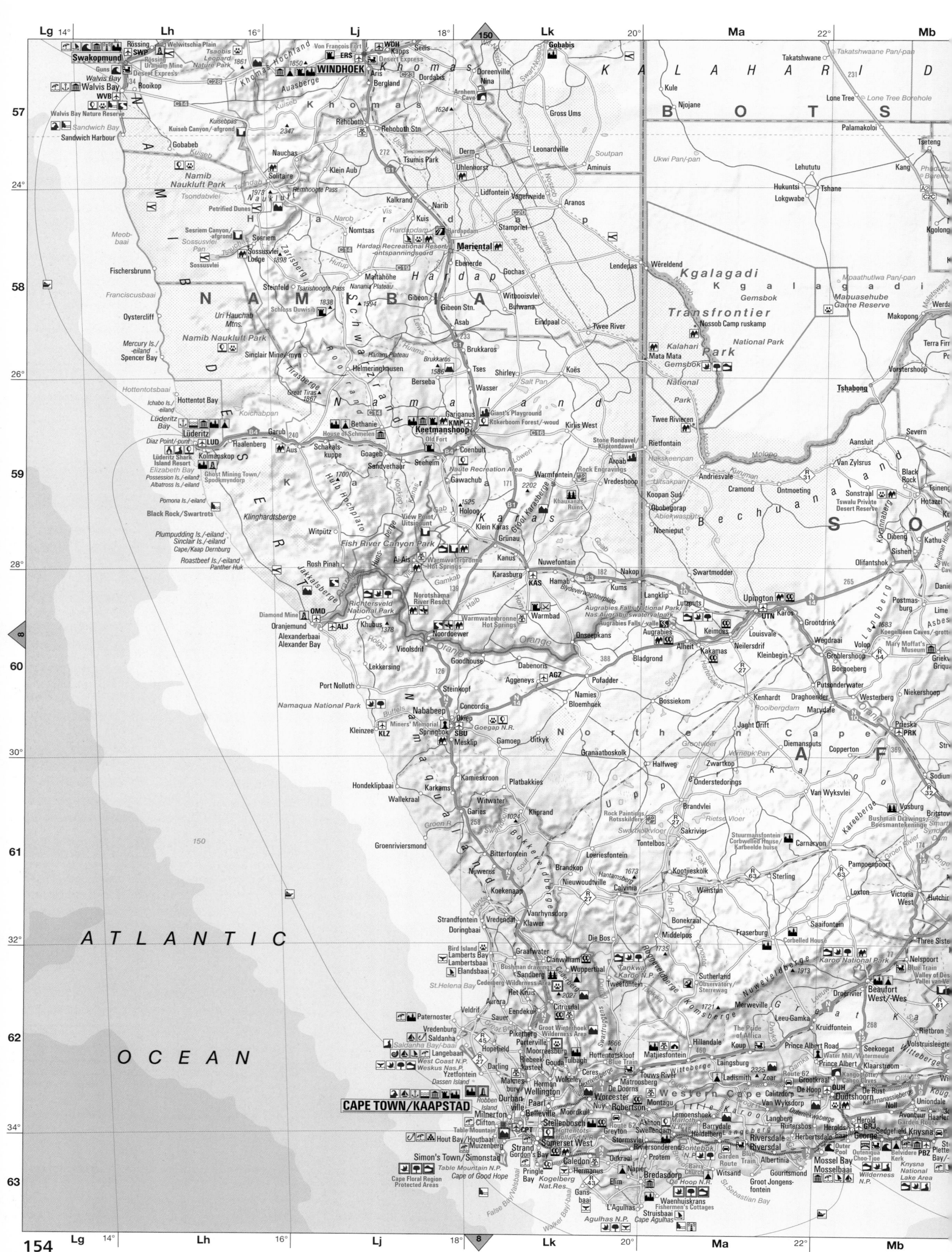

Madagascar, Réunion, Mauritius

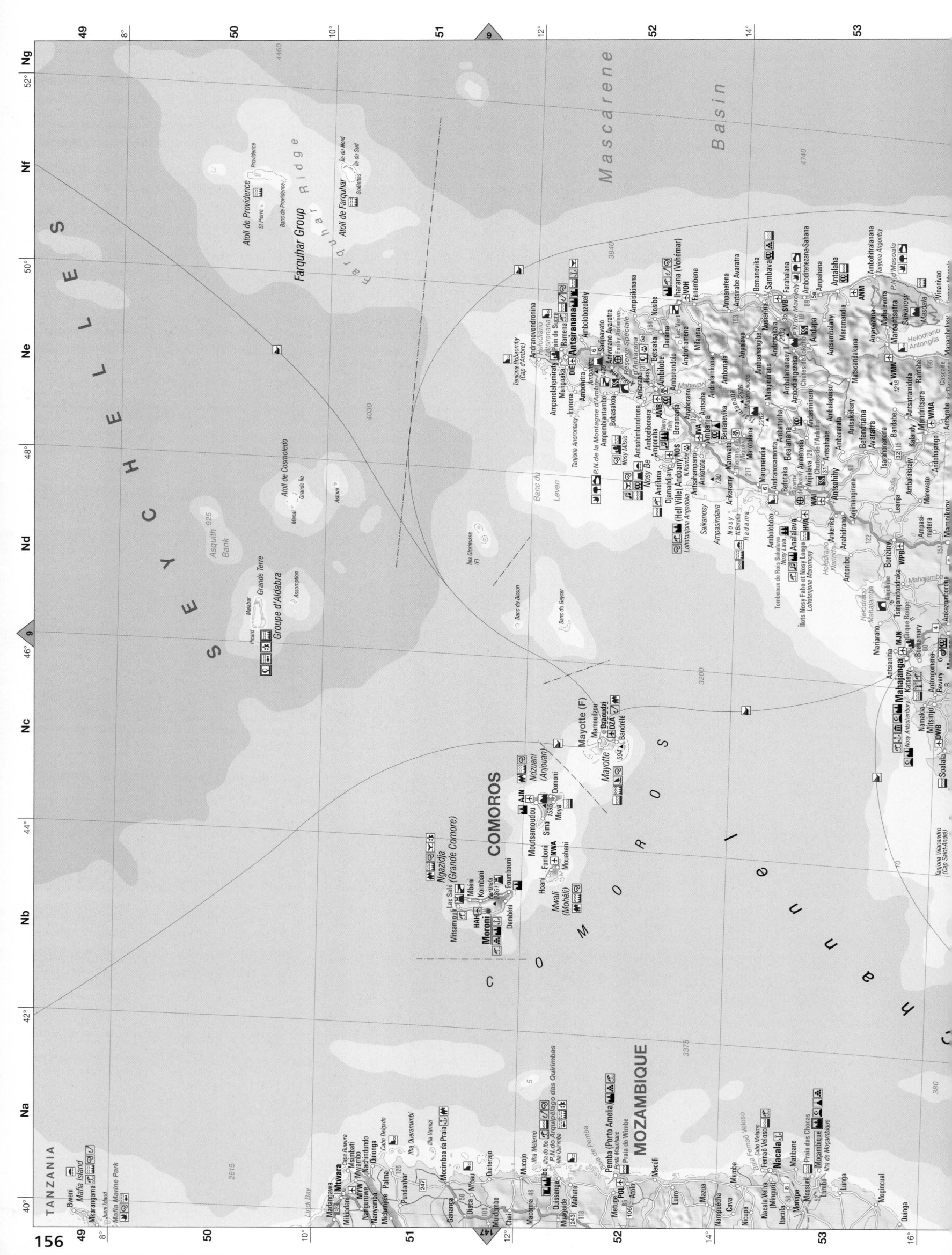

Scale 1:4,500,000

0 50 100 150 Kilometers
0 50 100 Miles

54 18° 55 20° 56 9 55 20° 56

Nk

INDIAN

OCEAN

Mascarene Plain

5350

Ng

Nf

Nh

Na

Mascarene Plateau

Mascarene Islands

MAURITIUS
Île Plate
Île d'Ambre
Pamplemousses
Port Louis
Beau-Bassin/Rose Hill
Curepipe
Goodlands
Flacq
Rivière Sud-Est
Mahébourg
MRU
Grand Rivière Noire
Souillac
Mauritius

INDIAN OCEAN

2350

Réunion (F)
Le Port
Saint-Denis
Saint-André
RUN
Saint-Benoît
Saint-Paul
Cilaos
Piton des Neiges
Piton de la Fournaise
Saint-Leu
Saint-Louis
Saint-Philippe
Saint-Pierre
Saint-Joseph
Réunion

4275

Nj

Nh

MADAGASCAR

Madagascar Basin

3020

Nf

Ne

Nd

Nc

Nb

INDIAN

OCEAN

Nosy Sainte-Marie

Toamasina

SMS

ANTANANARIVO

Antsirabe

Fianarantsoa

Toliara

Morondava

Mahajanga

Maevatanana

Antsohihy

Mananjary

Manakara

Vangaindrano

Farafangana

Tôlanaro

M o z a m b i q u e

Tropic of Capricorn

2440

18° 55 20° 56 153 57 22° 24° 58

157

The Virgin Islands are surrounded by beautiful tropical coasting.

Chicago: The modern skyline of the city glitters next to Lake Michigan.

NORTH AND CENTRAL AMERICA

THE NEW WORLD

The northern continent of the Western Hemisphere stretches from the Arctic Ocean to the Caribbean Sea. North America can be divided into three large geographic regions running from north to south. The western portion of the continent is dominated by the Cordilleras, a series of mountain ranges which contains Alaska's Mount McKinley (6,194 m), the continent's highest mountain. The Appalachian Mountains stretch through much of eastern North America. In between these two regions lie the vast Central Plains. One of the continent's most interesting geographic attractions is Death Valley, the lowest point on the planet's surface.

The Rocky Mountains, the largest mountain chain in North America, extend through the United States and Canada. In the American Southwest, the Rockies border the Sierra Madre mountain range, which extends through most of Mexico and into Central America. The Isthmus of Panama is only 50 kilometers wide. The islands of the Caribbean form a large chain running from Cuba to South America and are separated into two groups: the Lesser Antilles and the Greater Antilles.

In addition to the three large nations on the continent (Canada, Mexico, and the United States) there are numerous smaller North American nations. The indigenous people (Native Americans and Inuit) form only a small portion of the population in Canada and the United States, while most Mexicans and Central Americans are at least of partial indigenous descent.

Over the centuries millions of European immigrants settled in North America and most of the continent's population is of European descent. Millions of North Americans, mostly in the United States and the Caribbean, are of African descent. Canada and the USA attract a large number of immigrants every year, including many migrants from neighboring Mexico.

Hollow Water First Nation Land: Native reservation in Manitoba – on the southern shore of Lake Winnipeg.

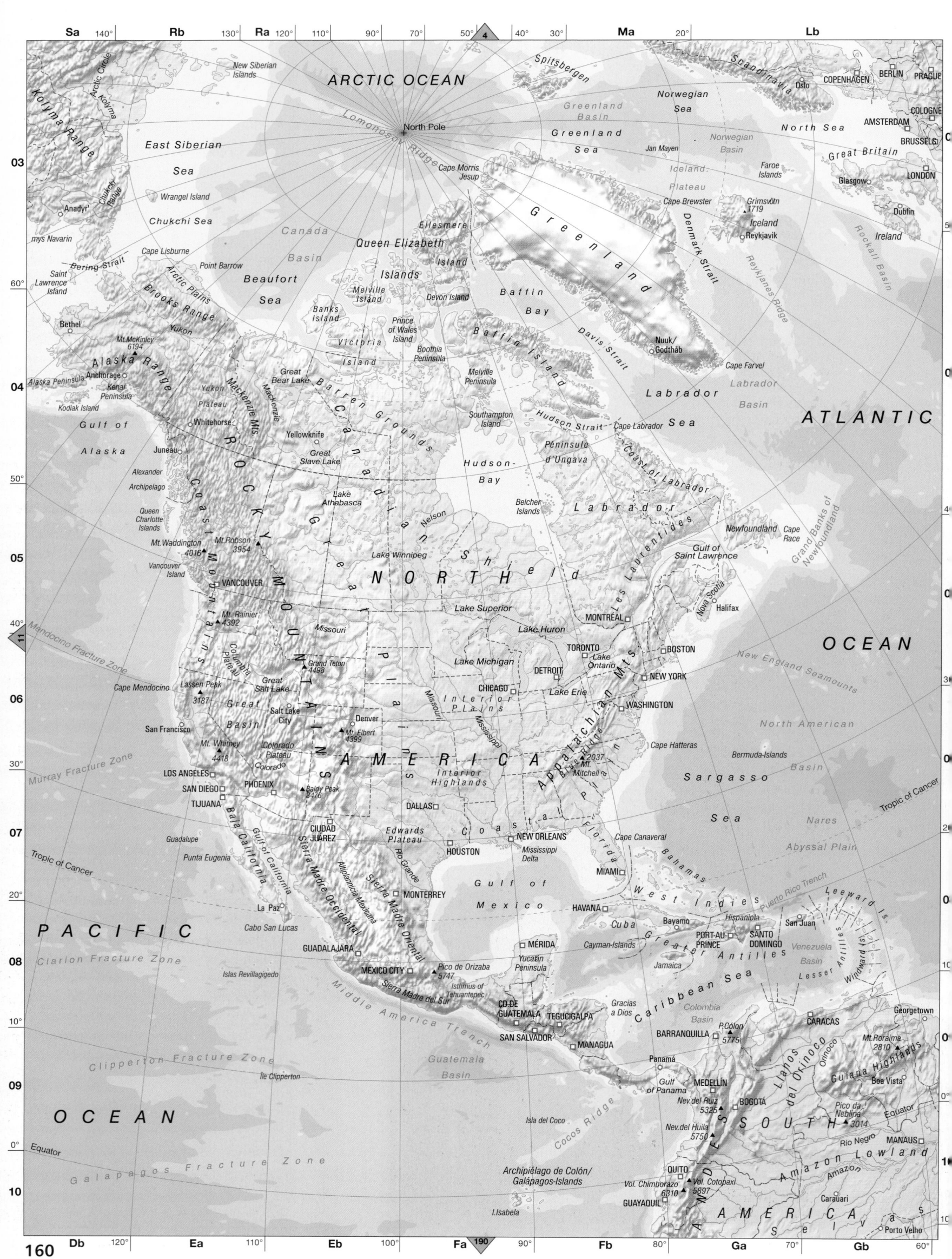

North and Central America

ARCTIC OCEAN

North Pole

East Siberian
Sea

Kolyma Range

Kolyma

New Siberian
Islands

Arctic Circle

Spitsbergen

Greenland
Basin

Norwegian
Sea

Scandinavia

Oslo   COPENHAGEN   BERLIN   PRAGUE

COLOGNE

Greenland
Sea

Jan Mayen

Norwegian
Basin

North Sea

AMSTERDAM

BRUSSELS

Anadyr'

Chukchi Range

Wrangel Island

Chukchi Sea

Cape Morris
Jesup

Iceland
Plateau

Faroe
Islands

Great Britain

Glasgow

LONDON

03

mys Navarin

Canada
Basin

Queen Elizabeth

Cape Brewster

Grimsvötn
1719

Iceland

Reykjavik

Dublin

Ireland

Rockall Basin

Saint
Lawrence
Island

Cape Lisburne

Bering Strait

Point Barrow

Arctic Plains

Beaufort
Sea

Ellesmere
Island

Islands

Greenland

Denmark Strait

Reykjanes Ridge

60°

Bethel

Brooks Range

Yukon

Melville
Island

Banks
Island

Devon Island

Prince
of Wales
Island

Baffin
Bay

Baffin Island

Davis Strait

Nuuk/
Godthåb

Labrador
Basin

5

Mt.McKinley
6194

Alaska Range

Anchorage

Kenai
Peninsula

Alaska Peninsula

Kodiak Island

Yukon
Plateau

Mackenzie Mts

Victoria
Island

Boothia
Peninsula

Melville
Peninsula

Cape Farvel

04

Gulf of
Alaska

Whitehorse

Juneau

Rocky

Mackenzie

Great
Bear Lake

Barren Grounds

Southampton
Island

Hudson Strait

Cape Labrador

Péninsule
d'Ungava

Labrador
Sea

ATLANTIC

Alexander
Archipelago

Coast Mountains

Yellowknife

Great
Slave Lake

Hudson-
Bay

Coast of Labrador

Queen
Charlotte
Islands

Mt.Waddington
4016

Mt.Robson
3954

Lake
Athabasca

Canadian

Belcher
Islands

Labrador

Newfoundland

Cape
Race

50°

Vancouver
Island

VANCOUVER

Mountains

Lake Winnipeg

NORTH

Shield

Grand Banks of
Newfoundland

05

Mt.Rainier
4392

Columbia
Plateau

Missouri

Nelson

Lake Superior

MONTRÉAL

Les Laurentides

Gulf of
Saint Lawrence

Nova Scotia

Halifax

4

Cape Mendocino

Lassen Peak
3187

Grand Teton
4498

Great
Salt Lake

Plateau

Lake Huron

TORONTO

Lake
Ontario

BOSTON

Appalachian Mts

3

Mandocino Fracture Zone

11

Great
Basin

Salt Lake
City

Denver

Interior
Plains

Lake Michigan

CHICAGO

DETROIT

Lake Erie

NEW YORK

WASHINGTON

New England Seamounts

OCEAN

San Francisco

Mt.Whitney
4418

Colorado
Plateau

Colorado

Mt.Elbert
4399

Missouri

AMERICA

Mississippi

Mt.
Mitchell

2037
Mt.

Cape Hatteras

North American

Bermuda-Islands

06

30°

LOS ANGELES

SAN DIEGO

TIJUANA

Phoenix

Baldy Peak
3476

Interior
Highlands

Coastal

Florida

Sargasso

Basin

07

CIUDAD
JUAREZ

Sierra Madre Occidental

Edwards
Plateau

Rio Grande

DALLAS

NEW ORLEANS

Plain

Cape Canaveral

Sea

Nares

Tropic of Cancer

Guadalupe

Punta Eugenia

Baja California

HOUSTON

Mississippi
Delta

MIAMI

Bahamas

Abyssal Plain

Tropic of Cancer

20°

PACIFIC

La Paz

Cabo San Lucas

Gulf of California

MONTERREY

Gulf of
Mexico

HAVANA

Cuba

West Indies

Leeward Is.

Puerto Rico Trench

Clarion Fracture Zone

Islas Revillagigedo

GUADALAJARA

MÉXICO CITY

Sierra Madre Oriental

Altiplanicie Mexicana

Pico de Orizaba
5747

MÉRIDA

Yucatán
Peninsula

Cayman-Islands

Bayamo

Jamaica

Greater
Antilles

Hispaniola

PORT-AU-
PRINCE

SANTO
DOMINGO

San Juan

Venezuela
Basin

Lesser Antilles

Windward Is.

08

10

Isla Revillagigedo

Middle America Trench

Isthmus of
Tehuantepec

Sierra Madre del Sur

CD.DE
GUATEMALA

SAN SALVADOR

TEGUCIGALPA

MANAGUA

Gracias
a Dios

Caribbean Sea

Colombia
Basin

BARRANQUILLA

P.Colón
5775

CARACAS

Georgetown

Mt.Roraima
2810

Boa Vista

Guiana Highlands

10°

Clipperton Fracture Zone

Île Clipperton

Guatemala
Basin

Panamá

Gulf
of Panama

MEDELLÍN

Nev.del Ruiz
5325

BOGOTÁ

Llanos del Orinoco

Orinoco

Pico da
Neblina
3014

09

OCEAN

Cocos Ridge

Isla del Coco

Nev.del Huila
5750

ANDES

Rio Negro

SOUTH

Equator

MANAUS

0°

Equator

Galapagos Fracture Zone

Archipiélago de Colón/
Galápagos-Islands

Vol. Chimborazo
6310

QUITO

Vol. Cotopaxi
5897

Amazon Lowland

Amazon

Carauari

10

I.Isabela

GUAYAQUIL

AMERICA

Porto Velho

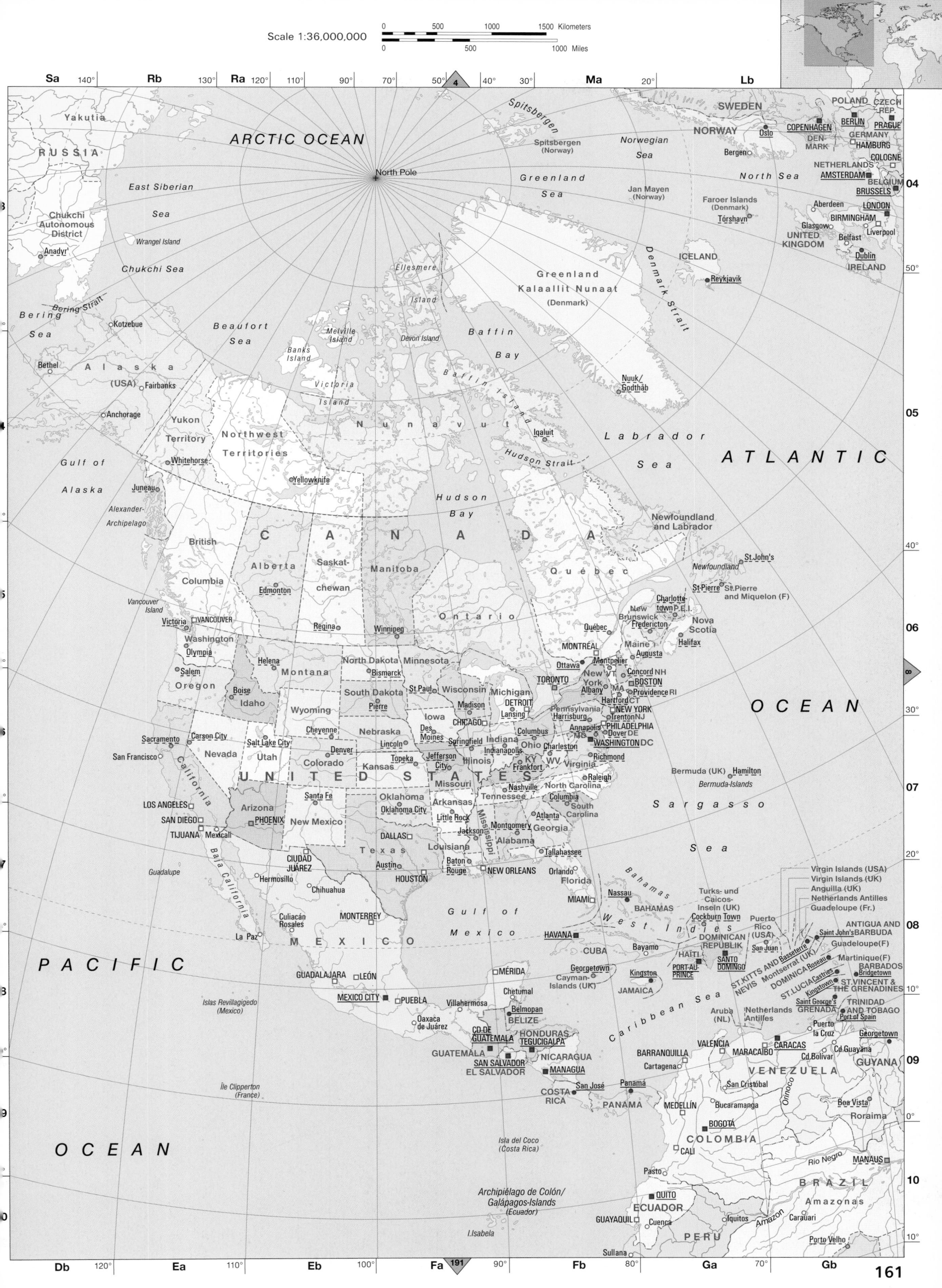

Alaska, Canada, Greenland

25°   20°   **Ka**   15°   **Kb**   10°   **Kc**   5°   **Kd**

Jan Mayen (N)   Faroe Islands (DK)
                                                          Tórshavn

G r e e n l a n d
Kap Morris Jesup   Kap Bismarck   Arctic Circle
Peary   Kronprins   Kap Bismarck
Land   Christian   Dove Bugt
              Land   **Icelandic**
                          Kap Bismarck   465
Cape   Kong Frederik VIII Land   **Sea**
Aldrich   **Plateau**   Seyðisfjörður
Alert   Lincoln   Dröning   627   Raufarhöfn   Höfn
Cape   Sea   Louise   Rifstangi Grímsvötn
Discovery   Kong Wilhelm   Ittoqqortoormiit/   1779 **ICELAND**
                            Land   Scoresbysund   Fontur
Point   Kong Christian X Land   Akureyri
            Ellesmere   Scoresby   Hornbjarg Sauðárkrókur
            Island   Kap Brewster   Land   Vík
Cape Discovery   Ísafjörður
                                                          Akranes Reykjavík
Norwegian Bjørne   Ólafsvík Hafnarfjörður
Bay   Pen.   Hayes Halvø   Keflavík
   Heiberg   **Greenland**   Kangerlussuaq
   Island   Grise Fiord Kap Parry   Kap Gustav Holm
             Jones Sound   Qaanaaq/   **Kalaallit Nunaat**   Breiðafjörður
                          Thule Uummannaq/
                                 Dundas   **(DK)**   832
                          Kap   Melville   Kap Gustav Holm
                          York   Bugt
Devon Island Cape Sherard   Ammassalik
                                Upernavik   Ikerssuaq
   Somerset   **Baffin**   Pikiutdleq/Køge Bugt
   Island Cape Crauford Bylot **Basin**   Guldenløves Fjord
           Lancaster Sound Island   Kap Møsting Tvillingøen   3125
Strait   Borden Arctic Bay Cape Graham Moore Ilulissat/   Kong   Tingmiarmiut Fjord
         Brodeur Pond Inlet Buchan Jakobshavn **Frederik IX**
         Peninsula   Gulf Cape Adair Disko Ø   **Land**
Boothia   Cape Christian Qeqertarsuaq/ Kangerlussuaq/
Peninsula Prince Regent Inlet Clyde   Godhavn   Søndrestrømfjord
Taloyoak   Gulf of Boothia   Cape Raper   Sisimiut/ **Dröning Ingrid**
         a   v   u   t Home   Holsteinsborg **Land**
Gjoa   Bay   Manitsoq/   Uummannarsuaq/
Haven   Committee Bay   Cape Dyer Sukkertoppen   Kap Farvel
        Hall Beach Prince   64   Nuuk/
        Melville Charles **Cumberland** Godthåb   2450
        Peninsula Island **Peninsula**   Narsarsuaq
Repulse Bay   Great Plain Pangnirtung 967 Paamiut/
         of the Nettiling   Frederikshåb   Qaqortoq/
         Koukdjuak Lake Cumberland Sound   Julianehåb

55°
07
08

L a b r a d o r   ATLANTIC
3115
S e a
                OCEAN
Basin   4374

N e w f o u n d l a n d   a n d   L a b r a d o r

25°

Fa 95° **Fb** 90° **Fc** 85° **Fd** 80° **Ga** 75° **Gb** 70° **Gc** 65° **Gd** 60° **Ha** **163**

Alaska

Ak 180° Ba 178° Bb 55 176° Bc 174° Bd 172° Be

RUSSIA

B e r i n g

Sireniki
Providenija Novoe 1158 Jandrakinot Raupeljan Lorino
Urelik Caplino Senjavina Mečigmenskij zaliv
mys Čukotskij PVX ostrov Lavrentija
Cecen Arakamčečen Nyglian
Caplino

ostrov
Rathmanova
(Big Diomede I.) Iñalik
Little Diomede I.
Inalik

16

Northwest Cape Gambell *B e r i n g S t r* Wales
Ningeehak Cape Prince Lopp
of Wales Lagoon Lost River
Powooiliak Camp Savoonga Brooks
King I. 883
673 Atuk Mtn. Point Spencer Port
Saint Lawrence I. Clarence Teller

Iveetok Camp

58° Southeast Cape 555 Lietnik Sinuk Kigluaik Mts. Pilgrim
Kinipaghulghat Northeast Cape Spring
Mts. Sinuk R.
Nome OME Eldorado Iron Cr. Casa

S e a Cape Nome

Hall I. 67 Bluff
450 White Mountain
Alaska Maritime Rocky Point Golovnin Bay
Wildlife Refuge Saint Matthew I. *N o r t o n* Cape
95 Darby
Cape Upright 18 *S o u n d*

Scammon C. Romanzof Waklarok Alakanuk Kwikpak Cape

17 20 Askinuk Mts. New Emmonak Kotlik Pastol Stuart I.
Hooper Bay 714 Knockhock Akulurak Bay
Chevak Scammon Hamilton Stebbins
Bay *Yukon Delta* New St. Michael
Cape Mohican Nunavakanuk Mountain Hamilton 701
Lake Village MOU Unalakleet
Nash Harbor Hazen Bay Chakaktolik Pitkas Pt. Andreafsky R. 1402
Yukon Delta Mekoryuk Cape Etolin Keyaluvik Kgun Pilot Station 396
Wildlife Refuge 283 *Nunivak I.* C. Vancouver Apropuk Lake
Tununak 451 Lake Cahkwaktolik Marshall Anvik Na
Cape Mendenhall Nightmare *Nelson I.* Chiftak *National* Stuyahok Yukon River Wildlif
Cape Corwin Baird Inlet Taksleskuk Ohogamiut Shageluk
Chefornak Kasigluk Lake Holy Cross
Kegum Kasigluk *Wildlife Refuge* Kalskag Flat
55 Kikegtek I. Kagati Nunavacnak Kuskokwim R.
Pingurbek I. Lake Lake BET Bethel Aniak Horn Mts. Crooked
Kipnuk Tuntutuliak Napakiak Akiachak Tuluksak ANI 1097 Creek George R.
56° Kwigillingok Eek Mt. Plummer *Kus*
Eek R. 1463 Whitefish Nogamut *kokw*
Kuskokwim Quinhagak Kisaralik R. Lake Taylor Mts.
Bay Kilbuck Mountains 1091
Carter Spit Nektok R. Mt. Oratia Holitna R.
Explorer Mtn. 1645 Chikmin
Platinum 811 Goodnews Bay Cairn Mts.
Goodnews Kukaklik R. *Togiak* Henolina R. 1158
Cape Newenham Mining Camp Manwak Lake *National* Niyakuk
Togiak *Wildlife Refuge* Lake *Ahklun Mountains* Swift R.
Calm Point Togiak Swift R.
Hagemeister Strait 544 Togiak Koliganek Ketok Mtn.
18 65 Hagemeister I. *Bay* High I. Lake 517
Crooked I. Nuyakuk Mulchatna R.
Walrus Is. Aleknagik Aleknagik Lake New Stuyahok Old Village
Kulukak Bay Nushagak Alaganik Telaquana *Lake Clark*
Peninsula Lake Lake *National Park*
DLG New *and Preserve*
Dillingham Nondalton Newhalen
Bristol Clarks Point Iliamna Redoubt
Cape Etolin Lake Pile Bay Vol. 3108
Bay Constantine Point Village
Hallersville *Chigmit Mountains*
A l a s k a P e n i n s u l a Kvichak Bay Iliamna Williamsport Iliamna Vol.
Naknek Iguigig Vol. 308-
54° Cape Cape Anvak AKN Sugarloaf Mtn. Chenik Sterling Highway
Sarichef Mordvinof Moffet King Salmon 745 Burr Pt. HOM
Unimak I. Pt. Izembek *Katmai* Kamishak 1196 English Bay Homer
Unimak Shishaldin Otter Pt. Wildlife Refuge *National Park* Bay Pt. Adam Seldovia
2862 Kudiakof Is. Cold Bay *and Preserve* Mt. Douglas Portlock *Kenai M*
Volcano CDB Lagoon Port Moller Pilot Point Becharof Mt. Katmai 2153 C. Douglas Chugach Is.
False Pass Point Strogonof Lake Mt. Peulik 2047 Gore Pt.
Pavlof Vol. Ilnik Point Port Heiden 1500 N.W.R. C. Nukshak
Deer I. 2504 Walrus I. AniaKchak *Range* Burr Pt.
King Cove Seal Is. *Alaska Peninsula* Mt. Kaguyak Afognak I.
Sanak I. Mt. Dana Veniaminof *Wildlife Refuge* Becharof Mt. Chiginagak Kanatak Marmot Tonki C.
Fawn Pt. 1310 Volcano Black 2144 Kamishak Marmot Bay
Dolgoi I. 2507 Lake Ugashik C. Kekurnoi C. Iktugitak Afognak
Sanak Islands Unga I. *A l e u t i a n* Bay Wide Bay Raspberry I. ADQ
Caton I. Sand Korovin I. Black C. Port Kodiak
Point Perryville Wide Bay Uganik I. Port Vita Shuyak I.
Popof I. Chignik C. Kunmik Amber Bay Pt. Banks
Kupreanof Chiach I. Chignik Bay *Shelikof Strait*
Shumagin Islands Pt. Castle C. Alaska Marine Highway William Alaska Marine Highway
Nagai I. Mitrofania I. Sutvik I. Foggy Karluk Raspberry I.
19 250 Big Koniuji I. Cape Kodiak Island Larsen Bay Pt. William *Gulf*
Chernabura I. Little Koniuji I. Aghiyuk I. Ikolik Low Cape *Kodiak* Fort Abercrombie Spruce I. *of*
Simeonof I. Semidi Is. Port Loins *National* State Historic Park Kodiak *Alaska*
Chowiet I. Akhiok *Wildlife Refuge* 1340 Chiniak Bay
Tugidak I. Old Harbor C. Chiniak
Bk 160° Ca 158° Cb 156° 11 Cc 154° Cd 152° Ce 150° Cf

164

Southern Alaska, Northwestern Canada

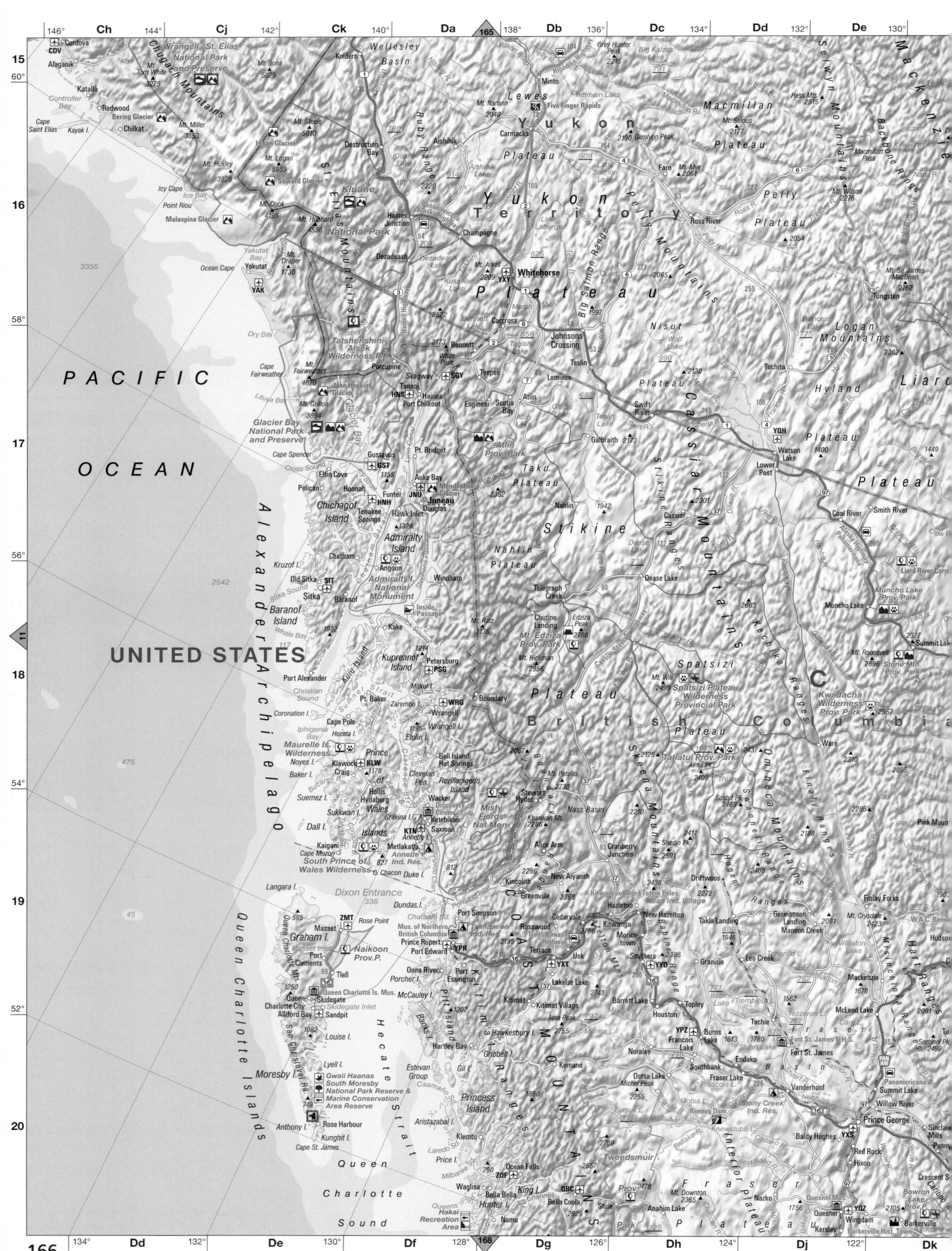

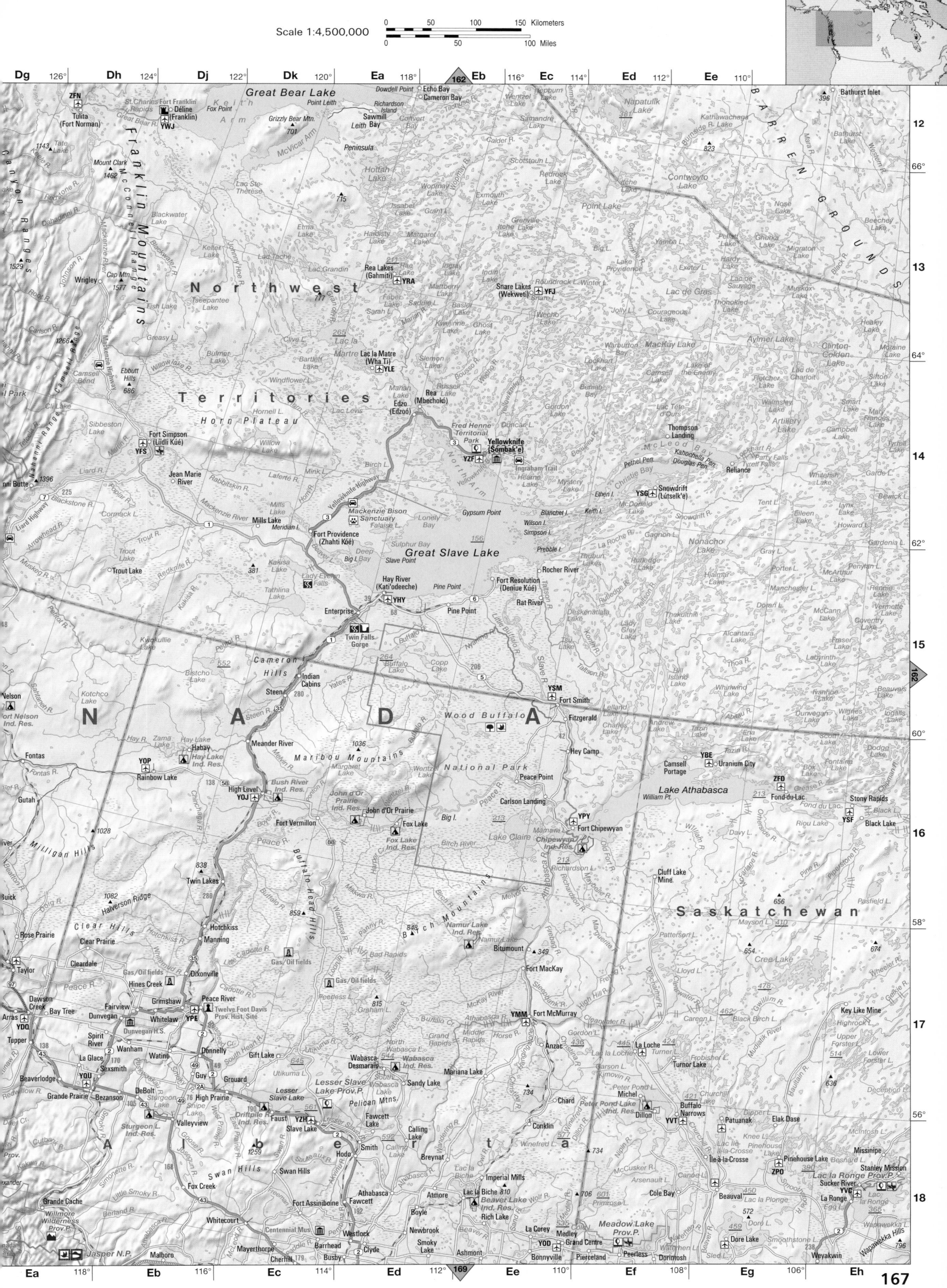

12

66°

13

64°

Great Bear Lake

N o r t h w e s t

T e r r i t o r i e s

14

62°

Great Slave Lake

15

162

C A N A D A

60°

Wood Buffalo

National Park

N

Lake Athabasca

S a s k a t c h e w a n

16

58°

17

A l b e r t a

56°

18

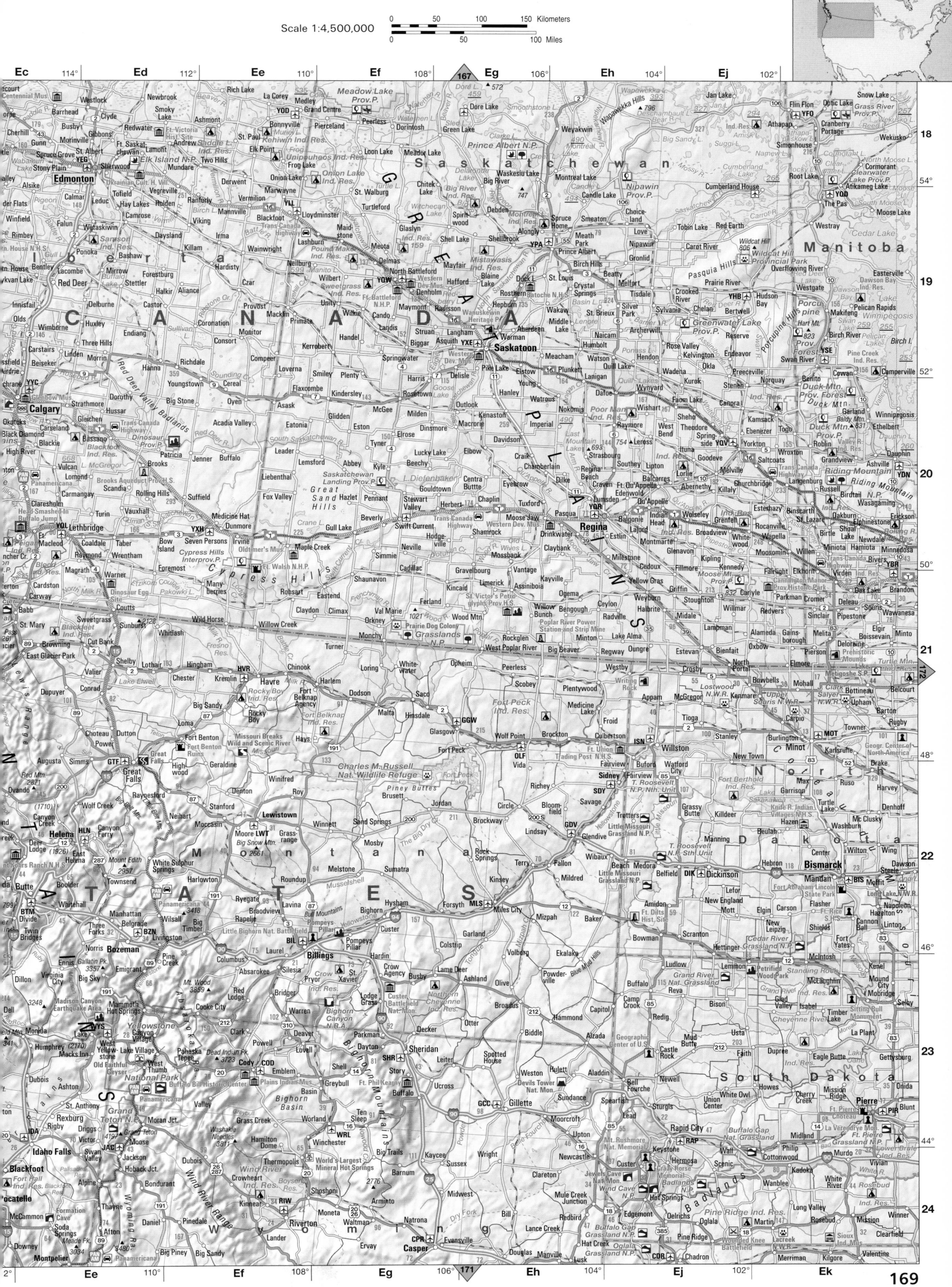

Scale 1:4,500,000

0   50   100   150 Kilometers

0   50   100 Miles

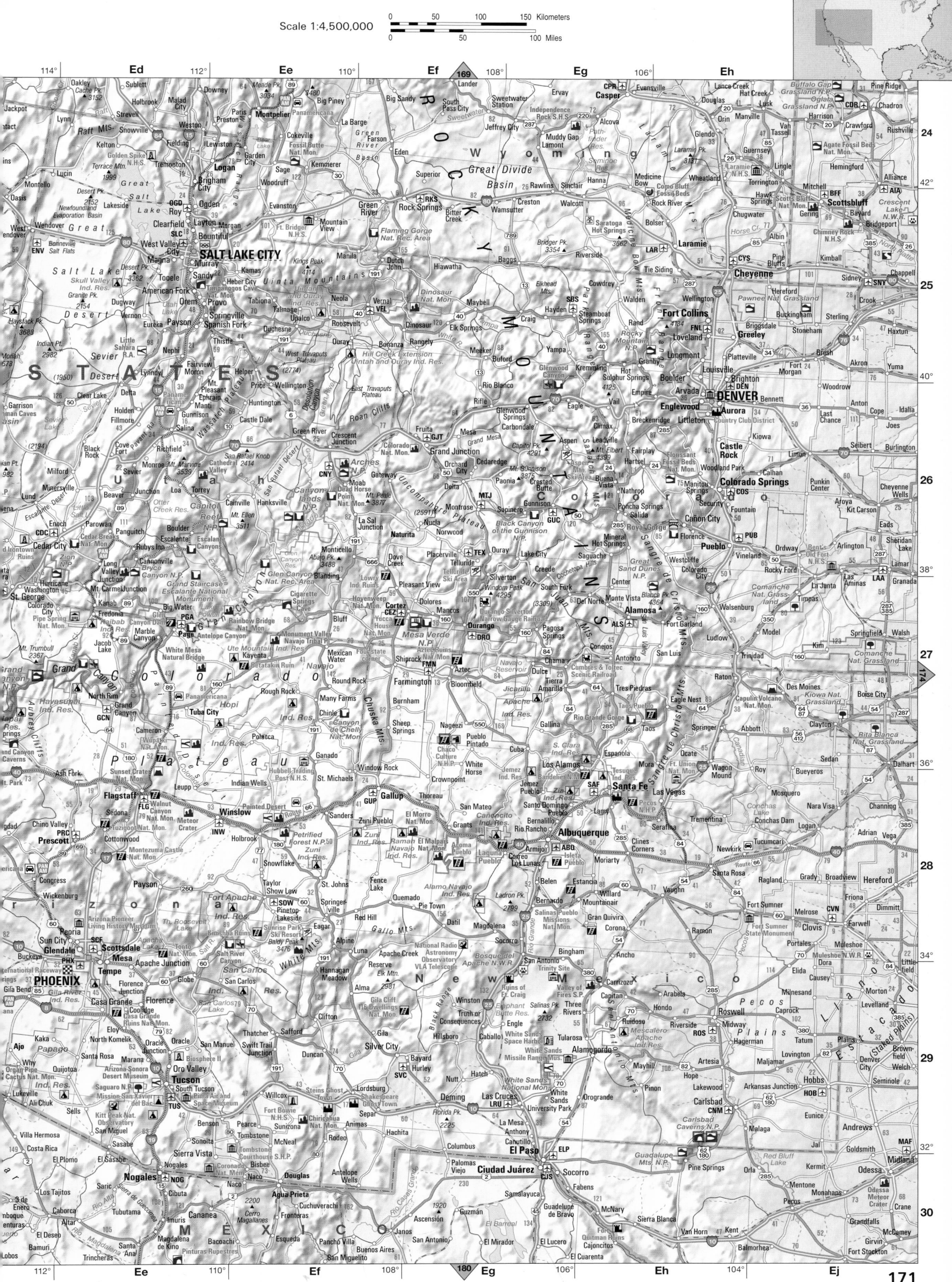

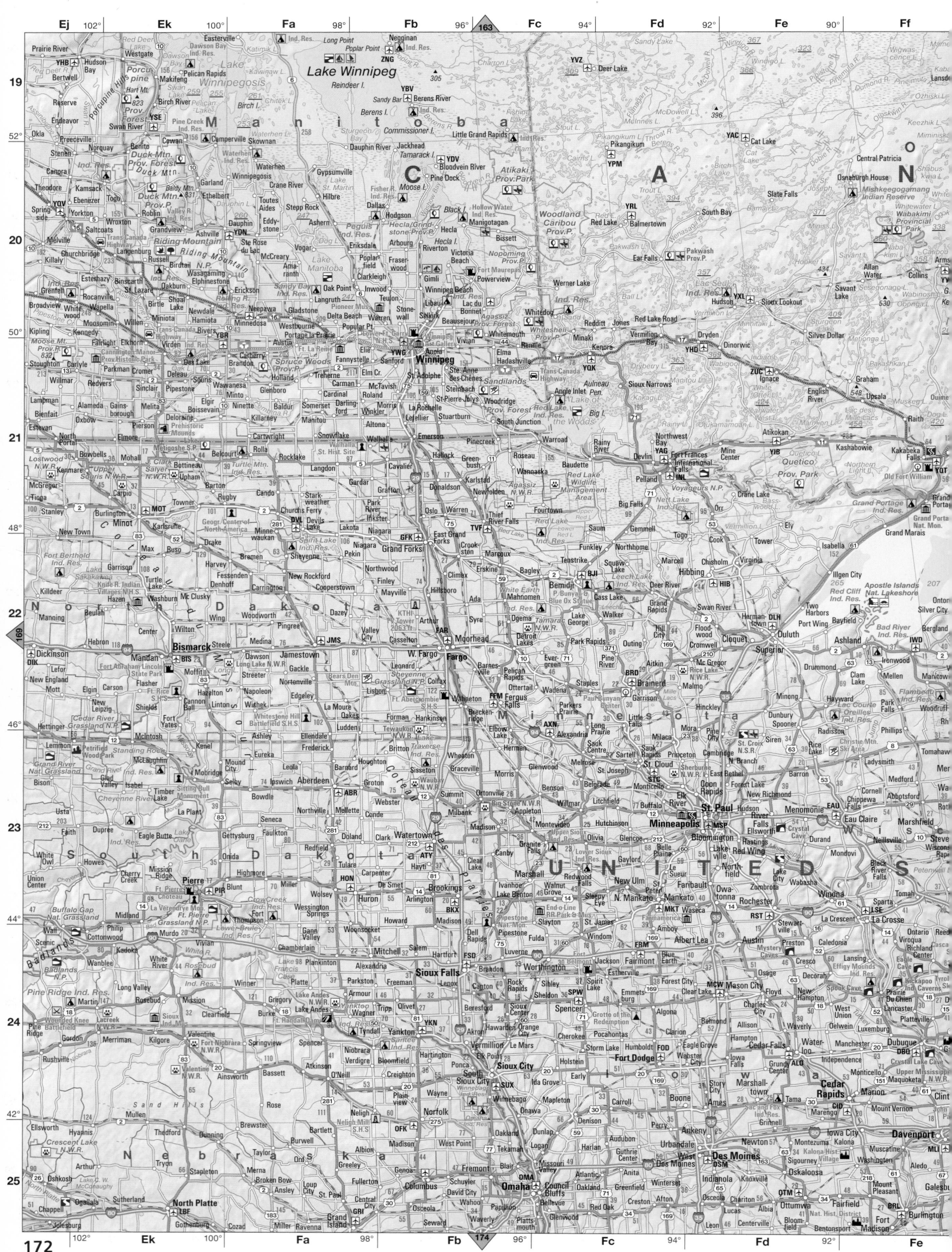

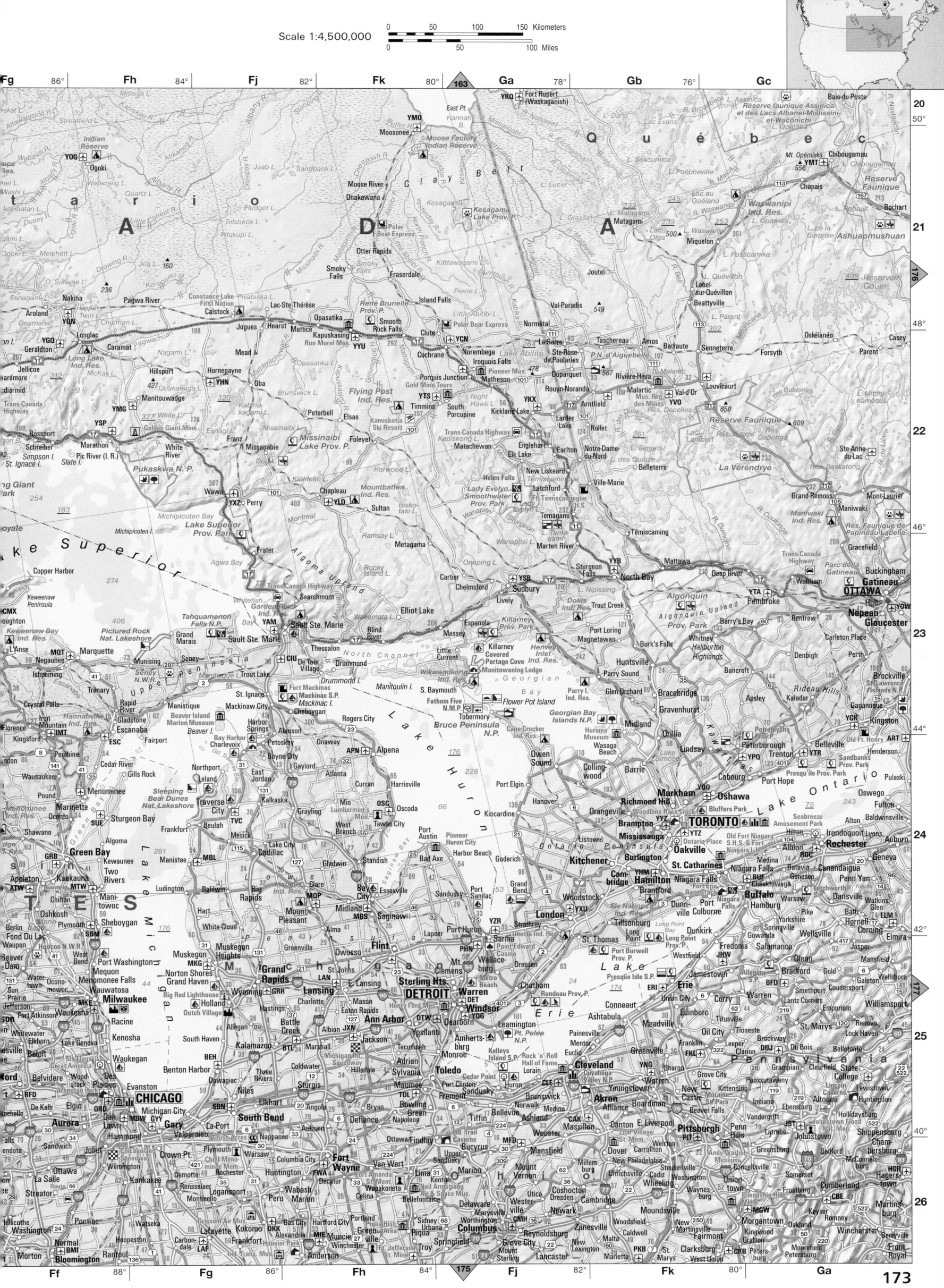

Scale 1:4,500,000

0   50   100   150 Kilometers

0   50   100 Miles

| Fg | 86° | Fh | 84° | Fj | 82° | Fk | 80° | Ga | 78° | Gb | 76° | Gc |

Québec

Ontario

Lake Superior

Lake Huron

Lake Michigan

Lake Erie

Lake Ontario

Georgian Bay

Pennsylvania

Ohio

TORONTO

OTTAWA

Gatineau

Nepean

Gloucester

DETROIT

CHICAGO

Milwaukee

Green Bay

Sault Ste. Marie

Sudbury

North Bay

Cleveland

Pittsburgh

Buffalo

Rochester

Hamilton

London

Windsor

Toledo

Columbus

Fort Wayne

Grand Rapids

Lansing

Flint

Ann Arbor

Kitchener

St. Catharines

Niagara Falls

Oshawa

Markham

Mississauga

Brampton

Oakville

Burlington

Akron

Erie

Marquette

Bloomington

| 20 | 50° |
| 21 |
| 22 |
| 23 |
| 24 |
| 25 |
| 26 |

| Ff | 88° | Fg | 86° | Fh | 84° | Fj | 82° | Fk | 80° | Ga |

175

176

177

173

Southern States

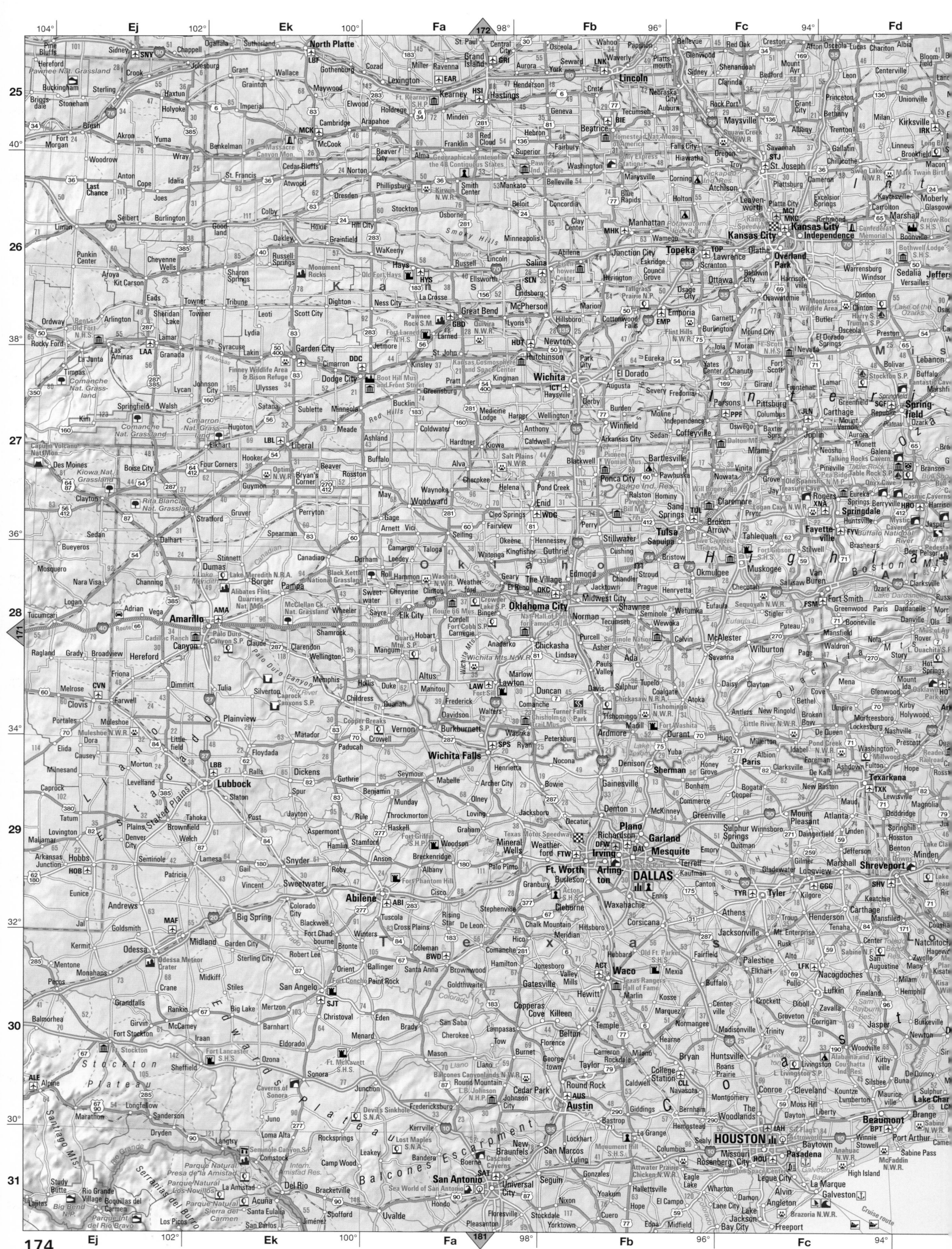

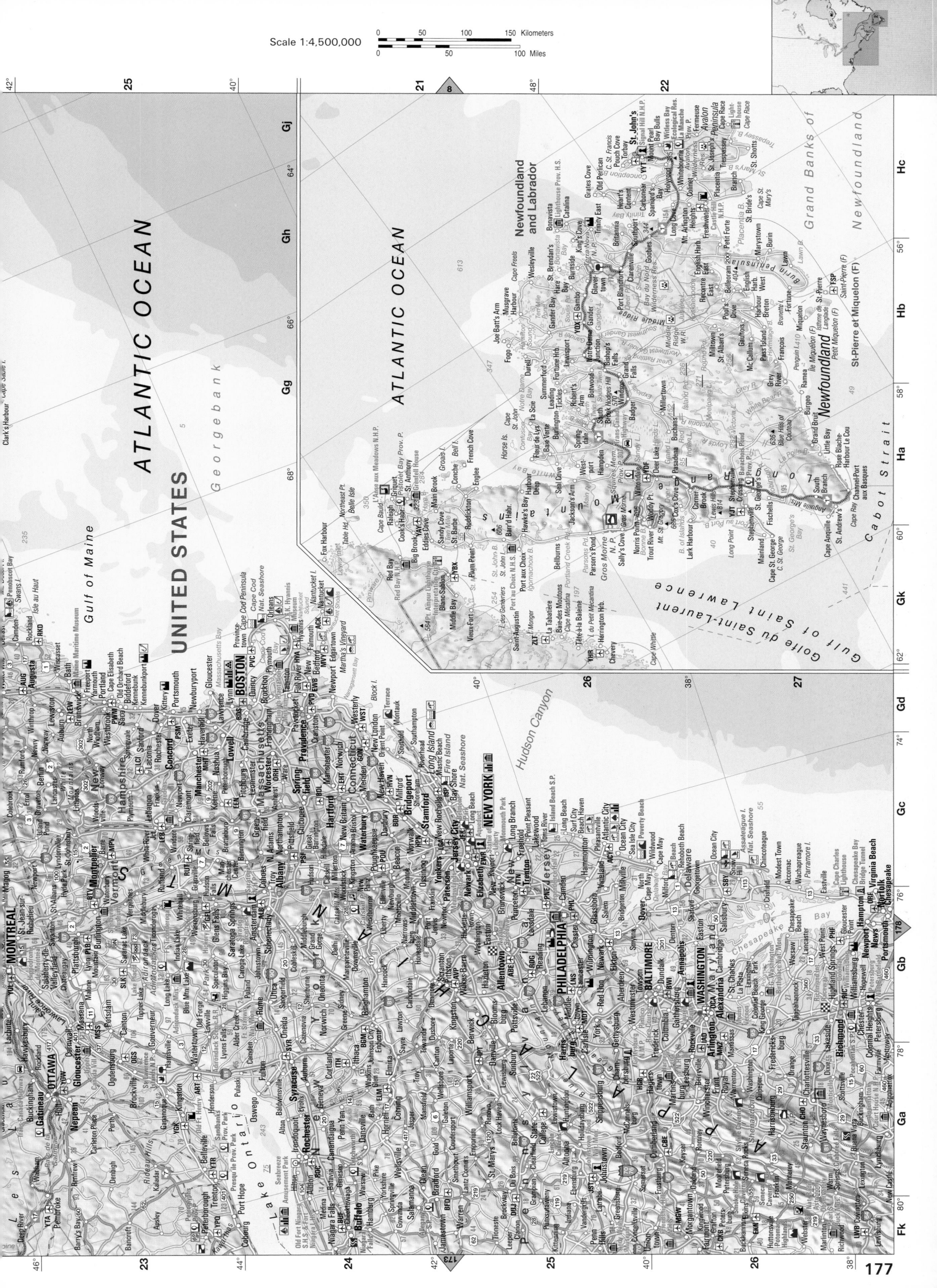

Scale 1:4,500,000

0   50   100   150 Kilometers
0   50   100 Miles

ATLANTIC OCEAN

UNITED STATES

Gulf of Maine

Georgebank

ATLANTIC OCEAN

Newfoundland and Labrador

Newfoundland

Grand Banks of Newfoundland

Cabot Strait

Golfe du Saint-Laurent
Gulf of Saint Lawrence

St. John's

St-Pierre et Miquelon (F)

BOSTON

NEW YORK

PHILADELPHIA

BALTIMORE

WASHINGTON

MONTREAL

OTTAWA

Lake Ontario

Hudson Canyon

Chesapeake Bay

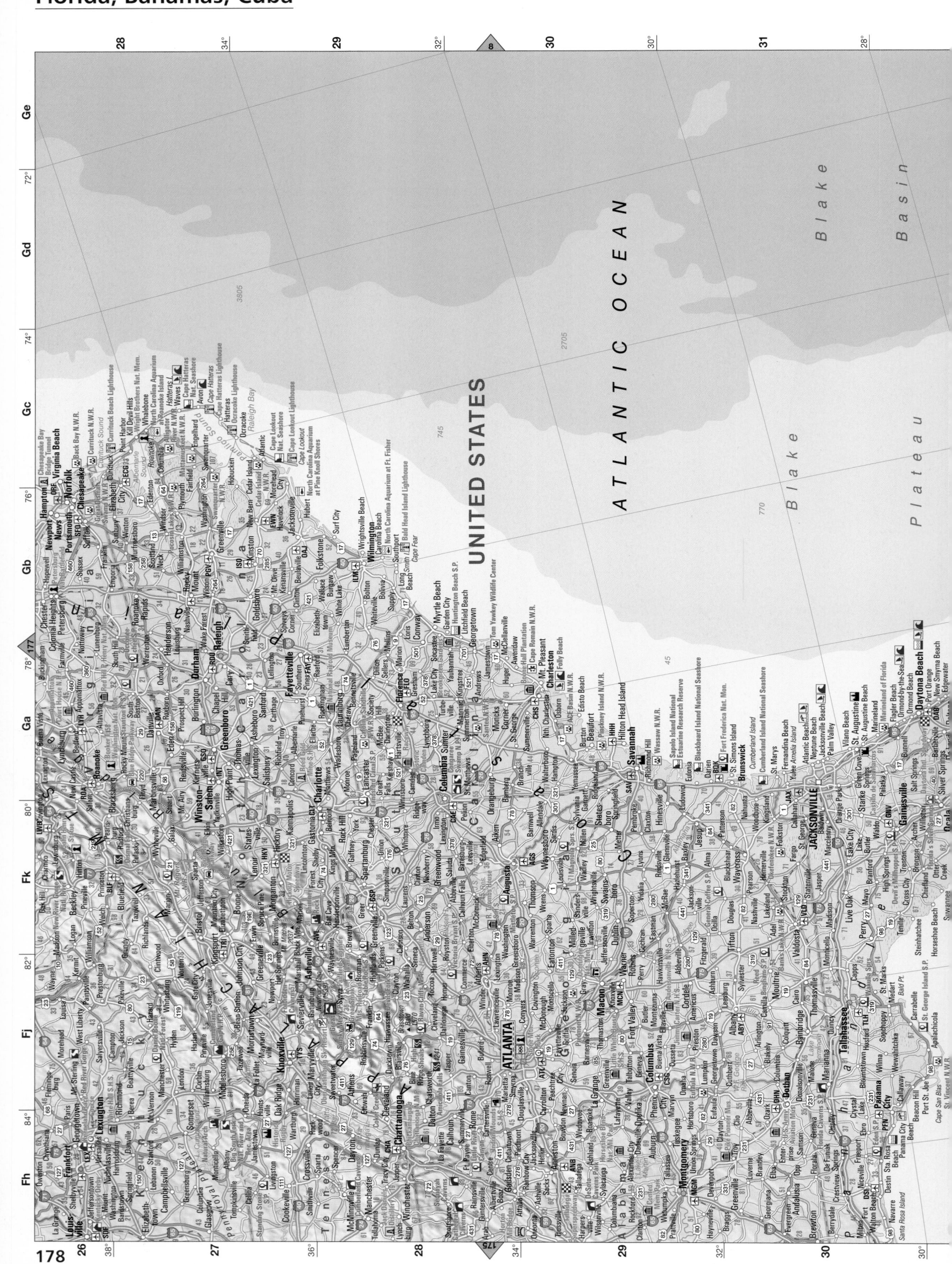

Scale 1:4,500,000

0   50   100   150   Kilometers
0   50   100   Miles

186

BAHAMAS

B a h a m a s

WEST INDIES

Walker's Cay
Fish Cays
Great Sale Cay
Mangrove Cay
Grand Bahama
Freeport
West End
Eight Mile Rock
Xanadu Beach
FPO
Lucaya

Great Guana Cay
Green Turtle Cay
Cedar Harbour
Cooper's Town
McLean's Town
Cross Cay
Water Cay
Moore's Island
Abaco Island
High Rock
MHH
Marsh Harbour
Great Harbour Cay
Cherokee Sound
Hope Town
Cherokee Rocks
Little Harbour
Sandy Point

Preacher's Cave
Dunmore Town
Glass Window Bridge
Alice Town
Current
Eleuthera Island
Spanish Wells
Governor's Harbour
Palmetto Point
ELH
Rock Sound
Powell Point
Tarpum Bay
RSD
East End Point

Northwest Point
San Salvador (Guanahani Island)
ZSA
Columbus Monument
Southwest Point
New Bight
Cat Island
Port Howe
Devil's Point
The Hermitage

Arthur's Town
Port Nelson
Colimbus Pt.
Stella Maris
Simms
LGI
Clarence Town
William's Town
Deadman's Cay
Mortimers
Long Island

Cay Verde
Cay Santo Domingo
Lloyd Rock (The Brothers)
Raccon Cay
Ragged Islands
Ragged Island Range
Duncan Town

Cockburn Town

Cabo Lucrecia
Cayo de María la Gorda
Gibara
Rafael Freyre
Banes
HOG
Holguín
Mayarí Arriba
Moa
Baracoa
SNU
Guantánamo
Santiago de Cuba

JAMAICA
Montego Bay
MBJ Río Bueno
Falmouth
Ocho Rios
Kingston
Negril
Savanna

CUBA
Matanzas
Cárdenas
VRA Varadero
LA HABANA (HAVANA)
Cienfuegos
CFG
Santa Clara
TND Trinidad
Sancti Spíritus
Camagüey
CMW

Cayman Islands (UK)
Grand Cayman
GCM
Georgetown
Seven Mile Beach

G r e a t e r   A n t i l l e s

Florida
MIAMI
Miami Beach
Fort Lauderdale
Hollywood
West Palm Beach
Coral Springs
Hialeah
MIA
Homestead
Key Largo
Marathon
EYW Key West
Big Pine Key
Florida Keys

Tampa
St. Petersburg
Clearwater
Sarasota
Bradenton
Fort Myers
Cape Coral
Naples

Gulf of Mexico

M e x i c a n   B a s i n

Straits of Florida

MÉXICO
Cancún
CUN
Isla Mujeres
Cozumel
CZM
Puerto Morelos
Playa del Carmen
Tulum

Yucatán Channel
Estrecho de Yucatán

185
183

179

Northern Mexico

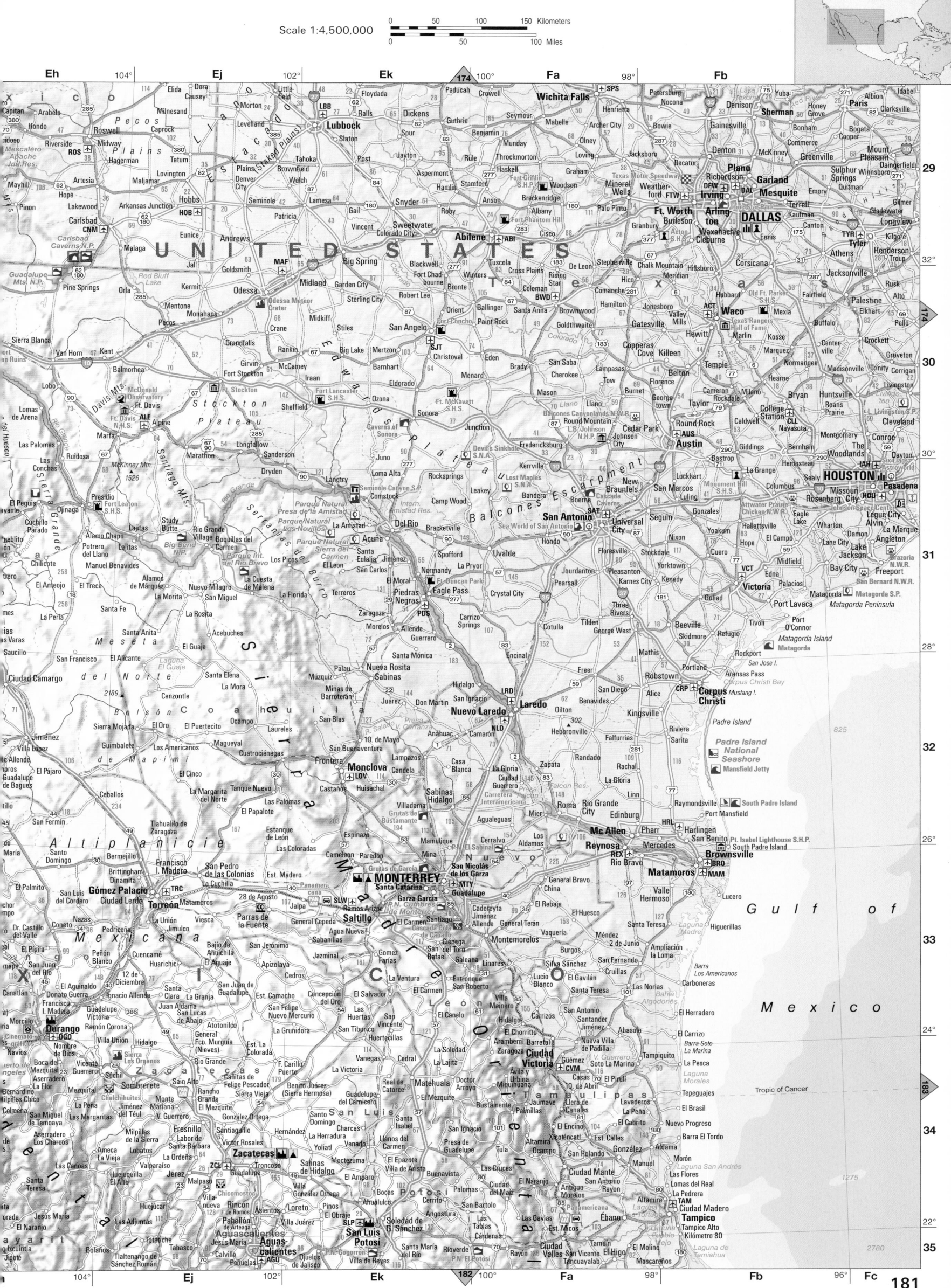

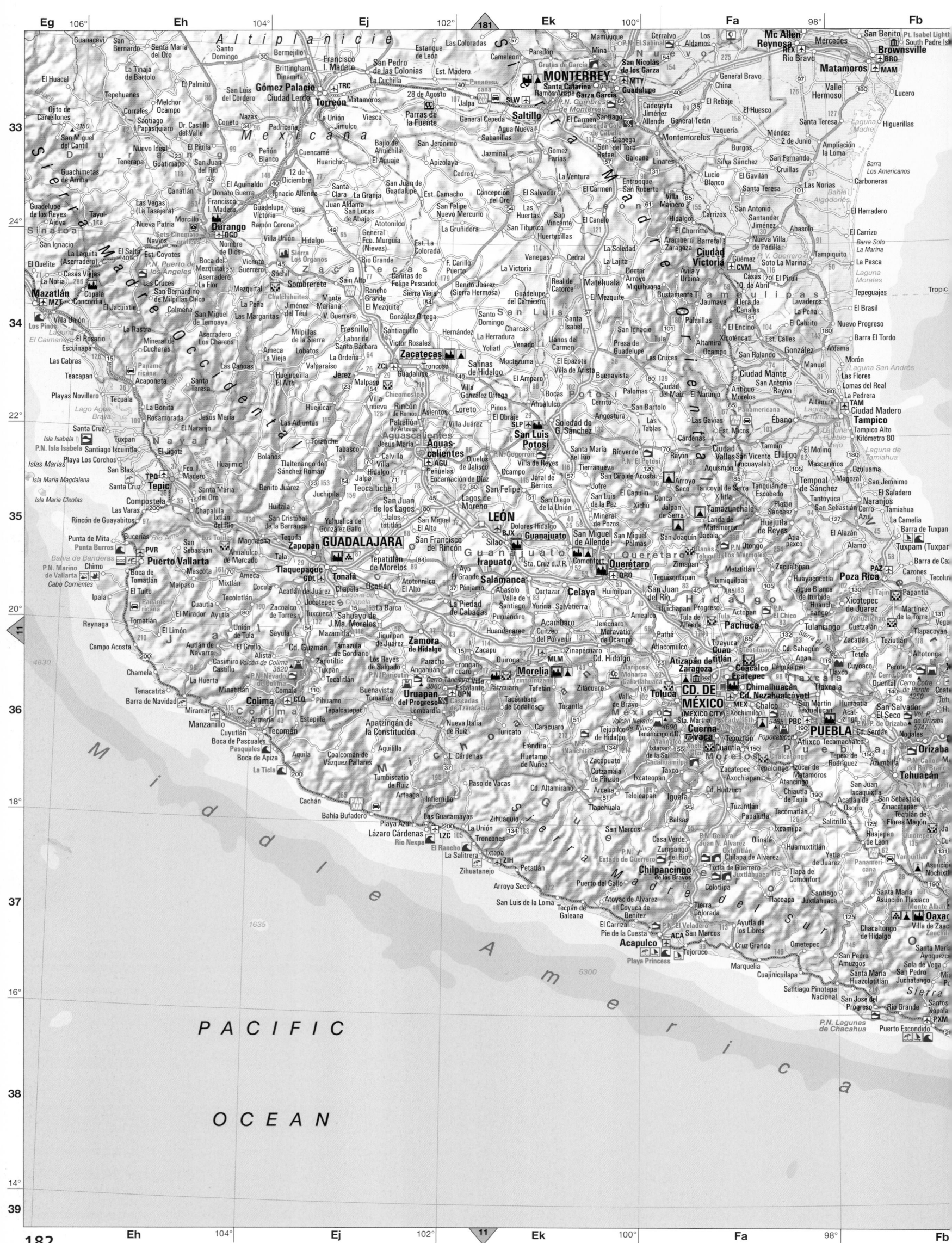

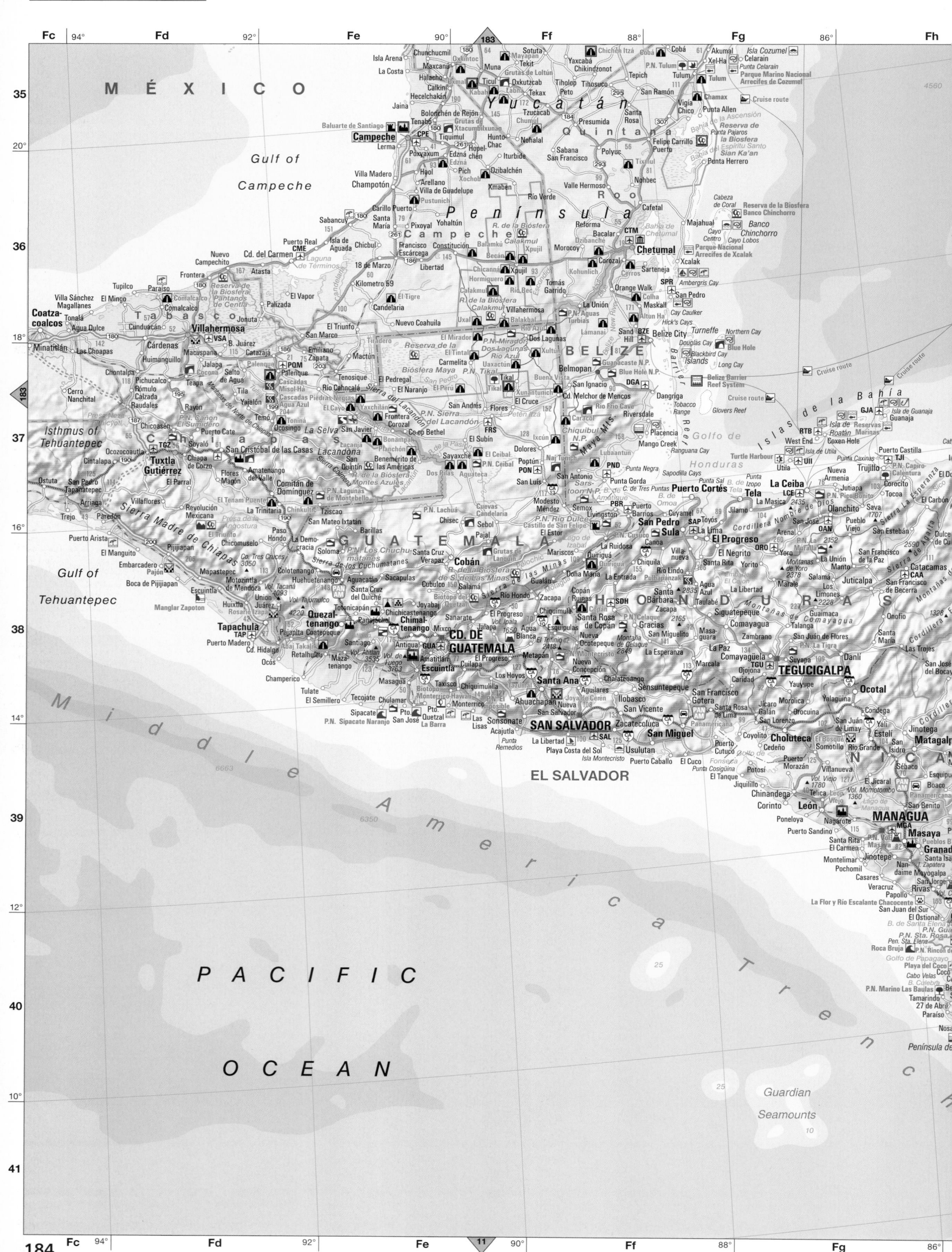

Scale 1:4,500,000

0   50   100   150 Kilometers

0   50   100 Miles

Cayman Ridge

Cayman Islands (UK)

West Bay   GCM
Seven Mile Beach
Georgetown
Grand Cayman
6270

440

26

Cayman Trench

Columbus
Landing 1494   Dunns River
MBJ Rio Bueno   Falls   Ocho Rios   Port Maria   Port Antonio   Cruise route
Montego Bay   Brown's   OCJ   Moneague   Annotto Bay   Long Bay Beach
Lucea   Falmouth   Town   Moneague   77   Manchioneal   18°
Negril Beach   Gourie   Lonstead   Beach Falls
Negril   Cambridge   Middlequaters   Spanish   Blue   Golden Grove
NEG   May Pen   Town   Morant
Savanna-la-Mar   Mandeville   Kingston   Bay   37
Black River   282   KIN
Treasure Beach   Lower   Portland
Great Pedro   Alligator   The Alley   Bight
Bluff   Pond   Portland
JAMAICA   Point   Morant
Cays

16°

Pedro Cays

28   Pedrobank

186

1030

Explorerbank

Rosalind-
bank
12   Bajo Nuevo
(CO.)   38

Banco de Serranilla (CO.)   East Cay
5   West Breaker

Cayos Cajones

Cayo Caratasca   Cayo Gorda
Cayo Becerro   Cayos
Cayo Vivorillo   Cocorocuma   C A R I B B E A N   S E A   Colombia   14°

Matano   Bancos del
Punta Patuca   Cabo Falso   Arrecifes de la
Laguna   Cayos Mayores   Media Luna   2150
de Brus   del Cabo Falso   Arrecife
ano   Ahuas   Alargado   Basin
Laguna
de Caratasca   Cabo Gracias   North Cay   39
Puerto Lempira   a Dios   Arrecife   Banco de
Sirsirtara   PEU   Edinburgh   Quitasueño   Banco de
Mocorón   Laguna   (CO.)   Serrana
de Colón   Bismuna   (CO.)
bila   South Cay
Waspan   Laguna   Cayos Morrison Dennis
Cocoland   Tabens   Punta   Cayos   Cayos de
Quaquel   Gorda   Cayos NASA   Roncador   12°
a de las   The Wittes   (CO.)
era   PUZ
nza   Puerto Cabezas
La Rosita   Laguna
Baká   Karatá
awas   Isla de Providencia   4220
Alamikamba   Laguna   (CO.)
Makataka   de Huaunta
San Pedro   Cayos Guerrero   40
del Norte   Río Grande   Isla de San Andrés (CO.) ADZ
Chile   Cayo Tyara   San Andrés   Cayos de E.S.E.
Cayos King   Punta Sur   (CO.)
Domingo   164   Laguna
Tomás   de   Cayos de
La Gateada   Perlas   Cayos de Perlas   Albuquerque
pa   Cordillera Chontaleña   Punta de Perlas   (CO.)
Nueva Guinea   Laguna de las Perlas   10°
GUA   I. de Maíz Pequeña
rrito   Punta Gorda   RNI   I. de Maíz Grande
San   BEF   El Bluff
Miguelito   Bluefields
icaragua   Bahía de
San Carlos   Bluefields
pala   El Castillo   San Juan del Norte   Bahía
LSL   Punta Castilla   Punta Gorda   2205
N. Val.   Indio-Maíz
ono   Los Chiles   P.N. Tortuguero   Isthmus of Panama   Archipiélago   Gulf of   41
San Rafael   Boca Arenal   Santa   de San Blas   Puerto Escondido
Arenal   Puerto Viejo   Palenque Isabel   El Porvenir   Darién
P.N. Vol.   P.N. J.C.   2745   Portobelo   El Valle   Arboletes
P.N. Vol.   Blanco   P.N. Braulio   Fuerte San Lorenzo   P.N. Portobelo   Carti Suitopo   Ailigandi   San Juán de Urabá
Juntas   Cairo   Carrillo   112   Colón   Salamanca   P.N. El Llano   PUE   San Fuerte
San Ramón   Matina   Puerto Limón   M.N. Isla Barro Colorado   Chilibre   Cordillera de San Blás   Puerto   San Bernardo
Alajuela   Guápiles   Boca de Río Indio   Chepo   Lago Bayano   Obaldia   del Viento   Monitos
Asunción   Gamboa   PAN   Acandi   Mulatos   170
San José   Penshurst   Cuipo   A   118   Cañazas   Santa Fé   Necoclé
LIO   Turrialba   La Arenosa   PTY   Chimán   192
SJO   Pandora   Bribri   Panamá   Meteti   Turbo   TRB
Cartago   Puerto Viejo   Balboa   Bahía   Yaviza
Santiago   San Mateo   BOC   La Chorrera   de Panamá   San Miguel   Golfo   8°
CA   138   Arch. de   Penonomé   Archipiélago   I. Pedro González   PYV   de Uraba
Jacó   Bocas   del Toro   Belén   P.N. Campana   1173   Isla de Rey   Púcuro
Parrita   XQP San Isidro   Almirante   Omar Torrijos - El Cope   El Cope   de   La Palma   Chigorodó
Quepos   de El General   I. Bastimentos   La Pintada   1173   San Carlos   las Perlas   Puerto Indio   P.N.
P.N. Manual Antonio   Buenos Aires   Santa Fé   Gatu   El Caño   Garachiné   Los   P.N. Paramillo
Dominical   178   Cerro   Santa Fé   Colobre   Río Hato   I. San José   Katios   2000
Punta Mala   Paso Real   Volcán   Punta   El Espinal   Golfo   de las Perlas   Garachiné   3400
COSTA RICA   Buenos Aires   Volcán   Boquete   Divisa   Puerto Piña   Mutatá   Murindó   Dabeiba
I. del Caño   Rincón   Río Claro   La Concepción   Horn-   San Bartolo   Santiago   Jaqué   Cupica   42
Peninsula de Osa   Palo Grande   DAV   concitos   San Francisco   Soná   Las Tablas   Punta Marzo
P.N. Corcovado   GLF Neily   David   Soná   Los Santos   R.V.S. Iguana   Bahía Solano   COLOMBIA   6°
Carate PJM   Puerto   Guabala   Cupica   (Ciudad Mutis)   Bebarama
Palma Sur   El María   Ponuga   Pedasi   P.N. Las
Puerto Armuelles   La Soledad   Pilón   Macaracas Pocrí   Punta Mala   Orquidias
Limones   Islas Secas   Llano   R.V.S. Canas
Punta Burica   Punta Cristo   Santa Catalina   Tonosí   Pto. Arquia
Isla de   Penal   Punta   Pto. Solano
Coiba   Colony   I. de   Cambutal
Cébaco
I. Montuosa   Punta Anegada   Punta
P.N. Isla Coiba   P.N. Cerro   Mariato
I. Jicarón   Hoya

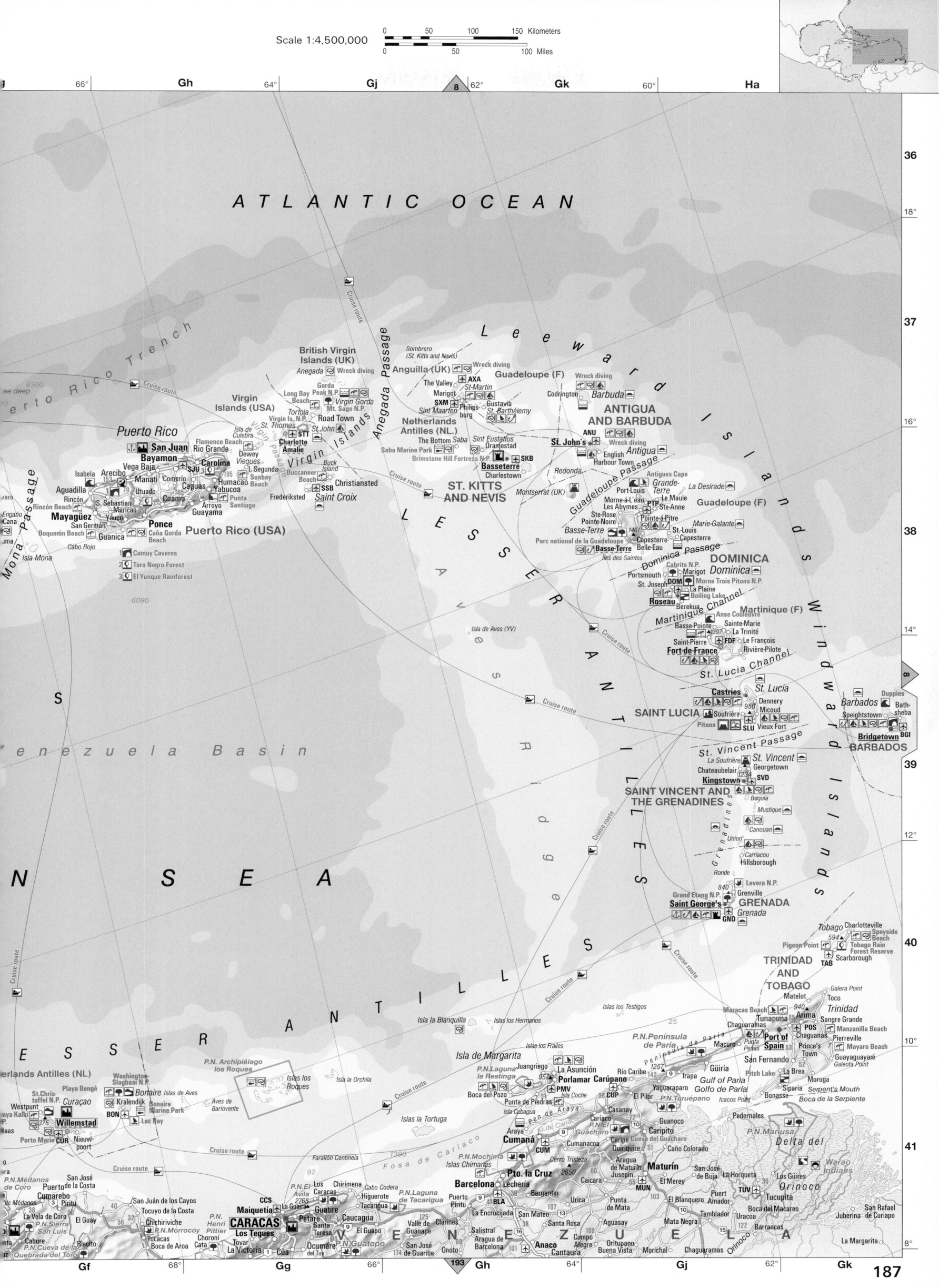

A rainbow spans the cascading Iguaçu falls amid the primeval forest.

Brazil's metropolis Rio de Janeiro: Copacabana and Sugarloaf Mountain.

SOUTH AMERICA

MAGNIFICENT PASSIONS, STUNNING LANDSCAPES

Compared to the other continents South America is a relatively compact landmass. It has smooth coastlines and a consistently flat relief – outside of the Andes. The southern continent of the western hemisphere is 7,500 kilometers long from north to south and the greatest distance from east to west measures 4,800 kilometers. The continent borders Central (and North) America at the Isthmus of Panama.

The Andes, the world's second highest mountain range after the Himalayas, rise to the east of the continent's Pacific coast. Aconcagua in Argentina is the highest mountain in the Western Hemisphere. Other significant mountain ranges in South America include the Pakaraima Mountains in the north and the Serra do Mar in Brazil. Between these two mountainous regions lies the vast basin of the Amazon River. With a length of 6,400 kilometers, the Amazon is the second longest river in the world after the Nile. The marshy land of the Gran Chaco is located north of the fertile Pampas and the sparsely populated region of Patagonia. The flat basin of the Orinoco River (2,140 km) occupies a large area in northern South America.

There are twelve independent nations in South America as well as French Guiana, a territory of France. South America is home to 304 million people, more than half of whom live in Brazil. Centuries of contact between Europeans, Amerindians and Africans has made the population of South America the most ethnically and racially mixed in the world. No other continent is as religiously homogeneous as South America. Almost 90 % of the continent's people are Roman Catholics. Migration from rural areas to cities continues to expand the population of cities in the region. In recent decades, the continent's cities have grown explosively. Most of South America's large cities are surrounded by large distirct of slums, home to the poorest members of society.

The Quechua live in the South American Andes.

South America

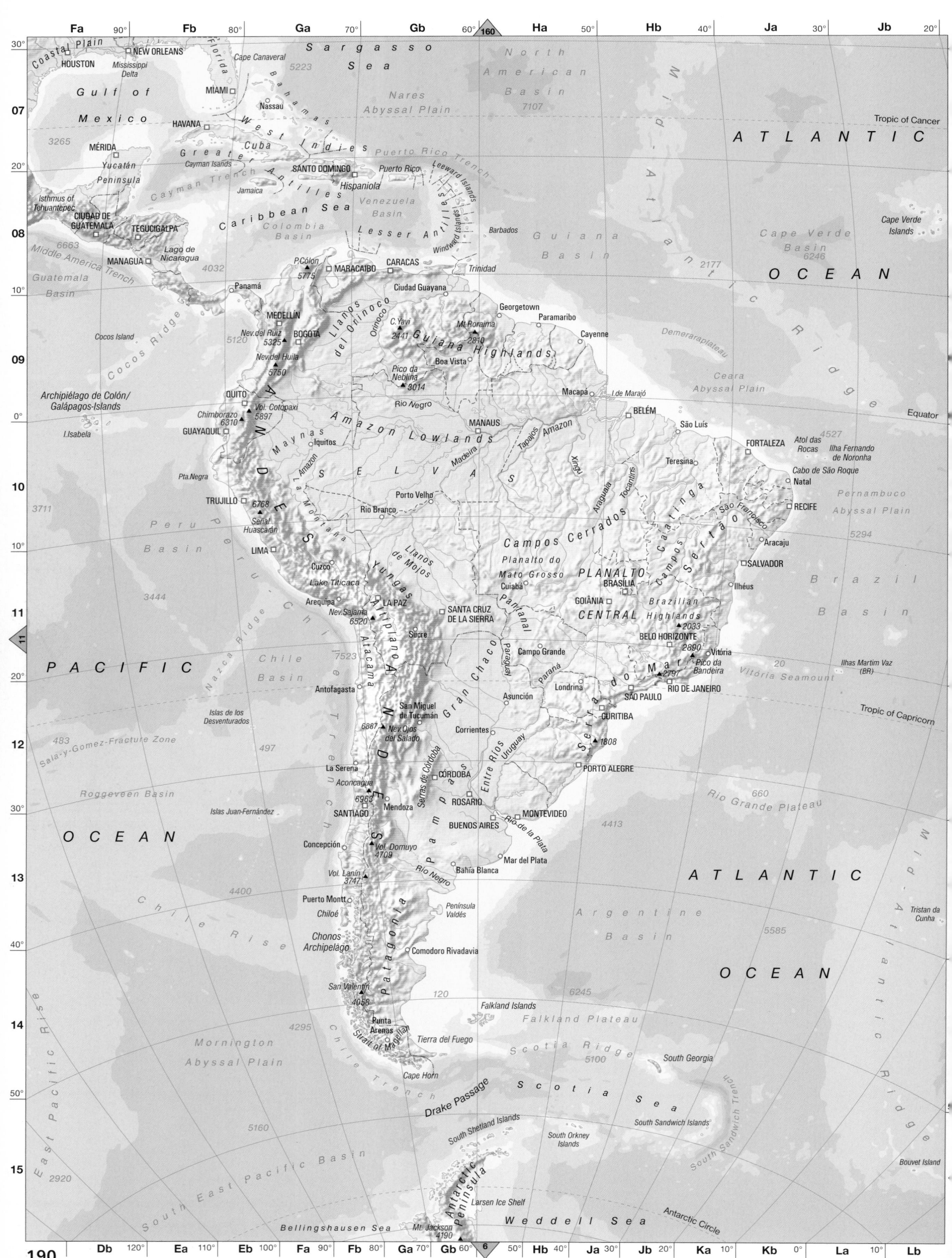

PACIFIC OCEAN

ATLANTIC OCEAN

Gulf of Mexico

Sargasso Sea

Caribbean Sea

Caribbean Sea

HOUSTON
NEW ORLEANS
Coastal Plain
Mississippi Delta
Cape Canaveral
5223
Florida
MIAMI
Bahamas
Nassau
MÉRIDA
3265
HAVANA
Cuba
Cayman Trench
Cayman Isands
Jamaica
Yucatán Peninsula
Isthmus of Tehuantepec
CIUDAD DE GUATEMALA
TEGUCIGALPA
MANAGUA
Lago de Nicaragua
6663
Middle America Trench
Guatemala Basin
Cocos Island
Cocos Ridge
4032
P.Cólon
5775
MARACAIBO
CARACAS
Trinidad
MEDELLÍN
Nev. del Ruiz
5325
Nev. del Huila
5750
BOGOTÁ
QUITO
Chimborazo
6310
Vol. Cotopaxi
5897
GUAYAQUIL
I.Isabela
Archipiélago de Colón/Galápagos-Islands
Pta.Negra
TRUJILLO
6768
Señal Huascarán
3711
LIMA
Peru Basin
3444
Arequipa
Cuzco
Lake Titicaca
Nev.Sajama
6520
LA PAZ
Sucre
Atacama
7523
Antofagasta
Nazca Ridge
Chile Basin
483
Sala-y-Gomez-Fracture Zone
497
San Miguel de Tucumán
6887
Nev Ojos del Salado
La Serena
Aconcagua
6963
Islas Juan-Fernández
Roggeveen Basin
Islas de los Desventurados
SANTIAGO
Mendoza
Concepción
Vol. Domuyo
4709
Vol. Lanín
3747
4400
Puerto Montt
Chiloé
Chonos Archipiélago
San Valentín
4058
Patagonia
4295
Punta Arenas
Strait of Magellan
5160
Mornington Abyssal Plain
2920
East Pacific Rise
Pacific Rise
South East Pacific Basin
Chile Rise
Chile Trench

Llanos del Orinoco
C.Yavi
2441
Mt Roraima
2810
Boa Vista
Pico da Neblina
3014
Rio Negro
Amazon Lowlands
MANAUS
Maynas
Iquitos
Amazon
S E L V A
Rio Branco
Porto Velho
Madeira
Tapajós
Xingu
Amazon
S
Llanos de Mojos
Cuiabá
Campos Cerrados
Planalto do Mato Grosso
Pantanal
SANTA CRUZ DE LA SIERRA
Gran Chaco
Paraguay
Campo Grande
Asunción
Corrientes
Paraná
Paraná
Pampas
Entre Rios
Uruguay
CÓRDOBA
Serras de Córdoba
ROSARIO
MONTEVIDEO
BUENOS AIRES
Río de la Plata
Mar del Plata
Rio Negro
Bahía Blanca
Península Valdés
Comodoro Rivadavia
120
Tierra del Fuego
Cape Horn
Falkland Islands

Orinoco
Ciudad Guayana
Georgetown
Paramaribo
Cayenne
Guiana Highlands
Macapá
I. de Marajó
BELÉM
São Luís
FORTALEZA
Atol das Rocas
4527
Ilha Fernando de Noronha
Teresina
Caatinga
Natal
Cabo de São Roque
RECIFE
São Francisco
Sertão
Aracaju
SALVADOR
Ilhéus
PLANALTO
BRASÍLIA
GOIÂNIA
CENTRAL Highlands
2033
Brazilian Highlands
BELO HORIZONTE
2890
Vitória
Pico da Bandeira
2797
Serra do Mar
1808
RIO DE JANEIRO
SÃO PAULO
Londrina
CURITIBA
PORTO ALEGRE
20
Vitória Seamount
Ilhas Martim Vaz (BR)

North American Basin
7107
Nares Abyssal Plain
Puerto Rico Trench
SANTO DOMINGO
Hispaniola
Puerto Rico
Leeward Islands
Lesser Antilles
Windward Islands
Barbados
Venezuela Basin
Guiana Basin
6246
Cape Verde Basin
Cape Verde Islands
2177
Demerara plateau
Ceara Abyssal Plain
Equator
Pernambuco Abyssal Plain
5294
Brazil Basin
Río Grande Plateau
660
4413
5585
Tristan da Cunha
Argentine Basin
6245
Falkland Plateau
Scotia Ridge
5100
South Georgia
Bouvet Island
Scotia Sea
South Sandwich Islands
South Sandwich Trench
South Orkney Islands
South Shetland Islands
Drake Passage
Antarctic Peninsula
Larsen Ice Shelf
Weddell Sea
Bellingshausen Sea
Mt. Jackson
4190
Antarctic Circle

ANDES

Tropic of Cancer
Tropic of Capricorn

A T L A N T I C   O C E A N

P A C I F I C   O C E A N

A T L A N T I C   O C E A N

Mid-Atlantic Ridge

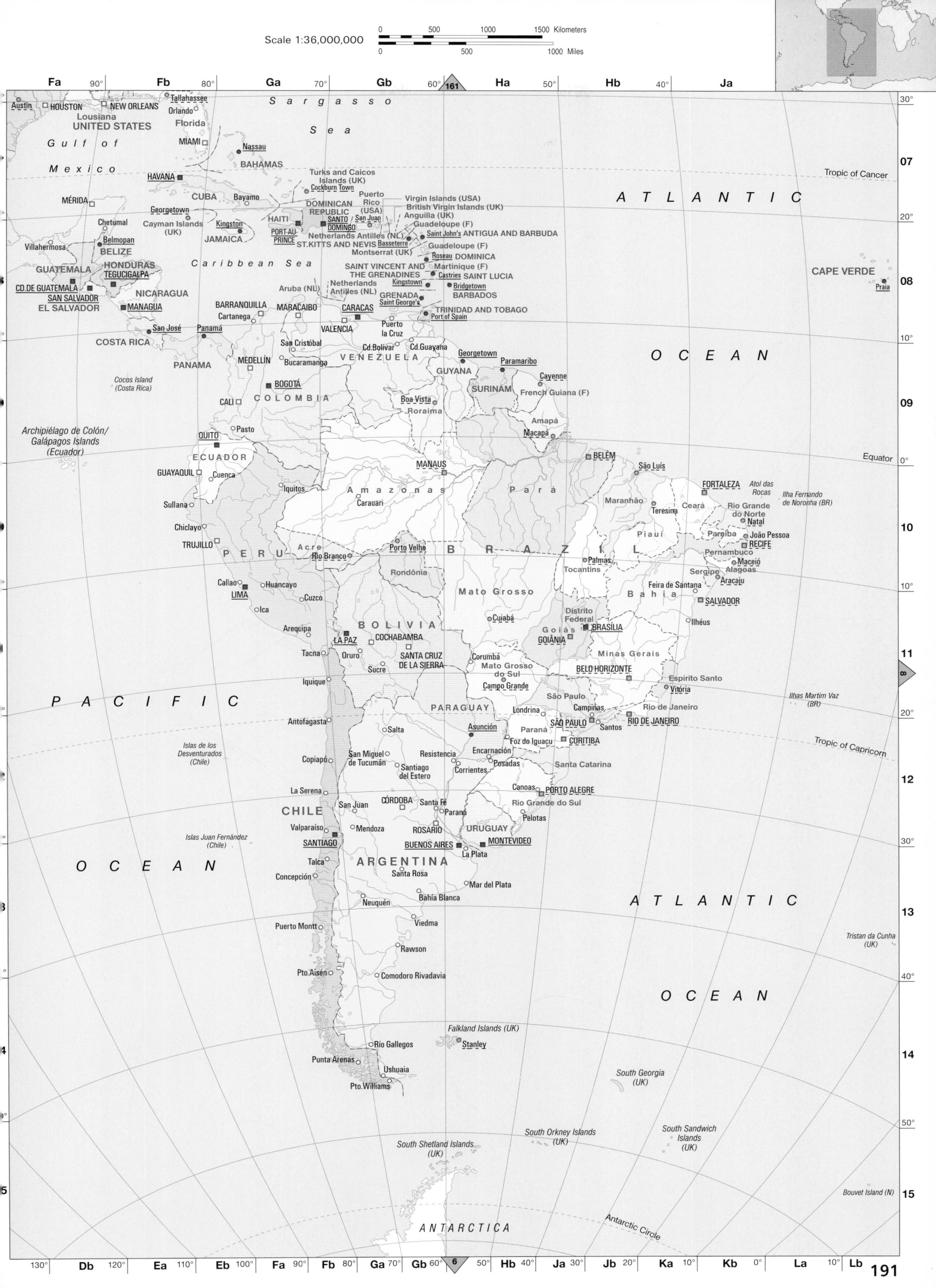

Scale 1:36,000,000

| 0 | 500 | 1000 | 1500 Kilometers |

| 0 | 500 | 1000 Miles |

Fa 90° **Fb** 80° **Ga** 70° **Gb** 60° 161 **Ha** 50° **Hb** 40° **Ja**

S a r g a s s o

Austin □ HOUSTON □ NEW ORLEANS • Tallahassee
Lousiana Orlando
UNITED STATES Florida
Gulf of MIAMI □
M e x i c o • Nassau
BAHAMAS

30°

S e a

A T L A N T I C

07 Tropic of Cancer

HAVANA □ Turks and Caicos
MÉRIDA □ Islands (UK)
• Cockburn Town
Chetumal □ CUBA • Bayamo Puerto
Georgetown □ Rico Virgin Islands (USA)
• Belmopan Cayman Islands Kingston (USA) British Virgin Islands (UK)
Villahermosa • BELIZE (UK) HAITI San Juan Anguilla (UK)
□ JAMAICA PORT-AU- DOMINICAN Guadeloupe (F)
GUATEMALA PRINCE REPUBLIC SANTO / San Juan Saint John's ANTIGUA AND BARBUDA
HONDURAS ST.KITTS AND NEVIS Basseterre Guadeloupe (F)
TEGUCIGALPA □ Netherlands Antilles (NL) Montserrat (UK) • Roseau DOMINICA
CD.DE GUATEMALA □ SAINT VINCENT AND Martinique (F)
SAN SALVADOR □ Aruba (NL) THE GRENADINES Castries SAINT LUCIA
EL SALVADOR □ MANAGUA Netherlands Kingstown • BARBADOS
NICARAGUA Antilles (NL) GRENADA Bridgetown •
BARRANQUILLA • Saint George's • BARBADOS
• San José MARACAIBO □ TRINIDAD AND TOBAGO
Panamá • Cartanega • CARACAS □ Port of Spain
COSTA RICA VALENCIA • Puerto
PANAMA San Cristóbal • la Cruz
MEDELLÍN □ Cd.Bolívar • Cd.Guayana •
• Bucaramanga V E N E Z U E L A Georgetown □ Paramaribo □
Cocos Island BOGOTÁ □ GUYANA SURINAM • Cayenne
(Costa Rica) CALI • Boa Vista • French Guiana (F)
COLOMBIA • Roraima

08 CAPE VERDE
Praia □

09

C a r i b b e a n   S e a

O C E A N

10°

QUITO □ Amapá •
Archipiélago de Colón/ Macapá •
Galápagos Islands ECUADOR • Pasto
(Ecuador) Equator **0°**

GUAYAQUIL • MANAUS □ BELÉM □ São Luís •
• Cuenca A m a z o n a s P a r á FORTALEZA □ Atol das
Sullana • • Carauari Maranhão Ceará Rocas Ilha Fernando
Chiclayo • • Teresina Rio Grande de Noronha (BR)
Iquitos • do Norte • Natal
TRUJILLO □ Acre Porto Velho • B R A Z I L Piauí Paraíba • João Pessoa
P E R U Rio Branco • Rondônia • Palmas RECIFE □
Callao □ Tocantins Pernambuco
• Huancayo Maceió •
LIMA □ • Cuzco M a t o   G r o s s o Sergipe Alagoas
• Ica Feira de Santana • • Aracaju
Arequipa • Cuiabá • B a h i a SALVADOR □
B O L I V I A Distrito
• Tacna LA PAZ □ COCHABAMBA Federal • Ilhéus
Oruro • Corumbá • G o i á s BRASÍLIA □
SANTA CRUZ Mato Grosso GOIÂNIA □
• Sucre DE LA SIERRA do Sul M i n a s   G e r a i s
Iquique • Campo Grande • BELO HORIZONTE □
Antofagasta • P A R A G U A Y Londrina • Campinas Espírito Santo
Salta • Asunción □ São Paulo • Vitória
Islas de los Paraná SÃO PAULO □ Rio de Janeiro •
Desventurados Copiapó • San Miguel Encarnación • Foz do Iguaçu • CURITIBA □ Santos RIO DE JANEIRO □
(Chile) de Tucumán • • Posadas Santa Catarina
• Resistencia • Corrientes Canoas • □ PORTO ALEGRE
La Serena • Santiago Rio Grande do Sul
del Estero CÓRDOBA □ Santa Fe • • Pelotas
San Juan • Paraná •
Islas Juan Fernández Valparaíso • • Mendoza ROSARIO □ URUGUAY
(Chile) SANTIAGO □ BUENOS AIRES □ □ MONTEVIDEO
• Talca A R G E N T I N A La Plata •
• Concepción Santa Rosa •
Neuquén • Bahía Blanca • Mar del Plata

10°

P A C I F I C

11

20° Tropic of Capricorn

12

30°

O C E A N

A T L A N T I C

• Puerto Montt • Viedma

13

Ilhas Martim Vaz
(BR)

Tristan da Cunha
(UK)

Pto.Aisén • • Comodoro Rivadavia

O C E A N

40°

Falkland Islands (UK)
• Río Gallegos • Stanley
Punta Arenas • • Ushuaia
Pto.Williams •

14

South Georgia
(UK)

50° South Orkney Islands
(UK)

South Sandwich
Islands
(UK)

South Shetland Islands
(UK)

Bouvet Island (N) **15**

A N T A R C T I C A Antarctic Circle

130° **Db** **120°** **Ea** **110°** **Eb** **100°** **Fa** **90°** **Fb** **80°** **Ga** **70°** **Gb** **60°** 6 **50°** **Hb** **40°** **Ja** **30°** **Jb** **20°** **Ka** **10°** **Kb** **0°** **La** **10°** **Lb**

191

Colombia, Venezuela

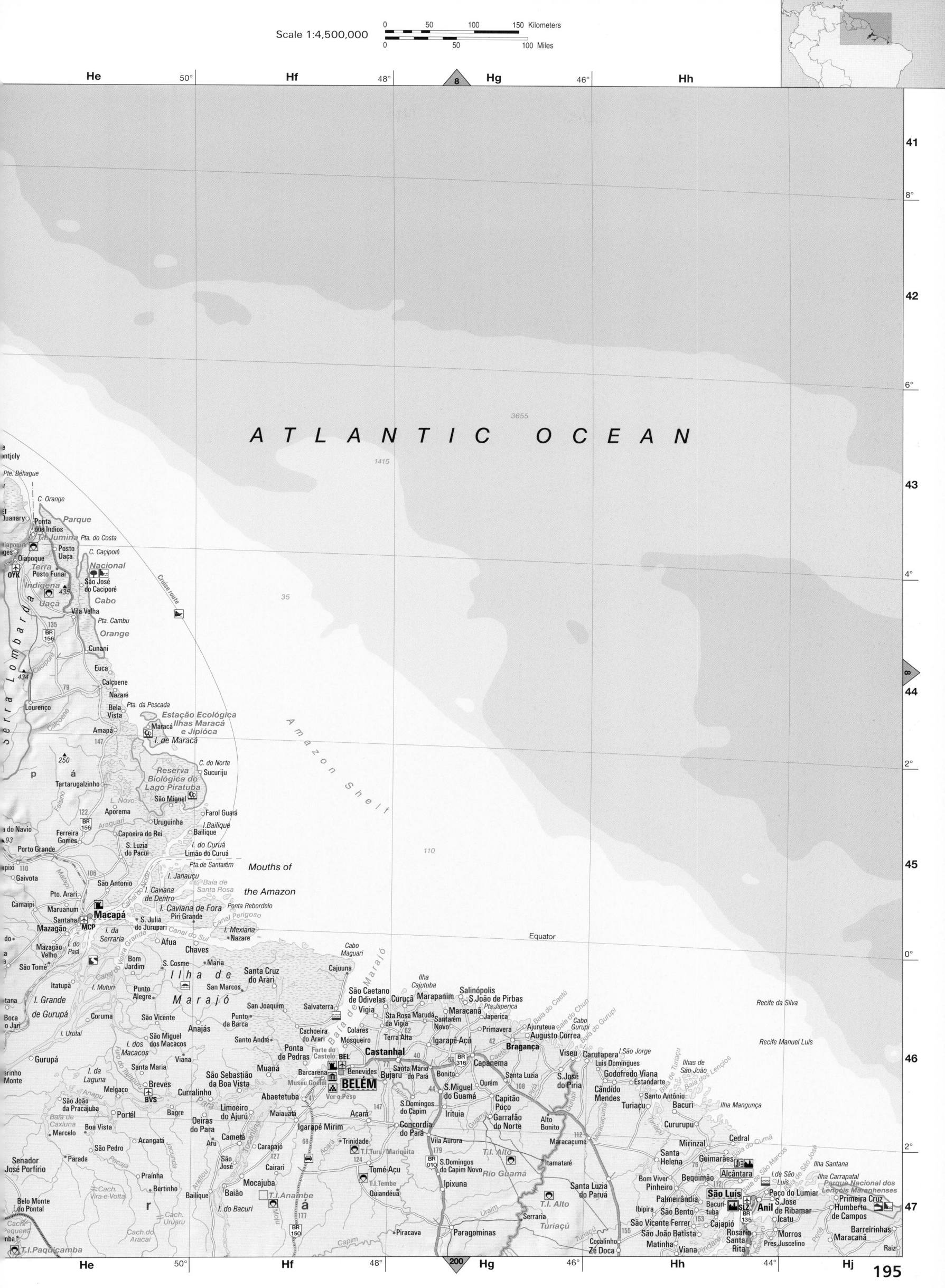

Scale 1:4,500,000

0 50 100 150 Kilometers
0 50 100 Miles

41

8°

42

6°

3655

43

ATLANTIC OCEAN

1415

Pte. Béhague
C. Orange
antjoly
luanary
Ponta
dos Indios Pta. do Costa
T.I.Jumina
Diapoque ges
C. Caçiporé
Posto
Uaça
Oiapoque
OYK Terra Posto Funai
Indigena
São José
do Caciporé 435
Uaçá
Vila Velha
Cabo
Pta. Cambu
135
BR 156
Orange
Pta. da Pescada
Cunani
Euca
434
Calçoene
Nazaré
Lourenço
79
Pta. da Pescada
Bela
Vista
Amapá
250 Maracá
Estação Ecológica
Ilhas Maracá
e Jipióca
I. de Maracá
147
p á
Tartarugalzinho
C. do Norte
Reserva
Biológica do
Lago Piratuba
Sucuriju
122 Aporema
São Miguel
BR 156
L. Novo.
Farol Guará
Uruguinha
Capoeira do Rei
I.Bailique
Bailique
Ferreira
Gomes
do Navio
S. Luzia
do Pacui
I. do Curuá
Limão do Curuá
93
Porto Grande
Pta.de Santarém
106
São Antonio
I. Janauçu
apixi 110
Gaivota
I. Caviana
de Dentro
Pto. Arari
Baía de
Santa Rosa
Camaipi
Maruanum
I. Caviana de Fora
Ponta Rebordelo
Santana
Macapá
S. Julia
Piri Grande
Mazagão
MCP
do Jurupari
Canal Perigoso
Mazagão
Velho
I. do Pará
I. da
Serraria
I. Mexiana
Nazare
São Tomé
Bom
Jardim
Chaves
Itatupã
I. Muturi
S. Cosme
Maria
Cabo
Maguari
I. Grande
de Gurupá
Punto
Alegre
Ilha de
San Marcos
Santa Cruz
do Arari
Cajuuna
Coruma
São Vicente
São Joaquim
Marajó
Ilha
Cajutuba
São Caetano
de Odivelas
Salinópolis
Curuçá Marapanim
S. João de Pirbas
Boca
do Jari
I. Urutaí
São Miguel
dos Macacos
Anajás
Punto
da Barca
Salvaterra
Vigia
Sta.Rosa Marudá
da Vigía
Maracanã
Pta.Japerica
Japerica
Gurupá
I. dos
Macacos
Santa Maria
Viana
Cachoeira
do Arari
Mosqueiro
Santo André
Ponta
de Pedras
Terra Alta
Igarapé-Açu
Primavera
Santarém
Novo
Augusto Correa
Ajuruteua
Bragança
I. da
Laguna
Melgaço
Forte do
Castelo
Muaná
Castanhal
Capanema
Viseu
Carutapera
Breves
São Sebastião
da Boa Vista
Barcarena
BEL
Benevides
Santa Mario
do Pará
BR 316
Santa Luzia
S.José
de Piria
I. São Jorge
Luis Domingues
Godofredo Viana
BVS
Curralinho
Museu Goeldi
BELÉM
Bujaru
Ver-o-Peso
Bonito
Qúrem
108
Cândido
Mendes
Estandarte
São João
da Pracajuba
Limoeiro
do Ajurú
Abaetetuba
S. Miguel
do Guamá
Capitão
Poço
Turiaçu
Santo Antônio
Portél
Bagre
Acará
147
S.Domingos
do Capim
Garrafão
do Norte
Bacuri
Oeiras
do Pará
Cametá
Igarapé Mirim
Iritúia
Vila Aurora
Alto
Bonito
Cururupu
Acangatá
Aru
Carapajó
68
Trinidade
179
Maracaçumé
112
Mirinzal
Cedral
São Pedro
São
José
124
T.I.Turu Mariquita
T.I. Alto
Santa
Helena
Guimarães
Praínha
Cairari
BR 010
S.Domingos
de Capim Novo
Rio Guamá
Itamataré
Bom Viver
Pinheiro
Alcântara
Ilha Santana
Bertinho
Mocajuba
Tomé-Açu
Ipixuna
T.I. Alto
Santa Luzia
do Paruá
Serraria
Cajapió
Ibipira
Palmeirândia
Bacuri-
tuba
I.de São
Luis
Parque Nacional dos
Lençóis Maranhenses
Bailique
Baião
T.I.Anambé
á
177
Quiandeúa
Turiaçú
155
São Bento
São Luís
Anil
Rosário
Paco do Lumiar
S.Jose
de Ribamar
Primeira
Cruz
T.I.Paquiçamba
BR 150
Piracava
Paragominas
Cocalinho
Zé Doca
Santa Luzia
do Paruá
São João Batista
Matinha
Santa
Rita
Morros
Pres. Juscelino
Humberto
de Campos
Maracanã
Barreirinhas
Raiz

Mouths of
the Amazon

Equator 0°

45

2°

46

Recife da Silva

Recife Manuel Luís

2°

47

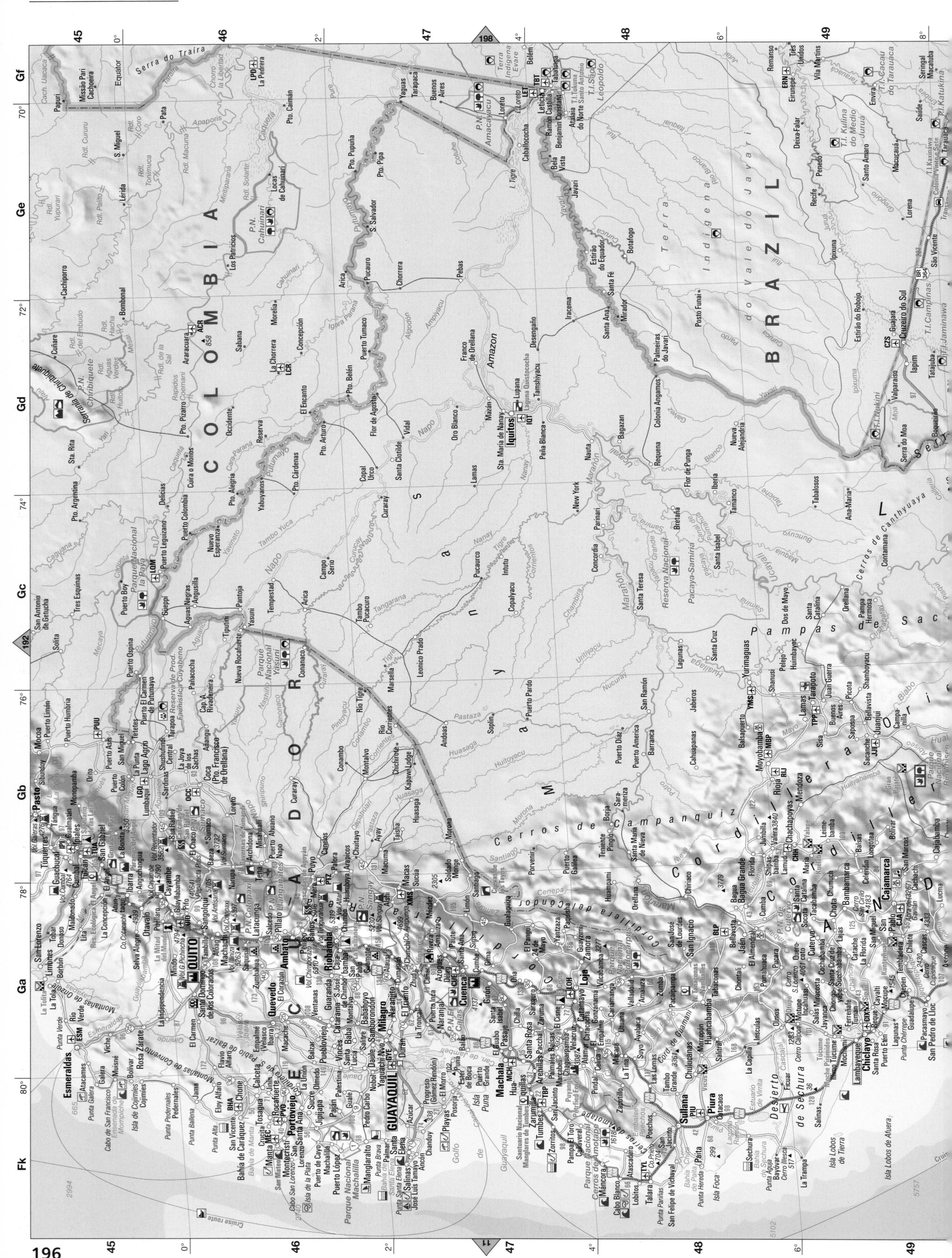

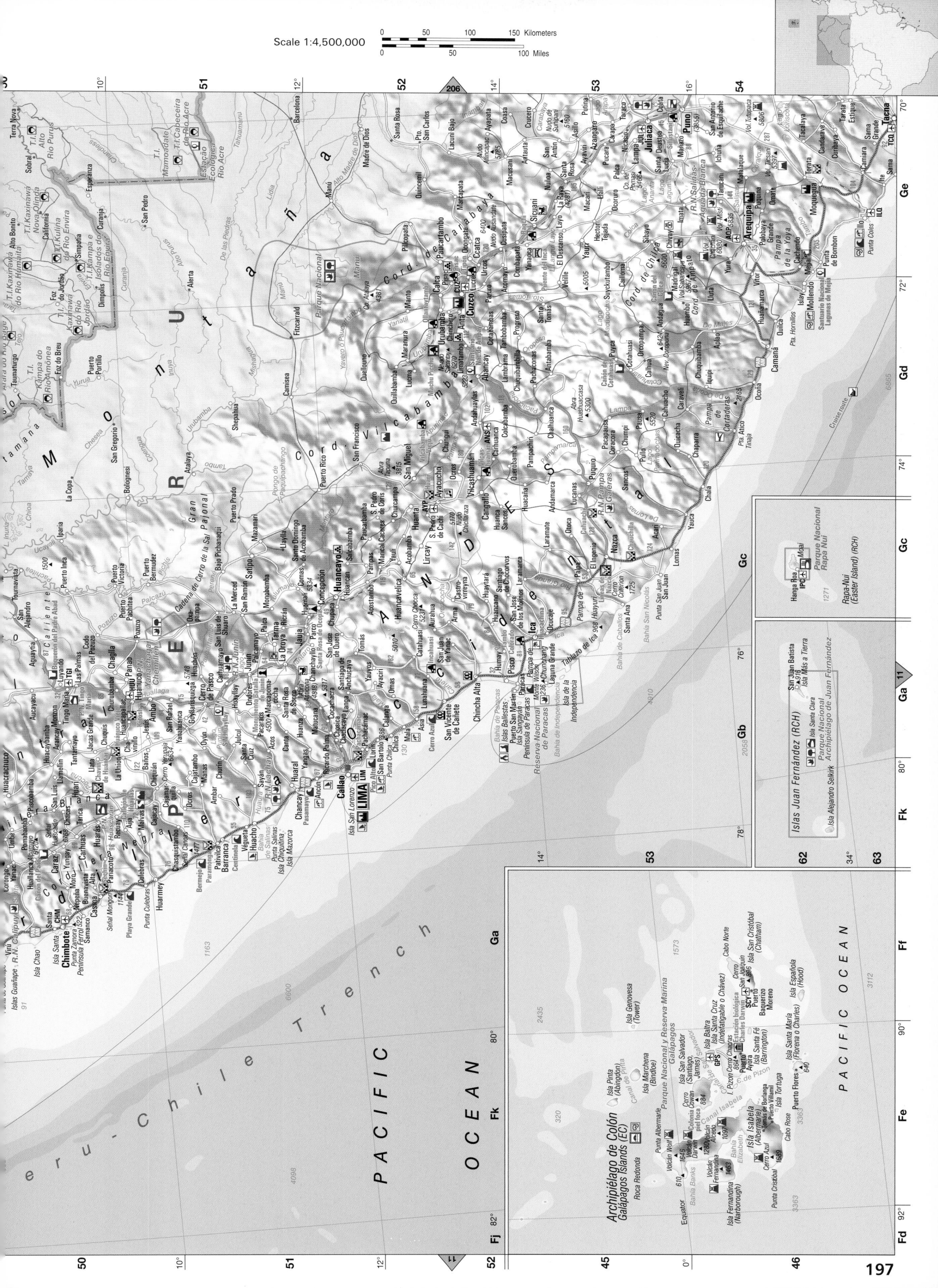

Amazon Lowlands

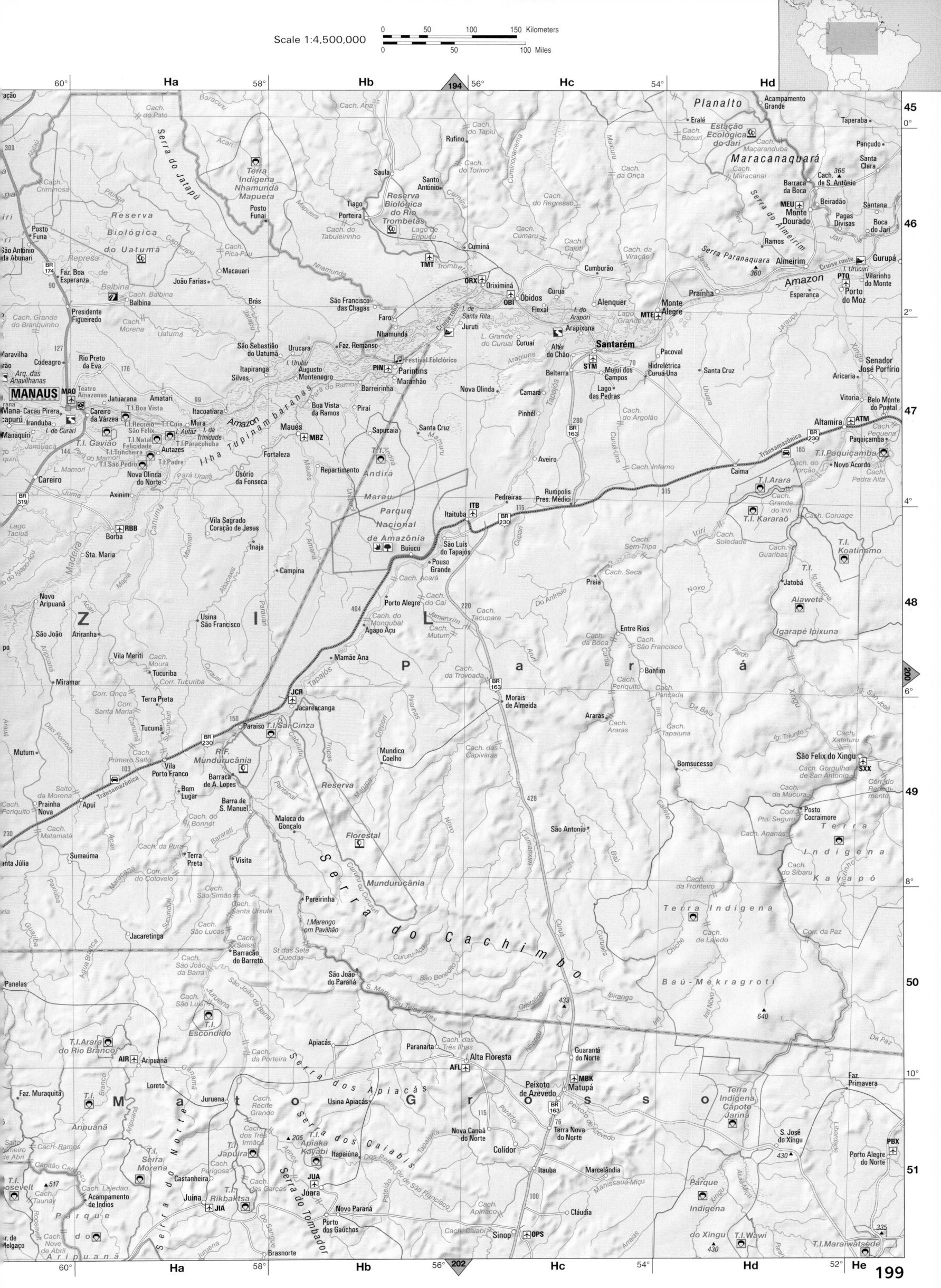

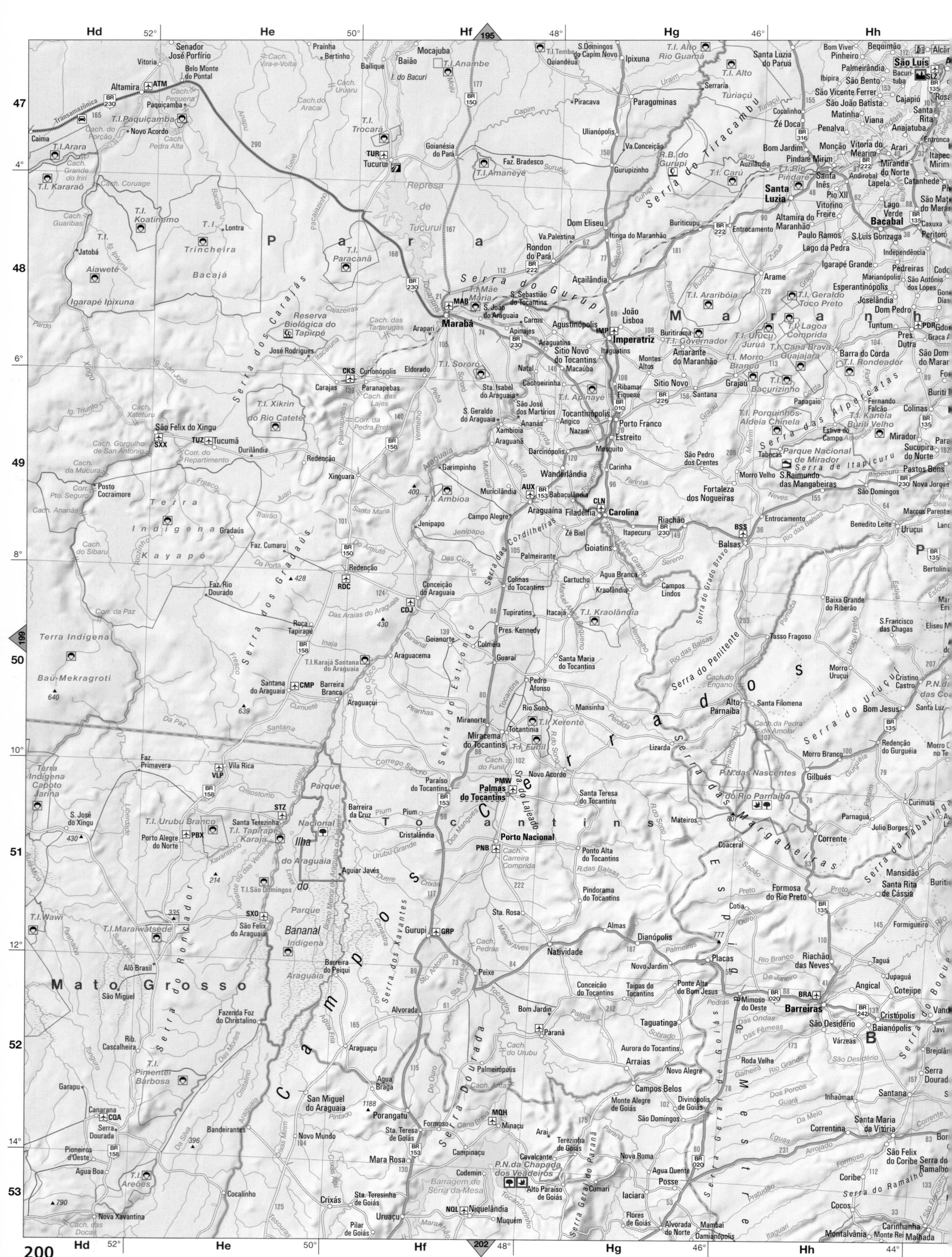

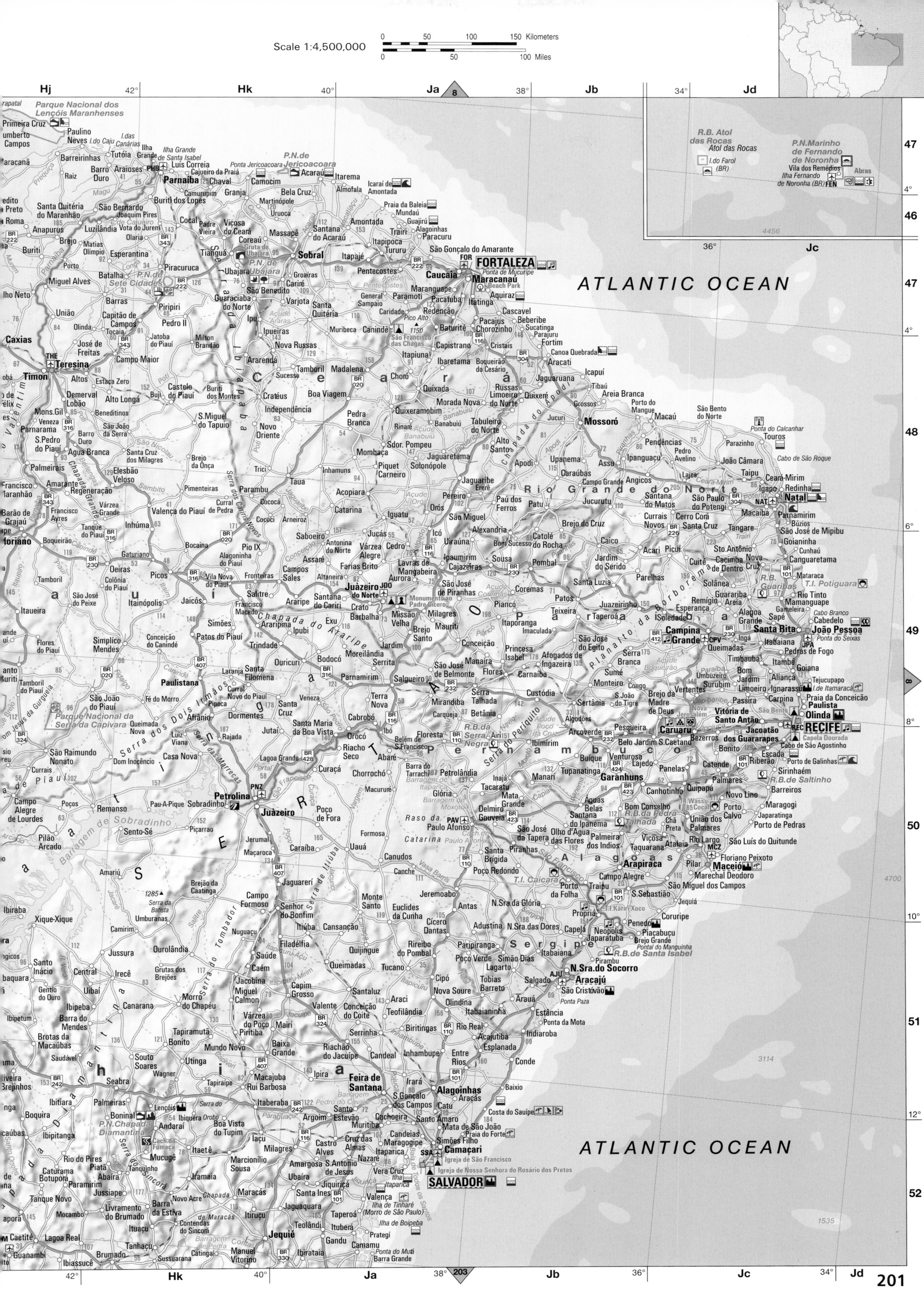

Scale 1:4,500,000

0 50 100 150 Kilometers
0 50 100 Miles

ATLANTIC OCEAN

ATLANTIC OCEAN

R.B. Atol das Rocas
Atol das Rocas
I.do Farol (BR)
P.N.Marinho de Fernando de Noronha
Vila dos Remédios
Ilha Fernando de Noronha (BR) FEN
Abras

Parque Nacional dos Lençóis Maranhenses

C e a r á

Rio Grande do Norte

P a r a í b a

P e r n a m b u c o

A l a g o a s

S e r g i p e

P i a u í

B a h i a

FORTALEZA
Caucaia
Maracanaú
Maranguape
Sobral
Parnaíba
Teresina
Timon
Caxias
Mossoró
Natal
Parnamirim
Macaíba
João Pessoa
Santa Rita
Campina Grande
Caruaru
Olinda
RECIFE
Jaboatão dos Guararapes
Paulista
Vitória de Santo Antão
Garanhuns
Arapiraca
Maceió
Aracaju
N.Sra.do Socorro
São Cristóvão
Petrolina
Juazeiro
Paulo Afonso
Feira de Santana
Alagoinhas
Camaçari
SALVADOR
Jequié
Juazeiro do Norte
Crato

Parque Nacional da Serra da Capivara
P.N.Chapada Diamantina
Barragem de Sobradinho

Pantanal, Eastern Brazil

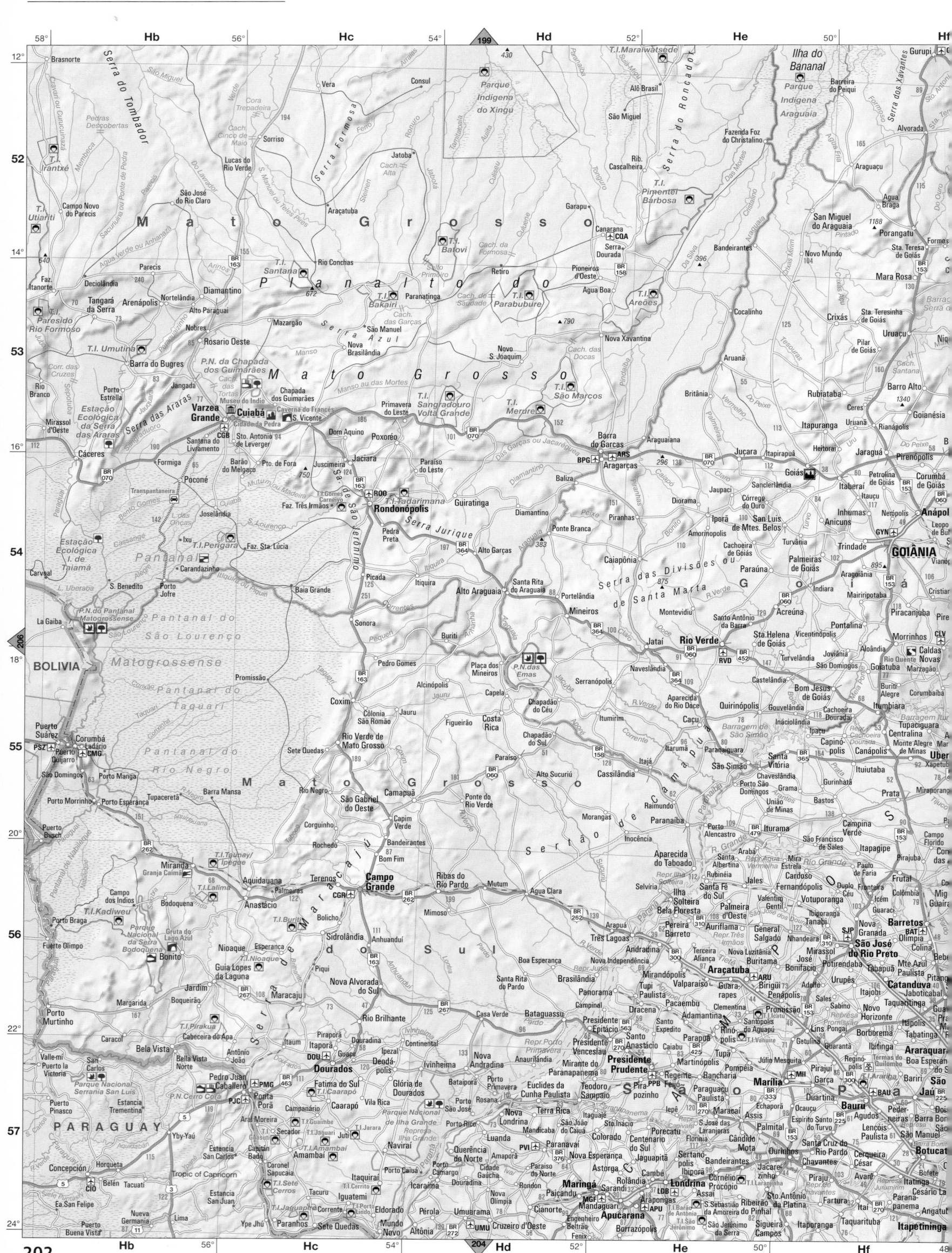

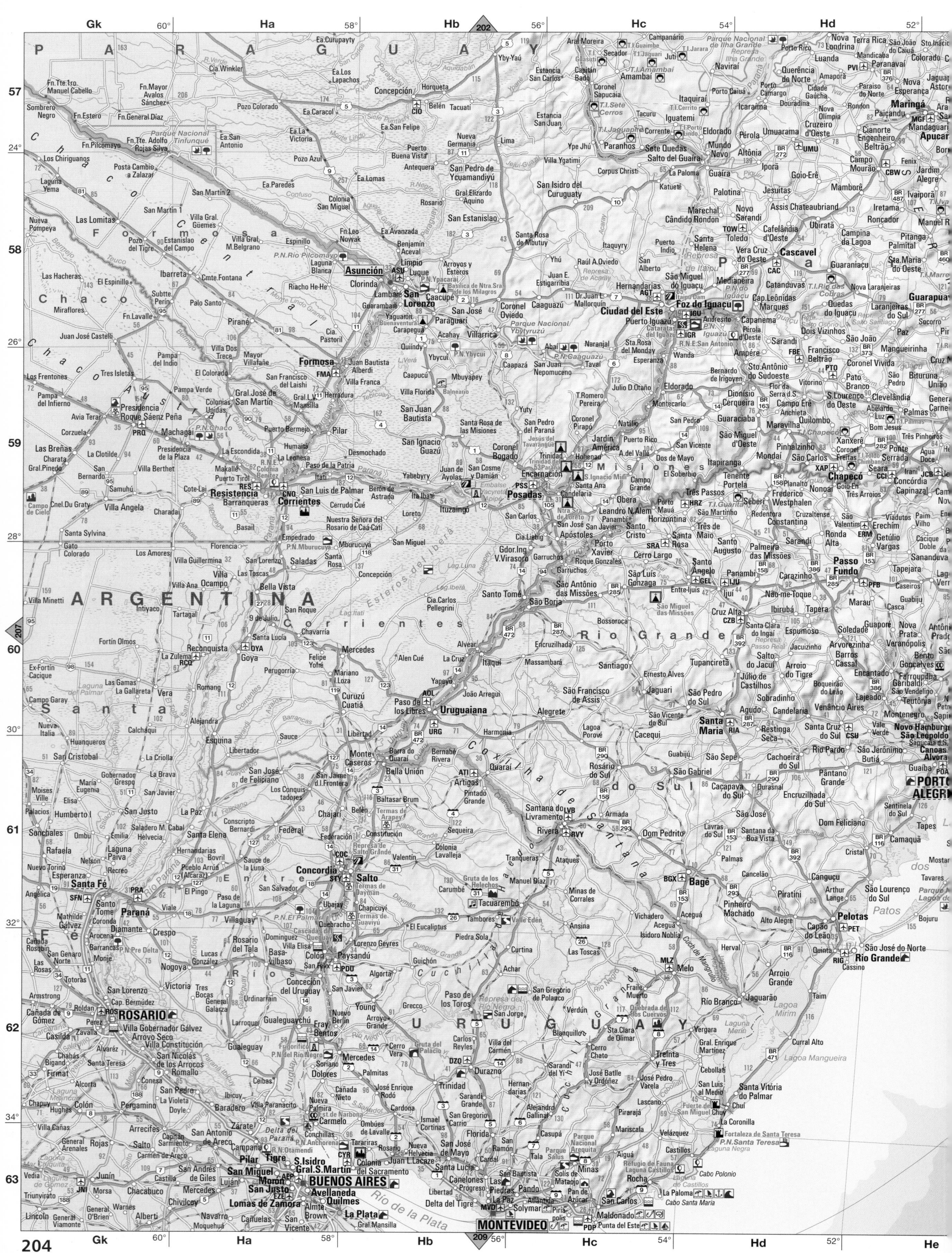

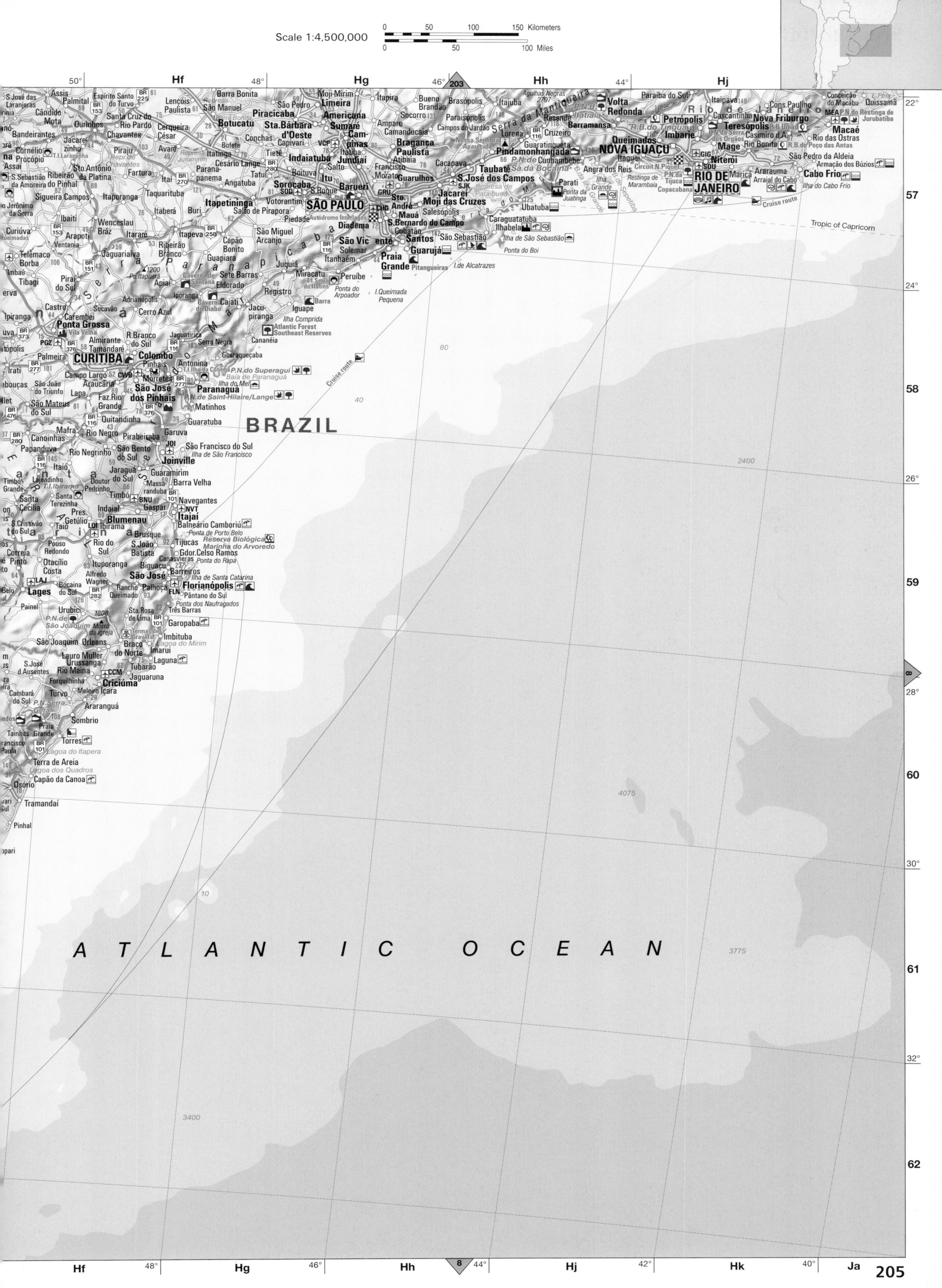

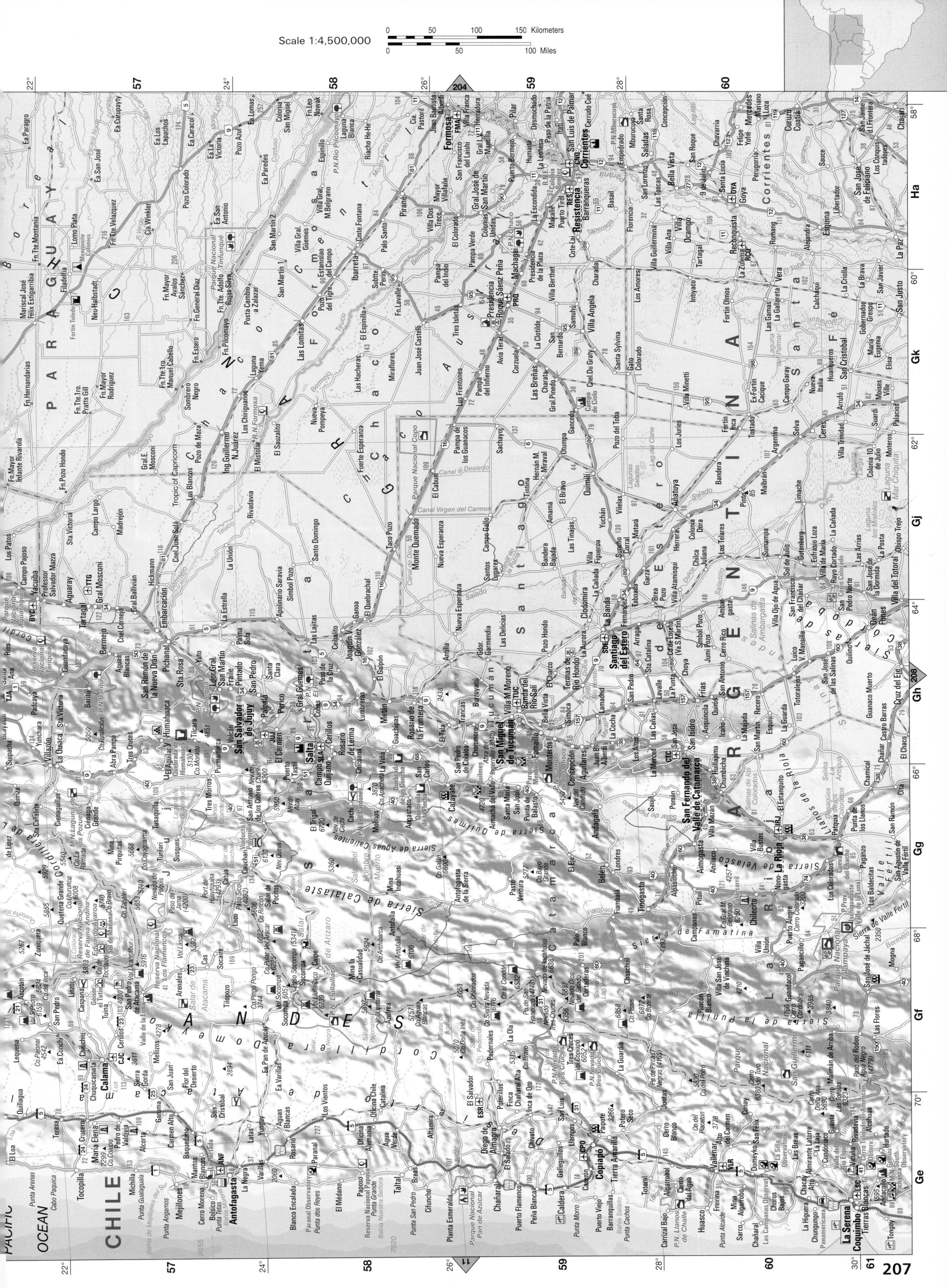

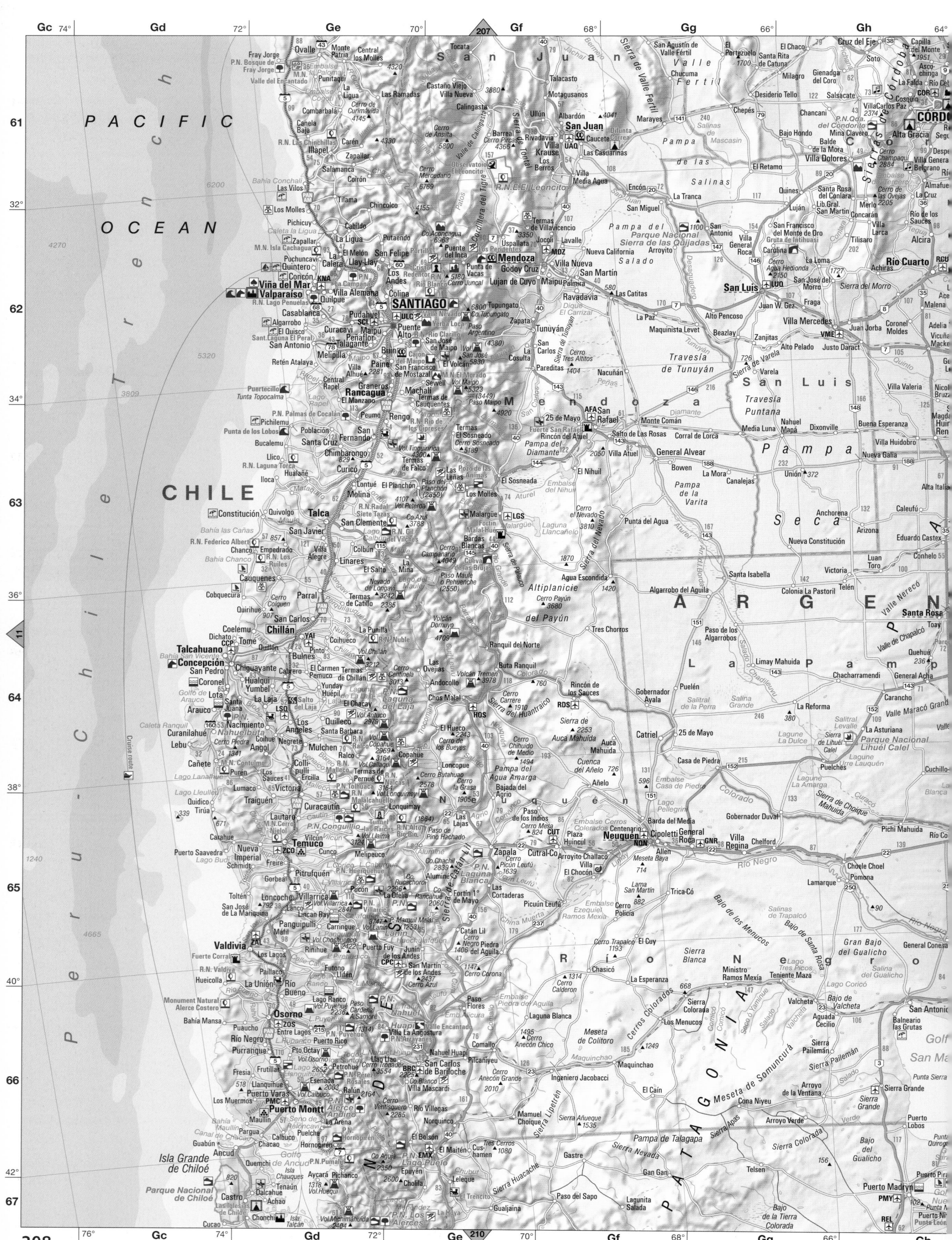

Gj   62°   Gk   60°   Ha   58°   204   Hb   56°   Hc

La Para   Miramar
Brinkmann   Sunchales
La Paz   Conscripto   Chajari   Belén   Santana do   LVR   Armada
Humberto I   La Paz   Bernardi   Federal   Sequeira   Livramento   RVY
Balnearia   Portena
Colonia Marina Freyre   Rafaela   Nelson   Saladero M. Cabal   Santa Elena   Federación   Tranqueras   Ataques   Dom Pedrito   Palmas   BR   Santana da   Boa Vista
La Rosa y Primera   Francisco   Esperanza   Recreo   Pueblo Arrúa   Constitución   COC   Colonia   Carumbé   Manuel Díaz   BGX   Bagé   BR 293   Cancelão
El Tío   Nuevo Torino   Santo   Concordia   Salto   Minas de Corrales   BR 153   Pinheiro   BRASIL
Santa Fé   Coronda   Paraná   STY   Termas de   Tacuarembó   Valle Edén   Ansina   Machado   Alto Alegre

62°   Gk   60°   Ha   58°   8   Hb   56°   Hc   54°   Hd   52° 209

ATLANTIC

OCEAN

BUENOS AIRES

MONTEVIDEO

URUGUAY

Rosario

Bahía Blanca

Mar del Plata

Río de la Plata

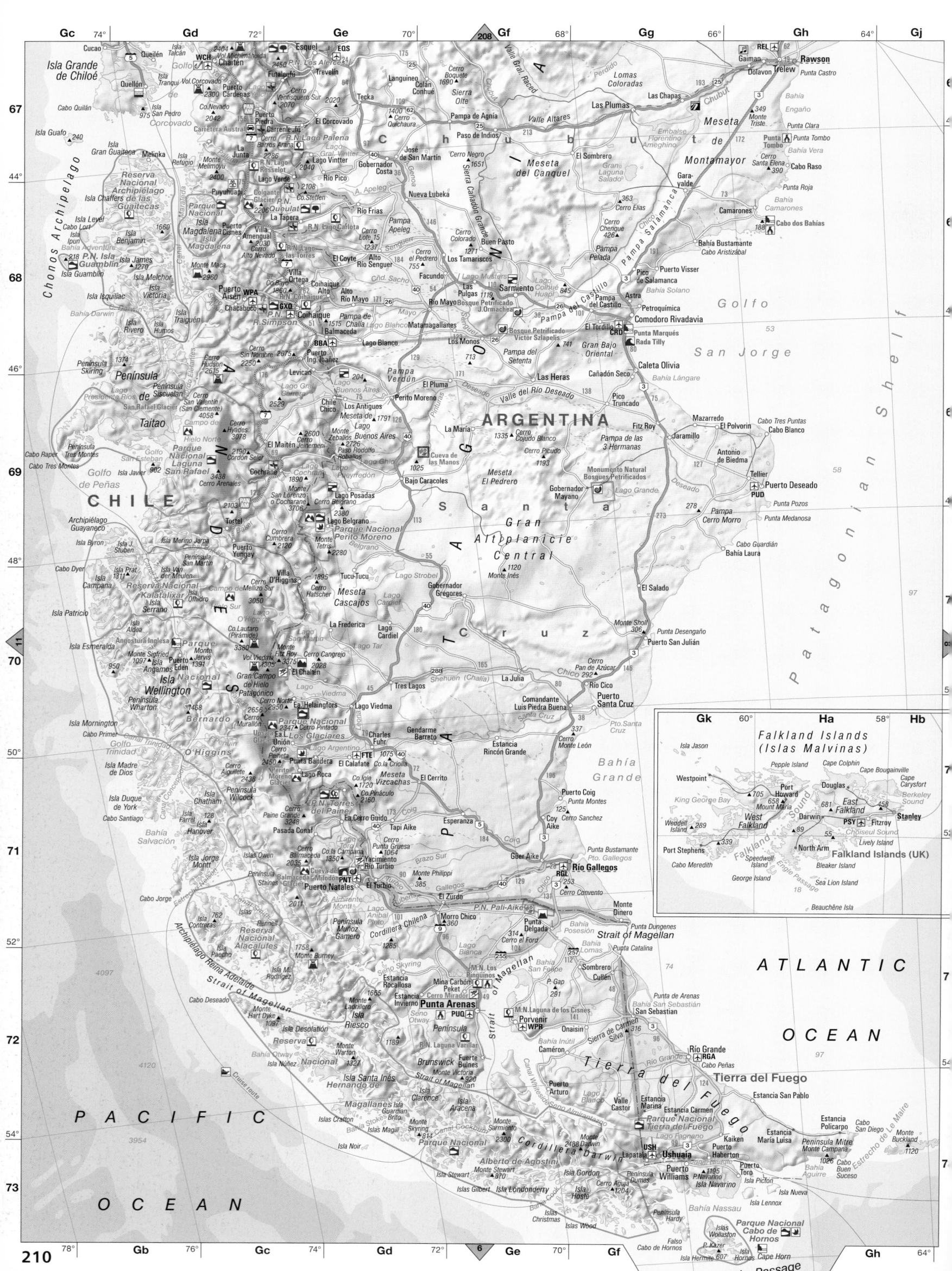

NATIONS OF THE WORLD

Facts and figures

There were 195 sovereign nations on six continents at the start of the 21st century. During the 20th century, the political makeup of our planet changed frequently and the borders of many nations were redrawn. Two world wars, the end of European colonialism, and the decline of communism led to the creation and collapse of numerous nations and political entities.

Although most of Africa was under the control of European powers at the start of the 20th century, it is now the continent with the most states: 54. Asia is only slightly behind Africa with 47 states, and is followed by Europe (45), North America (23), Australia/Oceania (14), and South America (12). Inhospitable Antarctica is the only "stateless" continent.

Index of local country names

Note on the use of this atlas:

The name of a country in international use may frequently differ from its English name (e.g. Albania = Shqipëri). The following index gives the English names of all countries in the first column and the official international names as employed by e.g. UNO in the second column. Entries in the atlas are strictly alphabetical and follow the order of the international names, regardless of their pronunciation and significance. When the English name of a country differs from its international name, a reference to the entry under the international name is given under the English name (e.g. Albania: see Shqipëri). Abbreviations: GDP = gross domestic product; GNP = gross national product; US$ = US dollars; m = million.

English	Local	Continent	Page	English	Local	Continent	Page
Afghanistan	Afghānistān	Asia	216	Cyprus	Kypros/Kibris	Europe	241
Albania	Shqipëria	Europe	260	Czech Republic	Česká Republika	Europe	226
Algeria	Al-Ğazā'ir/Algérie	Africa	216	Denmark	Danmark	Europe	229
Andorra	Andorra	Europe	218	Djibouti	Djibouti	Africa	230
Angola	Angola	Africa	218	Dominica	Dominica	Central America	230
Antigua and Barbuda	Antigua and Barbuda	Central America	218	Dominican Republic	República Dominicana	Central America	256
Argentina	Argentina	South America	219	East Timor	Timor-Leste	Asia	266
Armenia	Armenija (Hayastan)	Asia	219	Ecuador	Ecuador	South America	230
Australia	Australia	Australia	220	Equatorial Guinea	Guinea Ecuatorial	Africa	236
Austria	Österreich	Europe	253	Egypt	Al-Miṣr/Egypt	Africa	217
Azerbaijan	Azerbajdzan	Asia	220	El Salvador	El Salvador	Central America	232
Bahamas	Bahamas	Central America	220	Eritrea	Eritrea	Africa	232
Bahrain	Al-Bahrain	Asia	216	Estonia	Eesti	Europe	231
Bangladesh	Bangladesh	Asia	220	Ethiopia	Îtyopya	Africa	239
Barbados	Barbados	Central America	221	Fiji	Fiji	Australia/Oceania	233
Belarus	Belarus	Europe	221	Finland	Suomi/Finland	Europe	263
Belgium	België/Belgique	Europe	222	France	France	Europe	234
Belize	Belize	Central America	222	Gabon	Gabon	Africa	234
Benin	Benin	Africa	222	The Gambia	Gambia	Africa	234
Bhutan	Bhutan	Asia	222	Georgia	Gruzija (Sakartvelo)	Asia	235
Bolivia	Bolivia	South America	223	Germany	Deutschland	Europe	230
Bosnia-Herzegovina	Bosna i Hercegovina	Europe	223	Ghana	Ghana	Africa	234
Botswana	Botswana	Africa	223	Greece	Elláda (Hellás)	Europe	232
Brazil	Brasil	South America	224	Grenada	Grenada	Central America	234
Brunei	Brunei	Asia	224	Guatemala	Guatemala	Central America	235
Bulgaria	Bŭlgarija	Europe	224	Guinea	Guinée	Africa	236
Burkina Faso	Burkina Faso	Africa	224	Guinea-Bissau	Guinea-Bissau	Africa	236
Burundi	Burundi	Africa	225	Guyana	Guyana	South America	236
Cambodia	Kâmpŭchéa	Asia	240	Haiti	Haïti	Central America	236
Cameroon	Cameroun/Cameroon	Africa	225	Honduras	Honduras	Central America	237
Canada	Canada	North America	226	Hungary	Magyarország	Europe	244
Cape Verde	Cabo Verde	Africa	225	Iceland	Ísland	Europe	238
Central African Republic	République Centrafricaine	Africa	256	India	India (Bhărat)	Asia	237
Chad	Tchad	Africa	266	Indonesia	Indonesia	Asia	238
Chile	Chile	South America	226	Iraq	'Irāq	Asia	238
China	Zhongguo	Asia	272	Iran	Îrân	Asia	238
Colombia	Colombia	South America	227	Ireland	Éire/Ireland	Europe	231
Comoros	Comores	Africa	228	Israel	Yi'sra'el	Asia	271
Congo	Congo	Africa	228	Italy	Italia	Europe	239
Congo, Dem. Rep.	Congo, Rép. Démocratique	Africa	228	Ivory Coast	Côte d'Ivoire	Africa	228
Costa Rica	Costa Rica	Central America	228	Jamaica	Jamaica	Central America	240
Croatia	Hrvatska	Europe	237	Japan	Nippon/Nihon	Asia	252
Cuba	Cuba	Central America	229	Jordan	Urdunn	Asia	270

English	Local	Continent	Page	English	Local	Continent	Page
Kazakhstan	Kazahstan	Asia	240	Rwanda	Rwanda	Africa	257
Kenya	Kenya	Africa	240	Saint Kitts and Nevis	Saint Kitts and Nevis	Central America	257
Kiribati	Kiribati	Australia / Oceania	241	Saint Lucia	Saint Lucia	Central America	258
Korea, North	Choson	Asia	226	St. Vincent and the Grenadines	St. Vincent and the Grenadines	Central America	258
Korea, South	Taehan-Min'guk	Asia	264	Samoa	Samoa	Australia / Oceania	258
Kuwait	Al-Kuwait	Asia	216	San Marino	San Marino	Europe	258
Kyrgyzstan	Kyrgyzstan	Asia	241	São Tomé and Principe	São Tomé e Príncipe	Africa	259
Laos	Lao	Asia	242	Saudi Arabia	Al-Mamlaka	Asia	217
Latvia	Latvija	Europe	242		al-'Arabiya as-Sa'ūdiya		
Lebanon	Al-Lubnān	Asia	216	Senegal	Sénégal	Africa	259
Lesotho	Lesotho	Africa	242	Serbia	Srbija	Europe	262
Liberia	Liberia	Africa	242	Seychelles	Seychelles	Africa	260
Libya	Lîbîyâ	Africa	242	Sierra Leone	Sierra Leone	Africa	260
Liechtenstein	Liechtenstein	Europe	243	Singapore	Singapore	Asia	260
Lithuania	Lietuva	Europe	243	Slovakia	Slovenská Republika	Europe	261
Luxembourg	Luxembourg	Europe	243	Slovenia	Slovenija	Europe	260
Macedonia	Makedonija	Europe	244	Solomon Islands	Solomon Islands	Australia / Oceania	261
Madagascar	Madagasíkara	Africa	244	Somalia	Soomaaliya	Africa	262
Malawi	Malawi	Africa	244	South Africa	South Africa / Suid-Afrika	Africa	262
Malaysia	Malaysia	Asia	245	Spain	España	Europe	232
Maldives	Maldives (Divehi Rajje)	Asia	245	Sri Lanka	Şrī Laṅkā	Asia	262
Mali	Mali	Africa	245	Sudan	As-Sūdān	Africa	219
Malta	Malta	Europe	246	Suriname	Suriname	South America	263
Marshall Islands	Marshall Islands	Australia / Oceania	246	Swaziland	Swaziland (kaNgwane)	Africa	264
Mauritania	Mawrītāniyah	Africa	246	Sweden	Sverige	Europe	264
Mauritius	Mauritius	Africa	246	Switzerland	Suisse / Schweiz / Svizzera	Europe	262
Mexico	México	Central America	247	Syria	Sūriya	Asia	264
Micronesia	Micronesia	Australia / Oceania	247	Taiwan	Taiwan	Asia	265
Moldova	Moldova	Europe	248	Tajikistan	Tadžikistan	Asia	264
Monaco	Monaco	Europe	248	Tanzania	Tanzania	Africa	265
Mongolia	Mongol Ard Uls	Asia	248	Thailand	Muang Thai	Asia	249
Montenegro	Crna Gora	Europe	228	Togo	Togo	Africa	266
Morocco	Al-Maġrib / Maroc	Africa	217	Tonga	Tonga	Australia / Oceania	266
Mozambique	Moçambique	Africa	248	Trinidad and Tobago	Trinidad and Tobago	Central America	266
Myanmar (Burma)	Myanmar	Asia	249	Tunisia	Tūnisiyah / Tunisie	Africa	267
Namibia	Namibia	Africa	250	Turkey	Türkiye	Europe	267
Nauru	Nauru (Naoero)	Australia / Oceania	250	Turkmenistan	Turkmenistan	Asia	268
Nepal	Nepal	Asia	250	Tuvalu	Tuvalu	Australia / Oceania	268
Netherlands	Nederland	Europe	250	Uganda	Uganda	Africa	268
New Zealand	New Zealand	Australia / Oceania	251	Ukraine	Ukrajina	Europe	268
Nicaragua	Nicaragua	Central America	251	Uruguay	Uruguay	South America	270
Niger	Niger	Africa	252	Uzbekistan	Uzbekistan	Asia	270
Nigeria	Nigeria	Africa	252	Vanuatu	Vanuatu	Australia/Oceania	270
Norway	Norge	Europe	252	Vatican City	Città del Vaticano	Europe	227
Oman	Salṭanat 'Umān	Asia	258	Venezuela	Venezuela	South America	270
Pakistan	Pākistān	Asia	253	Vietnam	Viêt-Nam	Asia	271
Palau	Palau	Australia / Oceania	254	United Arab Emirates	Daulat al-Imārāt	Asia	229
Panama	Panamá	Central America	254		al-'Arabiya Al-Muttahida		
Papua New Guinea	Papua New Guinea	Australia / Oceania	254	United Kingdom	United Kingdom	Europe	268
Paraguay	Paraguay	South America	254	United States of America	United States of America	North America	269
Peru	Perú	South America	254	Western Sahara	Al-Saharaw	Africa	218
Philippines	Pilipinas	Asia	254	Yemen	Al-Yaman	Asia	218
Poland	Polska	Europe	255	Zambia	Zambia	Africa	272
Portugal	Portugal	Europe	255	Zimbabwe	Zimbabwe	Africa	272
Qatar	Qaṭar	Asia	256				
Romania	România	Europe	256				
Russia	Rossija	Europe	256				

Afghānistān Afghanistan

Teacher and disciple: Although Saudi Arabia, as a modern industrialized country, is provided with a fully developed and structured educational system (at one of the six universities in the country English is actually the language of instruction), getting instruction in the rules of the Koran is a very important matter for young Arabs. The Koran, together with the Sunna (traditions of the prophet Mohammed) serve as the country's constitution.

Afghānistān
Afghanistan

Area: 647,500 sq km
Population: 28.5 million
GDP per capita: 700 US$
Capital: Kabul
Government: Republic
Languages: Pushtu, Dari
Currency: 1 afghani = 100 puls

Geography: The mountainous interior includes the mighty Hindu Kush range, whose summits rise to over 7,000 meters culminating in Mount Tirich Mir on the Pakistan border. Great climatic differences exist in a relatively limited space, ranging from arid to subtropical and alpine climates depending on altitude. Tourist destinations include the Islamic buildings in Ghazni, the Caliph Mausoleums in Kabul and the pilgrimage sites of Kandahar and Mazar-e Sharif.

Politics: Settled by Iranian tribes since the 2nd millennium BC, Afghanistan has been under a succession of foreign dominations. The Afghan Emirate, established in 1747, later came under English influence. In 1919 it became a kingdom independent of Great Britain, and in 1973 a republic. The civil war from 1979 to 1992 and the struggle against the Russian army on its own soil to 1989 have brought lasting changes; the radical Islamist Taliban gained increasing influence from 1994. Their terror regime was overthrown at the end of 2001 in an offensive by the US and the Afghan Northern Alliance.

Economy: Afghanistan is one of the poorest countries in the world. Agriculture and fruit cultivation is practiced in the irrigated valleys, and livestock breeding in the mountain areas. Natural resources include coal, lapis lazuli, petroleum and natural gas. The continuous fighting has wreaked enormous damage on the economy – more than three quarters of the industrial plants lie in ruins today.

Al-Bahrain
Bahrain

Area: 665 sq km
Population: 677,800
GDP per capita: 17,100 US$
Capital: Al-Manama
Government: Emirate
Language: Arabic
Currency: 1 Bahrain dinar = 1,000 fils

Geography: The Emirate in the Persian Gulf is composed of 33 islands, 13 of which are inhabited. Bahrain, the main island, has a desert-like landscape with expansive salt marshes and sand dunes, whilst the archipelago enjoys a mild desert climate. Artesian wells permit oasis agriculture in the northern coastal area. Tourism is concentrated in the capital Al-Manama.

Politics: The city of Dilmun was a trading hub as early as the 3rd century BC. Occupied by the Portuguese in the 16th century and later by the Persians, the emirate was a British protectorate from 1816 to 1971 and joined the Arab League after declaring independence in 1971. The Emir in power since 1999 has ushered in political reforms including a constitution (in force since 2002), making the country a constitutional monarchy. Around 40% of Bahrain's population comprises non-nationals.

Economy: The rich petroleum reserves discovered in 1932 have provided a solid base for the country's economy, with the oil and gas sector generating 80% of exports but only 2% of employment. Because of the climatic conditions, the agricultural sector accounts for only 1% of GDP, while industry contributes 41%. The services sector (banking) plays an important role as part of diversification, anticipating the end of the oil reserves.

Albania see Shqipëria

Al-Ğazā'ir/Algérie
Algeria

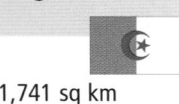

Area: 2,381,741 sq km
Population: 32.1 million
GDP per capita: 5,900 US$
Capital: Algiers
Government: Presidential republic
Language: Arabic
Currency: 1 Algerian dinar = 100 centimes

Geography: Settlements are concentrated in the Mediterranean climate of the fertile coastal areas to the north, extending along 1,300 kilometers of bays and inlets. 85% of the south is occupied by the

Saudi Arabia: The Ka'bah in Mecca, the religious center of the Islam.

Sahara. In addition to the Sahara's unique landscape and beautiful oases, other places of interest are the many cultural sites from the Roman and Phoenician eras.

Politics: First settled by the Phoenicians and later by Carthaginians and Romans, the coastal areas fell under Arab rule from the 7th to 15th centuries, were conquered by the French in 1830 and became French territory from 1881 to 1962. Although uprisings and resistance activities reached their peak in 1945 and 1958, political unrest continued after 1962 and terrorism by Islamic fundamentalists has increased since 1990, despite the election of a National Assembly in 1997.

Economy: Although constraints of climate and soil quality restrict agriculture to a narrow coastal area, it is the country's second largest industry. Algeria is among the world's largest cork exporters; the sparse forests are state-run. Natural gas and petroleum exports from the Sahara's extensive reserves form Algeria's main source of foreign currency. The country is now the world's second largest exporter of natural gas. Recent reforms may eventually help to diversify the economy, but Algeria's unemployment and poverty rates remain critically high.

Al-Kuwait
Kuwait

Area: 17,820 sq km
Population: 2.3 million
GDP per capita: 18,100 US$
Capital: Kuwait City
Government: Emirate
Language: Arabic
Currency: 1 Kuwait dinar = 100 dirhams = 1,000 fils

Geography: This emirate on the Persian Gulf consists of dry steppes and sandy deserts. Summers inland are extremely hot and dry, while the more humid coastal areas have some of the lowest precipitation on the planet. Destinations include the old town of Kuwait City as well as the Island of Faylakah (holiday facilities with beaches). The 1991 Gulf War left ecological devastation in its wake.

Politics: A British protectorate from 1899, Kuwait gained independence in 1961. Executive power lies with the Emir, a member of the Al Sabbah dynasty that has reigned since 1756, and has been elected by it; a house of representatives, elected in 1996, enjoys limited powers. Invaded and occupied by Iraq in 1990, Kuwait was freed by allied forces in the (first) Gulf War in early 1991.

Economy: 62% of the people living and working in Kuwait come from neighboring countries. Because of the terrain, agricultural use is limited to only 0.2% of the overall area where there is coastal irrigation. Most food is imported. Oil, drilled in Kuwait since 1946, accounts for the country's wealth. Kuwait has many large-scale oil harbors. Shrimps also form an important export. Kuwait does not levy taxes or social security contributions.

Al-Lubnān
Lebanon

Area: 10,452 sq km
Population: 3.8 million
GDP per capita: 4,800 US$
Capital: Beirut
Government: Republic
Languages: Arabic (official), French
Currency: 1 Lebanese pound = 100 piasters

Geography: Dominated by mountain ranges on the eastern edge of the Mediterranean, the country has only a narrow, fertile coastal strip, with a Mediterranean climate in this region and a continental climate in the hinterland, with high snowfalls in the winter. Tourist destinations include Baalbek (excavations of Roman sites), the old harbor city of Beirut, and Tripoli.

Politics: After the end of the Ottoman Empire, Lebanon came under a French mandate in 1920 until it gained independence in 1944. Since 1958 it has been continuously shaken by external political crises and internal conflicts, attributable to the overall Middle East conflict. After a peace treaty with neighboring Syria, Lebanon is also negotiating a comprehensive peace settlement with Israel.

Economy: The country's economic fabric and infrastructure was almost completely destroyed by the civil war. Agriculture covers only part of the country's needs. Fruit and vegetables are grown on the irrigated land on the coast. Industry is limited to products for domestic consumption. Services are the largest contributor to GDP.

Unveiled beauty: Although most of the Berber are Muslims, the women do not wear veils; their clothes are more colorful and decorated than those of the men. They enjoy more freedom than is usual for women in Arab countries. Berber society is based on the tribe and the clan, with blood relationships and the extended family of paramount importance.

Al-Maġrib/Maroc
Morocco

Area: 446,550 sq km
Population: 32.2 million
GDP per capita: 4,000 US$
Capital: Rabat
Government: Constitutional monarchy
Languages: Arabic, French (both official), Berber dialects
Currency: 1 dirham = 100 centimes

Geography: Fertile countryside with a Mediterranean climate extends to the Rif Mountains in the north. To the south of the coastal strip, three chains of the Atlas Mountains mark the transition to the steppes and deserts in the extreme southwest. The most popular tourist destinations are Agadir, Fès, Marrakesh, Meknès and Rabat.

Politics: Conquered by the Arabs in the 7th century, Morocco fell under the rule of Islamic dynasties until the end of the 19th century, became a French protectorate from 1912, and gained independence in 1956. The country's monarch is its political and spiritual leader. In 1996, the monarch Hassan II. then ushered in a phase of liberalization. Morocco's claim to the former Spanish colony of Western Sahara, source of a long-standing conflict, is still unresolved.

Economy: Agriculture accounts for less than 20% of GDP, with the chief exports being citrus fruit, wine, fruit and vegetables. Industry, though underdeveloped, contributes 32% of GDP. Morocco has the largest phosphate reserves in the world. Services, principally tourism, form the chief economic sector at 53%. Trade with Europe is an important economic factor for the country.

Al-Mamlaka al-'Arabiya as-Sa'ūdiya
Saudi Arabia

Area: 1,960,582 sq km
Population: 25.8 million
GDP per capita: 11,800 US$
Capital: Riyadh
Government: Islamic absolute monarchy (Koran and Sunna serve as constitution)
Language: Arabic

Currency: 1 Saudi riyal = 20 qirshes = 100 hallalas

Geography: The country's territory, covering a large part of the Arabian Peninsula, features stony and sandy deserts traversed by wadis (watercourses that flow only after rains), in a hot and dry climate. The only natural vegetation is found in the oases. Tourist destinations almost entirely concentrate to pilgrimages to the holy sites in Mecca and Medina.

Politics: The history of Saudi Arabia begins with the Prophet Mohammed, who in the 7th century not only founded the new religion of Islam, but also united various Arab tribes. The Ottomans conquered the north and west of the peninsula, as well as the holy sites, in the 16th century. The ruling Saud dynasty, still in power today, founded the Islamic State of the Wahhabites in the 18th century. The Kingdom of Saudi Arabia was proclaimed in 1932. Its ruler is also the head of government and Keeper of the Holy Places.

Economy: More than three-quarters of the almost exclusively Muslim population live in the cities. A small proportion engage in nomadic livestock breeding (sheep, camels, goats), and 13% generate nearly one-tenth of GDP through agriculture in the widely scattered oases. The gigantic petroleum and natural gas reserves in the Persian Gulf make Saudi Arabia the world's largest oil exporter. Water shortages and population growth represent areas of concern.

Al-Miṣr/Egypt
Egypt

Area: 1,001,450 sq km
Population: 76.1 million
GDP per capita: 3,900 US$
Capital: Cairo
Government: Presidential republic
Language: Arabic
Currency: 1 Egyptian pound =100 piasters

1 The Blue Mosque in Mazar-e Sharif, Afghanistan.

2 Egypt: The Sphinx near the Pyramid of Cheops in Gizeh, 2500 BC.

3 Carpet manufacturing is still highly estimated in Morocco. The most valuable pieces decorate the floors and walls of the mosques.

4 The emirate of Kuwait has become one of the richest Persian Gulf states by exporting petroleum and natural gas.

Heirs to a legend: The times when gauchos rode over the pampas are long gone. These skilled horsemen and cattle drovers led a nomadic life, but over time were replaced with poorly paid farm laborers by the Argentinian ranchers, who frequently mistrusted the gauchos' fiercely independent spirit and cavalier attitude to property.

Geography: The fertile Nile valley, between three and 20 kilometers wide and extending over 1,000 kilometers from the river delta in the north deep into the south, has been settled since earliest times. The Arabian Desert lies to the northwest, while the Libyan Desert in the west occupies one quarter of the country's area. Egypt is in a subtropical zone of high pressure, with only the Mediterranean coastal areas receiving rain in winter. The Aswan Dam enables the country's agricultural areas to be irrigated.

Politics: The cradle of one of the earliest major cultures from the 3rd millennium BC, Egypt fell under Libyan, Persian and Assyrian rule. At the turn of the millennium, the fertile Nile region was the granary of Ancient Rome. Islam took effect after the conquest by the Arabs in the 7th century. In 1517 the country came under Ottoman rule. British influence increased after the opening of the Suez Canal in 1869. Egypt became an independent kingdom in 1922. After conflicts with Israel over the latter's occupation of the Sinai peninsula in 1967, a peace treaty was concluded in 1979, and Sinai was returned in 1982.

Economy: The high level of education in the cities contrasts with the lifestyle of the nomads. Only the fertile Nile valley yields grain, sugar-cane and cotton – the latter being Egypt's principal export after oil. Agriculture accounts for 18% of GDP. The Suez Canal is a major source of revenue. Tourism is suffering from Islamic extremist acts of terrorism. Economic reforms in the 1990s led to an increase in foreign investment levels and growth rates.

Al-Saharaw
Western Sahara

Area: 266,000 sq km
Population: 267,000
GDP per capita: 9,300 US$
Capital: El Aaiún
Government: Republic/ annexed by Morocco in 1979
Languages: Arabic, Spanish, Hassani
Currency: Saharaui peseta; unofficial currency: 1 Moroccan dirham = 100 centimes

Geography: This almost uninhabited country largely consists of semi-desert. Rocky outcrops feature in the north, sand deserts in the south.

Politics: The territory belonged to the Islamic empires that ruled over what is now Morocco from the 11th century. It was declared Spanish in 1885 and became the overseas province of Spanish Sahara in 1958. The Polisario Liberation Front was founded in 1973. Spain withdrew in 1975 and designated Morocco and Mauretania as administrative powers. In 1979 Mauretania waived its share in favor of Polisario, only to have its share annexed by Morocco. After a UNO peace plan Polisario and Morocco agreed a cease-fire in 1991, to be followed by a referendum on independence planned for 2008 after a period of extensive autonomy. The country is recognized by 29 OAU states and 77 states worldwide.

Economy: The country has rich phosphate reserves and fishing grounds in coastal waters. Oasis cultivation and nomadic animal husbandry are practised as subsistence farming.

Al-Yaman
Yemen

Area: 527,970 sq km
Population: 20 million
GDP per capita: 800 US$
Capital: Sanaa
Government: Republic
Languages: Arabic (official), English
Currency: 1 Yemen rial = 100 fils

Geography: Yemen lies at the southwestern edge of the Arab peninsula. North Yemen occupies a coastal strip on the Red Sea, behind which rise highlands and the Rub al-Khali desert. The South extends behind a narrow, coastal area with high rainfall to meet a mountain plateau, giving way to the sandy desert in the north. The country enjoys a tropical desert climate. Tourists can visit numerous Islamic and ancient sites of the Kingdom of Sheba.

Politics: In pre-Christian times, Yemen belonged to the Kingdom of the Minoans and Shebans. In the 7th century it was conquered by the Abbasids, and in the 16th century became part of the Ottoman Empire. Under British control, the Kingdom of Yemen was created in 1918 in Northern Yemen, and became a republic in 1962. A socialist republic was created in South Yemen in 1967. The process of unification to the Republic of Yemen lasted from 1990 to 1994. The first direct presidential elections were held in 1999.

Economy: Yemen is one of the most underdeveloped countries in the world. Agriculture is still the most important sector. Nomads roam the hinterland and industrialization is still in its infancy, with the export of oil playing the most important role.

Andorra
Andorra

Area: 467.7 sq km
Population: 69,900
GDP per capita: 19,000 US$
Capital: Andorra la Vella
Government: Parliamentary principality
Language: Catalan (official), Spanish, French

Argentina: The Patagonian Andes in the southern part of the country.

Currency: 1 euro = 100 cents

Geography: The small principality of Andorra consists of three valleys surrounded by high mountains in the eastern Pyrenees (highest peak: Coma Pendrosa, 2,946 m). More than half of the country is above the tree line.

Politics: Several states vied for control of Andorra before the 13th century. An agreement in 1278 left the area under the joint control of the French monarchy and the bishops of d'Urgell in Catalonia. In 1993 Andorra was established as an independent parliamentary democracy.

Economy: Andorra's topography limited the growth of industrial activity and large-scale agriculture. Sheep herding and tourism are the country's largest industries.

Angola
Angola

Area: 1,246,700 sq km
Population: 11 million
GDP per capita: 1,900 US$
Capital: Luanda
Government: Republic
Languages: Portuguese (official), Bantu languages
Currency: 1 kwanza = 100 lwei

Geography: The high plateau is traversed by rivers and slopes steeply down to the rain forests along the narrow coastal region. The tropical climate of Angola's interior is moderated by the altitude. Savanna to the far southwest gives way to desert. Nine national parks and animal reserves provide protection for indigenous wildlife.

Politics: Discovered in 1483 by Diego Cao, Angola remained a Portuguese province. Its independence in 1975 triggered a civil war lasting more than 15 years. The country is currently ruled by UN mandate, but the peace process is making only slow progress. In 2002 a peace treaty was signed by the two warring factions, stabilizing the political situation. Angola now faces a long process of reconstruction.

Economy: The long civil war has ravaged the economy, and the population depends on foreign aid. Agricultural products are sisal, sugar and tobacco. Key exports are coffee, diamonds, petroleum, and iron ores. The small industrial sector primarily processes agricultural goods. Development of the country's poor infrastructure is desperately needed for greater economic progress.

Antigua and Barbuda
Antigua and Barbuda

Area: 442 sq km
Population: 68,300
GDP per capita: 11,000 US$
Capital: St. John's
Government: Constitutional monarchy within the Commonwealth
Languages: English (official), Creole
Currency: 1 Eastern Caribbean dollar = 100 cents

Geography: This tiny country in the Caribbean Ocean includes the islands of Antigua, Barbuda and Redonda in the Lesser Antilles. Uninhabited Redonda is part of the region's volcanic arc. In the south there are craggy mountains with lush vegetation. The climate is tropical, moderated by the sea winds but with frequent hurricanes. Beaches and ocean are ideal for bathing and diving, and the coastline is fringed by coral banks.

Politics: Discovered by Columbus in 1493, the islands were settled 150 years later by the English, who established plantations there. Antigua and Barbuda was a British colony from 1667 and did not gain independence until 1981. The country is governed by a bicameral parliament, elected every five years; the British monarch is the head of state.

Economy: The majority of the population is of African descent. Various plants are cultivated. The largest contribution to the economy comes from tourism. Exports include petroleum products.

Mysterious glances: Traditional dress is becoming rare in modern Yemen, but the veil is still an important part of women's clothing.

Many islamic women do not regard it as a symbol of suppression, but as an expression of their Muslim identity and growing autonomy in public life.

Argentina
Argentina

Area: 2,766,889 sq km
Population: 39.1 million
GDP per capita: 11,200 US$
Capital: Buenos Aires
Government: Federal republic
Language: Spanish
Currency: 1 Argentinian peso = 100 centavos

Geography: The country is around 3,700 kilometers long from north to south; the Andean mountains form its western border with Chile. To the southeast, the main settlement area is the treeless plains of the pampas, with their fertile steppes, giving way in the south to Patagonia's tableland. In the north, the pampas meets the densely wooded, rainy area between the Paraná and Uruguay rivers and the swamp forests along their banks, terminating in the Brazilian mountains. Favorite destinations are the beaches along the Atlantic Ocean, the ski resorts and nature reserves in the Andes and the game reserves on Tierra del Fuego.

Politics: The arrival of the Spanish in 1516 heralded two centuries of foreign rule that ended in 1816 with the Proclamation of Independence by the United Provinces. After conquering Patagonia in 1880, Argentina became a major destination for immigrants. Until 1982 the country was ruled by a succession of military juntas and conservative large-scale landowners. Argentina's defeat by Britain in the Falklands War led to the end of military rule and to free presidential elections in 1983. Since 1999 Argentina has faced a deep economic recession, resulting in the country's inability to pay back foreign debts and an exploding crime rate.

Economy: 90% of Argentina's population are descended from European immigrants. The country has extensive agricultural and industrial capacities. Agriculture (principally livestock) accounts for 8% of GDP, and services 63%. The country's industry concentrates on processing agricultural products and on mechanical engineering. Exports are primarily from the agricultural sector.

Armenija (Hayastan)
Armenia

Area: 29,800 sq km
Population: 3 million
GDP per capita: 3,900 US$
Capital: Yerevan
Government: Republic
Languages: Armenian (official), Russian, Kurdish
Currency: 1 dram = 100 luma

Geography: The Ararat highlands extend to the west, with the peaks of the Lesser Caucasus in the north. The central depression in the southeast is dominated by Lake Sevan.

The south has fertile farmlands and a favorable climate. Owing to the continental climate, steppe and semi-desert vegetation dominate. Armenia frequently suffers earthquakes and drought.

Politics: In the 7th century Turks and Persians contested the country; in the 19th century, Russia's attempt at conquest was repulsed. In 1922 Armenia was divided, with one part becoming a Soviet Republic, and the other remaining with Turkey. Armenia declared its independence in 1991, but retained the socialist-tinted constitution. The predominantly Christian enclave of Nagorno Karabakh has in recent times been the object of conflict with Armenia's Islamic neighbor Azerbaijan.

Economy: The economy is characterized by the difficult transition from the Soviet planned economy to a market economy. Half of GDP is generated by industry, only a fifth by services. Important exports

are light industry products and diamonds. The country imports oil, gas, and foodstuffs.

As-Sūdān
Sudan

Area: 2,505,813 sq km
Population: 39.1 million
GDP per capita: 1,900 US$
Capital: Khartoum
Government: Republic
Languages: Arabic (official),

1 Agriculture is the most important economic sector in Sudan. The south, however, is suffering from aridity and is therefore dependent on aid from the north.

2 The mini state of Antigua and Barbuda belongs to the "islands above the wind" (Lesser Antilles). The economy is mostly dependent on cruise tourism.

3 Argentina: Perito Moreno Glacier in Los Glaciares National Park.

4 The adobe houses of Wadi Hadramaut (UNESCO World Heritage Site) in the south of Yemen reach up to 30 meters high and are nearly 300 years old.

Land of the plains: In Bangladesh heavy rainfalls during monsoon periods flood the rivers. Like islands, dry spots are only accessible by boat. Paddies cover the fertile alluvial soil, the largest river delta of the world formed by the rivers of Ganges and Bramaputra. Sylhet in the north, surrounded by rolling hills on the border to the Indian province of Assam, houses the largest tea plantations of the country.

English, Hamitic, and Nilotic languages
Currency: 1 Sudanese pound = 100 piastres

Geography: The Sudan is the largest African country in terms of area. It is divided into north and south by the great swamps of the Sudd, a flood plain of the White Nile. Almost one-third of the country consists of barren sand desert, although rain forests grow in the mountainous southern regions. The climate is largely continental tropical. The game reserves in the south are the chief tourist destinations. Desertification is a major environmental issue throughout the country.

Politics: Sudan's early history was shaped by Egypt; an independent kingdom was not formed until 1000 BC. Christian empires ruled from the 6th century onwards until the country was Islamicized by Arab settlers at the end of the 13th century. Sudan was ruled by the British in the 19th and 20th centuries. Since Sudan acheived independence in 1956, religious and ethnic differences have led to frequent political unrest and armed conflicts; human rights violations and famine are commonplace in the country.

Economy: Subsistence agriculture and nomadic animal husbandry are practised. Agricultural products are the chief exports, comprising cotton, peanuts, sesame, and oilseed as well as 80% of the world's gum resin production. The small industrial sector, which did not begin its slow development until after independence, is rudimentary and employs 5% of the workforce. Services are the most significant sector, accounting for 50% of GDP, and the new oil industry boosts exports.

Australia
Australia

Area: 7,686,850 sq km
Population: 19.9 million
GDP per capita: 28,900 US$
Capital: Canberra
Government: Parliamentary democracy
Languages: English, Asian and Aboriginal languages

Currency: 1 Australian dollar = 100 cents

Geography: Deserts and semi-arid land cover around 70% of the world's smallest continent, including most of western and central Australia. The 3,000-kilometer-long Great Dividing Range stretches along the continent's east coast, while the Great Barrier Reef extends 2,000 kilometers from north to south, directly off the coast. Northern Australia features extensive grassy and forested savannas as well as humid rain forests along the coast. The Murray and Darling rivers in the south are Australia's most important rivers. The island state of Tasmania is located south of mainland Australia's southeastern coast. In addition to numerous national parks and wilderness areas, Australia also features countless beaches and diving sites open to tourists.

Barbuda: Sandy beaches make the Island a holiday paradise.

Politics: The Aborigines, Australia's indigenous inhabitants, arrived on the continent during the last ice age. In 1770, British captain James Cook claimed the colony of New South Wales for Great Britain. The colony served as a British penal colony until 1865. The first free settlers arrived – in the Sydney area – in 1793. The six Australian colonies united in 1901 to form the Commonwealth of Australia. In the following decades, Australia achieved increased political independence but the British monarch remains the country's official head of state. The Aborigines have been granted increased political rights in recent decades, including citizenship and voting rights after generations of political and social neglect.

Economy: Immigrants from more than 120 nations have settled in Australia during the past two centuries. The country's standard of living is one of the world highest. The country's leading export products include agricultural goods, and mineral resources such as iron, uranium, nickel, bauxite, raw diamonds, and opals. Australia, the world's leading wool and beef exporter, is also an important producer of grain, wine meat and dairy products. Around 25% of the country's labor force works in the manufacturing sector, while at least 70% of Australians now work in the service sector, including tourism.

Azerbajdzan
Azerbaijan

Area: 86,600 sq km
Population: 7.9 million
GDP per capita: 3,400 US$
Capital: Baku
Government: Republic
Languages: Azeri (official), Turkish, Russian
Currency: 1 manat = 100 gepik

Geography: Over half the country's area is covered by the Greater Caucasus (4,466 m) in the north, the Lesser Cau-

casus with Karabakh in the west, and the southern mountains extending to Iran. The plains of the Kura and Arax rivers in the east are bordered by the Caspian Sea in the south. The climate ranges from subtropical and humid to arid-dry. Large-scale irrigation is necessary for agriculture.

Politics: A settlement in early times, the area was briefly a Roman province. Islamization commenced in the 7th century. After 300 years of Mongol rule, Azerbaijan was besieged first by the Ottomans and then by the Russians, who in 1813 divided the country with the Persians. The Soviet Republic of Azerbaijan was founded in 1920. Ethnic conflicts over the Nagorno Karabakh enclave and its annexation by Armenia in 1988 led to the declaration of independence in 1991 and to a more pronounced turn towards Islam.

Economy: The economy concentrates on winemaking, cotton, tobacco, vegetables, olives, and tea. Canned fish products (caviar) from the Caspian Sea are exported. The country's real wealth, however, lies in its mineral resources such as oil, iron ore, copper, and manganese, for which development is planned. These resources form the basis of the remaining industry (chemical, mechanical engineering). The main oil fields lie in the Apseron peninsula and to the west of Baku. Environmental issues are an increasing concern.

Bahamas
Bahamas

Area: 13,939 sq km
Population: 300,000
GDP per capita: 16,800 US$
Capital: Nassau
Government: Parliamentary monarchy within the Commonwealth
Language: English
Currency: 1 Bahamian dollar = 100 cents

Geography: The island state comprises 30 large and 700 small to tiny islands, most with sandy beaches and thousands of reefs extending over 1,200 kilometers from Florida's east coast down to Haiti. Tourist centers with bathing or sailing

facilities can be found on the Exumas and around Nassau. Angling is popular around the Bimini Islands, and the Inagua Islands have a rich variety of tropical fauna.

Politics: It was here that Columbus first stepped onto American soil in 1492. The islands were depopulated by Spanish slave traders; the British established a crown colony in the 17th century. The Bahamas have been independent since 1973. The parliament is bicameral, modeled on its British counterpart, with elections held every five years.

Economy: Agriculture is restricted by the barrenness of the steppes. In addition to tourism, which accounts for around half of GDP, the economy is principally driven by the resale of imported petroleum and petroleum products, chiefly to the USA.

Bahrain see Al-Bahrain

Bangladesh
Bangladesh

Area: 144,000 sq km
Population: 141.3 million
GDP per capita: 1,900 US$
Capital: Dhaka
Government: Republic
Languages: Bengali (official), Urdu and Hindi
Currency: 1 taka = 100 poisha

Geography: The entire country consists of fertile lowlands in a monsoon region with high rainfall (June to October); the unprotected coast, with few harbors, is threatened by flooding, often with catastrophic consequences. The southwest at the Indian border comprises part of the flood plains of the Ganges and Brahmaputra. Tourist destinations include Dhaka with its interesting old town, and the coastal city of Chittagong for swimming. Part of the Sundarban National Park, with unique fauna, is on Bangladeshi territory.

Politics: The former Bengal belonged to the British colony of India (1757–1947). In the division that followed Indian independence, West Bengal

Dreamtime: The Aborigines of Australia inhabited the continent for 30,000 years. The myths of the semi-nomadic clans are evidence of their lifestyle in harmony with the forces of nature. Today many of the sacred landscapes of the Aborigines again carry their mythical names.

remained part of India, whereas East Bengal went to Pakistan. After bloody riots following the great flood of 1970, East Bengal separated from Pakistan, and the Republic of Bangladesh was declared in 1971. After 15 years of authoritarian presidential rule, characterized by frequent coups d'état, the first democratically elected government took office in 1991. Relations with neighboring India have visibly improved in recent years.

Economy: The education system has been seriously neglected, and only a quarter of the population is literate. One of the poorest national economies and highest population densities in the world, Bangladesh relies essentially on agriculture, which employs 66% of the working population in small companies and generates one third of GDP. The most important exports are rice, jute and seafood. 12% of the workforce are employed in industry, comprising small handicraft concerns (jute products, cotton yarn and fabrics, textiles, sugar, and tea), and generating about one third of GDP. Heavy industry processes the available raw materials (natural gas, oil, coal, and ores) but is of minor importance.

Barbados
Barbados

Area: 430 sq km
Population: 276,000
GDP per capita: 16,200 US$
Capital: Bridgetown
Government: Parliamentary monarchy within the Commonwealth
Languages: English (official), Bajan
Currency: 1 Barbados dollar = 100 cents

Geography: The easternmost island of the Lesser Antilles, 36 kilometers long and 24 kilometers wide, is volcanic in origin and largely (80%) composed of fossilized coral and fringed by coral reefs. The impermeable bedrock prevents the formation of watercourses. Only the north of the island has rolling hills, some up to 340 meters high. The island's climate and natural features make it a holiday paradise.

Politics: Discovered in the 16th century by Spain, Barbados became a British crown colony in 1652. In the 17th century the first settlers established sugar-cane plantations worked by imported African slaves; the slave economy ended in 1838. Barbados gained independence in 1966.

Economy: The traditional sugar-cane cultivation employs only 6% of the workforce and is dwindling in significance. The island is heavily dependent on imports, including foodstuffs, timber, consumer goods, paper, machinery, and crude oil. Its exports include sugar, cotton, and peanuts, but

also electronic components and petroleum from deposits in the interior and the north and east coasts. Services, principally tourism, contribute two-thirds of GDP. The island has an international airport and seaport.

Belarus
Belarus

Area: 207,600 sq km
Population: 10.3 million
GDP per capita: 6,000 US$
Capital: Minsk
Government: Republic
Language: Belarusian (official), Russian, minority languages
Currency: 1 Belarusian rouble = 100 kopecks

Geography: Belarus is located on the vast East European Plain and consists largely of flat lowlands. The country features numerous rivers, canals and lakes in all of its regions. The Palesse marsh in southern

Belarus is the largest marshland in Europe. The capital city of Minsk and the country's lakes are Belarus' principal tourist attractions.

Politics: The Slavic ancestors of the modern Belarusians were able to preserve their language and culture despite

 **The Great Barrier Reef** near the northeastern coast of Australia.

 **Uluru-kata Tjuta National Park** in Central Australia features the famous monolith Ayers Rock (Uluru) and other interesting natural attractions.

The Sydney Opera House is dominated by skyscrapers of the Australian metropolis. Port Jackson (also known as Sydney Harbour) saw the first penal colonists at the end of the 18th century.

België/Belgique Belgium

Caribbean joie de vivre: The small country of Belize is noted for its easy-going lifestyle, its snow-white beaches picturesquely fringed by coconut palms, and untouched tropical land-scapes in the interior.

The multi-ethnic population, augmented by Europeans and Americans, lives an unhurried, carefree life in tune with the tropical climate.

centuries of foreign domination by the Polish and Lithuanian Commonwealth. The country came under the control of the Russian Empire at the end of the 18th century. In 1922, Belarus became a Soviet republic in the USSR. Belarus was declared an independent republic in 1991, following the collapse of the Soviet Union. The repressive policies of Belarus' government have been repeatedly criticized by the European Union and numerous human rights organizations and have isolated the country.

Economy: Belarus faced a severe economic crisis, including high inflation rates and rising foreign debts, during most of the 1990s. The country has experienced stable growth in recent years, but the economy remains heavily regulated and is largely closed to foreign investment. The agricultural sector accounts for approximately one third of the country's GDP. Manufacturing produces just over half (56%) of the national GDP. The government has failed to implement the reforms neccesary for stable economic development.

België/Belgique
Belgium

Area: 30,528 sq km
Population: 10.3 million
GDP per capita: 29,000 US$
Capital: Brussels
Government: Parliamentary monarchy
Languages: French, Flemish, German
Currency: 1 euro = 100 cents

Geography: Belgium's smooth North Sea coast is lined by sand dunes and sandy beaches. The west and north are dominated by fertile marshy plains, polders, and moorlands. Farther south lies the central plateau, a region of fertile valley crossed by numerous rivers and canals. The third major region of Belgium, the Ardennes, is a heavily forested area of low mountains. Belgium's major tourist attractions include the historic towns of Flanders, the Ardennes countryside, and the capital city of Brussels.

Politics: The cities of Flanders were among Europe's leading

commercial and cultural centers during the late Middle Ages. From then, until the 19th century, Belgium was under the control of several foreign nations – Spain between the 16th and 17th centuries, followed by Austria, France, and finally the Netherlands. Belgium became an independent kingdom in 1833. Modern Belgium is a federal state divided into three distinct regions – Flanders, Brussels, and Wallonia, each of which has extensive political autonomy and its own government. The capital city of Brussels houses the European Union and NATO headquarters.

Economy: Belgium's highly productive agricultural sector produces less than 2% of the country's GDP. The industrial areas along the Sambre and Meuse (Maas) Rivers are important centers of the chemical, glass, and machinery industries. The expanding service sectors currently account for around 68% of the country's

Brussels: The city is the cultural and political center of Belgium.

annual GDP. Belgium has one of the world's most modern transportation networks.

Belize
Belize

Area: 22,965 sq km
Population: 273,000
GDP per capita: 4,900 US$
Capital: Belmopan
Government: Const. monarchy

Languages: English (official), Creole, Spanish, minorities
Currency: 1 Belize dollar = 100 cents

Geography: Belize, to the southeast of the Yucatán Peninsula, is composed of swampy coastland with large rivers and countless lagoons enclosing hilly landscapes (altitudes around 1,000 m) in the interior. Rain forests and dense mangrove forests flourish in the humid, tropical climate. A major natural phenomenon is an island chain of coral reefs extending 300 kilometers down the coastline. Hurricanes are frequent.

Politics: Before its discovery by Columbus in the 16th century and colonization by the Spanish conqueror Cortèz (1524/25) the region was the heartland of the Mayan civilization. Settled from the 17th century by British colonists, it became a crown colony in 1862 as British Honduras. Renamed Belize in 1973, it

gained independence in 1981. The Governor-General of Belize represents the British monarch.

Economy: While 38% of the area is suitable for cultivation, only around 12% is actually utilized. Citrus fruits, seafood, bananas, sugarcane, cocoa, and tropical hardwoods are key exports. The underdeveloped industrial sector employs 10% of

the workforce and is primarily oriented toward products for export, comprising sawmills, sugar factories, rum distilleries, and textiles. Services, including tourism, account for 57% of GDP.

Benin
Benin

Area: 112,622 sq km
Population: 7.2 million
GDP per capita: 1,100 US$
Capital: Porto Novo
Government: Presidential republic
Languages: French (official), Fon, Yoruba, and other tribal languages
Currency: 1 CFA franc = 100 centimes

Geography: Benin's coast along the Gulf of Guinea consists of humid, swampy lowlands fringed by lagoons. To the north fertile clay highlands rise to form a plateau. In the west the land slopes gently down to the Niger basin. Tourist destinations are the nature parks in the north, and the cities of Ouidah and Porto Novo in the south.

Politics: In the 17th century the kingdom of the Fon, based in the city of Aborney, increased in power. The Fon delivered slaves to European trading centers. In 1899 the region became part of the colony of French West Africa under the name Dahomey, and was decolonized and awarded independence in 1960. The Republic of Benin was established in 1975 after a coup d'ètat. Torn by tribal wars, the country held its first free parliamentary elections in 1991.

Economy: Benin is inhabited by more than 60 ethnic populations. Attempts to nationalize the economy in the 1970s failed. The country primarily lives from the agricultural sector, which produces for the domestic market, as well as coffee, oils, and cotton for export. The industrial and service sectors are both relatively undeveloped. Tourism is receiving increasing promotion. The country has experienced impressive growth rates in recent years but the high popu-

lation growth has prevented a significant rise in living standards.

Bhutan
Bhutan

Area: 47,000 sq km
Population: 2.2 million
GDP per capita: 1,300 US$
Capital: Thimphu
Government: Constitutional monarchy
Languages: Dzongkha (official), Tibetan dialects
Currency: 1 ngultrum = 100 chetrum

Geography: This small kingdom on the southern incline of the Himalayas is accessible only with extreme difficulty. The mighty mountain chains (Jomo Lhari, 7,314 m) flank the high plateau, which slopes down only gradually to the southern foothills on the Indian border. Interesting destinations include the monasteries and temples in the vicinity of the capital.

Politics: In a country initially ruled by Indian princes, Tibetan conquerors founded a lamaist state in the 9th century. In the wake of 19th century civil wars, a hereditary monarchy emerged under British influence, which today governs the land together with the National Assembly (parliament of estates). There is close cooperation with India over foreign affairs and defense. The country did not receive television until 1999 – a gift from the reigning monarch to his people.

Economy: Nearly half of GDP is generated by agriculture, which also accounts for 90% of all jobs and covers domestic needs. A few products (maize, wheat, cardamom) are also exported. Wood from the extensive forest is exported to India. The poorly developed industrial sector consists of small handicraft concerns (weaving, metalwork, mask carving). Bhutan has been open to tourism to a limited extent since 1974, and the 5,000 annual tourists are the most important source of foreign currency. Technical and mechanical work traditionally occupies a lowly status.

Mysterious: The people of Bhutan call their kingdom Druk Yul, "land of the thunder-dragon". White prayer banners and countless sacred buildings bear witness to the deeply religious nature of the mostly Buddhist popula-tion. The people of the almost inac-cessible valleys of the southern Himalayas have been able to preserve their traditional way of life. Nomadic yak-herds live in the upper regions.

Bolivia
Bolivia

Area: 1,098,581 sq km
Population: 8.7 million
GDP per capita: 2,400 US$
Capital: Sucre
Government: Presidential republic
Languages: Spanish, Quechua and Aymará (all official)
Currency: 1 boliviano = 100 centavos

Geography: The west of the country is taken up by the Bolivian Andes, divided by the Altiplano plateau with an aver-age altitude of 3,000–4,000 meters. The lowlands to the east of the Andes give way to the plain of La Plata in the south and the Amazon basin in the north. The climate ranges from cold to tropical. Tourist attrac-tions are Lake Titicaca, Inca sites in Tiahuanaco, and the ancient silver-mining center of Potosí.

Politics: Bolivia's history has always been closely linked to that of neighboring Peru. The end of the 18th century saw the first Indian uprisings against Spanish colonial rule, brought to an end in 1825 with the foundation of the republic. The present-day political situ-ation is marked by ideological conflicts, guerilla warfare and military coups. Bolivia has had around 200 governments since it was founded. The unicameral parliament, like the president, is elected every five years.

Economy: Almost 40% of the workforce supply 17% of GDP in agriculture on the plateau and in the valleys. The most important crop is probably illegal coca cultivation. Mining includes zinc, tin, lead, and precious metals. Petroleum and natural gas exports are an important economic factor. The processing industry pri-marily comprises small and medium-size enterprises (foodstuffs, textiles).

Bosna i Hercegovina
Bosnia-Herzegovina

Area: 51,129 sq km
Population: 4 million
GDP per capita: 6,100 US$ (estimated)

Capital: Sarajevo
Government: Republic
Languages: Bosnian, Croatian, Serbian (all official)
Currency: 1 mark

Geography: Bosnia-Herzego-vina is a largely mountainous country with large stretches of dense forests and a continen-tal climate. Because of poor soils and the mountainous ter-rain, only a few sections of the country, such as the Sava Val-ley, are suitable for large-scale agriculture.

Politics: Bosnia was domina-ted by foreign powers during most of its history. A large per-centage of Bosnia's popu-lation converted to Islam during the more than 400 years that the region was under the control of the Turkish Ottoman Empire from 1463. The region was ruled by the Austro-Hungarian Empire in the 19th century. Bosnia was part of the republic of Yugoslavia during most of the 20th century. Following the collapse of Yugoslavia, Bosnia experienced a period of ethnic conflict that escalated into a bloody war and widespread "ethnic cleansing." The coun-try has been divided into an ethnic Serb republic and a Croat-Muslim federation since 1995. Many refugees are now returning to the country des-pite continuing hostility be-tween the ethnic groups.

Economy: Most of the coun-try's infrastructure and indus-trial facilities were damaged in the civil war of the 1990s. Foreign aid remains important to the country, but post-war recovery is rapidly progressing.

Botswana
Botswana

Area: 600,370 sq km
Population: 1.6 million
GDP per capita: 8,800 US$
Capital: Gaborone
Government: Republic
Languages: Setswana, English (both official)
Currency: 1 pula = 100 thebe

Geography: The Kalahari semi-desert covers almost 80% of Botswana, which extends over the chiefly flat continental plateau (800–1,300 m). Agri-culture is restricted to small areas in the southeast. Around one-fifth of the country is a registered national park. The Okavango forms a freshwater delta on the northern rim of the Kalahari. The climate is subtropical and extremely dry, with maximum temperatures of 40° C in summer and 6° C in winter. Temperatures in the capital range from 13° C (July) to 26° C (January).

1 Marginal rainfall generated vast salt-pans in the Makarikari Basin of Botswana.

2 The impressive ruins of the Maya city Xunantunich, one of Belize's main attractions, perch on a mountain in the jungle.

3 The traditional ponchos and blankets of the Bolivian Indios are produced from naturally dyed llama or sheep's wool.

4 In the Kingdom of Bhutan, temples are not only places of worship but also administrative centers for the small country. The picture shows the 17th-century Paro Dzong.

At Carnival time in Brazil: Samba sets the pace. Processions may last for days and are crammed with gorgeous costumes that are lovingly fashioned throughout the year.

Politics: English missionary territory since 1820, Botswana became a British protectorate in 1885 because of its key strategic location to the north of the Boer state. The country was administered by the British Ambassador to South Africa from 1964, and gained independence in 1966 as the Republic of Botswana. The government comprises the National Assembly and the House of Chiefs.

Economy: 95% of the population are Bantu, with over 80% living outside the urban centers. Agriculture largely consists of extensive cattle farming, frequently beset by drought. However, the backbone of the economy are the rich diamond mines of the Kalahari, which have made Botswana the second largest exporter of these gems in the world. Iron ore and anthracite are also important export commodities. Botswana is a member of the Southern African Customs Union.

Brasil
Brazil

Area: 8,511,996 sq km
Population: 184 million
GDP per capita: 7,600 US$
Capital: Brasília
Government: Federative rep.
Languages: Portuguese (official), regional Indian languages
Currency: 1 real = 100 centavos

Geography: The Atlantic forms the eastern border of the world's fifth largest country; the narrow coastal strip is densely populated. To the north, in the mountains of Guyana, tropical rain forest dominates the landscape. Farther south is the rain forest area of the Amazon basin, home to a unique ecosystem with countless animal species. Tourist centers are Rio de Janeiro, the coastal regions, the Amazon and the southwestern Iguazú Falls.

Politics: Brazil was settled as early as the 8th century BC. The Spanish reached the coast in 1500, the first Europeans to do so; however, the region became a Portuguese colony in the 17th century. In 1825 Brazil declared independence, and

economic prosperity began as coffee exports grew. The military seized power in 1961; the first general elections were held in 1982, and the country had a civil president in 1985. The new constitution of 1988 confirmed the presidential system, although the military still retains extensive influence. Voting is compulsory between the ages of 18 and 69.

Economy: The country is inhabited by many ethnic groups, the smallest of which are the indigenous Indians. Agriculture is highly profitable; coffee, cocoa, soybeans, sugar, tobacco, maize, and cotton are cultivated in addition to livestock farming. Rich natural resources (iron, manganese) are as yet not fully exploited. Economic reforms introduced from the mid-1990s are showing initial success. The industrial sector of this highly industrialized country (textiles, leather goods) is dominated by the automotive industry and its suppliers. Other key exports are metals and metal products.

Brunei
Brunei

Area: 5,765 sq km
Population: 365,000
GDP per capita: 18,600 US$

Brunei comprises two non-adjoining territories on the northern coast of Borneo, surrounded by the Malaysian Sarawak mountains. The hill country, covered by tropical rain forests, is the habitat of a rich fauna. The densely settled coast consists of alluvial land with mangrove forests, broken by coral sand beaches. The country has an equatorial rainy climate. The capital with its old town, Sultan's palace and mosque, is worth visiting.

Politics: Muslim Malays founded the Sultanate of Brunei in the 15th century and it became a British protectorate in 1888. After Japanese occupation in 1941–1945, it became a British colony until the constitution of 1959, which initially guaranteed autonomy. Brunei finally gained independence in 1984. Enthroned in 1967, the Sultan took over the affairs of state in 1973, and has reigned as an absolute monarch since 1984, supported by a council. He is one of the world's richest men. The country has no political parties and no suffrage.

Economy: Islam plays an important role in the life of the predominantly Malay population, which, owing to the country's enormous riches, enjoys full social protection. Agricul-

Bŭlgarija
Bulgaria

Area: 110,910 sq km
Population: 7.5 million
GDP per capita: 7,600 US$
Capital: Sofia
Government: Republic
Language: Bulgarian
Currency: 1 lev = 100 stotinki

Geography: The marshy Danube basin forms the northern border of Bulgaria. South of this region lie vast fertile plains. Southern Bulgaria is largely mountainous: the Balkans, Rhodope Mountains, and other highlands cover over a third of the country. Bulgaria has a continental climate, with warm summers and cold winters. The country's major tourist attractions include the beaches along the Black Sea and the cities of Varna and Sofia, as well as the landscapes of Pirin National Park.

Politics: The first Bulgarian state was formed in the 7th century by Slavs and Bulgars from the Volga basin. Bulgaria was dominated by the Turkish Ottoman Empire for more than five centuries before it achieved independence in 1878. After decades as a kingdom, Bulgaria was declared a people's republic in 1947. The country was closely aligned to

transition to democracy in the early 1990s. The fall of the socialist government in 1996 was followed by fiscal discipline and economic reforms. Despite recent impressive growth and successful reforms, most Bulgarians still live in poverty. Manufacturing and services account for more than 75% of GDP. Major agricultural products include wine, fruits, and tobacco. Lignite, iron ore, lead, and zinc are mined. Key exports include chemicals and textiles.

Burkina Faso
Burkina Faso

Area: 274.200 sq km
Population: 13.6 million
GDP per capita: 1,100 US$
Capital: Ouagadougou
Government: Republic
Languages: French (official), Fulbe, More and other tribal languages
Currency: 1 CFA franc = 100 centimes

Geography: Wet savannas in the southwest give way to dry savannas in the country's center and main settlements. The Black Volta is the only river that carries water all year. Part of the Sahel desert region lies in the northeast, where a semi-desert climate reigns. Tourist centers are the cities of Ouagadougou and Bobo-Dioulasso and the national parks with their rich wildlife.

Politics: The heart of today's Burkina Faso was the state of Ouagadougou, founded in the 11th century by the Mossi and conquered by the French in the 19th century. The former colony of Upper Volta (1919–1960) was renamed Burkina Faso in 1984. After independence, Burkina Faso was weakened by frequent attempted coups followed by years of military dictatorship; the political situation seems to have stabilized.

Economy: Among the most densely populated countries in West Africa, Burkina Faso is inhabited by around 160 tribes, around half of whom practice natural religions. Illiteracy is high at around 80%. Despite regular periods of drought, the country's economy is based on

Rio de Janeiro: The Sugarloaf's peak towers 395 meters over Guanabara Bay.

Capital: Bandar Seri Begawan
Government: Sultanate
Languages: Malay (official), English
Currency: 1 Brunei dollar = 100 cents
Geography: The Sultanate of

ture is of subordinate importance. A large proportion of the foodstuffs are imported. Brunei has extensive petroleum and natural gas reserves and 56% of GDP is generated in this sector. Tourism is as yet limited.

the Soviet Union before 1991. Bulgaria is now a multi-party parliamentary republic and a candidate for EU membership.

Economy: Bulgaria has faced several economic crises since its

Tax-heaven: The vast wealth of the small Sultanate of Brunei is solely founded upon the exploitation of the country's petroleum resources.

Its inhabitants pay no taxes, enjoy free housing and receive a basic salary from the state.

agriculture, with 90% of the population practising subsistence farming to account for 35% of GDP. Small amounts of cotton are exported. Apart from gold, the rich natural resources are largely untapped. The country's poor infrastructure and widespread corruption have impaired development. 48% of GDP is generated by the services sector and 17% by industry.

Burundi
Burundi

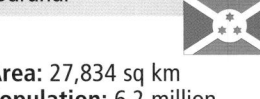

Area: 27,834 sq km
Population: 6.2 million
GDP per capita: 600 US$
Capital: Bujumbura
Government: Presidential republic
Languages: Kirundi, French (official), Kiswaheli
Currency: 1 Burundi franc = 100 centimes

Geography: Lying to the northeast of Lake Tanganyika, the country comprises uplands with wet and dry savannas in the interior and humid tropical rain forests to the northeast. The humid, tropical climate is moderated by the country's relatively high average elevation above sea level.

Politics: Tutsi tribes invaded the territory of Burundi in the 15th century and established feudal rule over the indigenous Hutus. In 1890, the country became part of the German colony of East Africa, and subsequently fell under Belgian administration. Since Burundi's independence in 1962, the political situation has been determined by repeated conflicts between the Hutu (85% of the population) and Tutsi (15%). Despite a new constitution (1992) and international efforts, the civil war cannot be regarded as over.

Economy: Agriculture is the chief economic sector. The mild climate favors tropical fruit farming and extensive animal husbandry. The industrial center around the city of Bujumbura produces textiles and small amounts of agricultural products for export, with coffee the most important of these. The government of Burundi is heavily dependent on foreign aid.

Cabo Verde
Cape Verde

Area: 4,033 sq km
Population: 415,000
GDP per capita: 1,400 US$
Capital: Praia
Government: Republic
Languages: Portuguese (official), Creole
Currency: 1 Cape Verde escudo = 100 centavos

Geography: Cape Verde, an archipelago off the west coast of Africa, comprises nine large islands and five uninhabited islets, all of volcanic origin. The landscape is dominated by bush, plains and semi-desert vegetation. Cape Verde has one of the lowest rainfalls in the world, and drought periods often last for years. The sandy beaches on Sal, Boa Vista, and Maio and the island of Fogo attract tourists.

Politics: After the islands' discovery by the Portuguese in 1460, it remained under Portuguese rule for more than 500 years. The slave trade with America brought long prosperity. Cape Verde did not become independent until 1975. The parliament, elected for a five-year term, elects the executive body and the President.

Economy: More than 70% of the population are descended from Portuguese immigrants and African slaves. More than 60% live and work abroad owing to the sparse natural resources. The rich fishing grounds off the coast account for 50% of export revenues, but almost all foodstuffs must be imported. There is a small textile industry. Most of the country's GDP is generated by the service sector. The country's local tourism industry is expanding.

Cameroun/Cameroon
Cameroon

Area: 475,442 sq km
Population: 16.1 million
GDP per capita: 1,800 US$
Capital: Yaoundé
Government: Presidential republic
Languages: French, English (both official), Bantu languages
Currency: 1 CFA franc = 100 centimes

Geography: The narrow coastal plain is covered by tropical rain forests that give way to wet savanna in the largely mountainous interior. To the north are dry grassland savannas that meet Lake Chad in the northeast and the Sahel to the far north. The highest point is the volcano Mount Cameroon (4,070 m). Cameroon's natural

1 The ritual dances and other traditions of eastern Africa arose as a way of making tribal territorial claims.

2 The Mosque of Bandar Seri Begawan, with its 44-meter-high minaret, lies amidst an artificial lagoon.

3 Burkina Faso is one of the poorest countries of the world.

4 The large monastery complex of Rila, most of which was reconstructed in the 19th century, is an important Bulgarian national monument.

Colombia: The year in this South American country is punctuated by numerous ethnic feasts: Five days before Ash Wednesday, Barranquilla turns into "the foolish city" and thousands of visitors come for the parades and dance competitions. Medellín is home to the second largest bullfighting arena in Latin America, where the popular corridas take place.

beauty and diversity of cultures offer a wide range of tourist attractions.

Politics: In the 15th century the coast of Cameroon was a center of the slave and ivory trade for European colonial powers. It became a German protectorate in 1884. From 1918 Britain and France shared the former colony under the mandate of the League of Nations, awarding the country independence in 1960. After a period as a federal republic, Cameroon became a presidential republic in 1972.

Economy: The population is composed of roughly 200 tribes. Agriculture plays a significant role, with coffee and cocoa, the principal exports. The country's petroleum resources brought only temporary economic growth. The industrial and services sectors are underdeveloped. Cameroon has experienced steady and strong growth in recent years and the country has made progress in reducing its foreign debt burden.

Central African Republic see République Centrafricaine

Chad see Tchad

Canada
Canada

Area: 9,984,670 sq km
Population: 32.5 million
GDP per capita: 29,700 US$
Capital: Ottawa
Government: Parliamentary monarchy in the Commonwealth
Languages: English, French (both official)
Currency: 1 Canadian dollar = 100 cents

Geography: Canada is the second largest country in the world, fringed to east and west by two great mountain chains. The foothills of the Appalachian Mountains extend to the Atlantic coast in the east, giving way in the west to the broad plains and lakes of the Great Plains and bounded by Hudson Bay to the north. The plains rise further to the west, meeting the Rocky Mountains (highest peak: Mt. Logan (6,050 m) at an altitude of 1,500 meters. To the far north, the Arctic islands border the North Polar Sea. 80% of the country consists of forests and tundra; the remainder is arable land and the polar islands. The continental climate fluctuates considerably, with average winter temperatures often falling below zero. Canada offers many tourist attractions: countless national parks of unspoiled scenery, Niagara Falls and cosmopolitan cities such as Toronto, Québec, Montreal, and Vancouver.

Politics: Up to the arrival of the first settlers in the 17th century, the country was inhabited by First Nations tribes and Inuit. Conflicts over British and French territorial claims were decided in 1763 by the British. Canada did not gain full political independence until 1931. The country is governed by a bicameral parliament, the lower house of which is elected every five years, with the British monarch as the formal Head of State. Given increasing calls for autonomy in the province of Québec (although the 1995 referendum narrowly rejected independence), a key goal of domestic politics is to achieve equilibrium between the French Canadian and English-speaking populations.

Prague: View of the Charles Bridge to the old town.

Economy: Canada is one of the world's most prosperous nations, with rich natural resources, forests and vast tracts of arable land. Agriculture employs 3% of the work-force; in addition to extensive livestock farming, grain (wheat, maize), and potatoes are cultivated. Ontario, Québec and British Columbia are the main industrial areas, where 22% of the workforce produces around 30% of GDP. Petroleum and natural gas drilling are important. The commercial and services sector accounts for 60% of GDP.

Cap Verde see Cabo Verde

Česká Republika
Czech Republic

Area: 78,866 sq km
Population: 10.2 million
GDP per capita: 15,700 US$
Capital: Prague
Government: Republic
Language: Czech (official), Slovakian
Currency: 1 Czech koruna = 100 haleru

Geography: The central plateau and the populous Bohemian basin are surrounded by the Sudetes, Bohemian forest, and the Ore Mountains. Moravia, in the east, is a fertile and largely hilly region. The Elbe and Vltava (Moldau) rivers are the most important waterways. The Czech Republic's leading tourist attractions include the historic towns of Bohemia, the natural landscapes of the country's mountainous regions, and the capital city Prague, one of Europe's most visited cities.

Politics: Great Moravia, a powerful Slavic state, emerged in the 9th century and was closely aligned to the German-dominated Holy Roman Empire for most of its history. Following the domination of the Hussites in the 15th century, the Czech lands were ruled by the Austrian Habsburg Empire. They united with Slovakia to form the first Czechoslovak republic in 1918 following the collapse of the Austro-Hungarian Empire. Czechoslovakia was occupied by Germany during the Second World War and assigned to the Soviet bloc in 1945. In 1948, Czechoslovakia was declared a socialist republic under the Communist party. An attempt at political liberalization during the Prague Spring of 1968 was brutally repressed by Soviet troops. Czechoslovakia was dissolved in 1993 and the Czech Republic joined the NATO in 1999 and the EU in 2004.

Economy: The Czech Republic is one of the most successful transition countries in Europe, with steady growth and an increase in living standards since the 1990s. Manufacturing accounts for a third of GDP, and services for more than 60%. Agriculture generates 5% of GDP. Leading industries include the production of textiles, glass, and metal. Coal, lignite, and metal ores are mined.

Chile
Chile

Area: 756,950 sq km
Population: 15.8 million
GDP per capita: 9,900 US$
Capital: Santiago de Chile
Government: Presidential republic
Language: Spanish
Currency: 1 Chilean peso = 100 centavos

Geography: Chile extends 4,230 kilometers along the west coast of South America, with an average width of only 176 kilometers. The country encompasses five highly diverse climatic zones. The northern desert zone is among the most arid places on earth; the semi-desert can only be cultivated with the help of irrigation. The main cities are in Central Chile between Illapel and Concepción; to their south is a panorama of lakes. The great forests of the south have high rainfall and a cold climate. The south also has many active volcanoes. The Easter Islands are a travel destination worth adding to Chile's many areas of natural beauty.

Politics: Conquered in 1544 by the Spanish, Chile gained independence in 1818 after a long struggle. The following decades were dominated by conflicts between the great landowners and farm workers. The socialist President Allende was overthrown in 1973 and power was seized by a military regime; after the brutal dictatorship of Pinochet, the country has faced the painful duty of addressing its political heritage since the process of democratization began in 1990. Chile has been a presidential republic since 1925, with a bicameral parliament. Voting is compulsory from age 18.

Economy: Only 23% of the area is fertile; in Central and South Chile fruit is grown for export and grain (wheat, maize) for subsistence. Yields from the rich fishing grounds are chiefly for export. Industry primarily consits of food processing (fishmeal, fish canning). Natural resources form the main economic sector (minerals, natural gas). Chile is the world's largest copper exporter (40% of foreign trade). Commerce and services account for more than half of GDP.

Choson
Korea, Democratic People's Republic

Area: 120,538 sq km
Population: 22.7 million
GDP per capita: 1,000 US$
Capital: Pyongyang
Government: People's democracy
Language: Korean
Currency: 1 won = 100 chon

Geography: The country covers the north of the Korean peninsula and a part of the Asian mainland. It is largely mountainous, with peaks of up to 2,541 meters (Gwammo), but becomes considerably flatter to the southwest. It has a cool, moderate monsoon climate. The country's flora and fauna have been seriously affected by industrialization.

Life in the polar region: The Inuit people of the eastern Canadian Arctic were highly skilled at surviving in the hostile environment. Isolated from other indiginous peoples, they developed a unique culture and *language. Today, they chiefly live in mixed settlements, and their traditional clothing, language, and customs are gradually being forgotten. They are in a minority in the population.*

Primary destinations for the scarcely developed tourist trade are Pyongyang and the old capital of Kaesong.

Politics: Owing to the country's geographic location, the history of Korea has always been influenced by the tensions between China and Japan. After the Japanese occupation (1910–1945), the north of the country was occupied by Soviet troops, and the Democratic People's Republic was established in 1948. The conflict with South Korea reached a climax during the Korean War (1950–1953). Initially close to China and the Soviet Union, the country has become increasingly isolated; relations with the USA are strained by Korea's nuclear arms programs.

Economy: The country has a Socialist planned economy. 65% of the population live in cities. Agriculture, which employs 34% of the workforce population and generates 20% of GDP, produces staples (rice, corn, potatoes) for domestic consumption. 7% of the industrial production is state run. The industrial sector generates two thirds of GDP; main branches include heavy industry (non-ferrous metals, coal), food, textiles, and increasingly the electrical goods industry. Reasons for the food shortages which led to a serious famine in 1997 include poor planning and enormous arms spending.

Città del Vaticano
Vatican City

Area: 0.44 sq km
Population: 920
GDP per capita: not available
Capital: Vatican City
Government: Sovereign diocese since 1929
Language: Latin, Italian
Currency: 1 euro = 100 cents, and own currency

Geography: The world's smallest sovereign state is located in the center of the Italian capital city, Rome. Vatican City's major tourist attractions include St. Peter's Basilica, St. Peter's Square, and the Sistine Chapel.

Politics: The history of the Vatican begins with the founding of the Roman Catholic

Church. For centuries, popes ruled the Papal States on the Italian peninsula. The territory of the Vatican and the popes was mostly lost in the creation of the modern Italian state. An agreement with Italy in 1928 guaranteed Vatican sovereignty. Vatican City, the center of the Roman Catholic church, is ruled by the Pope.

Economy: Vatican City's existence as a sovereign state is funded mostly by church investments and holdings as well as contributions from around the world. Tourism is also an important sources of income.

Croatia see Hrvatska

Cyprus see Kypros

Czech Republic
see Česká Republica

Colombia
Colombia

Area: 1,138,910 sq km
Population: 42.3 million
GDP per capita: 6,300 US$
Capital: Bogotá
Government: Republic
Language: Spanish
Currency: 1 Colombian peso = 100 centavos

Geography: The northern foothills of the Andes divide the country into a western coastal plain and eastern lowlands, extending in the far southeast into the Amazon basin through the pastures of Llanos del Orinoco. Tropical rain forests flourish here and on the Pacific coast. The main settlements are in the Andes basins. The

tropical climate has few temperature fluctuations. Tourist centers are the Caribbean coast to the north (Santa Marta), the pre-Colombian sites (San Augustín), and colonial cities (Cartagena, Bogotá).

Politics: Colombia was the site of early Indian civilizations. Discovered by the Europeans in

1 The llamas and alpacas of Chile's uplands were bred by the area's native Indians as hardy beasts of burden, but chiefly for their meat and wool.

2 Rio Magdalena and its tributaries in the coastal plains of Colombia were traditionally important trade routes.

3 Banff National Park in the Canadian Rockies: Founded in 1885, Canada's oldest nature reserve contains the glacial Lake Louise and Lake Moraine.

4 Lake Ontario and the Toronto skyline are dominated by the elegant CN Tower, the highest tower in the world.

Everyday life in Cuba: An essential for everyone is the "libreta," the supply booklet for cheap, state-subsidized food and clothing. Everyday life is fraught with organizational difficulties for Cuban families.

Equanimity is essential in Cuba. With public transportation almost always crammed, an old car is a precious asset; getting spare parts is an art in itself.

1499, it became a Spanish colony in the mid-16th century. After successfully fighting for independence under Simon Bolivar in 1819, the country gained its first republican constitution in 1886. Reforms in the 1930s were succeeded by years of bloody civil war. The military junta which took over power resigned in 1957; however, the uprisings and civil war which characterized the 1960s still recur today.

Economy: Agriculture accounts for 20% of GDP and employs 30% of the workforce. Colombia is the world's second largest coffee exporter, with bananas and flowers also cultivated for export. 30% of agricultural production is devoted to livestock farming. The industrial sector (automotive, foodstuffs, petroleum processing) accounts for 20% of GDP. Imports include machinery and chemicals. The rich natural resources (gold, iron ore, oil) are almost untouched. Services produce 40% of GDP.

Comores
Comoro Islands

Area: 2,170 sq km
Population: 652,000
GDP per capita: 700 US$
Capital: Moroni
Government: Islamic Presidential republic
Languages: Comorian, French (both official), minority languages
Currency: 1 Comorian franc = 100 centimes

Geography: The territory comprises the three large islands of Ngazidja, Ndzuani and Mwali and other islets off the East African coast. They are largely of volcanic origin, with the highest volcano the still-active Karthala (2,361 m). Rain forests cover the craggy mountain massifs. The narrow coastlines are fringed by coral reefs.

Politics: The islands fell under Persian and Arab rule from the 16th century. The colony founded by France in 1843 on the neighboring island of Mayotte was extended in 1912 to encompass the Comoro Islands. Most of the Islands declared their independence in 1975, while Mayotte remained French.

Economy: The educational, health and social security systems are inadequate (50% of the population are illiterate). 78% of the population work in agriculture which accounts for 41% of GDP. Large areas of the agricultural land are under state control. Major agricultural export commodities include vanilla, coconuts, and spices.

Congo
Congo

Area: 342,000 sq km
Population: 3 million
GDP per capita: 700 US$
Capital: Brazzaville
Government: Republic
Languages: French (official), Bantu languages
Currency: 1 CFA franc = 100 centimes

Geography: A narrow coastal plain where mangroves and tropical rain forests flourish gives way in the country's interior to rolling hills of an average height of 800 meters, with

Cuba: The Old City's colonial architecture.

savanna vegetation. The swampy lowlands of the Congo Basin are covered mostly by vast tropical rain forests.

Politics: After the Congo was discovered by Europeans in the 15th century, European explorers established trading posts there. The region did not become a French colony until 1880. After independence in 1960, the republic first modeled itself on France, but declared itself a Socialist People's Republic in 1970. 1991 saw the introduction of democracy and a multiple-party system.

Economy: The agricultural sector accounts for 12% of GDP, with crops being yams, plantains, and grain. Petroleum forms the basis of the economy, with drilling, processing and export bringing in around 80% of foreign currency. The country's industrial sector produces chemicals and foodstuffs. Services account for 51% of GDP. Political instability has been a major hindrance to economic development in Congo.

Congo, République Démocratique
Congo, Democratic Republic

Area: 2,345,410 sq km
Population: 58.3 million
GDP per capita: 600 US$
Capital: Kinshasa
Government: Republic
Language: French
Currency: 1 Congo franc

Geography: The third largest country in Africa is shaped by its location in the Zaire Basin, a plain at an altitude of 200–400 meters, which extends to the Central African rift valley in the east and is bounded to the west by the Congo and Kwango rivers. The highest peaks are the Virunga volcano (4,507 m) and the Ruwenzori (5,109 m). Tourism is restricted to the capital and the national parks. Tropical rain forests cover much of the country.

Politics: In 1885 the Congo was owned by the King of Belgium, but received independence in 1960 as Congo-Kinshasa. A military coup in 1965 was followed in 1971 by the foundation of the Republic of Zaire. The dictator Mobutu was finally overthrown in 1997 by rebels, whose leader Kabila proclaimed the Democratic Republic of Congo; after his murder in 2001, responsibility for solving the Congo conflict now lies with his son Joseph Kabila.

Economy: In agriculture, subsistence farming produces the bare minimum necessary, with coffee and rubber produced for export. The country is rich in natural resources, including copper, zinc, precious metals, diamonds, and petroleum.

Costa Rica
Costa Rica

Area: 51,100 sq km
Population: 3.9 million
GDP per capita: 9,000 US$
Capital: San José
Government: Presidential republic
Language: Spanish
Currency: 1 Costa Rica colón = 100 centavos

Geography: Humid savannas up to 700 meters in altitude and dry forest lie on the Pacific side of Costa Rica, while the main settlements are found in the Valle Central, with fertile land and a mild climate. Rain forests dominate the Caribbean coast.

Politics: Costa Rica was discovered by Columbus in 1502 and became a Spanish colony in the mid-16th century. It became a republic ten years after gaining independence (1838). The constitution of 1949 stipulates political neutrality. The country is governed by the parliament and a directly elected president. It has no army.

Economy: Costa Rica is one of Latin America's richest countries. The predominantly white population is relatively well-educated. Agriculture accounts for 16% of GDP and 64% of export revenues. The industrial sector contributes 26% of GDP from processing agricultural products, and textile and chemical production. Tourism is undergoing a dramatic increase.

Côte d'Ivoire
Ivory Coast

Area: 322,462 sq km
Population: 17.3 million
GDP per capita: 1,400 US$
Capital: Yamoussoukro
Government: Presidential republic
Languages: French (official), Dioula and further languages
Currency: 1 CFA franc = 100 centimes

Geography: From its 550 kilometers of coastline, fringed by lagoons to the east, the country rises to an altitude of 300–400 meters. Around half the country's area consists of tableland covered by wet savannas. Intensive farming is practiced along the coast. Tourist destinations include the animal reserves (Comoé, Nimba) and beaches.

Politics: Before its colonization by the French from 1893, the north belonged to the old kingdom of Mali and the south was ruled by the Ashanti. European influences were introduced by missionaries who traveled through the country from the 17th century. The Republic of the Ivory Coast gained independence in 1960.

Economy: 33% of national GDP is produced by the agriculture and fishery sectors, in which more than half of the workforce is employed. Ivory Coast is the world's fourth largest producer of coffee and has the highest level of industrialization in West Africa.

Crna Gora
Montenegro

Area: 13,812 sq km
Population: 620,000
GDP per capita: 3100 US$
Capital: Podgorica
Government: Republic
Language: Serbian, Albanian
Currency: 1 Euro = 100 cents

Geography: The highlands of central Montenegro are situated up to 2500 metres above sea level and extend to the country's coast along the Adriatic. Lake Skadar, the largest lake in the Balkans extends along the border with Albania.

Ethnic Variety: Côte d'Ivoire is populated by 60 clans that have developed and preserved their own traditions and contribute to the cultural variety of the nation. The Dan, who are settled in the West, are well known for their traditional masks. The Lobi, who live in the northeast, developed a certain kind of adobe architecture that is also common in West African countries.

Politics: Before 2006, Montenegro was united politically with neighbouring Serbia for more than 80 years. The country declared its independence after a referendum in May 2006.

Economy: The country's economy was greatly weakened by the break-up of Yugoslavia and the wars that followed during the 1990s. Tourism, the metals industry, agriculture, and sheep herding are the most important segments of the economy.

Cuba
Cuba

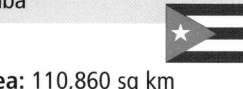

Area: 110,860 sq km
Population: 11.3 million
GDP per capita: 2,800 US$
Capital: La Habana
Government: Socialist republic
Language: Spanish
Currency: 1 Cuban peso = 100 centavos

Geography: The largest island of the Western Antilles, Cuba has an interior of craggy mountain chains (over 1,900 m) met by a swampy, fertile plain that gives way to the rain forests of the mountainous east. High, rolling hills dominate the west. Arable land and savannas have replaced much of the rain forests. The climate is tropical and humid. Tourist centers are La Habana (Havana), Trinidad, and Santiago de Cuba.

Politics: Discovered in 1492 by Columbus, the island was settled by the Spanish from 1511. In 1902 the republic of Cuba fell under the influence of the United States, but became a Socialist republic after Castro's revolution (1959). The disintegration of the USSR has caused Cuba many economic problems, particularly since the trade embargo by the USA, although the country has emerged from isolation since the end of the Cold War.

Economy: The healthcare and educational system are exemplary. 80% of agricultural operations are owned by the state. The main crop is sugarcane. The processing industry (textiles, leather, tobacco goods) accounts for 46% of GDP. Tourism is now the second largest source of foreign currency.

Danmark
Denmark

Area: 43,094 sq km; Greenland 2.176 million sq km; Faroe Islands 1,398 sq km
Population: 5.4 million; Greenland 55,400; Faeroes 43,700
GDP per capita: 31,200 US$
Capital: Copenhagen
Government: Parliamentary monarchy
Language: Danish
Currency: 1 Danish krone = 100 Øre

Geography: The Kingdom of Denmark consists of the Jutland peninsula and at least 400 islands located between the North and Baltic seas. Only a quarter of Denmark's islands are inhabited and 40% of the country's population live on the most populous island, Seeland. Denmark is a flat country and consists mostly of meadows, moorlands, sandy coastlines, and forests. The capital city, Copenhagen, and the beaches of Jutland are the country's major tourist attractions.

Politics: The history of the Danish kingdom begins around AD 800. In the 14th century, the Danish monarchy was able to expand its territory through a series of conquests and unions. The country was occupied by Germany during the Second World War. Both Greenland and the Faeroe Islands are currently administered by Denmark.

Economy: The generous welfare state of modern Denmark guarantees all Danish citizens access to excellent social services. Only around 5% of the country's population works in the agricultural sector. Textile, machinery, and metal production are among the country's leading industries. The service sector, including tourism, currently generates more than 70% of the country's annual GDP.

Daulat al-Imārāt al-'Arabiya Al-Muttahida
United Arab Emir.

Area: 82,880 sq km
Population: 2.5 million
GDP per capita: 23,200 US$
Capital: Abu Dhabi
Government: Federation of independent sheikdoms
Language: Arabic (official)
Currency: 1 dirham = 100 fils

Geography: The flat, coastal strip on the Persian Gulf is backed by salty clay plains inland, which meet the extensive dunes of Rub' al-Khali. On

1 In the rural districts of the United Arab Emirates camels are the most effective traditional means of transportation.

2 Copenhagen, Denmark's capital: The Nyhavn and Frederiksstaden district contain the city's old harbor, with its picturesque views and well-preserved historic buildings.

3 In Dubai the modern mosques are modeled on those of ancient Persia.

4 Costa Rica: The Central American Cordilleres are largely covered by tropical evergreen mountain and rain forests, with a wide variety of flora and fauna.

Ecuador: Most of the agricultural products of the smallest country in the Andes are sold at local markets, whereas the crops from the extensive plantations of bananas and cocoa are exported. The core of the economy, however, is provided by the export of petroleum which is driving ahead the development of the country.

the eastern border, the Al-Hajar mountains rise to 1,100 meters. Vegetation in this hot, dry climate is possible only in the irrigated coastal area. The chief tourist destination is the Emirate of Dubai.

Politics: The seven sheikdoms of Abu Dhabi, Dubai, Sharjah, Ajman, Umm-el-Qaiwain, Fudjaira, und Ras' al-Khaimah became a British protectorate in the 19th century. When the British withdrew, the emirates formed a federation in 1971. The seven emirates have constituted the Upper Council since the adoption of the constitution (1975), electing one of their number as president.

Economy: Three quarters of the inhabitants are migrant workers from the Indian subcontinent. Agriculture plays only a subordinate role, and contributes 2.5% to GDP. Oil has been drilled in the Persian Gulf since 1962. This industry employs 2% of the working population, and generates 40% of GDP. The modest processing industries produce textiles, leather goods and clothing.

East Timor see Timor-Leste

Geography: The northernmost region of Germany includes coastal areas along the North and Baltic seas and numerous islands. Germany's south is dominated by the Alps and Alpine foothills. Most of northern Germany consists of flat and fertile plains, bordering a series of mountains that stretch through much of central and eastern Germany. Farther south low rolling hills give way to the higher Alpine foothills and the Alps. The country's major waterways include the Rhine, Elbe, and Weser rivers. Germany's tourist

attractions include the capital city, Berlin, and the capital of Bavaria, Munich, as well as important cultural centers such as Dresden, Weimar, and Cologne. The Bavarian Alps, the Black Forest, and the coastal areas along the North and Baltic seas are also popular attractions.

Politics: Germany was originally settled by a variety of Germanic, Celtic, and later Slavic peoples. Large areas were controlled for centuries by the Romans, who founded many of Germany's oldest cities. Charlemagne was able to unite much of Germany into one empire during the 9th century. Between the 10th and 12th century, German nobles and the popes vied for control. During most of the Middle Ages, Germany was a collection of kingdoms known as the Holy Roman Empire, ruled by an elected Kaiser. The Thirty Years War, which devastated

The Brandenburg Gate: Symbol of Germany's new unified status.

Germany and left a third of its population dead, weakened the Holy Roman Empire and left Germany divided for many centuries. The formation of the German Empire in 1871 was followed by a period of rapid economic and social progress. Following Germany's defeat in the First World War, the Kaiser was forced to abdicate and the country became a republic. One of the darkest chapters in German history began in 1933 when the National Socialist party and Adolf Hitler came to power, leading the country to a devastating defeat in the Se-

cond World War and to the Holocaust. Following the Second World War, the country was divided into two states – East and West Germany. While West Germany, an ally of the USA, prospered under capitalism and democracy, the East was transformed into a repressive communist state. After the fall of communism, the two German states were reunited in 1990 and the country currently consists of sixteen federal states.

Economy: Germany is one of the world's wealthiest industrialized nations and has the largest economy in Europe. Agriculture plays only a marginal role in the national economy, while services (principal sectors include finance and insurance, commerce and transportion) and manufacturing account for most of Germany's GDP. Tourism is an important sector of the economy in several German regions.

Geography: The Tadjoura Basin, among the world's hottest areas, is covered by sand and

stony deserts in the interior. 95% of the country consits of steppe. Continuous vegetation (acacia and shrubs) is found only above 1,200 meters. Hot springs and active volcanos can be found throughout the country, and earthquakes are frequent.

Politics: In 1896, French protectorates on the Gulf of Aden were merged to form the state of Djibouti. Although the country became independent in 1977, the French army maintains a number of military bases there and is still responsible for national defense.

Economy: More than half the population are nomads. Djibouti has to cope with waves of Ethiopian refugees who make up almost one-fifth of the population. Frequent drought means that agriculture accounts for only around 2% of GDP, while industry contributes around 18%. The country aims to concentrate on services, which already account for 80% of GDP thanks to the French military presence. Djibouti has a large national debt and remains dependent on foreign aid. Its economy is based on its strategic location and status as free trade zone.

Egypt see Al-Misr

Equatorial Guinea see Guinea Ecuatorial

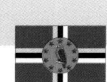
Geography: This volcanic island is part of the Lesser Antilles. It is predominantly mountainous (Morne Diablotins, 1,447 m), almost untouched at the center and covered with evergreen rain forests. The main settlements are on the coast. The climate is tropical and humid; cyclo-

nes may occur in the rainy season from June to November. The country's principal attraction is the Morne-Trois-Pitons National Park in the interior, with over 100 species of birds. The island has many hot springs and a crater lake giving evidence of its volcanic origins.

Politics: Discovered by Columbus on a Sunday ("Domingo") in 1493 (hence the name), Dominica successfully resisted all attempts at colonization into the 18th century. Faught over by the British and French, it became a British colony in 1805 and gained independence in 1978.

Economy: The economy is founded on agriculture, with 50% of export revenues produced by small farmers from banana cultivation. Other crops such as ginger, coconuts, copra, fruit juices, cocoa, and citrus fruits are industrially processed and contribute to exports. Plans to expand the underdeveloped industrial sector through incentives for foreign investors are under way. Trade and tourism generate 63% of GDP.

Geography: The country is divided into three main geographical zones: the densely settled coastal region on the Pacific, the mountainous Andean region (Chimborazo 6,310 meters, an extinct volcano) and the Oriente lowlands, in which tropical rain forests flourish up to the Peruvian border. The climate has no significant temperature fluctuations. Ecuador's territory includes the Galapagos Islands, around 1,000 kilometers away in the Pacific, with their unique animal life (tortoises, giant lizards, birds). The country's chief tour-

Ireland: In the 1970s the folk music group "The Dubliners" made traditional Irish folk music internationally known. Some of the traditional dance music is centuries old. Typical instruments are Irish bagpipes, fiddle, flute *and harp – the emblem of Ireland. The lively music can often be heard in Ireland's pubs.*

ist attractions are these islands, rain forest areas of natural beauty and the old colonial cities of Cuenca and Quito, today a world heritage site).

Politics: Ecuador was conquered in the 15th century, first by the Incas and 100 years later by the Spanish, who founded today's capital of Quito. The country received independence in 1822 but found only brief interludes of peace; not until the second half of the 20th century did Ecuador have long periods of political stability. The 1979 constitution appoints the parliament as the legislative power, elected every four years; the President is the head of government.

Economy: Agriculture accounts for 18% of GDP and employs one-third of the workforce. In addition to grain, potatoes, vegetables, and fruit as subsistence crops, coffee, cocoa, sugar-cane, and bananas are cultivated for export. Shrimp are also exported. A major source of foreign currency is the natural resources in the Amazon basin, where gold, silver, zinc, and copper are mined. Around 60% of the population live below the poverty line.

Area: 45,226 sq km
Population: 1.3 million
GDP per capita: 12,300 US$
Capital: Tallinn
Government: Parliamentary republic
Language: Estonian (official), Russian
Currency: 1 Estonian krone = 100 senti

Geography: Estonia consists primarily of low-lying plains, moorlands, and marshes. More than 1,500 islands are located off the country's coast. The cool temperate climate gives way to a continental climate in the country's interior. The country's principal tourist attractions are the capital city, Tallinn, and the cities of Narva and Tartu.

Politics: The small country on the Baltic Sea was conquered by the Danes in the 13th cen-

tury. During the 15th century it was ruled by Sweden and after 1721 by Russia. Estonia declared its independence from Russia in 1918 but was occupied by the Soviet Union in 1940. Estonia was declared an independent republic in 1991. The country is now a multiparty democracy with a unicameral parliament.

Economy: Estonia has been largely successful with its transition from a planned economy to free market capitalism. The country experienced strong growth and foreign investment

rates in the 1990s. The service sector now accounts for most of Estonia's GDP with agriculture and wood processing industries (paper, furniture) also key. Estonia is the world's second largest oil shale producer.

Éire/Ireland
Ireland

Area: 70,280 sq km
Population: 4 million
GDP per capita: 29,800 US$
Capital: Dublin
Government: Parliamentary republic
Language: Irish (Gaelic), English (both official)
Currency: 1 euro = 100 cents

Geography: Ireland is a medium-sized island in the North Atlantic with a temperate maritime climate. The country's terrain consists mostly of rolling hills, mea-

dows, and moorlands. The northern half of the island features numerous lakes. Ireland's historic monuments and attractive countryside are the island's leading tourist attractions.

Politics: Archeological finds show the island was settled by

1 Lough Corrib, the largest lake in Eire, offers great prospects for angling. It lies in the wild counties of Galway and Mayo amid spectacular scenery.

2 Today Tallinn's medieval city is a protected monument. The church of St. Nicholas was built in the 13th/14th century.

3 Quechua-speaking Indians in Peru and Ecuador live from potato farming and alpaca breeding. Woollen garments are their chief trade at city markets.

4 High above the Moselle in one of the largest winegrowing districts in Germany towers the restored Burg Cochem.

Corrida de toros: Today the classic corrida in its traditional form is solely held in Spain. It is separated into several parts; only in the last part, when the toreros have tantalized the bull to the limit, is it killed by the deadly stroke of the matador. In southern France and Portugal bloodless corridas are held. The bullfight is a complex ritual which many claim is central to Spain's culture.

Celts no later than the 3rd century BC. The island's people were converted to Christianity during the 5th century. The English conquest of Ireland in 1171 was followed by a series of revolts and centuries of British domination. Devastating famines in the mid-19th century decimated the population and caused thousands of people to emigrate, mostly to the United States. In 1921, the Republic of Ireland was declared an independent state, while several northern Irish countries in the province of Ulster remained within the United Kingdom. In 1937 Ireland became a sovereign state with its own constitution.

Economy: Traditionally one of the poorest regions of Western Europe, Ireland experienced a remarkable economic transition in the 1990s. The country is now one of Europe's richest due to foreign investment, competitive tax rates, and EU regional aid. While agriculture once dominated the Irish economy, services and manufacturing (primarily the computer, chemical and pharmaceuticals industries) now account for more than 90% of Ireland's GDP. Tourism is a key economic factor on the "Emerald Isle."

El Salvador
El Salvador

Area: 21,041 sq km
Population: 6.6 million
GDP per capita: 4,800 US$
Capital: San Salvador
Government: Presidential republic
Languages: Spanish (official), Indian languages
Currency: 1 El-Salvador colón = 100 centavos

Geography: El Salvador largely consists of fertile hills and grassland, apart from a narrow coastal strip of mangrove forest with a hot, humid climate. In the interior, a high plateau, with grassland enclosed by mountains, forms the main settlement area. Much of the natural vegetation has given way to arable land. The humid, hot climate extending to an altitude of 1,800 meters is ideal for agriculture. The country has one of the most frequent incidences of earthquakes in the world. Tourist destinations are the volcanoes and the Indian cult sites.

Politics: From the country's conquest in 1524 to its independence in 1821, El Salvador was part of the Spanish colony of Guatemala. Its history is marked by recurring periods of unrest, in which the economic and social situation deteriorated considerably. A military dictatorship ruled from 1931 to 1967. The military coup in 1979 resulted in 14 years of civil war, with a high toll of victims. The 1983 constitution states that the president is directly elected by the people for a term of five years.

Economy: 95% of the population of Central America's most densely populated country are mestizos. Agriculture employs 50% of the workforce and generates 14% of GDP. Rice, maize, beans, and millet are grown for domestic markets, and coffee, sugar, cotton, and more recently flowers and ornamental plants for export. The industrial sector chiefly comprises small and medium-size processing companies which account for 3% of GDP. Considerably more than half the population is employed in the services sector. The tourism industry is still in its infancy. High unemployment and government corruption are critical problems.

Elláda (Hellás)
Greece

Area: 131,940 sq km
Population: 10.6 million
GDP per capita: 19,900 US$
Capital: Athens
Government: Parliamentary republic
Language: Modern Greek
Currency: 1 euro = 100 cents

Geography: Greece consist of the large peninsula Peloponnese on the southern edge of the Balkans and numerous islands. Heavily forested mountains and hills cover more than three-quarters of the land. The Pindus Mountains occupy much of central and western mainland Greece. Most of the country has a warm Mediterranean climate, while the northernmost regions have a continental climate. Ancient monuments and the Greek islands are the country's main attractions.

Politics: The powerful Greek city-states of the classical era profoundly influenced European culture. Alexander the Great (356–323 BC) conquered vast territories and spread Greek (Hellenic) culture through the Near East and Mediterranean. Greece was a Roman province from 148 BC to 396 BC, then a province of the Byzantine Empire. Conquered by the Ottoman Turks in 1356, Greece remained an Ottoman province for almost five centuries. A sovereign Greek kingdom was created in 1832. After a military coup in 1967, the monarchy reintroduced in 1946 was abolished. Greece became a democratic republic in 1974 after several years of repressive dictatorship. Tension remains between Greece and Turkey over Cyprus.

Economy: Despite a move towards greater privatization a large segment of Greece's economy is under government control. Traditional crops

Mykonos: The best-known Cycladic island in the Aegean Sea.

including olives, wine, citrus fruits and tobacco account for more than a quarter of Greece's exports. Greece's manufacturing sector is dominated by small businesses. The rapidly growing service sector accounts for more than 60% of the country's GDP. Greece currently has the world's largest fleet of commercial sailing vessels. Its main trading partners are the European Union and the USA. Tourism remains an important sector of the economy. Greece joined the European currency union in 2000.

Eritrea
Eritrea

Area: 121,320 sq km
Population: 4.5 million
GDP per capita: 700 US$
Capital: Asmara
Government: Republic
Languages: Arabic, Tigrinja (official)
Currency: 1 birr = 100 cents

Geography: The Red Sea forms the country's northeastern border. The narrow coastal plain extends in the north to the Abyssinian Highlands, with mountains more than 2,600 meters in height. The main settlements are here because of the relatively high rainfall. Desert lowlands are found to the south in the foothills of the Denakil Mountains. The Dahlak Islands in the Red Sea also belong to Eritrea. Tourist destinations are Asmara, the nearby ancient city of Cohaito, the historic colonial architecture in Massawa and the coral reefs of the Dahlak archipelago.

Politics: What is today Eritrea was part of the Italian colony from 1890 to 1941, and subsequently under British administration until 1952. After ten years as an autonomous region within Ethiopia, it was annexed as the 14th province, finally gaining independence as a republic in 1993 after a long battle for freedom. The Provisional National Council, in power since 1991, is working on a democratic constitution and the establishment of a multiple-party system.

Economy: Illiteracy is around 80%. The war caused particularly extensive damage to agriculture; while 80% of the population are traditionally small farmers, millet, wheat, and pulse production is currently sufficient for only about 20% of the population. A current development program subsidizes coffee and tobacco farming for export. Industrial processing and consumer goods production account for 18% of GDP. Quarrying (marble) is planned for expansion. There are hopes of attracting foreign investors to support the reconstruction of the infrastructure, which was completely destroyed in the war. Tourism is in its infancy.

Ethiopia see Ityopya

España
Spain

Area: 504,782 sq km
Population: 40.3 million
GDP per capita: 22,000 US$
Capital: Madrid
Government: Parliamentary monarchy
Language: Spanish (Castilian), Catalan, Basque (Euskara), Galician
Currency: 1 euro = 100 cents

Geography: The Pyrenees mountains form a natural boundary between the mountainous Iberian Peninsula and the rest of Europe. Northern Spain is dominated by the plateaus of Castille, while the Sierra Nevada mountains stretch over much of the country's south. The south consists largely of semi-arid areas with steppe vegetation. The northernmost coastal areas have a distinct temperate climate with heavy rainfall. Spain is one of the world's most popular tourist destinations, with its leading attractions including islands such as Majorca in the Mediterranean or the Canary Islands, and large cities such as Barcelona.

South Seas: *In spite of the modern infrastructure due to tourism, the inhabitants of Fiji have preserved their traditional way of life to this day. On mostly small farms grain and fruit are cultivated for subsistence.*

In addition, the people on the Islands breed pigs and small livestock.

Politics: Spain was settled by a variety of European groups including Basques, Celts, and Iberians before the 3rd century BC. Most of Iberia became a Roman province in the 1st century BC. Large sections of the country fell under the control of Muslim Arabs during the 8th century. The Reconquista, a long military campaign led by Christian nobles, eventually succeeded in expelling the Arabs by 1492. Spain was Europe's most powerful nation by the 16th century and the ruler of vast territories in the Americas. By the 18th century, however, Spain was in a period of decline that culminated in the loss of its empire in the 19th century. A civil war between nationalists and Spanish republicans ended with a victory for the reactionary nationalists. The country returned to democracy following the dictator Franco's death in 1978.

Economy: After a period of high unemployment and rising foreign debts, the Spanish economy has become increasingly strong in recent years. Agriculture and fishing account for around one-tenth of the country's GDP, although this is falling. Manufacturing produces around a third of the GDP, and the service sector more than half. Tourism remains a major industry and provides employment for a large number of Spaniards.

Estonia see Eesti

Finland see Suomi

Fiji
Fiji

Area: 18,270 sq km
Population: 880,874
GDP per capita: 5,800 US$
Capital: Suva
Government: Republic
Languages: English, Fijian, Hindi
Currency: 1 Fijian dollar = 100 cents

Geography: Fiji consists of more than 320 islands, including volcanic and coral islands. Around 110 of the islands are inhabited. The mountains on the largest islands, Viti Levu and Vanua Levu, rise above 1,300 meters. Fiji is a major tourist attraction with a tropical climate and countless sandy beaches.

Politics: In 1643, Abel Tasman was the first European to visit the islands. More than a century later, James Cook claimed the islands for Great Britain. From 1874 to 1970 the islands were a British colony. Following independence, the country experienced periods of political instability including several military coups. A new constitution was created in 1997 in an attempt to ease tensions

between the country's indigenous Melanesian population and the large Indo-Fijian community. Political power is now divided between the Senate, House of Representatives, and President. Fiji's President, the official head of state, is chosen by the national council of chiefs, a non-elected body of mostly hereditary members. This council also appoints one-third of the country's senators. The role of the council is controversial because it excludes the country's Indo-Fijian majority. Elections to the House of Representatives are based on a mixture of universal direct elections and electoral rolls divided between the country's ethnic groups.

Economy: Around half of the Fijian labor force works in the country's large agricultural sector. Sugar and fish are among the country's main exports. The industrial sector consists primarily of sugar refining, rice milling, and textile production. Mining

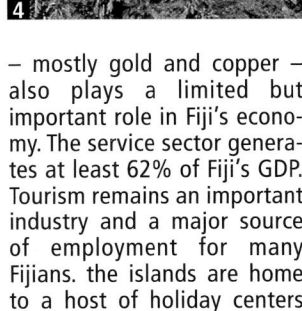

– mostly gold and copper – also plays a limited but important role in Fiji's economy. The service sector generates at least 62% of Fiji's GDP. Tourism remains an important industry and a major source of employment for many Fijians. the islands are home to a host of holiday centers and resorts.

1 The Parthenon on the Acropolis was founded in 3000 BC. The City, host of the 2004 Olympic Games, is home to more than four million residents.

2 The Straits of Gibraltar link the Atlantic Ocean and the Mediterranean Sea. The view extends to the North of Africa.

3 The construction of the late Gothic cathedral of Segovia started in 1525. The tower is 110 meters high.

4 Many of Fiji's Islands are covered by lush tropical rain forests.

French savoir-vivre: Since Roman times wine making has been common in France. Today the largest wine producing areas are to be found in Bordeaux, the Bourgogne, Champagne and Alsace, as well as the *Loire and Rhône valleys. The harvest and pressing lasts from September to December. Whether it is to accompany haute or rustic cuisine, wine is regarded as a staple in France.*

France
France

Area: 547,030 sq km
Population: 60.4 million
GDP per capita: 27,500 US$
Capital: Paris
Government: Parl. republic
Language: French
Currency: 1 euro = 100 cents

Geography: France is a mostly hilly country situated between the Atlantic Ocean, English Channel, and the Mediterranean Sea. Two high mountain ranges form natural borders along the country's edges – the Pyrenees in the south and the Alps in the east. Large basins cover a large segment of France's territory, including the densely populated Paris Basin. The Rhône, Seine, and Loire rivers are the country's principal rivers. France is an extremely popular tourist destination and its main attractions include the city of Paris, the Loire river valley, the French Riviera, and the country's Atlantic coast.

Politics: The history of modern France can be directly connected to the division of the Frankish Empire in the year AD 843. France emerged victorious from the Hundred Years' War (1338–1453) with England. In the centuries that followed, France greatly expanded its territory and was ruled by absolutist monarchs. The French Revolution of 1798 brought an end to the monarchy and established the first French republic. The French general Napoleon was declared emperor in 1804 and launched a series of military campaigns that changed the political structure of Europe. The country switched between monarchy and republicanism several times during the 19th century. The country was occupied by Germany during the Second World War. France is currently governed by the so-called Fifth Republic, a presidential democracy established in 1958.

Economy: France rapidly made the transition from a largely agricultural economy to an industrialized nation following the Second World War. Modern France is now one of the world's most affluent nations, with a diverse economy. Despite the country's wealth, unemploy-ment remains high and the French are heavily taxed. Tourism continues to play an important role in the national economy. The French government retains significant influence over the economy. The service sector now accounts for most of France's GDP.

Germany see Deutschland

Greece see Elláda (Hellás)

Hungary see Magyaroszag

Gabon
Gabon

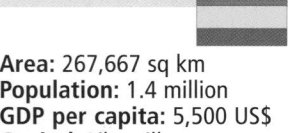

Area: 267,667 sq km
Population: 1.4 million
GDP per capita: 5,500 US$
Capital: Libreville
Government: Pres. republic
Languages: French (official), Bantu languages
Currency: 1 CFA franc = 100 cent.

The Eiffel Tower: Peak of civil engineering in the 19th century.

Geography: The landscape is marked by River Ogooué and its tributaries. The mangrove swamps and lagoons of the coastal lowlands give way to coastal savanna. The interior tableland with an altitude of up to 1,000 meters is largely covered with tropical rain forests (Birougou Mountains 1,190 m). There are dry savannas to the southeast. The climate is tropical. Tourist destinations are the capital city, the Albert Schweitzer Hospital in Lambaréné and the three national parks.

Politics: After the coast was discovered by the Portuguese in 1470, several European powers established trading points for raw materials principally ivory and exotic woods, and slave trading. The country became a French colony in 1885, and gained independence in 1960. Under the new constitution (1991), the National Assembly is elected for five years and the President is appointed by direct election.

Economy: Around half of the predominantly Bantu population lives in the cities. Agriculture accounts for only 8% of GDP; 20% of the country's area is taken up by subsistence crops of manioc, yams, plantains and maize, and coffee, cocoa, sugar-cane, and palms for export. Rain forest lumber is a major source of export revenue. The backbone of the economy, however, is the export of petroleum and refinery products, which accounts for 80% of GDP and makes Gabon one of Africa's richest countries. The mining industry produces uranium, manganese, iron ore, and gold. Tourism is relatively underdeveloped.

Gambia
The Gambia

Area: 11,295 sq km
Population: 1.5 million
GDP per capita: 1,700 US$
Capital: Banjul
Government: Pres. republic

Languages: English (official), Mandingo, Wolof, other local languages
Currency: 1 dalasi = 100 butut

Geography: Africa's smallest country, along the banks of the Gambia River, is completely enclosed by Senegal, and no more than 50 kilometers wide at its widest point. Mangrove swamps extend far inland from the Gambia delta. The Atlantic beaches, said to be the most beautiful in Africa, attract tourists. The national parks, with their rich fauna, are also popular.

Politics: In the 8th century a number of kingdoms arose in what is today The Gambia, and were annexed to the kingdom of Mali in the 12th century. The Gambia was discovered by the Portuguese in the 15th century and became a British colony in 1765, received independence in 1965 as a Commonwealth state and became a republic in 1970. The British-style constitution (1970) was repealed in 1994 after the military coup. Parliamentary elections were resumed in 1997.

Economy: The majority of the population are small farmers growing subsistence crops of millet, sorghum, rice, and maize; peanuts are the main export product, and like fishery products are processed by the underdeveloped industry. Tourism accounts for 15% of GDP and the industry has largely recovered from a major decline that followed a military coup in the 1990s.

Ghana
Ghana

Area: 239,460 sq km
Population: 20.8 million
GDP per capita: 2,2000 US$
Capital: Accra
Government: Presidential republic
Languages: English (official), over 70 further languages and dialects
Currency: 1 cedi = 100 pesewas

Geography: The 535-kilometer-long coastline along the Gulf of Guinea, rendered near-impassable by lagoons, forms a natural border to the south. From here, grassland gives way to the tropical rain forests that cover the Ashanti Highlands rising to the west. Lake Volta lies in the wet savanna to the east. The climate is tropical. Tourism concentrates on the partly preserved forts at the colonial trading outposts of Cape Coast, Elmina, and Accra.

Politics: The Ashanti people founded a powerful kingdom in what is now Ghana, engulfing neighboring tribes to extend their territory to the coast, from where they conducted slave trading with Europe from the 15th century. In 1850 the British conquered the country and founded the colony of Gold Coast. After early independence in 1957, the republic initially profited from its rich natural resources until economic decline set in from 1966. The new constitution (1993) is intended to promote the process of democratization by introducing a multiple-party system. Ghana has enjoyed a period of political stability since 1993 and is now one of the most open democracies in Africa.

Economy: Half of the population are small farmers, cultivating basic subsistence crops of rice, millet, yams, and plantains. 50% of the agricultural land is taken up by cocoa. Animal husbandry is primarily conducted in the north. Tropical rain forest lumber is exported. The mining industry supplies mineral raw materials (bauxite, manganese) and rich yields of gold. The small industrial processing sector produces foodstuffs, textiles, and shoes for the country's own needs. The service sector accounts for almost half of GDP.

Grenada
Grenada

Area: 344 sq km
Population: 89,300
GDP per capita: 5,000 US$
Capital: St. George's
Government: Constitutional monarchy
Languages: English (official), Patois
Currency: 1 East Caribbean dollar = 100 cents

Ancestor worship: While in the cities of western Africa the traditional beliefs are widely replaced by Islam and Christianity, in the countryside they are largely still alive. The numerous rites and dances are *evidence of a powerful community and closeness to the natural rhythms of life. They are to a large extent characterized by ancestor worship, which serves to foster cohesion within families.*

Geography: This volcanic island with countless crater-lakes, sulphur springs and earthquakes, is part of the Lesser Antilles. The highest peak in its mountainous interior (Mount St. Catherine) is 840 meters high. Mountain and rain forests grow in the mountainous interior. The climate is tropical, with an extended rainy season. The island's many beaches are visited primarily by cruise tourists.

Politics: Discovered in 1498 by Columbus, Grenada was first settled by the French. The island was occupied by the British in 1762 and remained a British crown colony until its independence in 1974. It was invaded by US American troops in 1983 following a Socialist revolution. According to the re-instated constitution of 1974, the parliament is composed of the Senate and the House of Representatives. The British monarch is the head of state.

Economy: The majority of Grenada's inhabitants are descended from African slaves. The country's flag depicts its main export: nutmeg (25% of the world's production), cultivated by small farmers in addition to bananas and cocoa. The underdeveloped industrial sector chiefly manufactures semi-luxury goods, but also electronic components and pharmaceuticals. Tourism is gaining a foothold.

Gruzija (Sakartvelo)
Georgia

Area: 69,700 sq km
Population: 4.7 million
GDP per capita: 2,500 US$
Capital: Tbilisi (Tiflis)
Government: Republic
Languages: Georgian (official), Russian, Ar
Currency: Lari

Geography: The western border is formed by the Black Sea coast, which runs into the Kura lowlands. The climate here is sub-tropical and humid. The north is dominated by the southern slope of the Greater Caucasus (Kasbe 5,033 m). The country extends into part of the Lesser Caucasus in the south. To the east of Tbilisi, the country is characterized by dry

forests in an increasingly continental climate, becoming grassy steppe. In addition to 15 nature reserves, winter sports, and hiking regions, towns such as Suchumi and Batumi on the Black Sea coast are very popular. Important historic sites are at Kutaisi and Mzcheta.

Politics: After the Roman era (from 65 BC), the country became part of the Byzantine Empire in the 4th century. In the 14th century it came under Mongol rule. Following the division of the country between the Ottomans, Persians, and Russians (1555), an Eastern Georgian Kingdom was founded in the 18th century and annexed by the Russian Empire (1801–1810). Georgia declared its independence in 1918, and the Soviet Socialist Republic of Georgia was founded in 1921. Since independence (1991), efforts towards autonomy by the Islam-oriented Republics of Abkhazia and South Ossetia have led to warring confrontations, largely settled with the aid of international intervention.

Economy: Most of the agricultural land consists of grain, beet and potato fields. In addition, tropical fruits, tea, tobacco, and grapes are cultivated, with eucalyptus, bamboo and bay trees on the coast. Mining yields coal, copper, manganese, barite, diatomite and semi-precious stones. The processing industry produces foodstuffs, wines and textiles. Chief exports are raw materials and foodstuffs. A third of the population lives from the traditional-

ly important sector of tourism.

Guatemala
Guatemala

Area: 108,889 sq km
Population: 14.3 million
GDP per capita: 4,100 US$

1 Mont Saint Michel monastery is on a small island off the coast of Normandy.

2 The steep, towering temples of Tikal in Guatemala are a relic of the mighty and powerful civilization of the Mayas.

3 Carriacou island, off the Caribbean island of Grenada; ideal for diving and swimming.

4 The 13th-century Metechi Church in Georgia's capital Tblisi.

Guinea Ecuatorial Equatorial Guinea

Ancient wisdom: In India there are many ascetics who have abjured the world for religious reasons and live off the alms of their fellow men. Hinduism, which esteems respect for all life and nonviolence as the highest values, teaches this way of life as a way to escape the eternal cycle of rebirth and gain salvation.

Capital: Guatemala City
Government: Presidential republic
Languages: Spanish (official), Maya languages
Currency: 1 quetzal = 100 centavos

Geography: The plains to the north are covered with tropical rain forests. The Central American Andes traverse the country's south from east to west. To the far south, the high plains of the Sierra Madre extend to the vertile Pacific coastal plains. Tourist attractions are the intact Indian cultures (Chichicastenango), sites of the Mayan civilizations (Tikal), and the colonial architecture in the cities of Antigua and Quezaltenango.

Politics: The center of the ancient Mayan culture was conquered by the Spanish in 1524 and remained a Spanish colony until its independence in 1821. Since then Guatemala has been ruled by a succession of military dictatorships. The government has been democratically elected since 1986, but the war led by the left-wing guerrilla movement URNG did not end until a peace treaty was signed in 1997.

Economy: More than half of the inhabitants work in agriculture; peas, broccoli, tobacco, and flowers are cultivated in addition to traditional export crops of coffee, sugar, bananas, and cardamom. Natural resources are largely untapped. The industrial sector processes foodstuffs, rubber, and textiles for export. Tourism is the main source of foreign revenue.

Guinea Ecuatorial
Equatorial Guinea

Area: 28,051 sq km
Population: 523,000
GDP per capita: 2,700 US$
Capital: Malabo
Government: Presidential republic
Languages: Spanish (official), pidgin English, Bantu languages
Currency: 1 CFA franc = 100 centimes

Geography: The country's territory comprises the mountainous region of Mbini and the volcanic islands of Bioko and Pagalu. The higher elevated areas of Mbini are covered with savanna and the rest with tropical rain forests, giving way to mangrove swamps on the coast. In the rainy season violent storms are frequent.

Politics: Discovered in 1470, Bioko and Pagalu became Spanish in 1778, and the mainland in 1885. After independence (1968) the country was ruled by a dictatorship until a military coup in 1979. The 1991 constitution's plans for a democratic multi-party system were limited prior to the country's first free elections in 1993.

Economy: The majority of the population are Bantu speakers and 85% are Catholic. The economy is founded on cocoa and coffee plantations and valuable lumber reserves. Livestock farming on the mainland is gaining in significance. 5% of the population is employed in industry, primarily processing agricultural products. Modest gold reserves are mined. The service sector accounts for 42% of employment but the export of oil now accounts for most economic growth.

India's Taj Mahal: Impressive mausoleum for a queen.

Guinea-Bissau
Guinea-Bissau

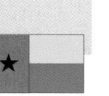

Area: 36,125 sq km
Population: 1.4 million
GDP per capita: 900 US$
Capital: Bissau

Government: Presidential republic
Languages: Portuguese (official), Creole, dialects
Currency: 1 Guinea peso = 100 centavos

Geography: The broad coastal plain traversed by rivers is bounded to the east by wet savanna and to the southeast by hills. Freshwater swamps in the interior give way to mangrove swamps at the coast. The country is rich in wildlife. Tourist attractions are the old colonial city of Bissau and the islands of the Bijagos Archipelago off the coast.

Politics: Portuguese outposts for the slave trade were founded in the 16th century. Guinea-Bissau was a Portuguese colony from 1879–1974 and later became a parliamentary democracy after gaining independence, which ended abruptly in a military coup. Following the approval of new parties in 1991, the first free elections of a National Assembly were held in 1994.

Economy: 80% of the population cultivate subsistence crops of rice, maize, and other grain. Animal husbandry accounts for nearly a third of GDP, and peanuts and cashews are significant exports. There are plans to attract foreign investors to tap the bauxite, phosphate, and petroleum reserves. The country's economy was thrown into a major crisis by a civil war in the late 1990s.

Guinée
Guinea

Area: 245,857 sq km
Population: 9.2 million
GDP per capita: 2,170 US$
Capital: Conakry
Government: Republic
Languages: French (official), tribal languages
Currency: 1 Guinea franc = 100 cauris

Geography: The coastal plain to the west gives way to the plateau of Fouta Djalon, up to 1,500 meters high and the source of the Senegal, Niger, and Gambia rivers, which slopes away to the east. The coast is swampy; the country's northeast is covered by savanna and the southeast by tropical rain forests.

Politics: For centuries, the Fulbe people defended their territory against the mighty kingdoms of Ghana and Mali. In the 19th century Guinea became a French colony. After independence in 1958 a single-party system was established which was overturned by a military coup in 1984. The republican constitution of 1991 led to the first democratic elections in 1995. Conflicts in neighboring states could threaten Guinea's current stability.

Economy: Three-quarters of the population live from agriculture, which barely covers domestic needs despite the extenive fertile areas. The country has rich natural resources and is the second largest bauxite producer in the world. Other mining products are iron ore, uranium, cobalt, gold. The small industrial sector produces foodstuffs and textiles.

Guyana
Guyana

Area: 214,969 sq km
Population: 706,000
GDP per capita: 4,000 US$
Capital: Georgetown
Government: Presidential republic within the Commonwealth
Languages: English (official), Hindi, Urdu, dialects
Currency: 1 Guyana dollar = 100 cents

Geography: The fertile coastal region gives way to mountain chains in the west and far south. Savannas dominate the southwest. 80% of the country is covered by largely untouched rain forest. Land reclamation for arable use has been practiced since the 17th century.

Politics: Guyana's history of colonization began in the early 17th century, when British colonizers were followed by French and Dutch. Following Dutch rule, the country returned to Great Britain, gaining independence in 1966 and adopting South America's only socialist constitution in 1980.

Economy: More than half the population is descended from Indian immigrants, who were imported in the 19th century to work in the plantations. A quarter of the workforce is employed in agriculture, cultivating the chief exports of cane sugar and rice. Hardwoods from the extensive forests, gold, sugar, bauxite, and manganese are the primary sources of export revenue. Trade, services, and transportation are underdeveloped. Regional airlines operate between the largest cities.

Haïti
Haiti

Area: 27,750 sq km
Population: 7.6 million
GDP per capita: 1,600 US$
Capital: Port-au-Prince
Government: Presidential republic
Languages: French (official), Creole
Currency: 1 gourde = 100 centimes

Geography: Haiti occupies the western third of the island of Hispaniola and includes the two neighboring islands of Gonâve and Tortue. The country is divided from east to west by four mountain chains, accounting for around 80% of the country's area. Vegetation is dominated by savannas, with the remaining tropical rain forests limited to a few mountain areas. Cruise ship tourism concentrates on the capital of Port-au-Prince.

Bidjogo: *The Bidjogo people on the Bissago Islands off the coast of Guinea-Bissau are said to be expert fishers, boat builders and craftspeople. Apart from cult objects and elaborate figures of ancestors, they* *also manufacture naturalistic animal masks, which they wear at initiation ceremonies.*

Politics: After its discovery by Columbus, Hispaniola was a Spanish colony; the western part became a French colony in 1697, rose to prosperity and declared its independence in 1804 as the Empire of Haiti. After an era of revolutions, dictatorships and civil war the country now appears to be gaining political stability. Democratic parliamentary elections were introduced in 1996.

Economy: Agriculture, although employing more than half the population, is barely at subsistence level. Sugar cane, coffee, coca, and sisal are exported. Industry principally comprises small trade companies operating for the national market. Raw materials and semifinished products (textiles, electrical goods) are processed for re-export. Services are also gaining in significance, although tourism figures have dropped in recent years.

Honduras
Honduras

Area: 112,088 sq km
Population: 6.8 million
GDP per capita: 2,600 US$
Capital: Tegucigalpa
Government: Pres. republic
Languages: Spanish (official), English, Indian languages
Currency: 1 lempira = 100 centavos

Geography: Honduras is bounded to the north by the Caribbean and to the southwest by the Pacific. Its territory includes the Bahía and Swan islands. The country is primarily mountainous, with only a narrow coastal strip along the Pacific, and rivers, lagoons and swamps on the Caribbean side. The main settlement area is concentrated in the valleys of the Central American Andes.

Politics: In 1524 the country was conquered by Spain; in 1821 Honduras proclaimed its independence and became an independent republic in 1838 after leaving the Central American Federation. Over 100 governments and military dictatorships have seized power as a result of coups to the present day. The 1982 constitution specifies a term of four years for

elected members of the National Assembly.

Economy: Agriculture primarily produces bananas and coffee for export, with seafood the second most important export. Extensive livestock farming also exports its surplus. The rich natural resources (lead, zinc, silver) are almost untapped. Industry is insignificant, directed chiefly at the domestic market.

Hrvatska
Croatia

Area: 56,542 sq km
Population: 4.5 million
GDP per capita: 10,700 US$
Capital: Zagreb
Government: Republic
Language: Croatian
Currency: 1 kuna = 100 lipa

Geography: Croatia borders the Adriatic Sea to the west. The country's narrow coastal stip stretches south from Dalmatia to the Bay of Kotor. Croatia's territory also includes at least 600 islands in the Adriatic. Northeastern Croatia is a largely mountainous region that borders the fertile plains between the Sava and Danube rivers. The Croatian coast is an increasingly popular tourist destination.

Politics: Croatia was first settled by Slavic groups in the 7th century. The first Croatian kingdom was established in the 9th century. The country came under the control of the Habsburg Empire in 1527. Between 1918 and 1991, Croatia was a republic in the kingdom and later socialist republic of Yugoslavia. The country's declaration of independence was followed by a brutal civil war that lasted until 1995.

Economy: Croatia's economy was severely affected by the war of the early 1990s but has since made a gradual recovery. Agriculture remains an important economic sector, although the service sector is the fastest growing segment of the economy. Key exports are engineering and shipping. Tourism declined dramatically during the violent breakup of Yugoslavia but the industry is now growing rapidly.

India (Bhărat)
India

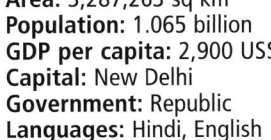

Area: 3,287,263 sq km
Population: 1.065 billion
GDP per capita: 2,900 US$
Capital: New Delhi
Government: Republic
Languages: Hindi, English
Currency: 1 Indian rupee = 100 paisa

1 Varanasi (Benares) is one of the most important sites of pilgrimage in India: devout Hindus purify themselves every year in the holy water of the Ganges with ritualistic ablutions.

2 Off the Honduran coast lie the mostly unspoiled Isles of Bahía, which stretch across one of the largest coral reefs in the world.

3 The Plitvic lakes and their surroundings in Croatia were declared a National Park in 1949. Since 1979 they have belonged to the UNESCO World Nature Heritage.

4 Rovinj, seaport and seaside resort in western Istria, is one of the most beautiful cities on the Croatian part of the Adriatic coast.

In the gods' honor: The temple dances of Bali employ fantastic masks and make-up and magnificent costumes to tell the traditional legends of the Hindu gods. The dances are performed at the islands' religious sites and shrines to entertain these gods. The Balinese value their ancient theater traditions, including Indonesian shadow plays.

Geography: The Indian subcontinent is divided into three regions: the mountain area of the Himalayas; the plain of the Indus and the Ganges; and the southern plateau, crossed by rivers, whose coasts are hemmed by wide plains. The climate is sub-tropical to tropical. In addition to nature reserves with a rich variety of fauna, India has countless cultural and historical monuments.

Politics: Aryan nomads displaced the Indus civilization from the 15th century BC. The Islamization of India began in the 12th century AD. The advance of the Europeans in the beginning of the 16th century led to the weakening of the Mogul rulers. In 1858 India was brought directly under the British crown. The struggle for independence started at the end of the 19th century, and inspired Mahatma Gandhi's movement after World War I. After Islamic Pakistan broke away, India finally gained independence in 1950. Although the country has enjoyed relative political stability since then, the conflict with Pakistan over Kashmir still continues until today.

Economy: The caste system dominates the life of the population. Three quarters of the inhabitants live from agriculture, generating some 32% of GDP. India is the world's number one tea exporter, and second largest exporter of dairy produce as well as a major fishing nation. The rich natural resources, which are little exploited, constitute the basis for the largely state-owned heavy industry. India has highly developed weapons, nuclear and space exploration industries. Tourism is an important branch of the services sector (40% of GDP).

Indonesia
Indonesia

Area: 1,919,440 sq km
Population: 238.4 million
GDP per capita: 3,200 US$
Capital: Jakarta
Government: Pres. republic
Languages: Indonesian (official), Javanese, other
Currency: 1 rupiah = 100 sen

Geography: More than 13,600 islands, about half of which are inhabited, span the Equator in a 5,000 kilometer arc. More than half the overall area is covered by forests, and the lowland plains of Sumatra and Borneo also feature extensive marsh and freshwater swamp forests. Chains of volcanoes (around 70 of which are active) extend through Western Sumatra. The climate is tropical and always humid. Indonesia is a popular tourist destination, especially Bali, the main island of Java, with Borobudur Temple, and the Lesser Sunda islands.

Politics: In early times, the country was under Hindu and Buddhist influence, becoming Islamic in the 13th century, with the exception of Hindu Bali. The Dutch took over the entire archipelago in the 16th–19th centuries to control the spice trade. In World War II,

The fertile fields of Bali yield two crops of rice every year.

Japan occupied the Dutch East Indies, which became independent in 1949 as the Republic of Indonesia. The country's history since then has been characterized by unrest and military coups. The military hold extensive power, and occupy several seats in the unicameral government.

Economy: The multiethnic state is predominantly inhabited by Malays, with Polynesian-Melanesian peoples in the eastern islands. More than half of the population work in agriculture, producing rice, corn, cassava, and sweet potatoes for domestic consumption, and coffee, cocoa, tea, and rubber from the plantations for export. Other important exports include wood, rattan and copal from the rain forest regions. Rich ore, mineral, oil and natural gas reserves form the basis of the highly developed heavy industry, which produces solely for export. Inland waterways are an important mode of transport.

Îrân
Iran

Area: 1,648,000 sq km
Population: 69 million
GDP per capita: 7,000 US$
Capital: Teheran
Government: Islamic republic
Languages: Farsi (official), Luri, Balochi, Kurdish
Currency: 1 rial = 100 dinar

Geography: Iran, between the Caspian Sea and the Persian Gulf, is bordered to the north by the Elburz Mountains (up to 5,064 m high), and the Zagros Mountains to the south. The arid highlands in the interior meet the Lût Desert in the east. In addition to the pilgrim cities of Qom and Masshad, popular destinations include the ancient ruins of Persepolis and Parsagadae, and the royal mosque in Isfahan.

Politics: The country's chequered history began with its settlement in the 2nd millennium BC by Iranians, who established the first Persian empire in the 6th century. Islamization began with the Arab conquest in the 7th century AD. In 1907 Russia and Great Britain divided the country into areas of influence. Extensive western-style reforms were introduced by Shah Pahlewi from 1925. The Islamic Revolution (1978) led to the flight of the Shah and the establishment of the Islamic Republic.

Economy: Only 10% of the area is used for agriculture through irrigation. In addition to wheat, barley, vegetables and sugar beet, tobacco, tea, pistachios, and dates are grown for export; the Caspian Sea yields caviar, whitefish, and ray. The country's heavy industry is based on rich petroleum and natural gas reserves, together with coal, copper, nickel, and chromium mining, and accounts for 85% of exports. Traditional crafts (e.g. carpetmaking) are declining.

'Îrāq
Iraq

Area: 437,072 sq km
Population: 25.3 million
GDP per capita: 1,600 US$
Capital: Baghdad
Government: Pres. republic
Language: Arabic
Currency: 1 Iraqi dinar = 1,000 fils

Geography: The heartland of the country in the northeast of the Arabian Peninsula is formed by the floodplain of the Tigris and Euphrates rivers, which turns into semi-desert and then desert to the west. There is a narrow access route to the Persian Gulf in the southeast. The sites of ancient Mesopotamia are of immense cultural and historical importance.

Politics: Mesopotamia was founded in the 3rd millennium BC by the Sumerians; in the 2nd and 1st millennium BC, the area was ruled by the Babylonians and Assyrians, and then conquered by the Persians in the 6th century BC. In the 7th century AD, the country fell under the Arabo-Islamic sphere of influence; the Ottomans ruled from the 16th to the 19th century. The monarchy established by the British in 1921 was overthrown by a bloody coup in 1958. Under the dictatorial president Saddam Hussein (in power from 1979), Iraq waged war with Iran over the oil regions from 1980–88. In 1990 Iraq annexed Kuwait. This led to the First Gulf War (1991), which ended with the defeat of Iraq by the US-led coalition. The conflict with the US escalated in 2002 when the latter suspected Iraq of harboring weapons of mass destruction. In 2003, the US, Great Britain and other countries launched a war which soon brought down the regime and investigated the democratic process.

Economy: Iraq has the third largest oil reserves in the world. The country is only slowly recovering from the consequences of the wars and from decades of a war economy, so economic reconstruction can only succeed with international help. Important industrial branches, other than the oil industry, are processing and construction.

Ísland
Iceland

Area: 103,000 sq km
Population: 294,000
GDP per capita: 30,900 US$
Capital: Reykjavik
Government: Republic
Language: Icelandic
Currency: 1 Icelandic krone = 100 aurar

Geography: Iceland is a volcanic island in the Atlantic Ocean. The northernmost sections of the country are located above the Arctic Circle. Most of the population is concentrated on the coast, while the rugged interior is largely uninhabited. Approximately 27 of the country's 140 volcanoes are active. Geysers, hot springs, lava, and ash fields are common throughout the country. About half of the island is covered by glaciers.

Multi-ethnic nation: Ethiopia is populated by more than 80 different ethnic groups which often differ widely. More than 90% of the inhabitants live from nomadic livestock breeding such as the small ethnic group of the Karo.

Among the most important peoples are the politically influential Oromo, the Amhara and the Tigrines.

Politics: Norwegians, the first permanent settlers of Iceland, arrived on the island during the 9th and 10th centuries. The Althing, an assembly of chiefs, was founded in 930 BC and exists to this day. The population of Iceland was converted to Christianity around AD 1000. The island was ruled by Denmark between the 13th century and 1944, when independence was declared.

Economy: Fishing and the manufacture of fish products is the largest industry in Iceland. Around a quarter of the workforce are directly or indirectly employed in the fishing industry. Livestock (sheep and horses) is also an important industry. The few mining operations are carefully regulated and limited. The economy has become increasingly diverse in recent years.

Israel see Yi'sra'el

Italia
Italy

Area: 301,230 sq km
Population: 58 million
GDP per capita: 26,800 US$
Capital: Rome
Government: Republic
Language: Italian
Currency: 1 euro = 100 cents

Geography: The Alps stretch along the northern border of Italy. Farther south, the Alpine foothills extend to the fertile Po River Valley. The Apennine Mountains stretch from north to south through the center of the Italian peninsula. In addition to mainland Italy, the country also consist of several large islands such as Sicily and Sardinia, and many smaller islands in the Mediterranean and Adriatic seas. The western coastline bears evidence of volcanic activity (Etna, Vesuvius). Italy is a popular tourist destination – major attractions include the country's ancient cities and coastal areas.

Politics: Italy was dominated by the Catholic Church for centuries following the collapse of the Roman Empire. Several Italian city-states – including Venice and Florence – emerged

as important centers of cultural and commercial progress during the late Middle Ages. The popes and several foreign powers vied for control of Italy between the 16th and 19th centuries. A united Italian kingdom was created in 1861 and Rome was declared the capital in 1870. A series of domestic crises led to the rise of Mussolini's fascist government in the 1920s. The country was occupied by German troops before the end of World War II. In 1946, Italy was declared a republic. Despite frequent changes in government during recent decades, Italy remains an open multi-party democracy.

Economy: The dramatic wealth gap between the industrialized north and the poorer, agricultural south of the country remains a major problem for Italy. Italy's highly productive agriculture sector now contributes less than 3% of the country's GDP, while the diverse service sector accounts for at least 70% of national GDP. Major exports include automobiles, electric goods, chemical products, textiles, and machinery. Tourism is a major industry in numerous Italian regions.

Îtyopya
Ethiopia

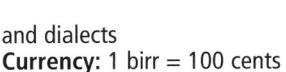

Area: 1,127,127 sq km
Population: 67.8 million
GDP per capita: 700 US$
Capital: Addis Ababa
Government: Federal republic
Languages: Amharic (official), 70 further languages

and dialects
Currency: 1 birr = 100 cents

Geography: The territory of Ethiopia extends over a mountain range divided by the East African Rift Valley. The north is dominated by desert and savanna, the south by rain forests. The chief tourist destinations are the landscapes and fauna of the national parks

1 The Roman Colloseum, which provided space for 50,000 spectators in the ancient world, was badly destroyed by an earthquake in 1348 and stripped of its decorations in subsequent centuries.

2 Italy: Vernazza on the Ligurian coast, one of five towns in the Cinque Terre region.

3 The north of Ethiopia encompasses vast dry savannas; water is a scarce commodity.

4 Jökulsá á Fjöllum, Iceland's second largest river, flows into the Greenland Sea.

Cyprus: The vast majority of the island's Greek inhabitants belong to the Greek Orthodox Church, which can trace its origins back to the 5th century. Starvo Abbey near Larnaca is one of Cyprus' numerous religious buildings, with mosques during established Osmanic times.

(Omo, Awash, Bale), the ruins at Axum and the Christian sites at Lalibela.

Politics: The legendary Kingdom of Sheba was succeeded in the 1st century by the mighty Axum, which lasted for more than 1,000 years, was Christianized as early as the 4th century and subsequently defied Islamization. Not until the 19th century did a mighty state again rise to resist colonialization. A Socialist people's republic was founded after the 1974 abdication of the last emperor; its leader was overthrown in 1991.

Economy: Agriculture accounts for more than half of GDP and employs 80% of the labor force, yet barely produces the basic foodstuffs. Coffee is the main export. The country's underdeveloped service industry primarily produces goods for the domestic market; a further obstacle is that the majority of large-scale companies are still state-owned.

Jamaica
Jamaica

Area: 10,990 sq km
Population: 2.7 million
GDP per capita: 3,800 US$
Capital: Kingston
Government: Parl. monarchy within the Commonwealth
Languages: English (official), Patois
Currency: 1 Jamaica dollar = 100 cents

Geography: The 235-kilometer-long island extends from east to west. The east is dominated by the volcanic Blue Mountains (up to 2,257 m); impenetrable gorges cleave the densely wooded western foothills. Rolling karst highlands in the west slope down to craggy sea cliffs. It's a Caribbean holiday paradise, with its tropical climate and idyllic sandy beaches.

Politics: Jamaica was discovered in 1494 by the Spanish, who eradicated the indigenous population and introduced slaves. The island was conquered by the British in 1655 and became a crown colony in 1866, one of the richest thanks to its sugar-cane and cocoa plantations. Jamaica has been independent since 1962 and has a bicameral parliament, with elections held every five years.

Economy: The educational and social systems are well-developed. Export crops are bananas, citrus fruits, coffee, cocoa, coconuts, and allspice, as well as large-scale sugar-cane plantations. Jamaica is the world's third largest bauxite supplier. The industrial sector comprises foodstuffs, electronics, and data processing products. Tourism is significant, accounting for just under 50% of GDP.

Japan see Nippon

Jordan see Urdunn

Kâmpŭchéa
Cambodia

Area: 181,035 sq km
Population: 13.4 million
GDP per capita: 1,700 US$
Capital: Phnom Penh
Government: Const. monarchy

Languages: Khmer (official), Vietnamese
Currency: 1 riel = 10 kak = 100 sen

Geography: The lowlands of the Tônlé-Sap basin and the Mekong Delta are bounded to the north by the Dangrek mountain range, and to the southwest by the Cardamom mountains, sloping down to the Gulf of Thailand. In the tropical, humid climate, vegetation ranges from mangrove forest swamps on the coast to monsoon forests in the central region and rain forests in the mountains. The most important travel destination is Angkor, the former capital of the old Khmer Empire.

Politics: The Khmer Empire was established in the 7th century and was overrun in the 17th century after repeated attacks by neighboring countries. In 1867 it was occupied by the French and incorporated into the Union of Indochina. The country gained independence in 1964. The civil war triggered in 1970 by the Indochina conflict was won by the communist forces of the Khmer Rouge. In 1975, they set up a terror regime, which was ended only when Vietnamese troops marched in. Despite free elections in 1993, the democratization process launched with the Vietnamese withdrawal and the introduction of a new constitution in 1989 has still not stabilized to the present day. The country is a constitutional monarchy.

Economy: The Agriculture accounts for 50% of GDP and employs 85% of the workforce, who, in addition to growing rice, cultivate soybeans, corn, and pepper for export. Tobacco, seafood, and valuable tropical hardwoods are also exported. The industrial sector comprises small companies and factories supplying the domestic market. Lack of infrastructure has hampered its growth. Tourism is an increasingly important sector.

Kazahstan
Kazakhstan

Area: 2,717,300 sq km
Population: 15.1 million
GDP per capita: 7,000 US$
Capital: Astana
Government: Republic
Languages: Kazakh, Russian
Currency: 1 tenge = 100 tiin

Geography: Much of the country, which comprises extensive steppes and deserts and includes part of the Tianshan Mountains in the southeast, has a continental, dry climate. The southwest border is formed by the Caspian Sea.

Politics: In the mid-18th century, the country, settled since the 6th century, came under Russian sovereignty, and was incorporated into the Czarist empire in 1873. The autonomous Socialist Republic was proclaimed in 1920 and joined the USSR in 1936. It again gained independence in 1991.

Economy: Grain, sugar beet, tobacco, and fruit are cultivated by means of irrigation, with vineyards in the northern mountain areas. Large copper and iron deposits, oil, and natural gas form the basis of the country's heavy industry. There are extensive road and rail networks and inland waterways. Pollution and ecological problems caused by industry and irrigation needs are a serious threat.

Kenya
Kenya

Area: 582,646 sq km
Population: 32 million
GDP per capita: 1,000 US$
Capital: Nairobi
Government: Pres. republic
Languages: Kiswaheli (official), English, tribal languages
Currency: 1 Kenya shilling = 100 Cents

Geography: Kenya on Africa's eastern coast, is divided into four distinct geographic zones: dry plains in the northeast; mountainous foothills around Lake Turkana to the northwest; southeastern savannas with forests and thorny scrub vegetation, and high plateaus in the west that rise to altitudes above 3,000 meters and then slope down to Lake Victoria.

Politics: The former British colony gained full independence in 1963, and proclaimed itself a republic. From 1982 the single-party system was gradually broadened in favor of democracy, at the urging of international aid contributors. The 2002 elections were a major transition in Kenyan politics and ended the decades of government by the KANU political party.

Economy: Kenya's agriculture produces tea, coffee, sisal, and sugar-cane for export. Cattle farming is practised at a high level. Processing industries (petroleum, agricultural products) account for 11% of GDP. The service sector, including tourism, is the largest segment of the national economy.

The west coast of Cyprus still offers unspoiled beaches.

Life in the savanna: In the arid lands in the north of Kenya, agriculture is all but impossible. The 80,000 or so Samburu who live here subsist from livestock, farming goats and cattle and more recently camels as well.

The Samburu National Park is home to numerous big game species and is said to be one of the most beautiful in Africa.

Kiribati
Kiribati

Area: 810.5 sq km
Population: 100,800
GDP per capita: 800 US$
Capital: Tarawa
Government: Presidential republic
Languages: I-Kiribati, English
Currency: 1 Australian dollar = 100 cents

Geography: Kiribati consists of 33 atolls scattered over an area of five million km² in the Pacific Ocean. Kiribati is generally divided into the Gilbert, Phoenix, and Line island groups. Most of the islands are unsuited for large scale agriculture because of their poor soils. The capital is located on the island of Tarawa.

Politics: The islands of Kiribati were first settled during the prehistoric era. During the 19th century, the first European traders arrived on the islands. They were declared a British protectorate in 1892, together with the Ellice Islands. After several decades as a British colony, the islands were granted independence in 1979.

Economy: The majority of Kiribati's population works in agriculture. Coconuts and fish are the leading exports. Manufacturing currently generates less than 10% of the country's gross domestic product. The country's geographic isolation is an obstacle to trade and increased foreign investments as is the shortage of skilled workers and weak infrastructure. Tourism accounts for around one-fifth of GDP. Aid from the industrialized countries, principally the UK and Japan, is an important source of income.

Kuwait see Al-Kuwait

Kypros/Kibris
Cyprus

Area: 9,250 sq km
Population: 776,000
GDP per capita: 16,000 US$
Capital: Nicosia
Government: Pres. republic

Language: Greek, Turkish (both official), English
Currency: 1 Cypriot pound = 100 cents

Geography: The island of Cyprus is in the Mediterranean Sea to the south of Turkey. Mesaoria, a large plain, stretches through central Cyprus and borders the Kyrenia mountains to the north. The Troodos Mountains, with Mount Olympus (1,953 m), stretch through most of southern and western Cyprus. Cyprus has a Mediterranean climate. The island is a popular tourist destination with many historic sites.

Politics: Cyprus has been dominated by numerous foreign powers throughout most of its history including Persians, Romans, Arabs, and Christian crusaders. It was a British colony (1925–1960). In 1974, Turkey occupied the northern sections of the island. Since then, the island has been divided between a Greek-speaking republic in the south and an ethnic Turkish state.

Economy: Greek Cyprus has experienced rapid growth in recent decades, while the Turkish north has stagnated due to its political isolation and corruption. The service sector dominates the economy of both areas and tourism is important.

Kyrgyzstan
Kyrgyzstan

Area: 198,500 sq km
Population: 5 million

GDP per capita: 1,600 US$
Capital: Biskek
Government: Presidential republic
Languages: Kyrghyz (official), Russian, and other minority languages
Currency: 1 Kyrghyzstan som = 100 tyin

1 Angkor has the largest complex of buildings in Southeast Asia, the Angkor Wat temple, began in the 12th century. From the 9th to the 15th centuries it was the religious and political center of the Khmer Empire.

2 Coconut palms are the predominant vegetation on Kiribati.

3 The majority of Jamaica's population are descended from slaves imported up to the mid-18th century to work in the country's many plantations.

4 The grassy savannas of the Serengeti cover a total of 14,500 square kilometers.

Laos: The majority of the inhabitants of Laos are Thai. In this communist country, Buddhism is joined by traditional tribal religions, particularly prevalent among the peasants. Nomadic cultivation is practised, with slash and burn methods causing damage to the tropical rainforest.

Geography: This Central Asian republic lies mostly in the Tianshan mountains. 50% of the landmass is at an altitude of above 3,000 meters, with only the western and northern promontories falling under 1,200 meters. At 3,000 meters, the landscape turns from desert and semi-desert into mountain steppes, meadows, and forests. The mountainous tundra lying beyond gives way to a glaciated region.

Politics: The country, settled early by nomadic peasants and hunters, achieved modern statehood only after the October Revolution of 1917. The Soviet Socialist Republic (from 1936) proclaimed its independence from the USSR in 1991. The amendment of the 1993 constitution granted far-reaching powers to the head of state.

Economy: Agriculture, which is possible in only 7% of the area, is the most important sector of the economy, accounting for 47% of GDP. In addition to grain and fodder for the extensive livestock breeding, fruit, vegetables, cotton, hemp, poppies, oil-giving plants, and tobacco are grown for export and for domestic consumption. Light industry is of great importance in this country with few natural resources.

Lao
Laos

Area: 236,800 sq km
Population: 6 million
GDP per capita: 1,700 US$
Capital: Vientiane
Government: People's republic
Languages: Lao (official), minority languages
Currency: 1 kip

Geography: The country is bordered in the north by the Tramin Plateau, which rises up to 2,820 meters, and in the south by the Boloven Plateau, about 2,000 meters high with a tropical monsoon climate. The rainy season (with temperatures of around 27° C) lasts from May to September. 40% of the area is covered by forests; dense deciduous growth gives way to rain forests at higher altitudes. The most important travel destination is Luang Prabang.

Politics: Buddhism was introduced in the 14th century with the establishment of the first Laotian Kingdom. After occupation by the Thais, Laos became a French protectorate in the 19th century and gained independence in 1954. During the Vietnam War, Communist revolutionary troops overran large parts of the country. The last king abdicated when the People's Republic was established in 1975.

Economy: Laos has experienced strong economic growth since 1986. Around 78% of the population work in agriculture, which accounts for 57% of GDP. A large part of the arable land comprises rice fields. Wood such as rattan and bamboo is felled for export.

Latvija
Latvia

Area: 64,589 sq km
Population: 2.3 million

Kyrghyzstan: Stock farming is run on the most remote high-pastures.

GDP per capita: 10,100 US$
Capital: Riga
Government: Republic
Language: Latvian (official), Russian
Currency: 1 lats = 100 santims

Geography: Latvia is bordered to the west by the Baltic Sea. The country's coast is mostly smooth and lined by wide sandy beaches. Latvia's interior is dominated by large fertile plains. Around 40% of the land area is covered by forests of birch, fir, and pine trees. Riga, the historic capital city, and Latvia's national parks are the country's leading tourist attractions.

Politics: The German speaking Teutonic Knights and the Hanseatic League dominated Latvia during the Middle Ages. Latvia was annexed by Russia in the 18th century and became independent in 1920. The country was reoccupied by Russia in 1940 and declared a republic of the USSR. Latvia declared its independence from the Soviet Union in 1991.

Economy: Agriculture and fishing remain important sectors of the Latvian economy and together account for around 10% of national GDP. The services sector now accounts for 66% of the country's GDP and is expanding. Major exports include agricultural produce, electronics, and machinery. Cargo handling in the Baltic ports is an important economic factor. The vast majority of former state enterprises have been privatized since 1991.

Lebanon see Al-Lubnān

Lesotho
Lesotho

Area: 30,355 sq km
Population: 1.9 million
GDP per capita: 3,000 US$
Capital: Maseru
Government: Constitutional monarchy within the Commonwealth
Languages: Sesotho, English
Currency: 1 loti = 100 lisente

Geography: Lesotho is completely enclosed by South Africa and is in the extreme south of the continent. There is little forest and scrub; the predominant forms of vegetation are grass savanna and mountain pastures. The country's territory consists largely of highlands and elevated plateaus.

Politics: The kingdom of the Basotho was formed in the 19th century and gained independence from British rule in 1966. It has been a constitutional monarchy since 1993. The close relationship to South Africa colors its political landscape.

Economy: Owing to the limited land area and repeated droughts, agriculture (maize, wheat, millet, and livestock) is poorly developed; supplies are imported. The majority of the country's GDP is derived from the wages of Lesotho citizens working in South Africa. Textile and leather processing is undergoing expansion.

Liberia
Liberia

Area: 111,369 sq km
Population: 3.4 million
GDP per capita: 1,000 US$
Capital: Monrovia
Government: Pres. republic
Languages: English (official), tribal languages
Currency: 1 Liberian dollar = 100 cents

Geography: The coastal areas are characterized by savanna, while much of the interior is covered by tropical rain forest. The climate is humid and tropical. The nature reserves in the Nimba Mountains were once tourist attractions, but the tourist industry is now virtually non-existent due to political instability.

Politics: Africa's oldest republic, Liberia was established in 1822 by freed American slaves. The country gained independence in 1847 but retained close ties to the USA for many years. After nine years of civil war following the 1990 fall of President Doe, the dictator who had ruled since 1986, a peacekeeping force was provided by ECOWAS.

Economy: Agriculture (rice, manioc) barely covers two-thirds of the country's needs. Large-scale plantations principally supply rubber for export. Other exports are coffee, cocoa, and palm kernels. Timber and iron ore are also exported. The services sector profits from the world's largest trading fleet in terms of tonnage.

Lîbîyâ
Libya

Area: 1,759,540 sq km
Population: 5.6 million
GDP per capita: 6,400 US$
Capital: Tripoli
Government: Islamic people's republic
Languages: Arabic (official), Berber dialects
Currency: 1 Libyan dinar = 1,000 dirham

Geography: The Mediterranean climate favors relatively lush vegetation along the narrow coastal region, which gives way in the south to plains and ultimately to the desert that cover 90% of the country's area. In the extreme south, foothills of the Tibesti Massif on the northern fringes of the Sahara reach altitudes of up to 2,285 meters. The ancient historical sites along the coast (Leptis Magna, Cyrene) and the capital of Tripoli are the main tourist destinations.

Politics: Settlements were established in the coastal regions by the 9th century BC, and fell to Roman rule in the 1st century AD. Libya was conquered by the Ottomans (1517) and ruled by an Islamic order in the 19th century. The country was an Italian protectorate for 40 years before receiving independence as a monarchy. The king was overthrown in 1969 by a military coup led by Colonel al-Gaddafi.

Economy: 90% of the population lives in the coastal area. Only 2% of the land is cultivatable, and the majority of farmland is irrigated. Privati-

Desert areas: While the densely populated coastal regions of Libya are sufficiently developed for traffic, travelling into the south of the country requires suitable cross-country vehicles to cope with the enormous distances *between the oasis settlements. Despite the exertions involved, the beauty of the landscape makes the journey well worth while.*

zation of most state-owned operations is planned to secure subsistence quantities of fruit, vegetables, grain, and fruit. The Libyan economy is centered on the country's enormous petroleum reserves, which produce 25% of the annual GDP.

Liechtenstein
Liechtenstein

Area: 160 sq km
Population: 33,400
GDP per capita: 25,000 US$
Capital: Vaduz
Government: Parliamentary monarchy
Language: German
Currency: 1 Swiss franc = 100 rappen

Geography: Liechtenstein is a small principality in the highlands of the Alps, located between Austria and Switzerland. The Rhine River forms the country's northwestern border. Liechtenstein is a year-round destination for skiers.

Politics: Liechtenstein's existence as a sovereign principality began in 1719. The country remained neutral during both world wars and joined a customs and monetary union with Switzerland in 1923. Liechtenstein's ruling monarch has broad sweeping powers in contrast to most other European constitutional monarchies.

Economy: Workers from neighbouring Switzerland, Germany and Austria form a third of the country's population. The majority of the country's people work in the service and manufacturing sectors. Modern Liechtenstein has a diverse and highly developed economy and its people enjoy a high standard of living.

Lietuva
Lithuania

Area: 65,200 sq km
Population: 3.6 million
GDP per capita: 11,200 US$
Capital: Vilnius
Government: Parliamentary republic
Language: Lithuanian (official), Russian

Currency: 1 litas = 100 centas

Geography: Lithuania has a 100-kilometer coastline along the Baltic Sea and the Curonian Lagoon. The country is largely flat. Most of the country's terrain is covered by forests, moorlands, and meadows. The coastal areas have a mild maritime climate, while the interior has a drier continental climate.

Politics: The Polish-Lithuanian Commonwealth ruled a vast territory stretching from the Baltic to the Black Sea during the 17th and 18th centuries. Lithuania came under the control of the Russian Empire in 1772. The country declared its independence from Russia in 1918 and was annexed by the Soviet Union in 1940. Lithuania became the first Soviet republic to declare its independence (1991).

Economy: Lithuania experienced a difficult transition to free market capitalism in the 1990s but the country has recently experienced strong growth levels. Although not plentiful in natural resources, Lithuania is developing an oil reserve discovered in the Baltic Sea. Agriculture accounts for 10% of Lithuania's GDP, while the service sector contributes approximately 66% of GDP.

Luxembourg
Luxembourg

Area: 2,586 sq km
Population: 462,700
GDP per capita: 55,100 US$
Capital: Luxembourg
Government: Constitutional monarchy
Language: Letzebuergesch, French, German (all official)
Currency: 1 euro = 100 cents

Geography: Luxembourg, one of the smallest states in Europe, shares borders with France, Germany, and Belgium. Northern Luxembourg is a heavily forested area with rolling hills while the south is dominated by river valleys. The country's main attractions include its river valleys and capital city.

Politics: Once a region of the German-dominated Holy

Roman Empire, Luxembourg came under the control of France in the 18th century. The country achieved its formal independence in 1867. It was occupied by the German army in both world wars and abandoned its neutrality when it joined the NATO defence alliance in 1949. The Grand Duke

1 Vast seas of dunes and sandy plains known as ergs cover large parts of the Libyan Sahara.

2 Riga, the capital city of Latvia, is near the country's Baltic Sea coast and boasts an attractive medieval city center.

3 The inhabitants of Lesotho paint their houses with colorful traditional patterns.

4 Monks are highly regarded in Laos, although it's a communist state; two-thirds of the population are Buddhists.

"Small Tiger": A booming economy led to the Islamic country of Malaysia being classified as one of the "four small tigers," Southeast Asia's most successful newly industrialized countries. The country is home to a range of Asiatic cultures which coexist largely peacefully; the population comprises two-thirds Malays and almost one-third Chinese, in addition to Indians and Pakistanis.

of Luxembourg is the country's official head of state.

Economy: Foreign workers – most from other EU countries – form more than a quarter of Luxembourg's population. The country's economy is heavily dependent on foreign trade. The steel industry was once the largest in the country, but the economy is now dominated by the service industries, including the large banking and financial services sector, in which around 70% of the workforce are employed. Luxembourg is the seat of the European Court of Auditors as well as other European organizations.

Madagasíkara
Madagascar

Area: 587,041 sq km
Population: 17.5 million
GDP per capita: 800 US$
Capital: Antananarivo
Government: Republic
Languages: Malagasy, French (both official official), Howa
Currency: 1 Madagascar franc = 100 centimes

Geography: The world's fourth largest island is largely composed of sloping mountains, with coastal plains to the west. The climate is tropical; the island's east has high rainfall and is covered with lush rain forest. The unique, partly endemic flora and fauna of the island is threatened by slash and burn agricultural techniques, cyclones, flooding, and earthquakes. Areas of tourist interest are the many nature reserves and the capital city.

Politics: Originally settled by South Asian peoples, the island was discovered in 1500 by the Portuguese, who established settlements with the French on the coast. The indigenous population successfully resisted colonization until 1896; then a colony of France, the country gained independence in 1960. Its 1992 constitution specifies a bicameral parliament, with elections held every five years.

Economy: Social and health-care services are as inadequate as the provision of basic foodstuffs. Agriculture forms the basis of existence for 75%

of the largely Malayan/Indonesian population, who cultivate rice, cassava, maize, sweet potatoes, mangos, bananas, and sugar cane in smallholdings. Key exports are coffee, vanilla, cotton, and tobacco. Shrimp, tuna and lobster are processed by the poorly developed industrial sector. The not inconsiderable natural resources are largely untapped. Recent political instability in the country has slowed economic growth. The government is now liberalizing the economy and challenging corruption.

Magyarország
Hungary

Area: 93,030 sq km
Population: 10 million
GDP per capita: 13,900 US$
Capital: Budapest

Kuala Lumpur: The economic and cultural center of Malaysia.

Government: Parliamentary republic
Language: Hungarian
Currency: 1 forint

Geography: The vast Pannonian plain/Carpathian Basin stretches over most of Hungary's national territory. Low mountains rising up to 1,000 meters stretch along the Slovakian border and through

northern Hungary. The Danube and Theiss river are the country's principal waterways. Budapest, Lake Balaton (the largest lake in Central Europe) and the pristine landscapes of Hortobagy National Park are the country's leading tourist attractions.

Politics: The Magyar ancestors of the Hungarians arrived in the Carpathian Basin during the 9th century. Hungary was one of Europe's most powerful states by the 13th century. The country was divided and controlled by the Habsburg Empire and Ottoman Turks during the 16th century. After a failed Hungarian revolution in 1867, the Habsburg Empire was reorganized into the Austro-Hungarian Empire. Hungary became an independent kingdom in 1918 at the end of the First World War and was governed by a reactionary nationalist government in the 1930s. Hungary was allied to the Axis powers in World War II and was placed in the Soviet sphere of influence after the war. Hungary was the first communist state in Eastern Europe to begin the transition to democracy and capitalism, and joined NATO in 1999 and the European Union in 2004.

Economy: Hungary is one of the wealthier transition countries in Europe. The country has privatized most former state industries and receives impressive levels of foreign investment. The service sector accounts for more than 62% of Hungary's GDP, while the manufacturing sector accounts for 34%.

Makedonija
Macedonia

Area: 25,333 sq km
Population: 2 million
GDP per capita: 6,700 US$
Capital: Skopje
Government: Republic
Language: Macedonian (official), Albanian, Turkish, Serbian
Currency: 1 Macedonian denar = 100 deni

Geography: The former Yugoslav republic of Macedonia is a largely mountainous republic with several peaks rising 2,000 meters or more. The southern sections of the country and the Vadar Valley have a Mediterranean climate, while the rest of the country has a cooler continental climate. More than a third of the country is covered by forests. The monasteries around Lake Ohrid, the country's national parks, and the almost Oriental-style capital city, Skopje, are Macedonia's leading attractions.

Politics: Macedonia was a region in the Ottoman Empire between the 14th and 19th centuries. The country was widely known as Vadarska before 1929 when it was renamed Macedonia. The country has been in dispute with Greece over the name Macedonia since its independence in 1991.

Economy: Macedonia was one of the poorer republics in Yugoslavia. The country's economy stagnated throughout the 1990s because of its poor infrastructure, conflicts in the Balkans, and a Greek embargo. Ethnic conflict and instability continue to undermine sustained economic development. Textiles, steel, and agricultural produce (the latter chiefly from small farms in the Pelargonija basin) are the country's lea-

ding export commodities. Services are gaining in importance in this transit country.

Malawi
Malawi

Area: 118,484 sq km
Population: 11.9 million
GDP per capita: 600 US$
Capital: Lilongwe
Government: Presidential republic within Commonwealth
Languages: Chichewa, English (both official), Chitumbuka, other Bantu languages
Currency: 1 Malawi kwacha = 100 tambala

Geography: The majority of the country's area is occupied by Lake Nyasa. The regions to the west and south of the lake are mountainous, with peaks of up to 2,670 meters (Nylka Plateau). Grasslands and dry forests are the principal forms of vegetation; dense forests can be found in the mountains. The rich animal life is protected in four national parks; tourist centers are Lake Nyasa and Blantyre, with its beautiful surroundings.

Politics: In 1891 the region surrounding Lake Nyasa became a British protectorate, and was incorporated into Rhodesia as Nyasaland in 1907. Malawi was declared independent in 1964. The president's extensive powers awarded by the Constitution in 1966 were repealed in 1993, partly at the urging of creditor countries. The first free elections were held in 1994.

Economy: 70% of Malawi's population lives from smallholder farming, producing 35% of GDP. Subsistence is threatened by periods of drought. 90% of export revenues are derived from coffee; other exports are tea, sugar, and tobacco. Subsistence fishing is practiced on the country's three lakes. The industrial sector processes domestic agricultural products (tea, beer, tobacco, textiles, shoes). Tourism is well-developed, contributing 25% to GDP. The service sector is underdeveloped but now contributes almost half of GDP. Malawi is heavily indebted and remains dependent on foreign aid.

The art of horsemanship: Although horse-breeding has diminished somewhat in importance, the herds of horses roaming the puszta are a typical image of traditional Hungarian life. Even today, the equestrian skills of the Magyars are a popular attraction at Hungary's numerous festivals and at circus performances all over the world.

Malaysia
Malaysia

Area: 329,758 sq km
Population: 23.5 million
GDP per capita: 9,000 US$
Capital: Kuala Lumpur
Government: Constitutional elected monarchy in the Commonwealth
Languages: Malay (official), Chinese, Tamil, Iban, English
Currency: 1 Malay ringgit = 100 sen

Geography: Malaysia extends over the southern part of the Malacca Peninsula and the northwestern part of the island of Borneo 600 kilometers away, separated by the China Sea. The predominantly mountainous country is largely covered by evergreen tropical rain forests, which flourish in lush abundance in the hot and humid climate with average temperatures of 27° C. Flora and fauna are highly varied. With many beaches, nature reserves and cities such as Kuala Lumpur or Malacca, Malaysia has a host of tourist destinations.

Politics: Malaysia was created in 1963 from the union of newly independent principalities on the Malacca peninsula, the British territories of Sabah and Sarawak, Borneo and Singapore, which, however, left the union two years later. The country is governed by a king elected from the Nine Sultans for a five-year term. The king then appoints the head of government, nominated by the lower house, and also appoints some members of the upper house. The more influential lower house is elected directly for a five-year term.

Economy: Exported forestry and agricultural products such as tropical hardwoods, rubber, palm oil, and coconut products, plus petroleum and natural gas, have helped Malaysia gain an economic upswing. The country is also the world's leading producer of tin. The backbone of Malaysia's economy is formed by the high-tech and automotive industries. The services sector, which has hitherto generated 20% of GDP, will gain in importance in future as the infrastructure of this emerging country expands.

Maldives (Divehi Rajje)
Maldives

Area: 298 sq km
Population: 339,300
GDP per capita: 3,900 US$
Capital: Malé
Government: Presidential republic in the Commonwealth
Languages: Divehi (official), English
Currency: 1 rufiyaa = 100 laari

Geography: The country's territory is divided into 19 atoll groups with about 2,000 islands, only about one tenth of which are inhabited. The tropical climate ensures an average annual temperature of 30° C. In contrast to the limited land fauna, there are many species of sea life in the coral reefs. The Maldives have a very well developed tourism industry, and a site of cultural and historical interest is the 17th-century mosque in the capital, Malé, as well as idyllic beaches.

Politics: The expansion of Islam, which has been the state religion since 1153, dates back to traveling Arab merchants of the 12th century. The British protectorate, on the other hand, which ruled from 1887 until independence in 1965, had little influence on the state system. The 1975 constitution vests the directly elected president with extensive powers. There are no political parties or parliamentary supervisory authorities.

Economy: A quarter of the population live in the capital. Owing to soil conditions, agriculture can only cover domestic needs (coconuts and betel nuts, cassava, onions, and chili peppers). Part of the fishing catches are processed for export, the second highest foreign currency earner after tourism. The Maldives have no railroad, and cars only on Malé and Gan. The most important economic sector on the Maldives is tourism, with 20% of GDP.

Mali
Mali

Area: 1,240,192 sq km
Population: 12 million
GDP per capita: 900 US$
Capital: Bamako
Government: Presidential republic
Languages: French (official), Bamakan, farther Mandé languages
Currency: 1 CFA franc = 100 centimes

Geography: Between Ségou and Timbuktu, the Niger forms

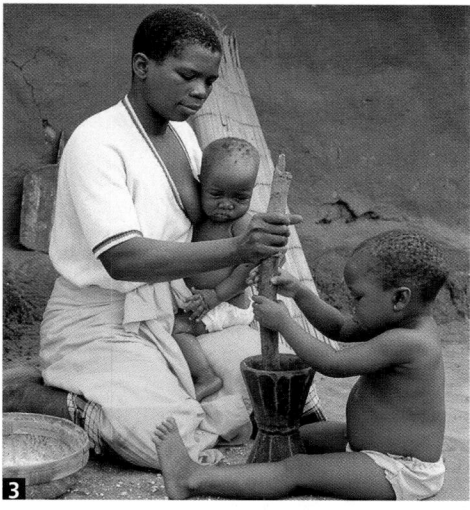

1 The capital city of Hungary is divided by the Danube River into two distinct sections, Buda in the west and Pest in the east.

2 Hardy plants like the coconut palm chiefly thrive in the sandy soil of the Maldives' 2,000-plus islands.

3 Malawi is chiefly populated by Bantu tribes and is among the most densely populated countries in Africa.

4 Sunset off the shore of Madagascar; the island, with its unique flora and fauna, is an increasingly popular destination.

Malta Malta

Pre-Colombian heritage: Indigenous communities, such as the Maya, make up only around ten percent of Mexico's 105 million inhabitants. As their numbers dwindle, their ancient cultural heritage and its legacy of countless archeological treasures has become an inspiration for contemporary artists and architects.

a large freshwater delta with fertile alluvial deposits. Mali's north is dominated by dry Saharan zones, while the south has tree savannas and gallery forests. These areas are home to a richly diverse range of wildlife. Tourist attractions are the areas of natural beauty and the ancient royal cities of Timbuktu, Mopti, and Bamako. Desertification is a major environmental issue in the country.

Politics: The legendary kingdom of the Mali arose in the 11th century. Its trading center – Timbuktu – became famous far beyond the borders of Africa in the 14th century. At the end of the 19th century the French conquered the country and incorporated it into the colony of French West Africa. The Republic of Mali gained independence in 1960 and was ruled by a dictatorship until 1991. After the first free elections in 1992, conflicts with the Tuareg were reconciled by the assurance of partial autonomy.

Economy: The north is inhabited only by the Tuareg, while 90% of the largely Islamic population live in the south. Because of Mali's poverty migration into neighboring countries is very high. Over 80% of the population subsists from agriculture. Desertification is reducing the amount of cultivatable land, and grain cultivation in the savannas is frequently affected by drought. Nomadic animal husbandry in the Sahel and fishing in the Niger delta and lakes are major contributions to subsistence. The industrial sector processes domestic agricultural products. Mali is heavily dependent on foreign aid, remittances from overseas workers, and global prices for agricultural goods. Government reforms have led to steady growth rates in recent years.

Malta
Malta

Area: 316 sq km
Population: 397,000
GDP per capita: 17,700 US$
Capital: Valletta
Government: Republic
Language: Maltese, English
Currency: 1 Maltese lira = 100 cents

Geography: The island republic of Malta in the southern Mediterranean, consists of three islands – Malta, Gozo, and Comino. The ancient islands are the remnants of a large land bridge that once stretched between North Africa and Europe. Malta has few freshwater sources and most of the islands consist of arid plains with poor soils. Most of Malta's indigenous vegetation was cleared during the Middle Ages. All of the Maltese islands have a distinctly Mediterranean climate with hot, dry summers and mild winters.

Politics: The ancient megaliths of Malta are remnants of an ancient stone age culture that once inhabited the islands. Malta was ruled by numerous foreign powers throughout its history, including the Romans, Egyptians, Phoenicians, Arabs, Spaniards, and the British. In the possession of the Knights of Malta, the country was an important center of the Christian wars against the Ottoman Turks between 1530 and 1798 and a bulwark of the West. It was a British colony from 1800 to 1964 and declared independence in 1974. Malta joined the EU in 2004.

Mexico City: The fourth largest city in the world.

Economy: Malta's agricultural sector consists mostly of small farms and produces less than 5% of the country's GDP. The services sector accounts for more than 74% of GDP. Tourism remains the single most important industry in the country and provides jobs for more than a quarter of the population. The country's leading export commodities include citrus fruits and machinery.

Marshall Islands
Marshall Islands

Area: 181 sq km
Population: 57,700
GDP per capita: 1,600 US$
Capital: Majuro
Government: Republic
Languages: Marshallese dialects, English
Currency: 1 US dollar = 100 cents

Geography: The Marshall Islands consist of two atolls that stretch over a distance of 1,200 kilometers. The Ratak island group comprises 16 atolls, while the large Ralik group consists of 18 atolls and more than 100 coral reefs. The Marshall Islands all have humid tropical climate with heavy rainfall.

Politics: The islands were first visited by Europeans in 1529 and became a German protectorate in 1884. After the First World War the islands were transferred to Japanese control. Between 1945 and 1980 they were administered by the United States. In 1980 the Marshall Islands were declared an independent state but the United States provides the country's defense and much development aid.

Economy: More than half of the Marshall Islands' population is concentrated on the islands of Ebeye and Majuro. Much of the population works in agriculture. Bananas, papayas, and coconuts are the most widely produced crops. The islands have few mineral resources, but phosphate is mined on the Ailinglaplap atoll. Coconuts and fish are the leading exports. Tourism is a small but important industry for the islands and the industrial sector consists mostly of fish processing. Development aid from the United States is the country's main source of government funding.

Mauritius
Mauritius

Area: 2,040 sq km
Population: 1.2 million
GDP per capita: 11,400 US$
Capital: Port Louis
Government: Republic
Languages: English (official), Creole, Hindi, Urdu
Currency: 1 Mauritius rupee = 100 cents

Geography: The tropical island, a volcanic formation in the Indian Ocean, has a humid tropical climate. Its highest mountain is the Cocotte (771 m) in the south. The white beaches of the coastline's many bays are fringed by lagoons. Parts of the original rain forest have survived only in the nature reserves. The island's capital is the center of its thriving tourism industry, and the nature reserves at Rivière Noire and Ile Aigrettes are easily accessible. The other islands in the group also attract holidaymakers and diving fans.

Politics: The island was conquered in the 16th century by the Dutch, who introduced plantation cultivation. The French took over the colony in the 18th century, while Mauritius came under British rule from 1810 until its independence in 1968. The Republic of Mauritius was founded in 1992, although the country remained a member of the Commonwealth.

Economy: Sugar-cane cultivation has primary importance, employing 14% of the labor force. Three-quarters of foodstuffs are imported; cultivation of potatoes, vegetables, bananas, and pineapple is subsidized. The country's industrial sector focuses on textile production and sugar-cane processing. 10% of the workforce are employed in the tourism sector. The island's infrastructure is well-developed, with road networks and shipping and air links to the other islands.

Mawrītāniyah
Mauritania

Area: 1,030,700 sq km
Population: 3 million
GDP per capita: 1,800 US$
Capital: Nouakchott
Government: Islamic presidential republic
Languages: Arabic (official), Niger-Congo languages
Currency: 1 ouguiya = 5 khoums

Geography: The eastern Atlantic coast gives way to flat coastal plains and extensive tableland with steppe vegetation. The majority of the country is occupied by the Sahara with sand and scree deserts. Its highest elevations are the plateaus of Adrar and Tagant, at around 500 meters. Owing to the extremely dry climate, palms and baobab flourish only in the far south in the savannas on the Senegal. Of interest for tourists are the cities of Chinguetti, Oualâta, Tîchît and Oudâne. The bird sanctuary of Djoudj and Banc d'Arguin national park are on the coast. Desertification is a major environmental problem in Mauritania.

Beautiful island: Beaches and lagoons make Mauritius a popular holiday destination. Today tourism is the most important source of income for the population. Two-thirds of them are descendants of the Indian plantation workers who were recruited in the 19th century for the dominant sugar-cane cultivation; the remainder are Creoles, Europeans, and Chinese.

Politics: The country, part of the wealthy Ghana Empire, was Islamicized by Arab settlers in the 11th century. It was ruled by Moorish sultans until the end of the 19th century. In 1902 the French acquired the territory and incorporated it into the colony of French West Africa in 1920. Mauritania gained independence in 1960. The new constitution of 1991 smoothed the path from dictatorship to democracy; the first elections were held in 1992.

Economy: Persistent droughts have reduced the proportion of traditional nomadic populations; urbanization is increasing. Only 0.2% of the country's area is cultivatable. The fertile land in the catchment area of the Senegal and the oases of the south is cultivated for subsistence agriculture supplying basic needs. Animal husbandry is practised in the southern steppe belt. Fishery accounts for the majority of export revenues, and forms the basis of a small processing industry. Iron ore exports are the major source of foreign currency.

México
Mexico

Area: 1,972,550 sq km
Population: 105 million
GDP per capita: 9,000 US$
Capital: Mexico City
Government: Presidential federal republic
Languages: Spanish (official), minority languages
Currency: 1 Mexican new peso = 100 centavos

Geography: Mexico lies between the Gulf of Mexico and the Pacific. A ridge of high mountains, with the Sierra Madre to the west, south and east, surround the tableland that comprises most of the country's interior, with the highest peak – Popocatépetl (5,452 m) – at its center. The peninsula of Yucatán, bordering the Caribbean in the southeast, is composed of a chalk layer. The southern foothills of the coastal American Cordilleras form the peninsula of Baja California, divided from the remaining territory by the Gulf of California. Northern Mexico has desert vegetation; tropical rain forests grow along the coast of the Gulf of Mexico. Tourist attractions are principally the capital, the many sites of ancient civilizations (Uxmal, Teotihuacán, Palenque) and the lively beaches (Acapulco, Tampico).

Politics: At the start of the 16th century the Spanish conquered the seat of the Maya and Aztec civilizations and plundered its rich silver reserves, overthrowing the native ruler to establish an extensive colony under Hernán Cortez. Mexico declared independence in 1821. The civil war in the following era culminated in 1911 in a bloody revolution, which ended in 1920 after the proclamation of a presidential federal republic. The country's states have their own constitutions, with a relatively high degree of autonomy. The president is elected by a bicameral parliament for a term of six years.

Economy: Agriculture forms the livelihood of half the population, with maize, wheat, pulses, vegetables and fruit grown for subsistence in smallholdings and private plantations cultivating coffee, tobacco and cotton for export. Extensive and largely untapped reserves of minerals and ores have already made Mexico a major supplier of silver, feldspar, and graphite. The rich petroleum and natural gas reserves make a significant contribution to the economy, accounting for around 30% of export revenues and forming the basis of the chemical industry. Tourism is well-developed and accounts for a large share of the services sector.

Micronesia
Micronesia

Area: 702 sq km
Population: 108,200
GDP per capita: 2,000 US$
Capital: Palikir
Government: Constitutional government

1 The Maya temple of Tulúm is picturesquely located on the Caribbean coast of Mexico in the northern part of the Yucatan peninsula.

2 Vast parts of Mauritania are occupied by dunes and rocky deserts; the country borders the Sahara to the northwest.

3 The storehouses and sanctuaries in the cliffs of Bandiagara, constructed some centuries ago of clay bricks, belong to the cultural heritage of the people of Dogon in Mali.

4 Ferries play an important role in the traffic system of Malta.

Moçambique Mozambique

Mongolian traditions: Although the majority of the Mongolian people have now settled, hunting and horse-riding are still living traditions among these former nomads and equestrians who once ruled the whole of Asia.

Today the various ethnic groups and tribes of the Mongols, who have a single language in common, live scattered over the national territories of Mongolia, China, and Russia.

Languages: English, local Polynesian and Micronesian languages
Currency: 1 US dollar = 100 cents

Geography: The territory of the Federated States of Micronesia are scattered over an area of 2.6 million km² in the Pacific Ocean. The country comprises four states – Chuuk (294 islands), Yap (145 islands), Kosrae (five islands), and Pohnpei (163 islands). The country consists of both volcanic and coral island groups. All of the islands have a humid tropical climate with heavy rainfall, and tropical storms are common in the regions. Ancient ruins and the diverse marine life in Micronesia's coral reefs are the country's main tourist attractions.

Politics: The islands of Micronesia were under Spanish control for centuries before they were sold to Germany in the 19th century. The islands were administered by Japan after the end of the First World War, and were transferred to the United States after the Second World War. Micronesia became an independent federal republic in 1990, although the United States continues to maintain responsibility for the country's defense. The constitution of 1979 applies. There are no formal political parties.

Economy: Small-scale farming of coconuts, cassava, and other crops provides most of Micronesia's food demands and employs a significant segment of the local population. The selling of fishing licenses to foreign companies, chiefly Japan, is an important source of income for the country. Tourism and the export of crops are both major industries in Micronesia.

Moçambique
Mozambique

Area: 801,590 sq km
Population: 18.8 Million
GDP per capita: 1,200 US$
Capital: Maputo
Government: Republic
Languages: Portuguese (official), Bantu languages
Currency: 1 metical = 100 centavos

Geography: The many bays of the coast along the Indian Ocean give way to savanna and dry forests inland. To the north are mountains of up to 2,000 meters. Mangrove forests grow in the swampy regions of the river deltas. In the summer, monsoons dominate the tropical climate. The once rich animal life (antelopes, gazelles, elephants, leopards) has been decimated by big game hunting. Tourism concentrates on nature reserves such as Gorongosa and the broad beaches, but also the old colonial cities of Moçambique and Maputo. The country's climate ranges from subtropical to tropical with significant differences between the coastal and interior regions. Severe flooding and periods of drought are common in many regions.

Politics: Occupied in the 16th century by the Portuguese, the country did not gain independence until 1975 after a long guerilla war. In the same year the liberation movement proclaimed a people's republic, which was replaced in 1990 by a parliamentary democracy with a new constitution. After a long civil war, a peace treaty was signed with the right-wing rebels in 1992.

Economy: Although the largest sector of the economy, agriculture is barely at subsistence level. Over half the export revenues are derived from shrimps, which are processed by the industrial sector. The rich natural resources (precious and semiprecious stones, iron ores, minerals, metals) are largely untouched. Improvements to the infrastructure since the 1990s have benefited the services sector as tourism and the cargo handling trade have increased.

Morocco see Al-Magrib/Maroc

Moldova
Republic of Moldova

Area: 33,700 sq km
Population: 4.4 million
GDP per capita: 1,800 US$
Capital: Chisinau
Government: Republic

Language: Moldovan (official), Russian
Currency: 1 Moldoan leu = 100 bani

Geography: The small country in Eastern Europe consists primarily of plains and marshes. Moldova is crossed by several rivers including the Danube, the Dniester, and the Prut. Most of the country is covered by grasslands, marshes, and deciduous forests. Tourism focuses on the capital, and on the historic castles.

Politics: The area of modern Moldova was part of the Principality of Moldovia during the Middle Ages. Moldova was conquered by the Ottomans in the 16th century. The eastern part of the country was annexed by Russia in 1812 and became a Soviet republic in 1918. The country declared its independence from the Soviet Union in 1991.

Economy: Moldova is one of the poorest states in Europe despite strong growth in recent years. The country has few mineral resources and agriculture contributes more than a quarter of national GDP and occupies over 70% of Moldova's area. The country's agricultural sector stagnated during the 1990s due to a loss of its traditional markets in the former Soviet republics. Privatization is progressing slowly. Moldova's service sector remains undeveloped and manufacturing is relatively unproductive. Major exports include fruits, grain, wine, tobacco, and machinery.

Monaco
Monaco

Area: 1.95 sq km
Population: 32,300
GDP per capita: 27,000 US$
Capital: Monaco City
Government: Constitutional hereditary monarchy
Language: French (official), Monegasque, Italian
Currency: 1 euro = 100 cents

Geography: Monaco is a small principality on the Mediterranean coast of Southern France. Most of the country's land area was created by reclaiming land from the sea. The densely populated country consists mostly of urban landscapes, although wines and olives are grown in a few areas. Monaco is a popular tourist destination.

Politics: The ruling Grimaldi dynasty gained control of Monaco in 1454. Monaco achieved complete independence in 1861 after periods of Spanish and French domination. Monaco lost most of its territory to France during the 19th century. The constitutions of 1911 and 1962 limited the power of Monaco's princes and transformed the country into a modern constitutional monarchy.

Economy: Only around 17% of Monaco's residents are citizens of the country. Monaco has a high standard of living and low taxes that attract many residents and investors. Tourism is an important industry for the country and the principality's famous casino in the Monte Carlo area is the country's largest single business. Other economic pillars are the real estate and financial sectors.

Mongol Ard Uls
Mongolia

Area: 1,565,000 sq km
Population: 2.8 million
GDP per capita: 1,800 US$
Capital: Ulan Bator
Government: Republic
Languages: Mongolian, Kazakh, Russian, other languages
Currency: 1 tugrik = 100 mongo

Geography: The country also known as Outer Mongolia is dominated in the west by the Altai Mountains, up to 4,300 meters in height, and the Changai Mountains (over 3,500 m). Highlands with peaks of 1,000–1,500 meters cover the east, and taiga vegetation grows in the northeast. The mountain desert and steppe vegetation that dominates the remaining area gives way to the Gobi Desert in the south.

Politics: Inhabited early by nomadic horsemen, Mongolia was united in 1206 by Genghis Khan and formed the core of a large empire with Beijing at its center. After the fall of the Mongolian imperial dynasty in 1368, the country fell under Chinese rule. In 1911, Outer Mongolia separated from China. The People's Republic of Mongolia was created in 1924. After the collapse of the USSR, a multi-party system was introduced and the Republic of Mongolia founded in 1992. The country has a unicameral parliament.

Economy: The population consists predominantly of Mongols, followed by Kazakhs, Chinese, and Russians. The transition from a socialist planned

Monaco: Tax haven on the Côte d'Azur.

"Golden triangle": The Shan people, Thai in origin, have populated northeastern Myanmar on the borders of Laos, Thailand, and China since the 13th century. Extensive smuggling of opium by troops of rebels from the world's largest production area has repeatedly led to armed conflict with the central government. Limited autonomy was granted to the Shan State in 1993, within a cease-fire agreement.

economy to a market economy has proved difficult. Traditional animal husbandry (goats, sheep, camels, and horses) predominates, as only 1% of the area can be used for agriculture (grains, vegetables, feedstuffs). The rich coal, copper, molybdenum, gold, and tin deposits are mined and form the basis of the industry. Tourism is almost non-existent; services account for 34% of GDP.

Montenegro see Crna Gora

Muang Thai
Thailand

Area: 513,115 sq km
Population: 64.8 million
GDP per capita: 7,400 US$
Capital: Bangkok
Government: Constitutional monarchy
Languages: Thai (official), English, Chinese dialects
Currency: 1 baht = 100 stangs

Geography: The west of the country consists of foothills of the Southeast Asian central mountain range, which reaches as far as the Malacca peninsula. The fertile lowland plain, running from north to south and watered by the Menam, is the most densely populated area of the country. The Korat plateau lies to the east, sloping gently into the Mekong. Rain and monsoon forests flourish in the tropical climate, with high temperatures all year round. In addition to tourist sites like Pattaya and Phuket, Thailand boasts numerous cultural sights such as Ayutthaya and Sukhotai. Rare animals can be seen in the Khao-Yai National Park.

Politics: The Kingdom of Siam was founded in the 13th century. Bangkok became its capital in 1782. In the 19th century, Siam ceded areas to France and Great Britain, without being colonized itself. In 1932, a coup d'état led to a constitutional monarchy. The emergence of a modern state since the Second World War has been delayed time and again by unrest. A new constitution has been in force since 1998, vesting power in a bicameral parliament. The monarch is the head of state and is much revered and respected. All but 5% of Thais are Buddhists.

Economy: 80% of the population live outside the cities. Some 60% of the workforce are employed in agriculture, cultivating rice, corn, manioc, sugar cane, and rubber. The country's main exports are rubber and tin. Illegal poppy growing is a not insignificant economic factor. In addition to foodstuffs, the industry produces paper, computer parts, building materials, and motor vehicles, and accounts for 40% of GDP. Tourism is the main branch of the services sector which contributes 50% of GDP.

Myanmar
Myanmar (Burma)

Area: 678,500 sq km
Population: 42.7 million
GDP per capita: 1,900 US$
Capital: Yangon
Government: Republic
Languages: Burmese (official), local languages
Currency: 1 kyat = 100 pyas

Geography: The land is surrounded by high mountains at the borders and opens up on the coast. The Arakan Mountains in the southwest (Hkakabo Razi, 5,881 m), covered with virgin forest, are foothills of the Himalayas. The Irawadi river valley flows through a densely populated lowland plain to the east, irrigating the world's largest rice-growing region. Myanmar belongs to the tropical monsoon zone. Popular tourist destinations include the Buddhist monuments in Yangon and Pagan and the beautiful landscapes on the Shan Plateau.

Politics: Settled by Burmese invaders from China in the 8th century, the country was conquered by the Mongols in the 13th century. Power struggles between the Arakan and Ava empires ended in 1752 with the union of the entire country under a Burmese dynasty. Burma was under British rule from 1866 to 1948. In the civil war that followed after independence, the military emerged victorious and has hampered all attempts at democratization since 1962 under a succession of leaders.

Economy: The leading economic sector of Myanmar is agriculture, the main products of which (rice, pulses, beans) are processed by the small-scale industrial sector for export. Forests yield hardwoods such as teak for export. Diamonds and natural gas reserves generate the highest export earnings. Illegal opium is grown in the area known

1 The Caroline Islands are the largest island group in Micronesia, with more than 963 islands, including some of volcanic origin and coral atolls. Archeological discoveries have indicated a long history of human settlement.

2 The buildings of the royal palace are in the center of Bangkok.

3 Predominantly Buddhist Myanmar is home to numerous important art treasures.

4 In agricultural Mongolia, the people primarily live from livestock breeding.

as the Golden Triangle. The country has well-developed rail and air networks.

Namibia
Namibia

Area: 825,418 sq km
Population: 1.9 million
GDP per capita: 7,100 US$
Capital: Windhoek
Government: Republic within Commonwealth
Languages: English (official), Afrikaans, German
Currency: 1 Namibian dollar = 100 cents

Geography: The sandy, rocky expanse of the Namib Desert extends parallel to the coast. A steep escarpment (Brandberg, 2,574 m) rises in the interior to rolling highlands that slope down in the east to the Kalahari basin at 1,000 meters. To the north is the Etoscha Pan, one of Africa's largest salt pans. The climate is subtropical. Around 7% of the country's area comprises animal reserves principally inhabited by antelopes, lions, and elephants. The country's major attractions include the seaside towns of Swakopmund and Walvis Bay as well the extensive desert wilderness in the interior.

Politics: European traders and missionaries first entered the country in the mid-19th century; Namibia became a German colony in 1884. It was occupied by South Africa during the First World War and was subsequently annexed as the Boer state's 5th province. The guerilla war that raged from the 1960s ended in a cease-fire in 1989; Namibia gained independence in 1990, and a democratic constitution followed. SWAPO, which led the resistance movement from the outset (1959), is today the most influential political force.

Economy: The economy is still suffering from the separation from South Africa, although it has retained close links with that country. Agriculture is the most important area, accounting for 73% of employment, and beef is the main agrarian export. Mining forms the backbone of the economy, with natural resources of diamonds, uranium, copper, zinc, and gold

contributing 20% to GDP and plentiful foreign exchange revenues. The profitable fishing industry is expanding further after the inclusion of the port of Walvis Bay in the country's territory (1994). Government reforms are now liberalizing the economy and privatizing many state industries.

Nauru (Naoero)
Nauru

Area: 21.3 sq km
Population: 12,800
GDP per capita: 5,000 US$
Capital: Yaren
Government: Parliamentary democracy
Languages: Nauruan, English
Currency: 1 Australian dollar = 100 cents

Geography: This small coral island is surrounded by a large reef. Nauru's coast consists of sandy beaches that border a broad strip of fertile land stretching between 150 and 300 meters inland. Most of the island is a plateau that rises 70 meters above sea level. Large sections of Nauru's interior are uninhabitable, covered with barren patches of land that are the result of phosphate mining. The island has neither rivers nor natural harbors.

Politics: In 1798, after centuries of isolation, European whale hunters arrived on the island. Nauru was incorpora-

ted into the German protectorate of the Marshall Islands in 1888. The island's first phosphate mining operation began in 1905. Nauru achieved independence in 1968 after decades of Japanese and later Australian administration. The country's parliament is directly elected every three years. The traditional Polynesian clan system is still in operation on the island.

Economy: The economy of Nauru is dominated almost entirely by phosphate mining. The local mining industry is controlled by the Nauru Phosphate Corporation, the country's largest company and employer and a major investor in fishing and tourism. With most of its phosphate deposits depleted, Nauru is now facing serious economic challenges that could threaten its survival as a viable independent nation.

Nederland
Netherlands

Area: 41,526 sq km
Population: 16.3 million
GDP per capita: 28,600 US$

Amsterdam's many canals are the most famous landmarks of the city.

Capital: Amsterdam
Government: Parliamentary monarchy
Language: Dutch
Currency: 1 euro = 100 cents

Geography: The Netherlands is situated on a vast plain that extends through large sections of western and central Europe. Reclaimed land that is below sea level comprises more than a quarter of the country's territory. The highest point in the country, the Vaalserberg hill, rises just 320 meters above sea level. Several major rivers flow through the country including the Rhine and the Meuse. Inland waters account for one sixth of its area. The Netherlands has a temperate-maritime climate with frequent precipitation throughout the year. The capital city, Amsterdam, is by far the most visited destination in the country.

Politics: The Netherlands gained its independence from the rulers of the German-dominated Holy Roman Empire in 1648. During much of the 16th and 17th centuries, the Dutch controlled Europe's most powerful trading and naval fleet. The country lost control of Belgium in 1831 but retained control of its largest overseas territories until the 1950s. The strictly neutral country was occupied by Germany during the Second World War. The Netherlands was one of the founding members of NATO and the EU. The Hague is the seat of government and the International Court of Justice.

Economy: The Netherlands has one of the most diverse and highly developed economies in the world. The people of the Netherlands enjoy one of the highest standards of living in Europe. Most of the country's population is concentrated in the heavily-populated Randstad, an urban conglomerate in the western section of the country. The country's service sector contributes more than 70% of national GDP. The Rhine Delta is one of the world's busiest centers of shipping and Rotterdam is the site of Europe's busiest harbor. Agriculture employs less than 4% of the workforce but is highly developed; the Netherlands is the world's third largest agricultural exporter, with major exports including flowers and hothouse vegetables. Fishing also remains an important industry. Machinery, electronics, and chemical products are important industrial exports.

Nepal
Nepal

Area: 140,800 sq km
Population: 27 million
GDP per capita: 1,400 US$
Capital: Kathmandu
Government: Constitutional monarchy
Languages: Nepali (official), Maithili, Bhojpuri
Currency: 1 Nepalese rupee = 100 paisa

Geography: Nepal consists of a narrow strip of land 853 kilometers long and 160 kilometers wide, on the southern slopes of the Central Himalayas. The flood plain of the Terai to the far south follows the Siwalik chain and the broad, medium-altitude Lower Himalayas. The national territory ends in the north at the crest of the Himalayas with some of the world's highest peaks (Mt. Everest, 8,846 m). The core economic and social region is the Kathmandu Valley, extending through the Fore-Himalayas for 30 kilometers in length and 25 kilometers breadth. Increasing numbers of Himalayan trekking tours are beginning to take their toll on the environment.

Politics: The principalities and tribal societies in the Valley of Kathmandu were united for the first time in 1756 under the rule of the Gurkhas. From the beginning of the 19th century, Great Britain exercised its influence on the Nepalese government. A constitutional monarchy followed a change of dynasty in 1951. The democratic constitution of 1959 was replaced in 1962 by a markedly monarchist constitution. Civil war has raged for years between the government and Maoist rebels. Political parties have been permitted since 1990, with representatives running for election to the National Assembly every five years.

Economy: The Nepalese economy is based on the poorly developed agricultural production (livestock breeding). Gold, copper, and iron ore deposits are mined and slate and limestone quarried for export. The modest industrial sector consists of textile companies, carpet weaving concerns, and brick-works, plus jute, tobacco,

Ovamboland: The largest population in Namibia is the Ovambo, a Bantu people from the fertile north of the country. They were leaders in the formation of the popular opposition movement SWAPO at the end of the

1950s. The organization fought a long and bitter guerilla war against the South African administration and military.

and grain processing. Tourism is emerging as the leading economic sector.

New Zealand
New Zealand

Area: 268,680 sq km
Population: 4 million
GDP per capita: 21,600 US$
Capital: Wellington
Government: Parliamentary democracy
Languages: English, Maori
Currency: 1 New Zealand dollar = 100 cents

Geography: New Zealand consists of two large islands (North and South Islands) separated by the Cook Strait, and several smaller islands. The terrain on both of the large islands is dominated by a series of mountain ranges. The North Island has several active volcanoes as well as numerous hot springs and geysers. The South Island features the 300-kilometer chain of the Southern Alps, New Zealand's largest mountain system. The country's largest mountain, Mount Cook, rises 3,764 meters. Most of New Zealand's virgin forests were cleared by settlers to create farmland. New Zealand is home to an array of unique flora and fauna, with a host of fascinating bird species including the Kiwi. The North Island has a mild subtropical climate, while the South Island features a cooler, more temperate climate.

Politics: The Polynesian ancestors of today's Maori first arrived in New Zealand during the 9th century. During the late 18th century, Captain James Cook explored the islands, and the first European settlers, mostly British, arrived on the islands shortly thereafter. The Treaty of Waitangi (1840) granted Great Britain control over most of New Zealand. A series of violent conflicts between the Maori and British forces was brought to an end in 1874. New Zealand achieved independence in 1931 but the British monarch remains the country's official head of state. New Zealand has one of the few unicameral parliaments in the world and elections are

held every three years. It was the first country in the world to introduce female suffrage.

Economy: New Zealanders of European descent comprise around 78% of the country's population. The country's advanced agricultural sector is one of the world's most productive. New Zealand is now the only developed nation which does not subsidize its domestic agricultural industry. Important crops include grains, fruits, and dairy products. The South Island has extensive sheep farming and wool production. The manufacturing and service sectors have both grown substantially

in recent decades. Important industrial exports include chemical, electronic, and wood products. The country's extensive hydroelectric resources are being increasingly exploited and could eventually have a major impact on New Zealand's economy.

Nicaragua
Nicaragua

Area: 129,494 sq km
Population: 5.3 million
GDP per capita: 2,200 US$
Capital: Managua
Government: Presidential republic
Languages: Spanish (official), Chibcha
Currency: 1 córdoba = 100 centavos

Geography: Central America's largest country is bounded to the west by the Pacific, to the

east by the Caribbean. Two-thirds of the population live on the plains of the Pacific coast. A 240-kilometer-long arc of volcanic mountains, 11 of which are active, lie to the east. Earthquakes are relatively frequent. The Caribbean coast is rich in lagoons and swamps, with savannas on the

 1 The Netherlands is traditionally the country of windmills. Their sails stand out amid the vast plains.

2 The Nepalis call the highest mountain in the world, first climbed in 1953, Sagarmatha or "King of Heaven."

3 The Namib desert extends along the Atlantic coast of Namibia.

4 The glaciers in the west of the Alps on New Zealand's South Island stretch almost to the coast of the Tasmanian Sea.

Priests of the mountains: Devotees of the popular Japanese faith of shugendo, a combination of Buddhist and Shinto elements, regularly go to the mountains to perform ascetic practices. They chant incantations, meditate and fast as a means of accumulating spiritual power.

Pacific coast. 40% of the country is covered by rain forests. Tourist destinations are the Pacific and Caribbean beaches, the capital Managua and the nearby Lake Nicaragua.

Politics: Nicaragua was discovered by Columbus in 1502 and conquered 20 years later by the Spanish. In the early 19th century the country joined the Central American Federation. Nicaragua was torn by civil war from the early 20th century; the overthrow of the dictator Somoza in 1979 after 40 years' rule triggered military conflict between the left-wing Sandinistas and the Contra rebel forces, which did not end until 1990. The first free democratic elections, won by the opposition party UNO, were held the same year.

Economy: Nicaragua suffers under a large foreign trade deficit. Agriculture supplies 28% of GDP and comprises basic food crops, but also coffee, sugarcane, cotton, and bananas for export. The industrial sector is poorly developed and chiefly processes foodstuffs. Tourism, although as yet in its infancy, is undergoing gradual expansion. 80% of the population live in poverty.

Niger
Niger

Area: 1,267,000 sq km
Population: 11.4 million
GDP per capita: 800 US$
Capital: Niamey
Government: Pres. republic
Languages: French (official), Haussa and further tribal languages
Currency: 1 CFA franc = 100 centimes

Geography: The country extends from the middle reaches of the Niger through the Sahel and deep into the Sahara. Oases are fed by rivers rising in the Aïr Mountains (1,944 m) to dry up in the desert. The north is dominated by sand and stony deserts, the south by dry savanna inhabited by elephants, lions and other wildlife. The chief settlement areas are the Niger and Komadougo basins. Popular tourist sights are the ancient city of Agadez, former hub of

caravan routes, prehistoric rock drawings in the Aïr Massif and the "W" nature reserve.

Politics: In the 16th century, the political structure that had stood in the Niger area since the 12th century came under Islamic influence before the country was conquered by the Fulbe in the 19th century. The French colony of Niger was founded in 1922. The constitution brought in after independence in 1960 was suspended until 1991. The National Assembly was dissolved in 1996 following a coup. A new constitution restored civilian rule to the country in 1999.

Economy: The country's economy is dominated by traditional nomadic animal husbandry and small-scale farming, principally in the Niger Valley and largely for subsistence. Fisheries and the fishing licence business are profitable. The mining industry supplies the country's main exports in the form of diamonds, copper, and uranium.

Nigeria
Nigeria

Area: 923,768 sq km
Population: 137.3 million
GDP per capita: 800 US$
Capital: Abuja
Government: Presidential federal republic
Languages: English (official), Arabic, tribal languages
Currency: 1 naira = 100 kobo

Geography: The country on the Gulf of Guinea has a humid tropical climate. The coast is fringed by a strip of mangroves 15–90 kilometers wide, which gives way to primeval forest farther inland. The plateau in the country's interior is marked by savannas, steppes and desert-like regions. Lake Chad lies to the northeast. The Niger flows through the country for 1,168 kilometers and ends in 24,000 km^2 of delta. Tourist destinations are the northern Haussa cities of Kano and Katsina.

Politics: The kingdoms of Nigeria, in existence since the early Middle Ages, were gradually conquered by the Fulbe. In 1885 the country was declared a British protectorate. Since its independence in 1960 Nigeria has been ravaged by military coups, unrest and religious conflict. The elections of 1992 were annulled by the country's leaders but the military dictatorship ended in 1999 with new elections.

A japanese landmark: The Torii in front of the Itsukushima-shrine.

Economy: Nigeria is inhabited by three major peoples: the Christian Yoruba and Igbo in the south, and the Muslim Haussa in the north. Agriculture consists of subsistence smallholdings and plantations that supply export goods such as cocoa and rubber. The main basis of the economy, at 90% of export revenue, is the petroleum and natural gas reserves that have been exploited since the 1970s.

Corruption and the poor infrastructure are major obstacles to the country's economic development. Tourism has been hampered by the unrest in the country, it is still a key source of foreign revenue.

Nippon/Nihon
Japan

Area: 377,801 sq km
Population: 127.3 million
GDP per capita: 28,000 US$
Capital: Tokyo
Government: Constitutional monarchy
Language: Japanese
Currency: 1 yen = 100 sen

Geography: Japan's territory comprises some 4,100 mainly mountainous islands, the peaks of an underwater mountain range. The highest mountain is the volcano Fuji (3,776 m); in addition to countless hot springs, there are also some 40 active volcanoes in this earthquake-prone country. Industrialization has almost completely destroyed the original natural landscapes. The extensive geographical area includes a variety of climates; the south is subtropical and hot, the north temperate and cool. Monsoon winds bring rain in summer, which falls as snow in winter. The numerous tourist destinations range from hot springs in the Beppu spa, to the ancient imperial cities of Nara and Kyoto and the metropolis Tokyo.

Politics: An early target for settlement, the country came under Chinese influence in the 6th–7th centuries, and was ruled by powerful warring clans from the 12th century. From the 16th to the 19th century, under the rule of the Tokugawa Shogunate, Japan moved into international isolation. After the restoration of imperial power (1868), the country underwent industrialization. At the end of World War II, two American atomic bombs were dropped on Japan (Hiroshima, Nagasaki). A new constitution was introduced in 1947, and the emperor is now only a figurehead.

Economy: Japan is one of the richest industrialized nations in the world. Agriculture (grains, rice, tea, fruit, and vegetables) is practiced primarily for

domestic consumption. The northern island of Hokkaido is the center of an extensive cattle breeding industry. Part of the fleet of this major fishing nation is stationed abroad. The highly developed industry of this country with little materials produces the most important export products: ships, cars, steel, computers, and artificial fibers and materials.

Norge
Norway

Area: 324,220 sq km
Population: 4.6 million
GDP per capita: 37,700 US$
Capital: Oslo
Government: Parliamentary monarchy
Language: Norwegian
Currency: 1 Norwegian krone = 100 Øre

Geography: Norway occupies the western section of the Scandinavian peninsula and has more than 2,650 kilometers of coastline. The northernmost sections are above the Arctic Circle. Most of Norway's landscapes were formed by glaciers during the last ice age. Large fjords cut deep into the country, and it is surrounded by numerous islands. Most of Norway's interior is dominated by mountains and hills. Northern Norway has a severe sub-arctic climate, and the far north consists of treeless tundras. Most of the country, however, has a mild maritime-temperate climate. The country's main tourist attractions include its impressive landscapes as well the cities of Bergen and Oslo.

Politics: Norway came under the control of the Danish monarchy in the late 14th century. The country was joined with Sweden in a political union between 1814 and 1915. Norway was neutral during the First World War but was occupied by Germany in the Second World War. The country was a founding member of NATO in the 1950s. Norway is a constitutional monarchy and a multiparty democracy.

Economy: Less than 3% of Norway's terrain consists of arable land. The agricultural sector is protected from for-

Fulbe: The largest ethnic group in Western Africa is composed of several peoples differing in economic, cultural, and religious aspects. The Bororo or Fulani people of Niger are traditionally nomadic cattle farmers, less Islamicized than the sedentary Fulbe people. They often form economic communities with farmers. The Bororo men are noted for their complex face painting.

eign competition by tariffs and subsidies. Oil from Norway's North Sea reserves is the country's most important export commodity, and the country is the third largest oil and natural gas exporter in the world. The service sector accounts for most of the country's GDP.

Oman see Saltanat 'Uman

Österreich
Austria

Area: 83,870 sq km
Population: 8.2 million
GDP per capita: 30,000 US$
Capital: Vienna
Government: Federal republic
Language: German
Currency: 1 euro = 100 cents

Geography: Austria is a small mountainous republic located in Central Europe. The Alps and Alpine foothills cover more than half of the country's terrain. A small section of the flat Carpathian Basin stretches through eastern Austria. The Danube and Inn rivers are the most important waterways. Austria's major tourist attractions include the capital city Vienna and the country's many excellent winter sports facilities.

Politics: Austria emerged as the center of the Habsburg Empire in the 13th century. The Habsburgs were able to rapidly expand their empire through numerous alliances and marriages. The vast multi-cultural empire was reorganized into the Austro-Hungarian Empire during the 19th century. The German-speaking provinces of the empire became the Republic of Austra in 1918. A second Austrian republic gained its sovereignty in 1955. Austria joined the European Union in 1995.

Economy: Austria has a highly developed and diverse economy. The country has attracted significant levels of foreign investment in recent years because of its proximity to the transition countries of Central Europe. The service sector contributes more than 65% of the national GDP. Tourism alone contributes 8% of Austria's GDP.

Pākistān
Pakistan

Area: 803,940 sq km
Population: 159.2 million
GDP per capita: 2,100 US$
Capital: Islamabad
Government: Islamic republic
Languages: Urdu (official), English, Punjabi, Sindhi, other minority languages
Currency: 1 Pakistani rupee = 100 paisa

Geography: Pakistan is bounded to the north by part of the Himalayas, the Hindu Kush and Karakorum, and to the West by the mountains bordering Iran and Afghanistan. The eastern part of the country is taken up by the Indus basin. The country has a high-altitude climate in the mountains, and a dry hot to arid climate in the Indus basin. Only 4% of the area is wooded. In addition to Lahore, possible tourist destinations include the ancient sites of Mohenjodaro and the northern mountains.

Politics: Pakistan was created in 1947 by the partition of former British India. After a civil war, the eastern part split off in 1971 as Bangladesh. Not even free elections since 1988 have succeeded in bringing peace to the country, which has been torn by politically motivated acts of violence since its independence. Atomic bomb tests and the Kashmir conflict affect relations with neighboring India.

Economy: Agriculture, which employs half the population, generates 25% of GDP. A fifth of the land is used for agriculture. The Indus basin has one of the largest irrigation systems in the world. In addition to wheat, cotton, and sugar cane, the main product is rice. The industrial sector, which is gaining in importance, processes agricultural products for export. The key exports are textiles, carpets, and clothing.

1 Architectural treasures from the baroque and classical eras are typical of the historic city of Salzburg.

2 Breathtaking Mount Fuji is Japan's highest mountain, at 3,776 meters. Every year the country's most sacred mountain attracts 4 million visitors.

3 Just recognizable under the decoration: a bus in Pakistan.

4 The seaport Ålesund, which is spread over a range of skerries off the west coast of Norway, is the fishing center of the country.

Highlands of the Andes: The majority of Peru's indigenous population are Quechuans. These breeders of llamas and alpacas inhabit the entire Andean highlands. Their religion and myths indicate the importance of their animals; for example, they believe that a decline in the size of their herds will indicate the end of the world, as the llamas return to their original homes under the earth.

Palau
Palau

Area: 458 sq km
Population: 20,000
GDP per capita: 9,000 US$
Capital: Koror
Government: Democratic state associated with the United States
Languages: Palauan, English, Japanese
Currency: 1 US dollar = 100 cents

Geography: Palau consists of 343 islands stretching over a distance of 200 kilometers. Most of the islands are volcanic in origin. Many of the country's coral islands feature extensive sand beaches and interesting diving sites, including numerous coral reefs.

Politics: The islands were settled as early as 1000 BC and were first visited by European explorers in the 18th century. Palau was administered by the German Empire at the beginning of the 20th century and came under Japanese control after 1914. The islands were under American administration between 1947 and 1982, when they became an independent republic with close ties to the United States.

Economy: Fishing and agriculture (fruit, manioc, coconuts) generate around half of Palau's GDP. Most of the country's national budget, however, is generated from annual payments from the United States government.

Panamá
Panama

Area: 78,200 sq km
Population: 3 million
GDP per capita: 6,300 US$
Capital: Panama City
Government: Presidential republic
Languages: Spanish (official), English
Currency: 1 balboa = 100 centésimos

Geography: The west of Panama is taken up by the foothills of the Central Cordilleras, with peaks of up to 3,475 meters, falling to the tropical lowlands of the Darien Jungle.

In the northern rain forests, rainfall is high owing to the climatic divide formed by the Cordilleras. Only 46 kilometers wide, the Panama isthmus is the narrowest point between the Atlantic and Pacific Oceans.

Politics: 1501 saw the first Spanish colonies on Panama coast. The country joined Greater Colombia in 1821. After the Panama Canal was completed, Panama became nominally independent in 1903 on intervention from the USA, and has been a sovereign state since 1982. The US military maintained a strong presence in the canal region (part of US territory until 1977) until 2000.

Economy: The commercial and services sector is the economy's largest at 70% of GDP, thanks to the Canal, opened in 1914, and the free trade area around Colón. Bananas, cane sugar, coffee, cocoa, shrimp, and tuna are the main exports. Industries process foodstuffs and petroleum.

Papua New Guinea
Papua New Guinea

Area: 462,840 sq km
Population: 5.4 million
GDP per capita: 2,200 US$
Capital: Port Moresby
Government: Democracy
Languages: Pidgin, English, Motu
Currency: 1 kina = 100 toea

Geography: Papua New Guinea comprises the eastern half of New Guinea, the Bismarck Archipelago, and numerous small Melanesian islands. The mainland is dominated by volcanic mountain ranges and large swampy plains. The majority of the population is concentrated in the central highlands. Vast tropical rainforests and savannas cover most of the islands.

Politics: The island of New Guinea has been continuously inhabited for at least 40,000 years. In 1884 the eastern section of the island was divided and occupied by Germany and Great Britain. In 1975, Papua New Guinea became an independent nation after decades of Australian administration.

Economy: A significant percentage of Papua New Guinea's population continues to live in isolated rural communities with little or no access to modern technology or education. At least 66% of the population works in the agricultural sector, which generates 33% of the country's GDP. Major export crops include coconuts, coffee, and tea. Around 80% of the country's income from exports is generated by mineral resources including gold, copper, and oil. Other major exports include timber and palm oil. Economic growth has slowed in recent years, but the government is now working to reform the economy.

The historic market square in Warsaw's scenic old town.

Paraguay
Paraguay

Area: 406,752 sq km
Population: 6.2 million
GDP per capita: 4,600 US$
Capital: Asunción
Government: Presidential republic
Languages: Spanish, Guaraní (all official)
Currency: 1 guaraní = 100 céntimos

Geography: The Río Paraguay divides Paraguay into an eastern region, with mountains and plateaus, and the western plains of Gran Chaco. The northwest has tropical rain forests giving way to savanna and grassland in the south. Tourist destinations are the areas of natural beauty and many sites dating from the colonial era.

Politics: Conquered by the Spanish in 1536, Paraguay housed a Jesuit state in the early 17th century until 1759. Paraguay became independent in 1811. 1989 saw the end of more than 30 years of dictatorship.

Economy: Agriculture is the principal economic sector, dominated by monocultures (livestock farming, coffee, rice, soybean, and cotton cultivation). The profitable export of tropical hardwoods has led to widespread clearing of rain forest areas. Industrial development has advanced little owing to lack of exploitation of the rich natural resources. River shipping is a popular transportation method in trading with neighboring countries.

Perú
Peru

Area: 1,285,216 sq km
Population: 27.5 million
GDP per capita: 5,200 US$
Capital: Lima
Government: Presidential republic
Languages: Spanish, Quechua (official), Aymará
Currency: 1 nuevo sol = 100 céntimos

Geography: The Andes Mountains (Nevado Huascarán, 6,768 m) in Peru's interior follow the coastline and slope down to the broad expanse of the Amazon basin in the northwest. Grasslands are found at higher altitudes. Tourist destinations are cultural monuments such as Machu Picchu and Chan-Chan, and colonial cities such as Lima and Trujillo. The coast comprises desert and steppes.

Politics: The Inca's kingdom was destroyed by Spanish conquerors in 1572. In 1821 Peru declared its independence from Spanish colonial rule, and since then the country has been ruled by a succession of military and civil governments. Moves towards neoliberalism have been met by social unrest.

Economy: The main agricultural crops are sugar-cane, maize, cotton, and coffee. Illegal coca cultivation is increasing dramatically. Fisheries account for 24% of export revenues; other key exports are copper, zinc, silver, and petroleum. The industrial sector processes textiles, foodstuffs, chemicals, and metals.

Pilipinas
Philippines

Area: 300,000 sq km
Population: 86.2 million
GDP per capita: 4,600 US$
Capital: Manila
Government: Presidential republic
Languages: Filipino (official), Spanish, English
Currency: 1 Philippine peso = 100 centavos

Geography: The Philippines extend along the northern part of the Malaysian Archipelago. The predominantly mountainous islands are often hit by earthquakes and volcanic eruptions. The humid climate favors tropical forests, which have largely been replaced by grass savanna as a result of land clearing. Primary tourist destinations are the scenic areas and the capital Manila.

Politics: The Philippines were under Spanish rule from the 16th to the 19th century. The colony was transferred to the United States in the late 19th century and granted independence in 1946. A 30-year dictatorship that ruined the country's economy was overturned in 1986.

Economy: 45% of the population live from agriculture, cultivating grains, vegetables, and coconut trees – the country is

Stone age: In the mountainous parts of the rainforests of Papua New Guinea there are still tribes living in complete isolation in neolithic-style settlements. These peoples largely practice ancestor worship and have systems of taboos. Many choose their leaders for their generosity and success in war.

the world's biggest producer of coconut products. The rich natural resources (copper, nickel, and petroleum) form the basis of a major industrial sector; high-tech electronic products generate the highest export revenues. The country's domestic air network is well developed.

Polska
Poland

Area: 312,685 sq km
Population: 38.6 million
GDP per capita: 11,000 US$
Capital: Warsaw
Government: Republic
Language: Polish
Currency: 1 zloty = 100 groszy

Geography: Poland consists mostly of vast plains and is bordered to the north by the Baltic Sea. A series of medium-height mountains stretches along the country's southern border. Several major rivers, including the Oder and the Vistula, flow through Poland. Poland's leading tourist attractions include the country's Baltic coast, the mountainous regions in the south, and historic cities such as Gdansk, Warsaw, and Krakow.

Politics: Poland emerged as a distinct nation around the 10th century. The country, together with Lithuania, ruled a vast empire that stretched from the Baltic to the Black Sea. Poland was divided between Prussia, Austria, and Russia in 1795 and did not exist as an independent state during most of the 19th century. The country regained its independence in 1918. Poland was occupied by Germany in the Second World War and 5 million Poles died during the war. The post-war period of communist rule was ended in 1989. Poland joined the EU in 2004.

Economy: Around 40% of the country's terrain is used for agricultural purposes. More than a quarter of the Polish labor force works in the agricultural sector, although agriculture contributes less than 5% of GDP. Major industries in the country include the chemical, steel, and shipbuilding industries. The rapidly growing service sector now contributes

more than half of the country's GDP. Reforms in the 1990s have opened the economy to increased foreign investment.

Portugal
Portugal

Area: 92,391 sq km
Population: 10.5 million
GDP per capita: 18,000 US$
Capital: Lisbon
Government: Republic
Language: Portuguese
Currency: 1 euro = 100 cents

Geography: Portugal occupies the westernmost section of the Iberian Peninsula. The

Sierra de Estrela mountain range stretches through the center of the country. The Tejo, Portugal's principal river, flows from Spain to its delta at the Atlantic Ocean near Lisbon. The country has a Mediterranean climate with hot, dry summers. In addition to the mainland, Portugal also consists of two island groups in the Atlantic Ocean: the Azores and Madeira Islands. Lisbon, the Algarve region, and the coastal areas are the country's most important tourist destinations.

Politics: Portugal was dominated by Arabs between the 8th and 13th centuries. The country gained its independence from the Spanish kingdom of Castille in the 12th century. Portugal was one of Europe's most powerful nations during the 15th and 16th centuries. Portugal was

declared a republic in 1910 but a military coup in 1926 left the country under military rule for decades. Portugal is now a multi-party democracy.

Economy: The areas between the Tejo and Duoro rivers are an important agricultural area

1 Machu Picchu, Peru's "Forgotten City" at an altitude of 2,900 meters. The countless artifacts give an insight into the ancient civilization.

2 Porto is one of the most beautiful cities of the Iberian peninsula.

3 Traditional island village off the coast of the island of Cebu at the heart of the Philippines.

4 The Iguaçu Falls cascade 70 meters down over two giant "steps."

The Caribbean: The Dominican Republic is one of the poorest countries in the Antilles. Its inhabitants have had to relearn subsistence agriculture since the prices of once-flourishing export crops such as sugar cane, tobacco, and coffee have dropped on the world market. Nevertheless, many economic refugees from Haiti immigrate to the country.

where wine, olives, and citrus fruits are produced. Maize, potatoes and livestock are the products of the rainy northern regions. The country's economy, which was once dominated by agriculture, has become increasingly diverse since the 1980s. Today, the service sector accounts for more than 65% of national GDP. Major exports include textiles, cork (for which Portugal supplies half the world's requirements), machinery and agricultural products. Tourism is taking on increasing significance.

Qaṭar
Qatar

Area: 11,437 sq km
Population: 840,00
GDP per capita: 21,500 US$
Capital: Doha
Government: Emirate (absolute monarchy)
Language: Arabic
Currency: 1 Qatar riyal = 100 dirham

Geography: The small peninsular country extends into the Persian Gulf from Arabia's east coast. Rolling hills about 100 meters high are found only in the east of this otherwise flat country, which has a hot, dry desert climate. Of the small islands off Qatar's coast, only Halul is inhabited.

Politics: The peninsula has been ruled by the al-Thani family since the 18th century. After interruptions by Ottoman (1872–1916) and British occupations (until 1971), members of the family have returned to reign over the stable country as a hereditary monarchy. Islam is the state religion, of which around 90% of Qatar's inhabitants are adherents.

Economy: More than 50% of the population are migrant workers from neighboring Arab states. Social security, health, and education systems are very good. Agriculture is insignificant; the majority of foodstuffs are imported. The economy as a whole is based on oil; Qatar's natural gas reserves are thought to be the largest in the world. The country is visited only by business travelers and has almost no tourism.

República Dominicana
Dominican Republic

Area: 48,730 sq km
Population: 8.8 million
GDP per capita: 6,000 US$
Capital: Santo Domingo
Government: Presidential republic
Language: Spanish
Currency: 1 Dominican peso = 100 centavos

Geography: The Dominican Republic covers two-thirds of the island of Hispaniola, and is bounded by Haiti to the west. The highest peaks of the four parallel mountains that cross the island are on Dominican territory. The dense forests have largely been replaced by sugar-cane plantations. Although frequently hit by earthquakes, the Dominican Republic is a popular tourist destination thanks to its beautiful beaches.

Politics: The island's history from the 17th century was dominated by colonial conflicts, revolutions and US military intervention, the latter continuing after independence (1844). The murder of the dictator Trujillo in 1961 led to a period of deceptive stability, but social tensions continually disrupt the peace.

Economy: 32% of the workforce is employed in the agricultural sector, with the main exports being sugar, honey, coffee, and cocoa. Despite rich natural resources (gold and silver ores, ferronickel) mining is poorly developed. The services sector (tourism) is the only growth industry and a major source of revenue; it accounts for 24% of jobs.

République Centrafricaine
Central African Republic

Area: 622,984 sq km
Population: 3.7 million
GDP per capita: 1,200 US$
Capital: Bangui
Government: Presid. republic
Languages: French, Sangho (both official), Bantu, and Sudan languages
Currency: 1 CFA franc = 100 centimes

Geography: The interior consists of low, rolling hills 500–1,100 meters in height, broken by isolated outcrops. Great rain forests flourish in the humid tropical climate of the south. The remaining country is covered by wet savannas, giving way to dry savanna in the northeast. Manovo-Gounda St. Floris National Park and the capital are the chief areas of interest for tourism, a sector that remains largely undeveloped. Floods are common throughout the country.

Politics: The French conquered the country and incorporated the region into what is now Chad; liberation movements gained the country's independence in 1960. The single-party system, in place since 1962, was

Dominican Republic: Idyllic sandy beaches.

replaced after a military coup in 1965 by a dictatorship under General Bokassa, who was overthrown in 1979. The country's first multi-party democratic elections were held in 1993.

Economy: Agriculture is primarily subsistence, with coffee and cotton cultivated for export. Small quantities of uranium, iron, copper, and nickel are mined, as are diamonds. The poorly developed industrial

sector produces foodstuffs, leather, and wood products. The service sector also remains largely undeveloped.

România
Romania

Area: 237,500 sq km
Population: 22.4 million
GDP per capita: 6,900 US$
Capital: Bucharest
Government: Republic
Language: Romanian (official), Hungarian, German
Currency: 1 leu = 100 bani

Geography: Romania is in southeastern Europe and borders the Black Sea in the east. The Transylvanian basin is surrounded by the Carpathian Mountains and other highland areas. Several large plains dominate the rest of the country including the hilly Moldavian plain in the north and fertile Wallachian plain in the south. The Danube flows along most of the country's southern border. Most of the country has a continental climate. The historic towns of Transylvania and the monasteries of Moldova are important tourist attractions.

Politics: The principalities of Moldavia, Wallachia, and Transylvania were conquered by the Ottoman Empire in the 14th century. In 1878, Wallachia and Moldavia united to form the Kingdom of Romania. The country was dominated by the Soviet Union after the Second World War and was declared a socialist republic in 1947. Romania was ruled by the dictator Nicolae Ceausescu for more than 24 years before he was overthrown in 1989. The country is now a candidate for membership in the EU.

Economy: Romania's economy is now gradually developing, after year of difficult transition to free market capitalism. The country's industry is largely antiquated and inefficient but the service sector now contributes more than half of Romania's GDP. Major exports include natural resources, machinery, and agricultural products.

Rossija
Russia

Area: 17,075,200 sq km
Population: 143.7 million
GDP per capita: 8,900 US$
Capital: Moscow
Government: Federated presidential republic
Language: Russian (official), other national languages
Currency: 1 rouble = 100 kopecks

Geography: Russia, the largest nation on Earth, stretches west from the Baltic Sea to the Pacific Ocean in the east and north from the Black Seato the Arctic Ocean in the north. The country's territory includes vast areas on two continents and a variety of climate and vegetation zones. The Caucasus Mountains stretch along the country's southeastern border while the Urals separate the European and Asian sections of Russia. Most of northern Russia consists of forested taiga areas and arctic tundras. Steppes and desert cover the southeast. Moscow and St. Petersburg, are the country's most popular tourist destinations.

Politics: The Kiev Rus, an alliance of Slavic groups, emer-

Siberia: The Yakuts who live in the north of Siberia subsist by breeding cattle, horses, and reindeer, hunting and fishing. Their language belongs to the Altaic-Turkic family of languages. The Yakuts have been members of the Russian Orthodox faith for nearly two centuries and adopted the Cyrillic script, yet still retain a number of shamanistic practices and believe in spirits.

ged in the 9th century and gained power and influence through its trade with the Byzantine Empire. Christianity arrived in Russia during the 10th century and encouraged the formation of a formal state. The duchy of Moscow gained increased political power in the 14th century. Russia developed into a vast empire in the following centuries. The imperial era, however, came to an end in 1918 during the Bolshevik Revolution. The Russian-dominated Soviet Union was one of the world's two superpowers before it collapsed in 1991. Russia is now a multi-party democracy consisting of 21 republics.

Economy: Russia has an incredible wealth of natural resources and a large manufacturing sector. Services are increasing in importance. The country faced a series of economic crises throughout the 1990s. The effects of a severe financial crisis in 1997 have mostly been overcome. High global oil prices and foreign investment have led to stable growth in recent years but the country's economy is still in need of major reforms. A particular problem is the underground economy.

Rwanda
Rwanda

Area: 26,338 sq km
Population: 7.9 million
GDP per capita: 1,300 US$
Capital: Kigali
Government: Presidential republic
Languages: Kinyarwanda, French (both official), Kiswaheli, English
Currency: 1 Rwanda franc = 100 centimes

Geography: The highest peaks in this mountainous country are the Virunga volcanoes (4,507 m) in the west. Much of central and eastern Rwanda consists of low, hilly tableland. Rain forests and wet savannas flourish in the humid tropical climate up to a height of 2,500 meters, giving way to bamboo forests at higher altitudes. Virunga National Park is the home of the mountain gorilla, a rare species that is now threatened with extinction due to widespread poaching.

Politics: In the 15th century the Tutsi people established feudal rule in the territory settled by the Hutu, which survived colonization by the Germans and Belgians. When the Tutsi (19% of the population) lost their position of power in the 1950s, sustained and bloody conflicts erupted that have continued to the present day and that reached a terrible climax in the 1994 massacres. Despite UNO's peace efforts, unrest continues.

Economy: A civil war that began in the spring of 1994 completely destroyed the economy in Africa's most densely populated country; rebuilding of the economy with foreign aid began in 1996. Coffee is the main export, followed by tea, pyrethrum, beans, maize, and bananas. The developing industrial sector mostly processes agricultural products in small and medium-sized enterprises.

Saint Kitts and Nevis
St. Kitts and Nevis

Area: 261.6 sq km
Population: 39,000
GDP per capita: 8,800 US$
Capital: Basseterre
Government: Federation/constitutional monarchy within the Commonwealth
Language: English
Currency: 1 East Caribbean dollar = 100 cents

Geography: The islands, five kilometers apart in the Eastern Caribbean, are volcanic in origin (Mount Liamuiga, 1,156 m; an extinct volcano with crater lake) and have many sulphurous springs. Rain forests grow at higher altitudes; the coastal plains are used for agriculture. The white, sandy beaches represent the main tourist attractions. The islands have a tropical climate, with high rainfall in the mountains.

1 The winter sports regions in the Caucasus Mountains are still largely unknown to vacationers.

2 The Kremlin, originally a fortress, is the seat of Russia's government.

3 The Winter Palace on the Neva River in St. Petersburg was built for Czar Peter the Great by the Italian architect Rastelli.

Windward Islands: The island states of Saint Lucia, Saint Kitts and Nevis lie in the crescent of the Lesser Antilles. Tourism is an increasingly important factor for all three countries, which present the perfect Caribbean idyll with their white sandy beaches and blue sea. While Saint Kitts has a well-developed tourist infrastructure, many of the Grenadine islands are largely undiscovered.

Politics: Discovered by Columbus in 1493, the islands were ruled for centuries by the Spanish, who enslaved the indigenous population. The islands became Britain's first West Indian colony in 1623. Long years of striving for independence were finally successful in 1983. A Governor-General still represents the British monarch. Nevis also has its own parliament and prime minister.

Economy: Illiteracy has been reduced to 10%, a key condition for advanced economic development. The islands' economy is principally based on agriculture (sugarcane) and tourism. Cruise passengers are the main source of foreign currency, so that the services sector employs 43.1% of the workforce. Exports are sugarcane and textiles.

Saint Lucia
Saint Lucia

Area: 616.3 sq km
Population: 164,000
GDP per capita: 4,500 US$
Capital: Castries
Government: Constitutional monarchy within the Commonwealth
Languages: English (official), Patois
Currency: 1 East Caribbean dollar = 100 cents

Geography: Located in the East Caribbean, St. Lucia is volcanic in origin. Agriculture is practiced in the coastal regions and in the broad mountain valleys in the north and south. Rain forests are confined to higher altitudes and are home to many species of birds. The climate, influenced by the northwest Trade winds, has average temperatures of 25–30° C. The main tourist destination is the cruise terminal of Pointe Seraphine in Castries.

Politics: The indigenous Caribbean inhabitants were wiped out by colonial rulers in the 17th century; the island was subsequently British and French in succession before finally becoming a British colony in 1814. A member of the West Indian Federation in 1958, St Lucia gained independence in 1979.

Economy: The economy chiefly consists of banana exports and tourism, with other exports being sugar and citrus fruits. While tourism has delivered around half of St. Lucia's foreign currency revenues since the early 1990s, banana cultivation and export is primarily practiced on smallholdings and is highly vulnerable to crises.

Saint Vincent and the Grenadines
St. Vincent and the Grenadines

Area: 389 sq km
Population: 117,000
GDP per capita: 2,900 US$
Capital: Kingstown
Government: Constitutional monarchy in the Commonwealth
Language: English

Saint Lucia: Picturesque view of Soufrière Bay.

Currency: 1 East Caribbean dollar = 100 cents

Geography: Part of the arc of the Lesser Antilles, the islands consist of the main island of St. Vincent, 345 km² in area, and the smaller Grenadine Islands, seven of which are inhabited. The active volcano Soufrière (1,234 m) lies in the north of St. Vincent. The mountains there are covered by tropical rain forests with a moist tropical climate: home to a rich variety of bird species, while the Grenadines are considerably drier. The land slopes down to the sea in the east.

Politics: St. Vincent was discovered by Christopher Columbus in 1498. Fought over by the French and English in the 17th century, in 1748 the island was initially awarded to the Carib Indians as neutral territory, before becoming a British colony in 1783. From 1958 to 1962 the islands joined the West Indian Federation, and became an Associated State of the British Commonwealth in 1969 it gained independence in 1979.

Economy: The islands' principal sources of revenue are agriculture and tourism, 28% of the area is given over to agriculture. The banana crop is frequently endangered by hurricanes. Other important exports are flour, cotton, and arrowroot. Tourism, primarily comprising cruise visitors and sailing enthusiasts, is increasing in importance as a source of foreign currency.

Salṭanat 'Umān
Oman

Area: 212,457 sq km
Population: 2.9 million
GDP per capita: 13,400 US$
Capital: Muscat
Government: Sultanate (absolute monarchy)
Languages: Arabic (official), Farsi, Urdu
Currency: 1 Omani rial = 1,000 baizas

Geography: Oman's natural borders are the Gulf of Oman in the east, the Arabian Sea in the south, and the Rub' al-Khali Desert in the west. 15 kilometers of fertile coast extend to the 3,000-meter-high Oman Mountains. The territory includes the Mussandam exclave, enabling Oman to control the Straits of Hormuz, the exit from the Persian Golf. Oman has an extreme desert climate, with temperatures of up to 50° C in summer, and a subtropical climate in the highlands. Monsoon rains fall in the south and west.

Politics: Settled around 2500 BC, the region fell under Islamic influence in the 7th century and became independent in 751. Ahmed bin Said founded the current reigning dynasty after the end of Portuguese rule, from the 16th century. Oman was a British protectorate from 1891 to 1951. Progress has been registered in all areas since Sultan Qabus became the ruling monarch in 1970.

Economy: Oman's economy is a liberal free market economy with some state influence. Only 5% of the national territory is inhabited. The oil sector has dominated the economy since oil was discovered in the 1950s, and registers a 38% share of GDP. As the oil reserves will be exhausted in 30 years at most, efforts are already under way to diversify the economy.

Samoa
Samoa

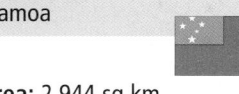

Area: 2,944 sq km
Population: 178,000
GDP per capita: 5,600 US$
Capital: Apia
Government: Constitutional monarchy
Languages: Somoan, English
Currency: 1 tala = 100 sene

Geography: Samoa consists of two large islands – Upoli and Savai'i – and seven small islands in the southern Pacific Ocean. All of Samoa's islands are of volcanic origin, and the country's tallest mountain, Silisili, rises to 1,857 meters. The island group has a tropical climate with high humidity and warm temperatures throughout the year. Tourist centers are the islands of Lifuka and Ha'apai.

Politics: Samoa was frequently visited by European traders and explorers throughout the 18th century. During the 19th century, the island was disputed between Germany, the United States, and Great Britain. Samoa became an independent nation in 1961, after decades under the administration of New Zealand. Samoa is now a constitutional monarchy, where local traditions play an important role in the nation's government, as befits what is probably Polynesia's oldest culture.

Economy: More than 70% of Samoa's people live on Upolu. Fishing and agriculture are the primary sources of income for most of the population. Coffee and bananas have traditionally been the leading export crops of Samoa but cocoa production is becoming increasingly important for the economy. Tourism is now a major source of income, but Samoa still maintains a large trade deficit.

San Marino
San Marino

Area: 61.2 sq km
Population: 28,500
GDP per capita: 34,600 US$
Capital: San Marino Città
Government: Republic
Language: Italian (official), Romagnol
Currency: 1 euro = 100 cents

Geography: The smallest republic in Europe is dominated by Mount Titano (756 m). The country comprises ten separate towns, including the small capital city San Marino Città. The principal rivers are the Marano and the Ausa. The country's small and historic capital city is a popular destination.

Politics: San Marino was first settled around AD 600. The country achieved its independence in 1400 and become a republic in 1600. San Marino's independence was affirmed at the Congress of Vienna in 1815. The neutral country was occupied by the German army and later the Allies during the

Samoa: The islands of the Samoan archipelago are home to probably the oldest Polynesian culture. Before the advent of colonialism, the social system comprised a complex network of family and social bonds. The head of *the family was also a member of the village council, which in turn appointed a representative to the regional council. Many of the ancient customs and traditional structures have been preserved in present-day Samoa.*

Second World War. San Marino's status as an Italian protectorate was ended in 1968. The country became a member of the Council of Europe in 1998 and of UNO in 1992.

Economy: Tourism and the sale of postage stamps are the two largest industries in San Marino, with tourist visits accounting for more than half of the country's GDP. Agriculture is entirely small scale and contributes little to the economy. San Marino has a relatively high standard of living and per capita GDP.

São Tomé e Príncipe
São Tomé and Príncipe

★★

Area: 1,001 sq km
Population: 182,000
GDP per capita: 1,200 US$
Capital: São Tomé
Government: Republic
Languages: Portuguese (official), Creole
Currency: 1 dobra = 100 centimos

Geography: The archipelago off the coast of Gabun near the Equator consists of the two main islands of São Tomé and Príncipe and some smaller islands, all volcanic in origin and part of the Cameroon line. The landscape is dominated by rain forests, favored by the climate and the numerous rivers. A leisure and sports fishing center was built in the north of Príncipe in 1992. Soil erosion due to farming is a major environmental issue in the country.

Politics: The islands were settled by the Portuguese from 1485, and from the 16th to the 18th centuries were the world's largest sugar suppliers and a center of the slave trade with Brazil. A Portuguese overseas province from 1951, the islands became independent in 1975. Recent years have seen major political reforms. In 1990 a multiple-party system was established and Príncipe received a statute of autonomy in 1995.

Economy: Cocoa, the principal crop from its introduction in the 19th century, is still almost the only significant economic factor, accounting for 78% of

export revenues. Agricultural land passed into state control in 1975 and was partly awarded to small farmers; foreign investors receive administration licences. Since 1987 the slump in world cocoa prices has generated structural reorganization initiatives supported by the World Bank. However, 80% of foodstuffs consumed in the country are imported. Portugal remains a key trading partner. Tourism and offshore oil reserves could both become important economic factors.

Saudi Arabia see Al-Mamlaka al-'Arabiya as-Sa'udiya

Serbia see Srbija

Sénégal
Senegal

★

Area: 196,722 sq km
Population: 10.8 million
GDP per capita: 1,600 US$
Capital: Dakar
Government: Presidential republic
Languages: French, Wolof
Currency: 1 CFA franc = 100 centimes

Geography: Senegal, bounded by the Senegal River and its tributary, the Falémé, is at the western extremity of the continent of Africa. Largely flat, it rises in the northeast to the Guinean Fouta Djalon. Senegal is in the Sahel zone; rainfall increases to the south, while Casamance has a humid tropical climate. Tourism is chiefly concentrated in Casamance, Dakar, and Petite Côte.

Politics: Home to European settlements, Senegal came un-

der French colonial rule from the 17th to the 19th centuries. In 1958 it was awarded autonomy within the French Communauté and became independent in 1960. Senegal became a single-party state in real terms in 1966; opposition parties were not permitted until 1975. The country joined with Gambia to form the confederation of Senegambia.

1 San Marino: The small capital city is 750 meters above sea level atop Mount Titato. The city has preserved most of its medieval character, including fascinating narrow lanes and historic buildings.

2 The island of Gorée off the coast of Senegal was one of the most important bases of the West African slavetraders.

3 Muscat: The seaport on the Gulf of Oman is the cultural and economic center of the sultanate.

4 The islands of Western Samoa are among the most unspoiled in the southern Pacific. The country also boasts a well-preserved and vibrant local culture.

Fruits of paradise: The main product in the Seychelles is coconuts, from which copra is extracted. In the valley of Mai, on the island of Praslin, gigantic palms known as "coco de mer" grow. Their fruits can reach weights of 25 kg and take up to ten years to ripen; they are governed by a special export licence.

Economy: Agriculture and fishery account for the majority of export revenues, with raw materials (gold, iron ore) increasing in significance. The service sector (tourism) is the country's primary economic focus, at 61% of GDP. Senegal realized full Internet connectivity in 1996, triggering a minor boom in information technology based services. Key economic tasks for the future are the reduction of subsidies and industrial privatization. Government reforms have led to strong growth rates in recent years and the country's government has successfully held inflation in check since the 1990s.

Seychelles
Seychelles

Area: 454 sq km
Population: 81,000
GDP per capita: 7,800 US$
Capital: Victoria
Government: Republic within the Commonwealth
Languages: English, French, Creole
Currency: 1 Seychelles rupee = 100 cents

Geography: The archipelago consists of more than 90 islands, fewer than half of which are inhabited. Only the larger islands are mountainous and covered with sparse vegetation. The climate is tropical marine. The territory covered by the archipelago includes more than a million km² in the Indian Ocean. The sandy beaches of Mahé, the nature reserve on Praslin, and the island of Silhouette are the primary tourist destinations.

Politics: Discovered by Vasco da Gama in 1501, the islands were colonized by the French from 1756 and by the British from 1794–1811, and became a British Crown colony in 1903. Independence in 1976 was followed by years of political unrest in which the constitution was overturned by a coup. Although other parties have been allowed since 1991, the Unity Party SPPF has held power since 1977.

Economy: The main exports continue to be fish, cinnamon, and copra. The greatest economic potential lies in tourism services. The economy has stagnated since 1991, leading to an extensive program of privatization intended to replace the previous government controls. The government is now attempting to diversify the economy by establishing the islands as a center for financial services and cargo handling.

Shqipëria
Albania

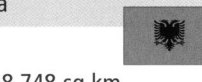

Area: 28,748 sq km
Population: 3.5 million
GDP per capita: 4,500 US$
Capital: Tirana
Government: Republic
Language: Albanian
Currency: 1 lek = 100 quindarka

Geography: Albania is in southeastern Europe along the Ionian and Adriatic Seas. The country is largely mountainous and features more than 40 peaks rising to more than 2,000 meters. Numerous rivers flow through the country, most of which are not navigable. The country's coast is bordered by expansive marshlands and swampy plains. Albania boasts several large man-made and natural

The Slovenian spa of Bled is in the Julian Alps.

lakes and reservoirs including Lake Ohrid.

Politics: The area of modern Albania was once a region of the Roman and later Byzantine Empire. Albania was dominated by the Ottoman Empire for several centuries after 1502.

The country declared its independence from the empire in 1913. Albania was occupied by German and Italian forces during the Second World War and was declared a communist republic in 1946. The country returned to democracy in 1991 after decades of dictatorship and repression.

Economy: Albania remains one of the poorest countries in Europe and has one of the continent's least developed infrastructures. Agriculture (grain, beans, cotton, and tobacco) is an important industry and contributes more than a third of GDP. The majority of the labor force works in agriculture.

Sierra Leone
Sierra Leone

Area: 71,740 sq km
Population: 5.9 million
GDP per capita: 500 US$
Capital: Freetown
Government: Republic within the Commonwealth
Languages: English (official), Creole
Currency: 1 leone = 100 cents

Geography: Sierra Leone is on Africa's west coast, and includes small islands off the flat, wooded coastal region with strips of alluvial deposits. The higher savannas in the country's interior are traversed by rivers that rise in the Talla and Falaba plateaus in the north and east. The tropical climate on the coast provides relatively constant temperatures.

Politics: England acquired land in the region from 1787–1788 and established settlements of freed slaves. The country was a British crown colony from 1808, and gained independence in 1961. A one-party state after 1973, Sierra Leone received a democratic constitution in 1991, shortly followed by a military coup and another in 1997. A system of parliamentary democracy was reintroduced in 1998.

Economy: Sierra Leone is one of the poorest countries in the world, with an economy originating from colonial times, based on raw materials and oriented to global markets. Mining products are titanium ore, diamonds, bauxite, and gold. Initial signs of economic stabilization were destroyed by the Liberian war. The industrial sector remains undeveloped, despite the country's mineral wealth. Destruction of the rain forests has caused severe environmental damage. Sierra Leone's service sector contributes one-fifth of national GDP and its development is blocked by political instability.

Singapore
Singapore

Area: 692.7 sq km
Population: 4.4 million
GDP per capita: 23,700 US$
Capital: Singapore
Government: Republic in the Commonwealth
Languages: Malay, English, Chinese, Tamil (all official)
Currency: 1 Singapore dollar = 100 cents

Geography: The main island of Singapore, with 54 smaller islands, only two dozen of which are inhabited, lies at the southern outlet of the Malacca Straits. The country is low-lying. A railroad and road causeway connects the main island with the Malaysian peninsula. The tropical flora and fauna have been seriously affected by settlement.

Politics: The first British trading settlement was founded in 1819, and in 1824 the East India Company took over Singapore. In 1955 the British crown colony was given a constitution with election rights for the entire population, as well as extensive self-government. After gaining autonomy in 1959 and independence in 1963, Singapore became a republic in 1965. Its president has been elected in general elections since 1991. The parliament is elected every five years.

Economy: Inhabited largely by Chinese, the city-state of Singapore is a leading industrial and service center, as well as an important air traffic hub in Asia. The agricultural sector today accounts for less than 1% of GDP, owing to rapid industrialization in the 1960s and 1970s. Export revenues are predominantly generated by electronic products in addition to tools, machinery, and shipbuilding. The services sector (banks) accounts for 62% of GDP.

Slovenija
Slovenia

Area: 20,273 sq km
Population: 2 million
GDP per capita: 18,300 US$
Capital: Ljubljana
Government: Republic
Language: Slovenian
Currency: 1 tolar = 100 stotin

Geography: The Julian Alps dominate much of northern Slovenia. More than half of the country is covered by forests, one of the highest ratios of woodland coverage in Europe. The flat Pannonian Plain covers sections of eastern Slovenia. Slovenia's narrow Adriatic coast has a Mediterranean climate, while the rest of the country has a cooler continental climate. The Slovenian Alps, Ljubljana, and the coast are all major tourist destinations.

Politics: The territory of modern Slovenia was under Austrian domination between the 13th century and 1918. Slovenia was joined in a united kingdom with Serbia, Croatia, and Macedonia after the First World War. The Yugoslav regions were reunited after the Second World War as a communist federation. Slovenia was the first Yugoslav republic to declare its independence, in 1991, with a constitution

Bounds: The Temne, an ethnic group consisting mostly of farmers, make up a third of Sierra Leone's population. Communities are governed by chiefs whose territories often include one large and several smaller villages.

Male and female social and community groups are formed according to traditions; here to organize religious ceremonies.

modeled on Western European democracy. The country is now a member of NATO and the EU.

Economy: Slovenia has a highly developed and diversified economy and a high standard of living. The country also boasts the highest GDP per capita of any former communist state in Europe. Agriculture and forestry contribute around 5% of national GDP, while the services sector accounts for 65%. Slovenia's major exports include machinery, electronic goods, and chemical products. Tourism is an important industry in several regions.

Slovenská Republika
Slovakia

Area: 48,845 sq km
Population: 5.4 million
GDP per capita: 13,300 US$
Capital: Bratislava
Government: Republic
Language: Slovakian (official), Hungarian, Ruthenian
Currency: 1 Slovakian krone = 100 heller

Geography: Slovakia is a largely mountainous country, its terrain dominated by the western Carpathian Mountains. Large basins separated by mountains also cover sections of the country. The Vah is the longest river, while the Danube flows along the country's southwestern border. Slovakia has a continental climate. The mountains and the towns of eastern Slovakia are the main tourist destinations.

Politics: Slovakia was settled by Slavs in the 6th century AD and came under the control of Hungary in 908. With Hungary, became a region of the Habsburg Empire in 1526. The country was merged with the Czech lands in 1918 to form Czechoslovakia. After the Second World War, Czechoslovakia became a communist state. Democracy was restored to Czechoslovakia in 1989 and Slovakia became an independent state in 1993.

Economy: Like many other former communist states in Europe, Slovakia experienced

a difficult transition to capitalism in the 1990s. Major reforms in recent years have opened the economy to foreign investment and led to stable growth. Most of the country's former state enterprises have been privatized and the service sector now contributes 60% of the country's GDP. High levels of unemployment are a major challenge for the country.

Solomon Islands
Solomon Islands

Area: 28,450 sq km
Population: 523,600
GDP per capita: 1,700 US$
Capital: Honiara
Government: Parliamentary democracy
Languages: Pidgin, English
Currency: 1 Solomon Islands dollar = 100 cents

Geography: The Solomon Islands comprise two long island chains stretching over 1,450 kilometers in the western Pacific. The largest islands – including Guadalcanal, San Cristobal, Santa Isabel, Malaita, New Georgia and Choiseul – are all of volcanic origin. The country also comprises numerous small coral islands and islets. Because of their tropical climate, heavy rainfall and high humidity are common throughout the year on the islands.

Politics: Originally settled more than 30,000 years ago, the Solomons are home to a blend of Polynesian and Melanesian cultures. The isolated island group was largely avoided by Europeans until the 19th century. Towards the end of that century, the islands were declared a British protectorate. Since independence in 1978, the Solomon Islands have experienced sporadic periods of political instability, including a coup in 2000. In response to civil unrest in 2003, international peacekeeping forces restored stability.

Economy: The economy of the Solomon Islands is dominated by agriculture, which generates 70% of the country's GDP. The most important crops include cocoa, coconuts, rice, and spices. Fishing accounts

for at least 25% of the country's gross domestic product and is a major source of foreign income. Forestry is a rapidly growing industry on the island, while the government strictly regulates the exploitation and export of mineral resources which include lead, zinc, nickel, and gold.

1 Mahé is the only island of the Seychelles with steep granite crags as well as palm-fringed beaches. The largest island is an ideal resort for divers.

2 The city-state of Singapore is characterized by contrasts. At the feet of the air-conditioned skyscrapers, rickshaws are a

common means of transportation in the narrow Chinese markets.

3 The High Tatra in the Slovakia was formed by glacial movement. Unique mountain flora and rare wildlife are protected in the Tatra National Park.

Soomaaliya Somalia

Soomaaliya
Somalia

Area: 637,657 sq km
Population: 8.3 million
GDP per capita: 500 US$
Capital: Mogadishu
Government: Republic
Languages: Somali (official), Arabic, English, Italian
Currency: 1 Somalia shilling = 100 centesimi

Geography: The largely steep, craggy coast of Somalia runs along the Gulf of Aden and Indian Ocean for more than 3,000 kilometers. The country's highest peak is Surud Add (2,408 m). The two largest rivers, Yuba and Shebeli, form great swamps along the flat southern coast. The climate is desert-like in the northwest, with monsoon conditions in other regions. Before the civil war, the beaches, natural landscapes and cultural heritage sites were important tourist destinations.

Politics: Following Portuguese and Turkish influences in the 16th century, the country came under the rule of the Sultan of Oman from the 17th to the 19th centuries. At the end of the 19th century the colonial territories of French and British Somaliland were founded on the Gulf of Aden, and Italian Somaliland on the Indian Ocean. The Republic of Somalia was founded in 1960. The military dictatorship in power from 1969 was overthrown in 1991. The civil war which has raged since then has resisted even UN intervention.

Economy: One of the world's poorest countries, Somalia has seen its animal husbandry and agriculture destroyed by drought and the long civil war. UN aid provided only temporary relief in the famines of 1992–1993. Political instability impedes substantial development.

South Africa/Suid-Afrika
South Africa

Area: 1,219,912 sq km
Population: 43.6 million
GDP per capita: 10,700 US$
Capital: Pretoria
Government: Republic

Languages: English, Afrikaans, Zulu, Bantu languages (all official)
Currency: 1 rand = 100 cents

Geography: South Africa is divided into three main regions: the plateau of the interior, the Rand ridge, and the coastal area. The extensive interior plateau of the Karoo (veld), 1,000–1,800 meters in height, is broken by isolated peaks and bordered by the Drakensberg mountains to the east. The coastal region, generally narrow and straight, joins this region farther east. The country has a warm, temperate subtropical climate. Krüger National Park and Cape Town are only two of South Africa's many tourist attractions.

Politics: The Dutch colony was founded in the 17th century. Conquered by the British in 1795, the region was divided into the crown colony of Natal and the Boer republics of Transvaal and Oranje, which were defeated in the Second

Sri Lanka: Flower sacrifice in front of the statue of the Aukana Buddha.

Boer War. The racist apartheid policy introduced in 1911 was fiercely opposed by the ANC. The policy of reconciliation launched in 1989 led in 1993 to a new constitution and the end of government-enforced racial discrimination.

Economy: Agriculture (citrus fruits, wine, fruit, wool, and cotton) accounts for only 4.6% of GDP and covers subsistence needs, but is increasing in importance for export. More than a third of exports come from mining; South Africa is the world's primary supplier of gold and platinum. The industrial sector (metal processing, automobiles, textiles) contributes 44% of GDP. The service sector now contributes most of country's GDP and provides employment for most of the labor force.

Spain see España

Srbija
Serbia

Area: 88,361 sq km
Population: 10.2 million
GDP per capita: 5,200 US$
Capital: Belgrade
Government: Federal republic
Language: Serbian (official)
Currency: Serbia: 1 novi dinar,

Geography: Landlocked Serbia is the largest of the former Yugoslav republics. The country encompasses both mountainous regions and flat lowlands on the Pannonian Plain. Kosovo is now under UN administration. The Danube is the country's most important waterway. Most of Serbia's regions have a continental climate, while the southernmost region has a warmer climate.

Politics: The first Serbian kingdom emerged in the 12th century and was later conquered by the Ottoman Empire. Serbia first regained its independence in the 19th century and formed a united kingdom with Croatia and Slovenia after the First World War. The communist Yugoslav federation existed from 1946 until its collapse in the 1990s. Slovenia and Croatia's separation from Yugoslavia unleashed a long period of violent conflict in the Balkans. The repression of Serbia's Albanian minority in Kosovo led to the Kosovo conflict, after which NATO forced Serbia to turn the region over to the control of the United Nations. A new constitution in 2003 abolished the name Yugoslavia and replaced it with the new title Serbia and Montenegro. Both republics enjoyed a high degree of autonomy but the union was finally dissolved after Montenegro declared its independence in June of 2006.

Economy: Agriculture (25% of GDP) and industry (45%) are the key economic sectors. The country has extensive natural resources. Serbia's economy stagnated throughout the 1990s due to international embargoes, corruption, and the country's political isolation. Increases in foreign investment and political stability are needed to help the country's economy recover.

Ṣrī Lankā
Sri Lanka

Area: 65,610 sq km
Population: 19.9 million
GDP per capita: 3,700 US$
Capital: Colombo
Government: Socialist presidential republic in the Commonwealth
Languages: Singhalese, Tamil
Currency: 1 Sri Lankan rupee = 100 cents

Geography: Sri Lanka is separated from the Indian subcontinent by the Palk Straits and the Gulf of Mannar. Its territory includes 22 smaller islands off its coasts. Extensive lowlands, broken by isolated peaks, join the coastal areas to the north and the east. The central mountain region rises over several terraces to the Pidurutalagala peak (2,524 m). The country has a monsoon-influenced tropical climate. The Buddhist sites of Kandy, Polonnaruva, and Dambulla are fascinating.

Politics: Settled by Tamils since the 2nd century, the island was discovered by the Portuguese in 1505. At the end of the 18th century, it became a British crown colony. The country gained its independence in 1948. Discrimination of Tamils by the Singhalese is destabilizing, resulting in terrorist acts and military conflict. Before the introduction of the republican constitution in 1972, Sri Lanka was named Ceylon.

Economy: Compared with the percentage of GDP generated by agriculture (tea and rubber plantations; 24%), industry (15%) is still insignificant, although steadily growing. The most important industrial exports are textiles. The services sector accounts for nearly half of GDP. However, the economic growth is threatened by its population explosion, crippling poverty and civil unrest.

Sudan see As-Sūdān

Suisse/Schweiz/Svizzera
Switzerland

Area: 41,290 sq km
Population: 7.3 million
GDP per capita: 32,800 US$
Capital: Bern
Government: Parliamentary federation
Languages: German, French, Italian, Rhaeto-Romance (all official)
Currency: 1 Swiss franc = 100 rappen/centimes

Geography: Switzerland is a mostly mountainous country and contains some of the highest peaks in Europe. The country consists of three distinct geographic regions: the Jura mountains, the central plateau, and the Alps. Several of Switzerlands's higher mountains rise to 4,000 meters or more, including the famous Matterhorn (4,478 m). The densely populated central plateau between the Jura mountains and the Alps is home to several large lakes including Lake Geneva and Lake Constance. Switzerland is a popular tourist destination with an excellent tourism infrastructure. Its climate is continental to alpine.

Somalia: *Since 1991 civil war has raged in the country between the warlords of the developed north and the tumultuous south. A humanitarian effort by the UN from 1993–95 alleviated some famine conditions, but could not restore order. Famine is a constant threat, and lining up for food is a way of life.*

Politics: In 1291, three German-speaking areas – Uri, Schwyz, Unterwalden – formed a confederation that would later evolve into Switzerland. The country later acquired French and Italian speaking regions in the 18th century. Switzerland became a federal republic in 1848 and maintained its neutrality through both world wars. The individual cantons maintain a large degree of sovereignty and referendums play an important role in Swiss democracy.

Economy: Switzerland is one of the world's wealthiest nations and its people enjoy a high standard of living. The small but productive agricultural sector accounts for less than 3% of the country's GDP. Despite its landlocked location, Switzerland is a major trading nation and an important center of the global banking and financial services industries. Major exports include timepieces, machinery, chemical products, and electronic goods. Tourism is an important industry in many Swiss regions.

Suomi/Finland
Finland

Area: 337,031 sq km
Population: 5.2 million
GDP per capita: 27,300 US$
Capital: Helsinki
Government: Republic
Language: Finnish, Swedish (both official)
Currency: 1 euro = 100 cents

Geography: Finland is in northern Europe and borders the Gulf of Bothnia in the east as well as the Gulf of Finland and Baltic Sea in the south. The country's terrain is dominated by forests and thousands of lakes and swamps. Its craggy coastline is lined with islets, with the Åland Islands to the southwest. The northernmost section of the country consist of treeless tundra with an arctic climate. While most of the country is flat, central and some eastern sections feature rolling hills. Finland's pristine landscapes attract numerous tourists to the country. Helsinki and the country's rural areas are its most popular tourist attractions.

Politics: Finland was under the control of the Swedish monarchy between the 12th and 18th centuries. Sweden relinquished control of the country to Russia after a series of wars. Finland achieved independence from Russia in 1918. Finland, a capitalist country, was closely aligned to its powerful neighbour, the USSR, after the Second World War. The country joined the EU in 1995.

Economy: Finland has a diverse and advanced free market economy. The country suffered a major economic crisis in the early 1990s but quickly rebounded and has experienced steady growth since then. Trade is vital for the Finish economy with exports accounting for around 15% of the national GDP. Major exports include paper, electronics, and machinery. Together with Russia, Finland is developing the petroleum and natural gas reserves to its northeast.

Suriname
Suriname

Area: 163,265 sq km
Population: 437,000
GDP per capita: 3,500 US$
Capital: Paramaribo
Government: Presidential republic
Languages: Dutch (official), Hindustani, Javanese, English
Currency: 1 Suriname guilder = 100 cents

Geography: Suriname, on the Caribbean, is named after the Suriname River that forms a great lake at Brokopondo before flowing into the Atlantic at Paramaribo. Behind the coastal plain, where around 80% of the population live, the interior rises to meet the Tumuc-Humac Mountains, covered with dense rain forest and largely unexplored. The climate is tropical and humid, moderated only by the northeastern trade winds.

Politics: After a turbulent colonial history from the 16th century, Suriname fell to the Dutch in 1814. In 1974 around 50,000 Surinamese utilized their Dutch citizenship to emigrate to Europe, after which, in 1975, Suriname became independent. Bitter ethnically motivated power struggles developed, as a result of which a third of the population continued to emigrate in the following years in search of a better life. The 1992 overthrow of Desi Bouterse, who had gained power in 1980 in a military coup, failed to restore

1 The majestic Matterhorn in the Valais Alps was first conquered in 1865.

2 South Africa's breathtaking Drakensberg Mountains reach heights of 3,376 meters. To the east, they slope dramatically down to the coastline.

3 The port, with its impressive neo-classical architecture, is the center of Finland's capital, Helsinki. The city's historic architecture was strongly influenced by the country's neighbours Sweden and Russia.

Chinese heritage: Traditional Korean education includes Confucianism, the Chinese philosophy that is widespread throughout Korea, and every other culture influenced by China. Confucian schools were introduced in the 4th century, serving as a reserve of resources for the civil service. Today, education is still held to be the key to a great career.

stability. Parliamentary elections are held every five years.

Economy: The agricultural sector produces key exports of rice, sugar, bananas, and coffee. Bauxite reserves, exploited almost exclusively by US companies, generate the majority of export revenues. The country also has some oil and gold reserves. Waterways are an important method of transportions. Tourism is almost non-existent. The consumer goods industry is directed solely at the home market. Since 85% of the country is wooded, forestry could be a potential factor, given appropriate development.

Sūriya
Syria

Area: 185,180 sq km
Population: 18 million
GDP per capita: 3,300 US$
Capital: Damascus
Government: Presidential republic
Languages: Arabic (official), Kurdish, Armenian
Currency: 1 Syrian pound = 100 piasters

Geography: 90% of Syria is uncultivated; while steppes dominate in the north and northwest, the Syrian Desert extends through the southeast. The remaining territory to the west is essentially mountainous (Mount Hermon, 2,814 m). Rising in Turkey, the Euphrates and its tributaries flow for 675 kilometers through the northeast. Syria lies at the transition zone between the Mediterranean climate, with its moist winters, and the continental dry climate. Chief travel destinations include important historical and cultural cities such as Damascus, Aleppo and Palmyra.

Politics: A Persian satrapy since the 6th century BC, the country became the centre of the Seleucid Empire in 323, and later came under Roman, Byzantine, Arab, and Ottoman rule. Declared part of the French mandate in 1922, Syria gained independence in 1946. The politically unstable years up to 1970 were marked by coups, a temporary union with Egypt and the Six Days' War in June 1967. The possibility of reconciliation with Israel did not emerge until the 1990s.

Economy: The socialist-planned economy provides for an amalgam of state, collective, and private ownership. Economic reforms and attempts at industrialization and diversification are progressing only slowly. Agriculture, which is still the mainstay of the economy at 28% of GDP, is dependent on highly fluctuating rainfall, and irrigation is employed to produce cotton and fruit for export in addition to grain. Oil extraction and processing account for the highest export revenues.

Sverige
Sweden

Area: 449,964 sq km
Population: 9 million
GDP per capita: 26,800 US$
Capital: Stockholm
Government: Constitutional monarchy

Seoul: More than 11 million people live in the metropolis.

Language: Swedish
Currency: 1 Swedish krone = 100 Ore

Geography: Sweden is in northern Europe between the Gulf of Bothnia and Norway. More than two-thirds of the country's land area is covered by forests. In addition to the mainland, Sweden also consists of numerous islands including Gotland and Oland. The country's interior has a continental climate with often severe winters, while the southern coasts have a milder maritime climate. The capital city of Stockholm as well as the country's many lakes and pristine forests are the most popular tourist destinations in Sweden.

Politics: Sweden was united with Norway and Denmark in the Kalmar Union between 1389 and 1520. The country emerged as a major European power during the 17th century. Sweden eventually lost its role as the leading power of northern Europe to Russia. The country remained neutral through both world wars, despite the occupation of its neighbors Finland and Denmark during the Second World War. Sweden joined the EU in 1995.

Economy: Sweden faced a major economic crisis in the 1990s but remains one of world's most prosperous nations. Citizens have access to a generous social network and an excellent public education system. Sweden has a modern infrastructure and a wealth of hydroelectric power sources and natural resources. The country's diverse service sector accounts for more than 70% of the Swedish national GDP.

Swaziland (kaNgwane)
Swaziland

Area: 17,363 sq km
Population: 1.2 million
GDP per capita: 4,900 US$

Capital: Mbabane
Government: Constitutional monarchy within the Commonwealth
Languages: English, Siswati (both official)
Currency: 1 lilangeni = 100 cents

Geography: Swaziland, enclosed by South Africa and Mozambique, is on the eastern side of the Drakensberg Mountains and has a warm, moderately subtropical climate. The country is divided into four zones of varying altitudes; the western highlands have large forestry plantations, while the main settlement area is the savanna of the adjacent Middle Veld, giving way to the Low Veld to the east on the border with Mozambique. The dry savanna of the Lebombo Plateaus is used for grazing. The mountains and game reserves (Mlilwane and Ehlane) are popular tourist destinations.

Politics: The area was settled by the Bantu people of Swazi from the mid-18th century before the first Boers entered the country in 1868, followed by the British in 1877. Swaziland was named a British protectorate in 1907 and gained independence in 1968. The constitution of 1978 gives the King extensive executive and legislative powers.

Economy: Swaziland's economy is dependent on global markets and its neighbor South Africa. It is traditionally dominated by the cultivation of agricultural and forestry products, which are processed by the industrial sector, contributing 38% to GDP. Services (tourism) account for 47% of GDP and are set to expand as a result of the changing economic structure. More than 75% of the population works in agriculture and animal husbandry.

Tadžikistan
Tajikistan

Area: 143,100 sq km
Population: 7 million
GDP per capita: 1,000 US$
Capital: Dushanbe
Government: Pres. republic
Language: Tajik
Currency: 1 Tajik rouble = 100 kopeks

Geography: An extremely mountainous land to the south of the CIS, 90% of which has an altitude of over 1,000 meters; almost the entire population lives in the narrow mountain valleys. In the southeast, the Pamir mountains cover an area of 64,000 km². The western mountain ranges boast the highest peaks of the CIS: Communism Peak (7,495 m), and Lenin Peak (7,134 m). The climate is continental, giving way to an arctic climate in the mountainous regions. Tourism is largely limited to trekking expeditions from the capital.

Politics: Settled as early as the 1st millennium BC, the region was ruled by the Persians, Greeks, Macedonians, and Arabs until the 9th century. After centuries of Mongol and Uzbek rule, the north of Tajikistan came under Russian control in 1870, and in 1918 became part of the Soviet Republic of Turkestan. In 1929, the Tajik Soviet Socialist Republic became part of the USSR, from which it broke away in 1991 to become an independent state and a member of CIS. It underwent changes of government and a civil war, before achieving relative stability.

Economy: Owing to poor infrastructure and the cotton monoculture of the USSR era, Tajikistan is today the poorest republic of the CIS. Agriculture still accounts for some 40% of GDP. The important industries are wool processing, foodstuffs and textiles. Raw materials include uranium and gold, and to a small extent petroleum, natural gas, lead, zinc, tungsten, and tin.

Taehan-Min'guk
Republic of Korea (South)

Area: 98,480 sq km
Population: 48.6 million
GDP per capita: 17,700 US$
Capital: Seoul
Government: Pres. republic
Language: Korean
Currency: 1 won = 100 chon

Geography: The landscape in the southern part of the Korean peninsula is predominantly mountainous. Unlike the east

Nordic nomads: *For the past 2,000 years, nomadic peoples from Lapland have inhabited the vast, sparsely populated marshy highlands of the tundra covering the north of Norway, Sweden, and Finland. They call them-selves Sami ("marsh people"), have their own language and subsist from breeding reindeer and fishing.*

coast, the south and west coasts are highly fragmented. A hilly, fertile basin in the south is traversed by the Naktong, with 50–100 kilometers of coastal plain to the west. Extensive coniferous forests dominate the landscape. The major rivers flow into the Yellow Sea and are only partly navigable. With the exception of the subtropical south, the climate is continental and cool to moderate. Cultural cities of interest other than Seoul include Taegu or Kyongju.

Politics: Tradition dates the founding of the Korean Empire to 2333 BC, although the date 57 BC is historically documen-ted. Under the influence of China and Japan, Korea has nonetheless developed its own independent culture. In 1910 Korea was annexed by Japan. In 1945, occupation by the USSR and the USA led to the division of the country, then in 1948 to the establishment of the Republic of Korea in the US-controlled south. After the Korean War (1950–53), the military held sway in South Korea. Democratization, launched in the mid 1980s, led to a new constitution in 1988.

Economy: Rice cultivation in smallholdings cannot meet domestic needs. Industrializa-tion has taken off in the last 30 years; initially in cheap, labor-in-tensive products, now export production is shifting from ma-nufactured products in the food, textile, and clothing industry to individualized technologies and brand articles for the automo-tive and electronics industry. In addition, the share of the finan-cial, service, and real-estate sec-tor in GDP is rising (48%).

Taiwan
Taiwan

Area: 35,980 sq km
Population: 22.7 million
GDP per capita: 23,400 US$
Capital: Taipei
Government: Republic
Language: Chinese
Currency: 1 New Taiwanese dollar = 100 cents

Geography: Taiwan lies off the southeast coast of China. The center has thickly wooded mountain ranges with more than 60 peaks above 3,000

meters in height (Jade Moun-tain or Yushan, 3,997 m). The climate is subtropical with high rainfall in the north, but tropical with winter monsoons in the south. In addition to the capital, chief tourist destina-tions are the magnificent inland and coastal landscapes.

Politics: Settled by the Chi-nese in the 9th century and the focus of colonization attempts by Portugal, Spain, and Holland, Taiwan became part of the Chinese Empire in 1661. China ceded the island to Japan in 1895, but it be-came Chinese territory again in 1945. Defeated in the civil war, the Kumointang moved its seat of government to Tai-

wan in 1949. Relations be-tween the People's Republic and Taiwan remain tense. Despite the constitution of 1946, the president retains significant political power.

Economy: Privatization is gradually replacing state econ-omic control. On this densely populated island with few natural resources, agriculture mainly produces rice to cover domestic needs. The core of this highly capitalist economy is its enormously productive in-dustry, primarily for export. While industry accounts for 37% of GDP, services generate 60%, and 50% of employment.

Tanzania
Tanzania

Area: 945,087 sq km
Population: 36.6 million

GDP per capita: 600 US$
Capital: Dodoma
Government: Federal Presidential republic
Language: Kiswaheli
Currency: 1 Tanzanian shil-ling = 100 cents

Geography: Situated on the Indian Ocean, the country rises

1 The historic province of Bohuslän on the Kattegat is one of Sweden's most popular holi-day regions.

2 The Chiang-Kai Shek Monu-ment, built 1980, commemora-tes Taiwan's first president.

3 Probably the oldest Christian monastery in the world, near the Syrian village of Ma'aloula.

4 Isolated umbrella thorn trees are typical of the Tanzanian Serengeti.

Caravans: The Tuareg call themselves Imushagh or "free men." They are noted for their head and face coverings. The Sahara and Sahel area is inhabited by a number of nomadic peoples. The resilient dromedaries are essential beasts of burden and means of transportations in the harsh climate. Although Islamicized at an early stage, the Tuareg have retained their belief in nature-spirits.

from the coast toward the west and is divided by highland plateaus and mountains. Its highest peak is Kilimanjaro (5,895 m). It is bordered by the three great lakes of Lake Victoria, Lake Nyasa and Lake Tanganyika. The territory also includes the islands of Zanzibar, Pemba, and Mafia. The climate is tropical, and temperate in the uplands. Tanzania is a popular safari destination.

Politics: In 1884 Tanganyika became the main constituent of the colony of German East Africa. The country was taken over by Britain in 1920 under a League of Nations mandate and became a UN trustee territory in 1946, and acheived independence in 1962. The presidential republic of Tanzania was formed in 1964 by merging Tanganyika and the British protectorate of Zanzibar, independent since 1963. The one-party system of the 1977 constitution was replaced by a multiple party system in 1992.

Economy: Agriculture, forestry and fishery account for around 53% of GDP and 60–70% of export revenue. Tanzania's food production is self-sufficient. Industry, at 4.3% of GDP, is insignificant, while services account for 23%. The government has endeavoured since 1986 to accelerate development in line with IMF requirements by restructuring the economy as a market economy. Major export commodities include gold and coffee. Government reforms have led to higher growth rates in recent years.

Tchad
Chad

Area: 1,284,000 sq km
Population: 9.5 million
GDP per capita: 1,200 US$
Capital: N'Djamena
Government: Presidential republic
Languages: French, Arabic (both official)
Currency: 1 CFA franc = 100 centimes

Geography: The Republic of Chad lies in the Sahara, Sahel, and Sudan regions along the east of the Chad Basin. The basin is broken by a few isolated peaks. Lake Chad to the west is an important source of water. Tourist centers include the national parks of Zakouma and Manda, the game reserves of Abou-Teflan, Siniaka-Minia, and Bahr-Salamat and the northern desert regions.

Politics: Chad was settled by Arabs, Berber, and Bantu from the 15th century and became a French protectorate in 1900. After gaining independence in 1960 the country was torn by military struggles. After international pressure the introduction of a multiple party system became possible.

Economy: The country today is one of the poorest and least-developed in the world. Agriculture is still at subsistence level, and is dominated by arable farming and animal husbandry. The economy is dependent on foreign aid, although the establishment of oil drilling and export offers a perspective for the future. The service industry is the main source of growth.

Istanbul: The Hagia Sophia was built in 532.

Thailand see Muang Thai

Timor-Leste
East Timor

Area: 15,007 sq km
Population: 1 million
GDP per capita: Estimated at 500 US$
Capital: Dili
Government: Republic
Languages: Indonesian, Portuguese
Currency: 1 US dollar = 100 cents

Geography: The island republic occupies the eastern part of the Lesser Sunda Island of Timor. The central mountains attain an altitude of 2,960 meters in Ramelan.

Politics: East Timor was a Portuguese colony from 1695; the west of the island was occupied by the Dutch. After World War II, this part was given to Indonesia. When the Portuguese withdrew in 1975, civil war broke out, with the Fretilin Party fighting for independence. Indonesia annexed East Timor in 1975/76, resulting in a bloody conflict with many lives lost. In 1999 the majority of the population voted for independence, and East Timor became a sovereign state in 2002.

Economy: There are great hopes for the petroleum and natural gas reserves in the Timor Sea. Hitherto the economy has relied on the cultivation of coffee, rice, manioc, and coconut palms.

Togo
Togo

Area: 56,785 sq km
Population: 5.5 million
GDP per capita: 1,500 US$
Capital: Lomé
Government: Presidential republic
Languages: French (official), Kabyé, Ewe
Currency: 1 CFA franc = 100 centimes

Geography: Togo lies in West Africa. Its narrow, 53-kilometer-long coastal region gives way to a 50-kilometer-wide strip of hills and a sandstone plateau traversed by the Togo-Atakora Mountains. The wet savanna in the south merges into dry savanna in the north. Forests are found only in the mountains and along the rivers. The major tourist destinations are the sandy beaches and former colonial cities such as Lomé.

Politics: Discovered by the Portuguese in 1481 and first settled by Europeans from the 16th century, Togo became a German protectorate in 1884. In 1922 the region was divided between the French and British under a League of Nations mandate, and became a UN territory of the French Union in 1946. Since its independence (1960) oppositional forces have battled for democracy. The 1992 constitution was planned as a transition from the dictatorship to a democratic republic.

Economy: The 40 or so tribes and peoples that make up Togo's population live in one of the poorest countries in the world. The less developed north is chiefly given over to subsistence farming. Agriculture accounts for 70% of employment, yet generates only 36% of GDP. Togo is highly dependent on the export of a few raw materials. Trade and services account for 42.7% of GDP.

Tonga
Tonga

Area: 748 sq km
Population: 110,200
GDP per capita: 2,200 US$
Capital: Nuku'alofa
Government: Constitutional monarchy
Languages: English, Tonga dialect
Currency: 1 pa'anga = 100 seniti

Geography: Tonga consist of two long island chains encompassing 172 islands in the southern Pacific. While the western islands are mostly of volcanic origin, the eastern chain mostly consits of flat coral islands. Tonga's capital city, Nuku'alofa, is located on Tongatapu, the country's largest and most populous island. Tonga has a tropical climate and the country's beaches and coral reefs attract many tourists.

Politics: Polynesian Tongans constitute 98% of the ethnically homogenous population. The Tongans once ruled vast sections of the southern Pacific. In 1793, the British Captain James Cook visited and explored the islands. During the 19th century European missionaries exerted major control on the islands and converted the majority of the population to Christianity. The islands became a British protectorate in 1900 and an independent kingdom in 1970.

Economy: Agriculture dominates the local economy. Key export crops are bananas and coconuts. Much of the country's food must be imported. Foreign aid and wages from Tongans working abroad are the country's two most important sources of income. Tourism remains minor and undeveloped.

Trinidad and Tobago
Trinidad and Tobago

Area: 5,128 sq km
Population: 1.1 million
GDP per capita: 9,600 US$
Capital: Port of Spain
Government: Presidential republic within the Commonwealth
Language: English
Currency: 1 Trinidad-and-Tobago dollar = 100 cents

Geography: The islands of Trinidad and Tobago, off the coast of Venezuela, form the southern end of the East Caribbean island arc. Trinidad's mountainous north has rain forests, while the flat east coast at the Gulf of Paria is mainly occupied by industrial plants and harbors. Tobago too has hilly rain forest country. The climate is tropical, with minor seasonal temperature fluctuations. Tourism focuses on Tobago as a diving paradise.

Politics: Discovered by Columbus in 1498, the islands were initially ruled by the Spanish before becoming a notorious center of piracy in the 17th century and a British crown colony in 1803. From 1958-

Joie de vivre: Trinidad's annual carnival is the island's major cultural event, with fascinating parades rivaling Rio de Janeiro in their riotously colorful, elaborate costumes. The origins lie in the Christian religion of the Spanish Colonialists but the exuberance is rooted in the African tradition: The descendants of African slaves represent the majority of the population.

1962 Trinidad and Tobago were members of the West Indian Federation, gaining independence in 1962 as a British Commonwealth state. The country received a republican constitution in 1976. Tobago has held autonomy since 1987. The islands have a bicameral parliament elected for a five-year term.

Economy: The population is heterogeneous, with 41% black and 41% Indian. Although export-oriented, agriculture (cocoa, sugar, citrus fruits) and fisheries contribute a mere 2.7% to GDP. Trinidad's economy remains dependent on petroleum and natural gas exports from the relatively small deposits in the country's ocean shelf, generating at least 23% of GDP. The country also has the world's largest natural asphalt deposits at Pitch Lake, a 38.5-hectare tar lake. Other exports include chemical products and rum. Tourism is also an important economic factor. The economy has grown at around 5% p. a. in recent years.

Tūnisiyah/Tunisie
Tunisia

Area: 163,610 sq km
Population: 9.9 million
GDP per capita: 6,900 US$
Capital: Tunis
Government: Pres. republic
Language: Arabic (official)
Currency: 1 Tunesian Dinar = 1000 Millimes

Geography: The Tell-Atlas Mountains, up to 1,200 m in height, join the north coast and give way to the Medjerda plain in the south, an agricultural area. Farther south is a central ridge of mountains up to 1,500 meters in height, which also marks the boundary of the humid Mediterranean climate. Beyond this border the south is characterized by dry steppes and deserts. Tourist centers are Tunis, Sousse, Kairouan, and Djerba.

Politics: A country with a great Carthaginian and Roman past, Tunisia experienced Arab and Turkish rule from the 7th century before becoming a French protectorate in 1881. Independent since 1956, Tunisia finally began to abandon the single-party system in 1981. The constitutional reform of 1987 was aimed at increasing democracy. Tunisia's largest political party, the Constitutional Democratic Assembly, has dominated politics since independence.

Economy: Agriculture accounts for around 15% of GDP and is export-oriented, cultivating grain, fruit, wine, and olives. Products from the textiles, food, and electrical engineering industries deliver around half of export revenues and have increased in importance over petroleum and natural gas exports. Phosphate mining has resulted in a network of narrow-gauge railroads for its transportation. The service sector, including the tourism industry, has a share of 50% of GDP.

Türkiye
Turkey

Area: 780,580 sq km
Population: 68.9 million
GDP per capita: 6,700 US$
Capital: Ankara
Government: Republic
Language: Turkish
Currency: 1 Turkish lira = 100 kurus

Geography: Turkey occupies the Anatolian peninsula, a small section of Europe, and numerous islands in the Mediterranean Sea. A large central plateau covers most of mainland Turkey and is surrounded by the Taurus and Pontus mountains. The country has a Mediterranean climate with mild winters, although some areas on the Black Sea coast have a distinctly humid subtropical climate. Turkey is a popular tourist destination and its major attractions include countless ancient historic sites and popular beach resorts.

Politics: The first Turkish state emerged around 552. The Ottoman Empire became one of the world's most powerful states in the centuries that followed. After centuries of conquest, however, the Ottoman Empire faced a series of military defeats and territorial losses in the 19th century. Mustafa Atatürk, a young soldier, founded the Turkish republic in 1923 after the country's defeat in the First World War. The republic has experienced several military coups in its history; the last took place in 1980.

Economy: Turkey is in the midst of a rapid transition from an agrarian economy to one centered on industry and services. Around 40% of the Turkish

1 Tourism on Tobago benefits from its unique diving and swimming locations.

2 Camels and dromedaries are still essential productive livestock in the vast desert regions of Chad.

3 The people of the Fulbe populate the whole western part of the Sudan. In the multiethnic state of Chad they are only a minority.

4 Antalya, center of tourism on the Turkish Mediterranean, has one of the most beautiful old towns in the country.

Clansmen: The Scots never ceased to stand up for their autonomy against their English neigbors. Clan membership is still very important to social life, including regular Clan Gatherings.

Apart from the surname, a person's clan can be identified by the patterns and colors of their tartan, worn, for instance, as the traditional kilt.

labor force currently works in the agricultural sector, which accounts for a fifth of the country's GDP. The rapidly growing service sector now accounts for just over half of GDP. The country's leading exports include both agricultural products and mineral resources. Other export areas are textiles and clothing, contributing one-third of GDP and primarily privately owned. Tourism is a rapidly growing industry in many parts of the country.

Turkmenistan
Turkmenistan

Area: 488,100 sq km
Population: 4.9 million
GDP per capita: 5,700 US$
Capital: Ashgabat
Government: Presidential republic
Language: Turkmen
Currency: 1 manat = 100 tenge

Geography: Turkmenistan is located between the Caspian Sea in the west and the Amu-Darja River on the Uzbek border in the east. 80% of the country is lowlands covered by the Karakum sand desert. The coastal area on the Caspian Sea is flat and sandy. The country has a continental desert climate with extreme temperature fluctuations.

Politics: Settled by Turkic peoples since the 5th century and Islamic since the 7th century, Turkmenistan became part of Czarist Russia during that country's expansion in 1877–1881. In 1918 it became a part of the Autonomous Soviet Republic of Turkestan and in 1991, after the dissolution of the USSR, an independent member of the CIS. However, the old Communist regime is still in power, even after the new constitution of 1992.

Economy: Turkmenistan's health and social services are well-developed. The economy shows little diversification; agriculture is concentrated around cotton production in irrigated areas. Formerly supplying raw materials to the USSR, industry is still underdeveloped. Key economic factors are the natural gas, petroleum, sulphur, and mineral reserves. The petrochemicals and textile sectors are also major industries in the country.

Tuvalu
Tuvalu

Area: 26 sq km
Population: 11,500
GDP per capita: 1,100 US$
Capital: Vaiaku (Funafuti)
Government: Constitutional monarchy
Languages: Tuvaluan, English
Currency: 1 Australian dollar = 100 cents

Geography: The island group in the southwestern Pacific consists of nine beautiful atolls and numerous coral islets. Most of the islands are surrounded by coral reefs and are just a few meters above sea level. Tuvalu has a hot and humid tropical climate.

London: Britain's Houses of Parliament with "Big Ben."

Politics: The population of Tuvalu was devastated by slave traders and diseases following the arrival of European traders and explorers in the 16th century. Great Britain declared the islands a protectorate in 1892 and officially annexed Tuvalu in 1916. Tuvalu was formally granted its independence from Great Britain in 1978.

Economy: The population of Tuvalu consists primarily of Polynesians and a Melanesian minority. Most of the country's people work as small-scale farmers. Fishing and the sale of postage stamps are major sources of income for Tuvalu but the country remains highly dependent on foreign aid. Export of mineral resources could help develop the country's economy, but the country's isolated location prevents the development of large-scale tourism and industry. A significant number of Tuvalan citizens now work in other countries and contribute to the economy through remittances. The licensing of the internet domain tv. has become another important source of income.

Uganda
Uganda

Area: 236,040 sq km
Population: 26.4 million
GDP per capita: 1,400 US$
Capital: Kampala

Government: Presidential republic within the Commonwealth
Languages: Kiswaheli, English (both official), Luganda
Currency: 1 Uganda shilling = 100 cents

Geography: Most of the country is made up of a high plateau from 1,000–3,000 meters, broken by isolated peaks. The highest elevations in this savanna landscape are Mount Elgon (4,321 m) to the east and the Ruwenzori Massif in the west, up to 5,119 meters high. Half of Lake Victoria lies within the southeast of Uganda's territory. The climate is temperate owing to the altitude. The rich wildlife of Ruwenzori National Park is a magnet for tourists.

Politics: A number of centralized African kingdoms had already existed for centuries in Uganda when the British conquered the country and declared it a protectorate in 1894. After independence (1962) the situation in the 1970s and 1980s under the terror regimes of Amin and Obote was characterized by civil war before the political situation stabilized in the 1990s.

Economy: Agricultural production dominates the economy, although half of agriculture's 50% share of GDP is accounted for by subsistence farming. Only 5% of agricultural products are exported, chiefly coffee (90% of export revenues), but also cotton, tea and tobacco. The industrial sector contributes only 11–12% to GDP. Since 1987 the government has applied a policy of economic liberalization in coordination with the IMF, and an economic community with Kenya and Tanzania has been in existence since 2001.

Ukrajina
Ukraine

Area: 603,700 sq km
Population: 47.7 million
GDP per capita: 5,300 US$
Capital: Kiev
Government: Republic
Language: Ukrainian (official), Russian
Currency: 1 hryvnia = 100 kopijken

Geography: Ukraine is in Eastern Europe and has a long coastline along the Black Sea. Most of the country consists of plains and scattered plateaus. The country is crossed by many significant rivers including the Dniepr, Donets, and Dnister. Odessa in southern Ukraine has one of the largest harbors on the Black Sea. The Crimean Peninsula is a popular destination for tourists from Ukraine and neighboring countries.

Politics: Much of Ukraine was once controlled by the Kievan Rus. Later the country came under the control of the Mongols, the Polish-Lithuanian Commonwealth, and eventually the Russian Empire. Ukraine was declared a Soviet Republic in 1922 and remained one of the most influential republics in the USSR up until the union's collapse in the 1990s. Ukraine declared independence in 1991.

Economy: Ukraine's economy has mostly stagnated since the country achieved independence in 1991. The economy remains largely closed to foreign investment and previous governments have been ineffective at implementing desperately needed reforms. Ukraine is rich in mineral resources and arable land; agriculture accounts for a large percentage of its national GDP. Russia is the country's leading trading partner and supplies most of its energy imports. Natural resources and agricultural products are the country's leading exports.

United Arab Emirates see Daulat al-Imārāt al-'Arabiya Al-Muttahida

United Kingdom
United Kingdom

Area: 244,820 sq km
Population: 60.3 million
GDP per capita: 27,700 US$
Capital: London
Government: Constitutional monarchy within Commonwealth
Language: English (official), Welsh, Scots Gaelic
Currency: 1 pound sterling = 100 pence

Geography: Great Britain is separated from mainland Europe by the English Channel and the North Sea. The United Kingdom consists of four main divisions: England, Wales, Scotland, and Northern Ireland. England, which comprises around two-thirds of Great Britain's land area, consists mostly of rolling hills. Scotland and Wales both feature

"People of the fireplaces": A member of the Potawatomie tribe is painted for a ritual. This nation lived south of the Great Lakes before it was forced to move to Oklahoma and Kansas in the 19th century.

Words like "wigwam," "moccasin," and "totem" derive from the language of the Algonquin people.

medium-height mountain systems and numerous valleys. The capital city of London and scenic rural areas such as the Scottish Highlands are the country's leading tourist destinations.

Politics: England was successfully invaded by a Norman army in 1066 AD. The end of the English Civil War left England without a monarchy before its restoration less than two decades later. England emerged as an important world power by the early 1700s and the 1800 Act of Union united Britain and Ireland. Great Britain was the world's premier power throughout the 19th century and ruled a vast empire with large territories on several continents. The country emerged exhausted but victorious from both world wars. Britain's vast colonial empire was gradually relinquished in the decades after the Second World War and Queen Elizabeth II was crowned in 1952. The country is now a member of NATO and the EU.

Economy: Britain was the world's first industrialized nation and the leading trading nation throughout much of the 19th century. The country experienced a painful transition during the 1970s and 1980s as it shifted from a manufacturing to a services-based economy. London is one of the world's most important financial services and banking centers. The country has a small but productive agricultural sector. The diverse service sector produces more than 70% of the country's GDP and provides employment for most of the population.

United States of America
United States
of America

Area: 9,631,418 sq km
Population: 293 million
GDP per capita: 37,800 US$
Capital: Washington
Government: Presidential federal republic
Languages: English (official), Spanish, tribal languages
Currency: 1 US dollar = 100 cents

Geography: The United States extend from the Canadian border in the north to the Carib-

bean Sea in the south, a distance of 2,500 kilometers; the country is 4,500 kilometers wide from the eastern Atlantic to the western Pacific coast. The USA can be divided into six major landforms: the coastal plains on the Atlantic and Gulf of Mexico, the craggy, low Appalachian Mountains, the inland plains, the high Rocky Mountains, the basins and plateaus of the west, and the Coastal Cordilleras. The country's territory includes the mountainous Arctic and sub-Arctic region of Alaska, and Hawaii, a group of tropical volcanic islands. Almost every climatic type, with the exception

of tropical, is represented. The USA offers an enormous variety of tourist destinations, from major cities such as New York, Chicago or Los Angeles to Florida's bathing beaches and the breathtaking scenery of the Colorado plateau.

Politics: Since the first European settlers arrived in the early 17th century, the country's history has been dominated by the rivaling interests of European colonists. The Declaration of Independence in 1776 heralded the USA's new status as an independent power. In the 19th century the country extended its territory significantly by waging war, acquiring lands and displacing the Native American population, and expanded toward the west coast. The civil war of 1861–1865 (War of Secession) led to the abolition of slavery. The USA became a military and economic superpower by entering the global political stage in both world wars. The Constitution of 1788 and Bill

of Rights of 1791 still determine the political system today. The country has a bicameral parliament, with direct elections to the House of Representatives held every two years. At the start of the new millennium, the USA regards itself as the world's economic and military leader and strives to implement western ideals of democracy

1 The peaks of the Rocky Mountains form a chain that stretches more than 4,300 kilometers from north to south.

2 For decades the Statue of Liberty, unveiled in 1886, saluted incoming ships bringing immigrants from Europe. The picture shows the skyline of New York as it was until

September 11, 2001, when the twin towers of the World Trade Center were destroyed in a terrorist attack.

3 The giant rocks (300–600 m) in Monument Valley in Arizona in the USA were shaped by erosion over millions of years.

The Promised Land: *Since 1948 the Jewish people, persecuted for centuries, have lived in their own country. The "Wailing Wall," the western wall of the ancient temple in Jerusalem, is a central sanctuary, not only for* *orthodox Jews. It has been open to the public again since 1967, a reminder of where King Solomon ordered the first temple to be built to house the Ark of the Covenant.*

and human rights throughout the world. The country was confronted by a new situation on September 11, 2001, when terrorists attacked the World Trade Center in New York and the Pentagon in Washington.

Economy: The country has the richest economy in the world. The geographical structure of the USA enables a variety of agriculture to be practiced in all areas, with large-scale livestock farming and highly mechanized grain cultivation (wheat, rice) playing key roles. Agriculture takes up around 47% of the country's total area. Vast natural resources (petroleum, coal, ores) have hastened the development of high-performance industries, particularly in the north (chemicals, mechanical engineering, automotive, electronics). In the USA's post-industrial economic structure, services account for almost 80% of GDP, employing an equivalent percentage of the workforce. The United States has around 13,400 airports, 180 of which are international.

Urdunn
Jordan

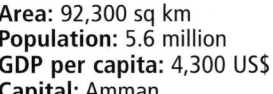

Area: 92,300 sq km
Population: 5.6 million
GDP per capita: 4,300 US$
Capital: Amman
Government: Constitutional monarchy
Language: Arabic
Currency: 1 Jordanian dinar = 1,000 fils

Geography: The Jordan valley separates the country at the northwest of the Arabian peninsula into a hilly landscape in the west, and a mountain range in the east, gradually sloping down to the Arabian desert. The twisting, non-navigable River Jordan flows into the Dead Sea. Jordan has an outlet to the Red Sea through a small coastal strip on the Gulf of Aqaba. Most areas have a desert climate, although the Mediterranean climate in the west enables agriculture. Tourist destinations, other than the capital Aqaba and Amman, include the ruins of Petra in the south.

Politics: Jordan's monarchy has existed since the country

gained independence in 1946. According to the constitution (since 1952), only the king exercises executive power, and in theory shares legislative power with the national assembly. In 1994 King Hussein concluded a peace treaty with Israel.

Economy: Jordan consists mostly of non-arable deserts and mountainous landscapes. Because it has no oil reserves, it is one of the poorest states in the Arab world. Economic activities concentrate in the services sector. Tourism is one of the most important sources of foreign revenue.

Uruguay
Uruguay

Area: 176,215 sq km
Population: 3.4 million
GDP per capita: 12,600 US$
Capital: Montevideo
Government: Presidential republic

Jerusalem is the holy City of three world religions.

Language: Spanish
Currency: 1 Peso Uruguayo = 100 centésimos

Geography: Uruguay lies to the north of the Río de la Plata. The foothills of the Brazilian highlands extend into the country from the north, creating rolling hills. Wet grasslands or pampas dominate the landscape at the coast and along the Uruguay River. Uruguay is the least forested country in South America. The climate is temperate, in-

fluenced by the ocean. March, April, October, and November are particularly good months to visit coastal resorts or the capital of Montevideo.

Politics: Discovered in 1515 by the Spanish, Uruguay was part of the viceroy of Rio de la Plata after 1777, passed to Brazil in 1817, and gained independence in 1830. In 1967, Uruguay regained the status of a presidential republic with a bicameral parliament, under its fifth constitution since its independence. A civil head of state was not elected until 11 years after the 1973 coup d'état. In the intervening period, two presidents were appointed by a "Council of Ministers."

Economy: Around 80% of Uruguay's land area is used for agriculture, mainly grazing. Despite this, only 8.5% of the population work in agriculture. Chief exports are agricultural products (beef, rice) and pro-

ducts from the processing industries (leather goods, wool, and textiles). The services sector accounts for 69% of GDP.

Uzbekistan
Uzbekistan

Area: 447,400 sq km
Population: 26.4 million
GDP per capita: 1,700 US$
Capital: Tashkent
Government: Pres. republic
Language: Uzbek

Currency: 1 Uzbek sum = 100 tijin

Geography: This Central Asian republic comprises the center of the Turan basin with the southwestern part of the Kysyl-Kum Desert. The Amu-Darja River flows through the desert on the southwest border and into the Aral Sea. In the east, the country is bounded by the foothills of the Tianshan and Altai mountains. The climate is continental.

Politics: When Uzbekistan was made a republic of the USSR (1924), the term "Uzbeks" was introduced for the Turkic speaking populations round Bukhara and Kokand. When the Soviet Union collapsed in 1991, Uzbekistan declared its independence.

Economy: Uzbekistan is an agricultural country with little industry. The cultivation of cotton plays a major role in the economy – Uzbekistan is the world's third largest exporter of cotton. Agriculture accounts for 32% of GDP and employs at least 44% of the workforce. Aside from the manufacture of cotton harvesting machinery, the industrial sector also produces fertilizers. Gold and oil production are becoming more important sectors.

Vanuatu
Vanuatu

Area: 12,190 sq km
Population: 203,000
GDP per capita: 2,900 US$
Capital: Port Villa
Government: Republic
Languages: English, French, Bislama
Currency: 1 vatu = 100 centimes

Geography: Vanuatu comprises 12 main islands and at least 70 smaller ones located 2,000 kilometers east of Australia. The country includes both coral islands and islands of volcanic origin, some still active. Except for the more arid islands of Eromanga and Aneityum in the south, most of Vanuatu has a humid tropical climate. The country's major tourist attractions include volcanic landscapes and beaches plus resorts such as the Mamanuca and Yasawa Islands.

Politics: The islands were visited by Portuguese explorers in 1606 and Captain James Cook in 1774, who named them the New Hebrides. In 1906, France and Great Britain agreed to jointly administer the islands. An independent state since 1980, Vanuatu is governed by an elected parliament and a council of local chiefs.

Economy: Agriculture and fishing are the most important segments of Vanuatu's economy and the sources of employment for most of the country's people. Cocoa and coconuts are the most important export crops produced on the islands, with sawmills for processing timber. The local service industry is rapidly expanding because of increased tourism. Vanuatu has become a minor financial services center because of its lax financial disclosure and tax laws, but the country has faced pressure to regulate the industry.

Venezuela
Venezuela

Area: 912,050 sq km
Population: 25 million
GDP per capita: 4,800 US$
Capital: Caracas
Government: Presidential federal republic
Language: Spanish
Currency: 1 bolívar = 100 céntimos

Geography: To the northwest is the oil-rich Maracaibo Basin with shallow Maracaibo Lake, 13,600 km² in area. These lowlands are bordered by the Cordillera de Mérida (Pico Bolívar, 5,002 m). To the southeast are the Orinoco lowlands and the Llanos, giving way in the south to the Guayana mountains, which occupy almost half the country's area. Canaima National Park is the main tourist attraction.

Politics: Discovered in 1498 by Columbus, Venezuela has been independent since 1830 following a succession of colonial and territorial claims. The 1961 constitution places legislative power with the National Congress, comprising the Senate and House of Representatives. The country

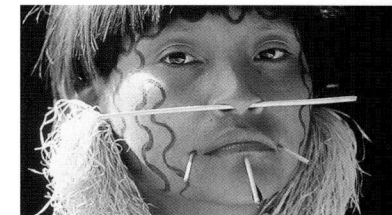

Endangered people: *The Yanomami live in the Amazon forests of Venezuela and Brazil. Landgrabbing and slash-and-burn clearance is threatening their homeland and lifestyle. Gold deposits have attracted countless treasure-hunters. Many Yanomami die of illnesses carried by outsiders, which their immune systems are not able to cope with.*

is still dogged by attempted coups, high crime and inflation and social unrest. General strikes in 2003 triggered an economic crisis and almost brought oil production to a standstill.

Economy: Long neglected, agriculture is now receiving new attention. Venezuela depends highly on its agricultural sector. The country has the potential to become a major exporter of coffee and cocoa. Petroleum and its derivates account for 71% of GDP. The government's efforts to promote industry have met with little success despite the country's rich natural resources.

Viêt-Nam
Vietnam

Area: 329,560 sq km
Population: 82.6 million
GDP per capita: 2,500 US$
Capital: Hanoi
Government: Socialist republic
Language: Vietnamese
Currency: 1 dong = 10 hào = 100 xu

Geography: The Red and Black River delta lies on the Gulf of Tongking. To the south extends the central region of Annam, formed by a deeply indented costal strip that is 40 kilometers wide at its narrowest point. In the south lies the Mekong Delta, 70,000 km² in area. In the long rainy season, tropical rain forests and mangrove forests flourish in the coastal areas. Vietnam has a host of cultural monuments in Ho Chi Minh City (Saigon) and Hue, plus areas of natural beauty.

Politics: In the 10th century, Vietnamese rebels drove out their Chinese overlords. Rivalries between two families caused a split in the country in the 15th century, which was reunited only in 1802 with French help. After World War II, the country was partitioned into communist-ruled North Vietnam, and dictator-led South Vietnam. The Vietnam War (1957/58–1975), in which the USA and the SEATO states played an important role, ended with the Vietcong taking power in South Viet-

nam and the unification of the country under communist leadership. The invasion of Cambodia in 1979 led to acts of war with China.

Economy: The transition from the socialist-planned economy has meant a surplus in rice production in recent years. Vietnam is today the world's third largest rice exporter. Wood and rubber reserves are industrially processed. Private companies are increasing, but the economy remains underdeveloped.

Yemen see Al-Yaman

Yi'sra'el
Israel

Area: 21,946 sq km
Population: 6.2 million
GDP per capita: 19,700 US$
Capital: Jerusalem
Government: Republic
Languages: Hebrew, Arabic (official), English
Currency: 1 new shekel = 100 agorot

Geography: The highlands of Galilee extend to the Mediterranean in the north, with a narrow, fertile coastal strip to the south that meets the Negev Desert, occupying the country's largest area. Israel is bounded to the east by the Red Sea and the Jordan plains. The coast has a Mediterranean climate, while a desert climate reigns to the south. Important tourist destinations, other than the Dead Sea scenery, are sites from Jewish, Roman, and Byzantine eras and the Crusades.

Politics: The Republic of Israel was proclaimed in 1948 at the end of the British Mandate in Palestine. A large number of the Arabs living in the national territory, who had fought for the creation of their own state thereupon left the country. Irreconcilable differences with their neighbors have led to a total of four Israeli-Arab wars. The peace process, initiated in 1993 by Arafat and Rabin with a mutual agreement to recognize Israel and the PLO, slowed down in 1996 when a conservative coalition came to power. Clashes escalated in 2001, and Palestinian suicide bombers aggrava-

ted the situation. The establishment of a Palestinian State has become the focus of international efforts, with a crucial aspect being how to draw the borders of a country when large areas are still under Israeli control. Time will tell whether the 2005 Israeli withdrawal from Gaza will help find a peaceful conclusion. The influence of PLO can scarcely be over-estimated.

1 Parts of the tropical rain forests in the mountainous parts of Vietnam have given way to terraced cultivated rice fields.

2 Impressive rock graves in Petra, Jordan, bear witness to the Nabatean culture of the 2nd century BC.

3 Vanuatu: The islands – formerly known as the New Hebri-des – have been settled by more than 100 Melanesian peoples.

4 The 3 million hectures of tropical forests in Venezuela's Canaima National Park are home to many endangered species. Countless waterfalls are typical of the landscape.

Picture perfect: The river Li in southern China, with its craggy mountains and cormorant fishers, is one of China's most popular holiday destinations. The more liberal economic policy that has developed in recent years allows culturally and scenically attractive, but commercially underdeveloped regions to benefit from tourist revenues.

Economy: Once solely agricultural, Israel is developing into a modern industrialized country; cooperative agriculture accounts for just 3% of GNP; industry for more than 30%. Important areas of industry include the food, metal, and aircraft industries. Tourism is the most reliable source of foreign exchange, at 2 billion US$.

Zambia
Zambia

Area: 752,614 sq km
Population: 10.4 million
GDP per capita: 800 US$
Capital: Lusaka
Government: Presidential republic within Commonwealth
Languages: English (official), Bantu languages
Currency: 1 kwacha = 100 ngwee

Geography: The high plateau (1,000–1,500 m) gradually rising from south to north is broken up by isolated outcrops and mountains of up to 2,300 meters. The basins of the Zambezi and Kafue rivers have shallow lakes and swamps. The altitude causes a moderately tropical climate; the highland savannas experience prolonged dry periods. Tourist attractions include Victoria Falls, Lake Tanganika and the national parks.

Politics: The country was formed from the original territories of Barotseland, Northwest Rhodesia and Northeast Rhodesia to the north of the Zambesi River, which were declared a British protectorate in 1911. In 1923 the region came under direct British colonial rule. From 1953 to 1963 North Rhodesia was part of the Central African Federation before gaining independence in 1964. Its president, K.D. Kaunda, established a single-party system in 1972–1973. National and international pressure for democracy led in 1990 to the approval of opposition parties. A new constitution guarantees the multi-party system and specifies the simultaneous holding of presidential and parliamentary elections. Forceful investigation into corruption has been championed by the current president, Levy Mwanawasa.

Economy: The majority of the African population, composed of 73 different ethnic groups, practices subsistence farming. Only the minority of European farmers use modern methods of cultivation. Zambia's economy is based on copper mining and export, which accounts for 65% of the total export volume. The government has privatized the country's largest mining company. Service industries, including tourism, are the country's fastest growing industries.

Zhongguo
China

Area: 9,596,960 sq km
Population: 1.3 billion.
GDP per capita: 5,000 US$
Capital: Beijing
Government: Socialist people's republic
Language: Mandarin Chinese

1

(official), Cantonese and other dialects
Currency: 1 yuan renminbi = 10 jiao = 100 fen

Geography: From the fertile lowlands in the east, the landscape rises to meet the Himalayas in the west. High plateaus and mountains of more than 1,000 meters occupy one third of the area. The coastline on the Yellow Sea is flat at the mouths of China's two major rivers, the Huanghe and the Yangze. The southern coast is mountainous, with many offshore islands. The testimonials to 5,000 years of civilization and a richly varied landscape offer a vast number of fascinating travel destinations. Rapid industrialization,

erosion and pollution have decimated the rich flora and fauna.

Politics: As early as 2000 BC, small states existed in what is now China. Since the formation of a united empire in 221 BC, accompanied by standardized systems for weights, measures and writing, China has twice fallen to foreign rule; the Mongols governed from 1280 to 1368, and the Manchurians from 1644 to 1911. The fall of the empire was followed by a republic in 1911. After the end of World War I, the country was the scene of repeated civil wars. In 1937 war broke out with Japan, and in 1941 China declared war on Germany. The Chinese civil war between Kuomintang and the communists ended in 1949 with the withdrawal of the Kuomintang to Taiwan, later the National Republic of China. In October 1949, the People's Republic of China was established under

2

Mao Tse Tung. In the 1960s internal struggles resulted in the Cultural Revolution. Since 1978, the communist leadership has been pursuing economic liberalization, although without relinquishing any of its political power. In 1997, China took over the former British crown colony of Hong Kong, undertaking to retain the existing economic system for another 50 years.

Economy: Most of the population lives and works in rural regions. Rice and grain cultivation covers basic needs, and surpluses are exported. The country is opening up to world markets and undergoing major structural upheavals as its economy develops. In a low-wage country such as China, the lion's share of exports is accounted for by processed goods, chiefly machinery and electronic appliances, but also textile products. Thanks to foreign

1 Tiananmen Square is of central significance for China; here Mao Tse Tung proclaimed the People's Republic in 1949.

2 Hong Kong: The breathtaking view from the 554-meter-high Victoria Peak to the peninsula of Kowloon.

trade and tourism, the services sector is gaining in importance.

Zimbabwe
Zimbabwe

Area: 390,757 sq km
Population: 12.6 million
GDP per capita: 1,900 US$
Capital: Harare
Government: Presidential republic
Languages: English (official), Bantu languages
Currency: 1 Zimbabwe dollar = 100 cents

Geography: Zimbabwe, bounded to the north by the Zambesi and to the south by the Limpopo lowlands, mainly consists of a high plateau belonging to the rim of the Kalahari Basin. The highlands of the interior consist of rolling tableland with rocky outcrops and savanna vegetation. The climate is tropical, but moderate thanks to the altitude. Tourist destinations include the nature reserves, Victoria Falls and the ruins of Great Zimbabwe.

Politics: A British protectorate from 1891, the country became the colony of Rhodesia in 1923, named after the British South African colonial politician Cecil Rhodes. In 1930 Rhodesia was divided into European and African territories, favoring the Europeans. After long negotiations and battles against minority rule, the country gained independence in 1980 under the name of Zimbabwe.

Economy: Zimbabwe's economy, with an export-oriented agriculture, well-developed processing industries and a variety of mineral resources, is more highly diversified than many other African countries. The main crops include sugar, maize, cotton, tobacco, tea, peanuts, and citrus fruits; livestock farming is also profitable. Important natural resources in the country, comparatively highly industrialized by African standards, include iron, nickel, chromium, gold, asbestos and anthracite. Government corruption and repression is now undermining the country's economy. The agricultural sector has deteriorated due to land seizures and emigration.

Secretary-Generals until 1981: The first Secretary-General of the UN was Tygve Lie from Norway (1946–1952, no picture) followed by the Swede Dag Hammersköld (1953–1961), Sihtu U Thant from Myanmar (1962–1971, pictured with John F. Kennedy), Kurt Waldheim from Austria (1972–1981).

UNO
United Nations Organization
Founded: 1945
Members: 192 countries
Headquarters: New York
In 1942, the effects of the Second World War moved 26 countries to form a joint organization. On October 24, 1945, 45 countries signed the United Nations Charter transforming the former war alliance into a global forum to replace the 1919 League of Nations.

The goals of the Organization are the establishment of world peace and international security, the promotion of human rights and basic freedoms "without distinction of race, sex, language or religion." In 1948 it formulated the Universal Declaration of Human Rights, under the heading of "all human rights for all." Peaceful resolution of conflicts is a key goal. The UN may not intervene in the right to self-determination of peoples.

The UN General Assembly (UNGA), in which each member is represented by one vote, meets annually. China, France, Great Britain, Russia, and the USA are permanent members of the Security Council, with ten further members elected for a two-year term. The Security Council acts on behalf of all members and awards and extends mandates of the UN forces. In 1988 the UN peace-keeping forces were awarded the Nobel Peace Prize.

IAEA
International Atomic Energy Agency
Founded: 1957
Members: 137 countries
Headquarters: Vienna
Monitoring of nuclear power plants and their waste disposal policies, plus compliance with the non-proliferation treaty of 1970.

IMF
International Monetary Fund
Founded: 1944
Members: 184 countries
Headquarters: Washington DC
Organization responsible for fostering monetary cooperation, facilitating international trade, monitoring the international currency system and promotion of development aid. The IMF also produces bi-annual reports on the international economic situation.

UNCTAD
United Nations Conference on Trade and Development
Founded: 1964
Members: 192 countries
Headquarters: Geneva
Promotion of international trade, particularly with developing countries, and interrelated issues of finance, technology, investment, and sustainable development.

UNDP
United Nations Development Programme
Founded: 1965
Headquarters: New York
Executive Council for the coordination and financing of technological and other forms of aid for developing countries. Its global network seeks to ensure the most effective use of UN and international aid resources. Voluntarily funded; largest multilateral source of grant technical assistance in the world.

UNEP
United Nations Environment Programme
Founded: 1972
Headquarters: Nairobi
Administrative council for international environmental issues, including those outside the UN system.

UNESCO
United Nations Educational, Scientific and Cultural Organization
Founded: 1946
Members: 190 countries
Headquarters: Paris
Special UN organization fostering cooperation with member states on cultural affairs and managing the continuously expanding "World Heritage List" of cultural and natural sites. Also contributes special support to educational and learning programs in developing countries and works on forging universal agreements on ethical issues.

UNHCR
United Nations High Commissioner for Refugees
Founded: 1949
Headquarters: Geneva
Assists those persecuted for reasons of race, religions or political views. Regular monitoring of refugee movements throughout the world and organization of aid campaigns. Leads and coordinates international action to protect refugees and internally displaced persons (IDPs) and resolve refugee problems worldwide.

UNICEF
United Nations International Children's Fund
Founded: 1946
Headquarters: New York
Secures food and medical supplies for children and mothers in need in around 160 countries and is largely financed by private donations. Demands ban on recruitment of "child sol-

Many UN organizations are headquartered in the Palace of Nations in Geneva.

diers." Educational, child development and training programs, promotion of children's rights, emergency assistance in crises.

World Bank Group
Headquarters: Washington
Comprises five institutions:

• IBRD
International Bank for Reconstruction and Development
Founded: 1944
Members: 184 countries

• IDA
International Development Association
Founded: 1959
Members: 163 countries

• IFC
International Finance Corporation
Founded: 1956
Members: 176 countries

• MIGA
Multilateral Investment Guarantee Agency
Founded: 1985
Members: 163 countries

• ICSID
International Centre for Settlement of Investment Disputes
Founded: 1966
Members: 154 countries
The World Bank Group supports economic development in less developed member countries by granting loans and supplying consulting and technical assistance, with the goals of combating poverty and improving the standard of living. The World Bank Group institutions are governed by a single president.

WHO
World Health Organization
Founded: 1948
Members: 193 countries
Headquarters: Geneva
WHO's objective, as set out in its constitution, is the attainment by all peoples of the highest possible level of health. Its constitution defines health as a state of complete physical, mental, and social well-being, and not merely the absence of disease or infirmity. The WHO maintains a global atlas of infectious diseases and is active in expanding medical research and care, for example in the struggle against Aids (UNAIDS Program). It also supplies emergency aid in disease outbreaks and crises.

Arab League
Founded: 1945
Members: 22 Arab countries in Africa and Asia
Headquarters: Cairo
Voluntary association of independent Arab countries fostering cooperation on cultural, economic, political, and scientific issues and representing common interests.

ASEAN
Association of South East Asian Nations
Founded: 1967
Members: Brunei, Cambodia, Indonesia, Malaysia, Philippines, Myanmar, Singapore, Thailand, Vietnam, Laos
Headquarters: Jakarta
Promotion of economic growth, social progress and political stability by means of political and security dialogue and cooperation. A free trade area is planned by 2010.

Commonwealth of Nations
Founded: 1931
Members: 53 countries
Headquarters: London
Fostering of political, economic, and cultural cooperation as well as the securing of democracy in the former territories of the British Empire. The foundation of the Commonwealth in 1931 coincided with the beginning of decolonization. Most colonies

International Organizations

Secretary-Generals since 1982: Javier Pérez de Cuéllar (1982–1991) from Peru and Boutros Boutros-Ghali from Egypt (1992–96). Seventh Secretary-General is Kofi Annan from Ghana. He took office in 1997 and was re-elected in June 2001.

had gained independence by 1984 but retained their close ties to Great Britain and the Commonwealth.

ECO
Economic Cooperation Organization
Founded: 1985
Members: Afghanistan, Azerbaijan, Iran, Kazakhstan, Kyrgyz Republic, Pakistan, Tajikistan, Turkey, Turkmenistan, Uzbekistan
Headquarters: Teheran
Cooperation of Islamic nations on economic, agricultural, industrial, transport, technological, scientific, and educational issues.

EFTA
European Free Trade Association
Founded: 1960
Members: Iceland, Liechtenstein, Norway, Switzerland
Headquarters: Geneva
Promotion of an extensive network of free trade agreements between member states and associated EU and non-EU countries.

EP
European Parliament
Founded: 1952
Members: total of 732 elected members from all EU countries
Headquarters: Strasbourg, Luxembourg, Brussels
The EP has far-reaching legislative powers and supervises the executive. Together with the European Council, it forms the EU budgetary authority and supervises budget spending. The EP also presides over EU issues of foreign and security policy and plays a key role in the enlargement discussion.

COE
Council of Europe
Founded: 1949
Members: 46 nations
Headquaters: Strasbourg
Organization with almost all European countries as members. Based on the law of nations and founded in London as a private initiative. Its goal is to foster cooperation, preserve items of common cultural heritage, defend human and minority rights as well as support the spread of democracy throughout Europe.

EU
European Union
Founded: 1993
Members: Germany, France, Great Britain, Finland, Italy, Spain, Netherlands, Belgium, Austria, Sweden, Denmark, Portugal, Greece, Ireland, Luxembourg, Latvia, Estonia, Lithuania, Hungary, Poland, Czech Republic, Slovakia, Slovenia, Malta, and Cyprus
Headquarters: Strasbourg, Brussels, Luxembourg
The EU is a development of the original European Coal and Steel Community, which joined with the European Economic Community (EEC) in 1957. In 1967, these bodies merged with the European Atomic Energy Commission (EURATOM) to form the European Community – renamed the EU in 1993. The organization strives toward a common foreign and security policy and fosters cooperation in issues of national policy and law.

European Court of Justice
Headquarters: Luxembourg
The highest legal institution in the EU deals with disputes involving EU law, ensuring that it is uniformly interpreted and applied throughout the Union. The Court hears actions against member countries, the EP, the Council or Commission. Its verdicts cannot be overturned by national courts. All member states are represented by one judge, presided over by a president.

FTAA
Free Trade Area of the Americas
Members: USA, Canada, all Latin and South American countries
Headquarters: none
The agreement signed in Miami in 1994 is aimed at interconnecting the planned North and South American free trade areas (NAFTA and Mercosur), with the goal of incorporating most countries in the Americas to create the world's largest international free trade zone by 2005.

CEFTA
Central European Free Trade Association
Founded: 1993
Members: Poland, Slovakian Republic, Slovenia, Czech Republic, Hungary, Bulgaria, Romania
Headquarters: none
The Free Trade Agreement came into force in 1993. The long-term goal of all members is EU and NATO membership, whereupon CEFTA would be dissolved.

IOC
International Olympic Committee
Founded: 1894
Members: 201 National Olympic Committees (NOCs)
Headquarters: Lausanne
International, non-governmental, non-profit organization and umbrella organization of the Olympic Movement. Decides the locations, rules and programs of the Summer and Winter Olympic Games and supervises their organization.

NATO
North Atlantic Treaty Organization
Founded: 1955
Members: 19
Headquarters: Brussels
The military pact was initiated by the USA and several Western European states in response to the formation of the Warsaw Pact during the Cold War. NATO has cooperated with the former Eastern Bloc countries since the early 1990s within the NATO Partnership for Peace. The organization has also extended membership to several former Warsaw Pact members. NATO's fundamental role is the safeguarding of its members' freedom and security by political and military means as well as upholding democracy, political stability and the rule of law.

OECD
Organization for Economic Cooperation and Development
Founded: 1961
Members: 30 countries
Headquarters: Paris
Successor to the Organization for European Economic Cooperation (OEEC) founded in 1948. Its goal is the economic development and improvement of living standards in member countries, fostering good governance and multilateral agreement. It produces individual country reviews and surveys, monitors trends and analyzes economic developments. It spearheads efforts to help countries respond to new economic challenges.

OPEC
Organization of Petroleum Exporting Countries
Founded: 1960
Members: 11 countries
Headquarters: Vienna
Oil cartel organization serving the interests of its member states with economies heavily reliant on oil. Aims to bring stability and harmony to the oil market by adjusting oil output to help ensure a balance between supply and demand.

OSCE
Organization for Security and Cooperation in Europe
Founded: 1975 (CSCE), since 1995 OSCE
Members: 56 countries
Headquarters: Vienna
The world's largest regional security organization, the Conference for Security and Cooperation in Europe, began its work with the signing of the Helsinki Final Act. It deals with many security and stability-related issues, early warning and crisis prevention and management. The OCSE has played an important role in assisting the former communist states of Europe in their transition to democracy.

WTO
World Trade Organization
Founded: 1995
Members: 149 countries and the EU Commission
Headquarters: Geneva
Replaced the GATT world trade agreement of 1947 and since then has supervised multilateral agreements concerning exchange of goods and services and agreements on patents and other property rights. The WTO also provides arbitration services in trade conflicts. Its promotion of global trade prompts many countries to apply for membership.

European Union: Parade of the banners of the members in front of the EU building in Brussels and in front of the European Parliament in Strasbourg.
25 countries are members of the European Union (EU) with a total of 450 million inhabitants.

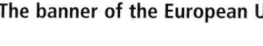
The banner of the European Union.

All of the places named on the maps in the atlas are listed in the atlas index. The place names are listed alphabetically. Special symbols and letters including accents and umlauts are ignored in the order of the index. For example, the letters Á, Ä, Å are all categorized under A, and è, °, Î are all treated as the standard Latin letter Z. Written characters consisting of two letters joined together (ligatures) are treated as two separate characters in the index: for example, words beginning with the character Æ would be indexed under AE.

The most commonly used abbreviations in the atlas – including N.P. for national park or N.W.R. for national wildlife refuge – are also used in the index. These abbreviations are listed and explained on this page (below). Generic geographic terms (sea, bay, etc.) and word articles (the, le, el, etc.)

were used in the order of the index: for example, the Gulf of Mexico is listed under G and Le Havre, France is listed under L.

A special aspect of the atlas is the detailed and specially developed system of pictograms it features. These pictograms highlight famous travel routes, scenic landscapes, natural attractions, man-made attractions, cultural sites, as well as sporting, vacation, and recreation facilities. These pictograms also appear in the index (up to three per place name). The pictograms provide a basic overview of the attractions featured in a particular area. The meanings of all of the pictograms featured in the atlas are explained on the following page. In addition to these pictograms, the index also features special symbols to provide information about the political status of certain

places including states, provinces, and capital cities. Virtually all of the places listed in the atlas have a country reference; these nations are identified by their international license (registration) plate codes. The various international license codes are identified on page 276. In the case of communities and areas that are located on or between the borders of two nations, the license

plate codes of both nations are listed and separated by a backslash.

The names of areas and geographic features that cannot be assigned to specific states, such as the Atlantic Ocean, are followed by the page number of a map featuring the area and the number of the map grid box in which the area is depicted on the map.

Antigua	⊟ ⊡ ⛰	AG	187	Gk37
Place name	Pictograms	Nation	Page	Map grid

Abbreviations

Abb.	Abbey, abbaye (French), abbadia (Span.), abbazia (Ital.)	Ind.	Indian/ Native Americans, First Nation	N.R.	Nature Reserve, Natuurreservaat (Dutch)	Sr.	Sredn -e, -ij, -jaja (Russian) = central, middle

Abb. — Abbey, abbaye (French), abbadia (Span.), abbazia (Ital.)
Abor. — Aboriginal (indigenous inhabitants of Australia)
Aborig. — Aboriginal (indigenous inhabitants of Australia)
Ad. — Adas (Turkish) = Island
Ág. — Ági -os, -a, -i (Greek) = Saint
A.L. — Aboriginal Land = Aboriginal land reserve in Australia
Ban. — Banjaran (Malaysian) = mountain range
Bol'. — Bol'-šoj, -šaja, -šoe (Russian) = large-
C. — Cape, cap (French), cabo (Span./Port.), capo (Ital.)
Can. — Canal
Cast. — Castle, castel (French.), castillo (Span.), castelo (Port.), castello (Ital.)
Cd. — Ciudad (Span.), cidade (Port.) = city
Co. — Cerro (Span.) = mountain, hill
Conv. — Convento (Span.) = monastery
Cord. — Cordillera (Span.) = mountain range
Corr. — Corrente (Port.), corriente (Ital./Span.) = river
Cr. — Creek
D. — Dake (Jap.) = mountain
D. — Danau (Indonesian) = lake
Dağ. — Dağlar, dağlari (Turkish) = mountain range
Ea. — Estancia (Span.) = estate
Emb. — Embalse (Span.), embassament (catalonian) = reservoir
Ens. — Ensenada (Span./Port.) = small bay
Erm. — Ermita (Span.) = hermitage
Est. — Estación (Span.) = train station
Faz. — Fazenda (Port.) = estate
Fl. — Fleuve (French) = river
Fs. — waterfalls
g. — gawa (Jap.) = river
G. — Gora (Russian), góra (Polish), gunung (Indonesian) = mountain
Gde. — Grande (Span./French) = large
Geb. — Gebirge (German), gebergte (Dutch) = mountain range
Grd. — Grand (French) = large
Gt. — Great-
Hist. — Historic, historical
Hr. — Hrebet (Russian) = high
Ht. — Haut (French) = high-
Hte. — Haute (French) = high-
Hts. — Haut -s, -es (French) = high-
Hwy. — Highway
I. — Isla (Span.), ilha (Port.) = island
Î. — Île (French) = island

Ind. — Indian/ Native Americans, First Nation
Ind.Res. — Indian Reservation = Native American land reserves in North America
Is. — Islands
Îs. — Îles (French) = islands
Jaz. — Jazovir (Bulg.) = reservoir
Jct. — Junction
Jez. — Jezioro (Pol.), jezero (Czech/Slovak./ Serb./Croat./Slov.) = lake
Kan. — Kanal (Turk./Rus.), kanaal (Dutch), kana (Pol.) = canal
Kep. — Kepulauan (Malaysian) = archipelago
Kg. — Kampong (Malaysian), kampung (Khmer) = village
Kör. — Körfezi (Turk.) = gulf, bay
L. — Lake, lac (French), lago (Ital./Span./ Port.), loch, lough (Gaelic)
M. — Mys (Rus./Ukr.) = cape
Mal. — Malo, -yj, -aja, -oe (Rus.) = small
Mem. — Memorial
Mon. — Monastery, monastère (French.), monasterio (Span.), monastero (Ital.)
M.P. — Milli Parki (Turk.) = national park
Mt. — Mount, mont (French)
Mta. — Montagna (Ital.), montaña (Span.) = mountain range
Mte. — Monte (Ital./Span./Port.), montagne (French) = mountain
Mtes. — Montes (Span./Port.), montagnes (French) = mountains
Mţi. — Munţii (Romanian) = mountain range
Mti. — Monti (Ital.) = mountain range
Mtn. — Mountain
Mtns. — Mountains
Mts. — Mountains, Monts (French)
Mus. — Musée (French), museo (Span.), museu (Port.) = museum
N. — North, Northern, Norte (Ital./Span./Port.), Norra (Swedish), Nørdre (Norwegian), Nørre (Danish), Nord (German)
Nac. — Nacional (Span.), Nacional'-nyj, -aja, -oe (Russian) = national
Naz. — Nazionale (Ital.) = national
N.B.C.A. — National Biodiversity and Conservation Area = protected natural area
Nev. — Nevado (Span.) = snow-covered mountain peaks
N.H.P. — National Historic Park
N.H.S. — National Historic Site
Niž. — Niž-e, -nij, -naja, -neje (Russian) = lower-
Nižm. — Nižmennost' (Rus.) = plain
N.M.P. — National Military Park
N.P. — National Park, Nationalpark (Swedish), nasjonal park (Norwegian), Nemzeti Park (Hungarian)

N.R. — Nature Reserve, Natuurreservaat (Dutch)
N.R.A. — National Recreation Area
N.S. — National Seashore
N.Sra. — Nossa Senhora (Port.) = our lady (Mary, the mother of Jesus)
Nva. — Nueva (Span.) = new-
Nvo. — Nuevo (Span.) = new-
N.W.R. — National Wildlife Refuge
o. — Ostrov (Rus.) = island
P. — Port (English and French), puerto (Span./Port.), porto (Ital.) = harbor
Peg. — Pegunungan (Indonesian) = mountain
Pen. — Peninsula, péninsule (franz.), península (Span.), penisola (Ital.)
Pk. — Peak
P.N. — Parc National (French), parque nacional (Span./Port.), parco nazionale (Ital.) = national park
p-ov. — Poluostrov (Rus.) = peninsula
Pres. — Presidente (Span./Port.) = president
Prov. — Provincial, Province
Pse. — Passe (French) = Pass
Pso. — Paso (Span.), passo (Ital.) = Pass
Pt. — Point
Pta. — Punta (Span./Port.) = point
Pte. — Pointe (French) = point
Pto. — Punto (Ital.) = point
Q.N.P. — Quasi National Park (Jap.) = national park
R. — River, rivière (French), río (Span.), ribeiro, rio (Port.), rîu (Romanian), reka (Bulgarian)
Ra. — Range
Rep. — Republic, république (French), república (Span./Port.), republicca (Ital.)
Repr. — Represa (Port.) = dam
Res. — Reserva (Span.), réserve (French) = nature reserve
Res. — Reservoir, réservoir (French)
Resp. — Respublika (Russian) = Republik
s. — San (Jap.) = mountain
S. — San (Span./Ital.), são (Port.) = saint
Sanc./ Sanct. — Sanctuary
Sd. — Sound, sund (German, Danish, Norwegian, Swedish)
Sel. — Selat (Indonesian) = strait
Sg. — Song (Vietnamese) = river
S.H.P. — State Historic Park
S.H.S. — State Historic Site
Sk. — Shuiku (Chinese) = reservoir
S.M. — State Monument
S.P. — State Park

Sr. — Sredn -e, -ij, -jaja (Russian) = central, middle
Sra. — Sierra (Span.), serra (Port./Ital.) = mountain range
St./St — Saint (English and French), sankt (German, Dutch)
Sta. — Santa (Span./Port./Ital.) = saint
Star. — Star -o, -yj, -aja, -oe (Russian) = old-
Ste — Sainte (French) = saint
Sth. — South, southern
St.Mem. — State Memorial
Sto. — Santo (Span./Port.) = Saint
Str. — Street, Strait, stretto (Italian), stræde (Danish), stret (Norwegian)
t. — tau (Kaz.) = mountain
T. — Take (Jap.) = peak, summit
T. — Temple
Tel. — Teluk (Indonesian) = bay
Tg. — Tanjung (Indonesian) = cape
T.I. — Terra Indígena (Port.), territorio indigena (Span.) = indigenous land reservation in Latin America
Vdhr. — Vodohranilišče (Russian) = reservoir
Vel. — Velik -o, -ij, -yki, -oe (Rus.) = large-
Verh. — Verhn -ee, -ie, -ij, -jaja (Rus.) = mountain
Vill. — Village
vlk. — Vulkan (Rus.) = volcano
Vol. — Volcano, volcan (French), volcán (Span.)
Vul. — Vulkan (German), Vulcano (Ital./Romanian) = volcano
W.A. — Wilderness Area
Wildl. — Wildlife
W.S. — Wildlife Sanctuary
Y. — Yama (Jap.) = mountain, mountain range
Zal. — Zaliv (Russian), zalew (Polish) = bay
Zap. — Zapovednik (Russian) = nature reserve
Z.B. — Nature reserve in the People's Republic of China
Zp. — Zapadn -e, -ji, -aja, -noe (Russian) = west, western

The index explained

International license (registration) plate code

A	Austria	CR	Costa Rica	GR	Greece	MD	Moldova	RCH	Chile	THA	Thailand
AFG	Afghanistan	CV	Cape Verde	GUY	Guyana	MEX	Mexico	RDC	Dem. Republic of the Congo	TJ	Tajikistan
AG	Antigua and Barbuda	CY	Cyprus	H	Hungary	MH	Marshall Islands	RG	Guinea	TLS*	East Timor
AL	Albania	CZ	Czech Republic	HN	Honduras	MK	Macedonia	RH	Haiti	TM	Turkmenistan
AND	Andorra	D	Germany	HR	Croatia	MNG	Mongolia	RI	Indonesia	TN	Tunisia
ANG	Angola	DARS	Western Sahara	I	Italy	MOC	Mozambique	RIM	Mauritania	TO	Tonga
ARM	Armenia	DJI	Djibouti	IL	Israel	MS	Mauritius	RL	Lebanon	TR	Turkey
AUS	Australia	DK	Denmark	IND	India	MV	Maldives	RM	Madagascar	TT	Trinidad and Tobago
AZ	Azerbaijan	DOM	Dominican Republic	IR	Iran	MW	Malawi	RMM	Mali	TUV	Tuvalu
B	Belgium	DY	Benin	IRL	Ireland	MYA	Myanmar (Burma)	RN	Niger	UA	Ukraine
BD	Bangladesh	DZ	Algeria	IRQ	Iraq	N	Norway	RO	Romania	UAE	United Arab Emirates
BDS	Barbados	E	Spain	IS	Iceland	NAM	Namibia	ROK	Korea, South	USA	United States of
BF	Burkina Faso	EAK	Kenya	J	Japan	NAU	Nauru	ROU	Uruguay		America
BG	Bulgaria	EAT	Tanzania	JA	Jamaica	NEP	Nepal	RP	Philippines	UZ	Uzbekistan
BH	Belize	EAU	Uganda	JOR	Jordan	NIC	Nicaragua	RSM	San Marino	V	Vatican City
BHT	Bhutan	EC	Ecuador	K	Cambodia	NL	Netherlands	RUS	Russia	VN	Vietnam
BIH	Bosnia and Herzegovina	ER	Eritrea	KIR	Kiribati	NZ	New Zealand	RWA	Rwanda	VU	Vanuatu
BOL	Bolivia	ES	El Salvador	KNA*	Saint Kitts and Nevis	OM	Oman	S	Sweden	WAG	Gambia
BR	Brazil	EST	Estonia	KS	Kyrgyzstan	P	Portugal	SD	Swaziland	WAL	Sierra Leone
BRN	Bahrain	ET	Egypt	KSA	Saudi Arabia	PA	Panama	SGP	Singapore	WAN	Nigeria
BRU	Brunei	ETH	Ethiopia	KWT	Kuwait	PAL	Palau	SCG**	Serbia and Montenegro	WD	Dominica
BS	Bahamas	F	France	KZ	Kazakhstan	PE	Peru	SK	Slovakia	WG	Grenada
BU	Burundi	FIN	Finland	L	Luxembourg	PK	Pakistan	SLO	Slovenia	WL	Saint Lucia
BY	Belarus	FJI	Fiji	LAO	Laos	PL	Poland	SME	Suriname	WS	Samoa
C	Cuba	FL	Liechtenstein	LAR	Libya	PNG	Papua New Guinea	SN	Senegal	WV	Saint Vincent and
CAM	Cameroon	FSM	Micronesia	LB	Liberia	PRK*	Korea, North	SOL	Solomon Islands		the Grenadines
CDN	Canada	G	Gabon	LS	Lesotho	PY	Paraguay	SP	Somalia	YE	Yemen
CH	Switzerland	GB	Great Britain	LT	Lithuania	Q	Qatar	STP	São Tomé and Príncipe	YV	Venezuela
CHN*	China	GCA	Guatemala	LV	Latvia	RA	Argentina	SUD	Sudan	Z	Zambia
CI	Cote d'Ivoire	GE	Georgia	M	Malta	RB	Botswana	SY	Seychelles	ZA	South Africa
CL	Sri Lanka	GH	Ghana	MA	Morocco	RC	Taiwan	SYR	Syria	ZW	Zimbabwe
CO	Colombia	GNB	Guinea-Bissau	MAL	Malaysia	RCA	Central Africa Republic	TCH	Chad		
COM	Comoros	GQ	Equatorial Guinea	MC	Monaco	RCB	Republic of the Congo	TG	Togo		

* Some countries do not have official vehicle registration codes. In these cases, the international three-letter code (ISO 3166) is shown.

** Montenegro and Serbia were without individual license plate codes at the time of publication. As a result, locations in these two countries are listed here under the code SCG.

Symbols used in the index

City
State
Capital
Province
Provincial Capital

Principal travel routes

Auto route
Rail road
Highspeed train
Shipping route

Remarkable landscapes and natural monuments

UNESCO World Natural Heritage
Mountain landscape
Rock landscape
Ravine/canyon
Extinct volcano
Active volcano
Geyser
Cave
Glacier
River landscape
Waterfall/rapids
Lake country
Desert
Oasis
Fossil site
Depression
Nature park
National park (landscape)
National park (flora)
National park (fauna)
National park (culture)
Biosphere reserve
Wildlife reserve
Whale watching

Turtle conservation area
Protected area for sea-lions/seals
Protected area for penguins
Zoo/safari park
Crocodile farm
Coastal landscape
Beach
Coral reef
Island
Underwater reserve

Remarkable Cities and cultural monuments

UNESCO World Cultural Heritage
Pre- and early history
Prehistoric rockscape
The Ancient Orient
Ancient Egypt
Ancient Egyptian pyramids
Minoan culture
Phoenecian culture
Early African culture
Etruscan culture
Greek antiquity
Roman antiquity
Nabatean culture
Vikings
Ancient India
Ancient China
Ancient Japan
Mayan culture
Inca culture
Aztec culture
Other ancient American cultures
Places of Jewish cultural interest
Places of Christian cultural interest
Places of Islamic cultural interest
Places of Buddhist cultural interest
Places of Hindu cultural interest

Places of Jainist cultural interest
Places of Sikh cultural interest
Places of Shinto cultural interest
Places of cultural interest to other religions
Places of cultural interest to indigenous peoples (native peoples)
Aborigine reservation
Places of Aboriginal cultural interest
Indian reservation
Indian Pueblo culture
Places of Indian cultural interest
Amazonian Indians/protected area
Cultural landscape
Historical city scape
Impressive skyline
Castle/fortress/fort
Caravanserai
Palace
Technical/industrial monument
Dam
Remarkable lighthouse
Remarkable bridge
Tomb/grave
Theater of war/battlefield
Monument
Memorial
Space mission launch site
Space telescope
Market
Festivals
Museum
Theater
World exhibition
Olympics

Sport and leisure destinations

Arena/stadium
Race track

Golf
Horse racing
Skiing
Sailing
Diving
Windsurfing
Surfing
Canoeing/rafting
Seaport
Deep-sea fishing
Waterskiing
Beach resort
Mineral/thermal spa
Amusement/theme park
Casino
Hill resort
Lodge

Special index pictograms

Bodies of Water
Canal
Other physical names
Pass
Underwater topography

2 de Junio ◻ MEX (TM) 181 Fa33
3 Castelli ◻ CH 34 Lk44
3 de Enero ◻ MEX (SO) 180 Ed30
9 de Julio ◻ RA (BA) 209 Gk63
9 de Julio ◻ RA (CR) 204 Ha60
10. de Abril ◻ MEX (TM) 182 Fa34
10. de Mayo ◻ MEX (COH)
181 Ek32
12 de Diciembre ◻ MEX (DGO)
183 Fe36
16 de Julio ◻ RA (BA) 209 Gk64
18 de Marzo ◻ MEX (CAM)
183 Fe36
24 de Mayo ◻ EC 196 Ga47
25 de Mayo ◻ RA (BA) 209 Gk63
25 de Mayo ◻ RA (LP) 208 Gd64
28 de Mayo ◻ RA (MD)
208 Gf63
27 de Abril ◻ CR 184 Fh40
27 de Enero ◻ MEX (BC) 180
Eb30
28 de Agosto ◻ MEX (COH)
181 Ej33
31 de Enero ◻ ANG 148 Lh49
70 Mile House ◻ CDN (BC)
168 Dk20
100 Mile House ◻ CDN (BC)
168 Dk20
108 Pagodas ◙ CHN 72 Qd26
150 Mile House ◻ CDN (BC)
168 Dk19

A

Å ◻ N 16 Lf14
A1-Ring ※ A 35 Lp43
Aabenraa ◻ DK 30 Lk35
Aabybro ◻ DK 30 Lk33
Aachen ◻ D 32 Lg40
Aadan Yabaal ◻ SP 145 Nd44
Aakirkeby ◻ DK 31 Lp35
Aalborg ◻ DK 30 Lk33
Aalen ◻ D 33 Ll42
Aalestrup ◻ DK 30 Lk34
Aalst ◻ B 23 Le41
Aalten ◻ NL 23 Lg39
Aalter ◻ B 23 Ld39
Aamudia ◻ SYR 57 Na27
Äänekoski ◻ FIN 38 Mf28
Aanslult ◻ ZA 154 Mb59
Aarau ◻ CH 34 Lj44
Aareschlucht ◙ CH 34 Lj44
Aars ◻ DK 30 Lk34
Aarschot ◻ B 23 Le40
Aarup ◻ DK 30 Ll35
Aba ◻ CHN (SCH) 72 Qa29
Aba ◻ RDC 144 Md43
Aba ◻ WAN 138 Ld43
Aba ad Dud ◻ KSA 59 Nc32
Abaco Island ◻ BS 179 Gb32
Abadan ◻ IR 59 Ne30
Abadeh ◻ IR 125 Kj30
Abaeté ◻ BR (MG) 203 Hh55
Abaetetuba ◻ BR (PA) 195 Hf46
Abag Qi ◻ CHN (NMZ) 71 Qh23
Abaí ◻ KZ 63 Oe25
Abaí ◻ PY 204 Hc58
Abaí ◻ RI 95 Qe48
Abaíra ◻ BR (BA) 201 Hk52
Abaji ◻ WAN 138 Lc42
Abajo Peak ◻ USA 171 Ef27
Abaj Takalik ◙ GCA 184 Fe38
Abakaliki ◻ WAN 138 Ld42
Abakan ◻ RUS 54 Pc08
Abakh Hoja Tomb ◙ CHN
66 Oj26
Abala ◻ RCB 148 Lh46
Abalak ◻ RN 132 Ld38
Abalessa ◻ DZ 132 Lc34
Ab Anbar ◻ IR 64 Nk32
Abancay ◻ PE 197 Gd52
Abanilla ◻ E 29 Ku52
Abanko ◻ RMM 131 La36
Abano Terme ◻ I 34 Lm45
Abapó ◻ BOL 206 Gj55
Abarán ◻ E 29 Ku52
Abaré ◻ BR (BA) 201 Ja50
Abashiri ◻ J 77 Sc23
Abasolo ◻ MEX (GJT) 182 Ek35
Abasolo ◻ MEX 181 Fa34
Abastumani ◻ GE 57 Nb26
Abau ◻ PNG 116 Sd24
Abay Wenz ◻ ETH 142 Mj40
Abay ◻ KZ 63 Oe24
Abbacyba ◻ BR 199 Hk52
Abbadia San Salvatore ◻ I
34 Lm48
Abba Kella ◻ ETH 142 Mj42
Abba-Omege ◻ WAN 138 Le42
Abbas Abad ◻ IR 57 Nf27
Abbas Abad ◻ IR 64 Nh30
Abbas Abad ◻ IR 62 Nj27
Abbasanta ◻ I 36 Lj50
Abbaye aux Dames de Saintes ◙
F 24 Ku45
Abbaye aux Hommes de Caen ◙
F 22 Ku41
Abbaye de Fontenay ◙ □ F
25 Le43
Abbaye de Fontfroide ◙ F
25 Lc47
Abbaye de Jumièges ◙ F 22 La41
Abbaye de la Chaise-Dieu ◙ F
25 Ld45
Abbaye de Saint-Benoit-sur-Loire
◙ F 25 Lc43
Abbaye de Saint-Guilhem-le-
Désert ◙ F 25 Ld47
Abbaye de Sénanque ◙ F 25 Lf47
Abbaye d'Orval ◙ B 23 Lf41
Abbaye Sainte-Foy ◙ F 25 Lc46
Abbaye Saint-Pierre ◙ F 24 Ku44
Abbazia della Trinità di Venosa ◙
I 37 Lq50
Abbazia di Casamari ◙ I 36 Lo49
Abbazia di Montecassino ◙ I
36 Lo49
Abbeville ◻ □ F 23 Lb40
Abbeville ◻ USA (AL) 175 Fh30
Abbeville ◻ USA (LA) 174 Fd31
Abbeville ◻ USA (WI) 172 Fa23
Abbeville ◻ USA (SC) 178 Fj29
Abbey ◻ CDN (SK) 169 Ef20
Abbeyfeale ◻ IRL 19 Kl38
Abbeyleix ◻ IRL 19 Ko38
Abbiategrasso ◻ I 34 Lj45
Abbotsford ◻ AUS (QLD)
109 Sd59
Abbot, Mount ◻ AUS (QLD)
107 Sd56
Abbotsbury ◻ GB 21 Ks40
Abbotsford ◻ CDN (BC) 168 Dj21
Abbottstown ◻ USA (WI) 172 Fa23
Abbott ◻ USA (NM) 171 En27
Abbottabad ◻ PK 65 Og28
Abd al-Kuri □ YE 61 Ng39
Abdallah bin Abbas Mosque ◙
KSA 60 Na35
Abdera ◙ GR 47 Me53
Abduccho ◻ ETH 143 Mg38
'Abdin ◻ SUD 134 Me39
Abdul Razzak Tomb ◙ AFG
65 Od29
Abease ◻ GH 137 Kk41
Abébé ◻ RMM 131 Kh39
Abeibara ◻ RMM 132 Lb37
Abejar ◻ E 28 Ks49
Abejukolo ◻ WAN 138 Ld41
Abelardo Luz ◻ BR (SC) 204
Hd59
Abel Erasmuspas ◙ ZA 155 Mf58
Abel Tasman N.P. ⓝ NZ 113 Tg66
Abemama ◻ ETH 142 Na41
Abemarire ◻ RI 115 Sa49

Abene ◻ GH 137 Kk42
Abengourou ◻ CI 137 Kj42
Abenójar ◻ E 27 Kq52
Abenberg ◻ D 33 Lm42
Abeokuta ◻ WAN 138 Lb42
Aberaeron ◻ GB 21 Kq38
Abercrombie Caves ◙ AUS
(NSW) 111 Se62
Aberdare N.P. ⓝ EAK 144 Mj46
Aberdare Range ◻ EAK 144 Mj46
Aberdeen ◻ CDN (SK) 169 Eg19
Aberdeen ◻ GB 20 Ks33
Aberdeen ◻ USA (MD) 175 Fh26
Aberdeen ◻ USA (MS) 175 Ff29
Aberdeen ◻ USA (SD) 172 Fa23
Aberdeen ◻ USA (WA) 168 Dj22
Aberdeen Road ◻ ZA 155 Mc62
Aberfeldy ◻ GB 20 Kr34
Aberfoyle ◻ GB 20 Kq34
Abergavenny ◻ GB 21 Ks39
Abergele ◻ ETH 142 Mk39
Abergele ◻ GB 21 Kr37
Aberjabon ◻ RI 95 Nf22
Abernethy ◻ CDN (SK) 169 Ej20
Abersoch ◻ GB 21 Kq38
Aberystwyth ◙ □ GB 21 Kq38
Abetone ◻ I 34 Ll46
Abetteh ◻ MA 124 Ke31
Ål Garm ◻ IR 57 Ne28
Abguê ◻ TCH 139 Lk40
Abha ◻ KSA 60 Nb36
Abhana ◻ IND (MPH) 82 Oh36
Abhanpur ◻ IND (CGH) 83 Pa35
Abhar ◻ IR 57 Ne27
Abhraw Bala ◻ IR 59 Ng30
Abico ◻ BR (AM) 198 Gh47
Abide ◻ TR 45 Mg50
Abide ◻ TR 47 Mk52
Abidjan ◙ CI 137 Kj43
Abi Hill ◻ WAN 138 Ld42
Abijatta-Shalla Lakes N.P. ⓝ ETH
142 Mk42
Abilene ◻ USA (KS) 174 Fb26
Abilene ◻ USA (TX) 174 Fa29
Abingdon = Isla Pinta □ EC
197 Fe45
Abingdon ◻ GB 21 Kt39
Abingdon Downs ◻ AUS (QLD)
107 Sb54
Abington ◻ GB 20 Kr35
Abinsi ◻ WAN 138 Le42
Abirem ◻ GH 137 Kk42
Abisko ◻ S 16 Lk11
Abisko Fjällstation ◙ S 16 Lk11
Abisko n.p. ⓝ S 16 Lk11
Abjorvosyma ◻ BY 41 Md38
Abkhazia □ GE (SA) 108 Rh59
Abmüm ◻ ET 129 Mf32
Abnûb ◻ ET 129 Mf32
Åbo = Turku □ FIN 38 Mc30
Aboa □ ANT (FIN) 6 Hb33
Aboboso ◻ CI 137 Kk43
Aboke ◻ EAU 144 Mg44
Abolones Beach ◙ USA (CA)
170 Dk28
Abomey ◻ DY 138 La42
Abomey Calavi ◻ DY 138 Lb42
Abomsa ◻ ETH 142 Na41
Abong Mbang ◻ CAM 139 Lg44
Aboni ◻ WAN 139 Lf42
Abony ◻ H 43 Lu43
Aborigen, Nevado de ◻ RA 207 Gg58
Abracom ◻ BR (AM) 198 Gh47
Abraham's Bay ◻ BS 186 Gd34
Abra Huashuaccasa ◻ PE
197 Gd53
Abraka ◻ WAN 138 Ld43
Abrantes ◻ □ P 27 Km51
Abra Pampa ◻ RA (PJ) 207 Gh57
Abra Tapuna ◻ PE 197 Gd52
Abra Campo ◻ BR (MG) 203 Hj56
Abrego ◻ CO 192 Gd41
Abrene = Pytalovo ◻ RUS
39 Mh33
Abreu ◻ MOC 153 Mj55
Abri de Koumbala ◻ RCA
140 Ma41
Abri de Toulou ◙ RCA 140 Ma41
Abritus ◙ BG 45 Mg47
Abrud ◻ RO 43 Md44
Abruka saar ◻ EST 39 Mc32
Abruzzo □ I 36 Lo48
Absaroka Range ◻ USA 175 Ff29
Abšaron, P.N. d' ◻ ◻ 36 Lo49
Abšaron, P.N. d' ◻ □ 36 Lo49
Absarokee ◻ USA (MT) 169 Ef23
Absarsoke Range ◻ USA 175
Ee23
Abšaroke ◻ USA (MT) 169 Ef23
Abtei Einsiedeln ◙ CH 34 Lj43
Abtei Stams ◙ A 34 Lm43
Ab Torsh ◻ IR 57 Ne27
Ab Touyour ◻ TCH 139 Lk40
Abu Ajram ◻ KSA 58 Mk31
Abu al-Abyadh □ UAE 61 Ng33
Abu al Khasib ◻ IRQ 59 Nd30
Abu 'Arish ◻ KSA 60 Nb36
Abu al Tabul ◻ OM 61 Nh35
Abu Ballas ◻ KSA 60 Nd35
Abu Dawn ◻ SUD 135 Mg38
Abu Deleig ◻ SUD 135 Mg38
Abu Dhabi ◻ UAE 61 Nh33
Abu Dhabi Icerink ◙ UAE
Nh33
Abu Durban ◻ ET 129 Mg31
Abu el Matâmir ◻ ET 129 Mf30
Abu Ghusun ◻ ET 129 Mh33
Abu Gabra ◻ SUD 134 Md40
Abu Gamel ◻ SUD 135 Mf38
Abu Ghirban ◻ SUD 135 Mg38
Abu Hadriyah ◻ KSA 59 Ne32
Abuhar ◻ IND 80 Oh31
Abu Hamed ◻ SUD 135 Mf37
Abu Hashim ◻ SUD 135 Mf40
Abu Hashim ◻ SUD 135 Mg36
Abu Higar ◻ SUD 135 Mf38
Abu Kabisa ◻ LAR 127 Lj30
Abu Kamal ◻ SYR 57 Na28
Abu Kebir ◻ ET 129 Mf30
Abuki Mausoleum ◙ RI 96 Ra47
Abu Matariq ◻ SUD 134 Md40
Abu Mina ◙ ET 129 Me30
Abu Mendi ◻ ET 142 Mj39
Abu Minqar ◻ ET 129 Me32
Abu, Mount = Guru Shikhar ◻
IND 82 Og33

Abunã ◻ BR (RO) 198 Gh50
Abu Na'im ◻ LAR 127 Lk31
Abu Ra's ◻ SUD 141 Mc42
Abu Road ◻ IND (RJT) 82 Og33
Abu Rudays ◻ ET 129 Mg31
Abu Saffar ◻ SUD 135 Mf35
Abu Simbel ◻ ET 129 Mf34
Abu Simbel ◙ ET 129 Mf34
Abu Sukhayr ◻ IRQ 59 Nc30
Abu Teeg ◻ ET 129 Mf32
Abut Head ◻ NZ 113 Tf67
Abu Tunaytin ◻ SUD 135 Mf38
Abu 'Uruq ◻ SUD 135 Mf38
Abu Uwayjilah ◻ ET 129 Mh30
Abuye Meda ◻ ETH 142 Mk40
Abuyog ◻ RP 90 Ra40
Abu Zabad ◻ SUD 134 Me39
Abu Zayyan ◻ SUD 134 Me39
Abu Zeyo Abad ◻ IR 57 Nf29
Abwong ◻ SUD 141 Mg41
Aby ◻ S 31 Lp32
Abyad ◻ SUD 134 Md39
Abyaneh ◙ IR 59 Nf29
Abyar 'Ali ◻ KSA 58 Mk33
Abyar ash Shuwayrif ◻ LAR
128 Le31
Abydos = El Âmirah ◙ ET
129 Mf32
Abyei ◻ SUD 141 Me41
Abyek ◻ IR 57 Nf27
Abyggeby ◻ S 31 Ls30
Abytorp ◻ S 31 Lp31
Ad-Dahna ◻ KSA 59 Nc32
Ad Dahra ◻ UAE 61 Nh33
Ad-Dhawah ◻ LAR 128 Ma33
Addi ◻ CAM 139 Lh42
Ad Dibdibah ◻ KSA 59 Nc32
Ad Dikakah ◻ KSA 61 Nf36
Ad Dilam ◻ KSA 61 Nf36
Ad Dir'iyah □ KSA 59 Nd33
Adis Ababa ◙ ETH 142 Mk41
142 Mk41
Addison ◻ USA (NY) 177 Ga24
Ad Diwaniyah ◻ IRQ 59 Nc30
Addo ◻ ZA 155 Mc62
Addo Elephant N.P. ⓝ ZA
200 Hf48
ad-Dabang ◻ SUD 135 Mg38
ad-Du'hayn ◻ SUD 134 Md40
Ad Dulaymiyah ◻ KSA 59 Nd33
Ad Dulu'iyah ◻ IRQ 57 Nc28
Ad Duqah ◻ KSA 60 Na36
Ad Dur'an ◻ KSA 59 Nb35
Ad-Duwayn ◻ SUD 135 Mg39
Adé ◻ TCH 134 Ma39
Adéane ◻ SN 136 Kb39
Adel ◻ USA (GA) 178 Fj30
Adel ◻ USA (GA) 178 Fj30
Ad Dari'o ◻ UAE 61 Ng34
Adelaide ◙ AUS (SA) 110
Rk63
Adelaide Island ◻ ANT 6 Gb33
Adelaide River ◻ AUS (NT)
106 Rf52
Adel Bagrou ◻ RIM 131 Kd38
Adelbert Range ◻ PNG 115 Sc48
Adelboden ◻ CH 34 Lh44
Adelbert Island ◻ AUS 102 Rb55
Adelia María ◻ RA (CD) 208
Gh62
Adelong ◻ AUS (NSW) 111 Se63
Adelong ◻ AUS (NSW) 111 Se63
Adely Land □ ANT 7 Rc32
Ademuz ◻ E 29 Kt50
Aden ◻ YE 60 Nc39
Adenau ◻ D 33 Lg40
Adendorp ◻ ZA 155 Mc62
Aderbissinat ◻ RN 132 Ld38
Adesar ◻ IND (GUJ) 82 Of34
Adet ◻ ETH 142 Mj40
Adéta ◻ TG 137 La42
Adhbay ◻ KSA 60 Nb37
Adhamara ◻ SUD (BIH) 83 Pb33
Adi Ar ◻ RI 114 Rg48
Adiake ◻ CI 137 Kk43
Adi Ark'ay ◻ ETH 142 Mj39
Adicora ◻ YV 193 Gf40
Adi Da'iro ◻ ETH 142 Mk38
Achberapakkam ◻ IND (TNU)
85 Ok40
Adi Gudom ◻ ETH 142 Mk39
Adigrat ◻ ETH 142 Mk39
Adikas ◻ ETH 144 Mh43
Adi Keyih ◻ ER 142 Mk38
Adi Kwala ◻ ER 142 Mk38
Adilabad ◻ IND (APH) 83 Ok36
Adilcevaz ◻ TR 57 Nb26
Adimi ◻ IR 64 Oa30
Adin ◻ USA (CA) 170 Dk25
Adimoone ◻ SP 143 Ne41
Adirampattinam ◻ IND (TNU)
85 Ok40
Adirondack Mountains ◻ USA
177 Gc24
Adirondack Museum ◙ USA
177 Gc24
Adirondack Park ◻ USA 177
Gc24
Adirondack Scenic R.R. ◙ USA
177 Gc24
Adis Ababa ◙ □ ETH 142 Mk41
Adis Alem ◻ ETH 142 Mk41
Adis Zemen ◻ ETH 142 Mj39
Adi Ugri ◻ ER 142 Mk38
Adjala Res. ◻ TR 56 Mk27
Adjengré ◻ TG 137 La42
Adjim ◻ TN 126 Lf29
Adje Kotoku ◻ GH 137 Kk42
Adjohon ◻ DY 138 Lb42
Adjud ◻ RO 49 Md22
Adler ◻ RUS 57 Na24
Admiralty I. National Monument ◙
USA 166 Dc17
Admiralty Islands ◻ PNG
116 Sd47
Admiralty Islands ◻ PNG
116 Sd47
Admjany ◻ SP 39 Mf36
Admont ◻ A 35 Lp43
Ado Awaiye ◻ WAN 138 La42
Ado-Ekiti ◻ WAN 138 Ld42
Adok ◻ SUD 141 Mf41
Adola ◻ ETH 143 Mk42
Adolfo González Chaves ◻ RA
(BA) 209 Ha64
Adolfo López Mateos ◻ MEX
(BCS) 180 Ed33
Adolfo López Mateos (La Junta)
◻ MEX (CHH) 180 Eg32
Adonara □ RI 97 Rb50
Adoni ◻ IND (APH) 82 Oj38
Adony ◻ H 43 Lu43
Adorf ◻ D 33 Ln40
Adoru ◻ WAN 138 Ld42
Adoumandjali ◻ RCA 140 Lh43
Adoumri ◻ CAM 139 Lg41
Adra ◻ E 27 Kr54
Adra ◻ SYR 56 Mk29
Adrano ◻ I 37 Lp53
Adrar ◻ DZ 132 La34
Adraskand ◻ AFG 64 Ob29
Adré ◻ TCH 134 Ma40
Adrar Adjelho ◻ DZ 132 Lc33
Adrar Ahellakane ◻ DZ 132 Lc33
Adrar Azzaouager ◻ RN 132 Le37
Adrar Bous ◻ RN 132 Le35

Adamova ◻ BY 39 Mj35
Adam's Bridge ◻ IND/CL
85 Ok41
Adams Lake ◻ CDN (BC)
168 Ea20
Adams, Mount ◻ USA 168 Dk22
Adam's Peak ◻ CL 85 Pa42
Adamstown ◻ (UK) 11 Ba56
Adamuz ◻ E 27 Kq52
'Adan ◻ YE 60 Nc39
Adana ◙ TR 56 Mh27
Adan as Sughra ◻ YE 60 Nc39
Adané ◻ G 148 Lf46
Adani ◻ WAN 138 Ld42
Adaouda ◻ DZ 132 Lc34
Adapazari = Sakarya ◻ TR
56 Mf25
Adare ◻ TCH 134 Ma40
Adarama ◻ SUD 135 Mg38
Adare ◻ IRL 19 Kl38
Adavale ◻ AUS (QLD) 109 Sc58
Adaz ◻ DZ 132 Lc33
ad-Dabba ◻ SUD 135 Mf36
Adraskand ◻ AFG 64 Ob29
Adrar ◻ DZ 132 La34
Adrar des Ifôrhas ◻ RMM
132 La36
Adrar Ikohahoëne ◻ DZ 126 Lc32
Adrar Ilebgane ◻ RMM 132 La36
Adrar Mariaou ◻ DZ 132 La34
Adrar n'Ahnet ◻ DZ 132 Lb33
Adrar-n-Aklim ◻ MA 125 Kg30
Adrar-n-Deren ◻ MA 125 Kg30
Adrar-n-Imchech ◻ MA 125 Kg30
Adrar-Ouzzeine ◻ RMM 132 La36
Adrar Souttouf ◻ DARS 130 Kc36
Adrar Tachtaket ◻ RIM 132 Ld36
Adrar Tedjorar ◻ DZ 132 Lc34
Adrar Tideridaouine ◻ DZ
132 La34
Adrar Tineliert ◻ DZ 126 Lb33
Adraskan ◻ AFG 64 Ob29
Adré ◻ TCH 134 Ma40
Adrian ◻ USA (MI) 173 Fh25
Adrian ◻ USA (TX) 174 Ek28
Adrianopolis ◻ BR (PR) 205 Hf58
Adriatic Sea ◻ 14 Lp35
Adršpašsko- teplické skály ◙
CZ 42 Lq40
Adul ◻ SUD 141 Me41
Ad Darb ◻ KSA 60 Nb36
Ad-Dariz ◻ OM 61 Nj34
Ad Dawadami ◻ KSA 59 Nc33
Ad Dawwah ◻ Q 59 Nf33
Ad Dawr ◻ IRQ 57 Nc28
Ad Dhaid ◻ UAE 61 Nh33
Ad-Dhawah ◻ LAR 128 Ma33
Addi ◻ CAM 139 Lh42
Adamawa, Mount ◻ USA 168 Dk22

Adar des Ifôrhas ◻ RMM
132 La36
Adrar Ikohahoëne ◻ DZ 126 Lc32
Agia Varvára ◻ GR 47 Mf55
Agighiol ◻ RO 45 Mj45
Ağil Apóstoli ◻ GR 45 Md54
Ağıl M'Lila ◻ GR 126 Ld27
Agla'i ◻ ETH 142 Mk39
Aglagal ◻ GR (AGB) 71 Qh20
Aglona ◻ RO 43 Mh45
Agiokambos ◻ GR 46 Mc51
Agiokambos ◻ GR 44 Md52
Agiokambos ◻ GR 46 Mc53
Agios Andréas ◻ GR 46 Mc53
Agios Charalampos ◻ GR
45 Mf50
Agios Christós ◻ GR 46 Mc50
Agios Dimítrios ◻ □ GR 46 Mc50
Agios Dimítrios ◻ GR 46 Mc51
Agios Efstrátios ◻ GR 47 Mf51
Agios Efstrátios □ GR 47 Mf51
Agios Geórgios ◻ GR 46 Mc52
Agios Kirikos ◻ GR 47 Mg53
Agios Mámas ◻ GR 46 Mc53
Agios Nikolaos ◻ GR 46 Mb51
Agios Nikolaos ◻ GR 46 Mc51
Agios Nikolaos ◻ □ GR
47 Mf55
Agios Pétros ◻ GR 46 Mc53
Agios Stéfanos ◻ GR 46 Mc51
Agios Stéfanos ◻ GR 47 Mf54
Agios Theodoros = Çayırova ◻
CY 56 Mh28
Agira ◻ I 34 Ln45
Agirwal ◻ ER 142 Mk38
Agjert ◻ RIM 130 Kf37
Aglagal ◻ RMM 131 Kj37
Aglou ◻ MA 124 Ke30
Agnantiá ◻ GR 46 Mb51
Agnes Lodge ◻ SOL 117 Sj50
Agnew ◻ AUS (WA) 104 Ra60
Agnone ◻ I 37 Lp49
Ago ◻ J 79 Rj28
Ago-Are ◻ WAN 138 La41
Agogo ◻ GH 137 Kk42
Agogo ◻ RP 91 Rc41
Agôlai ◻ IND (RJT) 80 Og32
Agona-Sweru ◻ GH 137 Kk43
Agoo ◻ RP 90 Ra37
Agordo ◻ I 34 Ln44
Agou ◻ TG 137 La42
Agouna ◻ DY 138 La42
Agouni Jefal ◻ RMM 131 Kj37
Agoutí ◻ MA 125 Kg30
Agra ◻ IND (UPH) 81 Oj32
Agra Fort ◙ IND 81 Oj32
Agrahanskij poluostrov ◻ RUS
57 Nd24
Agrelia ◻ GR 46 Mb51
Agrélia ◻ GR 46 Mb51
Agri ◻ I 28 Kt49
Agrianí ◻ TR 57 Nb26
Ağrı Dağı ◻ TR 57 Nc26
Agrigento ◻ □ I 36 Lo53
Agrinio ◻ GR 46 Mb52
Agriovótano ◻ GR 47 Me52
Agrópoli ◻ I 37 Lp50
Agtos ◻ WAN 138 Lc43
Agua Azul ◻ HN 184 Fg38
Agua Blanca ◻ GCA 184 Ff38
Agua Blanca de Iturbide ◙ MEX
(HDG) 182 Fa35
Agua Boa ◻ BR (MT) 202 Hc53
Agua Boa ◻ BR (GO) 200 Hf52
Agua Braga ◻ BR (GO) 200 Hg49
Agua Branca ◻ BR (PI) 201 Hj48
Agua Caliente ◻ PE 197 Gc50
Aguacatán ◻ GCA 184 Fe38
Aguachica ◻ CO 192 Gd41
Agua Comprida ◻ BR (SP)
203 Hg56
Aguada Cecilio ◻ RA (RN)
208 Gh66
Aguada de Pasajeros ◻ C
179 Fk34
Agua Dulce ◻ CO 192 Gc43
Agua Dulce ◻ MEX (VC) 183 Fc36
Agua Escondido ◻ RA (MD)
208 Gf64
Agua Grande ◻ MEX (SO)
180 Ee31
Agua Hedionda, Cerro ◻ RA
180 Ef31
Agua Negras ◻ CDN 169 Ed21
Agua Nueva ◻ MEX (COH)
181 Ek33
Agua Petra Inari, T.I. ◙ BR
198 Gg49
Agua Quente ◻ BR (GO) 200
Hg52
Aguaraguá, P.N. ◙ BOL
207 Gj56
A Guarda ◻ E 26 Km49
Aguarico ◻ EC 196 Gb46
Agua Verde ◻ MEX (SL) 180 Ee33
Agua Viva ◻ YV 192 Ge41
Aguayita ◻ PE 197 Gc50
Aguá ◻ PY 204 Hb59
Agudal ◻ RIM 130 Ke35
Agudos ◻ BR (SP) 204 He56
Aguelhok ◻ RMM 132 Lb36
Aguia Branca ◻ BR (ES) 203 Hk55
Aguiar ◻ E 27 Kp51
Aguié ◻ RN 133 Le39
Águila, Cerro □ MEX (QR)
183 Fg36
Aguilar ◻ E 27 Kq53
Aguilar de Campóo ◻ E 26 Kq48
Aguilas ◻ E 29 Kt54
Aguililla ◻ MEX (MHC) 182 Ej36
Aguja, Cerro □ RA/RCH 210
Ge67
Aguascalientes ◙ MEX (AGS)
182 Ej35
Aguascalientes □ MEX 182 Ek35
Aguchao ◻ BR (RS) 204 Hd60
Aguchila ◻ BR (PI) 201 Hj49
Aguas Belas ◻ BR (PE) 201 Jb50
Aguas Belas, T.I. ◙ BR 203 Ja54
Ailly-sur-Noye ◻ F 23 Lc41

Agia Varvára ◻ GR 47 Mf55
Aguirre Cerda ◻ ANT (RCH)
6 Gd31
Aguja, Cerro □ RA/RCH 210
Ge67
Aguinaldo ◻ RP 90 Ra37
Aguirre Cerda ◻ ANT (RCH)
Aguja, Cerro □ RA/RCH 210
Aguçadoura □ P 26 Km49
Agunj-jima □ J 79 Rd32
Aguní-jima □ J 79 Rd32
Agustinópolis ◻ BR (TO)
200 HH48
Aigawa Island ◻ RP 90 Ra40
Agva ◻ TR 45 Mk49
Agwarra ◻ WAN 138 Lc41
Agweri ◻ WAN 138 Ld40
Agwit ◻ SUD 141 Md41
Ahaberge ◻ NAM 151 Mb55
Ahad Rafidah ◻ KSA 60 Nb36
Aha Hills ◻ RB 151 Mb55
Ahakeye (Ti-Tree) A.L. ◙ AUS
103 Rg57
Aharan ◻ IR 57 Nd26
Ahar ◻ IR 57 Nd26
Ahaus ◻ D 32 Lh38
Åheim ◻ N 17 Lc14
Ahenkto ◻ GH 137 La42
Ahero ◻ EAK 144 Mh46
Ahipara Bay ◻ NZ 112 Tg63
Ahitii ◻ NZ 113 Th65
Ahlaf ◻ RIM 130 Kf37
Ahladiá ◻ GR 45 Me49
Ahladóri ◻ GR 44 Md49
Ahlainen ◻ FIN 38 Mb29
Ahlainen ◻ FIN 38 Mb29
Ahlbeck ◻ D 32 Lp37
Ahlen ◻ D 32 Lh39
Ahmadi ◻ KWT 59 Ne31
Ahmadnagar ◻ IND (MHT) 82 Oj36
Ahmadpur ◻ PK 65 Of30
Ahmadpur East ◻ PK 65 Of31
Ahmad Shah Durrani Tomb ◙
AFG 65 Od29
Ahmad Wal ◻ PK 65 Oc31
Ahmar Mountains ◻ ETH
142 Na41
Ahmedabad ◻ IND (GUJ) 82
Og34
Ahmednagar ◻ IND (MHT)
82 Oh36
Ahmeti ◻ TR 47 Mh52
Ahoada ◻ WAN 138 Ld43
Ahome ◻ MEX (SL) 180 Ee33
Ahoskie ◻ USA (NC) 178 Gb27
Ahram ◻ IR 59 Nf31
Ahrensbök ◻ D 32 Ll37
Ahrensburg ◻ D 32 Ll37
Ahsu ◻ AZ 57 Nd25
Ahtamar ◻ TR 57 Nb26
Ähtäri ◻ FIN 38 Me28
Ahtari ◻ FIN 38 Mh31
Ahtopol ◻ BG 45 Mh48
Ahu ◻ IRQ (UPH) 81 Oh32
Ahu ◻ RP 91 Rc42
Ahu ◻ IR 59 Ne30
Ahuacapan ◻ ES 184 Ff39
Ahualulco de Mercado ◻ MEX
(JLC) 182 Ej35
Ahuano ◻ EC 196 Gb46
Ahuas ◻ HN 185 Fh38
Ahuasbila ◻ HN 185 Fh38
Ahun ◻ F 25 Lc44
Ahus ◻ RI 94 Oj44
Ahvar ◻ IR 59 Ne30
Ahvenanmaa = Åland □ FIN
38 Lu30
Ai ◻ IND (GUJ) 82 Of35
Aihava ◻ YE 60 Nd39
Ai-Ais Hot Springs ◙ NAM
154 Lj59
Ai-Ais Warmwaterbronne ◙ NAM
154 Lj59
Aiaktalik Island ◻ USA 164 Cd17
Aiapuá ◻ BR (AM) 198 Gj46
Aiawete Igarapé Ipixuna, T.I. ◙
BR 199 Hd48
Aibar ◻ E 28 Kt48
Aibonito ◻ USA (PR) 195 Gg36
Aichach ◻ D 33 Lm42
Aiduna ◻ RI 114 Rh48
Aiere ◻ WAN 138 Lc42
Aigamas Caves ◙ NAM 150 Lj55
Aigen ◻ A 35 Lp42
Aigen mekeni ◻ KZ 63 Oe23
Aigialii ◻ GR 47 Mf54
Aígina ◻ □ GR 46 Md53
Aígina □ GR 46 Md53
Aígio ◻ GR 46 Mc52
Aigle ◻ CH 34 Lg44
Aigoual, le-Duc ◻ F 25 Ld46
Aigrefeuille-d'Aunis ◻ F 24 Ku44
Aigua ◻ ROU 209 Hc63
Aiguá ◻ ROU 209 Hc63
Aiguebelle, P.N. d' ◙ CDN
173 Ga21
Aigues-Mortes ◻ □ F 25 Le47
Aiguilles de Sindou ◙ BF
138 Kh40
Aiguille du Midi ◻ F 34 Lg45
Aiguilles ◻ F 34 Lg46
Aiguilles de Sindou ◙ BF
138 Kh40
Aiha ◻ SUD 141 Mf41
Ailao Shan ◻ CHN 87 Qa34
Aileron ◻ AUS (NT) 108 Rg57
Ailigandi ◻ PA 185 Ga41
Ailinglaplap Atoll □ MH 10 Ta09
Ailly-sur-Noye ◻ F 23 Lc41

Aguja, Cerro □ RA/RCH 210
Akkeshi ◻ J 77 Sc24
„Akko" ◻ □ IL 56 Mh29
Akkol ◻ KZ 63 Of24
Akkoursoulbak ◻ RCA 140 Ma41
Akköy ◻ TR 56 Mg26
Akköy ◻ TR 47 Mh53
Ak Kupruk = Keshendeh ◻ AFG
63 Od27
Akkus ◻ TR 56 Mj25
Aklampa ◻ DY 138 Lb41
Aklera ◻ IND (RJT) 82 Oj33
Akmektep ◻ KZ 66 Pb22
Akmola ◻ KZ 63 Oe22
Akmenrags ◻ LV 39 Mb34
Akmeqit ◻ CHN (XUZ) 66 Og27
Akniste ◻ LV 39 Mf34
Aknoul ◻ MA 125 Kj29
Ako ◻ J 79 Rh28
Akodiya ◻ IND (MPH) 82 Oh34
Akokan ◻ RN 132 Ld37
Akoke ◻ SUD 141 Mj47
Akoko ◻ SUD 141 Mf41
Akokpo ◻ SUD 141 Me41
Akola ◻ IND (MHT) 82 Oj35
Akolica ◻ BY 39 Mh36
Akoma ◻ PNG 115 Sc49
Akonio ◻ CAM 139 Li44
Akonolinga ◻ CAM 139 Lg44
Akop ◻ SUD 141 Me41
Akorabi ◻ GUY 194 Ha43
Akordat ◻ ER 142 Mj38
Akören ◻ TR 56 Mg27
Akören ◻ TR 57 Kk43
Akosombo ◻ GH 137 Kk43
Akosombo Dam ◙ □ GH
137 La42
Akot ◻ IND (MHT) 82 Oj35
Akot ◻ SUD 141 Mf42
Akoupé ◻ CI 137 Kj43
Akpara □ TG 137 La42
Akpinar ◻ TR 56 Mg26
Akplabnya ◻ GH 137 La43
Akqi ◻ CHN (XUZ) 66 Og25
Akrabah ◻ TM 62 Oa26
Akraberg ◻ FR (DK) 18 Kp29
Akrahamn ◻ N 30 Lf31
Akrai ◻ I 37 Lp53
Akranes ◻ IS 18 Js26
Ak ◻ IRQ 57 Nb27
Åkrehamn ◻ N 30 Lf31
Åkrestrømmen ◻ N 17 Lf15
Akrîtiri ◻ GR 47 Mf55
Akropolis ◙ □ GR 47 Md53
Akropolis ◙ GR 47 Md53
Akropong ◻ GH 137 Kk43
Akrotíri ◻ □ GR 47 Mf55
Akrotíri Agios Ioánnis ◻ GR
47 Mf55
Akrotíri Ákrathos ◻ GR 45 Me50
Akrotíri Araxos ◻ GR 46 Mb52
Akrotíri Doukáto ◻ GR 46 Ma52
Akrotíri Drépano ◻ GR 45 Md51
Akrotíri Kassándra ◻ GR 44
Md51
Akrotíri Kilini ◻ GR 46 Mb53
Akrotíri Kithnos ◻ GR 46 Me53
Akrotíri Kriós ◻ GR 45 Md55
Akrotíri Lithino ◻ GR 47 Mf55
Akrotíri Maléas ◻ GR 46 Md54
Akrotíri Murzeflos ◻ GR 47 Mf51
Akrotíri Palioúri ◻ GR 45 Me51
Akrotíri Sidonikiós ◻ GR 45
Me52
Akrotíri Soúnio ◻ GR 47 Me53
Akrotíri Ténaro ◻ GR 46 Mc54
Aksla ◻ RUS 70 Qb28
Aksaj ◻ RUS 49 Mk22
Aksakal ◻ TR 56 Mh26
Aksakovo ◻ RUS 53 Nh09
Aksay ◻ CHN (GSU) 69 Ph26
Aksay ◻ CHN 68 Pd28
Aksdal ◻ N 30 Lf31
Aksehir ◻ TR 56 Mf27
Aseki ◻ TR 56 Mf27
Akshyghanak ◻ KZ 63 Oe24
Aksoran tau ◻ KZ 66 Oh21
Ajoda ◻ WAN 138 Lc43
Aksaj ◻ MEX (SL) 180 Eg33
Aksu ◻ CHN (XUZ) 66 Og25
Aksu ◻ KZ 63 Of24
Aksu ◻ KZ 67 Pb21
Aksu Canyon ◻ KZ 63 Of24
Aksum ◙ ETH 142 Mk38
Ashutayic royal city of Kohaito ◙
ER 142 Mk38
Aku-Zhabaghly Nature Reserve
◙ KZ 63 Of23
Ak-Syjak ◻ KS 66 Oh25
Ak Tag ◻ CHN 68 Pc27
Ak-Tal ◻ KS 66 Oh25
Ak-Eze □ WAN 138 Lf43
Akterek ◻ KZ 66 Oh23
Aktogaj ◻ KZ 63 Oe22
Aktogaj ◻ KZ 66 Oj22
Aktogay ◻ KZ 66 Oh23
Aktsé ◻ SUD 142 Mh42
Aktsé ◻ SUD 142 Mh42
Aktobe ◻ KZ 63 Of22
Aktobe ◻ KZ 63 Oe21
Aktubinsk ◻ RUS 63 Nj21
Aku ◻ N 17 Lt15
Akure ◻ WAN 138 Lc42
Akureyri ◻ IS 18 Kb25
Akuseki-jima □ J 79 Re31
Akutukpa ◻ WAN 138 Le43
Hávi ◻ GR 47 Mf55
Akyab = Sittwe ◻ MYA 86 Pg35
Akyáka ◻ GUY 194 Ha43
Akyazi ◻ TR 56 Mf25
Akzhal ◻ KZ 66 Oh23
Akzhar ◻ KZ 66 Oh23
Akzhar ◻ KZ 66 Oh23
Al A'amiyah ◻ IRQ 57 Nc29
Al-Anan Balusa ◻ KSA 60 Nb37
Ala-Archa Canyon ◻ □ KS
66 Oh24
Ala-Archa N.P. ⓝ KS 66 Oh24
Alabama □ USA 175 Fg29
Alabama and Coushatta Ind. Res.
◙ USA 174 Fc30
Alabaster Island ◙ RP 90 Rb38
al-'Abbasiya ◻ LAR 127 Lk30
Alabel ◻ RP 91 Rc42
Al Abu ◻ KSA 60 Na35
Ala-Buka ◻ KS 63 Og24
Alacahöyük ◙ TR 56 Mh25
Alaçam ◻ TR 56 Mh25
Alaca ◻ TR 56 Mh25
Alaca Dağlari ◻ TR 47 Mj53
Alaçatı ◻ TR 47 Mg52
Alaçatı ◻ TR 47 Mg52
Alagir ◻ RUS (SOA) 57 Nc24
Alagna Valésia ◻ I 34 Lh45

Amélie-les-Bains ☐ F 24 Lc48
Amelinghausen ☐ D 32 Lf37
Amélioland ☐ F 24 Lc44
Amelup ☐ AUS (WA) 104 Qk63
Amendolara ☐ I 37 Lr51
Ameng ☐ CHN (YUN) 87 Qc34
Amentego ☐ SUD 135 Mf36
Ameri ☐ IR 59 Nf30
America ☐ BR (AM) 198 Gh49
Americana ☐ BR (SP) 203 Hg57
American Falls ☐ USA (ID) 168 Ed24
American Fork ☐ USA (UT) 171 Ee25
American Samoa ☐ USA 101 Bb11
Americus ☐ USA (GA) 175 Fh29
Amersfoort ☐ NL 23 Lf38
Amersfoort ☐ ZA 155 Me59
Amery ☐ ANT (AUS) 7 Oc32
Ameya ☐ ETH 142 Mj42
Amfiklia ☐ GR 46 Mc53
Amfilohia ☐ GR 46 Mb52
Amfissa ☐ GR 46 Mc52
Amfiteatri ☐ AL 44 Lu49
Amga ☐ RUS 55 Rc06
Amga ☐ RUS 55 Rc06
Amgala ☐ DARS 124 Ke32
Amgaon ☐ IND (MHR) 83 Pa35
Amgu ☐ RUS 77 Rj23
Amguid ☐ DZ 126 Le33
Amherst ☐ CDN (NS) 86 Ph32
Amherst = Kyaikkami ☐ MYA 88 Pj37
Amherst ☐ USA 177 Gd24
Amhertzburg ☐ CDN (ON) 173 Fj24

Ariguani ☐ CO 192 Gc41
Ariha ☐ JOR 58 Mh30
Ariha ☐ SYR 56 Mj28
Arikawa ☐ J 79 Re29
Arikok N.P. ☐ NL 192 Gf39
Arilje ☐ SCG 44 Ma47
Arima ☐ TT 187 Gk34
Arimu Mine ☐ GUY 194 Ha42
Arinagour ☐ GB 20 Ko34
Aringay ☐ RP 90 Ra37
Ariniş ☐ RO 43 Md43
Arinos ☐ BR (MG) 203 Hg53
Arinos ☐ BR 199 Hb51
Arinthod ☐ F 25 Lf44
Ariogala ☐ LT 39 Md35
Aripuana ☐ BR (MT) 199 Ha50
Aripuaná ☐ BR 199 Gk48
Aripuaná, T.I. ☐ BR 199 Gj50
Ariquemes ☐ BR (RO) 198 Gj50
Ariquida ☐ RCH 206 Gf55
Ariranha ☐ BR (AM) 199 Ha48
Aris ☐ NAM 150 Lj57
Arisaig ☐ GB 20 Ko34
Ariseman Ancient City ☐ IR 64 Ng29
Arismendi ☐ YV 193 Gf41
Arissa ☐ ETH 142 Na40
Aristazabal Island ☐ CDN 166 Df19
Aristóbulo del Valle ☐ RA (MI) 204 Hc59
Aritao ☐ RP 90 Ra37
Arite ☐ SOL 117 Ta50
Aritzo ☐ I 36 Lk51
Arivonimamo ☐ RM 157 Nd55
Ariyalur ☐ IND (TNU) 85 Ok40
Ariza ☐ E 29 Ks49
Arizona ☐ AUS (QLD) 107 Sa55
Arizona ☐ RA (SL) 208 Gh53
Arizona ☐ USA 171 Ed29
Arizona Pioneer Living History Museum ☐ USA 171 Ee29
Arizona Sonora Desert Museum ☐ USA 171 Ee29
Arizpe ☐ MEX (SO) 180 Ee30
'Arjah ☐ KSA 59 Nc31
Ärjäng ☐ S 30 Ln31
Arjan Lake ☐ IR 64 Ng31
Arjeplog ☐ S 16 Lj12
Arjo ☐ ETH 142 Mj41
Arjona ☐ CO 192 Gc40
Arjona ☐ E 27 Kq53
Arjuni ☐ IND (CGH) 83 Pb35
Arkadak ☐ RUS 48 Nb18
Arkadelphia ☐ USA (AR) 174 Fd28
Arkadia ☐ PL 41 Ma38
Arkalyk ☐ KZ 54 Ob08
Arkansas ☐ USA 174 Ek27
Arkansas ☐ USA 174 Fc27
Arkansas City ☐ USA (AR) 175 Fe29
Arkansas City ☐ USA (KS) 174 Fb27
Arkássa ☐ GR 47 Mh55
Arkatag ☐ CHN 68 Pd27
Arkell, Mount ☐ CDN 166 Dc15
Arkesini ☐ GR 47 Mf54
Arkhangay ☐ MNG 70 Pk22
Arkhut ☐ IND (TNU) 84 Oj39
Arki ☐ IND (HP) 80 Oh31
Arkitsa ☐ GR 44 Md52
Arklow ☐ IRL 19 Ko38
Arkö ☐ S 31 Lr32
Arkösund ☐ S 31 Lr32
Arkoudi ☐ GR 46 Mc52
Arktikum ☐ FIN 16 Mc12
Ärla ☐ S 31 Lr31
Arlanc ☐ F 25 Ld45
Arles ☐ F 25 Le47
Arli ☐ BF 137 La40
Arlit ☐ RN 132 Ld36
Arlon ☐ B 23 Lf41
Arma ☐ GR 45 Md52
Arma ☐ PE 197 Gc52
Armadale ☐ AUS (WA) 104 Qj62
Armagh ☐ GB 19 Ko36
Armando Bermúdez, P.N. ☐ DOM 186 Ge36
Armant ☐ ET 129 Mg33
Armenia ☐ ARM 57 Nc25
Armenia ☐ CO 192 Gc43
Armenis ☐ RO 44 Mc45
Armentières ☐ F 23 Lc40
Armidale ☐ AUS (NSW) 109 Sf61
Armijo ☐ USA (NM) 171 Eg28
Arminto ☐ USA (WY) 169 Eg24
Armjans'k ☐ UA 49 Mg22
Armori ☐ IND (MHT) 83 Ok35
Armour ☐ USA (SD) 172 Fa24
Armraynald ☐ AUS (QLD) 107 Rk55
Armstrong ☐ CDN (ON) 172 Ff20
Armstrong ☐ RA (SF) 209 Gk62
Armur ☐ IND (APD) 82 Ok36
Armutlu ☐ TR 47 Mg51
Arnautovo ☐ TR 47 Mg51
Arnac-Pompadour ☐ F 24 Lb45
Arnavutli ☐ S 38 Lf27
Arnavutköy ☐ TR 47 Mh50
Arnay-le-Duc ☐ F 25 Le43
Arnéa ☐ GR 45 Md50
Arnedo ☐ E 28 Ks48
Arneroz ☐ BR (CE) 201 Hk49
Årnes ☐ IS 18 Jt25
Årnes ☐ N 30 Lm30
Arnett ☐ USA (OK) 174 Fa27
Arnhem ☐ NL 23 Lf39
Arnhem Bay ☐ AUS 106 Rj52
Arnhem Cave ☐ NAM 154 Lk57
Arnhem Land ☐ AUS 106 Rg52
Arnhem Land Aboriginal Reserve ☐ AUS 106 Rh52
Arni ☐ IND (TNU) 85 Ok40
Arnissa ☐ GR 46 Mc50
Arno ☐ AUS (QLD) 109 Sb58
Arno ☐ S 31 Lq32
Arno ☐ USA (ID) 109 Sb58
Arnold ☐ USA (MO) 175 Fe26
Arnsberg ☐ D 32 Lj39
Arnstadt ☐ D 32 Ll40
Arnstein ☐ D 33 Lk41
Arnfield ☐ CDN (QC) 173 Ga21
Aroa ☐ YV 193 Gf40
Aroab ☐ NAM 154 Lk58
Aroland ☐ CDN (ON) 173 Fg20
Aroma ☐ PNG 116 Se61
Aroma ☐ SUD 135 Mg38
Aron ☐ IND (MPH) 82 Oj32
Arona ☐ I 34 Lj45
Aroostook Hist. & Art Mus. ☐ USA 176 Gf22
Aropa ☐ PNG 117 Se57
Arorae ☐ KIR 120 Tb11
Arosa ☐ CH 34 Lk44
Arosbaya ☐ RI 95 Qg49
Äreysund ☐ N 30 Li31
Arpajon le Norville ☐ F 23 Lc42
Arpaşu de Jos ☐ RO 43 Me45
Arpino ☐ I 36 Lo49
Arqu ☐ SUD 135 Mf36

Bachmač ⬛ UA 48 Mg20
Bacho ⬛ THA 89 Qa42
Bachórz ⬛ PL 41 Mc41
Bach Thong ⬛ VN 87 Qc34
Bachu ⬛ CHN (XUZ) 66 Ok26
Bachuo ⬛ CAM 138 Le43
Bačina ⬛ SCG 44 Md47
Baciu ⬛ RO 43 Md44
Baciuty ⬛ PL 41 Mc37
Bačka Palanka ⬛ SCG 44 Lu45
Bačka Topola ⬛ SCG 44 Lu45
Back Bay N.W.R. ⬛ USA 178 Gc27
Backbone Ranges ⬛ CDN 166 Df14
Bäckebo ⬛ S 31 Lr34
Bäckefors ⬛ S 30 Ln32
Bachhammar ⬛ S 31 Lp31
Backnang ⬛ D 33 Lk42
Bačko Novo Selo ⬛ SCG 44 Lu45
Bačkovski manastir ⬛ BG 45 Me49
Backstairs Passage ⬛ AUS 110 Rk63
Backwaters ⬛ IND 84 Oj41
Bac Lieu ⬛ VN 89 Qc41
Bac Ninh ⬛ VN 87 Qd35
Bacnotan ⬛ RP 90 Ra39
Baco ⬛ RP 90 Ra39
Bacoachi ⬛ MEX (SO) 180 Ef30
Bacobampo ⬛ MEX (SO) 180 Ef32
Bacolod ⬛ RP 90 Rb40
Bacon ⬛ RP 90 Rc39
Baconao, P.N. ⬛ C 186 Gc36
Bacopari ⬛ BR (RS) 205 He61
Bacoparé ⬛ RP 90 Rc41
Bacuit Archipel ⬛ RP 90 Qk40
Bacungan ⬛ RP 90 Ra40
Bacuri ⬛ BR (MA) 195 Hh46
Bacuritinha ⬛ BR (MA) 195 Hh46
Bacurizinho, T.I. ⬛ BR 200 Hh48
Bada ⬛ RUS 70 Qe20
Bada Barabil ⬛ IND (ORS) 83 Pc34
Badagangshan Z.B. ⬛ CHN 74 Qe31
Badagiri ⬛ WAN 138 Ld42
Bad Abling ⬛ D 33 Lm43
Badai-Tugai Nature Reserve ⬛ UZ 62 Oa25
Badajós ⬛ BR (AM) 198 Gj47
Badaling ⬛ CHN 73 Qh25
Badalona ⬛ E 29 Lc49
Badami ⬛ IND (KTK) 82 Oh38
Badami ⬛ IND 82 Oh38
Badanga ⬛ TCH 139 Lj40
Bad Arolsen ⬛ D 32 Lk39
Bad Aussee ⬛ A 35 Lo43
Bad Axe ⬛ USA (MI) 173 Fj24
Bad Bederkesa ⬛ D 32 Lj37
Bad Bentheim ⬛ D 32 Lh38
Bad Bergzabern ⬛ D 33 Lj41
Bad Berka ⬛ D 32 Lm40
Bad Bevensen ⬛ D 32 Ll32
Bad Bibra ⬛ D 32 Ln39
Bad Bramstedt ⬛ D 32 Lk37
Bad Brückenau ⬛ D 33 Lk40
Bad Camberg ⬛ D 33 Lj40
Bad Gleichenberg ⬛ A 35 Lq44
Bad Griesbach ⬛ D 33 Lo42
Bad Hall ⬛ A 42 Lp42
Bad Hersfeld ⬛ D 32 Lk40
Bad Hofgastein ⬛ A 35 Lo43
Bad Homburg ⬛ D 33 Lj40
Bad Honnef ⬛ D 32 Lh40
Bad Iburg ⬛ E 29 Lc51
Badiakanam ⬛ GH 137 Kk42
Badiar, P.N. de ⬛ RG 136 Kd39
Badme ⬛ ETH 142 Mj38
Badir ⬛ PK 65 Oe31
Badiraguato ⬛ MEX (SL) 180 Eg33
Bad Ischl ⬛ A 35 Lo43
Badjao-Seanomads ⬛ RP 91 Qk43
Badjer ⬛ CAM 139 Lg42
Bad Karlshafen ⬛ D 32 Lk39
Badkhyz Nature Reserve ⬛ TM 62 Oa28
Bad Kissingen ⬛ D 33 Ll40
Bad Kleinen ⬛ D 32 Lm37
Bad Königshofen ⬛ D 33 Ll40
Bad Kreuznach ⬛ D 33 Lh41
Bad Laasphe ⬛ D 32 Lj40
Badlands ⬛ USA 169 Ej24
Badlands N.P. ⬛ USA 169 Ej24
Bad Langensalza ⬛ D 32 Ll39
Badlapur ⬛ IND (UPH) 83 Pb33
Bad Lausick ⬛ D 32 Ln39
Bad Lauterberg ⬛ D 32 Ll39
Bad Leonfelden ⬛ A 42 Lp42
Bad Liebenwerda ⬛ D 32 Lo39
Bad Mergentheim ⬛ D 33 Lk41
Bad Münstereifel ⬛ D 32 Lg40
Bad Muskau ⬛ D 32 Lp39
Bad Nauheim ⬛ D 33 Lj40
Badnawar ⬛ IND (MPH) 82 Oh34
Badnor ⬛ IND (MHT) 82 Og33
Bad Neuenahr-Ahrweiler ⬛ D 32 Lh40
Bad Neustadt ⬛ D 33 Ll40
Bad Oeynhausen ⬛ D 32 Lj38
Bad Oldesloe ⬛ D 32 Ll37
Badong ⬛ CHN (HUB) 74 Qf30
Ba Dong ⬛ VN 89 Qd41
Badonville ⬛ F 23 Lg42
Badou ⬛ TG 137 La42
Badoumbé ⬛ RMM 136 Kd40
Badoussa ⬛ DZ 125 La39
Badplaas Mineral Spring ⬛ ZA 155 Mf58
Bad Pyrmont ⬛ D 32 Lk39
Bad Radkersburg ⬛ A 35 Lq44
Badrah ⬛ IRQ 59 Nc29
Badrah ⬛ PK 65 Od32
Bad Reichenhall ⬛ D 33 Ln43
Bad Hunayn ⬛ KSA 58 Mj37
Badrinath ⬛ IND (UTT) 81 Ok32
Badrinath ⬛ IND 81 Ok30

Bad River Ind. Res. ⬛ USA 172 Fc22
Bad Säckingen ⬛ D 33 Lh43
Bad Salzuflen ⬛ D 32 Lj38
Bad Salzungen ⬛ D 32 Ll40
Bad Sankt Leonhard ⬛ A 35 Lp44
Bad Saulgau ⬛ D 33 Lk42
Bad Schönborn ⬛ D 33 Lj41
Bad Schwalbach ⬛ D 33 Lj40
Bad Schwartau ⬛ D 32 Ll37
Bad Segeberg ⬛ D 32 Ll37
Bad Sobernheim ⬛ D 33 Lh41
Bad Sülze ⬛ D 32 Ln36
Bad Tölz ⬛ D 33 Lm43
Badu ⬛ CHN (JGX) 75 Qh32
Badu Island ⬛ AUS 107 Sb51
Badulla ⬛ CL 85 Pa42
Badvel ⬛ IND (APH) 85 Ok38
Bad Vöslau ⬛ A 35 Lr43
Bad Waldsee ⬛ D 33 Lk43
Bad Wildungen ⬛ D 32 Lk39
Bad Wurzach ⬛ D 33 Lk43
Badzéré ⬛ CAM 139 Lh43
Baedaem ⬛ RIM 130 Ke38
Baena ⬛ E 27 Kq53
Baependi ⬛ BR (MG) 203 Hh57
Baeza ⬛ EC 196 Gb46
Bafang ⬛ CAM 139 Lf43
Bafatá ⬛ GNB 136 Kc39
Baffin Basin ⬛ 163 Gd04
Baffin Bay ⬛ 163 Gc04
Baffin Island ⬛ CDN 163 Ga04
Bafia ⬛ TG 137 La41
Bafing ⬛ RG 136 Ke40
Bafing ⬛ RMM 136 Ke39
Bafing-Makana ⬛ RMM 136 Ke39
Bafodia ⬛ WAL 136 Ke41
Bafoulabé ⬛ RMM 136 Kd40
Bafoussam ⬛ CAM 138 Lf43
Bafra ⬛ TR 64 Nh30
Bafra Burnu ⬛ TR 56 Mh25
Baft ⬛ IR 64 Nj31
Bafu Bay Town ⬛ LB 136 Kf43
Bafut ⬛ CAM 138 Lf42
Bafwabalinga ⬛ RDC 141 Md45
Bafwabogbo ⬛ RDC 141 Md45
Bafwasende ⬛ RDC 141 Md45
Baga ⬛ WAN 138 Lh40
Bagaces ⬛ CR 185 Fh40
Bagagem ⬛ RP 90 Ra37
Bagabag Island ⬛ PNG 115 Sd48
Bagamanoc ⬛ RP 90 Rc39
Bagamoyo ⬛ EAT 147 Mk49
Bagan ⬛ MYA 86 Ph35
Bagandou ⬛ RCA 140 Lj44
Baganga ⬛ RP 91 Rd42
Bagani ⬛ NAM 151 Ma55
Bagansiapiapi ⬛ RI 93 Qa44
Bagansinembah ⬛ RI 93 Qa44
Baganuur ⬛ MNG 70 Qe22
Bāgarasi ⬛ TR 47 Mh53
Bagaré ⬛ BF 137 Kk40
Bagaroua ⬛ RN 132 Lc38
Baga Sola ⬛ TCH 133 Lh39
Bagassi ⬛ BF 137 Kk40
Bagata ⬛ BF 137 Kk40
Bagata ⬛ RDC 149 Lj47
Bagdad ⬛ USA (AZ) 171 Ed28
Bagdad ⬛ GE 57 Nb25
Bagdogra ⬛ IND (WBG) 86 Pe32
Bagé ⬛ BR (RS) 204 He61
Bag-e-Eram ⬛ IR 64 Ng31
Bagega ⬛ WAN 138 Lc40
Bag-e Malek ⬛ IR 59 Ne30
Bagenalstown ⬛ IRL 19 Ko38
Bagepalli ⬛ IND (KTK) 84 Oj39
Bagerhat ⬛ BD 86 Pe34
Bageya ⬛ WAN 138 Lh40
Bagla ⬛ CHN (GZH) 74 Qd22
Baggs ⬛ USA (WY) 171 Eg25
Baghain ⬛ IND (MPH) 82 Oh34
Baghdad ⬛ IRQ 57 Nc29
Bagh-e-Chenar ⬛ IR 64 Nj31
Baghel Boland ⬛ IR 59 Ne30
Baghelkhand Plateau ⬛ IND 83 Pb34
Bagheria ⬛ I 36 Lo52
Baghin ⬛ IR 64 Nj30
Baghlan ⬛ AFG 63 Oe27
Bagienice ⬛ PL 41 Mc37
Bagnan ⬛ IND (ASM) 86 Pg32
Bagnara Cálabra ⬛ I 37 Lq52
Bagnacavallo ⬛ I 34 Lm46
Bagnères-de-Bigorre ⬛ F 24 Lb48
Bagnères-de-Luchon ⬛ F 24 Lb48
Bagni Contursi ⬛ I 37 Lq50
Bagno di Romagna ⬛ I 34 Lm47
Bagno Lavoir, P.L. ⬛ PL 41 Mc37
Bagnoles-de-l'Orne ⬛ F 22 Ku42
Bagnoli del Trigno ⬛ I 37 Lp49
Bagnols-sur-Cèze ⬛ F 25 Le46
Bago ⬛ RP 90 Rb40
Bagodar ⬛ IND (JKD) 83 Pc33
Bagodara ⬛ IND (GUJ) 82 Og34
Bagoé ⬛ CI 137 Kh41
Bagolino ⬛ I 34 Ll45
Bagoso ⬛ GH 137 Kj43
Bago Yoma ⬛ MYA 86 Ph36
Bagpat ⬛ IND (UPH) 81 Oj31
Bagrami ⬛ AFG 65 Oe28
Bagrationovsk = Eylau ⬛ PL 41 Ma36
Bagua ⬛ BR (PA) 195 He46
Bagsara ⬛ IND (GUJ) 82 Of35
Bagua Grande ⬛ PE 196 Ga48
Baguineda ⬛ RMM 137 Kg39
Baguio ⬛ RP 90 Ra37
Baguirmi ⬛ TCH 139 Lj40
Bagulhaghat ⬛ IND (ASM)
Bagyurda ⬛ TR 47 Mh52
Bahadur Abad ⬛ IR 64 Ng31
Bahadurganj ⬛ IND (BIH) 83 Pd32
Bahala ⬛ IND (ORS) 83 Pd34
Bahama Islands ⬛ 179 Gb32
Bahamas ⬛ 179
Bahí ⬛ ET 129 Me31
Baharia Oasis ⬛ ET 129 Me31
Baharu ⬛ IR 64 Ng31
Bahaur ⬛ RI 95 Qh47
Bahawalnagar ⬛ PK 65 Oh31
Bahawalpur ⬛ PK 65 Of31
Baheri ⬛ IR 57 Ne28
Baherí ⬛ IND (UPH) 81 Ok31
Bahía Adventure ⬛ RCH 210
Bahía Aguirre ⬛ RA/RCH 210 Gg73
Bahía Algodones ⬛ MEX 181 Fb33

Bahia Anegada ⬛ RA 209 Gj66
Bahía Blanca ⬛ MEX 180 Ec31
Bahía Blanca ⬛ RA (BA) 209 Gj65
Bahía Bufadero ⬛ MEX (MHC) 182 Ej36
Bahía Bustamante ⬛ RA (CB) 210 Gg68
Bahía Camarones ⬛ RA 210 Gg63
Bahía Chanco ⬛ RCH 208 Gd68
Bahía Chiquinta ⬛ RCH 206 Ge56
Bahía Colonet ⬛ MEX 180 Eb30
Bahía Conchalí ⬛ RCH 208 Ge61
Bahía Cook ⬛ RCH 210 Ge73
Bahía Coyote ⬛ RA (RN) 209 Gj66
Bahía Creek ⬛ RA (RN) 209 Gj66
Bahía Culebra ⬛ CR 184 Fh40
Bahía Darwin ⬛ RCH 210 Gc68
Bahía de Adair ⬛ MEX 180 Ed30
Bahía de Amatique ⬛ GCA 184 Ff38
Bahía de Banderas ⬛ MEX 182 Eh35
Bahía de Bluefields ⬛ NIC 185 Fj41
Bahía de Buenaventura ⬛ CO 192 Gb44
Bahía de Caballos ⬛ PE 197
Bahía de Caráquez ⬛ EC 196 Fk46
Bahía de Chetumal ⬛ MEX 183 Fg36
Bahía de Coronado ⬛ CR 185 Fj41
Bahía de Corrientes ⬛ C 179 Fh35
Bahía de Guadiana ⬛ C 179 Fh34
Bahía de Independencia ⬛ PE 197 Gb53
Bahía de la Ascensión ⬛ MEX 183 Fg36
Bahía del Espíritu Santo ⬛ MEX 183 Fg36
Bahía de Lobos ⬛ MEX (SO) 180 Ee32
Bahía de Loreto, P.N. ⬛ MEX (BCS) 180 Ee32
Bahía de los Angeles ⬛ MEX (BCN) 180 Ed31
Bahía de Manta ⬛ EC 196 Fk46
Bahía de Mejillones del Sur ⬛ RCH 207 Ge57
Bahía de Ocoa ⬛ DOM 186 Ge36
Bahía de Omoa ⬛ HN 184 Ff38
Bahía de Paita ⬛ PE 196 Fk48
Bahía de Palmas ⬛ MEX 180 Ef34
Bahía de Panamá ⬛ PA 185 Ga41
Bahía de Paracas ⬛ PE 197 Gb52
Bahía de Portete ⬛ CO 192 Gd39
Bahía de Salinas ⬛ PE 197 Gb51
Bahía de Samaná ⬛ DOM 186 Gf36
Bahía de San Esteban ⬛ MEX 180 Ef33
Bahía de San Quintín ⬛ MEX 180 Eb30
Bahía de Santa Elena ⬛ CR 184 Fh40
Bahía de Santa Elena ⬛ EC 196 Fk46
Bahía de Santa Ines ⬛ MEX 180 Ee32
Bahía de Santa María ⬛ MEX 180 Ef33
Bahía de Sechura ⬛ PE 196 Fk48
Bahía de Sepetiba ⬛ BR 205 Hh57
Bahía de Tablazo ⬛ YV 192 Ge40
Bahía de Tela ⬛ HN 184 Fg38
Bahía de Tepoca ⬛ MEX 180 Ed31
Bahía de Tortugas ⬛ MEX (BCS) 180 Ec32
Bahía Elizabeth ⬛ EC
Bahía Engaño ⬛ RA 210 Gh67
Bahía Escocesa ⬛ DOM 186 Gf36
Bahía Grande ⬛ RA 210 Gf71
Bahía Honda ⬛ C 179 Fj34
Bahía Honda ⬛ CO 192 Ge39
Bahía Inútil ⬛ RCH 210 Gf72
Bahía Kino ⬛ MEX (SO) 180 Ee32
Bahía Laura ⬛ RA (SC) 210 Gg70
Bahía Lomas ⬛ RCH 210 Gf72
Bahía Magdalena ⬛ MEX 180 Ed33
Bahía Mansa ⬛ RCH 208 Gd66
Bahía Maullín ⬛ RCH 208 Gd66
Bahía Morena ⬛ RCH 207 Ge57
Bahía Nassau ⬛ RCH 210 Gg73
Bahía Negra ⬛ PY 206 Ha56
Bahía Nuestra Señora ⬛ RCH 207 Ge58
Bahía Otway ⬛ RCH 210 Ge72
Bahía Posesión ⬛ RCH 210 Gf72
Bahía Puerto de Lobos ⬛ MEX 180 Ed30
Bahía Punta Gorda ⬛ NIC 185 Fj41
Bahía Rosario ⬛ MEX 180 Ec31
Bahía Salado ⬛ RCH 208 Ge59
Bahía Salvación ⬛ RCH 210 Gc71
Bahía Samborombón ⬛ RA 209 Hb63
Bahía San Blas ⬛ RA (BA) 209 Gj66
Bahía San Carlos ⬛ MEX 180 Ec31
Bahía San Felipe ⬛ RCH 210 Gf72
Bahía San Jorge ⬛ MEX 180 Ed30
Bahía San Luis Gonzaga ⬛ MEX 180 Ee31
Bahía San Nicolás ⬛ PE 197 Gc53
Bahía San Sebastián ⬛ RA 210 Gf72
Bahía San Vicente ⬛ RCH 208 Gd64
Bahías de Huatulco, P.N. ⬛ MEX 182 Fb37
Bahía Sebastián Vizcaíno ⬛ MEX 180 Ec31
Bahía Solano ⬛ CO 192 Gb42
Bahía Stokes ⬛ RCH 210 Gd72
Bahía Vera ⬛ RA 210 Gh68
Bahii ⬛ ET 129 Me31
Bahir Dar ⬛ ETH 142 Mj40
Bahla ⬛ OM 61 Nj34
Bahla Fort ⬛ OM 61 Nj34
Bahir ⬛ IND (MPH) 82 Oj33
Bahraich ⬛ IND (UPH) 81 Pa32
Bahrain ⬛ BRN 59 Nf32
Bahrain ⬛ 59 Nf32
Bahrain Al-Arab ⬛ SUD 141 Me41
Bahr-el-Ghazal ⬛ SUD 141 Md41
Bahr el Ghazal ⬛ TCH 133 Lh39
Bahri ⬛ RCA 140 Lj44
Bahía Grande do Ribeirão ⬛ BR 201 Hk51
Bai Xang ⬛ VN 87 Qc36
Baixio ⬛ BR (BA) 201 Jb52

Baixo Guandu ⬛ BR (ES) 203 Hk55
Baixo Licungo ⬛ MOC 153 Mj54
Baixo Longa ⬛ ANG 150 Lk53
Baiyer River ⬛ PNG 115 Sc48
Baiyü ⬛ CHN (SCH) 69 Pk30
Baja ⬛ H 43 Lt44
Baja California ⬛ MEX 180 Eb33
Baja California Norte ⬛ MEX 180 Ec30
Baja California Sur ⬛ MEX 180 Ed32
Bajada del Agrio ⬛ RA (NE) 208 Gf65
Baja de Maputo ⬛ MOC 155 Mg58
Baja de Marajó ⬛ BR 195 Hf46
Baja de Paranaguá ⬛ BR 205 Hf58
Baía de Pemba ⬛ MOC 147 Na52
Baía de Santa Rosa ⬛ BR 195 Hf45
Baía de São José ⬛ BR 195 Hj47
Baía de São Marcos ⬛ BR 195 Hh47
Baía de Todos os Santos ⬛ BR 201 Ja52
Baía de Turiaçu ⬛ BR 195 Hh46
Baía de Varela ⬛ GNB 136 Kb39
Baía do Bengo ⬛ ANG 148 Lg50
Baía de Caeté ⬛ BR 195 Hg46
Baía do Chun ⬛ BR 195 Hg46
Baía do Cumá ⬛ BR 195 Hh47
Baía do Gurupi ⬛ BR 195 Hg46
Baía dos Lençóis ⬛ BR 195 Hh46
Baía dos Tigres ⬛ ANG 150 Lf54
Baía Farta ⬛ ANG 150 Lg52
Baía Fernão Veloso ⬛ MOC 153 Na53
Baía Grande ⬛ BR (MT) 202 Hc54
Baía Mare ⬛ RO 43 Md43
Baião ⬛ BR (PA) 195 Hf47
Baía Sprie ⬛ RO 43 Md43
Baicheng ⬛ CHN (JLN) 71 Rb23
Baicheng ⬛ CHN (XUZ) 66 Pa25
Bàicoli ⬛ RO 43 Me45
Baïdi Cheng ⬛ CHN 74 Qe30
Bai Duc Thon ⬛ VN 87 Qc36
Baie de Concarneau ⬛ F 22 Kq43
Baie de Cortisco ⬛ GQ 148 Le45
Baie de Gaspé ⬛ CDN 176 Ha23
Baie-deHenne ⬛ RH 186 Gd36
Baie des Chaleurs ⬛ CDN 176 Ha23
Baie-des-Sables ⬛ CDN 176 Gg22
Baie du Mont-Saint-Michel ⬛ F 22 Kt42
Baie-Johan-Beetz ⬛ CDN 176 Gj20
Baie-du-Poste ⬛ CDN (QC) 176 Gd20
Baie-Saint-Paul ⬛ CDN 176 Ge21
Baigneux-les-Juifs ⬛ F 25 Le43
Baihanchang ⬛ CHN (YUN) 87 Qa32
Baihe ⬛ CHN (MPH) 83 Pa34
Baie San ⬛ CHN (SAA) 72 Qf29
Baijiang ⬛ CHN (GSU) 72 Qc29
Baijnath ⬛ CHN (GZG) 74 Qd34
Bai Khem Beach ⬛ VN 89 Qa40
Baikonyr ⬛ KZ 62 Oa23
Bailkunthapur ⬛ IND (CGH)
Baïla ⬛ SN 136 Kb39
Bailadila ⬛ CHN (GZH) 74 Qd22
Baile Felix ⬛ RO 43 Md43
Bâile Govora ⬛ RO 43 Me45
Bâile Herculane ⬛ RO 44 Mc46
Bailén ⬛ E 27 Kr52
Bâile Olănești ⬛ RO 43 Me45
Bâilești ⬛ RO 44 Md46
Bailey Ice Stream ⬛ 6 Jb35
Bailieborough ⬛ IRL 19 Ko37
Bailique ⬛ BR (AP) 195 He45
Bailique ⬛ BR (PA) 195 Hf47
Bailleul ⬛ F 23 Lc40
Bai Ma St ⬛ CHN (TIB) 68 Pe31
Bailong ⬛ CHN (TIB) 68 Pd31
Bailundo ⬛ ANG 150 Lh52
Baimajing ⬛ CHN (HAN) 75 Qe36
Bai Ma Sò ⬛ CHN (TIB) 68 Pg31
Baimuru ⬛ PNG 115 Sc49
Bainang ⬛ CHN (TIB) 68 Pe31
Bainbridge Island ⬛ USA 165 Cf15
Baines-Bretagne ⬛ F 22 Kt43
Baines' Baobab ⬛ RB 151 Mc56
Baines Drift ⬛ RB 152 Me57
Bainet ⬛ RH 186 Gd36
Baingoin ⬛ CHN (TIB) 68 Pf30
Baining Mountains ⬛ PNG 116 Sg48
Bainsa-les-Bains ⬛ F 25 Lg42
Baïoga ⬛ WAN 139 Lg42
Baiona ⬛ E 26 Km48
Baiquan ⬛ CHN (HLG) 76 Rd22
Baira ⬛ IND (BIH) 83 Pc32
Baird Bay ⬛ AUS 110 Rh62
Baird Inlet ⬛ USA 164 Bj15
Baird Mountains ⬛ USA 165 Bk12
Bairiki ⬛ KIR 101 Tb09
Bairin Qiao ⬛ CHN (NMZ) 71 Qk24
Bairin Youqi ⬛ CHN (NMZ) 71 Qk24
Bairin Zuoqi ⬛ CHN (NMZ) 71 Qk24
Bairnsdale ⬛ AUS (VIC) 111 Sd64
Bais ⬛ RP 90 Rb41
Baisha ⬛ CHN (CGQ) 74 Qd31
Baisha ⬛ CHN (SAA) 72 Qe28
Baishan ⬛ CHN (JLN) 76 Rd24
Bai Shan ⬛ CHN 67 Pg25
Baishizhen ⬛ CHN 75 Qh32
Baishlzhou Z.B. ⬛ CHN 75 Qf25
Baishuijiang Z.B. ⬛ CHN 72 Qc29
Baishuitai Terraces ⬛ CHN 87 Qa32
Baisogala ⬛ LT 39 Md35
Baitadi ⬛ NEP 81 Pa31
Baía Pagoda ⬛ CHN 76 Rb25
Bait Na'aman ⬛ OM 61 Nj34
Baitarammam Grand Mosque ⬛ RI 92 Pna3
Baixa Grande ⬛ BR (BA) 201 Hk51

Balandou ⬛ RG 136 Kf40
Balangala ⬛ RDC 140 Lk45
Balangala ⬛ RP 90 Ra38
Balangiga ⬛ RP 90 Rc40
Balao ⬛ EC 196 Ga47
Balapur ⬛ IND (MHT) 82 Oj35
Balashov ⬛ RUS 48 Na20
Balasore ⬛ IND (ORS) 83 Pd35
Balassagyarmat ⬛ H 43 Lu42
Balat ⬛ ET 129 Me31
Balāt ⬛ TR 47 Mg52
Balatan ⬛ RP 90 Rb39
Balaton ⬛ H 42 Ls44
Balatonfüred ⬛ H 42 Ls44
Balatonfüzfő ⬛ H 42 Ls44
Balatonkeresztúr ⬛ H 42 Ls44
Balatonlelle ⬛ H 42 Ls44
Balatopar ⬛ KZ 66 Oh23
Bālāurți ⬛ RO 43 Me44
Balaxe ⬛ DZ 127 Kk50
Balbi, Mount ⬛ PNG 117 Sh48
Balbriggan ⬛ IRL 19 Ko37
Balcad Nature Reserve ⬛ SP 145 Nc44
Balcanoona ⬛ AUS (SA) 108 Rk61
Balcarce ⬛ RA 209 Ha64
Balçova ⬛ TR 47 Mg52
Balçık ⬛ BG 45 Mi47
Balclutha ⬛ NZ 113 Te69
Baldchieser ⬛ USA 181 Ej30
Bald Head Island Lighthouse ⬛ USA 178 Gb29
Bald Knob ⬛ USA (AR) 175 Fe28
Bald Knob M.W.R. ⬛ USA 175 Fe28
Bald Mtn. ⬛ USA 170 Ec27
Baldone ⬛ LV 39 Me34
Baldos ⬛ RP 91 Qk43
Baldur ⬛ CDN (MB) 172 Fa21
Baldwin ⬛ USA (FL) 178 Fk30
Baldwin ⬛ USA (MI) 173 Fh24
Baldwin City ⬛ USA (KS) 174 Fc26
Baldwin Peninsula ⬛ USA 165 Bj12
Bale ⬛ TR 47 Mh51
Balen ⬛ B 23 Lf39
Balena ⬛ RP 90 Rb39
Bálti ⬛ MD 49 Mf22
Bale Sea ⬛ 14 Lb04
Baler ⬛ RP 90 Ra38
Baler Bay ⬛ RP 90 Ra38
Balesberg ⬛ ZA 154 Mf59
Balessne ⬛ DOM 186 Ge36
Baley ⬛ RUS 70 Qe20
Baley Guerrero ⬛ DOM 186 Ge36
Balfes Creek ⬛ AUS (QLD)
Balfour ⬛ CDN (BC) 168 Eb21
Balfour ⬛ ZA 155 Me61
Balfour Downs ⬛ AUS (WA) 102 Ra54
Baltagoonde ⬛ IRL 19 Km37
Balgo A.L. ⬛ AUS 103 Re56
Balguntay ⬛ CHN (XUZ) 67 Pd24
Balhaf ⬛ YE 60 Ne39
Bali ⬛ RI 95 Qh49
Bali Barat N.P. ⬛ RI 95 Qh50
Balibago ⬛ RP 90 Ra38
Balibo ⬛ TLS 97 Rc50
Balie ⬛ RP 90 Rb39
Baliem Valley ⬛ RI 114 Rk48
Balige ⬛ RI 93 Pk44
Balikesir ⬛ TR 47 Mh51
Balikpapan ⬛ RI 95 Qh46
Balilihan ⬛ RP 90 Rb41
Balimbing ⬛ RI 93 Qb48
Balimila Res. ⬛ IND 83 Pb36
Balimo ⬛ PNG 115 Sb50
Balinao ⬛ RP 90 Ra37
Balingasag ⬛ RP 91 Rc41
Balingen ⬛ D 33 Lj42
Balingeo ⬛ GB 20 Kq35
Balingup ⬛ AUS (WA) 104 Qh63
Baling ⬛ MAL 92 Qa43
Bali Sea ⬛ RI 95 Qh49

Ballenas Whale watching ⬛ MEX 180 Ed32
Ballencrieff Castle ⬛ GB 20 Ks33
Ballesreros ⬛ RA (CD) 209 Gj62
Ballia ⬛ IND (UPH) 83 Pc33
Ballidu ⬛ AUS (WA) 104 Qh62
Ballina ⬛ AUS (NSW) 111 Sg60
Ballina ⬛ IRL 19 Ki36
Ballina ⬛ IRL 19 Km37
Balling ⬛ DK 30 Lj34
Ballinger ⬛ USA (TX) 174 Fa30
Ball Island ⬛ PNG 115 Sc47
Ball, Mount ⬛ AUS 103 Rd65
Ballon d'Alsace ⬛ F 25 Lg43
Balloul ⬛ DZ 125 La28
Ballsh ⬛ AL 46 Lu50
Ballstad ⬛ N 16 Lg11
Ballybofey ⬛ IRL 19 Kn36
Ballybunnion ⬛ IRL 19 Kj38
Ballycastle ⬛ GB 19 Ko35
Ballycastle ⬛ IRL 19 Ki36
Ballyclare ⬛ GB 19 Ko36
Ballyhaunis ⬛ IRL 19 Km37
Ballylongford ⬛ IRL 19 Kj38
Ballymahon ⬛ IRL 19 Kn37
Ballymena ⬛ GB 19 Ko36
Ballymoney ⬛ GB 19 Ko35
Ballyshannon ⬛ IRL 19 Km36
Ballyvaughan ⬛ IRL 19 Kl37
Balmaceda, Cerro ⬛ RCH 210 Gd71
Balmaceda ⬛ RCH 210 Ge68
Balmazújváros ⬛ H 43 Mb43
Balmertown ⬛ CDN 172 Fd20
Balmoral ⬛ AUS (VIC) 110 Sa64
Balmoral Castle ⬛ GB 20 Ks33
Balmorhea ⬛ USA (TX) 181 Ej30
Balneario ⬛ RA (CD) 209 Gj61
Balneario Camborió ⬛ BR (SC) 205 Hf59
Balneario de la Mora ⬛ RA (CD) 208 Gh61
Balneario Massini ⬛ RA (RN) 209 Gj65
Balneario Oriente ⬛ RA (BA) 209 Gj65
Balneario de Panticosa ⬛ E 28 Lc48
Balneario las Grutas ⬛ RA (RN) 208 Gh65
Baloa ⬛ RI 96 Rb46
Balochistan ⬛ PK 64 Oa31
Balodabazar ⬛ IND (CGH) 83 Pb35
Baloda Bazar ⬛ IND (CGH) 83 Pb35
Balombe ⬛ ANG 150 Lh52
Balong ⬛ CHN (QHI) 69 Pk29
Balonne River ⬛ AUS 109 Se60
Balorzee ⬛ RMM 156 Nd51
Balotra ⬛ IND (RJT) 82 Og33
Baložii ⬛ LV 39 Md34
Balpyk Bi ⬛ KZ 66 Ok23
Balrampur ⬛ IND (UPH) 83 Pb32
Bals ⬛ RO 44 Me46
Balsapuerto ⬛ PE 196 Gb48
Balsas ⬛ BR (MA) 200 Hg49
Balsas ⬛ EC 196 Ga47
Balsas ⬛ MEX (GUR) 182 Fa36
Balsas ⬛ PE 196 Gb49
Balta ⬛ UA 49 Mf22
Baltanás ⬛ E 26 Kq49
Baltasar Brum ⬛ ROU 204 Hb61
Balta ⬛ IT 57 Mk26
Baltatim ⬛ ET 129 Me31
Baltic Sea ⬛ 14 L004
Baltijsk ⬛ RUS 39 Lu36
Baltim ⬛ ET 129 Me31
Baltimore ⬛ IRL 19 Kj39
Baltimore ⬛ USA (MD) 177 Gb26
Baltinglass ⬛ IRL 19 Ko38
Baltit Fort ⬛ PK 80 Oh27
Baltoro Glacier ⬛ 80 Oj27
Baluan Island ⬛ PNG 116 Sd47
Baluarte de Santiago ⬛ MEX (CAM) 183 Fe36
Balud ⬛ RP 90 Rb39
Baluchaung ⬛ MYA 86 Ph36
Baluk ⬛ CHN (JLN) 76 Rd22
Baluran N.P. ⬛ RI 95 Qh49
Balurghat ⬛ IND (WBG) 86 Pe33
Balut Island ⬛ RP 91 Rd42
Balvi ⬛ LV 39 Mf33
Balya ⬛ TR 47 Mh51
Balychy ⬛ KS 66 Oj24
Balykchy ⬛ KZ 67 Pd21
Balzar ⬛ EC 196 Ga46
Balzola ⬛ I 34 Lj46
Bám ⬛ TCH 140 Li41
Bama ⬛ CHN 137 Kj41
Bama ⬛ WAN 139 Lg40
Bamaga ⬛ AUS (QLD) 107 Sb51
Bamaji L. ⬛ CDN 172 Fd20
Bamako ⬛ RMM 137 Kf39
Bamanalli ⬛ IND (MHT) 83 Pa36
Bamba ⬛ CHN (GZG) 74 Qd33
Bamba ⬛ RMM 131 Kg37
Bambama ⬛ RCB 148 Lg47
Bambamarca ⬛ PE 196 Gb49
Bambara-Maoundé ⬛ RMM 131 Kj38
Bambari ⬛ RCA 140 Lk42
Bambas ⬛ E 26 Kq48
Bambel ⬛ RI 93 Qb45
Bamberg ⬛ D 33 Ll41
Bamberg ⬛ USA (SC) 178 Fk29
Bambesa ⬛ RDC 141 Md44
Bambey ⬛ SN 130 Kb38
Bambili ⬛ RDC 141 Md44
Bambio ⬛ RCA 140 Lj44
Bamboesberg ⬛ ZA 155 Md61
Bamboo Creek ⬛ AUS (WA)
Bamboo Springs ⬛ AUS (WA) 105 Rb62
Bamboo Temple ⬛ CHN 87 Qb33
Bambouk ⬛ RMM 136 Kd40
Bambui ⬛ BR (MG) 203 Hh55
Bambuka ⬛ WAN 139 Lg42
Bamburi ⬛ EAK 147 Na48
Bamburgh ⬛ GB 19 Ks35
Bamenda ⬛ CAM 138 Lf42
Bamendjing ⬛ CAM 138 Lf43
Bamfield ⬛ CDN (BC) 168 Dh21
Bami ⬛ TM 62 Nj24

Bamian ⬛ AFG 65 Od28
Bamiancheng ⬛ CHN (LNG) 76 Rb24
Bamiantong ⬛ CHN (HLG)
Baminghi-Bangoran, P.N. du ⬛ RCA 140 Lk42
Baminghi-Bangoran ⬛ RCA 140 Lk42
Bamingui ⬛ RCA 140 Ma42
Bamoa ⬛ MEX (SL) 180 Ef33
Bamo ⬛ 186 Gc35
Bampton ⬛ GB 21 Kr40
Bamuri ⬛ MEX (SO) 180 Ef33
Bamusso ⬛ CAM 138 Le43
Ban ⬛ BF 137 Kj38
Bana ⬛ RCA 140 Lj43
Banaba Island ⬛ KIR 10 Ta10
Banabuiú ⬛ BR (CE) 201 Ja48
Banadia ⬛ CO 192 Gd43
Banalia ⬛ RDC 141 Md45
Banamba ⬛ RMM 137 Kf39
Banana ⬛ RDC 148 Lf47
Banana ⬛ AUS (QLD) 109 Sf58
Banana Islands ⬛ WAL 136 Kd41
Banana Range ⬛ AUS 109 Sf58
Bananal ⬛ CI 137 Kg41
Bananandje ⬛ CI 137 Kg41
Banankoro ⬛ RG 136 Kf40
Banankoro ⬛ RMM 136 Kf40
Bananeiras ⬛ BR (PB) 201 Jb49
Bananga ⬛ IND 84 Pg43
Bananga ⬛ RCA 140 Mb43
Banani ⬛ RMM 131 Kj38
Banapur ⬛ IND (ORS) 83 Pc35
Banaras = Varanasi ⬛ IND (UPH) 83 Pb33
Banarli ⬛ TR 45 Mg49
Banas ⬛ IND 82 Og33
Banat ⬛ RO 43 Ma44
Banatski Karlovac ⬛ SCG 44 Mb45
Banavie ⬛ GB 20 Kq34
Banaz ⬛ TR 56 Mi26
Banbridge ⬛ GB 19 Ko36
Banbury ⬛ GB 21 Kt38
Banc Africain ⬛ SY 145 Nj48
Banc d'Arguin, P.N. du ⬛ RIM 130 Kb37
Banc du Geyser ⬛ RM 156 Nd51
Bancea ⬛ RI 96 Ra47
Ban Chamrung ⬛ THA 89 Qb39
Ban Chang ⬛ THA 89 Qb39
Ban Chiang ⬛ THA 87 Qb37
Banchory ⬛ GB 20 Ks33
Banco Chinchorro ⬛ MEX 183 Fg36
Banco de Quitasueño ⬛ CO 185 Fk38
Banco de Serrana ⬛ CO 185 Fk38
Banco de Serranilla ⬛ CO 185 Ga38
Banco, P.N. du ⬛ CI 137 Kh43
Bancoran Island ⬛ RP 91 Qk42
Bancos del Cabo Falso ⬛ HN 185 Fj38
Bancroft ⬛ CDN (ON) 177 Gb23
Banda ⬛ RDC 149 Mb50
Banda ⬛ IND (MPH) 83 Pa34
Banda ⬛ IND (UPH) 83 Pa33
Bandama ⬛ CI 137 Kh41
Bandama Blanc ⬛ CI 137 Kh42
Bandana ⬛ IND (APH) 85 Ok38
Banda Aceh ⬛ RI 92 Pj43
Bandar ⬛ IND (ORS) 83 Pc34
Bandar-Abbas ⬛ IR 64 Nj32
Bandar-e-Anzali ⬛ IR 57 Ne27
Bandar-e-Busher ⬛ IR 59 Nf31
Bandar-e-Charak ⬛ IR 64 Nh32
Bandar-e-Deylam ⬛ IR 59 Ne30
Bandar-e-Emam Khomeyni ⬛ IR 59 Ne30
Bandar-e-Gonaveh ⬛ IR 59 Nf31
Bandar-e-Hamiran ⬛ IR 64 Nh33
Bandar-e-Khamir ⬛ IR 64 Nh32
Bandar-e Lengeh ⬛ IR 64 Nh32
Bandar-e-Mahshar ⬛ IR 59 Ne30
Bandar-e-Moqam ⬛ IR 64 Nh32
Bandar-e-Rig ⬛ IR 59 Nf31
Bandar-e Taheri ⬛ IR 64 Ng32
Bandar-e-Torkaman ⬛ IR 62 Nh27
Bandar Lampung ⬛ RI 93 Qc48
Bandar Murcaayo ⬛ SP 145 Nf40
Bandarpunch ⬛ IND 81 Ok30
Bandar Sri Aman ⬛ MAL 94 Qf45
Bandawe ⬛ MW 153 Mh53
Bande ⬛ E 26 Km48
Bandeira ⬛ RI 97 Re48
Banda Nkwanta ⬛ GH 137 Kj41
Bandeirantes ⬛ BR (MS) 202 Hd55
Bandeirantes ⬛ BR (PR) 202 He57
Bandera ⬛ RA 207 Gk59
Bandera ⬛ USA (TX) 181 Fa31
Bandera, la ⬛ YV 192 Gh42
Banderliepkop N.M. ⬛ ZA 152 Me57
Bandi ⬛ IND (RJT) 82 Og32
Bandiagara ⬛ RMM 131 Kj38
Bandikui ⬛ IND (RJT) 82 Oj32
Bandipur ⬛ IND (KTK) 84 Oj40
Bandirma ⬛ TR 45 Mh50
Bandon ⬛ IRL 19 Kl39
Bandon ⬛ USA (OR) 168 Dg24
Bandundu ⬛ RDC 149 Lj47
Bandung ⬛ RI 95 Qd49

Banea ⬛ EAK 145 Nb46
Baneh ⬛ IR 57 Nc27
Banes ⬛ C 186 Gc35
Baneza ⬛ RO 45 Mg46
Banfèle ⬛ RG 136 Kf40
Banff ⬛ CDN (AB) 168 Ec20
Banff ⬛ GB 20 Ks33
Banff N.P. ⬛ CDN 168 Eb20
Banfora ⬛ BF 137 Kh40
Banga ⬛ RCA 140 Li42
Banga ⬛ ANG 148 Lh50
Banga ⬛ RDC 141 Lk48
Banga ⬛ RP 91 Rc42
Banganga ⬛ IND (KTK) 84 Oj39
Bangaluda ⬛ IND (ORS) 83 Pb36
Bangangté ⬛ CAM 138 Lf43
Bangar ⬛ RP 90 Rc41
Bangarapet ⬛ IND (KTK) 84 Oj39
Bangar ⬛ IND 81 Og30
Bangassou ⬛ RCA 141 Mb43
Bangba ⬛ RCA 140 Lj42
Bangbali ⬛ RI 92 Pk46
Banghazi ⬛ LAR 127 Lg29
Banggai ⬛ RI 96 Rb46
Banggai Islands ⬛ RI 96 Rb46
Banggi ⬛ MAL 94 Qj42
Banghara ⬛ RI 91 Rc45
Bangka ⬛ RI 93 Qc46
Bangkala ⬛ RI 95 Qj48
Bangkalan ⬛ RI 95 Qf49
Bangkaru ⬛ RI 92 Pj45
Bangli ⬛ RI 95 Qh49
Bangolo ⬛ CI 137 Kg42
Bangong Co ⬛ CHN 68 Oh29
Bangong Co ⬛ IND 68 Oj29
Bangor ⬛ GB 19 Kp37
Bangor ⬛ GB 19 Ko36
Bangor ⬛ USA (ME) 177 Ge23
Bangoran ⬛ RCA 140 Ma41
Bangourain ⬛ RCB 148 Lf47
Bangouya ⬛ RG 136 Kd40

Bangued ⬛ RP 90 Ra37
Bangui ⬛ RCA 140 Lj43
Bangui ⬛ RP 90 Ra36
Bangui-Motaba ⬛ RCB 140 Li44
Bangula ⬛ MW 153 Mh55
Banguru Swamps ⬛ Z 146 Mf51
Bangxi ⬛ CHN (HAN) 75 Qe36
Ban Hat ⬛ LAO 87 Qd37
Ban Hat Lek ⬛ THA 89 Qb40
Ban Heu ⬛ LAO 87 Qd37
Banhine, P.N. de ⬛ MOC 152 Mg57
Ban Huayma ⬛ LAO 87 Qc37
Bani ⬛ BF 137 Kk39
Bani ⬛ DOM 186 Ge36
Bani ⬛ RCA 140 Lk43
Bani ⬛ RP 90 Ra37
Bani Amer ⬛ KSA 60 Nb36
Banian ⬛ IR 64 Ng31
Banian ⬛ RN 132 Lb38
Bani Bangou ⬛ RN 132 Lb38
Banica ⬛ RH 186 Gd36
Bani Hadi ⬛ KSA 60 Na36
Bani Khatmah ⬛ KSA 60 Na37
Bani Mal'al ⬛ KSA 60 Na36
Bani Mazar ⬛ ET 129 Mf31
Bani Mukasir ⬛ KSA 60 Nc36
Bani Walid ⬛ LAR 127 Lg30
Bani Yas ⬛ UAE 61 Nh33
Banja ⬛ BIH 35 Ls46
Banjaran Timur ⬛ MAL 92 Qb43
Banjaran Bintang ⬛ MAL 92 Qa43
Banjar Brassey ⬛ MAL 94 Qj43
Banjar Crocker ⬛ MAL 94 Qh44
Banjaran Tama Abu ⬛ MAL 94 Qh44
Banjaran Titiwangsa ⬛ MAL 92 Qa43
Banjarbaru ⬛ RI 95 Qg47
Banjarmasin ⬛ RI 95 Qf47
Banjoewangi ⬛ RI 95 Qh49
Banjul ⬛ WAG 136 Kb39
Banka ⬛ AZ 57 Ne26
Ban Kabong ⬛ THA 89 Qb41
Banka Banka ⬛ AUS (NT)
Bankaji ⬛ RI 93 Qa44
Ban Katang ⬛ THA 88 Pk42
Bankawalurugu ⬛ RI 96 Qk48
Bankeryd ⬛ S 31 Lo33
Ban Khlong Kua ⬛ THA 88 Pk43
Ban Khlong Son ⬛ THA 89 Qb40
Bankilaré ⬛ RN 132 La38
Ban Khao ⬛ LAO 87 Qd36
Ban Khok Kloi ⬛ THA 88 Pj42
Banks Island ⬛ AUS (NT)
Banks Islands ⬛ VU 118 Td53

Belet Weyne ☒ SP 143 Nc43
Belev ☒ RUS 48 Mj19
Běleya ☒ RG 136 Ke40
Belezma, P.N. de ☒ DZ 126 Lc28
Belfast ☒ GB 19 Kg36
Belfast ☒ USA (MA) 177 Gf23
Belfast ☒ RO 43 Mh44
Belfield ☒ USA (ND) 169 Ej22
Belfir ☒ RO 43 Mh44
Belfodiyo ☒ ETH 142 Mh40
Belford ☒ GB 20 Kt35
Belfort ☒ F 25 Lg43
Belgachhi ☒ IND (BIH) 83 Pd33
Belgaum Fort ☒ IND (KTK)
82 Oh38
Belgern ☒ D 32 Lo39
Belgium ■ B 23 Le40
Belgodère ☒ F 34 Lk48
Belgorod ☒ RUS 48 Mj20
Belgrade ● ☒ SCG 44 Ma46
Belgrade ☒ USA (MT) 169 Ee23
Belgrano, Cerro ▲ RA 210 Ge69
Belgrano II ☒ ANT (RA) 6 Ha34
Belhar ☒ IND (BIH) 83 Pd33
Belhatti ☒ IND (KTK) 82 Oh38
Belhirane ☒ DZ 126 Ld30
Beli Izvor ☒ BG (DAG) 57 Ne25
Belifang ☒ CAM 138 Lf42
Beli Manastir ☒ HR 35 Lt45
Belin-Béliet ☒ F 24 Ku46
Belinga ☒ G 139 Lg45
Belinyu ☒ RI 92 Qd34
Beliş ☒ RO 43 Md44
Beliščice ☒ HR 35 Lt45
Belitsaka ☒ RM 157 Nc54
Belitung ▲ RI 95 Qd47
Belize ☒ ANG 148 Lh49
Belize ★ 184 Ff37
Belize Barrier Reef System ≈
BH 184 Ff37
Belize City ☒ BH 184 Ff37
Beljanovo ☒ BG 45 Mf47
Belkhera ☒ IND (MPH) 83 Ok34
Bel'ki ☒ BY 39 Mh35
Bel'kovo ☒ RUS 48 Mg19
Belk (QLD) 109 Sf59
Beller ☒ CAM 138 Lf44
Belleek ☒ DZ 126 Ld30
Belledère ☒ DOM 186 Ge36
Bella Flor ☒ BOL 198 Gg51
Belláglo ☒ F 34 Lk46
Bellária ☒ AUS (QLD) 108 Sb59
Bellária-Igea Marina ☒ I 34 Ln46
Bella Unión ☒ ROU 204 Hb61
Bellavista ☒ CO 192 Ga50
Bella Vista ☒ RA (CR) 204 Ha62
Bella Vista ☒ PE 196 Gb49
Bella Vista Norte ☒ PY 202 Hb57
Bell Brook ☒ AUS (NSW)
109 Sg61
Bellburns ☒ CDN (NF) 177 Hb20
Belle Anse ☒ RH 186 Gd36
Belleden Ker N.P. ☒ AUS (QLD)
107 Sc54
Bellefontaine ☒ USA (OH)
173 Fj25
Bellefonte ☒ USA (PA) 177 Gd25
Belle Glade ☒ USA (FL) 179 Fk32
Belle-île ☒ F 24 Ks43
Belle Isle ☒ CDN 177 Hc20
Bellème ☒ F 22 Ls42
Bellenden Ker N.P. ☒ AUS (QLD)
107 Sc54
Belleoram ☒ CDN (NF) 177 Hc22
Belle Plaine ☒ USA (MN)
172 Fd25
Belleterre ☒ CDN (QC) 173 Ga22
Belleville ☒ CDN (ON) 173 Gb22
Belleville ☒ F 25 Le44
Belleville ☒ USA (IL) 175 Fe26
Belleville ☒ USA (KS) 174 Fb26
Belleville-sur-Vie ☒ F 24 Kt44
Bellevue ☒ AUS (QLD) 107 Sc54
Bellevue ☒ USA (ID) 168 Ec24
Bellevue ☒ USA (OH) 173 Fj25
Bellevue ☒ F 25 Li45
Belle Yella ☒ LB 136 Kf42
Bellfield ☒ AUS (QLD) 107 Sb55
Bell Fourche ☒ USA (SD)
169 Ej23
Bellingham ☒ USA (WA) 168 Dj21
Bellingwedde Gardens ☒ USA
175 Fi30
Bellingshausen ☒ ANT (RUS)
6 Ha30
Bellingshausen Sea ≋ ANT
6 Fd32
Bellinzona ☒ CH 34 Lk44
Bell Island ☒ CDN 177 Hc20
Bell Island Hot Springs ☒ USA
(AK) 166 De18
Bello ☒ CO 192 Gc42
Bellocq ☒ RA (BA) 209 Gk63
Bellows Falls ☒ USA (VT)
177 Gd24
Belpat ☒ PK 65 Od31
Bell Peninsula ☒ CDN 163 Fd06
Belle ☒ F 29 Lb49
Bell River ☒ CDN (YT) 165 Db12
Bell Rock ☒ USA 159 Ee27
Bellrose ☒ AUS (QLD) 108 Sd59
Bells Beach ☒ AUS (VIC)
111 Sd65
Bellville ☒ ZA 154 La62
Belmez ☒ E 27 Kp42
Belmond ☒ USA (IA) 172 Fd24
Belmont ☒ GB 20 Ku31
Belmont ☒ AUS (NC) 178 Fk28
Belmont ☒ ZA 155 Mc60
Belmonte ☒ BR (BA) 203 Ja53
Belmonte ☒ E 29 Ks45
Belmonte de Miranda ☒ E
Belmonte ☒ P 26 Kn42
Belmopan ■ BH 184 Ff37
Belmore Park ☒ AUS (QLD)
AUS 104 Qb61
Belmopan ■ BH 184 Ff37
Belmore Falls ☒ AUS (NSW) 110 Sa62
Belmullet ☒ IRL 19 Kl36
Belo ☒ RM 157 Nc55
Belo Campo ☒ BR (BA) 203 Hk53
Belœil ☒ B 23 Ld40
Belogradčik Skali ▲ BG
44 Mc47
Belo Horizonte ● ☒ BR (MG)
203 Hj55
Belogradec ☒ RUS (WI) 174 Fa26
Belojarovo ☒ RUS 71 Re20
Belojarskij ☒ RUS 54 Ob06

Béloko ☒ RCA 140 Lh43
Belo Monte ☒ BR (OM) 198 Gh49
Belo Monte do Pontal ☒ BR (PA)
195 He47
Belonge ☒ RDC 149 Ma47
Belorado ☒ E 28 Kr48
Beloreč enk ☒ RUS 48 Mk23
Belot ☒ USA 175 Lq46
Belotinci ☒ BG 44 Mc47
Belo Tsiribihina ☒ RM 157 Nc55
Belovodskoe ☒ KS 66 Oh24
Belpasso ☒ I 37 Lp53
Belper ☒ GB 21 Kt37
Belpre (OH) 175 Fk26
Belsay ☒ GB 20 Kt35
Beltana ☒ AUS (PA) 108 Rk61
Belterra ☒ BR (PA) 199 Hc47
Beltiug ☒ RO 43 Md43
Belton ☒ USA (SC) 178 Fj28
Belton ☒ USA (TX) 174 Fb30
Beluguppa ☒ IND (APH) 84 Oj38
Beluran ☒ MAL 94 Qh44
Beluru ☒ MAL 94 Qh44
Belvedere Marittimo ☒ I 37 Lq51
Belvès ☒ F 24 La46
Belvidere ☒ USA (IL) 173 Ff24
Belvidere Kerk ☒ ZA 154 Mb63
Belvy ☒ RUS 48 Mg19
Belz ☒ UA 41 Me41
Belzig ☒ D 32 Ln38
Belzoni ☒ USA (MS) 175 Fe29
Bełżyce ☒ PL 41 Mc39
Béma ☒ RMM 130 Kf38
Bema, P.N. de ☒ CAM 139 Lf41
Bénoye ☒ TCH 140 Lj41
Ben Quang ☒ VN 87 Qd37
Ben B'Bour ☒ DZ 126 Lc28
Benakou ☒ DY 138 Lb40
Benakou ☒ DY 138 Lb40
Ben-Slimane ☒ MA 125 Kg29
Benson ☒ USA (AZ) 171 Ee30
Benson ☒ USA (MN) 172 Fc23
Ben Starav ☒ GB 20 Kq34
Benté ☒ RI 64 Nk22
Benteng ☒ RI 96 Ra49
Benteng Belgica ☒ RI 97 Rf48
Bentia ☒ RMM 131 La38
Bentick Island ☒ AUS (QLD)
106 Rk55
Bentinck Island ☒ AUS (QLD)
Bentiu ☒ SUD 141 Me41
Bentley ☒ USA (IN) 173 Fg26
Bento Gonçalves ☒ BR (RS)
204 He60
Bernáscio ☒ BR (RS) 204 Hd58
Benton ☒ USA (AR) 174 Fd28
Benton ☒ USA (CA) 170 Ea27
Benton ☒ USA (IL) 175 Ff27
Bentong ☒ MAL 92 Qa44
Benton Harbor ☒ USA (MI)
173 Fg24
Bentonsport ☒ USA (MO)
172 Fe25
Bentota Beach ☒ CL 85 Ok42
Bentuang Karimun Nature
Reserve ☒ RI 94 Qg45
Benty ☒ RG 136 Kd41
Benua ☒ RI 95 Qd45
Benue ☒ WAN 138 Ld41
Ben Wyvis ▲ GB 20 Kq33
Benwee Head ☒ IRL 19 Kl36
Bencubbin ☒ AUS (LNG) 76 Rb25
Benz ☒ USA (OR) 168 Dk23
Benza ☒ ANG 148 Lg49
Beo ☒ RI 91 Rd43
Beograd ● ☒ SCG 44 Ma46
Beograd-Surčin ☒ SCG 44 Ma46
Béoumi ☒ CI 137 Kh42
Beowawe ☒ USA (NV) 170 Eb26
Beppu ☒ J 79 Rf29
Beqa ☒ FJI 119 Tk55
Bequia ☒ WV 187 Gk39
Bequimão ☒ BR (MA) 195 Hh47
Ber ☒ RMM 131 Kj37
Berahle ☒ ETH 142 Mk39
Bereketa ☒ RM 157 Nd57
Berakit Beach ☒ RI 93 Qc45
Beramanja ☒ RM 156 Ne52
Bérandjokou ☒ RCB 140 Lj44
Berangang ☒ RI 93 Qb46
Berasia ☒ IND (MPH) 82 Oj34
Beraspapan ☒ RI 92 Qh46
Berastagi ☒ RI 92 Pk44
Berat ☒ AL 46 Lu50
Berat Forteresse ☒ AL 46 Lu50
Beravina ☒ RM 157 Nc55
Beravy ☒ RM 157 Nd57
Berazino ☒ BY 48 Me19
Berazino ☒ BY 39 Mj36
Berbak National Park ☒ RI
93 Qb46
Berber ☒ SUD 135 Mg36
Berbera ☒ SP 143 Nc40
Berbérati ☒ RCA 140 Lh43
Berbinzana ☒ E 28 Kt48
Berceto ☒ I 34 Ll46
Berchtesgaden ☒ D 33 Ln43
Berck-Plage ☒ F 23 Lb40
Berdale ☒ SP 145 Nb44
Berdale ☒ SP 143 Nd44
Berdia ☒ E 26 Km48
Berdjans'k ☒ UA 49 Mg22
Berdychiv ☒ UA 48 Me21
Bere ☒ TCH 140 Lj41
Berea ☒ USA (KY) 175 Fh27
Béréba ☒ BF 137 Kj40
Berebere ☒ RI 91 Rd44
Berega ☒ EAT 147 Mj49
Berehove ☒ UA 43 Mc42
Berehomet ☒ UA 43 Mf42
Bereku ☒ EAT 147 Mh48
Bereku ☒ WAT 147 Mh48
Berendi ☒ TR 56 Mj27
Berenice ☒ ET 129 Mh34
Berens ☒ CDN (MB)
Berens River ☒ CDN (MB)
Beresford ☒ USA (SD) 172 Fb24
Berestečko ☒ UA 41 Me40
Berettyóújfalu ☒ H 43 Mb43
Berezanskaja ☒ RUS 49 Mk23
Berežany ☒ UA 41 Mf41
Berezani ☒ UA 43 Mf42
Berezna ☒ UA 48 Mf20
Berezne ☒ UA 41 Mf40
Bereznehuvate ☒ UA 49 Mf22
Bereznik ☒ RUS 54 Nd07
Bereżnica ☒ PL 41 Md39
Berezniki ☒ RUS 54 Nd08
Berga ☒ D 32 Ln39
Bergama ☒ TR 47 Mh51
Bergamo ☒ I 34 Lk45
Bergantín ☒ YV 193 Gh41
Bergantiños ☒ E 26 Km47
Bergara ☒ E 28 Kr47
Bergby ☒ S 31 Ls30
Bergeijk ☒ NL 23 Lf39
Bergen ☒ D 32 Ln40
Bergen ☒ N 30 Lg31
Bergen auf Rügen ☒ D 32 Lo36
Bergen op Zoom ☒ NL 23 Le39
Bergenshamn ☒ S 31 Lt31
Bergisch ☒ D 32 Lh40
Bergomanville ☒ USA
Bergsjö ☒ S 17 L t35
Bergville ☒ ZA 155 Me60
Berhait ☒ IND (JKD) 83 Pd33
Beringga ☒ NAM (WA) 104 Qj59
Beringen ☒ B 23 Lf39
Bering Glacier ☒ USA 166 Cj15
Bering Land Bridge National
Preserve ☒ USA 166 Ba06
Bering Sea ≋ USA/RUS 162
Ba06
Bering Strait ≋ USA/RUS
160 Ba03
Berisu ☒ IR 57 Nc27
Berja ☒ E 27 Ks54
Berkåk ☒ N 16 Lf14
Berkane ☒ MA 125 Lc28
Berkeley ☒ USA (CA) 170 Dj27
Berkh ☒ MNG 70 Qf22
Berkner Island ☒ 6 Hc34
Berkovica ☒ BIH 44 L147
Berlanga ☒ E 27 Kp52
Berlanga de Duero ☒ E
28 Ks49
Berlenga ☒ P 27 Kl51
Berlevåg ☒ N 16 Me10
Berlin ● CO 192 Gd42
Berlin ☒ D 32 Lo38
Berlin ☒ USA (WI) 177 Gb24
Berlin, Mount ▲ 6 Da34
Bermagui ☒ AUS (NSW) 111 Sf64
Bermejillo ☒ MEX (DGO)
181 Ej33
Bermejo ☒ BOL 207 Gh57
Bermejo ☒ BOL 207 Gh57
Bermejo ☒ PE 197 Gb51
Bermejo ☒ RA 207 Gf61
Bermeo ☒ E 28 Kr47
Bermillo de Sayago ☒ E 26 Ko49
Bermuda ☒ RN 132 Ld38
Bermuda ■ GB 161 Gb06
Bernalda ☒ I 37 Lr50
Bernalillo ☒ USA (NM) 171 Ee28
Bernardo ☒ E 186 Gc35
Bernardo de Irigoyen ☒ RA (MI)
204 Hd59
Bernardo O'Higgins, P.N. ☒ RCH
210 Gc70
Bernartice ☒ CZ 42 Lp41
Bernasdale ☒ GB 20 Ko33
Bernau ☒ D 32 Lo38
Bernau ☒ D 33 Ln43
Bernay ☒ F 22 La41
Bernburg ☒ D 32 Lm39
Berne ☒ USA (IN) 173 Fh25
Berner Alpen ▲ CH 34 Lj44
Bernerray ☒ GB 20 Kn33
Bernham ☒ USA (TX) 174 Fb30
Bernier Island ☒ AUS 104 Qg58
Bernkastel-Kues ☒ D 33 Lh41
Bérnon de Astrada ☒ RA (CR)
204 Hb59
Beronovo ☒ BG 45 Mg48
Berón de Astrada ☒ RA (CR)
204 Hb59
Berounka ☒ CZ 42 Lo41
Berri ☒ AUS (SA) 110 Sa63
Berriane ☒ DZ 126 La29
Berridale ☒ AUS (NSW) 111 Se63
Berrigan ☒ AUS (NSW) 111 Sc63
Berrouaghia ☒ DZ 126 La27
Berrydale ☒ USA (FL) 175 Fg30
Berry Islands ☒ BS 179 Gb33
Berryville ☒ USA (AR) 174 Fd27
Bersăd ☒ UA 49 Me21
Bersenbrück ☒ D 32 Lh38
Bertești de Jos ☒ RO 45 Mh46
Berthoud ☒ USA (CO) 169 Eh25
Bertincourt ☒ F 23 Lc40
Bertinho ☒ BR (PA) 195 He47
Bertolínia ☒ BR (PI) 201 Hj49
Bertoua ☒ CAM 139 Lg43
Bertrix ☒ B 23 Lf41
Bertwell ☒ CDN (SK) 169 Ej19
Berunai ☒ UZ 62 Oa25
Beruni ☒ UZ 62 Oa25
Beruri ☒ BR (AM) 198 Gk47
Berwala ☒ CL 85 Ok42
Berwick ☒ AUS (TAS) 111 Sd64
Berwick ☒ CDN (NB) 176 Gh23
Berwick ☒ USA (PA) 177 Gd25
Berwick-upon-Tweed ☒ GB
20 Ks35
Berzasca ☒ RO 44 Mb46
Berzence ☒ H 42 Lr44
Berzpils ☒ LV 39 Mh34
Besakih ☒ RI 95 Qh50
Besalampy ☒ RM 157 Nc54
Besalú ☒ E 28 Lc48
Besançon ☒ F 25 Lf43
Besançkivci ☒ BY 48 Me18
Besar ☒ MAL 92 Qa44
Besar ☒ RI 96 Rb50
Besar, Gunung ▲ RI 95 Qg48
Besasesil ☒ DY 138 Lb40
Besckhoky tau ☒ KZ 62 Ng23
Besedino ☒ RUS 48 Mj20
Besenyszög ☒ H 43 Ma43
Beshar ☒ IR 62 Ng27
Beshariq ☒ UZ 63 Of25
Beshkent ☒ UZ 63 Oe26
Beshton ☒ UZ 62 Nh24
Bère Regis ☒ GB (SD) 172 Fa26
Besir ☒ RI 97 Rf46
Beskid Wysoki ▲ PL 41 Lu41
Beslan ☒ RUS (SOA) 57 Nc24
Besni ☒ TR 56 Mj27
Bessa Monteiro ☒ ANG 148 Lg49
Bessarabia ☒ MD 43 Mh43
Bessbrook ☒ GB 19 Ko36
Bessé ☒ F 25 Lg46
Bessèges ☒ F 25 Le46
Bessenuhvate ☒ UA 175 Fg29
Bessoung Kang ☒ CAM 138
Le43
Best ☒ NL 23 Lf39
Bestavarराppu ☒ IND (APH)
Bestwig ☒ D 32 Lj39
Betania ☒ CO 192 Gd42
Bétania ☒ BR (PE) 201 Ja50

Bergheim ☒ D 32 Lg40
Bergland ☒ USA (MI) 172 Ff21
Bergland ☒ NAM 154 Lj57
Bergo ☒ FIN 38 Mb28
Bergsamra ☒ S 31 Lt31
Bergsig ☒ NAM (MH) 172 Fg22
Bergsjö ☒ S 17 Lj15
Bergula ☒ D 23 Lc40
Bergville ☒ ZA 155 Me60
Berhait ☒ IND (JKD) 83 Pd33
Beringarra ☒ AUS (WA) 104 Qj59
Beringen ☒ B 23 Lf39
Bering Glacier ☒ USA 166 Cj15
Bering Land Bridge National
Preserve ☒ USA 166 Ba06
Bering Sea ≋ USA/RUS 162
Ba06
Bering Strait ≋ USA/RUS
160 Ba03
Berisu ☒ IR 57 Nc27
Berja ☒ E 27 Ks54
Berkåk ☒ N 16 Lf14
Berkane ☒ MA 125 Lc28
Berkeley ☒ USA (CA) 170 Dj27
Berkh ☒ MNG 70 Qf22
Berkner Island ☒ 6 Hc34
Berkovica ☒ BIH 44 L147
Berlanga ☒ E 27 Kp52
Berlanga de Duero ☒ E
28 Ks49
Berlenga ☒ P 27 Kl51
Berlevåg ☒ N 16 Me10
Berlin ● CO 192 Gd42
Berlin ☒ D 32 Lo38
Berlin ☒ USA (WI) 177 Gb24
Berlin, Mount ▲ 6 Da34

Betanzos ☒ BOL 206 Gh55
Betanzos ☒ E 26 Km47
Betararaca ☒ VU 118 Te53
Bétaré Oya ☒ CAM 139 Lh43
Betatakin Ruin ☒ USA 171 Ee27
Bete Hor ☒ ETH 142 Mk40
Betein ☒ WAN 138 Ld40
Betela ☒ ZA 155 Ne59
Betety Bay ☒ BS 186 Gd34
Bethal ☒ ZA 155 Me59
Bethanie ☒ NAM 154 Lj59
Bethanien ☒ D 32 Lo39
Bethanye ☒ USA (OK) 174 Fa27
Bethel ☒ USA (AK) 164 Bk15
Bethel ☒ USA (ME) 177 Ge23
Bethel ☒ USA (OH) 173 Fj26
Bethlehem ☒ IL 58 Mh30
Bethlehem ☒ ZA 155 Me60
Bethulie ☒ ZA 155 Mc61
Béthune ☒ F 23 Lc40
Betio ☒ KIR 119 Tc47
Betioky ☒ RM 157 Nc57
Betita ☒ DZ 126 Ld28
Betong ☒ MAL 94 Qf44
Betong ☒ THA 89 Qa43
Berkåk ☒ N 16 Lf14
Berkane ☒ RCB 140 Lk44
Betpak Dala ☒ KZ 54 Ob09
Betpaquitatam ☒ KZ 62 Nj21
Betretka ☒ RM 157 Nd54
Betsaa ☒ RI 91 Rh55
Betsiaka ☒ RM 156 Ne52
Bettiah ☒ IND (BIH) 83 Pc32
Bettié ☒ CI 137 Kj42
Betül ☒ IND (MPH) 82 Oj36
Betulia ☒ CO 192 Gb42
Betung ☒ RI 93 Qc47
Betws-y-Coed ☒ GB 21 Kr37
Betzdorf ☒ D 32 Lh40
Béu ☒ ANG 148 Lh49
Beulah ☒ AUS (VIC) 110 Sb63
Beulah ☒ USA (MI) 173 Fg23
Beuvray, Mont ▲ F 25 Le44
Bevalville ☒ USA (MC) 178 Gb28
Beveren ☒ B 23 Le39
Beverley ☒ AUS (WA) 104 Qj62
Beverley ☒ GB 21 Ku37
Beverlø ☒ B 23 Lf39
Beverly ☒ CDN (SK) 169 Eg19
Beverly Hills ☒ USA (FL) 179 Fj31
Beverly Springs ☒ AUS (WA)
Beverungen ☒ D 32 Lk39
Beverwijk ☒ NL 23 Le38
Bewani ☒ PNG 115 Sa47
Bewar ☒ IND (UPH) 81 Ok33
Beyan Alpen ▲ CH 34 Lj44
Beyazcepme Şelâlesi ☒ TR
57 Nb26
Beyazcaym ☒ TR 45 Mg50
Beydağ ☒ TR 47 Mj52
Beyköz ☒ TR 45 Mh49
Beyla ☒ RG 136 Kf41
Beylaqan ☒ AZ 57 Nd26
Beylul ☒ ER 142 Na39
Beypazarı ☒ TR 56 Me25
Beypore ☒ IND (KER) 84 Oh40
Beyram ☒ IR 61 Ng31
Beyşehir ☒ TR 56 Md27
Beyşehir Gölü ☒ TR 56 Mf27
Beytüşşebap ☒ TR 57 Nb28
Bezahia ☒ RM 157 Nc57
Bezau ☒ A 34 Lk43
Bežanica ☒ RUS 48 Me17
Bezançon ☒ DB (AB) 167 Ea18
Bezau ☒ A 34 Lk43
Bezerros ☒ BR (PE) 201 Jc50
Béziers ☒ F 25 Ld47
Bez'va ☒ RUS 38 Mj32
Bhabbar ☒ IND (GUJ) 82 Of33
Bhabua ☒ IND (BIH) 83 Pb33
Bhadaur ☒ IND (PJB) 80 Oh30
Bhadasar ☒ IND (RJT) 80 Oh32
Bhabhua ☒ IND (MPH) 83 Pb34
Bhadohi ☒ IND (UPH) 83 Pb33
Bhadra ☒ IND (RJT) 80 Oh31
Bhadra W.S. ☒ IND 84 Oh39
Bhadreswar ☒ IND (WBG)
86 Pe34
Bhadra ☒ PK 65 Od31
Bhag ☒ PK 65 Od31
Bhagalpur ☒ IND (BIH) 83 Pd33
Bhagamandala ☒ IND (KTK)
Bhaguapura ☒ IND (MPH)
20 Ks35
Bhai ☒ USA (WA) 49 Mg22
Bhairab Bazar ☒ BD 86 Pf33
Bhairamgarh ☒ IND (CGH)
Bhairi Hol ▲ PK 65 Oc33
Bhaisa ☒ IND (APH) 82 Oj36
Bhakrapeta ☒ IND (APH)
85 Ok39
Bhakkar ☒ PK 65 Of30
Bhaktapur ☒ NEP 81 Pc32
Bhaktapur ☒ IND (KTK) 82 Oj37
Bhalki ☒ IND (KTK) 82 Oj37
Bhalwal ☒ PK 65 Og29
Bhamo ☒ MYA 86 Ph33
Bhandara ☒ IND (MPH) 83 Ok35
Bhander ☒ IND (MPH) 83 Ok33
Bhanga ☒ BD 86 Pf34
Bhanjanagar ☒ IND (ORS)
83 Pc36
Bhanupratappur ☒ IND (CGH)
83 Pa35
Bhaptiali ☒ IND (BIH) 83 Pc33
Bharatpur ☒ IND (RJT) 81 Ok32
Bharatpur National Park ☒
IND 81 Ok32
Bharuch ☒ IND (GUJ) 82 Og35
Bharthana ☒ IND (UPH) 81 Ok33
Bhatapara ☒ IND (CGH) 83 Pb35
Bhatapara ☒ IND (BIH) 83 Pd33
Bhatgaon ☒ IND (APH) 82 Oj38
Bhatinda ☒ IND (PJB) 80 Oh30
Bhatkal ☒ IND (KTK) 84 Oh39
Bhatpara ☒ IND (WBG) 86 Pe34
Bhatpur ☒ PK 65 Og29
Bhatti na ☒ IND (NGL) 86 Ph33
Bhatwari ☒ IND (UTT) 81 Ok30
Bhaunagar ☒ IND (GUJ) 82 Og35
Bhauli ☒ IND (UPH) 81 Pa32
Bhavani ☒ IND (TNU) 84 Oj40
Bhawanipatna ☒ IND (ORS)
83 Pb36

Bheemunipatnam Beach ☒ IND
83 Pb37
Bhera ☒ PK 65 Og29
Bherdaghat Marble Rocks ☒ IND
83 Ok34
Bhigvan ☒ IND (MHT) 82 Oh36
Bhikamkor ☒ IND (RJT) 80 Og32
Bhilai ☒ IND (CGH) 83 Pa35
Bhilwara ☒ IND (RJT) 82 Oh33
Bhim ☒ IND (RJT) 82 Oh33
Bhimavaram ☒ IND (APH)
83 Pa37
Bhimber ☒ PK 65 Og29
Bhimbetka ☒ IND 82 Oj34
Bhimpur ☒ IND (MPH) 82 Oj35
Bhind ☒ IND (MPH) 83 Ok32
Bhinmal ☒ IND (RJT) 82 Og33
Bhojpur ☒ IND (MPH) 82 Oj34
Bhojpur ☒ NEP 81 Pd32
Bhokar ☒ IND (MHT) 82 Oj36
Bhola ☒ BD 86 Pf34
Bhongaon ☒ IND (UPH) 81 Ok33
Bhongir ☒ IND (APH) 83 Ok37
Bhopal ☒ IND (MPH) 83 Pa36
Bhoramdeo ☒ IND (CGH)
83 Pa34
Bhor ☒ IND (BIH) 83 Pc32
Bhorvadi ☒ IND (MHT) 82 Oh36
Bhuban ☒ IND (ORS) 83 Pc35
Bhubaneswar ☒ IND (ORS)
83 Pc35
Bhuj ☒ IND (GUJ) 82 Oe34
Bhusawal ☒ IND (MHT) 82 Oh35
Bhutan ■ BHT 86 Pf32
Biadola ☒ IND (WBG) 86 Pe33
Biafra ☒ WAN 138 Ld41
Biafra ☒ IND (BIH) 83 Pc33
Biaford ☒ WAN 138 Ld41
Biak ☒ RI 114 Rh46
Biak Utara Nature Reserve ☒ RI
114 Rh46
Biała Piska ☒ PL 41 Mc37
Biała Podlaska ☒ PL 41 Md38
Biao ☒ WAN 138 Lc41
Biała Rawska ☒ PL 41 Ma39
Białobrzegi ☒ PL 41 Ma39
Białobrzegi ☒ PL 41 Mb38
Białogard ☒ PL 40 Lq36
Białopole ☒ PL 41 Md40
Białowieża ☒ PL 41 Md38
Białowieża N.P. ☒ PL 41 Md38
Biały Bór ☒ PL 40 Lr37
Białystok ☒ PL 41 Md37
Biancavilla ☒ I 37 Lp53
Bianco ☒ I 37 Lr52
Bianga ☒ RCA 140 Ma43
Biankouma ☒ CI 137 Kg42
Bia N.P. ☒ GH 137 Kj42
Biao ☒ WAN 138 Ld41
Biaora ☒ IND (MPH) 82 Oj34
Biara ☒ RDC 149 Lk45
Biaro ☒ RI 91 Rd44
Biarritz ☒ F 24 Kt47
Bíča ☒ CH 34 Lj44
Bičevaja ☒ RUS 77 Rh22
Bichena ☒ ETH 142 Mk40
Bicheno ☒ AUS (TAS) 111 Se66
Bichura ☒ RUS 71 Qf20
Bichvinta ☒ GE 57 Na24
Bickerton Island ☒ AUS 106 Rk52
Bicol N.P. ☒ RP 90 Rb39
Bidache ☒ F 24 Kt47
Bicuar, P.N. do ☒ ANG
150 Lh53
Bid ☒ WAN 138 Ld41
Bida ☒ WAN 138 Ld41
Bidar ☒ IND (KTK) 82 Oj37
Bidbid ☒ OM 61 Nk34
Bidde ☒ SP 145 Nb34
Biddeford ☒ USA (ME) 177 Ge24
Bideford ☒ GB 21 Kq39
Bidgemia ☒ AUS (WA) 104 Qh59
Bidokhti ☒ IR 64 Nk28
Bidon V ☒ DZ 132 La34
Bidukbiduk ☒ RI 95 Qj45
Bidzan ☒ IND (GUJ) 82 Oe33
Biel ☒ CH 34 Lj43
Biel = Bienne ☒ CH 34 Lj43
Bielefeld ☒ D 32 Lj38
Bielawa ☒ PL 40 Lr40
Bielice ☒ PL 41 Lu37
Bieler See ☒ CH 34 Lj43
Bielsk ☒ PL 41 Lu38
Bielsko-Biała ☒ PL 41 Lu41
Bielsk Podlaski ☒ PL 41 Md38
Bien Hoa ☒ VN 89 Qd40
Bienków ☒ PL 41 Lu41
Biegany ☒ PL 41 Mc39
Bieńkowice ☒ PL 40 Lt40
Biecz ☒ PL 41 Mb41
Biedenkopf ☒ D 32 Lj40
Biei ☒ J 77 Sb24
Biek ☒ IND (MHT) 82 Of35
Biel ☒ CH 34 Lj43
Biella ☒ I 34 Lj45
Bielefeld ☒ D 32 Lj38
Bielawy ☒ PL 41 Lu38
Bielefeld ☒ D 32 Lj38
Bielice ☒ PL 41 Lu37
Biélitz ☒ PL 41 Lu41
Bień ☒ PL 41 Mc39
Bieruń ☒ PL 41 Lu41
Bierutów ☒ PL 40 Lr39
Biesieswuar ☒ PL 40 Lu40
Biewry ☒ PL 41 Me41
Biga ☒ TR 45 Mg50
Biga Yarımadası ☒ TR 45 Mg50
Bigadiç ☒ TR 47 Mj51
Big Ambergris Cay ☒ GB
186 Ge36
Bigand ☒ RA (SF) 209 Gk62

Biga Yarımadası ☒ TR 45 Mg50
Billa Kalina ☒ AUS (SA) 108 Rj60
Billdal ☒ S 30 Lm33
Billengarrah ☒ AUS (NT) 106
Rh53
Billinuna ☒ AUS (WA) 103 Rd55
Billinghurst ☒ AUS (WA)
Billinooka ☒ AUS (WA)
Bilogora ☒ HR 35 Ls45
Billings ☒ USA (MT) 169 Ef23
Billings ☒ USA (OK) 174 Fb27
Bill of Portland ☒ GB 21 Ks40
Billom ☒ F 25 Ld45
Billum ☒ AUS (QLD) 108 Sd59
Billung ☒ IND (RJT) 80 Oh31
Biloela ☒ AUS (QLD) 109 Sf58
Bilohors'k ☒ UA 49 Mg23
Bilokurakyne ☒ UA 48 Mk21
Biloli ☒ IND (MHT) 82 Oj37
Biloxi ☒ USA (MS) 175 Ff30
Bilqās Qism Auwal ☒ ET 129
Mf30
Bilteen ☒ TCH 134 Ma38
Biltine ☒ N 16 Ma11
Biltugyan ☒ MYA 88 Pj37
Bilungala ☒ RI 91 Rd45
Bilverdil ☒ IR 57 Nd26
Bilwi = Puerto Cabezas ☒
NIC 185 Fj38
Bimba ☒ ANG 148 Lh49
Bimbe ☒ ANG 150 Lh51
Bimbéréke ☒ DY 138 Lb40
Bimbiya ☒ WA 100 Qk60
Bimbo ☒ RCA 140 Lk43
Bimini Islands ☒ BS 179 Ga33
Bina-Etawa ☒ IND (MPH) 83 Ok33
Binalbagan ☒ RP 90 Rb40
Binanga ☒ RI 93 Pk45
Binarowa ☒ PL 41 Mb41
Binauhan Falls ☒ RP 90 Rc39
Binbee ☒ AUS (QLD) 108 Se57
Binche ☒ B 23 Le40
Binchuan ☒ CHN (YUN) 87 Qa33
Binder ☒ BF 137 Kk40
Bindi ☒ AUS (VIC) 111 Se63
Bindki ☒ IND (UPH) 83 Pa32
Bindloe = Isla Marchena ☒ EC
197 Fe45
Bingam ☒ NEP 81 Pd32
Bingadi ☒ IND (CGH) 83 Pa35
Bingara ☒ AUS (NSW) 109 Sf60
Bing Bong ☒ AUS (NT) 106 Rj53
Bingen ☒ D 33 Lh41
Bingham ☒ GB 21 Ku38
Bingham ☒ USA (OK) 174 Fa28
Bingham ☒ USA (MA) 176 Gf23
Bingham ☒ USA (NM) 171 Eg29
Binghamton ☒ USA (NY) 177
Gc24
Bingöl ☒ TR 57 Na26
Binh ☒ VN 87 Qd38
Binh Dai ☒ VN 89 Qd40
Binh Gia ☒ VN 87 Qe35
Binh Long ☒ VN 89 Qd40
Binh Son ☒ VN 89 Qe38
Binic ☒ F 22 Ks42
Binitata ☒ RP 90 Rb38
Binjai ☒ RI 92 Pk44
Binka ☒ IND (ORS) 83 Pb35
Binnaway ☒ AUS (NSW) 109
Se61
Binningen ☒ CH 34 Lj43
Bintulu ☒ MAL 94 Qg44
Binzhou ☒ CHN (SDG) 73 Qj27
Bio Addo ☒ SP 145 Nc44
Bioča ☒ SCG 44 Lu48
Biougra ☒ MA 124 Kf30
Bippen ☒ D 32 Lh38
Biquinhas ☒ BR (MG) 203 Hh55
Bira Beach Resort ☒ RI
96 Ra48
Bir al 'Abd ☒ ET 129 Mg30
Bir al 'Akkariyah ☒ LAR 127 Lh30
Bir al 'Alaqah ☒ LAR 127 Lg30
Bir al Ghanam ☒ LAR 127 Lg30
Bir al Guzayyil ☒ LAR 128 La33
Bir al Jadid ☒ LAR 127 Lg31
Bir al Kammuniyah ☒ LAR
127 Lj31
Bir al Mastutah ☒ LAR 127 Lh31
Bir al Muwaylih ☒ LAR 128 La32
Bir al Qaf ☒ LAR 127 Lg32
Bir al Uwaynat ☒ LAR 128 La33
Bir al Wash ☒ LAR 127 Lg30
Biranabagan ☒ IND (WBG) 86 Pe33
Birandhanagar ☒ NEP 81 Pa31
Biratnagar ☒ NEP 81 Pd32
Biratori ☒ J 77 Sb24
Birbhum ☒ IND (WBG) 86 Pe33
Birch ☒ USA (AK) 165 Cf14
Birch Creek ☒ USA (AK) 165
152 Mg55
Birchenough Bridge ☒ ZW
152 Mg55
Birchip ☒ AUS (VIC) 111 Sb63
Birchi ☒ WAN 138 Ld38
Birch Hills ☒ CDN (SK) 169 Eh19
Birchi ☒ WAN 138 Ld38
Birch Island ☒ CDN 172 Fa19
Birch Mountains ☒ CDN (AB)
167 Ed17
Birch River ☒ CDN (MB) 169
Ek19
Bircot ☒ ETH 143 Nb42
Birch ☒ PL 41 Mc41
Bir Di ☒ SUD 141 Me42
Bird Island ☒ île aux Vaches ☒
SY 145 Nh47
Bird Island ☒ ZA 154 Lk62
Bir Djedid ☒ DZ 126 Ld29
Bir Dolmane ☒ DZ 126 Lc28
Bird Rock Lighthouse ☒ BS
186 Gc34
Birdsville ☒ AUS (QLD) 108 Rk58
Birdsville Race ☒ AUS 108 Rk58
Birdtail ☒ CDN (MB) 172 Fa20
Birein ☒ IL 58 Mg31
Bir el Amdar ☒ DZ 126 Ld29
Bir El-Ater ☒ DZ 126 Lc28
Bir el Fakama ☒ SUD 135 Mg37
Bir el Gâreb ☒ RMM 130 Kb35
Bir el Gorofa ☒ SUD 129 Mh34
Bir el Hasa ☒ SUD 129 Mh34
Birendranagar ☒ NEP 81 Pa31
Bir en Nugeim ☒ SUD 135 Mh36
Biretwa ☒ EAK 144 Mh45
Birfel ☒ DZ 126 Lc28
Bir Fadoid ☒ SUD 135 Mh36
Binchuan ☒ CHN (YUN) 87 Qa33
Bir Faysan ☒ KSA 60 Nd35
Bir Fegoussi ☒ TN 126 Le30
Birféla'd ☒ RUS (YAO) 76 Rg21
Bir Furawiya ☒ SUD 134 Md38
Bir Gandouz ☒ DARS 130 Kb35
Birganj ☒ NEP 81 Pc32
Bir gigel ☒ TR 47 Mj52
Birgudil ☒ IND (CGH) 83 Pa35
Bir Hadi ☒ KSA 61 Nh36
Birham ☒ ETH 142 Mj40
Birhan ☒ ETH 142 Mj40
Birhanu ☒ EAT 147 Mj49
Bir Hatab ☒ SUD 129 Mg30
Bir Hismet 'Umar ☒ ET 129
Mh35
Biri ☒ N 17 Lf15
Birigüi ☒ BR (SP) 202 He56
Biri Island ☒ RP 90 Rc39
Birin ☒ DZ 126 La28
Birjand ☒ IR 64 Nk29
Bir Jaydah ☒ KSA 58 Mj32
Bir Jidid ☒ MA 125 Kg29
Bir Jubni ☒ LAR 128 Mc30
Birka ☒ S 31 Ls31
Birkat al 'Aqabah ☒ LAR 128 Mc31
Birkat al Jumaymah ☒ KSA
60 Nd33
Birkat Dagran ☒ SP 145 Nb33
Birkat Saira ☒ SUD 134 Mb39
Birkeland ☒ N 30 Lh32
Birkeland ☒ N 30 Lh32
Birkeland ☒ SN 130 Kc38
Birkenau ☒ PL 41 Lu41
Birkenfeld ☒ D 33 Lh41
Birkenhead ☒ GB 21 Kr37
Birkered ☒ DK 30 La35
Bi'r Khalaf Allah ☒ LAR 127 Lg32
Bir Kiau ☒ SUD 135 Mh37
Bir Labasoi ☒ SUD 129 Mh35
Birkolo ☒ WAL 136 Ke41
Birmenstorf ☒ CH 34 Lj43
Birmingham ☒ GB 21 Ks38
Birmingham ☒ USA (AL) 175
Fg29
Birmitrapur ☒ IND (ORS) 83 Pc34
Bir Mogrein ☒ RIM 124 Ke33
Bir'l Mudakim ☒ LAR 127 Lg32
Bir Nawari ☒ SUD 135 Mh35
Bir Nazsirah ☒ LAR 124 Le33
Bir Nawari ☒ SUD 135 Mh35
Birni-Kebbi ☒ WAN 138 Lb40
Birnin ☒ RN 132 Le38
Birnin Gaouré ☒ RN 132 Lc39
Birnin Konni ☒ RN 132 Lc38
Birnin Kudu ☒ WAN 138 Ld40
Birnin Lallé ☒ RN 132 Ld38
Birnin-Yauri ☒ WAN 138 Lc40
Birniwa ☒ WAN 138 Ld39
Birni ☒ DY 138 La41
Biron ☒ DY 138 La41
Birqash ☒ ET 129 Mf30
Birtle ☒ CDN (MB) 172 Fa20
Bir Oumäne ☒ RMM 131 Kh35
Birparára ☒ IND (WBG) 86 Pe32
Biqueño ☒ IND (WBG) 86 Pe32
Qar'at ad Dibah ☒ LAR
126 Le31
Bir'r Qaryas ☒ LAR 127 Lj31
Bir Tabankourt ☒ LAR 127 Lj31
Bir Tanjdar ☒ LAR 127 Lg30
Bir'r Taqiet ☒ LAR 127 Lg31
Bir Tam-Tam ☒ MA 125 Kh29
Bir'r Terfawi ☒ SUD 134 Md36
Bir'r Awyan ☒ LAR 127 Lj30
Bir al Banaksih ☒ LAR 127 Lg30
Birthday Camp ☒ AUS (NT)
IND 82 Oe35
Birthplace of Mahatma Gandhi ☒
IND 82 Oe35
Birthplace of Sun Yat-sen ☒ CHN
75 Qg34
Birti ☒ SUD 135 Mg37
Bir'Tin Abunda ☒ LAR 127 Lh31
Bir'r Ticheln ☒ LAR 127 Lj31
Bir Ali Ben Khlifa ☒ TN 126 Le29
Bir al Jadid ☒ LAR 127 Lg31
Bir'r Tuhab ☒ LAR 127 Ma29
Biruaca ☒ YV 114 Rh48
Birufu ☒ RI 114 Rh48
Biruintsa ☒ MD 43 Mh42
Biruwa ☒ SUD 141 Me41
Birżai ☒ LT 39 Me34
Birżebbuġa ☒ M 37 Lp55
Birżi ☒ LV 39 Mf34
Bisacco ☒ I 37 Lq50
Bisaccia ☒ I 37 Lq50
Bisagana ☒ IND (ORS) 83 Pd34
Bisalehra ☒ IND (CGH)
83 Pa34
Bisalpur ☒ IND (UPH) 81 Ok31
Bisanadi National Reserve ☒
EAK 145 Na45
Bisane ☒ IR 59 Nf34
Bisáu ☒ IR 59 Nf31
Bisauli ☒ IND (UPH) 81 Ok31

Bisaurin ◻ E 28 Ku48
Bisbee ◻ USA (AZ) 171 Ef30
Biscarrosse ◻ F 24 Ki46
Biscayne N.P. ◻ USA 179 Fk33
Biscéglie ◻ I 37 Lr49
Bischofshofen ◻ A 35 Lo43
Bischofsheim ◻ D 32 Lp39
Bischwiller ◻ F 23 Lh42
Biscoe Islands ◻ 6 Gc32
Biscucuy ◻ YV 193 Gf41
Biselia ◻ SUD 141 Md42
Biserula ◻ EAU 144 Mf45
Bilevo ◻ AR 35 Lq48
Bisha ◻ ER 142 Mj38
Bishkek ● KS 66 Oh24
Bisho ◻ ZA 155 Md62
Bishop ◻ USA (CA) 170 Ea27
Bishop Auckland ◻ GB 21 Kt36
Bishop Hill S.H.S. ◻ USA 172 Fe25
Bishop's Falls ◻ CDN (NF) 177 Hc21
Bishop's Stortford ◻ GB 21 La39
Bishnur ◻ LAR 127 Lk30
Bishunpur ◻ IND (JKD) 83 Pc34
Bishu Shanzhuang ◻ CHN 73 Qj25
Biskra ◻ DZ 126 Lc28
Biskuplec ◻ PL 41 Ma37
Bisilig ◻ RP 91 Rd41
Bismarck ◻ USA (ND) 172 Ek22
Bismarck Archipelago ◻ PNG 116 Se47
Bismarck Sea ◻ PNG 116 Sd48
Bismark ◻ D 32 Lm38
Bismark ◻ TN 57 Na27
Bismo ◻ N 17 Lh51
Biso ◻ EAU 144 Mf45
Bison ◻ USA (SD) 169 Ej23
Bisonò ◻ DOM 186 Ge36
Bisotun ◻ IR 57 Nd28
Bisotun ◻ IR 57 Nd28
Bisogården ◻ S 16 Lj14
Bissau ● GNB 136 Kc40
Bissett ◻ CDN (MB) 172 Fc22
Bissikrima ◻ RG 136 Ke40
Bissorã ◻ GNB 136 Kc39
Bistret ◻ RO 44 Md47
Bistrica ◻ BIH 35 Ls46
Bistrica ◻ SCG 44 Lu47
Bistrica ◻ SCG 44 Lu48
Bistrița ◻ RO 43 Md44
Bisungarh ◻ IND (JKD) 83 Pc33
Bisunah ◻ IND (UPH) 81 Pa32
Bisztynek ◻ PL 41 Ma36
Bitam ◻ G 139 Lj44
Bitangor ◻ MAL 94 Qf44
Bitata ◻ ETH 145 Mk43
Bitburg ◻ D 33 Lg41
Bitchabé ◻ TG 137 La41
Bitche ◻ F 23 Lh41
Bitčvinta ◻ GE 57 Na24
Bithoor ◻ IND 83 Pa32
Bitigliu ◻ ETH 142 Na41
Bitilifondi ◻ RCA 141 Md43
Bisunagarh ◻ IND (JKD) 83 Pc33
Bittis ◻ TR 57 Nb26
Bitola ◻ MK 44 Mb49
Bitonto ◻ I 37 Lr49
Bitou ◻ BF 137 Kk40
Bitoutouek ◻ CAM 138 Lf44
Bitragunta ◻ IND (APH) 85 Ok38
Bitra Island ◻ IND 84 Oh38
Bittencourt ◻ BR (AM) 198 Gf46
Bitter Creek ◻ USA (WY) 171 Ef25
Bitterfeld ◻ D 32 Ln39
Bitterfontein ◻ ZA 154 Lj62
Bitterroot Range ◻ USA 168 Ec22
Bitti ◻ I 36 Lk50
Bittuang ◻ RI 96 Qf43
Bitumount ◻ CDN (AB) 167 Ee17
Bitung ◻ RI 97 Rc45
Bituruna ◻ BR (PR) 204 He59
Biu ◻ WAN 139 Lg42
Biu Plateau ◻ WAN 139 Lg40
Bivona ◻ I 36 Lo53
Biwat ◻ PNG 115 Sd48
Biwinapada ◻ RI 96 Qh46
Bixby ◻ USA (MO) 175 Fe27
Biyang ◻ CHN (HNN) 73 Qg29
Bíye K'obe ◻ ETH 143 Nb40
Biyoley ◻ SP 145 Nc44
Bizana ◻ ZA 155 Me61
Bizen ◻ J 79 Rh28
Bizerte ◻ TN 126 Le27
Bjahoml' ◻ BY 39 Mj36
Bjala ◻ BG 45 Mg48
Bjala ◻ BG 45 Mh48
Bjala čerkva ◻ BG 45 Me49
Bjala Slatina ◻ BG 44 Md47
Bjalynicy ◻ BY 48 Me19
Bjarézina ◻ BY 39 Mg36
Bjargtangar ◻ IS 18 Jp25
Bjarnerya ◻ IS 18 Kt25
Bjärnum ◻ S 31 Lo34
Bjarozavka ◻ BY 41 Mf37
Bjasta ◻ S 38 Lo27
Bjelakinca ◻ BIH 44 Lt47
Bjelovar ◻ HR 35 Lr45
Bjerkvik ◻ N 16 Lj32
Bjerringbro ◻ DK 30 Lk34
Bjötbo ◻ S 31 Lo30
Bjorkelangen ◻ N 30 Lm31
Bjorklinge ◻ S 31 Ls31
Björkö ◻ S 31 Lt31
Bjorkoby ◻ FIN 38 Mb27
Bjorkon ◻ S 38 Mb27
Bjorksele ◻ S 16 Lt33
Bjorko ◻ S 38 Lt27
Bjorneborg ◻ S 31 Lp31
Bjorne Peninsula ◻ CDN 163 Fo03
Björnlandets n.p. ◻ S 16 Lk14
Bjurholm ◻ S 16 Lk14
Bjurslatt ◻ S 17 Lh15
Bjuv ◻ S 30 Ln34
Bla ◻ RMM 137 Kh39
Blåa Iónió ◻ IS 18 Jz27
Blace ◻ SCG 44 Mc47
Blackall ◻ AUS (QLD) 109 Sc58
Black and White Pagoda ◻ CHN 87 Qa34
Blackbeard Island National Seashore ◻ USA 178 Fk30
Blackbird Cay ◻ BH 184 Fg37
Black Braes ◻ AUS (QLD) 107 Sc55
Blackbull ◻ AUS (QLD) 107 Sa54
Blackburn ◻ GB 21 Ks37
Blackbutt ◻ AUS (QLD) 109 Sg59
Black C. ◻ USA 164 Cd16
Black Canyon of the Gunnison N.P. ◻ USA 171 Eg26
Black Diamond ◻ CDN (AB) 169 Ec20
Blackdown ◻ AUS (QLD) 107 Sa54
Blackdown Tableland N.P. ◻ AUS 109 Sd57
Blackfeet Ind. Res. ◻ USA 169 Ed21
Blackfellows ◻ AUS 110 Rh62
Blackfoot ◻ CDN (AB) 169 Ee19
Blackfoot ◻ USA (ID) 169 Ed24
Blackfoot Ind. Res. ◻ USA 169 Ed20
Blackfoot Res. ◻ USA 169 Ee24
Black Forest ◻ D 33 Lh43
Black Gate ◻ AUS (NSW) 111 Sb62
Black Head ◻ IRL 19 Kl37
Black Lake ◻ CDN (SK) 167 Eh16
Black Island ◻ CDN 172 Fc20
Black Mountain ◻ IND 86 Pf32

Black Mountain ◻ USA (NC) 178 Fj28
Black Mountain N.P. ◻ BHT 86 Pf32
Black Mountains ◻ GB 21 Kr39
Black Point ◻ BS 179 Gb33
Blackpool ◻ GB 21 Kr37
Black Range ◻ USA 171 Eg29
Black River ◻ JA 186 Gb36
Black River ◻ VN 87 Qb35
Black River Falls ◻ USA (WI) 172 Fe23
Black Rock ◻ NAM 154 Lh59
Black Rock ◻ USA (UT) 171 Ed26
Black Rock ◻ ZA 154 Mb59
Black Rock Desert ◻ USA
Blacksburg ◻ USA (VA) 178 Fk27
Black Sea ◻ 14 Mb05
Blackshear ◻ USA (GA) 178 Fj30
Black Volta ◻ GH/BF 137 Kj40
Blackwater ◻ AUS (QLD) 109 Se57
Blackwell ◻ USA (OK) 174 Fb27
Blackwell ◻ USA (TX) 174 Ek29
Blacktown ◻ AUS (QLD) 109 Sb57
Bladel ◻ NL 23 Lf39
Bladensburg N.P. ◻ AUS (QLD) 108 Sb57
Blaenavon ◻ GB 21 Kr39
Blaenau ◻ GBI 35 Sa47
Blagodarnyj ◻ RUS 48 Na48
Blagoevgrad ◻ BG 44 Md48
Blagoveščenka ◻ RUS 49 Oh21
Blagoveščensk ◻ RUS 71 Rd20
Blahovešcenky raion ◻ UA
Blain ◻ F 22 Kt43
Blaine Lake ◻ CDN (SK) 169 Eg19
Blair ◻ USA (NE) 172 Fb25
Blair Athol ◻ AUS (QLD) 109 Sd57
Blairbeth ◻ ZA 155 Md58
Blair Castle ◻ GB 20 Kr34
Blairgowrie ◻ GB 20 Ks34
Blairquhan Castle ◻ GB 20 Ks33
Blairmore ◻ CDN (AB) 169 Ec21
Blairsville ◻ USA (GA) 170 Dk26
Blairsville ◻ USA (GA) 178 Fj28
Blaj ◻ RO 43 Md44
Blå Jungfrun ◻ S 31 Lr33
Blå Jungfrun n.p. ◻ S 31 Lr33
Blawa Laodem ◻ RN 133 Lg35
Blakely ◻ RN 41 Mc36
Blake Basin ◻ 178 Gc31
Blakely ◻ USA (GA) 175 Fh30
Blake Plateau ◻ 178 Ga30
Blakstad ◻ N 30 Lk32
Blambala ◻ WAL 136 Ke42
Blambangan ◻ RI 93 Qc48
Blåmont ◻ F 23 Lg42
Blanca Aurora Falls ◻ RP 90 Rc40
Blanca Flor ◻ BOL 198 Gg51
Blancagrande ◻ RA (BA) 209 Gk44
Blanca Peak ◻ USA 171 En27
Blanchard Springs Caverns ◻ USA 175 Fd28
Blanche Channel ◻ SOL 117 Sj50
Blanche Marievallen ◻ SME
Blanchet Island ◻ CDN 167 Ed15
Blanchetown ◻ AUS (SA) 110 Rk63
Blanco ◻ USA (TX) 174 Fa30
Blanco-Sablon ◻ CDN 177 Hb20
Blandford Forum ◻ GB 21 Ks40
Blanding ◻ USA (UT) 171 Ef27
Blanes ◻ E 29 Lc49
Blanfla ◻ CI 137 Kh42
Blangkejeren ◻ RI 92 Pj43
Blangkeruan ◻ RI 92 Ph44
Blangy-sur-Bresle ◻ F 23 Lb41
Blankahom ◻ S 31 Lr33
Blankenberge ◻ B 23 Ld39
Blankenburg ◻ D 32 Lm39
Blankenheim ◻ D 32 Lg40
Blanquillo ◻ ROU 204 Hd62
Blantyre ◻ MW 153 Mh53
Blanzac ◻ F 24 Ls45
Blarney ◻ IRL 19 Km39
Blarney Castle ◻ IRL 19 Kk38
Blasket Islands ◻ IRL 19 Kk38
Blaszki ◻ PL 40 Lt39
Blatnica ◻ BIH 35 Ls46
Blato ◻ HR 35 Ls48
Blaubeuren ◻ D 33 Lk42
Blaufelden ◻ D 33 Lk41
Blåvand ◻ DK 30 Lj35
Blåvands Huk ◻ DK 30 Lj35
Blawwag ◻ RI 95 Qh50
Blaye ◻ F 24 Ks45
Blayney ◻ AUS (NSW) 111 Se62
Bo'al ◻ CHN (YUN) 74 Qd34
Boajibu ◻ WAL 136 Ke41
Bleberg ◻ A 35 Lp44
Bleasa ◻ LV 39 Me33
Bleaker Island ◻ GB 210 Ha72
Blebo ◻ LB 136 Kg43
Bled ◻ SLO 42 Lp44
Blega ◻ RI 95 Qg49
Bleiburg ◻ A 35 Lp44
Bleikvassli ◻ N 16 Lg32
Blejsko jezero ◻ SLO 42 Lp44
Blekinge ◻ S 31 Lq34
Bléneau ◻ F 25 Lc43
Blenheim ◻ AUS (QLD) 109 Se59
Blenheim ◻ NZ 113 Tg66
Blenheim Palace ◻ GB
21 Kt39
Blérê ◻ F 24 La43
Blerick ◻ NL 23 Lf39
Blesansposo ◻ ZA 155 Mc59
Bletterans ◻ F 25 Lf44
Blida ◻ DZ 126 Lb27
Blieskastel ◻ D 33 Lh41
Blimbing ◻ RI 95 Qj46
Blina ◻ AUS (WA) 103 Rc54
Blinaodi ◻ CI 137 Kh42
Blind Channel ◻ CDN (BC) 168 Dh20
Blind River ◻ CDN (ON) 173 Fj22
Blinman ◻ AUS (SA) 108 Rk61
Blinnenhorn ◻ CH 34 Lj44
Blitar ◻ RI 95 Qg50
Blitta ◻ TG 137 La41
Block Island ◻ USA 177 Ge25
Bloemfontein ● ZA 155 Md60
Bloemhoek ◻ ZA 154 Lk60
Bloemhof ◻ ZA 155 Mc59
Bloemhof Dam Nature Reserve ◻ ZA 155 Md59
Blois ◻ F 24 La43
Blokhus ◻ DK 30 Lk33
Blolékin ◻ CI 136 Kg42
Blombacka ◻ S 31 Lo31
Blonduós ◻ IS 18 Ka25
Blongas ◻ RI 96 Qj50
Bloody Foreland ◻ IRL 19 Km35
Bloomfield ◻ CDN 169 Ed21
Bloomfield ◻ USA (IN) 175 Fg26
Bloomfield ◻ USA (MT) 169 Eh22
Bloomfield River ◻ AUS (QLD) 107 Sc53
Bloomington ◻ USA (IL) 175 Ff25

Bloomington ◻ USA (MN) 172 Fd23
Bloomington ◻ USA (PA) 177 Gb35
Bloomsbury ◻ AUS (QLD) 107 Se56
Blora ◻ RI 95 Qf49
Blossom Village ◻ GB 179 Fk36
Blouberg ◻ PL 40 Lg37
Bloukrans Bridge ◻ ZA 154
Blountstown ◻ USA (FL) 175 Fh30
Blowholes ◻ OM 61 Ng37
Blowholes (Quobba) ◻ AUS 104 Qg58
Blubber Bay ◻ CDN (BC) 168 Dh21
Bludenz ◻ A 34 Lk43
Blue Dam ◻ AUS (SA) 108 Rh61
Blue Earth ◻ USA (MN) 172 Fc24
Blue Nile ◻ ETH 135 Mh40
Blue Nile S ◻ SUD 142 Mf40
Blue Grotto ◻ M 37 Lp55
Blue Hills of Couteau ◻ CDN 177 Hb22
Blue Hole ◻ BH 184 Fg37
Blue Hole N.P. ◻ BH 184 Ff37
Blue Lagoon N.P. ◻ Z 152 Me54
Blue Lake ◻ AUS 110 Sa64
Blue Lake ◻ USA (CA) 168 Dj25
Blue Mountain ◻ USA (NY) 177 Gc24
Blue MountainLake ◻ USA (NY) 177 Gc24
Blue Mountains ◻ USA 168 Ea23
Blue Mountains ◻ USA 178 Fk27
Blue Mountains N.P. ◻ AUS (NSW) 111 Sf62
Blue Mountains N.P. ◻ JA 186 Gb36
Blue Mud Hills ◻ USA 169 Ef22
Blue Nile ◻ ETH 135 Mh40
Blue Nile S ◻ SUD 122 Mf40
Blue Nile Canyon ◻ ETH 142 Mk40
Blue Nile Falls = Tis Isat Falls ◻ ETH 142 Mj40
Blue Rapids ◻ USA (KS) 174 Fb26
Blue Ridge ◻ USA (GA) 175 Fh28
Blue Ridge ◻ USA 178 Fk27
Blue Ridge Parkway ◻ USA 178 Fk27
Blue River ◻ CDN (BC) 168 Ea19
Blue Stack Mountains ◻ IRL 19 Km36
Blue Train ◻ USA 134 Lk62
Blue Train (Garden Route) ◻ ZA 155 Mc62
Bluewater ◻ AUS (QLD) 107 Sd55
Bluff ◻ AUS (QLD) 109 Se57
Bluff ◻ NZ 113 Te69
Bluff ◻ PA 185 Fj41
Bluff ◻ USA (AK) 164 Bj13
Bluff ◻ USA (UT) 171 Ef27
Bluff Downs ◻ AUS (QLD) 107 Sc55
Bluffers Park ◻ CDN 173 Ga24
BluffFace Range ◻ AUS 103 Rd54
Bluff Point ◻ AUS 104 Qh59
Blukwa ◻ RDC 144 Mf45
Blumberg ◻ D 33 Lj43
Blumenau ◻ BR (SC) 205 Hf59
Blup Blup Island ◻ PNG 115 Sc47
Blyde River Canyon Nature Reserve ◻ ZA 155 Mf58
Blyth ◻ GB 20 Kt35
Blythe ◻ USA (CA) 170 Ec29
Blytheville ◻ USA (AR) 175 Ff28
Bni-Boufrah ◻ MA 125 Kj27
Bo ◻ WAL 136 Ke41
Bo ◻ WAL 136 Ke41
Boa ◻ RCA 141 Lk43
Boana ◻ PNG 115 Sd49
Boanamary ◻ RM 156 Nd53
Boanda ◻ CAM 138 Lf43
Boang Island ◻ PNG 116 Sg47
Boa Nova ◻ BR (BA) 203 Hk53
Boardman ◻ USA (OH) 173 Fk25
Boardman ◻ USA (OR) 168 Ea22
Boat Basin ◻ CDN (BC) 168 Dg21
Boat of Garten ◻ GB 20 Kr33
Boa Viagem ◻ BR (CE) 201 Ja48
Boa Vista ◻ BR (AM) 198 Gh46
Boa Vista ◻ BR (AM) 198 Gj48
Boa Vista ◻ BR (BA) 201 Ja49
Boa Vista ◻ BR (PA) 195 Hd47
Boa Vista ◻ BR (RR) 193 Gk44
Boa Vista da Ramos ◻ BR (AM) 199 Hb47
Boa Vista do Tupim ◻ BR (BA) 203 Hj52
Boa Vista, T.I. ◻ BR 199 Ha47
Boa Island ◻ RP 90 Qk38
Boac ◻ RP 90 Ra39
Boaco ◻ NIC 184 Fh39
Boal ◻ E 26 Ko47
Boana ◻ PNG 115 Sd49
Boardman ◻ USA (OH) 173 Fk25
Boardman ◻ USA (OR) 168 Ea22
Boat Basin ◻ CDN (BC) 168 Dg21
Bobadah ◻ AUS (NSW) 111 Sd62
Bobai ◻ CHN (GZG) 74 Qf34
Bobâlna ◻ RO 43 Md44
Bobasakoa ◻ RM 156 Ne52
Bobbejaanland ◻ B 23 Le39
Bobbili ◻ IND (APH) 83 Pc36
Bobé ◻ DY 138 Lb41
Bobi ◻ CI 137 Kg42
Bobia ◻ E 26 Ko47
Bobigny ◻ F 23 Lc42
Bobilla ◻ RDC 140 Ma44
Bobingen ◻ D 33 Ll43
Böblingen ◻ D 33 Lk42
Boblice ◻ PL 40 Lr37
Bobonong ◻ RB 152 Me56
Boboye ◻ PNG 115 Sd48
Bobr ◻ BY 39 Mh36
Bobrov ◻ RUS 48 Na20
Bobrowice ◻ PL 40 Lp38
Bobures ◻ YV 192 Ge41
Bobute ◻ SCG 45 Lt48
Boca Arenal ◻ CR 185 Fh41
Boca Barranca ◻ CR 185 Fh41
Bočac ◻ BIH 35 Ls46

Boca Candelaria ◻ CO 192 Gb44
Boca Caragua ◻ CO 192 Gb43
Boca Chica ◻ CO 186 Gb36
Boca de Anaro ◻ YV 192 Ge42
Boca de Apiza ◻ MEX (COL) 182 Ej36
Boca de Aroa ◻ YV 193 Gf40
Boca de la Serpiente ◻ YV 193 Gk41
Boca de la Vinorama ◻ MEX (BCS) 180 Ef34
Boca del Macareo ◻ YV 193 Gk41
Boca del Mezquital ◻ MEX (DGO) 181 Eh34
Boca del Pao ◻ YV 193 Gh41
Boca del Pozo ◻ YV 193 Gk40
Boca del Río ◻ MEX (VC) 183 Fb36
Boca de Pascuales ◻ MEX (COL) 182 Ej36
Boca de Pijjiapan ◻ MEX (CHP) 183 Fd38
Boca de Río Indio ◻ PA 185 Fk41
Boca de Tomatlán ◻ MEX (JLC) 182 Eh35
Boca de Yuma ◻ DOM 187 Gf36
Boca do Acre ◻ BR (AM) 198 Gg50
Boca do Acre, T.I. ◻ BR 198 Gg50
Boca do Capanã ◻ BR (AM) 198 Gk48
Boca do Jaco ◻ BR (AM) 198 Gk48
Boca do Jari ◻ BR (AP) 195 He46
Boca do Mutum ◻ BR (AM) 198 Gh48
Boca Grande ◻ YV 193 Gk41
Boca Iglesia ◻ MEX (QTR) 183 Fg35
Bocaina ◻ BR (PI) 201 Hk49
Bocaina do Sul ◻ BR (SC) 205 Hf59
Bocaiúva ◻ BR (MG) 203 Hj54
Boca Mavaca ◻ YV 193 Gh44
Bocanda ◻ CI 137 Kh42
Bocaranga ◻ RCA 140 Lk42
Boca Raton ◻ USA (FL) 179 Fk32
Bocas ◻ MEX (SLP) 182 Ek34
Bocche di Bonifacio ◻ F/I 36 Lk48
Bochart ◻ CDN (QC) 176 Gd21
Bochinche ◻ YV 193 Gk42
Bochnia ◻ PL 41 Ma41
Bocholt ◻ D 32 Lg39
Bochum ◻ D 32 Lh39
Bockenem ◻ D 32 Ll38
Böcki ◻ PL 41 Mc38
Bocoio ◻ ANG 150 Lh52
Boconó ◻ YV 192 Ge41
Boconoíto ◻ YV 192 Ge41
Boco-Songho ◻ RCB 148 Lg48
Boça ◻ PL 40 Mc45
Bocsig ◻ RO 43 Mb44
Bod ◻ BD 86 Pe32
Boda ◻ RCA 140 Lk43
Boda ◻ S 17 Lh35
Bodailang ◻ RDC 140 Mb44
Bodalla ◻ AUS (NSW) 111 Sf64
Bodallin ◻ AUS 104 Qk61
Bodani ◻ SCG 44 Lu45
Bodators ◻ S 31 Lq33
Bodaybo ◻ RUS 55 Rc07
Bodélé ◻ TCH 133 Lj37
Boden ◻ S 16 Ma13
Bodensee ◻ D 33 Lk43
Bodê-Shadu ◻ WAN 138 Lc41
Bodhan ◻ IND (APH) 82 Oj36
Bodhgaya ◻ IND 83 Pc33
Bodi ◻ DY 138 La41
Bodi ◻ GH 137 Kj42
Bodi ◻ MNG 70 Qa23
Bodinayakkanur ◻ IND (TNU) 84 Oj40
Boditi ◻ ETH 142 Mj42
Bodjokola ◻ RDC 140 Ma44
Bodmin ◻ GB 21 Kq40
Bôdô ◻ N 16 Lh12
Bodocó ◻ BR (AM) 199 Ja49
Bodocó ◻ BR (PE) 201 Ja49
Bodoni ◻ EAK 145 Na46
Bodoquena ◻ BR (MS) 202 Hb56
Bodoukpa ◻ RCA 140 Lk43
Bodrost ◻ BG 44 Md48
Bodrum ◻ TR 47 Mh53
Boduna ◻ RM 157 Nd57
Bodzentyn ◻ PL 41 Ma40
Boende ◻ RDC 149 Ma46
Boende ◻ RDC 149 Ma46
Boerne ◻ USA (TX) 181 Fa31
Boesmanstekeninge ◻ ZA 154 Mb61
Bofete ◻ BR (SP) 202 Hf57
Boffa ◻ RG 136 Kc40
Bofossou ◻ RG 136 Kf41
Bogale ◻ MYA 88 Ph37
Bogalusa ◻ USA (LA) 175 Ff30
Bogamgon ◻ RCA 141 Lh43
Bogandé ◻ BF 137 Kk39
Bogané ◻ DY 138 La41
Bogangolo ◻ RCA 140 Lk43
Bogantungan ◻ AUS (QLD) 109 Sd57
Bogarella ◻ AUS (QLD) 109 Sd58
Bogarra ◻ E 27 Ks52
Bogata ◻ USA (TX) 174 Fc29
Bogatynia ◻ PL 40 Lp39
Bogazici ◻ TR 47 Mh52
Bogazici Köprüsü ◻ TR 45 Mk49
Boğazkale ◻ TR 56 Mn25
Boğazkale Milli Parkı ◻ TR 56 Mn25
Bogda ◻ PNG 115 Sd48
Bogbonga ◻ RDC 140 Ma44
Bogda Feng ◻ CHN 67 Pe24
Bogdan Shan ◻ CHN 67 Pe24
Bogé ◻ DY 138 La41
Bogg Uul ◻ MNG 67 Pk22
Bogí ◻ AL 44 Lu49
Bogi ◻ PNG 116 Sf50
Boğ, ◻ RN 133 Lh38
Bogodukhiv ◻ UA 48 Mg20
Bogol ◻ SUD 135 Mf41
Bogoroditsk ◻ RUS 48 Mk19
Bogoric ◻ SCG 44 Lt48
Bogoslof Island ◻ USA 164 Bf19
Bogoso ◻ GH 137 Kj42
Bogoste ◻ YV 192 Gb46
Bogotá ● CO 192 Gc44
Bogovina ◻ SCG 44 Mc47
Bogra ◻ BD 86 Pe33

Bogučar ◻ RUS 48 Na21
Boguda ◻ RDC 140 Ma44
Boguila ◻ RCA 140 Lj42
Boguila Kota ◻ RCA 140 Lj42
Bogunda ◻ RDC (DRC) 109 Sc56
Bogutovac ◻ SCG 44 Mb47
Bo Hai ◻ CHN 73 Qk26
Bo Hai Haixia ◻ CHN 73 Ra26
Bohain-en-Vermandois ◻ F 23 Ld41
Bohai Shangjing-Longquanfu ◻ CHN 76 Re24
Bohdalov ◻ CZ 42 Lq41
Böhler ◻ USA (WY) 171 Eh25
Böhmer Wald ◻ D 33 Ln41
Bohodukhiv ◻ UA 48 Mh20
Bohol ◻ RP 90 Rc41
Bohol Strait ◻ RP 90 Rb41
Bohonal de Ibor ◻ E 27 Kp51
Bohong ◻ RCA 140 Lk42
Bohonye ◻ H 42 Ls44
Böhöröt ◻ MNG 70 Qe33
Bohotleh ◻ SP 143 Nc42
Boi ◻ WAN 138 Le41
Boiaçu ◻ BR (RR) 198 Gk46
Boijoon ◻ RP 90 Rb41
Boila ◻ BG 45 Mf47
Boiling Lake ◻ WD 187 Gk34
Boina ◻ RM 156 Nd53
Boing ◻ MM (ORS) 83 Pc36
Boiro ◻ E 26 Km48
Boise City ◻ USA (OK) 174 Ej27
Bois-le-Roi ◻ F 23 Lc42
Boltaña ◻ E 28 La44
Bois pétrifié de Tn Ouřassène ◻ DZ 126 Lb36
Boissevain ◻ CDN (MB) 172 Ek21
Boituva ◻ BR (SP) 205 Hg57
Boizenburg ◻ D 32 Ll37
Bojana ◻ D 32 Ls42
Bojano ◻ I 37 Lp49
Bojanovo ◻ BG 45 Mh48
Bojanowo ◻ PL 41 Mb40
Boma ◻ CN 46 Mj58
Bomadi ◻ WAN 138 Lc43
Boma ◻ RDC 148 Lg48
Bójka ◻ BG 45 Mf47
Bojnický zámok ◻ SK 42 Lt42
Bojnik ◻ SCG 44 Mc47
Bojo ◻ IR 62 Nj27
Bojonegoro ◻ RI 95 Qf49
Boju ◻ WAN 138 Ld42
Boju-Ega ◻ WAN 138 Ld42
Bojuru ◻ BR (RS) 204 He61
Bo'ka ◻ UZ 63 Oe25
Boka Kotorska ◻ SCG 44 Lt48
Böka ◻ RDC 140 Lk43
Bokada ◻ RDC (ASM) 86 Pg32
Bokakhat ◻ IND (ASM) 86 Pg32
Bokani ◻ WAN 138 Ld41
Bokaro tog'lari ◻ UZ 62 Ob24
Boke ◻ KZ 66 Oj24
Bokele ◻ RDC 149 Ma46
Boken ◻ RDC 140 Kk39
Boking ◻ WAN 138 Le42
Bokna ◻ RDC 140 Mb44
Bokol Plain ◻ EAK 145 Mk44
Bokoli ◻ RDC 140 Ld44
Bokolo ◻ RDC 149 Ld45
Bokolobo ◻ RDC 140 Mb45
Bokonbaji ◻ KS 66 Oj24
Bokondo ◻ RDC 140 Lk45
Bokoro ◻ TCH 139 Lj39
Bokoro ◻ RDC 149 Ma46
Bokter Muzbel ◻ KZ 62 Nb24
Bol ◻ HR 35 Ls47
Bol ◻ TCH 133 Lh39
Bolafa ◻ RDC 140 Md45
Bolaiti ◻ RDC 140 Md45
Bolama ◻ GNB 136 Kc40
Bolangir ◻ IND (ORS) 83 Pb35
Bolama-Bijagós ◻ GNB 136 Kc40
Bolaños ◻ MEX (JLC) 182 Ej35
Bolaños de Calatrava ◻ E 27 Kr52
Bolanpass ◻ PK 65 Od31
Bolaven Plateau ◻ LAO 89 Qd38
Bolayir ◻ TR 45 Mg50
Bolbec ◻ F 22 La41
Boldesti Scăeni ◻ RO 45 Mg45
Bolderaja ◻ LV 39 Md33
Bôle ◻ ETH 142 Mj42
Boleko ◻ RDC 140 Mb45
Bolekhiv ◻ UA 43 Me41
Bolena ◻ RDC 140 Md45
Bolentio ◻ I 34 Lm46
Bolestawiec ◻ PL 40 Lp39
Bolewicko ◻ PL 40 Lr38
Bolgatanga ◻ GH 137 Kk40
Bolhov ◻ RUS 48 Mj19
Boli ◻ CHN (HLG) 76 Rb24
Boli ◻ SUD 141 Md42
Boli ◻ RDC 140 Lk44
Bolia ◻ RDC 149 Ma46
Bolívar ◻ CO 192 Gc42
Bolívar ◻ EAK 145 Na46
Bolívar ◻ RA (BA) 209 Gk44
Bolívar ◻ PE 196 Gb49
Bolívar ◻ CO 174 Fd27
Bolívar 802, Cerro ◻ YV 193 Gj42
Bolivia ◻ C 179 Ga34
Bolivia ◻ BS 179 Ga34
Bolkow ◻ PL 40 Lr40
Bollène ◻ F 25 Le46
Bollebygd ◻ S 30 Ln32
Bollnäs ◻ S 17 Ls28
Bollon ◻ AUS (QLD) 109 Sd60
Bolmen ◻ S 31 Lo34
Bolnisi ◻ GE 57 Nc25
Bologna ◻ I 37 Kg40
Bolobo ◻ RDC 149 Lj47
Boločevka-2-ja ◻ RUS (YAO)
76 Rn21
Bolod ◻ MNG 70 Qb23
Bologoïye ◻ RUS 48 Mg17
Bologu ◻ RDC 140 Lc44
Bolomba ◻ RDC 140 Ma44
Bolombo ◻ RDC 149 Ma47
Bolongo ◻ RDC 140 Mb44

Bolona ◻ CI 137 Kg40
Bolongolava ◻ RM 157 Nc55
Bolonguera ◻ ANG 148 Lh50
Bolonguera ◻ ANG 150 Lg52
Bonham ◻ USA (TX) 174 Fb29
Bonhicon ◻ DY 138 La42
Bonifacio ◻ F 36 Lk49
Bonifacio ◻ F 36 Lk49
Boni National Reserve ◻ EAK 145 Na46
Bonin Islands ◻ J 10 Sa07
Bonin Trench ◻ J 10 Sa06
Bonita Springs ◻ USA 179 Fk32
Bonito ◻ BR (BA) 201 Hk51
Bonito ◻ BR (MS) 202 Hb56
Bonito ◻ BR (PA) 195 Hg46
Bonito ◻ BR (PE) 201 Ja50
Bonito de Minas ◻ BR (MG) 203 Hh53
Bonkoukou ◻ RN 133 Lb38
Bonn ● D 32 Lh40
Bonners Ferry ◻ USA (ID) 168 Eb21
Bonnétable ◻ F 22 La42
Bonnet Plume River ◻ CDN 165 Dd13
Bonneval ◻ F 23 Lb42
Bonneville ◻ F 25 Lg44
Bonneville Salt Flats ◻ USA 171 Ed25
Bonney Downs ◻ AUS (WA) 102 Qk57
Bonnie Rock ◻ AUS (WA) 104 Qk61
Bonny ◻ WAN 138 Ld44
Bonnyrigg ◻ RI 114 Rd16
Bonnyville ◻ CDN (AB) 169 Ee18
Bonoi ◻ RI 114 Rh46
Bonoua ◻ CI 137 Kh43
Bonyera ◻ GI 34 Lm45
Bonyhád ◻ H 43 Lt44
Bon Zone ◻ MYA 86 Pg34
Boo ◻ S 31 Lt31
Boodarie ◻ AUS (WA) 104 Qk60
Boogardie ◻ AUS (WA) 104 Qj60
Booligal ◻ AUS (NSW) 111 Sc62
Boola ◻ RG 136 Kf41
Boolaboola ◻ AUS (SA) 108 Sa61
Boologooro ◻ AUS (WA) 104 Qh58
Boomi ◻ AUS (NSW) 111 Se60
Boonah ◻ AUS (QLD) 109 Sg60
Boone ◻ USA (IA) 172 Fc24
Boone ◻ USA (NC) 178 Fj27
Boorabbin ◻ AUS (WA) 104 Ra61
Boorabbin N.P. ◻ AUS (WA) 104 Ra61
Boorindarrie ◻ AUS (WA) 104 Qk61
Booroorban ◻ AUS (NSW) 111 Sc62
Boorowa ◻ AUS (NSW) 111 Se63
Boosaaso ◻ SP 143 Ne40
Boot Hill Mus. and Front Street ◻ USA 174 Fa27
Booti Booti N.P. ◻ AUS (NSW) 111 Sg62
Bootle ◻ GB 21 Ks37
Booué ◻ G 148 Lf46
Bopako ◻ RDC 140 Ma45
Bopfingen ◻ D 33 Ll42
Boppard ◻ D 33 Lh40
Bopolu ◻ LB 136 Ke42
Boqueirão ◻ BR (SP) 202 Hf56
Boqueirão ◻ BR (UT) 157 Lc50
Boqueirão ◻ BR (RS) 205 He60
Boqueirão ◻ BR (MG) 203 Hg54
Boqueirão ◻ BR (PI) 201 Hj50
Boquerón del Padre Abad ◻ PE 197 Gc50
Boquete ◻ PA 185 Fj41
Boquilla, Cerro ◻ RA 210 Gf67
Boquillas del Carmen ◻ MEX (COH) 181 Ej31
Bor ◻ CZ 42 Ln41
Bor ◻ RUS 54 Pb06
Bor ◻ SCG 44 Mc46
Bor ◻ SUD 141 Mf43
Bor ◻ TR 56 Mn27
Bora ◻ SUD 141 Md41
Bora Peak ◻ USA 168 Ed23
Borah Peak ◻ USA 168 Ed23
Borakalalo N.P. ◻ ZA 155 Md58
Borankul ◻ KZ 57 Ng22
Borås ◻ S 31 Ln33
Borba ◻ BR (AM) 199 Ha48
Borba ◻ P 27 Ko52
Borbonema ◻ BR (PB) 201 Jb49
Bordeaux ◻ F 24 Ks45
Bordj ◻ DZ 126 Lc31

Bongo Island ◻ RP 91 Rb42
Bongolava ◻ RM 157 Nc55
Border Peninsula ◻ CDN 163 Fd04
Border City Lodge ◻ USA (AK) 165 Ck14
Border Downs ◻ AUS (NSW) 108 Sa61
Border Ranges N.P. ◻ AUS 109 Sg60
Bordertown ◻ AUS (SA) 110 Sa64
Bordesholm ◻ D 32 Ll36
Borðeyri ◻ IS 18 Jt25
Bordighera ◻ I 34 Lh46
Bordj Bou-Arreridj ◻ DZ 126 Lc27
Bordj Bounaama ◻ DZ 126 Lb28
Bordj Bourgoulba ◻ TN 126 Le30
Bordj el Haoues ◻ DZ 132 Le33
Bordj Flye Sante Marie ◻ DZ
Bordj Foucauld ◻ DZ 132 Lc34
Bordj Machehed Salah ◻ TN 126 Lf29
Bordj M'Chiguig ◻ TN 126 Lf30
Bordj Messouda ◻ DZ 126 Le31
Bordj Mokhtar ◻ DZ 132 Lb35
Bordj Omar Driss ◻ DZ 126 Ld31
Bordolini ◻ IND (ASM) 86 Pg32
Borðoy ◻ DK 18 Ko28
Bordžomi ◻ GE 57 Nb25
Borðeyri ◻ IS 18 Jt25
Boreda ◻ ETH 142 Mj42
Borek Wielkopolski ◻ PL 40 Ls39
Borensberg ◻ S 31 Lq32
Boreray ◻ GB 20 Km33
Bosworth ◻ AUS (SA) 108 Rj61
Bósznéta ◻ H 42 Ls44
Botad ◻ IND (GUJ) 80 Of34
Botafogo ◻ BR (AM) 196 Gk48
Borgentreich ◻ D 32 Lj39
Borger ◻ NL 23 Lg38
Borger ◻ USA (TX) 174 Ek28
Borgholm ◻ S 31 Lr34
Borgomanero ◻ I 34 Lj45
Borgorosso ◻ I 36 Lm49
Borgo San Dalmazzo ◻ I 34 Lh46
Borgo San Lorenzo ◻ I 34 Lm47
Borgosésia ◻ I 34 Lj45
Borgo Val di Taro ◻ I 34 Lk46
Borgo Valsugana ◻ I 34 Lm44
Borj de Bel Frissate ◻ MA 125 Kj29
Borjhar ◻ IND (MPH) 82 Oh34
Borkavichy ◻ BY 39 Mg34
Borkum ◻ D 32 Lg38
Borkou ◻ TCH 133 Lk36
Borlänge ◻ S 31 Lq30
Bormes-les-Mimosas ◻ F 25 Lg47
Borna ◻ D 32 Ln39
Borne ◻ NL 23 Lg38
Bornheim ◻ D 32 Lg40
Bornholm ◻ DK 31 Lr35
Bornova ◻ TR 47 Mh52
Boroatu ◻ RM 157 Nd55
Borodinskoe ◻ RUS 38 Mk29
Borohoro Shan ◻ CHN 66 Pb23
Boromata ◻ RCA 134 Lh43
Boromo ◻ BF 137 Kj40
Boron ◻ CI 137 Kg41
Borongan ◻ RP 91 Rd40
Boroughbridge ◻ GB 21 Ku36
Borovan ◻ BG 44 Md47
Borovenets ◻ BG 45 Mg48
Borovsk ◻ RUS 39 Mg35
Borroloola ◻ AUS (NT) 106 Rj54
Borsa ◻ RO 43 Me43
Borščovočnyj hrebet ◻ RUS 71 Qk20
Borsec ◻ RO 43 Mf43
Borsippa ◻ IRQ 59 Nc29
Børsu ◻ MNG 70 Qa20
Bort-les-Orgues ◻ F 25 Lc45
Boru ◻ RI 96 Rb49
Borujerd ◻ IR 57 Ne29
Bör-Üzüür ◻ MNG 67 Pg23
Borve ◻ GB 20 Ko33
Børeya-Bata ◻ IR 57 Ne29
Borýslav ◻ UA 43 Me41
Boryslav ◻ UA 48 Md41
Boryspil ◻ UA 48 Mf20
Borzonasco ◻ I 34 Lk46
Borzya ◻ RUS 71 Qk20
Bosa ◻ I 36 Lj51
Bosanci ◻ HR 35 Lq45
Bosanska Dubica ◻ BIH 35 Lr45
Bosanska Gradiška ◻ BIH 35 Ls45
Bosanska Kostajnica ◻ BIH 35 Lr45
Bosanska Krupa ◻ BIH 35 Lr46
Bosanski Brod ◻ BIH 35 Ls45
Bosanski Novi ◻ BIH 35 Lr45
Bosanski Petrovac ◻ BIH 35 Lr46
Bosanski Šamac ◻ BIH 35 Lt45
Bosco Chek Prey ◻ K 89 Qc39
Bosco ◻ CI 192 Gd40
Boscone ◻ I 34 Lm46
Bose ◻ CHN (GZG) 74 Qe34
Bosilegrad ◻ SCG 44 Mc48
Boskovice ◻ CZ 42 Lr41
Bosna ◻ BIH 35 Ls46

Bosobolo ◻ RDC 140 Lk43
Bosohanto ◻ J 79 Sa28
Bosossama ◻ RDC 141 Lh43
Bosporus ◻ TR 45 Mk49
Bosque de Fray Jorge, P.N. ◻ RCH 208 Ge61
Bosque del Apache N.W.R. ◻ USA 171 Eg29
Bosque Petrificado J.Ormachea ◻ RA 210 Gf68
Bosque Petrificado Victor Szlapelis ◻ RA 210 Gf68
Bosra ◻ SYR 56 Mj29
Bossangoa ◻ RCA 140 Lj42
Bossaria ◻ RCA 140 Lj43
Bossembélé ◻ RCA 140 Lj43
Bossentelé ◻ RCA 140 Lj43
Bossey Bangou ◻ RN 137 La39
Bosso ◻ RN 132 Lg38
Bossô Mts. ◻ BR (AM) 199 Ha47
Bostan ◻ IR 59 Nd30
Bostan ◻ PK 65 Od30
Bostan ◻ IR 57 Nd27
Bostanabad ◻ IR 57 Nd27
Bostankum ◻ KZ 62 Ng24
Bostn ◻ RP 91 Rd42
Bostoen ◻ USA (MA) 177 Ge24
Bo'ston ◻ UZ 62 Oa25
Bo'ston Bay ◻ CDN (BC) 168 Dk21
Boston Mts. ◻ USA 174 Fd28
Bostan ◻ SCG 44 Lu46
Bosworth ◻ AUS (SA) 108 Rj61
Bósznéta ◻ H 42 Ls44
Botad ◻ IND (GUJ) 80 Of34
Botafogo ◻ BR (AM) 196 Gk48
Botev ◻ BG 44 Mf48
Botevgrad ◻ BG 44 Md48
Bothaápo ◻ RB 151 Mb56
Bothaville ◻ ZA 155 Md59
Bothnia, Gulf of ◻ 16 Ma28
Bothwell ◻ AUS (TAS) 111 Sd67
Bothwell Lodge S.H.S. ◻ USA
Boticas ◻ P 26 Kn49
Botímenbongo ◻ RDC 149 Lk46
Botíz ◻ RO 43 Md43
Botlhapatlou ◻ RB 155 Mc57
Botlih ◻ RUS (DAG) 57 Nd24
Bot Makak ◻ CAM 138 Lf43
Botolan ◻ RP 90 Ra38
Botou ◻ BF 137 La39
Botou ◻ CHN (HBI) 73 Qj26
Bo Trach ◻ VN 87 Qd37
Botro ◻ CI 137 Kh42
Botswana ◻ 133 Ma12
Bottineau ◻ USA (ND) 172 Ek21
Bottle Creek ◻ GB 186 Ge35
Bottrop ◻ D 32 Lg39
Botucatu ◻ BR (SP) 202 Hf57
Botum Sakor N.P. ◻ K 89 Qb40
Botuna ◻ RDC 149 Ma46
Botwood ◻ CDN (NF) 177 Hc21
Bouaflé ◻ CI 137 Kh42
Bou-Ahmed ◻ MA 125 Kh28
Bou Akba ◻ DZ 125 Kj28
Bou Alek ◻ RIM 131 Kf37
Boualem ◻ DZ 125 La29
Bou Ali ◻ DZ 125 Kk32
Bouam ◻ CAM 139 Lg43
Bouânane ◻ MA 125 Kj29
Bouandougou ◻ CI 137 Kh41
Bouanila ◻ RCB 140 Lj45
Bouanrí ◻ SY 138 Ld42
Bouar ◻ RCA 140 Lj43
Bouba Ndjida, P.N. du ◻ CAM 139 Lh41
Boubin ◻ CZ 42 Lo41
Boubon ◻ ANG 150 Lk54
Boudoua ◻ RCA 140 Lj42
Boudenib ◻ MA 125 Kj29
Boudry ◻ CH 34 Lh44
Boufarik ◻ DZ 126 Lb27
Boufssa ◻ MA 125 Kg29
Bougaa ◻ DZ 126 Lc27
Boú Gâdoûm ◻ RIM 131 Kg38
Bougainville ◻ PNG 117 Sh48
Bougainville Island ◻ PNG 117 Sh48
Bougainville Reef ◻ AUS (QLD) 107 Sd53
Bougainville Strait ◻ SOL 117 Sj49
Bougeaa ◻ DZ 126 Lc27
Boughessa ◻ RMM 137 Kl37
Bougoumb ◻ DY 138 La42
Bougouni ◻ RCA 140 Lh43
Bougouni ◻ RMM 137 Kg40
Bougousso ◻ CI 137 Kg40
Bou Guettara ◻ RIM 130 Kc36
Bou Hadjra ◻ TN 126 Le28
Bou-Hanifia ◻ DZ 125 La28
Bouhana, P.N. de ◻ TN 126 Le28
Bouheina Downs ◻ AUS (NT) 106 Rh54
Boukoula ◻ CAM 139 Lg40
Boukra ◻ DARS 124 Kc32
Boulal ◻ RMM 137 Kf38
Boulanouar ◻ RIM 130 Kb36
Boulari ◻ SN 130 Kc38
Boulanko ◻ RCB 148 Lh47
Bou Lanouâr ◻ RIM 130 Kb36
Boulay ◻ MA 125 Kg29
Bou Kadir ◻ DZ 126 Lb27
Bou Lanouâr ◻ RIM 130 Kb36
Boulazac ◻ F 24 La45
Boulder ◻ USA (CO) 171 Eh25
Boulder ◻ USA (MT) 169 Ed22
Boulder ◻ USA (NV) 170 Ec27
Boulder City ◻ USA (NV) 170 Ec27
Boulel ◻ RMM 131 Kf38
Boulen ◻ RMM 131 Kf38
Boulsa ◻ BF 137 Kk39
Boulevard ◻ USA (CA) 170 Eb29
Boulia ◻ AUS (QLD) 108 Rk57
Boulogne-Billancourt ◻ F 23 Lc42

Boulogne-sur-Gesse F 24 La47
Boulogne-sur-Mer F 23 Lb40
Bouloire F 22 La43
Boulonnais F 23 Lb40
Boulouba RCA 140 Ma42
Boultham F 118 Td56
Boulsa BF 137 Kk39
Boultoum RN 132 Lf38
Boumalne Dadès MA 125 Kh30
Boumango G 148 Lg47
Bouma N.P. FJI 119 Ua54
Boumbou RMM 131 Kk38
Boundett RIM 130 Ke37
Boumerdès DZ 126 Lb27
Boumia RCA CI 137 Kf41
Bou Mrega CI 137 Kh42
Boû Nâga RMM 131 Kj36
Bouna CI 137 Kf41
Bounafla CI 137 Kh42
Boû Nâga RMM 131 Kj36
Bouquet RA (SF) 209 Gk62
Boura BF 137 Kh39
Boura RMM 137 Kh39
Bourail CI 118 Tc56
Bourbon-Lancy F 25 Lf43
Bourbon-l'Archambault F 25 Ld44
Bourbonne-les-Bains F 25 Lf43
Bourbriac F 22 La42
Bourdeaux F 25 Lf46
Boureïmi CI RN 132 Lb39
Bourem RMM 131 Kf37
Bourem-Inali RMM 131 Kj37
Bourganeuf F 24 Ld45
Bourg-Argental F 25 Le45
Bourg-en-Bresse F 25 Lf44
Bourges F 25 Ld43
Bourg-et-Comin F 23 Ld41
Bourg-Madame F 24 Lb48
Bourgneuf-en-Retz F 24 Kt43
Bourgoin-Jallieu F 25 Lf45
Bourg-Saint-Andéol F 25 Lf46
Bourg-Saint-Maurice F 25 Lg45
Boû Rjeïmât RIM 130 Kc37
Bourke AUS (NSW) 109 Sc61
Bourndа N.P. AUS (NSW) 111 Se64
Bournemouth GB 21 Kt40
Bourou TCH 140 Lf41
Bouroum BF 137 Kh39
Bouroum-Bouroum BF 137 Kj40
Bourrah CAM 139 Lg40
Bourscheid L 23 Lg41
Bourzanga BF 137 Kk39
Bou Saâda DZ 126 Lc28
Bou Salem TN 126 Le27
Bousse F 23 Lc44
Boussé BF 137 Kk39
Bousso TCH 139 Lj40
Boussou BF 137 Kk39
Boussouma BF 137 Kk39
Boutilimit RIM 130 Kc37
Boutiller D RH 186 Gd36
Boutougou Fara SN 136 Kd39
Bouvet Island U 10 La15
Bouzwiller D 23 Lh42
Bouza RN 132 Ld38
Bouzghaïa DZ 126 Ld27
Bovalino Mare I 37 Lr52
Bova Marina I 37 Lq53
Bovbjerg Fyr DK 30 Lj34
Bovenden D 32 Lk39
Boves F 23 Lc41
Bovino I 37 Lq49
Bovril RA 204 Ha61
Bowa Falls AUS 155 Md62
Bowdle USA (SD) 172 Fa23
Bowdie D USA 175 Fh29
Bowdon USA (GA) 175 Fh29
Bowen RA (MD) 208 Gg63
Bowerville AUS 109 Sf59
Bowers CI 28 Kt36
Bow Island CDN (AB) 169 Ej21
Bowling Green USA (KY) 175 Fg27
Bowling Green USA (MO) 175 Fe26
Bowling Green USA (OH) 173 Fj25
Bowling Green Bay N.P. AUS (QLD) 107 Sd55
Bowman USA (ND) 169 Ej22
Bowman GB 20 Ko35
Bowning AUS (NSW) 111 Se63
Bowraville AUS 109 Sg61
Bowron Lake Prov. Park CDN 168 Dk19
Bowser CDN (BC) 168 Dh21
Bowwood Z 152 Md54
Boxberg D 32 Lk41
Boxholm S 31 Lq32
Boxmeer NL 23 Lg39
Boxtel NL 23 Lf39
Boxwood Hill AUS (WA) 104 Qj63
Boyabat TR 56 Mh25
Boyaca RDC 140 Lk44
Boyaca CO 192 Gd43
Bo Yai Hot Spring LAO 87 Qb36
Boyalali RI 95 Qf49
Boysun UZ 63 Od26
Boyuibe BOL 206 Gj56
Boyup Brook AUS (WA) 104 Qj62
Boyuyo BOL 198 Gf51
Boza EAT 147 Mk49
Bozanbai KZ 62 Nb23
Bozava HR 35 Lq46
Bozcaada TR 47 Mf54
Bozcaada TR 47 Mg51
Bozdoğan TR 47 Mj53
Bozeman USA (MT) 169 Ee23

Cay Lobos – Chennakeshava Temple

Cay Lobos C 179 Gb34
Caylus F 24 Lb46
Cayman Brac GB 179 Ga36
Cayman Islands GB 179 Fk36
Cayman Ridge 179 Fj36
Cayman Trench 179 Fk36
Cay Marino 94 Qh41
Caynabo SP 143 Nd41
Cayo Arenas MEX 183 Fe34
Cayo Becerro HN 185 Fj38
Cayo Becerro HN 185 Fj38
Cayo Caballones C 179 Ga35
Cayo Cabeza del Este C 179 Ga35
Cayo Cantiles C 179 Fj35
Cayo Caratasca HN 185 Fj37
Cayo Caratasca HN 185 Fj37
Cayo Centro MEX 183 Fg36
Cayo Coco C 179 Ga34
Cayo del Rosario C 179 Fj35
Cayo de Santa María C 179 Ga34
Cayo Fragoso C 179 Ga34
Cayo Gorda HN 185 Fj38
Cayo Gorda HN 185 Fj38
Cayo Grande C 179 Ga35
Cayo Guajaba C 179 Gb35
Cayo Guillermo C 179 Ga34
Cayo Largo C 179 Fj35
Cayo Largo C 179 Fk35
Cayo Lobos MEX 183 Fg36
Cayo Mambi C 186 Gc35
Cayo Nuevo MEX 183 Fd35
Cayo Ramona C 179 Fk34
Cayo Romano C 179 Gb34
Cayo Sabinal C 179 Gb35
Cayos Anctitas C 179 Ga35
Cayos Blancos del Sur C 179 Fk34
Cayos Cajones HN 185 Fj37
Cayos Cajones HN 185 Fj37
Cayos Cinco Balas C 179 Ga35
Cayos Cocorocuma HN 185 Fj38
Cayos Cocorocuma HN 185 Fj38
Cayos de Albuquerque CO 185 Fk39
Cayos de E.S.E. CO 185 Fk39
Cayos de Perlas NIC 185 Fj39
Cayos de Roncador CO 185 Fk39
Cayos de San Felipe C 179 Fj35
Cayos Guerrero NIC 185 Fj39
Cayos King NIC 185 Fj39
Cayos los Indios C 179 Fj35
Cayos Mayores del Cabo Falso HN 185 Fj38
Cayos Mayores del Cabo Falso HN 185 Fj38
Cayos Miskitos NIC 185 Fj38
Cayos Morrison Dennis NIC 185 Fj38
Cayos NASA NIC 185 Fj38
Cayo Tyara NIC 185 Fj39
Cayo Vivorillo HN 185 Fj38
Cayo Vivorillo HN 185 Fj38
Cay Sal BS 179 Fk34
Cay Santo Damingo BS 186 Gc35
Cay Verde BS 186 Gc35
Cazage ANG 151 Ma51
Cazalla de la Sierra E 27 Kp53
Čažaši GE 57 Nb24
Cazaubon F 24 Ku47
Cazenovia USA (NY) 177 Gc24
Cazin BIH 35 Lq46
Čazma HR 35 Lr45
Cazombo ANG 151 Mb51
Cazones MEX (VC) 182 Fb35
Cazorla E 27 Ks53
Cazorla YV 193 Gg41
Cazula MOC 152 Mg53
Cazuza Ferreira BR (RS) 205 He60
Ccatca PE 197 Ge52
Cea E 26 Kq48
Ceahlău, P.N. RO 49 Mc22
Ceanu Mare RO 43 Md44
Ceará BR 191 Hb10
Ceara Abyssal Plain 190 Hb09
Ceará-Mirim BR (RN) 201 Jc48
Ceará-Mirim BR 201 Jc48
Ceatalchioi RO 45 Mj45
Ceballos MEX (DGO) 181 Eh32
Čeboksary RUS (CHU) 48 Nd17
Cebollatí ROU 204 Hd62
Cebreros E 27 Kq50
Cebu RP 90 Rb40
Cebu RP 90 Rc40
Čečava BIH 35 Ls46
Ceccano I 36 Lo49
Cece H 43 Lt44
Čečel'nyk UA 49 Me21
Čechtice CZ 42 Lq41
Cecil Plains AUS (QLD) 109 Sf59
Cécina I 34 Ll47
Cedar Bay N.P. AUS 107 Sc53
Cedar Bluffs USA (KS) 174 Ek26
Cedar Breaks Nat. Mon. USA 171 Ed27
Cedar City USA (UT) 171 Ed27
Cedaredge USA (CO) 171 Eg26
Cedar Falls USA (IA) 172 Fd24
Cedar Grove USA (CA) 170 Ea27
Cedar Harbour BS 179 Gb32
Cedar Island USA (NC) 178 Gb28
Cedar Island N.W.R. USA 178 Gb28
Cedar Key USA (FL) 178 Fj31
Cedar Lake CDN 169 Ek19
Cedar Park USA (TX) 174 Fb30
Cedar Point USA 173 Fj25
Cedar Rapids USA (IA) 172 Fe24
Cedar River USA (MI) 173 Fg23
Cedar River Grassland N.P. USA 172 Ek22
Cedartown USA (GA) 175 Fh29
Cedarvale CDN (BC) 166 Df18
Cedarville USA (CA) 168 Dk25
Cedarville ZA 155 Me61
Cedeira E 26 Km47
Cedeño HN 184 Fg39
Cederberg ZA 154 Lk62
Cederberg Wilderness Area ZA 154 Lk62
Cedillo E 27 Kn51
Cedoux CDN (SK) 169 Ej21
Cedral BR (MA) 195 Hh46
Cedral MEX (SLP) 182 Ek34
Cedrillas E 29 Ku50
Cedro BR (CE) 201 Ja49
Cedros MEX (ZCT) 181 Ek33
Cedros Trench 180 Eb32
Ceduna AUS (SA) 110 Rg62
Cée E 26 Kl48
Ceek SP 143 Nc41
Ceel Afweyn SP 143 Nd41
Ceelayo SP 143 Ne40
Ceel Baxay ETH 143 Nb40
Ceelbur = El Bur SP 145 Nd43
Ceel Dhaab SP 143 Nd41
Ceeldheer SP 145 Nd44
Ceeldhere SP 145 Nd43
Ceel Duubo SP 145 Nc44
Ceel Gaal SP 143 Nf40
Ceel Gaan SP 145 Nd43
Ceel Garas SP 145 Nc43
Ceel Huur SP 143 Ne43
Cefalù I 37 Lp52
Cegléd H 43 Lu43
Céglie Messápica I 37 Ls50
Cehegín E 29 Kt52
Ceheng CHN (GZH) 87 Qc33
Čehov RUS 48 Mj18
Cehu Silvaniei RO 43 Md43
Ceibalito RA (SA) 207 Gh58
Ceibal, P.N. GCA 183 Ff37
Ceibas RA (ER) 204 Ha62
Céide Fields IRL 19 Kl36
Čejč CZ 42 Lr42
Çekerek TR 56 Mh25
Čekiškė LT 39 Md35
Čekurdah RUS 55 Sb04
Celano I 36 Lo48
Celanova E 26 Kn48
Celaque, P.N. HN 184 Ff38
Celarain MEX (QTR) 183 Fg35
Celaya MEX (GJT) 182 Ek35
Celbridge IRL 19 Ko37
Celebes RI 52 Ra10
Celebes Basin RP 91 Ra44
Celebes Sea RI 52 Ra09
Čelebići BIH 44 Lt47
Celendin PE 196 Ga49
Celestún MEX (YT) 183 Fe35
Čelić BIH 44 Lt46
Celica EC 196 Ga48
Celilabad AZ 57 Ne26
Celina RUS 49 Na22
Celina USA (OH) 173 Fh25
Celina USA (TN) 175 Fh27
Čelinac Donji BIH 35 Ls46
Čeljabinsk RUS 54 Oa07
Celjachany BY 41 Mf38
Celje SLO 42 Lq44
Cella E 29 Kt50
Celldömölk H 42 Ls43
Celle D 32 Ll38
Celle Lígure I 34 Lj46
Celorico da Beira P 26 Kn50
Čel'ovce SK 43 Mb42
Celtic Sea 19 Kn40
Cemaru, Gunung RI 94 Qh45
Cemerno BIH 44 Lt47
Çemişgezek TR 57 Mk26
Čemolgan KZ 66 Oj24
Cenderawasih Marine Reserve RI 114 Rh47
Cenovo BG 45 Mf47
Centani ZA 155 Me62
Centelles E 29 Lc49
Centenario RA (NE) 208 Gf65
Centenario do Sul BR (PR) 202 He57
Centenary ZW 152 Mf54
Centennial Museum, Barrhead CDN 167 Ec18
Center USA (CO) 171 Eg27
Center USA (ND) 172 Ek22
Center USA (TX) 174 Fc30
Centerville USA (IA) 174 Fd25
Centerville USA (MO) 175 Fe27
Centerville USA (TN) 175 Fg28
Centerville USA (TX) 174 Fc30
Centinela PE 197 Gb51
Centinela PE 197 Gb51
Centinela, Cerro RA 208 Ge64
Cento I 34 Lm46
Centovalli Express CH/I 34 Lj44
Centra Buttte CDN (SK) 169 Eg20
Central BR (BA) 201 Hj51
Central RB 151 Mc56
Central African Republic 123 Lb09
Central Australia A.L. AUS 103 Re57
Central Balkan, N.P. BG 45 Me48
Central Brahui Range PK 65 Od31
Central City USA (KY) 175 Fg27
Central City USA (NE) 172 Fa25
Central Desert A.L. AUS 103 Rf55
Central Eastern Rainforest Reserves AUS 109 Sg60
Centralia USA (IL) 175 Ff26
Centralia USA (WA) 168 Dj22
Centralina BR (MG) 202 Hf55
Central Island EAK 144 Mj44
Central Island N.P. EAK 144 Mj44
Central Kalahari Game Reserve RB 151 Mb57
Central Karakorum N.P. PK 81 Oj28
Central los Molles RCH 208 Ge61
Central Makran Range PK 65 Oc32
Central Mosque (Pattani) THA 89 Qa42
Central Mount Wedge AUS 103 Rf57
Central'nojakutskaja ravnina RUS 55 Qd06
Central'notungusskoe plato RUS 54 Pd06
Central Pacific Basin 10 Ba08
Central Patricia CDN (ON) 172 Fe20
Central Range LS 155 Me60
Central Range PNG 115 Sb48
Central Rapel RCH 208 Ge62
Central Reserve A.L. AUS 105 Re58
Central Siberian Plateau RUS 54 Pc05
Centre F 22 Lb43
Centre USA (AL) 175 Fh28
Centre Island AUS 106 Rj53
Centre minier de Lewarde F 23 Ld40
Centre Spatial Guyanais F 194 Hd43
Centreville USA (AL) 175 Fg29
Centreville USA (MS) 175 Fe30
Cenxi CHN (GZG) 74 Qf34
Cenzontle MEX (COH) 181 Ej32
Čepigovo MK 44 Mb49
Čepin HR 35 Lt45
Cepu RI 95 Qf49
Cer MK 44 Mb49
Cerachovka BY 48 Mf19
Ceram RI 97 Re47
Ceram Sea RI 97 Rd47
Cerbère F 25 Ld48
Cercal P 27 Km53
Cercle mégalithique SN 136 Kc39
Cerdeira P 26 Kn50
Cereal CDN (AB) 169 Ee20
Cerejeiras BR (RO) 206 Gk52
Čeremhovo RUS 70 Qb19
Ceremošnja Pecina SCG 44 Mb46
Čerencovo RUS 48 Mg16
Čerepiški manastir BG 44 Md47
Ceres BR (GO) 202 Hf53
Ceres RA (SF) 207 Gk60
Ceres ZA 154 Lk62
Čereševo BG 45 Mg47
Ceresole Reale I 34 Lh45
Céret F 24 Lc48
Cerete CO 192 Gc41
Cerezo de Abajo E 26 Kr49
Cerfontaine B 23 Le40
Cerignola I 37 Lq49
Çerıklı TR 56 Mg26
Cerillos RA (SA) 207 Gh58
Cerillos RCH 207 Gf57
Cérilly F 25 Lc44
Cerizay F 24 Ku44
Čerkasovo RUS 38 Mj30
Čerkasy UA 49 Mg21
Çerkeş TR 56 Mg25
Čerkessk RUS (KCH) 57 Nb23
Cerkev Marijinega oznanjanja SLO 42 Lp44
Çerkezköy TR 45 Mj49
Cerknica SLO 42 Lp45
Cermei RO 43 Mb44
Çermik TR 57 Mk26
Čern' RUS 48 Mj19
Cerna HR 35 Lt45
Cerna RO 45 Mj45
Cerna Domogled, P.N. RO 44 Mc46
Cerna-Sat RO 44 Mc45
Černava RUS 48 Mk19
Černava RUS 48 Mk19
Cernavodă RO 45 Mj46
Cernay F 25 Lh43
Cernégula E 28 Kr48
Černëvo RUS 38 Mj32
Cernica RO 45 Mg46
Černihiv UA 48 Mf20
Černivci UA 49 Mc21
Černjachiv UA 49 Me20
Černjaevo RUS 71 Rd19
Černjahovsk RUS 39 Mb36
Černjanka RUS 48 Mj20
Černovice CZ 42 Lp41
Černyševsk RUS 71 Qj19
Černyškovskij RUS 48 Nb21
Cerovačke Špilje HR 35 Lq46
Cerovica SCG 44 Mc47
Cerqueira César BR (SP) 202 Hf57
Cerralvo MEX (NL) 181 Fa32
Cerrigydrudion GB 21 Kr37
Cërrik AL 44 Lu49
Cerrito CO 192 Gd42
Cerrito MEX (SLP) 182 Ek34
Cerrito, T.I. BR 202 Hc57
Cerro Aconcagua RA 208 Ge62
Cerro Agua Hedionda RA 208 Gg62
Cerro Aguas Blancas RA/RCH 207 Gf58
Cerro Aguja RA/RCH 208 Ge67
Cerro Aguja RCH 210 Gf73
Cerro Aiguilete RCH 210 Gd71
Cerro Alto Nevado RCH 210 Gd68
Cerro Anecón Chico RA 208 Gf66
Cerro Anecón Grande RA 208 Ge66
Cerro Apacheta RA 207 Gg58
Cerro Archibarca RA 207 Gg58
Cerro Arenales RCH 210 Gd69
Cerro Atajaña RCH 206 Ge55
Cerro Atalaya PE 197 Ge52
Cerro Aucanquilcha RCH 206 Gf56
Cerro Avispa BR/YV 193 Gh45
Cerro Ayapunga PE 196 Gc47
Cerro Azanaques BOL 206 Gg55
Cerro Azul BR (PR) 205 Hf58
Cerro Azul EC 197 Fe46
Cerro Azul MEX (VC) 182 Fb35
Cerro Azul PE 197 Gb52
Cerro Azul RA 208 Ge66
Cerro Azul RCH 208 Ge63
Cerro Balmaceda RCH 210 Gd71
Cerro Barros Arana RCH 210 Gd67
Cerro Bayo RCH 210 Gd68
Cerro Bayo Grande RA 207 Gg59
Cerro Belgrano RA 210 Ge69
Cerro Blanco RA 208 Ge66
Cerro Blanco RCH 207 Ge60
Cerro Bolívar 802 YV 193 Gj42
Cerro Bonete RA 207 Gf59
Cerro Boquete RA 210 Gf67
Cerro Bravo BOL 207 Gg57
Cerro Bravo BOL 206 Gh54
Cerro Bravo RCH 207 Gf59
Cerro Butahuao RA 208 Ge65
Cerro Calderon RA 208 Gf66
Cerro Calpon PE 196 Ga49
Cerro Caltama BOL 206 Gf56
Cerro Campanario RA/RCH 208 Ge63
Cerro Cangrejo RA 210 Gd70
Cerro Carrere RA 208 Gf64
Cerro Centinela RA 208 Ge64
Cerro Cerrón YV 192 Ge40
Cerro Chachil RA 208 Ge65
Cerro Chacras EC 197 Fe46
Cerro Champaqui RA 208 Gh61
Cerro Chato ROU 204 Hc62
Cerro Chenque RA 210 Gg68
Cerro Chihuido de Medio RA 208 Gf64
Cerro Chocca PE 197 Gc52
Cerro Chulluncani BOL 206 Gh55
Cerro Cibaray BOL 206 Gf55
Cerro Cirque BOL 206 Gf54
Cerro Cofre de Perote MEX 182 Fb36
Cerro Cofre, P.N. MEX 182 Fb36
Cerro Coipasa BOL 206 Gf55
Cerro Cojudo Blanco RA 210 Gf69
Cerro Colorado MEX (SO) 180 Ef32
Cerro Colorado RA 210 Gf68
Cerro Colorado RA 207 Gg60
Cerro Colorado RA 207 Gj61
Cerro Colorados RA/RCH 207 Gf59
Cerro Colquen RCH 208 Gd64
Cerro Colupo RCH 207 Ge57
Cerro Convento RA 210 Gf71
Cerro Copa BOL/RCH 206 Gf56
Cerro Coposa RCH 206 Gf56
Cerro Corá BR (RN) 201 Jb49
Cerro Corá RA (MI) 204 Hc59
Cerro Corá, P.N. PY 202 Hb57
Cerro Cordobés RA 207 Gf60
Cerro Corona RA 208 Ge66
Cerro Cotacachi CO 192 Ga45
Cerro Cowan EC 197 Fe46
Cerro Coyaguaima RA 207 Gg57
Cerro Criterion PE 197 Gc53
Cerro Cumbrera RCH 210 Gd69
Cerro Cupisnique PE 196 Ga49
Cerro de Ansilta RA 208 Gf61
Cerro de Curimávida RCH 208 Ge61
Cerro de la Neblina EC 196 Fk46
Cerro de las Ovejas RA 208 Gh62
Cerro Delgado-Chalbaud BR/YV 193 Gj44
Cerro del Inca BOL/RCH 207 Gf56
Cerro de los Bueyes RA 208 Ge64
Cerro del Placeton RCH 207 Ge60
Cerro del Potro RA/RCH 207 Gf60
Cerro del Toro RA/RCH 207 Gf60
Cerro de Pasco PE 197 Gb51
Cerro de Pomasi PE 197 Ge53
Cerro de Tocopuri BOL 207 Gg57
Cerro Doña Ana RCH 207 Ge60
Cerro Doña Inés RCH 207 Gf59
Cerro Duida YV 193 Gh44
Cerro el Condór RA 207 Gf59
Cerro el Ford RCH 210 Ge72
Cerro Elias RA 210 Gg68
Cerro el Nevado RA 208 Gf63
Cerro el Pedrero RA 210 Ge68
Cerro Fundición RA 207 Gh57
Cerro Galán RA 207 Gg59
Cerro Gallinero YV 193 Gg43
Cerro General M. Belgrano RA 207 Gg60
Cerro Guanay YV 193 Gg43
Cerro Hatscher RA 210 Gd70
Cerro Hoya, P.N. PA 185 Fk42
Cerro Huanchaca BOL 206 Gg56
Cerro Hudson RCH 210 Gd69
Cerro Hyades RCH 210 Gd69
Cerro Igle RA 210 Gd71
Cerro Illesca PE 196 Fk49
Cerro Jeinemeni RCH 210 Gd69
Cerro Juncal RA/RCH 208 Gf62
Cerro la Campana RCH 210 Gd71
Cerro la Criolla RA 210 Ge71
Cerro la Grasa RA 208 Ge65
Cerro La Ramada BOL/RA 207 Gg57
Cerro Largo BR (RS) 204 Hc60
Cerro Las Torolas RA/RCH 207 Gf60
Cerro Lautaro RCH 210 Gd70
Cerro Leiva CO 193 Gf44
Cerro León PY 206 Gk56
Cerro Lique BOL 206 Gh56
Cerro Lliscaya BOL/RCH 206 Gf55
Cerro Lote 15 RA 210 Ge68
Cerro Magallanes MEX 180 Ef30
Cerro Mellizo Sur RCH 210 Gd70
Cerro Mercedario RA 208 Ge61
Cerro Mesa RA 208 Gf65
Cerro Mina CO 192 Gd41
Cerro Mirador RCH 210 Ge72
Cerro Monte León RA 210 Gf71
Cerro Morado RA 207 Gh57
Cerro Moreno RCH 207 Ge57
Cerro Murallón RA/RCH 210 Gd70
Cerrón, Cerro YV 192 Ge40
Cerro Nanchital MEX (VC) 183 Fc37
Cerro Napa BR/RCH 206 Gf56
Cerro Negro RA 208 Ge65
Cerro Negro RA 210 Gf68
Cerro Nevado RCH 210 Gd67
Cerro Norte RA 210 Gd70
Cerro Ovana YV 193 Gg43
Cerro Paine Grande RCH 210 Gd71
Cerro Pajonal RCH 207 Gf56
Cerro Pan de Azúcar RA 210 Gf70
Cerro Paroma BOL/RCH 206 Gf56
Cerro Payún RA 208 Gf64
Cerro Peineta RA 210 Gd71
Cerro Picudo RA 210 Gf69
Cerro Picún Leufú RA 208 Gf65
Cerro Piedra RCH 208 Gd64
Cerro Pináculo RA 210 Gd71
Cerro Pingo Pongo RCH 207 Gf58
Cerro Pintado RA 210 Gd70
Cerro Pircas RA 208 Gf61
Cerro Pissis RA 207 Gf59
Cerro Policía RA (RN) 208 Gf65
Cerro Prieto PE 196 Fk48
Cerro Pular RCH 207 Gf58
Cerro Punta PA 185 Fj41
Cerro Punta Gruesa RA 210 Ge71
Cerro Quichaura RA 210 Ge67
Cerro Rancahué RA 208 Ge65
Cerro Rico BOL 206 Gh55
Cerro Rico RA (SE) 207 Gh60
Cerro Rincón RA/RCH 207 Gg58
Cerro Rucachoroi RA 208 Ge65
Cerros BH 183 Ff36
Cerro Sanchez RA 210 Gf71
Cerro San Cirilo PE 196 Ga49
Cerro San Joaquín EC 197 Ff46
Cerro San Lorenzo PE 196 Ga49
Cerro Santa Elena RA 210 Gh68
Cerro San Valentín RCH 210 Gd69
Cerro Saroche, P.N. YV 193 Gf40
Cerros Colorados RA 208 Gf66
Cerros de Amotape PE 196 Fk48
Cerros de Amotape, P.N. PE 196 Fk48
Cerros de Bala BOL 206 Gg53
Cerros de Campanquiz PE 196 Gb48
Cerros de Canthyuaya PE 196 Gc49
Cerro Sierra Nevada RCH/RA 207 Gf59
Cerro Sin Nombre RCH 210 Gd68
Cerro Sosneado RA 208 Gf63
Cerro Steffen RA/RCH 210 Ge68
Cerro Tamaná CO 192 Gb43
Cerro Tatajachura RCH 206 Gf55
Cerro Tazna BOL 206 Gg56
Cerro Tetari CO/YV 192 Gd40
Cerro Tololo Inter-American Observatory RCH 207 Ge61
Cerro Trapalco RA 208 Gf65
Cerro Tres Altitos RA 208 Gf62
Cerro Tres Cruces MEX 183 Fd38
Cerro Tres Picos RA 209 Gj65
Cerro Tristeza YV 193 Gj40
Cerro Tronador RA/RCH 208 Ge66
Cerro Tunapa BOL 206 Gg55
Cerro Tupungato RA/RCH 208 Gf62
Cerro Turagua YV 193 Gh42
Cerro Uturuncu BOL 207 Gg57
Cerro Ventisquero RA 208 Ge66
Cerro Ventisquero Sur RCH 210 Ge67
Cerro Vera ROU 204 Hb62
Cerro Yarvicoya RCH 206 Gf56
Cerro Yerupaja PE 197 Gb51
Cerro Zapaleri BOL/RA/RCH 207 Gg57
Cerrudo Cué RA (CR) 204 Hb59
Čerskij RUS 55 Ta05
Certaldo I 34 Lm47
Cértegui CO 192 Gb43
Čertižné SK 43 Mb41
Čertkovo RUS 48 Na21
Certosa di Padula I 37 Lq50
Certosa di Pavia I 34 Lk45
Čerusti RUS 48 Na18
Cervales E 27 Kp51
Cervantes AUS (WA) 104 Qh61
Cervantes RP 90 Ra37
Čėrven' BY 48 Me19
Červená Skala SK 43 Ma42
Červená Voda CZ 42 Lr40
Červen Brjag BG 45 Me47
Cervera E 29 Lb49
Cervera del Río Alhama E 28 Kt48
Cervera de Pisuerga E 26 Kq48
Cervéteri I 36 Ln49
Cérvia I 34 Ln46
Cervignano di Friuli I 35 Lo45
Červonohrad UA 41 Me40
Čėrykav BY 48 Mf19
Cesário Lange BR (SP) 205 Hg57
Češavlja BY 41 Mf37
Cesena I 34 Ln46
Cesenático I 34 Ln46
Cēsis LV 39 Mf33
Česká Kamenice CZ 42 Lp40
Česká Kubice CZ 42 Ln41
Česká Lípa CZ 42 Lp40
České Budějovice CZ 42 Lp42
České Švýcarsko, N.P. CZ 42 Lp42
České Velenice CZ 42 Lp42
Český Brod CZ 42 Lp40
Český Dub CZ 42 Lp40
Český Krumlov CZ 42 Lp42
Český ráj CZ 42 Lq40
Český Těšín CZ 42 Lt41
Çeşme TR 47 Mg52
Čěšskaja guba RUS 54 Nb05
Cessnock AUS (NSW) 111 Sf62
Cestos Point LB 136 Kf43
Cesvaine LV 39 Mg34
Cêtar CHN (QHI) 72 Qa27
Cetatea de Baltă RO 43 Me44
Cetatea Heracleea RO 45 Mj46
Cetăţeni RO 45 Mf45
Cetingrad HR 35 Lq45
Cetinje SCG 44 Lt48
Çetinkaya TR 56 Mj26
Çetinkaya TR 57 Na27
Cetraro I 37 Lq51
Ceuta E 125 Kh28
Ceuta E 125 Kh28
Ceuta YV 192 Ge41
Ceva I 34 Lj46
Cevedale = Zufallspitze I 34 Ll44
Cévennes F 25 Ld46
Cévennes, P.N. des F 25 Ld46
Cevicos DOM 186 Gf36
Cevizli TR 56 Mf27
Cewice PL 40 Ls36
Ceyhan TR 56 Mh27
Ceyhan Nehri TR 56 Mj27
Ceylanpınar TR 57 Na27
Ceylon CDN (SK) 169 Eh21
Ceylon CL 52 Pa09
Chaacha TM 62 Oa27
Cha-am THA 88 Pk39
Cha'anpu CHN (HUN) 74 Qf31
Chabahar IR 64 Oa33
Chabanais F 24 La45
Chabás RA (SF) 209 Gk62
Chabet el Akra DZ 126 Lc27
Chabeuil F 25 Lf46
Chabi IND (MPH) 83 Pa34
Chablis F 25 Ld43
Chaboksar IR 57 Nf27
Chabovičy BY 41 Me38
Chabris F 25 Lb43
Chacabuco RA (BA) 209 Gk63
Chacabuco RCH 210 Gd68
Chacaltaya BOL 206 Gf54
Chacaltongo de Hidalgo MEX (OAX) 182 Fb37
Chacane MOC 153 Mh58
Chacao RCH 208 Gd66
Chacarilla RCH 206 Gf56
Chacas PE 197 Gb50
Chaca Sur RCH 206 Gf55
Chacay Alto RCH 207 Ge60
Chachani, Volcán PE 197 Ge54
Chachapoyas PE 196 Gb49
Chacharan PK 65 Of31
Chacharramendi RA (LP) 208 Gh64
Chaché GH 137 Kj41
Chachil, Cerro RA 208 Ge65
Chachoengsao THA 88 Qa39
Chachro PK 65 Of33
Chaclacayo PE 197 Gb52
Chaco RA 207 Gj58
Chaco Austral RA 207 Gk59
Chaco Boreal PY 207 Gk56
Chaco Central RA 207 Gk58
Chaco Culture N.H.P. USA 171 Ef28
Chacoma BOL 206 Gf55
Chaco, P.N. RA 204 Ha59
Chacras, Cerro EC 197 Fe46
Chad 123 Lb08
Chadakori RN 132 Ld39
Chadaouanka RN 132 Ld38
Chad Basin N.P. WAN 139 Lg39
Chadegan IR 59 Nf29
Chadiza Z 152 Mg53
Chadron USA (NE) 171 Ej24
Chadyang CHN (GDG) 75 Qj34
Chae Hom THA 87 Pk36
Chaek KS 66 Oh25
Chaeryong PRK 78 Rc26
Chae Son N.P. THA 87 Pk36
Chafe WAN 138 Ld40
Chafo WAN 138 Lc40
Chagai PK 65 Oc31
Chagai Hills PK 65 Ob31
Chagalamarri IND (APH) 85 Ok38
Chaghalvandi IR 57 Ne29
Chaghcharan AFG 65 Oc28
Chaglla PE 197 Gc50
Chagne ETH 142 Mj40
Chagny F 25 Le44
Chagos Archipelago GB 52 Ob10
Chagos-Laccadive Ridge 52 Ob11
Chagres, P.N. PA 185 Ga41
Chaguanas TT 187 Gk40
Chaguaramas TT 187 Gk40
Chaguaramas YV 193 Gg41
Chaguaramas YV 193 Gj41
Chaguarpamba EC 196 Ga47
Chagyl TM 62 Nh25
Chahar Borjak AFG 64 Ob30
Chahar Rustal IR 59 Nf31
Chahbounia DZ 126 Lb28
Chahe CHN (YUN) 87 Qb32
Chah-e Ab AFG 63 Oe27
Chah-e-Mosafar IR 64 Nj28
Chahjam IR 62 Nh28
Chah Kavr IR 64 Nh30
Chah Pahn IR 59 Nf32
Chah Sagak IR 64 Oa29
Chah Sorkh IR 64 Ng31
Chah Zardar IR 64 Nk32
Chah Zebar IR 64 Nh31
Chai MOC 147 Na51
Chai Badan THA 88 Qa38
Chaibasa IND (JKD) 83 Pc34
Chail IND (UPH) 83 Pa33
Chaillé-les-Marais F 24 Kt44
Chainat THA 88 Qa38
Chaîne de l'Atakora DY 137 La40
Chaîne des Biban DZ 126 Lc27
Chai Pra Kan THA 87 Pk36
Chaiqiao CHN (ZJG) 75 Ra31
Chaitanya Temple BD 86 Pf33
Chaitén RCH 210 Gd67
Chaiwopu CHN (XUZ) 67 Pd24
Chaiya THA 88 Pk41
Chaiyaphum THA 89 Qb38
Chajarí RA (ER) 204 Ha61
Chajian CHN (AHU) 78 Qk29
Chakai IND (BIH) 83 Pd33
Chakaktolik USA (AK) 164 Bj15
Chakari ZW 152 Me55
Chakavel IND (KTK) 84 Ok39
Chak Chak IR 64 Nh29
Chakchoka IND (WBG) 86 Pe32
Chakdaha IND (WBG) 86 Pe34
Chake Chake EAT 147 Mk48
Chakhansur AFG 64 Ob30
Chak Kompong Som K 89 Qb40
Chakkrarat THA 89 Qb38
Chakradharpur IND (JKD) 83 Pc34
Chakrata IND (UTT) 81 Oj30
Chaksu IND (RJT) 80 Oh32
Chak Swari 65 Og29
Chakur IND (MHT) 82 Oj36
Chakwal PK 65 Og29
Chakwale EAT 147 Mj48
Chakwenga Z 152 Me53
Chala EAT 146 Mf49
Chala MOC 153 Mh52
Chala PE 197 Gc53
Chalais F 24 La45
Chalakudi IND (KER) 84 Oj40
Chalalou PNG 116 Sd47
Chalamera E 29 La49
Chalamont F 25 Lf45
Chalatenango ES 184 Ff38
Chalaua MOC 153 Mk54
Chalbi Desert EAK 144 Mj44
Chalcatzingo MEX 182 Fa36
Chalchihuites MEX 182 Ej34
Chalco MEX (MEX) 182 Fa36
Chalengkou CHN (QHI) 69 Pg26
Châlette-sur-Loing F 23 Lc42
Chalhuanca PE 197 Gd53
Chaling CHN (HUN) 75 Qg32
Chalinze EAT 147 Mk49
Chalisgaon IND (MHT) 82 Oh35
Chalk Mountain USA (TX) 174 Fb29
Chalky Inlet NZ 113 Td69
Chalkyitsik USA (AK) 165 Cj12
Challa AUS (WA) 104 Qk60
Challa BOL 206 Gg54
Challakere IND (KTK) 84 Oj38
Challans F 24 Kt44
Challapalle IND (APH) 83 Pa37
Challapata BOL 206 Gg55
Challenger Deep 10 Sa08
Challis USA (ID) 168 Ec23
Cha Lo VN 87 Qc37
Chaloem Rattanakosin N.P. THA 88 Pk38
Châlons-en-Champagne F 23 Le42
Chalon-sur-Saône F 25 Le44
Chalt 80 Oh27
Cha Lugela MOC 153 Mj54
Châlus F 24 La45
Chalus IR 57 Nf27
Cham CH 34 Lj43
Cham D 33 Ln41
Chama USA (NM) 171 Eg27
Chama Z 146 Mg51
Chamah, Gunung MAL 92 Qa43
Chamama MW 146 Mg52
Chaman PK 65 Od30
Chaman Soltan IR 59 Ne29
Chamax MEX 183 Fg36
Chamba EAT 147 Mj51
Chamba IND (HPH) 81 Oj29
Chamba MOC 153 Mj53
Chambal IND 83 Ok32
Chambarak ARM 57 Nc25
Chamberlain CDN (SK) 169 Eh20
Chamberlain USA (SD) 172 Fa24
Chamberlain Lake USA 176 Gf22
Chambersburg USA (PA) 177 Gb26
Chambers Pillar AUS 108 Rg58
Chambéry F 25 Lf45
Chambishi Z 146 Me52
Chambley F 23 Lf41
Chambly F 23 Lc41
Chambo EC 196 Ga46
Chambord CDN (QC) 176 Gd21
Chambord F 24 Lb43
Chamburi Kalat PK 65 Oc32
Chamchamal IRQ 57 Nc28
Chamela MEX (JLC) 182 Eh36
Chametengo MOC 153 Mh54
Chameza CO 192 Gd43
Châmi RIM 130 Kc35
Chamical RA (LR) 207 Gg61
Cham Ka THA 87 Pk36
Cham Kabud IR 59 Nd29
Chamkani AFG 65 Oe29
Chamoli IND (UTT) 81 Ok30
Chamonix-Mont-Blanc F 25 Lg45
Champa IND (CGH) 83 Pb34
Champagne CDN (YT) 166 Db15
Champagne F 23 Le42
Champagne-Ardenne F 23 Ld42
Champagne-Mouton F 24 La45
Champagne Pools NZ 113 Tj65
Champagnole F 25 Lf44
Champagny Island AUS 103 Rc53
Champai IND (MZR) 86 Pg34
Champaign USA (IL) 175 Ff25
Champaner-Pavagadh Archaeological Park IND (GUJ) 82 Og34
Champaqui, Cerro RA 208 Gh61
Champasak LAO 89 Qc38
Champerico GCA 184 Fe38
Champhon LAO 89 Qc37
Champlitte-et-le-Prélot F 25 Lf43
Champotón MEX (CAM) 183 Fe36
Chamrajanagar IND (KTK) 84 Oj40
Chamursi IND (MHT) 83 Ok36
Chana THA 89 Qa42
Chañar RA (LR) 207 Gh61
Chañaral RCH 207 Ge59
Chañaral RCH 207 Ge60
Chanaran IR 62 Nk27
Chanasma IND (GUJ) 82 Og34
Chancani RA (CD) 208 Gh61
Chancay PE 197 Gb51
Chan-Chan PE 197 Ga50
Chanchayllo PE 197 Gc51
Chancho ETH 142 Mk41
Chanchra BD 86 Pf34
Chanco RCH 208 Gd63
Chanda IND (UPH) 83 Pb32
Chandaler USA (AK) 165 Cf12
Chandama EAT 147 Mj48
Chandarpur IND (CGH) 83 Pb35
Chandausi IND (UPH) 81 Ok31
Chandbali IND (ORS) 83 Pd35
Chandeleur Islands USA 175 Ff31
Chandeleur Sound USA 175 Ff31
Chandeokgung Palace ROK 78 Rd27
Chanderi IND (MPH) 83 Ok33
Chandernagore IND (WBG) 86 Pe34
Chandia IND (MPH) 83 Pa34
Chandigarh IND (PJB) 81 Oj30
Chandil IND (JKD) 83 Pd34
Chandina BD 86 Pf34
Chandipur IND (ORS) 83 Pd35
Chandipur Beach IND 83 Pd35
Chandla IND (MPH) 83 Pa33
Chandler CDN (QC) 176 Gh21
Chandler USA (OK) 174 Fb28
Chandmani MNG 70 Qf23
Chandmeni MNG 67 Pj21
Chandpur BD 86 Pf34
Chandpur BD 86 Pf34
Chandpur IND (UPH) 81 Ok31
Chandraghona BD 86 Pg34
Chandrakona IND (WBG) 83 Pd34
Chandranath Temple BD 86 Pf34
Chandraprabha Wildlife Sanctuary IND 83 Pb33
Chandrapur IND (MHT) 83 Ok36
Chandrasekbarapuram IND (APH) 85 Ok38
Chandreshwar Bhutnath IND 82 Oh38
Chandui IND (UPH) 83 Pb33
Chanduy EC 196 Fk47
Chandvad IND (MHT) 82 Oh35
Chandwa IND (JKD) 83 Pc34
Chane BOL 206 Gj54
Changa Z 152 Me54
Changadae Dan PRK 78 Re26
Changanacherry = Changanassery IND (KER) 84 Oj41
Changanassery IND (KER) 84 Oj41
Changara MOC 152 Mg54
Changbai CHN (JLN) 76 Re25
Changbai Shan CHN/PRK 76 Rd25
Changbaishan Z.B. CHN 76 Rd24
Changchun CHN (JLN) 76 Rc24
Changchunpu CHN (GZH) 87 Qc32
Changdao CHN (SDG) 73 Ra27
Changde CHN (HUN) 74 Qf31
Changfeng CHN (AHU) 78 Qj29
Changgi Gap ROK 79 Re27
Changhang ROK 78 Rd27
Chang Hap K 89 Qd39
Chang He CHN 78 Qj30
Changhua RC 75 Ra33
Changhung PRK 76 Rd25
Changji CHN (XUZ) 67 Pd24
Changjiang CHN (HAN) 75 Qe36
Chang Jiang CHN 74 Qe30
Chang Jiang Cruise route CHN 74 Qd31
Chang Jiang Da Qiao CHN 75 Qh30
Chang Jiang Da Qiao CHN 78 Qk29
Changjin PRK 76 Rd25
Changjue Temple CHN 72 Qe28
Changle CHN (FJN) 75 Qk33
Changle CHN (SCH) 74 Qd30
Changli CHN (HBI) 73 Qk26
Changling CHN (JLN) 76 Rc23
Changlinggang CHN (HUB) 73 Qg30
Changlun MAL 92 Qa42
Changming CHN (GZH) 74 Qd32
Changning CHN (HUN) 74 Qg32
Changning CHN (YUN) 87 Pk33
Changpin RC 75 Ra34
Changping CHN (BJG) 73 Qj25
Changsan Got PRK 78 Rc26
Changsha CHN (HUN) 75 Qg31
Changshan CHN (ZJG) 75 Qk31
Changshan Qundao CHN 73 Rb26
Changshou CHN (CGQ) 74 Qd31
Changshoujie CHN (HUN) 75 Qg31
Changshu CHN (JGS) 78 Ra30
Changshun CHN (GZH) 74 Qd33
Changsong ROK 78 Rd28
Changtai CHN (FJN) 75 Qj33
Changtai CHN (SCH) 69 Pk30
Changting CHN (FJN) 75 Qj33
Changtu CHN (LNG) 76 Rc24
Ch'angwon ROK 79 Re28
Changwu CHN (GZG) 74 Qf34
Changwu CHN (HLG) 76 Rc23
Changxing CHN (ZJG) 78 Qk30
Changxing Dao CHN 73 Ra26
Changyon PRK 78 Rc26
Changyuan CHN (CGQ) 74 Qc31
Changyuan CHN (HNN) 73 Qh28
Chang Yuchun, Tomb of = Imperial Tombs of the Ming and Qing Dynasties CHN (JGS) 78 Qk29
Changzhi CHN (SAX) 73 Qg27
Changzhou CHN (JGS) 78 Qk30
Chañi, Nevado de RA 207 Gh58
Chanka Z 146 Mg50
Channagiri IND (KTK) 84 Oh39
Channapatna IND (KTK) 84 Oj39
Channarayapatna IND (KTK) 84 Oj39
Channel Country AUS 108 Sa58
Channel Islands GB 22 Ks41
Channel Islands USA 170 Ea29
Channel Islands National Park USA 170 Ea29
Channel-Port aux Basques CDN (NF) 177 Ha22
Channel Rock BS 179 Gb34
Channel Tunnel F/GB 23 Lb40
Channing USA (TX) 174 Ej28
Chansura IND (MPH) 83 Pa34
Chantada E 26 Kn48
Chantelle F 25 Ld44
Chanthaburi THA 89 Qb39
Chantilly F 23 Lc41
Chanto GNB 136 Kc40
Chantongia IND (NGL) 86 Ph32
Chantonnay F 24 Kt44
Chantulo MW 153 Mh53
Chanu Daro PK 65 Oe32
Chanute USA (KS) 174 Fc27
Chaohu CHN (AHU) 78 Qj30
Chaouïa MA 125 Kg29
Chaource F 23 Le42
Chaoyang CHN (LNG) 76 Ra25
Chaozhou CHN (GDG) 75 Qj34
Chapada de Maracás BR 201 Hk52
Chapada Diamantina BR 201 Hj52
Chapada Diamantina, P.N. BR 201 Hk52
Chapada do Apodi BR 201 Jb48
Chapada do Araripe BR 201 Hk49
Chapada dos Guimarães BR (MT) 202 Hc53
Chapada dos Guimarães, P.N.da BR 202 Hc53
Chapada dos Parecis BR 206 Gk52
Chapada dos Veadeiros, P.N. da BR 200 Hg52
Chapada Grande BR 201 Hj49
Chapadão do Céu BR (GO) 202 Hd55
Chapadão do Sul BR (MS) 202 Hd55
Chapadinha BR (MA) 201 Hj47
Chapais CDN (QC) 176 Gc21
Chapala MEX (BC) 180 Ec31
Chapala MEX (JLC) 182 Ej35
Chapalilla MEX (NYT) 182 Eh35
Chapara IND (APH) 83 Pc36
Chaparra CO 192 Gc44
Chaparra PE 197 Gd53
Chaparrito CO 192 Ge43
Chapcha BHT 86 Pe32
Chapeau napoléon MA 124 Kf31
Chapecó BR (SC) 204 Hd59
Chapecó, T.I. BR 204 Hd59
Chapel Hill USA (NC) 178 Ga28
Chapel Island Ind. Res. CDN 176 Gk23
Chapfuche ZW 152 Mf56
Chapicuyí ROU 204 Hb61
Chapleau CDN (ON) 173 Fj22
Chaplin CDN (SK) 169 Eg20
Chappell USA (NE) 174 Ej25
Chapra IND (MPH) 82 Oj34
Chã Preta BR (AL) 201 Jc50
Chapuru SOL 117 Sk50
Chapuy RA (SF) 209 Gk62
Châr RIM 130 Kd35
Charadai RA (CH) 204 Ha59
Charagua BOL 206 Gj55
Charalá CO 192 Gd42
Charama IND (CGH) 83 Pa35
Charaña BOL 206 Gf54
Charara Safari Area ZW 152 Me54
Charata RA (CH) 207 Gk59
Charcas MEX (SLP) 182 Ek34
Chard CDN (AB) 167 Ee18
Charente F 24 Ku45
Ch'arents'avan ARM 57 Nc25
Chargarbazar SYR 57 Na27
Chari TCH/CAM 139 Lh39
Charikar AFG 65 Oe28
Chariton USA (IA) 172 Fd25
Charity GUY 194 Ha42
Charkhai BD 86 Pg33
Charkhari IND (UPH) 83 Ok33
Charkhari IND (UPH) 83 Ok33
Charkhi Dadri IND (HYA) 80 Oj31
Charkiv UA 48 Mj21
Charleroi B 23 Le40
Charlesbourg CDN (QC) 176 Ge22
Charles City USA (IA) 172 Fd24
Charles Fort IRL 19 Km39
Charles Fuhr RA (SC) 210 Ge71
Charles Lake CDN (AB) 167 Ee16
Charleston NZ 113 Tf66
Charleston USA (MO) 175 Ff27
Charleston USA (SC) 178 Ga29
Charleston USA (WV) 175 Fk26
Charlestown IRL 19 Km37
Charlestown KNA 187 Gj37
Charlestown USA (IN) 175 Fh26
Charleville AUS (QLD) 109 Sd59
Charleville IRL 19 Km38
Charleville-Mézières F 23 Le41
Charlevoix USA (MI) 173 Fh23
Charlieu F 25 Le44
Charlotte USA (MI) 173 Fh24
Charlotte USA (NC) 178 Fk28
Charlotte Amalie USA (VI) 187 Gh36
Charlotte Bank 89 Qd42
Charlotte Bank 100 Tb11
Charlottenberg S 30 Ln31
Charlotte Plains AUS (QLD) 109 Sd60
Charlottesville USA (VA) 177 Ga26
Charlottetown CDN (PE) 176 Gj22
Charlotteville TT 187 Gk40
Charlston USA (IL) 175 Ff26
Charlton AUS (VIC) 111 Sb64
Charmco USA (WV) 175 Fk26
Charmes F 23 Lg42
Charminar IND 82 Ok37
Charny F 25 Ld43
Charolles F 25 Le44
Charost F 25 Lc44
Charouïne DZ 125 Kk31
Char Rah AFG 64 Ob29
Charrud IR 64 Nj30
Charsadda PK 65 Of28
Charshanga TM 63 Oc27
Charters Towers AUS (QLD) 107 Sd56
Chartres F 23 Lb42
Chas IND (JKD) 83 Pd34
Chasanga EAT 146 Mg48
Chasaya Z 146 Mf50
Chaschuil RA (CA) 207 Gf59
Chascomús RA (BA) 209 Ha63
Chasicó RA (BA) 209 Gj65
Chasicó RA (RN) 208 Gf66
Chasquistambo PE 197 Gb51
Chatarpur IND (MPH) 83 Ok33
Château-Arnoux F 25 Lg46
Chateaubelair WV 187 Gk39
Châteaubourg F 22 Kt42
Châteaubriant F 22 Kt43
Château-Chinon F 25 Ld43
Château de Brissac F 24 Ku43
Château de Chillon CH 34 Lg44
Château de Peyrepertuse F 24 Lc48
Château de Versailles F 23 Lc42
Château-du-Loir F 22 La43
Châteaudun F 22 Lb42
Château fortifié = Aney RN 133 Lg36
Chateaugay USA (NY) 177 Gc23
Châteaugiron F 22 Kt42
Château-Gontier F 22 Ku43
Château-Landon F 23 Lc42
Château-la-Vallière F 24 La43
Château-l'Evêque F 24 La45
Châteaulin F 22 Kq42
Châteaumeillant F 25 Lc44
Châteauneuf-de-Randon F 25 Ld46
Châteauneuf-du-Faou F 22 Kr42
Châteauneuf-en-Thymerais F 22 Lb42
Châteauneuf-la-Forêt F 24 Lb45
Châteauneuf-sur-Charente F 24 Ku45
Châteauneuf-sur-Cher F 25 Lc44
Châteauneuf-sur-Loire F 25 Lc43
Châteauneuf-sur-Sarthe F 22 Ku43
Châteauponsac F 24 Lb44
Château-Porcien F 23 Le41
Château-Renault F 24 La43
Châteauroux F 24 Lb44
Château-Salins F 23 Lg42
Château- Thierry F 23 Ld41
Châteauvillain F 25 Le42
Châtelaillon-Plage F 24 Kt44
Châtel-Censoir F 25 Ld43
Châtelet B 23 Le40
Châtelguyon F 25 Ld45
Châtellerault F 24 La44
Châtelus-Malvaleix F 25 Lc44
Châtenois F 23 Lf42
Chatgaon IND (MHT) 83 Pa35
Chatham = Miramichi CDN (NB) 176 Gh22
Chatham CDN (ON) 173 Fj24
Chatham = Isla San Cristóbal EC 197 Ff46
Chatham GB 21 La39
Chatham USA (AK) 166 Dc17
Chatham USA (LA) 175 Fd29
Chatham Islands 100 Ba14
Chatham Rise 100 Tb14
Châtillon I 34 Lh45
Châtillon-Coligny F 25 Lc43
Châtillon-en-Bazois F 25 Ld43
Châtillon-sur-Chalaronne F 25 Le44
Châtillon-sur-Indre F 24 Lb44
Châtillon-sur-Loire F 25 Lc43
Châtillon-sur-Marne F 23 Ld41
Châtillon-sur-Seine F 25 Le43
Chatom USA (AL) 175 Ff30
Chatra IND (JKD) 83 Pc33
Chatrapur IND (ORS) 83 Pc36
Chatsworth AUS (QLD) 108 Sa56
Chatsworth USA (GA) 175 Fh28
Chatsworth House GB 21 Kt37
Chattanooga USA (TN) 175 Fh28
Chatthin Wildlife Sanctuary MYA 86 Ph35
Chatturat THA 89 Qa38
Chatyn' BY 39 Mh36
Chaua ANG 149 Lk50
Cha-Uat THA 88 Qa42
Chauchilla PE 197 Gc53
Chaudes-Aigues F 25 Ld46
Chau Doc VN 89 Qc40
Chauffailles F 25 Le44
Chauk MYA 86 Ph35
Chaukundi Necropolis PK 65 Od33
Chaul IND 82 Og36
Chaumergy F 25 Lf44
Chaumont F 24 Lb43
Chaumont F 25 Lf42
Chaung-U MYA 86 Ph35
Chaung wa MYA 86 Pj33
Chauny F 23 Ld41
Chauparan IND (JKD) 83 Pc33
Chaur IND 81 Oj30
Chauradadar IND (MPH) 83 Pa34
Chaurai IND (MPH) 83 Ok35
Chaura Island IND 88 Pg41
Chauri IND (GOA) 82 Oh38
Chautauqua N.W.R. USA 175 Ff25
Chauvigny F 24 La44
Chavakachcheri CL 85 Pa41
Chavakkad IND (KER) 84 Oj40
Chaval BR (CE) 201 Hk47
Chavantes BR (SP) 202 Hf57
Chavarría RA (CR) 204 Ha60
Chaves BR (PA) 195 Hf46
Chaves P 26 Kn49
Chaveslândia BR (MG) 202 He55
Chavín de Huántar PE 197 Gb50
Chavinillo PE 197 Gb50
Chavuma Z 151 Mb52
Chavuma Falls Z 151 Mb52
Chavuna EAT 146 Mg48
Chaweng Beach THA 88 Qa41
Chazelles-sur-Lyon F 25 Le45
Chazón RA (CD) 209 Gj62
Chbar K 89 Qd39
Cheadle GB 21 Ks37
Cheakamus Ind. Res. CDN 168 Dj21
Cheb CZ 42 Ln40
Chebba TN 126 Lf28
Chebeba DZ 126 Lb31
Cheboygan USA (MI) 173 Fh23
Chebwe MYA 86 Pk33
Ché Ché GNB 136 Kc40
Checheng RC 75 Ra34
Chechenia RUS 57 Nc24
Chech'on ROK 78 Re27
Chęciny PL 41 Ma40
Checotah USA (OK) 174 Fc28
Chedaba = Man'aung MYA 86 Pg36
Cheektowaga USA (NY) 173 Ga24
Cheepie AUS (QLD) 109 Sc59
Cheerigaabo SP 143 Nd40
Cheeseman Peak AUS 105 Rf59
Chef-Boutonne F 24 Ku44
Chefchaouen MA 125 Kh28
Chefferie Baffoussam CAM 138 Lf43
Chefornak USA (AK) 164 Bh15
Chegarachi UZ 63 Od27
Chegga DZ 126 Lc28
Chegga RIM 125 Kh33
Chegge RIM 130 Ke36
Chegutu ZW 152 Mf55
Chegutu Safari Area ZW 152 Me54
Chehalis USA (WA) 168 Dj22
Chehe CHN (GZG) 74 Qd33
Cheia RO 45 Mf45
Cheile Bicazului-Hăşmaş, P.N. RO 49 Mc22
Cheile Nerei-Beuşniţa, P.N. RO 44 Mb46
Cheju ROK 78 Rd29
Cheju Do ROK 78 Rd29
Chelago ETH 145 Na43
Chelak UZ 63 Od26
Chelan CDN (SK) 169 Ej19
Chelan USA (WA) 168 Dk22
Cheleken TM 62 Ng26
Cheles E 27 Kn52
Chelford RA (RN) 208 Gg65
Chelghoum-El Aïd DZ 126 Ld27
Cheline MOC 153 Mh57
Chellal DZ 126 Lc28
Chełm PL 41 Md39
Chełmno PL 40 Lt37
Chelmsford CDN (ON) 173 Fk22
Chelmsford GB 21 La39
Chelmsford Public Resort Nature Reserve ZA 155 Me59
Chełmża PL 40 Lt37
Cheltenham GB 21 Ks39
Chelva E 29 Ku51
Chelvai IND (APH) 83 Pa36
Chemaïa MA 125 Kf29
Chemax MEX (YT) 183 Fg35
Chemba MOC 153 Mh54
Chembe Z 146 Me51
Chemillé F 24 Ku43
Chemin de Saint-Jacques-de-Compostelle F 24 Kt47
Chemnitz D 32 Ln40
Chemtou TN 126 Le27
Chenachane DZ 125 Kh32
Chena Hot Springs USA (AK) 165 Cg13
Chena River State Recreation Area USA 165 Cg13
Chenar Shahijan IR 59 Nf31
Chen Barag Qi CHN (NMZ) 71 Qk21
Chencha ETH 142 Mj42
Chénerailles F 25 Lc44
Cheney USA (WA) 168 Eb22
Chengalpattu IND (TNU) 85 Ok39
Chengam IND (TNU) 85 Ok39
Chengbu CHN (HUN) 74 Qf32
Chengcheng CHN (SAA) 72 Qe28
Chengde CHN (HBI) 73 Qj25
Chengdu CHN (SCH) 74 Qc30
Chenggong CHN (YUN) 87 Qb33
Chenggou CHN (SAA) 72 Qd29
Chenghai CHN (GDG) 75 Qj34
Chengmai CHN (HAN) 75 Qf36
Chengqian CHN (SDG) 78 Qj28
Chengshan Jiao CHN 73 Rb27
Chengwu CHN (SDG) 73 Qh28
Chengxi CHN (HUN) 74 Qf31
Cheng Xian CHN (GSU) 72 Qc29
Chengyang Bridge CHN 74 Qe33
Chenik USA (AK) 164 Cc16
Chenini TN 126 Lf29
Chenjiagang CHN (JGS) 78 Qk28
Chennai IND (TNU) 85 Pa39
Chennakeshava Temple IND 84 Oh39

Chenonceaux ◻ F 24 Lb43
Chenôve ◻ F 25 Le43
Chenpur ◻ NEP 81 Pa31
Chenque, Cerro ▲ RA 210 Gg68
Chenxi ◻ CHN (CGG) 74 Qd30
Chenzhou ◻ CHN (HUN) 75 Qg33
Cheo Reo ◻ VN 89 Qe39
Chepen ◻ PE 196 Ga49
Chepés ◻ RA (LR) 208 Gg61
Chepo ◻ PA 185 Ga61
Chepsikunya ◻ EAU 144 Mh45
Cheptow ◻ GB 21 Ks39
Cher ◻ F 24 Lb43
Cheranchi ◻ WAN 132 Ld39
Cherangani ◻ EAK 144 Mh45
Cherangany Hills ▲ EAK 144 Mh45
Cherating Beach ◻ MAL 92 Qb43
Cheraw ◻ USA (SC) 178 Ga28
Cherbourg-Octeville ◻ F 22 Kt41
Cherchell ◻ DZ 126 Lb27
Cherhill ◻ CDN (AB) 169 Ec19
Chéri ◻ RN 133 Lf39
Cheria ◻ DZ 126 Lb27
Cheripon ◻ GH 137 La40
Chernobyl ◻ UA 48 Mf20
Chernyshev shyghanagh ◻ KZ 62 Nk25
Cherokee ◻ USA (IA) 172 Fc24
Cherokee ◻ USA (OK) 174 Fa27
Cherokee ◻ USA (TX) 174 Fa29
Cherokee Sound ◻ BS 179 Gb32
Cheroy ◻ F 23 Ld42
Cherry Creek ◻ USA (NV) 170 Ec26
Cherry Creek ◻ USA (SD) 172 Ek23
Cherryfield ◻ USA (ME) 176 Gg23
Cherryville ◻ CDN (BC) 168 Ea20
Cherskiy Range ▲ RUS 55 Rd05
Cherson ◻ UA 49 Mg22
Chersonesus ◻ UA 49 Mg23
Cheru Konda ▲ IND 83 Pb37
Chesapeake ◻ USA (VA) 178 Gb27
Chesapeake Bay ◻ USA 177 Gb26
Chesapeake Bay Bridge Tunnel ▲ USA 178 Gc27
Chesapeake Beach ◻ USA (VA) 177 Gb27
Cheshmeh Malek ◻ IR 64 Nk30
Chesht-e Sharif ◻ AFG 65 Ob28
Chesmeh Kabud ◻ IR 57 Nd29
Cheste ◻ E 29 Ku51
Chester ◻ CDN (NS) 176 Gh23
Chester ◻ GB 21 Ks37
Chester ◻ USA (IL) 175 Ff27
Chester ◻ USA (MT) 169 Ee21
Chester ◻ USA (PA) 177 Gc26
Chester ◻ USA (SC) 178 Fk28
Chester ◻ USA (VA) 178 Gb27
Chesterfield ◻ GB 21 Kt37
Chesterfield Inlet ◻ CDN 163 Fb06
Chesterton Range ▲ AUS (QLD) 109 Sd58
Chesterton Range N.P. ▲ AUS 109 Sd59
Chetaibi ◻ DZ 126 Ld27
Chete ☐ ZW 152 Md54
Chete Safari Area ☐ ZW 152 Md54
Cheticamp ◻ CDN (NS) 176 Gk22
Chet Korkora ◻ RIM 131 Kh37
Chetlat Island ▲ IND 84 Og40
Chetput ◻ IND (TNU) 85 Ok39
Chetumal ◻ MEX (QTR) 183 Ff36
Chetwynd ◻ CDN (BC) 168 Dh18
Chevak ◻ USA (AK) 164 Bh15
Chevanceaux ◻ F 24 Ku44
Cheverny ▲ F 24 Lb43
Cheviot ◻ NZ 113 Tg67
Chew Bahir ☐ ETH 144 Mj43
Chewelah ◻ USA (WA) 168 Eb21
Chewore Safari Area ☐ ZW 152 Me53
Cheyenne ◻ USA (OK) 174 Fa28
Cheyenne ◻ USA (WY) 171 Eh25
Cheyenne ◻ USA 169 Eg23
Cheyenne River Ind. Res. ▲ USA 172 Ek23
Cheyenne Wells ◻ USA (CO) 174 Ej26

Chichagof Island ▲ USA 166 Dc17
Chichaoua ◻ MA 124 Kf30
Chichawatni ◻ PK 65 Og30
Chicheng ◻ CHN (HBI) 73 Qj25
Chichén Itzá ◻ MEX 183 Ff35
Chichester ◻ GB 21 Ku40
Chichibu ◻ J 77 Rk27
Chichibu-Tama N.P. ◻ J 79 Rk28
Chichicastenango ◻ GCA 184 Fe38
Chichihualco ◻ MEX (GUR) 182 Fa36
Chichiriviche ◻ YV 193 Gf40
Chicholi ◻ IND (MPH) 83 Ok35
Chickaloon ◻ USA (AK) 165 Ch15
Chickamauga & Chattanooga N.M.P. ◻ USA 175 Fh28
Chickasaw N.R.A. ◻ USA 174 Fb28
Chickasaw N.W.R. ◻ USA 175 Ff28
Chickasha ◻ USA (OK) 174 Fa28
Chicken Cr. Summit ◻ USA 170 Eb25
Chiclana de la Frontera ◻ E 27 Ko54
Chiclayo ◻ PE 196 Ga49
Chico ◻ MOC 152 Mg56
Chico ▲ RA 210 Gf70
Chicoa ◻ MOC 152 Md53
Chicoana ◻ RA (SA) 207 Gh58
Chicoasén ◻ MEX (CHP)
Chicoca ◻ ANG 151 Mb54
Chicomba ◻ ANG 150 Lj53
Chicomo ◻ MOC 152 Mf56
Chicomostoc ◻ MEX 182 Ej34
Chicomuselo ◻ MEX (CHP) 183 Fd38
Chicopee ◻ USA (MA) 177 Gd24
Chicoral ◻ CO 192 Gc43
Chicotte ◻ CDN (QC) 176 Gj21
Chicoutimi ◻ CDN (QC) 176 Ge21
Chicualacuale ◻ MOC 152 Mf57
Chicundo ◻ ANG 150 Lj52
Chicupa ◻ ANG 150 Lk53
Chicuti ◻ MOC 153 Mh52
Chidambaram ◻ IND (TNU) 85 Ok40
Chidenguele ◻ MOC 152 Mh58
Chidu ◻ ROK 78 Rd28
Chidya ◻ EAT 147 Mk51
Chiede ◻ ANG 150 Lk54
Chiefland ◻ USA (FL) 178 Fj31
Chief Menominee Mem. ◻ USA 173 Fg25
Chief's Island ☐ RB 151 Mb55
Chiemsee ☐ D 33 Ln43
Chieng Cang ◻ VN 87 Qb35
Chiengi ◻ Z 146 Me50
Chiengo ◻ ANG 151 Lj53
Chieri ◻ I 34 Lh46
Chiesa di San Pio ◻ I 37 Lq49
Chieti ◻ I 37 Lp48
Chifango ◻ ANG 150 Lj53
Chifeng ◻ CHN (NMZ) 71 Qk24
Chiftak ◻ USA (AK) 164 Bj15
Chifukwe Hills ▲ Z 152 Me53
Chifunde ◻ Z 146 Mg51
Chifunde ◻ MOC 152 Mg53
Chig ☐ RIM 131 Kg36
Chigamane ◻ MOC 152 Mg57
Chigasaki ◻ J 79 Rk28
Chigicho ◻ ETH 142 Mk41
Chigirin ◻ UA 49 Mf21
Chignecto, Mount ▲ USA 173 Fc23
Chignik Mountains ▲ USA 164 Cd15
Chignik ◻ USA (AK) 164 Ca17
Chigongwe ◻ EAT 146 Mh49
Chigorodó ◻ CO 192 Gb42
Chiguana ◻ BOL 206 Gg54
Chiguana, Volcán ▲ BOL 206 Gg56
Chiguayante ◻ RCH 208 Gd64
Chigubo ◻ MOC 152 Mg57
Chigugu ◻ EAT 147 Mk49
Chigwell ◻ GB 21 La39
Chihil Zina ◻ AFG 65 Oc30
Chihsing Yen ◻ RC 75 Ra35
Chihuahua ◻ MEX (CHH) 180 Eg31
Chihuahua ◻ MEX 180 Eg31
Chihuido de Medio, Cerro ▲ RA 208 Gf64
Chihuíl ◻ BOL 206 Gg54
Chijinpani ◻ BOL 206 Gg54
Chikali Kalan ◻ IND (MPH) 83 Ok37
Chikamewani ◻ IND (APH) 84 Oj39
Chikhli ◻ IND (GUJ) 82 Og35
Chikhli ◻ IND (MHT) 82 Oj35
Chikindzonot ◻ MEX (YT) 183 Ff35
Chikmagalur ◻ IND (KTK) 84 Oh39
Chikodi ◻ IND (KTK) 82 Oh37
Chikombedzi ◻ ZW 152 Mf56
Chikupale ◻ IND (APH) 84 Pa38
Chikupo Cave ◻ ZW 152 Mf54
Chikwawa ◻ MW 153 Mh54
Chikwawa ◻ Z 146 Mf51
Chila ◻ ANG 150 Lh53
Chilakalurupeti ◻ IND (APH) 83 Pa37
Chilamatamani ◻ IND (KTK) 84 Oh39
Chilanko Forks ◻ CDN (BC) 166 Dh19
Chilapa de Alvarez ◻ MEX (GUR) 182 Fa37
Chilapa ◻ IND 82 Oh32
Chilaw ◻ CL 85 Ok42
Chilca, Juliana ◻ RA (SE) 207 Gj60
Chilcoot ◻ USA (CA) 170 Dk26
Childers ◻ AUS (QLD) 109 Sg58
Chile ■ RCH 205 Gb58
Chile Basin ◻ 190 Ga12
Chile Chico ◻ RCH 210 Ge69
Chilecito ◻ RA (LR) 207 Gg60
Chilembwe ◻ Z 146 Mg51
Chile Rise ◻ 190 Fa13
Chilete ◻ PE 196 Ga49
Chilibre ◻ PA 185 Ga61
Chilicote ◻ MEX (CHH) 181 Eh31
Chililka Lake ☐ IND 83 Pc36
Chililabombwe ◻ Z 151 Md52
Chilkat ◻ USA (AK) 166 Dc16
Chilla ◻ EC 196 Ga47
Chillagoe-Mungana Caves N.P. ◻ AUS (QLD) 107 Sc54
Chillán ◻ RCH 208 Gd64
Chillán, Volcán ▲ RCH 208 Gd64
Chilla Well ◻ AUS (NT) 103 Rf56
Chillicothe ◻ USA (IL) 175 Ff25
Chillicothe ◻ USA (MO) 174 Fd26
Chillicothe ◻ USA (OH) 175 Fj26
Chillihué ◻ J 80 Oh27
Chilongozi ◻ Z 146 Mf51
Chiloé, P.N. de ◻ RCH 208 Gc67
Chiloma ◻ MOC 153 Mh54
Chilombo ◻ ANG 151 Mb53
Chilombola ◻ EAT 147 Mj50
Chilongoshi ◻ Z 146 Mf51
Chiloquin ◻ USA (OR) 168 Dk24

Chilpancingo de los Bravos ◻ MEX (GUR) 182 Fa37
Chilpi ◻ IND (MPH) 83 Pa34
Chiltern ◻ AUS (VIC) 111 Sd64
Chiltern Hills ▲ GB 21 Ku39
Chilton ◻ USA (WI) 173 Ff23
Chiluage ◻ ANG 149 Ma50
Chilumba ◻ MW 146 Mh51
Chilumbwa ◻ Z 151 Md52
Chilung ◻ RC 75 Ra35
Chimala ◻ EAT 146 Mh51
Chimaltenango ◻ GCA 184 Fe38
Chimán ◻ PA 185 Ga61
Chimanimani ◻ ZW 152 Mg55
Chimanimani N.P. ◻ ZW 152 Mg55
Chimay ◻ B 23 Le40
Chimbarongo ◻ RCH 208 Gd63
Chimbarongo ◻ ANG 150 Lj52
Chimbinde ◻ ANG 150 Lk52
Chimborazo, Volcán ▲ EC 196 Ga46
Chimbote ◻ PE 197 Ga50
Chimboy ◻ UZ 62 Nk24
Chimbwingombi ◻ Z 146 Mf52
Chimney Rock ◻ USA 171 Ej25
Chimney Rock N.H.S. ◻ USA 171 Ek25
Chimoio ◻ MEX (JLC) 182 Eh35
Chimoio ◻ MOC 152 Mf55
Chimpamba ◻ MW 146 Mh51
Chimur ◻ IND (MHT) 83 Ok35
Chimusimike ◻ ZW 152 Me54
China ◻ CHN 53 Pa06
Chin Hills ▲ MYA (NL) 181 Fa33
Chinácota ◻ CO 192 Gd42
Chinák-merü ◻ YV 193 Gk43
Chincha Alta ◻ PE 197 Gb52
Chinchero ▲ PE 197 Gd52
Chinchilla ◻ AUS (QLD) 109 Sf59
Chinchilla de Monte Aragón ◻ E 29 Kt52
Chinchina ◻ CO 192 Gc43
Chinchin Straits ◻ THA/MAL 88 Pk42
Chincholi ◻ IND (KTK) 82 Oj37
Chincoteague ◻ USA (VA) 177 Gc27
Chinchorro, Reserva de la Biosfera Banco ◻ MEX 183 Fg36
Chinchwad ◻ IND (MHT) 82 Og36
Chincolco ◻ RCH 208 Ge62
Chincoteague ◻ USA 177 Gc27
Chinde ◻ MOC 153 Mj55
Chin Do ▲ ROK 78 Rd28
Chindo ◻ ROK 78 Rd28
Chindrikir ◻ J 81 Oj27
Chindwin ◻ MYA 86 Ph33
Chingaza, P.N. ▲ CO 192 Gd43
Chingo ◻ ANG 150 Lj53
Chingola ◻ Z 151 Md52
Chinguar ◻ ANG 150 Lj52
Chinguetti ◻ RIM 130 Kd35
Chinhae ◻ ROK 78 Re28
Chinhanda ◻ MOC 152 Mg55
Chinhanguanine ◻ MOC 155 Mg58
Chin Hills ▲ MYA 86 Pg35
Chinhoyi ☐ ZW 152 Mf54
Chinhoyi Caves ◻ ZW 152 Mf54
Chinida ◻ Z 152 Mg53
Chinivasso ◻ I 34 Lh45
Chinjan ◻ PK 65 Oc30
Chinle ◻ USA (AZ) 171 Ef27
Chinmen Tao ▲ RC 75 Qk33
Chinnur ◻ IND (APH) 83 Ok36
Chinobampo ◻ MEX (SL) 180 Ef32
Chinook ◻ USA (MT) 169 Ef21
Chino Valley ◻ USA (AZ) 171 Ed28
Chinsali ◻ Z 146 Mg51
Chinsura ◻ IND (WBG) 83 Pd34
Chintalapudi ◻ IND (APH) 83 Pa37
Chintalnar ◻ IND (CGH) 83 Pa36
Chintamani ◻ IND (KTK) 84 Oj39
Chintapalle ◻ IND (APH) 83 Pb37
Chintheche ◻ MW 146 Mh51
Chinú ◻ CO 192 Gc41
Chinunje ◻ EAT 147 Mj51
Chinyama Litapi ◻ Z 151 Mb52
Chioco ◻ MOC 152 Mg54
Chióggia ◻ I 34 Ln45
Chiojdu ◻ RO 45 Mg45
Chiona ◻ EAT 147 Mj50
Chipaka ◻ Z 151 Mc52
Chipande ◻ ANG 151 Ma53
Chipasanse ◻ Z 146 Mf50
Chipata ◻ Z 152 Mg53
Chipego ◻ Z 152 Mg53
Chipego ◻ Z 146 Me53
Chipewyan Ind. Res. ◻ CDN (AB) 167 Ee16
Chiphen Hot Springs ◻ RC 75 Ra34
Chipindo ◻ ANG 150 Lj52
Chiping ◻ CHN 73 Qj27
Chipinga Safari Area ☐ ZW 152 Mg55
Chipiona ◻ E 27 Ko54
Chipinge ◻ ZW 152 Mg55
Chiplun ◻ IND (MHT) 82 Og37
Chipman ◻ CDN (NB) 176 Gh22
Chipogola ◻ EAT 147 Mj49
Chipoia ◻ ANG 150 Lk51
Chipole ◻ EAT 147 Mj50
Chippewa Falls ◻ USA (WI) 172 Fe23
Chiprana ◻ E 29 Ku49
Chipungo ◻ Z 146 Mf52
Chiputa ◻ MOC 152 Mg53
Chiputneticook Lakes ◻ USA 176 Gg23
Chiquián ◻ PE 197 Gb51
Chiquilá ◻ MEX (QTR) 183 Ff35
Chiquimula ◻ GCA 184 Ff38
Chiquimulilla ◻ GCA 184 Fe39
Chiquinquirá ◻ CO 192 Gd42

Chiricahua Nat. Mon. ◻ USA 171 Ef29
Chiriguana ◻ CO 192 Gd41
Chirimena ◻ YV 193 Gg40
Chiriqui Grande ◻ PA 185 Fj41
Chiri San ▲ ROK 78 Rd28
Chirisan N.P. ◻ ROK 78 Rd28
Chirisa Safari Area ☐ ZW 152 Me54
Chirivel ◻ E 27 Ks53
Chirochi ◻ Z 152 Mg53
Chiripó, P.N. ◻ CR 185 Fj41
Chirumanzu ◻ ZW 152 Mf55
Chirundu ◻ Z 152 Me53
Chirundu ◻ ZW 152 Me53
Chisamba ◻ Z 151 Md53
Chisapa ◻ Z 146 Mg51
Chisana ◻ USA (AK) 165 Ck14
Chisasibi ◻ CDN (QC) 163 Ga08
Chisec ◻ GCA 184 Fe38
Chisekesi ◻ Z 152 Md54
Chisenga ◻ MW 146 Mg51
Chishui ◻ CHN 172 Fd22
Chisinau ☐ MD 49 Me22
Chislaz ◻ RO 43 Mc43
Chisoso ◻ Z 146 Mf51
Chissano ◻ MOC 155 Mg58
Chissibuca ◻ MOC 152 Mh56
Chissiguane ◻ MOC 152 Mh56
Chistian Mandy ◻ PK 65 Og31
Chisumbanje ◻ ZW 152 Mg55
Chisvingo ◻ ZW 152 Mf55
Chita ◻ CO 192 Gd42
Chita ◻ RUS
Chitado ◻ ANG 150 Lh54
Chitalwana ◻ IND (RJT) 82 Of33
Chitanda ◻ Z 152 Md53
Chi Tanh ◻ VN 89 Qd39
Chitero ◻ MW 146 Mg52
Chitila ◻ MEX (JLC) 182 Eh35
Chitembo ◻ ANG 150 Lj52
Chitengo ◻ MOC 152 Mg55
Chitga ◻ Z 152 Md54
Chitipa ◻ MW 146 Mg50
Chitobe ◻ MOC 152 Mg56
Chitonga ◻ Z 152 Md54
Chitose ◻ J 77 Sa24
Chitradurga ◻ IND (KTK) 84 Oj38
Chitrakot ◻ IND (CGH) 83 Pa36
Chitrakut ◻ IND (UPH) 83 Pa33
Chitré ◻ PA 185 Fk42
Chittagong ◻ BD 86 Pf34
Chittaranjan ◻ IND (JKD) 83 Pd34
Chittaurgarh ◻ IND (RJT)
Chittaurgarh Fort ◻ IND (RJT) 82 Oh33
Chittoor ◻ IND (APH) 85 Ok39
Chittor = Chittaurgarh ◻ IND (RJT) 82 Oh33
Chitungwiza ◻ ZW 152 Mf54
Chitute ◻ MOC 152 Mg55
Chityal ◻ IND (APH) 83 Ok36
Chiuchiu ◻ RCH 207 Gf57
Chium ◻ ANG 151 Ma53
Chiumbo ◻ ANG 149 Ma50
Chiume ◻ ANG 151 Mb53
Chiure Novo ◻ MOC 147 Mk52
Chiure Velho ◻ MOC 147 Mk52
Chiusa = Klausen ◻ I 34 Lm44
Chiusi ◻ I 34 Lm47
Chiuta ◻ MOC 153 Mh53
Chiva ◻ E 29 Ku51
Chivacoa ◻ YV 193 Gf40
Chivasso ◻ I 34 Lh45
Chivato ◻ RCH 207 Ge59
Chivay ◻ PE 197 Ge53
Chive ◻ BOL 206 Gf52
Chivhu ◻ ZW 152 Mf55
Chivilcoy ◻ RA (BA) 209 Ha63
Chiviricó ◻ C 179 Gb36
Chizarira Hills ▲ ZW 152 Md53
Chizarira N.P. ▲ ZW 152 Md54
Chizu ◻ J 79 Rh28
Chizwina ◻ RB 152 Md56
Chlef ◻ DZ 126 Lb27
Chludowo ◻ PL 41 La38
Chlumec nad Cidlinou ◻ CZ 42 Lq40
Chmel'nyc'kyj ◻ UA 49 Md21
Chmielnik ◻ PL 41 Ma40
Chmil'nyk ◻ UA 49 Md21
Choam Khsant ◻ K 89 Qc38
Choam Sla ◻ K 89 Qb40
Choba ◻ RB 151 Mc55
Chobe ◻ RB/NAM 151 Mc54
Chobe N.P. ◻ RB 151 Mc55
Choca, Cerro ▲ RP 90 Rc41
Chocianów ◻ PL 40 Lq39
Chociwel ◻ PL 40 Lq37
Chocolate Hills ▲ RP 90 Rc41
Chocolate Mts. ▲ USA 170 Ec29
Choconta ◻ CO 192 Gd43
Chocope ◻ PE 196 Ga49
Choctaw N.W.R. ◻ USA 175 Ff30
Chodavaram ◻ IND (APH) 83 Pb37
Chodecz ◻ PL 41 Lu38
Cho Do ▲ PRK 78 Rc26
Chodoriv ◻ UA 43 Me41
Chodov ◻ CZ 42 Ln40
Chodová Planá ◻ CZ 42 Ln41
Chodzież ◻ PL 41 Lr38
Choele Choel ◻ RA (RN) 208 Gg65
Chofombo ◻ MOC 152 Mf53
Choharwa ◻ NEP 83 Pd32
Choiceland ◻ CDN (SK) 169 Eh19
Choicó Day ◻ BS 179 Gb34
Choirokoitia ◻ CY 56 Mg28
Choiseul ◻ SOL 117 Sj49
Choix ◻ MEX (SL) 180 Ef32
Chojbalsan ◻ MNG 71 Qm21
Chojnice ◻ PL 40 Lp38
Chojnów ◻ PL 40 Lq39
Chokai-Q.N.P. ◻ J 77 Rk26
Chokai-san ▲ J 77 Sa26
Chok Chai ◻ THA 89 Qb38
Chokwé ◻ MOC 155 Mg58

Chongjin ◻ PRK 76 Re25
Chongju ◻ PRK 76 Rc26
Ch'ongju ◻ ROK 78 Rd28
Chongli ◻ CHN (SCH)
Chongming Dao ▲ CHN 74 Qc31
Chongoene ◻ MOC 155 Mg58
Chongoni Rock Art ◻ MW 153 Mh53
Chongoroi ◻ ANG 150 Lg52
Chongoyape ◻ PE 196 Ga49
Chong'yong ◻ PRK 76 Rd26
Chongqing ◻ CHN (CGQ)
Chongqing ◻ CHN 74 Qd31
Chongren ◻ CHN (JGX) 75 Qj32
Chong Samui ◻ THA 88 Pk41
Chongsan Do ◻ ROK 78 Rd28
Chongsŏn ◻ ROK 78 Re27
Chongwe Monastery ◻ CHN 87 Qa33
Chongwe ◻ Z 152 Me53
Chongzuo ◻ CHN (GZG) 74 Qd34
Chonju ◻ ROK 78 Rd28
Chonogol ◻ MNG (ARP) 86 Pj32
Chonos Archipelago ▲ RCH 210 Gc68
Chontali ◻ PE 196 Ga48
Chontalpa ◻ MEX (TB) 183 Fd37
Chon Thanh ◻ VN 89 Qd40
Cho Oyu ▲ NEP/CHN 81 Pd31
Chopan ◻ IND (UPH) 83 Pb33
Chopan ◻ IND (MHT) 82 Oh35
Choqa Zanbil ◻ IR 59 Ne29
Chorea ◻ MA 125 Kh30
Chorkenp ◻ IND (MNP)
Chorol ◻ UA 49 Mg21
Chorolque, Nevado ▲ BOL 206 Gh56
Choroma ◻ RA (TU) 207 Gh59
Choroni ◻ YV 193 Gg40
Choros Bajos ◻ RCH 207 Ge60
Choroszcz ◻ PL 41 Mc37
Chorozinho ◻ BR (CE) 201 Ja48
Chorrera ◻ PE 196 Ga47
Chorrochó ◻ BR (BA) 201 Ja50
Chorro de Maita ◻ C 186 Gc35
Chorro El Indio, P.N. ▲ YV 192 Gd41
Chorzele ◻ PL 41 Ma37
Chorzów ◻ PL 41 Lt40
Ch'osan ◻ PRK 76 Rc25
Choshuenco, Volcán ▲ RCH 208 Gd65
Chos Malal ◻ RA (NE) 208 Ge64
Chosong ◻ PRK 76 Rd25
Chota ◻ PE 196 Ga49
Chota Nagpur Plateau ▲ IND 83 Pa34
Chota Udaipur ◻ IND (GUJ) 82 Oh34
Chotilsko ◻ CZ 42 Lp41
Chott Ech Chergui ◻ DZ 125 Lb28
Chott el Fedjadj ◻ TN 126 Le28
Chott el Gharbi ◻ DZ 125 Kk29
Chott el Gharsa ◻ TN 126 Le28
Chott el Hodna ◻ DZ 126 Lc28
Chott el Jerid ◻ TN 126 Le29
Chott el Malah ◻ DZ 125 La29
Chott Mehrir ◻ DZ 126 Ld28
Chott Merouane ◻ DZ 126 Ld29
Chotyn ◻ UA 49 Md21
Chou ▲ RL 56 Mh29
Choûm ◻ RIM 130 Kd35
Chowchilla ◻ USA (CA) 170 Dk27
Choya ◻ RA (SE) 207 Gh60
Choyr ◻ MNG 70 Qf22
Chrám ◻ CZ 42 Lq40
Chréa ◻ DZ 126 Lb27
Chréa, P.N. de ◻ DZ 126 Lb27
Chrerik ◻ RIM 130 Kd35
Chris Ammoudia ◻ GR 45 Me50
Chrisman ◻ USA (IL) 175 Fg26
Christchurch ◻ GB 21 Kt40
Christchurch ◻ NZ 113 Tg67
Christiana ◻ ZA 155 Mc59
Christiansburg ◻ GUY 194 Ha42
Christiansborg ◻ USA (VA) 178 Fk27
Christiansfeld ◻ DK 30 Lk35
Christiansø ▲ N 30 Lt32
Christiansted ◻ USA (VI) 187 Gh37
Christina ◻ MYA 88 Pj41
Christie Mtn. Ski Area ◻
Christina Lake ◻ CDN (BC)
Christmas Creek ◻ AUS (WA) 103 Rc55
Christmas Ridge ◻ 10 Bb08
Christmas Valley ◻ USA (OR) 168 Dk24
Christoval ◻ USA (TX) 174 Ek30
Chrudim ◻ CZ 42 Lq41
Chrysopolí ◻ GR 45 Mf50
Chrzanów ◻ PL 41 Lu40
Chu ◻ KS 66 Oa24
Chu = Shu ◻ KZ 63 Oe23
Chuadanga ◻ BD 86 Pe34
Chuang ◻ PNG 115 Sc49
Chuave ◻ PNG 115 Sc49
Chubu-Sangaku N.P. ◻ J 79 Rj27
Chubut ◻ RA 210 Gg67
Chucuito ◻ PE 206 Ge54
Chucunaque ◻ PA 185 Gb61
Chuda ◻ IND (GUJ) 82 Og34
Chugach Is. ▲ USA 164 Ce16
Chugach Mountains ▲ USA 165 Ch15
Chugiak ◻ USA (AK) 165 Ch15
Chugwater ◻ USA (WY) 171 Eh25
Chuhloma ◻ RUS 48 Nb17
Chuhubo ◻ Z 152 Md53
Chu'i ◻ BR (RS) 204 Hd62
Chui ▲ USA 165 Ch15
Chuina ◻ PE 196 Ga46
Chuitayo ◻ EC 196 Ga46
Chujiang ◻ CHN 74 Qf32
Chukai ◻ MAL 92 Qb43
Chukchi Autonomous District ◻ RUS 55 Tb05
Chukchi Plateau ◻ 10 Ba08
Chukchi Sea ◻ RUS/USA 55 Uc04
Chukhloma ◻ RUS 48 Nb17
Chuknagar ◻ BD 86 Pe34
Chukotsk Peninsula ▲ RUS 55 Ub05
Chukudukraal ◻ RB 152 Mb56
Chukwani ◻ EAT 147 Mk49
Chulakivka ◻ UA 49 Mg22
Chula Vista ◻ USA (CA) 170 Eb29
Chulman ◻ RUS 55 Rb07
Chulucanas ◻ PE 196 Fk48
Chulumani ◻ BOL 206 Gg54
Chuma ◻ BOL 206 Gf53

Chumba ◻ ETH 144 Mk43
Chumbicha ◻ RA (CA) 207 Gg60
Chumbo ◻ BR (MG) 203 Hg55
Chumda ◻ CHN (QHI) 69 Pj29
Chumet Kal ◻ K 89 Qb39
Chumphon ◻ THA 88 Pk40
Chumphon Buri ◻ THA 89 Qb38
Chum Phuang ◻ THA 89 Qb38
Chumunjin ◻ ROK 78 Re27
Chumuco ◻ PE 196 Ga49
Chumui ◻ MEX 183 Fd36
Chuna ◻ IR 64 Nh29
Chunal ◻ MEX 181 Eg34
Chunchi ◻ EC 196 Ga47
Chunchucmil ◻ MEX 183 Fe35
Chundale ◻ ANG 151 Ma53
Chunga ◻ Z 151 Mc53
Chunga ◻ Z 146 Mg51
Chungang ◻ PRK 76 Rc25
Chunga Rest Camp ◻ Z 151
Ch'ungju ◻ ROK 78 Rd27
Ch'ungmu ◻ ROK 79 Re28
Chungu ◻ PE 197 Gb52
Chungungo ◻ RCH 207 Ge60
Chungyang Shanmo ▲ RC 75 Ra34
Chunhuhub ◻ MEX (QTR) 183 Ff36
Chunhui ◻ CHN (HNN) 73 Qg29
Chunian ◻ PK 65 Og30
Chunwan ◻ CHN (GDG) 74 Qf34
Chuor Phnom Kravanh ▲ K 89 Qb39
Chuor Phnom Dangrek ▲ K 89 Qc38
Chupaca ◻ PE 197 Gc52
Chupanan ◻ IR 64 Nh29
Chupara ◻ VN 89 Qd39
Chu Prong ▲ VN 89 Qd39
Chuquibamba ◻ PE 197 Gd53
Chuquibambilla ◻ PE 197 Gd53
Chuquicamata ◻ RCH 207 Gf57
Chuquis ◻ PE 197 Gb50
Chur ◻ CH 34 Lk44
Churachandpur ◻ IND (MNP) 86 Pg34
Churapcha ◻ RUS 55 Rd06
Churchill ◻ CDN 163 Fa07
Churchill Falls ◻ CDN 163 Fd07
Churchill Lake ◻ CDN 167 Ef17
Churchill Mountains ▲ 7 Sc35
Churchill River ◻ CDN 167 Ef18
Churchs Ferry ◻ USA (ND)
Churia Range ▲ NEP 81 Pa31
Churi ◻ IND (CGH) 83 Pb34
Churu ◻ IND (RJT) 80 Oh31
Churubamba ◻ PE 197 Gb50
Chu Se ◻ VN 89 Qd39
Chushal ◻ IND (JAK)
Chu Ta ◻ VN 87 Qb34
Chusovoj ◻ RUS 54 Nh07
Chute-des-Passes ◻ CDN (QC) 176 Ge21
Chutes d'Abourou ◻ RCA 140 Mb43
Chutes d'Antafofo ◻ RM 157 Nd55
Chutes de Béla ◻ RCB/RDC 148 Lh44
Chutes de Betsiboka ◻ RM 157 Nd54
Chutes de Billy ◻ RMM 136 Kf39
Chutes de Boali ◻ RCA 140 Lk43
Chutes de Bouenza ◻ RCB 148 Lg47
Chutes de Dibouangui ◻ G 148 Lf46
Chutes de Félou ◻ RMM 136 Ke39
Chutes de Gouina ◻ RMM 130 Ke38
Chutes de Gozobangui ◻ RCA 140 Mb43
Chutes de Kinkon ◻ RG 136 Kd40
Chutes d'Ekom ◻ CAM 138 Lf43
Chutes de Kongou ◻ G 148 Lg45
Chutes de Kotto ◻ RCA 140 Ma43
Chutes de la Kagera ◻ BU 146 Me47
Chutes de la Kiubo ◻ RDC 146 Md50
Chutes de la Lobé ◻ CAM 138 Le44
Chutes de la Lofoi ◻ RDC 146 Md51
Chutes de la Lufira ◻ RDC 146 Md51
Chutes de la Madeleine ◻ F 118 Td57
Chutes de Lancrenon ◻ CAM 139 Lh42
Chutes de l'Ankofia ◻ RM 156 Ne53
Chutes de l'Ivindo et Tsengué Leledi ◻ G 148 Lg46
Chutes de Livingstone ◻ RDC 148 Lg48
Chutes de Lokoho ◻ RM 156 Ne53
Chutes de Loufoulakari ◻ RCB/RDC 148 Lh48
Chutes de Lubi ◻ RDC 149 Mb49
Chutes de Mataki ◻ RCA 140 Ma43
Chutes de Mbi ◻ RCA 140 Lj43
Chutes de Mingouli ◻ G 148 Lg45
Chutes de Nachtigal ◻ CAM 139 Lf43
Chutes de Ngolo ◻ RCA 140 Mb43
Chutes de Papara ◻ RMM 130 Ke38
Chutes de Poubara ◻ G 148 Lg45
Chutes de Sakalona ◻ RM 157 Nd56
Chutes de Tanougou ◻ DY 137 La40
Chutes de Tinkisso ◻ RG 136 Ke40
Chutes de Touboutou ◻ RCA 140 Ma43
Chutes de Zongo ◻ RCB/RDC 148 Lh48
Chutes d'Inga ◻ RDC 148 Lg48
Chutes du Tello ◻ CAM 139 Lg42
Chutes Gauthiot ◻ TCH 140 Lh41
Chutes Johnston ◻ RDC 146 Me51
Chutes Tembo ◻ RDC 149 Lj48
Chutine Landing ◻ CDN (BC)
Chuvashia ◻ RUS 48 Nd18
Chuxiong ◻ CHN (YUN) 87 Qa33
Chuy ◻ ROU 204 Hd62
Chuzhou ◻ CHN (AHU) 78 Qk29
Chwaka ◻ EAT 147 Mk49

Chwaszczyno ◻ PL 40 Lt36
Chynów ◻ PL 41 Mb39
Chynthiana ◻ USA (KY) 175 Fh26
Chyriv ◻ UA 43 Mc41
Chyulu Hills N.P. ◻ EAK 144 Mj47
Ciamis ◻ RI 95 Qd49
Cianjur ◻ RI 95 Qd49
Cianorte ◻ BR (PR) 202 Hd57
Ciawi ◻ RI 95 Qd49
Cibadak ◻ RI 95 Qd49
Cibatu ◻ RI 95 Qd49
Cibola, Cerro ▲ BOL 206 Gf55
Cibitoung ◻ RI 95 Qd49
Cibit ◻ RUS (ALT) 67 Pd20
Cicciano ◻ I 37 Lp49
Çiçekdağı ◻ TR 56 Mg26
Cicia ▲ FJI 119 Ua54
Cícero Dantas ◻ BR (BA) 201 Ja51
Çiçevac ◻ SCG 44 Mb47
Cícheng ◻ CHN (ZJG) 75 Ra31
Çifteler ◻ TR 56 Me26
Çifte Minare Medresesi ◻ TR 57 Na26
Cifuentes ◻ C 179 Fk34
Cifuentes ◻ E 29 Ks50
Cifunchu ◻ PE 207 Ge58
Cigarro ◻ BR (AM) 198 Gj47
Cigel'ka ◻ SK 43 Mb41
Cigliano ◻ I 34 Lh45
Cihanbeyli ◻ TR 56 Mf26
Cihanbeyli Yaylası ▲ TR 56 Mg26
Cijawang ◻ RI 93 Qc49
Cijulang ◻ RI 95 Qd49
Cikalong ◻ RI 95 Qd49
Cikampek ◻ RI 95 Qd49
Cikarang ◻ RI 95 Qd49
Cikatomas ◻ RI 95 Qd49
Cikobia ▲ FJI 119 Ua53
Cikói, Khrebet ▲ RUS 70 Qe20
Cilacap ◻ RI 95 Qd49
Cilaos ▲ F 157 Nh56
Çıldır ◻ TR 57 Nb25
Ciledug ◻ RI 95 Qd49
Cilegon ◻ RI 95 Qd49
Ciléungsi ◻ RI 37 Lq50
Cilento e Vallo di Diano, P.N. del ◻ I 37 Lq50
Cili ◻ CHN (HUN) 74 Qf31
Cillas ◻ E 29 Kt50
Cilleros ◻ E 27 Ko50
Cillium ◻ TN 126 Le28
Cima ◻ USA (CA) 170 Ec28
Cimahi ◻ RI 95 Qd49
Cimarron Nat. Grassland ◻ USA 174 Ek27
Çımkent ◻ KZ 63 Oc24
Çımenlik ◻ TR 45 Mg50
Çimeniyaylası ◻ TR 56 Mf27
Cimetières des Dinosaures de Gadafaoua ◻ RN 132 Le37
Cimislia ◻ MD 49 Me22
Çimmaly ◻ TR 56 Me25
Çınarcık ◻ TR 45 Mk50
Çınar ◻ TR 57 Na27
Cinaruco-Capanaparo, P.N. ◻ YV 193 Gg42
Cincinnati ◻ USA (OH) 175 Fh26
Çine ◻ TR 47 Mj53
Çiney ◻ B 23 Lf40
Cinfães ◻ P 26 Km49
Cingoli ◻ I 35 Ln47
Cinque Island ▲ IND 88 Pg40
Cinque Terre ▲ I 34 Lk46
Cinque Terre, P.N. delle ◻ I 34 Lk46
Cintalapa ◻ MEX (CHP) 183 Fd37
Cintegabelle ◻ F 24 Lb47
Cintra ◻ RA (CD) 209 Gj62
Ciobanesti ◻ RO 43 Mf44
Ciocîle ◻ RO 45 Mh45
Ciochina ◻ RO 45 Mh46
Cioclovina ◻ RO 44 Md45
Ciorani ◻ RO 45 Mg45
Ciorãsti ◻ RO 45 Mh45
Cipa ◻ RUS 55 Qd07
Cipatujah ◻ RI 95 Qd49
Cipatu ◻ BR (BA) 201 Ja51
Cipó ◻ BR (BA) 201 Ja51
Cipolletti ◻ RA (RN) 208 Gg65
Cipó, Serra do ▲ BR 203 Hh55
Cira Island ◻ IRL 19 Km39
Circeo, P.N. del ◻ I 36 Ln49
Circle ◻ USA (AK) 165 Ch13
Circle ◻ USA (MT) 169 Eh22
Circleville ◻ USA (OH) 175 Fj26
Circuit de Catalunya ◻ E 29 Lc49
Circuit Nelson Piquet ◻ BR 205 Hj57
Circuito de Jerez ◻ E 27 Kp54
Circuito Ricardo Tormo ◻ E 29 Ku51
Cirebon ◻ RI 95 Qd49
Cirema, Gunung ▲ RI 95 Qd49
Cirencester ◻ GB 21 Kt39
Cirey-sur-Vezouze ◻ F 23 Lg42
Ciri ◻ PA 185 Fk41
Cîr Kud ◻ SP 145 Nd44
Círò Marina ◻ I 37 Lr51
Çırpan ◻ BG 45 Mf48
Cirque de Jaffar ▲ MA 125 Kh30
Cirque de Navacelles ◻ F
Cirque Rouge ▲ RM 156 Nd53
Cìrsa ◻ USA (TX) 174 Fa29
Cisláu ◻ RO 45 Mg45
Cismigiu ◻ MD 49 Me22
Cisneros ◻ CO 192 Gc42
Cisowsko-Orłowiański Park Krajobrazowy ◻ PL 41 Ma40
Cissna ◻ USA (IL) 175 Fg25
Cistern Point ▲ BS 179 Gb34
Cisterna di Latina ◻ I 36 Ln49
Cisternas ◻ RA (LR) 208 Gf61
Cistierna ◻ E 26 Kp48
Citeureup ◻ RI 93 Qd49

Çitluk ◻ BIH 35 Ls47
Citronelle ◻ USA (AL) 175 Ff30
Citrusdal ◻ ZA 154 Lk62
Citrus Heights ◻ USA (CA) 170 Dk26
Città Alta di Bergamo ◻ I 34 Lk45
Cittadella ◻ I 34 Lm45
Città della Pieve ◻ I 34 Ln48
Città del Palladio ◻ I 34 Lm45
Città di Castello ◻ I 34 Ln47
Città Sant'Angelo ◻ I 34 Lp48
City Palace (Jaipur) ◻ IND 80 Oh32
City Palace (Udaipur) ◻ IND 82 Oh33
Ciucea ◻ RO 43 Mc44
Ciucurova ◻ RO 45 Mj46
Ciudad Altamirano ◻ MEX (GUR) 182 Ek36
Ciudad Bolívar ◻ YV 193 Gj41
Ciudad Bolivia ◻ YV 192 Ge41
Ciudad Camargo ◻ MEX (CHH) 181 Eh32
Ciudad Constitución ◻ MEX (BCS) 180 Ed33
Ciudad Cortés ◻ CR 185 Fj41
Ciudad de Guatemala ■ GCA 184 Fe38
Ciudad del Carmen ◻ MEX (CAM) 183 Fe36
Ciudad del Este ◻ PY 204 Hc58
Ciudad del Maíz ◻ MEX (SLP) 182 Fa34
Ciudad de Loreto ◻ RA (SE) 207 Gh60
Ciudad de México ● ■ MEX 182 Fa36
Ciudad de México ◻ MEX (MEX) 182 Fa36
Ciudad de Nutrias ◻ YV 192 Ge41
Ciudad Encantada ▲ E 29 Ks50
Ciudad Guayana ◻ YV 193 Gj41
Ciudad Guerrero ◻ MEX (TM) 181 Fa32
Ciudad Guzmán ◻ MEX (JLC) 182 Eh36
Ciudad Hidalgo ◻ MEX 183 Fd38
Ciudad Hidalgo ◻ MEX (MHC) 182 Ek36
Ciudad Huitzuco ◻ MEX (GUR) 182 Fa36
Ciudad Insurgentes ◻ MEX (BCS) 180 Ee33
Ciudad Ixtepec ◻ MEX (OAX) 183 Fc37
Ciudad Juárez ◻ MEX (CHH) 180 Eg30
Ciudad Lerdo ◻ MEX (DGO) 181 Eg33
Ciudad Lerdo de Tejada ◻ MEX (VC) 183 Fc36
Ciudad Madero ◻ MEX (TM) 182 Fb34
Ciudad Mante ◻ MEX (TM) 182 Fa34
Ciudad Melchor de Mencos ◻ GCA 183 Ff37
Ciudad monumental de Cáceres ◻ E 27 Ko51
Ciudad Mutis = Bahía Solano ◻ CO 192 Gb43
Ciudad Nezahualcóyotl ◻ MEX (MEX) 182 Fa36
Ciudad Obregón ◻ MEX (SO) 180 Ee32
Ciudad Ojeda ◻ YV 192 Ge40
Ciudad Perdida ▲ CO 192 Gd40
Ciudad Piar ◻ YV 193 Gj42
Ciudad Real ◻ E 27 Kr52
Ciudad Rodrigo ◻ E 26 Ko50
Ciudad Sahagún ◻ MEX (HDG) 182 Fa36
Ciudad Serdán ◻ MEX (PUE) 182 Fb36
Ciudad Valles ◻ MEX (SLP) 182 Fa35
Ciudad Victoria ◻ MEX (TM) 182 Fa34
Ciuperceni ◻ RO 44 Md46
Ciutadella ◻ E 29 Le50
Civil'sk ◻ RUS (CHV) 48 Nd18
Civita Castellana ◻ I 36 Ln48
Civitanova Marche ◻ I 35 Lo47
Civitavecchia ◻ I 36 Lm48
Civitella del Tronto ◻ I 35 Lo48
Civitella Roveto ◻ I 36 Lo49
Civry ◻ F 24 La44
Cixi ◻ CHN (ZJG) 78 Ra30
Cixian ◻ CHN (HBI) 73 Qh27
Çizre ◻ TR 57 Nb27
Çizurquín's ◻ USA 49 Mg22
Cjakovec ◻ KS 66 Oj25
Ćki-Naryn ◻ KS 66 Oj25
Clacton-on-Sea ◻ GB 21 La39
Clairview ◻ AUS (QLD) 109 Se57
Clamecy ◻ F 25 Ld43
Clam Lake ◻ USA (WI) 172 Fe22
Clan Donald Centre ◻ GB 20 Kp33
Clanton ◻ USA (AL) 175 Fg29
Clanwilliam ◻ ZA 154 Lk62
Claonaig ◻ GB 20 Kp35
Claquato Church ◻ USA 168 Dj22
Clara Island ▲ MYA 88 Pj42
Clara, Mount ▲ NZ 113 Tg67
Clara City ◻ USA (MN) 172 Fb23
Claraville ◻ BR (PR) 204 Hd59
Clare ◻ AUS (SA) 110 Rj62
Claremont ◻ USA (NH) 177 Gd24
Claremont Point ▲ AUS (QLD) 107 Sb53
Claremore ◻ USA (OK) 174 Fc27
Clarence ◻ RO (FO) 204 Hb58
Clarence Strait ◻ AUS 106 Rf52
Clarence Town ◻ BS 186 Gc34
Clarendon ◻ USA (TX) 174 Ek28
Clarens ◻ ZA 155 Md60
Claresholm ◻ CDN (AB) 169 Ec20
Clarion ◻ USA (IA) 172 Fd24
Clarion ◻ USA (PA) 177 Ga25
Clarion Fracture Zone ◻ 11 Cb08
Clark ◻ USA (SD) 172 Fb23
Clark Fork ◻ USA (ID) 168 Eb21
Clark Fork ◻ USA (MT) 168 Eb22
Clarke River ◻ AUS (QLD) 107 Sc54
Clarks Harbour ◻ CDN (NS) 176 Gh24
Clarks Point ◻ USA (AK) 164 Ca16
Clarksburg ◻ USA (WV) 173 Fk26
Clarksdale ◻ USA (MS) 175 Fe28
Clarkson ◻ ZA 155 Mc63
Clarks Point ◻ BS 179 Gb34
Clarksville ◻ USA (AR) 174 Fd28
Clarksville ◻ USA (TN) 175 Fg27
Clarksville ◻ USA (TX) 174 Fc29

Claro dos Poções ◻ BR (MG) 203 Hh54
Claromecó ◻ RA (BA) 209 Gk65
Classical Gardens ◻ CHN 78 Ra30
Claudio ◻ BR (MG) 203 Hh56
Clausthal-Zellerfeld ◻ D 32 Ll39
Claveria ◻ RP 90 Ra38
Claveria ◻ RP 90 Rb39
Clay ◻ USA (WV) 175 Fk26
Claybank ◻ CDN (SK) 169 Eg20
Clay Center ◻ USA (KS) 174 Fb26
Claydon ◻ CDN (SK) 169 Ef21
Clayton ◻ AUS (SA) 108 Rk60
Clayton ◻ USA (AL) 175 Fh30
Clayton ◻ USA (ID) 168 Ed23
Clayton ◻ USA (NM) 174 Ej27
Clayton ◻ USA (NC) 178 Ga28
Clayton ◻ USA (OK) 174 Fc28
Cleardale ◻ CDN (AB) 167 Ea17
Clearfield ◻ USA (PA) 177 Ga25
Clearfield ◻ USA (UT) 171 Ed25
Clear Hills ◻ CDN (AB) 167 Ea17
Clear Lake ◻ USA (IA) 172 Fd24
Clear Lake ◻ USA (SD) 172 Fb23
Clear Lake ◻ USA (WI) 172 Fd23
Clear Prairie ◻ CDN (AB) 167 Ea17
Clearwater ◻ CDN (BC) 168 Dk20
Clearwater ◻ USA (FL) 178 Fj32
Clearwater Lake Prov. Park ◻ CDN 169 Ek18
Clearwater Mountains ▲ USA 168 Ec22
Cle Elum ◻ USA (WA) 168 Dk22
Cleethorpes ◻ GB 21 Ku37
Clejani ◻ RO 45 Mf46
Clelles ◻ F 25 Lf46
Clementina ◻ BR (SP) 202 He56
Clemson ◻ USA (SC) 178 Fj28
Cleopatra Needle ▲ RP 90 Qk40
Cleo Springs ◻ USA (OK)
Clerke Reef ▲ AUS 102 Qk54
Clermont ◻ AUS (QLD) 109 Sd57
Clermont ◻ F 23 Lc41
Clermont ◻ USA (FL) 179 Fk31
Clermont-en-Argonne ◻ F 23 Lf41
Clermont-Ferrand ◻ F 25 Ld45
Clermont-l'Hérault ◻ F 25 Ld47
Clerval ◻ F 25 Lg43
Clervaux ◻ L 23 Lg40
Cles ◻ I 34 Lm44
Cleugh Passage ◻ IND 88 Pg39
Cleve ◻ AUS (SA) 110 Rj62
Clevedon ◻ GB 21 Ks39
Cleveland ◻ GB 21 Kt36
Cleveland ◻ USA (GA) 175 Fj29
Cleveland ◻ USA (MS) 175 Fe29
Cleveland ◻ USA (OH) 173 Fj25
Cleveland ◻ USA (TN) 175 Fh28
Cleveland ◻ USA (TX) 174 Fc30
Clevelan Pen. ▲ USA 166 Dd18
Cleveleys ◻ GB 21 Ks37
Clew Bay ◻ IRL 19 Km37
Clewiston ◻ USA (FL) 179 Fk32
Clifden ◻ IRL 19 Kk36
Cliffdell ◻ USA (WA) 168 Dk22
Clifford ◻ USA (AZ) 171 Ef29
Clifton ◻ AUS (QLD) 109 Sf59
Clifton ◻ USA (AZ) 171 Ef29
Clifton ◻ USA (TX) 174 Fb30
Clifton ◻ ZA 154 Lk62
Clifton Bridge ◻ GB 21 Ks39
Clifton Hills ◻ AUS (SA) 108 Rk59
Climax ◻ CDN (SK) 169 Ef21
Climax ◻ USA (CO) 171 Eg26
Climax ◻ USA (MN) 172 Fb22
Clinch Mts. ▲ USA 178 Fj27
Clines Corners ◻ USA (NM)
Clinton ◻ CDN (BC) 168 Dk20
Clinton ◻ USA (AR) 174 Fd28
Clinton ◻ USA (IA) 175 Fe25
Clinton ◻ USA (IL) 175 Ff25
Clinton ◻ USA (MO) 174 Fd26
Clinton ◻ USA (NC) 178 Ga28
Clinton ◻ USA (OK) 174 Fa28
Clinton-Colden Lake ◻ CDN 167 Eg13
Clintwood ◻ USA (VA) 178 Fj27
Clío ◻ USA (AL) 175 Fh30
Clipperton Fracture Zone ◻ 11 Cb09
Clitheroe ◻ GB 21 Ks37
Cliza ◻ BOL 206 Gg54
Clodomira ◻ RA (SE) 207 Gh59
Clogher Head ▲ IRL 19 Ko37
Clogherhead ◻ IRL 19 Ko37
Clonakilty ◻ IRL 19 Km39
Cloncurry ◻ AUS (QLD) 107 Sa56
Clonmacnoise ◻ IRL 19 Kn37
Clonmel ◻ IRL 19 Kn38
Cloppenburg ◻ D 32 Lj38
Cloquet ◻ USA (MN) 172 Fd22
Clorinda ◻ RA (FO) 204 Hb58
Cloudy Mount ▲ USA 165 Cb14
Clovelly ◻ GB 21 Kq40
Cloverdale ◻ USA (CA) 170 Dj26
Clovis ◻ USA (CA) 170 Ea27
Clovis ◻ USA (NM) 174 Ej28
Cloyes-sur-le-Loir ◻ F 23 Lb43
Clucellas ◻ RA (SF) 209 Gj61
Cluff Lake Mine ◻ CDN (SK) 167 Ef16
Cluj-Napoca ◻ RO 43 Md44
Clun ◻ GB 21 Ks38
Cluny ◻ F 25 Le44
Clusone ◻ I 34 Lk45
Clute ◻ USA (TX) 174 Fc31
Clutha ◻ NZ 113 Td69
Clwyd ◻ GB 21 Kr37
Clyde ◻ CDN (AB) 167 Ed18
Clyde ◻ USA (TX) 174 Fa29
Clydebank ◻ GB 20 Kq35
Clyde River ◻ CDN 177 Gh24
Coal Creek ◻ CDN (AB) 169 Ed21
Coaldale ◻ CDN (AB) 169 Ee21
Coal Harbour ◻ CDN (BC) 168 Df20
Coalinga ◻ USA (CA) 170 Dk27
Coal River ◻ CDN (BC) 166 Dg16
Coamo ◻ USA (PR) 187 Gg36
Coaraci ◻ BR (BA) 203 Ja53
Coari ◻ BR (AM) 198 Gj48
Coast Mountains ◻ CDN/USA 160 Db04

Crocodile Camp □ RB 151 Mh56
Crocodile Farm ☒ AUS 106 Rf52
Crocodile Pond ⬚ GH 137 Kk40
Crocq ☒ F 25 Lc45
Croissilles ☒ F 23 Lc40
Cromarty ☒ GB 20 Kq33
Cromer ☒ GB 21 Lb38
Cromwell ☒ NZ 113 Te68
Cromwell ☒ USA (MN) 172 Fd22
Cronulla Point ☒ AUS 109 Sf58
Crook ☒ (CO) 174 Ej25
Crooked Creek ☒ USA (AK) 164 Ca15
Crooked Island ☒ BS 186 Gc34
Crooked Island ☒ USA 164 Bb16
Crooked Island Passage ☒ BS 186 Gc34
Crooked River ☒ CDN (SK) 169 Ej19
Crookhaven ☒ IRL 19 Ki39
Crookston ☒ USA (MN) 172 Fb22
Crookwell ☒ AUS (NSW) 111 Se63
Crosby ☒ USA (MS) 175 Fe30
Crosby ☒ USA (ND) 169 Ej21
Cross City ☒ BS 179 Ga32
Cross City ☒ USA 179 Ga32
Cross Creek ☒ USA (FL) 178 Fj31
Cross Creeks N.W.R. ☒ USA 175 Fg27
Crossett ☒ USA (AR) 175 Fe29
Cross Fell ☒ GB 21 Ks36
Crossfield ☒ CDN (AB) 169 Ec21
Cross Hands ☒ GB 21 Kq39
Crossing Rocks ☒ BS 179 Gb32
Crossmore ☒ AUS (QLD) 109 Sc57
Crosson Ice Shelf ⬚ 6 Ec33
Cross Plains ☒ USA (TX) 174 Fa29
Crossville ☒ USA (TN) 175 Fh28
Crotone ☒ I 37 Ls51
Crow Agency ☒ USA (MT) 169 Eg23
Crow Creek Ind. Res. ☒ USA 172 Fa23
Crowder Lake S.P. ☒ USA 174 Fa28
Crowdy Bay N.P. ☒ AUS 109 Sg61
Crowell ☒ USA (TX) 174 Fa29
Croweheart ☒ USA (WY) 169 Ef23
Crow Ind. Res. ☒ USA 169 Ef23
Crowley ☒ USA (LA) 173 Fd25
Crown Island ☒ PNG 115 Sd48
Crown Point ☒ USA (IN) 173 Fg25
Crown Point ☒ USA (NM) 171 Ef28
Crown Prince Frederik Land ⬚ PNG 117 Sh49
Crowpara ☒ BD 86 Pg34
Crows Nest ☒ AUS (QLD) 109 Sg59
Crownnest Pass ☒ CDN 168 Ec21
Croydon ☒ SD 155 Mf59
Crozet Islands ⬚ 9 Nb14
Crozet Plateau ⬚ 9 Na14
Crozon ☒ F 22 Kq42
Crucea ☒ RO 45 Mj46
Crucero ☒ PE 206 Ge33
Crucero ☒ RCH 207 Gf57
Cruces ☒ C 179 Fk34
Crucita ☒ EC 196 Fk46
Cruden Bay ☒ GB 20 Kt33
Cruillas ☒ MEX (TM) 181 Fa33
Cruise Route ☒ 184 Fh37
Cruise route ☒ GB 186 Gc34
Cruise route ☒ SB 186 Gc34
Cruise route (Irrawaddy) ☒ MYA 86 Ph35
Cruz Alta ☒ BR (RS) 204 Hd60
Cruz Alta ☒ RA (CD) 209 Gd62
Cruz das Almas ☒ BR (RS) 204 Hd59
Cruzamento de Pegões ☒ P 27 Km52
Cruz das Almas ☒ BR (BA) 201 Ja52
Cruz del Eje ☒ RA (CD) 207 Gh61
Cruzeiro ☒ BR (SP) 205 Hh57
Cruzeiro ☒ MOC 153 Mh54
Cruzeiro d'Oeste ☒ BR (PR) 202 Hd57
Cruzeiro do Sul ☒ BR (AC) 196 Gd49
Cruz Grande ☒ MEX (GUR) 182 Fa37
Cruzilia ☒ BR (MG) 203 Hh56
Cruz Machado ☒ BR 204 He59
Crveni čot ☒ SCG 44 Lu45
Cryon ☒ AUS (NSW) 109 Se60
Crysdale, Mount ☒ CDN 166 Dj17
Crystal Brook ☒ AUS (SA) 110 Rk62
Crystal Cave ☒ USA 172 Fd23
Crystal City ☒ USA (TX) 181 Fa31
Crystal Falls ☒ USA (MI) 172 Ff22
Crystal Lake ☒ USA (FL) 175 Fh30
Crystal Lake Cave ☒ USA 172 Fe24
Crystal River ☒ USA (FL) 178 Fj31
Crystal River N.W.R. ☒ USA 178 Fj31
Crystal Springs ☒ CDN (SK) 169 Eh19
Crystal Springs ☒ USA (MS) 175 Fe30
Csákvár ☒ H 42 Lt43
Csányelek ☒ H 43 Ma44
Csaroda ☒ H 43 Mc42
Csatalja ☒ H 43 Lu44
Csenger ☒ H 43 Mc43
Csesznek ☒ H 42 Ls43
Csigar-heg ☒ H 43 Ma44
Csongrád ☒ H 43 Ma44
Csorna ☒ H 42 Ls43
Csorvás ☒ H 43 Ma44
Csót ☒ H 42 Ls43
Ctesiphon ☒ IRQ 59 Nc29
Cúa ☒ YV 193 Gg40
Cuacaña ☒ YV 193 Gh43
Cuajinicuilapa ☒ MEX (GUR) 182 Fa37
Cuamato ☒ ANG 148 Lj50
Cuamba ☒ MOC 153 Mj53
Cuando ☒ RB 151 Mb54
Cuangar ☒ ANG 150 Lk54
Cuango ☒ ANG 148 Lj49
Cuango ☒ ANG 150 Lk54
Cuango ☒ ANG 148 Lj49
Cuango ☒ ANG 150 Lj52
Cuanza ☒ ANG 150 Lh53
Cuanza ☒ ANG 150 Lj52
Cuárenta Casas ☒ MEX 180 Ef31
Cuarinemba ☒ CO 193 Gf44
Cuarteron Reef ☒ 94 Qg47
Cua Song Cuu Long ☒ 89 Qd41
Cuatrociénegas ☒ MEX (COH) 181 Ej32
Cuauhtémoc ☒ MEX (CHH) 180 Eg31
Cuautitlan ☒ MEX (MEX) 182 Fa36
Cuautla ☒ MEX (JLC) 182 Eh35
Cuautla ☒ MEX (MOR) 182 Fa36
Cuba ☒ C 179 Fk35
Cuba ☒ USA (AL) 175 Ff29
Cuba ☒ USA (NM) 171 Eg27
Cu Bai ☒ VN 87 Qd38
Cubal ☒ ANG 150 Lh52
Cubango ☒ ANG 150 Lh53
Cubango ☒ ANG 150 Lk54
Cubatão ☒ BR (SP) 205 Hg57
Cubao ☒ C 192 Gd42
Cubao ☒ RCH 210 Gd67

Cuchagua ☒ BOL 206 Gg55
Cuchi ☒ ANG 150 Lj53
Cuchilla de Haedo ☒ ROU 204 Hb61
Cuchilla de Mangrullo ☒ ROU 204 Hd62
Cuchilla Grande ☒ ROU 204 Hc62
Cuchillo-Co ☒ RA (LP) 208 Gh65
Cuchillo Parado ☒ MEX (CHH) 181 Eh31
Cuckadoo ☒ AUS (QLD) 108 Sa57
Čučkovo ☒ RUS 48 Na18
Cuc Phuong N.P. ☒ VN 87 Qc35
Cucui ☒ BR (AM) 193 Gg45
Cucurital ☒ YV 193 Gh43
Cucurpé ☒ MEX (SO) 180 Ee30
Cúcuta ☒ CO 192 Gd42
Cudalore ☒ IND (TNU) 85 Ok40
Cuddapah ☒ IND (APH) 85 Ok38
Cudillero ☒ E 26 Ko47
Čudnik ☒ UA 49 Me20
Čudnilo Parado ☒ MEX (SO) 180 Ef30
Cue ☒ AUS (WA) 104 Qj59
Cuéllar ☒ E 26 Kq49
Cuemba ☒ ANG 150 Lk52
Cuenca ☒ E 29 Ks50
Cuenca ☒ EC 196 Ga47
Cuenca del Añelo ☒ RA 208 Gf65
Cuencamé ☒ MEX (DGO) 181 Ej33
Cuernavaca ☒ MEX (MOR) 182 Fa36
Cuero ☒ USA (TX) 181 Fa31
Cuerva ☒ E 27 Kq51
Cuestecitas ☒ CO 192 Gd40
Cueto ☒ C 186 Gc35
Cuetzalán ☒ MEX (PUE) 182 Fa35
Cueva de Altamira ⬚ E 26 Kq47
Cueva de Ambrosio ⬚ C 179 Fk34
Cueva de la Quebrada del Toro, P.N. ☒ YV 193 Gf40
Cueva de las Brujas ☒ RA 208 Gh63
Cueva de las Manos ☒ RA 210 Ge69
Cueva del Chacho ☒ RA 207 Gg61
Cueva del Elefante ☒ YV 193 Gj42
Cueva del Guácharo ☒ YV 193 Gj40
Cueva del Milodón ☒ RCH 210 Gd71
Cueva de los Guácharos, P.N. ☒ CO 192 Gb45
Cueva de Nerja ☒ E 27 Kr54
Cuevas Bellamar ☒ C 179 Fk34
Cuevas Candelaria ☒ GCA 184 Fe38
Cuevas del Almanzora ☒ E 29 Kt53
Cuevas de los Tayos ⬚ EC 196 Ga47
Cugir ☒ RO 44 Md45
Cugnaux ☒ F 24 Lb47
Čuhujiv ☒ UA 48 Mj21
Cuijk ☒ NL 23 Lf39
Cuilapa ☒ GCA 184 Fe38
Cuillin Hills ☒ GB 20 Kp34
Cuilo-Futa ☒ ANG 150 Lh49
Cuilo Pombo ☒ ANG 148 Lh49
Cuima ☒ ANG 150 Lh52
Cuimba ☒ ANG 148 Lh49
Cuito ☒ ANG 150 Lh52
Cuipo ☒ PA 185 Fk41
Cuira o Monos ☒ CO 196 Gd46
Cuiseaux ☒ F 25 Lf44
Cuisery ☒ F 25 Lf44
Cuité ☒ BR (PB) 201 Jb49
Cuito Cuanavale ☒ ANG 150 Lk53
Cuitzeo del Porvenir ☒ MEX (MHC) 182 Ek36
Cuiyun Lang ☒ CHN 72 Qc29
Cuijabá ☒ BR (MT) 199 Qk50
Cukurca ☒ TR 57 Nd27
Çukurköprü ☒ TR 56 Mh27
Cukurova ☒ TR 56 Mh29
Culagat ☒ ANG 148 Lj49
Culan ☒ F 25 Lc44
Cu Lao Cham ☒ VN 89 Qe38
Cu Lao Re ☒ VN 89 Qe38
Cu Lao Thu = Phu Quy ☒ VN 89 Qe40
Cula Sancai ☒ ETH 142 Mh40
Culasi ☒ RP 90 Rb40
Culasian ☒ RP 94 Qj41
Culbertson ☒ USA (MT) 169 Eh21
Culburra ☒ AUS (NSW) 109 Sc60
Culcairn ☒ AUS (NSW) 111 Sd63
Culebras ☒ PE 197 Ga50
Culemborg ☒ NL 23 Lf39
Culfa ☒ AZ 57 Nc28
Culgoa River N.P. ☒ AUS 109 Se60
Culiacán ☒ MEX (SL) 180 Eg33
Culion ☒ RP 90 Ra40
Culion Island ☒ RP 90 Qj40
Cúllar-Baza ☒ E 27 Ks53
Cullen ☒ GB 20 Ks33
Cullen ☒ RCH 210 Gf72
Cullera ☒ E 29 Ku51
Cullinan ☒ ZA 155 Me58
Cullman ☒ USA (AL) 175 Fg28
Cullompton ☒ GB 21 Kr40
Culluleraine ☒ AUS (VIC) 110 Sa63
Culpeper ☒ USA (VA) 177 Gb26
Culross Island ☒ USA 165 Cg15
Culuene ☒ BR 202 Hd52
Culuwuru Island ☒ AUS 106 Rj51
Culverden ☒ NZ 113 Tg67
Culym ☒ RUS 54 Pa07
Culzean Castle ☒ GB 21 Kq36
Culzean Castle ☒ USA 180 Kq35
Cumae ☒ I 37 Lp50
Cumana ☒ YV 193 Gh40
Cumanacoa ☒ YV 193 Gj40
Cumandá ☒ EC 196 Ga47
Cumar ☒ SP 145 Nc44
Cumari ☒ BR (GO) 203 Hg53
Cumaribo ☒ CO 193 Gf43
Cumba ☒ PE 196 Ga48
Cumbal ☒ CO 192 Gb44
Cumbal, Volcán ☒ CO 192 Gb45
Cumberland ☒ USA (MD) 177 Ga26
Cumberland Caverns ☒ USA 175 Fh28
Cumberland Gap N.H.P. ☒ USA 178 Fj27
Cumberland House ☒ CDN 169 Ej19

Cumberland Island ☒ USA 178 Fk30
Cumberland Island National Seashore ☒ USA 178 Fk30
Cumberland Islands ☒ AUS 107 Se56
Cumberland Peninsula ☒ CDN 163 Gd05
Cumberland Sound ☒ CDN 163 Gd05
Cumbi ☒ ANG 148 Lj49
Cumborah ☒ AUS (NSW) 109 Sd60
Cumbres, Cerro ☒ RCH 210 Gd69
Cumbres de Majalca, P.N. ☒ MEX 180 Eg31
Cumbres de Monterrey, P.N. ☒ MEX 181 Ek33
Cumbres & Toltec Scenic Railroad ☒ USA 171 Eg27
Cumbrian Mountains ☒ GB 21 Kr36
Cumburão ☒ BR (PA) 194 Hc46
Čumečki ☒ BG 45 Mf48
Čumić ☒ SCG 44 Ma46
Čumikan ☒ RUS 55 Rd08
Čudovo ☒ RUS 48 Mf16
Čudzin ☒ BY 41 Mg38
Cue ☒ AUS (WA) 104 Qj59
Cumi ☒ F 25 Ld45
Cumnock ☒ GB 20 Kq35
Cumpas ☒ MEX (SO) 180 Ef31
Cumra ☒ TR 56 Mg27
Cunani ☒ BR (AP) 195 He44
Cuñare ☒ CO 192 Gc43
Cunco ☒ RCH 208 Gd65
Cunday ☒ CO 192 Gc43
Cundeelee ☒ AUS (WA) 105 Rb61
Cunderdin ☒ AUS (WA) 104 Qj61
Cunduacán ☒ MEX (TB) 183 Fd36
Cunene ☒ ANG 150 Lg54
Cunene ☒ ANG 150 Lh53
Cúneo ☒ I 34 Lh46
Cunhambebe ☒ BR (RJ) 205 Hh57
Cunhaú ☒ BR (RN) 201 Jc49
Cunjamba ☒ ANG 150 Ma53
Cunlhat ☒ F 25 Ld45
Cunnamulla ☒ AUS (QLD) 109 Sd59
Cunningham Islands ☒ AUS 106 Rj51
Cuntima ☒ GNB 136 Kc39
Cunyu ☒ AUS (WA) 104 Ra59
Cuorgne ☒ I 34 Lh45
Cupar ☒ GB 20 Kr34
Cupica ☒ CO 192 Gb42
Cupica, Cerro ☒ PE 196 Ga49
Cupixi ☒ BR (AP) 195 He45
Cúprija ☒ SCG 44 Mb47
Curaçá ☒ BR (BA) 201 Ja51
Curaçao ☒ NL 193 Gf39
Curacautín ☒ RCH 208 Ge65
Curacaví ☒ RCH 208 Ge62
Curachi ☒ GUY 194 Gk42
Curahuara de Carangas ☒ BOL 206 Gg55
Curale ☒ ETH 143 Nc42
Cural Velho ☒ CV 136 Jj37
Curanilahué ☒ RCH 208 Gd64
Curanja ☒ PE 197 Ge50
Curaray ☒ EC 196 Gb46
Curaray ☒ PE 196 Gb48
Curaru ☒ RA (SA) 209 Gh64
Curburr ☒ AUS (WA) 104 Qh53
Curdimurka ☒ AUS (SA) 108 Rj60
Curepipe ☒ MS 157 Nj56
Curia ☒ P 26 Km50
Curiapo ☒ YV 193 Gk41
Curicó ☒ RCH 208 Ge63
Curicó ☒ RCH 208 Ge63
Curimatá ☒ BR (PI) 200 Hh51
Curimávida, Cerro de ☒ RCH 208 Ge61
Curionópolis ☒ BR (PA) 200 Hf48
Curitiba ☒ BR (PR) 205 Hf58
Curitiba ☒ BR (PR) 205 Hf58
Curitibanos ☒ BR (SC) 205 He59
Curiúva ☒ BR (PR) 205 He58
Curly Cut Cay ☒ BS 179 Gb34
Currane ☒ AUS (SA) 108 Rk61
Curragh Racetrack ☒ IRL 19 Ko37
Currais ☒ BR (PI) 201 Hj50
Currais Novos ☒ BR (RN) 201 Jb49
Cural Alto ☒ BR (RS) 204 Hd62
Curral de Pedra ☒ BR (PI) 201 Hk49
Curralinho ☒ BR (PA) 195 Hf46
Curral Novo do Piauí ☒ BR (PI) 201 Hk50
Curralinho ☒ BR (MI) 173 Fj23
Currant ☒ USA (NV) 170 Ec26
Curranyalpa ☒ AUS (NSW) 109 Sc61
Currawilla ☒ AUS (QLD) 108 Sa58
Currawinya N.P. ☒ AUS (QLD)
Currawinya N.P. ☒ AUS 109 Sc60
Currie ☒ AUS (NSW) 111 Sd63
Currie ☒ AUS (TAS) 111 Sb65
Curtbra ☒ IND (APH) 83 Ok37
Curtis Beach Lighthouse ☒ USA 178 Gc27
Currituck N.W.R. ☒ USA 178 Gc27
Curtain Springs ☒ AUS (NT) 105 Rf58
Curtea de Argeş ☒ RO 43 Md45
Curtici ☒ RO 43 Mb44
Curtina ☒ ROU 204 Hb62
Curtis Island ☒ AUS (QLD) 111 Sd65
Curtis Island ☒ NZ 112 Ua61
Curuá ☒ BR (PA) 194 Hc46
Curuaí ☒ BR (PA) 199 Hc47
Curuçá ☒ BR (PA) 195 Hg46
Curuçu Sewu ☒ RI 95 Qe49
Curuzú ☒ RI 93 Qd47
Curuzú Cuatiá ☒ RA (CR) 204 Ha60
Curvelo ☒ BR (MG) 203 Hh55
Cushamen ☒ RA (CB) 208 Ge67
Cushing ☒ USA (OK) 174 Fb28
Cusihuiriáchic ☒ MEX (CHH) 180 Eg32
Cuspáta ☒ CO 192 Gd42
Cusset ☒ F 25 Ld44
Cusseta ☒ USA (GA) 175 Fh29
Cússia ☒ USA (MT) 169 Eg22
Cushavan ☒ DJI 143 Nb39
Cust ☒ NZ 113 Tg67
Custer ☒ USA (SD) 169 Ej23
Custer Battlefield Nat. Mon. ☒ USA 169 Eg23
Custódia ☒ BR (PE) 201 Jb50
Cusuco, P.N. ☒ HN 184 Ff38
Cutaio ☒ ANG 150 Lj53
Cutato ☒ ANG 150 Lj53
Cutervo ☒ PE 196 Ga49
Cutervo, P.N. de ☒ PE 196 Ga49
Cuthbert ☒ USA (GA) 175 Fh30
Çütleri ☒ TR 56 Mh28
Čútove ☒ UA 48 Mh21
Cutral-Co ☒ RA (NE) 208 Gf65
Cutro ☒ I 37 Lr51

Cuttack ☒ IND (ORS) 83 Pc35
Cutta Cutta Caves ☒ AUS 106 Rg53
Cutzamala de Pinzón ☒ MEX (GUR) 182 Ek36
Cuvelar ☒ ANG 150 Lh53
Cuvette de Doany ☒ RM 156 Nd53
Cuvier Island ☒ NZ 112 Th64
Cuxhaven ☒ D 32 Lj37
Cuya ☒ RCH 206 Gf55
Cuyagua ☒ YV 193 Gg40
Cuyagua ☒ YV 193 Gg40
Cuyahoga Valley N.P. ☒ USA 173 Fk25
Cuyamá ☒ USA 170 Ea28
Cuyamel ☒ HN 184 Ff38
Cuyo ☒ RP 90 Ra40
Cuyoaco ☒ MEX (PUE) 182 Fb36
Cuyo 'English Game' Subterranean N.P. ☒ RP 90 Ra40
Cuyo Islands ☒ RP 90 Ra40
Cuyo Islands ☒ RP 90 Ra40
Cuyo West Passage ☒ RP 90 Ra40
Cuyuni ☒ GUY 194 Ha42
Cuyutlán ☒ MEX (COL) 182 Eh36
Cuzco ☒ PE 197 Ge52
Cwmcarn ☒ GB 21 Kr39
Cyangugu ☒ RWA 146 Me47
Cybinka ☒ PL 40 Lo38
Cyclades ☒ GR 47 Md53
Cyclops Mountains ☒ RI 115 Sa47
Čyhyryn ☒ UA 49 Mg21
Cylinder ☒ AUS 109 Sg59
Cynthia ☒ AUS (QLD) 109 Sf58
Cypress Gardens ☒ USA 179 Fj31
Cypress Hills ☒ CDN 169 Ef21
Cypress Hills Interprov. Park ☒ CDN 169 Ee21
Cyprus ☒ CY 56 Mg28
Cyran ☒ BY 41 Mg37
Cyrenaica al Akhdar ☒ LAR 127 Ma31
Cyrene = Shahhat ☒ LAR 127 Ma29
Cyrrhus ☒ SYR 56 Mj27
Cytherea ☒ AUS 109 Sd59
Czaplinek ☒ PL 40 Lr37
Czar ☒ CDN (AB) 169 Ee19
Czarna ☒ PL 41 Mc41
Czarna Białostocka ☒ PL 41 Md37
Czarna Dąbrówka ☒ PL 40 Ls36
Czarnków ☒ PL 40 Lr38
Czarny Dunajec ☒ PL 41 Lu41
Czchów ☒ PL 41 Ma41
Czechowice-Dziedzice ☒ PL 41 Lt40
Czech Republic ☒ CZ 42 Lp41
Czekarzewice ☒ PL 41 Mb39
Czermno ☒ PL 41 Ma39
Czerniawska ☒ PL 41 Mc38
Czerwionka-Leszczyny ☒ PL 40 Lt40
Czerwony Dwór ☒ PL 41 Mc36
Częstochowa ☒ PL 41 Lu40
Człopa ☒ PL 40 Lr37
Czyżew-Osada ☒ PL 41 Mc38

D

Da'an ☒ CHN (JLN) 76 Rc23
Daanbantayan ☒ RP 90 Rc40
Daan Viljoen Game Park ☒ NAM 150 Lj57
Dabaga ☒ EAT 147 Mh50
Dabaga ☒ RN 132 Le37
Dabagram ☒ IND (WBG) 86 Pe34
Dabai ☒ WAN 138 Le39
Dabaka ☒ IND (ASM) 86 Pg32
Dabaka ☒ CI 137 Kh41
Dabakala ☒ CI 137 Kh41
Dabar Shan ☒ CHN 72 Qa27
Dabaro ☒ SP 143 Ne42
Daba Shan ☒ CHN 72 Qa27
Dabbagh ☒ KSA 58 Mj31
Dabbas ☒ IR 43 Lu43
Dabeiyuan Monastery ☒ CHN 73 Qj26
Dabenoris ☒ ZA 154 Lk60
Dabhoi ☒ IND (GUJ) 82 Og34
Dąbie ☒ PL 40 Lr38
Dąbie ☒ PL 40 Lo38
Dabie Shan ☒ CHN 73 Qh30
Dabilja ☒ MK 44 Mc49
Dabiss ☒ RG 136 Kc40
Dabnou ☒ RN 132 Lc38
Dabo ☒ RI 93 Qc46
Dabokong ☒ CHN (HBI) 73 Qj26
Dabola ☒ RG 136 Kd40
Dabolatounka ☒ RG 136 Ke40
Daboya ☒ GH 137 Kk41
Dabqig ☒ CHN (NMZ) 72 Qf26
Dabrabanay ☒ BY 41 Mg38
Dąbrowa Górnicza ☒ PL 41 Lu40
Dąbrowa Tarnowska ☒ PL 41 Ma40
Dabrynéva ☒ BY 39 Mh37
Dabugam ☒ IND (ORS) 83 Pb36
Dabuk ☒ RI 93 Qd47
Dabuleni ☒ RO 45 Md47
Dabwa ☒ TCH 133 Lg38
Dac Glei ☒ VN 89 Qd38
Dac To ☒ VN 89 Qd38
Dada ☒ EAK 145 Na45
Dadanawa ☒ GUY 194 Ha44
Daddato ☒ DJI 143 Nb39
Dade City ☒ USA (FL) 179 Fj31
Dadégudié ☒ CI 137 Kh42
Dadeville ☒ USA (AL) 175 Fh29
Dadou ☒ F 24 Lc47
Dadong ☒ CHN (GZG) 74 Qe34
Dadong H.P. ☒ CHN (HBI) 73 Qj26
Dadra and Nagar Haveli ☒ IND 82 Og35
Dadra and Nagar Haveli ☒ IND 82 Og35
Dadu ☒ CHN (JGX) 75 Qh33
Daet ☒ RP 90 Rb38
Dafang ☒ CHN (GZH) 72 Qd32
Dafangshi ☒ CHN (NMZ) 72 Qf26
Dafeng ☒ CHN (JGS) 78 Ra29
Dáfni ☒ GR 46 Mc53

Dafni ☒ GR 45 Md53
Dafni ☒ GR 45 Me50
Dafoe Si ☒ CHN 72 Qa26
Dagaari ☒ SP 143 Nd42
Dagabule ☒ ETH 144 Mj43
Dagagh ☒ SN 130 Ld30
Dagana ☒ SN 130 Kc37
Dagapost ☒ SUD 142 Mg41
Dagardı ☒ TR 47 Mj51
Dagash ☒ SUD 135 Mg38
Dagdere ☒ TH 47 Mj52
Dagestan ☒ RUS 57 Nd24
Dagestanskij zapovednik ☒ RUS 57 Nd23
Daghabij ☒ SN 144 Mk38
Dag Hammarskjöld Memorial ☒ 147 Md44
Dagla Game Reserve ☒ WAN 138 Lc41
Daglah ☒ ET 129 Mh30
Daglung ☒ CHN (TIB) 68 Pf31
Dagomys ☒ RUS 49 Mk24
Dagon ☒ CHN 72 Qd34
Dal'negorsk ☒ RUS 77 Rh23
Dal'nerečensk ☒ RUS 76 Rg23
Dagua ☒ CO 192 Gb44
Dagupan ☒ RP 90 Ra37
Daguragu A.L. ☒ AUS 106 Rf54
Daguragu A.L. ☒ AUS 106 Rf54
Dagworth ☒ AUS (QLD) 107 Sb54
Dagzê ☒ CHN (TIB) 68 Pf30
Dahaban ☒ KSA 58 Mk35
Dahab ☒ IND (MHT) 82 Og36
Dahanu Beach ☒ IND 82 Og35
Dahanu ☒ IND (MHT) 82 Og35
Dahebian ☒ CHN (SCH) 87 Qa31
Daheqiu ☒ CHN (GSU) 72 Qd27
Dahinsara ☒ IND (GUJ) 82 Of34
Dahiri ☒ CI 137 Kh43
Dahlak Marine N.P. ☒ ER 142 Na38
Dahlonega ☒ USA (GA) 178 Fj28
Dahmani ☒ TN 126 Le28
Dahme ☒ D 32 Ln39
Dahn ☒ D 33 Lh41
Dahomey = Taalintehdas ☒ FIN 38 Mc30
Dahra ☒ DZ 126 Lc27
Dahra Oil Field ☒ LAR 127 Lj31
Dahr Oualâta ☒ RIM 131 Kf36
Dahuk ☒ CHN (GZG) 74 Qe34
Dahuk ☒ IRQ 57 Nb27
Dai Dao ☒ CHN 78 Rb30
Dai Mai ☒ VN 89 Qd39
Daik Lamb Beach ☒ VN 89 Qe39
Daikeh ☒ NEP 84 Pa31
Daimiel ☒ E 27 Kr51
Dainzú ☒ MEX 183 Fb37
Daireaux ☒ RA 209 Gk64
Dairo ☒ CI 137 Kk41
Dairût ☒ ET 129 Mf32
Dairy Creek ☒ AUS (WA) 104 Qh58
Dai-sen ☒ J 79 Rg28
Daisetsuzan N.P. ☒ J 77 Sa25
Daisen-Oki N.P. ☒ J 79 Rg27
Daisetsuzan N.P. ☒ J 77 Sb24
Daisy ☒ USA (OK) 174 Fc28
Daishi ☒ USA (SAA) 72 Qe28
Dai Xian ☒ CHN (SAX) 73 Qg26
Daiyun Shan ☒ CHN 75 Qj33
Dajabón ☒ DOM 186 Ge36
Dajarra ☒ AUS (QLD) 108 Rk56
Dajing ☒ CHN (GSU) 72 Qd27
Dakao ☒ CHN 78 Rb30
Dakak ☒ EAU 147 Mg44
Dakawa ☒ EAT 147 Mh49
Dakar ☒ SN 130 Kb38
Dakar ☒ SN 130 Kb38
Dakawa ☒ EAT 147 Mh49
Da Kharga Sharif Ziarat Mosque ☒ AFG 65 Oc30
Dakhla ☒ RIM 130 Kc34
Dakhla ☒ RIM 130 Kc34
Dakhla Oasis ☒ ET 129 Me33
Dakhlet Nouâdhibou ☒ RIM 130 Kb35
Dakingari ☒ WAN 138 Lc40
Daki Takwas ☒ WAN 138 Lc40
Dak ☒ VN 89 Qd39
Dakoank ☒ IND (AAN) 88 Pg42
Dakoro ☒ RN 132 Ld38
Dakovica ☒ SCG 44 Ma48
Dakovo ☒ HR 35 Lt45
Katedrala u Đakovu ☒ HR 35 Lt45
Dakpam ☒ GH 137 Kk41
Dakshin Gangotri ☒ ANT (IND) 7 Nc34
Daksum ☒ 80 Oh29
Daku, Gunung ☒ RI 91 Ra45
Dala ☒ ANG 149 Ma50
Dala ☒ ANG 149 Ma50
Dalaba ☒ RG 136 Kc40
Dalaba ☒ RG 136 Kc40
Dalaba ☒ RG 136 Kc40
Dalada Maligawa (Kandy) ☒ CL 85 Pa42
Dalad Qi ☒ CHN (NMZ) 72 Qf26
Dalafi ☒ SN 136 Kd39
Dalai Nur ☒ CHN (NMZ) 72 Qf26
Dalai Shan ☒ CHN 78 Rb30
Dalaki ☒ IR 59 Nf31
Dalälven ☒ S 31 Lq30
Dalaman ☒ TR 47 Mj54
Dalama ☒ SUD 135 Mf40
Dalar ☒ WAN 138 Le39
Dalbandin ☒ PK 65 Oc32
Dalbeattie ☒ GB 20 Kr36
Dal Bilo ☒ WAN 138 Le40
Dalby ☒ AUS (QLD) 109 Sf59
Dalby Söderskog n.p. ☒ S 31 Lo35
Dalgaranga Homestead ☒ AUS 104 Qj59
Dalgonally ☒ AUS 107 Sb55
Dalhart ☒ USA (TX) 174 Ej27
Dalhousie ☒ CDN (NB) 176 Gg21
Dalhousie Springs ☒ AUS (SA) 108 Rh59
Dali ☒ CHN (SAA) 72 Qe28
Dali = Xiaguan ☒ CHN (YUN) 87 Qa33
Dali ☒ RMM 131 Kg38
Dalian ☒ CHN 73 Ra26
Dalianhe ☒ CHN (HLG) 76 Re22
Dalias ☒ E 27 Ks54
Dali Museum (Saint Petersburg) ☒ USA 179 Fj32
Dali Sharafat ☒ SUD 135 Mg38
Dalj ☒ HR 35 Lt45
Daljá ☒ ET 129 Mf32
Dalkeith ☒ GB 20 Kr35
Dalkhaki ☒ IND (WBG) 83 Pd33
Dalkola ☒ IND (WBG) 83 Pd33
Dalkola ☒ IND 86 Pe33
Dalli ☒ WAN 138 Le40
Dan Gorayo ☒ SP 143 Ne41
Dangriga ☒ BH 184 Ff37
Dangriga ☒ BH 184 Ff37
Dangshan ☒ CHN (AHU) 78 Qj28
Dangtu ☒ CHN (AHU) 78 Qj28
Damoh ☒ IND (MPH) 83 Ok34
Daman ☒ IND (DAD) 82 Og35
Daman ☒ IND 82 Og35
Damanhûr ☒ ET 129 Mf30
Damar ☒ AI 97 Re49
Damar ☒ AI 97 Re49
Damaramalanda ☒ WAN 132 Ld40
Damardatar ☒ CI 95 Qh47
Damar Laut ☒ MAL 92 Qa43
Damas Cays ☒ BS 179 Fk34
Damasak ☒ WAN 133 Lg39
Damascus ☒ SYR 56 Mj29
Damaskínia ☒ GR 46 Mb50
Damaturu ☒ WAN 139 Lh39
Damauli ☒ NEP 81 Pc32
Dao Co To ☒ VN 87 Qd35
Dambva ☒ AFG 65 Oe27
Dali ☒ UAE 61 Ng33
Dalmacija ☒ HR 35 Lq46
Dalmally ☒ GB 20 Kq34
Dalmatia ☒ 14 Ls05
Dalmellington ☒ GB 21 Kq36
Dalmine ☒ I 34 Lk45
Daloa ☒ CI 137 Kg42
Dalol Crater ☒ ER 142 Na38
Dalol Saltlake and Hot Springs ☒ ETH 142 Na38
Dalong ☒ CHN (HUN) 74 Qe32
Dalou Shan ☒ CHN 72 Qd32
Dalrymple, Mount ☒ AUS 109 Se56
Dalsbruk = Taalintehdas ☒ FIN 38 Mc30
Dalsjöfors ☒ S 30 Lo33
Dalton ☒ USA (GA) 175 Fh28
Dalton Mus. ☒ USA 174 Fc27

Damavand, Mount ☒ IR 62 Ng27
Damba ☒ ANG 148 Lh49
Damba Island ☒ EAU 146 Mf46
Dambar ☒ WAN 138 Lf40
Dambat ☒ TR 45 Mh51
Dambel ☒ RN 139 Lh39
Dambai Waterfall ☒ IND (APH) 86 Ph31
Dambulla ☒ CL 85 Pa42
Damenge ☒ CHN (YUN) 87 Pk34
Dao Timi ☒ RN 133 Lf38
Dao Vay ☒ VN 89 Qd41
Damietta ☒ ET 129 Mf30
Dapa ☒ RP 91 Rd42
Dapango = Dapaong ☒ TG 137 La40
Dapaong ☒ TG 137 La40
Dapdiap ☒ RP 90 Rb38
Dapélogo ☒ BF 137 Kk39
Dapengwan ☒ CHN (GZG) 74 Qe34
Dapitan ☒ RP 91 Rb41
Daporijo ☒ IND (ARP) 86 Ph31
Dao-Bello ☒ RN 139 Lh39
Daqaidam ☒ CHN (QHI) 69 Pg27
Daqaq ☒ CHN (TIB) 69 Ph29
Daqing ☒ CHN (HLG) 76 Rc22
Daqing Shan ☒ CHN 72 Qe26
Daqu ☒ CHN 78 Rb30
Dara ☒ SN 130 Kc38
Dar ☒ IND (ASM) 86 Pf32
Darab ☒ IR 62 Ng31
Darab ☒ SP 143 Ne41
Daraban ☒ PK 65 Of30
Darabani ☒ RO 43 Me43
Daraga ☒ RP 90 Rb39
Dar-al-Hajar ☒ YE 60 Nc38
Daram ☒ RP 90 Rc40
Daram Island ☒ RP 90 Rc40
Daran ☒ IR 62 Ng29
Darasa ☒ ETH 143 Nc41
Darasun ☒ RUS 71 Qf20
Daravica ☒ SCG 44 Ma48
Daraw ☒ ET 129 Mg33
Darāzo ☒ WAN 138 Lf40
Darāzo ☒ WAN 138 Lf40
Darband-i Khan ☒ IRQ 57 Nc28
Darband Sari ☒ IR 57 Nf27
Darbanga ☒ IR (BIH) 83 Pc32
Darbat Tegh ☒ MA 125 Kf29
Dar Caid-Hadji ☒ MA 124 Kf30
Dar Chioukh ☒ DZ 126 Ld28
Dar Barto ☒ ETH 142 Na39
Dardara ☒ SUD 134 Mc39
Darfur ☒ SUD 134 Mc39
Darganata ☒ TM 62 Ob25
Dargaville ☒ NZ 112 Tg63
Dargaz ☒ IR 63 Nk28
Dargecit ☒ TR 57 Nb27
Dargol ☒ RN 132 Lb39

Dafni ☒ GR 45 Md53
Dargol ☒ RN 132 La39
Dargosław ☒ PL 40 Lq36
Darhala ☒ CI 137 Kh41
Darhan Muminggan Lianheqi ☒ CHN (NMZ) 72 Qf25
Darica ☒ TR 56 Mj26
Darica ☒ TR 45 Mk50
Darién ☒ CO 192 Gb44
Darien ☒ PA 185 Ga42
Darién, P.N. del ☒ PA 185 Gb42
Darién (ARP) 86 Ph31
Dario Meira ☒ BR (BA) 203 Ja53
Darmang ☒ GH 137 Kk42
Darmaraopet ☒ BR (MG) 77 Pg22
Darnah ☒ LAR 127 Ma29
Darnety ☒ F 25 Lc42
Daroca ☒ E 29 Kt49
Darou-Mousti ☒ SN 130 Kb38
Darrahne ☒ AFG 65 Oc30
Darrah Wildlife Sanctuary ☒ IND 82 Oh33
Dawson City ☒ CDN (YT) 165 Da13
Dawson Creek ☒ CDN (BC) 167 Dk13
Dawson Landing ☒ CDN (BC) 168 Dg20
Dawson Range ☒ CDN 165 Da14
Dawson River ☒ AUS 109 Sf58
Dawson Springs ☒ USA (KY) 175 Fg27
Dawson Tibur ☒ CHN (HUB) 73 Qh30
Dawu ☒ CHN (SCH) 69 Qa30
Dawu ☒ WAL 136 Ke42
Dawson Bay Ind. Res. ☒ CDN 169 Fa19
Dax ☒ F 24 Kt47
Daxian ☒ CHN (SCH) 74 Qd30
Daxin ☒ CHN (GZG) 74 Qd34
Daxing ☒ CHN (YUN) 87 Qa32
Daxue Shan ☒ CHN 69 Qa30
Dayang Buntig ☒ MAL 92 Pk42
Dayangshu ☒ CHN (NMZ) 71 Rc21
Dayao ☒ CHN (YUN) 87 Qa32
Dayca ☒ SP 143 Nd40
Daylesford ☒ AUS (VIC) 111 Sc64
Daysland ☒ CDN (AB) 169 Ee19
Dayton ☒ USA (OH) 175 Fh26
Dayton ☒ USA (TX) 174 Fc30
Darwin ☒ AUS (NT) 106 Rf52
Darwin, Volcán ☒ EC 197 Fe46
Daryacheh-ye-Maharlu ☒ IR 64 Ng31
Daryacheh-ye-Namak ☒ IR 57 Nf28
Dayyinah ☒ UAE 61 Ng33
Dazafilu ☒ J 79 Rf29
Dazey ☒ USA (ND) 172 Fa22
Dazhu ☒ CHN (GZG) 74 Qe34
Dazu ☒ CHN (SCH) 74 Qd30
Dazu Rock Carvings ☒ CHN (CGQ) 74 Qc31
Dchira ☒ MA 124 Kd32
De Aar ☒ ZA 155 Mb61
Deadhorse ☒ USA (AK) 165 Cf10
Dead Horse Point Nat. Mon. ☒ USA 171 Ef27
Dead Indian Peak ☒ USA 169 Ef23
Deadman's Cr. Ind. Res. ☒ CDN 168 Dk20
Dead Sea ☒ IL 58 Mh30
Deakin ☒ AUS (WA) 105 Re61
Deal ☒ GB 21 Lb39
Dealesville ☒ ZA 155 Mc60
Deaulille Silvaniei ☒ RO 43 Mc43
De'an ☒ CHN (JGX) 75 Qh31
Deán Funes ☒ RA (CD) 207 Gh61
Dearborn ☒ USA (MI) 173 Fj24
Dease Lake ☒ CDN (BC) 166 Df16
Dease Strait ☒ CDN 162 Ed05
Death Valley ☒ USA (CA) 170 Ec27
Death Valley Junction ☒ USA (CA) 170 Ec27
Death Valley N.P. ☒ USA 170 Eb27
Deauville ☒ F 22 La41
Debal'ceve ☒ UA 49 Mk21
Debano ☒ RI 95 Qh49
Debaoxh Mts. ☒ USA 165 Ca13
Debay ☒ SUD 141 Md41
Debayomma ☒ ER 142 Mk39
Deb-Deb ☒ DZ 126 Le31
Debelo ☒ MA 125 Kg23
Debelo brdo ☒ SCG 44 Ma47
Debepare ☒ IND 115 Sa50
Debiapur ☒ IND (UPH) 83 Ok32
Debica ☒ PL 41 Ma40
Debica ☒ PL 41 Ma40
Debin ☒ RUS 55 Sc06
Debliza Kaszubska ☒ PL 40 Ls36
Debno ☒ PL 40 Lp38
Debo ☒ CI 137 Kf42
Debolt ☒ CDN (AB) 167 Ea18
DeBorgia ☒ USA (MT) 169 Ec22
Debre Birhan ☒ ETH 142 Mk40
Debre Bizen ☒ ER 142 Mk38
Debre Damo ☒ ETH 142 Mk39
Debre Libanos Gedam ☒ ETH 142 Mk41
Debre Markos ☒ ETH 142 Mj40
Debre Sina ☒ ETH 142 Mk39

Eemshaven ☐ NL 23 Lg37
Eendekuil ☐ ZA 154 Lk62
Eenhana ☐ NAM 150 Lj54
Éfaté ☐ VU 118 Te54
Effigy Mounds Ind. Res. ☐ USA 172 Fe24
Effingham ☐ USA (IL) 175 Ff26
Efkarpia ☐ GR 45 Md50
Eflâni ☐ TR 56 Me24
Efon Alaye ☐ WAN 138 Lc42
Eforie ☐ RO 45 Mj46
Efremov ☐ RUS 48 Mk19
Efteling ☐ NL 23 Lf39
Eg ☐ MNG 70 Qf21
Egayit ☐ MYA 89 Ph36
Egg ☐ WAN 138 Lc41
Egbunda ☐ RDC 141 Md44
Egbunda ☐ RDC 141 Me44
Egby ☐ S 31 Lr34
Egeln ☐ D 32 Lm39
Eger ☐ H 43 Ma43
Egersund ☐ N 30 Lg32
Egeskov ☐ DK 30 Lk30
Eggedal ☐ N 30 Lk30
Eggenburg ☐ A 42 Lq42
Eggenfelden ☐ D 33 Lm42
Egg ☐ D 32 Lp37
Egg Lagoon ☐ AUS (TAS) 111 Sb65
Eghola ☐ SOL 117 Sj50
Eghra ☐ IND (JKD) 86 Pd33
Eglisstaðir ☐ IS 18 Kf25
Egina ☐ GR 45 Md53
Egina ☐ GR 45 Md53
Eginio ☐ GR 46 Mc50
Egio ☐ GR 46 Mc52
Eğirdir Gölü ☐ TR 56 Mf26
Eğirdir ☐ TR 56 Mf27
Egito Praia ☐ ANG 150 Lg51
Egletons ☐ F 24 Lc45
Egmond aan Zee ☐ NL 23 Le38
Egor'e ☐ RUS 48 Mj18
Egor'evsk ☐ RUS 48 Mk18
Goorlykskaja ☐ RUS 49 Na21
Egosthena ☐ GR 45 Md52
Egra ☐ IND (WBG) 83 Pd35
Egtved ☐ DK 30 Lk35
Egum Atoll ☐ PNG
Egvekinot ☐ RUS 55 Ua05
Egyed ☐ H 42 Ls43
Egyek ☐ H 43 Ma43
Eha-Amufu ☐ WAN 138 Lc42
Ehi ☐ GH 137 La42
Ehingen ☐ D 33 Lk42
Ehinos ☐ GR 45 Me49
Ehrenbreitstein ☐ D 33 Lh40
Ehrwald ☐ A 34 Ll43
Eibar ☐ E 26 Kr47
Eibergen ☐ NL 23 Lg38
Eibiswald ☐ A 35 Lq44
Eichenried ☐ D 33 Lm42
Eichstätt ☐ D 33 Lm42
Eidar ☐ IS 18 Kf25
Eider ☐ D 32 Lk36
Eidfjord ☐ N 30 Lk30
Eidsvag ☐ N 16 Le14
Eidsvold ☐ AUS (QLD) 109 Sf58
Eidsvoll ☐ N 30 Ll30
Eifel ☐ D 33 Lg40
Eigersøya ☐ N 30 Lf32
Eigg ☐ GB 20 Ko34
Eight Degree Channel ☐ IND 84 Og42
Eight Mile Rock ☐ BS 179 Ga32
Eights Coast ☐ 6 Fa33
Eighty Mile Beach ☐ AUS 102 Ra55
Eijsden ☐ D 23 Lf40
Eik ☐ N 30 Lh32
Čikoknskij hrebet ☐ MNG 70 Qe21
Eilal ☐ SOL 117 Sj50
Eilean Donan Castle ☐ GB 20 Kp33
Eilerts de Haangeberge ☐ SME 194 Hb44
Eil Malk ☐ PAL 90 Rh42
Eilsleben ☐ D 32 Lm38
Eina ☐ N 30 Ll30
Einasleigh ☐ AUS (QLD) 107 Sc55
Einbeck ☐ D 32 Lk39
Eindayaza ☐ MYA 88 Pk38
Eindhoven ☐ NL 23 Lf39
Eindpaal ☐ NAM 150 Lk53
Ein Mansur ☐ SUD 134 Md38
Einme ☐ MYA 88 Ph37
Eire ☐ 15 Ko04
Eirikjökull ☐ IS 18 Jz26
Eirikstaðir ☐ IS 18 Jz25
Eirunepé ☐ BR (AM) 198 Gf49
Eisenach ☐ D 32 Ll40
Eisenach ☐ D 32 Ll40
Eisenberg ☐ D 32 Lm40
Eisenerz ☐ A 35 Lp43
Eisenerzer Alpen ☐ A 35 Lp43
Eisenhower Center ☐ USA 174 Fb26
Eisenhüttenstadt ☐ D 32 Lp38
Eisenstadt ☐ A 35 Lr43
Eisenwurzen ☐ A 35 Lp43
Eisfeld ☐ D 33 Ll40
Eišiškės ☐ LT 39 Mf36
Eisenwerelt ☐ A 35 Lo43
Eitorf ☐ D 32 Lh40
Eivissa = Ibiza ☐ E 29 Lb51
Eivissa ☐ E 29 Lb52
Ejaji ☐ ETH 142 Mj41
Ejea de los Caballeros ☐ E 28 Kt48
Ejeda ☐ RM 157 Nc58
Ejer Bavnehøj ☐ DK 30 Lk35
Ejido ☐ YV 192 Ge41
Ejidogari ☐ WAN 138 Lc41
Ejido La Concha ☐ MEX (CHH) 180 Eg31
Ejin Horo Qi ☐ CHN (NMZ) 72 Qe26
Ejin Qi ☐ CHN (NMZ) 72 Qa25
Ejirin ☐ WAN 138 Ld42
Ejisu ☐ GH 137 Ka42
Ejouj ☐ RIM 130 Kf37
Ejsk ☐ RUS 49 Mk22
Ejura ☐ GH 137 Ka42
Ejura ☐ GH 137 Kk42
Ekalaka ☐ USA (MT) 169 Eh23
Ekamour ☐ RIM 130 Kd37
Ekang ☐ WAN 138 Le42
Ekata ☐ G 140 Lh45
Ekaterinoslavka ☐ RUS 71 Re20
Ekaterinovka ☐ RUS 48 Mk16
Ekaterinovka ☐ RUS 48 Nc19
Ekaterinskij dvorec ☐ RUS 48 Mf16
Ek Balám ☐ MEX 183 Ff35
Ekeby ☐ S 30 Ln35
Ekenäs = Tammisaari ☐ FIN 38 Md31
Ekenäs ☐ S 30 Lo32
Ekenäs skärgårds n.p. = Tammisaaren saariston kansallispuisto ☐ FIN 38 Md31
Ekerö ☐ S 31 Lr31
Eket ☐ WAN 138 Ld43
Eketahuna ☐ NZ 113 Th66
Ekibastuz ☐ KZ 63 09c08
Ekimchán ☐ RUS 48 Lg38
Ekisu ☐ WAN 138 Lf36
Ekimane ☐ RM 157 Lg38
Eklutna Village Hist. Park ☐ USA 165 Cf15

Ekombe ☐ RDC 140 Ma45
Ekondo Titi ☐ CAM 138 Le43
Ekor ☐ RI 91 Rd45
Ekouata ☐ G 140 Le46
Ekrafane ☐ RN 132 Lb38
Ekshärad ☐ S 31 Lo30
Eksi džamija ☐ BG 45 Mf49
Eksjö ☐ S 31 Lp33
Ekuku ☐ WAN 138 Lc43
Ekukola ☐ RDC 140 Ma45
Ekumakoko ☐ RDC 149 Mb47
Ekuropon ☐ GH 137 Kj43
Ekwa ☐ CAM 139 Lg44
Ekwendeni ☐ MW 146 Mg51
Ekylamentusom ☐ GH 137 Kk42
Ekzarh Antinovo ☐ BG 45 Mg48
El-Abiodh-Sidi-Cheikh ☐ DZ 125 La29
El Abred ☐ ETH 145 Nc43
El Adeb Larache ☐ DZ 126 Le32
Elafónissos ☐ GR 46 Mc54
El-Aguia ☐ GR (COH) 181 Ej33
El Aguia ☐ RA (PJ) 207 Gh57
El Aguilar ☐ RA (JUY) 207 Gh57
El Aguinaldo ☐ MEX (DGO) 181 Eh33
Elahera ☐ CL 85 Pa42
Elaidia ☐ SUD 135 Mg36
El Ain ☐ TN 126 Le34
El-Alamein ☐ ET 129 Me30
El-Alamein War Cemetery ☐ ☐ ET 129 Me31
El Alazán ☐ MEX (VC) 182 Fb35
El Alicante ☐ MEX (CO) 181 Ej32
El Almendral ☐ PE 196 Ga48
El Alto ☐ MEX (JLC) 182 Ej35
Elamanchili ☐ IND 83 Pb37
El Ámirah ☐ ET 129 Mf32
El Amparo ☐ MEX (SLP) 182 Ek34
El Amparo ☐ YV 193 Gf41
El Amparo de Apure ☐ YV 192 Ge42
Elan' ☐ RUS 48 Nb20
Elan Bank ☐ 7 Ob30
Elandsbaai ☐ ZA 154 Lk62
Elands Height ☐ ZA 155 Me61
Elandslaagte ☐ ZA 155 Mf61
El Ángel ☐ EC 196 Gb45
Elan'-Kolenovskij ☐ RUS 48 Na20
El Anteojo ☐ MEX (CHH) 181 Eh31
El Aouinet ☐ DZ 126 Ld28
El Aqaba ☐ JOR 58 Mh31
El-Araïche ☐ MA 125 Kg28
El Arar ☐ SP 145 Nd44
El Arco ☐ MEX (BC) 180 Ed31
El Arco ☐ MEX (BC) 180 Ec30
El Argoub ☐ DARS 130 Kc34
El Arihal ☐ RIM 131 Kh37
El Aricha ☐ DZ 125 Kk28
El Arish ☐ ET 129 Mg30
El Astillero ☐ E 28 Kr47
Elat ☐ IL 58 Mh31
El Ataya ☐ TN 126 Le29
Elátia ☐ GR 46 Mc52
El Dorado ☐ HN 184 Fh38
El Dorado ☐ MEX (COH) 181 Ej32
El Dorado ☐ MEX (MI) 204 Hc59
El Dorado ☐ RA (SC) 209 Gj61
El Dorado ☐ USA (AR) 175 Fd29
El Dorado ☐ USA (KS) 174 Fb27
El Dorado ☐ YV 193 Gj43
Eldorado River ☐ USA 164 Bh13
El Dorado Springs ☐ USA (MO) 174 Fc27
Eldoret ☐ EAK 144 Mh45
Eldzhurt ☐ TM 62 Oa36
El Duncan ☐ EAK 144 Mh45
Elec ☐ RUS 48 Mk19
Eléftheres ☐ GR 45 Me50
Elefthereopóli ☐ GR 45 Me50
Eleja ☐ LV 39 Md34
El Eje ☐ RA (CA) 207 Gg59
Elektostal ☐ RUS 48 Mk18
Elektrénai ☐ LT 39 Me36
Elela ☐ BR (PR) 194 Gk43
Eles ☐ USA (IN) 173 Fh25
El Empalme ☐ EC 196 Ga46
El Empedrado ☐ YV 192 Ge41
Elena ☐ BG 45 Mf48
El Encanto ☐ CO 196 Gd46
El Encino ☐ MEX (TM) 182 Fa34
Elephantos ☐ GR 46 Mc53
Elephanta Island ☐ ☐ IND 82 Og36
Elephant Butte Res. ☐ USA 171 Eg29
Elephant Island ☐ 6 Hb31
Elephant Island ☐ USA (AK) 165 Bk12
Elephant Trading Centre ☐ RI 93 Qd48
Elbag ☐ PL 41 Lu36
El Blanquero ☐ YV 193 Gj41
El Bluff ☐ NIC 185 Fj39
El Bolsón ☐ RA (RN) 208 Ge66
El Bonillo ☐ E 27 Kr51
El Bordj ☐ DZ 125 La28
El Bordo ☐ CO 192 Gb44
El Borma ☐ TN 126 Le30
El-Borouj ☐ MA 125 Kg29
El Bosque ☐ NIC 184 Fh38
El Bouz ☐ RIM 130 Kf38
El Brasil ☐ BR (TM) 182 Fb34
El Bravo ☐ RA (SC) 210 Gd70
El'brus ☐ RUS (KBA) 57 Nb24
El Burgo de Osma ☐ E 26 Kr49
Elburgon ☐ EAK 144 Mh46
El Burro ☐ YV 193 Gg42
El Burumbul ☐ ET 129 Mf31
Elburz Mountains ☐ IR 62 Nf27
El Cabrito ☐ MEX (TM) 182 Fa34
Elbistan ☐ TR 56 Mj26
El Caburé ☐ RA (SE) 207 Gh59
El-Cajón, P.N. ☐ HN 184 Fg37
El Cajas, P.N. ☐ EC 196 Ga47
El Cajon ☐ RA (SC) 210 Gd71
El Calafate ☐ RA (SC) 210 Gd71
El Callao ☐ YV 193 Gj42
El Campo ☐ USA (TX) 181 Fb31
El Campo ☐ CO 192 Gd43
El Campo ☐ MEX (TX) 181 Fb31
El Caño ☐ PA 185 Fk41
El Cantón ☐ YV 192 Ge42
El Capulin ☐ MEX (GUT) 182 Ek35
El Carmen ☐ BOL 198 Gh50
El Carmen ☐ BOL 206 Gj53
El Carmen ☐ BOL 206 Gj54
El Carmen ☐ CO 192 Gb43
El Carmen ☐ CO 192 Gd44
El Carmen ☐ EC 196 Ga46
El Carmen ☐ MEX (BC)
El Carmen ☐ MEX (NL) 181 Ek33
El Carmen ☐ MEX (NIC 184 Fg37
El Carmen ☐ RA (PJ) 207 Gh58
El Carrizal ☐ MEX (CHH)
El Carrizo ☐ MEX (GUR) 182 Ek37
El Castillo ☐ MEX (SLP) 182 Fa35
El Cayo ☐ MEX 183 Fe37

El Cayuco ☐ MEX (BCS) 180 Ee33
El Centro ☐ USA (CA) 170 Ec29
El Cerrito ☐ CO 192 Gb44
El Cerrito ☐ RA (CR) 210 Ge71
El Cerro de Concepción ☐ BOL 206 Gk54
El Chacay ☐ RCH 208 Ge44
El Chaco ☐ EC 196 Gb46
El Chaco ☐ RA (SA) 206 Gd61
El Chaltén ☐ RA (SC) 210 Gd70
El Chaparro ☐ YV 193 Gh41
El Charco ☐ RA (SE) 207 Gh59
Elche ☐ E 29 Ku52
Elche de la Sierra ☐ E 27 Ks52
El Chico, P.N. ☐ MEX 182 Fa35
El Chile ☐ NIC 185 Fh39
El Chinero ☐ MEX (BC) 180 Ec30
Elcho Island ☐ AUS 106 Rh51
El Chorro ☐ MEX (TM) 181 Fa33
El Chorro ☐ BOL 198 Gj51
El Cien ☐ MEX (BCS)
El Cinco ☐ MEX (COH) 181 Ej32
El Cisne ☐ EC 196 Ga47
El Cisne ☐ EC 196 Ga47
El Cobre ☐ MEX (BCS)
El Cocuy ☐ CO 192 Gd42
El Cocuy, P.N. ☐ CO 192 Gd42
El Colorado ☐ RA (FO) 204 Ha59
El Comitán ☐ MEX (BCS)
El Cope ☐ PA 185 Fk41
El Corazón ☐ EC 196 Ga46
El Corcovado ☐ RA (CB) 210 Ge67
El Corozo ☐ YV 193 Gh41
El Coyote ☐ MEX (BCS) 180 Ee32
El Coyote ☐ MEX (SO) 180 Ef31
El Coyote ☐ RA (SC) 210 Ge71
El Crispín ☐ RA (CD) 209 Gj61
El Cruce ☐ GCA 183 Ff37
El Crucero ☐ MEX (SLP) 182 Ek34
El Cuarenta ☐ MEX (CHH)
El Cubo de Tierra del Vino ☐ E 26 Kp49
El Cuco ☐ ES 184 Ff39
El Cuy ☐ RA (RN) 208 Gf65
El Cuyo ☐ MEX (YT) 183 Fg35
El Dab'ah ☐ ET 129 Me30
El Dabb'ah ☐ ET 128 Md30
El Deir ☐ ET 129 Mf32
Eldersile ☐ AUS (QLD) 108 Sb57
El Descanso ☐ PE 197 Ge53
El Desemboque ☐ MEX (SO) 180 Ed30
El Desemboque ☐ MEX (SO) 180 Ed31
El Deseo ☐ MEX (SO) 180 Ed30
El Divisadero ☐ MEX (CHH) 180 Eg32
El Divisorio ☐ RA (BA) 209 Gk65
El Djem ☐ TN 126 Le29
El Djezair ☐ DZ 126 Lc27
Eldon Hazlet S.P. ☐ USA 175 Ff26
El Jigote ☐ MEX (NYT) 182 Eh35
El Jordán ☐ CO 192 Gd43
Efk ☐ PL 41 Mc37
El Kab ☐ SUD 135 Mg36
El Kab (Nekheb) ☐ ET 129 Mg33
El Kala ☐ DZ 126 Le27
El Kala, P.N. d' ☐ DZ 126 Le28
El Kantara ☐ DZ 126 Lc28
El Karaib ☐ SUD 135 Mg36
Elk City ☐ USA (ID) 168 Ec23
Elk City ☐ USA (OK) 174 Fa28
Elk Creek ☐ USA (CA) 170 Dj26
El Kebab ☐ MA 125 Kh29
Elkedra ☐ AUS (NT) 106 Rh56
El Kef ☐ TN 126 Ld29
El-Kelaa-des-Sraghna ☐ MA 125 Kg30
El Kere ☐ ETH 145 Nb43
Elkford ☐ CDN (BC) 168 Ec20
Elk Grove ☐ USA (CA) 170 Dk26
El Khanka ☐ ET 129 Mf30
El Kharga ☐ ET 129 Mf32
Elkhart ☐ USA (IN) 173 Fh25
Elkhart ☐ USA (KS) 174 Fa28
Elkhart ☐ USA (TX) 174 Fc30
El Khattara ☐ ET 129 Mg30
El Khnâchich ☐ RMM 131 Kh35
Elkhorn ☐ CDN (MB) 172 Fa21
Elkhorn ☐ USA (WI) 173 Ff24
El Khroub ☐ DZ 126 Ld27
El Khufrah ☐ LAR 128 Mb33
Elkin ☐ USA (NC) 178 Fk27
El Kiswa ☐ ET 129 Mg30
Elko ☐ USA (NV) 170 Eb25
Elk Point ☐ CDN (AB) 169 Ee19
Elk Point ☐ USA (SD) 172 Fb24
Elk River ☐ USA (ID) 168 Ec22
Elk River ☐ USA (MN) 172 Fd23
El Kseur ☐ DZ 126 Lc27
El-Ksiba ☐ MA 125 Kh29
Elk Springs ☐ USA (CO) 171 Ef25
Elkton ☐ USA (MD) 177 Gc26
El Kuntilla ☐ ET 129 Mh31
Elkwe ☐ GH 137 Kk43
El Lánuru ☐ IND (APH) 84 Ok38
Ella Valla ☐ AUS 104 Qh58
Ellaville ☐ USA (GA) 175 Fh30
El Leh ☐ ETH 145 Mk44
Elléloyéd ☐ TCH 133 Lk37
El Lel ☐ ETH 145 Nb44
Ellendale ☐ AUS (WA) 103 Rd54
Ellendale ☐ USA (ND) 172 Fa22
Ellenburg ☐ USA (WA) 168 Dk22
Ellenville ☐ USA (NY) 177 Gc25
El León ☐ MEX (NC) 181 Ek31
Ellère Racecourse ☐ NZ 180 Ec34
Ellesmere Island ☐ CDN 163 Fd02
El Limón ☐ MEX (JLC) 182 Eh36
Ellingia ☐ USA (MO) 175 Fe27
Elliot ☐ ZA 155 Md61
Elliot ☐ ZA 155 Me62
Elliot Heads ☐ AUS (QLD) 109 Sg58
Elliot Key ☐ USA 179 Fk33
Elliot Lake ☐ CDN (ON) 173 Fj22
Elliott ☐ AUS (NT) 106 Rg54
Ellis Park ☐ USA (KY) 175 Fg27
Ellisras ☐ ZA 152 Md57
El Llobregat ☐ E 28 La49
El Portezuelo ☐ RA (LR) 208 Gg60

El Guapo ☐ YV 193 Gh40
El Guay ☐ YV 193 Gf40
El Guayabo ☐ YV 192 Gd41
El Guérara ☐ DZ 125 Lb29
El Guettar ☐ TN 126 Le29
El Guettara ☐ RMM 131 Kj36
El Hadjar ☐ DZ 126 Ld27
El Hagounia ☐ DARS 124 Kd32
El-Hajeb ☐ MA 125 Kh29
El Hamel ☐ DZ 126 Lb28
El Hamma ☐ TN 126 Le29
El Hammam ☐ ET 129 Me30
El Hammam ☐ ET 129 Mf32
El Hank ☐ RIM/RMM 131 Kg33
El Haouaria ☐ TN 126 Lf27
El-Haoufta ☐ DZ 126 Lb29
El-Harcha ☐ SUD 135 Mh39
El Herradero ☐ MEX 181 Fb33
El Higo ☐ MEX (VC) 182 Fa35
El Homr ☐ DZ 125 La31
Elhovo ☐ BG 45 Mg48
El Hueco ☐ RA (NE) 208 Ge64
El Huesco ☐ MEX (NL) 181 Fa33
El Humurre ☐ SP 143 Ne42
Elía ☐ GR 46 Mb53
Elias, Cerro de ☐ RA 210 Gg68
El-Idríssia ☐ DZ 126 Lb28
Elie ☐ CDN (MB) 172 Fb21
Eliki Gounda ☐ RN 132 Ld38
El Indio ☐ USA (TX) 181 Ek31
Elimäki ☐ FIN 38 Mg30
El Imposible, P.N. ☐ ES 184 Ff39
El Ingenio ☐ PE 197 Gc53
Elin Pelin ☐ BG 44 Md48
Elionka ☐ RUS 48 Mj19
Elisa ☐ RDC 140 Mc46
Elisa ☐ BR (RO) 206 Gj52
Elisa ☐ SP (207) 200 Hj50
El Iskandariya ☐ ET 129 Mf30
Eliye Springs ☐ EAK 144 Mj44
Elizabeth ☐ GUY 194 Ha42
Elizabeth ☐ USA (NJ) 177 Gc25
Elizabeth City ☐ USA (NC) 106 Rf52
Elizabeth Downs ☐ AUS (NT) 106 Rf52
Elizabeth Harbour ☐ BS 186 Gc34
Elizabethtown ☐ USA (TN) 178 Fj27
Elizabethtown ☐ USA (KY)
Elizabethtown ☐ USA (NC) 175 Fh27
El Jacuixtle ☐ MEX (DGO) 181 Eh33
El-Jadida ☐ MA 125 Kg29
El Jadidah ☐ ET 129 Me31
El Jicaro ☐ NIC 184 Fg39
El Kab ☐ SUD 135 Mg36
El-Kelaa-des-Sraghna
Elliot ☐ ZA 155 Me62
El Pilar ☐ YV 193 Gj40
El Pilar ☐ YV 193 Gj40
El Pilar de la Mola ☐ E 29 Lb52
El Pinar ☐ YV 192 Ge42
El Pingo ☐ RA (ER) 204 Ha61
El Pípila ☐ MEX (DGO) 181 Eh33
El Planchón ☐ RCH 208 Ge63
Elliott ☐ AUS (NT) 106 Rg54
Ellore ☐ AUS (VIC) 111 Sc64
Elmore ☐ USA (SK) 172 Fa21
El Morrión ☐ MEX (CHH) 181 Eh31
El Morro ☐ EC 196 Fk47
El Morro Nat. Mon. ☐ USA 171 Ef28
El Morro = San Pedro de la Roca Castle ☐ C 186 Gc35
El Sombrero ☐ YV 193 Gh41
El Sosneado ☐ RA (MD) 208 Ge64
El Mreiti ☐ RIM 131 Kg34
El Mreïyé ☐ RIM 131 Kg35
Elmshorn ☐ D 32 Lk37
El Munia ☐ ET 129 Mf33
El Muti'a ☐ ET 129 Mf32
El Mzereb ☐ RMM 131 Kg33
El Nakhl ☐ ET 129 Mg31
El Naranjo ☐ GCA 183 Ff37
El Naranjo ☐ MEX (NYT) 181
El Naranjo ☐ MEX (SLP) 182 Fa34
El Nawawra ☐ ET 129 Mf32
El Nbeiket el Ahouâch ☐ RIM 131 Kh37
Elne ☐ F 25 Lc48
El Negrito ☐ HN 184 Fg38
El Nido ☐ RP 90 Qk40
El Nihuil ☐ RA (MD) 208 Gf63
El'nja ☐ RUS 48 Mg18
El Novillo ☐ MEX (SO) 180 Ef31
El Nula ☐ YV 192 Ge42
El Oasis ☐ MEX (BC) 180 Ec30
El Oasis ☐ MEX (SO) 180 Ed31
Elsa ☐ CDN (YT) 166 Db15
El Obraje ☐ MEX (ZCT) 182 Ek34
Elogbatindi ☐ CAM 138 Lf44
El Ogla ☐ DZ 126 Ld28
El Ogla Gasses ☐ DZ 126 Ld28
Elogo ☐ RCB 140 Lj45
Eloko ☐ USA (VA) 177 Gb27
El Koran ☐ ETH 145 Nc43
El Koul ☐ DZ 126 Ld29
Elk Point ☐ CDN (AB) 169 Ee19
El Oro ☐ MEX (COH) 181 Ej32
El Oro ☐ MEX (DGO) 181 Eh33
Elorza ☐ YV 193 Gf41
El Oso ☐ YV 193 Gg41
El Ostíonal ☐ NIC 184 Fh40
El Ouatia ☐ DZ 125 La33
El Ouatia ☐ MA 124 Ke31
El Palmar ☐ YV 193 Gj42
El Palmar ☐ USA (KY) 175 Fg27
El Palmar, P.N. ☐ RA 204 Ha61
El Palmito ☐ MEX (DGO) 181 Eh33
El Panguï ☐ EC 196 Ga47
El Paraíso ☐ BOL 206 Gk53
El Paraíso ☐ HN 184 Fg38
El Pardo ☐ E 27 Kr50
El Paso ☐ USA (IL) 175 Ff25
El Paso ☐ USA (TX) 171 Eg30
Ellensburg ☐ USA (WA) 168 Dk22
El Paso de los Libres ☐ RA 204 Ha60
El Pedregal ☐ MEX (TB) 183 Fe37
El Pedroso ☐ E 27 Kp53
El Pensamiento ☐ BOL 206 Gk53
Elos ☐ GR 46 Mc54
El Perú ☐ GCA 183 Fe37
Elsersile Racecourse ☐ NZ
Eldía Fonfou ☐ PN (MX) 175 Fh27

Ellsworth ☐ USA (MA) 177 Gf23
Ellsworth ☐ USA (ME) 172 Fj25
Ellsworth ☐ USA (WI) 172 Ej25
Ellsworth Land ☐ ANT 6 Fc34
Ellsworth Mountains ☐ 6 Fc34
El Lucero ☐ MEX (CHH) 180 Ed31
Elwangen ☐ D 33 Ll42
Elm ☐ D 32 Ll38
Elma ☐ CDN (MB) 172 Fc21
El Maad ☐ DZ 126 Lc27
El Macao ☐ DOM 186 Gf36
El Maestrat ☐ E 28 Ku49
El-Mahalla-al-Kubra ☐ ET 129 Mf30
El Mahamid ☐ ET 129 Mg33
El Maïa ☐ DZ 126 Lb29
El Maïtén ☐ RA (CB) 208 Ge67
El Maïtén ☐ RCH 210 Gd69
El Mahab ☐ DZ 126 Ld29
El Malpais Nat. Mon. ☐ USA 171 Eg28
El Mamouel ☐ RMM 131 Kj36
El Maï'soûr ☐ ET 129 Mf32
El Ma'moûr-Ighicharene ☐ RMM 131 Kj36
El Manguïto ☐ MEX (CHP) 183 Fd38
El Mannsour ☐ DZ 125 Kk32
El-Mansoura ☐ ET 129 Mf30
El-Mansûra ☐ YV 193 Gf41
El Manteco ☐ YV 193 Gj42
El Manzano ☐ RCH 208 Ge63
El Marâgha ☐ ET 129 Mf32
El Maria ☐ PA 185 Fk41
El Matariyah ☐ ET 129 Mf30
El May ☐ TN 126 Lf29
Elm Creek ☐ CDN (MB) 172 Fb21
El Médano ☐ PE 207 Ge58
El Medo ☐ ETH 145 Na43
El Meghaïer ☐ DZ 126 Ld29
El-Méhaïa ☐ DZ 126 Lb30
El Merey ☐ YV 193 Gj41
El Meselemiya ☐ SUD 135 Mg38
El Mezquite ☐ MEX (SLP)
El Mezquite ☐ MEX (ZCT) 182 Ek34
El Mhaïjrât ☐ RIM 130 Kb36
El Miamo ☐ YV 193 Gk42
El Milia ☐ DZ 126 Ld27
Elmina ☐ GH 137 Kk43
El Mingo ☐ MEX (TB) 183 Fd36
El Minya ☐ ET 129 Mf31
El Minshah ☐ ET 129 Mf32
Elmira ☐ CDN (PE) 176 Gj22
Elmira ☐ USA (NY) 177 Gb24
El Mirador ☐ MEX (JLC) 182 Eh35
El Mistolar ☐ RA (FO) 207 Gk58
El Moïnâne ☐ RIM 130 Kb36
El Molinillo ☐ E 27 Kp51
El Molino ☐ MEX (CHH) 180 Eg32
El Molino ☐ MEX (VC) 182 Fa35
El Monterey ☐ E 29 Ku51
El Moral ☐ E 27 Ks53
El Moro ☐ EC 196 Fk47
Elmore ☐ AUS (VIC) 111 Sc64
El Sibu Temple ☐ ET 129 Mg34
El Socorro ☐ MEX (BC) 180 Ec30
El Socorro ☐ CO 192 Gd42
El Socorro ☐ YV 193 Gh41
El Sombrero ☐ YV 193 Gh41
El Sombrero ☐ YV 193 Gh41
Elsterwerda ☐ D 32 Lo39
Elstow ☐ CDN (SK) 169 Ee20
Eltisley ☐ GB 21 Ku38
Elton ☐ USA (IA) 172 Fd24
El Tordillo ☐ RA (CB) 210 Gg68
El Toro ☐ E 29 Ku51
El Transcantábrico ☐ E 28 Kr47
El Trece ☐ MEX (CHH) 181 Ej32
El Trencito ☐ RA 208 Ge67
El Trifinio = ES/GCA/HN 184 Ff38
El Trigal ☐ RA (SA) 207 Sa23
El Triunfo ☐ EC (TB) 183 Fd37
El Triunfo ☐ MEX 183 Fd38
El Troncal ☐ CO 192 Gc42
El Tuito ☐ MEX (JLC) 182 Eh35
El Tuparro, P.N. ☐ CO 192 Ge43
El Turbio ☐ RA (SC) 210 Gd71
Eltville ☐ D 33 Lj40
Eluru ☐ IND (APH) 83 Pa37
El Vado ☐ E 27 Kr49
El Valle ☐ CO 192 Gb43
El Vapor ☐ CAM) 183 Fe36
El Vedrell ☐ E 29 La49
El Vendó ☐ E 29 Ku52
El Vigia ☐ YV 192 Ge41
El Villar de Arnedo ☐ E 28 Ks48
El Vínculo ☐ YV 193 Gf39
El Viso ☐ E 27 Kq52
El Vívero ☐ YV 192 Ge42
El Volcán ☐ RCH 208 Ge63
El Wak ☐ EAK 145 Na44
El Wâsitah ☐ ET 129 Mf31
Elwood ☐ USA (IN) 174 Fg26
Elx ☐ E 29 Ku52
Ely ☐ GB 21 Ku38
Ely ☐ USA (MN) 172 Fe22
Ely ☐ USA (NV) 170 Ec26
Elyria ☐ USA (OH) 173 Fj25

El Potosí, P.N. ☐ MEX 182 Fa35
El Potrero ☐ MEX (CHH) 181 Eh31
El Progreso ☐ GCA 184 Ff38
El Progreso ☐ GCA 184 Ff38
El Progreso ☐ HN 184 Fg38
El Progreso ☐ MEX (BC) 180 Ed31
El Puente ☐ BOL 206 Gk54
El Puerto ☐ MEX (CO) 181 Ek31
El Puerto de Santa María = E 27 Kp51
El Puerto de Santa María = E 27 Ko54
El-Qahira ☐ ET 129 Mf30
El Qasr ☐ ET 129 Me33
El Quebracha ☐ RA (SA) 207 Gh58
El Quelite ☐ MEX (SL) 180 Eg33
El Questro ☐ AUS (WA) 103 Re53
El Quiaco ☐ RCH 208 Ge62
El Qûsiya ☐ ET 129 Mf32
El Rancho ☐ MEX (CHH) 181 Eh31
El Rastro ☐ YV 193 Gg41
El Real de la Jara ☐ E 27 Kp53
Real de San Vicente ☐ E 27 Kq50
El Rebaje ☐ MEX (NL) 181 Fa33
El Re'ia ☐ ET 129 Mg33
El Refugio ☐ MEX (CHH) 180 Eg32
El Retamo ☐ RA (SL) 208 Gg62
El Rey, P.N. ☐ RA 207 Gh58
El Ridisiya Bahari ☐ ET 129 Mg33
El Rocío ☐ E 27 Ko53
El Rubio ☐ E 27 Kq53
El Sabinal, P.N. ☐ RA 184 Fa32
El Saff ☐ ET 129 Mf31
El Saladero ☐ MEX (VC) 182 Fb35
El Salado ☐ MEX (CA) 170 Eb29
El Salado ☐ RA (SC) 210 Gg70
El Salitre ☐ MEX (CHH) 181 Eh31
El Salto ☐ MEX (DGO) 181 Eh34
El Salto ☐ RCH 208 Ge63
El Salvador ☐ MEX (ZCT) 181 Ek33
El Salvador ☐ RCH 207 Gf59
El Santo ☐ C 179 Ga34
El Sargento ☐ MEX (BCS) 180 Ee33
El Sauce ☐ CHN (TB) 69 Pj30
El Sasabe ☐ MEX (SO) 180 Ee30
El Saucejo ☐ E 27 Kp53
El Sauzalito ☐ RA (CH) 204 Gk59
El Seibo ☐ DOM 186 Gf36
El Semillero ☐ GCA 184 Ff38
El Shatt ☐ ET 129 Mg31
El Socorro ☐ MEX (BC) 180 Ec30
El Tala ☐ RA (SA) 207 Gh59
El Tamango ☐ NIC 184 Fg38
El Tambo ☐ CO 192 Gb44
El Tanque ☐ MEX (SL) 180 Eg33
El Tarf ☐ DZ 126 Le27
El Tebol ☐ RA (SF) 209 Gk62
El Tejar ☐ RA (BA) 209 Gk63
El Tenam Puente ☐ MEX 183 Fd37

Emam Abbas ☐ IR 57 Nc28
Emam Hasan ☐ IR 57 Nf31
Emam Saheb ☐ AFG 63 Oe27
Emam Taqi ☐ ZA 155 Mg59
Emangusi ☐ ZA 155 Mg59
Emas, P.N. das ☐ BR 202 Hb55
Emaniel ☐ USA (ID) 168 Ed24
Emiganuru ☐ IND (APH) 82 Oj38
Emmonak ☐ USA (AK) 164 Bh14
Emory ☐ USA (TX) 174 Fc29
Embalse Casa de Piedra ☐ RA 207 Gh58
Embalse Camatagua ☐ YV 193 Gg41
Embalse Cerros Colorados ☐ RA 207 Gh58
Embalse Cogotí ☐ RCH 208 Ge61
Embalse de Aguilar de Campóo ☐ E 26 Kq48
Embalse de Alange ☐ E 27 Ko51
Embalse de Alarcón ☐ E 29 Ks51
Embalse de Alcántara ☐ E 27 Ko51
Embalse de Almendra ☐ E 26 Ko49
Embalse de Arbón ☐ E 26 Ko47
Embalse de Belesar ☐ E 26 Kn48
Embalse de Bembézar ☐ E 27 Kp53
Embalse de Buendía ☐ E 29 Ks50
Embalse de Cijara ☐ E 27 Kq51
Embalse de Contreras ☐ E 29 Ks51
Embalse de El Cajon ☐ HN 184 Fg38
Embalse de El Grado ☐ E 28 La48
Embalse de Entrepeñas ☐ E 29 Ks50
Embalse de Gabriel y Galán ☐ E 27 Ko50
Embalse de García de Sola ☐ E 27 Kp51
Embalse de Giribaile ☐ E 27 Kr52
Embalse de Guadalcacín ☐ E 27 Kp54
Embalse de Guadalhorce ☐ E 28 Kt49
Embalse de Guri ☐ YV 193 Gj42
Embalse de Jándula ☐ E 27 Kr52
Embalse de la Serena ☐ E 27 Kp52
Embalse de las Portas ☐ E 26 Kn48
Embalse del Cenajo ☐ E 29 Kt52
Embalse del Chanza ☐ E 27 Kn53
Embalse del Ebro ☐ E 28 Kr47
Embalse del Guárico ☐ YV 193 Gg41
Embalse del Nihuil ☐ RA 208 Gf63
Embalse del Pintado ☐ E 27 Kp52
Embalse del Porma ☐ E 26 Kp48
Embalse del Rumblar ☐ E 27 Kr52
Embalse del Tercero ☐ RA 208 Gh62
Embalse de Mediano ☐ E 28 La48
Embalse de Mequinenza ☐ E 29 La49
Embalse de Negratín ☐ E 27 Kr53
Embalse de Orellana ☐ E 27 Kp52
Embalse de Santa Teresa ☐ E 27 Kp50
Embalse de Sierra Boyera ☐ E 27 Kp52
Embalse de Sierra Brava ☐ E 27 Kp51
Embalse de Urrunaga ☐ E 28 Kr47
Embalse de Valdecañas ☐ E 27 Kp51
Embalse de Valdemojón ☐ E 27 Kr52
Embalse Ezequiel Ramos Mexia ☐ RA 208 Gf64
Embalse Florentino Ameghino ☐ RA 210 Gg67
Embalse la Paloma ☐ RCH 208 Ge61
Embalse Paso de las Piedras ☐ RA 209 Gk65
Embalse Peñol ☐ CO 192 Gc42
Embalse Piedra del Aguila ☐ RA 208 Ge66
Embalse Poechos ☐ PE 196 Fk48
Embalse Río Hondo ☐ RA 207 Gh59
Embalse Yacyretá Apipé ☐ PY/RA 204 Ha59
Embarcación ☐ RA (SA) 207 Gh57
Embarcadero ☐ MEX (CHP) 183 Fc37
Embarras ☐ CDN (IN) 175 Fg26
Embi ☐ KZ 54 Nd09
Embleton ☐ GB 21 Ks36
Embrun ☐ F 25 Lg46
Embu ☐ EAK 144 Mj46
Emeck ☐ TR 47 Mh54
Emei Shan ☐ ☐ CHN (SCH) 74 Qb31
Emeishan Sacred Mountains ☐ CHN 74 Qb31
Emerald ☐ AUS (QLD) 109 Se57
Emerald Mound ☐ USA 175 Fe30
Emerau Point ☐ AUS 102 Rb54
Emery ☐ USA (UT) 171 Ee27
Emerado ☐ BR (BA) 199 Ja51
Emi Fezzane ☐ RN 133 Lj35
Emi Koussi ☐ TCH 133 Lk36
Emiliano Zapata ☐ MEX (CHP) 183 Fd37
Emilia-Romagna ☐ I 34 Ll46
Emina ☐ FIN 16 Mb11
Emi Lulu ☐ RN 133 Lh36
Emory ☐ USA (TX) 174 Fc29

Emmeloord ☐ NL 23 Lf38
Emmen ☐ CH 34 Lj43
Emmen ☐ NL 23 Lg38
Emmendingen ☐ D 33 Lj42
Emmerich ☐ D 32 Lg39
Emmet ☐ AUS (QLD) 109 Sc57
Emmett ☐ USA (ID) 172 Fc24
Emmonak ☐ USA (AK) 164 Bh14
Emory ☐ USA (TX) 174 Fc29
Emonak ☐ USA (AK) 164 Bh14
Emory ☐ USA (TX) 174 Fc29
Empalme ☐ MEX (SO) 180 Ee31
Empangeni ☐ ZA 155 Mf60
Emparré ☐ EC 196 Ga46
Emperor Range ☐ PNG 117 Sh48
Emporia ☐ USA (KS) 174 Fb26
Emporia ☐ USA (VA) 178 Gb27
Emporium ☐ USA (PA) 173 Ga25
Empress ☐ CDN (AB) 169 Ee20
Empress Augusta Bay ☐ PNG 117 Sh49
Empress Mine ☐ ZW 152 Me55
Ems ☐ D 32 Lh38
Emsdetten ☐ D 32 Lh38
Emu-Jade-Kanal ☐ D 32 Lh37
Emu Park ☐ AUS (QLD) 109 Sf57
Ena ☐ J 79 Rj28
Ena ☐ RUS 16 Mj17
Enånger ☐ S 17 Ll15
Enangiperd ☐ EAK 144 Mh46
Enarotali ☐ RI 114 Rj47
En-a-san Tunnel ☐ J 79 Rj28
Enawene-Nawe, T.I. ☐ BR 206 Ha52
Enbebess ☐ ETH (RS) 204 He60
Encantado ☐ BR (RS) 204 He60
Encarnación ☐ PY 204 Ha59
Encarnación de Díaz ☐ MEX (JLC) 182 Ej35
Enckeler ☐ TR 47 Mj52
Encinal ☐ USA (TX) 170 Ed29
Encinitas ☐ USA (CA) 170 Eb29
Encío ☐ E 28 Kr48
Encoje ☐ ANG 148 Lh49
Encón ☐ RA (SJ) 208 Gg62
Encruzilhada ☐ BR (BA) 203 Hk53
Encruzilhada ☐ BR (RS) 204 Hc60
Encruzilhada do Sul ☐ BR (RS) 204 Hd61
Enda ☐ CHN (TIB) 69 Pj30
Endakot ☐ EAT 146 Mh50
Endau ☐ CDN (BC) 169 Ee19
Endasak ☐ EAT 146 Mh48
Endau ☐ EAK 145 Mh46
Endau Rompin N.P. ☐ MAL 92 Qb44
Endeavor ☐ CDN (SK) 169 Ej19
Endeavour Strait ☐ AUS 107 Sb51
Endelave ☐ DK 30 Ll35
Enderbury ☐ CDN (SK) 168 Ea20
Enderby Land ☐ ANT 7 Na32
Enderlin ☐ USA (ND) 172 Fa22
Endicott ☐ USA (NY) 177 Gb24
Endicott Mountains ☐ USA 165 Cd12
End-of-Line RR Park & Mus. ☐ USA 172 Fb21
Endom ☐ CAM 138 Lf44
Endoma ☐ AUS (WA) 104 Qe60
Energía ☐ RA (BA) 209 Ha65
Enerhodar ☐ UA 49 Mh22
Enez ☐ TR 45 Mg50
Enfield ☐ CDN (NS) 176 Gj23
Enfield ☐ GB 21 Ku39
Engadi ☐ CA 54 Nd09
Engan ☐ N 16 Le14
Engaru ☐ J 77 Sb23
Engcobo ☐ ZA 155 Md61
Engdad ☐ TR 56 Mk26
Engenheiro Beltrão ☐ BR (PR) 202 Hd57
Engenheiro Dolabela ☐ BR (MG) 203 Hj54
Enger ☐ D 32 Lj38
Engganu ☐ RI 93 Qb48
Engler ☐ CHN (NMZ) 71 Qb21
Engineer Group ☐ PNG 116 Sf51
Engkilili ☐ MAL 94 Qf45
Engku ☐ ☐ RI 91 Rd46
Englee ☐ CDN (NF) 177 Hb24
Englefield ☐ AUS (WA) 105 Rd60
Englehart ☐ CDN (ON) 173 Ga22
Englewood ☐ USA (CO) 171 Eh26
English Channel ☐ 22 Kr41
English Coast ☐ 6 Gb33
English Fort ☐ GB 137 Kk43
English Harbour Town ☐ AG 187 Hc22
English River ☐ CDN (ON) 172 Fe21
Engoobo ☐ ZA 155 Md61
Engozero ☐ RUS 16 Mh16
Engoi ☐ ☐ RDC 141 Md44
Engure ☐ LV 39 Md33
Enguri ☐ GE 57 Na24
Enham ☐ TCH 134 Mb39
Enid ☐ USA (OK) 174 Fb27
Eniwaki ☐ J 77 Sb24

Enoch ☐ USA (UT) 171 Ed27
Enonkoski ☐ FIN 38 Mj28
Enontekiö ☐ FIN 16 Mb11
Enping ☐ CHN (GDG) 74 Qg34
Enrekang ☐ RI 96 Qk47
Enrique ☐ RP 90 Ra07
Enriquillo ☐ DOM 186 Ge37
Enschede ☐ NL 23 Lg38
Ensenada ☐ MEX (BC) 180 Ec30
Ensenada de Calabozo ☐ YV 192 Ge40
Ensenada de Garachiné ☐ PA 185 Ga41
Ensenada de la Broa ☐ C 179 Fj34
Ensenada de Mompiche ☐ EC 196 Fk45
Ensenada de Tumaco ☐ CO 192 Ga45
Ensenada Los Muertos ☐ MEX (BCS) 180 Ef33
Ensenada Pabellones ☐ MEX 180 Ef32
Ensheim ☐ D 33 Lh41
Ensisheim ☐ F 25 Lh43
Entebbe ☐ EAU 144 Mf45
Enterprise ☐ CDN 167 Ed15
Enterprise ☐ USA (AL) 175 Fh30
Enterprise ☐ USA (OR) 168 Ed23
Enterprise ☐ USA (UT) 171 Ed27
Entrague-sur-Truyère ☐ F 25 Ld46
Entre Ríos ☐ BR (BA) 203 Ja53
Entre-Ijuis ☐ BR (RS) 204 Hc60
Entre Lagos ☐ RCH 208 Gd66
Entre-os-Rios ☐ P 26 Kn49
Entre Ríos ☐ BOL 207 Gh56
Entre Ríos ☐ BR (BA) 201 Ja51
Entre Ríos ☐ PA 199 Ho48
Entre Ríos ☐ RA 204 Ha61
Entre Ríos de Minas ☐ BR (MG) 203 Hh56
Entrevaux ☐ F 25 Lg47
Entrocamento ☐ BR (MA) 200 Hg48
Entrocamento ☐ BR (MA) 200 Hh49
Entronque San Roberto ☐ MEX (NL) 181 Ek33
Entrop ☐ RI 115 Sa47
Entumeni ☐ ZA 155 Mf60
Entwistle ☐ CDN (AB) 169 Ec19
Enugu ☐ WAN 138 Ld42
Enugu Ezike ☐ WAN 138 Ld42
Enumclaw ☐ USA (WA) 168 Dj22
Envermeu ☐ F 23 Lb41
Envigado ☐ CO 192 Gc42
Enviken ☐ S 17 Ll15
Envira ☐ BR (AC) 196 Ge49
Enxudé ☐ GNB 136 Kc40
Enyélié ☐ RCB 140 Lj44
Enz ☐ D 33 Lj42
Epako ☐ NAM 150 Lj56
Epe ☐ NL 23 Lg38
Epe ☐ WAN 138 Ld42
Épernay ☐ F 23 Ld41
Épernon ☐ F 23 Lb42
Epényi ☐ F 23 Ld41
Ephesos ☐ TR 47 Mh53
Ephraim ☐ USA (UT) 171 Ee26
Ephrata ☐ USA (WA) 168 Ea22
Epi ☐ RDC 141 Md44
Epi ☐ VU 118 Te54
Épidavros ☐ GR 46 Md53
Épila ☐ E 28 Kt49
Épinal ☐ F 25 Lg42
Épinay ☐ RDC 141 Me45
Episkopí ☐ GR 47 Me55
Epirana ☐ BOL 206 Gh54
Epoanda ☐ CHN (NMZ) 71 Qb21
Epping ☐ GB 21 Ku39
Epping Forest ☐ AUS (QLD) 109 Sd57
Epsom ☐ GB 21 Ku39
Epukiro ☐ NAM 150 Lk56
Epupa Falls ☐ NAM 150 Lh54
Epuyén ☐ RA (CB) 208 Ge67
Equator Monument ☐ RI 95 Qe45
Équeurdreville-Hainneville ☐ F 22 Kt41
Eraballi ☐ IND (KTK) 84 Oj38
Eraclea Minoa ☐ I 36 Lo53
Eragudur ☐ IND 84 Oj41
Eralié ☐ BR (PA) 194 Hd45
Eranti ☐ IND (APH) 83 Ok37
Erap ☐ PNG 115 Sc48
Erárica ☐ GR 46 Mc54
Erasmia ☐ EST 38 Mj31
Erave ☐ PNG 115 Sb48
Erawan Cave ☐ THA 89 Qb37
Erawan N.P. ☐ THA 88 Pk38
Erbaa ☐ TR 56 Mh25
Erbach ☐ D 33 Lj41
Erbaut ☐ D 33 Ll42
Erbe Lugang ☐ CHN (AHU) 75 Qk30
Erbent ☐ TM 62 Nk26
Erbeskopf ☐ D 33 Lh41
Erçek Gölü ☐ TR 57 Nb26
Erciş ☐ TR 57 Nb26
Erciyas Dağı ☐ TR 56 Mh26
Erd ☐ H 43 Lt43
Erdaobaihe ☐ CHN (JLN) 76 Re24
Erdek ☐ TR 45 Mh50
Erdemli ☐ TR 56 Mh27
Erdemli ☐ TR 56 Mg27
Erdemli ☐ TR 56 Mg27
Erdenet ☐ MNG 70 Qc21
Erdene Zuu Monastery ☐ MNG 70 Qe22
Erdeven ☐ F 22 Kr43
Erdut ☐ TCH 134 Mb36
Erdut ☐ HR 35 Lt45
Eré ☐ CI 137 Kj42
Erebus, Mount ☐ 7 Tc34
Erebato ☐ YV 193 Gh43
Erechim ☐ BR (RS) 204 Hd60
Ereği ☐ TR 56 Mg26
Ereğli ☐ TR 56 Mg26
Ereğli Ovasi ☐ TR 56 Mg27
Ereli ☐ TCH 134 Mb36
Erenhot ☐ CHN (NMZ) 72 Qg24
Erenler Dağları ☐ TR 56 Mg27
Erentepe ☐ TR 57 Nb26
Erer ☐ ETH (RS) 201 Ja48
Erta Gök ☐ TR 47 Mk52
Eressós ☐ GR 47 Mf51
Erétria ☐ GR 46 Md52
Erg Atoulia ☐ RMM 131 Kk34
Erg Azennezal ☐ DZ 132 Ld34
Erg Bourahhet ☐ DZ 126 Le32
Erg Chech ☐ DZ 125 Kj33
Erg d'Admer ☐ DZ 126 Le32
Erg du Djourab ☐ TCH 133 Lk37
Erg du Ténéré ☐ RN 133 Lh35
Erg el Atchane ☐ DZ 125 Kk31
Erg Iguidi ☐ DZ/RMM 131 Kj33
Erg Raoui ☐ DZ 125 Kj31

Glória ☐ BR (BA) 201 Ja50
Gloria ☐ RP 90 Ra39
Glória de Douradas ☐ BR (MS) 202 Hc57
Glossa ☐ GR 45 Md51
Gloucester ☐ AUS (NSW) 111 Sf62
Gloucester ☐ CDN (ON) 177 Gc23
Gloucester ☐ GB 21 Ks39
Gloucester ☐ USA (MA) 177 Ge24
Gloucester Island ▲ AUS 107 Se56
Gloucester Point ☐ USA (VA) 177 Gb27
Glovertown ☐ CDN (NF) 177 Hc21
Główczyce ☐ PL 40 Ls36
Głowno ☐ PL 41 Lu39
Głożenski manastir ☒ BG 45 Me48
Głubczyce ☐ PL 40 Ls40
Głuboki ☐ RUS 48 Na21
Głuchołazy ☐ PL 40 Ls40
Głuchowo ☐ PL 41 Lu38
Glückstadt ☐ D 32 Lk37
Gluhove ☐ RUS 48 Nb18
Glymur ⌕ IS 18 Jt26
Gmünd ☐ A 35 Lo44
Gmünd ☐ A 42 Lp42
Gmunden ☐ A 35 Lo43
Gnadenkapelle Altötting ✠ D 33 Ln42
Gnaraloo ☐ AUS (WA) 104 Qg57
Gnarp ☐ S 17 Lj14
Gnarrenburg ☐ D 32 Lj37
Gnesmeason ☐ DY 138 La40
Gnesta ☐ S 31 Ls31
Gniazdowo ☐ PL 41 Mb38
Gniben ▲ DK 30 Lm34
Gnibi ☐ SN 132 Kc26
Gniew ☐ PL 40 Ls37
Gnieżen ☐ LB 136 Ke42
Gniezno ☐ PL 40 Ls38
G'nit ☐ SN 130 Kc37
Gnjilane ☐ SCG 45 Mb48
Gnoien ☐ D 32 Ln37
Gnonamorikou ☒ RG 136 Kf41
Gnosjö ☐ S 31 Lo33
Gnowangerup ☐ AUS (WA) 104 Qk62
Goa ☐ IND 82 Og38
Goa ☐ RP 90 Rb39
Goageb ☐ NAM 154 Lj59
Goal Mtn. ▲ USA 154 Lf59
Goalpara ☐ IND (ASM) 86 Pf32
Goaltor ☐ IND (WBG) 83 Pd34
Goan ☐ RMM 131 Kc49
Goari ☐ GH 137 Kj42
Goaso ☐ GH 137 Kj42
Goat Fell ▲ GB 20 Kp35
Goat Horn Mosque (Chahar Borjak) ☒ AFG 64 Ob30
Goba ☐ ETH 142 Mk42
Goba ☐ MOC 155 Mg59
Gobabeb ☐ NAM 150 Lh57
Gobabis ☐ NAM 150 Lh57
Gobe ☐ PNG 116 Se50
Gobernador Ayala ☐ RA (LP) 208 Gg64
Gobernador Costa ☐ RA (CB) 210 Gd68
Gobernador Duval ☐ RA (LP) 208 Gg65
Gobernador Gregores ☐ RA (SC) 210 Ge70
Gobernador Grespo ☐ RA (SF) 207 Gk61
Gobernador Mayano ☐ RA (SC) 210 Gf69
Gobesh ☐ AL 46 Ma50
Gobi Desert ☒ CHN 72 Qa25
Gobindpur ☐ IND (JKD) 83 Pd33
Gobindpur ☐ IND (ORS) 83 Pc34
Gobo ☐ J 79 Rh28
Gobo ☐ ZW 152 Mf55
Gobobosebberge ▲ NAM 150 Lh58
Gobra Nawapara ☐ IND (CGH) 83 Pa35
Gobur ☐ SUD 144 Mf43
Göçbeyli ☐ TR 47 Mh51
Goce Delčev ☐ BG 44 Md49
Goce Delčev ☐ BG 45 Md49
Goch ☐ D 32 Lg39
Gochang Dolmen Site ☒ ROK 78 Rd28
Gochas ☐ NAM 154 Lk58
Go Cong Dong ☐ VN 89 Qd40
Göd ☐ H 43 Lu43
Godafoss ⌕ IS 18 Kc25
God-e Alizak ☐ IR 62 Nj27
Godatair ☐ SUD 141 Md41
Godavari ☐ IND 83 Pa37
Godawarari ☐ NEP 81 Pa31
Godbout ☐ CDN (QC) 176 Gg21
Godby ☐ FIN 38 Lu30
Godda ☐ IND (JKD) 83 Pd33
Goodalir ☐ IS 18 Ka25
Goddo ☐ SME 194 Hc43
Gode ☐ BF 137 Kj39
Gode ☐ ETH 143 Nb42
Godeanu ▲ RO 44 Mc46
Godeč ☐ BG 44 Md47
Godegode ☐ EAT 147 Mj49
Godeli ☐ ETH 143 Nb42
Goderich ☐ CDN 173 Fk24
Godeskov ☐ S 31 Lo32
Godhi ☐ IND (UPH) 81 Pa32
Godhavn = Qeqertarsuaq ☐ DK 163 Hb05
Godhra ☐ IND (GUJ) 82 Og34
Godinlabe ☐ SP 145 Nd43
Godofredo Viana ☐ BR (MA) 195 Hh46
Gödöllő ☐ H 43 Lu43
Godong ☐ RI 95 Qf49
Godoy Cruz ☐ RA (MD) 208 Gf62
Gods Lake ☐ CDN 163 Fb08
Gods Lake Narrows ☐ CDN (MB) 163 Fb08
Gothåb = Nuuk ☐ DK 163 Hb06
Godwin Austen, Mount ▲ PK 81 Oj28
Goe ☐ PNG 115 Sa50
Goegap Nature Reserve ☒ ☐ ZA 154 Lk60
Goilettes ☐ SY 156 Nf51
Goes ☐ NL 23 Ld39
Gog ☐ ETH 142 Mg44
Gogango ☐ AUS (QLD) 109 Se57
Gogo ☐ AUS (WA) 103 Rc55
Gogo ☐ RI 92 Qf47
Gogo ☐ WAN 138 Le44
Gogonagogo ☐ RM 157 Nc48
Gogoro ☐ MOC 152 Mg56
Gogorón ▲ MEX 182 Ek35
Gogrial ☐ SUD 141 Md41
Goh ☐ IND (BIH) 83 Pc33
Gohana ☐ IND (HYA) 80 Oj31
Gohitafla ☐ CI 137 Kg42
Gohren ☐ D 32 Lo36
Goiana ☐ BR (PE) 201 Jc49
Goiandira ☐ BR (GO) 203 Hf53
Goiânia ☐ BR (GO) 203 Hf53
Goianésia do Pará ☐ BR (PA) 195 Hf47
Goiânia ☐ BR (GO) 202 He53
Goianinha ☐ BR (RN) 201 Jc49
Goianorte ☐ BR (TO) 200 Hf49
Goiás ☐ BR (GO) 202 He52
Goiás ☐ BR (GO) 202 Hf52
Goiatins ☐ BR (TO) 200 Hg49

Goidhoo Atoll ▲ MV 84 Og43
Goilkera ☐ IND (JKD) 83 Pd34
Goio-En ☐ BR (SK) 204 Hd59
Goio-Erê ☐ BR (PR) 204 Hd58
Goi-Pula ☐ RDC 146 Md49
Góis ☐ P 26 Km41
Goito ☐ I 34 Ll46
Gojra ☐ PK 65 Og30
Gojyo ☐ J 79 Rh28
Gokak ☐ IND (KTK) 82 Oh37
Gokavaram ☐ IND (APH) 83 Pa37
Gökceada ▲ TR 45 Mf50
Gökcedağ ☐ TR 47 Mj51
Gökcek ☐ TR 47 Mh52
Gök Medrese ☒ TR 56 Mj26
Gökçen ☐ TR 47 Mh52
Gökova Körfezi ☐ TR 47 Mh54
Göksu ☐ TR 57 Nb26
Göksu Milli Park ☒ TR 56 Mg27
Göksun ☐ TR 56 Mj26
Göktepe ☐ TR 47 Mj53
Gokwe ☐ ZW 152 Me55
Gol ☐ N 17 Lj15
Gola ☐ IND (JKD) 83 Pd34
Golaghat ☐ IND (ASM) 86 Ph32
Gola Hills ▲ WAL 136 Kd42
Golapalle ☐ IND (APH) 83 Pa37
Golasheranî ☐ IR 64 Nj31
Golbaf ☐ IR 64 Nj31
Gölhisar ☐ TR 56 Me27
Golbasi ☐ TR 56 Mg26
Golbasi ☐ TR 56 Mj27
Gölbegui ☐ RN 132 La38
Golconda ☐ USA (NV) 170 Eb25
Golconda Fort ☒ IND 82 Ok37
Gölcük ☐ TR 56 Me25
Gölcük ☐ TR 56 Mj25
Gölcük ☐ TR 47 Mh51
Gölcük ☐ TR 57 Nb26
Golcuv Jenikov ☐ CZ 42 Lq41
Golczewo ☐ PL 40 Lp37
Gold Beach ☐ USA (OR) 168 Dh24
Goldberg ☐ D 32 Ln37
Gold Bridge ☐ CDN 168 Dj20
Gold Coast ✈ AUS (QLD) 109 Sg66
Gold Coast ☐ AUS (QLD) 109 Sh59
Gold Coast ☐ AUS 137 Kk43
Goldcreek ☐ USA (MT) 169 Ed22
Golddust ☐ USA 175 Ff28
Golden ☐ CDN (BC) 168 Eb20
Golden Beach ☐ AUS (VIC) 111 Sd65
Goldendale ☐ USA (WA) 168 Dk23
Golden Ears Prov. Park ☒ CDN 168 Dj21
Golden Fleece ☐ GUY 194 Ha42
Golden Gate ☐ USA (FL) 179 Fk32
Golden Gate Bridge ☒ USA 170 Dj27
Golden Gate Highlands N.P. ☒ ZA 155 Me60
Golden Giant Mine ☐ CDN 173 Fh21
Golden Spike N.H.S. ☒ USA 171 Ed25
Golden Temple = Jindian ☒ CHN 87 QD33
Golden Temple (Amritsar) ☒ IND 80 Oh30
Golden Triangle ☐ LAO/MYA/THA 87 Qa35
Golden Triangle Express ☐ MYA 86 Pj34
Golden Valley ☐ ZW 152 Me55
Goldfield ☐ USA (NV) 170 Eb27
Gold Mine Tours ☒ CDN 173 Fk21
Gold River ☐ CDN (BC) 168 Dg21
Goldsboro ☐ USA (NC) 178 Ga28
Goldsmith ☐ USA (TX) 181 Ej30
Goldsworthy ☐ AUS (WA) 102 Qk56
Goldthwaite ☐ USA (TX) 174 Fa30
Gölé ☐ TR 57 Nb25
Golelnov ☐ PL 40 Lp37
Golestan ☐ AFG 65 Oc30
Golf de l'Ajaccio ☐ F 36 Lj49
Golfe de Gabès ☐ TN 126 Lf28
Golfe de Hammamet ☐ TN 126 Lf27
Golfe de la Gonâve ☐ RH 186 Gd36
Golfe de Porto ☐ F 34 Lj48
Golfe de Sagone ☐ F 36 Lj48
Golfe de Saint-Florent ☐ F 34 Lk48
Golfe de Saint-Malo ☐ F 22 Ks42
Golfe de Saint-Tropez ☐ F 25 Lg47
Golfe de Tadjoura ☐ DJI 143 Nd40
Golfe de Tunis ☐ TN 126 Lf27
Golfe de Valinco ☐ F 36 Lj49
Golfe du Lion ☐ F 25 Ld47
Golfe du Morbihan ☐ F 22 Ks43
Golfe du Saint-Laurent ☐ CDN 176 Gj21
Golfe de Coro ☐ YV 193 Gd40
Golfete de Coro ☐ YV 193 Gd40
Golfo Almirante Montt ☐ RCH 210 Gd71
Golfo Aranci ☐ I 36 Lk49
Golfo de Almería ☐ E 27 Ks54
Golfo de Ana María ☐ C 179 Ga35
Golfo de Ancud ☐ RCH 208 Gd66
Golfo de Arauco ☐ RCH 208 Gd64
Golfo de Batabanó ☐ C 179 Fj34
Golfo de Cádiz ☐ E 27 Kn54
Golfo de Cariaco ☐ YV 193 Gh40
Golfo de Cazones ☐ C 179 Fk35
Golfo de Chiriquí ☐ PA 185 Fj41
Golfo de Corcovado ☐ RCH 210 Gd67
Golfo de Cupica ☐ CO 192 Gb42
Golfo de Fonseca ☐ ES/HN/NIC 184 Fg39
Golfo de Guanacayabo ☐ C 179 Gb35
Golfo de Guayaquil ☐ EC 196 Fk47
Golfo de Honduras ☐ HN 184 Fg37
Golfo de Humboldt ☐ CO 192 Gb42
Golfo de la Masma ☐ E 26 Kn47
Golfo de los Mosquitos ☐ PA 185 Fk41
Golfo de Morrosquillo ☐ CO 192 Gc41
Golfo de Nicoya ☐ CR 185 Fh41
Golfo de Papagayo ☐ CR 184 Fh40
Golfo de Paria ☐ YV 193 Gj40
Golfo de Parita ☐ PA 185 Ga42
Golfo de Peñas ☐ RCH 210 Gc69
Golfo de San Blás ☐ PA 185 Ga41
Golfo de San Miguel ☐ PA 185 Gb41
Golfo de Tribugá ☐ CO 192 Gb43

Goodenough Island ▲ PNG 116 Sf50
Good Hope ☐ CDN (BC) 168 Dg20
Good Hope ☐ RB 155 Mc58
Goodhouse ☐ ZA 154 Lk60
Goodluck Inlet (ID) 168 Ec24
Goodland ☐ USA (KS) 174 Ek26
Goodlands ☐ MS 157 Nj56
Goodnews Bay ☐ USA (AK) 164 Bk16
Goodnews Mining Camp ☐ USA (AK) 164 Bk16
Goodooga ☐ AUS (NSW) 109 Se60
Goodooga ☐ AUS (NSW) 109 Se60
Goombobokie ☐ AUS (NSW) 109 Se60
Goongarrie ☐ AUS (WA) 104 Ra61
Goongarrie N.P. ☒ ☐ AUS 104 Ra61
Goonyella Mine ☒ AUS (QLD) 108 Sd57
Goonyella ☐ AUS 109 Se56
Goongoola Mine ☒ AUS (QLD) 104 Qj61
Goomeri ☐ AUS (QLD) 109 Sg59
Goondiwindi ☐ AUS (QLD) 109 Sf60
Goondoola ☐ AUS (NSW)
Goonoo Goonoo ☐ AUS (NSW)
Goole ☐ GB 21 Ku37
Googlwol ☐ AUS (NSW) 111
Gora ☐ RUS 48 Mk17
Goradiz ☐ AZ 57 Nd26
Goragorsk ☐ RUS 48 Mj20
Gorakh ☐ TR (QH) 69 Pb27
Gorakhpur ☐ IND (UPH) 81 Pb32
Gorap ☐ IND (ORS) 83 Pd36
Gorapalganj ☐ IND (UPH) 81 Pa32
Goratwar-on-Sea ☐ CO (COH) 179
Gorazde ☐ BIH 35 Lt47
Gorda Peak N.P. ☒ GB 187 Gh36
Gördes ☐ TR 47 Mj52
Gördil ☐ TCH 140 La41
Gordion ☐ TR 56 Mg26
Gordo ☐ USA (AK) 165 Ck11
Gordon ☐ USA (NE) 172 Ej24
Gordon Downs ☐ AUS (WA) 103 Re55
Gordon, Mount ▲ AUS 104 Ra62
Gordon's Bay ☐ ZA 154 Lk63
Gordonvale ☐ AUS 107 Sc54
Gore ☐ ETH 142 Mh41
Gore ☐ NZ 113 Td69
Gore ☐ TCH 140 Lh41
Gore Highway ⛖ AUS 109 Sf59
Goreé ☐ BF 131 Kk38
Gorelki ☐ RUS 48 Mj18
Göreme Milli Parkı ☒ TR 56 Mh26
Gore Pt. ▲ USA 164 Cc16
Gorey ☐ IRL 19 Ko38
Gorgadji ☐ BF 131 Kk38
Gorgan ☐ IR 62 Nh27
Gorges d'Aouli ☒ MA 125 Kh29
Gorges de la Pipi ☐ RCA 140
Gorges de l'Ardèche ☒ F 25 Le46
Gorges de la Restonica ☒ F 34 Lk48
Gorges de l'Asco ☒ F 34 Lk48
Gorges de l'Oued Seldja ☒ TN 126 Ld29
Gorges de l'Oudingueur ☒ TCH 133 Lj35
Gorges de Lukwila ☒ RDC
Gorges de Spelunca ☒ F 34 Lj48
Gorges de Talari ☒ RMM
Gorges de Tighanimine ☒ DZ 126 Lc28
Gorges Diasso ☒ RCB 148 Lg48
Gorges du Dadès ☒ MA 125 Kh30
Gorges du Kadéï ☒ RCA 140 Lh44

Gorges du Keran ☒ TG 137 La41
Gorges du Prunelli ☒ F 36 Lk49
Gorges du Tarn ☒ F 25 Ld46
Gorges du Todra ☒ MA 125 Kh29
Gorgoram ☐ WAN 139 Lf39
Gori ☐ GE 57 Nc25
Gori ☐ PK 65 Of33
Gorica ☐ AL 46 Ma50
Goricy ☐ RUS 48 Mh18
Gorinchem ☐ NL 23 Le39
Goris ☐ ARM 57 Nd26
Goritsá ☐ GR 46 Mc53
Gorizia ☐ I 35 Lo45
Gorizkij monastýr ☒ RUS 48 Mk17
Gorjakij Ključ ☐ RUS 49 Mk23
Gorkha ☐ NEP 81 Pc31
Gorki ☐ RUS 38 Mk31
Gørlev ☐ DK 30 Lm35
Görlitz ☐ D 32 Lp39
Gorman ☐ USA (CA) 170 Ea28
Gormanston ☐ IRL 19 Ko37
Gorna Beševica ☐ BG 44 Md47
Gorna Orjahovica ☐ BG 45 Mf47
Gorna Studena ☐ BG 45 Mf47
Gorni Okol ☐ BG 44 Md48
Gornjacki ☐ RUS 49 Na21
Gornja Radgona ☐ SLO 42 Lq44
Gornja Sabanta ☐ SCG 44 Ma47
Gornje Peulje ☐ BIH 35 Ls46
Gornji Jabolčište ☐ MK 44 Mb49
Gornji Vakuf = Uskoplje ☐ BIH 35 Ls47
Górno ☐ PL 41 Ma40
Gorno-Altaj ☐ RUS 54 Pb08
Gorno-Altajsk ☐ RUS 132 La33
Gornovodnoe ☐ RUS 77 Sa22
Goro ☐ ETH 142 Na42
Goroch'an ▲ ETH 142 Mj41
Gorodec ☐ RUS 48 Nc19
Gorogoro ☐ RI 97 Rd46
Goroka Show ☐ PNG 115 Sc49
Goromonzi ☐ ZW 152 Mf55
Goron-Gorom ☐ BF 131 Kk38
Gorong ▲ RI 97 Rf47
Gorongosa ☐ MOC 152 Mh55
Gorongoza, P.N. de ☒ MOC 153 Mh55
Gorontalo ☐ RI 91 Rb45
Gorovo Hawkckie ☐ PL 41 Ma36
Goyllarisquizga ☐ PE 197 Gb51
Goyum ☐ CAM 139 Lg43
Goz-Beida ☐ TCH 134 Ma39
Gozdnica ☐ PL 41 Lq39
Gözne ☐ TR 56 Mh27
Goz Regeb ☐ SUD 135 Mh37
Gozo = M ▲ M 27 Lp54
Graaff-Reinet ☐ ZA 155 Mc62
Graafwater ☐ ZA 154 Lj62
Graalubo ☐ S 31 Lq30
Grabarka ☒ PL 41 Mc38
Graben-Neudorf ☐ D 33 Lj41
Gräbo ☐ S 31 Lo32
Gräboč ☐ A 43 Lq44
Graborovo ☐ RUS 48 Mk17
Gračac ☐ HR 35 Lq46
Gračanica ☒ BIH 35 Lt46
Gračanica ☐ BIH 35 Lt46
Gračanica ☐ SCG 44 Mb48
Graçay ☐ F 25 Lb43
Gracefield ☐ CDN (QC) 173 Gb22
Gracemere ☐ AUS (QLD) 109 Sf57
Graceville ☐ USA (MN) 172 Fb23
Gracias ☐ HN 184 Ff38
Gradac ☐ HR 35 Ls47
Gradacac ☐ BIH 44 Lt46
Gradaús ☐ BR (PA) 200 He49
Gradec ☐ BG 45 Mf47
Gradefes ☒ E 26 Kp48
Gradina ☐ BG 45 Mf47
Gradinari ☐ RO 44 Md46
Gradiste ☐ HR 44 Lt45
Gradiste ☐ RO 44 Md45
Gradiška ☐ BIH 35 Ls45
Grado ☐ E 26 Kp47
Grado ☐ I 35 Lo45
Gradojević ☐ SCG 44 Ma46
Gradski bedemi ☒ MK 44 Mb48
Grafenau ☐ D 33 Ln42
Grafenhainichen ☐ D 32 Ln39
Gräfenthal ☐ D 33 Lm41
Gräfjell ▲ N 30 Lk30
Grafton ☐ AUS (NSW) 109 Sg60
Grafton ☐ USA (ND) 172 Fb21
Grafton ☐ USA (WV) 177 Ga26
Graham ☐ USA (TX) 174 Fa29
Graham Island ▲ CDN 166 Dd19
Graham Lake ☐ G
Grahamstad ☐ ZA 155 Md62
Grahamstown ☐ ZA 155 Md62
Graiguenamanagh ☐ IRL 19 Ko38
Grain Coast ☐ LB 136 Ke43
Grainfield ☐ USA (KS) 174 Ek26
Grainton ☐ USA (NE) 174 Ek25
Grajagan ☐ RI 95 Qh50
Grajaú ☐ BR (MA) 200 Hg48
Grajewo ☐ PL 41 Mc37
Grama ☐ BR (MG) 202 He56
Gramada ☐ BR (RS) 204 He60
Grammchele ☐ I 37 Lp53
Gramalote ☐ CO 192 Gd42
Grammichele ☐ I 37 Lp53
Gramphu ☐ IND (HPH) 81 Oj29
Grampian ☐ USA (PA) 177 Ga25
Grampianfjella ▲ N 16 Lf06
Grampian Mountains ▲ GB 20 Kp34
Grampians N.P. ☒ ☐ AUS 110 Sb64
Gramsh ☐ AL 46 Ma50
Gramzow ☐ D 32 Lo38
Gran ☐ N 30 Ll30
Granada ☐ CO (COR) 192 Gc43
Granada ☐ E 27 Kr53
Granada ☐ NIC 184 Fh40
Granada ☐ USA 173 Gb22
Granada ☒ E 27 Kr53
Granadilla de Abona ☐ E 124 Kc32
Granalanga ☐ S 31 Lo31
Granby ☐ CDN (QC) 177 Ge23
Granby ☐ USA (CO) 171 Eh25

Granard ☐ IRL 19 Kn37
Granites Mine, The ☒ AUS (NT) 103 Rf56
Granitis ☐ GR 45 Md49
Granja ☐ BR (CE) 201 Hk48
Granjon ☐ SME 194 Hc44
Granbury ☐ USA (TX) 174 Fb29
Gränna ☐ S 31 Lp32
Grannas ☐ S 16 Lt13
Granollers ☐ E 29 Lc49
Gran Pajaten ☒ PE 196 Gb46
Gran Pajonal ☒ PE 197 Gc51
Gran Paradiso ▲ I 34 Lh45
Gran Paradiso, P.N. del ☒ I 34 Lh45
Gran Pilastro = Hochfeiler ▲ A/I 34 Lm44
Gran Quivira ☒ USA (NM) 171 Eg28
Gran Sasso d'Italia ▲ I 35 Lo48
Gran Sasso e Monti della Laga, P.N. del ☒ I 35 Lo48
Grantham ☐ GB 21 Ku38
Grant-Kohrs Ranch N.H.S. ☒ USA 169 Ed22
Grants ☐ USA (NM) 171 Eg28
Grants Pass ☐ USA (OR) 168 Dj24
Granville ☐ AUS (QLD) 109 Sc59
Granville ☐ F 22 Ks42
Granville ☐ USA (NY) 177 Gd24
Grão Mogol ☐ BR (MG) 203 Hj54
Grão-Pará ☐ BR (SC) 204 He60
Grasse ☐ F 25 Lg47
Grass Patch ☐ AUS (WA) 104 Ra62
Grass Range ☐ USA (MT) 169 Ef22
Grass Valley ☐ USA (CA) 170 Dk26
Grassy ☐ AUS (TAS) 111 Sc66
Grassy Butte ☐ USA (ND) 169 Ej22
Grassy Island N.H.S. ☒ CDN 176 Gj22
Grästorp ☐ S 30 Ln32
Grates Cove ☐ CDN (NF) 177 Hd21
Gratwein ☐ A 35 Lp43
Graulhet ☐ F 24 Lb47
Graus ☐ E 28 La48
Gravatá ☐ BR (PE) 201 Jc49
Gravelbourg ☐ CDN (SK) 172 Eh21
Gravelines ☐ F 23 Lc40
Gravelotte ☐ ZA 152 Mf57
Gravesend ☐ GB 21 La39
Graviá ☐ GR 46 Mc52
Gravina di Puglia ☐ I 37 Lr49
Gravina Island ▲ USA 166 Dd18
Gravity ☐ USA (NA)
Gravina Junction ☐ USA (CA)
Gravures rupestres (Aozou) ☒ TCH 133 Lj35
Gravures rupestres (Bambari) ☒ RCA 140 Ma43
Gravures rupestres de Dabous ☒ RN 132 Ld37
Gravures rupestres de Gonoa ☒ TCH 133 Lj35
Gravures rupestres de Laghouat ☒ DZ 126 Lb29
Gravures rupestres de Mertoutek ☒ DZ 132 Lc33
Gravures rupestres (Lengo) ☒ RCA 140 Mb43
Gravures rupestres (Mapé) ☒ RCA 140 Mb43
Gravures rupestres (Nzako) ☒ RCA 140 Mb43
Gravures rupestres (Oued Mengao) ☒ BF 137 Kk39
Gravures rupestres (Pobé Ouani) ☒ DZ 126 Le32
Gravures rupestres (Taghit) ☒ DZ 125 Kj30
Gravures rupestres (Zouar) ☒ TCH 133 Lj35
Gray ☐ F 25 Lf43
Gray ☐ USA (GA) 178 Fj29
Grayling ☐ USA (AK) 165 Ck12
Grayling ☐ USA (MI) 173 Fh24
Grayling Fork ☐ USA/CDN (AK/YT) 165 Ck12
Grays ☐ GB 21 La39
Grayville ☐ USA (IL) 175 Ff27
Great Artesian Basin ▲ AUS 100 Sa53
Great Astrolabe Reef ☒ FJI 119 Tk55
Great Australian Bight ☐ AUS 100 Ra13
Great Ayton ☐ GB 21 Kt36
Great Bahama Bank ☐ BS 179 Ga33
Great Barrier Island ▲ NZ 112 Th64
Great Barrier Reef ☒ AUS 100 Sa11
Great Barrier Reef Marine Park ☒ AUS 107 Sc52
Great Barrington ☐ USA (MA) 177 Gd24
Great Basalt Wall N.P. ☒ AUS 107 Sc54
Great Basin N.P. ☒ USA 171 Ec26
Great Bear Lake ☐ CDN 162 Dd05
Great Belt ☐ DK 30 Ll35
Great Bend ☐ USA (KS) 174 Fa26
Great Bitter Lake ☐ ET 129 Mg30
Great Britain ▲ GB 14 La04
Great Channel ☐ IND 88 Pf42
Great Coco Island ▲ MYA
Great Dismal Swamp N.W.R. ☒ USA 178 Gb27
Great Divide Basin ▲ USA 171 Ef25
Great Dividing Range ▲ AUS 100 Sa11
Great Eastern Erg ☐ DZ 126 Lc30
Great Eastern Highway ⛖ AUS 104 Qj61

Greater Hinggan Range ▲ CHN 52 Qb05
Greater Sunda Islands ▲ RI 52 Qa10
Great Exhibition Bay ☐ NZ 112 Tg63
Great Exuma Island ▲ BS 179 Gb34
Great Falls ☐ USA (MT) 169 Ee22
Great Falls ☐ USA (SC) 178 Fk28
Great Fish River Reserves ☒ ZA 155 Md62
Great Malvern ☐ GB 21 Ks39
Great Guana Cay ▲ BS 179 Gb32
Great Harbour Cay ▲ BS 179 Ga32
Great Himalayan N.P. ☒ IND 81 Oj29
Great Inagua Island ▲ BS 186 Gd35
Great Isaac ☒ BS 179 Ga32
Great Karoo ▲ ZA 154 Ma62
Great Keppel Island ▲ AUS 109 Sf57
Great Limpopo Transfrontier Park ☒ ZW/ZA/MOC 152 Mf57
Great Mercury Island ▲ NZ 112 Th64
Great Mosque ☒ CHN 72 Qf25
Great Nicobar Island ▲ IND 88 Pg42
Great North East Channel ☐ AUS 107 Sb51
Great Northern Highway ⛖ AUS 102 Qk57
Great Northern Highway ⛖ AUS 103 Rd54
Great Ocean Road ⛖ AUS
Great Ormes Head ▲ GB 21 Kr37
Great Oyster Bay ☐ AUS 111 Se67
Great Palm Island ▲ AUS (QLD) 107 Sd55
Great Papuan Plateau ▲ PNG 115 Sb49
Great Pedro Bluff ▲ JA 186 Gb37
Great Plain of the Koukdjuak ▲ CDN 163 Gb05
Great Plains ☐ CDN/USA 160 Ea04
Great Rift Valley ▲ USA 122 Ma10
Great Rift Valley ▲ EAT 142 Mh10
Great Ruaha ☐ EAT 147 Mj49
Great Salt Lake ☐ USA 171 Ed25
Great Salt Lake Desert ▲ USA 171 Ed25
Great Sand Dunes N.P. ☒ USA 171 Eh27
Great Sand Hills ▲ CDN 169 Ef20
Great Sandy Desert ▲ AUS 100 Ra12
Great Sandy Desert ▲ USA
Great Sandy N.P. ☒ AUS 109 Sg58
Great Sea Reef ☒ FJI 119 Tk54
Great Sea Reef ☒ FJI 119 Tk54
Great Slave Lake ☐ CDN
Great Smoky Mts. N.P. ☒ USA 178 Fj28
Great Smoky Mts. Railroad ⛖ USA 178 Fj28
Great Tiras ▲ NAM 154 Lj59
Great Valley ▲ USA 154 Lf
Great Victoria Desert ▲ AUS 100 Ra13
Great Victoria Desert Nature Reserve ☒ AUS 106 Re60
Great Wall ☒ ANT 6 Ha30
Great Western Erg ☐ DZ
Great Western Tiers ▲ AUS (TAS) 111 Sd66
Great White Heron N.W.R. ☒ USA 179 Fk33
Great Yarmouth ☐ GB 21 Lb38
Great Zab ☐ IRQ 57 Nb28
Great Zimbabwe National Monument ☒ ZW 152 Mf56
Grebbestad ☐ S 30 Lm32
Greboċin ☐ PL 40 Ls37
Grebów ☐ PL 41 Mb40
Greci ☐ RO 45 Mh45
Greece ☐ 15 Ma06
Greelandia ▲ 15
Greeley ☐ USA (CO) 171 Ek25
Greeley ☐ USA (NY) 173 Fg23
Greely ☐ USA (NE) 172 Fa25
Green ☐ USA 171 Ee26
Greenbush ☐ USA (MN) 172 Fb21
Green Cape Lighthouse ☒ AUS 111 Se64
Green Cay ▲ BS 179 Gb33
Green Cove Springs ☐ USA (FL) 178 Fk31
Greene ☐ USA (NY) 177 Gc24
Greenfield ☐ USA (CA) 170 Dk27
Greenfield ☐ USA (IA) 175 Fd25
Greenfield ☐ USA (IN) 175 Fh26
Greenfield ☐ USA (MO) 174 Fd27
Greenfield ☐ USA (OH) 175 Fj26
Green Head ☐ AUS (WA) 104 Qh60
Greenhill Island ▲ AUS 106 Qf51
Greenland ▲ DK 163 Hd03
Greenland ☐ DK 14 Kb02
Greenland Sea ☐ 14 Kb06
Greenlaw ☐ GB 20 Ks35
Green Mts. ▲ USA 177 Gd24
Greenock ☐ GB 20 Kq35
Greenodd ☐ GB 21 Kr36
Greenough ☐ AUS (WA) 104 Qh60
Green Point ☐ ZA 155 Mf61
Green River ☐ PNG 115 Sa47
Green River ☐ USA (UT) 171 Ee26
Green River ☐ USA (WY) 171 Ef25
Green River Basin ▲ USA 171 Ef24
Greensboro ☐ USA (AL) 175 Fg29
Greensboro ☐ USA (NC) 178 Ga27
Green Turtle Cay ▲ BS 179 Gb33
Greenvale ☐ AUS (QLD) 107 Sc55

Greenview – Hajjah

Greenview USA (CA) 168 Dj25
Greenville CDN (BC) 166 Df18
Greenville LB 136 Kf43
Greenville USA (AL) 175 Fg30
Greenville USA (GA) 175 Fh29
Greenville USA (KY) 175 Fg27
Greenville USA (MA) 176 Gf23
Greenville USA (MI) 173 Fh24
Greenville USA (MO) 175 Fe27
Greenville USA (MS) 175 Fe29
Greenville USA (NC) 178 Gb28
Greenville USA (OH) 173 Fh25
Greenville USA (PA) 173 Fk25
Greenville USA (SC) 178 Fj28
Greenville USA (TX) 174 Fb29
Greenwater USA (WA) 168 Dk22
Greenwater Lake Prov. Park CDN 169 Ej19
Greenwich GB 21 La39
Greenwood AUS (WA) 104 Qj59
Greenwood CDN (BC) 168 Ea21
Greenwood USA (AR) 174 Fc28
Greenwood USA (IN) 175 Fg26
Greenwood USA (MS) 175 Fe29
Greenwood USA (SC) 178 Fj28
Greer USA (ID) 168 Eb22
Greer USA (SC) 178 Fj28
Greetsiel D 32 Lh37
Gregbeu CI 137 Kg42
Gregory USA (SD) 172 Fa24
Gregory Downs AUS (QLD) 106 Rk55
Gregory N.P. AUS 106 Rf53
Gregory N.P. AUS 106 Rf54
Gregory Range AUS (QLD) 107 Sb55
Gregory Range AUS 102 Ra56
Gregory Springs AUS (QLD) 107 Sc55
Greifenburg A 35 Lo44
Greifswald D 32 Lo36
Greifswalder Bodden D 32 Lo36
Grein A 42 Lp42
Greiz D 33 Ln40
Gremiha RUS 54 Md05
Gremjač'e RUS 48 Mk20
Grenaa DK 30 Ll34
Grenada CO 192 Gc41
Grenada USA (MS) 175 Ff29
Grenada WG 187 Gk40
Grenada 187 Gk39
Grenade F 24 Lb47
Grenade-sur-l'Adour F 24 Ku47
Grenadines WV 187 Gk39
Grenchen CH 34 Lh43
Grendill IS 18 Ke26
Grenen DK 30 Ll33
Grenfell AUS (NSW) 111 Se62
Grenfell CDN (SK) 169 Ej20
Grenfell House CDN 177 Hc20
Grenivík IS 18 Kb25
Grenoble F 25 Lf45
Grenville WG 187 Gk39
Gresford AUS (NSW) 111 Sf62
Gresham USA (OR) 168 Dj23
Gresham USA (SC) 178 Ga29
Gresham ZW 152 Mf54
Gresik RI 95 Qg49
Gressåmoen n.p. N 16 Lg13
Gressoney-la-Trinité I 34 Lh45
Gretna Green GB 20 Kr36
Greve in Chianti I 34 Lm47
Greven D 32 Lh38
Grevená GR 46 Mb50
Grevenbroich D 32 Lg39
Grevenmacher L 23 Lg41
Grevesmühlen D 32 Lm37
Greve Strand DK 30 Ln35
Grevie S 30 Ln34
Greybull USA (WY) 169 Ef23
Grey Cairns GB 20 Kr32
Grey Hunter Peak CDN 165 Dc14
Greylingstad ZA 155 Me59
Grey Mare's Tail GB 20 Kr35
Greymouth NZ 113 Tf67
Grey Range AUS 108 Sb60
Grey Range AUS 109 Sc59
Grey River CDN (NF) 177 Hb22
Greystone ZW 152 Me56
Greystones IRL 19 Ko37
Greyton ZA 154 Lk63
Greytown ZA 155 Mf60
Grgurnica MK 44 Mb49
Grianan of Aileach IRL 19 Kn35
Gribanovskij RUS 48 Na20
Gribbelt Island CDN 166 Df19
Gridley USA (CA) 170 Dk26
Griekwastad ZA 154 Mb60
Grieskirchen A 42 Lo42
Griffin CDN (SK) 169 Ej21
Griffin USA (GA) 175 Fh29
Griffin Point USA (AK) 165 Cj10
Griffith AUS (NSW) 111 Sd63
Grigor'evskoe RUS 48 Nb17
Grigoriopol MD 49 Me22
Grik MAL 92 Qa43
Grillby S 31 Ls31
Grillon, Mount USA 166 Db16
Grimari RCA 140 Ma43
Grimma D 32 Ln39
Grimmen D 32 Lo36
Grimsby GB 21 Ku37
Grimsey IS 18 Kb24
Grímsey IS 18 Kb24
Grimshaw CDN ( ) 167 Eb17
Grímsstaðir IS 18 Kd25
Grimstad N 30 Lj32
Grimsvötn IS 18 Kc26
Grindavík IS 18 Js27
Grindelwald CH 34 Lj44
Grindsted DK 30 Lj35
Grinkiškis LT 39 Md35
Grinnell USA (IA) 172 Fd25
Grinnel Peninsula CDN 163 Fb03
Grintavec SLO 42 Lp44
Gripsholm S 31 Ls31
Griquatown ZA 154 Mb60
Griquet CDN 177 Hc20
Grise Fiord CDN 163 Fc03
Griškabūdis LT 39 Md36
Grisolles F 24 Lb47
Grisslehamn S 31 Lt30
Grissom Air Mus. USA 173 Fg25
Grivenskaja RUS 49 Mk23
Grivița RO 45 Mh46
Grizzly Bear Mountain CDN 167 Dk13
Grjady RUS 48 Mf16
Grjazi RUS 48 Mk19
Grmeč BIH 35 Lr46
Groaíras BR (CE) 201 Hk47
Groais Island CDN 177 Hc20
Grobiņa LV 39 Mb34
Groblersdal ZA 155 Me58
Groblershoop ZA 154 Mb60
Grobniza BG 45 Mf48
Grocka SCG 44 Ma46
Gródek PL 41 Md37
Gröditz D 32 Lo39
Gródki PL 41 Ma37
Gródki PL 41 Mc40
Grodków PL 40 Ls40
Grodziczno PL 41 Lu37
Grodzisk Mazowiecki PL 41 Ma38
Grodzisk Wielkopolski PL 40 Lr38
Groeninge-Museum B 23 Ld39
Groenriviersmond ZA 154 Lj61
Groesbeek ZA 152 Me57
Groix F 22 Kr43
Groix F 22 Kr43
Grójec PL 41 Ma39
Grombalia TN 126 Lf27
Grömitz D 32 Ll36
Gromnik PL 41 Ma41
Gröna Lund S 31 Ls31
Gronau D 32 Lh38
Grong N 16 Lg13
Grong Grong AUS (NSW) 111 Sd63
Gröningen D 32 Lm39
Groningen NL 23 Lg37
Groningen SME 194 Hc43
Groninger Museum NL 23 Lg37
Gronlid CDN (SK) 169 Eh19
Grønligrotta N 16 Lh12
Grönskåra S 31 Lq33
Grootberg NAM 150 Lh55
Grootdrink ZA 154 Ma60
Groote Eylandt AUS 106 Rj53
Groote Eylandt A.L. AUS 106 Rj53
Grootfontein NAM 150 Lk55
Groot Henar SME 194 Hb43
Groot Jongensfontein ZA 154 Ma63
Groot Karasberge NAM 154 Lk59
Grootkraal ZA 154 Mb62
Groot Marico ZA 155 Md58
Grootrivierhoogte ZA 154 Mb62
Groot Waterberg NAM 150 Lj55
Grootwinterhoekberge ZA 155 Mc62
Groot Winterhoek Wilderness Area ZA 154 Lk62
Gropeni RO 45 Mh45
Gros Morne CDN 177 Hb21
GrosMorne RH 186 Gd36
Gros Morne N. P. CDN 177 Hb21
Gross Barmen NAM 150 Lj57
Gross Barmen Hot Springs NAM 150 Lj57
Großenhain D 32 Lo39
Großenkneten D 32 Lj38
Großer Arber D 33 Lo41
Großer Beerberg D 32 Ll40
Großer Feldberg D 33 Lj40
Großer Garten D 32 Lk38
Großer Inselsberg D 32 Ll40
Großer Peilstein A 42 Lq42
Großer Plöner See D 32 Ll36
Großer Pyhrgas A 35 Lp43
Großer Rachel D 33 Lo42
Grosses AUS (SA) 108 Rh61
Große Sandspitze A 35 Ln44
Grosseto I 34 Lm47
Grosseto Prugna F 36 Lj49
Groß-Gerau D 33 Lj41
Groß Gerungs A 42 Lp42
Großglockner A 35 Ln43
Großglockner Straße A 35 Ln43
Grossos BR (RN) 201 Jb48
Großpetersdorf A 35 Lr43
Großräschen D 32 Lo39
Gross Ums NAM 154 Lk57
Großvenediger A 34 Ln43
Grosuplje SLO 42 Lp45
Groton USA (SD) 172 Fa23
Grotta Azzurra I 37 Lp50
Grotta del Genovese I 36 Ln52
Grotta di Nettuno I 36 Lj50
Grotta di San Michele I 36 Lk50
Grottáglie I 37 Ls50
Grottaminarda I 37 Lq49
Grottammare I 35 Lo47
Grotte de Clamouse F 25 Ld47
Grotte de Grand-Roc F 24 La46
Grotte de Lascaux F 24 Lb45
Grotte de Niaux F 24 Lb48
Grotte de Pech Merle F 24 Lb46
Grotte des Demoiselles F 25 Ld47
Grotte de Villars F 24 La45
Grotte di Castellana I 37 Ls50
Grotte di Catullo I 34 Ll45
Grotte di Frasassi I 35 Ln47
Grotte du Mas-d'Azil F 24 Lb47
Grottes (Bangbali) RCA 140 Ma41
Grottes d'Azé F 25 Le44
Grottes de Beni-Add DZ 125 Kk28
Grottes de Bétharram F 24 Ku47
Grottes de Bongolo G 148 Lf47
Grottes de Dimba et Ngovo RDC 148 Lh48
Grottes de Matupi RDC 141 Me45
Grottes de Missirikoro RMM 137 Kh40
Grottes de Remouchamps B 23 Lf40
Grottes de Yambala RCA 140 Ma42
Grottes du Galo Boukoy RCA 140 Lh43
Grotto of the Redemption USA 172 Fc24
Grouard CDN (AB) 167 Eb18
Groumania CI 137 Kj42
Groundbirch CDN (BC) 167 Dk18
Groupe d'Aldabra SY 156 Nd50
Grov N 16 Lj11
Grove USA (OK) 174 Fc27
Grove City USA (OH) 173 Fj26
Grove City USA (PA) 173 Fk25
Grove Hill USA (AL) 175 Fg30
Grove Mountains 7 Oc32
Groveton USA (NH) 177 Ge23
Groveton USA (TX) 174 Fc30
Grožnjan HR 35 Lo45
Groznyj RUS (CHE) 57 Nc24
Grube GH 137 Kk41
Grube Messel D 33 Lj41
Grubišno Polje HR 35 Ls45
Grudusk PL 41 Ma37
Grudziądz PL 40 Lt37
Grumento Nova I 37 Lq50
Grums S 30 Lo31
Grünau NAM 154 Lk59
Grünberg D 32 Lj40
Grundarfjörður IS 18 Jr26
Grundkallen 31 Lt30
Grundy USA (VA) 178 Fj27
Grundy Center USA (IA) 172 Fd24
Grünstadt D 33 Lj41
Grunwald PL 41 Ma37
Grupe GH 137 Kj41
Gruppo di Sella I 34 Lm44
Gruszka PL 41 Ma39
Gruta de Intihuasi RA 208 Gh62
Gruta de la Paz EC 196 Gb45
Gruta de las Maravillas E 27 Ko53
Gruta de los Helechos ROU 204 Hb61
Gruta del Palacio ROU 204 Hb62
Gruta de Ubajara BR 201 Hk47
Gruta do Lago Azul BR 202 Hb56
Grutas de Bustamante MEX 181 Ek32
Grutas de García MEX 181 Ek33
Grutas de Lanquin GCA 184 Ff38
Grutas de Loltún MEX 183 Ff35
Grutas de Xtacumbilxunán MEX 183 Fe36
Grutas dos Brejões BR (BA) 201 Hk51
Grutas Lázaro Cárdenas MEX 183 Fc37
Gruver USA (TX) 174 Ek27
Gruža SCG 44 Ma47
Gruzdžiai LT 39 Md34
Grybów PL 41 Ma41
Grycksbro S 31 Lq30
Gryfice PL 40 Lq37
Gryfino PL 40 Lp37
Gryfów Śląski PL 40 Lq39
Grykë AL 46 Lu50
Gryllefjord N 16 Lj11
Gryt S 31 Lr32
Grythyttan S 31 Lp31
Gstaad CH 34 Lh44
Gua EAT 146 Mg49
Guabalá PA 185 Fk41
Guabijú BR (RS) 204 Hc61
Guabiju BR (RS) 204 He60
Guabún RCH 208 Gd66
Guacamayas CO 192 Gc44
Guacamayas CO 192 Ge43
Guacara YV 193 Gg40
Guacautey YV 193 Gk43
Guachara YV 193 Gf42
Gua Charah MAL 92 Qb43
Guachimetas de Arriba MEX (DGO) 180 Eg33
Guachipas RA (SA) 207 Gh58
Guachochi MEX (CHH) 180 Eg32
Guachucal CO 192 Gb45
Guaco CO 192 Ge44
Guaçu BR (MS) 202 Hc57
Guaçuí BR (ES) 203 Hk56
Guadalajara E 27 Kr50
Guadalajara MEX (JLC) 182 Ej35
Guadalcanal E 27 Kp52
Guadalcanal SOL 117 Sk50
Guadalest E 29 Ku52
Guadalupe BR (PI) 201 Hj49
Guadalupe MEX (NL) 181 Ek33
Guadalupe MEX (ZCT) 182 Ej34
Guadalupe PE 196 Ga49
Guadalupe USA (CA) 170 Dk28
Guadalupe de Bagues MEX (CHH) 181 Eh32
Guadalupe Mts. N.P. USA 171 Eh30
Guadalupe y Calvo MEX (CHH) 180 Eg32
Guadeloupe F 187 Gk37
Guadeloupe Passage 187 Gk37
Guadelupe de Bravo MEX (CHH) 180 Eg30
Guadelupe del Carnicero MEX (SLP) 182 Ek34
Guadelupe de los Reyes MEX (SL) 180 Eg33
Guadelupe Victoria MEX (BC) 180 Ec29
Guadelupe Victoria MEX (DGO) 181 Eh33
Guadix E 27 Kr53
Guaduas CO 192 Gc43
Guafera Ye Terara Senselet ETH 142 Mh42
Guahaja, T.I. BR 198 Gg49
Guaíba BR (RS) 204 He61
Guaimaca HN 184 Fg38
Guáimaro C 179 Gb35
Guaimbe, T.I. BR 202 Hc57
Guaina YV 193 Gj43
Guaíra BR (PR) 204 Hc58
Guaíra BR (SP) 202 Hf56
Guajará BR (AM) 196 Gd49
Guajará-Mirim BR (RO) 198 Gh51
Guajirú BR (CE) 201 Ja47
Gualán GCA 184 Ff38
Gualaquiza EC 196 Ga47
Gualdo Tadino I 34 Ln47
Guale EC 196 Fk46
Gualeguay RA (ER) 204 Ha62
Gualeguaychú RA (ER) 204 Ha62
Gualjaina RA (CB) 208 Ge67
Guallatiri RCH 206 Gf55
Guallatiri, Volcán RCH 206 Gf55
Gualmatán CO 192 Gb45
Guam USA 101 Sa08
Guama YV 193 Gf40
Guamal CO 192 Gc41
Guamal San Martin CO 192 Gd44
Gua Mampu RI 96 Ra48
Guamini RA (BA) 209 Gj64
Guamo CO 192 Gc43
Guamote EC 196 Ga46
Guamúchil MEX (SL) 180 Ef33
Gua Musang MAL 92 Qb43
Gu'an CHN (HBI) 73 Qj26
Guanabo C 179 Fj34
Guanacaste N.P. BH 184 Ff37
Guanacaste, P.N. CR 184 Fh40
Guanacevi MEX (DGO) 180 Eh33
Guanaco Muerto RA (CD) 207 Gh61
Guanahani Island = San Salvador BS 186 Gc33
Guanaja HN 184 Fh37
Guanajay C 179 Fj34
Guanajuato MEX (GJT) 182 Ek35
Guanajuato MEX 182 Ek35
Guanajuña YV 193 Gj43
Guanambi BR (BA) 203 Hj53
Guanare YV 193 Gf41
Guanarito YV 193 Gf41
Guanay BOL 206 Gg53
Guanay, Cerro YV 193 Gg43
Guancheng CHN (ZJG) 78 Ra30
Guandacaya BOL 207 Gh57
Guandacol RA (LR) 207 Gf60
Guandiping CHN (HUN) 74 Qf31
Guandong CHN 75 Qg34
Guang'an CHN (SCH) 74 Qd30
Guangang CHN (AHU) 75 Qj31
Guangba CHN (SCH) 72 Qd29
Guangchang CHN (JGX) 75 Qj32
Guangde CHN (AHU) 78 Qk30
Guangdong CHN 75 Qg34
Guangfenghai CHN (GZH) 87 Qc32
Guanghai CHN (GDG) 75 Qg35
Guangmao Shan CHN 87 Qa32
Guangnan CHN (YUN) 87 Qc33
Guangning CHN (GDG) 74 Qg34
Guangrao CHN (SDG) 73 Qk27
Guangshan CHN (HNN) 73 Qh30
Guangsheng Si CHN 72 Qf27
Guangshui CHN (HUB) 73 Qh30
Guangshuishi CHN (HUB) 73 Qg30
Guangshun CHN (GZH) 74 Qd32
Guangtong CHN (YUN) 87 Qa33
Guangxi Zhuangzu Zizhiqu CHN 74 Qd33
Guangyuan CHN (SCH) 72 Qc29
Guangze CHN (FJN) 75 Qj32
Guangzhou CHN 75 Qg34
Guanhães BR (MG) 203 Hj55
Guaní CO 192 Gd44
Guaniamo YV 193 Gg42
Guanica USA (PR) 187 Gg37
Guanling CHN (GZH) 87 Qc33
Guanoco YV 193 Gj40
Guanqiao CHN (NHZ) 72 Qc27
Guanta RCH 207 Ge60
Guantánamo C 186 Gc35
Guantanamo Bay US Naval Base USA 186 Gc36
Guantao CHN (HBI) 73 Qh27
Guanyun CHN (JGS) 78 Qk28
Guapé BR (MG) 203 Hh56
Guapi CO 192 Gb44
Guapiara BR (SP) 205 Hf58
Guápiles CR 185 Fj40
Guaporé BOL 206 Gk52
Guaporé BR (RS) 204 He60
Guaporé BR 206 Ha53
Guaporé BR 204 Hd60
Guaqui BOL 206 Gf54
Guará BR (SP) 203 Hg56
Guara E 28 Ku48
Guaraci BR (SP) 202 Hf56
Guaraciaba BR (SC) 204 Hd59
Guaraciaba do Norte BR (CE) 201 Hk48
Guaraí BR (TO) 200 Hf50
Guaramacal, P.N. YV 192 Ge41
Guarambaré PY 204 Hb58
Guaramirim BR (SC) 205 Hf59
Guaramuri GUY 194 Ha42
Guaranda EC 196 Ga46
Guaraní BOL 206 Gj56
Guaraniaçu BR (PR) 204 Hd58
Guarantã BR (SP) 202 Hf56
Guarantã do Norte BR (MT) 199 Hc50
Guarapari BR (ES) 203 Hk56
Guarapuava BR (MG) 203 Hg54
Guarapuava BR (PR) 204 He58
Guaraqueçaba BR (PR) 205 Hf58
Guararapes BR (SP) 202 He56
Guarariba BR (PB) 201 Jc49
Guaratinga BR (BA) 203 Ja54
Guaratingueta BR (SP) 205 Hh57
Guaratuba BR (PR) 205 Hf58
Guarayos BOL 206 Gf52
Guarda P 26 Kn50
Guardalavaca C 186 Gc35
Guardamar del Segura E 29 Ku52
Guarda-Mor BR (MG) 203 Hg54
Guardiagrele I 37 Lp48
Guardia Mitre RA (RN) 209 Gj66
Guardian Seamounts 184 Fg41
Guardo E 26 Kq48
Guareña E 27 Ko52
Guarento YV 193 Gj42
Guari PNG 115 Sd50
Guariba BR (SP) 202 Hf56
Guarita, T.I. BR 204 Hd59
Guarujá BR (SP) 205 Hg58
Guarulhos BR (SP) 205 Hg57
Guasave MEX (SL) 180 Ef33
Guasca CO 192 Gd43
Guasdualito YV 192 Ge42
Guasipati YV 193 Gk42
Guasizaco MEX (CHH) 180 Ef32
Guasopa PNG 116 Sg50
Guastalla I 34 Ll46
Guasuti, T.I. BR 202 Hc57
Guatacondo RCH 206 Gf56
Guataqui CO 192 Gc43
Guatemala 184 Fe38
Guatemala Basin 160 Fa08
Guatimape MEX (DGO) 181 Eh33
Guatire YV 193 Gg40
Guatopo, P.N. YV 193 Gg40
Guatraché RA (LP) 209 Gj64
Guaviare CO 193 Gf44
Guaxupé BR (MG) 203 Hg56
Guayabal C 179 Gb35
Guayabones YV 192 Ge41
Guayaguayaré TT 187 Gk40
Guayama USA (PR) 187 Gg37
Guayaquil EC 196 Ga47
Guayaquil MEX (BC) 180 Ec31
Guayaramerín BOL 198 Gh51
Guayllabamba EC 196 Ga46
Guaymas MEX (SO) 180 Ee32
Guayubin DOM 186 Ge36
Guayzimi EC 196 Ga48
Guba ETH 142 Mh40
Guba RDC 146 Md51
Guban SP 143 Nb40
Gubat RP 90 Rc39
Gubatsaa Hills RB 151 Mc55
Gúbbio I 34 Ln47
Guben D 32 Lp39
Gubi WAN 138 Le40
Gubin PL 40 Lp39
Gubio WAN 139 Lg39
Gubkin RUS 48 Mj20
Gubra IND (MPH) 83 Ok34
Guča SCG 44 Ma47
Gucheng CHN (HUB) 72 Qf29
Gucheng CHN (SAX) 72 Qf28
Guci Hot Water Spring RI 95 Qe49
Gudalur IND (TNU) 84 Oj40
Gudauta GE 57 Na24
Gudbrandsdalen N 17 Le15
Guder ETH 142 Mj41
Guder Falls ETH 142 Mj41
Gudermes RUS (CHE) 57 Nd24
Guderup DK 30 Lk36
Gudgaon IND (MPH) 82 Oj35
Gudha IND (RJT) 80 Oj32
Gudhjem DK 31 Lp35
Gudi WAN 138 Le41
Gudivada IND (APH) 83 Pa37
Gudiyattam IND (TNU) 85 Ok39
Gudong CHN (YUN) 87 Pk33
Gudur IND (APH) 85 Ok38
Guéassou RG 136 Kf41
Guebwiller F 25 Lh43
Guechémé RN 132 Lb39
Guéckédou RG 136 Ke41
Guelb El Makhsar RIM 131 Kf36
Guelb El Rhein RIM 130 Kd34
Guelb er Richât RIM 130 Ke35
Guelb Makhrouga RIM 131 Kf36
Guelb Ragoum RIM 131 Kf36
Guelb Zednes RIM 130 Ke33
Guéléhé TCH 140 Lk41
Guélengdeng TCH 139 Lh40
Guellala TN 126 Lf29
Guelltat Sidi Saad DZ 126 La28
Guelma DZ 126 Ld27
Guelmim MA 124 Ke31
Guelta d'Archei TCH 134 Ma37
Guémar DZ 126 Ld29
Guémené-Penfao F 22 Kt43
Guémené-sur-Scorff F 22 Kr42
Güémez MEX (TM) 182 Fa34
Guemour DZ 126 Lc32
Guènt Paté SN 130 Kc38
Guépaouo CI 137 Kh42
Güeppí PE 196 Gc46
Guer F 22 Ks43
Güer Aike RA (SC) 210 Gf71
Guérande F 22 Ks43
Guerara DZ 126 Lc29
Guercif MA 125 Kj28
Guéréda TCH 134 Mb38
Guerende LAR 128 Ma34
Guéret F 24 Lb44
Guerguarat DARS 130 Kb35
Guérin-Kouka TG 137 La41
Guermessa TN 126 Lf29
Guerneville USA (CA) 170 Dj26
Guernsey GB 22 Ks41
Guernsey USA (WY) 171 Eh24
Guérou RIM 130 Ke37
Guerrero MEX (CHH) 180 Eg31
Guerrero MEX (COH) 181 Ek31
Guerrero MEX 182 Ek36
Guerrero Negro MEX (BCS) 180 Ec32
Guerzim DZ 125 Kk31
Gueskérou RN 133 Lg39
Guéssabo CI 137 Kg42
Guésséyo CI 137 Kg42
Guessou South DY 138 Lb40
Gueugnon F 25 Le44
Guéyo CI 137 Kg43
Guézaoua RN 132 Le38
Guffertspitze A 34 Lm43
Gufudalur IS 18 Js25
Guge, Mount ETH 142 Mj42
Gugești RO 45 Mh45
Guglionesi I 37 Lp49
Guguang, Gunung RI 94 Qj44
Gugu, Mount ETH 142 Mk41
Gugurtli UZ 62 Ob25
Guhagar IND (MHT) 82 Og37
Guia Lopes da Laguna BR (MS) 202 Hb56
Guiana Basin 190 Ha08
Guiana Highlands 190 Gb09
Guiana Plateau 194 Hc41
Guiarote BOL 206 Gj55
Guibaré BF 137 Kk39
Guibéroua CI 137 Kg42
Guicán CO 192 Gd42
Guichi CHN (AHU) 78 Qj30
Guichón ROU 204 Hb62
Guidan-Roumji RN 132 Ld39
Guidari TCH 140 Lj41
Guider CAM 139 Lg41
Guidiguir RN 132 Le39
Guidiguis CAM 139 Lh40
Guidimaka RIM/RMM 130 Ke38
Guidimouni RN 132 Le39
Guiding CHN (GZH) 74 Qd32
Guidjiba CAM 139 Lg41
Guidong CHN (HUN) 75 Qg32
Guiembé CI 137 Kh41
Guiendana CI 137 Kh41
Guiengola MEX 183 Fc37
Guiffa RCA 140 Lk42
Guigang CHN (GZG) 74 Qe34
Guiglo CI 137 Kg42
Güigüe YV 193 Gg40
Guihua Temple CHN 69 Pk31
Guihuayuan CHN (SCH) 74 Qc30
Guihulñgan RP 90 Rb40
Guijuelo E 27 Kp50
Guilderton AUS (WA) 104 Qh61
Guildford GB 21 Ku39
Guilin CHN (GZG) 74 Qf33
Guillaumes F 25 Lg46
Guillestre F 25 Lg46
Guilmara DY 137 La40
Guilvinec F 22 Kq43
Guimarães BR (MA) 195 Hh47
Guimarães P 26 Km49
Guimaras Island RP 90 Rb40
Guimba RP 90 Ra38
Guimbalete MEX (COH) 181 Ej32
Guimiliau F 22 Kr42
Guinagourou DY 138 Lb41
Guinchos Cay BS 179 Ga34
Guindulman RP 90 Rc41
Guinea 123 Ka08
Guinea Basin 122 Kb10
Guinea-Bissau 123 Ka08
Güines C 179 Fj34
Guînes F 23 Lb40
Guingamp F 22 Kr42
Guinguineo SN 130 Kc38
Guipavas F 22 Kq42
Guiping CHN (GZG) 74 Qf34
Guir RMM 131 Kj36
Güira de Melena C 179 Fj34
Guiratinga BR (MT) 202 Hd54
Guiri CAM 139 Lh40
Güiria YV 193 Gj40
Guirwas SN 130 Kc38
Guisa C 179 Gb35
Guisborough GB 21 Kt36
Guiscard F 23 Ld41
Guise F 23 Ld41
Guishi Shuiku CHN 74 Qf33
Guissat RN 132 Le37
Guissèr MA 125 Kg29
Guissona E 29 Lb49
Guitiriz E 26 Kn47
Guitri CI 137 Kh43
Guiuan RP 90 Rc40
Guiyang CHN (GZH) 74 Qd32
Guiyang CHN (HUN) 75 Qg33
Gui Yuan Si CHN 75 Qh30
Guizhou CHN (HUB) 74 Qf30
Guizhou CHN 74 Qc32
Gujan-Mestras F 24 Kt46
Gujarat IND 82 Of34
Gujar Khan PK 65 Og29
Gujba WAN 139 Lf40
Gujiao CHN (SAX) 72 Qg27
Gujranwala PK 65 Oh29
Gujrat PK 65 Oh29
Gujri IND (MPH) 82 Oh34
Gukovo RUS 49 Mk21
Gulabgarh 81 Oj29
Gulagambone AUS (NSW) 109 Se61
Gulang CHN (GSU) 72 Qb27
Gulangyu CHN 75 Qk33
Gulbarga IND (KTK) 82 Oj37
Gulbarga Fort IND 82 Oj37
Gulbene LV 39 Mg33
Gul'ca KS 63 Og25
Guledagud IND (KTK) 82 Oh38
Gulf Islands National Seashore USA 175 Ff30
Gulf of Aden 52 Na08
Gulf of Alaska USA 162 Cc07
Gulf of Aqaba ET/KSA 58 Mh31
Gulf of Arab ET 129 Me30
Gulf of Bahrain KSA 59 Nf33
Gulf of Bone RI 96 Ra48
Gulf of Boothia CDN 163 Fc05
Gulf of Bothnia S/FIN 17 Lk15
Gulf of California MEX 180 Ed31
Gulf of Carpentaria AUS 106 Rk53
Gulf of Corinth GR 46 Mc52
Gulf of Darién PA/CO 185 Gb41
Gulf of Finland 38 Md31
Gulf of Gdansk PL 41 Ltu6
Gulf of Genoa I 34 Lj46
Gulf of Guinea 122 La09
Gulf of Hikma ET 128 Me30
Gulf of Kachchh IND 82 Oe34
Gulf of Khambhat IND 82 Og35
Gulf of Liaotung CHN 76 Ra25
Gulf of Lingayan RP 90 Ra37
Gulf of Maine USA 177 Gf24
Gulf of Mannar IND/CY 85 Ok41
Gulf of Martaban MYA 88 Pj38
Gulf of Masirah OM 61 Nk35
Gulf of Mexico 160 Fa07
Gulf of Oman 52 Nb07
Gulf of Panama PA 185 Ga42
Gulf of Papua PNG 115 Sc50
Gulf of Paria YV 193 Gj40
Gulf of Riga EST/LV 39 Md33
Gulf of Saint Lawrence CDN 176 Gj21
Gulf of Sallum ET 128 Mc30
Gulf of Salonica GR 46 Mc50
Gulf of Sirte LAR 127 Lj30
Gulf of Suez ET 129 Mg31
Gulf of Taranto I 37 Ls50
Gulf of Tehuantepec MEX 183 Fc38
Gulf of Thailand T 88 Qa40
Gulf of Tolo RI 96 Rb47
Gulf of Tomini RI 96 Ra46
Gulf of Tonkin VN/CHN 87 Qd36
Gulf of Valencia E 29 La51
Gulf of Venezuela YV 192 Ge40
Gulf of Venice I 35 Ln45
Gulfport USA (MS) 175 Ff30
Gulf Saint Vincent AUS 110 Rk63
Gulfstream Park USA (FL) 179 Fk33
Gulganj IND (MPH) 83 Ok33
Gulgong AUS (NSW) 111 Se62
Gulioni EAT 147 Mk49
Gulir RI 97 Rf48
Guliston UZ 63 Oe25
Guljanci BG 45 Me47
Gul Kach PK 65 Oe30
Gul'keviči RUS 49 Na23
Gullbrandstorp S 30 Ln34
Gullfoss IS 18 Ju26
Gull Lake CDN (SK) 169 Ef20
Gullspång S 31 Lp32
Güllü TR 47 Mk52
Güllü Dağları TR 57 Na25
Güllük TR 47 Mh53
Gulmarg IND 80 Oh28
Gülpınar TR 47 Mg51
Gulshat KZ 66 Oh22
Gulsvik N 30 Lk30
Gulu EAU 144 Mg44
Gulumba Gana WAN 139 Lh40
Gulwe EAT 147 Mj49
Guma = Pishan CHN (XUZ) 66 Ok27
Gumaca RP 90 Ra39
Gumare RB 151 Mb55
Gumba ANG 150 Lh51
Gumba RDC 140 Ma44
Gumbardo AUS (QLD) 109 Sc59
Gumbiro EAT 146 Mh51
Gumdag TM 62 Nh26
Gumel WAN 138 Le39
Gumgarhi NEP 81 Pb31
Gumi RI 91 Rd45
Gumiel de Hizán E 26 Kr49
Gumine PNG 115 Sc49
Gumla IND (JKD) 83 Pc34
Gumlu AUS (QLD) 107 Sd55
Gummersbach D 32 Lh39
Gummi WAN 138 Lc39
Gumsi WAN 132 Lf39
Gümüldür TR 47 Mh52
Gümüşçay TR 45 Mh50
Gümüşhane TR 57 Mk25
Gumu Uen SP 145 Nb45
Gumzai RI 114 Rh48
Guna IND (MPH) 82 Oj33
Guna Terare ETH 142 Mk40
Gunbad-e-Haruniyeh IR 62 Nk27
Gundabooka N.P. AUS (NSW) 109 Sc61
Gundardehi IND (CGH) 83 Pa35
Gundelfingen D 33 Ll42
Gundji RDC 140 Ma44
Gundulpet IND (KTK) 84 Oj40
Güney TR 47 Mj52
Güney TR 47 Mk52
Güney Doğu Toroslar TR 56 Mj26
Gunga ANG 150 Lk53
Gungadei AUS (NSW) 111 Se63
Gungi RDC 149 Lk49
Gungo ANG 150 Lh51
Gungu RDC 149 Lk48
Gungure MOC 147 Mk51
Guniujiang Z.B. CHN 75 Qj31
Gunlom A.L. AUS 106 Rg52
Gunn CDN (AB) 169 Ec19
Gunna SUD 141 Md42
Gunnaur IND (UPH) 81 Ok31
Gunnebo S 31 Lr33
Gunnedah AUS (NSW) 109 Sf61
Gunnerus Ridge 7 Mc32
Gunning AUS (NSW) 111 Se63
Gunnison USA (CO) 171 Eg26
Gunnison USA (UT) 171 Ee26
Gunnison, Mount USA 171 Eg26
Gunpowder AUS (QLD) 106 Rk55
Guns NAM 150 Lh57
Günsang CHN (TIB) 68 Pb30
Gunta WAN 138 Le40
Guntakal IND (APH) 84 Oj38
Guntersville USA (AL) 175 Fg28
Guntin de Pallares E 26 Kn48
Guntur IND (APH) 83 Pa37
Gununa AUS (QLD) 106 Rk54
Gunungagung RI 93 Qc48
Gunung Ambang Reserve RI 91 Rc45
Gunung Angemuk RI 114 Rk47
Gunung Antares RI 115 Sa48
Gunungapi RI 97 Rd49
Gunungapi RI 97 Rd49
Gunung Api RI 97 Re48
Gunung Argopuro RI 95 Qg49
Gunung Bakayan RI 94 Qj44
Gunung Balease RI 96 Ra47
Gunung Basakan RI 94 Qj44
Gunung Batubrok RI 94 Qh45
Gunung Batukau RI 95 Qh50
Gunung Besar RI 95 Qg48
Gunung Bromo RI 95 Qg49
Gunung Butak RI 95 Qg49
Gunung Cemaru RI 94 Qh45
Gunung Chamah MAL 92 Qa43
Gunung Cirema RI 95 Qe49
Gunung Daku RI 91 Ra45
Gunung Dempo RI 93 Qb47
Gunung Dom RI 114 Rj47
Gunung Gading N.P. MAL 94 Qe45
Gunung Gagau MAL 92 Qb43
Gunung Gambuta RI 91 Rb45
Gunung Gandadiwata RI 96 Qk47
Gunung Guguang RI 94 Qj44
Gunung Halimun RI 95 Qd49
Gunung Harden RI 94 Qh43
Gunung Irau RI 114 Rg46
Gunung Kambuno RI 96 Ra47
Gunung Katoposo RI 96 Ra46
Gunung Kemal RI 94 Qj45
Gunungkembang RI 93 Qb47
Gunung Kerihun RI 94 Qh45
Gunung Kerinci RI 93 Qa46
Gunung Kinabalu MAL 94 Qj42
Gunung Kujat RI 94 Qj44
Gunung Kwoka RI 114 Rg46
Gunung Lawit RI 94 Qg45
Gunung Lawu RI 95 Qf49
Gunung Leuser N.P. RI 92 Pj44
Gunung Liangmangari RI 95 Qg46
Gunung Liangpran RI 94 Qh45
Gunung Liman RI 95 Qf49
Gunung Loi RI 94 Qg45
Gunung Lompobatang RI 96 Ra48
Gunung Lumaku MAL 94 Qh43
Gunung Lumut RI 95 Qh46
Gunung Malabar RI 95 Qd49
Gunung Malea RI 93 Pk45
Gunung Malino RI 91 Ra45
Gunung Masurai RI 93 Qa47
Gunung Mata Bia TLS 97 Rd50
Gunung Mebo RI 114 Rg46
Gunungmegang RI 93 Qb48
Gunung Meja Reserve RI 114 Rg46
Gunung Mekongga RI 96 Ra47
Gunung Menyapa RI 94 Qj45
Gunungmeraksa RI 93 Qc47
Gunung Merapi RI 95 Qf49
Gunung Merapi RI 95 Qh50
Gunung Mulu N.P. MAL 94 Qh43
Gunung Muria RI 95 Qf49
Gunung Mutis RI 97 Rc50
Gunung Nanti RI 93 Qb48
Gunung Niut RI 94 Qe45
Gunung Noring MAL 92 Qa43
Gunung Pancungapang RI 94 Qh45
Gunung Pangrango RI 95 Qd49
Gunung Payang RI 94 Qh45
Gunung Ranakah RI 96 Ra50
Gunung Rantemario RI 96 Ra47
Gunung Ratai RI 93 Qc48
Gunung Raung RI 95 Qh50
Gunung Raya RI 93 Qa47
Gunung Raya RI 95 Qg46
Gunung Rinjani RI 96 Qj50
Gunung Saran RI 95 Qf46
Gunung Sebayan RI 95 Qf46
Gunung Seblat RI 93 Qb47
Gunung Semeru RI 95 Qg50
Gunungsitoli RI 93 Pj45
Gunung Slamet RI 95 Qe49
Gunung Tahan MAL 92 Qb43
Gunung Takan RI 96 Qj50
Gunung Tamborra RI 96 Qj50
Gunung Tampu Inanajing RI 93 Pk45
Gunung Tata Mailau = Mount Ramelau TLS 97 Rc50
Gunung Tebak RI 93 Qc48
Gunung Tenamatua RI 96 Ra46
Gunung Tentolomatinan RI 91 Rb45
Gunung Tibau RI 94 Qh45
Gunung Trus Madi MAL 94 Qj43
Gunungtua RI 93 Pk45
Gunung Tuham RI 94 Qg45
Gunung Ubia RI 114 Rj48
Gunung Umsini RI 114 Rg46
Gunung Wanggamet RI 96 Ra51
Gunung Welirang RI 95 Qg49
Gunupur IND (ORS) 83 Pb36
Gunupur IND (ORS) 83 Pb36
Gunwara IND (MPH) 83 Pa33
Günz D 33 Ll42
Günzburg D 33 Ll42
Gunzenhausen D 33 Ll41
Guocheng CHN (GSU) 72 Qc27
Guodao CHN (SAX) 73 Qg27
Guoquanyan CHN 72 Qb30
Guoyang CHN (AHU) 78 Qj29
Guozhen CHN (SAA) 72 Qd28
Gupeng CHN (GZG) 74 Qe34
Gupis 80 Og27
Guptapur IND (ORS) 83 Pc36
Guraghe, Mount ETH 142 Mk41
Gura Haitii RO 43 Mf43
Gurahonț RO 43 Mc44
Gura Humorului RO 49 Mc22
Gurais 80 Oh28
Gurampod IND (APH) 83 Ok37
Guran IR 64 Nh32
Gurasada RO 44 Mc45
Gurbantünggüt Shamo CHN 67 Pd23
Gurdaspur IND (PJB) 80 Oh29
Gurdim IR 64 Oa33
Gurdžaani GE 57 Nc25
Güre TR 47 Mk52
Gur'evsk RUS 39 Ma36
Gurgaon IND (HYA) 80 Oj31
Gurguéia BR 200 Hj49
Gurig N.P. & Cobourg Marine Park AUS 106 Rg51
Guri Hatnur IND (APH) 82 Ok36
Gurin WAN 139 Lg41
Gurinhatã BR (MG) 202 Hf55
Gurk A 35 Lp44
Gurkovo BG 45 Mf48
Gurktaler Alpen A 35 Lo44
Gurlan UZ 62 Oa25
Gurmatkal IND (KTK) 82 Oj37
Gurner AUS (NT) 103 Rf57
Guro MOC 152 Mg54
Güroymak TR 57 Nb26
Gürpınar TR 45 Mj50
Gurramkonda IND (APH) 85 Ok39
Gurri SUD 134 Mb39
Gursahaiganj IND (UPH) 81 Ok32
Gursarai IND (UPH) 83 Ok33
Guruapin RI 91 Rd45
Guru Chantal Monastery IND 81 Oj29
Gurué MOC 153 Mj53
Gurun MAL 92 Qa43
Gürün TR 56 Mj26
Gurupá BR (PA) 195 He46
Gurupi BR (TO) 200 Hf51
Gurupi BR 195 Hg46
Gurupizinho BR (PA) 200 Hg47
Guru Sai Baba IND 84 Oj38
Guru Shikhar IND 82 Og33
Guruve ZW 152 Mf54
Gurvan Saykhan MNG 70 Qb24
Gurvan Saykhan N.P. MNG 70 Qa24
Gury AUS (NSW) 109 Se60
Gurziwan AFG 63 Oc28
Gusau WAN 138 Ld39
Gusev RUS 39 Mc36
Gushan CHN (LNG) 73 Rb26
Gushan CHN 75 Qk32
Gushi CHN (HNN) 73 Qh29
Gushi CHN (TIB) 69 Pj30
Gushiago GH 137 Kk41
Gushikawa J 79 Rd32
Gush Laghar IR 62 Oa28
Gus'-Hrustal'nyj RUS 48 Na18
Gusi RI 114 Rg47
Gusinje SCG 44 Lu48
Gusinoozërsk RUS (BUR) 70 Qd20
Guskhara IND (WBG) 83 Pd34
Gúspini I 36 Lj51
Gusselby S 31 Lq31
Güssing A 35 Lr43
Gustavfjellet N 16 Lj06
Gustavia F 187 Gj37
Gustavsberg S 31 Lt31
Gustavus USA (AK) 166 Dc16
Gustav V Land N 16 Lk05
Gustine USA (CA) 170 Dk27
Güstrow D 32 Ln37
Gusum S 31 Lr32
Gus'-Železnyj RUS 48 Na18
Gutah CDN (BC) 167 Dk17
Gutcher GB 20 Ku30
Gutenberg RA (CD) 207 Gj60
Gutenko Mountains 6 Gd33
Gütersloh D 32 Lj39
Gutha AUS (WA) 104 Qh60
Guthalungra AUS (QLD) 107 Sd55
Guthrie USA (OK) 174 Fb28
Guthrie USA (TX) 174 Ek29
Guthrie Center USA (IA) 172 Fc25
Gutian CHN (FJN) 75 Qk32
Gutierrez BOL 206 Gj55
Gutland L 23 Lf41
Gutsuo CHN (TIB) 68 Pd31
Gutu ZW 152 Mf55
Gutulia n.p. N 17 Lg14
Gützkow D 32 Lo37
Guuija MOC 155 Mg58
Guwahati IND (ASM) 86 Pf32
Guwayr SUD 135 Mg37
Guwer IRQ 57 Nb27
Guy CDN (AB) 167 Eb18
Guya ZW 152 Me56
Guyana 191 Ha09
Guyang CHN (NMZ) 72 Qf25
Guyi ETH 142 Mh41
Guymon USA (OK) 174 Ek27
Guyra AUS (NSW) 109 Sf61
Guyuan CHN (HBI) 73 Qh25
Guyuan CHN (NHZ) 72 Qd28
Güzelçamlı TR 47 Mh53
Güzelsu TR 57 Nb26
Güzelyurt = Morfou CY 56 Mg28
Guzhang CHN (GZG) 87 Qc33
Guzhen CHN (AHU) 78 Qj29
Guzhou CHN (GZH) 74 Qe33
Guzmán MEX (CHH) 180 Eg30
G'uzor UZ 63 Od26
Gvardejsk RUS 39 Mb36
Gvarv N 30 Lk31
Gvasjugi RUS 77 Rj22
Gvozd HR 35 Lq45
Gwa MYA 88 Ph37
Gwaai ZW 152 Md55
Gwabegar AUS (NSW) 109 Se61
Gwada WAN 138 Ld41
Gwadar PK 64 Ob33
Gwadar East Bay PK 64 Ob33
Gwagwalada WAN 138 Ld41
Gwaidam IND (UTT) 81 Ok30
Gwaii Haanas South Moresby National Park Reserve & Marine Conservation Area Reserve CDN 166 De19
Gwalior IND (MPH) 83 Ok32
Gwalior Fort IND 83 Ok32
Gwalishtap PK 64 Ob31
Gwamba WAN 138 Lc40
Gwambara WAN 138 Lc39
Gwanda ZW 152 Me56
Gwane RDC 141 Mc43
Gwara IND (MPH) 83 Pa34
Gwaram WAN 138 Le40
Gwarif RI 114 Rk47
Gwarzo WAN 138 Ld40
Gwasero WAN 138 Lb41
Gwatar Bay PK 64 Oa33
Gwayi River ZW 152 Md55
Gwembe Z 152 Md54
Gweru ZW 152 Me55
Gweta RB 151 Mc56
Gwi WAN 138 Ld41
Gwoza WAN 139 Lg40
Gy F 25 Lf43
Gyaca CHN (TIB) 69 Pg31
Gyál H 43 Lu43
Gyali GR 47 Mh54
Gyangze CHN (TIB) 68 Pe31
Gyaring Hu CHN 69 Pj28
Gydanskaja guba RUS 54 Od04
Gydanskij Poluostrov RUS 54 Od04
Gydanskiy Poluostrov RUS 54 Od04
Gyekiti GH 137 La42
Gyeongju ROK 79 Re28
Gyeongju Historic Areas ROK 79 Re28
Gyirong CHN (TIB) 68 Pc31
Gyitang CHN (TIB) 69 Pj30
Gyldenløvehøj DK 30 Lm35
Gylien S 16 Mb12
Gympie AUS (QLD) 109 Sg59
Gyobingauk MYA 86 Ph36
Gyokusendo J 79 Rd32
Gyomaendrőd H 43 Ma44
Gyömrő H 43 Lu43
Gyöngyös H 43 Lu43
Győr H 42 Ls43
Győrtelek H 43 Mc43
Gypsum Point CDN 167 Ec15
Gypsumville CDN (MB) 172 Fa20
Gyraspur IND 83 Ok34
Gysinge S 31 Lr30
Gysum Palace AUS (NSW) 111 Sc62
Gyttorp S 31 Lp31
Gyula H 43 Mb44
Gyumri ARM 57 Nb25
Gyzylarbat TM 62 Nj26
Gyzylsu TM 62 Ng26
Gžatsk RUS 48 Mh18

H

Haa-Alifu Atoll MV 84 Og42
Häädemeeste EST 39 Me32
Haa-Dhaalu Atoll MV 84 Og42
Haag am Hausruck A 42 Lo42
Haag in Oberbayern D 33 Ln42
Haag, Niederösterreich A 42 Lp42
Haag Nunataks 6 Ga34
Haakon VII Land N 16 Lg06
Haaksbergen NL 23 Lg38
Haalenberg NAM 154 Lh59
Haamstede NL 23 Ld39
Haanja körgustik EST 39 Mg33
Ha'apai Group TO 10 Ba11
Haapsalu EST 38 Md32
Haarlem NL 23 Le38
Haarlem ZA 154 Mb62
Haast NZ 113 Te67
Haastberget N 16 Ma06
Haast Bluff AUS (NT) 103 Rf57
Haasts Bluff A.L. AUS 103 Rf57
Haaway SP 145 Nb45
Habahe CHN (XUZ) 67 Pd21
Habalah Mountain Village KSA 60 Nb36
Ha Baroana Rock Paintings LS 155 Md60
Habarovsk RUS 76 Rh21
Habarut OM 61 Ng37
Habaswein EAK 145 Mk45
Habay CDN (AB) 167 Ea16
Habay-la-Neuve B 23 Lf41
Habban YE 60 Nd38
Habiganj BD 86 Pf33
Habirag CHN (NMZ) 73 Qh24
Habo S 31 Lp33
Habor Cirir SP 145 Nd43
Haboro J 77 Sa23
Habshan UAE 61 Ng34
Hachcholli IND (KTK) 82 Oj38
Hachenburg D 32 Lh40
Hachijo-jima J 79 Rk29
Hachinohe J 77 Sa25
Hachita USA (NM) 171 Ef30
Hacıbektaş TR 56 Mh26
Hacıömer TR 57 Na26
Haci Zeynalabdin AZ 57 Ne25
Hackås S 16 Lh14
Hackettstown USA (NJ) 177 Gc25
Hack, Mount AUS 108 Rk61
Hackney GUY 194 Ha42
Haco ANG 148 Lh51
Hacufera MOC 152 Mg56
Haczów PL 41 Mb41
Hadaaftimo SP 143 Ne40
Hadagalli IND (KTK) 84 Oh38
Hadakta RUS 70 Qg20
Hadaluma ETH 143 Nb42
Hadamar D 33 Lj40
Hadar (site of Lucy) ETH 142 Na39
Hadashville CDN (MB) 172 Fc21
Hadat CHN (NMZ) 71 Qk21
Hadbin OM 61 Nh37
Hadda AFG 65 Of28
Hadda' KSA 58 Mk35
Hadda PK 63 Of28
Haddad Bani Malik KSA 60 Na35
Had-des-Oulad-Frej MA 125 Kf29
Haddington GB 20 Ks35
Hadejia WAN 138 Lf39
Hadera IL 56 Mh29
Haderslev DK 30 Lk35
Hadgaon IND (MHT) 82 Oj36
Hadhah KSA 60 Na34
Hadh Bani Zaynan KSA 60 Ne35
Hadhdhunmathee Atoll = Laamu Atoll MV 84 Og45
Hadiboh YE 61 Ng39
Hadihui CHN (SAX) 72 Qf27
Hadilik CHN (XUZ) 68 Pd27
Hadım TR 56 Mg27
Hadımköy TR 45 Mj49
Hadjač UA 48 Mh20
Hadjer Bandala TCH 134 Ma40
Hadjer el Hamis TCH 139 Lh39
Hado Dan PRK 76 Rd26
Hadramawt YE 60 Ne38
Hadraniyah IRQ 57 Nb28
Hadrian's Wall GB 20 Ks36
Hadseløya N 16 Lh11
Hadsten DK 30 Ll34
Hadsund DK 30 Ll34
Haduyangratu RI 93 Qc48
Hadžići BIH 44 Lt47
Hae THA 87 Qa36
Hægeland N 30 Lh32
Haeinsa Temple ROK 78 Re28
Haeju PRK 78 Rc26
Hae-nam ROK 78 Rd28
Haenertsburg ZA 152 Me57
Haéré Lao SN 130 Kc37
Hafar al 'Atk KSA 59 Nd32
Hafar al Batin KSA 59 Nc31
Hafford CDN (SK) 169 Eg19
Haffouz TN 126 Le28
Hafik TR 56 Mj26
Hafirat al Ayda KSA 58 Mk32
Hafirat Nisah KSA 59 Nd33
Hafizabad PK 65 Og29
Hafiz Sa'adi IR 64 Ng31
Hafjell alpincenter N 17 Lf15
Hafnaberg IS 18 Js27
Hafnarfjörður IS 18 Jt26
Hafnir IS 18 Js27
Hafratindur IS 18 Jt25
Haftgel IR 59 Ne30
Haft Tappeh IR 59 Ne29
Hag Abdullah SUD 135 Mg38
Hagadera EAK 145 Na45
Hagar Banga SUD 134 Mb40
Hagar Nish Plateau ER 135 Mj37
Hagelberg D 32 Ln38
Hagemeister Island USA 164 Bk16
Hagen D 32 Lh39
Hagenow D 32 Lm37
Hage Qaltan Pir Gandom Beryan IR 64 Oa30
Hagere Hiywot ETH 142 Mj41
Hagerman USA (ID) 168 Ec24
Hagerman USA (NM) 171 Eh29
Hagerstown USA (MD) 177 Gb26
Hagetmau F 24 Ku47
Hagewood USA (LA) 174 Fd30
Hagfors S 31 Lo30
Häggenås S 16 Lh14
Hagi J 79 Rf28
Ha Giang VN 87 Qc34
Hagia Sophia TR 45 Mj49
Hagia Sophia (Trabzon) TR 57 Mk25
Hagondange F 23 Lg41
Hagonoy RP 90 Ra38
Hagonoy RP 91 Rc42
Haguenau F 23 Lh42
Hahndorf AUS (SA) 110 Rk63
Hahót H 42 Lr44
Haia PNG 115 Sc49
Hai'an CHN (GDG) 74 Qf35
Hai'an CHN (JGS) 78 Ra29
Haibao Ta CHN 72 Qd26
Haibei CHN (HLG) 76 Rd22
Haïbongo RMM 131 Kj37
Haicheng CHN (LNG) 76 Rb25
Haidargarh IND (UPH) 83 Pa32
Hai Dong VN 87 Qc35
Haidra TN 126 Le28
Hai Duong VN 87 Qd35
Haifa IL 56 Mh29
Haifeng CHN (GDG) 75 Qh34
Haig AUS (WA) 105 Rd61
Haiger D 32 Lj40
Haikang CHN (GDG) 74 Qf35
Haikou CHN (HAN) 75 Qf35
Ha'il KSA 58 Na32
Hailakandi IND (ASM) 86 Pg33
Hailar CHN (NMZ) 71 Qk21
Hailey USA (ID) 168 Ec24
Hailin CHN (HLG) 76 Re23
Hailing Dao CHN 74 Qf35
Hailun CHN (HLG) 76 Rd22
Hailuoto FIN 16 Mc13
Hailuoto FIN 16 Mc13
Haima OM 61 Nj36
Haimen CHN (JGS) 78 Ra30
Hainan CHN 75 Qe36
Hainan Dao CHN 75 Qf35
Hainan Strait CHN 74 Qe35
Hainburg A 42 Lr42
Haindi LB 136 Ke42
Haines USA (AK) 166 Dc16
Haines USA (OR) 168 Eb23
Haines City USA (FL) 179 Fk31
Haines Highway CDN 166 Db16
Haines Junction CDN (YT) 166 Db15
Hainfeld A 42 Lq42
Haingsisi RI 97 Rb51
Hainichen D 32 Lo40
Hainich, N.P. D 32 Ll39
Haining CHN (ZJG) 78 Ra30
Hainleite D 32 Ll39
Haiphong VN 87 Qd35
Haitan Dao CHN 75 Qk33
Haití C 179 Gb35
Haiti RH 186 Gd36
Haitou CHN (HAN) 75 Qe36
Hai Van VN 89 Qe37
Haiyan CHN (QHI) 72 Qa27
Haiyan CHN (ZJG) 78 Ra30
Haiyuan CHN (NHZ) 72 Qc27
Hajar KSA 58 Mk34
Hajdarkan KS 63 Of26
Hajdúböszörmény H 43 Mb43
Hajdúnánás H 43 Mb43
Hajdúsámson H 43 Mb43
Hajdúszoboszló H 43 Mb43
Hajeb el Aïdun TN 126 Le28
Hájek CZ 42 Ln40
Hajganj BD 86 Pf34
Haji Abad IR 64 Nh31
Haji Abad IR 64 Nk29
Haji Jafar Shahid PK 65 Oe32
Hajiki-saki J 77 Rk26
Hajin SYR 57 Na28
Hajipur IND (BIH) 83 Pc33
Hajjah YE 60 Nb37
Hajjah YE 60 Nb38

Hajnówka ○ PL 41 Md38
Hajo ○ IND (ASM) 86 Pf32
Hajo Do ○ NAM 78 Rd28
Hajós ○ H 43 Lu44
Hajrah ○ KSA 60 Na35
Hajyr ○ RUS 59 Rc04
Hakai Recreation Area ◫ ◫ CDN 168 Df20
Hakha ○ MYA 86 Pg34
Hakkâri ○ TR 57 Nb27
Hakkâri Dağları ▲ TR 57 Nb27
Haken-sen ◫ J 79 Rt28
Hakodate ○ J 77 Sa25
Hakui ○ J 77 Rj27
Hakusan N.P. ◫ J 79 Rj27
Hala ○ PK 65 Oe33
Halaib ○ SUD 129 Mj34
Halali ○ NAM 150 Lj55
Halástra ○ GR 46 Mc50
Halat 'Ammar ○ KSA 58 Mj31
Halawa ○ FIN (old) 170 Cb35
Halberstadt ○ D 32 Lm39
Halbrite ○ CDN (SK) 169 Ej21
Halden ○ N 30 Ld34
Haldensleben ○ D 32 Lm38
Haldia ○ IND (WBG) 86 Pe34
Haldibari ○ IND (BIH) 83 Pd32
Haldwani ○ IND (UTT) 81 Ok31
Hale ○ EAT 147 Mk48
Haleakala N.P. ◫ USA 170 Cb35
Halebid ○ IND 84 Oj39
Haleji Bird Reserve ◫ PK 65 Od33
Halembe ○ EAT 146 Me48
Hale, Mount ▲ USA 164 Qj58
Halesworth ○ GB 21 Lb38
Half Assini ○ GH 137 Kj43
Halfawiyah al-Muluk ○ SUD 135 Mg38
Halfmoon Bay ○ CDN (BC) 168 Dj21
Halfmoon Bay ○ NZ 113 Te68
Half Moon Shoal ◰ 94 Qj41
Halfweg ○ ZA 154 Ma61
Halgen ○ SP 145 Nc43
Haliburton Highlands ▲ CDN 173 Ga23
Halič ○ UA 43 Me41
Halidon ○ AUS (SA) 110 Sa63
Halifax ○ AUS (QLD) 107 Sd55
Halifax ○ CDN (NS) 176 Gj23
Halifax ○ GB 21 Kt37
Halifax Bay ≋ AUS (QLD) 107 Sd55
Halikarnassos ∴ TR 47 Mh53
Halikko ○ FIN 38 Md30
Haliluik ○ RI 97 Rc50
Halimun, Gunung ▲ RI 95 Qd49
Haliyal ○ IND (KTK) 82 Oh38
Haljala ○ EST 38 Mg31
Halke Shan ▲ CHN 66 Pa24
Hálki ○ GR 47 Mh54
Halkida ○ GR 45 Md52
Halkidhiki ◫ GR (AK) 169 Ed19
Halkirk ○ CDN (AB) 169 Ed19
Halland ▲ S 30 Lo33
Hallandale ○ USA (FL) 179 Fk33
Hallands Väderö ◫ S 30 Ln34
Hallasan ▲ ROK 78 Rd29
Hallasan N.P. ◫ ROK 78 Rd29
Halle ○ B 23 Le40
Halleck ○ USA (NV) 170 Ed25
Hälleforss ○ S 31 Lp31
Hälleforsnäs ○ S 31 Lp31
Hallein ○ A 35 Lo43
Hällekis ○ S 31 Lo32
Hallen ○ S 16 Lh14
Hallersville ○ USA (AK) 164 Cb16
Halle (Saale) ○ D 32 Lm39
Hallett ○ AUS (SA) 110 Rk62
Hallettsville ○ USA (TX) 181
Halley ◰ ANT (UK) 6 Jc34
Halligen ◫ D 32 Lj36
Hallingdal ▲ N 30 Lk30
Hällingsåfallet ≈ S 16 Lh13
Hall in Tirol ○ A 34 Lm43
Hall Islands ◫ FSM 10 Sb09
Hallnäs ○ S 16 Lk13
Hallock ○ USA (MN) 172 Fd21
Hallormsstaður ○ IS 18 Ke32
Hall Peninsula ◫ CDN 163 Gc06
Hall Point ○ AUS 103 Rc53
Hall Point ○ AUS 106 Rg51
Halls ○ USA (TN) 175 Ff28
Hallsberg ○ S 31 Lq31
Halls Creek ○ AUS (WA) 103
Halls Gap ○ AUS (VIC) 110 Sb64
Hallsta ○ S 31 Lr31
Hallstahammar ○ S 31 Lq31
Hallstatt ▲ A 35 Lo43
Hallstatt-Dachstein Salzkammergut ◫ △ A 35 Lo43
Hallstätter See ≋ A 35 Lo43
Hallstavik ○ S 31 Lt30
Hallyo Haesang N.P. ◫ ROK 79 Rd28
Halmahera ◫ RI 91 Re45
Halmahera See ≋ RI 97 Re46
Halmstad ○ S 30 Ln34
Halol ○ IND (GUJ) 82 Og34
Halong Bay ◫ VN 87 Qd35
Halong City ○ VN 87 Qd35
Hals ○ DK 30 Ll34
Hal Saflieni Hypogeum ∴ M 37 Lp55
Hal'sany ○ BY 39 Mg36
Hälsingland ▲ S 17 Lh15
Halsön ○ FIN 38 Mb28
Halstead ○ GB 21 La39
Halsteren ○ NL 23 Le39
Halsur ○ IND (KTK) 82 Oj37
Halten Bank ◰ 16 Lf13
Haltern ○ D 32 Lh39
Haltwhistle ○ GB 21 Kr36
Haluaghat ○ BD 86 Pf33
Halul ▲ Q 61 Ng33
Halvad ○ IND (GUJ) 82 Of34
Halvardgårdarna ○ S 31 Lq30
Halverson Ridge ▲ CDN (AB) 167 Ea17
Halvmåneøya ◫ N 16 Mb07
Ham ◰ F 23 Ld41
Hama ○ TCH 139 Lh43
Hama ○ SYR 56 Mj28
Hamada ○ NAM 154 Lk60
Hamada ○ J 79 Rg28
Hamada al Hamrah ◫ LAR 126 Lf31
Ham ada de la Dao ura ◫ DZ 125 Kj31
Hamada de Tindouf ◫ DZ 124 Kf32
Hamada de Tinrhert ◫ DZ 126 Ld31
Hamada du Drâa ◫ DZ 125 Kh30
Hamada du Guir ◫ DZ 125 Kj30
Hamada ed Douakel ◫ DZ 124 Kg32
Hamada el Harich ◫ RMM 131 Kh34
Hamada Marzuq ◫ LAR 127 Lg32
Hamada Mangeni ◫ RN 133 Lg34
Hamada Tounassine ◫ DZ 125 Kg31

Hamadat Tingarat ◫ LAR 126 Lf31
Hamada Zegher ◫ LAR 126 Lf32
Hamadet el Atchane ◫ DZ 125 Kk30
Hamaguir ○ DZ 125 Kj31
Hamamah ○ LAR 127 Ma29
Hamamatsu ○ J 79 Rj28
Hamamatsu ○ J 79 Rj28
Hamam ○ CAM 139 Lg43
Haman-sen ◫ J 79 Rt28
Hamarro Hadad ○ ETH 143 Nb42
Hamasaka ○ J 79 Rh28
Hama-Tombetsu ○ J 77 Sb23
Hambantota Conservation Park ◫ AUS 110 Rh62
Hamburg ○ D ◫ ◫ 32 Lk37
Hamburg ○ USA (AR) 175 Fe29
Hamburg ○ USA (IA) 175 Fc25
Hamburg ○ USA (NY) 173 Ga24
Hamdah ○ KSA 60 Na36
Hamdallay ○ RMM 131 Kh38
Hamdallay ○ RN 132 Lb39
Hamdanah ○ KSA 60 Na36
Hamdibey ○ TR 47 Mh51
Hämeenkyrö ○ FIN 38 Md29
Hämeenlinna ○ FIN 38 Md29
Hämeenselkä ▲ FIN 38 Me28
Hämeenkangas ▲ FIN 38 Md29
Hamelin Bay ≋ AUS (WA) 104 Qh59
Hameln ○ D 32 Lk38
Hamersley Gorge ◫ AUS 102 Qk57
Hamersley Range ▲ AUS 102 Qj57
Hamhung DR 78 Re26
Hami ○ CHN (XUZ) 67 Pg24
Hamid ○ IR 59 Ne30
Hamid ○ SUD 135 Mf35
Hamidiye ○ TR 45 Mg49
Hamidiyeh ○ IR 59 Ne30
Hamilton ○ AUS (TAS) 111 Sd67
Hamilton ○ AUS (VIC) 111 Sb64
Hamilton ○ CDN (ON) 173 Ga24
Hamilton ○ GB 20 Kq35
Hamilton ○ NZ 112 Th64
Hamilton ○ USA (AK) 164 Bj14
Hamilton ○ USA (AL) 175 Fg28
Hamilton ○ USA (IL) 175 Fe25
Hamilton ○ USA (OH) 175 Fh26
Hamilton ○ USA (TX) 181 Fb30
Hamilton ○ USA (WA) 168 Dj21
Hamilton Dome ○ USA (WY) 169 Ef24
Hamilton Downs ○ AUS (QLD) 108 Sb56
Hamilton Hotel ○ AUS (QLD) 108 Sb54
Hamilton Island ○ AUS 107 Se56
Hamilton, Mount ▲ USA 170 Ec26
Hamilton River ○ AUS (QLD) 108 Sa57
Hamilton Sound ≋ CDN 177 Hc21
Hamim ○ UAE 61 Nh34
Hamina ○ FIN 38 Mh30
Hamirpur ○ CDN (MB) 172 Ek20
Hamirpur ○ IND (HPH) 81 Oj30
Hamirpur ○ IND (UTP) 83 Pa33
Hamju ○ DPR 76 Rd26
Hamlin ○ USA (TX) 181 Fa29
Hamlin ○ USA (WV) 175 Fj26
Hamm ○ D 32 Lh39
Hamm ◰ F 11 Cb11
Hammam al Alil ○ IRQ 57 Nb27
Hammam ○ YE 60 Nc38
Hammam Meskoutine ○ DZ 126 Ld27
Hammam-Righa ○ DZ 126 Ld27
Hammam Salahine ○ DZ 126 Lc28
Hammarön ◫ S 31 Lo32
Hammarsund ○ S 31 Lp35
Hammar ○ DK 30 Lk34
Hammenhög ○ S 31 Lp35
Hammerdal ○ S 16 Lh14
Hammeren ○ DK 31 Lo35
Hammerfest ○ N 16 Mb10
Hamminkeln ○ D 32 Lg39
Hammonasset ○ USA (CT) 177 Ge23
Hammond ○ USA (IL) 173 Fg25
Hammond ○ USA (IN) 173 Fg25
Hammond ○ USA (LA) 175 Fe30
Hammond ○ USA (MT) 169 Eh23
Hammond Island ▲ AUS 107 Sb51
Hammonton ○ USA (NJ) 177 Gc26
Hamnvik ○ N 16 Lj11
Hamoir ○ B 23 Lf40
Hamón ○ MEX 130 Ke38
Hamra ○ S 31 Lp32
Hamrarön ◫ S 31 Lo31
Hampden ○ NZ 113 Tf68
Hampi ∴ IND 82 Oj38
Hampton ○ CDN (NB) 176 Gh23
Hampton ○ USA (AR) 175 Fd29
Hampton ○ USA (IA) 172 Fd24
Hampton ○ USA (SC) 178 Fk29
Hampton ○ USA (VA) 178 Gb27
Hamra ○ SUD 135 Me40
Hamra n.p. ◫ S 17 Lh15
Hamrat al-Wuzz ○ SUD 135 Mf38
Hamrat as Shaykh ○ SUD 134 Md38
Hamrlya ○ UAE 61 Nh33
Ham Tan ○ VN 89 Qd40
Ham Thuam Nam ≈ VN 89 Qe40
Hamtic ○ RP 90 Ra40
Hamuku ○ RI 114 Rh47
Hamum-e-Jazmuriyan ≋ IR 64 Nk32
Han Nam N.P. ◫ IR 64 Oa30
Ham Yen ○ VN 87 Qd35
Hamyški ○ RUS (ADY) 49 Na23
Hanahai ○ RB 154 Ma58
Hanagal ○ IND (KTK) 84 Oj38
Hanahan ○ USA (SC) 178 Ga29
Hanak ○ TR 57 Nb25
Hanalei Bay ≋ USA (HI) 170 Ca34
Hanamaki ○ J 77 Sa26
Hanamkonda ○ IND (APH) 83 Ok36
Hanang ▲ EAT 147 Mh47
Hananui ▲ VN 87 Qd35
Hanau ○ D 33 Lk40
Hanawa ○ J 77 Sa25
Hanbogd ○ MNG (OD) 70 Qe24
Hancock ○ USA (MD) 177 Ga26
Hancock ○ USA (MI) 173 Ff22
Hancock ○ USA (NY) 177 Gc24
Handa ○ J 79 Rj28
Handalan ○ IND (HBI) 73 Qh27
Handan ○ CHN (ORS) 83 Pc35
Handel ○ CDN (SK) 169 Eh19
Handeni ○ EAT 147 Mk48
Handewitt ○ D 33 Lk41
Handha ○ SP 143 Nf40
Handova ○ SK 43 Lt42
Handwara ○ IND (JKT) 81 Oh29
Handyga ○ RUS 55 Rd06
Hanford ○ USA (CA) 170 Ea27
Hanga Roa ○ RCH 197 Gc54
Hang Chat ○ THA 87 Qa36
Hanggin Houqi ○ CHN (NMZ) 72 Qd25

Hanggin Qi ○ CHN (NMZ) 72 Qe26
Hanging Rock ▲ AUS 102 Ra57
Hanging Trail ▲ LB 136 Kf43
Hangö = Hanko ○ FIN 38 Mc31
Hangu ○ CHN (TJN) 73 Qj26
Hangu ○ PK 65 Of29
Hangzhou ○ CHN (ZJG) 78 Ra30
Hanhowuz ○ TM 62 Oa27
Hani ○ TR 57 Na26
Hanidh ○ KSA 59 Ne32
Hanidtis ○ GR 45 Md50
Han Island ▲ PNG 117 Sh48
Hankasalmi ○ FIN 38 Mg28
Hankensbüttel ○ D 32 Ll38
Hanker ○ IND (CGH) 83 Pa35
Hankey ○ ZA 155 Mc62
Hankinson ○ USA (ND) 172 Fb22
Hankö = Hangö ○ FIN 38 Mc31
Harkány ○ H 42 Lt45
Harkidum ○ IND (UTT) 81 Ok30
Harlan ○ USA (IA) 172 Fc25
Harlan ○ USA (KY) 178 Fj27
Harlau ○ RO 43 Md22
Harlech Castle ◫ ◫ GB 21 Kq38
Harleigh Farm ○ ZW 152 Me35
Härlev ○ DK 30 Ln35
Harlin ○ AUS (QLD) 109 Sg59
Harlingen ○ NL 23 Lf37
Harlingen ○ USA (TX) 181 Fb32
Harlow ○ GB 21 La39
Harlowton ○ USA (MT) 169 Ef22
Harmancik ○ TR 47 Mh51
Härmänkylä ○ FIN 16 Me13
Harmanli ○ BG 45 Mf49
Harmil ▲ ER 142 Nd37
Harmonia ○ BR (RS) 204 Hb60
Harnai ○ PK 65 Od30
Harnai ○ IND (MHT) 82 Og37
Härnösand ○ S 17 Lj14
Harney Basin ◫ USA 168 Ea24
Harney, Lake ≋ USA 168 Ea24
Harney Peak ▲ USA 171 Ek24
Haro ○ E 24 Ks47
Haro Shiikh ○ SP 143 Nc41
Harpanahalli ○ IND (KTK) 84 Oh38
Harper ○ LB 136 Kg43
Harper ○ USA (KS) 174 Fa27
Harper, Mount ▲ USA 165 Cj13
Harper, Mount ▲ USA 165 Cj13
Harpers Ferry N.H.P. ◫ USA 175 Fg27
Harperville ○ USA (AL) 175 Ff29
Harpeth Narrows Historic Area ▲ USA 175 Fg27
Harput Kalesi ▲ TR 57 Mk26
Harqin Qi ○ CHN (NMZ) 73 Qk25
Harqin Zuoyi ○ CHN (NMZ) 73 Qk25
Harrat al Buqum ◫ KSA 60 Na35
Harrat el Kishb ◫ KSA 60 Na34
Harrat al ,Uwayrid ◫ KSA 58 Mj32
Harriman ○ USA (TN) 175 Fh28
Harrington ○ USA (DE) 177 Gc26
Harrington ○ AUS (NSW) 109 Sg61
Harripur ○ PK 65 Og29
Harris ○ GB 20 Ko33
Harrisburg ○ USA (AR) 175 Fe28
Harrisburg ○ USA (IL) 175 Ff27
Harrisburg ▲ USA (PA) 177 Gb25
Harrismith ○ ZA 155 Me60
Harris, Mount ▲ AUS 103 Re58
Harrison ○ USA (AR) 175 Fd27
Harrison ○ USA (NE) 171 Ej24
Harrisonburg ○ USA (VA) 178 Ga27
Harrisville ○ USA (MO) 174 Fc26
Harrisville ○ LB 136 Ke42
Harrisville ○ USA (WI) 173 Fg23
Harrisville ○ USA (NY) 177 Gc23
Harrodsburg ○ USA (KY) 175 Fh27
Harrogate ○ CDN (BC) 168 Eb20
Harrogate ○ GB 21 Kt37
Harrow ○ AUS (VIC) 110 Sa64
Harry S. Truman S.P. ◫ USA 174 Fc26
Harsani ○ IND (RJT) 82 Of33
Harsefeld ○ D 32 Lk37
Harsin ○ IR 57 Nd28
Harsor ○ IND (RJT) 80 Oh32
Harsova ○ RO 45 Mg46
Harsovo ○ BG 45 Mg47
Harstad ○ N 16 Lj11
Harsud ○ IND (MHT) 82 Oj34
Harsum ○ D 32 Lk38
Harsvallbukta ≋ N 16 Mb07
Hart ◰ CDN (ABI) 173 Fg24
Hartberg ▲ A 35 Lq43
Hartbeesfontein ○ ZA 155 Md59
Hartenbos ○ ZA 155 Mb62
Harter Lake ◫ F 157 Nh56
Hart, Mount ▲ AUS 103 Rd54
Hart Mount ▲ CDN 169 Ek19
Hartford ○ USA (CT) 177 Gd25
Hartford ○ USA (MI) 173 Fh25
Hartford ○ USA (SD) 172 Fb24
Hârtigești ○ RO 45 Mf45
Hartington ○ USA (NE) 172 Fb24
Hartland ○ CDN (NB) 176 Gh22
Hartland Covered Bridge ◫ CDN 176 Gh22
Hartland Point ▲ GB 21 Kq39
Hartlepool ○ GB 21 Kt36
Hartley Bay ○ CDN (BC) 166 Df19
Hartmannberge ▲ ◫ NAM 150 Lg56
Hartmannsdorf ○ D 32 Lo39
Hartola ○ FIN 38 Mg29
Harts Range ▲ AUS 108 Sc56
Hartsdale ○ CDN (NF) 177 Hc22
Hartselle ○ USA (AL) 175 Fg28
Hartshorne ○ USA (OK) 174 Fc28
Hartsville ○ USA (SC) 178 Ga28
Hartsville ○ USA (TN) 175 Fg27
Hartswater ○ ZA 155 Mc60
Hartville ○ USA (WY) 169 Eh24
Hartwell ○ USA (GA) 178 Fj28
Haru ○ RI 97 Rc49
Haruku ▲ RI 97 Rd47
Harun = Gunung Harden ▲ RI 94 Qh43
Harunabad ○ PK 65 Og31
Haruru ○ IND (MHT) 82 Oj37
Harvel ○ USA (IL) 175 Ff26
Harvey ○ AUS (WA) 104 Qh62
Harvey ○ CDN (NB) 176 Gh22
Harvey ○ USA (ND) 172 Fa22
Harvey ○ USA (NF) 177 Hd21
Harwich ○ GB 21 Lb39
Haryana ◫ IND 80 Oj33

Hašaat ○ MNG 70 Qc23
Hargele ○ ETH 145 Nb43
Hargeysa ○ SP 143 Nc41
Hasasama ○ J 77 Sa26
Hasan ○ RUS 76 Rf24
Hasanabad ○ IND (APH) 83 Ok36
Hasan Abad ○ IR 57 Nf28
Hasan Abad ○ IR 64 Ng29
Hasan Abad ○ IR 64 Nk28
Hasancelebi ○ TR 56 Mj26
Hasankale ▲ TR 57 Na26
Hasankeyf ○ TR 57 Na27
Hasan Kuleh ○ AFG 64 Oa23
Hasan Langi ○ IR 64 Ng32
Harisal ○ IND (MHT) 82 Oj35
Hasan Paşa Kümbet ▲ TR 57 Nb26
Hasanpur ○ IND (UPH) 81 Ok31
Hasawnah ○ KSA 60 Nb34
Hasdargg Reserve ◫ TM 62 Nj26
Hasavjurt ○ RUS (DAG) 57 Nd24
Haselünne ○ D 32 Lh38
Hashab ○ SUD 134 Mc39
Hashtrud ○ IR Nd27
Hasik ○ OM 61 Nh37
Hasil ▲ RI 97 Re46
Hasht ○ PK 65 Og31
Haskanit ○ SUD (Dar) 134 Md40
Haskovo ○ BG 45 Mf49
Hasle ○ DK 31 Lo35
Haslev ○ DK 30 Lm35
Harlin ○ AUS (QLD) 109 Sg59
Hasnal ○ BD 86 Pf33
Hasparren ◰ F 24 Kt47
Hassa ○ TR 56 Mj27
Hassan ○ IND (KTK) 84 Oj39
Hassel ▲ S 17 Lj14
Hassela ○ S 17 Lj14
Hasselt ○ B 23 Lf40
Hasselt ○ NL 23 Lg38
Haßfurt ○ D 33 Ll40
Hassi Bahbah ○ DZ 126 Lb28
Hassi Baroudia ○ DZ 126 Lb30
Hassi Bel Guebbour ○ DZ 126 Ld31
Hassi Benmira ○ DZ 126 Lb29
Hassi-Bou-Allala ○ DZ 125 Kj30
Hassi Daoula ○ DZ 126 Lc29
Hassi Defla ○ DZ 125 Kj29
Hassi-Delaa ○ DZ 126 Lb29
Hassi el Behar ○ DZ 126 Lb30
Hassi el Ghella ○ DZ 125 Kk28
Hassi el-Hadjar ○ DZ 126 Lc30
Hassi el Khannfous ○ DZ 126 Ld31
Hassi el-Khenig ○ DZ 126 Lb32
Hassi el Klebi ○ DZ 125 Kh31
Hassi el Mouni ○ DZ 125 Kh31
Hassi-Fahl ○ DZ 126 Lb29
Hassi Fouani ○ RIM 131 Kg37
Hassi Fouini ○ RIM 131 Kg37
Hassi Habadra ○ DZ 126 Lc29
Hassi Hadhour ○ DZ 126 Lc30
Hassi Hassane ○ MA 125 Kg30
Hassi Ifertas ○ DZ 126 Ld31
Hassi Inifel ○ DZ 126 Lc30
Hassi Ismoulaye ○ DZ 126 Le31
Hassi Issendjel ○ DZ 126 Le32
Hassi Karkabane ○ DZ 131 Kk27
Hassi Kord Myriem ○ DZ 125 Kj31
Hassi-Mahzez ○ DZ 125 Kh31
Hassi Marraket ○ DZ 126 Lb30
Hassi Messaoud ○ DZ 126 Lc29
Hassi Mouissa ○ DZ 125 La31
Hassi Ntsel ○ DZ 126 Ld32
Hassi Ramad ○ DZ 126 Ld31
Hassi Rei el Erg ○ DZ 126 Lc31
Hassi-R'Mel ○ DZ 126 Lb29
Hassi Safiet Iniguel ○ DZ 126 Lb30
Hassi Tabankort ○ DZ 126 Ld31
Hassi Tabelbalet ○ DZ 126 Le32
Hassi Tartrat ○ DZ 124 Kg32
Hassi Touil ○ RIM 131 Kh37
Hasskah ○ SYR 57 Mk28
Hasslö ▲ S 31 Lq34
Hasslö ○ S 31 Lq34
Hassu ○ RI 97 Rc50
Hastavena ○ S 31 Lo35
Hastings ○ GB 21 La40
Hastings ○ NZ 113 Tj65
Hastings ○ USA (MI) 173 Fh24
Hastings ○ USA (NE) 172 Fb25
Hastings ▲ MYA 88 Pk40
Hastings Island ▲ PNG 116 Sf51
Hastveda ○ S 31 Lp34
Hasy Haguě ○ LAR 128 Lg32
Hasy in Aguel ○ LAR 128 Lf32
Hasy Tissan ○ LAR 127 Lg31
Hasy Uigh el-Kebir ○ LAR 128 Lf31
Hat Chao Mai N.P. ◫ THA 88 Pk42
Hatches Creek ○ AUS (NT) 106 Rh56
Hatchie N.W.R. ◫ USA 175 Fe28
Hat Creek ○ USA (WY) 171 Eh24
Hat Creek Hist. Ranch ◫ CDN 168 Dk20
Hatęg ○ RO 44 Mc45
Hatfield ○ AUS 111 Sb62
Hatfield ○ AUS 111 Sb62
Hat Gamar ◫ IND (KTK) 83 Pa34
Hathazari ○ BD 86 Pf34
Hat Head N.P. ◫ AUS 109 Sg61
Hatherleigh ○ GB 21 Kq40
Hatia ○ IND (KTK) 83 Pc35
Hatia ○ BD 86 Pf34
Hatibi ○ THA 88 Pk41
Hatta ○ UAE 61 Nh33
Hatta ○ IND (MPH) 83 Ok33
Hattah ○ AUS (VIC) 110 Sb63
Hattah Kulkyne N.P. ◫ AUS 111 Sb63
Hatteras ○ USA (NC) 178 Gc28
Hatteras Abyssal Plain ◰ 160 Gb06
Harts Range ◫ AUS 108 Rh57
Hartsville ○ USA (SC) 178 Fk28
Hattfjelldal ○ N 16 Lh13
Hat Thai Muang N.P. ◫ THA 88 Pk41
Hattieesburg ○ USA (MS) 175 Ff30
Hattigudur ○ IND (KTK) 82 Oj37
Hattingen ○ D 32 Lh39
Hatton-Dikoya ○ CL 85 Pa42
Hatton ○ USA (WA) 168 Ea22
Hatuaga ○ RI 97 Rb49
Hat Yai ○ THA 88 Qa42
Hatyn ○ PNG 115 Sc48
Hat'yul ○ ETH 143 Nd41
Haugastøl ○ N 30 Lj30
Hauge ○ N 30 Lh31
Hauge ○ N 30 Lh31
Hauge ○ N 30 Lh31
Hauho ○ FIN 38 Me29
Haukeligrend ○ N 30 Lj31
Haukeliseter ○ N 30 Lj31
Haukivuori ○ FIN 38 Mh28

Hauraha ○ SOL 117 Ta51
Hauraki Gulf ≋ NZ 112 Th64
Hausach ○ D 33 Lj42
Hausdiha ○ IND (JKD) 83 Pd33
Hausen ○ IND (JKD) 83 Pd33
Haut Atlas ▲ MA 124 Kf30
Haut Camopi ◰ F 194 Hd44
Hauteclair ◰ F 24 Lb45
Hautes Fagnes ▲ B 23 Lf40
Hautes Plateaux de l'Ouest ◫ WAN 138 Le42
Hauzenberg ○ D 33 Lo42
Havalí ○ AZ 57 Nd26
Havana ○ RF ◫ F j34
Havana ○ USA (FL) 175 Fh25
Havana ○ USA (IL) 175 Fe25
Havana ○ USA (ND) 172 Fb22
Havasu Ind. Res. ◫ USA 171 Ed27
Havdhem ○ S 31 Lt33
Havdrup ○ DK 30 Ln35
Have Etoe ○ GH 137 La42
Havel ≈ D 32 Ln38
Havelberg ○ D 32 Ln38
Havelí Lakkha ○ PK 65 Og30
Haveland ▲ D 32 Ln38
Havelock ○ USA (NC) 178 Gb28
Havelock Island ▲ IND 88 Pg40
Haven ○ IND (KTK) 84 Oh38
Haverhill ○ GB 21 La39
Haverhill ○ USA (MA) 177 Ge24
Hăverud ○ S 30 Lo32
Havlah ○ KSA 60 Nb35
Havíov ○ CZ 43 Lt41
Havøysund ○ N 16 Mc10
Havran ○ TR 47 Mh51
Havrán ○ IND (MBT) 82 Of34
Havre ○ USA (MT) 169 Ef21
Havre-Aubert ○ CDN (QC) 176 Gk22
Havre-Saint-Pierre ○ CDN (QC) 176 Gj21
Havrylivka ○ UA 49 Mj41
Havsa ○ TR 45 Mg49
Havsa ○ TR 56 Mj25
Hawai ○ USA (HI) 170 Cc36
Hawai'i ◫ USA 170 Ca35
Hawaii ○ KWT 59 Nd31
Hawaiian Ridge ◰ 170 Bk34
Hawaii Volcanoes N.P. ◫ USA 170 Cb36
Hawalli ○ KWT 59 Nd31
Hawarden ○ USA (IA) 172 Fb24
Hawarden ○ CDN (SK) 169 Eh19
Hawea, Lake ≋ NZ 113 Te67
Hawera ○ NZ 112 Tg65
Hawesville ○ USA (KY) 175 Fg27
Hawi ○ USA (HI) 170 Cc35
Hawick ○ GB 20 Ks35
Hawke Bay ≋ NZ 113 Tj65
Hawker ○ AUS (SA) 108 Rk61
Hawke's Bay ◫ CDN 177 Ha20
Hawke's Bay ○ CDN 177 Ha20
Hawkesbury ○ CDN (ON) 173 Gc23
Hawkesbury Island ▲ CDN 166 Df19
Hawke Nest ○ AUS (NSW) 111 Sg62
Hawk Inlet ○ USA (AK) 166 Dc16
Hawkins Island ▲ USA (AK) 165 Cg15
Hawkinsville ○ USA (GA) 178 Fj29
Hawke's Head Lookout ◫ AUS 104 Qh59
Haw Springs ○ USA (WY) 171 Eh25
Hawrah ○ YE 60 Ne38
Hawtat Sudayr ○ KSA 59 Nc33
Hawthorne ○ USA (FL) 170 Ea26
Haxtun ○ USA (CO) 174 Ej25
Hay ○ AUS (NSW) 111 Sc63
Haya ○ SUD 135 Mj36
Hayar'er ○ CHN (HLG) 69 Pg27
Hayanga ○ CHN (AHU) 75 Qk31
Hayange ◰ F 23 Lg41
Hejaz ○ KSA 58 Mj32
Hayden ○ USA (AZ) 171 Ee29
Hayden ○ USA (CO) 171 Eg25
Haydere ○ TR 56 Me27
Haydock Park ◫ GB 21 Ks37
Hayes Creek ○ AUS (NT) 106 Rf52
Hayes, Mount ▲ USA 165 Cg14
Hayeswater ▲ IND 84 Ok39
Hayfield ○ PNG 115 Sb49
Hayk ○ ETH 142 Mj38
Hayling Island ◫ GB 21 Kt40
Hay Lake Ind. Res. ◫ CDN 167 Ea16
Hay Lakes ○ CDN (AB) 169 Ed19
Haymana ○ TR 56 Mg26
Hay, Mount ▲ AUS 103 Rg57
Haynes ○ USA (ND) 172 Ek23
Hay Point ○ AUS (QLD) 109 Se56
Hayrabolu ○ TR 45 Mh49
Hay River ○ CDN 167 Ec15
Hays ○ USA (KS) 174 Fa26
Hays ○ USA (MT) 169 Ef22
Hays ○ YE 60 Nb39
Hays Mountains ▲ 6 Jc34
Haysville ○ USA (KS) 174 Fb27
Haysyn ○ UA 41 Me42
Hayter ○ CDN (AB) 169 Eg19
Hayton ○ AUS (QLD) 107 Sd56
Haywards Heath ○ GB 21 Ku39
Hayward ○ USA (CA) 170 Dk26
Hayward ○ USA (WI) 172 Fe22
Hayy ○ IRQ 57 Nc28
Hazan ○ IRQ 57 Nb28
Hazard ○ USA (KY) 178 Fj27
Hazaré ○ IND 84 Oj39
Hazar Gölü ≋ TR 57 Mk26
Hazarasp ○ UZB 62 Oa25
Hazareeni N.P. Markhor Leopard ◫ PK 65 Od32
Hazaribagh ○ IND (JKD) 83 Pc34
Hazaribagh N.P. ◫ IND 83 Pc33
Hazar Sum ▲ AFG 63 Oe27
Hazebrouck ◰ F 23 Lc40
Hazelton ○ USA (ND) 172 Ek22
Hazelton ○ CDN (BC) 166 Df18
Hazen Bay ≋ USA 164 Bh15
Hazen Strait ≋ CDN 162 Ec03
Hazards Castle ◫ IR 64 Nj32
Hazel ○ USA (KY) 178 Fg27
Hazell ○ USA (AZ) 171 Ee28
Hazleton ○ USA (PA) 177 Gc25
Hazm al-Udayd ◫ KSA 58 Mk32
Hazor ∴ IL 56 Mh29
Hazratguda Mausoleum ◫ IRQ 57 Nb27
Hazro ○ TN 126 Le29
Hazu ○ TR 57 Nb28
Headingley ○ AUS (QLD) 106 Rk56
Heading Inn ◫ ZW 152 Mg55
Head of Bight ≋ AUS 105 Rf61
Head-Smashed-In Buffalo Jump ◫ ∴ CDN 169 Ed21
Heanor ○ GB 21 Kt38
Heard ▲ 9 Lb16
Hearne ○ USA (TX) 174 Fb30
Hearst ○ CDN (ON) 173 Fj21
Hearst San Simeon S.H.M. ◫ USA 170 Dk28
Heart's Content ○ CDN (NF) 177 Hd22

Hebbe Falls ◫ IND 84 Oh39
Hebbel ○ CHN 73 Qh26
Hebei ◫ CHN (HEI) 73 Qh28
Hebel ○ AUS (QLD) 109 Sd60
Hebenshausen ○ D 32 Lh40
Heber ○ D 32 Lh39
Heber ○ USA (CA) 170 Eb29
Heber City ○ USA (UT) 171 Ee25
Heberides ▲ GB 14 Ko04
Heber Springs ○ USA (AR) 175 Fe28
Hebi ○ CHN (HNN) 73 Qh28
Hebo ○ USA (OR) 168 Dj23
Hebrides ▲ GB 14 Ko04
Hebron ○ CDN 163 Gd07
Hebron ○ IL 58 Mh30
Hebron ○ USA (ND) 169 Ej22
Hebron ○ USA (NE) 174 Fb25
Heby ○ S 31 Lr31
Hecate Strait ≋ CDN 166 De19
Hecelchakán ○ MEX (CAM) 183 Fe35
Heceta Island ▲ USA (AK) 166 Dd18
Hechford Bank ◰ 88 Pj40
Hechi ○ CHN (GXZ) 74 Qd33
Hechingen ○ D 33 Lj42
Hechuan ○ CHN (CGQ) 74 Qd30
Hecla ○ CDN (MB) 172 Fb20
Hecla/Grindstone Prov. Park ◫ CDN 172 Fb20
Hecla Island ▲ CDN 172 Fb20
Hector ○ USA (AR) 175 Fe28
Hectorspruit ○ ZA 155 Mf58
Hector Island ▲ IND 88 Pg40
Haverfordwest ○ GB 21 Kq39
Haverhill ○ GB 21 La39
Hédé ◰ F 22 Kt42
Heddal stavkirke ◫ ◫ N 30 Lk31
Hédé ◰ F 22 Kt42
Hede ○ S 17 Lg14
Hedensa ○ S 31 Lq30
Hedesunda ○ S 31 Lr30
Heek ○ D 32 Lh38
Heerde ○ NL 23 Lg38
Heerenveen ○ NL 23 Lf38
Heerhugowaard ○ NL 23 Le38
Heerlen ○ NL 23 Lg40
Hefa ○ IL 56 Mh29
Hefeng ○ CHN (HUB) 74 Qf31
Heflin ○ USA (AL) 175 Fh29
Hegang ○ CHN (HLG) 76 Rf22
Hegura-jima ▲ J 79 Rj27
Hegyfalu ○ H 42 Lq43
Hegysúr ○ H 42 Lr43
Heho ○ MYA 86 Ph35
Hei Shan ▲ CHN 73 Qg26
Heian ○ CHN (HUB) 74 Qf30
Heidal ○ N 30 Lk30
Heide ○ D 32 Lk37
Heidelberg ○ D 33 Lj41
Heidelberg ○ USA (MS) 175 Ff30
Heidelberg ○ ZA 154 Ma63
Heidelberg ○ ZA 155 Me59
Heidenau ○ D 32 Lo40
Heidenheim ○ D 33 Ll42
Heidenreichstein ○ A 42 Lq42
Heide-Park ◫ D 32 Ll37
Heiðin há ▲ IS 18 Jc27
Heijiang ○ CHN (HLG) 71 Rd20
Heijiang ○ CHN (GZG) 74 Qf35
Heikendorf ○ D 32 Ll36
Heilbron ○ ZA 155 Md59
Heilbronn ○ D 33 Lk41
Heiligenbeil ○ D 35 Lm43
Heiligenblut ○ A 35 Lo43
Heiligenhafen ○ D 32 Ll36
Heilongjiang ◫ CHN 53 Ra05
Heilong Jiang ≈ CHN 76 Rf22
Heimaey ▲ IS 18 Ji27
Heinävesi ○ FIN 38 Mg28
Heinerscheid ○ L 23 Lg41
Heinola ○ FIN 38 Mg29
Heinsberg ○ D 32 Lg39
Heinze ○ USA (WA) 88 Pg38
Heishantou ○ CHN (LNG) 76 Rb25
Heishantou ○ CHN (NMZ) 71 Qk20
Heishui ○ CHN (SCH) 72 Qb29
Heitoral ○ BG (QO) 202 Hf53
Hejiang ○ CHN (SCH) 74 Qd31
Hejing ○ CHN (XUJ) 66 Pd24
Hejaz ○ KSA 58 Mj32
Hejian ○ CHN (HBI) 73 Qj28
Hejin ○ CHN (SAX) 73 Qg28
Hejing ○ CHN (SAX) 72 Qf28
Hekimhan ○ TR 56 Mj26
Hekla ▲ IS 18 Jc27
Hekla ▲ IS 18 Jc27
Hekou ○ CHN (GSU) 72 Qd27
Hekou ○ CHN (SCH) 74 Qd31
Hekou ○ CHN (YUN) 87 Qc34
Hel ○ PL 37 Ls36
Hel Abad ○ IR 57 Nf29
Helan Shan ▲ CHN 72 Qd27
Helena ○ USA (AR) 175 Fe28
Helena ▲ USA (MT) 169 Ee22
Helensburgh ○ GB 20 Kq34
Helen Springs Roadhouse ○ AUS (NT) 106 Rg55
Helensville ○ NZ 112 Th64
Helgoland ▲ D 32 Lj36
Helgoländer Bucht ≋ D 32 Lj36
Heliodoro ○ MEX (AHU) 78 Qe38
Heliolandia ○ BR (SP) 205 Hh57
Heliopolis ∴ ET 129 Mf32
Hell ○ CHN (JLN) 76 Rd24
Hella ○ IS 18 Jc27
Hellendoorn ○ NL 23 Lg38
Hellesvikan ○ N 16 Le14
Helligdomsklipperne ◫ DK 31 Lp35
Hellín ○ E 25 Ks52
Hells Canyon ◫ USA 168 Eb23
Hells Canyon Nat. Rec. Area ◫ USA 168 Eb23
Hells Gate Airtram ◫ CDN 168 Dk21
Hell Ville = Andoany ○ RM 157 Nb37
Helmand ≈ AFG 64 Oa30
Helmand ◫ AFG 64 Ob30
Helmeringhausen ○ NAM 150 Lj58
Helmond ○ NL 23 Lf39
Helmsdale ○ GB 20 Kr32
Helmstedt ○ D 32 Lm38
Helong ○ CHN (JLN) 76 Re25
Helper ○ USA (UT) 171 Ee26
Helsby ○ GB 21 Ks37
Helsingborg ○ S 30 Ln34
Helsingør ○ DK 30 Ln34
Helsinki = Helsingfors ▲ FIN 38 Me30

Helston ○ GB 21 Kp40
Heltermaa ○ EST 38 Md32
Helvécia ○ BR (BA) 203 Ja54
Helvécia ○ RA (SF) 209 Gk61
Helvetinjärven kansallispuisto ◫ FIN 38 Md28
Hemau ○ D 33 Lm41
Hemavan ○ S 16 Lh13
Hemel Hempstead ○ GB 21 Ku39
Hemer ○ D 32 Lh39
Hemet ○ USA (CA) 170 Eb29
Hemingford ○ USA (NE) 171 Ej24
Hemis Monastery ◫ IND 81 Oj29
Hemling ○ S 16 Lk14
Hemmoor ○ D 32 Lk37
Hemnes ○ N 30 Lm31
Hemnesberget ○ N 16 Lg12
Hemphill ○ USA (TX) 174 Fd30
Hempstead ○ USA (TX) 174 Fb30
Hemse ○ S 31 Lt33
Hemsedal ○ N 30 Lk30
Hemyš ○ CHN 73 Qg29
Hemyock ○ GB 21 Kr40
Henan ◫ CHN (HNN) 73 Qg28
Henares ≈ E 27 Ks51
Henashi-zaki ▲ J 77 Rk25
Henbury ○ AUS (NT) 108 Rg58
Henbury Meteorite Craters ◫ AUS 108 Rg58
Henderiksdale ○ ZA 154 Ma62
Henderadura ○ E 27 Ko51
Henderson ○ USA 207 Gj59
Henderson ○ RA (BA) 209 Gk61
Henderson ○ USA (KY) 175 Fg27
Henderson ○ USA (NC) 178 Ga27
Henderson ○ USA (NV) 170 Ec28
Henderson ○ USA (TN) 175 Ff28
Henderson ○ USA (TX) 174 Fd29
Henderson ○ USA (NY) 177 Gb24
Hendorabi ▲ IR 64 Ng32
Hendon ○ CDN (SK) 169 Ej19
Hengelo ○ NL 23 Lg38
Heng Shan ▲ CHN (HUN) 75 Qh32
Henganofi ○ PNG 115 Sc49
Hengchun ○ RC 75 Ra34
Hengduan Shan ▲ CHN 87 Pk32
Hengelo ○ NL 23 Lg38
Hengoed ○ GB (HUN) 75 Qh32
Hengshan ○ CHN 74 Qg32
Hengshan ○ CHN 73 Qg27
Hengshui ○ CHN (HBI) 73 Qh27
Heng Xian ○ CHN (GZG) 74 Qe34
Hengyang ○ CHN (HUN) 74 Qg32
Henices'k ○ UA 49 Mh22
Hénin-Beaumont ◰ F 23 Lc40
Henley ○ CDN 163 Fa07
Henley-on-Thames ○ GB 21 Kt39
Hennebont ◰ F 22 Kr43
Hennef ○ D 32 Lh40
Hennenman ○ ZA 155 Md59
Hennessey ○ USA (OK) 174 Fb27
Hennigsdorf ○ D 32 Lo38
Henningsvær ○ N 16 Lh11
Hennop's River ◫ ZA 155 Md58
Henribourg ○ CDN (SK) 169 Eh18
Henrietta ○ USA (TX) 174 Fb29
Henrietta Maria, Cape ◫ CDN 163 Fc08
Henryetta ○ USA (OK) 174 Fc28
Henry Ford Museum ◫ USA (Dearborn, MI) 173 Fj24
Henry Lawrence Island ▲ IND 88 Pg39
Hevea ◫ H 43 Ma43
Hevi ◫ GH 137 La42
Hévíz ○ H 42 Lr44
Hevron ○ IL 58 Mh30
Hewart Downs ○ AUS (NSW) 108 Sa60
Hewitt ○ USA (TX) 174 Fb30
Hexham ○ GB 21 Ks36
Hexian ○ CHN (SCH) 87 Qb32
Hexigten Qi ○ CHN (NMZ) 73 Qj24
Hexrivierberge ▲ ZA 154 Lk62
Heyang ○ CHN (SAX) 72 Qf28
Hey Camp ○ CDN (AB) 167 Ee16
Heydalír ▲ IS 18 Kf26
Heydon ○ ZA 155 Mc61
Heyrieux ◰ F 25 Lf45
Heysham ○ GB 21 Ks36
Heyuan ○ CHN (GDG) 75 Qh34
Heywood ○ AUS (VIC) 110 Sa65
Heywood ○ AUS 103 Rc53
Heze ○ CHN (SDG) 73 Qh28
Hezhang ○ CHN (GZH) 87 Qc32
Hezhou ○ CHN (GSU)
Hhohho ◫ SD 155 Mf58
Hialeah ○ USA (FL) 179 Fk33
Hian ○ GB 137 Kj40
Hiawatha ○ USA (GA) 178 Fj28
Hiawatha ○ USA (KS) 171 Eh25
Hibbard ○ IRQ 57 Nb28
Hibberdene ○ ZA 155 Mf61
Hibbing ○ USA (MN) 172 Fd22
Hibernia Reef ◫ AUS 102 Rb52
Hickman ○ USA (KY) 175 Ff27
Hickory ○ USA (NC) 178 Fk28
Hickory Motor Speedway ◫ USA 178 Fk28
Hico ○ USA (WV) 175 Fa30
Hico ○ USA (TX) 174 Fa30
Hidaka ○ J 77 Sb24
Hidalgo ○ MEX (COH) 180 Eg30
Hidalgo ○ MEX (MCH) 183 Fd36
Hidalgo ○ MEX (TAM) 182 Fb33
Hidalgo ○ MEX (ZCT) 182 Ej34
Hidalgo del Parral ○ MEX (CHH) 180 Eh32
Hida-sammyaku ▲ J 79 Rj27
Hiddensee ▲ D 32 Lo36
Hiddenvale ○ AUS (QLD) 106 Rg54
Hidden Valley ○ AUS (QLD) 107 Rd54
Hidden Valley ○ AUS (QLD) 107 Sd55
Hidden Valley N.P. = Mirima National Park ◫ AUS 103 Re53
Hidra ▲ N 30 Lg32
Hidrelétrica Curuá-Una ◫ BR (PA) 193 Hc47
Hieflau ○ A 35 Lp43
Hien ○ VN 89 Qd38
Hienghène ◰ F 118 Tc56
Hien Luong Bridge ◫ VN 89 Qe37
Higashine ○ J 77 Rk26
Higgins ○ USA (TX) 174 Fa28
Higginsville ○ AUS (WA) 104 Ra61
Highborn Cay ▲ BS 179 Gb34
Highbury ○ AUS (QLD) 107 Sb53
Highbury ○ AUS (QLD) 109 Se59
Highbury ○ GUY 194 Hc42
Highcraft ○ ZA 155 Mf61
Highflats ○ ZA 155 Mf61
High Island ▲ USA 164 Bk16
Highland Plains ○ AUS (NT) 106 Rj55

Hvanneyri – Isla de los Riachos

Hvanneyri IS Jt26
Hvanngiljafoss IS 18 Ka26
Hvar HR 35 Lr47
Hvar HR 35 Lr47
Hvastovići RUS 48 Mh19
Hveragerði IS 18 Jt27
Hveravellir IS 18 Ka26
Hvide Sande DK 30 Lj33
Hvittingfoss N 30 Lk31
Hvolsvöllur IS 18 Jt27
Hwali ZW 152 Mf56
Hwange ZW 152 Md55
Hwange N.P. ZW 152 Md55
Hwaseong Fortress ROK 78 Rd27
Hwasun Dolmen Site ROK 78 Rd27
Hwedza ZW 152 Mf55
Hwelziyeh SYR 57 Na27
Hyades, Cerro RCH 210 Gd69
Hyannis USA (MA) 177 Ge25
Hyannis USA (NE) 172 Ek25
Hydaburg USA (AK) 166 Dd18
Hyden AUS (WA) 104 Qk62
Hyden USA (KY) 178 Fj27
Hyde Park USA (VT) 177 Gd23
Hyder USA (AK) 166 De18
Hyderabad IND (APH) 82 Ok37
Hyderabad PK 65 Oe33
Hyères F 25 Lg27
Hyesan PRK 78 Re25
Hyland Plateau CDN 166 Df15
Hyères F 25 Lg27
Hyrax Hill EAK 144 Mk46
Hysham USA (MT) 169 Eg22
Hyuga J 79 Rf29
Hyvinkää FIN 38 Me30

I

Ia GR 47 Mf54
Iaciara BR (GO) 203 Hg53
Iaçu BR (BA) 201 Hk52
Iagain Island PNG 117 Sh48
Iaguareté BR (AM) 193 Gf45
Iakora RM 157 Nd57
Íamara PNG 115 Sb50
Ianabinda RM 157 Nc57
Ianakafy RM 157 Nc57
Ianapera RM 157 Nc57
Ianca RO 45 Mh45
Iapim BR (AC) 196 Gd49
Iaripo BR (PA) 194 Hc45
Iaşi RO 45 Mh44
Iasmos GR 45 Mf49
Iba RP 90 Qk38
Ibacari BR (BA) 203 Ja53
Ibadan WAN 138 Lc42
Ibague CI 192 Gc43
Ibaiti BR (PR) 205 He57
Ibaïé EAL 44 Lc48
Ibanda EAU 144 Mf46
Ibanda Game Reserve EAT 144 Mf46
Ibanga RDC 146 Md47
Ibarantih BR (BA) 201 Ja48
Ibaretama BR (CE) 201 Ja48
Ibarra EC 196 Ga45
Ibarreta RA (FO) 204 Ha58
Ibatiba BR (ES) 203 Hk56
Ibb YE 60 Nc39
Ibbenbüren D 32 Lh38
Ibeas de Juarros E 28 Kr48
Ibembo RDC 141 Mb44
Iberia USA (MO) 172 Fd26
Iberia E 196 Ge45
Ibertioga BR (MG) 203 Hj56
Ibi E 29 Ku52
Ibi WAN 138 Le41
Ibiá BR (MG) 203 Hg55
Ibiaí BR (MG) 203 Hj53
Ibiassucê BR (BA) 203 Hj53
Ibibobo BR 207 Gj56
Ibicuí BR (BA) 201 Ja50
Ibicuy RA (ER) 204 Ha62
Ibimirim BR (PE) 201 Jb50
Ibindy RM 157 Nd56
Ibipeba BR (BA) 201 Hj51
Ibipetum BR (BA) 201 Hj51
Ibipira BR (BA) 195 Hh47
Ibipitanga BR (BA) 203 Hj54
Ibiporã BR (PR) 202 He57
Ibiporanga BR (SP) 202 Hf56
Ibiquera BR (BA) 201 Hj51
Ibiraci BR (BA) 201 Hj51
Ibiracu BR (ES) 203 Hk56
Ibirama BR (SC) 205 Hf59
Ibirama, T.I. BR 205 Hf59
Ibiranhém BR (BA) 203 Hk54
Ibirataiá BR (BA) 201 Ja53
Ibirité BR (BA) 203 Hh56
Ibirubá BR (RS) 204 Hd60
Ibitiara BR (BA) 201 Hj52
Ibitinga BR (SP) 202 Hf56
Ibiza = Eivissa E 29 Lb51
Ibiza = Eivissa E 29 Lb52
Ibo BR (BA) 201 Ja50
Ibo MOC 147 Na52
Ibohamane RN 132 Lc38
Iboih Beach RI 84 Pc42
Ibolo RDC 149 Lk46
Ibologelo EAT 146 Mg48
Ibonma RM 114 Rg47
Ibotirama BR (BA) 201 Hj52
Ibra OM 61 Nk34
Ibrce J 79 Rr30
Ibusuki J 79 Rf30
Ibra PE 197 Ge53
Icabarú YV 193 Gk43
Icacos Point YV 193 Gj40
Içana BR (AM) 193 Gf45
Icaño RA (CA) 207 Gh60
Icapuí BR (CE) 201 Jb48
Içara BR (SC) 205 Hf60
Icaraí de Amontada BR (CE) 201 Ja47
Icatiara BR (PR) 202 Hd57
Icatu, T.I. BR 202 Hd56
Ice Caves USA 168 Dk23
Icefield Ctr. CDN 168 Eb19
Icel TR 56 Mf27
Iceland IS 18 Ju24
Iceland IS 18 Ju24
Iceland Basin 14 Jb04
Iceland Faroe Rise 163 Kb06
Icelandic Plateau 160 Ka03
Içeyçume RI 56 Mg27
Ice Stream A 6 Cd35
Ice Stream B 6 Cd35
Ice Stream C 6 Cd35
Ice Stream D 6 Cd35
Ice Stream E 6 Cd35
Ichalkaranji IND (MHT) 82 Oh37
Ichchapuram IND (APH) 83 Pc36
Iche MA 125 Kb29
Ichenhausen D 33 Ll42
Icheu WAN 138 Ld42
Ichhawar IND (MPH) 82 Oj34
Ichinomiya J 79 Rj28
Ichinos J
Ichkeul, P.N. de TN 126 Le27
Ich'on PRK 78 Rd26
Ich'on ROK 78 Rd27

Iclod RO 43 Md44
Içmeler TR 47 Mf54
Icnja UA 48 Mg20
Icó BR (CE) 201 Ja49
Icoca ANG 148 Lg43
Icy Cape USA (AK) 165 Bk10
Icy Cape USA (AK) 165 Cc11
Icy Reef USA (AK) 165 Cc11
Ida SP 145 Nb45
Idabato CAM 138 Le43
Idabel USA (OK) 174 Fc29
Idafe ETH 142 Na42
Idaga Hamus ETH 142 Mk38
Ida Grove USA (IA) 172 Fc24
Idah WAN 138 Ld42
Idaho USA 168 Ec24
Idaho Falls USA (ID) 169 Ed24
Idalia N.P. AUS (QLD) 109 Sc58
Idalion GE 57 Nc25
Ida-Oumarkt MA 124 Kf31
Ida Valley AUS (WA) 104 Ra60
Idd al-Ghanam SUD 134 Mc40
Idelès DZ 132 Lc34
Idenao CAM 138 Le43
Idgaon BD 86 Pg35
Idhan WAN 138 Lc42
Idi WAN 138 Lc42
Idini RIM 130 Kc37
Idiofa RDC 149 Lk48
Id-Kah-Mosque CHN 66 Oj26
Idlib SYR 56 Mg28
Idoani WAN 138 Lc42
Idodi WAN 138 Lc42
Idodoma EAT 147 Mj49
Idongo RCA 140 Ma42
Idra GR 45 Md53
Idrefjäll S 17 Lg15
Idrija SLO 42 Lp45
Idstein D 33 Lj40
Idudma RDC 149 Ma47
Idutywa ZA 155 Me62
Idvor SCG 44 Ma45
Iecava LV 39 Me34
Ie-jima J 79 Rd32
Iepê BR (SP) 202 He57
Ierápetra GR 47 Mf55
Ierissós GR 45 Md50
Iernut RO 43 Me44
Ieud RO 43 Md43
Ifakara EAT 147 Mj50
Ifaki WAN 138 Lc42
Ifanadiana RM 157 Nd56
Ifanirea RM 157 Nd57
Ifaty RM 157 Nb57
Ife WAN 138 Lc42
Ifenat TCH 133 Lk39
Iferouâne RN 139 Le36
Ifetedo WAN 138 Lc42
Ifetesene DZ 126 Lc33
Iffezheim D 33 Lj42
Ifford N 16 Md10
Ifon WAN 138 Lc42
Ifumbe EAT 146 Mg49
Igabi WAN 138 Ld40
Igalukula EAT 146 Mg48
Igalulu EAT 146 Mg45
Iganga EAU 144 Mg45
Igangan WAN 138 Lc42
Igaporã BR (BA) 201 Hj52
Igapora BR (RN) 201 Ja48
Igarapava BR (SP) 203 Hg56
Igarapé BR (MG) 203 Hh56
Igarapé-Açú BR (PA) 195 Hg46
Igarapé Capana, T.I. BR 196 Gc50
Igarapé Grande BR (MA) 200 Hh48
Igarapé Lages, T.I. BR 198 Gh51
Igarapé Lourdes, T.I. BR 196 Gf50
Igarapé Mirim BR (PA) 195 Hf46
Igarapé Ribeirão, T.I. BR 198 Gh51
Igarka RUS 54 Pb05
Igarra WAN 138 Lc42
Igatpuri IND (MHT) 82 Og36
Igbara WAN 138 Lc41
Igbetti WAN 138 Lc41
Igbo WAN 138 Lc41
Igbo-Ora WAN 138 Lc42
Igboho WAN 138 Lc41
Igbo-Ukwu WAN 138 Ld42
Igdir TR 57 Nb26
Ighil Izane DZ 126 Lb28
Ighiu RO 43 Md44
Igichuk Hills USA 165 Bj12
Igina RDC 141 Md44
Igiugig USA (AK) 164 Cc16
Igle, Cerro RA 210 Gd71
Iglesias I 36 Lj51
Ignace CDN (ON) 172 Fe21
Ignacio Allende MEX (DGO) 181 Ej33
Ignalina LT 39 Mg35
Ignarasü I 36 Lp50
Ignasino RUS 71 Rb19
Igneada TR 45 Mh48
Igoma EAT 146 Mg50
Igoto MOC 152 Mg53
Igreja de Boroma MOC 152 Mg53
Igreja de Nossa Senhora do Rosário dos Pretos BR 201 Ja52
Igreja de São Francisco BR 201 Ja52
Igrita WAN 138 Ld43
Iguaçu, P.N. do BR 204 Hc58
Iguaí BR (BA) 203 Hk53
Iguala MEX (GUR) 182 Fa36
Igualada E 29 Lb49
Iguatemi BR (MS) 202 Hc57
Iguatu BR (CE) 201 Ja49
Iguazú, P.N. BR/RA 204 Hc58
Iguéla G 148 Lc46
Igüeña E 26 Ko48
Iguguno EAT 146 Mg48
Igüidi Ouan Kasa LAR 133 Lf33
Igunga EAT 146 Mg48
Igusule EAT 144 Mg47
Iharana RM 157 Ne54
Iharosberény H 42 Lr44
Iheya J 79 Rd32
Iheya-jima J 79 Rd32
Ihiala WAN 138 Ld43
Ihosy RM 157 Nd56
Ihtiman BG 44 Md48
Ihu PNG 115 Sc49
Ihumbu EAT 147 Mh49

Iisalmi FIN 16 Md14
Iittala FIN 38 Me29
Ij IND (APH) 82 Oj37
Iáfenes RIM 131 Kf35
Ijebu-Igbu WAN 138 Lc42
Ijebu-Ode WAN 138 Lc42
Ijev-Merapi Maelang Reserves RI 95 Qh50
Ijevan ARM 57 Nc21
IJmuiden NL 23 Le38
Ijoubban RIM 131 Kg34
Ijouksk MA 125 Kh34
IJssel NL 23 Lg38
IJsselmeer NL 23 Lf38
IJsselstein NL 23 Lf38
Ijui BR (RS) 204 Hd60
Ikaalinen FIN 38 Md29
Ikali ND 145 Na42
Ikalto Monastery GE 57 Nc25
Ikanbujimal CHN (XUZ) 67 Pe26
Ikanda RDC 149 Ma47
Ikang EAK 144 Mk46
Ikaria GR 47 Mg53
Ikast DK 30 Lk34
Ikauna IND (UPH) 83 Pa32
Ikeda J 77 Sb24
Ikeja WAN 138 Lc42
Ikela RDC 149 Mb46
Ikelenge Z 151 Mc51
Ikenan SP 145 Na42
Ikengué G 148 Lc46
Ikerre WAN 138 Lc42
Ikh Bogd Uul MNG 70 Qa33
Ikh Bulag MNG 70 Qc22
Ikh Gazaryn Chuluu MNG 70 Qd23
Ikh Khayrkhan MNG 70 Qc22
Ikh Khenteyn Nuruu MNG 70 Qe21
Ikh Nuuruudyn Khotgor MNG 67 Ph21
Iki-shusuji MNG 70 Qd21
Iki J 79 Re29
Ikire WAN 138 Lc42
Iko WAN 138 Ld43
Ikoko RDC 149 Lk46
Ikoma WAN 138 Lb41
Ikom WAN 138 Le42
Ikongo RDC 140 Lk45
Ikot Ekpene WAN 138 Ld43
Ikoto SUD 144 Mf45
Ikskile LV 39 Me34
Ikuba EAT 146 Mf49
Ikutha EAK 144 Mk47
Ilagan RP 90 Ra37
Ilaiyankudi IND (TNU) 84 Ok41
Ilaji WAN 138 Ld42
Ilaka Atinanana RM 157 Nd56
Ilakaka RM 157 Nc55
Ilam NEP 83 Pd32
Ilan RC 75 Ra33
Ilangali EAT 146 Mh49
Ilaro WAN 138 Lc42
Ila-Orangun WAN 138 Lc41
Ilara WAN 138 Lc41
Ilaura EAT 144 Mg47
Ilave PE 206 Gf54
Ilawa PL 41 Lu37
Ilawe WAN 138 Lc42
Ilbilbie AUS (QLD) 109 Se56
Ilbisil EAK 144 Mj47
Ilchester GB 21 Ks40
Il'ča UA 43 Mg40
Ildir TR 47 Mg52
Ile KZ 66 Ok24
Ile-à-la-Crosse CDN 167 Eg18
Ile-Ala-Tonga KS 63 Qg26
Ile Aoba VU 118 Td53
Ile Aride F 23 Lc41
Ile Art F 118 Td57
Ile aux Serpents MS 157 Nj55
Ile-Bé-Vache SY 145 Nh47
Ile-Bé-Vache RH 186 Gd36
Ile Baabn F 118 Tc56
Ile Balabio F 118 Tc56
Ile-à-la-Gonâve RH 186 Gd36
Ile de la Tortue RH 186 Gd35
Ile Denis SY 145 Nh47
Ile-d'Entrée CDN (QC) 176 Hb22
Ile des Genévriers CDN 176 Ha20
Ile des Pins F 118 Td57
Ile Desroches SY 145 Ng48
Ile de Tiagba CI 137 Kh43
Ile de Tumba MA 124 Kd41
Ile d'Orléans CDN 176 Gd21
Ile du Diable F 194 Hd43
Ile du Nord SY 145 Nf51
Ile du Nord SY 145 Nh47
Ile du Petit Mécantina CDN 176 Ha20
Ile d'Yeu F 24 Kt44
Ile Esumba RDC 140 Ma45
Ile Europa F 153 Na57
Ile Joinville 6 Hb31
Ile Roxa GNB 136 Kd40
Ile Kötomo F 118 Td57
Ile Lamèque Island CDN 176 Gg21
Ile Matthew F 10 Tb12
Ile Miquelon F 177 Hd23
Ile Miscou Island CDN 176 Gg21
Ile Monger F 118 Ha20
Ile Moucha DJI 143 Nb40
Ile Plate SY 145 Nh48
Ile Pot F 118 Tb55
Iles Belep F 118 Tb55
Iles Chausey F 24 Kt42
Iles Daos F 118 Tb55
Iles de Glénan F 22 Kr43
Iles de Kerkenah TN 126 Lf28
Iles de la Madeleine, P.N. SN 130 Kb38
Iles de Los RG 136 Kd41
Iles des Saintes F 187 Gk38
Iles d'Hyères F 25 Lg44
Iles du Rapeau F 11 Cb11

Îles du Salut F 194 Hd43
Îles Ehotilés, P.N. des CI 137 Kj43
Ilgar TR 56 Mg25
Ilgaz Dağları TR 56 Mg25
Ilgaz Dağı Milli Parkı TR 56 Mf26
Ilgın TR 56 Me25
Ilha Aaratuba BR 199 Gk47
Ilha Autaz BR 199 Ha47
Ilha Bailique BR 195 Hd45
Ilhabela BR (SP) 205 Hh57
Ilha Cajutuba BR 195 Hg46
Ilha Caravela BR 201 Jb49
Ilha Caravelas BR 203 Ja54
Ilha Carrapatal BR 195 Hj47
Ilha da Caviana de Dentro BR 195 He45
Ilha da Caviana de Fora BR 195 He45
Ilha Cipotuba BR 198 Gj47
Ilha Comprida BR 205 Hg58
Ilha Cuxiuara BR 198 Gh48
Ilha da Boa Vista CV 136 Jj37
Ilha da Botija BR 198 Gj47
Ilha da Conteiga, T.I. BR 205 Hf55
Ilha da Inhaca MOC 155 Mg59
Ilha de Benguerra MOC 153 Mh56
Ilha de Boipeba BR 201 Ja52
Ilha de Bolama GNB 136 Kc40
Ilha de Brava CV 136 Jh38
Ilha de Curari BR 199 Gk47
Ilha de Fogo CV 136 Jj38
Ilha de Itamaracá BR 201 Jc49
Ilha de Jeta GNB 136 Kc40
Ilha de Maio CV 136 Jj38
Ilha de Maracá BR 195 Hd44
Ilha de Marajó BR 195 He46
Ilha de Moçambique MOC 153 Mh55
Ilha de Orango GNB 136 Kc40
Ilha de Orangozinho GNB 136 Kc40
Ilha de Pecixe BR 136 Kb40
Ilha de Santa Catarina BR 205 Hf59
Ilha de Santa Luzia CV 136 Jh37
Ilha de Santa Rita BR 199 Hc47
Ilha de Santiago CV 136 Jj38
Ilha de Santo Antão CV 136 Jh37
Ilha de São Francisco BR 205 Hf59
Ilha de São Luís BR 195 Hh47
Ilha de São Nicolau CV 136 Jh37
Ilha de São Sebastião CV 205 Hh57
Ilha de São Vicente CV 136 Jh37
Ilha do Bazaruto MOC 153 Mh56
Ilha do Cabo Frio BR 203 Hk57
Ilha do Caju BR 201 Hj47
Ilha do Coro BR 198 Gj47
Ilha do Corumbau BR 195 Hf45
Ilha do Faroli BR 201 Jb49
Ilha do Faroli BR 201 Jd47
Ilha do Ibo MOC 147 Na52
Ilha do Mel BR 205 Hf58
Ilha do Mexiana BR 195 He45
Ilha do Porto Santo P 124 Kb29
Ilha dos Macacos BR 195 He46
Ilha Fernando de Noronha BR 201 Jd47
Ilha Fernando de Noronha BR 201 Jd47
Ilha Formosa GNB 136 Kc40
Ilha Grande BR (PI) 201 Hk47
Ilha Grande BR 205 Hh57
Ilha Grande de Gurupá BR 195 He46
Ilha Grande de Santa Isabel BR 201 Hk47
Ilha Ipixuna BR 198 Gj47
Ilha Itapuaica BR 201 Ja52
Ilha Jamaucu BR 195 He46
Ilha Loreto BR (PI) 201 Hk47
Ilha Magaruque MOC 153 Mh56
Ilha Mangunça BR 195 Hh46
Ilha Marengo em Pavilhão BR 199 Hb50
Ilha Metemo MOC 147 Na52
Ilha Mexiana BR 195 He45
Ilha Muturi BR 195 He46
Ilhanköy TR 45 Mh50
Ilha Panamim BR 198 Gj47
Ilha Queimada Pequena BR 205 Hg58
Ilha Queremimbi MOC 147 Na51
Ilha Quirimba MOC 147 Na52
Ilha Roxa GNB 136 Kc40
Ilha Santa Carolina MOC 153 Mh56
Ilha Santana BR 195 Hh46
Ilha São Jorge BR 195 Hh46
Ilhas de Barlovento CV 136 Jh37
Ilhas Desertas P 124 Kb29
Ilhas de Sotavento CV 136 Jj38
Ilhéu Martins BR (PR) 205 He58
Ilha-à-Adiatafene DZ RMM 131 Kj38
Ilha Afetaheim BR 199 Ha48
Ilha Urubu BR 199 Hd47
Ilha Urucuri BR 199 Hd46
Ilhavo P 26 Km50
Ilha Vamizi MOC 147 Na52
Ilhéo A BR (PE) 201 Jb49
Ilhéu Bugio BR 199 Hb48
Ilhéu de Barlavento CV 136 Jh38
Ilhéu Razo CV 136 Jh37
Ilhéus Secos e Rombo CV 136 Jh38
Ilhota da Maloca Arori BR (PA) 194 Hd45

Iliç TR 57 Mk26
Iliça TR 47 Mh51
Ilıca IND (MG) 203 Hh56
Iligan RP 91 Rc41
Iliigan Bay RP 91 Rb41
Ilih BHR 44 L47
Iliki USA 165 Sd50
Ilim Island RP 90 Ra39
Il'ino RUS 48 Mf18
Il'inovka RUS 71 Re21
Iliokomi GR 45 Me50
Ilirska Bistrica SLO 42 Lp45
Il'ja SY 39 Mh36
Ilkal IND (KTK) 82 Oj38
Ilkeston RCH 208 Ge61
Ilkley GB 21 Kt37
Illapel RCH 208 Ge61
Il-Tanoute MA 124 Kf31
Il-Léla RN 132 Lc39
Il-Léla RN 132 Lc39
Illertissen D 33 Ll42
Illescas, Cerro PE 196 Fk49
Illescas E 27 Kr50
Ile-sur-Têt F 24 Lc48
Illgen City USA (MN) 172 Fe22
Illiers-Combray F 22 Lb42
Illimani, Nevado del BOL 206 Gg54
Illimo Yucume PE 196 Ga49
Illinois, Volcán EC 196 Ga46
Illinois USA 175 Fe25
Illizi DZ 126 Le32
Ilm D 32 Lm39
Ilm enau D 33 Ll40
Ilm inster GB 21 Ks40
Ilmk GR 47 Md49
Ilobu WAN 138 Lc42
Ilobasco ES 184 Ff39
Iloc RCH 208 Gd63
Ilofa WAN 138 Lc41
Ilok D 84 Pg40
Iloilo RP 90 Ra40
Ilok C 44 Lu45
Ilomantsi FIN 16 Md15
Ilonga EAT 147 Mj50
Ilongero EAT 146 Mh49
Ilorin WAN 138 Lc41
Ilovays'k UA 49 Mj22
Ilpohefen D 33 Ll42
Ilsko S 17 Lj15
Iluka AUS 109 Sg60
Ilükste LV 39 Mg35
Ilulissat = Jakobshavn DK 163 Hc05
Ilupu IND (ARP) 86 Ph31
Ilur RI 97 Rd44
Ilushi WAN 138 Ld42
Ilwa Mare RO 43 Me43
Ilwaco USA (WA) 168 Dh22
Ilwaki RI 97 Rd49
Ilwendo Z 151 Mc54
Ilža PL 41 Mb39
Imabari J 79 Rg28
Imachrakeksti BR (PB) 201 Jb49
Imaichi J 79 Rk27
Imakane J 77 Sb24
Imajo J 79 Rj28
Imajó BR (RJ) 205 He57
Imali MEX (SL) 180 Eg33
Imam al Hamzah IRQ 59 Nc30
Imam-gung ROK 78 Rd27
Imamoğlu TR 56 Mf27
Imam Zadeh Ali IR 64 Ng28
Imam Zadeh Qolam Rasuli IR 64 Oa33
Imamzadeh Jafar IR 57 Nf28
Imanombo EAT 157 Nd56
Imari J 79 Re29
Imaruí BR (SC) 205 Hf60
Imasa SUD 135 Mj36
Imata PE 197 Ge54
Imatong Mountains SUD 144 Mg43
Imatra FIN 38 Mg29
Imavere EST 38 Mf32
Imbaú BR (PR) 205 He58
Imbituba BR (SC) 205 Hf60
Imbituva BR (PR) 205 He58
Imbé BR 203 Hh57
Imenas RMM 157 Ne54
Imerimandroso RM 157 Ne54
Imênsa RDC 140 La44
Imérodo SY 145 Nf51
Imi ETH 142 Nb42
Imi-Tanoute MA 124 Kf30
Imi-n'Ouasif MA 125 Kg30
Imar IR 57 Nf20
Imarui SUD 135 Mj36
Imjin Do ROK 78 Rd28
Imlay USA (NV) 170 Eb25
Immendstadt D 33 Ll43
Immokalee USA (FL) 179 Fk32
Imola I 34 Lm46
Imotski HR 35 La47
Impasugong RP 91 Rc41
Imperatriz BR (MA) 200 Hg48
Imperatriz BR 195 He46
Imperial USA (NE) 174 Ek25
Imperial Mills USA 167 Ee18
Imperial Palace CHN 73 Qj25
Imperial Palace CHN 76 Rc24
Imperiase Reef AUS (SA) 108 Rh58
Impfondo RCB 148 Lk44
Imphal IND (MNP) 86 Ph33
Imphy F 25 Ld44
Imrali Adasi TR 45 Mj50
Imralı TR 45 Mj50
Imroz AUS 154 Mb39

In A'mguel DZ 132 Lc34
Inangahua NZ 113 Tf66
In-Azaoua DZ 132 Lc37
In-Belbel DZ 125 La30
Inca, Cerro del BOL/RCH 207 Gf56
Inca E 29 Lc51
Inca de Oro RCH 207 Ge61
Incahuasi BOL 206 Gh56
Incahuasi PE 196 Ga49
Incahuasi, Nevado de RA/RCH 207 Gf58
Incallajta BOL 206 Gh54
Incaracay BOL 206 Gg56
Ince Burnu TR 56 Mf26
Ince Burnu TR 56 Mg24
Incekum Burnu TR 56 Mg27
Incebel Dağları TR 56 Mj26
Incesu TR 56 Mf26
Inchaden MA 124 Kf30
Inchbonnie NZ 113 Tf67
Inchnadamph GB 20 Kq35
Inchon = Incheon ROK 78 Rd27
Inchope MOC 152 Mg54
Inciems LV 39 Me33
Incirliova TR 47 Mh53
Incudine, M. F 34 Lk48
Indaiá BR (MG) 203 Hh52
Indaiabira BR (BA) 200 Hh52
Indalsälven S 16 Lh14
Indapur IND (MHT) 82 Oh36
Indau MYA 86 Ph33
Indaw MYA 86 Pj33
Indaw MYA 86 Pj35
Indawgyi Lake Wildlife Sanctuary MYA 86 Ph35
Indefatigable Bank 21 Lc37
Indefatigable o Chávez = Isla Santa Cruz EC 197 Ff46
In-Délimane RMM 132 La38
In-Délimane RMM 132 La38
Independence USA (IA) 172 Fe24
Independence USA (KS) 174 Fc27
Independence USA (KY) 175 Fh26
Independence USA (MO) 174 Fc26
Independence USA (OR) 168 Dj23
Independence Hall USA 177 Gc26
Independence Mine USA 165 Cf15
Independence Rock S.H.S. USA 171 Eg24
Independência BOL 206 Gg54
Independência BR (CE) 201 Hk48
Independência BR (MA) 200 Hh48
Inderaba SUD 135 Mg39
Inderborskij KZ 54 Nc09
India IND (KTK) 82 Oh37
India USA (NT) 108 Rh57
Indiana AUS (VIC) 111 Sc65
Indiana USA 175 Fg26
Indiana N.P. USA 175 Fg26
Indiana Territory S.H.S. USA 175 Fg26
Indiana Transportation Mus. USA 173 Fg25
Indian Cabins CDN (AB) 167 Eb16
Indian Grave Mountain USA (AK) 165 Cf15
Indian Head SD 169 Ed23
Indian Lake CDN 172 Fe21
Indian Lake USA (NY) 177 Gc24
Indian Mosque USA 169 Eg26
Indian Mounds S.H.S. (Etowah) USA 175 Fh28
Indian Ocean 9 Nb13
Indianola USA (IA) 172 Fd25
Indianola USA (MS) 175 Fe29
Indianópolis BR (MG) 203 Hg55
Indianola USA 175 Fe27
Indian-Pacific (Western Australia) AUS 105 Rg61
Indian-Pacific (South Australia) AUS 105 Rg61
Indian Pt. USA 171 Eg26
Indian Pt. USA 171 Ed26
Indian Res. 159 CDN 169 Ef19
Indian Springs USA (NV) 170 Ec27
Indiantown CI 179 Fk32
Indian Township Ind. Res. USA 176 Gg23
Indian Trail Caverns USA 173 Fj25
Indian Wells USA (AZ) 171 Ee28
Indiara BR (GO) 202 Hf54
Indiaroba BR (BA) 201 Jb51
Indigirka RUS 55 Sb05
Indija SCG 44 Ma45
Indio USA (CA) 170 Eb29
Indio-Maíz, Reserva de Biosfera NIC 185 Fh40
Indio Rico RA (BA) 209 Gk65
Indispúr IND (ORS) 83 Pd35
Indira Gandhi Canal IND 80 Og31
Indira Sagar Reservoir IND 82 Oj34
Interior Highlands USA 174 Fc27
Indoebas Grande USA 165 Kc11
Indochina Peninsula 10 Qa08
Indombo G 148 Lg45
Indonesia RI 83 Qa10
Indonesia AUS (SA) 108 Rj57
Indore IND (MPH) 82 Oh34
Indramayu RI 95 Qd49
Indre Arna N 17 Lc15
Indri F 34 Li46
Indunjat RI 91 Md37
Indur IND 60 Nc39
Indus PK 65 Of31
Indus IND (APH) 82 Ok37
Indwe ZA 155 Md61

Ingeniero Guillermo N.Juárez RA (FO) 207 Gk57
Ingeniero Jacobacci RA (RN) 208 Gf66
Ingeniero Mora BOL 206 Gj55
Ingeniero Woudagemaal NL 23 Lf38
In Ghar DZ 125 La32
Inginiyagala CL 85 Pa42
Ingleward USA (CO) 170 Eb28
Ingoka Bum MYA 86 Pj33
Ingólfshöfði IS 18 Kd27
Ingoldstadt D 33 Ll42
Ingomar AUS (SA) 108 Rh60
Ingonish Beach CDN (NS) 176 Gg22
Ingozih GB 136 Kc39
Ingram USA (WI) 172 Fe23
Ingraham Trail CDN 167 Ed14
Ingraj Bazar IND (WBG) 86 Pd33
Ingushetia RUS 57 Nc24
Ingwe Z 151 Mc54
Inhafenga MOC 152 Mg53
Inhambane BR (BA) 201 Ja51
Inhaminga MOC 153 Mh55
Inhamitanga MOC 153 Mh55
Inhamuns BR (CE) 201 Hk48
Inhapim BR (MG) 203 Hj55
Inharrime MOC 153 Mh56
Inhaúma BR (BA) 200 Hh52
Inhauma, Volcán BR 200 Hh52
Inhaúnho MOC 152 Mh56
In Herene LAR 126 Lf32
Inobim BR (BA) 203 Hh53
Inhúma BR (PI) 201 Hk49
Inhumas BR (GO) 202 Hf54
Inió FIN 38 Mb30
Inishbofin IRL 19 Kj37
Inishkea IRL 19 Kj36
Inishman IRL 19 K37
Inishmore IRL 19 Kk37
Inishowen IRL 19 Kn35
Inishtrahull IRL 19 Kn35
Inishturk IRL 19 Kj37
Inja IS 67 Pd20
Injarah RG 57 Nc28
Injibara ETH 142 Mj40
Injune AUS (QLD) 109 Se59
Inkauk MYA 86 Pj37
Inkerman AUS (QLD) 107 Sa54
Inkosso, T.I. BR 198 Gd49
Inkoo = Ingå FIN 38 Mc30
Inkouélé RCB 148 Lh46
Inkster CDN (ND) 172 Fb21
Inland Kaikoura Range NZ 113 Tg67
Inlandsbanan S 16 Lh13
Inlandsbanan S 17 Lh15
Inle Lake MYA 86 Pj35
Inman KS 174 Fb27
I-n-Milach RMM 131 Kk37
Innamincka AUS (SA) 104 Ra59
Innamincka Regional Reserve AUS 108 Sa59
Innbygda N 16 Lh12
Inndyr N 16 Lh12
Inner Hebrides GB 20 Kr35
Inner Mongolia CHN 53 Qb05
Inner Silver Pit GB 21 La37
Inner Sister Island AUS (VIC) 111 Sd65
Inner Sound GB 20 Kp33
Innerleithen GB 20 Kr35
Innernsuen AUS (NSW) 109 Rj63
Innisfail AUS (QLD) 107 Sd54
Innisfail CDN (AB) 169 Ed19
Innisvale CDN (SK) 169 Sd61
Innoko N.W.R. USA 164 Cb14
Innsbruck A 34 Lm43
Innset N 16 Lj11
Inngiyda N 16 Lh12
Inocência BR (MS) 202 Hf55
Inobí G 46 Mb53
Inongo RDC 149 Lk46
Inoni ZW 152 Mf55
Inoro ZW 152 Mf55
Inoucdjouac = Inukjuak CDN (QC) 173 Ga17
Inoué RI 41 Ma39
Inowrocław PL 40 Lt38
I-n-Quezzam DZ 132 Lc35
Inowville ID AUS 209 Gd64
Inseln shuban CDN 149 Lj46
Insein MYA 86 Pj37
Iznik Iskenderun TR 56 Mg27
Inside Passage USA 166 Dd17
Insjön S 109 Sg58
Inskip Point AUS 109 Sg58
Insula Mică a Brăilei, P.N. RO 45 Mh46
Insúrate DARS 130 Kc34
Inta RUS 54 Nj05
Intamachi EAT 147 Mh49
Intelewa DZ 126 Le28
Interlaken CH 34 Lh44
International Amistad Reasional USA 181 Ek31
International Falls USA (MN) 172 Fc21
Interview Island IND 88 Pg39
Intipucá ES 142 Mk38
Intíu'ó ETH 142 Mk38
In-Tillit RMM 132 La38
Intorsura Buzaului RO 45 Mg45
Intu J 79 Ra28
Inuarajit PE 197 Ge53
Inubo-saki J 79 Sa28
Inúbia-Paulista BR (SP) 202 He56
Inukjuak CDN (QC) 173 Ga17
Inú River USA (MI) 176 Dd05
Inuvik CDN 162 Db05
Invercagill NZ 113 Td69
Invercargill AUS 109 Sf60
Inverell AUS (NSW) 109 Sf60
Invergordon GB 20 Kq33
Inverloch AUS (VIC) 111 Sc65
Invermoriston GB 20 Kq33
Inverness CDN (NS) 176 Gg22
Inverness GB 20 Kq33
Inverness USA (MS) 175 Fe29
Inverurie GB 20 Ks33
Inverway AUS (NT) 103 Re54
Inverway Channel MYA 88 Pj40

Investigator Passage MYA 88 Pj39
Investigator Shoal 94 Qh41
Investigator Strait AUS 110 Rj65
Inwood CDN (MB) 172 Fb20
Inyala EAT 152 Mg55
Inyanga ZW 152 Mg55
Inyanyen ZW 152 Mg55
Inyathi ZW 152 Me55
Inychek Glacier KS 66 Pa24
Inyokern USA (CA) 170 Eb28
Inyonga EAT 146 Mg49
Inza RUS 48 Nb19
In Ziza DZ 132 Lb34
Ioánnina GR (KS) 174 Fc27
Io-jima J 79 Rf30
Iola USA (KS) 174 Fc27
Iona GB 20 Ko34
Iona ANG 150 Lg54
Iona N.P. ANG 150 Lg54
Iongo ANG 149 Lj50
Ionian Islands GR 46 Lu51
Ionian Sea 14 Lb06
Ion Roată RO 45 Mg46
Ios GR 47 Mf54
Iowa USA 175 Fd24
Iowa City USA (MO) 172 Fe25
Iowa Falls USA (IA) 172 Fd24
Iowanga RDC 149 Mb46
Ipaçu BR (MG) 202 Hf55
Ipala WAN (JLC) 182 Fa35
Ipala, Volcán HN 184 Ff38
Ipameri BR (GO) 203 Hf54
Ipanu-Esa WAN 138 Lc41
Ipanema BR 201 Jb50
Ipanguaçu BR (RN) 201 Jb48
Ipao VU 118 Tf55
Iparia PE 197 Gc50
Ipatinga BR (MG) 203 Hj55
Ipatjevskij monastyr RUS 48 Na17
Ipaumirim GR (CE) 201 Ja49
Iperu WAN 138 Lc42
Ipetu-Ijesha WAN 138 Lc42
Ipiales CO 196 Gb45
Ipiaú BR (PR) 205 He58
Ipiranga BR (PR) 205 He58
Ipixuna BR (AM) 196 Ge49
Ipixuna, T.I. BR 198 Gj47
Ipogoro EAT 146 Mh50
Ipoh MAL 92 Qa43
Iporá BR (GO) 202 He54
Iporã BR (PR) 204 Hd58
Iporanga BR (SP) 205 Hf58
Ipota VU 118 Te55
Ipsvich GB 21 Ld38
Ipswich AUS (QLD) 109 Sg59
Ipu CI BR (SP) 202 Hf56
Ipueiras BR (CE) 201 Hk48
Ipupiara BR (BA) 201 Hj52
Iput RUS 48 Mg20
Iqaluit CDN 163 Gc06
Iqe CHN (QH) 69 Ph26
Iquique RCH 206 Ge56
Iquitos PE 196 Gd47
Iraan USA (TX) 174 Ek30
Ira Banda RCA 140 Mb43
Iracema BR (CE) 201 Ja49
Iracoubo F 194 Hd43
Iraka WAN 138 Le40
Iráklia GR 44 Mf54
Iráklia GR 47 Mf55
Iráklio GR 47 Mf55
Iran IR 53 Nb06
Iranduba BR (AM) 198 Gh48
Irani BR (SC) 204 He59
Iran Shahr IR 64 Oa32
Irau, Gunung MAL 94 Qa44
Irbeni RY V 39 Mb33
Irbid JOR 56 Mh29
Irbit RUS 54 Oa07
Irece BR (BA) 201 Hj51
Irécé BR 201 Hj51
Irede USA (IA) 172 Fe24
Irene RA (BA) 209 Gk65
Iretama BR (PR) 204 Hd58
Irgakly RUS 57 Nd23
Irgiz KZ 63 Oc09
M'Goun USA 154 Mb39
Iri = Iksan ROK 78 Rd27
Irian Jaya RI 114 Rk46
Iriba TCH 134 Mb38
Iribo RCH 208 Gd67
Iriga RP 90 Rb39
Irigul RMM 131 Kh37
Irimote Jima J 79 Rb33
Iringa EAT 147 Mh49
Irinjalakuda IND (KER) 84 Oj40
Iriona HN 184 Fh38
Iriri BR 194 Hd44
Irish Sea 21 Kr37
Irirn BR (RS) 204 Hd60
Irituia BR (PA) 195 Hg46
Irkeštam CHN (XUZ) 66 Og28
Irklijiv UA 49 Mg21
Irklineskoe vodohranilišče RUS 48 Na08
Irkutsk RUS 70 Qc19
Irma CDN (AB) 169 Ee19
Iroise, Mer d' F 22 Kq42
Iron River USA (MI) 173 Ff22
Ironton USA (MO) 175 Fe27
Irorogwakubwe GB 20 Kq34
Iron Gate GB 45 La46
Iron Knob AUS (SA) 110 Rj62
Iron Mountain USA (MI) 173 Fg23
Iron Range N.P. AUS 107 Sb52
Irosin RP 90 Rb39
Ir Ovot IS 58 Mh30
Irrawaddy MYA 86 Ph36
Irrisé RMM 157 Nc57
Irshad Pass PK 65 Oh27
Irshava UA 43 Md43
Irtysh RUS 54 Oc07
Iryna = Ertis 154 Od08
Irumu RDC 141 Me45
Irún E 28 Kt47
Iruña E 28 Kt47
Irupana BOL 206 Gg54
Irurita E 28 Kt47

Irurzun E 28 Kt48
Irvine CDN (AB) 169 Ee21
Irvine GB 20 Kq35
Irvinestown GB 19 Kn36
Irwin USA (CA) 178 Fb29
Irwinton USA (GA) 178 Fj29
Isa WAN 132 Ld39
Isabel USA (SD) 172 Ek23
Isabela USA RP 90 Rb40
Isabela RP 90 Qh40
Isabela de Sagua C 179 Fj34
Isabela de Sagua C 179 Fj34
Isabella USA (MN) 172 Fe22
Isabella Ind. Res. USA 173 Fh24
Isabel Pass USA 165 Ch14
Isabel Rubio C 179 Fh34
Isaccea RO 45 Mj45
Isafjörður IS 18 Jr24
Isagarh IND (MPH) 83 Oj33
Isahaya J 79 Rf29
Isaka EAT 146 Mg47
Isa Khel PK 65 Of30
Isala RM 157 Nc57
Isalo, P.N. de l' RM 157 Nc57
Isambe RDC 141 Md46
Isandhiwana ZA 155 Mf60
Isandja RDC 149 Ma46
Isanga RDC 141 Md45
Isanga RDC 149 Mb46
Isangano N.P. Z 146 Mf51
Isanlu WAN 138 Ld41
Isanlu-Esa WAN 138 Lc41
Isar D 33 La42
I Sassi di Matera I 37 Lr50
Iscar E 26 Kq49
Iscayachi BOL 207 Gh56
Iscehisar TR 56 Me26
Ischgl A 34 Ll43
Ischia I 36 Lo50
Isebania EAK 144 Mh46
Iselin Bank ANT 6 Ba33
Iseo I 34 Ll45
Iseramagazi EAT 146 Mg48
Iserlohn D 32 Lh39
Isérnia I 37 Lp49
Ise-shima N.P. J 79 Rj28
Isesy RM 156 Ne52
Iseyin WAN 138 Lc42
Isfjord Radio N 16 Lg06
Isha PK 65 Or29
Ishaka EAU 144 Mf46
Ishak Paşa Sarayı TR 57 Nc26
Ishasha RDC 149 Md47
Isherton GUY 194 Ha44
Ishiara EAK 144 Mk46
Ishigaki Jima J 79 Rc33
Ishikari J 77 Sa24
Ishikawa J 77 Sa24
Ishinomaki J 77 Sa26
Ishishi RDC 149 Ma47
Ishizuchi-san J 79 Rg28
Ishotellet S 16 Ma12
Ishpeming USA (MI) 173 Fg22
Ishtgaæ-ha'n IR 64 Ng29
Ishtixon UZ 63 Od26
Ishurdi BD 86 Pd32
Ishwara S 16 Ma12
Isibooro Secure, P.N. BOL 206 Gh54
Isidoro Noblía ROU 204 Hc61
Isigny-sur-Mer F 22 Kt41
Isikari-santi J 77 S24
Isikari-wan J 77 Sa24
Isili I 36 Lk51
Isil'kul' SU 54 Oc08
Ísim RUS 54 Ob07
Isimila EAT 147 Mh49
Isimu D 91 Rd45
Isinya EAK 144 Mj47
Isiolo EAK 144 Mk45
Isipingo ZA 155 Mf60
Isiro RDC 141 Md44
Isisford AUS (QLD) 109 Sc58
Isissysten N 16 Md06
Iskagundam J 79 Rj28
Iskenderun TR 56 Mg27
İskenderun Körfezi TR 56 Mf27
İskilip TR 56 Mf25
Iskushuban SP 143 Nh40
Isla MEX (VC) 183 Fc36
Isla Aji C 179 Fj34
Isla Aldea RCH 210 Gc70
Isla Alejandro Selkirk RCH 197 Fk62
Isla Amantani PE 206 Gf53
Isla Angamos RCH 210 Gc70
Isla Ángel de la Guarda MEX 180 Ee31
Isla Antica YV 193 Gj40
Isla Aracena RCH 210 Ge73
Isla Arena MEX (CAM) 183 Fe35
Isla Baltra EC 197 Fe46
Isla Barro Colorado, Monumento Nacional PA 185 Fk41
Isla Beata DOM 186 Ge37
Isla Benjamin RCH 210 Gc68
Isla Blanca MEX 183 Fg35
Isla Blanquilla YV 187 Gg40
Isla Byron RCH 210 Gc69
Isla Cabritos, P.N. DOM 186 Ge36
Isla Campana RCH 210 Gc70
Isla Cañas MEX 180 Ee32
Isla Cayambe E 197 Ff45
Isla Cedros MEX 180 Ed31
Isla Cerralvo MEX 180 Ee33
Isla Chaffers RCH 210 Gd69
Isla Chao E 196 Fk50
Isla Chatham E 197 Fg46
Isla Chiquitina E 197 Ff46
Isla Coiba, P.N. PA 185 Fj41
Isla Coiba PA 185 Fj41
Isla Colón PA 185 Fj41
Isla Contreras RCH 210 Gc71
Isleo E 197 Ff46
Isla Corocoro YV 194 Gk41
Isla Coronados MEX 180 Ee32
Isla Cozumel MEX 183 Fg35
Isla de Aguada MEX (CAM) 183 Fe36
Isla de Altamura MEX 180 Ef33
Isla de Bioko GQ 138 Ld43
Isla de Cebaco E 21 Lc37
Isla de Cébaco PA 185 Fk42
Isla de Coiba PA 185 Ga42
Isla de Coiba E 196 Gc46
Isla de Corisco GQ 138 Lc44
Isla de Culebra USA (PR) 187 Gg36
Isla de Guajaba C 179 Fk34
Isla de la Independencia PE 197 Gb53
Isla de la Juventud C 179 Fh35
Isla del Alburión RCH 210 Gc71
Isla del Caño CR 185 Fj41
Isla del Caño E 196 Gc46
Isla de los Césares RA 209 Gj66
Isla de los Riachos RA 209 Gj66

302

Jew Town ⊠ IND 84 Oj41
Jeypur ⊠ IND (ORS) 83 Pb36
Jeziorany ⊡ PL 41 Na37
Jezioro Bukowo ◪ PL 40 Lr36
Jezioro Jamno ◪ PL 40 Lr36
Jezioro Jeziorsko ◪ PL 41 Lu37
Jezioro Kopan ◪ PL 40 Lr36
Jezioro Lebsko ◪ PL 40 Ls36
Jezioro Mamry ⊠ PL 41 Nb36
Jezioro Śniardwy ⊠ PL
   41 Nb37
Jezioro Wicko ◪ PL 40 Lr36
Jezzine ⊠ RL 56 Mn29
Jhabua ⊠ IND (MPH) 82 Oh34
Jhajha ⊠ IND (BIH) 83 Pd33
Jhajjar ⊠ IND (HYA) 80 Oj31
Jhal ⊠ PK 65 Od31
Jhalakati ⊠ BD 86 Pe34
Jhalawar ⊠ IND (RJT) 82 Oj33
Jhalida ⊠ IND (WBG) 83 Pd34
Jhang ⊠ PK 65 Og30
Jhanjharpur ⊠ IND (BIH) 83 Pd32
Jhansi Fort ⚑ IND 83 Ok33
Jhansi ⊠ IND (ASM) 86 Pg32
Jhargram ⊠ IND (WBG) 83 Pd34
Jharol ⊠ IND (RJT) 82 Og33
Jharsuguda ⊠ IND (ORS)
   83 Pc34
Jhatpat ⊠ PK 65 Oe31
Jhelum ⊠ PK 65 Og29
Jhenaidah ⊠ BD 86 Pe34
Jhimpir ⊠ PK 65 Od33
Jhudo ⊠ PK 65 Od33

Ji'an ⊠ IND (RJT) 80 Oh31
Jiachuan ⊠ CHN (SCH) 72 Qd31
Jiading ⊠ CHN (SHG) 78 Ra30
Jiamusi ⊠ CHN (HLG) 76 Rf22
Jiajiang ⊠ CHN (SCH) 74 Qb31
Ji'an ⊠ CHN (JGX) 75 Qb32
Jian ⊠ IR 64 Ng30
Jianchang ⊠ CHN (LNG) 73
   Qk25
Jianchaxi ⊠ CHN (GZH) 74 Qe31
Jianchi ⊠ CHN (HUB) 74 Qe30
Jianchi ⊠ CHN (YUN) 87 Pk32
Jiande ⊠ CHN (ZJG) 75 Qk31
Jiang'an ⊠ CHN (SCH) 74 Qc31
Jiangbei ⊠ CHN (CGQ) 74 Qd31
Jiangcheng ⊠ CHN (YUN)
   87 Qa32
Jiangchuan ⊠ CHN (YUN)
   87 Qa33
Jiangdi ⊠ CHN (YUN) 87 Qb32
Jiange ⊠ CHN (SCH) 72 Qc29
Jiangjjin ⊠ CHN (CGQ) 74 Qd31
Jiangjunmiao ⊠ CHN (XUZ)
   67 Pf23
Jiangkou ⊠ CHN (CGQ) 74 Qd31
Jiangkou ⊠ CHN (GZH) 74 Qe32
Jiangling ⊠ CHN (FJN) 75 Qj32
Jiangling ⊠ CHN (HUB)
   74 Qg30
Jiangmen ⊠ CHN (GSU) 74 Qg34
Jiangshan ⊠ CHN (ZJG) 75 Qk31
Jiangshan ⊠ CHN (ZJG) 75 Ra31
Jiangxi ⊡ CHN 75 Qh32
Jiangxin ⊠ CHN 78 Qk29
Jiangyong ⊠ CHN (HNA) 74 Qf33
Jiangyin ⊠ CHN (JGS) 78 Ra30
Jianhu ⊠ CHN (JGS) 78 Qk29
Jianli ⊠ CHN (HUB) 75 Qg32
Jian'ou ⊠ CHN (FJN) 75 Qk32
Jianping ⊠ CHN (LNG) 73 Qk25
Jianshui ⊠ CHN (YUN)
   87 Qb34
Jianyang ⊠ CHN (FJN) 75 Qk32
Jianyang ⊠ CHN (SCH) 74 Qc30
Jiaohe ⊠ CHN (HBI) 73 Qj27
Jiaohe ⊠ CHN (JLN) 76 Rd24
Jiaohe Gucheng ⚑ CHN 67 Pe24
Jiaojiang ⊠ CHN (ZJG) 75 Ra31
Jiaokou ⊠ CHN (SAX) 72 Qf27
Jiaoling ⊠ CHN (GDG) 75 Qj33
Jiaonan ⊠ CHN (SDG) 73 Qj28
Jiaotelo ⊠ CHN (TIB) 68 Pd31
Jiaozhou ⊠ CHN (SDG) 73 Ra27
Jiaozuo ⊠ CHN (YUN) 87 Qa33
Jiashan ⊠ CHN (AHU) 78 Qj29
Jiashan ⊠ CHN (HNN) 73 Ra30
Jiashi ⊠ CHN (XUZ) 66 Oj26
Jia Xian ⊠ CHN (HNN) 73 Qh28
Jia Xian ⊠ CHN (SAA) 72 Qf28
Jiaxing ⊠ CHN (ZJG) 78 Ra30
Jiayin ⊠ CHN (HLG) 76 Rf21
Jiayuguan ⊠ CHN (GSU) 69 Pk26
Jibert ⊠ RO 43 Mf45
Jiberu ⊠ WAN 139 Lg41
Jibiya ⊠ WAN 132 Ld39
Jibjaat ⊠ OM 61 Ni37
Jiba ⊠ YE 60 Nb39
Jibóia ⊠ BR (AM) 193 Gf45
Jibsh ⊠ IND 84 Nd43
Jicarilla Apache Ind. Res. ⚑ USA
   171 Eg27
Jícaro Galán ⊠ HN 184 Fg39
Jichang ⊠ CHN (GZH) 87 Qc32
Jichang ⊠ CHN (GZH) 74 Qd33
Jičín ⊠ CZ 42 Lq40
Jiddah ⊠ KSA 58 Mk35
Jiddat al-Harasis ◪ OM 61 Nh36
Jiele Golden Pagoda ⚑ CHN
   87 Pj34
Jielong ⊠ CHN (CGQ) 74 Qd32
Jieshi ⊠ CHN (GDG) 75 Qh34
Jieshou ⊠ CHN (AHU) 73 Qh29
Jiexiu ⊠ CHN (SAX) 72 Qf27
Jiexiu ⊠ CHN (SAX) 72 Qf28
Jieznas ⊠ LT 39 Me36
Jigalong ◪ AUS (WA) 102 Ra57
Jigalong Aboriginal Reserve ◪
   AUS 102 Ra57
Jiggs ⊠ USA 170 Ec25
Jigme Dorji N.P. ⚑ BHT 86 Pe32
Jiguani ⊠ C 179 Gb35
Jihanah ⊠ YE 60 Nc38
Jihlava ⊠ CZ 42 Lq41
Jijel ⊠ DZ 126 Ld27
Jijia ⊡ CHN (YUN) 87 Qb34
Jijiga ⊠ ETH 143 Nb41
Jijona = Xixona ⊠ E 29 Ku52
Jiju ⊠ CHN (SCH) 87 Qa31
Jilamo ⊠ HN 184 Fg38
Jilian ⊠ IR 62 Nh27
Jilevele ⊠ RD 45 Mg46
Jilibadji Nature Reserve ◪ AUS
   (WA) 104 Qk61
Jilib ⊠ SP 145 Nb45
Jilin ⊡ CHN 76 Rd24
Jilin Hada Ling ◪ CHN 76 Rd24
Jima ⊠ ETH 142 Mj42
Jim Abad ⊠ IR 62 Nh26
Jimani ⊠ DOM 186 Ge36
Jimata ⊠ ETH 142 Mj41

Jimbe ⊠ ANG 151 Mb51
Jimbolia ⊠ RO 44 Ma45
Jimda ⊠ CHN (TIB) 69 Pg31
Jimena de la Frontera ⊠ E
   27 Kp54
Jiménez ⊠ MEX (CHH) 181 Eh32
Jiménez ⊠ MEX (COH) 181 Ek33
Jiménez ⊠ MEX (BA) 200
   Hg48
Jiménez del Téul ⊠ MEX (ZCT)
   182 Ej34
Jimeno ⊠ MEX (MG)
Jimenoa Waterfall ⚑ DOM
   186 Ge36
Jimeta ⊠ WAN 139 Lg41
Jim Falls ⊠ USA 175 Fd23
Jimmy Carter N.H.S. ⚑ USA
   175 Fh29
Jimnice ⊠ PL 41 Mc40
Jimsar ⊠ CHN (XUZ) 67 Pe24
Jimulco ⊠ MEX (COH) 181 Eh33
Jinan ⊠ CHN (SDG) 73 Qj27
Jinchai ⊠ CHN (GZG) 74 Qe33
Jincheng ⊠ CHN (SAX) 72 Qg28
Jincheng ⊠ CHN (YUN) 87 Qb33
Jinchuan ⊠ CHN (SCH) 72 Qb30
Jinci ⊠ CHN 72 Qf27
Ji'an ⊠ IND (HYA) 80 Oj31
Jinabpwne ⊠ AUS (NSW)
   111 Se64
Jindarre ⊠ AUS (NT) 106 Rf33
Jindian ⊠ CHN 87 Pk32
Jindřichov ⊠ CZ 42 Lq41
Jindřichův Hradec ⊠ CZ 42 Lq41
Jinfo Shan ◪ CHN 74 Qd31
Jing'an ⊠ CHN (JGX) 75 Qh31
Jingbian ⊠ CHN (SAA) 72 Qe27
Jingchuan ⊠ CHN (GSU) 72
   Qd28
Jingde ⊠ CHN (AHU) 78 Qk30
Jingdezhen ⊠ CHN (JGX)
   75 Qj31
Jinggang ⊠ CHN (YUN) 87 Qa33
Jinggelic ⊠ AUS (BIH) 83 Pd32
Jingmarra ⊠ AUS (NSW) 111 Sd63
Jogyue ⊠ CHN (JLN) 76 Rd24
Jinggangshan ⊠ CHN 75 Qh32
Jinggu Daizu ⊠ CHN (YUN)
   87 Qa34
Jinghong ⊠ CHN (YUN) 87 Qa34
Jingjiang ⊠ CHN (JGS) 78 Ra29
Jingle ⊠ CHN (SAX) 72 Qf26
Jingmen ⊠ CHN (HUB) 74 Qg30
Jingning ⊠ CHN (GSU) 72 Qd28
Jingshan ⊠ CHN (HUB) 74 Qg30
Jingtai ⊠ CHN (GSU) 72 Qc27
Jingxi ⊠ CHN (GSU) 72 Qc27
Jingxian ⊠ CHN (AHU) 78 Qk30
Jingtie Shan ◪ CHN 69 Pj26
Jingxi ⊠ CHN 74 Qd34
Jing Xian ⊠ CHN (AHU) 78 Qk30
Jingxiang ⊠ CHN (SDG) 73 Qj28
Jingxing ⊠ CHN (HBI) 71 Rb22
Jingyu ⊠ CHN (JLN) 76 Rd24
Jingyuan ⊠ CHN (GSU) 72 Qc27
Jingyu Nao ⊠ CHN 72 Qe29
Jingzhou ⊠ CHN (HUN) 74 Qe32
Jinhe ⊠ CHN (NMZ) 71 Ra20
Jinhua ⊠ CHN (ZJG) 75 Qk31
Jining ⊠ CHN (NMZ) 73 Qg25
Jining ⊠ CHN (SDG) 73 Qj28
Jinja ⊠ EAU 144 Mg45
Jinja War Cemetery ⚑ EAU
   144 Mg45
Jinjiang = Panzhihua ⊠ CHN
   (SCH) 87 Qa32
Jinka ⊠ ETH 144 Mj43
Jinkou ⊠ CHN (HUB) 75 Qh30
Jinniu ⊠ CHN (HUB) 75 Qh31
Jinning ⊠ CHN (YUN) 87 Qb33
Jinotega ⊠ NIC 184 Fg40
Jinotepe ⊠ NIC 184 Fg40
Jinping ⊠ CHN (GZH) 74 Qe32
Jinping ⊠ CHN (YUN) 87 Qb34
Jinping ⊠ CHN (YUN) 87 Qb34
Jinpu ⊠ CHN (JGS) 78 Pa29
Jinsha ⊠ CHN (GZH) 74 Qd32
Jinsha Jiang ◪ CHN 87 Qb32
Jinshan ⊠ CHN (SHG) 78 Ra30
Jinshanlin ⚑ CHN 73 Qj25
Jinshi ⊠ CHN (SAX) 73 Qg28
Jinshi ⊠ CHN (HUN) 74 Qf32
Jinshiajang ⊠ CHN (YUN) 87 Qb32
Jinta ⊠ CHN (GSU) 69 Pk26
Jintan ⊠ CHN (JGS) 78 Qk30
Jintololo Channel ◪ RP 90 Rb40
Jintur ⊠ IND (MHT) 82 Oj36
Jinxi ⊠ CHN (JGX) 75 Qj32
Jinxian ⊠ CHN (JGX) 75 Qj32
Jinyang ⊠ CHN (SCH) 87 Qb32
Jinyun ⊠ CHN (ZJG) 75 Ra31
Jinzhou ⊠ CHN (LNG) 76 Ra25
Jinzhou ⊠ CHN (LNG) 73 Ra25
Ji-Paraná ⊠ BR (RO) 198 Gk51
Jipijapa ⊠ EC 196 Fk46
Jiquilillo ⊠ NIC 184 Fg40
Jiquipilan de Juárez ⊠ MEX
   (MCH) 182 Ej35
Jiquiriçá ⊠ BR (BA) 201 Ja52
Jirampal ⊠ IND (CGH) 83 Pb36
Jirga Main ⊠ PK 65 Oe30
Jiri ⊠ NEP 81 Pd32
Jirjir ⊠ IR 64 Nj37
Jiroft ⊠ IR 64 Nj37
Jirriban ⊠ SP 143 Ne42
Jirwan ⊠ KSA 61 Nf34
Jishan ⊠ CHN (SAX) 72 Qf28
Jishou ⊠ CHN (HUN) 74 Qe31
Jishui ⊠ CHN (JGX) 75 Qh32
Jitarning ⊠ AUS (WA) 104 Qj62
Jítía ⊠ RO 45 Mg45
Jitian ⊠ CHN (SCH) 74 Qc30
Jitra ⊠ MAL 92 Qa43
Jitzamurri ⊠ MEX (SL) 180 Ef32
Jiucai Ling ◪ CHN (GZH) 74 Qe32
Jiuding Shan ◪ CHN (SCH) 72 Qb30
Jiuhuashan ◪ CHN 78 Qj30
Jiujiang ⊠ CHN (JGX) 75 Qj31
Jiuling Shan ◪ CHN 75 Qj31
Jiujiang = Kowloon ⊠ CHN
   (HKG) 75 Qh34
Jiumu ⊠ EAT 146 Mf49
Jiuquan ⊠ CHN (GSU)
   73 Rb27
Jiutai ⊠ CHN (JLN) 76 Rc23
Jiuxu ⊠ CHN (GZG) 74 Qd33
Jiuyishnan ◪ CHN (HUN)
   72 Qf29
Jiuzhaigou ⊠ CHN (GSU)
   72 Qb29
Jiuzhaigou ⚑ CHN 72 Qb29
Jiuzhaigou ⊠ CHN (HLG) 71 Rd20
Jiwani ⊠ PK 64 Oa34
Jiwika ⊠ RI 114 Rk47
Jixi ⊠ CHN (AHU) 78 Qk30
Jixian ⊠ CHN (HLG) 76 Rf23
Jixian ⊠ CHN (LNG) 76 Rc25
Ji Xian ⊠ CHN (SAX) 72 Qf28
Jiyang ⊠ CHN (SDG) 73 Qj27
Jizan ⊠ KSA 60 Nb37
Jizax ⊠ UZ 63 Od25

Joal-Fadiout ⊠ SN 130 Kb38
João Arregui ⊠ BR (RS) 204
   Hb60
João Câmara ⊠ BR (RN)
   201 Jc48
João Chagas ⊠ BR (AM) 193 Gf45
João Farias ⊠ BR (AM) 194 Ha46
João Lisboa ⊠ BR (MA) 200
   Hg48
João Monlevade ⊠ BR (MG)
   203 Hj55
João Neiva ⊠ BR (ES) 203 Hk55
João Pataço ⊠ MOC 153 Mh55
João Pessoa ⊠ BR (PB)
   201 Jc49
João Pinheiro ⊠ BR (MG)
   203 Hg54
Joaquim Pires ⊠ BR (PI)
   201 Hj47
Joaquín V. González ⊠ RA (SA)
   207 Gg58
Joara ⊠ BR (MPH) 203 Hk54
Jobabo ⊠ C 179 Gb35
Jocotepec ⊠ MEX (JLC) 182 Ej35
Jocoli ⊠ RA (MD) 208 Gf62
Jódar ⊠ E 27 Kr53
Jodensavanna ⊠ SME 194 Hc43
Jodhpur ⊠ IND (RJT) 82 Og32
Jodiya ⊠ IND (GUJ) 82 Of34
Jodoigne ⊠ B 23 Le40
Joe Batt's Arm ⊠ CDN (NF)
   177 Hc27
Joensuu ⊠ FIN 38 Mk28
Joetsu ⊠ J 77 Rk27
Jofane ⊠ MOC 152 Mh54
Jöf il Montásio ◪ I 35 Lo44
Joffre, Mount ◪ CDN 168 Ec20
Joésilndia ⊠ BR (MT) 202 Hb54
José Luís Tamayo ⊠ EC 196
   Fk47
Jogbani ⊠ IND (BIH) 83 Pd32
José Panganiban ⊠ RP 90 Rb38
Jog Falls ⚑ IND 84 Oh38
Joghara ⊠ IND (BIH) 83 Pb34
Jogdan ⊠ IR 64 Nj32
Joginder Nagar ⊠ IND (HPH)
   81 Oj29
Jogues ⊠ CDN (ON) 173 Fj21
Johanna Beach ◪ AUS
   106 Rh55
Johannesburg ⊠ ZA
   170 Eb28
Johannsengenstadt ⊠ D
   33 Ln40
Jogtie Shan ◪ CHN 69 Pj26
John Day ⊠ USA 168 Dk23
John Day Fossil Beds Nat.
   Mon. Clarno Unit ⚑ USA
John Day Fossil Beds Nat. Mon.
   Painted Hills Unit ⚑ USA
   168 Dk23
John Day Fossil Beds Nat. Mon.
   Sheep Rock Unit ⚑ USA
   168 Dk23
John Deere H.S. ⚑ USA 173 Ff24
John Deere Pavilion ⚑ USA (IL)
   172 Fe25
Johndilbil ⊠ LB 136 Kf42
John D'Or Prairie ⊠ CDN (AB)
John Flynn Memorial ⚑ AUS
   106 Rh55
John Fitzgerald Kennedy
   Hyannis Museum ⚑ USA
   177 Ge25
John Flynn Memorial ⚑ AUS
   177 Ge25
John Henry Statue ⚑ USA
   178 Fz27
John Hopkins Glacier ◪ USA
   (AK) 166 Db16
John o'Groats ⊠ GB 20 Kr32
John Pennekamp Coral Reef S.P.
   ⚑ USA 179 Ga33
Johnson City ⊠ USA (KS)
   174 Ek27
Johnson City ⊠ USA (NY)
   177 Gb24
Johnson City ⊠ USA (TX)
   174 Fa30
Johnson N.H.P. ⚑ USA 174 Fa30
Johnson River ⊠ CDN 167 Dh14
Johnsons ⊠ USA (CA) 168 Dj23
Johnsons Crossing ⊠ CDN (YT)
   166 Dd14
Johnson Space Center ⚑ USA
   174 Fc31
Johnston Atoll ⊠ USA 10 Bb08
Johnstone ⊠ AUS (QLD) 107
   Sc54
Johnstown ⊠ AUS (QLD) 109
   Se60
Johnstown ⊠ GB 20 Kq35
Johnstown ⊠ USA (NY) 177 Gc24
Johnstown ⊠ USA (PA) 173 Ga26
Johnstown Flood Nat. Mon. ⚑
   USA 173 Ga25
Johnsville ⊠ USA (CA) 170 Dk26
John W. Kyle S.P. ⚑ USA
   175 Ff28
Johor Baru ⊠ MAL 93 Qb45
Johvi ⊠ EST 38 Mh31
Joigny ⊠ F 25 Ld43
Joinville ⊠ BR (SC) 205 Hf59
Joinville ⊠ F 23 Lf42
Joita ⊠ RO 45 Mf46
Jokau ⊠ SUD 142 Mg41
Jokhang = Dazhao S.P. ⚑ CHN
   (TIB) 69 Pf31
Jokkmokk ⊠ S 16 La12
Jökulsarlón ◪ IS 18 Kf26
Jolfa ⊠ IR 57 Nc26
Jolié ⊠ USA (IL) 173 Ff25
Joliette ⊠ CDN (QC) 176 Gd22
Jolo ⊠ RP 91 Ra42
Jolo Group ◪ RP 91 Ra43
Jolo Island ◪ RP 91 Ra42
Jombala ⊠ FIN 38 Lu48
Jombang ⊠ RI 95 Qg49
Jomboy ⊠ UZ 63 Oc26
Jomda ⊠ CHN (TIB) 69 Pg30
Jomu ⊠ EAT 146 Mf49
Jonai Bazar ⊠ IND (ASM)
   86 Ph32
Jonava ⊠ LT 39 Me36
Jonč ⊠ CHN (NMZ) 72 Qe27
Jonê ⊠ CHN (GSU) 72 Qb28
Jondal ⊠ N 30 Lg30
Jonesboro ⊠ USA (LA) 175 Fe29
Jonesboro ⊠ USA (AR) 175 Fe28
Jones Islands ◪ USA (AK)
   165 Ck10
Jones Mountains ◪ 6 Fb33
Jones Sound ◪ CDN 163 Fd13
Jonesville ⊠ USA (VA) 178 Fj27
Jongeld ⊠ IQ 62 Nd25
Jonggol ⊠ RI 95 Qd49
Jonglei ⊠ SUD (LNG) 76 Rc25
Jøngø Shrine ⚑ ROK
   78 Rd27
Joniškēlis ⊠ LT 39 Me34
Joniškis ⊠ LT 39 Me34
Jonker ⊠ CDN (NWS) 111 Se33
Jonquières ⊠ F 25 Le46
Joaçaba ⊠ BR (SC) 205 He59
Joachimsthal ⊠ D 32 Lo38
Joaíma ⊠ BR (MG) 203 Hk54

Joplin ⊠ USA (MO) 174 Fc27
Jora ⊠ IND (MPH) 80 Oj32
Jordan ⊠ USA 36 Mh29
Jordan ⊠ JOR 58 Mj30
Jordan ⊠ RP 90 Rb40
Jordán ⊠ BR (AM) 194 Ha46
Jordânia ⊠ BR (MG) 203 Hk53
Jordanów ⊠ PL 41 Lu41
Jordan Valley ⊠ USA (ID)
Jordão ⊠ IND (ORS) 83 Pb34
Jordbro ⊡ S 31 Lt31
Jorf ⊠ MA 125 Kh30
Joriapani ⊠ NEP 81 Pa31
Jörn ⊠ S 16 Ma13
Joroinen ⊠ FIN 38 Mh28
Jörpeland ⊠ N 30 Lg31
Joru ⊠ WAL 136 Ke42
Jos ⊠ WAN 138 Le39
José Abad Santos ⊠ RP 91 Rc43
José Batlle y Ordóñez ⊠ ROU
   204 Hc62
José Bonifacio ⊠ BR (SP)
   202 Hf55
José Cardel ⊠ MEX (VC)
   183 Fb36
José de Freitas ⊠ BR (PI)
   201 Hj48
José del Carmen Ramírez, P.N.
   ⚑ DOM 186 Ge36
José de San Martín ⊠ RA (CB)
   210 Ge68
José Enrique Rodó ⊠ ROU
   204 Hb62
Joselândia ⊠ BR (MA) 200 Hh48
Joselândia ⊠ BR (MT) 202 Hb54
Jumba la Mtwana ⚑ EAK
   145 Mk47
Jumbe Foume ⊠ EAT 147 Mj51
Jumbilla ⊠ PE 196 Ga48
Jumbo ⊠ ZA 146 Mh50
Jumeaux ⊠ F 25 Ld45
Jumentos Cays ◪ BS 186 Gc34
Jumilla ⊠ E 29 Kt52
Jumira, T.I. ◪ BR 195 He43
Jumi Pozo ⊠ RA (SE) 207 Gh60
Jumla ⊠ NEP 81 Pb31
Jumma Masjid (Gulbarga) ⚑
   IND 82 Oj37
Jumurda ⊠ LV 39 Mf34
Jun Abad ⊠ IR 64 Oa31
Juna Downs ◪ AUS (WA)
   102 Qk57
Junagadh ⊠ IND (GUJ) 82 Of35
Junagarh ⊠ IND (ORS) 83 Pb36
Junan ⊠ CHN (SDG) 73 Qk28
Juncal, Cerro ◪ RA/RCH
   208 Gf62
Junction ⊠ USA (TX) 171 Ek29
Junction ⊠ USA (UT) 171 Ed26
Junction ⊠ AUS (NSW) 109 Rg51
Junction City ⊠ USA (KS)
   174 Fb26
Junction City ⊠ USA (LA)
   174 Fe29
Junction City ⊠ USA (OR)
Junction, Mount ◪ AUS 103
   Re55
Jundah ⊠ AUS (QLD) 108 Sb58
Jundee ⊠ AUS (WA) 104 Ra59
Jundiaí ⊠ BR (SP) 203 Hg57
Junee ⊠ AUS (NSW) 111 Se63
Jungapeo ⊠ MEX (MCH) 182 Ek36
Jungfrau ◪ CH 34 Lh44
Jungfraubahn ⚑ CH 34 Lh44
Jungoley Canal ◪ SUD 141 Mf41
Jungu ⊠ EAT 146 Mf49
Jungua ⊠ ANG 150 Lh51
Junín ⊠ CO 192 Ga45
Junín ⊠ RA (BA) 209 Gk63
Junín de los Andes ⊠ RA (NE)
   208 Ge65
Junin Dunes Wilderness ◪
   USA 168 Ea22
Juniper Forests ◪ PK 65 Od30
Juniyah ⊠ RL 56 Mn29
Junlerl ⊠ WAN 139 Lf41
Junlian ⊠ CHN (SCH) 74 Qc31
Junnar ⊠ IND (MHT) 82 Og36
Junqlong ⊠ SUD 141 Mf41
Junsele ⊠ S 16 Lj14
Juntas ⊠ CR 185 Fh40
Juntura ⊠ USA (OR) 168 Ea24
Junyun ⊠ CHN (JGX) 75 Qj33
Jupiter ⊠ BR (BA) 200 Hh51
Jupiter ⊠ USA (FL) 179 Fk32
Juquiá ⊠ BR (SP) 205 Hg58
Jura ⊡ SUD 141 Md41
Jura ⊡ CH 34 Lg43
Juracidáti ⊠ BR (BA) 201 Ja52
Jurado ⊠ CO 192 Gb42
Juramento ⊠ BR (MG) 203 Hj54
Jurbarkas ⊠ LT 39 Mc35
Jurbec ⊠ RUS 48 Na17
Jurev-Pol'skij ⊠ RUS 48 Mk17
Jürgenstorf ⊠ D 33 Ln38
Juribelá ⊠ BR (MG) 203 Hh53
Jurien ⊠ AUS (WA) 104 Qh61
Jurilovca ⊠ RO 45 Mj46
Jurino ⊠ RUS 48 Nd17
Jurjevka ⊠ UA 49 Mj21
Jurkáine ⊠ LV 39 Mc33
Jürmala ⊠ LV 39 Md34
Jurmo ⊠ FIN 38 Ma30
Juromenha ⊠ P 27 Kn52
Jurong ⊠ CHN (JGS) 78 Qk30
Jurongk'a ⊠ CHN 87 Pk32
Juruá ⊠ BR (AM) 198 Gd47
Juruena ⊠ BR (MT) 199 Ha50
Jusepín ⊠ YV 193 Gj41
Juškino ⊠ RUS 38 Mh32
Jussey ⊠ F 25 Lf43
Justiniano Posse ⊠ RA (CD)
   209 Gj62
Justo Daract ⊠ RA (SL) 208

Juzzak ⊠ PK 64 Oa31
Jwalamukhi Temple ⚑ IND
   81 Oj29
Jwaneng ⊠ RB 155 Mc58
Jyderup ⊠ DK 30 Lm35
Jylland Bank ◪ DK 30 Lh34
Jyväskylä ⊠ FIN 38 Mf28

K

K2 ◪ PK 81 Oj28
Kaaba ⚑ KSA 58 Mk35
Kaap Dernburg ◪ NAM 154 Lh59
Kaapmuiden ⊠ ZA 155 Mf58
Kaapstad ⊠ ZA 154 Lk62
Kaaresuvanto ⊠ FIN 16 Mb11
Kaarina ⊠ FIN 38 Mc30
Kaashidhoo ⊠ MV 84 Og43
Kaavi ⊠ FIN 38 Mh28
Kaba ⊠ H 43 Mb43
Kabaena ◪ RI 96 Rb48
Kabage ⊠ G 148 Lg46
Kabah ⚑ MEX 183 Ff35
Kabakly ⊠ TM 62 Ob26
Kabala ⊠ WAL 136 Ke41
Kabaena ⊠ SN 136 Kb39
Kabale ⊠ EAU 144 Me46
Kabalebostuwmeer (projected) ◪
   SME 194 Hb43
Kabalega Falls N.P. = Murchison
   Falls N.P. ◪ EAU 144 Mf44
Kabalo ⊠ RDC 146 Me49
Kabambare ⊠ RDC 146 Md48
Kabanbai ⊠ KZ 66 Pa25
Kabanbai ⊠ RP 91 Rb42
Kabanjahe ⊠ RI 92 Pk44
Kabba ⊠ WAN 138 Le42
Kabdalis ⊠ S 16 Ma12
Kabetovik ⊠ RUS (AK) 165 Cj10
Kabelvåg ⊠ N 16 Lh11
Kaberamaido ⊠ EAU 144 Mg45
Kabetan ⊠ RI 91 Ra45
Kabeya ⊠ RDC 146 Md49
Kabi ⊠ ETH 142 Mh44
Kabile ⊠ LV 39 Mc34
Kabinburi ⊠ THA 89 Qa38
Kabinda ⊠ RDC 146 Md49
Kabir ⊠ RI 97 Rc50
Kabirzizi ⊠ EAU 144 Mf45
Kabna ⊠ SUD 135 Mg36
Kabobo ⊠ RDC 146 Me47
Kabompo ⊠ Z 151 Mb52
Kabompo ⊠ Z 151 Mc52
Kabondo-Dianda ⊠ RDC 149
   Mc50
Kabong ⊠ MAL 94 Qf45
Kabongo ⊠ RDC 146 Mc49
Kabou ⊠ TG 137 La41
Kabourja ⊠ RCA 140 Ma43
Kabrai ⊠ IND (UPH) 83 Pa33
Kabud Gonab ◪ IR 62 Nk27
Kabud Rahang ⊠ IR 57 Ne28
Kabugao ⊠ RP 90 Ra37
Kabul ◪ AFG 65 Oc28
Kabumbu ⊠ RDC 146 Md48
Kabunda ⊠ RDC 146 Md50
Kabunduk ◪ RI 96 Qk50
Kaburuang ◪ RI 91 Rc44
Kabushiya ⊠ SUD 135 Mg37
Kabuyemi ⊠ RI 93 Qb48
Kabuzala Island ◪ MYA 88 Pj39
Kabwe ⊠ Z 152 Me53
Kabwum ⊠ PNG 115 Sd49
Kačanik ⊠ SRB 44 Mb48
Kachanovka ◪ UA 48 Mh20
Kachchh, Gulf of ◪ IND 82 Oe34
Kachessly ⊠ RUS 39 Mk33
Kachikau ⊠ RB 152 Mb55
Kachin ⊡ MYA 86 Ph34
Kachug ⊠ RUS 70 Qd20
Kadan Kyun ◪ MYA 89 Pk39
Kadaň ⊠ CZ 42 Ln40
Kadanai ⊠ AFG 65 Ob30
Kadavu ◪ FJI 119 Tc55
Kade ⊠ GH 137 Kk43
Kadeji ⊠ SUD 135 Mf40
Kadi ⊠ IND (GUJ) 82 Og34
Kadina ⊠ AUS (SA) 110 Rj62
Kadınhanı ⊠ TR 56 Mf27
Kadiolo ⊠ RMM 137 Kh40
Kadir ⊠ IND (APH) 85 Ok38
Kadiri ⊠ IND (APH) 85 Ok38
Kadirli ⊠ TR 56 Mj27
Kadnikov ⊠ RUS 48 Na16
Kadoka ⊠ USA (SD) 172 Ek24
Kadoma ⊠ ZW 152 Me55
Kadubandi ⊠ RI 96 Rb49
Kaduna ⊠ WAN 138 Le39
Kadungan Agung ⊠ MYA 86 Pg32
Kaduru ⊠ IND (KTK) 84 Oj39

Kadyi ⊠ RUS 48 Nb17
Kadziidło ⊡ PL 41 Mb38
Kaech'on ⊠ PRK 78 Rc26
Kaédi ⊠ RIM 130 Kd38
Kaélé ⊠ CAM 139 Lh40
Kaena Point ◪ USA (HI) 170 Cb34
Kaeng Khlo ⊠ THA 89 Qb37
Kaeng Krachan N.P. ◪ THA
   88 Pk39
Kaeng Tana N.P. ◪ THA 89 Qc38
Kaeo ⊠ NZ 112 Tg63
Kaesong ⊠ PRK 78 Rd27
Kaevanga ⊠ SOL 117 Sk50
Kaew Kho Rum Cave ⚑ THA
   88 Pk40
Kaf ⊠ KSA 58 Mk30
Kafakumba ⊠ RDC 149 Mb50
Kafar-Jar-Ghar Range ◪ AFG
   65 Oc29
Kaffin-Saru ⊠ WAN 138 Ld41
Kaffrine ⊠ SN 130 Kc38
Kafia Kingi ⊠ SUD 141 Mc41
Kafin-Chana ⊠ WAN 132 Lc39
Kafindibei ⊠ SUD 141 Mc41
Kafiné ⊠ CI 137 Kh41
Kafin Hausa ⊠ WAN 138 Lf39
Kåfjord ⊠ N 16 Mc10
Kafolo ⊠ CI 137 Kh41
Kafountine ⊠ SN 136 Kb39
Kafr el-Dauwār ⊠ ET 129 Mf30
Kafr el-Sheikh ⊠ ET 129 Mf30
Kafu ⊠ Z 146 Me52
Kafue ⊠ Z 146 Me53
Kafunzo ⊠ EAU 144 Me46
Kafura ⊠ EAT 144 Mf47
Kafwala ⊠ Z 152 Md53
Kaga ⊠ J 79 Rg28
Kaga Bandoro ⊠ RCA 140 Lk42
Kagadi ⊠ EAU 144 Mf45
Kagan ⊠ PK 63 Og28
Kagan ⊠ PK 65 Og28
Kagara ⊠ BF 137 Kh39
Kagarko ⊠ WAN 138 Le40
Kağızman ⊠ TR 57 Nb25
Kagmara ⊠ NEP 81 Pb31
Kaglama ⊠ IND (ORS) 83 Pb36
Kagnal ⊠ TCH 140 Lj41
Kagologolo ⊠ EAU 144 Mf45
Kagopal ⊠ TCH 140 Lj41
Kagora, Mount ◪ WAN 138 Le41
Kagoshima ⊠ J 79 Rf30
Kagoshima wan ◪ J 79 Rf30
Kagu ⊠ ET 129 Mg33
Kagugla ⊠ EAU 144 Mf45
Kaha ⊠ ETH 143 Nd47
Kahal Tabebala ◪ DZ 125 Kj31
Kahama ⊠ EAT 146 Mf47
Kahani ⊠ IND (MPH) 83 Ok34
Kaharlyk ⊠ UA 49 Mf21
Kahatola ◪ RI 96 Rc46
Ka-Hem = Malyj Enisej ◪ RUS
   67 Pj20
Kahemba ⊠ RDC 149 Lk49
Kahir ⊠ IR 64 Oa33
Kahla ⊠ D 32 Lm40
Kahler Asten ◪ D 32 Lj39
Kahmmoo ⊠ AUS (QLD) 109 Sc60
Kahnuj ⊠ IR 64 Nj32
Kahone ⊠ SN 130 Kc38
Kahoolawe ◪ USA 170 Cb35
Kahramanmaraş ⊠ TR 129
   Mg34
Kahror Pakka ◪ PK 65 Of31
Kahuku Point ◪ USA 170 Cb35
Kahului ⊠ USA (HI) 170 Cb35
Ka Lae ◪ USA 170 Cc36
Kalaero ⊠ RI 96 Rb48
Kahurangi ⊠ NZ 113 Tg66
Kahurangi Point ◪ NZ 113 Tg66
Kahurestan ⊠ IR 64 Nh32
Kahuzi-Biega, P.N. du ◪ RDC
   146 Md47
Kai ⊠ RI 114 Rg48
Kaiama ⊠ PNG 115 Sd49
Kaiama ⊠ WAN 138 Ld41
Kabraii ◪ PNG 115 Sd49
Kaiau ⊠ NZ 112 Tg64
Kaibab Ind. Res. ◪ USA 171 Ed27
Kai Beab ⊠ RI 114 Rk49
Kaibola ⊠ PNG 116 Sf50
Kaichui, Mount ◪ SOL 117 Ta50
Kaichun ⊠ CHN (HLG) 76 Re23
KaiDulan ⊠ RI 114 Rk48
Kaiemothia ⊠ SUD 144 Mh43
Kaieteur Fall ◪ GUY 194 Ha43
Kaieteur National Park ◪ GUY
   194 Ha43
Kaifeng ⊠ CHN (HNN) 73
   Qh28
Kaihua ⊠ CHN (ZJG) 75 Qk31
Kaikalur ⊠ IND (APH) 85 Pa37
Kaikohe ⊠ NZ 112 Tg63
Kaikoura ⊠ NZ 113 Tg67
Kaikoura Peninsula ◪ NZ
   113 Tg67
Kailahun ⊠ WAL 136 Ke41
Kailas = Kangrinboqê Feng ◪
   CHN 81 Pa30
Kaili ⊠ CHN (GZH) 74 Qe32
Kailu ⊠ CHN (NMZ) 76 Ra24
Kailua-Kona ⊠ USA (HI) 170
   Cc36
Kailas, Mount ◪ CHN 68 Pa30
Kaili ⊠ CHN (NMZ) 76 Ra24
Kaimana ⊠ RI 114 Rg47
Kaimanawa Forest Park ◪ NZ
   112 Th65
Kaimganj ⊠ IND (UPH) 81 Ok32
Kaimur Range ◪ IND 83 Pb33
Kaina ⊠ EST 38 Mc32
Kainantu ⊠ PNG 115 Sc49
Kainar ⊠ KZ 66 Oh24
Kainchanaburi ⚑ THA 88 Pk38
Kainji Dam ⚑ WAN
   138 Ld40
Kainji Lake N.P. ◪ WAN
   138 Lc40
Kainji Reservoir ◪ WAN 138
   Lc40
Kaintragarh ⊠ IND (ORS) 83 Pc35
Kaipara Harbour ◪ NZ 112 Tg64
Kaiparowits Plateau ◪ USA
   171 Ee27
Kaipen ⊠ MYA 86 Pj33
Kaipichig ⊠ WAN 138 Lg41
Kairaki ⊠ NZ 113 Tf67
Kairouan ⊠ TN 126 Lf28
Kairuku ⊠ PNG 116 Sd50
Kaiserslautern ⊠ D 33 Lh41
Kaisiadorys ⊠ LT 39 Me36
Kaisut Desert ◪ EAK 144 Mj45
Kaitaia ⊠ NZ 112 Tg63
Kaitangata ⊠ NZ 113 Te69
Kaithar ◪ IND 83 Pd33
Kaitumbar ⊠ S 16 Lj11
Kaitum älv ◪ S 16 Lk11
Kaiwi Channel ◪ USA 170 Cb35
Kaixin ⊠ CHN (GDG) 74 Qf34
Kaiyuan ⊠ CHN (LNG) 76 Rc24
Kaiyuan ⊠ CHN (YUN) 87 Qb34
Kaiyuan Temple ⚑ CHN 75 Qk33
Kaizerka ⊠ RUS 48 Nd17
Kaja ⊠ MYA 86 Pg33
Kajaani ⊠ FIN 16 Mg13
Kajabbi ⊠ AUS (QLD) 107 Sa55
Kajakï ⊠ AFG 65 Ob29
Kajang ⊠ MAL 92 Qa44
Kajeray ⊠ AFG 65 Oe29
Kajiado ⊠ EAK 144 Mj46
Kajiastuj ⊠ RUS 71 Qk21
Kajo Kaji ⊠ SUD 144 Mf44
Kajuru ⊠ WAN 138 Le40
Kaka ⊠ TM 62 Nk27
Kaka ⊠ USA (AZ) 171 Ed29
Kakabeka Falls ⚑ CDN (ON)
   172 Ff21
Kakadu A.L. ◪ AUS 106 Rg52
Kakadu A.L. ◪ AUS 106 Rg52
Kakadu N.P. ◪ AUS 106 Rg52
Kakamas ⊠ ZA 154 Mb60
Kakamega ⊠ EAK 144 Mh45
Kakamega Forest National
   Reserve ◪ EAK 144 Mh45
Kakdwip ⊠ IND (WBG) 86 Pe35
Kake ⊠ J 79 Rg28
Kake ⊠ USA (AK) 166 Dd17
Kakegawa ⊠ J 79 Rk28
Kakhovka ⊠ UA 49 Mg22
Kakia ⊠ RB 154 Mb58
Kakira ⊠ EAU 144 Mg45
Kakira ⊠ IND (ORS) 83 Pb36
Kakiri ⊠ EAU 144 Mf45
Kakisa ⊠ CDN 167 Ec16
Kakkar ⊠ PK 65 Oe30
Kakkirigumma ⊠ IND (ORS) 83
   Pb36
Kakogawa ⊠ J 79 Rh28
Kakoma ⊠ EAT 146 Mf48
Kakoro ⊠ EAT 146 Mg50
Kakosi ⊠ EAT 146 Mg50
Kakpin ⊠ CI 137 Kj41
Kaksa ⊠ RI 96 Rb49
Kaktovik ⊠ USA (AK) 165 Cj10
Kakumiri ⊠ CI 146 Md48
Kakuma ⊠ EAK 144 Mh44
Kakumbi ⊠ Z 146 Mf52
Kakum N.P. ◪ GH 137 Kk43
Kakunodate ⊠ J 77 Sa25
Kakwa Prov. Rec. Area ◪ CDN
   167 Ea18
Kala ⊠ EAK 145 Mk46
Kalaallit Nunaat ⊡ DK 163 Hd03
Kalaat Kasbah ⚑ TN 126 Le28
Kalabahi ⊠ RI 97 Rc50
Kalabáka ⊠ GR 46 Mb51
Kalabáki ⊠ GR 44 Mb50
Kalabagh ⊠ PK 65 Of29
Kalabo ⊠ Z 151 Mb53
Kalabrezë ⊠ RDC 146 Mb48
Kalač ⊠ RUS 48 Na20
Kalač-na-Donu ⊠ RUS 48 Na21
Kalae = Ka Lae ◪ USA 170 Cc36
Kalach ⊠ RUS 48 Na21
Kalaeloa ⊠ USA (HI) 170 Cb35
Kalaeloa ⊠ USA (HI) 170 Cb35
Kalajoki ⊠ FIN 16 Md14
Kalajoki ◪ FIN 16 Md13
Kalakan ⊠ RUS 71 Qj19
Kalakazhdan ⊠ RUS 38 Mk33
Kalakwani ⊠ EAK 145 Mk46
Kalalusi ⊠ Z 146 Me53

Kalumburu ☑ AUS (WA) 103 Rd53
Kalumburu A.L. ☑ AUS 103 Rd53
Kalundborg ☑ DK 30 Lm35
Kalundu ☑ RDC 146 Me47
Kalundwe ☑ RDC 149 Mc49
Kalur Kot ☑ PK 65 Of29
Kaluš ☑ UA 43 Me41
Kaluvaye ☑ IND (APH) 85 Ok38
Kalvåg ☑ N 17 Lc15
Kalvola ☑ FIN 38 Me29
Kalvarija ☑ LT 39 Md36
Kalvitsa ☑ FIN 38 Me29
Kalwakurti ☑ IND (APH) 82 Ok37
Kalwaria Zebrzydowska ☑ ▲
PL 41 Lu41
Kalyan ☑ IND (MHT) 82 Og36
Kalyandrug ☑ IND (APH) 84 Oj38
Kalynivka ☑ UA 49 Me21
Kalzhat ☑ KZ 66 Pa24
Kama ☑ RMM 136 Ke39
Kamablon ☑ RMM 136 Kf40
Kamada ☑ TCH 133 Lj37
Kamaday ☑ TCH 134 Ma40
Kamaishi ☑ J 77 Sa26
Kamakura ☑ J 79 Rk28
Kamakusa ▲ GUY 194 Mf45
Kamakwie ☑ WAL 136 Kd41
Kamal ☑ RI 95 Qg40
Kamalpur ☑ PK 65 Og30
Kamalpur ☑ IND (TRP) 86 Pf33
Kamana ☑ TR 56 Mg26
Kamanga ☑ EAT 144 Mg47
Kamaran ☑ YE 60 Nb38
Kamarang ☑ GUY 194 Mg43
Kamareddi ☑ IND (APH) 82 Ok36
Kamáres ☑ GR 46 Mb52
Kamáres ☑ GR 47 Me53
Kamári ☑ GR 47 Mf54
Kamarino ☑ RUS 38 Mk32
Kamarod ☑ PK 65 Od29
Kamarhati ☑ IND (WB) 86 Pe34
Kamaron ☑ WAL 136 Ke41
Kamaru ☑ RI 97 Rd48
Kamas ☑ USA (UT) 171 Ee25
Kamasin ☑ IND (UTT) 83 Pa32
Kamatvi ☑ ZW 152 Md53
Kamba ☑ ETH 142 Mj42
Kamba ☑ WAL 136 Kd41
Kamba Kota ☑ RCA 140 Lj42
Kambalda ☑ AUS (WA) 104 Ra61
Kambam ☑ IND (TNU) 84 Oj40
Kambambe ▲ ANG 148 Lh50
Kambánis ☑ GR 46 Mb50
Kambe ☑ PK 65 Od32
Kambeng ☑ IND (ARP) 86 Ph31
Kamberatoro ☑ PNG 115 Sa47
Kambia ☑ WAL 136 Kd41
Kambiakoto ☑ EAT 146 Mg49
Kambode ☑ RI 97 Rb48
Kambolé ☑ TG 137 La41
Kámbos ☑ GR 46 Mc54
Kambove ☑ RDC 146 Md51
Kambubu ☑ PNG 116 Sg48
Kambuno, Gunung ▲ RI 96 Ra47
Kamburu ☑ EAK 144 Mh46
Kambut ☑ LAR 128 Mc30
Kambwata ☑ Z 151 Mb51
Kamchatka Peninsula ▲ RUS
55 Sc07
Kamčija ☑ BG 45 Mh47
Kamčija ☑ BG 45 Mh47
Kamdara ☑ IND (JKD) 83 Pc34
Kamdeysh ☑ AFG 63 Of28
Kameel ☑ ZA 155 Mc59
Kameeldrif ☑ ZA 155 Mc59
Kameme ☑ MW 146 Mg50
Kameno ☑ BG 45 Mh47
Kamen Nyboloo ☑ RUS 76 Rg23
Kamenskoe ☑ RUS 55 Tb06
Kamensk-Šahtinskij ☑ RUS
49 Na21
Kamensk-Ural'skij ☑ RUS
54 Oa07
Kamenka ☑ RUS 48 Mk20
Kamenka ☑ RUS 48 Nb19
Kamen'-na-Ob'☑ RUS 54 Pa08
Kamennite gábi ▲ BG 45 Mh47
Kamennogorsk ☑ RUS 38 Mk30
Kamenz ☑ D 32 Lo39
Kamenice ☑ SCG 44 Ma44
Kamenica ☑ SCG 44 Lu46
Kamenice nad Lipou ☑ CZ
42 Lq41
Kamenka ☑ RUS 48 Mk20
Kamenka ☑ RUS 48 Nb19

Kamphaeng Phet Historical Park
□ ▲ THA 88 Pk37
Kamphambale ☑ MW 146 Mg52
Kamphnoski P.N. ▮ PL 41 Ma38
Kampli ☑ IND (KTK) 82 Oj38
Kampong Padawan ☑ MAL
94 Qf45
Kampong Sirik ☑ MAL 94 Qf44
Kampong Sralao ☑ K 89 Qc39
Kampong Taben ☑ K 89 Qc39
Kampot ☑ K 89 Qc40
Kampti ☑ BF 137 Kj40
Kampumbu ☑ Z 146 Mg51
Kangaroo Hills ☑ AUS (QLD)
107 Sc55
Kangalampi ☑ FIN 38 Mj28
Kanganiemi ☑ FIN 38 Mg29
Kangavar ☑ IR 57 Nd28
Kangayam ☑ IND (TNU) 84 Oj40
Kangasniemi ☑ FIN 38 Mg29
Kangchow ☑ EAU 144 Mh45
Kangding ☑ CHN (SCH) 69 Qa30
Kangdong ☑ PRK 78 Rd26
Kangean ☑ RI 96 Qk48
Kangerlussuaq ≈
Søndrestrømfjord ☑ DK
163 Hb05
Kangeta ☑ EAK 144 Mj45
Kanggye ☑ PRK 78 Rd26
Kanghwa ☑ ROK 78 Rd27
Kanghwa Do ☑ ROK 78 Rd27
Kangil ☑ SUD 141 Md41
Kangki ☑ WAN 138 La39
Kangkir ☑ CHN (XUZ) 68 Ok27
Kangmar ☑ CHN (TIB) 68 Pe31
Kangnung ☑ ROK 78 Re27
Kango ☑ G 148 Lf45
Kangopriog ☑ CHN (LNG) 76 Rb24
Kangra ☑ IND (HPH) 80 Oj28
Kangrinboqê Feng ▲ CHN
68 Pa30
Kangto ☑ CHN/IND 86 Pg32
Kangpu Plains ▲ Z 151 Mc54
Kangxian ☑ CHN (GSU) 72 Qc29
Kan Gyi ☑ MYA 86 Ph35
Kangz'gyai ▲ CHN 69 Pj36
Kanha N.P. ▮ IND 83 Pa34
Kani ☑ CI 137 Kg41
Kani ☑ J 79 Rk28
Kani ☑ MYA 86 Ph34
Kaniasso ☑ CI 137 Kg41
Kani-Gogouna ☑ IND (APH) 85 Ok38
Kanioume ☑ RMM 131 Kj38
Kanisa ☑ SUD 135 Mf36
Kanita ☑ J 77 Sa25
Kaniv ☑ UA 49 Mf21
Kaniya ☑ IND (VIC) 110 Sa64
Kaniya ☑ PNG 115 Sa48
Kanjan Cham ☑ IR 59 Nd29
Kanjanka ☑ EAT 146 Mg43
Kanjed ☑ IND (GUJ) 83 Pa36
Kanji-dong ☑ PRK 76 Re25
Kanjiroba ▲ NEP 81 Pb31
Kanjiža ☑ SCG 44 Ma44
Kanker ☑ IND 146 Mh49
Kankaanpää ☑ FIN 38 Mc29
Kankakee ☑ USA (IL) 173 Fg25
Kankalab ☑ BF 137 Kh40
Kankalaha ☑ BF 137 Kh40
Kankara ☑ WAN 138 Ld40
Kankan ☑ RI 95 Qh49
Kankelduang ☑ MYA 88 Ph37
Kankeng ☑ WAN 146 Mf46
Kanna ☑ MYA 86 Pf32
Kannack ▲ VN 89 Qe38
Kannad ☑ IND (MHT) 82 Oh35
Kannapolis ☑ USA (NC) 178
Fk28
Kannauj ☑ IND (UPH) 81 Ok32
Kanniyakumari ☑ IND (TNU)
84 Oj41
Kannod ☑ IND (MPH) 82 Oj33
Kannur ☑ IND (KER) 84 Oh40
Kano ☑ J 79 Rf28
Kano ☑ NAM 150 Lk55
Kano ☑ WAN 138 Le40
Kanona ☑ Z 146 Mf52
Kanoni ☑ RDC 146 Md51
Kanosh ☑ USA (UT) 171 Ee27
Kanoura ☑ J 79 Rf30
Kanowit ☑ MAL 94 Qg44
Kanowna ☑ AUS (WA) 104 Ra61
Kanpur ☑ IND (UPH) 83 Pa32
Kanpur ☑ IND (UPH) 83 Pa32
Kansanshi ☑ Z 151 Mc52
Kansas ☑ USA 174 Ek26
Kansas City ☑ USA (KS) 174
Fc26
Kansas City ☑ USA (MO)
174 Fc26
Kansas Cosmosphere and
Space Center ☑ USA 174 Fa27
Kansenia ☑ RDC 146 Md51
Kanseth ☑ IND 83 Pa35
Kanshengel ☑ KZ 66 Oh23
Kansk ☑ RUS 54 Pd07
Kant ☑ KS 66 Oh24
Kantaji Temple ☑ BD 86 Pe33
Kantala ☑ FIN 38 Mh28
Kantanagar Temple ☑ BD
86 Pe33
Kantbalu ☑ MYA 86 Ph34
Kantchari ☑ BF 137 La39
Kantemirovka ☑ RUS 48 Mk31
Kantharalak ☑ THA 89 Qc38
Kantishna ☑ USA (AK) 165 Ce14
Kantishna ☑ USA (AK) 165 Ce14
Kantunilkin ☑ MEX (QTR)
183 Fg35
Kanturk ☑ IRL 19 Km38
Kanuku Mountains ▲ GUY
194 Ha44
Kanum Monastery ▮ IND
81 Ok30
Kanun ☑ IND (MPH) 82 Oh34
Kanungu ☑ EAU 144 Mf46
Kanus ☑ NAM 154 Lk59
Kanuti National Wildlife Refuge
▮ USA 165 Ce12
Kanwa Woralaksaburi ☑ THA
88 Pk37
Kanwat ☑ IND (RJT) 80 Oh32
Kanyamaza ☑ Z 146 Md50
Kanye ☑ RB 155 Mc58
Kanyemba ☑ ZW 152 Mf53
Kanyi-kayi ☑ IND (MHT) 82 Oj35
Kanyü ☑ Z 147 Mk47
Kanye ☑ RB 155 Mc58
Kanzenze ☑ RDC 151 Mc51
Kao ☑ RI 96 Rd46
Kaoshen ☑ CHN 132 Lc36
Kao Chaison ☑ THA 88 Qa43
Kaohsiung ☑ RC 75 Ra34
Kaokoveld ▲ NAM 150 Lg54
Kaolack ☑ SN 130 Kb39
Kaoma ☑ Z 151 Mb53
Kaouara ☑ CI 137 Kg40
Kao Yai ▲ THA 89 Qc39
Kapaa ☑ USA (HI) 170 Ca34
Kapen ☑ PY 204 Hc58
Kapemba ☑ RDC 146 Mc49
Kapena ☑ SME 194 Hb44
Kapenga ☑ Z 151 Mc52
Kapenguria ☑ EAK 144 Mh45
Kapetáni ☑ GR 46 Mb51

Káto Nevrokópi ☑ GR 45 Md49
Katonga Game Reserve ▮ EAU
144 Mf45
Katonkaraghaj ☑ KZ 67 Pc21
Katoomba ☑ AUS (NSW)
111 Sf62
Katopasa, Gunung ▲ RI 96 Ra46
Katorku hhoi Darvoz ☑ TJ
63 Of26
Katorkuhhoi Quarama ☑ TJ
63 Oe25
Katorkuhhoi Turkistan ☑ TJ
63 Oe26
Katorkuhhoi Zarafšon ☑ TJ
63 Oe26
Katoto ☑ Z 146 Mf47
Káto Vlassía ☑ GR 46 Mb52
Katowice ☑ PL 41 Lt40
Katrineholm ☑ S 31 Lr32
Kâtse ☑ EAK 144 Mk46
Katse Dam ☑ LS 155 Me60
Katsepy ☑ RM 156 Nd53
Katsina ☑ WAN 138 Ld39
Katsina-Ala ☑ WAN 138 Le41
Katsumoto ☑ J 79 Rd28
Katsuta ☑ J 77 Sa27
Katsuura ☑ J 79 Sa28
Kattaqo'rg'on ☑ UZ 63 Od26
Kattavia ☑ GR 47 Mh55
Kattegat ☑ 30 Ll34
Kattwigscaettreit ☑ DK 30 Lt34
Katthammarsvik ☑ S 31 Lt33
Katumuwadi ☑ IND (TNU)
85 Ok40
Katuende ▮ PY 204 Hc58
Katukina, T.I. ☑ BR 196 Ge50
Katumbi ☑ MW 146 Mg51
Katun Abad ☑ IR 64 Nh30
Katunayaka ☑ CL 85 Ok42
Katunda ☑ Z 151 Mc54
Katunguru ☑ EAU 144 Mf46
Katunskij hrebet ▲ RUS/KZ
67 Pc21
Katupon ☑ RI 96 Ra46
Katuria ☑ IND (BIH) 83 Pd33
Katwe ☑ EAU 144 Mf46
Katwijk aan Zee ☑ NL
23 La38
Katy Wrocławskie ☑ PL 41 Ls39
Katzenbuckel ▲ D 33 Lk41
Kaual ☑ USA 170 Ca34
Kauai Channel ☑ USA 170 Ca35
Kaufbeuren ☑ D 33 Ll43
Kaukau ☑ USA (HI) 174 Fa29
Kaufungen ☑ D 32 Lk39
Kauhajoki ☑ FIN 38 Mc28
Kauhanevan-Pohjankankaan
kansallispuisto ▮ FIN 38
Mc28
Kaukaveld ▲ NAM/RB 151 Ma53
Kaukel ☑ KZ 63 Oe29
Kaula ☑ USA 170 Bk35
Kaulakahi Channel ☑ USA
170 Bk35
Kaulshishi ☑ Z 152 Me53
Kaulsdorf ☑ D 33 Lm40
Kaumalapau ☑ USA (HI) 170
Cb35
Kaunakakai ☑ USA (HI) 170 Cb35
Kaunas ☑ LT 39 Md36
Kaunos ☑ TR 47 Mj54
Kaupanga ☑ PNG 115 Sd49
Kaurai ☑ PNG 116 Sg50
Kau Rainforest Museum ☑ PNG
115 Sc48
Kaure-Namoda ☑ WAN 138 Ld39
Kaurissalo ☑ FIN 38 Mb30
Kausala ☑ FIN 38 Mg30
Kaut ☑ RI 95 Qe42
Kava-Ye Island ▲ MYA 88 Pg37
Kavaci ☑ YV 193 Gj43
Kavacik ☑ TR 47 Mj51
Kavadarci ☑ MK 44 Mc49
Kavajë ☑ AL 44 Lu49
Kaval ☑ WAN 138 La39
Kavála ☑ GR 45 Me49
Kavalerovo ☑ RUS 77 Rk23
Kavali ☑ IND (APH) 85 Ok38
Kavaratti ☑ IND 84 Og40
Kavarna ☑ BG 45 Mj47
Kavenge ▲ RG 136 Kd40
Kavieng ☑ PNG 116 Sf47
Kavinga ☑ Z 146 Mg52
Kavir, Daryacheh ▲ IR 64 Ng30
Kavir National Park ▮ IR
64 Nh28
Kavkazkij zapovednik ▮ RUS/GE
52 Na23
Kavos ☑ GR 46 Ma51
Kawachi-Nagano ☑ J 79 Rg28
Kawagebo ☑ J 79 Rj28
Kawagoe ☑ J 79 Rk28
Kawai ☑ IND (RJT) 82 Oj33
Kawaihae ☑ USA (HI) 170 Cc36
Kawaikini ▲ USA 170 Ca34
Kawala ☑ EAT 146 Mf49
Kawalo ☑ EAT 146 Mh50
Kawambwa ☑ Z 146 Me50
Kawanoe ☑ J 79 Rg28
Kawardha ☑ IND (CGH) 83 Pa34
Kawarthas ☑ CDN 173 Ga23
Kawau ☑ NZ 113 Tg64
Kawawachikamach ☑ CDN
166 Gg20
Kawéni ☑ RCA 140 Ma41
Kechika Ranges ▲ CDN 166
Dg16
Kawempe ☑ EAU 144 Mf45
Kawhia ☑ NZ 113 Tg65
Kawich Peak ☑ USA 170 Ea27
Kawimbe ☑ Z 146 Mf50
Kawio ☑ RI 97 Rc45
Kawkareik ☑ MYA 88 Pj37
Kawm Umbu ☑ ET 129 Mg33
Kawthaung ☑ MYA 88 Ph39
Kaya ☑ BF 137 Kk39
Kayaapu ☑ RI 93 Qb48
Kaya Island ▲ USA 166 Ch16
Kayan ☑ RI 93 Qc47
Kayangel ☑ USA 112 Sd45
Kayanhara ☑ RI 96 Me50
Kayan Bung ▲ IND 86 Ph31
Kayan-Sungai Mentarang ▮ RI
94 Qf44
Kayance ☑ RI 94 Qh44
Kayapa ☑ TR 47 Mh51
Kayapó, T.I. ☑ BR 200 He49
Kayar ☑ IND (MHT) 83 Ok36
Kayar ☑ SN 130 Kb38
Kaycee ☑ USA (WY) 169 Eg24
Kayeli ☑ RI 97 Rd47
Kayembe Mukulu ☑ RDC 149
Mc49
Kaye, Mount ▲ AUS 111 Se64
Kayenta ☑ USA (AZ) 171 Ee27
Kayenze ☑ EAT 144 Mg46
Kayes ☑ RCB 148 Lg47
Kayes ☑ RMM 130 Ke38
Kayima ☑ WAL 136 Ke41
Kaymakçi ☑ TR 47 Mj52
Kaymor ☑ SN 136 Kc39
Kayna-Bayonga ☑ RDC 141
Me46
Kayra ☑ RI 91 Rd45
Kayogoro ☑ BU 146 Me48
Kayombo ☑ Z 151 Mb52
Kayonza ☑ RWA 144 Mf46
Kay Point ☑ CDN (YT) 165 Ck11
Kayrunnera ☑ AUS (NSW)
108 Sb61
Kayserdgebege ☑ TR 56 Mh26
Kayserberg ☑ F 25 Lh42
Kayuadi ☑ RI 96 Ra49
Kayuagung ☑ RI 93 Qa47
Kayuaro ☑ RI 93 Qa46
Kayuyu ☑ WAL 136 Le42
Kayuwaru ☑ RI 95 Qd44
Kayville ☑ CDN (SK) 169 Eh21
Kazačka ☑ RUS 48 Na21
Kazakhstan ▮ KZ 53 Oa05
Kazakh Uplands ▲ KZ 54 Ob09
Kazak shyghanaghy ☑ KZ
62 Nf24
Kazaki ☑ KZ 62 Nh23
Kazanka ☑ UA 49 Mg22
Kazan-rettò ▲ BG 45 Mh48
Kazanskaja ☑ RUS 48 Na21
Kazarman ☑ KS 66 Oh25
Kazerun ☑ IR 59 Nf31
Kazi Kazi ☑ EAT 146 Mg48
Kazikli ☑ TR 47 Mh54
Kazimierza Wielka ☑ PL 41 Ma40
Kazimierz Dolny ☑ PL 41
Mb39
Kazimkarabekir ☑ TR 56 Mg27
Kazincbarcika ☑ H 43 Ma42
Kaziranga N.P. ▮ IND 86 Pg32
Kaziza ☑ RDC 151 Md52
Kazlu Ruda ☑ LT 39 Md36
Kazoo ☑ PNG 115 Sd49
Kaznėjov ☑ CZ 42 Lo41
Kazya Pann N.P. ▮ ZW 151
Mc55
Kazumba ☑ RDC 149 Mb49
Kazuno ☑ J 77 Sa25
Kazwama ☑ EAT 144 Mg46
Kazyghurt ☑ KZ 63 Oe25
Kbombole ☑ SN 130 Kb38
Kbor Roumia ▮ DZ 126 Lb38
Kčynia ☑ PL 40 Ls38
Kdyné ☑ CZ 42 Lo41
Kéa ☑ GR 47 Me53
Kéa ☑ GR 47 Me53
Keaau ☑ USA (HI) 170 Cc36
Keahole Point ☑ USA 170 Cb36
Keanae ☑ USA (HI) 170 Cc35
Kearney ☑ USA (NE) 174 Fa25
Keatchie ☑ USA (LA) 174 Fc29
Keating Point ☑ AUS 106
Rk52
Kébaly ☑ RG 136 Kd40
Kebban ☑ TR 57 Mk26
Keban Baraji ☑ TR 57 Mk26
Kebara ☑ WAN 138 Lh47
Kebbe ☑ WAN 138 Lc40
Kébémèr ☑ SN 130 Kb38
Kebili ☑ TN 126 Le29
Kebitigollewa ☑ CL 85 Pa41
Kebnekaise ▲ S 16 Lk12
Kebri Dehar ☑ ETH 143 Nd42
Kebumen ☑ RI 95 Qd49
Kéché ☑ RCA 140 Ma41
Kechika Ranges ▲ CDN 166
Dg16
Kecskemét ☑ H 43 Lu44
Kedainiai ☑ LT 39 Md36
Kedah ☑ IND (UTT) 81 Ok30
Kedarnath (Hindu shrine) ☑ IND
81 Ok30
Kedarnath Sanctuary ▮ IND
81 Ok30
Kédédéssé ☑ TCH 139 Lj40
Kedgaon ☑ IND (MHT) 82 Oh36
Kédougou ☑ SN 130 Kc40
Kedgwick ☑ CDN (NB) 176 Gg22
Kediet ej Jill ▲ RIM 130 Kd34
Ke Dinh ☑ VN 87 Qc36
Kedrovyj ☑ RUS 54 Pc06
Kédidi ☑ RI 91 Ra49
Kedondong ☑ CHN (HLG) 76 Rd22
Keelung ☑ RC 75 Ra33
Kee
Keele Peak ▲ CDN 165 Db14
Keeley Lake ☑ CDN (SK) 169 Ed18
Keeler ☑ USA (CA) 170 Eb27
Keeling Islands ☑ AUS 112 Pb49
Keene ☑ USA (NH) 177 Gd24
Keeneland Race Course ▮ USA
(KY) 175 Fh26
Keeroongooloo ☑ AUS (QLD)
108 Sb58
Keetmanshoop ☑ NAM
154 Lk59
Kefalonía ☑ GR 46 Ma52
Kefamenanu ☑ RI 97 Rb50
Kefar Sava ☑ IL 58 Mh29
Keffeti ☑ WAN 138 Le41
Kef Mimouna ☑ DZ 126 La31
Keftya ☑ ETH 142 Mj39
Kegalla ☑ CL 85 Pa42
Kégérti ☑ KS 63 Oh25
Kegeyli ☑ UZ 62 Nk24
Kehancongrong-Kozio ☑ PL 40 Ls40
Kehl ☑ D 33 Lh42
Kehra ☑ EST 38 Mf31
Keibul Lam Jao N.P. ▮ IND
86 Pg33

Kitami-Yamato-tai – Kremlin

Kitami-Yamato-tai J 77 Sc23
Kita-Nagato Q.N.P. J 79 Rf28
Kitanda RDC 146 Md49
Kitangari EAT 147 Mk51
Kitani EAK 144 Mj47
Kitaotao RP 91 Rc42
Kit Carson USA (CO) 174 Ej26
Kitchener AUS (WA) 105 Rc61
Kitchener CDN (ON) 173 Fk24
Kiteba RDC 149 Mc49
Kitee FIN 38 Ml28
Kitembé RCB 148 Lh47
Kitendwe RDC 146 Me49
Kitenga RDC 148 Lj48
Kitengo RDC 149 Mc49
Kiteto EAT 147 Mj48
Kitgum EAU 144 Mg44
Kithairónas Óros GR 45 Md52
Kíthira GR 46 Mc54
Kíthnos GR 47 Me53
Kíthnos GR 47 Me53
Kitika RCA 140 Mb43
Kitimat CDN (BC) 166 Df18
Kitimat Ranges CDN 166 Df19
Kitimat Village CDN (BC) 166 Df18
Kitiu GH 137 Kk40
Kitmore Range AUS 103 Re57
Kitob UZ 63 Od26
Kitomanga EAT 147 Mk50
Kitou J 79 Rh29
Kítros GR 46 Mc50
Kitsuki J 79 Rf29
Kittelfjäll S 16 Lh13
Kittenning USA (PA) 173 Ga25
Kittilä FIN 16 Mc12
Kitt Peak Nat. Observatory USA 171 Ee30
Kitui EAK 144 Mj46
Kitumbia EAT 147 Mk50
Kitunda EAT 146 Mg49
Kitunga RDC 149 Mc50
Kitutu RDC 146 Me47
Kitwancool Totem Poles CDN 166 Dg18
Kitwanga CDN (BC) 166 Dg18
Kitwanga EAU 144 Mg45
Kitwe Z 146 Me52
Kitzbühel A 34 Ln43
Kitzbüheler Alpen A 34 Ln43
Kitzingen D 33 Ll41
Kiumbila RDC 146 Md48
Kiunga EAK 145 Na46
Kiunga PNG 115 Sa49
Kiunga Marine National Reserve EAK 145 Na46
Kiuruvesi FIN 16 Md14
Kivalina USA (AK) 165 Bh12
Kiverci UA 41 Mf40
Kivijärvi FIN 38 Mf27
Kivik S 31 Lp35
Kiviks marknad S 31 Lp35
Kiviõli EST 38 Mg31
Kivotós GR 46 Mb50
Kiwai Island PNG 115 Sb50
Kiwale EAT 146 Mg50
Kiwalik USA (AK) 165 Bk12
Kiwayu Island EAK 145 Na47
Kiwirrkurra A.L. AUS 103 Rd57
Kiworo RI 114 Rk49
Kiyamaki Dagh IR 57 Nd26
Kiyasar IR 62 Ng27
Kiyawa WAN 138 Le40
Kiyembwe RDC 146 Md47
Kıyıköy TR 45 Mj49
Kızbeyi TR 57 Mk27
Kızılcahamam TR 56 Mg25
Kızıldağ Milli Parkı TR 56 Mf27
Kızılırmak TR 56 Mg25
Kiziljurt RUS (DAG) 57 Nd24
Kizil Kala TM 62 Nh25
Kizil Qianfo Dong CHN 66 Pb25
Kızıltepe TR 57 Na27
Kizimbani EAT 147 Mk50
Kizimkazi EAT 147 Mk49
Kižinga RUS (BUR) 70 Qe20
Kız Kalesi TR 56 Mh27
Kizljar RUS (DAG) 57 Nd24
Kjahta RUS (BUR) 70 Qd20
Kjellerup DK 30 Lk34
Kjellmyra N 30 Ln30
Kjøllefjord N 16 Md10
Kjölur IS 18 Ka26
Kjustendil BG 44 Mc48
Klaarbeck RI 97 Re46
Klaarstroom ZA 154 Mb62
Klabat RI 91 Rc45
Kladanj BIH 44 Lt46
Kladar RI 114 Rj50
Kladnica SCG 44 Ma47
Kladno CZ 42 Lp40
Kladovo SCG 44 Mc46
Klaeng THA 89 Qa39
Klagenfurt A 35 Lp44
Klaipėda LT 39 Mb35
Klakah RI 95 Qg49
Klaksvík DK 18 Ko28
Klamath USA (CA) 168 Dj25
Klamath Falls USA (OR) 168 Dk24
Klamath Mountains USA 168 Dj25
Klamono RI 97 Rf46
Klampa RI 94 Qj45
Klanac HR 35 Lq46
Klarälven S 31 Lo31
Klaserie Nature Reserve ZA 155 Mf58
Klasies River Caves ZA 155 Mc63
Klášterec nad Ohří CZ 42 Lo40
Klasztor Paulinów PL 41 Lu40
Klasztor Świętej Anny PL 40 Lt40
Klatovy CZ 42 Lo41
Klausen = Chiusa I 34 Lm44
Klawer ZA 154 Lk61
Klawock USA (AK) 166 Dd18
Kle LB 136 Ke42
Kleck BY 41 Mg37
Kłecko PL 40 Ls38
Kleena CDN (BC) 168 Dh20
Klein Aub NAM 154 Lj57
Kleinbegin ZA 154 Ma60
Klein Karas NAM 154 Lk59
Kleinpoort ZA 155 Mc62
Kleinwalsertal D/A 33 Ll43
Kleinzee ZA 154 Lj60
Klekovača BIH 35 Lr46
Kléla RMM 137 Kh40
Klemtu CDN (BC) 166 Df19
Klenovac BIH 35 Lr46
Kleppe N 30 Lf32
Klerksdorp ZA 155 Md59
Klerkskraal ZA 155 Md59
Klery Creek USA (AK) 165 Bk12
Klésso BF 137 Kj40
Kleszczele PL 41 Md38
Kletnja RUS 48 Mg19
Kletskij RUS 48 Nb21
Klevan' UA 41 Mg40
Kleve D 32 Lg39
Klezevo RUS 39 Mh33
Kličav BY 48 Me19
Klička RUS 71 Qj20
Kličkinskij hrebet RUS 71 Qj20
Kliczków PL 40 Lq39
Klimavičy BY 48 Mf19
Klimovo RUS 48 Mg19
Klimovsk RUS 48 Mj18
Klin RUS 48 Mj17
Klincy RUS 48 Mg19
Klingenthal D 33 Ln40
Klinghardtsberge NAM 154 Lh59
Klingnau CH 34 Lj43
Kliniča Sela HR 35 Lq45
Klintehamn S 31 Lt33
Klipfontein ZA 155 Mc62
Klippan S 30 Lo34
Klipplaat ZA 155 Mc62
Kliprand ZA 154 Lk61
Kliprondawel NAM 154 Lk59
Klipskool ZA 155 Mf58
Klissoúra GR 46 Ma51
Klisura BG 45 Me48
Klitmøller DK 30 Lj33
Klitoría GR 46 Mc53
Kljajićevo SCG 44 Lu45
Kljavica BY 39 Mf36
Ključ BIH 35 Lr46
Ključevskaja Sopka, vulkan RUS 55 Ta07
Kłobuck PL 41 Lt40
Kłodawa PL 40 Lt38
Kłodzko PL 40 Lr40
Kløfta N 30 Lm30
Klokkarvik N 30 Lf30
Kłomnice PL 41 Lu40
Klondike Highway CDN 165 Db14
Klondike Plateau CDN 165 Da14
Klondike River CDN (YT) 165 Db13
Klos AL 44 Ma49
Kloštar Ivanić HR 35 Lr45
Kloster CH 34 Lk44
Kloster Corvey D 32 Lk39
Klosterkirche in Weingarten D 33 Lk43
Klosterkirche Jerichow D 32 Ln38
Kloster Lehnin D 32 Ln38
Kloster Lorsch D 33 Lj41
Kloster Maulbronn D 33 Lj41
Kloster Müstair CH 34 Ll44
Klosterneuburg A 42 Lr42
Klosterruine Chorin D 32 Lo38
Kloster Säben = Monastero di Sabiona I 34 Lm44
Kloster Sankt Gallen CH 34 Lk43
Klosterwappen A 35 Lq43
Kloster Zinna D 32 Lo38
Kloten CH 34 Lj43
Kloten S 31 Lq31
Klötze D 32 Lm38
Klouékanmé DY 138 La42
Kluane Lake CDN 166 Da15
Kluane National Park CDN 166 Da15
Kluang MAL 93 Qb44
Kluczbork PL 40 Lt40
Klütz D 32 Lm37
Knäred S 31 Lo34
Knaresborough GB 21 Kt36
Knarvik N 17 Lc15
Knee Lake CDN 167 Eg18
Kneža BG 45 Me47
Knežev dvor HR 35 Lt48
Kneževici Sušica SCG 44 Lu47
Kneževi Vinogradi HR 35 Lt45
Knićanin SCG 44 Ma45
Knidos TR 47 Mh54
Knife R. Indian Villages N.H.S. USA 172 Ek22
Knight Island USA 165 Cg15
Knighton GB 21 Kr38
Knin HR 35 Lr46
Knislinge S 31 Lp34
Knittelfeld A 35 Lp43
Knivsta S 31 Ls31
Knjaževac SCG 44 Mc47
Knjaze-Volkonskoe RUS 77 Rh21
Knjažiha RUS 48 Nd18
Knocklong IRL 19 Km38
Knokke-Heist B 23 Ld39
Knollsgrund 31 Ls33
Knossós GR 47 Mf55
Knox Coast 7 Qa32
Knoxville USA (GA) 178 Fj29
Knoxville USA (IA) 172 Fd25
Knoxville USA (TN) 178 Fj28
Knud Rasmussen Land DK 163 Hb02
Knüll D 32 Lk40
Knurów PL 40 Lt40
Knurowiec PL 41 Mb38
Knuthenborg DK 30 Lm36
Knutsford GB 21 Ks37
Knysna ZA 154 Mb63
Knysna National Lake Area ZA 154 Mb63
Knyszyn PL 41 Mc37
Koaba DY 138 La40
Ko Adang THA 88 Pk42
Koagas RI 114 Rg47
Koala BF 137 Kk39
Koamb CAM 139 Lg44
Koatinemo, T.I. BR 199 Hd48
Koba RI 95 Qd47
Kobadié RN 132 La39
Kobadja RCA 140 Lk43
Kobarid SLO 42 Lo44
Kobayashi J 79 Rf29
Kobe J 79 Rh28
Kobe RI 91 Rd45
Kobédaigouré CI 137 Kh43
Kobeljaky UA 49 Mh21
Kobenni RIM 130 Kf38
Kobero BU 146 Mf47
Kobi CAM 139 Lh43
Kobi WAN 139 Lg41
Koblagué TCH 140 Lj41
Koblenz D 33 Lh40
Kobli DY 137 La40
K'obo ETH 142 Mk39
Koboko EAU 144 Mf44
Kobou RMM 131 Kk38
Koboža RUS 48 Mh16
Kobroor RI 114 Rh49
Kobryn BY 41 Me38
Kobuk USA (AK) 165 Cb12
Kobuk Valley National Park USA 165 Ca12
Kobuleti GE 57 Na25
Kobylin PL 40 Ls39
Kocaeli TR 56 Me25
Kocaeli Yarımadası TR 56 Me25
Kočani MK 44 Mc49
Koçarlı TR 56 Md27
Koceljevo SCG 44 Lu46
Kočerin BIH 35 Ls47
Kočetovka RUS 48 Na19
Kočevje SLO 42 Lp45
Koch'ang ROK 78 Rd28
Ko Chang THA 88 Pk41
Ko Chang THA 89 Qb40
Koch Bihar IND (WBG) 86 Pe32
Kocher D 33 Lk42
Kochi IND (KER) 84 Oj41
Kochi J 79 Rg29
Kochkorka KS 66 Oh24
Kock PL 41 Mc39
Kočkor-Bazar-Korgon KS 63 Og25
Kocsola H 42 Lt44
Kócsújfalu H 43 Ma43
Kočubej RUS (DAG) 57 Nd23
Kodachad IND 84 Oh39
Kodad IND (APH) 83 Ok37
Kodaikanal IND (TNU) 84 Oj40
Kodala IND (ORS) 83 Pc36
Kodari NEP 81 Pc32
Kodarma IND (JKD) 83 Pc33
Kode S 30 Lm33
Kodeń PL 41 Md39
Kodiak USA (AK) 164 Cd17
Kodiak Island USA 164 Cd17
Kodiak National Wildlife Refuge USA 164 Cd17
Kodinar IND (GUJ) 82 Of35
Kodinsk RUS 54 Pd07
Kodjari BF 138 La40
Kodlipet IND (KTK) 84 Oh39
Kodok SUD 141 Mg41
Kodrąb PL 41 Lu39
Kodumuru IND (APH) 82 Oj38
Kodungallur IND (KER) 84 Oj40
Koduru IND (APH) 85 Ok39
Kodyma UA 49 Me21
Koébonou CI 137 Kj41
Koegelbeen Caves ZA 154 Mb60
Koegelbeengrotte ZA 154 Mb60
Koekenaap ZA 154 Lk61
Koelwar IND (BIH) 83 Pc33
Koës NAM 154 Lk58
Kofa N.W.R. USA 170 Ed29
Kofarnihon TJ 63 Oe26
Kofçaş TR 45 Mh49
Kofele ETH 142 Mk42
Koffi-Amankro CI 137 Kj42
Koffiefontein ZA 155 Mc60
Kofiau RI 97 Re46
Köflach A 35 Lq43
Koforidua GH 137 Kk42
Kofu J 79 Rg28
Kofu J 79 Rk28
Koga J 77 Rk27
Kogan AUS (QLD) 109 Sf59
Køge DK 30 Ln35
Køge Bugt = Pikiutdleq DK 163 Ja06
Køge Bugt DK 30 Ln35
Kogelberg Nature Reserve ZA 154 Lk63
Koghaly KZ 66 Ok23
Kogon UZ 63 Oc26
Kogula EST 39 Mc32
Koguryo, Capital Cities and Tombs of the Ancient Kingdom CHN 76 Rd25
Koguryo Tombs, Complex of PRK 76 Rd25/Rd26
Koguva EST 39 Md32
Kogyae Strict Nature Reserve GH 137 Kk42
Kohalpur NEP 81 Pa31
Kohan PK 65 Od32
Koh Ang Tong THA 88 Pk41
Kohat PK 65 Of29
Kohila EST 38 Me31
Kohima IND (NGL) 86 Ph33
Koh-i-Patandar PK 65 Oc32
Koh Kong K 89 Qb40
Kohler Range 6 Eb33
Kohlu PK 65 Oe31
Kohma RUS 48 Na17
Kohol RI 97 Rd47
Koh Phaluai THA 88 Pk41
Koh Phangan THA 88 Qa41
Kohrud IR 62 Ng27
Koh Rung K 89 Qb40
Koh Rung Samloem K 89 Qb40
Koh Samui THA 88 Qa41
Koh Tang K 89 Qb40
Koh Tao THA 88 Pk40
Koh Thmei K 89 Qb40
Kohtlajärve EST 38 Mh31
Kohung ROK 78 Rd28
Kohunlich MEX 183 Ff36
Koidern CDN (YT) 166 Ck15
Koidu-Sefadu WAL 136 Ke41
Koil Island PNG 115 Sc47
Koilkundla IND (APH) 85 Ok38
Koilovci BG 45 Me47
Koimbani COM 156 Nb51
Koindu WAL 136 Ke41
Koi Sanjaq IRQ 57 Nc27
Koito EAK 145 Mk47
Koivu FIN 16 Mc12
Koivulahti FIN 38 Mb27
Kojandytau KZ 66 Ok23
Koje Do ROK 79 Re28
Kojetín CZ 42 Ls41
Kojin ROK 78 Re26
Kojonup AUS (WA) 104 Qj62
Kojtas KZ 67 Pc21
Koka ETH 142 Mk41
Kokand UZ 63 Of25
Kökar FIN 38 Ma31
Kökar FIN 38 Ma31
Kokaral tübegi KZ 62 Nk22
Kokas RI 114 Rg47
Kokatha AUS (SA) 108 Rh61
Kokcha UZ 62 Oa25
Kokemäki FIN 38 Mb29
Kokemäki FIN 38 Mc29
Kokenau RI 114 Rj48
Kokerboom Forest NAM 154 Lk59
Kokerboomwoud NAM 154 Lk59
Kokerit GUY 194 Ha42
Ko Kho Khao THA 88 Pk41
Kokinombléa GR 45 Md52
Kokish CDN (BC) 168 Dg20
Kok-Jangak KS 63 Og25
Kókkines Pétres GR 44 Md50
Kokkola FIN 16 Mb14
Koklot FIN 38 Mb27
Koknese LV 39 Mf34
Koko ETH 142 Mj40
Koko WAN 138 Lc40
Koko WAN 138 Lc42
Kokoda PNG 115 Sd50
Kokofata RMM 136 Kf39
Kokologo BF 137 Kk39
Kokolopozo CI 137 Kg43
Kokomo USA (IN) 173 Fg25
Kokopo PNG 116 Sg48
Kokore DY 138 Lb41
Kokosa ETH 142 Mk42
Kokoso GH 137 Kk43
Kokotí GR 46 Mc51
Kokpek KZ 66 Ok24
Kokpekti KZ 66 Pb21
Kökpınar TR 57 Na26
Kokqakam CHN (XUZ) 68 Pd26
Kokrajhar IND (ASM) 86 Pf32
Kokrines Hills USA 165 Cc13
Kokruagarok USA (AK) 165 Cd10
Kokšajsk RUS (MEL) 48 Nd17
Koksan PRK 78 Rd26
Koksara IND (ORS) 83 Pb36
Koksarai KZ 63 Oe24
Köksengir tau KZ 62 Nj23
Köksengir tau KZ 63 Oc23
Kokstad ZA 155 Me61
Koktal KZ 66 Ok23
Koktebel' UA 49 Mh23
Koktokay CHN (XUZ) 67 Pe22
Koktuma KZ 66 Pa23
Kokubo J 79 Rf30
Kokuj RUS 71 Qj19
Kokum Do ROK 78 Rd28
Ko Kut THA 89 Qb40
Kol PNG 115 Sc48
Kola LB 136 Kg42
Kola RI 114 Rh48
Kola RI 114 Rh48
Kola RUS 16 Mg11
Kolaba Fort IND 82 Og36
Kołacze PL 41 Md39
Kolaghat IND (WBG) 83 Pd34
Kolahun LB 136 Ke41
Kolaka RI 96 Ra48
Kolana RI 97 Rc50
Ko Lanta THA 88 Pk42
Ko Lanta Marine N.P. THA 88 Pk42
Kola Peninsula RUS 14 Mb03
Kolar IND (KTK) 84 Ok39
Kolari FIN 16 Mb12
Kolárovo SK 42 Ls43
Kolasava BY 41 Mg37
Kolåsen S 16 Lg14
Kolašin SCG 44 Lu48
Kolbäck S 31 Lr31
Kolbai KZ 66 Pa23
Kolbio EAK 145 Na46
Kolbu N 30 Ll30
Kolbudy Grn. PL 40 Lt36
Kolbuszowa PL 41 Mb40
Kol'čugino RUS 48 Mk17
Kolda SN 136 Kc39
Koldaga TCH 140 Lj41
Kolding DK 30 Lk35
Koldinghus DK 30 Lk35
Kole RDC 149 Mb47
Kole RDC 141 Mc44
Kolebira IND (JKD) 83 Pc34
Kolen IR 59 Ne30
Kolèntèn RG 136 Kd40
Kölesd H 43 Lt44
Kolga-Jaani EST 38 Mf32
Kolgaon IND (MHT) 82 Oh36
Kolgompja RUS 38 Mj31
Kolhan Upland IND 83 Pc34
Kolhapur IND (APH) 82 Ok37
Kolhapur IND (MHT) 82 Oh37
Kolhar IND (KTK) 82 Oh37
Kolho FIN 38 Me28
Kolhozabad TJ 63 Oe27
Kolhumadulu Atoll = Thaa Atoll MV 84 Og44
Kolia CI 137 Kg41
Ko Libong THA 88 Pk42
Koliganek USA (AK) 164 Cb16
Kolín CZ 42 Lq40
Kolin kansallispuisto FIN 16 Me14
Koljučinskaja guba RUS 55 Ua05
Kolka LV 39 Mc33
Kolkasrags LV 39 Mc33
Kolkata IND 86 Pe34
Kolkhetis Nakrdzali GE 57 Na24
Kolky UA 41 Mf39
Kollafjarðarnes IS 18 Jt25
Kollam IND (KER) 84 Oj41
Kölleda D 32 Lm39
Kollegal IND (KTK) 84 Oj39
Kollo RN 132 Lb39
Kollur IND (KTK) 84 Oh39
Kolmanskop NAM 154 Lh59
Kolmården S 31 Lr32
Köln D 32 Lg40
Kolno PL 41 Mb37
Kolo EAT 147 Mh48
Koło PL 40 Lt38
Kolobane SN 130 Kc38
Kolobeke RDC 149 Lk46
Kołobrzeg PL 40 Lq36
Koločava UA 43 Md42
Kolofata CAM 139 Lh40
Kolokani RMM 137 Kf39
Koloko BF 137 Kh40
Kolokondé DY 138 La41
Kolombangara SOL 117 Sj49
Kolomenskye RUS 48 Mj18
Kolomna RUS 48 Mk18
Kolomonyi RDC 149 Mb48
Kolomyja UA 43 Mf42
Kolon CI 137 Kh41
Kolondiéba RMM 137 Kg40
Kolongotomo RMM 137 Kh39
Kolono RI 96 Rb48
Kolonodale RI 96 Ra46
Koloro, V. = Pamporovo BG 45 Me49
Kolosib IND (MZR) 86 Pg33
Koloveden kansallispuisto FIN 38 Mj28
Kolpaševo RUS 54 Pa07
Kolpny RUS 48 Mj19
Kólpos Agiou Órous GR 44 Md50
Kólpos Alkyonídon GR 44 Md52
Kólpos Hanión GR 45 Md55
Kólpos Ierissoú GR 45 Md50
Kólpos Kassándras GR 45 Md50
Kólpos Kaválas GR 45 Me50
Kólpos Kissámou GR 45 Md55
Kólpos Messarás GR 47 Me55
Kólpos Mirambélou GR 47 Me56
Kólpos Orfanoú GR 45 Md50
Kólpos Petalion GR 47 Me53
Kolpur PK 65 Od31
Kolskij Poluostrov RUS 54 Md05
Kolsva S 31 Lq31
Koltur DK 18 Kn29
Kolufoss IS 18 Ju25
Koluli ER 142 Na38
Kolur IND (CGH) 83 Pa36
Koluszki PL 41 Lu39
Kolwezi RDC 151 Mc51
Kolyčivka UA 48 Mf20
Kolyma RUS 55 Sc05
Kolyma Range RUS 55 Sc06
Kolymskaja nizmennost' RUS 55 Sd05
Kolyšlej RUS 48 Nc19
Koma ETH 142 Mj41
Komadougou Yobe RN/WAN 133 Lg39
Komaio PNG 115 Sb49
Komaki J 79 Rj28
Komako PNG 115 Sc49
Komańcza PL 41 Mc41
Komanda RDC 141 Me45
Komandorskie ostrova RUS 55 Ta07
Komárno SK 42 Lt43
Komarno UA 43 Md41
Komárom H 42 Lt43
Komarówka Podlaska PL 41 Mc39
Komatipoort ZA 155 Mf58
Komatlapeta IND (ORS) 83 Pb36
Komatsu J 79 Rj27
Komba RI 97 Rb49
Kombat NAM 150 Lj55
Kombe RDC 149 Mc48
Kombissiri BF 137 Kk39
Kombo ZW 152 Me55
Kombo-Itindi CAM 138 Le43
Kombone CAM 138 Le43
Kombong IND (ARP) 86 Ph31
Kombongou BF 138 La40
Komborodougou CI 137 Kh41
Koméayo CI 137 Kg42
Kome Island EAT 144 Mg47
Kome Island EAU 144 Mg46
Komejan IR 57 Ne28
Kom el Ahmar (Nekhen) ET 129 Mg33
Komenda GH 137 Kk43
Komfane RI 114 Rh48
Komga ZA 155 Md62
Komha IND (ORS) 83 Pb35
Komi 53 Nb03
Kominternivs'ke UA 49 Mf22
Komin-Yanga BF 137 La40
Kôm Ishqaw ET 129 Mf32
Komiža HR 35 Lr47
Komló H 42 Lt44
Kommunar RUS 38 Ml31
Komniná GR 46 Mb50
Komo PNG 115 Sb49
Komodo RI 96 Qk50
Komodo RI 96 Qk50
Komodo N.P. RI 96 Qk50
Komodou RG 136 Kf41
Kôm Ombo ET 129 Mg33
Komono RCB 148 Lg47
Komoran RI 114 Rk50
Komoro J 77 Rk27
Komorzno PL 40 Lt39
Komosi RDC 140 Lk43
Komosomol'sk RUS 48 Na17
Komotini GR 45 Mf49
Kompia WAL 136 Kd41
Kompiam PNG 115 Sb48
Kompina PL 41 Ma38
Komponaone RI 97 Rb48
Kompong Cham K 89 Qc40
Kompong Chhnang K 89 Qc39
Kompong Som = Sihanoukville K 89 Qb40
Kompong Speu K 89 Qc40
Kompong Thom K 89 Qc39
Kompong Trach K 89 Qc40
Kompot RI 91 Rc45
Komsberge ZA 154 Ma62
Komsomolabad TJ 63 Oe26
Komsomol'sk RUS 39 Ma36
Komsomol'sk TM 62 Ob26
Komsomol'skaja ANT (RUS) 7 Pd33
Komsomol'skij RUS (DAG) 57 Nd24
Komsomol'skij RUS (KAL) 57 Nd23
Komsomol'skij RUS (MOR) 48 Nc18
Komsomol'sk-na-Amure RUS 55 Rd08
Komsomolskoye KZ 63 Oe25
Komsomol'sk Zapovednik RUS 39 Ma36
Komun Do ROK 78 Rd28
Kömür Burnu TR 47 Mg52
Kömürlimanı TR 45 Mf50
Kon CAM 139 Lf43
Kona BF 137 Kj39
Kôna RN 132 Le39
Kona WAN 139 Lf41
Konada IND (APH) 83 Pb36
Konak SCG 44 Ma45
Konakovo RUS 48 Mj17
Konakpınar TR 47 Mh51
Konandikro CI 137 Kh42
Konankro CI 137 Kh42
Konapeta IND (APH) 85 Ok38
Konarak IR 64 Oa33
Konare BG 45 Mj47
Konark IND (ORS) 83 Pd36
Konark Beach IND 83 Pd36
Konarzyny PL 40 Lr37
Konch IND (UPH) 83 Ok33
Konda RI 97 Rf46
Kondagaon IND (CGH) 83 Pa36
Kondakamberu IND (ORS) 83 Pb36
Kondanar IND (CGH) 83 Pa36
Kondavidu IND 83 Pa37
Kondembia WAL 136 Ke41
Kondhali IND (MHT) 83 Ok35
Kondinin AUS (WA) 104 Qk62
Kondio = Kombongou BF 138 La40
Kondoa EAT 147 Mh48
Kondol' RUS 48 Nc19
Kondolovo BG 45 Mh48
Kondrovo RUS 48 Mh18
Kondue RDC 149 Mb48
Konduga WAN 139 Lg40
Koné F 118 Tc56
Koneng RI 92 Pj43
Koneurgench TM 62 Nk24
Kong CAM 139 Lg43
Kong CI 137 Kh41
Kongasso CI 137 Kg42
Kongbo RCA 140 Ma43
Kong Christian IX Land DK 163 Ja05
Kong Christian X Land DK 163 Jb4
Kongelai EAK 144 Mh45
Kong Frederik IX Land DK 163 Hc05
Kong Frederik VIII Land DK 163 Jc03
Kong Frederik VI Kyst DK 163 Hd06
Kong Karls Land N 16 Md06
Kong Krailat THA 88 Qa37
Konglong CHN (HUB) 75 Qh31
Kongo LB 136 Ke42
Kongolo NAM 151 Mb54
Kongolo RDC 146 Md48
Kongor SUD 141 Mf42
Kongoussi BF 137 Kk39
Kongsberg N 30 Lk31
Kongsøya N 16 Me06
Kongsten fort N 30 Ll31
Kongsvege Kongbreen N 16 Lg06
Kongsvinger N 30 Lm30
Kongtal IND (MNP) 86 Pg34
Kongur Shan CHN 66 Oh26
Kongwa EAT 147 Mj49
Kong Wilhelm Land DK 163 Jd03
Koni RDC 146 Md51
Konibodom TJ 63 Of25
Konice CZ 42 Lr41
Königsbrück D 32 Lo39
Königsbrunn D 33 Ll42
Königsee D 32 Lm40
Königstein D 33 Lj40
Königstein D 32 Lp40
Königswiesen A 42 Lp42
Königswinter D 32 Lh40
Königs Wusterhausen D 32 Lo38
Konimex UZ 63 Oc25
Konin PL 40 Lt38
Konina RMM 137 Kg39
Konio RMM 137 Kh39
Kónitsa GR 46 Ma50
Köniz CH 34 Lh44
Konj BIH 35 Lr47
Konjed Jan IR 59 Nf29
Konjic BIH 35 Ls47
Konko RDC 146 Md51
Konkoma ETH 145 Mk43
Konkouré RG 136 Kd40
Konkwesso WAN 138 Lc40
Konna RMM 131 Kj38
Könnern D 32 Lm39
Kono PNG 116 Sg47
Konobougou RMM 137 Kg39
Konodimini RMM 137 Kg39
Konopiště CZ 42 Lp41
Konopki PL 41 Ma38
Konos PNG 116 Sf47
Konoša RUS 54 Na06
Konosu J 77 Rk27
Konotop PL 40 Lq39
Konotop UA 48 Mg20
Kon Plong VN 89 Qe38
Konrra IND (JKD) 83 Pc34
Konsankoro RG 136 Kf41
Konséguéla RMM 137 Kh39
Końskie PL 41 Ma39
Konsmo N 30 Lh32
Konso ETH 144 Mj43
Konsotami RG 136 Kd40
Konstancin-Jeziorna PL 41 Mb38
Konstantin BG 45 Mg48
Konstantinovka RUS 71 Rd21
Konstantinovsk RUS 49 Na22
Konstantinovy Lázně CZ 42 Ln41
Konstantynów PL 41 Md38
Konstantynów Łódzki PL 41 Lu39
Konstanz D 33 Lk43
Konta IND (CGH) 83 Pa37
Konta WAL 136 Kd41
Kontagora WAN 138 Lc40
Kontcha CAM 139 Lg42
Kontilola Cave RI 114 Rk47
Kontiolahti FIN 38 Mk28
Kon Tum VN 89 Qe38
Konya Ovası TR 56 Mg27
Konyrat KZ 66 Oh22
Konz D 33 Lg41
Konza EAK 144 Mj46
Konza RMM 131 Kj38
Konzo CI 137 Kh42
Koobi Fora EAK 144 Mj43
Kookynie AUS (WA) 104 Ra60
Koolan Island AUS 102 Rb54
Koolatah AUS (QLD) 107 Sb53
Kooline AUS (WA) 102 Qj57
Koolpinyah AUS (NT) 106 Rf52
Koombooloombah AUS (QLD) 107 Sc54
Koonalda AUS (SA) 105 Re61
Koondoo AUS (QLD) 109 Sc58
Koongie Park AUS (WA) 103 Rd55
Kooniba AUS (SA) 108 Rg61
Koonmarra AUS (WA) 104 Qj59
Koopan Sud ZA 154 Ma59
Koopmansfontein ZA 155 Mc60
Koo Puay Noi THA 89 Qb38
Koor RI 114 Rg46
Koorawatha AUS (NSW) 111 Se63
Koorda AUS (WA) 104 Qj61
Koosa EST 38 Mh32
Kooskia USA (ID) 168 Ec22
Kootenay Bay CDN (BC) 168 Eb21
Kootenay Ind. Res. CDN 168 Ec21
Kootenay Lake CDN 168 Eb21
Kootenay N.P. CDN 168 Eb20
Kootenay River USA 168 Ec21
Kootingal AUS (NSW) 109 Sf61
Kootjieskolk ZA 154 Ma61
Kopa KZ 66 Oh24
Kopa Z 146 Mf51
Kopalnia Soli PL 41 Lu40
Kopaonik SCG 44 Ma47
Kopaonik, N.P. SCG 44 Ma47
Kopargo DY 138 La41
Kópasker IS 18 Kd24
Kópavogur IS 18 Jt26
Ko Payang THA 88 Pj41
Kopbirlik KZ 66 Oj22
Kopejsk RUS 54 Oa07
Koper SLO 42 Lo45
Kopervik N 30 Lf31
Ko Pha Yam THA 88 Pk41
Ko Phi THA 88 Pk42
Ko Phuket THA 88 Pk42
Kopiago PNG 115 Sb48
Kopidlno CZ 42 Lq40
Köping S 31 Lq31
Kopingue CI 137 Kj41
Koplik i Poshtëm AL 44 Lu48
Kopmanholmen S 38 Lt27
Kopong RB 155 Mc58
Kopor'e RUS 38 Mk31
Koporokenité-Na RMM 131 Kj38
Koppa IND (KTK) 84 Oh39
Koppal IND (KTK) 82 Oj38
Koppang N 17 Lf15
Kopparberg S 31 Lp31
Kopparstenarne 31 Lu32
Koppe Dag IR/TM 62 Nj27
Kopperå N 16 Lf14
Koppies ZA 155 Md59
Koppom S 30 Ln31
Ko Prah Thong THA 88 Pk41
Koprivna BIH 44 Lt46
Koprivnica HR 35 Lr44
Kopřivnice CZ 42 Lt41
Koprivštica BG 45 Me48
Köprübaşı TR 47 Mj52
Köprülü Kanyon Milli Parkı TR 56 Mf27
Kõpu EST 38 Mc32
Koputh EAU 144 Mh44
Kopyčynci UA 43 Mf41
Kora IND (BIH) 83 Pd33
Ko Ra THA 88 Pk41
Korab SCG/AL 44 Ma49
Korablino RUS 48 Mk19
Ko Racha Noi THA 88 Pk42
Ko Racha Yai THA 88 Pk42
Koraghaty KZ 66 Og24
K'orahe ETH 143 Nc42
Korand IR 62 Nh27
Korangal IND (APH) 82 Oj37
Korannaberg ZA 154 Mb59
Kora N.P. EAK 145 Mk46
Koraput IND (ORS) 83 Pb36
Korasa SOL 117 Sj49
Koratagere IND (KTK) 84 Oj39
Ko Rawi THA 88 Pk42
Korba IND (CGH) 83 Pb34
Korba TN 126 Lf27
Korbach D 32 Lj39
Korbol TCH 140 Lj41
Korbous TN 126 Lf27
Korçe AL 46 Ma50
Korčevka RUS 48 Nd18
Korčula HR 35 Lr48
Korčula HR 35 Ls48
Kordai KZ 66 Oh24
Kordkuy IR 62 Nh27
Korea 10 Ra06
Korea Bay 73 Rb26
Korean Folk Village ROK 78 Rd27
Korea Strait 79 Re29
Korec' UA 49 Md20
Koregaon IND (MHT) 82 Oh37
Korem ETH 142 Mk39
Koré Maïroua RN 132 Lb39
Korenevo RUS 48 Mh20
Korenica HR 35 Lq46
Korenovsk RUS 49 Mk23
Koréra-Koré RMM 130 Kf38
Korf RUS 55 Tb06
Korfantów PL 40 Ls40
Korff Ice Rise 6 Gb34
Korgas KZ 66 Pa23
Korgen N 16 Lg12
Korgom RN 132 Le39
Korhogo CI 137 Kh41
Koria FIN 38 Mg30
Koribundu WAL 136 Ke42
Korientzé RMM 131 Kj38
Korifási GR 46 Mb53
Korim RI 114 Rj46
Korinós GR 46 Mc50
Kórinthos GR 46 Mc53
Korioume RMM 131 Kj37
Koripobi PNG 117 Sh49
Korita BIH 44 Lt47
Korita SCG 44 Lu48
Koriyama J 77 Sa27
Korjakskaja Sopka, vulkan RUS 55 Sd08
Korjukivka UA 48 Mg20
Korkuteli TR 56 Mf27
Korla CHN (XUZ) 67 Pd25
Körmen TR 47 Mh54
Körmend H 42 Lr43
Kornaka RN 132 Ld38
Kornat HR 35 Lq47
Kornati, N.P. HR 35 Lq47
Korneuburg A 42 Lr42
Kórnik PL 40 Ls38
Kornofolia GR 45 Mg49
Kornwestheim D 33 Lk42
Koro CI 137 Kg41
Koro FJI 119 Tk54
Koro RMM 131 Kj38
Koroba PNG 115 Sb48
Korobo GH 137 Kk42
Koroča RUS 48 Mj20
Korodiga EAT 147 Mj48
Korodziba ZW 152 Md55
Köroğlu Dağları TR 56 Mf25
Köroğlu Tepe TR 56 Mf25
Korogwe EAT 147 Mk48
Korohane RN 132 Ld38
Korohouita CI 137 Kh41
Korolevu FJI 119 Tj55
Koroli Desert EAK 144 Mj44
Koromačno HR 35 Lp46
Koronadal RP 91 Rc42
Korondougou CI 137 Kg41
Koronga RMM 131 Kg38
Koróni GR 46 Mb54
Koronowo PL 40 Ls37
Korop UA 48 Mg20
Koror PAL 90 Rh42
Korort-Darasun RUS 71 Qg20
Koro Sea FJI 119 Tk54
Körösladány H 43 Mb44
Körös-Maros N.P. H 43 Ma43
Korosten' UA 48 Me20
Korostyšiv UA 49 Me20
Koroth IND (KER) 84 Oh40
Koro Toro TCH 133 Lk37
Koroviha RUS 48 Nc17
Korovin Island USA 164 Bk18
Korovniki RUS 48 Mk17
Korovou FJI 119 Tk54
Korovou SOL 117 Sh49
Koroyanitu N.P. FJI 119 Tj54
Korpilahti FIN 38 Mf28
Korpiselka RUS (KAR) 38 Mm28
Korpo = Korppoo FIN 38 Mb30
Korppoo FIN 38 Mb30
Korppoo = Korpo FIN 38 Mb30
Korreh IR 64 Ng30
Korsakow RUS 77 Sb22
Korsberga S 31 Lq33
Korsimoro BF 137 Kk39
Korsnäs FIN 38 Mb28
Korsør DK 30 Lm35
Korsun'-Ševčenkivs'kyj UA 49 Mf21
Korsze PL 41 Mb36
Kortala SUD 135 Mf39
Korten BG 45 Mf48
Kortesjärvi FIN 38 Md27
Kórthio GR 47 Me53
Kortrijk B 23 Ld40
Korucu TR 47 Mh51
Korup, P.N. de CAM 138 Le43
Koruyeh IR 59 Nf30
Koryak Autonomous District RUS 55 Tb06
Koryak Range RUS 55 Tb06
Koryčany CZ 42 Ls41
Korycin PL 41 Md37
Korzybie PL 40 Lr36
Kós GR 47 Mh54
Kós GR 47 Mh54
Kosa ETH 142 Mj42
Koš-Agač RUS (ALT) 67 Pe21
Kosaja Gora RUS 48 Mj18
Ko Samet N.P. THA 89 Qa39
Kosanica SCG 44 Lu47
Košarovce SK 43 Mb41
Kosava BY 41 Mf38
Kościan PL 40 Lr38
Kościelec PL 40 Lt38
Kościerzyna PL 40 Ls36
Kościół Mariacki PL 40 Lr36
Kościół Sytersów PL 40 Lr40
Kosciusko USA (MS) 175 Ff29
Kosciuszko, Mount AUS 111 Se64
Kosciuszko N.P. AUS (NSW) 111 Se63
Koš-Dëbë KS 66 Oh25
Kose EST 38 Mf31
Köse TR 57 Mk25
Köse Dağları TR 56 Mj25
Kosgi IND (APH) 82 Oj37
Kosha SUD 135 Mf35
Koshi RDC 149 Lk48
Koshikijima-retto J 79 Re30
Koshk AFG 64 Ob28
Koshk-e Kohneh AFG 64 Ob28
Koshoba TM 62 Nh25
Ko Si THA 88 Pk42
Kosi Bay Nature Reserve ZA 155 Mg59
Košice SK 43 Mb42
Košická Belá SK 43 Mb42
Kosihovce SK 43 Lu42
Ko Similan THA 88 Pj41
Ko Similan N.P. THA 88 Pj41
Kosjerić SCG 44 Lu46
Koška HR 35 Lt45
Koskenpää FIN 38 Mf28
Koski FIN 38 Md30
Koskolovo RUS 38 Mj31
Koskue FIN 38 Mc28
Kosmás GR 46 Mc53
Koson UZ 63 Oc26
Kosong PRK 78 Re26
Kosonsoy UZ 63 Of25
Kosovska Mitrovica SCG 44 Ma48
Kosów Lacki PL 41 Mc38
Kosrae FSM 10 Ta09
Kosrayi IR 57 Nc28
Kosse USA (TX) 174 Fb30
Kosso CI 137 Kh43
Kossol Reef PAL 90 Rh42
Kossuth-Múzeum H 43 Lu43
Kosta S 31 Lq34
Kostanaj KZ 54 Oa08
Kostanjevica SLO 42 Lo45
Kostanjevica na Krki SLO 42 Lq45
Kostelec nad Černými Lesy CZ 42 Lp41
Kostelec na Hané CZ 42 Ls41
Kostenec BG 45 Md48
Koster ZA 155 Md58
Kosteröarna S 30 Lm32
Kostinbrod BG 44 Md48
Kostjantynivka UA 49 Mj21
Kostomłoty PL 40 Lr39
Kostomukša RUS (KAR) 16 Mf13
Kostopil' UA 41 Mg40
Kostroma RUS 48 Na17
Kostryna UA 43 Mc42
Kostrzyn PL 40 Lp38
Kosubosu WAN 138 Lb41
Kosubuke RDC 149 Mb48
Ko Sukong THA 88 Pk42
Ko Surin Nua THA 88 Pj41
Ko Surin Tai THA 88 Pj41
Koszalin PL 40 Lr36
Kőszeg H 42 Lr43
Koszuty PL 40 Ls38
Kota IND (CGH) 83 Pb34
Kota IND (RJT) 82 Oh33
Kota Agung RI 93 Qc48
Kotabangun RI 95 Qj46
Kotabaru RI 93 Qa46
Kotabaru RI 93 Qa46
Kotabaru RI 95 Qj47
Kotabatu RI 93 Qb48
Kota Belud MAL 94 Qj42
Kota Bharu MAL 92 Qb42
Kotabumi RI 93 Qc48
Kot Addu PK 65 Of30
Kotagad IND (ORS) 83 Pb36
Kotagaroterminal RI 93 Qa45
Kotakapur RI 93 Qc47
Kota Kinabalu MAL 94 Qj43
Kota Lenggong MAL 92 Qa43
Kotamobagu RI 91 Rc45
Kota Nopan RI 93 Pk45
Kotanopan RI 93 Pk45
Kotapinang RI 93 Qa45
Kotaringin RI 93 Qb45
Ko Tarutao THA 88 Pk42
Kota Tinggi MAL 93 Qb45
Kota Tinggi Waterfalls MAL 93 Qb45
Kot Diji PK 65 Oe32
Kotdwara IND (UTT) 81 Ok31
Kotel BG 45 Mg48
Kotel'skij RUS 38 Mj31
Kotel'va UA 48 Mh20
Koteshwar IND (GUJ) 82 Oe34
Kotgajah RI 93 Qc48
Kotgal IND (MHT) 83 Pa35
Kothakota IND (APH) 82 Oj37
Kothapet IND (APH) 83 Ok36
Kothari IND (MHT) 83 Ok36
Köthen D 32 Lm39
Kothili IND (UPH) 83 Pb32
Kotiari Naoudé SN 136 Kd39
Kotido EAU 144 Mh44
Kotikawatta CL 85 Ok42
Kotira PK 65 Od32
Kotka FIN 38 Mg30
Kot Kapura IND (PJB) 80 Oh30
Kotlas RUS 54 Nb06
Kotlenski Prohod BG 45 Mg48
Kotli 65 Og29
Kotlik USA (AK) 164 Bj14
Kotly RUS 38 Mj31
Kot Mumin PK 65 Og29
Kotobi CI 137 Kh42
Kotongoro II TCH 140 Lk41
Koton-Karifi WAN 138 Ld41
Koton-Koro WAN 138 Lc40
Kotor SCG 44 Lt48
Kotoriba HR 35 Lr44
Kotor Katedrala SCG 44 Lt48
Kotorsko BIH 44 Lt46
Kotor Varoš BIH 35 Ls46
Kótosh PE 197 Gb50
Kotouba CI 137 Kj41
Kotoula CI 137 Kg40
Kotovsk RUS 48 Na19
Kotovs'k UA 49 Me22
Kot Putli IND (RJT) 80 Oj32
Kotri PK 65 Oe33
Kótronas GR 46 Mc54
Kötschach A 35 Lo44
Kottagudem IND (APH) 83 Pa37
Kottai Malai IND 84 Oj41
Kottampatti IND (TNU) 84 Ok40
Kottappatti IND (TNU) 85 Ok40
Kottarakara IND (KER) 84 Oj41
Kottayam IND (KER) 84 Oj41
Kotto RCA 140 Ma43
Kottur IND (KTK) 84 Oj38
Kotuj RUS 55 Qa05
Koturdepe TM 62 Ng26
Kotwa ZW 152 Mg54
Kotzebue USA (AK) 165 Bj12
Kotzebue Sound USA 165 Bj12
Kötzting D 33 Ln41
Kouadio-Prikro CI 137 Kh42
Kouakourou RMM 131 Kh38
Kouandé DY 137 La40
Kouango RCA 140 Ma43
Kouankan RG 136 Kf41
Kouassikro CI 137 Kj42
Kouba Olanga TCH 133 Lk38
Koubia RG 136 Ke40
Koubo Abou Azraq TCH 134 Ma40
Kouchibouguac CDN (NB) 176 Gh22
Kouchibouguac N. P. CDN 176 Gh22
Koudougou BF 137 Kj39
Kouéré BF 137 Kh40
Koufália GR 46 Mc50
Koufey RN 133 Lg38
Koufonísi GR 47 Mg56
Kougaberge ZA 154 Mb62
Kougnohou TG 137 La42
Kougouleu G 148 Le45
Kouhezi CHN (NMZ) 76 Ra24
Kouibli CI 137 Kg42
Kouka BF 137 Kh40
Kouki RCA 140 Lj42
Koukia = Bentia RMM 131 La38
Koukou TCH 134 Mb40
Koukourou RCA 140 Ma42
Koula RMM 137 Kg39
Koula RMM 137 Kh39
Koulbo TCH 134 Ma39
Koulbous SUD 134 Mb38
Koulé RG 136 Kf41
Koulé Ekou DY 138 Lb41
Koulikoro RMM 137 Kg39
Koulou RN 138 Lb39
Koulouan CI 136 Kg42
Koum CAM 139 Lh41
Kouma RCA 140 Lk42
Koumac F 118 Tc56
Koumaïra RMM 131 Kj38
Koumala AUS (QLD) 109 Se56
Koumameyong G 148 Lf45
Koumantou RMM 137 Kg40
Koumbal RCA 140 Mb41
Koumbala CI 137 Kh41
Koumbala RCA 140 Ma41
Koumbia BF 137 Kj40
Koumbia RG 136 Kd40
Koumbili BF 137 Kk40
Koumbi Saleh RIM 131 Kf38
Koumbri BF 137 Kj39
Koumia RMM 137 Kh39
Koumogo TCH 140 Lk41
Koumpentoum SN 130 Kc38
Koumra TCH 140 Lj41
Kounahiri CI 137 Kh42
Kounávi GR 47 Mf55
Koundara RG 136 Kd39
Koundé RCA 140 Lh42
Koundessong CAM 139 Lg44
Koundian RG 136 Kf40
Koundian RMM 136 Ke39
Koundijourou TCH 133 Lk39
Koundougou BF 137 Kh40
Koúndouros GR 47 Me53
Koun-Fao CI 137 Kj42
Koungheul SN 136 Kc39
Koungi BF 137 Kj39
Koungouri TCH 139 Lk40
Kouniana RMM 137 Kh39
Kounkane SN 136 Kc39
Kounoupítsa GR 45 Md53
Kounsitel RG 136 Kd40
Kountze USA (TX) 174 Fc30
Kouoro RMM 137 Kh39
Koup ZA 154 Ma62
Koupéla BF 137 Kk39
Kouragué RMM 136 Ke39
Kouré RN 132 Lb39
Kourémalé RMM 136 Kf40
Kourgou TCH 139 Lj40
Kouri BF 137 Kj39
Kouri RMM 137 Kh39
Kouri Kouri TCH 133 Lj39
Kourion CY 56 Mg28
Kourkéto RMM 130 Ke38
Kourou F 194 Hd43
Kourouba CI 136 Kg41
Kourouba RMM 136 Kf39
Koûroudjél RIM 130 Ke37
Kouroukoto RMM 136 Ke39
Kourouma BF 137 Kh40
Kourouninkoto RMM 136 Kf39
Kouroussa RG 136 Kf40
Kousrosh Palace IR 59 Nf31
Koussa Arma RN 133 Lg37
Koussanar SN 136 Kc39
Koussané RMM 130 Ke38
Koussane SN 130 Kd38
Kousseri CAM 139 Lh39
Koussountou TG 137 La41
Koutaba CAM 138 Lf43
Koutalás GR 47 Me53
Koutammakou TG 137 La40
Koutia Gaïdi SN 130 Kc38
Koutiala RMM 137 Kh39
Kouto CI 137 Kg41
Koutougou TG 137 La40
Kouvola FIN 38 Mg30
Kovačevci BG 44 Md48
Kovačica SCG 44 Ma45
Kovada Gölü Milli Parkı TR 56 Mf27
Kovalam IND (KER) 84 Oj41
Kovalam Beach IND 84 Oj41
Kovancılar TR 57 Mk26
Kov-Ata TM 62 Nj26
Kovdor RUS 16 Mf12
Kovel' UA 41 Me39
Kovernino RUS 48 Nb17
Kovero FIN 38 Ml28
Kovilpatti IND (TNU) 84 Oj41
Kovrov RUS 48 Na17
Kovvur IND (APH) 83 Pa37
Kovylkino RUS (MOR) 48 Nb18
Kowal PL 41 Lu38
Kowale Oleckie PL 41 Mc36
Kowangge RI 96 Qk50
Kowanyama AUS (QLD) 107 Sa53
Kowares NAM 150 Lh55
Kowary PL 40 Lq40
Kowloon CHN (HKG) 75 Qh34
Kowon PRK 76 Rd26
Kowt-e Ashrow AFG 65 Oe28
Koxlax CHN (XUZ) 66 Pa26
Koya WAN 132 Ld39
Koyama RG 136 Kf42
Ko Yao Yai THA 88 Pk42
Koyasan sacred site (Koya) J 79 Rh28
Köyceğiz TR 47 Mj54
Koygolo RN 132 Lb39
Koyuk USA (AK) 165 Bk13
Koyukuk USA (AK) 165 Cb13
Koyukuk National Wildlife Refuge USA 165 Cb13
Koyulhisar TR 56 Mj25
Koyyuru IND (APH) 83 Pb37
Koza CAM 139 Lg40
Kozak TR 47 Mh51
Kozaklı TR 56 Mh26
Kozan TR 56 Mh27
Kozáni GR 46 Mb50
Kozara BIH 35 Lr45
Kozara, N.P. BIH 35 Lr46
Kozel'sk RUS 48 Mh19
Kozha Akhmed Yasaui Mausoleum KZ 63 Oe24
Kozhikode IND (KER) 84 Oh40
Koziegłowy PL 41 Lu40
Kozienice PL 41 Mb39
Koziki BY 41 Mf38
Kozjak German MK 44 Mc48
Kozjatyn UA 49 Me21
Kozloduj BG 44 Md47
Kozłów PL 41 Lu40
Kozlu TR 56 Mf25
Kozluk TR 57 Na26
Kozlupınar TR 57 Mk26
Koźmin PL 40 Ls39
Koźminek PL 40 Lt39
Koźminiec PL 40 Ls39
Koz'modem'jansk RUS (MEL) 48 Nd17
Kożuchów PL 40 Lq39
Kozu-jima J 79 Rk28
Kozyn UA 41 Mf40
Kpagto GH 137 Kk41
Kpalbusi GH 137 Kk41
Kpalimé TG 137 La42
Kpando GH 137 La42
Kparigu GH 137 Kk40
Kpaso GH 137 La41
Kpassagon DY 138 Lb42
Kpatawe Falls LB 136 Kf42
Kpatinga GH 137 Kk41
Kpèssi TG 137 La41
Kpetoe GH 137 La42
Kpetuo LB 136 Kf42
Kpeve GH 137 La42
Kraankuil ZA 155 Mc60
Krabi THA 88 Pk41
Kra Buri THA 88 Pk40
Krafla IS 18 Kd25
Kraftstation S 16 Lk12
Kragenæs DK 30 Lm36
Kragerø N 30 Lk32
Kragujevac SCG 44 Ma46
Krajište SCG 44 Mc48
Krajnovka RUS (DAG) 57 Nd24
Krakatau Island = Rakata RI 93 Qc49
Krakatau Volcano RI 93 Qc49
Kraké DY 138 Lb42
Kräklingbo S 31 Lt33
Krakorum GH 137 Kj42
Krakovec' UA 43 Md41
Kraków PL 41 Lu40
Krakow am See D 32 Ln37
Kralendijk NL 193 Gf39
Králický Sněžník PL 40 Lr40
Kraljevica HR 35 Lp45
Kraljevo SCG 44 Ma47
Kralovice CZ 42 Lo41
Král'ovský Chlmec SK 43 Mb42
Kralupy nad Vltavou CZ 42 Lp40
Kramators'k UA 49 Mj21
Kramfors S 16 Lj14
Kramjanica BY 41 Me37
Kranídi GR 45 Md53
Kranj SLO 42 Lp44
Kranji SGP 93 Qb45
Kranjska Gora SLO 42 Lo44
Kranovodskoye plato TM 62 Ng25
Kransfontein ZA 155 Me60
Kranskop ZA 155 Mf60
Kranuan THA 89 Qb37
Kraolândia BR (TO) 200 Hg50
Kraolândia, T.I. BR 200 Hg50
Krapina HR 35 Lq44
Krapinske Toplice HR 35 Lq44
Krapkowice PL 40 Ls40
Krasaesin THA 88 Qa42
Kraskino RUS 76 Rf24
Krāslava LV 39 Mh35
Kraslice CZ 42 Ln40
Krasnae BY 39 Mh36
Krásna Hôrka SK 43 Ma42
Krasnaja Gora RUS 48 Mf19
Krasnaja Gorbatka RUS 48 Na18
Krasnaja Jaruga RUS 48 Mh20
Krásna nad Hornádom SK 43 Mb42
Kraśnik PL 41 Mc40
Krasnoarmejsk RUS 48 Mk17
Krasnoarmijs'k UA 49 Mj21
Krasnobród PL 41 Md40
Krasnodar RUS 49 Mk23
Krasnodarskoe Vodohranilišče RUS 49 Mk23
Krasnodon UA 49 Mk21
Krasnoe RUS 39 Mb36
Krasnoe RUS 48 Mk19
Krasnogorodskoe RUS 39 Mj34
Krasnohorivka UA 49 Mj21
Krásnohorské Podhradie SK 43 Ma42
Krasnohrad UA 49 Mh21
Krasnohvardijs'ke UA 49 Mh23
Krasnojarovo RUS 71 Re20
Krasnojarsk RUS 54 Pc07
Krasnojil's'k UA 43 Mf42
Krasnokamensk RUS 71 Qk20
Krasnokuts'k UA 48 Mh20
Krasnomajskij RUS 48 Mh17
Krasnopavlivka UA 49 Mj21
Krasnoperekops'k UA 49 Mg23
Krasnopillja UA 48 Mh20
Krasnosel'e RUS 39 Mc36
Krasnosielc PL 41 Mb37
Krasnoslobodsk RUS (MOR) 48 Nb18
Krasnotorovka RUS 39 Lu36
Krasnovolja UA 41 Mf39
Krasnoye Znamya TM 62 Ob27
Krasnoznamensk RUS 39 Mc36
Krasnye Baki RUS 48 Nc17
Krasnyj Holm RUS 48 Mj16
Krasnyj Luč UA 49 Mk21
Krasnyj Manyč RUS 49 Na22
Krasnystaw PL 41 Md40
Krastë AL 44 Ma49
Krasti LV 39 Me34
Krasyliv UA 49 Md21
Krathing Falls THA 89 Qb39
Kratie K 89 Qd39
Kratke Range PNG 115 Sc49
Kratovo MK 44 Mc48
Krau RI 115 Sa47
Kražiai LT 39 Mc35
Krėva BY 39 Mg36
Kreb Bekati el Bâss RMM 132 La35
Krefeld D 32 Lg39
Kregbé CI 137 Kj42
Krek K 89 Qc40
Krekenava LT 39 Me35
Kremenčuc'ke vodoschovyšče UA 49 Mg21
Kremenčuk UA 49 Mg21
Kremenec' UA 41 Mf40
Kremikovci BG 44 Md48
Kreml RUS 48 Mj18
Kremlin USA (MT) 169 Ee21

Lansdale ◻ USA (PA) 177 Gc25
Lansdowne ◻ USA (WA) 103 Rd54
Lansdowne ◻ IND (UTT) 81 Ok31
Lansdowne House ◻ CDN (ON) 172 Fg19
L'Anse ◻ USA (MI) 173 Ff22
L'Anse aux Meadows N.H.P. ◻ CDN 177 Hc20
Länsi-Aure ◻ FIN 38 Md29
Lansing ◻ USA (IA) 172 Fe24
Lansing ◻ USA (MI) 173 Fh24
Länskroun ◻ CZ 42 Lm31
Lanslebourg-Mont-Cenis ◻ F 25 Lg45
Lantau ◻ CHN 75 Qh34
Lantewa ◻ WAN 139 Lf39
Lantian ◻ CHN 72 Qh34
Lantuy Nai ◻ LAO 87 Qa34
Lants Corners ◻ USA (PA) 173 Ga25
Lanu ◻ RI 91 Ra45
Lanusei ◻ I 36 Lk51
Lanxi ◻ CHN (HLG) 76 Rd22
Lanxi ◻ CHN (ZJG) 75 Qh31
Lan Xian ◻ CHN (SAX) 72 Qf26
Lanya ◻ CZ 42 Lm40
Lany ◻ PL 40 Lt40
Lanyu ◻ RC 75 Ra34
Lanyu ◻ RC 75 Ra34
Lanza ◻ BOL 198 Gg51
Lanzai ◻ WAN 139 Lf39
Länzhöu ◻ CHN (GSU) 72 Qb27
Lanzo Torinese ◻ I 34 Lh45
Laoag ◻ RP 90 Ra36
Laoang ◻ RP 90 Rc39
Laobie Shan ◻ CHN 87 Pk34
Lao ◻ CHN 87 Qb34
La Ofelia ◻ RA (NE) 208 Gd65
Laokas ◻ TCH 140 Lt44
La Ola ◻ RCH 207 Gf59
Laon ◻ F 23 Ld41
Lao Ngam ◻ LAO 89 Qd38
Laonmais ◻ F 23 Ld41
Laora ◻ RI 96 Ra44
Laora ◻ RI 96 Rb48
La Ordeña ◻ MEX (ZCT) 182 Ej34
La Oroya ◻ PE 197 Gc51
Laos ◻ LAO 53 Qa08
Laoshan ◻ CHN 73 Ra27
Laoshunku ◻ CHN (YUN) 87 Pk33
Laotieshan Shedao Z.B. ✿ CHN 73 Ra26
Lapa ◻ BR 205 Hf58
La Paca ◻ E 29 Kt53
La Pacaudière ◻ F 25 Ld44
Lapac Island ◻ RP 91 Ra43
Lapai ◻ WAN 138 Ld41
Lapala ◻ MOC 153 Mk53
Lapalisse ◻ F 25 Ld44
La Palma ◻ C 179 Fj34
La Palma ◻ CO 192 Go43
La Palma ◻ PA 185 Ga41
La Palma del Condado ◻ E 27 Ko53
La Palmarita ◻ C 179 Ga35
La Palmita ◻ CO 192 Ge43
La Paloma ◻ PY 204 Hc58
La Paloma ◻ ROU 209 Hc63
La Pampa ◻ RA 208 Gg64
La Para ◻ RA (CD) 209 Gg61
Laparan Island ◻ RP 91 Ra43
La Pargua ◻ YV 193 Gj42
Lapatapia ◻ RA (TF) 210 Gf73
Lapeek ◻ PNG 116 Sf48
la Paya, P.N. ⚘ CO 196 Gc45
La Paz ◻ BOL 206 Gf54
La Paz ◻ HN 184 Fg38
La Paz ◻ MEX (BCS) 180 Ee33
La Paz ◻ RA (MD) 208 Gg63
La Paz ◻ ROU 209 Hb63
La Paz ◻ RA (SE) 207 Ga58
La Paz ◻ YV 192 Gd40
Lapchaura ◻ IND (MPH) 82 Oj33
La Pedrera ◻ CO 198 Gf46
La Pedrera ◻ RA (SF) 207 Gf58
Lapeer ◻ USA (MI) 173 Fj24
Lapela ◻ BR (MA) 200 Hd47
La Peña ◻ MEX (DGO) 181 Eh34
La Perla ◻ RCH 207 Ge59
La Perla ◻ MEX (CHH) 181 Eh31
Perouse Strait ⊟ J/RUS 77 Sa23
La Pesca ◻ MEX (TM) 182 Fb34
La Piedad de Cabadas ◻ MEX (MHC) 182 Ej34
La Pine ◻ USA (OR) 168 Dd24
Lapin Island ◻ RP 90 Rc40
La Pintada ◻ PA 185 Fk41
La Pintada (Rock paintings) ☆ ☐ MEX 182 Ed32
Laplace ◻ USA (LA) 175 Fe30
La Plagne ◻ F 25 Lg45
La Plaine ◻ WD 187 Gk38
Lapland ◻ S/FIN 16 Lj12
La Plant ◻ USA (SD) 172 Ek23
La Plata ◻ CO 192 Gc44
La Plata ◻ RA (BA) 209 Hb63
La Plata ◻ USA (MO) 174 Fd26
La Pobla de Segur ◻ E 28 La48
La Pocatière ◻ CDN (QC) 176 Gf22
La Pola de Gordón ◻ E 26 Kp48
Laponia ◻ S 16 Lj12
La Port ◻ USA (IN) 173 Fg25
La Portada ◻ RCH 207 Ge57
Laporte ◻ USA (PA) 177 Gb25
La Portera ◻ E 29 Kt51
Lapoş ◻ RO 45 Mg44
La Posta ◻ SCG 44 Mb46
Lapovo ◻ SCG 44 Mb46
La Poyata ◻ CO 192 Gc43
Lappajärvi ◻ FIN 38 Md27
Lappajärvi ◻ FIN 38 Md27
Läppe ◻ S 31 Lg31
Lappeenranta ◻ FIN 38 Mj29
Lappersdorf ◻ D 33 Ln41
Lappfjärd = Lapväärtti ◻ FIN 38 Mb28
Lappi Tä FIN 38 Mb29
Lappohja = Lappvik ◻ FIN 38 Md31
Lappuobball ◻ N 16 Mb11
Lapptrask = Lappohja ◻ FIN 38 Md31
Lappvik = Lappohja ◻ FIN 38 Md31
Laprida ◻ RA (BA) 209 Gk64
La Pryor ◻ USA (TX) 181 Fa31
Läpseki ◻ TR 45 Mg49
Lapteyo ◻ RUS 39 Mj34
Lapua ◻ FIN 38 Md28
La Puebla de Cazalla ◻ E 27 Kp53
La Puebla del Río ◻ E 27 Ko53
La Puebla de Montalbán ◻ E 29 Kq50
La Puebla de Valverde ◻ E 29 Kt50
La Puerta ◻ MEX (BC) 180 Ed28
La Puerta ◻ RA (CD) 209 Gj61
La Punta ◻ MEX (DGO) 181 Eh31
La Punta ◻ YV 192 Ge41
La Punilla ◻ RCH 208 Ge64
La Punta ◻ C 179 Ga33
La Punta ◻ MEX (BCS) 180 Ee32
La Punta ◻ RA (SE) 207 Gh60
La Purisima ◻ MEX (BCS) 180 Ed32

Las Conchas ◻ BOL 206 Ha54
Las Conchas ◻ MEX (CHH) 181 Eh31
Las Cortaderas ◻ RA (NE) 208 Ge65
Las Cruces ◻ MEX (DGO) 181 Eh34
Las Cruces ◻ MEX (TM) 182 Fb34
Las Cruces ◻ MEX (SJ) 171 Eg29
Las Cuatas ◻ MEX (CHH) 180 Ed34
Las Dawaco ◻ SP 143 Ne40
Las Delicias ◻ CO 192 Gd43
Las Delicias ◻ RA (SA) 207 Gh59
La SelvaLacandona ◻ MEX 183 Fe37
Lasem ◻ RI 95 Qf49
La Sénia ◻ E 29 La50
La Serena ◻ E 27 Kp52
La Serena ◻ RCH 207 Ge60
Las Estrellas ◻ RA (NE) 208 Gd65
La Seu de Palma de Mallorca ◻ ◻ ◻ E 28 Lb48
La Seu d'Urgell ◻ ◻ ◻ E 28 La48
La Seyne-sur-Mer ◻ F 25 Lf47
Las Flores ◻ MEX (TM) 182 Fb34
Las Flores ◻ RA (BA) 209 Ha64
Las Flores ◻ RA (SJ) 207 Gf61
Las Galeras ◻ DOM 186 Gf37
Las Gamas ◻ RA (SF) 207 Gb60
Las Gavias ◻ MEX (SL) 180 Eh34
La Raya ◻ PE 197 Gd52
Lärba ◻ DZ 126 Lb27
Las Glorias ◻ MEX (SL) 180 Ef33
Las Guacamayas ◻ MEX (MHC) 182 Ej36
Las Hacheras ◻ RA (CH) 207 Gk58
Lärbro ◻ S 31 Lt33
Larderello ◻ I 34 Ln47
Larder Lake ◻ CDN (ON) 173 Ga21
las Hermosas, P.N. ⚘ CO 192 Gc44
Lashio ◻ MYA 86 Pj34
Lashkar Gah ◻ AFG 65 Oc30
Lashkari Bazar ☆ AFG 65 Oc30
Lash ◻ PK 63 Og27
Las Huertas ◻ MEX (ZCT) 180 Ee31
Lasia ◻ RI 93 Pj44
Las Iglesias Beach ◻ RI 97 Rb51
Las Iglesias de Chiloé ◻ ◻ RCH 208 Gd67
L'Asile ◻ RH 186 Gd36
La Silla Observatory ⚘ RCH 207 Ge60
Lasimaseop ✿ FIN 38 Me30
Lask ◻ PL 41 Lu37
Laskarzew ◻ PL 41 Mb39
Laskowice ◻ PL 40 Lt37
La Lajas ◻ RA (NE) 208 Ge65
La Lajitas ◻ RA (SJ) 180 Ef32
La Lajitas ◻ RA (SA) 207 Gh58
Las Leñas ◻ RA (MD) 208 Ge63
Las Lisas ◻ GCA 184 Fe39
Las Lomas ◻ PE 196 Fk48
Las Lomitas ◻ RA (FO) 207 Gk58
Las Margaritas ◻ MEX (DGO) 181 Eh34
Las Marismas ◻ E 27 Ko53
Las Martinas ◻ C 179 Fh35
Las Médulas ◻ E 26 Ko48
Las Mercedes ◻ YV 193 Gg41
Las Minas ◻ PA 185 Fk42
Las Navas ◻ RP 90 Rc39
Las Navas de la Concepción ◻ E 27 Kp53
Las Negras ◻ E 29 Kt54
Las Nieves ◻ E 27 Ko51
Las Norias ◻ MEX (TM) 181 Fa33
Las Nubes ◻ RA (BA) 209 Ha65
La Solana ◻ E 27 Kr52
La Soledad ◻ MEX (DGO) 180 Eg33
La Soledad ◻ MEX (NL) 181 Ek33
Las Flats ◻ RP 35 Fk42
Las Orquideas, P.N. ⚘ CO 192 Gc42
La Sortija ◻ RA (BA) 209 Gk65
Las Piedras ◻ PE 198 Gd50
Las Piedras ◻ ROU 209 Hb63
Las Plumas ◻ RA (CT) 210 Gf68
Las Pulgas ◻ PA 185 Ga41
Las Ramadas ◻ RCH 208 Ge61
Las Rosas ◻ RA (SF) 209 Ha62
Lassance ◻ BR (MG) 203 Hh54
l'Assekrem ◻ DZ 132 Lc34
Lassen Volcanic N.P. ⚘ USA (CA) 170 Dk26
Las Tablas ◻ PA 185 Fk42
Las Tablas ◻ MEX (SLP) 182 Fa34
Las Tinajas ◻ RA (SJ) 207 Gf61
Las Torolas, Cerro ▲ RA/RCH 207 Gf60
Las Toscas ◻ RA (BA) 209 Gk65
Las Toscas ◻ RCH (SA) 204 Ha60
Las Toscas ◻ ROU 204 Hc62
Las Tres ◻ RA (SF) 207 Gb60
Las Tunas ◻ C 179 Gb35
Las Tunitas ◻ MEX (BCS) 180 Ee33
La Suze-sur-Sarthe ◻ F 23 La43
Las Varas ◻ MEX (CHH) 180 Ef31
Las Varillas ◻ RA (CD) 209 Gj61
Las Vegas ◻ RA (NM) 171 Eh28
Las Vegas ◻ USA (NV) 182 Fa34
Las Vegas (La Tasajera) ◻ MEX (DGO) 181 Eh34
Las Ventas con Peña Aguilera ◻ E 27 Kp51
Las Vilos ◻ RCH 208 Gd61
Las Vírgenes, Volcán ▲ MEX 180 Ed32
La Tabatière ◻ CDN (QC) 176 Ha20
Lascelles ◻ AUS (VIC) 110 Sb63
Las Chapas (BC) 210 Gdp67
Lady Island ◻ C 179 Fh35
Latakia = Al Lādhiqīyah ◻ SYR 56 Mh28
Latakia ◻ RI 97 Rd46
La Scie ◻ CDN (NF) 177 Hd20
La Scieri ◻ SCG 14 Ld45
Las Claritas ◻ YV 193 Gh42
Las Coloradas ◻ MEX (COH) 181 Ek32

Latchford ◻ CDN (ON) 173 Ga22
Låtefossen ◻ N 30 Lg31
Latehar ◻ IND (JKD) 83 Pc34
Laterza ◻ I 37 Lr50
Latgale ▲ LV 39 Mg34
Latham ◻ AUS (WA) 104 Qj60
La Tigra, P.N. ⚘ HN 184 Fg38
La Ticla ◻ MEX 182 Ej36
La Tigra, P.N. ⚘ HN 184 Fg38
La Tinaja ◻ PE 196 Ga44
La Tinaja ◻ MEX (VC) 182 Fb36
La Tinaja de Bartolo ◻ MEX (DGO) 181 Eh33
La Trampa ◻ RP 90 Rc39
La Tranca ◻ RA (SL) 208 Gg62
La Tranche-sur-Mer ◻ F 24 Kt44
La Tremblade ◻ F 24 Kt45
La Trimouille ◻ F 24 Lb44
La Trinidad ◻ YV 193 Gf41
La Trinidad de Orichuna ◻ YV 193 Gf42
La Trinitaria ◻ MEX (CHP) 183 Fd37
La Trinité ◻ F 187 Gk38
La Trinité-Porhoët ◻ F 22 Ks42
Latrobe ◻ USA (PA) 173 Ga26
La Troncal ◻ EC 196 Ga47
Latrónico ◻ I 37 Lq50
Latundo-Lompo ◻ RI 96 Ra49
La Tunia ◻ CO 192 Gd45
La Tuque ◻ CDN (QC) 176 Gd22
Latur ◻ IND (MHT) 82 Oj36
Latvia ◻ LV 39 Mc34
Lat Yao ◻ THA 88 Pk38
Latyr ◻ PNG 116 Sf48
La WAN 139 Lf41
Lauca, P.N. ⚘ RCH 206 Gf55
Lauchhammer ◻ D 32 Lo39
Lauda-Königshofen ◻ D 33 Lk41
Lauda, Gunung ▲ RI 96 Ra48
Lauderdale ◻ AUS (TAS) 111 Sd67
Laudio-Llodio ◻ E 28 Ks47
Laudona ◻ LV 39 Mg34
Lauenburg ◻ D 32 Ll37
Lauf ◻ D 33 Lm43
Lauffen (Neckar) ◻ D 33 Lk41
Laugar ◻ IS 18 Kc25
Laugarbakki ◻ IS 18 Ju25
Laugarvatn ◻ IS 18 Ju26
Lauhanvuoren kansallispuisto ✿ FIN 38 Mc28
Laujar de Andarax ◻ E 27 Ks54
Lauka ◻ EST 38 Md31
Laukuva ◻ LT 39 Mc35
Laun ◻ THA 88 Pk40
Launceston ◻ AUS (TAS) 111 Sd66
Launglon ◻ MYA 88 Pk38
La Unión ◻ CO 192 Gb44
La Unión ◻ EC 196 Fk46
La Unión ◻ HN 184 Fg38
La Unión ◻ MEX (DGO) 181 Ej33
La Unión ◻ MEX (GUR) 182 Ej37
La Unión ◻ MEX (QTR) 183 Ff37
La Unión ◻ MEX (SLP) 182 Fa34
La Unión ◻ RA (SA) 207 Gh58
La Unión ◻ RCH 208 Gd66
La Unión ◻ YV 193 Gg41
Launionken Islands ◻ MYA 88 Pj39
Lupheim ◻ D 33 Lk42
Laura ◻ AUS (QLD) 107 Sc55
Laura ◻ AUS (SA) 110 Rk62
La Urbana ◻ YV 193 Gg42
Laurel ◻ USA (MS) 175 Ff30
Laurel ◻ USA (MT) 169 Ef23
Laureles ◻ MEX (COH) 181 Ej32
Laurel Park ◻ USA (NY) 177 Gb26
Laurencekirk ◻ GB 20 Ks34
Laurens ◻ USA (SC) 178 Fj28
Laurentians = Les Laurentides ◻ CDN 173 Gd22
Lauri ◻ IND (MPH) 83 Pa33
La Uribe ◻ CO 192 Gd44
La Uribe ◻ CO 192 Gc44
Lau Ridge ◻ FJI 119 Tb56
Laurinburg ◻ USA (NC) 178 Fk28
Lauriya Mandangarh ◻ IND (BIH) 83 Pc32
Lauro de Freitas ◻ BR (BA) 201 Ja52
Lauru Muller ◻ BR (SC) 205 Hf60
Lauro Sodré ◻ BR (AM) 198 Gj47
Lausanne ◻ CH 34 Lg44
Lauscha ◻ D 32 Lp40
Laut, Pulau ▲ RI 94 Qh43
Laut ◻ RI 94 Qe43
Lautaporras ◻ FIN 38 Md30
Lautaro ◻ RCH 208 Gd65
Lautaro, Cerro ▲ RCH 210 Gd70
Lauterach ◻ D 33 Lk41
Lauterbach (Hessen) ◻ D 32 Lk40
Lauterecken ◻ D 33 Lh41
Lautoka ◻ FJI 119 Tj54
Lauwersoog ◻ NL 23 Lg37
Lauzerte ◻ F 24 Lb46
Lava Beds Nat. Mon. ⚘ USA 170 Dg24
Lavaca ◻ E 29 Ku51
Lavagh More ▲ IRL 19 Km37
la Vall d'Uixó ◻ E 29 Ku51
Lavamünd ◻ A 35 Lp44
Lavant ◻ RI 94 Qe43
Lavapié, Punta ◻ RCH 208 Gc64
Lavardac ◻ F 24 La46
Lava Tubes ◻ AUS (QLD) 107 Sc55
Lavaur ◻ F 24 Lb47
Lávdas ◻ GR 46 Mb50
La Vega ◻ CO 192 Gc43
La Vega ◻ DOM 186 Ge36
La Vela de Coro ◻ YV 193 Gf40
Lavello ◻ I 37 Lq49
Laveno ◻ I 34 Lj45
La Ventura ◻ MEX (COH) 181 Ek33
La Verendrye Mon. ◻ USA 172 Fa22
La Victoria ◻ MEX (SLP) 182 Ek34
La Victoria ◻ YV 192 Ge42

La Victoria ◻ YV 193 Gf40
La Vieille-Lyre ◻ F 22 La42
La Vila Joiosa ◻ E 29 Ku52
La Viña ◻ RA (SA) 207 Gh58
La Viña ◻ YSlo, P.N. ⚘ RM 186 Gd36
La Violeta ◻ RA (BA) 209 Gk62
La Vôge ▲ F 25 Lg42
La Voulte-sur-Rhône ◻ F 25 Le46
La Viuda ◻ YV 193 Gj41
Lavras ◻ BR (MG) 203 Hh56
Lavras da Mangabeira ◻ BR (CE) 201 Ja49
Lavras do Sul ◻ BR (RS) 204 Hd61
La Tina ◻ PE 196 Ga44
La Tinaja de Bartolo ◻ MEX (DGO) 181 Eh33
Lavre ◻ P 27 Km52
Lavrentiya ◻ RUS 55 Ub05
Lavrio ◻ GR 47 Me55
Lavumisa ◻ SD 155 Mf56
Lawahi ◻ FJI 119 Tk54
Lawarai Pass ◻ PK 63 Og28
Lawdar ◻ YE 60 Nc39
Latoma ◻ RI 96 Ra47
Latoma ◻ RI 96 Ra47
Lawe Sigalagala ◻ RI 93 Pj44
Laweueng ◻ RI 92 Ph43
Lawik Reef ◻ PNG 116 Sg51
Lawit, Gunung ▲ MYA 92 Qg45
La Tranca ◻ RA (SL) 208 Gg62
Lawley River N.P. ⚘ AUS (WA) 103 Rc53
Lawn Hill ◻ AUS (QLD) 106 Rk55
Lawn Hill N.P. ⚘ AUS (QLD) 106 Rk55
Lawqah ◻ KSA 59 Nb31
Lawra ◻ GH 137 Kj40
Lawrence ◻ NZ 113 Te68
Lawrence ◻ USA (KS) 174 Fc26
Lawrence ◻ USA (MA) 177 Gd24
Lawrenceburg ◻ USA (TN) 175 Fg28
Lawrence House ◻ CDN 176 Gj23
Lawrenceville ◻ USA (GA) 178 Fj29
Le Faou ◻ F 22 Kq42
Le Faouët ◻ F 22 Kr42
Lawrence Wells, Mount ◻ AUS 104 Ra59
Lawson ◻ AUS (NSW) 111 Sf62
Lawson ◻ USA (OK) 174 Fa28
Lawu, Gunung ▲ RI 95 Qf49
Laxá ◻ S 31 Lq32
Laxenburg ▲ A 42 Lr42
Laxford Bridge ◻ GB 20 Kq32
Laxman Jhoola ◻ IND 81 Ok30
Lay ◻ BF 137 Kk39
Laya ◻ RI 96 Rc48
Laya Dula ◻ RI 96 Ra48
Layang-Layang ◻ MAL 94 Qg42
La Yarada ◻ PE 206 Ge55
Laybo ◻ KSA 60 Nd34
Layou ◻ RP 147 Sa55
Layshi ◻ MYA 86 Ph33
Layton ◻ USA (UT) 171 Ee25
Laytonville ◻ USA (CA) 170 Dj26
Lazarevac ◻ SCG 44 Ma46
Lazarevskoe ◻ RUS 49 Mk24
Lázaro Cárdenas ◻ MEX (BC) 180 Ec30
Lázaro Cárdenas ◻ MEX (MHC) 182 Ej37
Lazaropore ◻ MK 44 Ma49
Lazdijai ◻ LT 39 Md36
Lázio ◻ I 36 Ln48
Lazo ◻ RUS 55 Rd05
Lazo ◻ RUS 77 Rg24
La Zulema ◻ RA (SF) 207 Gb60
Lazuri de Beiuş ◻ RO 43 Mc44
Lead ◻ USA (SD) 169 Ej23
Leadore ◻ USA (ID) 168 Ed23
Leadville ◻ USA (CO) 171 Eg26
Leaf Rapids ◻ CDN (MB) 165 Ee17
Leahy ◻ USA (WA) 168 Ea22
Leakesville ◻ USA (MS) 175 Ff30
Lealui ◻ Z 151 Mb55
Leamington ◻ CDN (ON) 173 Fj24
Le'an ◻ CHN (JGX) 75 Qh32
Leander ◻ CDN (BC) 168 Eb20
Leander Point ◻ AUS 104 Qh60
Leandra ◻ ZA 155 Me59
Leandro N.Alem ◻ RA (MI) 204 Hc59
Leang-Leang ◻ RI 96 Qk48
Leang Temple ◻ IND 83 Pc33
Leanja ◻ RM 156 Nd53
Leamorth ◻ AUS (WA) 102 Qh57
Leavenworth ◻ USA (KS) 174 Fc26
Leavenworth ◻ USA (WA) 168 Dk22
Leichlingen ◻ D 32 Lh39
Leie ◻ NL 23 Le38
Leie ◻ EST 38 Mf31
Leigh ◻ NZ 112 Th64
Leigh Creek ◻ AUS (SA) 108 Rk61
Leine ◻ D 32 Lk38
Leinefelde ◻ D 32 Ll39
Leinster ◻ AUS (WA) 104 Ra59
Leinster Downs ◻ AUS (WA) 104 Ra59
Leinster, Mount ▲ IRL 19 Ko38
Leipaligis ◻ LT 39 Md36
Leipzig ◻ D 32 Ln39
Leira ◻ N 16 Le14
Leira ◻ N 17 Lg35
Leirvik ◻ DK 18 Kd28
Leirvik ◻ N 30 Lf31
Leisi ◻ EST 39 Mc32
Leisler, Mount ◻ AUS 103 Re57
Leitchfield ◻ USA (KY) 175 Fg27
Leiter City ◻ USA (WY) 169 Eg23
Leitha ▲ A 42 Lr43
Leith Peninsula ◻ CDN 167 Ea13
Leitre ◻ PNG 115 Sc47
Leiva, Cerro ▲ CO 193 Gf44
Leivonmäen kansallispuisto ✿ FIN 38 Mf29
Leixlip ◻ IRL 19 Ko37
Leiyang ◻ CHN (HUN) 75 Qg32

Lecheria ◻ YV 193 Gh40
Le Chesne ◻ F 23 Le41
Le Cheylard ◻ F 25 Le46
Lechinta ◻ RO 43 Me43
Le Vila, P.N. ⚘ RH 186 Gd36
Leciana ◻ E 28 Ku49
Lecino ◻ PL 41 Mb37
Leck ◻ D 32 Lj36
Le Conquet ◻ F 22 Kq42
Le Creusot ◻ F 25 Le44
Le Croisic ◻ F 22 Kr43
Le Crotoy ◻ F 23 Lc40
Lectoure ◻ F 24 La47
Łęczna ◻ PL 41 Mc39
Łęczyca ◻ PL 41 Lu38
Ledesma ◻ E 26 Kp49
Lédignan ◻ F 25 Le46
Ledmore ◻ GB 20 Kr32
Le Malzieu-Ville ◻ F 25 Ld46
Leman Bank ◻ GB 21 Lb38
Lednico-Valtice ◻ CZ 42 Lr42
Ledong ◻ CHN (HAN) 75 Qe36
Le Donjon ◻ F 25 Ld44
Le Dorat ◻ F 24 Lb44
Ledu ◻ CHN (QHI) 72 Qb27
Ledyczek ◻ PL 40 Lr37
Leedey ◻ USA (OK) 174 Fa28
Leeds ◻ GB 21 Kt37
Leeds ◻ GUY 194 Hb42
Leek ◻ GB 21 Ks37
Leek ◻ NL 23 Lg37
Leeland ◻ USA (NF) 177 Hd27
Leeman ◻ AUS (WA) 104 Qh60
Leeming ◻ CDN (NF) 177 Hc22
Leenh Range ◻ USA 158 Ec23
Leesburg ◻ USA (FL) 178 Fk31
Leesburg ◻ USA (VA) 175 Fh30
Leesburg ◻ USA (VA) 177 Gb26
Leesi ◻ EST 38 Mf31
Leesville ◻ USA (LA) 174 Fd30
Leeudoringstad ◻ ZA 155 Md59
Leeu-Gamka ◻ ZA 154 Mb62
Leeupoort ◻ ZA 155 Md58
Leeuwarden ◻ NL 23 Lf37
Leeuwen-Naturaliste N.P. ⚘ AUS 104 Qh62
Lee Vining ◻ USA (CA) 170 Ea27
Leeward Islands ◻ 187 Gj36
Le Faou ◻ F 22 Kq42
Le Faouët ◻ F 22 Kr42
Lefellier ◻ CDN (MB) 172 Fb21
Lefkáda ◻ GR 46 Ma52
Lefkáda ◻ GR 46 Ma52
Lefká Óri ▲ GR 47 Me55
Lefkí ◻ GR 46 Ma51
Lefkímmi ◻ GR 46 Lu52
Lefkosa ▲ CY 56 Mg28
Lefkosia ◻ CY 56 Mg28
Lefor ◻ USA (ND) 172 Ej22
Lefroux ◻ RCB 148 Lg47
Léogane ◻ RH 186 Gd36
Legazpi ◻ RP 90 Rb39
Legden ◻ D 32 Lh38
Legé ◻ F 24 Kt44
Legend Island ◻ AUS 102 Qj56
Legendre Island ◻ AUS 102 Qj56
Leggett ◻ USA (CA) 170 Dj26
Legionowo ◻ PL 41 Ma38
Legkovo ◻ RUS 48 Mk16
Le Grand-Quevilly ◻ F 23 Lb41
Legrad ◻ HR 35 Lr44
Le Grand-Lucé ◻ F 24 La43
Léguan Island ◻ GUY 194 Ha42
Le Guéroulet ◻ RN 132 Fc31
Le Guérouel ◻ RN 132 Ld38
Leguna ◻ AUS (NT) 103 Re53
Legutiano ◻ E 28 Ks48
Le Havre ◻ F 22 La41
Lehigh Acres ◻ USA (FL) 175 Fk32
Lehliu-Gară ◻ RO 45 Mg46
Lehman Caves ☆ USA 171 Ec26
Lehnin ◻ D 32 Ln38
Lehre ◻ D 32 Ll38
Lehrte ◻ D 32 Lk38
Lehtimäki ◻ FIN 38 Md28
Lehtula ◻ FIN 38 Mh29
Lehututu ◻ RB 154 Mb57
Lehu ◻ PK 65 Of30
Leibnitz ◻ A 35 Lq44
Leibo ◻ CHN (SCH) 74 Qb31
Leicester ◻ GB 21 Kt38
Leichhardt Range ◻ AUS (QLD) 107 Sd56
Leichhardt River ◻ AUS (QLD) 107 Rk55
Leichlingen ◻ D 32 Lh39
Leicester ◻ USA (MA) 177 Gc24

Leleasca ◻ RO 45 Me46
Lélehoy ◻ RMM 131 La38
Lelehudi ◻ PNG 116 Sf51
Leleque ◻ RA (CB) 208 Ge67
Leling ◻ CHN (SDG) 73 Qj27
Lepokole Hills ◻ RB 152 Me56
Le Pont-de-Beauvoisin ◻ F 25 Lf45
Le Porge ◻ F 24 Kt46
Le Portel ◻ F 23 Lc40
Leppävesi ◻ FIN 38 Mf28
Leppävirta ◻ FIN 38 Mh28
Lelystad ◻ NL 23 Lf38
Lepsi Magna = Labdah ☆ LAR 127 Lh29
Le Puy-en-Velay ◻ F 25 Ld45
Leqceiba ◻ RIM 130 Kd37
Leqceiba ◻ RIM 130 Kd37
Le Quesnoy ◻ F 23 Ld40
Lequena ◻ RCH 207 Gf55
Leven ◻ GB 21 Kt35
Levaris N.P. ◻ WG 187 Gk38
Le Verdon-sur-Mer ◻ F 24 Kt45
Leverkusen ◻ D 32 Lh39
Levet ◻ F 25 Lc44
Lerbäck ◻ S 31 Lg32
Lercara Friddi ◻ I 36 Lo53
Léré ◻ RMM 131 Kh38
Lere ◻ WAN 138 Le40
Léré ◻ TCH 140 Lh41
Lere ◻ WAN 138 Le41
Léré ◻ CI 34 Lm44
Lévico Terme ◻ I 34 Lm44
Léré ◻ RMM 131 Kh38
Levie ◻ SK 43 Lt42
Lérida = Lleida ◻ E 28 La49
Lévis ◻ CDN (QC) 176 Gf22
Lévico Terme ◻ I 34 Lm44
Lerik ◻ AZ 57 Ne26
Le Vigan ◻ F 25 Ld46
Lerma ◻ E 28 Kr48
Levin ◻ NZ 113 Th66
Lerma ◻ MEX (CAM) 183 Fe36
Levis ◻ CDN (QC) 176 Gf22
Lermontovo ◻ RUS 48 Nb19
Levirtha ▲ GR 47 Mg54
Lerma ◻ CDN (NF) 177 Hc22
Le Voile de la Mariée ☆ RG 136 Kd41
Leros ▲ GR 47 Mg53
Levroux ◻ F 24 Lb44
Le Rozier-Peyreleau ◻ F 25 Ld46
Lévuka ◻ FJI 119 Tk54
Lerum ◻ S 30 Ln33
Le Russey ◻ F 25 Lg43
Levice ◻ SK 43 Lt42
Lervik ◻ N 30 Lf31
Lewes ◻ GB 21 La40
Lerwick ◻ GB 20 Kt30
Lewes Plateau ◻ CDN 166 Db14
Ler Zerai ◻ SUD 134 Md40
Lewisburg ◻ USA (PA) 177 Gb25
Lemon Grove ◻ USA (CA) 170 Eb29
Lewisburg ◻ USA (TN) 175 Fg28
Les ◻ RO 43 Md44
Lewiston ◻ USA (ID) 168 Eb22
Les Abers ◻ F 22 Kq42
Lewiston ◻ USA (ME) 176 Ge23
Les Abymes ◻ F 187 Gk37
Lewiston ◻ USA (UT) 171 Ee25
Les Aix-d'Angillon ◻ F 25 Lc43
Lewistown ◻ USA (IL) 174 Fe26
Lešak ◻ SCG 44 Ma47
Lewistown ◻ USA (MT) 169 Ef22
Les Andelys ◻ F 23 Lb41
Lewistown ◻ USA (PA) 177 Gb25
Lešani ◻ MK 44 Ma49
Lewisville ◻ USA (AR) 174 Fd29
Les Arcs ◻ F 25 Lg47
Lexington ◻ USA (AL) 175 Fg28
Les Arènes de Nîmes ☆ F 25 Le47
Lexington ◻ USA (KY) 175 Fh27
Les Arènes de Saintes ☆ F 24 Ku45
Lexington ◻ USA (MS) 175 Fe29
Le Sauze ◻ F 25 Lg46
Lexington ◻ USA (NE) 174 Fa25
Les Baux-de-Provence ◻ F 25 Le47
Lexington ◻ USA (TN) 175 Fe28
Les Borges Blanques ◻ E 28 La49
Lexington ◻ USA (VA) 177 Fk27
L'Escarla ◻ E 29 Ld48
Lexington Park ◻ USA (MD) 177 Gb26
La Calanche ◻ F 34 Lj48
Les Calanques ◻ F 25 Lf47
Les Cayes ◻ RH 186 Gd36
L'Escarène ◻ F 25 Lh47
Leybucht ◻ D 32 Lg37
Les Cayes ◻ RH 186 Gd36
Leydsdorp ◻ ZA 155 Mf58
Les Corniches ◻ F 25 Lh47
Leyburn ◻ GB 21 Kt36
Lescun ◻ F 24 Ku48
Leyburn ◻ AUS (QLD) 109 Sf60
Les Deux-Alpes ◻ F 25 Lg46
Leye ◻ CHN (GZG) 74 Qd33
Le Neubourg ◻ F 22 La42
Leyre ◻ RP 90 Rc40
Les Echelles ◻ F 25 Lf45
Leyte ◻ RP 90 Rc40
Les Essarts ◻ F 24 Kt44
Lezajsk ◻ PL 41 Mc40
Les Eyzies-de-Tayac ◻ F 24 Lb46
Lézardrieux ◻ F 22 Kr42
Lesh ◻ F 24 Lb44
Lezay ◻ F 24 La44
Les Herbiers ◻ F 24 Kt44
Lezhë ◻ AL 44 Lu49
Lesjöfors ◻ S 31 Lp31
Lezhi ◻ CHN (SCH) 74 Qc30
Leskovac ◻ SCG 44 Mb48
Lézignan-Corbières ◻ F 25 Lc47
Leskovik ◻ AL 46 Ma50
Lezno ◻ PL 41 Lu36
Les Laurentides ◻ CDN 176 Gd21
Lézignan-Corbières ◻ F 25 Lc47
Leslie ◻ AR) 174 Fd28
L'govo ◻ RUS 48 Mk20
Leslie ◻ USA (ID) 168 Ed24
Lhari ◻ CHN (TIB) 69 Pg30
Les Méchins ◻ CDN (QC) 176 Gg21
Lhasa ◻ CHN (TIB) 68 Pd31
Lesneven ◻ F 22 Kq42
Lhaviyani Atoll ◻ MV 84 Og43
Lesnoe ◻ RUS 39 Ma36
Lhaze ◻ CHN (TIB) 68 Pd31
Lesnoi ◻ RUS 48 Nh16
Lhokkruet ◻ RI 92 Ph43
Lesnoj Gorodok ◻ RUS 70 Qg20
Lhoknga ◻ RI 92 Ph43
Lesnozavodsk ◻ RUS 76 Rg23
L'Hôpital Dr.Schweitzer ☆ G 148 Lf46
Lesosibirsk ◻ RUS 54 Pc07
Lhorong ◻ CHN (TIB) 69 Pg30
L'Hospitalet ◻ F 24 Lb48
Lhotse ◻ CHN (TIB) 68 Pe31
L'Hospitalet ◻ F 24 Lb48
Lhotse I.AI NEP/CHN 81 Pd32
Lesotho ◻ LS 155 Md60
Leperre-Médoc ◻ F 24 Kt45
Lhünzë ◻ CHN (TIB) 69 Pg31
L'Esperance Rock ◻ NZ 112 Ua61
L'Esperou ◻ F 25 Ld46
Liak ◻ PNG 116 Sg51
Les Ponts-de-Cé ◻ F 24 La43
Liakov ◻ RUS 55 Rc04
Les Portes de Fer ◻ DZ 126 Lc27
Liang ◻ RI 97 Rd46
Les Riceys ◻ F 25 Le43
Lianga ◻ RP 91 Rd41
Les Sables-d'Olonne ◻ F 24 Kt44
Liangcheng ◻ CHN (NMZ) 72 Qg25
Lessau ◻ PNG 116 Sd47
Lianghe ◻ CHN (SDG) 78 Qk29
Lesse et Lomme, P.N. de ✿ B 23 Lf40
Lianghe ◻ CHN (GGQ) 74 Qa33
Lesser Antilles ◻ 187 Gj37
Lianghe ◻ CHN (GZH) 87 Qc33
Lesser Caucasus ▲ 57 Nb25
Lianghe ◻ CHN (YUN) 87 Pk33
Lesser Hinggan Range ▲ CHN 71 Rd20
Lianghekou ◻ CHN (GSU) 72 Qc29
Lesser Slave Lake ◻ CDN 162 Ed17
Liangpan ◻ RI 95 Qd40
Lesser Slave Lake ◻ CDN 167 Ec18
Liangpran, Gunung ▲ RI 94 Qh45
Lesser Slave Lake Prov. Park ✿ CDN 167 Ec18
Lianhua ◻ CHN (SDG) 78 Qg32
Lesser Sunda Islands ▲ RI 52 Qb10
Lianjiang ◻ CHN (FJN) 75 Qk33
Lessini ◻ SCG 46 Ma49
Lianjiang ◻ CHN (GDG) 74 Qf33
Leominster ◻ GB 21 Ks38
Lianokládi ◻ GR 46 Mc52
Leominster ◻ USA (MA) 177 Gd24
Liannan ◻ CHN (GDG) 75 Qg33
León ◻ E 26 Kp48
Lianshui ◻ CHN (JGS) 78 Qk29
León ◻ MEX (GJT) 182 Ek35
Liantang ◻ CHN (GZG) 74 Qd33
León ◻ NIC 184 Fg39
Liantang ◻ CHN (JGX) 75 Qg33
Leon ◻ USA (IA) 174 Fc25
Lian Xian ◻ CHN (GDG) 75 Qg33
León, Cerro ▲ PY 206 Gk56
Lianyin ◻ CHN (HUN) 74 Qg32
Leonard ◻ USA (TX) 174 Fb29
Lianyuan ◻ CHN (JGS)
Leonarisso ◻ NAM 154 Lh58
Lianyungang ◻ CHN 78 Qk28
Leondari ◻ GR 46 Mc53
Lianyungang ◻ CHN (JGS)
Leonforte ◻ I 37 Lp53
Liaocheng ◻ CHN (SDG) 73 Qh27
León, Golfo de ◻ F 25 Ld47
Liaodong Peninsula ◻ CHN 73 Ra26
Leonico Prado ◻ PE 196 Gc47
Liaoning ◻ CHN (LJN) 76 Rb25
Leonidio ◻ GR 46 Mc53
Liaoyang ◻ CHN (LJN) 76 Rc24
Leonora ◻ AUS (WA) 104 Ra60
Liaoyuan ◻ CHN (JLN) 76 Rc24
Léon Viejo ◻ NIC 184 Fg39
Liaozhong ◻ CHN 76 Rb25
Léopold and Astrid Coast ◻ 7 Pa32
Liard ◻ CDN 166 Df17
Leopold Downs A.L. ◻ AUS 103 Rc54
Liard Highway ◻ CDN 167 Dj16
Leopoldina ◻ BR (MG) 203 Hj56
Liard Plateau ◻ CDN 166 Dg15
Leopoldo de Bulhões ◻ BR 202 Hf54
Liard River ◻ CDN 167 Dj16
Lepar ▲ RI 93 Qd46
Liard River Corridor ◻ CDN
Lepe ◻ E 27 Kn53
Liard River ◻ CDN

Lepel' ◻ BY 48 Me18
Lepsy ◻ KZ 66 Oh23
Leping ◻ CHN (JGX) 75 Qj31
Leu ◻ K 89 Qd39
Leting ◻ CHN (HBI) 73 Qj27
Letycitv ◻ UA 49 Md21
Lacina ◻ E 28 Ka49
Le Lion-d'Angers ◻ F 22 Ku43
Le Locle ◻ CH 34 Lg43
Lelogama ◻ RI 97 Rc50
Le Loroux-Bottereau ◻ F 24 Kt43
Lélouma ◻ RG 136 Kd40
Le Lude ◻ F 24 La43
Lelydorp ◻ SME 194 Hc43
Lelygebergte ▲ SME 194 Hc43

(column continues cut off)

Liberator General San Martin – Los Reyes de Salgado

Liberator General San Martin RA (SL) 208 Gh62
Liberec CZ 42 Lp40
Liberia CR 184 Fh40
Liberia 123 Ka09
Libertad MEX (CAM) 183 Fe36
Libertad RA (CR) 204 Hb61
Libertad ROU 209 Hb63
Libertad YV 193 Gf41
Libertad YV 193 Gf41
Libertador RA (CR) 204 Ha61
Libertador General San Martín RA (PJ) 207 Gh57
Liberty USA (NY) 177 Gc25
Liberty USA (TX) 174 Fc30
Libiąż PL 41 Lu40
Libina CZ 42 Ls41
Libjo RP 90 Rc40
Libmanan RP 90 Rb39
Libo CHN (GZH) 74 Qd33
Libode ZA 155 Me61
Libohovë AL 46 Ma50
Liboi EAK 145 Na45
Liboko RDC 140 Ma44
Libon RP 90 Rb39
Libona RP 91 Rc41
Libourne F 24 Ku46
Libramont-Chevigny B 23 Lf41
Libreville G 148 Le45
Libya 123 Lb07
Libyan Desert LAR/ET 128 Mc31
Licancábur, Volcán RCH 207 Gg57
Licata I 36 Lo53
Lice TR 57 Na26
Lich D 33 Lj40
Licheng CHN (JGS) 78 Qk29
Licheng CHN (SAX) 73 Qg27
Lichinga MOC 146 Mh52
Lichtenau D 32 Lj39
Lichtenburg ZA 155 Md59
Lichtenfels D 33 Lm40
Lichtenvoorde NL 23 Lg39
Lichuan CHN (HUB) 74 Qe30
Lichuan CHN (JGX) 75 Qj32
Liciro MOC 153 Mj54
Licking USA (MO) 175 Fe27
Lički Osik HR 35 Lq46
Ličko Lešće HR 35 Lq46
Lida BY 41 Mf37
Liden S 17 Lj14
Lidfontein NAM 154 Lk58
Lidhult S 31 Lo34
Lidingö S 31 Lt31
Lidjombo RCA 140 Lj44
Lidköping S 30 Lo32
Lido RN 132 Lb39
Lido di Jésolo I 35 Ln45
Lido di Metaponto I 37 Lr50
Lidoríki GR 46 Mc52
Lidzbark PL 41 Lu37
Lidzbark Warmiński PL 41 Ma36
Liebenburg D 32 Ll38
Liebenthal CDN (SK) 169 Ef20
Liebenwalde D 32 Lo38
Lieberose D 32 Lp38
Liebig, Mount AUS 103 Rf57
Liechtenstein FL 34 Lk43
Liechtensteinklamm A 35 Lo43
Liège B 23 Lf40
Lieksa FIN 16 Mf14
Lielauce LV 39 Mc34
Lielstraupe LV 39 Me33
Lielvārde LV 39 Me34
Liemianzhen CHN (SCH) 74 Qc30
Lienz A 35 Ln44
Liepāja LV 39 Mb34
Liepene LV 39 Mb33
Liepna LV 39 Mh33
Lier B 23 Le39
Lierbyen N 30 Ll31
Liesjärven kansallispuisto FIN 38 Md30
Liestal CH 34 Lh43
Liești RO 49 Md23
Lietnik USA (AK) 164 Bf14
Lieto FIN 38 Mc30
Lievestuore FIN 38 Mg28
Liévin F 23 Lc40
Liezen A 35 Lp43
Lifamatola RI 97 Rd46
Liffol-le-Grand F 23 Lf42
Lifford IRL 19 Kn36
Lifou F 118 Td56
Lifupa MW 146 Mg52
Liganga EAT 146 Mh51
Ligao RP 90 Rb39
Ligar TCH 140 Lj41
Ligera EAT 147 Mh51
Lighthouse Prov. H.S. CDN 177 Hd21
Lightning Ridge AUS (NSW) 109 Sd60
Lignano Sabbiadoro I 35 Lo45
Lignières F 25 Lc44
Ligny-en-Barrois F 23 Lf42
Ligny-le-Châtel F 25 Ld43
Ligowola EAT 147 Mj51
Ligueil F 24 La43
Ligui MEX (BCS) 180 Ee33
Ligunga EAT 147 Mj51
Ligúria I 34 Lj46
Ligurian Sea I/F 34 Lj47
Lihangwa EAT 147 Mk50
Lihás GR 46 Mc52
Lihir Group PNG 116 Sg47
Lihir Island PNG 116 Sg47
Lihoslavl' RUS 48 Mh17
Lihovskoj RUS 49 Na21
Lihue USA (HI) 170 Ca35
Lihuél Calel, P.N. RA 208 Gh64
Lihula EST 38 Md32
Liídli Kúé = Fort Simpson CDN 167 Dk15
Liinahamari RUS 16 Mf11
Lijiang CHN (YUN) 87 Qa32
Lijiang CHN 74 Qf33
Lijiang River cruises CHN 74 Qf33
Likala RDC 140 Lk45
Likasi RDC 146 Md51
Likati RDC 141 Mb44
Likely CDN (BC) 168 Dk19
Likely USA (CA) 168 Dk25
Likete RDC 149 Ma46
Likhmisar IND (RJT) 80 Og32
Liki RI 93 Qa46
Likisia TLS 97 Rc50
Liknes N 30 Lg32
Likódimo GR 46 Mb54
Likoma Island MW 146 Mh51
Likoto RDC 149 Mc46
Likovskoe RUS 38 Mj31
Liku RI 94 Qe45
Likum PNG 116 Sd47
Likupang RI 91 Rc45
Likuyu EAT 147 Mj51
Lilarea AUS (QLD) 109 Sc57
l'Île de Zembra, P.N. TN 126 Lf27
Lilienfeld A 42 Lq42
Lilienthal D 32 Lj37
Liling CHN (HUN) 75 Qg32
Liljendal FIN 38 Mg30
Lilla Creek AUS (NT) 108 Rh58
Lilla Edet S 30 Ln32
Lillärdal S 17 Lh15
Lille F 23 Ld40
Lillebonne F 22 La41
Lillehammer N 17 Lf15
Lillers F 23 Lc40
Lillesand N 30 Lj32
Lillestrøm N 30 Lm31
Lilli EST 39 Mf33
Lillie Marleen ANT (D) 7 Tc33
Lillo E 27 Kr51
Lillooet CDN (BC) 168 Dk20
Lilong IND (MNP) 86 Ph33
Lilongwe MW 146 Mg52
Liloy RP 91 Rb41
Lilydale AUS (SA) 110 Rk62
Lima PE 197 Gb52
Lima PY 202 Hb57
Lima USA (OH) 173 Fh25
Limache RA (CD) 207 Gj60
Lima Duarte BR (MG) 203 Hj56
Limah OM 61 Nj33
Limanáki GR 46 Mb52
Liman, Gunung RI 95 Qf49
Limanowa PL 41 Ma41
Limão do Curuá BR (AP) 195 He45
Limar RI 97 Rd49
Limas RI 93 Qc45
Limasawa Island RP 90 Rc41
Limassa RCA 140 Mb43
Limassol CY 56 Mg28
Limatambo PE 197 Gd52
Limavady GB 19 Ko35
Limay RA 208 Gf65
Limay RP 90 Ra38
Limay Mahuida RA (LP) 208 Gg64
Limba EAT 146 Mg49
Limbani PE 206 Gf53
Limbasa RDC 140 Mb43
Limbaži LV 39 Me33
Limbda IND (GUJ) 82 Of35
Limbdi IND (GUJ) 82 Of34
Limbé CAM 138 Le43
Limbe MW 153 Mh53
Limbé RH 186 Gd36
Limboto RI 91 Rb45
Limbuak MAL 94 Qj42
Limbung RI 96 Qk47
Limbunya AUS (NT) 103 Re54
Limburg D 33 Lj40
Lime Acres ZA 154 Mb60
Limeira BR (SP) 203 Hg57
Liménas Géraka GR 45 Md54
Liménas Hersonissou GR 47 Mf55
Limerick CDN (SK) 169 Eg21
Limerick IRL 19 Km38
Limes D 33 Lj40
Limestone Cliffs (Middle Caicos) GB 186 Ge35
Limestone Plateau ET 129 Mf33
Limfjorden DK 30 Lk34
Liminangcong RP 90 Qk40
Limmared S 31 Lo33
Limmen Bay AUS 106 Rh53
Limmen Bight River AUS 106 Rh53
Límnes GR 46 Mc53
Límni GR 45 Md52
Límni Kastoriás GR 46 Mb50
Límni Kerkínis GR 44 Md49
Límni Mikrí Préspa GR 46 Mb50
Límni Vouliagménis GR 46 Mc52
Límnos GR 47 Mf51
Limoeiro BR (PE) 201 Jc49
Limoeiro do Ajurú BR (PA) 195 Hf46
Limoeiro do Norte BR (CE) 201 Ja48
Limoges F 24 Lb45
Limón EC 196 Ga47
Limon USA (CO) 174 Ej26
Limone Piemonte I 34 Lh46
Limones EC 196 Ga45
Limones PA 185 Fj41
Limousin F 24 Lb45
Limousin F 24 Lb45
Limoux F 24 Lc47
Limpio PY 204 Hb58
Limpopo ZA 152 Me57
Limpopo ZA/ZW 152 Mf57
Limski kanal HR 35 Lo45
Limulunga Z 151 Mb53
Limuru EAK 144 Mj46
Lin AL 44 Ma49
Linah KSA 59 Nb31
Linapacan Island RP 90 Qk40
Linares E 27 Kr52
Linares MEX (NL) 181 Fa33
Linares RCH 208 Ge63
Linariá GR 47 Me52
Linbana S 16 Lk13
Lincang CHN (YUN) 87 Qa34
Lincan Ray RCH 208 Gd65
Linchang CHN (SAA) 72 Qe29
Linchuan CHN (JGX) 75 Qj32
Lincoln GB 21 Ku37
Lincoln RA (BA) 209 Gk63
Lincoln USA (CA) 170 Dk26
Lincoln USA (IL) 175 Ff25
Lincoln USA (KS) 174 Fa26
Lincoln USA (MA) 176 Gf23
Lincoln USA (NE) 174 Fb25
Lincoln Birthplace N.H.S. USA 175 Fh27
Lincoln Caverns USA 173 Ga25
Lincoln City USA (OR) 168 Dj23
Lincoln Highway AUS 110 Rj62
Lincoln Log Cabin S.H.S. USA 175 Ff26
Lincoln N.P. AUS 110 Rj63
Lincoln Sea CDN/DK 163 Ha02
Lincolnshire Wolds GB 21 Ku37
Lincoln's New Salem S.H.S. USA 175 Ff26
Lincoln's New Salem S.H.S. USA 175 Ff26
Lincoln Tomb S.H.S. USA 175 Ff26
Lincoln Tomb S.H.S USA 175 Ff26
Lincolnton USA (NC) 178 Fk28
Lind DK 30 Lj34
Lind USA (WA) 168 Ea22
Lindås N 17 Lc15
Lindau D 33 Lk43
Linde LV 39 Me34
Linde RUS 55 Ra05
Lindela MOC 153 Mh58
Lindelse DK 30 Ll36
Lindeman Group AUS 107 Se56
Lindeman Islands N.P. AUS 107 Se56
Linden CDN (AB) 169 Ed20
Linden D 32 Lj40
Linden GUY 194 Ha42
Linden USA (AL) 175 Fg29
Linden USA (TN) 175 Fg28
Linden USA (TX) 174 Fc29
Linderödsåsen S 31 Lo35
Lindesberg S 31 Lq31
Lindesnes N 30 Lh33
Lindesnes N 30 Lh33
Lindholm Høje DK 30 Lk33
Lindi EAT 147 Mk50
Lindi RDC 141 Md45
Lindian CHN (HLG) 76 Rc22
Lindi Bay EAT 147 Mk50
Lindis Valley NZ 113 Te68
Lindley ZA 155 Md59
Lindleyspoort ZA 155 Md58
Lindome S 30 Ln33
Lindos GR 47 Mj54
Lindoso P 26 Km49
Lindow D 32 Lo38
Lindsay CDN (ON) 173 Ga23
Lindsay USA (CA) 170 Ea27
Lindsay USA (MT) 169 Eh22
Lindsay USA (OK) 174 Fb28
Lindsborg USA (KS) 174 Fb26
Lindsdal S 31 Lr34
Linduri VU 118 Td53
Líneas de Nazca PE 197 Gc53
Line Islands 11 Bb09
Linfen CHN (SAX) 72 Qf27
Lingadaw MYA 86 Ph35
Lingal IND (APH) 82 Ok37
Lingala IND (APH) 85 Ok38
Linga Linga MOC 153 Mh57
Lingaraja Temple IND 83 Pc35
Lingayen RP 90 Ra38
Lingbao CHN (HNN) 72 Qf28
Lingbi CHN (AHU) 78 Qj29
Lingbim CAM 139 Lh43
Lingen D 32 Lh38
Lingga RI 93 Qc46
Lingga Karo Batak Village RI 92 Pk44
Linggi MAL 92 Qb44
Linghai CHN (LNG) 76 Ra25
Linghem S 31 Lq32
Lingig RP 91 Rd41
Lingi Point AUS 106 Rf51
Lingle USA (WY) 171 Eh24
Lingomo RDC 140 Mb45
Lingomo RDC 149 Mb46
Lingqi Dong CHN 75 Qk31
Lingqiu CHN (SAX) 73 Qh26
Lingshan CHN (GZG) 74 Qe34
Lingshan Dao CHN 78 Ra28
Lingshan Han Tombs CHN 73 Qh26
Lingshi CHN (SAX) 72 Qf27
Lingshui CHN (HAN) 75 Qf36
Ling Shui CHN 74 Qe34
Lingsugur IND (KTK) 82 Oj37
Lingtai CHN (GSU) 72 Qd28
Lingtou CHN (HAN) 75 Qe36
Linguaglossa I 37 Lq53
Linguèr SN 130 Kc38
Lingwu CHN (NHZ) 72 Qd26
Ling Xian CHN (HUN) 75 Qg32
Lingyan Si CHN 73 Qj27
Lingyin Si CHN 78 Qk30
Lingyuan CHN (LNG) 73 Qk25
Lingyun CHN (GZG) 74 Qd33
Linhai CHN (HLG) 71 Rc20
Linhai CHN (ZJG) 75 Ra31
Linhares BR (ES) 203 Hk55
Linhe CHN (NMZ) 72 Qd25
Linhemo ANG 150 Lj52
Linia PL 40 Ls36
Linjiang CHN (JLN) 76 Rd25
Linji Temple CHN 73 Qh27
Linköping S 31 Lq32
Linkou CHN (HLG) 76 Rf23
Linkuva LT 39 Md34
Linli CHN (HUN) 74 Qf31
Linlithgow GB 20 Kr35
Linn USA (TX) 181 Fa32
Linna FIN 38 Mc30
Linnansaaren kansallispuisto FIN 38 Mj28
Linneus USA (MO) 174 Fd26
Linnoitus FIN 38 Mj30
Linping CHN (ZJG) 78 Ra30
Linqing CHN (SDG) 73 Qh27
Linqu CHN (SDG) 73 Qk27
Linquan CHN (AHU) 73 Qh29
Lins BR (SP) 202 Hf56
Linsan RG 136 Kd40
Linshu CHN (SDG) 78 Qk28
Linshui CHN (SCH) 74 Qd30
Linshuize CHN (YUN) 87 Qc33
Linstead JA 186 Gb36
Lintan CHN (GSU) 72 Qb28
Lintao CHN (GSU) 72 Qb28
Linté CAM 139 Lf43
Linton USA (IN) 175 Fg26
Linton USA (ND) 172 Ek22
Lintong CHN (SAA) 72 Qe28
Linxi CHN (HBI) 73 Qk26
Linxi CHN (NMZ) 71 Qk24
Linxia CHN (GSU) 72 Qb28
Lin Xian CHN (HNN) 73 Qg27
Lin Xian CHN (SAX) 72 Qf27
Linxiang CHN (HUN) 75 Qg31
Linyanti RB 151 Mc55
Linyanti Camp RB 151 Mb55
Linyanti Swamp NAM/RB 151 Mb55
Linyi CHN (SDG) 73 Qj27
Linyi CHN (SDG) 78 Qk28
Linying CHN (HNN) 73 Qg29
Linz A 42 Lp42
Linz D 32 Lh40
Linze CHN (GSU) 72 Qa26
Linzhen CHN (SAA) 72 Qe27
Linzolo RCB 148 Lh48
Linzor RCH 207 Gf57
Lioma MOC 153 Mj53
Lions Den ZW 152 Mf54
Lioppa RI 97 Rd49
Lioto RCA 140 Ma43
Lioua TCH 133 Lh39
Liouesso RCB 140 Lh45
Lipa RP 90 Ra39
Lipany SK 43 Ma41
Liparamba EAT 146 Mh51
Lípari I 37 Lp52
Lipari Islands I 37 Lp52
Lipeck RUS 48 Mk19
Liperi FIN 38 Mk28
Lipiany PL 40 Lp37
Lipica SLO 42 Lo45
Lipicy-Zybino RUS 48 Mj19
Lipik HR 35 Ls45
Lipka PL 40 Ls37
Lipki RUS 48 Mj19
Lipljan SCG 44 Mb48
Lipniak PL 41 Md36
Lipnica PL 40 Ls36
Lipnica Murowana PL 41 Ma41
Lipnidki BY 41 Mf37
Lipník nad Bečvou CZ 42 Ls41
Lipno PL 41 Lu38
Lipoba Z 151 Mb53
Lipoche Olivença MOC 146 Mh51
Lipolist SCG 44 Lu46
Lipova RO 43 Mb44
Lipovcy RUS 76 Rf23
Lipovljani HR 35 Lr45
Lippstadt D 32 Lj39
Lipsí GR 47 Mg53
Lipsk PL 41 Md37
Lipsko PL 41 Mb39
Lipson AUS (SA) 110 Rj63
Lipton CDN (SK) 169 Ej20
Liptougou BF 137 La39
Liptovský Hrádok SK 43 Lu41
Lipu CHN (GZG) 74 Qf33
Lique, Cerro BOL 206 Gh56
Lira EAU 144 Mg44
Liranga RCB 149 Lj46
Lirangwe MW 153 Mh53
Lircay PE 197 Gc52
Lisala RDC 140 Ma44
Lisboa P 27 Kl52
Lisbon P 27 Kl52
Lisbon USA (ND) 172 Fb22
Lisbon Falls ZA 155 Mf58
Lisburn GB 19 Ko36
Lisburne Peninsula USA (AK) 165 Bh11
Liscomb Game Sanctuary CDN 176 Gj23
Lisdoonvarna IRL 19 Kl37
Liseberg S 30 Ln33
Lishan CHN (SCH) 74 Qd30
Lishan Z.B. CHN 72 Qf28
Lishi CHN (SAX) 72 Qf27
Lishizhen CHN (CGQ) 74 Qd31
Lishu CHN (JLN) 76 Rc24
Lishui CHN (JGS) 78 Qk30
Lishui CHN (ZJG) 75 Qk31
Lisieux F 22 La41
Lisitu EAT 146 Mh50
Liskeard GB 21 Kq40
Liski RUS 48 Mk20
L'Isle-Adam F 23 Lc41
L'Isle-en-Dodon F 24 La47
L'Isle-Jourdain F 24 La44
L'Isle-Jourdain F 24 Lb47
L'Isle-sur-la-Sorgue F 25 Lf47
L'Isle-sur-le-Doubs F 25 Lg43
Lismore AUS (NSW) 109 Sg60
Lismore AUS (QLD) 109 Sf59
Lismore AUS (VIC) 111 Sb64
Lismore GB 20 Kp34
Lismore IRL 19 Kn38
Lisnaskea GB 19 Kn36
Lišov CZ 42 Lp41
Lissadell AUS (WA) 103 Re54
Lissenung Island Resort PNG 116 Sf47
Lissington AUS (NSW) 109 Sd60
List D 32 Lj36
Listafjorden N 30 Lg32
Lister, Mount 7 Ta34
Listowel CDN (ON) 173 Fk24
Listowel IRL 19 Kl38
Listvjanka RUS 70 Qc20
Lita EC 196 Ga45
Litang CHN (GZG) 74 Qe34
Litang CHN (SCH) 69 Qa31
Litawa Flats Z 151 Mb53
Litchfield USA (MN) 172 Fc23
Litchfield Beach USA (SC) 178 Ga29
Litchfield N.P. AUS 106 Rf52
Lithgow AUS (NSW) 111 Sf62
Lithuania LT 39 Mc35
Lití GR 46 Mc50
Litija SLO 42 Lp44
Litipara IND (JKD) 83 Pd33
Lítla Dímun DK 18 Ko29
Litóhoro GR 46 Mc50
Litoměřice CZ 42 Lp40
Litomyšl CZ 42 Lr41
Litoral RO 45 Mj46
Litovel CZ 42 Ls41
Little Aden = 'Adan as Sughra YE 60 Nc39
Little Andaman IND 88 Pg40
Little Avalon AUS 111 Sf62
Little Barrier Island NZ 112 Th64
Little Bay CDN (NF) 177 Ha22
Little Belt DK 30 Lk35
Little Belt Mts. USA 169 Ee22
Little Bighorn Nat. Battlefield USA 169 Ef23
Little Cayman GB 179 Fk36
Little Coco Island MYA 88 Pg39
Little Colorado USA 171 Ee28
Little Current CDN (ON) 173 Fk23
Little Desert AUS 110 Sa64
Little Desert N.P. AUS 110 Sa64
Little Diomede Island USA (AK) 164 Bf13
Little Exuma Island BS 186 Gc34
Little Falls USA (MN) 172 Fc23
Littlefield USA (TX) 174 Ej29
Little Fort CDN (BC) 168 Dk20
Little Gombi WAN 139 Lg40
Little Grand Rapids CDN (MB) 172 Fc19
Little Harbour BS 179 Gb33
Little Inagua Island BS 186 Gd35
Little Lake USA (CA) 170 Eb28
Little Missouri USA 169 Ej22
Little Missouri Grassland N.P. USA 169 Ej22
Little Nicobar Island IND 88 Pg42
Little Ragged Island BS 186 Gc34
Little River Canyon USA 175 Fh28
Little River N.W.R. USA 174 Fc28
Little Rock USA (AR) 175 Fd28
Little Sahara R.A. USA 171 Ed26
Little Sandy Desert AUS 104 Ra58
Little San Salvador Is. BS 186 Gc33
Littleton USA (CO) 171 Eh26
Littleton USA (NH) 177 Ge23
Little White House S.H.S. USA 175 Fh29
Little Zab IRQ 57 Nb27
Lituhu EAT 146 Mh51
Litunde MOC 146 Mh52
Litvínov CZ 42 Lo40
Liuba CHN (SAA) 72 Qd29
Liuchiu Yü RC 75 Ra34
Liuhe CHN (JLN) 76 Rc24
Liuheng Dao CHN (ZJG) 75 Rb31
Liujiachang CHN (HUB) 74 Qf30
Liujiang CHN (GZG) 74 Qe33
Liujing CHN (GZG) 74 Qf34
Liujixia Shiku CHN 72 Qb28
Liuku CHN (YUN) 87 Pk33
Liuli EAT 146 Mh51
Liulin CHN (SAX) 72 Qf27
Liuliu SOL 117 Sj49
Liupan Shan CHN 72 Qc28
Liupanshan Z.B. CHN 72 Qd28
Liupanshui CHN (GZH) 87 Qc32
Liupo MOC 153 Mk53
Liurongsi Huata CHN 75 Qg34
Liushi CHN (ZJG) 75 Ra31
Liushilipu CHN (AHU) 73 Qh29
Liuwa Plain Z 151 Mb53
Liuwa Plain N.P. Z 151 Mb53
Liuxu CHN (GZG) 74 Qe34
Liuyang CHN (HUN) 75 Qg31
Liuzhai CHN (GZG) 74 Qd33
Liuzhou CHN (GZG) 74 Qe33
Liuzhuang CHN (JGS) 78 Ra29
Livada RO 43 Md43
Livaderó GR 46 Mb50
Livaderó GR 45 Me49
Livádi GR 47 Me53
Livadiá GR 46 Mc52
Livadia Palats UA 49 Mh23
Livadohóri GR 47 Mf51
Līvāni LV 39 Mg34
Livari SCG 44 Lu48
Livarot F 22 La42
Lively CDN (ON) 173 Fk22
Lively Island GB 210 Ha72
Livengood USA (AK) 165 Cf13
Live Oak USA (FL) 178 Fj30
Liverpool AUS (NSW) 111 Sf62
Liverpool CDN (NS) 176 Gh23
Liverpool GB 21 Ks37
Liverpool Range AUS 109 Sf61
Livigno I 34 Ll44
Livingston CDN 163 Gc08
Livingston GB 20 Kr35
Lívingston GCA 184 Ff38
Livingston USA (MT) 169 Ee23
Livingston USA (TN) 175 Fh27
Livingston USA (TX) 174 Fc30
Livingstone Z 151 Mc54
Livingstone Church ZA 155 Mb60
Livingstonegrot RB 155 Mc58
Livingstonekerk ZA 155 Mb60
Livingstone Memorial Z 146 Mf52
Livingstone Mountains EAT 146 Mh50
Livingstone's Cave RB 155 Mc58
Livingstonia MW 146 Mh51
Livingston Island 6 Gd31
Livizile RO 43 Md44
Livno BIH 35 Lr47
Livny RUS 48 Mj19
Livonia USA (MI) 173 Fj24
Livorno I 34 Ll47
Livramento do Brumado BR (BA) 201 Hk52
Livron-sur-Drôme F 25 Le46
Liw PL 41 Mb38
Liwa OM 61 Nj33
Liwa RI 93 Qc48
Liwale EAT 147 Mj50
Liwa Oasis UAE 61 Ng34
Imperial Tombs of the Ming and Qing Dynasties (Nanjing) CHN (JGS) 78 Qk29
Li Wenzhong, Tomb of = Imperial Tombs of the Ming and Qing Dynasties CHN (JGS) 78 Qk29
Liwonde MW 153 Mh53
Liwonde N.P. MW 153 Mh53
Li Xian CHN (GSU) 72 Qc28
Li Xian CHN (HUN) 74 Qf31
Li Xian CHN (SCH) 74 Qb30
Lixin CHN (AHU) 78 Qj29
Lixoúri GR 46 Ma52
Lixus MA 125 Kg28
Liyang CHN (JGS) 78 Qk30
Li Yubu SUD 141 Md43
Lizarda BR (TO) 200 Hg50
Lizard Island AUS 107 Sc53
Lizard Point GB 21 Kp41
Lizespasts LV 39 Mg33
Lizotte CDN (QC) 176 Gd21
Lizums LV 39 Mg33
Ljachavičy BY 41 Mg37
Ljady RUS 38 Mj32
Ljangar TJ 63 Og27
Ljaplëvka BY 41 Md39
Ljig SCG 44 Ma46
Ljørndalen N 17 Lg15
Ljuban' BY 48 Me19
Ljuban' RUS 48 Mf16
Ljubar UA 49 Md21
Ljubča BY 41 Mg37
Ljubešiv UA 41 Mf39
Ljubija BIH 35 Lr46
Ljubim RUS 48 Na16
Ljubinje BIH 44 Lt48
Ljubiš SCG 44 Lu47
Ljubljana SLO 42 Lp44
Ljuboml' UA 41 Me39
Ljubovija SCG 44 Lu46
Ljubuški BIH 35 Ls47
Ljubymivka UA 49 Mj22
Ljubytino RUS 48 Mg16
Ljudinovo RUS 48 Mh19
Ljugarn S 31 Lt33
Ljukkum KZ 66 Oj22
Ljung S 30 Lo33
Ljunga S 31 Lr32
Ljungby S 31 Lp34
Ljungbyhed S 30 Lo34
Ljungbyholm S 31 Lr34
Ljunghusen S 30 Ln35
Ljungsbro S 31 Lq32
Ljungskile S 30 Lm32
Ljusdal S 17 Lj15
Ljusfallshammar S 31 Lq32
Ljusterö S 31 Lt31
Ljutomer SLO 42 Lr44
Lkhachinvandad Uul Nature Reserve MNG 71 Qh23
Llagostera E 29 Lc49
Llaima, Volcán RCH 208 Ge65
Llallagua BOL 206 Gg55
Llalli PE 197 Ge53
Llamellin PE 197 Gb50
Llampos RCH 207 Ge59
Llanberis GB 21 Kq37
Llandeilo GB 21 Kr39
Llandovery GB 21 Kr39
Llandrindod-Wells GB 21 Kr38
Llandudno GB 21 Kr37
Llanelli GB 21 Kq39
Llanes E 26 Kq47
Llanganates, P.N. EC 196 Ga46
Llangollen GB 21 Kr38
Llangurig GB 21 Kr38
Llanidloes GB 21 Kr38
Llano USA (TX) 174 Fa30
Llanobajo CO 192 Gb44
Llano de Magdalena MEX 180 Ee33
Llano Estacado USA 174 Ej29
Llano Mariato PA 185 Fk42
Llanos de Challe, P.N. RCH 207 Ge60
Llanos de Chiquitos BOL 206 Gk55
Llanos de Guarayos BOL 206 Gj53
Llanos de la Rioja RA 207 Gg60
Llanos del Carmen MEX (SLP) 182 Ek34
Llanos del Orinoco CO/YV 192 Ge42
Llanos de Mojos BOL 206 Gh53
Llanquihue RCH 208 Gd66
Llanrheidol AUS (QLD) 108 Sa57
Llanrwst GB 21 Kr37
Llanwddyn GB 21 Kr38
Llanwrtyd Wells GB 21 Kr38
Llao Llao RA (RN) 208 Ge66
Llata PE 197 Gb50
Llaylla PE 197 Gc51
Llay-Llay RCH 208 Ge62
Lleida E 29 La49
Llera de Canales MEX (TM) 182 Fa34
Llerena E 27 Ko52
Lleyn GB 21 Kq38
Llica BOL 206 Gf55
Llico RCH 208 Gd63
Llifén RCH 208 Gd66
Llíria E 29 Ku51
Lliscaya, Cerro BOL/RCH 206 Gf55
L'Ile-Rousse F 34 Lj48
Llorente RP 90 Rc40
Lloret de Mar E 29 Lc49
Lloydminster CDN (SK) 169 Ef19
Lloyd Rock BS 186 Gc35
Lloyds Camp RB 151 Mc55
Llucena E 29 Ku50
Llucmajor E 29 Lc51
Llullaillaco, P.N. RCH 207 Gf58
Llullaillaco, Volcán RCH/RA 207 Gf58
Lluta PE 197 Gd54
Lnáře CZ 42 Lo41
Loa USA (UT) 171 Ee26
Loajanan RI 95 Qj46
Loakulu RI 95 Qj46
Loanda G 148 Le46
Loango RCB 148 Lf48
Loango RDC 148 Lg48
Loango, P.N. de G 148 Le47
Loano I 34 Lj46
Loay RP 90 Rc41
Lobatos MEX (ZCT) 182 Ej34
Lobatse RB 155 Mc58
Löbau D 32 Lp39
Lobay RCA 140 Lj43
Lobcovo RUS 48 Na17
Lobenstein D 33 Lm40
Lobería RA (BA) 209 Ha65
Löberöd S 31 Lo35
Łobez PL 40 Lq37
Lobi MW 153 Mh53
Lobira SUD 144 Mg43
Lobito ANG 150 Lg52
Lobitos PE 196 Fk48
Lobo RI 114 Rh47
Lobo RP 90 Ra39
Lobo USA (TX) 181 Eh30
Loboko RCB 148 Lj46
Lobos RA (BA) 209 Ha63
Lobougoula RMM 137 Kh40
Loburg D 32 Ln38
Łobżenica PL 40 Ls37
Locarno CH 34 Lj44
Locas de Cahuinarí CO 196 Ge46
Lochaline GB 20 Kp34
Lochboisdale GB 20 Kn33
Loché MEX (YT) 183 Ff35
Lochearnhead GB 20 Kq34
Lochem NL 23 Lg38
Loches F 24 Lb43
Lochgilphead GB 20 Kp34
Lochiel ZA 155 Mf59
Lochinvar N.P. Z 152 Md53
Lochinver GB 20 Kp32
Loch Lilly AUS (NSW) 110 Sa62
Loch Lomond GB 20 Kq34
Loch Lomond and The Trossachs N.P. GB 20 Kq34
Lochmaddy GB 20 Kn33
Loch Maree GB 20 Kp33
Loch Ness GB 20 Kq33
Łochów PL 41 Mb38
Lochranza GB 20 Kp35
Loch Sport AUS (VIC) 111 Sd65
Lochvycja UA 48 Mg20
Lociel AUS (SA) 110 Rk62
Lock AUS (SA) 110 Rh62
Lockeport CDN (NS) 176 Gh24
Lockerbie GB 20 Kr35
Lockesburg USA (AR) 174 Fc29
Lockhart AUS (NSW) 111 Sd63
Lockhart USA (TX) 181 Fb31
Lockhart Lake CDN 167 Ed14
Lockhart River AUS (QLD) 107 Sb52
Lockhart River CDN 167 Ef14
Lockhart River A.L. AUS 107 Sb52
Lock Haven USA (PA) 177 Gb25
Lockichokio EAK 144 Mh43
Löcknitz D 32 Lp37
Lockwood USA (CA) 170 Dk28
Lockwood Hills USA 165 Cc12
Locminé F 22 Ks43
Loc Ninh VN 89 Qd40
Locri I 37 Lr52
Locri Epizefiri I 37 Lr52
Locronan F 22 Kq42
Loctudy F 22 Kq43
Lod IL 58 Mh30
Lodein SUD 142 Mg42
Löderup S 31 Lp35
Lodève F 25 Ld47
Lodge Corner USA (AR) 175 Fe28
Lodge Grass USA (MT) 169 Eg23
Lodhran PK 65 Of31
Lodi I 34 Lk45
Lodi RDC 149 Ma48
Lodi USA (CA) 170 Dk26
Løding N 16 Lh12
Lødingen N 16 Lj11
Lodja RDC 149 Mb47
Lodosa E 28 Ks48
Lödöse S 30 Ln32
Lodoyo RI 95 Qg50
Lodrani IND (GUJ) 82 Of34
Lodungokwe EAK 144 Mj45
Lodwar EAK 144 Mh44
Łódź PL 41 Lu39
Loei THA 88 Qa37
Loeng Nok Tha THA 89 Qc37
Loeriesfontein ZA 154 Lk61
Løfallstrand N 30 Lg30
Lofé SN 130 Kc38
Lofer A 35 Ln43
Lofoten N 16 Lg12
Lofoten Basin 14 La03
Lofsdalen S 17 Lg14
Loftahammar S 31 Lr33
Lofthus N 30 Lg30
Lofty Range AUS 104 Qk58
Lofty Ranges, Mount AUS 110 Rk63
Loga RN 132 Lb39
Loga SUD 144 Mf43
Logan USA (IA) 172 Fc25
Logan USA (NM) 174 Ej28
Logan USA (OH) 175 Fj26
Logan USA (UT) 171 Ee25
Logan USA (WV) 178 Fk27
Logan Cave N.W.R. USA 174 Fc27
Logan Glacier CDN 166 Ck15
Logan, Mount CDN 166 Ck15
Logan Mountains CDN 166 Df15
Logan Pass USA 168 Ec21
Logansport USA (IN) 173 Fg25
Logatec SLO 42 Lp45
Logeloge EAT 147 Mk49
Logobou BF 137 La40
Logoforok SUD 144 Mg44
Logone CAM/TCH 139 Lh40
Logone Birni CAM 139 Lh40
Logone Gana TCH 139 Lh40
Lógos GR 46 Mc52
Logozohe DY 138 Lb42
Logroño E 28 Ks48
Logrosán E 27 Kp51
Løgstør DK 30 Lk34
Løgumkloster DK 30 Lj35
Lohaghat IND (UTT) 81 Pa31
Lohals DK 30 Ll35
Lohara IND (CGH) 83 Pa35
Lohardaga IND (JKD) 83 Pc34
Lohatanjona Angadoka RM 156 Nd52
Lohatanjona Antsirakakambana RM 157 Nf54
Lohatanjona Fenambosy RM 157 Nc58
Lohatanjona Maromony RM 156 Nd53
Lohatanjona Vohibato RM 157 Ne54
Lohawat IND (RJT) 80 Og32
Lohikoski FIN 38 Mj29
Lohja FIN 38 Me30
Lohmar D 32 Lh40
Lohne D 32 Lj38
Lohr D 33 Lk40
Loi PNG 116 Sd47
Loibltunnel A/SLO 35 Lp44
Loiborsoit EAT 147 Mj48
Loi, Gunung RI 94 Qg45
Loi-kaw MYA 86 Pj36
Loikisale EAT 144 Mj47
Loi-lawm MYA 86 Pj34
Loimaa FIN 38 Md30
Loima Hills EAK 144 Mh44
Loir F 22 Ku43
Loire F 24 Ku43
Loire F 24 Lb43
Loiro Poco BR (AM) 193 Gf45
Loi Sang MYA 86 Pj35
Loi Song MYA 86 Pj34
Loita Plains EAK 144 Mh46
Loi Tawngkyaw MYA 86 Pj34
Loitz D 32 Lo37
Loiyangalani EAK 144 Mj44
Loja E 27 Kq53
Loja EC 196 Ga47
Lojanice SCG 44 Lu46
Lojsthajd S 31 Lt33
Lokači UA 41 Me40
Lokalema RDC 140 Mb45
Lokandu RDC 149 Mc47
Lokapur IND (KTK) 82 Oh37
Lokata RI 97 Rf46
Lökbetan AZ 57 Ne25
Løken N 30 Lm31
Lokeren B 23 Ld39
Loket CZ 42 Ln40
Lokgwabe RB 154 Ma58
Lokichar EAK 144 Mh44
Lokichar EAU 144 Mh44
Lokitanyaly EAK 144 Mh44
Lo Kitaung EAK 144 Mh43
Loknja RUS 48 Mf17
Loko WAN 138 Ld41
Lokofe RDC 149 Mb46
Lokoja WAN 138 Ld42
Lokolama RDC 149 Lk47
Lokolia RDC 149 Ma46
Lokomby RM 157 Nd57
Lokomo CAM 139 Lh44
Lokon RI 91 Rc45
Lokono PNG 116 Sf47
Lokori EAK 144 Mj45
Lőkösháza H 43 Mb44
Lokossa DY 138 La42
Lokot' RUS 48 Mh19
Lokoti CAM 139 Lh42
Loksa EST 38 Mf31
Loksado RI 95 Qh47
Lokutu RDC 141 Mb45
Lol SUD 141 Md41
Lol SUD 141 Me42
Lola ANG 150 Lg53
Lola RG 136 Kf42
Lolela USA (CA) 168 Dh25
Lolengi RDC 140 Ma45
Lolgorien EAK 144 Mh46
Loliondo EAT 144 Mh47
Lolland DK 30 Lm36
Lollar D 32 Lj40
Lolo USA (MT) 168 Ec22
Loloata Resort PNG 115 Sd50
Lolobau Island PNG 116 Sf48
Lolodorf CAM 138 Lf44
Lolo Hot Springs USA (MT) 168 Ec22
Lolokadan IR 64 Oa31
Lolui Island EAU 144 Mg46
Lolwane ZA 155 Mb59
Lolworth AUS (QLD) 107 Sc56
Lom BG 44 Md47
Lom N 17 Le15
Loma ETH 142 Mj42
Loma USA (MT) 169 Ee22
Loma Alta USA (TX) 181 Ek31
Loma Bonita MEX (VC) 183 Fc36
Loma de Cabrera DOM 186 Ge36
Lomaloma FJI 119 Ua54
Lomami RDC 149 Mb46
Lomami RDC 141 Mc45
Loma Mountains Forest Reserve WAL 136 Ke41
Lomas PE 197 Gc53
Lomas Coloradas RA 210 Gg67
Lomas de Arena BOL 206 Gj54
Lomas de Arena MEX (CHH) 181 Eh30
Lomas del Real MEX (TM) 182 Fb34
Lomas de Zamora RA (BA) 209 Ha63
Lomaum ANG 150 Lh52
Lombadina AUS (WA) 102 Rb54
Lombadina Point AUS 102 Rb54
Lombardía MEX (MHC) 182 Ej36
Lombardy I 34 Lk45
Lombe ANG 148 Lj50
Lombe RI 96 Rb48
Lombez F 24 La47
Lomblen RI 97 Rb50
Lombok RI 96 Qj50
Lombol SN 130 Kb38
Lombolo RCB 148 Lh48
Lomci BG 45 Mg47
Lomé TG 137 La42
Lomela RDC 149 Ma46
Lomela RDC 149 Mb47
Łomianki PL 41 Ma38
Lomié CAM 139 Lg44
Loming SUD 144 Mg43
Lomma S 30 Lo35
Lommel B 23 Lf39
Lom nad Rimavicou SK 43 Lu42
Lomond CDN (AB) 169 Ed20
Lomonosov RUS 38 Mk31
Lomonosov Ridge 4 Hb01
Lomo Plata PY 207 Ha57
Lomphat K 89 Qd39
Lomphat W.S. K 89 Qd39
Lompobatang, Gunung RI 96 Ra48
Lompoc USA (CA) 170 Dk28
Lom Sak THA 88 Qa37
Łomża PL 41 Mc37
Lonand IND (MHT) 82 Oh36
Lonar IND (MHT) 82 Oj36
Lonavala IND (MHT) 82 Og36
Lonavala Hill Resort IND 82 Og36
Lončakovo RUS 76 Rh22
Loncoche RCH 208 Gd65
Loncopue RA (NE) 208 Ge65
Londa IND (KTK) 82 Oh38
Londa Tana-Toraja RI 96 Qk47
Londela-Kayes RCB 148 Lg48
Londengo ANG 150 Lg52
Londiani EAK 144 Mh46
Londolovit PNG 116 Sg47
London CDN (ON) 173 Fk24
London GB 21 Ku39
London USA (KY) 175 Fh27
Londonderry GB 19 Kn36
London Reefs 94 Qg41
Londres RA (CA) 207 Gg59
Londrina BR (PR) 202 He57
Lone Butte CDN (BC) 168 Dk20
Lone Pine USA (CA) 170 Ea27
Lone Pine Ind. Res. USA 170 Eb27
Lone Star Park USA (TX) 174 Fb29
Lone ton MYA 86 Pj33
Lone Tree RB 154 Mb57
Long THA 87 Pk36
Longa ANG 150 Lk53
Longadambau RI 94 Qh45
Long'an CHN (GZG) 74 Qd34
Long'an CHN (SAA) 72 Qe27
Longana VU 118 Td53
Long'anqiao CHN (HLG) 76 Rc22
Longarone I 34 Ln44
Longavi, Nevado de RCH 208 Ge64
Longbawan RI 94 Qh44
Long Bay Beach GB 187 Gh36
Long Bay Beach JA 186 Gb36
Long Beach USA (CA) 170 Ea29
Long Beach USA (MS) 175 Ff30
Long Beach USA (NC) 178 Ga29
Long Beach USA (NJ) 177 Gc26
Long Beach USA (NY) 177 Gd25
Long Beach Pen. USA 168 Dh22
Long Branch USA (NJ) 177 Gc25
Long Branch S.P. USA 174 Fd26
Long Cay BH 184 Fg37
Longchamp F 23 Lc42
Longchang CHN (GZH) 74 Qd32
Longchang CHN (SCH) 74 Qc31
Longchuan CHN (GDG) 75 Qh33
Longchuan CHN (YUN) 87 Pk33
Long Cove CDN (NF) 177 Hd22
Long Creek USA (OR) 168 Ea23
Long Dat VN 89 Qd40
Longeau F 25 Lf43
Longfellow USA (TX) 181 Ej30
Longfellow, Mount NZ 113 Tg67
Longford AUS (TAS) 111 Sd66
Longford IRL 19 Kn37
Long Gaij RI 94 Qh45
Longgang CHN (CGQ) 74 Qc31
Longgang Shan CHN 76 Rd24
Longgong Cave CHN 87 Qc32
Longgun CHN (HAN) 75 Qf36
Long Hai Beach VN 89 Qd40
Longhe CHN (HLG) 71 Rb19
Longhua CHN (HBI) 73 Qj25
Longhui CHN (HUN) 74 Qf32
Longhurst, Mount 7 Sd34
Longido EAT 144 Mj47
Longikis RI 95 Qj46
Longiram RI 95 Qh46
Long Island AUS 102 Qh56
Long Island AUS 109 Se57
Long Island BS 186 Gc34
Long Island CDN 176 Gg23
Long Island PNG 115 Sd48
Long Island USA 177 Gd25
Longjiang CHN (HLG) 71 Rb22
Longjing CHN (JLN) 76 Re24
Longkou CHN (SDG) 73 Ra27
Longku IND (ASM) 86 Pg33
Longlac CDN (ON) 173 Fg21
Long Lake USA (NY) 177 Gc24
Long Lake Ind. Res. CDN 173 Fg21
Long Lake N.W.R. USA 172 Fa22
Long Lama MAL 94 Qh44
Longleat House GB 21 Ks39
Long Lellang MAL 94 Qh44
Longli CHN (GZH) 74 Qd32
Longlin CHN (GZG) 87 Qc33
Longling CHN (YUN) 87 Pk33
Longlinjie CHN (GZG) 74 Qd34
Longmen CHN (GDG) 74 Qf35
Longmen CHN (GDG) 75 Qh34
Longmen Shan CHN 72 Qb30
Longmen Shiku CHN 73 Qg28
Long Men Xia CHN 74 Qe30
Longmont USA (CO) 171 Eh25
Longnah RI 94 Qj45
Longnan CHN (JGX) 75 Qh33
Longnawang RI 94 Qh45
Longo CI 137 Kh41
Longo G 148 Lg46
Longo RCB 140 Lj45
Longobucco I 37 Lr51
Longonjo ANG 150 Lh52
Longotea PE 196 Gb49
Longozabe RM 157 Ne55
Long Palai MAL 94 Qh44
Long Point CDN (ON) 173 Fk24
Long Point CDN 172 Fa19
Long Point CDN 177 Ha21
Long Point Prov. Park CDN 173 Fk24
Long Prairie USA (MN) 172 Fc23
Long Preston GB 21 Ks36
Longquan CHN (GZH) 74 Qd32
Longquan CHN (ZJG) 75 Qk31
Long Range Mountains CDN 177 Hb21
Longreach AUS (QLD) 109 Sc57
Longs Creek CDN (NB) 176 Gg23
Long Seridan MAL 94 Qh43
Longshan CHN (GDG) 75 Qg34
Longshan CHN (HUN) 74 Qe31
Long Shan CHN 72 Qa26
Long Shan Si CHN 75 Qk33
Longsheng CHN (GZG) 74 Qf33
Longtanshan Park CHN 76 Rd24
Long Thanh VN 89 Qd40
Longtian CHN (FJN) 75 Qk33
Long Tompas ZA 155 Mf58
Longton AUS (QLD) 107 Sc56
Longtown GB 20 Ks35
Longué-Jumelles F 24 Ku43
Longueuil CDN (QC) 177 Gd23
Longuyon F 23 Lf41
Long Valley USA (SD) 172 Ek24
Long Valley Junction USA (UT) 171 Ed27
Longview CDN (AB) 169 Ec20
Longview USA (TX) 174 Fc29
Longview USA (WA) 168 Dj22
Longwa EAT 147 Mj48
Longwangmiao CHN (HLG) 76 Rg23
Longwarry AUS (VIC) 111 Sc65
Longwy F 23 Lf41
Longxi CHN (GSU) 72 Qc28
Long Xian CHN (SAA) 72 Qd28
Longxing Temple CHN 73 Qh26
Long Xuyen VN 89 Qc40
Longyan CHN (FJN) 75 Qj33
Longyao CHN (HBI) 73 Qh27
Longyearbyen N 16 Lh06
Longyou CHN (ZJG) 75 Qk31
Longzhen CHN (HLG) 71 Rd21
Longzhou CHN (GZG) 74 Qd34
Löningen D 32 Lh38
Łoniów PL 41 Mb40
Lonkintsy RM 157 Ne54
Lonoke USA (AR) 175 Fe28
Lonquimay RA (LP) 209 Gj64
Lonquimay RCH 208 Ge65
Lonquimay, Volcán RCH 208 Ge65
Lonrong RI 96 Ra48
Lönsboda S 31 Lp34
Lons-le-Saunier F 25 Lf44
Lontar RI 97 Re48
Lontar RI 97 Rf48
Lontou RMM 130 Ke38
Lontra BR (PA) 200 He48
Lontué RCH 208 Ge63
Loogootee USA (IN) 175 Fg26
Lookout Mount USA 165 Cd12
Lookout Ridge USA 165 Ca11
Loolmalassin EAT 144 Mj47
Looma AUS (WA) 103 Rc55
Loon RP 90 Rb41
Loongana AUS (WA) 105 Rd61
Loon Lake CDN (SK) 169 Ef18
Loonse en Drunense Duinen, N.P. NL 23 Lf39
Loop Head IRL 19 Kl38
Loosdrechtse Plassen NL 23 Lf38
Lop CHN (XUZ) 68 Pa27
Lopar HR 35 Lp46
Lopary RM 157 Nd57
Lopătari RO 45 Mg45
Lopatovo RUS 39 Mj33
Lopatyn UA 41 Me40
Lop Buri THA 88 Qa38
Lopé, P.N. de la G 148 Lf46
Lopez CO 192 Gb44
Lopez RP 90 Rb39
Lop Nur = Yuli CHN (XUZ) 67 Pd25
Lop Nur CHN 67 Pf25
Lopori RDC 140 Ma45
Lopou CI 137 Kh43
Loppi FIN 38 Me30
Lopuhinka RUS 38 Mk31
Lora del Río E 27 Kp53
Lorain USA (OH) 173 Fj25
Loralai PK 65 Oe30
Lorca E 29 Kt53
Lorch D 33 Lh40
Lordegan IR 59 Nf30
Lord Howe Island AUS 100 Sb13
Lord Howe Rise 100 Ta12
Lord Howe Seamounts 100 Sb12
Lord Loughborough Island MYA 88 Pj40
Lordsburg USA (NM) 171 Ef29
Lore TLS 97 Rd50
Lore Lindu N.P. RI 96 Ra46
Lorena BR (AM) 196 Ge49
Lorena BR (SP) 205 Hh57
Lorengau PNG 116 Sd47
Lorentz RI 114 Rk48
Lorentz N.P. RI 114 Rj48
Lorenzo Geyres ROU 204 Hb62
Loreto BOL 206 Gh53
Loreto BR (MT) 199 Ha51
Loreto CO 196 Ge47
Loreto EC 196 Gb46
Loreto I 35 Lo47
Loreto MEX (BCS) 180 Ee32
Loreto MEX (ZCT) 182 Ek34
Loreto RA (CR) 204 Hb59
Loreto RP 90 Rc40
Loreto Aprutino I 35 Lo48
Lorgues F 25 Lg47
Lorica CO 192 Gc41
Lorient F 22 Kr43
Lőrinci H 43 Lu43
Loring USA (MT) 169 Eg21
Loriol-sur-Drôme F 25 Le46
Loris USA (SC) 178 Ga29
Lorlie CDN (SK) 169 Ej20
Lormes F 25 Ld43
Lormi IND (CGH) 83 Pa34
Lorna Glen AUS (WA) 104 Ra59
Lorne AUS (VIC) 111 Sb65
Lorneville CDN (NB) 176 Gg23
Loronyo SUD 144 Mg43
Loropéni BF 137 Kj40
Lörrach D 33 Lh43
Lorraine AUS (QLD) 107 Rk55
Lorraine F 23 Lf41
Lorraine F 23 Lf42
Lorris F 25 Lc43
Loruk EAK 144 Mj45
Lorzot TN 126 Lf30
Los S 17 Lh15
Losai N.P. EAK 144 Mj45
Los Aldamos MEX (NL) 181 Fa32
Los Alerces, P.N. RA 210 Ge67
Los Almos USA (NM) 171 Eg28
Los Altos RA (CA) 207 Gh60
Los Americanos MEX (COH) 181 Ej32
Los Amores RA (SF) 204 Ha60
Los Andes = Sotomayor CO 192 Gb45
Los Andes RCH 208 Ge62
Los Angeles RCH 208 Gd64
Los Angeles USA (CA) 170 Ea28
Los Ánimas MEX (CHH) 180 Eg31
Los Antiguos RA (SC) 210 Ge69
Los Arcos E 28 Ks48
Losari RI 95 Qe49
Los Arrieros MEX (SO) 180 Ee31
Los Asientos PA 185 Fk42
Los Azabaches MEX (BCS) 180 Ee33
Los Baldecitas RA (SJ) 207 Gg61
Los Banos USA (CA) 170 Dk27
Los Barrancos YV 193 Gj41
Los Barriles MEX (BCS) 180 Ef34
Los Barrios E 27 Kp54
Los Berros RA (SJ) 208 Gf61
Los Blancos RA (SA) 207 Gj57
Los Caracas YV 193 Gg40
Los Cardones, P.N. RA 207 Gg58
Los Caribes YV 193 Gk43
Los Chiles CR 185 Fh40
Los Chiriguanos RA (FO) 207 Gk58
Los Chuchumatanes, P.N. GCA 184 Fe38
Los Cocos YV 193 Gg40
Los Cocos YV 193 Gg40
Los Colorados RA (LR) 207 Gg60
Los Colorados, P.N. CO 192 Gc40
Los Conquistadores RA (ER) 204 Ha61
Los Corozos YV 193 Gg42
Los Corrales de Buelna E 26 Kq47
Los Cortijos de Arriba E 27 Kq51
Los Cristianos E 124 Kb31
Losesia EAK 144 Mj45
Los Flamencos CO 192 Gd40
Los Frailes MEX (CHH) 180 Eg33
Los Frentones RA (CH) 207 Gk59
Los Gatuzos NIC 185 Fh40
Los Glaciares, P.N. RA 210 Gd70
Los Güires YV 193 Gk41
Los Haïtises, P.N. DOM 186 Gf36
Losheim D 33 Lg41
Los Hoyos GCA 184 Fe38
Los Hoyos MEX (SO) 180 Ef30
Łosice PL 41 Mc38
Los Indios C 186 Gc35
Lošinj HR 35 Lp46
Losiny ostrov N.P. RUS 48 Mj18
Los Jobillos DOM 186 Ge36
Los Juríes RA (SE) 207 Gj60
Los Katíos, P.N. CO 192 Gb42
Loskop Dam Nature Reserve ZA 155 Me58
Los Lagos RCH 208 Gd65
Los Limones HN 184 Fg38
Los Llanos de Aridane E 124 Kb31
Los Lunas USA (NM) 171 Eg28
Los Mármoles, P.N. MEX 182 Fa35
Los Médanos MEX (SO) 180 Ee32
Los Menucos RA (RN) 208 Gf66
Los Mochis MEX (SL) 180 Ef33
Los Molles RCH 208 Ge62
Los Monasterios de Suso y Yuso E 28 Ks48
Los Monos RA (SC) 210 Gf69
Los Muermos RCH 208 Gd66
Los Navalmorales E 27 Kq51
Los Negrones YV 192 Ge40
los Nevados, P.N. CO 192 Gc43
Løsning DK 30 Lk35
Losogonoi Plateau EAT 147 Mj48
Los Ojitos MEX (SL) 180 Ef32
Losomba RDC 149 Mc47
Los Osos USA (CA) 170 Dk28
Los Palacios y Villafranca E 27 Kp53
Los Palos RH 186 Ge36
Los Patos BOL 207 Gj56
Lospatos TLS 97 Rd50
Los Patricios CO 196 Ge46
Los Pedales YV 192 Gd40
Los Penitentes RA 208 Gf62
Los Picos MEX (COH) 181 Ej31
Los Pijiguaos YV 193 Gg42
Los Pinos C 179 Fj34
Los Pinos MEX 180 Eg34
Los Puentes MEX (SL) 180 Eg33
Los Reyes de Salgado MEX (MHC) 182 Ej36

Mahbubnagar ☐ IND (APH) 82 Oj37
Mahdah ☐ OM 61 Nh33
Mahdalynka ☐ UA 49 Mh21
Mahdia ☐ GUY 194 Ha43
Mahdia ☐ TN 126 Lf28
Mahdi's Tomb ☒ MA 125 Kg28
Mahdija-Plage ☐ MA 125 Kg28
Mahé ☐ IND 79 Qd44
Mahé ☒ SY 145 Nh48
Mahebourg ☐ MS 157 Rj56
Mahendragarh ☐ IND (CGH) 83 Pb34
Mahendragarh ☐ IND (HYA) 82 Oj34
Mahenge ☐ EAT 147 Mh50
Mahe Pondicherry ☐ IND 84 Oh40
Maheshwar ☐ IND (MPH) 82 Oh34
Maheshkali Island ☐ BD 86 Pf35
Mahfuzbhendaru ☐ IND (APH) 83 Pe36
Mahgawan ☐ IND (MPH) 83 Ok32
Mahia Peninsula ☒ NZ 113 Tj65
Mahibadhoo ☐ MV 79 Qd44
Mahidasht ☐ IR 57 Nd28
Mahin ☐ SYR 56 Mj28
Mahin ☐ RDC 146 Me48
Mahilëv ☐ BY 48 Mf19
Mahin ☐ IND 138 Lc42
Mahisama ☐ IND (APH) 82 Ok37
Mahitsy ☐ RM 157 Nd55
Mahlab ☐ LAR 127 Lh29
Mahlaing ☐ MYA 86 Ph35
Mahmiya ☐ SUD 135 Mg37
Mahmudabad ☐ IND (UPH) 83 Ok32
Mahmud Abad ☐ IR 62 Ng27
Mahmud-e 'Eraqi ☐ AFG 65 Oe28
Mahmud Jiq ☐ IR 57 Nd27
Mahnar Bazar ☐ IND (BIH) 83 Pc33
Mahneh ☐ IR 64 Nk28
Mahneh ☐ IR 57 Nd27
Mahnomen ☐ USA (MN) 172 Fc22
Mahoba ☐ ☒ IND (UPH) 83 Ok33
Maholi ☐ IND (UPH) 81 Pa32
Mahón = Maó ☐ ☒ E 29 Le51
Mahou ☐ SYR 56 Mj28
Mahora Abd ☐ IR 83 Pa34
Mahoua ☐ RMM 137 Kh39
Mahoua ☐ TCH 139 Lk40
Mahrauni ☐ IND (UPH) 83 Ok33
Mahrès ☐ TN 126 Lf28
Mahri ☐ PK 65 Od32
Mahru Mosque ☒ IR 59 Ne29
Mahur ☐ IND (MHA) 86 Pg33
Mahura ☐ UA 43 Md42
Mahur Island ☒ IND (RJT) 80 Oj32
Maiala ☐ E 29 La49
Maiama ☐ PNG 115 Sd49
Maiauata ☐ BR (PA) 195 Hi46
Maibo ☐ TCH 140 Lk41
Mãicãnteşti ☐ RO 45 Mh45
Mai Chau ☐ VN 87 Qc35
Maiche ☐ F 25 Lg43
Maici ☐ BR (AM) 198 Gj49
Maidanshar = Kowt-e Ashrow ☐ AFG 65 Oe28
Maidenhead ☐ GB 21 Ku39
Maiden, Mount ☒ AUS 104 Rb59
Maiden, Mount ☒ AUS (NT) 106 Rh53
Maidi ☐ RI 91 Rd45
Maidstone ☐ CDN (SK) 169 Ef19
Maidstone ☐ GB 21 La39
Maiduguri ☐ WAN 138 Lf40
Maidukuru ☐ IND (APH) 85 Ok38
Maiela, P.N.della ☒ I 37 Lp48
Mãieruş ☐ RO 45 Mf45
Maigatari ☐ WAN 138 Le39
Maigudo, Mount ☒ ETH 142 Mj42
Maihar ☐ IND (MPH) 83 Pa33
Maiichic ☐ WAN 138 Ld39
Maijishan Shiku ☒ ☐ CHN 72 Qc28
Maikala Range ☒ IND 83 Pa34
Maikapshaghai ☐ KZ 67 Pc22
Maiko ☐ RDC 141 Md46
Maikonkele ☐ WAN 138 Ld41
Maiko, P.N.de la ☒ RDC 141 Md46
Maikoro ☐ TCH 140 Lj41
Mailani ☐ IND (UPH) 81 Pa31
Mailepalli ☐ IND (APH) 83 Ok37
Mailly-le-Camp ☐ F 23 Le42
Maimi ☐ PK 65 Og31
Mainana = Meymaneh ☐ AFG 63 Oc28
Maimón ☐ DOM 186 Ge34
Main ☐ D 33 Lk41
Mainaguri ☐ IND (WBG) 86 Pe32
Mainamati ☒ BD 86 Pf34
Main Brook ☐ CDN 177 Hb20
Mainburg ☐ D 33 Lm42
Main Camp ☐ ZW 152 Md55
Main-Donau-Kanal ☐ D 33 Lm41
Maine ☒ F 22 Ku42
Maine ☐ USA 177 Ge23
Maine Maritime Museum ☒ USA 177 Gf24
Mainé-Soroa ☐ RN 138 Lf39
Maing Kwan ☐ MYA 86 Pj32
Mainit ☐ RP 90 Rc41
Mainland ☒ CDN (NF) 177 Ha21
Mainland ☒ GB 20 An30
Mainling ☐ CHN (TIB) 69 Ph31
Mainoru ☐ AUS (NT) 106 Rh53
Mainpuri ☐ IND 81 Ok32
Main Range ☒ AUS
109 Sg59
Maintenon ☐ F 23 Lb42
Maintirano ☐ RM 157 Nc55
Mainz ☐ D 33 Lj40
Maiparu ☐ YV 193 Ga42
Maipo, Volcán ☒ RCH/RA 208 Gf63
Maipú ☐ RA (MD) 208 Gf62
Maipú ☐ RA (BA) 209 Gk62
Maiqui ☐ RCH 208 Ge62
Maiquetía ☐ YV 193 Gd40
Mairi ☐ BR (BA) 201 Hk51
Mairiripotaba ☐ BR (GO)
201 Hf54
Mairwa ☐ IND (BIH) 83 Pc32
Maisandra ☐ IND (KTK) 84 Oj39
Maisan-e-Imam ☒ IR 59 Nf29
Maisi ☐ C 186 Gc35
Maiṣiagala ☐ LT 39 Mf36
Maisome Island ☒ EAT 144 Mg47
Maison Carrée de Nîmes ☒ F
25 Le47
Maisonnette ☐ CDN (NB)

Majanpek ☐ SCG 44 Mb46
Majenang ☐ RI 95 Qe49
Majes ☐ RI 96 Qk47
Majete Game Reserve ☒ MW
153 Mh53
Majevica ☐ BIH 44 Lt46
Majgaon ☐ IND (MPH) 83 Pb34
Majhgawan ☐ IND (MPH)
83 Pa33
Majhaon ☐ IND (JKD) 83 Pb33
Majholi ☐ IND (MPH) 83 Pa33
Maji ☐ ETH 142 Mh42
Majiahewan ☐ CHN (NHZ)
72 Qc27
Majie ☐ CHN (YUN) 87 Qb33
Majilovac ☐ SCG 44 Mb46
Majimalu ☐ EAT 146 Mf48
Majagón ☐ E 27 Kr51
Majalahar ☐ RI 96 Ra50
Majkop ☐ RUS 49 Na23
Majli-Saj ☐ KS 63 Og25
Majors Place ☐ USA (NV)
170 Ec26
Majskij ☐ RUS (KBA) 57 Nc24
Majuba Hill ☒ ZA 155 Me59
Majuro Atoll ☒ MH 10 Tb09
Majz ☐ YE 60 Nb37
Maka ☐ RI 96 Qk47
Maka ☐ SN 130 Kb37
Maka ☐ SN 130 Kc39
Makabana ☐ RCB 148 Lg47
Makadó ☐ ZW 152 Me56
Maka Gouye ☐ SN 130 Kb37
Makaha ☐ USA (HI) 170 Ca35
Makah Ind. Res. ☒ USA (WA)
168 Dh21
Makak ☐ CAM 139 Lf44
Makaka ☐ RCB 148 Lg47
Makalamabedi ☐ RB 151 Mb56
Makale ☐ RI 91 Ra44
Makalehi ☒ RI 91 Rc44
Makalé ☐ RA (CH) 204 Ha59
Makalogo ☐ MOC 146 Mh52
Makalondi ☐ RN 132 La39
Makalu-Barun N.P. ☒ NEP
81 Pd32
Makalu I ☒ NEP/CHN 81 Pd32
Makami ☐ EAT 146 Mf48
Makami ☐ EAT 146 Mf48
Makanshy ☐ KZ 66 Pe23
Makantaka ☐ NIC 185 Fh39
Makapuu Valley ☒ ZA Me58
Makaranangang ☒ RI 96 Qk47
Makarev'evyj ☐ UA 41 Mf39
Makarfi ☐ WAN 138 Ld40
Makari ☐ CAM 139 Lh39
Makari ☐ GUY 194 Ha43
Makaroa ☐ NZ 113 Te68
Makarov Basin ☒ 4 Ec01
Makarovo ☐ RUS 48 Nb19
Makarska ☐ HR 35 Ls47
Makarska ☐ Z 146 Mf50
Makassar ☐ RI 96 Qk48
Makassar Strait ☐ RI 96 Qj47
Makawo ☒ MYA 86 Pj32
Makay ☒ RM 157 Nc56
Makedaden ☐ TLS 97 Rc50
Makedonien ☐ GR 46 Mb50
Makekeda ☐ RDC 141 Md44
Makekeda ☐ RDC 141 Me44
Makemo Atoll ☒ F 11 Db11
Makere ☐ WAL 136 Ke41
Makere ☐ EAT 146 Mf48
Maketu ☐ NZ 112 Tj64
Makgadikgadi Pans ☒ RB
Makgadikgadi Pans N.P. ☒ RB
Makhmur ☐ IRQ 57 Nb28
Makhtal ☐ IND (APH) 82 Oj37
Makhu ☐ IND (PUB) 80 Oh30
Maki ☐ RI 114 Rh47
Makiefeng ☐ CHN (MB) 169 Ek19
Makijivka ☐ UA 49 Mk21
Makinba ☐ SOL 117 Ta52
Makindu ☐ EAK 144 Mj47
Makingeny Cave ☒ EAK 144
Mk47
Makira ☒ SOL 117 Ta51
Makiya ☐ Z 151 Md52
Makkah ☐ KSA 58 Mk35
Makkovik ☐ CDN 163 Ha08
Makkura ☐ IND (APH) 83 Pb36
Makli Hills ☒ PK 65 Od32
Makoassy ☐ TR 126 Lg38
Mako ☐ H 43 Ma44
Mako ☐ SN 136 Kd39
Makojo ☐ EAT 144 Mg48
Makokou ☐ G 148 Lg45
Makonde ☐ EAT 146 Mh51
Makonde Plateau ☒ EAT 147
Mk51
Makongo ☐ GH 137 Kk41
Makongolosi ☐ EAT 146 Mg50
Makoor ☐ CAM 139 Lf43
Makos ☐ RDC 146 Me49
Makose ☐ ZW 152 Md55
Makotipoko ☐ RCB 148 Lj46
Makou ☐ CHN (HUB) 75 Qg30
Makoua ☐ RCB 148 Lh46
Makovo ☐ SK 42 Lu41
Makovo ☐ MK 44 Mb49
Mąkowarsko ☐ PL 40 Ls37
Maków Mazowiecki ☐ PL
41 Mb38
Makrakómi ☐ GR 46 Mc52
Makran Coast Range ☒ PK
65 Ob33
Makrany ☐ BY 41 Me39
Makrigialós ☐ GR 47 Mf55
Makrinitsa ☐ GR 44 Md51
Makróni ☐ GR 47 Md53
Maksatiha ☐ RUS 48 Mh17
Maksi ☐ IND (MPH) 82 Oh34
Maksudangarh ☐ IND (MPH)
82 Oj33
Maktau ☐ EAK 144 Mk47
Makthar ☐ TN 126 Le28
Makuende ☐ RDC 146 Me49
Makukabu ☐ RDC 149 Mc50
Makum ☐ RDC (ASM) 86 Pk32
Makumbako ☐ EAT 146 Mf50
Makunda ☐ RDC 149 Ma48
Makundurwe ☐ EAT 147 NA49
Makungo ☐ RDC 146 Me49
Makunguvilo ☐ EAT 147 Mf51
Makungwe ☐ Z 146 Mf51
Makurazaki ☐ J 79 Rf30
Makurdi ☐ WAN 138 Le42
Makusi Island ☒ Z 153 Mf54
Makutano ☐ EAK 144 Mh46
Makutano ☐ EAK 144 Mh46
Makutano ☐ EAK 144 Mh48
Makutano ☐ EAK 144 Mh48
Makuti ☐ ZW 152 Me54
Makuyuni ☐ EAT 144 Mh47
Makwero ☐ ZW 152 Md54
Mala ☐ RIM 130 Kd37
Mala ☐ RI 96 Qk49
Mala A.L. ☒ AUS 103 Rf56
Mala ☐ GR 43 Kb48
Mala A.L. ☒ E

Malabo ☐ ☒ GQ 138 Le44
Malabo ☐ RI 96 Qk47
Malabugan ☐ RP 94 Qj41
Malacacheta, T.I. ☒ BR (MG)
203 Hj54
Malacacheta ☐ IND (AAN) 88 Pg41
Malacca ☐ MAL 93 Qb44
Malacky ☐ SK 42 Lr42
Malad City ☐ USA (ID) 171 Ed24
Maladzeczna ☐ BY 39 Mg36
Malá Fatra, N.P. ☒ SK 43 Lu41
Málaga ☐ CO 192 Gd42
Málaga ☐ ☒ E 27 Kq54
Malaga ☐ USA (NM) 171 Eh29
Malain Head ☒ IRL 19 Kn35
Malinliec ☐ PL 40 Lt38
Maline ☐ SN 136 Kd39
Malino, Gunung ☒ RI 91 Ra45
Malino ☐ HR 35 Lp45
Malino ☐ RI 96 Qk48
Malinyi ☐ EAT 146 Mf50
Malipari ☐ IND (WBG) 86 Pe32
Malita ☐ AL 46 Ma50
Mal i Çarrishtë ☒ AL 44 Ma49
Mala Mari ☒ EAK 145 Na43
Mala Mari N.P. ☒ EAK 145 Na43
Malkangiri ☐ IND (ORS)
83 Pa36
Malkawka ☐ CDN (BC) 168 Ea20
Malkera ☐ PNG 115 Sc48
Malakal ☐ SUD 141 Mf38
Malakand ☐ PK 63 Of28
Malakanta ☐ PNG 116 Se46
Malakheti ☐ NEP 81 Pa31
Mala Kladuša ☐ BIH 35 Lq45
Mal'kovo ☐ RUS 59 Mj34
Malala ☐ PNG 115 Sc48
Malalamai ☐ PNG 115 Sd50
Malalaua ☐ PNG 115 Sd50
Malambo ☐ EAT 144 Mh47
Malambo ☐ EAT 146 Mf49
Mala Mechet ☒ UA 45 Mj45
Mala Serdoba ☐ RUS 48 Nc19
Malatya ☐ TR 56 Mk26
Malau'i ☐ IND (PJB) 80 Oh30
Malavalli ☐ IND (KTK) 84 Oj39
Malavi ☐ IR 59 Nd29
Mala Vyska ☐ UA 49 Mf21
Malawali ☐ MAL 94 Qj42
Malawiyia ☐ SUD 135 Mj38
Malay ☐ RP 90 Ra40
Malaybalay ☐ RP 91 Rc41
Malay ☐ IR 57 Ne28
Malay Peninsula ☒ MAL 92 Qc43
Malaybel ☐ SN 93 Qa09
Malazgirt ☐ TR 57 Nb26
Malbaza ☐ RN 132 La39
Malbebale Plain ☒ EAK 145
Mk47
Malbhanguwa ☐ NEP 81 Pa31
Malbon ☐ AUS (QLD) 107 Sa56
Malbon Vale ☐ AUS (QLD)
107 Rk54
Malbooma ☐ AUS (SA) 108 Rh61
Malborghetto ☐ I 34 Lo44
Malbork ☐ PL 40 Lu36
Malbran ☐ RA (SA) 207 Gj60
Malbuisson ☐ F 25 Lg44
Malca Rie ☐ SP 145 Na44
Malcésine ☐ I 34 Ll45
Malchin ☐ D 32 Lm37
Malchow ☐ D 32 Lm37
Malcolm ☐ AUS (WA) 104 Ra60
Maldegem ☐ B 23 Ld39
Malden ☐ USA (MO) 175 Ff27
Maldives ☒ MV 52 Ob09
Maldives ☒ MV 79 Qd44
Maldon ☐ AUS (VIC) 111 Sb63
Maldon ☐ GB 21 La39
Maldonado ☐ EC 196 Ga45
Maldonado ☐ ROU 209
Hc63
Maldybaj ☐ KZ 66 Og24
Maldyty ☐ PL 41 Lu37
Malé ☐ I 34 Ll44
Malea, Gunung ☒ RI 93 Pk45
Maleaea ☐ LS 155 Md60
Male Downs ☐ AUS (WA)
110 Sa64
Male Gacno ☒ PL 40 Lt37
Malegaon ☐ IND (MHT) 82 Oh35
Malegaon Jahagir ☐ IND (MHT)
82 Oj35
Malei ☐ MOC 153 Mj54
Malek ☐ SUD 141 Mf42
Malekan ☐ IR 57 Nd27
Malé Karpaty ☒ CZ 42 Ls42
Malélé ☐ RCB 148 Lg48
Malema ☐ MOC 153 Mh53
Malé Malé ☐ RN 132 La39
Malemba-Nkulu ☐ RDC 146
Md50
Mãlesco ☐ Z 151 Mb59
Malente ☐ D 32 Ll36
Malesherbes ☐ F 23 Lc42
Malestan ☐ AFG 65 Oe29
Malestroit ☐ F 22 Ks43
Malexander ☐ S 31 Lp32
Maléyer ☒ RUS 70 Qe20
Malgobek ☐ RUS (ING) 57 Nc24
Malgrat de Mar ☐ E 29 Lc49
Malha ☐ SUD 134 Md38
Malhanskij hrebet ☒ RUS
70 Qe20
Malhia ☐ YV 193 Gj43
Mali ☐ RDC 146 Md47
Mali ☐ EAK 144 Mk46
Mali ☐ MYA 87 Pk33
Mali ☐ GR 47 Kb48
Mália La ☒ GR 47 Mf55
Malibu ☐ USA (CA) 170 Ea28
Mali Derdap ☐ SCG 44 Mb46
Maligaya ☐ RP 90 Ra40
Malihabad ☐ IND (UPH) 83 Pa32
Mali Island ☒ RI 96 Qk49
Malik ☐ SUD 135 Mf38
Malili ☐ RI 96 Ra47
Malilla ☐ S 31 Lq33
Málila ☐ S 31 Lp33

Mali Lošinj ☐ ☒ HR 35 Lp46
Maliman de Arriba ☐ RA (SJ)
207 Gf60
Malimbong ☐ ZW 152 Me55
Malinalco ☒ MEX 182 Fa36
Malinau ☐ RI 94 Qj44
Malindang, Mount ☒ RP 91 Rb41
Malindi ☐ EAT 147 Mk48
Malindi Marine N.P. ☒ EAK
145 Na47
Malingping ☐ RI 95 Qd49
Malin Head ☒ IRL 19 Kn35
Maliniec ☐ PL 40 Lt38
Maline ☐ SN 138 Kd39
Malino, Gunung ☒ RI 91 Ra45
Malino ☐ HR 35 Lp45
Malino ☐ RI 96 Qk48
Malinyi ☐ EAT 146 Mf50
Malipari ☐ IND (WBG) 86 Pe32
Malita ☐ AL 46 Ma50
Mal i Çarrishtë ☒ AL 44 Ma49
Mala Mari ☒ EAK 145 Na43
Mala Mari N.P. ☒ EAK 145 Na43
Malkangiri ☐ IND (APH) 82 Ok37
Malkapur ☐ IND (MHT) 82 Oj35
Malkawka ☐ IND (ORS)
83 Pa36
Malkawka ☐ VU 118 Td54
Malkwa Tárnovo ☐ BG 45 Mj49
Mal'kovo ☐ RUS 59 Mj34
Mal'kovo ☐ IND (KTK) 82 Oj37
Mallacoota ☐ AUS (VIC)
111 Se64
Mallacoota Inlet ☒ AUS 111 Se64
Malla'is ☐ AUS (SA) 108 Rk63
Mallanganee ☐ AUS (NSW)
109 Sg60
Mallaoua ☐ RN 132 Le39
Mallawi ☐ ET 129 Mf32
Mallee Cliffs N.P. ☒ AUS
Mallee Highway ☒ AUS 110 Sa63
Málles Venosta = Mals im
Vinschgau ☐ I 34 Ll44
Mallorca ☒ E 29 Ld51
Mallorca ☐ E 29 Ld51
Mallow ☐ IRL 19 Km38
Mallwyd ☐ GB 21 Kr38
Malm ☐ N 16 Lk11
Malmberget ☐ S 16 Ma12
Malmesbury ☐ GB 21 Ks39
Malmesbury ☐ ZA 154 Lk62
Malmköping ☐ S 31 Lq31
Malmö ☐ ☒ S 30 Lo35
Malmo ☐ USA (MN) 172 Fd22
Malmslätt ☐ S 31 Lp32
Malngin A.L. ☒ AUS 103 Re54
Maloca ☐ BR (PA) 194 Hc45
Maloca Macu ☐ BR (RR)
193 Gj44
Maloe ☐ BY 41 Me37
Maloelap Atoll ☒ MH
10 Tb09
Malof ☐ RP 90 Ra38
Malojaroslavec ☐ RUS 48 Mj18
Malokuril'skoe ☐ RUS 77 Sa24
Malole ☐ Z 146 Mf51
Malolo ☒ FIJI 119 Tj54
Malolos ☐ RP 90 Ra38
Malolo Plantation Lodge ☒
PNG 115 Sc48
Malolotja Nature Reserve ☒
SD 155 Mf59
Malombo ☐ PL 40 Lu39
Malomice ☐ PL 40 Lq39
Malonda ☐ RDC 149 Mc50
Malong ☐ CHN (YUN) 87 Qb33
Malonga ☐ RDC 149 Mb51
Małopolska ☒ PL 41 Ma40
Mal Pais - Santa Teresa ☐ CR
185 Fh41
Malpartida de Plasencia ☐ E
27 Ko51
Malpas Hut ☐ AUS (QLD)
107 Sb55
Malpaso ☐ MEX (JLC) 182 Eh35
Malpaso ☐ MEX (ZCT) 182 Ej34
Malpe Beach ☐ AUS 84 Oh39
Malpica de Bergantiños ☐ E
26 Km47
Malpils ☐ LV 39 Me33
Malprabha ☐ IND (RJT) 80 Oh32
Maluku ☐ RDC 148 Lh46
Mals im Vinschgau = Málles
Venosta ☐ I 34 Ll44
Malta ☐ I 37 Lp55
Malta ☐ LV 39 Mh34
Malta ☒ M 37 Lp55
Malta ☐ USA (MT) 169 Eg21
Malta ☒ 173 Fk26
Maltahöhe ☐ NAM 154 Lj59
Maltat ☐ A 35 Lo44
Maltby ☐ GB 21 Ku36
Malton ☐ GB 21 Ku36
Maluhusu ☐ CHN 72 Qd35
Maluhusu ☐ RI 91 Rd45
Malu ☐ RI 91 Rc44
Maluku ☒ RI 96 Rc46
Malukalukuang ☒ RI 96 Qj48
Maluku ☐ RDC 148 Lh46
Malumfashi ☐ WAN 138 Ld40
Malunga ☐ RI 96 Qk49
Malungi ☐ RI 96 Qk49
Malungi ☐ RDC 146 Md51
Maluso ☐ RP 91 Rb42
Malut ☐ SUD 135 Mg40
Malutu ☐ RI 96 Qk49
Maluszyn ☐ PL 41 Lu40
Malvan ☐ IND (MHT) 82 Oh37
Malvasia ☐ PE 197 Gb50
Malvern ☐ GB 21 Ks38
Malvernia ☐ AR) 174 Fd28
Maly Ciel ☐ USA 117 Tako
Malý Čurašević ☐ RUS 48 Nd18
Malyj Jenisej ☐ RUS 67 Pj20
Malyj Naryn ☐ KS 66 Oj25
Malyj ☐ UA 48 Mg20
Maly Ptsch ☐ PL 41 Mc37
Malý Anjui ☐ RUS 45 Na18
Mamae Ana ☐ BR (PA) 199 Hb48
Mama Hatun Türbesi ☒ TR
57 Na26
Mamala ☐ RO 45 Mj46
Mamallapuram ☐ IND (TNU)
85 Pa39
Mamantel ☐ MEX (CAM) 183 Ff37
Mamara ☐ RI 96 Qk47

Mamâri ☐ SN 130 Kd38
Manastir Sopoćani ☐ ☒ SCG
54 Ma47
Manastir Studenica ☐ ☒ SCG
54 Ma47
Manastir Žiča ☐ ☒ SCG 54 Ma47
Manat ☐ KZ 67 Pb21
Manat ☐ C 179 Gb35
Manat ☐ C 179 Ga34
Manati ☐ USA (PR) 187 Gg36
Manatuto ☐ TLS 97 Rc50
Manaus ☐ C 192 Gd40
Manaus ☐ BR (AM) 199 Gk48
Manaure ☐ CO 192 Gd40
Man'aung ☐ RI 114 Rj45
Manaure ☐ CO 192 Gd40
Manavat ☒ TR 56 Mf27
Manavat Seläesi ☒ TR 56 Mf27
Manawar ☐ IND (MPH) 82 Oh34
Manawgat ☒ TR 56 Mf27
Mamba C ☐ EAK 146 Mh48
Mamba ☐ LB 136 Ke42
Mamba ☐ RDC 146 Md47
Mambajao ☐ RP 91 Rc41
Mambali ☐ CAM 139 Lg42
Mambasa ☐ RDC 146 Me46
Mamberamo ☐ RI 114 Rj46
Mamberamo Delta ☒ RI 114 Rj46
Mamberamo-Foja Mountains-
Rouffaer Reserves ☒ RI
114 Rk47
Mambil ☐ RN 138 Lf40
Mambia ☐ RG 136 Kd41
Mambila Plateau ☒ CAM/
WAN 139 Lf42
Mambilima Falls ☒ Z 146 Me51
Mamboma ☐ RMM 136 Kf39
Mambolo ☐ WAL 136 Kd41
Mamboré ☐ BR (PR) 204 Hd58
Mambova ☐ Z 151 Mc54
Mamili N.P. ☒ NAM 151 Mb55
Mamirauá ☐ BR 198 Gj47
Mamre ☐ ZA 155 Na40
Mammoth Cave ☒ USA 175 Fg27
Mammoth Cave N.P. ☐ ☒ USA
(WY) 169 Le27
Mammoth Hot Springs ☒ USA
175 Fg27
Mammoth Lakes ☐ USA (CA)
170 Ea27
Mammoth Springs ☐ USA (AR)
175 Ff27
Mamoodate, T.I. ☒ BR (PA)
197 Gd51
Mamoeiro ☐ BR (AC) 198 Gf50
Mamonas ☐ BR (MG) 203 Hj53
Mamonovo ☐ RUS 39 Lu36
Mamoré ☐ BOL (PB) 198 Gh51
Mamoria ☐ BR (AM) 198 Gh51
Mamoudzou ☒ F (MYT) 156 Nc52
Mampikony ☐ RM 156 Nd54
Mampodre ☒ E 26 Kp47
Mampong ☐ GH 137 Kk42
Mampongtin Range ☒ GH
137 Kk42
Mamu ☐ WAN 138 Ld40
Mamudo ☐ WAN 138 Lf40
Mamuil Choique ☐ RA (RN)
208 Ge66
Mamum Malal, P. ☐ RA/RCH
208 Ge65
Mamuliqe ☒ ZW 152 Me55
Mamuno ☐ RB 150 Ma57
Mamure Kalesi ☒ TR 56 Mg27
Mamuras ☐ AL 44 Lu48
Man ☐ CI 137 Kg42
Man ☐ RCA 140 Lh42
Mana Camp ☐ ZW 152 Me53
Manacapurú ☐ BR (AM) 199
Gk47
Manacor ☐ E 29 Ld51
Manadhoo ☐ MV 84 Oc43
Manado ☐ RI 91 Rc45
Managua ☒ NIC 184 Fg39
Manain ☐ OM 61 Nj34
Manakara ☐ RM (PB) 201 Ja49
Manajiv ☐ UA 43 Md41
Manakamana ☐ NEP 81 Pc31
Manakara ☐ RM 157 Nd54
Manambaro ☐ RM 157 Nd57
Manam Island ☒ PNG 115
Sc48
Manamo ☐ YV 193 Gj42
Mananara Avaratra ☐ RM
156 Ne54
Mananjary ☐ RM 157 Nd56
Manankoro ☐ RMM 137 Kg40
Manantali ☐ RMM 136 Ke39
Manantenina ☐ RM 157 Nd57
Manapari ☐ IND (KER)
84 Oj40
Manapire ☐ YV 193 Ge41
Manapouri ☐ NZ 113 Tc68
Manapools N.P. ☐ ☒ ZW
152 Me53
Manaqil ☐ SUD 135 Mg39
Manár ☒ TR 56 Mg27
Manari ☐ IND (MPH) 82 Oh34
Manas ☐ PE 197 Gb51
Manas ☐ SUD 135 Mf38
Manas Hcat ☐ IND (BIH) 86 Pe32
Manatei ☐ IND (KTK) 84 Oj39
Manasquan ☐ IND (KER)
84 Oj40
Manaslu ☒ NEP 81 Pc31
Manaus ☐ RA (AV) 177 Gd26
Manassa ☒ Tiger Reserve ☒ IND
86 Pf32
Manastir Đurdevi Stupovi ☐
SCG 54 Ma48
Manastir Gračanica ☐ SCG
54 Ma48
Manastir Gradac ☐ ☒ SCG
54 Ma47
Manastir Kalenić ☐ SCG 44
Ma47
Manastir Manasija ☐ ☒ SCG
44 Mb47
Manastir Mileševa ☐ SCG
44 Lu47
Manastir Ostrog ☐ SCG 44 Lt48
Manastir Ravanica ☐ SCG
44 Mb47

Mangango ☐ Z 151 Mc53
Manganti ☐ RI 93 Qa46
Mangaon ☐ IND (MHT) 82 Og36
Mangarwar ☐ IND (RJT) 82 Oh33
Mangawan ☐ IND (MPH) 83 Pa33
Mangbwalu ☐ RDC 146 Me46
Mangchang ☐ CHN (GZG)
74 Qf32
Mangdangshan ☒ CHN (FJN) 75 Qj28
Mange ☐ PNG 115 Sd49
Mange ☐ WAL 136 Kd41
Mangen ☐ SN 130 Kb37
Manggar ☐ RI 95 Qe47
Manggasi ☐ RI 114 Rg47
Manggetangan ☐ CHN (GSU) 72 Qe26
Manggopoh ☐ RI 93 Qa46
Mangial ☐ IND (MHT) 82 Oh34
Mangindrano ☐ RM 156 Ne53
Mang'it ☐ UZ 62 Oa24
Manglaralto ☐ EC 196 Fk46
Manglares ☐ CO 192 Ga43
Manglar Zapoton ☒ MEX
183 Fd38
Mangnai ☐ CHN (QHI) 69 Pf27
Mangnai Zhen ☐ CHN (QHI)
69 Pf26
Mangoaka ☐ RM 156 Ne52
Mangochi ☐ MW 153 Mh53
Mango Creek ☐ BH 184 Ff37
Mangok'y ☐ RM 157 Nc56
Mangole ☐ RI 97 Rc46
Mangombe ☐ RDC 141 Md46
Mangoneï ☐ NZ 112 Tg63
Mangoro ☐ BF 137 Kh41
Mangoro ☐ RM (JU) 82 Or35
Mangrove Cay ☐ BS 179 Ga33
Mangrul Pir ☐ IND (MHT)
82 Oj35
Mangshan ☒ CHN 73 Qg28
Mangualde ☐ P 26 Kn50
Mangueigne ☐ TCH 134 Ma40
Mangueira, T.I. ☒ BR 193 Gk44
Mangueirinha ☐ BR (PR) 204 Hd58
Manguel Creek ☒ AUS (WA)
102 Rb54
Manguito ☐ C 179 Fk34
Mangum ☐ USA (OK) 174 Fa28
Mangungu ☐ RDC 148 Lj48
Mangunza ☐ Z 152 Md54
Mangwe ☐ ZW 152 Md55
Mang'o ☐ PRK 76 Rd25
Mangoustou ☒ BF 137 Kh41
Manpur ☐ IND (CGH) 83 Pa35
Mansfield ☐ USA (LA) 174 Fe29
Mansfield ☐ USA (PA) 177 Gb25
Mansfield Jetty ☒ AUS (TA)
181 Fb32
Manticao ☐ RP 91 Rc41
Manu ☐ PE 197 Gd52
Manú ☐ PE 197 Gd51

Maranguape ☐ BR (CE) 201 Ja47

313

Maranhão ○ BR (AM) 199 Hb47
Maranhão ○ BR 191 Hb10
Maranhão ○ BR 202 Hf53
Maranhoto ○ BR (AM) 198 Gj47
Maranhon ○ BR 196 Gc48
Marans F 24 Ku44
Maranura PE 197 Gd52
Marapanim ○ BR (PA) 195 Hg46
Marapi ○ BR 194 Hb45
Mara Rosa ○ BR (GO) 200 Hf52
Marasefi RO 49 Md23
Marasu RO 45 Mh46
Marat UZ 63 Oc24
Marataízes ○ BR (ES) 203 Hk56
Marateca ◇ I 37 Lg46
Marathon ○ CDN (ON) 173 Fg21
Marathon ○ USA (FL) 179 Fk33
Marathon ○ USA (TX) 181 Ej30
Marathónas ○ GR 47 Mj44
Maraú ○ BR (BA) 203 Ja53
Maraú ○ BR (RS) 204 Hd60
Maraudeur ◇ F (GF) 194 Hd44
Maravato de Ocampo ○ MEX (MHC) 182 Ek36
Maravilha ○ BR (AM) 199 Gk47
Maravilha ○ BR (SC) 204 Hd59
Maravilhas ○ BR (MG) 203 Hh55
Maravilla ○ BOL 198 Gg51
Marawah LAR 127 Ma29
Marawi ○ RP 91 Rc41
Marawi SUD 135 Mf36
Maravo Patá ○ BR (PA) 194 Hb45
Marayes ○ RA (SJ) 208 Gg61
Marayoun ○ RL 56 Mh29
Mar'ayt ○ YE 61 Nf37
Marazion ○ GB 21 Kp40
Marbach ○ D 33 Lj41
Marbella ○ E 37 Kq44
Marble Bar ○ AUS (WA) 102 Qk56
Marble Bar Road ⬛ AUS 102 Ra56
Marble Canyon ○ USA (AZ) 171 Ee27
Marble Hall ○ ZA 155 Me58
Marble Hill ○ USA (MO) 175 Ff27
Marble Point ○ ANT (USA) 7 Tb34
Marburg ○ D 32 Lj40
Marcabelí ○ EC 196 Ga47
Marcala ○ HN 184 Fg38
Marcali ○ H 42 Ls44
Marcaltő ○ H 42 Ls43
Marčana ○ HR 35 Lo46
Marcapata ○ PE 197 Ge52
Marcapomacocha ○ PE 197 Gb51
Marcelândia ○ BR (MT) 199 Hc51
Marcelino ○ BR (AM) 199 Gg45
Marcelino ○ BR (AM) 194 Ha55
Marcelo ○ USA (MN) 172 Fc22
Marcelo D ○ BR (PA) 195 He47
March ○ GB 21 La38
Marchagaz ○ AUS (WA) 104 Qj61
Marche ○ I 35 Lo47
Marche-en-Famenne ○ B 23 Lf40
Marchena ○ E 37 Kq44
Marchenoir ○ F 24 La43
Marchinbar Island ⬛ AUS 106 Rj51
Marciac ○ F 24 La47
Marcigny ○ F 25 Le44
Marcilhac ○ RP 90 Ra39
Marcillac-la-Croisille ○ F 24 Lc45
Marcinkonys ○ LT 39 Me36
Marcinkowice ○ PL 41 Ma41
Marcionilio Sousa ○ BR (BA) 201 Hk52
Marco ○ CL 23 Ld40
Marco D ○ USA (FL) 179 Fk33
Marco de Canaveses ○ P 26 Kn49
Marconi N.H.S. ● CDN 176 Ha22
Marco Rondon ○ BR (RO) 198 Gj50
Marcos Juárez ○ RA (CD) 209 Gj62
Marcos Parente ○ BR (PI) 200 Hj49
Marcoux ○ USA (MN) 172 Fb22
Marcus Baker, Mount ▲ USA (AK) 165 Cg15
Mard Abad ○ IR 57 Nf28
Mardan ○ PK 65 Og28
Mar de Ajó ○ RA (BA) 209 Hb64
Mar de Espanha ○ BR (MG) 203 Hj56
Mar del Plata ☆ RA (BA) 209 Hb65
Mardie ○ AUS (WA) 102 Qh56
Mardie Island ⬛ AUS 102 Qh56
Mardin ○ TR 57 Na27
Mardin Dağları ▲ TR 57 Na27
Mardie ○ NCL 118 Td56
Mare ○ RI 96 Rb44
Marea del Portillo ○ C 179 Gb39
Mare aux Crocodiles de Doukou ◆ BF 137 Kj39
Mare aux Crocodiles de Sabou ◆ BF 137 Kj39
Marechal Cândido Rondon ○ BR (PR) 204 Hc58
Marechal Deodoro ○ BR (AL) 201 Jc50
Mareeba ○ AUS (QLD) 107 Sc54
Mareeq ○ SP 145 Nd44
Marema ○ RI 96 Qk49
Marena ○ RMM 130 Kd38
Marenge ○ RDC 146 Md48
Marengo ○ USA (IA) 172 Fd25
Marennes ○ F 24 Ku45
Marerano ○ RM 157 Nc56
Mareth ○ TN 126 Lf29
Mareuil-sur-Lay ○ F 24 Kt44
Marfa ○ M 37 Lp55
Marfa ○ USA (TX) 181 Eh30
Margao ○ IND (GOA) 82 Og38
Margaret Forks ○ CDN (NS) 176 Gk22
Margaret ○ AUS (QLD) 108 Sb59
Margaret ⬛ USA (NY) 102 Qj57
Margaretville ○ USA (NY) 177 Gd24
Margarida ○ BR (MS) 202 Hb56
Margarita ○ PNG 116 Sb48
Margariti ○ GR 46 Mb50
Margaritove ○ RUS 49 Mk22
Margasari ○ RI 94 Qg47
Margate ○ GB 21 Lb39
Margate ○ USA (FL) 179 Fk33
Margate ○ ZA 155 Mf61
Margecany ○ SK 43 Mb42
Margherita ○ IND (ASM) 86 Ph32
Margherita di Savoia ○ I 37 Lr49
Margilan ○ UZ 63 Oe25
Margjol ○ IR 57 Na29
Margone ○ G 24 Lh45
Margos ○ PE 197 Gb51
Margosatubig ○ RP 91 Rb42
Marguerite ○ CDN (BC) 168 Dj19
Margyang ○ CHN (TIB) 68 Pe31
Marhamat ○ UZ 63 Oe25
Marhanec' ○ UA 48 Mj22
Marhoum ○ DZ 125 Kh28
Mari ○ BR (AM) 198 Gh49
Mari ○ PNG 115 Sa50
Mari ○ SYR 56 Na28
Maria ○ MOC 153 Mj54
Maria ○ PE 196 Gb49
Maria Aurora ○ RP 90 Ra38
Maria Elena ○ RCH 207 Gf57
Maria Eugenia ⬛ RA (SF) 207 Gk61

Markham ○ CDN (ON) 173 Ga24
Markham, Mount ▲ 7 Tb35
Markhu ○ PK 80 Oc27
Marki ○ PL 41 Mb38
Markit ○ CHN (XUZ) 66 Oj26
Markivka ○ UA 48 Mk21
Markkleeberg ○ D 32 Ln39
Markópoulo ○ GR 45 Md53
Marko de ⬛ BG 45 Mh47
Markov ○ BF 131 Kk38
Markovo ○ RUS (MA) 54 Td06
Marksewo ○ PL 41 Mb37
Marksville ○ USA (LA) 175 Fe30
Markt Indersdorf ○ D 33 Lk41
Markt Indersdorf ○ D 33 Lk41
Marktredwitz ○ D 33 Lm40
Mark Twain Birthplace S.H.S ● USA 174 Fd26
Mark Twain Boyhood Home & Museum ● USA 175 Fe26
Mark Twain National Forest ● USA 175 Fe27
Mark Twain N.W.R. ● USA 175 Fe26
Mark Twain S.P. ● USA 175 Fe26
Markudi ○ SUD 134 Mb40
Markwassie ○ ZA 155 Md59
Marl ○ D 32 Lh39
Marla ○ AUS (SA) 108 Rh58
Marlborough ○ AUS (QLD) 109 Se57
Marlborough ○ GB 21 Ks39
Marlborough ○ GUY 194 Ha42
Marlborough Sounds ⬛ NZ 113 Th66
Marle ○ F 23 Ld41
Marlin ○ USA (TX) 174 Fb30
Marlinton ○ USA (WV) 175 Fk27
Marl Island ⬛ PNG 115 Sc46
Marlo ○ AUS (VIC) 111 Se64
Marloth Nature Reserve ● ZA 154 Ma62
Marlow ○ GB 21 Ku39
Marlow ○ USA (OK) 174 Fb28
Marmande ○ F 24 La46
Marmara ○ TR 45 Mh50
Marmara Adası ⬛ TR 45 Mh50
Marmaraereglisi ○ TR 45 Mh50
Marmaris Gölü ⬛ TR 47 Mj52
Marmaris ○ TR 47 Mj54
Mármol ○ GF 47 Mg52
Mar Menor ◎ E 27 Kr53
Mar Menor ◎ E 27 Kr53
Marmora ○ CDN (ON) 173 Ga23
Marmore ● I 35 Lo47
Marmot Island ⬛ USA 164 Ce16
Marne ○ D 32 Lj37
Marne ◇ F 23 Ld42
Marne ○ USA (OH) 175 Fg24
Marneuli ○ GE 57 Nb25
Marniu ○ IND (ARP) 86 Ph32
Marnoo ○ AUS (VIC) 110 Sb63
Maro ○ TCH 140 Lh41
Marve ○ YV 193 Gg44
Maroantsetra ○ RM 156 Ne53
Marobi Raghza ○ PK 65 Oe29
Marod ○ IND (CGH) 83 Pa35
Marofandilia ○ RM 157 Nc56
Maroharatra ○ RM 157 Nd56
Marojejy, P.N.de ● RM 156 Ne53
Marol ○ IND 81 Oj28
Marolambo ○ RM 157 Ne56
Maromandia ○ RM 156 Ne53
Maromokotro ▲ RM 156 Ne53
Marondera ☆ ZW 152 Mf55
Maronga ○ AUS (QLD) 109 Se59
Maronvato ○ RM 156 Ne52
Maronvato ○ RM 156 Ne53
Maronvoay ○ RM 156 Nd54
Marovoo ○ RI 96 Ra46
Marqadeh Gharbiyeh ○ SYR 57 Na28
Marquand ○ USA (MO) 175 Ff27
Marquard ○ ZA 155 Md60
Marquelia ○ MEX (GUR) 182 Fa37
Marquesas Islands ⬛ 11 Cb10
Marquesas Keys ⬛ USA 179 Fj33
Marquette ○ USA (MI) 173 Fg22
Marquise ○ F 23 Lb40
Marquq ○ SUD 141 Md41
Marracas ○ MOC 153 Mh54
Marracuene ○ MOC 153 Mj58
Marradong ○ AUS (WA) 104 Qj62
Marradi ○ I 34 Lm46
Marrakba ○ KSA 64 Na38
Marrakba ○ USA (AL) 175 Fg29
Marrakush ○ MA 125 Kf30
Marrakush ○ MA 125 Kf30
Marrawah ○ AUS (TAS) 111 Sc66
Marrée, T.I. ○ BR (AM) 198 Gg49
Marrero ○ USA (LA) 175 Ff31
Marromeu ○ MOC 153 Mh55
Marroqui ○ BR 140 Qh58
Marrua ○ BR 147 Mc49
Marsa ○ M 37 Lp55
Marsa Ben-Mehidi ○ DZ 125 Kj28
Marsabit ○ EAK 144 Mj44
Marsabit National Reserve ● EAK 144 Mj44
Marsa Darur ○ SUD 135 Mj36
Marsa Delwein ○ SUD 122 Nb11
Marsala ○ I 36 Ln53
Marsa Matruh ○ ET 128 Md30
Marsa Mubārak ○ ET 129 Mh33
Marsa Salak ○ SUD 135 Mj35
Marsa Shin'ab ○ SUD 135 Mj35
Marsberg ○ D 32 Lj39
Mars Bay ○ BS 179 Gb34
Marsberg ○ D 32 Lj39
Mars Bay ○ BS 179 Gb34

Marsh Island ⬛ USA 175 Fe31
Mársico Nuovo ○ I 37 Lq50
Marsoui ○ CDN (QC) 176 Gg21
Marssac ◇ B 31 Ls31
Marstal ○ DK 30 Lm36
Marstrand ○ S 31 Lm33
Martaban ○ MYA 88 Pj37
Martap ○ CAM 139 Lg42
Martapura ○ RI 93 Qc48
Martapura ○ RI 94 Qg47
Marte ○ WAN 139 Lg43
Martelange ○ B 23 Lf41
Marten River ○ CDN (ON) 173 Ga22
Martensoya ⬛ N 16 Ma05
Martfu ○ H 43 Ma43
Martí ○ C 179 Fk34
Martigné-Ferchaud ○ F 22 Kt43
Martigny ○ CH 34 Lh44
Martigues ○ F 25 Lf47
Martil ○ MA 125 Kg28
Martin ○ SK 43 Ls41
Martin ○ USA (SD) 172 Ek24
Martin ○ USA (TN) 175 Ff27
Martina Franca ○ I 37 Ls50
Martinborough ○ NZ 113 Th66
Martinborough ○ NZ 113 Th66
Martínez de la Torre ○ MEX (VC) 182 Fb35
Martinho Campos ○ BR (MG) 203 Hh55
Martinique ◆ F 187 Gk38
Martinique Channel ◇ 187 Gk38
Martinópole ○ BR (CE) 201 Hk47
Martinópolis ○ BR (SP) 202 He57
Martinsburg ○ USA (WV) 177 Ga26
Martinsville ○ USA (IN) 175 Fg26
Martinsville ○ USA (VA) 178 Ga28
Martins Well ○ AUS (SA) 108 Rk61
Martin ○ RA (SL) 209 Gg61
Martorell ○ E 27 Lb49
Martos ○ E 27 Kr53
Martuni ○ ARM 57 Nc25
Marudá ○ BR (AP) 195 Hg46
Marudi ○ MAL 94 Qh43
Maruf ○ AFG 65 Oc30
Marum ○ USA (NSW) 111 Se63
Marum, Mount ▲ VU 118 Te54
Marungu ▲ EAT 146 Mf48
Marutea ○ F 10 Bb11
Maru'ura ○ SOL 117 Ta50
Marvão ○ P 27 Kn51
Marv Dasht ○ IR 64 Ng30
Marve Beach ○ IND 82 Og36
Marvejols ○ F 25 Ld46
Marvik ○ N 30 Lg31
Marwa, Mount ▲ GB 20 Ka34
Marvin ○ USA (AR) 175 Fe28
Marvo Lagoon ○ SOL 117 Sk50
Marwah ○ AFG 64 Ob28
Marwar ○ IND 82 Og36
Marwayne ○ CDN (AB) 169 Ee19
Marwick Head ▲ GB 20 Ks33
Marwil ○ TM 62 Oa27
Maryal Bai ○ SUD 141 Md41
Mary Anne Group ⬛ AUS 102 Qh56
Mary Anne Passage ◇ AUS 102 Qh56
Maryborough ○ AUS (QLD) 109 Sg58
Maryborough ○ AUS (VIC) 111 Sb64
Marydale ○ ZA 154 Mb60
Maryland ◇ USA (WA) 168 Dk23
Mary Kathleen uranium deposit ○ AUS (QLD) 107 Rk56
Maryland ◇ USA 177 Gb26
Maryport ○ GB 20 Kr36
Marystown ○ CDN (NF) 177 Hc22
Marysville ○ USA (CA) 170 Dk26
Marysville ○ USA (KS) 174 Fb26
Marysville ○ USA (OH) 173 Fj25
Maryvale ○ AUS (VIC) 107 Sd55
Maryville ○ USA (MO) 174 Fc25
Maryville ○ USA (TN) 178 Fj28
Marzabotto ○ I 34 Lm46
Marzagão ○ BR (GO) 202 Hf54
Marzan Abad ○ IR 57 Nf27
Marzūq ○ LAR 127 Lg33
Masaguro ○ GCA 184 Fe38
Masa guara ○ HN 184 Fg38
Masahunga ○ EAT 144 Mg47
Masai-Mbia ○ RDC 146 Mc47
Masai Steppe ⬛ EAT 147 Mj48
Masaki ○ EAT 147 Mk48
Masalembo besar ⬛ RI 95 Qh48
Masalembo kecil ⬛ RI 95 Qh48
Masalima ⬛ RI 96 Qj48
Masaliti ○ AZ 57 Nd26
Masamba ○ RI 96 Ra47
Masan ○ ROK 79 Re28
Masanga ○ RI (JKD) 83 Pd33
Masanjor ○ IND (JKD) 83 Pd33
Masapin ○ RI 96 Ra46
Masara ○ EAT 147 Mh45
Masaurhi ○ IND (BIH) 83 Pc33
Masaya ○ NIC 184 Fg40

Masia ○ RDC 148 Lj47
Masiaca ○ MEX (SO) 180 Ef32
Masindi ○ EAU 144 Mf45
Masigo ○ EAT 146 Mf49
Masi-Manimba ○ RDC 149 Lj48
Masin ○ RI 96 Qk46
Masindi ○ EAU 144 Mf45
Masindi Port ○ EAU 144 Mg45
Masinga Reservoir ⬛ EAK 144 Mj46
Masingbi ○ WAL 136 Ke41
Masinloc ○ RP 90 Qk38
Masirah ○ OM 61 Nk35
Masirah Channel ◇ OM 61 Nk35
Masis ○ ARM 57 Nc26
Masis ○ SN 49 Nf30
Masisea ○ PE 197 Gc50
Masisi ○ RDC 149 Me47
Masjed-e Soleymān ○ IR 64 Nk31
Masjed Neger ○ AFG 65 Oc28
Masjid Basar ○ RI 92 Ra44
Masjid-e Jame ○ IR 57 Nc26
Masjid-e Jami ○ IR 59 Nf29
Masjid Zahir ◆ MAL 92 Qa42
Maskall ○ BH 184 Ff37
Maskana Minaret ● SYR 56 Mk28
Maski ○ IND (KTK) 82 Oj38
Maskinonge ○ CDN 173 Gd22
Masmak Fort ● KSA 59 Nd33
Masoala, P.N.d'e ● RM 156 Nf53
Masoarivo ○ RM 157 Nc55
Masokut ○ RI 93 Pk46
Masomeloka ○ RM 157 Ne56
Masoni ○ IND (MPH) 83 Ok32
Masoni ○ IND (TN) 174 Fa24
Mason ○ USA (TX) 174 Fa30
Masontown ○ USA (WV) 175 Fk26
Masoyi ○ ZA 155 Mf58
Maspalomas ○ E 124 Kc32
Maspero ○ YV 192 Ge41
Masqat ● OM 61 Nk34
Masrakh ○ IND (BIH) 83 Pc32
Massa ○ I 34 Ll46
Massaango ○ ANG 148 Lj50
Massaca ○ BR (AM) 199 Gk50
Massaguaçu ○ BR 203 Hh57
Massalassef ○ TCH 139 Lj40
Massama ○ WAN 138 Ld39
Massa Marittima ○ I 34 Ll47
Massambará ○ BR (RS) 204 Oh39
Massambará ○ BR (SC) 205 H59
Massangano ○ CAM 139 Lh43
Massangana ○ ANG 148 Lh50
Massangano ○ MOC 152 Mg56
Massangulo ○ MOC 153 Mh53
Massantola ○ RMM 137 Kg39
Massapê ○ BR (CE) 201 Hk47
Massarossa ○ I 34 Ll46
Massassi ○ EAT 147 Mj49
Massatiele ○ ZA 155 Me61
Massawa ○ ER 142 Mk38
Massenya ○ TCH 139 Lj40
Masseube ○ F 24 La47
Massey ○ CDN (ON) 173 Fj22
Massey ○ USA (MD) 177 Ga26
Massi ○ ANG 150 Ma51
Massif Central ● F 25 Ld45
Massif d'Abo ▲ TCH 133 Lh35
Massif d' Alafa ▲ RN 133 Lh34
Massif de Dahra ▲ DZ 126 Lg27
Massif de Chaîne ▲ CAM 139 Lh42
Massif de l'Adrar ▲ DZ 132 Ld33
Massif de l'Aurès ▲ DZ 126 Le28
Massif de la Vanoise ● F 25 Lg45
Massif de l'Esterel ● F 25 Lg47
Massif de l'Ouarsenis ▲ DZ 126 La28
Massif des Bongo ▲ RCA 140 Md41
Massif des Maures ▲ F 25 Lg47
Massif de Taghouaji ▲ RN 132 Le37
Massif de Tchingou ▲ F (NCL) 118 Tc56
Massif de Termit ▲ RN 133 Lf37
Massif du Humboldt ▲ F (NCL) 118 Td56
Massif du Kapka ▲ TCH 134 Ma38
Massif du Manengouba ▲ CAM 138 Le43
Massif du Sud ou de la Hotte ▲ RH 186 Gc36
Massif du Tamqué ▲ RG 136 Kd39
Massilon ○ USA (OH) 173 Fj25
Massillon ○ USA (OH) 173 Fk25
Massina ○ RP 90 Rb40
Massing ○ MOC 153 Mh57
Massinga ○ MOC 153 Mj57
Massingir ○ MOC 153 Mh57

Matadi ○ RDC 148 Lg48
Mata do Buçaco S.P. ● DE 26 Km50
Matador ○ USA (TX) 174 Ek28
Mataga ○ ZW 152 Mf56
Matagalpa ○ NIC 184 Fh39
Matagami ○ CDN (QC) 173 Gb21
Matagorda ○ USA (TX) 181 Fc31
Matagorda ▲ USA (TX) 181 Fc31
Matagorda Island ⬛ USA (TX) 181 Fb31
Matagorda Peninsula ⬛ USA (TX) 181 Fc31
Mata Grande ○ BR (AL) 201 Jb50
Matak ○ C 179 Fk34
Matak ○ KZ 66 Oh25
Matak ⬛ RI 92 Qe44
Makana Island ⬛ NZ 112 Tk64
Matakana Point ▲ NZ 112 Th64
Matakawa ○ NZ 112 Th64
Matala ○ ANG 150 Lh53
Matala ○ GR 47 Me56
Matalam ○ RP 91 Rc42
Mata Lama ○ EAK 145 Mk44
Matalaque ○ PE 197 Ge54
Matam ○ SN 130 Kd38
Matamata ○ NZ 112 Th65
Matamela ○ DR (AM) 198 Gg48
Mata Mata ⬛ ZA 154 Mb58
Matambo ○ EAT 147 Mj49
Matamey ○ RN 132 Le39
Matamoros ○ MEX (COH) 181 Ej33
Matamoros ○ MEX (TM) 181 Fa33
Matandu ○ EAT 147 Mj49
Matane ○ CDN (QC) 176 Gg21
Mata Negra ○ YV 193 Gg41
Matanga ○ RM 157 Nd56
Matanni ○ PK 65 Oe29
Mataniko Falls ● SOL 117 Ta50
Matankari ○ RN 132 Lc39
Matanuska Glacier ⬛ USA 165 Cg15
Matanzas ○ C 179 Fk34
Matanzas ○ YV 193 Gj41
Matão ○ BR (SP) 202 Hf56
Matateco ○ RI 96 Rc44
Matapédia ○ CDN (QC) 176 Gg22
Matara ○ CL 85 Pa43
Matara ○ ER 142 Mk38
Matara ○ IND 82 Og36
Mataracá ○ BR (PB) 201 Jc49
Mataral ○ BOL 206 Gh55
Mataram ☆ RI 96 Qj50
Matarka ○ AUS (NT) 106 Rg53
Mata Redonda ○ MEX (VC) 182 Fb36
Mataró ○ E 27 Lc49
Mata Roma ○ BR (MA) 201 Hj47
Matarombeo Mountains ▲ RI 96 Rb47
Matassat ○ F 24 Ld48
Matasse ○ ANG 148 Lj49
Matawa ○ ER 142 Mk38
Matawai ○ NZ 113 Tj65
Matawil ○ DOM 186 Gd36
Matching Green ○ GB 21 La39
Matehuala ○ MEX (SLP) 182 Ek34
Mateguá ○ BOL 206 Gj52
Matela ○ MEX (SLP) 182 Ek34
Matelot ○ TT 187 Gk40
Matema ○ MOC 153 Mj53
Matera ○ I 37 Lr50
Matétsi ○ ZW 152 Md55
Mateur ○ TN 126 Le27
Matha ○ F 24 Ku45
Mathabiane Pt. ▲ CDN 168 Dg21
Mathews Range ▲ EAK 144 Mj45
Mathilda ○ RA (SF) 209 Gk62
Mathiston ○ USA (MS) 175 Ff29
Mathoura ○ AUS (NSW) 111 Sc63
Mathura ○ IND (UPH) 81 Oj32
Mathura ▲ RP 91 Rd42
Matiakoali ○ BF 131 Kk39
Matian ○ USA (IN) 175 Fg26
Matias Cardoso ○ BR (MG) 201 Hj53
Matias Olimpio ○ BR (PI) 201 Hk47
Matías Romero ○ MEX (OAX) 183 Fc37
Matibane ○ MOC 153 Na53
Matienzo ○ ANT (RA) 6 Ha32
Matihani ○ IND (BIH) 83 Pd33
Matii ○ CHN (JGX) 75 Qj33
Matina ○ CR (LIM) 185 Fj41
Matinhos ○ BR (PR) 205 Hf58
Matisi ○ CHN 69 Pk26
Matjiesfontein ○ ZA 154 Mb61

Matsari ○ CAM 139 Lg43
Matsieng Footprints ● RB 155 Mc58
Matsoandakana ○ RM 156 Ne53
Matsu ○ J 79 Rg28
Matsue ☆ J 79 Rg28
Matsu Lietao ⬛ RC 75 Ra32
Matsumae ○ J 77 Sa25
Matsumoto ○ J 79 Rj27
Matsu Temple ● RC 75 Ra34
Matsusaka ○ J 79 Rh28
Matsuyama ○ J 79 Rg29
Mattamuskeet N.W.R. ● USA 178 Gb28
Mattawa ○ CDN (ON) 173 Ga22
Matterhorn ▲ CH/I 34 Lh45
Matterhorn ▲ USA 170 Ec25
Mattersburg ○ A 35 Lr43
Matthew Town ○ BS 186 Gd35
Matthews Ridge ○ GUY 194 Gk42
Matthew Town ○ BS 186 Gd35
Mattice ○ CDN (ON) 173 Fj21
Mattighofen ○ A 42 Lo42
Matto ○ J 79 Rj27
Mattoon ○ USA (IL) 175 Ff26
Mattusona ○ RM 156 Ne53
Matu ○ MAL 94 Qf44
Matua ⬛ RI 95 Qf47
Matubara ○ PNG 115 Sc48
Matucana ○ PE 197 Gb51
Matumbo ○ Z 146 Mg51
Matumbo ○ Z 146 Mg51
Matupá ○ BR (MT) 199 Hc51
Matupi ○ BR 194 Hc48
Matupika ○ NZ 113 Tg66
Matuq ○ SUD 135 Mg38
Maturin ☆ YV 193 Gj41
Matusadona N.P. ● ZW 152 Me54
Matutuang ⬛ RI 91 Rc43
Matveev Kurgan ○ RUS 49 Mk22
Maty-Centre ○ RCB 148 Lh47
Matyli ○ BY 41 Me37
Mau ○ IND (MPH) 83 Ok32
Mau ○ IND (UPH) 83 Pa34
Mau ○ RI 95 Qf47
Maubara ○ EAK 144 Mj45
Maubeuge ○ F 23 Ld40
Maubin ○ MYA 88 Ph37
Maubourguet ○ F 24 La47
Maude ○ USA (NSW) 111 Sc63
Maudaha ○ IND (UPH) 83 Pa32
Maude ○ AUS (NSW) 111 Sb63
Maudheimvidda ▲ 6 Kc33
Maués ○ BR (AM) 199 Hb47
Maugris ○ RM 130 Kd36
Mauhar ○ IND (UPH) 83 Pa32
Maui ⬛ USA (HI) 170 Cb35
Maul ○ RI 95 Qd49
Maullín ○ RCH 208 Gd66
Maumee ○ USA (OH) 173 Fj25
Maumelle ○ USA (AR) 175 Fe28
Maumere ○ RI 96 Rb50
Maun ☆ RB 151 Mb55
Maunabo ○ USA (PR) 187 Gh36
Maunagala ○ RI 91 Rd43
Maunalua ○ USA (HI) 170 Cb35
Maungala ○ USA 170 Cb36
Maunath Bhanjan ○ IND (UPH) 83 Pa33
Maungdaw ○ MYA 86 Ph35
Maungmagan Islands ⬛ MYA 88 Pj38
Maunoir, Lac ◎ CDN 165 Df12
Maupihaa ⬛ F 10 Ba10
Maupin ○ USA (OR) 168 Dk23
Mauragedo Velho ○ BR (AM) 195 He46
Maura ○ RI 95 Qd49
Maurawan ○ IND (UPH) 83 Pa32
Maure-de-Bretagne ○ F 22 K143
Maurelie Is. Wilderness ● USA 166 Dd18
Mauriac ○ F 25 Lc45
Mauriceville ○ USA (TX) 174 Fd30
Mauricie, P.N. de la ● CDN 176 Gd22
Mauriti ○ BR (CE) 201 Ja49
Mauritius ■ MS 157 Nf59
Mauritshuis ◆ NL 23 Le38
Maury ○ F 25 Lc48
Maury Mts. ▲ USA 168 Dk23
Mauterndorf ○ A 35 Lo43
Mauthausen ○ A 42 Lp42
Mauze-sur-le-Mignon ○ F 24 Ku44
Mauvelin ○ F 24 La47
Mavengue ○ ANG 150 Lk54
Mavericks ⬛ USA (CA) 170 Dj27
Mavila ○ PE 206 Gf51
Mavila ○ PE 206 Gf51
Mavita ○ MOC 152 Mf56
Mavrovoúni ▲ GR 46 Mc51
Mavrovoúni ▲ MK 44 Mb49
Mavouri ○ RI 96 Rb48
Mavrélli ○ GR 46 Mb51
Mavrovo ○ MK 44 Ma49
Mavinzi ○ LV 39 Mf33

Mbanza-Ngungu ○ RDC 148 Lh48
Mbar ○ SN 130 Kc38
Mbarangandu ○ EAT 147 Mj50
Mbarara ☆ EAU 144 Mf46
Mbargué ○ CAM 139 Lg43
Mbarizunga Game Reserve ● SUD 141 Md43
Mbaswana ○ ZA 155 Mg59
Mbawa ○ RCA 140 Lk44
Mbati ○ Z 146 Mf50
Mbatto ○ CI 137 Kh43
Mbatto ○ CI 137 Kh43
Mbé ○ CAM 139 Lg43
Mbé ○ RCB 148 Lg47
Mbé ○ RCB 148 Lg47
Mbebou ○ CAM 138 Le43
Mbebo ▲ RCA 140 Ma43
Mbéli ○ RCB 148 Lg48
Mbengué ○ CI 137 Kh40
Mbengwi ○ CAM 138 Ld42
Mbengwi ○ CAM 138 Ld42
Mbérengwa ○ ZW 152 Me56
Mbesumba Ranch ○ Z 146 Mg51
Mbet ○ CAM 139 Lg43
Mbéti = Alayo ○ RCA 140 Md43
Mbéwé ○ CAM 139 Lg42
Mbeya ○ Z 146 Mg50
Mbeya, Mount ▲ EAT 146 Mg50
Mbiama ○ WAN 138 Ld43
Mbié ○ RCB 148 Lg47
Mbigou ○ G 148 Lf47
Mbinda ○ RCB 148 Lg47
Mbinga ○ EAT 146 Mh49
Mbini ○ GQ 138 Le44
Mbire ○ EAT 144 Mg46
Mbirizi ○ EAU 144 Mf46
Mbizi Mountains ▲ EAT 146 Mf50
Mbo ○ RCA 140 Lk43
Mbo ○ RCB 148 Lg48
Mboké ○ CAM 139 Lg43
Mbokonimbeti Island ⬛ SOL 117 Sk50
Mbomo ○ RCB 148 Lg46
Mbomou ○ RCA 141 Mb43
Mbon ○ RCB 148 Lf47
Mboné ○ RG 136 Ke40
Mbongé ○ CAM 138 Le43
Mboro Nduekat ○ SN 130 Kb38
Mbouda ○ CAM 138 Lf43
Mboula ○ CAM 139 Lg42
Mboumi ○ G 148 Lf47
Mboung-Ouaka ○ RCA 140 Ma43
Mboune ○ RMM 131 Kf37
Mbour ○ SN 130 Kb38
Mbout ○ RIM 130 Kd37
Mbozi ○ EAT 146 Mf50
Mbrès ○ RCA 140 Ma42
Mbuba ○ RCA 140 Ma43
Mbuba ○ CAM 139 Lg42
Mbudi ○ RDC 149 Lk46
Mbulu ○ EAT 144 Mh47
Mbulu ○ EAT 144 Mh47
Mbuma ○ RCA (CR) 204 Ha60
Mburucuyá, P.N. ○ RA 204 Ha59
Mbuti ○ EAT 147 Mh50
Mbuyi-May ○ RDC 149 Lk46
Mbuyapey ○ PY 204 Hb59
Mbuyuni ○ EAT 147 Mj48
Mbwewe ○ EAT 147 Mk49
McAdam N.P. ○ PNG 115 Sd49
Mc Alester ○ USA (OK) 174 Fc28
Mc Allen ○ USA (TX) 181 Fa32
Mc Arthur Lake ○ CDN 167 Eg15
McBee ○ USA (SC) 178 Ga28
McBride ○ CDN (BC) 168 Dk19
McCall ○ USA (ID) 168 Dk23
Mc Camey ○ USA (TX) 181 Ej30
Mc Cammon ○ USA (ID) 169 Ed24
Mc Carthy ○ USA (AK) 165 Cj15
Mc Cauley Island ⬛ CDN 166 Dd18
Mc Clellan Ck. Nat. Grassland ● USA 174 Ek28
McClintock Channel ◇ CDN 163 Ea04
McClintock, Mount ▲ 7 Tb34
McClintock Range ▲ AUS 103 Rd55
Mc Clure Strait ◇ CDN 162 Ea04
Mc Clusky ○ USA (ND) 172 Ek22
Mc Comb ○ USA (MS) 175 Fe30
Mc Connell Range ▲ CDN 167 Dj13
Mc Connell Range ▲ CDN 167 Dj13
Mc Connelsburg ○ USA 177 Ga26
Mc Cook ○ USA (NE) 174 Ek25
Mc Creary ○ CDN (MB) 172 Fa20
Mc Donald ○ USA (KS) 174 Ek26
McDonald Observatory ● USA 181 Eh30
Mc Donough ○ USA (GA) 175 Fh29
McDouall Peak ○ AUS (SA) 108 Rh60
McDowell Lake ○ CDN 172 Fd19
Mcensk ○ RUS 48 Mj19
McFaddin N.W.R. ● USA 174 Fc31
Mc Gee ○ USA (SK) 169 Ed20
McGill ○ USA (NV) 170 Ec26
McGraw Brook ○ CDN 176 Gg22
Mc Gregor ○ USA (MN) 172 Fd22
Mc Gregor ○ USA (ND) 169 Ej21
Mc Gregor Range ▲ AUS (QLD) 108 Sa58
McGuire, Mount ▲ USA 168 Ec23
Mcherrah ▲ DZ 125 Kh32
Mchinga ○ EAT 147 Mk49
Mchinji ○ MW 146 Mg52
Mc Intosh ○ USA (SD) 172 Ek23
Mc Kenzie Bridge ○ USA (OR) 168 Dj23
Mc Kinlay ○ AUS (QLD) 108 Sa56
Mc Kinley, Mount ▲ USA 165 Ce14
Mc Kinney Mts. ▲ USA 181 Eh31
Mc Kinney Mts. ▲ USA 181 Eh31
Mc Laren Vale ○ AUS (SA) 110 Rk63
Mc Laughlin ○ USA (SD) 172 Ek23
Mc Lean's Town ○ BS 179 Gb33
Mc Leod Bay ◇ CDN 167 Ee14
Mc Leod Lake ○ CDN (BC) 166 Dj18
McLeod River ○ CDN 168 Dj19

McLoughlin, Mount ⌂ USA 168 Dj24
Mc Minnville ⊡ USA (OR) 168 Dj23
McMinnville ⊡ USA (TN) 175 Fh28
Mc Murdo ⊡ ANT (USA) 7 Tb34
McMurdo Sound ≋ 7 Ta34
McMurray ⊡ USA (WA) 168 Dj21
McNary ⊡ USA (TX) 171 Eh30
McNeal ⊡ USA (AZ) 171 Ef30
McPherson ⊡ USA (KS) 174 Fb26
McRae ⊡ USA (GA) 175 Fj29
McTavish ⊡ CDN (MB) 172 Fb21
Mdantsane ⊡ ZA 155 Md62
Mdiq ⊡ MA 27 Kp45
M'Doukal ⊡ DZ 126 Lc28
Mdr ⊡ BY 41 Mg37
M'drac ⊡ VN 89 Qe39
Mdsagawen ⊡ CAM
Mead ⊡ CDN (SK) 169 Eh19
Meacham ⊡ USA (OR) 168 Ea22
Mead ⊡ USA (KS) 174 Ek27
Mé Adéo ⊡ F (NCL) 118 Tc56
Meade ⊡ USA 169 Ee24
Meade Peak ⌂ USA 169 Ee24
Meadji ⊡ CI 137 Kg43
Meadow ⊡ CDN (SK) 169 Eh18
Meadow ⊡ AUS 104 Qh59
Meadowbank ⊡ AUS (QLD) 107 Sc55
Meadow Creek ⊡ CDN (BC)
Meadow Lake Prov. Park ⊕ CDN 169 Ef18
Meadowlands Racetrack ⊞ USA (NJ) 177 Gc25
Meadville ⊡ USA (MS) 175 Fe30
Meadville ⊡ USA (PA) 173 Fk25
Meandarra ⊡ AUS (QLD) 109 Se59
Meander River ⊡ CDN (AB) 167 Eb16
Meane Baba Mausoleum ⊞ TM 62 Nk27
Meath Park ⊡ CDN (SK) 169 Eh19
Meaux ⊡ F 23 Lc42
Mebo, Gunung ⌂ RI 114 Rg46
Mebridege ⊡ ANG 148 Lh49
Mebsi ⊡ RI (BIH) 83 Pd37
Mecambelas ⊡ MOC 153 Mh53
Mecca ⊡ KSA 58 Mk35
Mechang ⊡ MAL 92 Qb43
Mechara ⊡ ETH 142 Na41
Mechcheri ⊡ IND (TNU) 84 Oj40
Mechelen ⊡ B 23 Le39
Mécheria ⊡ DZ 125 Kk28
Mechra-Benâbbou ⊡ MA 125 Kg29
Mechra-Ben-Ksiri ⊡ MA 125 Kh28
Mechra-Hassi-Bouédienne ⊡ DZ 125 Kj30
Mechroha ⊡ DZ 126 Ld27
Mecidiye ⊡ TR 45 Mg50
Mecitözü ⊡ TR 56 Mh25
Mečka ⊡ BG 45 Mf47
Meckering ⊡ AUS (WA) 104 Qj61
Mecklenburg-Vorpommern ⊡ D 32 Ln37
Mecklenburg Bay ≋ D 32 Ln37
Mecklenburgische Seenplatte ⌂ D 32 Ln37
Meconta ⊡ MOC 153 Mk53
Mecubúri ⊡ MOC 147 Na52
Mecula ⊡ MOC 147 Mj52
Medak ⊡ IND (APH) 82 Ok36
Medak Church ⊞ IND 82 Ok36
Medak Fort ⊞ IND 82 Ok37
Medale ⊡ ETH 142 Na42
Medan ⊡ RI 92 Pk44
Medang ⊡ RI 93 Qa44
Médanos ⊡ RA (BA) 209 Gj65
Médanos de Coro, T.I. ⌂ YV 193 Gf40
Medaramella ⊡ IND (APH) 83 Ok38
Medawachchiya ⊡ CL 85 Pa41
Medd Allah ⊡ RMM 131 Kh38
Mede ⊡ I 34 Lj45
Médéa ⊡ DZ 126 Lc27
Medeina ⊞ TR 126 Le28
Medeiros ⊡ BR (MG) 203 Hg54
Medeiros Neto ⊡ BR (BA) 203 Hk54
Medellin ⊡ CO 192 Gc42
Medeltidsbyeckan ⊞ S 31 Lt33
Medenblik ⊡ NL 23 Lf38
Medenine ⊡ TN 126 Lf29
Medenýci ⊡ UA 43 Md41
Meder ⊡ ER 142 Na38
Méderdra ⊡ RIM 130 Kc37
Medeu ⊞ KZ 66 Oj24
Medeyal ⊡ SY 31 Ls32
Medford ⊡ USA (OR) 168 Dj24
Medford ⊡ USA (WI) 172 Fe23
Medgidia ⊡ RO 45 Mj46
Medgyesegyháza ⊡ H 43 Mb44
Medhane Alem ⊞ ETH 142 Mj39
Medi ⊡ SUD 144 Mf43
Media Luna ⊡ RA (SL) 208 Gg53
Medianera ⊡ BR (PR) 204 Hc58
Medias ⊡ RO 43 Me44
Medical Springs ⊡ USA (OR) 168 Eb23
Medicina ⊡ I 34 Lm46
Medicine Bow ⊡ USA (WY) 171 Eg25
Medicine Bow Mts. ⌂ USA (WY) 171 Eg25
Medicine Hat ⊡ CDN (AB) 169 Ee20
Medicine Lake ⊡ USA (MT) 169 Eh21
Medicine Lodge ⊡ USA (KS) 174 Fa27
Medijana ⊡ SCG 44 Mb47
Medina ⊡ BR (MG) 203 Hk54
Medina ⊡ KSA 58 Mk33
Medina ⊡ USA (ND) 172 Fa22
Medina ⊡ USA (NY) 173 Ga24
Medina ⊡ USA (OH) 173 Fk25
Medinaceli ⊡ E 29 Ks49
Medina del Campo ⊡ E 26 Kq49
Medina de Pomar ⊡ E 28 Kr48
Medina de Rioseco ⊡ E 26 Kp49
Medina Gounas ⊡ SN 136 Kd39
Medina Sidonia ⊡ E 27 Kp54
Médina-Yorofoula ⊡ SN 136 Kc39
Medinet el'Ameriya el Guedida ⊡ ET 129 Me30
Médinet el-Faijûm ⊡ ET 129 Mf31
Medinet Sahara ⊡ ET 129 Md31
Medininkai ⊞ LT 39 Mf36
Medio Río Negro I, T.I. ⌂ BR 198 Gj46
Medjana ⊡ MA 125 Kg29
Mediterranean Sea ≋ 14 Lb06
Medje ⊡ RDC 141 Md44
Medjedel ⊡ DZ 126 Lc28
Medjez el Bab ⊡ TN 126 Le27
Medley ⊡ CDN (AB) 169 Ee18
Medoc ≋ F 24 Ku45
Medora ⊡ USA (ND) 169 Ej22
Medrissa ⊡ DZ 126 Lb28
Meðugorje ⊞ BIH 35 Ls47
Meðurječje ⊡ SCG 44 Ma47
Medveda ⊡ SCG 44 Mb48
Medvedja ⊡ RUS 48 Mj20

Medvenka ⊡ RUS 48 Mj20
Medyka ⊡ PL 41 Mc41
Medze ⊡ LV 39 Mb34
Medžhid tabija ⊞ SK 43 Mb41
Medzilaborce ⊡ SK 43 Mb41
Meeandah ⊡ AUS (WA) 104 Qh58
Meekatharra ⊡ AUS (WA) 104 Qj58
Meeker ⊡ USA (CO) 171 Eg25
Meeladeen ⊡ SP 143 Ne40
Meeline ⊡ AUS (WA) 104 Qj59
Meenakshi Temple ⊞ IND 84 Oj41
Meerane ⊡ D 32 Ln40
Meersburg ⊡ D 33 Lk43
Meerut ⊡ IND (UPH) 81 Oj31
Meerzorg ⊡ SME 194 Hc43
Mega ⊡ ETH 145 Mk44
Mega ⊡ IND (ARP) 86 Ph31
Mega Escarpment ⌂ ETH
Mega ⊡ RI 97 Rf46
Megáli Panagía ⊡ GR 45 Md50
Megáli Stérna ⊡ GR 44 Mc49
Megálo ⊞ I 35 Lq51
Megalithic Temples ⊞ M 37 Lp55
Megáli Vríssi ⊡ GR 44 Mc49
Megalo ⊡ ETH 142 Nb42
Megalohóri ⊡ GR 46 Mb51
Megalo Horio ⊡ GR 47 Mh54
Megalópoli ⊡ GR 46 Mc53
Megalópoli ⊞ GR 46 Mc53
Megamo ⊡ RI 97 Rf46
Meganissi ⌂ GR 46 Mb52
Mégara ⊡ GR 45 Md52
Mega Spileo ⊞ GR 46 Mc52
Megauda ⊡ SUD 135 Mf36
Megeitia ⊡ SUD 135 Mf38
Megève ⊡ F 25 Lg45
Megezez ⌂ ETH 142 Mk41
Meghalaya ⊡ IND 86 Pf33
Megiddo ⊞ IL 56 Mh29
Meghna ⊡ ARM 57 Nd26
Mégué ⊡ BF 137 Kk39
Meguidene ⊡ DZ 125 La31
Mehakit ⊡ RI 95 Qh47
Meharry, Mount ⌂ AUS 102 Qh57
Mehdawal ⊡ IND (UPH) 83 Pc33
Mehdia ⊡ DZ 126 Lc28
Mehdi Šahr ⊡ IR 62 Ng28
Mehelata ⊡ RI 97 Re46
Meherpur ⊡ BD 86 Pe34
Mehesana ⊡ IND (GUJ) 82 Og34
Mehezangulu ⊡ EAT 147 Mh48
Mehikoorma ⊞ EST 39 Mh32
Mehkar ⊡ IND (MHT) 82 Oj35
Mehrabpur ⊡ PK 65 Od31
Mehran ⊡ IR 64 Nd29
Mehranpark Fort ⊞ IND 80 Og32
Mehrawan ⊡ IND (UPH) 83 Pb33
Mehrgarh ⊞ PK 65 Od31
Mehriz ⊡ IR 62 Nh29
Mehsana ⊡ IND
Mehrz ⊡ IR 64 Ng28
Mehmeg ⊡ RI (JTG) 95 Qf49
Meicheng ⊡ CHN (ZJG) 75 Qk31
Meidougou ⊡ CAM 139 Lh42
Meiganga ⊡ CAM 139 Lh42
Meigu ⊡ CHN (JLN) 76 Rc24
Meiktila ⊡ MYA 86 Ph35
Meilen ⊡ CH 34 Lj43
Meill ⊞ CHN 87 Pk33
Meinersen ⊡ D 32 Ll38
Meinhardt ⊡ D 33 Ll40
Meiningen ⊡ D 33 Ll40
Meinmagwe ⌂ MYA 86 Pg36
Meinmahla Kyun Wildlife Sanctuary ⊕ MYA 88 Pf37
Meira ⊞ E 26 Kn47
Meiringen ⊡ CH 34 Lj44
Meishan ⊡ CHN (AHU) 73 Qh30
Meishan ⊡ CHN (SCH) 74 Qb30
Meißner ⌂ D 32 Lk39
Meitan ⊡ CHN (GZH) 74 Qd32
Mei Xian ⊡ CHN (ISAA) 72 Qd28
Meiyu ⊡ CHN (JLN) 71 Pa23
Meiyu ⊡ CHN (SCH) 87 Qa32
Meizhou ⊡ CHN (GDG) 75 Qj33
Meizhou Dao ⌂ CHN 75 Qk30
Meja Reserve, Gunung ⊕ RI 114 Rg46
Mejillones ⊡ RCH 207 Ge57
Mejo ⊡ YV 193 Gg41
Meka ⊡ AUS (WA) 104 Qj59
Mékambo ⊡ G 148 Lg45
Mekane Selam ⊡ ETH 142 Mk40
Mekdela ⊞ ETH 142 Mk40
Mékel ⊡ CAM 139 Lh44
Mékhé ⊡ SN 130 Kb38
Mekhtar ⊡ PK 65 Oe30
Mekmene Ben Amar ⊡ DZ 125 Kk29
Meknès ⊡ MA 125 Kh29
Meko ⊡ WAN 138 Lb42
Mekomo ⊡ CAM 139 Lh44
Mekong ⊡ 89 Qc40
Mekong Delta ⌂ VN 89 Qd40
Mekonga, Gunung ⌂ RI 96 Ra47
Mekoryuk ⊡ USA (AK) 164 Bg15
Mektib ⊡ EAT 147 Mh48
Meladanga ⊡ RI 96 Rb47
Melaje ⊡ SCG 44 Ma47
Melak ⊡ RI 95 Qh46
Melaka ⊡ MAL 92 Qb43
Melalahti ⊡ FIN 38 Mf28
Melali ⊡ MAL 94 Qd43
Melalih ⊡ RI 97 Rf46
Melanesia ⌂ 100 Sa10
Melanesian Basin ≋ 100 Ta10
Melanesian Basin ≋ 100 Ta10
Melati ⊡ RI 94 Qd45
Melates ⊡ GR 46 Mb51
Melbourne ⊡ AUS (VIC)
Melbourne ⊞ USA (FL) 179 Fk31
Melchor Ocampo ⊡ MEX (DGO) 181 Eh33
Meld ⊡ I 34 Lk36
Meldo ⊡ RCA 140 Ma41
Melegnano ⊡ I 34 Lk45
Meleni ⊡ SQ 205 Hf60
Melenci ⊡ SCG 44 Ma45
Meleuz ⊡ RUS 48 Nb18
Melfi ⊡ I 37 Lq50
Melfi ⊡ TCH 139 Lk39
Melfort ⊡ ZW 152 Me55
Melfort ⊡ CDN (SK) 169 Eh19
Melfort ⊡ ZW 152 Me55

Melinka ⊡ RCH 210 Gd67
Melipeuco ⊡ RCH 208 Ge65
Melipilla ⊡ RCH 208 Ge62
Mélisae ⊡ GR 46 Mc51
Mélito de Porto Salvo ⊡ I 37 Lq54
Melitón Albánez ⊡ MEX (BCS) 180 Ee34
Melitopol ⊡ UA 49 Mh22
Melivia ⊡ GR 46 Mc51
Melk ⊡ A 42 Lq42
Melka Guba ⊡ ETH 145 Mk43
Melka Kuntre ⊞ ETH 142 Mk41
Melka Marl ⊞ ETH 142 Mk41
Melka Teko ~ Gode ⊡ ETH 143 Nb42
Melkrivier ⊡ ZA 155 Me58
Melkosa ⊡ ZA (NSW) 111 Sb62
Meningie ⊡ AUS 110 Rk63
Menkerja ⊡ RUS 55 Ra05
Menku, T.I. ⊠ BR 206 Hb33
Mennonite Colonies ⌂ PY 207 Ha57
Menongue ⊡ ANG 150 Lj53
Menorca ⌂ E 29 Ld50
Mentakab ⊡ MAL 92 Qb44
Mentana ⊡ I 36 Ln48
Mentasta Pass ≋ USA 165 Cj14
Menton ⊡ F 25 Lh47
Mentone ⊡ USA (TX) 181 Ej30
Mentone ⊡ AUS (WA) 104 Ra60
Menzies, Mount ⌂ 7 Oa33
Meo Vac ⊡ VN 87 Qd34
Meongkung ⊡ RI 95 Qa46
Menxing ⊡ CHN (YUN) 87 Qa35
Menyamya ⊡ PNG 115 Sd49
Menyapa, Gunung ⌂ RI 94 Qj45
Menyuan ⊡ CHN (QHI) 72 Qa27
Menza ⊡ RUS 70 Qc31
Menzel Bourguiba ⊡ TN 126 Le27
Menzel Chaker ⊡ TN 126 Lf28
Menzel Temime ⊡ TN 126 Lf27
Menzies ⊡ AUS (WA) 104 Ra60
Menzies, Mount ⌂ 7 Oa33
Meobbi ⊡ MEX (CHH) 181 Eh31
Meoqui ⊡ MEX (CHH) 181 Eh31
Meos Num ⊡ RI 114 Rf46
Meppel ⊡ NL 23 Lg38
Meppen ⊡ D 32 Lh38
Mequinenza ⊡ E 29 La49
Mera ⊡ EC 196 Ga46
Merak ⊡ RI 93 Qc48
Merakan ⊡ RI 115 Sa50
Merauke ⊡ RI 114 Rk49
Merbein ⊡ AUS (NSW) 110 Sb63
Merca = Marka ⊡ SP 145 Nc45
Mercaderes ⊡ CO 192 Gb45
Mercantour ⊠ F/I 25 Lh46
Mercantour, P.N.du ⊕ F 25 Lh46
Mercato Saraceno ⊡ I 34 Ln47
Merced ⊡ USA (CA) 170 Dk27
Mercedario, Cerro ⌂ RA 208 Ge61
Mercedes ⊡ RA (BA) 209 Ha63
Mercedes ⊡ RA (CR) 204 Ha60
Mercedes ⊡ ROU 204 Ha61
Mercedes ⊡ USA (TX) 181 Fb32
Mercuryeiland ⌂ NAM 154 Lh58
Mercury Island ⌂ NAM 154 Lh58
Merdinac ⊡ F 22 Ks42
Meredoua ⊡ DZ 125 Lc29
Merefa ⊡ UA 48 Mj21
Merek ⊡ RO 45 Mg45
Merek ⊡ RI 93 Pk44
Mere Lava ⌂ VU 118 Te53
Mererale ⊡ ETH 143 Nc42
Mereichic ⊡ MEX (SO) 180 Ee30
Mereuch ⊡ K 89 Qd39
Merewa ⊡ ETH 142 Mj42
Merga = Nukhayla ⊡ SUD 134 Md36
Mergui ⊡ MYA 88 Pk39
Mergui Archipelago ⌂ MYA 88 Pk39
Méri ⊡ CAM 139 Lh41
Méri ⊡ SN 130 Kc37
Meribah ⊡ AUS 110 Sa63
Mérida ⊡ E 25 Kp51
Mérida ⊞ MEX (YT) 183 Ff35
Mérida ⊞ YV 192 Ge41
Meridian ⊡ RI 93 Qa45
Meridian ⊡ USA (CT) 177 Gd25
Meridian Island ⌂ CDN 167 Eb15
Mérida ⊡ DZ 125 Kj30
Mérignac ⊡ F 24 Ku46
Mérihas ⊡ GR 47 Me53
Merikarvia ⊡ FIN 38 Mb29
Merimbula ⊡ AUS (NSW)
Mering ⊡ WAN 139 Lg40
Meringur ⊡ AUS (VIC) 110 Sa63
Merino Downs ⊡ NZ 113 Te69
Merir Island ⌂ PAL 90 Rg43
Merij ⊡ MAL 94 Qd44
Merivale ⊡ AUS (QLD) 109 Se58
Merke ⊡ KZ 66 Og24
Merlo ⊡ RA (SL) 208 Gg62
Merluna ⊡ AUS (QLD) 107 Sb52
Mermaid Reef ⊠ AUS 102 Qk54
Mermerna Pecina ⊞ SCG

Mengshan ⊡ CHN (GZG) 74 Qf33
Menguémé ⊡ CAM 139 Lh44
Mengui ⊡ RI 95 Qh50
Menguan ⊡ CHN (GZH) 74 Qe32
Mengyin ⊡ CHN (SDG) 78 Qj28
Mengyou ⊡ CHN (YUN) 87 Qb33
Mengzi ⊡ CHN (YUN) 87 Qb34
Menhir de Champ-Dolent ⊞ F 22 Kt42
Menid ⊡ GR 46 Mb51
Menindee ⊡ AUS (NSW) 111 Sb62
Menindee ⊡ AUS 110 Rk63
Menkerja ⊡ RUS 55 Ra05
Merta ⊡ IND (RJT) 80 Oh32
Merthyr Tydfil ⊡ GB 21 Kr39
Merti ⊡ EAK 145 Mk45
Merti Plateau ⌂ EAK 145 Mk45
Mértola ⊡ P 27 Kn53
Merton ⊡ AUS (TAS) 111 Sd66
Mertoutek ⊡ DZ 132 Lb32
Mertule Maryam ⊡ ETH 142 Mk40
Merty Merty ⊡ AUS (SA) 108 Sa60
Mertz Glacier ≋ 7 Sb32
Mertzon ⊡ USA (TX) 174 Ek30
Meru ⊡ EAK 144 Mj45
Meru ⊡ F 23 Lc41
Merume Mountains ⌂ GUY 194 Ha42
Meru, Mount ⌂ EAT 144 Mj47
Merure, T.I. ⊠ BR 202 Hd53
Merville ⊡ ZA 154 Ma52
Merveveille ⊡ ZA 154 Ma52
Méry ⊡ BY 39 Mh35
Meryemana ⊞ TR 47 Mh53
Merzifon ⊡ TR 57 Mh25
Merzig ⊡ D 33 Lg41
Mezouga ⊡ MA 125 Kh30
Mesa ⊡ USA (AZ) 171 Ee29
Mesa, Cerro ⌂ RA 208 Gf65
Mesa ⊡ USA (AZ) 171 Ee29
Mesa ⊡ CO 171 Ef26
Mesa de Coloradas ⌂ MEX (DGO) 180 Eg32
Mesa del Huracán ⌂ MEX (CHH) 180 Ef31
Mesa del Seri ⊡ MEX (SO) 180 Ee31
Mesagne ⊡ I 37 Ls50
Mesaieed ⊡ Q 59 Nf33
Mesanga ⊡ RI 96 Rd46
Mesa Mountain ⌂ USA 171 Eg27
Mesa Verde N.P. ⊕ ⊞ USA 171 Ef27
Mescalero Apache Ind.Res. ⊠ USA 171 Ef29
Meschede ⊡ D 32 Lj39
Mescit Dağlan ⌂ TR 57 Na25
Meselefors ⊡ S 16 Lj13
Meseta Baya ⌂ RA 208 Gf65
Meseta Cascajos ⌂ RA 210 Ge70
Meseta de Colitoro ⌂ RA 208 Gf66
Meseta de Icutú ⌂ YV 193 Gh42
Meseta de Jáua ⌂ YV 193 Gh43
Meseta de Lago Buenos Aires ⌂ RA 210 Gd68
Meseta del Canquel ⌂ RA 210 Gf68
Meseta del Norte ⌂ MEX 181 Ej31
Meseta de Montamayor ⌂ RA 210 Gg68
Meseta de Somuncurá ⌂ RA 208 Gg66
Meseta El Pedrero ⌂ RA 210 Gf69
Meseta Vizcachas ⌂ RA 210 Ge71
Mesfinto ⊡ ETH 142 Mj39
Mesgouez S.P. ⊠ USA 175 Fe26
Mesgouez S.P. ⊠ USA 175 Fe26
Merampal ⊡ RI 114 Rj48
Merano = Meran ⊡ I 34 Lm44
Merano = Meran ⊡ I 34 Lm44
Meratus, Gunung ⌂ RI 95 Qf49
Merapi, Gunung ⌂ RI 95 Qf50
Meratus Mountains ⌂ RI 95 Qf49
Merauke ⊡ RI 114 Rk49
Merauwah ⊡ UAE 61 Ng33

Meuse ⊟ B 23 Lf40
Meuselwitz ⊡ D 32 Ln39
Méwéguébé ⊡ BF 137 Kk39
Mewat ⊡ IND (RJT) 80 Oh32
Mexia ⊡ USA (TX) 174 Fb30
Mexicali ⊞ MEX (BC) 170 Ec28
Mexican Basin ≋ 183 Fd33
Mexican Plateau ⌂ MEX 181 Eh32
Mexican Water ⊡ USA (AZ) 171 Ef27
México ⊞ MEX 161 Eb07
México ⊡ MEX 182 Fa36
Mexico City = Ciudad de México ● ⊞ MEX 182 Fa36
Mexiko ⊡ RP 90 Rb38
Meyanodas ⊞ ETH 142 Na40
Meybod ⊡ IR 64 Ng29
Meydancik ⊡ TR 57 Nb25
Meyenburg ⊡ D 32 Ln37
Meyer Range, H. ⌂ PNG 116 Sg48
Meymac ⊡ F 25 Lc45
Meymand ⊡ IR 59 Nf30
Méyo Centre ⊡ CAM 139 Lf44
Meyomessala ⊡ CAM 139 Lg44
Meyrueis ⊡ F 25 Ld46
Meyzieu ⊡ F 25 Lf45
Mezali ⊡ MYA 86 Ph35
Mezalingon ⊡ MYA 86 Pg34
Mézaranil ⊡ BG 45 Mf47
Mezdra ⊡ BG 44 Md47
Mezek ⊞ BG 45 Mg49
Mezen' ⊡ RUS 54 Na05
Mezenc ⊡ PL 41 Mc37
Mézessé ⊡ CAM 139 Lg44
Mežica ⊡ SLO 42 Lp44
Mezökövesd ⊡ H 43 Ma44
Mežotnes-Brenne ⊠ F 24 Lb44
Mezieres-sur-Issoire ⊡ F 24 La44
Mézín ⊡ F 24 La46
Mezöberény ⊡ H 43 Ma43
Mezöcsát ⊡ H 43 Ma43
Mezökovácsháza ⊡ H 43 Ma44
Mezökövesd ⊡ H 43 Ma44
Mézos ⊡ F 24 Kt46
Mezötne ⊡ LV 39 Me34
Mezötúr ⊡ H 43 Ma43
Mezra ⊡ TR 57 Mk27
Mfango Island ⌂ EAU 144 Mg46
Mfinga ⊡ EAT 146 Mj49
Mfou ⊡ CAM 139 Lg44
Mfouati ⊡ RCB 148 Lg47
Mfum ⊟ WAN 138 Le43
Mgahinga Gorilla N.P. ⊕ ⊞ EAU 141 Md46
Mgbidi ⊡ WAN 138 Ld43
Mgeta ⊡ EAT 147 Mj50
Mgodi ⊡ Z 146 Mc49
Mgori ⊡ EAT 146 Mh48
M'Guiden ⊡ DZ 125 Kh31
Mhabri ⊡ SYR 56 Mj29
Mhamid ⊡ MA 125 Kg30
Mhangura ⊡ ZW 152 Me54
Mhasvad ⊡ IND (MHT) 82 Oh37
Mhemieden ⊡ SYR 57 Na28
Mhow ⊡ IND (MPH) 82 Oh34
Mi-jima ⌂ J 79 Rd24
Miajadas ⊡ E 27 Kp51
Miajlar ⊡ IND (RJT) 80 Of32
Miamere ⊡ RCA 140 Lk43
Miami ⊡ USA (AZ) 171 Ee29
Miami ⊞ USA (FL) 179 Fk33
Miami ⊡ USA (OK) 174 Fc27
Miami Beach ⊡ USA (FL) 179 Fk33
Mian Channun ⊡ PK 65 Og30
Miandrivazo ⊡ RM 157 Nc55
Miane ⊡ DZ 126 Lc28

Milano ⊞ I 34 Lk45
Milano ⊡ USA (TX) 174 Fb30
Milas ⊡ TR 47 Mh53
Milavidy ⊡ BY 41 Mf38
Milazzo ⊡ I 37 Lq52
Milbank ⊡ USA (SD) 172 Fb23
Mildmay ⊡ CDN (ON) 173 Fk24
Mildred ⊡ USA (MT) 169 Eh22
Mildura ⊡ AUS (VIC) 110 Sb63
Mile ⊡ ETH 142 Na40
Mile ⊡ GR 46 Mb51
Milepa ⊡ MOC 147 Mj51
Miles ⊡ USA 109 Sf59
Miles City ⊡ USA (MT) 169 Eh22
Mile Serdo Reserve ⊕ ETH 142 Na40
Mileševo ⊡ SCG 44 Lu45
Mifeso ⊡ ETH 142 Na41
Milestone ⊡ CDN 169 Eh20
Milford ⊡ IRL 19 Km38
Milet ⊞ TR 47 Mh53
Mileto ⊡ I 37 Lr52
Mileševo ⊡ SCG 44 Lu45
Milford ⊡ MA 125 Kh29
Milford ⊡ USA (CT) 177 Gd25
Milford ⊡ USA (DE) 177 Gc26
Milford ⊡ USA (UT) 171 Ed26
Milford ⊡ USA (UT) 171 Ed26
Milford Haven ⊡ GB 21 Kp39
Milford Sound ⊡ NZ 113 Td68
Milford Sound ⌂ NZ 113 Td68
Mili ⊡ J 79 Re28
Milgarra ⊡ AUS (QLD) 107 Sa55
Miliana ⊡ DZ 126 Lc27
Milici ⊡ BIH 44 Lu46
Milicz ⊡ PL 40 Ls39
Milimbu ⊡ AUS (NT) 106 Rf51
Milin ⊡ CZ 42 Lp41
Milin ⊡ AUS (WA) 104 Qj61
Milina ⊡ GR 46 Mc51
Mineral del Chico ⊡ MEX (HDG) 182 Fa36
Mineral de Pozos ⊡ MEX (GJT) 182 Ak55
Mineral Hot Springs ⊡ USA (CO) 171 Eh26
Mineral'nye Vody ⊡ RUS 57 Sc54
Mineral Springs ⊡ ZA 152 Mf57
Millas ⊡ F 24 Lc48
Millau ⊡ F 25 Ld46
Milledgeville ⊡ USA (GA) 178 Fk29
Millicent ⊡ AUS 110 Sa65
Millington ⊞ USA (TN) 175 Fe28
Millinocket ⊡ USA (ME) 176 Gf23
Millinocket ⊡ USA (ME) 176 Gf23
Million Dollar Point ⌂ VU 118 Td53
Millmerran ⊡ AUS (QLD) 109 Sf59
Millom ⊡ GB 21 Kr36
Millport ⊡ USA (AL) 175 Ff29
Millthorpe ⊡ AUS 109 Se62
Mills Lake ⊟ CDN 167 Ea15
Millstatter See ⊟ A 35 Lo44
Millstream-Chichester N.P. ⊕ AUS 102 Qh56
Milltown ⊡ USA (WV) 175 Fk26
Millungera ⊡ AUS (QLD) 107 Sa55
Millwood ⊡ USA (SA) 104 Qh59
Millwood S.P. ⊠ USA 174 Fd29
Milly Milly ⊡ AUS (WA) 104 Qj59
Milne Bay ≋ PNG 116 Se50
Milngavie ⊡ GB 20 Kq34
Milo ⊡ RG 136 Kf40
Milo ⊡ USA (ME) 176 Gf23
Milolii ⊡ USA (HI) 170 Cc36
Milolii ⊡ USA (HI) 170 Cc36
Miłomłyn ⊡ PL 41 Ma37
Milos ⌂ GR 47 Me54
Milove ⊡ UA 48 Mk21
Miłparinka ⊡ AUS (NSW) 108 Sb61
Milly Milly ⊡ AUS (WA) 104 Qj59
Milpitas de la Sierra ⊡ MEX (ZCT) 182 Ej34
Milrin ⊞ SCG
Milton ⊡ USA (FL) 175 Fg30
Milton ⊡ NZ 113 Te69
Milton ⊡ USA (PA) 177 Gb25
Milton Brandão ⊡ BR (PI) 201 Hk48
Milton Freewater ⊡ USA (OR) 168 Ea22

Minas Gerais ⊡ BR 191 Hb11
Minas Novas ⊡ BR (MG) 203 Hj54
Minattitlán ⊡ MEX (COL) 182 Eh36
Minaya ⊡ E 29 Ks51
Minbya ⊡ MYA 86 Pf35
Minbyar ⊡ MYA 86 Pg35
Minch, The ≋ GB 20 Kp32
Minchinabad ⊡ PK 65 Og30
Mincha ⊡ AZ 57 Nd26
Mindanao ⌂ RP 91 Rd42
Mindanao Sea ≋ RP 90 Rc41
Mindelheim ⊡ D 33 Ll42
Mindelo ⊡ CV 136 Jh37
Minden ⊡ D 32 Lj38
Minden ⊡ USA (LA) 174 Fd29
Minden ⊡ USA (NE) 174 Fa25
Minderoo ⊡ AUS (WA) 102 Qh56
Mindif ⊡ CAM 139 Lh41
Mindik ⊡ PNG 115 Sd49
Mindiptana ⊡ RI 114 Sa49
Mindik ⊡ EC 196 Ga46
Mine ⊡ J 79 Re28
Minehead ⊡ GB 21 Kr39
Mineiros ⊡ BR (GO) 202 Hd54
Mineiros do Tietê ⊡ BR (SP)
Mineola ⊡ USA (TX) 174 Fc29
Mineola ⊡ USA (NY)
Mine Head ⌂ IRL 19 Kn39
Mineral del Chico ⊡ MEX (HDG)
Minecourt ⊡ F 25 Lf41
Mine Center ⊡ CDN (ON) 172 Fc21
Minehead ⊡ GB 21 Kr39
Minehead ⊡ USA 126 Lb28
Mineiros do Tietê ⊡ BR
Miners' Memorial ⊞ ZA 154 Lj60
Miners' Mus. ⊞ CDN 176 Gh23
Minersville ⊡ USA (UT) 171 Ed26
Mineral de Pozos ⊡ MEX
Mineral Water Spring ⌂ MNG 70 Qc22
Mineral Water Springs ⌂ MNG 70 Qc22
Mineral Wells ⊡ USA (TX) 174 Fa29
Minervino Murge ⊡ I 37 Lr49
Minfeng ⊡ CHN (XUZ) 68 Pb27
Mingá ⊡ RDC 146 Md47
Mingala ⊡ RCA 140 Ma43
Mingan ⊡ CDN (QC) 176 Gh20
Mingaora ⊡ PK 63 Og28
Mingary ⊡ GB 20 Kp34
Mingenew ⊡ AUS (WA) 104 Qh59
Minggang ⊡ CHN (HNN) 73 Qh29
Mingfoshan ⊡ CHN (GSU) 67 Pk25
Mingin ⊡ MYA 86 Pg34
Mingin Taung ⌂ MYA 86 Pg33
Minglanilla ⊡ E 29 Kt51
Mingoyo ⊡ EAT 147 Na51
Mingshashan ⊡ CHN 69 Ph26
Mingshul ⊡ CHN (HLG) 76 Rc22
Ming Tombs ⊞ CHN 73 Qj25
Mingxi ⊡ CHN (FJN) 75 Qj32
Mingxian ⊡ AUS (SA) 110 Rj63
Minhla ⊡ MYA 86 Pg35
Miniota ⊡ CDN (MB) 169 Ek20
Minidoka ⊡ USA (ID) 168 Ed24
Minigwal, L. ⊟ AUS (WA) 104 Ra59
Minilya Roadhouse ⊡ AUS 104 Qg57
Minineron ⊡ BR 202 Hd54
Minipi Lake ⊟ CDN 176 Gg22
Minjilang ⊡ AUS (NT) 106 Rg51
Minkébé, P.N.de ⊕ G 148 Lg45
Minlaton ⊡ AUS (SA) 110 Rj63
Minnamoolka ⊡ AUS 107 Sc54
Minneapolis ⊡ USA (KS) 174 Fa26
Minneapolis ⊡ USA (MN) 172 Fd24
Minnedosa ⊡ CDN (MB) 172 Fa20
Minnesota ⊡ USA 174 Fc24
Minnewaukan ⊡ USA (ND) 172 Fa21
Minnie Downs ⊡ AUS (QLD) 109 Sc58
Minnies ⊡ AUS (QLD) 107 Sb54
Mino ⊡ E 26 Kn47
Minong ⊡ USA (WI) 172 Fe22
Minority Village ⊞ CHN 87 Qb35
Minot ⊡ USA (ND) 172 Ek21
Minqin ⊡ CHN (GSU) 72 Qc26
Minquan ⊡ CHN (HNN) 73 Qh28
Min Shan ⌂ CHN 72 Qb28
Minsk ● BY 39 Mh37
Minsk Mazowiecki ⊡ PL 41 Mb38
Mintaka Umm Khuwayt ⊡ LAR 128 Mb30
Mintirib ⊡ OM 61 Nj34
Mintlaw ⊡ GB 20 Ks33
Minto ⊡ CDN (NB) 176 Gg22
Minto ⊡ CDN (ON) 172 Fc19
Minton ⊡ CDN (SK) 169 Eh21

Minas Gerais ⊡ BR 191 Hb11
Minatitlán ⊡ MEX (VC) 183 Fc37
Min Buri ⊡ THA 88 Qa39
Mindanao ⌂ RP 91 Rd42
Mindanao Sea ≋ RP 90 Rc41
Mindelheim ⊡ D 33 Ll42
Mindif ⊡ CAM 139 Lh41
Mindik ⊡ PNG 115 Sd49
Mine Center ⊡ CDN (ON)
Minbya ⊡ MYA 86 Pf35
Mineiros ⊡ BR (GO) 202 Hd54
Mino ⊡ E 26 Kn47
Minya ⊞ ET 129 Mf31
Miomo ⊡ J 34 Lj48
Mió ⊡ J 79 Rf29
Miomo ⊡ CDN (SK) 169 Eh21
Mioulane, Mount ⌂ T 7
Miquelon ⊡ F (SPM) 176 Hc22
Miquihuana ⊡ MEX (TM) 182 Fa34
Mir ⊞ BY 39 Mg37
Mir Abad ⊡ IR 64 Oa31
Mirabel ⊡ CDN (QC) 177 Gc23

Mirabela ☐ BR (MG) 203 Hh54
Miracatu ☐ BR (SP) 205 Hg58
Miracema ☐ BR (RJ) 203 Hj56
Miracema do Tocantins ☐ BR (TO) 200 Hf50
Miradoira ☐ PE 196 Ga49
Mirador ☐ BR (AM) 196 Gd48
Mirador ☐ BR (MA) 200 Hh49
Mirador- Dos Lagunas- Río Azul, P.N. ☐ GCA 183 Ff37
Mira Estrela ☐ BR (SP) 202 He55
Miraflores ☐ BR (AM) 198 Gh47
Miraflores ☐ CO 192 Gd48
Miraflores ☐ CO 192 Ge45
Miraflores ☐ CH 207 Gk58
Miragoâne ☐ RH 186 Gd36
Miraí ☐ BR (MG) 203 Hj56
Miraj ☐ IND (MHT) 82 Oh37
Miramar ☐ BR (AM) 199 Gk48
Miramar ☐ MEX (COL) 182 Eh36
Miramar ☐ RA (BA) 209 Hb65
Miramar ☐ F (CA) 209 Gj61
Miramar ☐ F 25 Le47
Mirambeau ☐ F 24 Ku44
Miramichi ☐ CDN (NB) 176 Gh22
Miramichi Bay ☐ CDN 176 Gh22
Miramont-de-Guyenne ☐ F 24 La46
Miran Shah ☐ PK 65 Oe29
Miran ☐ CHN (XUZ) 67 Pe26
Miran ☐ PK 65 Of30
Miranda ☐ BR (MS) 202 Hb56
Miranda ☐ MOC 146 Mh52
Miranda de Ebro ☐ E 28 Ks48
Miranda do Douro ☐ P 26 Ko49
Miranda do Norte ☐ BR (MA) 200 Hh47
Miranda Downs ☐ AUS (QLD) 107 Sa54
Mirande ☐ F 24 La47
Mirandela ☐ P 26 Kn49
Mirandiba ☐ BR (PE) 201 Ja50
Mirandola ☐ I 34 Lm46
Mirandópolis ☐ BR (MG) 203 Hk53
Mirandópolis ☐ BR (SP) 202 He55
Mirani ☐ IND (UPH) 83 Pc32
Mirani ☐ AUS (QLD) 109 Se56
Miranorte ☐ PE 196 Ge54
Mirani ☐ OM 61 Nk34
Miranle da Sura ☐ BR (RO) 198 Gj51
Mirano ☐ I 34 Lm45
Miranorte ☐ BR (TO) 200 Hf50
Mirante ☐ BR (BA) 203 Hk52
Mirante do Paranapanema ☐ BR (SP) 202 Hd57
Mirapo ☐ PNG 115 Sd50
Miraporanga ☐ BR (MG) 202 Hf55
Mira-por-vos Cays ☐ BS 186 Gc54
Mira-por-vos Passage ☐ BS 186 Gc34
Mirassol ☐ BR (SP) 202 Hf56
Mirassol d'Oeste ☐ BR (MT) 206 Ha53
Miratu, T.I. ☐ BR 198 Gh47
Miravalles ☐ E 26 Ko48
Mir Bachech Kowt ☐ AFG 65 Oe28
Mirbat ☐ OM 61 Nh37
Mirce ☐ PL 41 Md40
Mirebalais ☐ RH 186 Gd36
Mirebeau ☐ F 24 La44
Mirebeau-sur-Bèze ☐ F 25 Lf43
Mirecourt ☐ F 23 Lg42
Mirepoix ☐ F 24 Lb47
Mirgani ☐ IND (BIH) 83 Pc32
Miri ☐ MAL 94 Qg43
Miri ☐ RN 132 Le39
Miriala guda ☐ IND (APH) 83 Ok37
Miriam Vale ☐ AUS (QLD) 109 Sf58
Mirikata ☐ AUS (SA) 108 Rh60
Mirima National Park ☐ AUS (WA) 103 Re53
Mirina Kástro ☐ GR 47 Mf51
Mirinzal ☐ BR (MA) 195 Hh47
Mir Javeh ☐ IR 64 Oa31
Mirlerft ☐ F 24 Ku44
Mir Mövsum Aĝa ☐ AZ 57 Ne26
Miroč ☐ MNE 44 Mb49
Miroğl ☐ AV (RUS) 7 Pc32
Miro ☐ SCG 44 Mc46
Mirogi ☐ EAK 144 Mh46
Mirong ☐ CHN (YUN) 87 Qb34
Mirool ☐ AUS (NSW) 111 Sd63
Mirosławiec ☐ PL 40 Lr37
Mirotice ☐ CZ 42 Lp41
Mirovice ☐ CZ 42 Lp41
Miro ☐ D 32 Lc37
Mirpur Batoro ☐ PK 65 Oe33
Mirpur Khas ☐ PK 65 Oe33
Mirpur Mathelo ☐ PK 65 Oe31
Mirpur Sakro ☐ PK 65 Od33
Mirote ☐ MOC 153 Mk52
Mirrow ☐ CDN (AB) 169 Ed19
Mirsale ☐ SP 145 Nd43
Mirski zamak ☐ BY 41 Mg37
Mirtna ☐ AUS (QLD) 109 Sd56
Mirto ☐ I 37 Lr51
Mirtos ☐ GR 47 Mf55
Miruro ☐ MOC 152 Mf53
Mirzapur ☐ IND (UPH) 83 Pb33
Mirzapur Hills ☐ IND 83 Pb33
Misahualli ☐ EC 196 Gb46
Misali ☐ EAT 146 Mh48
Misamis ☐ F 79 Rb29
Misaki ☐ J 79 Rg29
Misantla ☐ MEX (VC) 182 Fb36
Misau ☐ WAN 138 Lf40
Misawa ☐ J 77 Sa25
Mischii ☐ RO 44 Md46
Miscou Centre ☐ CDN (NB) 176 Gh22
Misele ☐ RDC 149 Lj48
Misery, Mount ☐ NZ 113 Tf67
Mishaleyi ☐ CHN (XUZ) 66 Pa26
Mishamo ☐ EAT 146 Mf48
Mishan ☐ CHN (HLG) 76 Rf23
Mishan ☐ IR 59 Ne30
Mishkeegogamang Indian Reserve ☐ CDN 172 Fe20
Misiki ☐ PNG 115 Sb49
Misima ☐ EAT 147 Mk48
Misima Island ☐ PNG 116 Sg55
Misinchinka Ranges ☐ CDN 166 Dj18
Misiones ☐ RA 204 Hc59
Misiones franciscanas de la Sierra Gorda de Querétaro = Arroyo Seco, Jalpan de Serra, Landa de Matamoros ☐ ☐ MEX 182 Fa35
Misión Platanal ☐ YV 193 Gh44
Misión San Fernando de Velicatá Adac ☐ MEX 180 Ed31
Misión Santa Gertrudis ☐ MEX (BC) 180 Ed31
Misión Santa María de los Angeles ☐ MEX 180 Ec31
Miski ☐ KSA 58 Nb33
Miski ☐ SUD 134 Mc38
Mismar ☐ SUD 135 Mh36
Misinjak ☐ HR 35 Lp46
Misoumin ☐ EAT 146 Mh49
Misratah ☐ LAR 127 Lh29
Misri Shah ☐ IND (UPH) 81 Pa32
Missanabie ☐ CDN (ON) 173 Fh21

Missara ☐ SN 136 Ke39
Misséni ☐ RMM 137 Kg40
Missinaibi Lake ☐ CDN 173 Fj21
Missinaibi Lake Prov. Park ☐ CDN 173 Fj21
Missinaibi River ☐ CDN 173 Fj20
Missinipe ☐ CDN 167 Eh18
Mission ☐ CDN (BC) 168 Dj21
Mission ☐ USA (SD) 172 Ek24
Mission Beach ☐ USA (SD) 107 Sd54
Mission Ridge ☐ USA (SD) 172 Ek23
Mission San Buenaventura ☐ USA 170 Ea28
Mission San Juan Capistrano ☐ USA 170 Ea28
Mission San Luis Obispo ☐ USA 170 Ea28
Mission Santa Barbara ☐ USA 170 Ea28
Mission San Xavier del Bac ☐ USA 171 Ed29
Misso ☐ EST 39 Mh33
Missoula ☐ USA (MT) 168 Ed22
Missour ☐ MA 125 La28
Missouri ☐ USA 174 Fd27
Missouri Breaks Wild and Scenic River ☐ USA 169 Ef22
Missouri City ☐ USA (TX) 174 Fc31
Missouri Valley ☐ USA (IA) 172 Fb24
Mistawasis Ind. Res. ☐ CDN 169 Eg19
Mistelbach ☐ A 42 Lr42
Misterbianco ☐ I 37 Lp53
Misterei ☐ SUD 134 Mb39
Misterhult ☐ S 31 Lr33
Misti, Volcán ☐ PE 197 Ge54
MistelToe S.P. ☐ USA 178 Fj29
Mistras ☐ GR 46 Mc53
Mistretta ☐ I 37 Lp53
Misty Fjords Nat. Mon. ☐ USA 166 De18
Misurata ☐ LAR see Misratah
Mita-Mirim ☐ BR (AM) 198 Gh46
Mita Mita ☐ AUS (VIC) 111 Sd64
Mitan ☐ OM 61 Nj36
Mitatib ☐ SUD 135 Mj37
Mitchell ☐ CDN (ON) 173 Fh21
Mitchell ☐ USA (NE) 171 Ej25
Mitchell ☐ USA (OR) 168 Dk23
Mitchell ☐ USA (SD) 172 Fa24
Mitchell ☐ USA (SD) 172 Ek24
Mitchell and Alice Rivers N.P. ☐ AUS 107 Sb53
Mitchell Falls ☐ AUS 103 Rc53
Mitchell Highway (Queensland) ☐ AUS 109 Sd61
Mitchell, Mount ☐ USA 178 Fj28
Mitchell Highway (New South Wales) ☐ AUS 109 Sd61
Mitchell River ☐ AUS (WA) 103 Rc53
Mitchell River ☐ AUS 107 Sb53
Mitchell River N.P. ☐ AUS 103 Rc53
Mitchelstown ☐ IRL 19 Km38
Miteja ☐ EAT 147 Mk50
Mithankot ☐ PK 65 Of31
Mithi Tiwana ☐ PK 65 Og29
Mithimna ☐ GR 47 Mg51
Mithi ☐ PK 65 Oe33
Mitiamo ☐ AUS (VIC) 111 Sc64
Mitikas ☐ GR 46 Mb52
Mitkof Island ☐ USA 166 Dd17
Mitla ☐ MEX 183 Fb37
Mitly ☐ J 77 Sa27
Mitoko ☐ RDC 140 Ma44
Mitole ☐ EAT 147 Mk50
Mitra ☐ G 148 Lk45
Mitrašinci ☐ MK 44 Mc49
Mitrofania Island ☐ USA 164 Cb17
Mitrovica ☐ RUS 48 Mk21
Mitrovica ☐ SCG 44 Ma47
Mitsamiouli ☐ COM 156 Nb51
Mitsinjo ☐ RM 156 Nd56
Mitsiwa ☐ ER 142 Mk38
Mitsuishi ☐ J 77 Sb24
Mittelandkanal ☐ D 32 Lk38
Mittelrheintal ☐ ☐ D 33 Lj43
Mittenwald ☐ D 33 Lm43
Mitterill ☐ A 34 Ln43
Mitterteich ☐ D 33 Ln41
Mittweida ☐ D 32 Ln40
Mitu ☐ CO 192 Gd46
Mitundu ☐ MW 152 Mg53
Mitunguu ☐ EAK 144 Mj46
Mitwaba ☐ RDC 146 Md50
Mitzic ☐ G 148 Lh45
Miura-hanto ☐ J 79 Rk28
Miuri ☐ EAT 147 Mk50
Mixco ☐ GCA 184 Fe38
Mixtlán ☐ MEX (JLC) 182 Eh35
Miya ☐ WAN 138 Le40
Miyako ☐ J 77 Sa27
Miyake ☐ J 79 Rk28
Miyako Jima ☐ J 79 Rc33
Miyakonojo ☐ J 79 Rf30
Miyandoab ☐ IR 57 Nd27
Miyandasht ☐ IR 59 Ng28
Miyazaki ☐ J 79 Rf30
Miyazu ☐ J 79 Rh28
Miyun ☐ CHN (BJG) 73 Qj25
Mizan Teferi ☐ ETH 142 Mh42
Mizdah ☐ LAR 127 Lg30
Mizen Head ☐ IRL 19 Kj39
Mizevicy ☐ BY 41 Mf38
Mizhhir'ya ☐ UA (SAJ) 72 Qf27
Mizil ☐ RO 45 Mg45
Mizoč ☐ UA 41 Mg40
Mizoram ☐ IND 86 Pg34
Mizpah ☐ USA (MT) 169 Eh22
Mizque Ramon ☐ BOL (COCH) 206 Gh54
Mizuho ☐ ANT (J) 7 Nb32
Mizur ☐ RUS (SO) 57 Nc24
Mizusawa ☐ J 77 Sa26
Mjadzel ☐ BY 39 Mg36
Mjanji ☐ EAU 144 Mg45
Mjanji ☐ EAT 144 Mg45
Mjanje ☐ AL 46 Ma50
Mjøby ☐ S 31 Lq32
Mjönäs ☐ S 31 Lp32
Mjøndalen ☐ N 30 Lk31
Mkalamo ☐ EAT 147 Mk48
Mkanshi Nature Reserve ☐ ZA 155 Nd46
Mkanga ☐ EAT 146 Mh47
Mkangira ☐ EAT 147 Mj50
Mkarangama ☐ EAT 147 Mk49
Mkasi ☐ Z 146 Mg50
Mkasu ☐ RDC 140 Lk44
Mkata ☐ EAT 147 Mk49
Mkhaya Nature Reserve ☐ SD 155 Mf59
Mkhota ☐ MW 146 Mg52
Mkoani ☐ EAT 147 Mk49
Mkokotoni ☐ EAT 147 Mk49
Mkomazi Game Reserve ☐ EAT 144 Mj47
Mkombe ☐ EAT 146 Mh49
Mkuchika ☐ EAT 147 Mk50
Mkushi Boma ☐ Z 146 Me52
Mkushi River ☐ Z 146 Me52
Mkuze ☐ ZA 155 Mg50

Mkuze Game Reserve ☐ ☒ ZA 155 Mg59
Mkwaja ☐ EAT 147 Mk48
Mkwasine ☐ ZW 152 Mf56
Mladá Boleslav ☐ CZ 42 Lq40
Mladá Vožice ☐ CZ 42 Lq41
Mladenovac ☐ SCG 44 Ma46
Mlandizi ☐ EAT 147 Mk49
Mlandzi ☐ EAT 147 Mk49
M'Lang ☐ RP 91 Rc42
Mtawa ☐ PL 41 Ma37
Mlawula Nature Reserve ☐ SD 155 Mf59
Millwane Wildlife Sanctuary ☐ SD 155 Mf59
Mlinište ☐ BIH 35 Lr46
Mljet ☐ HR 35 Ls48
Mljet, N.P. ☐ ☒ HR 35 Ls48
Mlowka ☐ EAT 147 Mk49
Mtynary ☐ PL 41 Ma37
Mtynarze ☐ PL 41 Mb38
Mlyniv ☐ UA 41 Mf40
Mmabatho ☐ ZA 155 Mc58
Mmadinare ☐ RB 152 Md57
Mmamabula ☐ RB 152 Md57
Mmashoro ☐ RB 152 Md56
Mmathethe ☐ RB 155 Mc58
Mmatshumo ☐ RB 151 Mc56
Mnarani Ruins ☐ EAK 145 Mk47
Mnísek nad Hnilcom ☐ SK 43 Ma42
Mnyani ☐ EAT 146 Mh49
Mo ☐ N 30 Lm30
Moa ☐ BR 196 Gd49
Moa ☐ EAT 147 Mk48
Moa ☐ RI 96 Ra66
Moa ☐ RI 97 Re50
Moa ☐ WAL 136 Ke42
Moab ☐ USA (UT) 171 Ef26
Moacsa ☐ RO 45 Mf45
Moa Island ☐ AUS 107 Sb51
Moala ☐ FJI 119 Tk55
Mo'alleman ☐ IR 64 Nh28
Moama ☐ AUS (NSW) 109 Sc61
Moamba ☐ MOC 153 Mf58
Moanda ☐ G 148 Lh46
Moanda R. Ind. Res. ☐ USA 170 Ec27
Moara Vlăsiei ☐ RO 45 Mg46
Moate ☐ IRL 19 Km37
Moatize ☐ MOC 146 Mg52
Moba ☐ RDC 146 Me49
Mobaye ☐ RCA 79 Sa28
Mobayi-Mbongi ☐ RDC 140 Lk44
Mobdoua ☐ RIM 131 Kg38
Moberly ☐ USA (MO) 174 Fd26
Moberly ☐ USA (MO) 174 Fd26
Mobile ☐ USA (AL) 175 Fg30
Mobridge ☐ USA (SD) 172 Ek23
Moca ☐ DOM 186 Ge36
Mocajuba ☐ BR (PA) 195 Hf47
Mocambinho ☐ BR (MG) 203 Hh53
Moçambique ☐ MOC 153 Nb53
Moçâmedes = Namibe ☐ ANG 150 Lg53
Mocanaqua ☐ USA (PA) 177 Gc25
Moccasin ☐ CA (MT) 169 Ef22
Moc Chau ☐ VN 87 Qc36
Moce ☐ FJI 119 Ua55
Mocha ☐ YE 60 Nb39
Moche Pirámides ☐ PE 197 Ga50
Moche Pirámides (Túcume) ☐ PE 196 Ga49
Mochima, P.N. ☐ ☒ YV 193 Gh40
Mochpo ☐ VN 89 Qc40
Mochong ☐ CHN (ZJG) 74 Qd32
Mochudi ☐ RB 155 Md58
Mochumi ☐ PE 196 Ga49
Mociu ☐ RO 44 Md44
Mociu ☐ PL 40 Lr38
Mocimboa da Praia ☐ ☐ ☒ MOC 147 Na51
Mocimboa do Rovuma ☐ MOC 147 Mk51
Mockern ☐ D 32 Lm38
Mockfjärd ☐ S 31 Lp30
Möckmühl ☐ D 33 Lk41
Mo Co ☐ ANG 150 Lh52
Mocoa ☐ CO 192 Gb45
Mocoa ☐ BR (SP) 203 Hg56
Mocoduene ☐ MOC 153 Mh57
Mocorito ☐ MEX (SIN) 180 Eg33
Mocuba ☐ HN 185 Fh38
Moctezuma ☐ MEX (SLP) 182 Ek34
Moctezuma ☐ MEX (SO) 180 Ef31
Mocuba ☐ MOC 153 Mj54
Mocuba ☐ PE 196 Ga49
Modafferi San Rock Paintings ☐ USA 170 Ed28
Modena ☐ USA (CO) 171 Ee27
Modena ☐ I 34 Lm46
Modena ☐ USA (UT) 171 Ee27
Modena ☐ USA (CA) 170 Dk27
Modesto Méndez ☐ GCA 184 Ff38
Modest Town ☐ USA (VA) 177 Gc27
Modhera Sun Temple ☐ IND 82 Og34
Módica ☐ I 37 Lp54
Modigliana ☐ I 34 Lm46
Modinagar ☐ IND (UPH) 81 Oj31
Modjigo ☐ RN 133 Lg37
Modliborzyce ☐ PL 41 Mc40
Mödling ☐ A 42 Lr42
Modoc ☐ USA (SC) 178 Fj29
Modogu ☐ MNG 70 Qe22
Modoh spila ☐ HR 35 Lr48
Modrica ☐ BIH 44 Lt46
Mödrudalur ☐ IS 18 Ke25
Modugno ☐ I 37 Lr49
Modwebi ☐ ☐ AUS (WA) 108 Sb60
Moéfeté ☐ LT 39 Mf35
Moela ☐ PL 40 Lr38
Moelan ☐ F 24 Kr43
Moen ☐ N 16 Ld14
Modo-Too ☐ KS 66 Oh25
Moen ☐ N 16 Ld14
Moengo ☐ SME 194 Hc43
Moeraki Boulders ☐ NZ 113 Tf68
Moerkeskung ☐ CHN (TIB) 68 Pg30
Moero ☐ D 32 Lg39
Moeraki ☐ GB 20 Kr35
Moffat ☐ IND (SAJ) 172 Ek22
Moffin ☐ RO 43 Mc43
Moffa ☐ RI 146 Mf51
Moga ☐ USA (UPH) 80 Oh30
Mogadore ☐ F 26 Kh49
Mogadoudo ☐ F 26 Kh49
Mogadishu = Muqdisho ☐ ☒ SP 145 Nd44
Mogalu ☐ RDC 140 Lk44
Mogalakwena ☐ ZA 155 Me57
Mogadouro ☐ P 26 Kn49
Mogán ☐ E 124 Kb31
Mogadishu ☐ SP 145 Nc44
Mogalu ☐ RDC 140 Lk44
Mogabi ☐ EC 196 Gb48
Mogaung ☐ MYA 86 Ph33
Mogguli ☐ RI 114 Rh46
Mogelin ☐ D 32 Ln38
Mogi das Cruzes ☐ BR (SP) 205 Hg57
Mogi-Guaçu ☐ BR (SP) 203 Hg57
Mogi-Mirim ☐ BR (SP) 203 Hg57
Mogiquiçaba ☐ BR (BA) 203 Ja54
Mogl ☐ ETH 142 Mk41
Moglj ☐ RUS (KAR) 38 Mk34
Mojokerto ☐ RI 95 Qg49
Mogocha ☐ RUS (CTA) 71 Qj20
Mogocin ☐ RUS (CTA) 71 Qj20
Mogaon ☐ IND (MPH) 82 Oh34
Mogod ☐ TN 34 Le48
Mogocha ☐ RUS (CTA) 71 Qj20
Mogodé ☐ CAM 139 Lg40
Mogoch ☐ RUS 55 Ra08
Mogo-Tog ☐ RUS 207 Gf61
Mogoca ☐ RUS (CTA) 71 Qj20
Mogoga ☐ RP 90 Ra35
Mogaung ☐ MYA 86 Ph33

Mogorjelo ☐ BIH 35 Ls47
Mogosoaia ☐ RO 45 Mf46
Mogosoia ☐ RO 45 Mg46
Mogotio ☐ EAK 144 Mh45
Mogpog ☐ RP 90 Ra35
Mogrum ☐ TCH 139 Lh40
Moguer ☐ E 27 Ko53
Mogumber ☐ AUS (WA) 104 Qj61
Mogwase ☐ ZA 155 Md58
Mogzon ☐ RUS 70 Qg20
Mohács ☐ H 43 Lt44
Mohadi ☐ IND 83 Pa35
Mohale's Hoek ☐ LS 155 Md61
Mohali ☐ IND (ND) 172 Ek21
Mohammad Abad ☐ IR 64 Oa30
Mohammad Abad ☐ IR 64 Nh31
Mohammad Agha ☐ AFG 65 Oe28
Mohenbenzéfé ☐ RCB 148 Lj45
Mohammad Hasan Khaan Bridge ☐ IR 62 Ng27
Mohamedia ☐ DZ 125 La28
Mohana ☐ IND (ORS) 83 Pc36
Mohanganj ☐ BD 86 Pf33
Mohania ☐ IND (BIH) 83 Pb33
Mohanlalganj ☐ IND (UPH) 83 Pa32
Mohanpur ☐ NEP 83 Pd32
Moharli ☐ IND (MH) 83 Ok35
Mohdra ☐ IND (MPH) 83 Ok33
Mohe ☐ CHN (HLG) 71 Rb19
Mohe ☐ CHN (HLG) 71 Rb19
Mohe ☐ IND (AAN) 88 Pg42
Moheli = Mwali ☐ COM 156 Nb52
Mohelnice ☐ CZ 42 Lr41
Mohen ☐ FSM 101 Sb09
Mohenjo Daro ☐ ☐ PK 65 Oe32
Möhne ☐ D 32 Lj39
Möhnesee ☐ D 32 Lj39
Mohnyin ☐ MYA 86 Ph33
Moho ☐ PE 206 Gf53
Mohol ☐ IND (MHT) 82 Oh35
Mohon ☐ IND (MHT) 82 Oh37
Mohora ☐ H 43 Lu43
Moho R. Ind. Res. ☐ USA 170 Ec27
Mohyliv-Podil's'kyj ☐ UA 49 Me21
Moi ☐ N 30 Lg32
Moiben ☐ EAK 144 Mh45
Moi Hoa Binh Pagoda ☐ VN 89 Qc41
Moila Point ☐ PNG 117 Sh49
Moimba ☐ ANG 150 Lg54
Moincêr ☐ CHN (TIB) 68 Pa30
Moinii Hills ☐ AT 37 Lm52
Moineşti ☐ RO 45 Mg44
Mõisaküla ☐ EST 39 Mf32
Moisie Ville ☐ RA (SF) 207 Gk61
Moisie ☐ CDN (QC) 176 Gg20
Moissac ☐ F 24 La46
Moisson ☐ F 24 Lc47
Môizan ☐ RI 95 Qg49
Mojakoré ☐ RI 95 Qg49
Mojacar ☐ E 29 Kt53
Mojados ☐ E 26 Kq49
Mojave ☐ USA 170 Ea28
Mojave Desert ☐ USA 170 Ea28
Mojave National Preserve ☐ USA 170 Ec28
Mojiang ☐ CHN (YUN) 87 Qa34
Mojjo das Cruzes ☐ BR (SP) 205 Hg57
Moji-Guaçu ☐ BR (SP) 203 Hg57
Mojikit ☐ CDN 172 Fg19
Môkko ☐ LS 155 Md61
Moklakoré ☐ RI 95 Qg49
Mokattam ☐ SUD 135 Mh37
Mokolo ☐ CAM 139 Lg40
Mokau ☐ NZ 113 Tg64
Mokpho ☐ ROK 78 Rd28
Mokre ☐ PL 40 Ls37
Mokran ☐ IR 64 Oa31
Mokšan ☐ RUS 48 Nc19
Môktama Kwe ☐ MYA 88 Pj38
Mokuti ☐ EAK 140 Lk49
Mokwa ☐ WAN 138 Le41
Mola ☐ RDC 140 Lk44
Mola di Bari ☐ I 37 Ls49
Molalatau ☐ RB 152 Md57
M'lali botig't ☐ UZ 63 Oc25
Molaly ☐ KZ 66 Oe23
Molalaman ☐ IND (PUB) 80 Og31
Molat ☐ HR 35 Lp46
Molatedi ☐ RB 155 Md57
Molave ☐ RP 91 Rb41
Mold ☐ GB 21 Kr37
Moldau = Vltava ☐ CZ 42 Lp41
Modde ☐ N 16 Ld14
Moldova ☐ MD 49 Me22
Moldoveanu ☐ RO 43 Md44
Mole ☐ RDC 140 Ma43
Mole N.P. ☐ IND 82 Oh38
Mole N.P. ☐ GH 137 Kk41
Molepolole ☐ RB 155 Mc58
Môle-SaintNicolas ☐ RH 186 Gd36
Molesworth ☐ AUS (VIC) 111 Sd65
Moletai ☐ LT 39 Mf35
Molfetta ☐ I 37 Ls49
Molibagu ☐ RI 91 Rb45
Molina ☐ RCH 208 Ge62
Molina de Segura ☐ E 29 Kt52
Molimo ☐ LS 155 Md61
Moline ☐ USA (KS) 174 Fb27
Moline ☐ USA (IL) 174 Fe25
Molinella ☐ I 34 Lm46
Molinggapoto ☐ RI 91 Rb45
Molina de Aragón ☐ E 29 Kt50
Molis ☐ I 37 Lq49
Môllan ☐ S 31 Lo31
Molkom ☐ S 31 Lo31
Mollagara ☐ TR 45 Mk50
Mollafeneri ☐ TR 45 Mk50
Mollagara ☐ TM 62 Ng25
Mollagariny ☐ RB 152 Md57
Mollafossen ☐ N 16 Ma11
Mollendo ☐ PE 197 Ge54
Mollerussa ☐ E 28 La49
Mollina ☐ E 27 Kq53
Mölltorp ☐ S 31 Lp32
Mölln ☐ D 32 Ll37
Mol ☐ MYA 86 Pj34
Moloti ☐ RUS 16 Mk22
Moloti ☐ RUS 38 Ms10
Mologitong ☐ CHN (TIB) 69 Pk31
Molokai ☐ USA 170 Cc34
Molong ☐ AUS (NSW) 111 Sd62
Molong ☐ IND (ASM) 86 Pg33

Molopo ☐ RB/ZA 155 Mc58
Moloporivier ☐ ZA 155 Mc58
Mólos ☐ GR 46 Mc52
Moloundou ☐ CAM 139 Lh44
Molsheim ☐ F 23 Lh42
Molteno ☐ ZA 155 Md61
Moluccas = Maluku ☐ RI 96 Re46
Molucca Islands ☐ RI 10 Ra10
Molucca Sea ☐ RI 96 Rb46
Molumbo ☐ MOC 153 Mj53
Molunat ☐ HR 35 Lt48
Molwe ☐ RDC 151 Mc51
Mona ☐ MOC 153 Mk54
Monaca ☐ USA (WI) 173 Ff23
Monaco ☐ ☐ ☐ MC 25 Lh47
Monaghan ☐ IRL 19 Ko36
Monahans ☐ USA (TX) 181 Ej30
Mona Passage ☐ DOM/USA 186 Gf36
Monapo ☐ MOC 153 Na53
Mona Quimbundo ☐ ANG 149 Lk50
Monarch Mtn. ☐ CDN 168 Dh20
Monari ☐ RCB 65 Oe29
Monasterace Marina ☐ I 37 Lr52
Monasterio de Guadalupe ☐ E 27 Ko51
Monasterio de Leyre ☐ E 28 Kt49
Monasterio de Piedra ☐ E 28 Kt50
Monasterio de San Juan de la Peña ☐ E 28 Ku49
Monasterio de Veruela ☐ E 28 Kt49
Monasterio de Yuste ☐ E 27 Kp50
Monasterio di Sabiona = Kloster Säben ☐ I 34 Lm44
Monastery of Saint Anthony ☐ ET 129 Mg31
Monastery of Saint Catherine ☐ ET 129 Mg31
Monastery of Saint Paul ☐ ET 129 Mg31
Monastery of Saint Simeon ☐ ET 129 Mg33
Monastir ☐ F 23 Ld44
Monastir ☐ TN 126 Lf28
Monastyryśće ☐ UA 49 Me21
Monastyrys'ka ☐ UA 43 Me41
Monatélé ☐ CAM 139 Lf43
Monbroé ☐ CAM 139 Lh41
Moncalieri ☐ I 34 Lh46
Moncalvo ☐ I 34 Lh46
Monção ☐ BR (MA) 200 Hh47
Monção ☐ E 26 Km49
Mončegorsk ☐ RUS 16 Mj12
Mönchengladbach ☐ D 32 Lg39
Monchy ☐ SDN (SK) 169 Eg21
Moncks Corner ☐ USA (SC) 178 Fk29
Monclova ☐ MEX (COH) 181 Ek32
Moncontour ☐ F 22 Ks42
Moncqu ☐ F 24 Lb46
Mondego ☐ P 26 Kn50
Mondéjar ☐ E 27 Kr50
Mondello ☐ I 36 Lo52
Mon Desir ☐ NAM 150 Lh55
Mondim de Basto ☐ P 26 Kn49
Mondjamboli ☐ RDC 140 Ma44
Mondjigo ☐ RDC 149 Mb46
Mondo ☐ EAT 147 Mk49
Mondo ☐ TCH 133 Lh38
Mondocino ☐ USA (CA) 170 Dh26
Mondolfo ☐ I 35 Lo47
Mondombe ☐ RDC 149 Mb46
Mondoñedo ☐ E 26 Ko47
Mondonguillo ☐ CR 185 Fj40
Mondovì ☐ I 34 Lh46
Mondoubleau ☐ F 22 Lb43
Mondra ☐ MNG (IM) 72 Qf23
Mondragone ☐ I 36 Lp49
Mondriz ☐ E 26 Ko47
Mondy ☐ RUS (BUR) 70 Qa20
Moneague ☐ JA 186 Gb36
Moneasa ☐ RO 43 Mc44
Monein ☐ F 24 Ku47
Monemvassía Kástro ☐ GR 46 Mc54
Monesterio ☐ E 27 Ko52
Monestir de Montserrat ☐ E 28 La49
Monestir de Santes Creus ☐ E 29 La49
Moneta ☐ USA (WY) 169 Eg24
Monett ☐ USA (MO) 174 Fc27
Monfalcone ☐ I 35 Ln45
Monforte de Lemos ☐ E 26 Kn48
Monforte ☐ P 26 Kn51
Mongagua ☐ BR (SP) 205 Hg58
Mongalla Game Reserve ☐ SUD 144 Mh43
Mongalow ☐ RDC 144 Mf45
Mongar ☐ BD 86 Pf33
Mongemputu ☐ RDC 149 Ma47
Monggui ☐ RI 114 Rh46
Mongo ☐ TCH 133 Lj39
Mongol Daguo ☐ MNG 73 Qh22
Mongo ☐ TCH 133 Lj39
Mongol Daguan Nature Reserve ☐ MNG 71 Qh21
Mongol Els ☐ MNG 53 Pb05
Mongolia ☐ MNG 53 Pb05
Mongomo ☐ GQ 139 Lg44
Mongororo ☐ TCH 134 Mb39
Mongotong ☐ CHN (TIB) 69 Pk31
Môngpawng ☐ MYA 86 Pj34
Mongu ☐ Z 151 Mb53
Mongua ☐ ANG 150 Lh54
Mönguel ☐ RIM 130 Kd37
Mông Yai ☐ MYA 87 Pk35
Mông Yang ☐ MYA 87 Pk35
Mông Yawng ☐ MYA 87 Qa35
Mông Yu ☐ MYA 86 Pk34
Mónistir ☐ D 33 Ll42
Mönistir ☐ D 33 Lg40
Moni ☐ RI 96 Ra50
Monika ☐ MYA 86 Pk34
Moni Agios Ioanni Theologou ☐ GR 47 Mg53
Moni Arkádi ☐ GR 47 Mf55
Mónica ☐ USA (WI) 173 Ff23
Monikie ☐ GB 17 Kq35
Moni Dochiariu ☐ GR 45 Me50
Monimpébougou ☐ RMM 131 Kh38
Moni Simonos Pétras ☐ GR 46 Me50
Môniste ☐ EST 39 Mg33
Monivong (AB) 169 Ej19
Monivong (AB) 169 Ej19
Monkayo ☐ RP 91 Rd42
Monkey Bay ☐ MW 153 Mh53
Monkey Mia ☐ AUS (WA) 104 Qg58
Mönkhbulag ☐ MNG 70 Qd22
Mónki ☐ PL 41 Mc37
Monkoto ☐ RDC 149 Mb46
Monmouth ☐ GB 21 Ks39
Monmouth Park ☐ USA (NJ) 177 Gc25
Monnow ☐ GB 21 Ks39
Mono ☐ TG 137 Lb42
Monocacy ☐ USA (MD) 177 Gb26
Monolithos ☐ GR 47 Mh54
Monolithos ☐ GR 47 Mh54
Monomoy ☐ USA (NY) 177 Gc25
Monopoli ☐ I 37 Ls49
Monou ☐ TCH 134 Md37
Monowai ☐ NZ 113 Td68
Monreal del Campo ☐ E 29 Kt50
Monreale ☐ I 36 Lo52
Monroe ☐ USA (LA) 175 Fe29
Monroe ☐ USA (GA) 178 Fj29
Monroe ☐ USA (UT) 171 Ee26
Monroe ☐ USA (MI) 173 Fj25
Monroe ☐ USA (WA) 168 Dj22
Monroe ☐ USA (NC) 178 Fk28
Monroe ☐ USA (NY) 177 Gc25
Monroe City ☐ USA (MO) 174 Fd26
Monroeville ☐ USA (AL) 175 Fg30
Mons ☐ B 23 Ld40
Monsaras ☐ P 27 Kn52
Monsaraz ☐ P 27 Kn52
Monselice ☐ I 34 Lm45
Monsenhor Gil ☐ BR (PI) 201 Hj48
Mons Klint ☐ DK 30 Lm36
Mönsterås ☐ S 31 Lr33
Mont Abourak ☐ RMM 132 La37
Montagnac ☐ F 25 Ld47
Montagnana ☐ I 34 Lm45
Montagne Azul Paulista ☐ BR (SP) 202 Hd57
Montagne d'Ambre, P.N.de la ☐ ☐ RM 156 Ne52
Montagne de Lure ☐ F 25 Lf46
Montagne de Nganha ☐ CAM 139 Lh42
Montagne du Lubéron ☐ F 25 Lf47
Montagne Noire ☐ F 24 Lc47
Montagnes Arawa ☐ F 194 Hd44
Montagnes del'Afdé ☐ RIM 130 Kd37
Montagnes Trinité ☐ F 194 Hd43
Mont Agou ☐ TG 137 La42
Montague ☐ USA (TX) 174 Fb29
Montague ☐ CDN (PE) 176 Gj22
Montague ☐ CA 154 Ma62
Montalbán ☐ E 29 Ku50
Montalcino ☐ I 34 Lm47
Montalegre ☐ ANG 148 Lj52
Montalegre ☐ P 26 Kn49
Montalieu-les-Bains ☐ F 24 Ki45
Montalto di Castro ☐ I 34 Lm48
Montalto Uffugo ☐ I 37 Lr51
Montalvánia ☐ BR (MG) 203 Hh53
Montalvo ☐ EC 196 Gb46
Montamarta ☐ E 26 Kp49
Montana ☐ BG 44 Md47
Montana ☐ USA 169 Ee22
Montaña de Celaque ☐ HN 184 Ff38
Montaña de Comayagua ☐ HN 184 Ff38
Montaña Punta Piedra ☐ HN 184 Fh38
Montañas de Colón ☐ HN 185 Fh38
Montañas de Comayagua ☐ HN 184 Ff38
Montañas de Convento ☐ EC 196 Ga46
Montañas del Norte de Chiapas ☐ MEX 183 Fd37
Montañas de Onzole ☐ EC 196 Ga45
Montañas de Patuca ☐ HN 184 Fh38
Monta̅nas de Yoro ☐ HN 184 Fh38
Montañas de Yoro ☐ HN 184 Fg38
Montanha ☐ BR (ES) 203 Hk55
Montargil ☐ P 26 Km51
Montargis ☐ F 25 Ld43
Montataire ☐ F 23 Lc41
Montauban ☐ F 24 Lb47
Montauban-de-Bretagne ☐ F 22 Ks42
Montauk ☐ USA (NY) 177 Gd25
Montbard ☐ F 25 Le43
Mont Bata ☐ RCA 140 Mb43
Montbazillac ☐ F 24 La46
Montbazon ☐ F 24 La44
Montbéliard ☐ F 25 Lg43
Mont Bélo ☐ RCB 148 Lh46
Mont Birougou ☐ ☐ G 148 Lg46
Mont Birougou, P.N.de ☐ ☐ ☐ G 148 Lg46
Montblanc ☐ F/I 25 Lg45
Montbrison ☐ F 25 Le45
Montbron ☐ F 24 La45
Monteau-les-Mines ☐ F 25 Le44
Monthermé ☐ F 23 Le41
Monção ☐ BR (MA) 200 Hh47

Montes de Oca ☐ RA (BA) 209 Gj65
Montes de Toledo ☐ E 27 Kq51
Monte Senes ☐ I 36 Lk50
Montes des Ksour ☐ DZ 125 Kk29
Monte Sholl ☐ I 36 Lk50
Monte Sigfried ☐ RA (QLD) 109 Gc70
Mont-Dore ☐ F (NCL) 118 Td57
Mont Douan ☐ CI 136 Kg42
Monte Sírino ☐ I 37 Lr50
Mont du Métal ☐ DZ 132 Le35
Montesquieu-Volvestre ☐ F 24 La47
Monte Skyring ☐ RCH 210 Gd73
Montespluga ☐ I 34 Lk44
Montebello Islands ☐ AUS 102 Qh56
Monte Stewart ☐ RCH 210 Ge73
Monte Tetris ☐ RA 210 Gd73
Monte Triste ☐ RA (PA) 194 Hd47
Monte Urtigu ☐ I 34 Lj50
Monte Alben, P.N.de ☐ GQ 138 Lf45
Monte Vettore ☐ I 35 Lo48
Monte Viso ☐ I 34 Lh46
Montevarchi ☐ I 34 Lm47
Montevedeo ☐ ROU 209 Hb63
Monte Velino ☐ I 34 Lo48
Monte Victoria ☐ RCH 210 Gd72
Monte Vigía ☐ RCH 210 Gc72
Monte Vulture ☐ I 37 Lq50
Monts de la Medjerda ☐ DZ/TN 126 Le27
Monts de Ouled Nail ☐ DZ 126 Ld28
Monts des Nementcha ☐ DZ 126 Le28
Monts des Traras ☐ DZ 125 Kk28
Monts de Tébessa ☐ DZ 126 Le28
Monts de Tlemcen ☐ DZ 125 Kk28
Monts du Cantal ☐ F 25 Lc45
Monts du Hodna ☐ DZ 126 Lc28
Monts du Hombori ☐ RMM 131 Kj38
Monts du Muzâl ☐ DZ 132 Ld33
Monts du Zab ☐ DZ 126 Lc28
Montségur ☐ F 24 Lb48
Montseny ☐ E 29 Lc49
Montserrat ☐ GB 187 Gk37
Montserrat ☐ GB 187 Gj37
Monts Grouix ☐ CDN 176 Gg20
Montsinery ☐ F (GF) 194 Hd43
Monts Kabyé ☐ TG 137 La41
Monts Manding ☐ RMM 136 Kf39
Monts Marungu ☐ RDC 146 Me49
Monts Mitumba ☐ RDC 146 Me48
Monts Mugila ☐ RDC 146 Me49
Monts Notre-Dame ☐ CDN 176 Gg22
Monts Otish ☐ CDN 176 Ge19
Monts Totomal ☐ RN 133 Lh35
Montsúirs ☐ F 22 La42
Mont Ténibre ☐ F 25 Lg46
Mont Teza ☐ BU 146 Me47
Mont Tonkoui ☐ CI 136 Kg42
Mont Toussoro ☐ RCA 140 Mb43
Mont Tremblant ☐ F 176 Gc22
Montverde ☐ I 29 Lc51
Mont Ventoux ☐ F 25 Lf46
Monument Hill S.H.S. ☐ USA 181 Fb31
Monument Natural Alerce Costero ☐ RCH 208 Gd66
Monumento ao Padre Cícero ☐ BR (CE) 201 Ja49
Monumento Natural de Junín ☐ PE 197 Gc51
Monumento Natural Ballena Franca Austral ☐ I ☐ RA 209 Gj67
Monumento Natural Bosques Petrificados ☐ RA 207 Gd68
Monumento Natural Cerro Ñielol ☐ RCH 208 Gd65
Monumento Natural Contumo ☐ RCH 208 Gd64
Monumento Natural Dos Lagunas ☐ RCH 210 Ge68
Monumento Natural Isla Cachagua ☐ RCH 208 Ge62
Monumento Natural Laguna de los Cisnes ☐ RCH 210 Ga73
Monumento Natural Laguna de los Pozuelos ☐ RA 207 Gh57
Monumento Natural Los Pingüinos ☐ ☐ RCH 210 Ge72
Monumento Natural Pichasca ☐ RCH 207 Ge61
Monumento Natural Salar de Surire ☐ RCH 206 Gf55
Monumento Natural Valle del Encantado ☐ RCH 208 Ge61
Monument Rocks ☐ USA 174 Ek26
Monuments romains et romans d'Arles ☐ F 25 Le47
Monument Valley Navajo Tribal Park ☐ USA 171 Ee27
Monywa ☐ MYA 86 Ph34
Monze ☐ Z 152 Md54
Monzón ☐ PE 197 Gb50
Monzón ☐ E 28 La49
Mooketsi ☐ ZA 152 Mf57
Moola ☐ Z 151 Mb54
Moolawatana ☐ AUS (SA) 108 Rk60
Mooloogool ☐ AUS (WA) 104 Qk58
Moolooha Wharf ☐ AUS 109 Sg59
Mooloo Downs ☐ AUS (WA) 104 Qh58
Moomba ☐ AUS (SA) 108 Sa60
Moonan Flat ☐ AUS (NSW) 109 Sf61
Moonaree ☐ AUS (SA) 108 Rh61
Moonee Valley Racecourse ☐ AUS (VIC) 111 Sc64
Moonshine Beach ☐ USA (CA) 170 Dk28
Moon ☐ AUS (WA) 104 Qj61
Moonyoonooka ☐ AUS (WA) 104 Qh60
Moora ☐ AUS (WA) 104 Qj61
Moorarie ☐ AUS (WA) 104 Qj58
Moorcroft ☐ USA (WY) 169 Eh23
Moordkuil ☐ ZA 154 La62
Moore ☐ USA (MT) 169 Ef22
Moore ☐ USA (ID) 171 Ea24
Moore Islands, Sir G. ☐ AUS 103 Rd52
Moore Park ☐ AUS (QLD) 109 Sg58
Moore River Estuary ☐ AUS 104 Qh61
Moore's Island ☐ BS 179 Ga32
Moorea ☐ F 11 Ca11
Moorhead ☐ USA (MN) 172 Fb22
Mooroongga Island ☐ AUS 106 Rj51
Moorosi, Mount ☐ LS 155 Me61
Moorsburg ☐ D 33 Lm42
Moosburg ☐ D 33 Lm42
Moose ☐ USA (WY) 171 Ee24
Moose Creek ☐ USA (AR) 175 Fd29
Moosehead Lake ☐ USA 176 Gf23
Moose Jaw ☐ CDN (SK) 169 Eg21
Moose Lake ☐ CDN (MB) 172 Fa20
Moose Law ☐ CDN (SK) 169 Eh20
Moose Mountain Prov. Park ☐ CDN 169 Ej21
Moose Mountain Ski Resort ☐ USA (AK) 165 Cg13
Moose River ☐ CDN 173 Fk20
Moosomin ☐ CDN (SK) 172 Ek20
Moosonee ☐ CDN (ON) 173 Fk20
Mootwingee ☐ AUS (NSW) 109 Sb61
Mop ☐ IND (MHT) 82 Oj36
Mopeia ☐ MOC 153 Mk54
Mopipi ☐ RB 151 Mc56
Mopti ☐ RMM 131 Kh38

Moqatta ☐ SUD 135 Mh38

Moqor – Muhu

Moqor AFG 65 Od29
Moquegua PE 197 Ge54
Moquehuá RA (BA) 209 Ha63
Mór H 42 Lt43
Mora CAM 139 Lh40
Mora E 27 Kr51
Mora GUY 194 Ha42
Mora P 27 Km52
Mora S 17 Lh15
Mora USA (MN) 172 Fd23
Mora USA (NM) 171 Eh28
Morabgi IND (MHT) 82 Oh37
Morača klisura SCG 44 Lu48
Moradabad IND (UPH) 81 Ok31
Morada Nova BR (CE) 201 Ja48
Morada Nova de Minas BR (MG) 203 Hh55
Mora de Rubielos E 29 Ku50
Moradlu IR 57 Ne26
Morado, Cerro RA 207 Gh57
Morafeno RM 157 Nd54
Morafenobe RM 157 Nc54
Morąg PL 41 Lu37
Mórahalom H 43 Lu44
Morai RI 114 Rh49
Moraine St. Park USA 173 Ga25
Morais de Almeida BR (PA) 199 Hc49
Morakovo SCG 44 Lu48
Morakowo PL 40 Ls38
Móra la Nova E 29 La49
Moral de Calatrava E 27 Kr52
Moraleja E 27 Ko50
Moralinta RM 157 Nc58
Moramanga RM 157 Ne55
Moramo Bay RI 96 Rb48
Moramo Waterfall RI 96 Rb48
Moran USA (KS) 174 Fc27
Morangas BR (MS) 202 Hd55
Moran Junction USA (WY) 169 Ee24
Morant Cays JA 186 Gb37
Morar IND (MPH) 83 Ok32
Morarano RM 157 Nd56
Morarano Chrome RM 157 Ne54
Morărești RO 43 Me45
Moratalla E 29 Kt52
Moratuwa CL 85 Ok42
Morava CZ 42 Ls41
Moravița RO 44 Mb45
Morávka CZ 42 Lt41
Moravská Třebová CZ 42 Lr41
Moravské Budějovice CZ 42 Lq41
Moravské Lieskové SK 42 Ls42
Moravský Beroun CZ 42 Ls41
Moravský kras CZ 42 Lr41
Moravský Krumlov CZ 42 Lr41
Morawa AUS (WA) 104 Qj60
Morawhanna GUY 193 Gk41
Morawica PL 41 Ma40
Moray Downs AUS (QLD) 109 Sd56
Moray Firth GB 20 Kr33
Morbach D 33 Lh41
Morbanipari, Mount PNG 115 Sb48
Morbarakeh IR 59 Nf29
Mörbylånga S 31 Lr34
Morcego BR (AM) 198 Gj47
Morcenx F 24 Ku46
Morcheh Khort IR 59 Nf29
Morcillo MEX (DGO) 181 Eh33
Morcone I 37 Lp49
Mordaga CHN (NMZ) 71 Ra20
Mordelles F 22 Kt42
Morden AUS (NSW) 108 Sb61
Mordogan TR 47 Mg52
Mordovo RUS 48 Na19
Mordvinia RUS 48 Nb18
Mordy PL 41 Mc38
Morecambe GB 21 Ks36
Morecambe Bay GB 21 Ks36
Moreda E 27 Kr53
Moree AUS (NSW) 109 Se60
Morée F 22 Lb43
Morehead PNG 115 Sa50
Morehead USA (KY) 175 Fj26
Morehead City USA (NC) 178 Gb28
Moreilândia BR (PE) 201 Ja49
Moreli CDN (PE) 176 Gj22
Morelia CO 192 Gc45
Morelia CO 196 Gd46
Morelia MEX (MHC) 182 Ek36
Morella AUS (QLD) 109 Sb57
Morella E 29 Ku50
Morelos MEX (COH) 181 Ek31
Morelos MEX (SO) 180 Ee31
Morelos MEX 182 Fa36
Moremi Game Reserve RB 151 Mb55
Moremi Gorge RB 152 Md57
Morena IND (MPH) 83 Oj32
Moreni RO 45 Mf46
Móres I 36 Lj50
Moresby Island CDN 166 Dd19
Moreton AUS (QLD) 107 Sb52
Moreton-in-Marsh GB 21 Kt39
Moreton Island AUS 109 Sg59
Moreton Island N.P. AUS 109 Sg59
Moret-sur-Loing F 23 Lc42
Moreuil F 23 Lc41
Morez F 25 Lg44
Morfou = Güzelyurt CY 56 Mg28
Morgan AUS (SA) 110 Rk63
Morgan USA (UT) 171 Ee25
Morgan City USA (LA) 175 Fe31
Morganfield USA (KY) 175 Fg27
Morgan Hill USA (CA) 170 Dk27
Morganito YV 193 Gg43
Morganton USA (NC) 178 Fk28
Morgantown USA (KY) 175 Fg27
Morgantown USA (WV) 177 Ga26
Morgan Vale AUS (SA) 110 Sa62
Morgenzon ZA 155 Me59
Morges CH 34 Lg44
Morgins CH 34 Lg44
Morgongåva S 31 Lr31
Morgos RO 43 Md44
Morgram IND (WBG) 86 Pe33
Morgun-Tajga RUS 67 Pf20
Morhange F 23 Lg42
Mori CHN (XUZ) 67 Pf24
Mori J 77 Sa24
Moriah, Mount USA 171 Ec26
Moriani-Plage F 34 Lk48
Moriarty USA (NM) 171 Eg28
Morib MAL 92 Qa44
Moribaya RG 136 Kf41
Morib Beach MAL 92 Qa44
Moricetown CDN (BC) 166 Dg18
Morichal YV 193 Gj41
Morichal Viejo CO 192 Ge44
Morigbadougou RG 136 Kf41
Morija LS 155 Md60
Morijo EAK 144 Mh46
Moriki WAN 132 Ld39
Morin Dawa CHN (NMZ) 71 Rc21
Morinville CDN (AB) 169 Ed19
Morioka J 77 Sa26
Morire MOC 153 Mh54
Moritzburg D 32 Lo39
Morjärv S 16 Mb12
Morlaàs F 24 Ku47
Morlaix F 22 Kr42
Morley CDN (AB) 169 Ec20
Mörlunda S 31 Lq33
Morne-à-L'eau F (GL) 187 Gk37
Morne Seychellois N.P. SY 145 Nh48
Morne Trois Pitons N.P. WD 187 Gk38
Morney AUS (QLD) 108 Sa58
Mornington Abyssal Plain 190 Fa15
Mornington Island AUS (QLD) 106 Rk54
Mornington Islands A.L. Trust AUS (QLD) 107 Rk54
Moro PE 197 Ga50
Moro PK 65 Od32
Moro USA (OR) 168 Dk23
Morobe PNG 115 Sd49
Morobo SUD 144 Mf44
Morocco 123 Kb06
Moročne UA 41 Mf39
Morococala BOL 206 Gg55
Morocoy MEX (QTR) 183 Ff36
Morodougou RG 136 Kf40
Morogoro EAT 147 Mj49
Moro Gulf RP 91 Rb42
Moroiemu RI 114 Rk49
Morokweng ZA 155 Mb59
Morolaba BF 137 Kh40
Morolica HN 184 Fg39
Moromaho RI 97 Rc49
Morombe RM 157 Nb56
Morón C 179 Ga34
Morón MEX (TM) 182 Fb34
Mörön MNG 70 Qa21
Mörön MNG 70 Qf22
Morón RA (BA) 209 Ha63
Moron USA (UT) 171 Ee26
Morón YV 193 Gf40
Morona EC 196 Gb47
Morondava RM 157 Nc56
Morón de Almazán E 28 Ks49
Morón de la Frontera E 27 Kp53
Moroni COM 156 Nb51
Moronou CI 137 Kh42
Morotai RI 91 Re44
Moroto EAU 144 Mh44
Moroto, Mount EAU 144 Mh44
Morotuto YV 192 Gd41
Morouba RCA 140 Ma42
Morowali Reserve RI 96 Ra46
Morozovsk RUS 48 Na21
Morpará BR (BA) 201 Hj51
Morpeth GB 20 Kt35
Morphettville Racecourse AUS (SA) 110 Rk63
Morretes BR (PR) 205 Hf58
Morrilton USA (AR) 174 Fd28
Morrin CDN (AB) 169 Ed20
Morrinhos BR (GO) 202 Hf54
Morris CDN (MB) 172 Fb21
Morris USA (MN) 172 Fc23
Morris, Mount AUS 105 Rf59
Morristown USA (TN) 178 Fj27
Morrito NIC 185 Fh40
Morro Agudo BR (SP) 202 Hf56
Morro Bay USA (CA) 170 Dk28
Morro Branco BR (PI) 200 Hh50
Morro Branco, T.I. BR 200 Hg48
Morro Cabeça no Tempo BR (PI) 200 Hj50
Morro Chico RCH 210 Ge72
Morrocoy, P.N. YV 193 Gf40
Morro da Igreja BR 205 Hf60
Morro de São Paulo = Ilha de Tinharé BR 201 Ja52
Morro do Chapéu BR (BA) 201 Hk51
Morro do Padre BR 203 Hg54
Morro Jable E 124 Kc31
Morropón PE 196 Ga48
Morros BR (MA) 195 Hh47
Morro Uruçui BR (PI) 200 Hh50
Morro Velho BR (MA) 200 Hg49
Morrow USA (LA) 175 Fe30
Mörrum S 31 Lp34
Morrumbala MOC 153 Mh54
Morrumbene MOC 153 Mh57
Morrungolo MOC 153 Mh57
Mors DK 30 Lj34
Morsa RA (BA) 209 Gk63
Moršansk RUS 48 Na19
Morsi IND (MHT) 82 Ok35
Mörsil S 16 Lg14
Morskoj RUS 39 Ma35
Mörskom = Myrskylä FIN 38 Mf30
Morskoy aral KZ 62 Nf23
Morsovo RUS 48 Nb19
Morstone AUS (QLD) 106 Rk55
Mørsvik N 16 Lh12
Mørsvikfjorden N 16 Lh12
Mortagne-au-Perche F 22 La42
Mortagne-sur-Sèvre F 24 Ku44
Mortain F 22 Ku42
Mortara I 34 Lj45
Morteau F 25 Lg43
Mortesoro SUD 135 Mh40
Mortimers BS 186 Gc34
Mortlake AUS (VIC) 111 Sb65
Mortlock Islands FSM 10 Sb09
Mortlock Islands PNG 117 Sj48
Morton USA (IL) 175 Ff25
Morton USA (MS) 175 Ff29
Morton USA (TX) 174 Ej29
Morton USA (WA) 168 Dj22
Morton N.P. AUS 111 Sf63
Mortrée F 22 La42
Moruga TT 187 Gk40
Morundah AUS (NSW) 111 Sd63
Moruongole EAU 144 Mh44
Morupule RB 152 Md57
Moruya AUS (NSW) 111 Sf63
Morven AUS (QLD) 109 Sd59
Morvi IND (GUJ) 82 Of34
Morwell AUS (VIC) 111 Sd65
Moryna BY 41 Mf37
Morzhovoi Bay USA (AK) 164 Bj18
Morzine F 25 Lg44
Morzyczyn PL 40 Lp37
Mosa PNG 116 Sf48
Mosal'sk RUS 48 Mh18
Mosbach D 33 Lk41
Mosby N 30 Lh32
Mosby USA (MT) 169 Eg22
Moscheea mare RO 45 Mj46
Moscow RUS 48 Mj18
Moscow USA (ID) 168 Eb22
Moscow University Ice Shelf 7 Qd32
Mosel D 33 Lg41
Moselle F 23 Lg42
Moser River CDN (NS) 176 Gj23
Moses Lake USA (WA) 168 Ea22
Moses, Mount USA 170 Eb25
Moses Point USA (AK) 164 Bj13
Mosetse RB 152 Md56
Mosfellsbær IS 18 Jt26
Mosgiel NZ 113 Tf68
Moshaneng RB 155 Mc58
Moshesh's Ford ZA 155 Md61
Moshi EAT 144 Mj47
Moshi Z 152 Md53
Moshófito GR 46 Mb51
Mosi WAN 138 Lb41
Mosina PL 40 Lr38
Mosi Oa Tunya N.P. Z 151 Mc54
Mosite RDC 141 Mb45
Mosjøen N 16 Lg13
Moskenesøya N 16 Lg12
Mosko BIH 44 Lt48
Moskva RUS 48 Mj18
Moslavina Podravska HR 35 Ls45
Mosomane RB 152 Md57
Mosongoie RDC 149 Mc50
Mosonmagyaróvár H 42 Ls43
Mosopo RB 155 Mc58
Mosqueiro BR (PA) 195 Hf46
Mosquera CO 192 Ga44
Mosquero USA (NM) 174 Ej28
Mosquitia HN 185 Fh38
Mosquito BR (TO) 200 Hg49
Mosquito BR 203 Hk53
Mosquito PY 207 Ha57
Mosquito River USA 165 Cj13
Moss N 30 Ll31
Mossaka RCB 148 Lj46
Mossbank CDN (SK) 169 Eh21
Moss Bluff USA (LA) 174 Fd30
Mossburn NZ 113 Te68
Mosselbaai ZA 154 Mb63
Mossel Bay ZA 154 Mb63
Mossendjo RCB 148 Lg47
Mossgiel AUS (NSW) 111 Sc62
Moss Hill USA (TX) 174 Fc30
Moss Landing USA (CA) 170 Dk27
Mossman AUS (QLD) 107 Sc54
Mossman Gorge AUS (QLD) 107 Sc54
Mossoró BR (RN) 201 Jb48
Mossuril MOC 153 Na53
Moss Vale AUS (NSW) 111 Sf63
Most CZ 42 Lo40
Mostaganem DZ 125 La28
Mostar BIH 35 Ls47
Mostardas BR (RS) 204 He61
Mosteiro da Batalha P 27 Km51
Mosteiro de Alcobaça P 27 Kl51
Mosteiro dos Jerónimos P 27 Kl52
Mosteiros CV 136 Jh38
Most na družbata BG 45 Mf47
Móstoles E 27 Kr50
Mosty PL 41 Md39
Mostys'ka UA 43 Md41
Mot'a ETH 142 Mj40
Mota del Cuervo E 29 Ks51
Mota del Marqués E 26 Kp49
Motagusanos RA (SJ) 208 Gf61
Motaha RI 96 Rb48
Motal BY 41 Mf38
Motala S 31 Lq32
Mota Lava VU 118 Td52
Motatán YV 192 Ge41
Moter IND (ORS) 83 Pb36
Moteros RA (CD) 209 Gk61
Moth IND (UPH) 83 Ok33
Motherwell GB 20 Kq35
Motihari IND (BIH) 83 Pc32
Motilla del Palancar E 29 Kt51
Motinala IND (MPH) 83 Pa34
Motlhabaneng RB 152 Me56
Motloutse Ruins RB 152 Me57
Motobu J 79 Rd32
Motokwe RB 154 Mb58
Motozintla de Mendoza MEX (CHP) 183 Fd38
Motril E 27 Kr54
Motru RO 44 Mc46
Mott USA (ND) 169 Ej22
Mottugudiam IND (CGH) 83 Pa36
Motueka NZ 113 Tg66
Motuhora Island NZ 112 Tj64
Motul MEX (YT) 183 Ff35
Motu One F (PYF) 10 Ca11
Motupe PE 196 Ga49
Motupena Point PNG 117 Sh49
Motygino RUS 54 Pc07
Mouahani COM 156 Nb52
Moučadz' BY 41 Mf37
Mouchoirbank 186 Ge35
Mouchoir Passage BS 186 Ge35
Moudjéria RIM 130 Kd37
Moudon CH 34 Lg44
Moúdros GR 47 Mf51
Mougamou G 148 Lg46
Mougins F 25 Lg47
Mougna RMM 137 Kh39
Mouhijärvi FIN 38 Md29
Mouila G 148 Lf46
Moujia RN 132 Lc38
Mouka RCA 140 Ma42
Moukabou G 148 Lf46
Moukalaba-Doudou, P.N.de G 148 Lf47
Moukoundou G 148 Lf47
Moul RN 133 Lg38
Moulamein AUS (NSW) 111 Sc63
Moulay Bouâzza MA 125 Kg29
Moulay-Bousselham MA 125 Kg28
Moulay-Idriss MA 125 Kh28
Mould Bay CDN 162 Dd03
Mouléngui Binza G 148 Lf47
Moulhoulé DJI 143 Nb39
Mouli Gbangba RCB 140 Lj44
Moulins F 25 Ld44
Moulmein = Maulamyaing MYA 88 Pj37
Moulmeingyun MYA 88 Ph37
Moulton USA (AL) 175 Fg28
Moultrie USA (GA) 178 Fj30
Moulvouday CAM 139 Lh40
Moumba G 148 Lf47
Mounanko CAM 138 Le44
Mound City USA (KS) 174 Fc26
Mound City USA (SD) 172 Fa23
Moundou TCH 140 Lj41
Moundsville USA (WV) 173 Fk26
Moundville USA (AL) 175 Fg29
Moundville Archaeological Park USA 175 Fg29
Moungoundou-Sud RCB 148 Lg47
Moung Russei K 89 Qb39
Mounguel CAM 139 Lg42
Mount Abbot AUS 107 Sd56
Mount Aborlan RP 91 Qk41
Mount Abu IND (RJT) 82 Og33
Mount Abu = Guru Shikhar IND 82 Og33
Mount Abu Wildlife Sanctuary IND 82 Og33
Mount Adams USA 168 Dk22
Mountainair USA (NM) 171 Eg28
Mountain Ash GB 21 Kr39
Mountain City USA (NV) 170 Ec25
Mountain City USA (TN) 178 Fk27
Mountain Grove USA (MO) 175 Fd27
Mountain Home USA (AR) 175 Fd27
Mountain Home USA (ID) 168 Ec24
Mountain Nile SUD 141 Mf42
Mountain Pass USA (CA) 170 Ec28
Mountain Railway IND 84 Oj40
Mountain View USA (AR) 175 Fd28
Mountain View USA (MO) 175 Fe27
Mountain View USA (WY) 171 Ee25
Mountain Village USA (AK) 164 Bj14
Mountain Zebra N.P. ZA 155 Mc62
Mount Aiome PNG 115 Sc48
Mount Airy USA (NC) 178 Fk27
Mount Ajax NZ 113 Tg67
Mount Albert Edward PNG 115 Sd50
Mount Alfred AUS (QLD) 109 Sc59
Mount Alma AUS (QLD) 109 Sf58
Mount Amara ETH 142 Mj41
Mount Amhurst AUS (WA) 103 Rd55
Mount Amungwiwa PNG 115 Sd49
Mount Anglem NZ 113 Td69
Mount Anne AUS 111 Sd67
Mount Aoraki NZ 113 Tf67
Mount Apo RP 91 Rc42
Mount Ararat = Ağri Daği TR 57 Nc26
Mount Arkell CDN 166 Dc15
Mount Arlington Heights CDN (NF) 177 Hd22
Mount Aspiring NZ 113 Te68
Mount Aspiring N.P. NZ 113 Te68
Mount Assiniboine CDN 168 Ec20
Mount Atouat VN 89 Qd38
Mount Augustus AUS 104 Qj58
Mount Augustus N.P. AUS 104 Qj58
Mount Aylift ZA 155 Me61
Mount Ayr USA (IA) 174 Fc25
Mount Baco RP 90 Ra39
Mount Bajimba AUS 109 Sg60
Mount Baker USA 168 Dk21
Mount Balbi PNG 117 Sh48
Mount Ball AUS 103 Rd55
Mount Bangeta PNG 115 Sd49
Mount Barker AUS (WA) 104 Qj63
Mount Barnett AUS (WA) 103 Rc54
Mount Barrington AUS 111 Sf62
Mount Barry AUS (SA) 108 Rh60
Mountbatten Ind. Res. CDN 173 Fj22
Mount Beauty AUS (VIC) 111 Sd64
Mount Bellew IRL 19 Km37
Mountbenger GB 20 Kr35
Mount Berlin 6 Da34
Mount Bintumani WAL 136 Ke41
Mount Boggola AUS 102 Qj57
Mount Bona USA 165 Ck15
Mount Bonaparte USA 168 Ea21
Mount Bosavi PNG 115 Sb49
Mount Brassey AUS 108 Rh57
Mount Brazeau CDN 168 Eb19
Mount Brockman AUS 102 Qj57
Mount Bruce AUS 102 Qk57
Mount Bryan AUS 110 Rk62
Mount Buffalo National Park AUS (VIC) 111 Sd64
Mount Buller AUS 111 Sd64
Mount Busa RP 91 Rc42
Mount Cairns AUS 106 Rh56
Mount Calavite RP 90 Ra39
Mount Callaghan USA 170 Eb26
Mount Capoas RP 90 Qk40
Mount Capotoan RP 90 Rc39
Mount Carleton CDN 176 Gg22
Mount Carleton Prov. Park CDN 176 Gg22
Mount Carmel USA (IL) 175 Fg26
Mount Carmel Junction USA (UT) 171 Ed27
Mount Carter AUS 107 Sb52
Mount Chamberlin USA (AK) 165 Ch11
Mount Chiginagak USA 164 Cb17
Mount Chilalo ETH 142 Mk41
Mount Clara NZ 113 Tg67
Mount Clark CDN 167 Dh13
Mount Clemens USA (MI) 173 Fj24
Mount Columbia CDN 168 Eb19
Mount Connor AUS 103 Rd53
Mount Cook AUS 104 Qj62
Mount Cook CDN 166 Ck15
Mount Cook NZ 113 Tf67
Mount Cook = Mount Aoraki NZ 113 Tf67
Mount Cook N.P. NZ 113 Tf67
Mount Coolon AUS (QLD) 109 Sd56
Mount Cornish AUS 103 Rd56
Mount Crysdale CDN 166 Dj17
Mount Currie Ind. Res. CDN 168 Dj20
Mount Dalrymple AUS 109 Se56
Mount Dana USA 164 Bk18
Mount Darwin ZW 152 Mf54
Mount Davis AUS 105 Re59
Mount de Babel CDN 176 Gf20
Mount Deering AUS 103 Re58
Mount Denison AUS (NT) 103 Rg57
Mount Desert Island USA 177 Gf23
Mount Djebobo GH/TG 137 La41
Mount Dockrell AUS 103 Rd55
Mount Dora USA (FL) 178 Fk31
Mount Douglas AUS (QLD) 109 Sd56
Mount Douglas USA (AK) 164 Cd16
Mount Downton CDN 166 Dh19
Mount Draper USA 166 Da16
Mount Dremsel PNG 116 Sd47
Mount Eba AUS (SA) 108 Rh61
Mount Ebenezer Roadhouse AUS (NT) 103 Rg58
Mount Edgar AUS 102 Ra56
Mount Edith USA 169 Ee22
Mount Eduni CDN 166 Df13
Mount Edward AUS 103 Rf57
Mount Edward 6 Gc34
Mount Edziza Prov. Park CDN 166 De17
Mount Elbert USA (CO) 171 Eg26
Mount Elgon EAU/EAK 144 Mh45
Mount Elgon N.P. EAU/EAK 144 Mh45
Mount Ellen USA 171 Ee26
Mount Elliot AUS (QLD) 107 Sd55
Mount Elsie AUS (QLD) 107 Sd56
Mount Elvire AUS 102 Qj56
Mount Enterprise USA (TX) 174 Fc30
Mount Erebus 7 Tc34
Mount Essendon AUS 104 Ra58
Mount Etna Caves N.P. AUS 109 Sf57
Mount Everest NEP/CHN 81 Pd31
Mount Fairweather CDN 166 Db16
Mount Farnham CDN 168 Eb20
Mount Farquharson AUS 106 Rf54
Mount Field N.P. AUS 111 Sd67
Mount Fletcher ZA 155 Me61
Mount Frakes 6 Ea34
Mount Frankland N.P. AUS 104 Qj63
Mount Fraser AUS (WA) 104 Qk58
Mount Frederick A.L. AUS 103 Re55
Mount Frederick No2 A.L. AUS 103 Re56
Mount Freeling AUS (SA) 108 Rk60
Mount Frere ZA 155 Me61
Mount Fridtjof Nansen 6 Bd36
Mount Gambier AUS (SA) 110 Sa64
Mount Garnet AUS (QLD) 107 Sc54
Mount Gede-Pangrango N.P. RI 95 Qd49
Mount Gelia AUS (WA) 105 Rb60
Mount Gerdine USA (AK) 165 Cd15
Mount Geureudong RI 92 Pj43
Mount Gilruth AUS 106 Rg52
Mount Godwin Austen PK 81 Oj28
Mount Gordon AUS 104 Ra62
Mount Goura WAN 138 Le40
Mount Graham International Observatory USA (AZ) 171 Ef29
Mount Grenfell Aboriginal Cave Paintings AUS (NSW) 109 Sc61
Mount Grillon USA 166 Db16
Mount Guge ETH 142 Mj42
Mount Gugu ETH 142 Mk41
Mount Guide AUS (QLD) 106 Rk56
Mount Gunnison USA 171 Eg26
Mount Guraghe ETH 142 Mk41
Mount Hack AUS 108 Rk61
Mount Hagen PNG 115 Sc48
Mount Hagen Show PNG 115 Sc48
Mount Hale AUS (WA) 104 Qj59
Mount Hale AUS 104 Qj58
Mount Halimun N.P. RI 95 Qd49
Mount Hamilton USA 170 Ec26
Mount Hamlet USA (AK) 165 Bh11
Mount Hanang EAT 146 Mh48
Mount Hann AUS 103 Rc53
Mount Harper USA (AK) 165 Cj13
Mount Harris AUS 103 Re58
Mount Hart CDN 165 Ck14
Mount Hay AUS 103 Rg57
Mount Hayes USA (AK) 165 Cg14
Mount Hebron USA (CA) 168 Dk25
Mount Hermon RL 56 Mh29
Mount Hickman CDN 166 De17
Mount Hinkley AUS 105 Re59
Mount Hollister AUS 102 Qg57
Mount Hood USA 168 Dk23
Mount Hope AUS (NSW) 111 Sc62
Mount Hope AUS (SA) 110 Rh63
Mount Hopeless AUS (SA) 108 Rk60
Mount House AUS (WA) 103 Rc54
Mount Howe 6 Ca36
Mount Howitt AUS (QLD) 108 Sb59
Mount Howship AUS 106 Rg52
Mount Hubbard CDN 166 Da15
Mount Hutt NZ 113 Tf67
Mount Hutton AUS (QLD) 109 Se58
Mount Huxley NZ 113 Te68
Mount Huxley USA 166 Ck15
Mount Ida AUS (WA) 104 Ra60
Mount Ida USA (AR) 174 Fd28
Mount Illbillee AUS 105 Rg59
Mount Isa AUS (QLD) 106 Rk56
Mount Ive AUS (SA) 110 Rj62
Mount Jackson AUS (WA) 104 Qk61
Mount Jackson 6 Gd33
Mount Jacques Cartier CDN 176 Gh21
Mount James A.L. AUS 104 Qj58
Mount Jefferson USA 168 Dk23
Mount Jefferson USA 170 Eb26
Mount Joffre CDN 168 Ec20
Mount Joyce 7 Sd34
Mount Junction AUS 103 Re55
Mount Kadam EAU 144 Mh45
Mount Kagora WAN 138 Le41
Mount Kaichui SOL 117 Ta50
Mount Kaka ETH 142 Mk42
Mount Kalourat SOL 117 Ta50
Mount Kaputar AUS 109 Sf61
Mount Kaputar N.P. AUS 109 Sf61
Mount Karimui PNG 115 Sc49
Mount Karoma PNG 115 Sb48
Mount Katmai USA 164 Cc16
Mount Kaye AUS 111 Se64
Mount Keith AUS (WA) 104 Ra59
Mount Kendall NZ 113 Tg66
Mount Kenya EAK 144 Mj46
Mount Kenya N.P. EAK 144 Mj46
Mount Kilal EAK 144 Mj44
Mount Kimball USA (AK) 165 Ch14
Mount Kirkpatrick 7 Ta35
Mount Klotz CDN (YT) 165 Da13
Mount Kosciuszko AUS 111 Se64
Mount Kusiwigasi PNG 115 Sa48
Mount Labo RP 90 Rb39
Mount Lacy AUS 103 Rc54
Mount Lambell AUS 106 Rg53
Mount Lamington PNG 116 Se50
Mount Larcum AUS (QLD) 109 Sf57
Mount Lawrence Wells AUS 104 Ra59
Mount Lebanon RL 56 Mh29
Mount Leichhardt AUS 103 Rg56
Mount Leinster IRL 19 Ko38
Mount Leisler AUS 103 Re57
Mount Lembu RI 92 Pj43
Mount Lesueur AUS 104 Qh61
Mount Leuser RI 92 Pj44
Mount Lewis AUS (NSW) 109 Sd61
Mount Liebig AUS 103 Rf57
Mount Lister 7 Ta34
Mount Lofty Ranges AUS 110 Rk63
Mount Logan CDN 166 Ck15
Mount Longfellow NZ 113 Tg67
Mount Longhurst 7 Sd34
Mount Longonot N.P. EAK 144 Mj46
Mount Luke AUS 104 Qj59
Mount Lulworth AUS 104 Qj59
Mount Lyall NZ 113 Td68
Mount Lyndhurst AUS (SA) 108 Rk61
Mount Ma'an CHN 87 Pk33
Mount Macdonald VU 118 Te54
Mount Madden AUS (WA) 104 Qk62
Mount Madley AUS 103 Rb58
Mount Magnet AUS (WA) 104 Qj60
Mount Mago ETH 144 Mj43
Mount Maiden AUS 104 Rb59
Mount Maigudo ETH 142 Mj42
Mount Maitabi SOL 117 Sj49
Mount Malindang RP 91 Rb41
Mount Manning Range AUS 104 Qk60
Mount Mantalingajan RP 94 Qj41
Mount Marcus Baker USA (AK) 165 Cg15
Mount Margaret AUS (WA) 105 Rb60
Mount Margaret AUS 102 Qj57
Mount Maria GB 210 Ha71
Mount Markham 7 Tb35
Mount Marum VU 118 Te54
Mount Marvine USA 171 Ee26
Mount Maunganui NZ 112 Tj64
Mount Mbeya EAT 146 Mg50
Mount McClintock 7 Sd34
Mount McGuire USA 168 Ec23
Mount McKinley USA (AK) 165 Ce14
Mount McLoughlin USA 168 Dj24
Mount Meharry AUS 102 Qk57
Mountmellick IRL 19 Kn37
Mount Mengam PNG 115 Sc48
Mount Menzies 7 Oa33
Mount Meru EAT 144 Mj47
Mount Michael PNG 115 Sc49
Mount Miller USA 166 Cj15
Mount Miller 7 Tb35
Mount Minto 7 Tc33
Mount Misery NZ 113 Tf67
Mount Mitchell USA 178 Fj28
Mount Molloy AUS (QLD) 107 Sc54
Mount Moorosi LS 155 Me61
Mount Morbanipari PNG 115 Sb48
Mount Morgan AUS (QLD) 109 Sf57
Mount Moriah USA 171 Ec26
Mount Moroto EAU 144 Mh44
Mount Morris AUS (QLD) 109 Sc58
Mount Morris AUS 105 Rf59
Mount Moses USA 170 Eb25
Mount Mulgrave AUS (QLD) 107 Sb54
Mount Mulligan AUS (QLD) 107 Sc54
Mount Mulya AUS (NSW) 109 Sc61
Mount Murchinson NZ 113 Tf67
Mount Mye CDN 166 Dd14
Mount Nansen CDN 166 Db14
Mount Nasi ETH 142 Mh41
Mount Nebo JOR 58 Mh30
Mount Nellie AUS 103 Rc54
Mount Nicholson AUS (QLD) 109 Se58
Mount Norman AUS (QLD) 107 Sb55
Mount Northampton 7 Tb33
Mount Nott AUS 110 Rh62
Mount Okora WAN 138 Ld42
Mount Olga AUS 105 Rf58
Mount Olive USA (NC) 178 Ga28
Mount Olympus USA 168 Dj22
Mount Opémiska CDN 176 Gc20
Mount Oratia USA 164 Bk16
Mount Ord AUS 103 Rc54
Mount Ossa AUS (TAS) 111 Sd66
Mount Padbury AUS (WA) 104 Qk58
Mount Palgrave AUS 102 Qh57
Mount Panshan CHN 73 Qj25
Mount Parker AUS 103 Re54
Mount Patterson CDN 165 Dc13
Mount Patullo CDN 166 Df17
Mount Peale USA 171 Ef26
Mount Pearl CDN (NF) 177 Hd22
Mount Penot VU 118 Td54
Mount Perry AUS (QLD) 109 Sf58
Mount Petras 6 Dc34
Mount Peuetsagoe RI 92 Pj43
Mount Peulik USA 164 Cb17
Mount Pfizner AUS 108 Rh57
Mount Pinapan RI 93 Pk44
Mount Pinatubo RP 90 Ra38
Mount Pinos USA 170 Ea28
Mount Pleasant USA (MI) 173 Fh24
Mount Pleasant USA (MO) 172 Fe25
Mount Pleasant USA (SC) 178 Ga29
Mount Pleasant USA (TX) 174 Fc29
Mount Pleasant USA (UT) 171 Ee26
Mount Plummer USA 164 Ca15
Mount Popa MYA 86 Ph35
Mount Popomanaseu SOL 117 Ta50
Mount Pulog N.P. RP 90 Ra37
Mount Pye NZ 113 Te69
Mount Queen Bess CDN 168 Dh20
Mount Ragang RP 91 Rc42
Mount Rainier N.P. USA 168 Dk22
Mount Ramelau TLS 97 Rc50
Mount Ranai RI 94 Qe43
Mount Ratz CDN 166 Dd17
Mount Rebecca AUS (WA) 104 Qh59
Mount Remarkable AUS (QLD) 107 Rk56
Mount Remarkable AUS 103 Rd54
Mount Remarkable N.P. AUS 110 Rk62
Mount Revelstoke N.P. CDN 168 Eb20
Mount Robe AUS 108 Sa61
Mount Robinson AUS 102 Qk57
Mount Robson CDN 168 Ea19
Mount Robson Prov. Park CDN 168 Ea19
Mount Rogers N.R.A. USA 178 Fk27
Mount Roosevelt CDN 166 Dh16
Mount Roraima GUY/YV 194 Gk43
Mount Ruapehu NZ 113 Th65
Mount Rungwe EAT 146 Mh50
Mount Rupert ZA 155 Mc60
Mount Rushmore Nat. Memorial USA 169 Ej24
Mount Russell USA (AK) 165 Ce14
Mount Ryan AUS 111 Se62
Mount Sage N.P. GB 187 Gh36
Mount Saint Gregory CDN 177 Ha21
Mount Saint Helens Nat. Volcanic Mon. USA 168 Dj22
Mount Salisbury USA (AK) 165 Cg11
Mount Sandiman AUS (WA) 104 Qh58
Mount Sandiman AUS 104 Qh58
Mount Sanford USA (AK) 165 Ch14
Mount Sankanbiaiwa WAL 136 Ke41
Mount Sasari SOL 117 Sk50
Mount Saunders 7 Tb36
Mount Seelig 6 Ed35
Mount Selinda ZW 152 Mg56
Mount Selous CDN 166 Dd14
Mount Sembuang RI 92 Pj43
Mount Shasta USA (CA) 168 Dj25
Mount Shasta USA 168 Dj25
Mount Sicapoo RP 90 Ra37
Mount Sidley 6 Dc34
Mount Siple 6 Dc33
Mount Sir James MacBrien CDN 166 Dg14
Mount Skinner AUS (NT) 108 Rh57
Mount Somers NZ 113 Tf67
Mount Spokane S.P. USA 168 Eb22
Mount Stanley EAU/RDC 144 Mf45
Mount Steele CDN 166 Ck15
Mount Sterling USA (IL) 175 Fe25
Mount Sterling USA (KY) 175 Fj26
Mount Sterling USA (OH) 173 Fj26
Mount Stevens NZ 113 Tg66
Mount Stewart AUS (QLD) 107 Sc56
Mount Stewart CDN 165 Da14
Mount Stinear 7 Ob33
Mount Strong PNG 115 Sd49
Mount Stuart AUS (WA) 102 Qj57
Mount Sturgeon AUS (QLD) 107 Sc56
Mount Suckling PNG 116 Se50
Mount Sulen PNG 115 Sb47
Mount Sullivan AUS 106 Rf54
Mount Surprise AUS (QLD) 107 Sc55
Mount Tabletop AUS 109 Sd57
Mount Takahe 6 Eb34
Mount Taknan PNG 117 Sh49
Mount Taranaki NZ 113 Th65
Mount Tavani VU 118 Te54
Mount Thuillier IND 88 Pg42
Mount Tipton USA 170 Ec28
Mount Tip Tree AUS (QLD) 107 Sc54
Mount Tobin USA 170 Eb25
Mount Tom White USA 165 Cj15
Mount Tops AUS 108 Rg56
Mount Trumbull USA 171 Ed27
Mount Tutoko NZ 113 Te68
Mount Ulbanep PNG 115 Sb47
Mount Unbunmaroo AUS (QLD) 108 Sa57
Mount Vangunu SOL 117 Sj50
Mount Vernon AUS (WA) 104 Qk58
Mount Vernon USA (AL) 175 Fg30
Mount Vernon USA (IL) 175 Ff26
Mount Vernon USA (KY) 175 Fh27
Mount Vernon USA (MO) 172 Fe25
Mount Vernon USA (MO) 174 Fd27
Mount Vernon USA (OH) 173 Fj25
Mount Vernon USA (OR) 168 Ea23
Mount Vernon USA (WA) 168 Dj21
Mount Victor 7 Mc33
Mount Victoria MYA 86 Pg35
Mount Victoria NZ 113 Tg67
Mount Victoria PNG 115 Sd50
Mount Victory PNG 116 Se50
Mount Waddington CDN 168 Dh20
Mount Walton AUS 104 Qk61
Mount Warning AUS 109 Sg60
Mount Washington USA (KY) 175 Fh26
Mount Wechecha ETH 142 Mk41
Mount Wedge AUS (SA) 110 Rh62
Mount Wells AUS 103 Rd54
Mount Wharton 7 Ta35
Mount Whitney USA 170 Ea27
Mount Wilhelm PNG 115 Sc48
Mount Will CDN 166 Df17
Mount William AUS 111 Sb64
Mount William N.P. AUS 111 Se66
Mount Wiloughby AUS (SA) 108 Rh59
Mount Wilson CDN 166 Df14
Mount Windsor AUS (QLD) 108 Sa57
Mount Wittenoon AUS (WA) 104 Qj59
Mount Wood USA 169 Ee23
Mount Woodroffe AUS 105 Rf59
Mount Yawatoutou GH/TG 137 La42
Mount Zeil AUS 103 Rg57
Mouping CHN (SDG) 73 Ra27
Moura AUS (QLD) 109 Se58
Moura BR (AM) 198 Gk46
Moura P 27 Kn52
Mourão P 27 Kn52
Mouray TCH 134 Ma40
Mourdiah RMM 131 Kg38
Mourenx F 24 Ku47
Mouri Mountains WAN 139 Lf41
Mourmelon-le-Grand F 23 Le41
Mourne Mountains GB 19 Kp36
Mouroungoulay TCH 140 Lj41
Mousa GB 20 Kt30
Mousa Broch GB 20 Kt30
Mouscron B 23 Ld40
Mousgougou TCH 139 Lj40
Moussa Castle RL 56 Mh29
Moussafoyo TCH 140 Lk41
Moussaya RG 136 Kd41
Moussaya RG 136 Ke40
Moussoro TCH 133 Lj39
Moustiers-Sainte-Marie F 25 Lg47
Moutamba RCB 148 Lg47
Mouthe F 25 Lg44
Mouths of the Amazon BR 195 Hf45
Mouths of the Ganges IND 86 Pe35
Mouths of the Indus PK 65 Od33
Mouths of the Irrawaddy MYA 88 Ph38
Mouths of the Krishna IND 83 Pa38
Mouths of the Mekong 89 Qd41
Moutier CH 34 Lh43
Moûtiers F 25 Lg45
Moutindi G 148 Lf47
Moutong RI 91 Ra45
Mouton Rothschild F 24 Ku45
Moutouroua CAM 139 Lh40
Moutsamoudou COM 156 Nc52
Moutsoúna GR 47 Mf53
Mouy F 23 Lc41
Mouyondzi RCB 148 Lg47
Mouzáki GR 46 Mb51
Mouzarak TCH 133 Lh39
Mouzon F 23 Lf41
Movie World AUS 109 Sg59
Movila Miresii RO 45 Mh45
Movilița RO 45 Mg46
Mowanjum AUS (WA) 102 Rb54
Mowanjum A.L. AUS 102 Rb54
Mowasi GUY 194 Ha43
Möwe Bay NAM 150 Lg55
Moya COM 156 Nc52
Moyale EAK 145 Mk44
Moyale ETH 145 Mk44
Moyamba WAL 136 Kd41
Moyen Atlas MA 125 Kh29
Moyeni LS 155 Md61
Moyenne Sido RCA 140 Lk41
Moyhu AUS (VIC) 111 Sd64
Moyie CDN (BC) 168 Ec21
Moyie Springs USA (ID) 168 Eb21
Mo'ynoq UZ 62 Nk24
Moyo EAU 144 Mf44
Moyo RI 96 Qj50
Moyobamba PE 196 Gb49
Moyogalpa NIC 184 Fh40
Moyowosi Game Reserve EAT 146 Mf48
Moyto TCH 139 Lj39
Moyu CHN (XUZ) 68 Ok27
Moyuela E 29 Ku49
Mozăceni RO 45 Mf46
Mozaffar Abad-e Kur Gol IR 57 Nf28
Možajsk RUS 48 Mj18
Mozambique 123 Mb11
Mozambique Basin 122 Mb12
Mozambique Channel 122 Na11
Mozambique Plateau 122 Mb11
Mozambique Ridge 122 Mb13
Mozdok RUS (SOA) 57 Nc24
Mozduran IR 62 Oa27
Mozia I 36 Ln53
Mozirje SLO 42 Lp44
Mozogo-Gokoro, P.N.de CAM 139 Lg40
Mozuli RUS 39 Mj34
Mpagwe EAT 146 Mf48
Mpaha GH 137 Kk41
Mpakani EAT 147 Mk49
Mpal SN 130 Kb38
Mpala RDC 146 Me49
Mpanda EAT 146 Mf49
Mpandaamatenga RB 151 Mc55
Mpanga EAT 147 Mj49
Mpanta Z 146 Me51
Mpase RDC 149 Ma46
Mpataba GH 137 Kj43
Mpatora EAT 147 Mk50
Mpé RCB 148 Lh47
Mpesao Hills GH 137 Kj42
Mpessoba RMM 137 Kh39
Mphaki LS 155 Me61
Mphoengs ZW 152 Md56
Mphwayungu EAT 146 Mh49
Mpiéla RMM 137 Kg39
Mpigi EAU 144 Mg45
Mpika Z 146 Mf51
Mpili Z 152 Md53
Mpo RDC 149 Lk48
Mpomgwe Z 146 Me52
Mponela MW 146 Mg52
Mporokoso Z 146 Mf50
Mpouya RCB 148 Lj47
Mpraeso GH 137 Kk42
Mpui EAT 146 Mf50
Mpulungu Z 146 Mf50
Mpumalanga ZA 155 Me59
Mpumalangao ZA 155 Mf60
Mpume RDC 149 Lk48
Mpurukasese EAT 147 Mj51
Mpwapwa EAT 147 Mj49
Mrągowo PL 41 Mb37
M'Rara DZ 126 Lc29
Mrauk-U MYA 86 Pg35
Mrčajevci SCG 44 Ma47
Mrežičko MK 44 Mc49
Mrikula Devi Temple IND 81 Oj29
Mrirt MA 125 Kh29
Mrkonjić Grad BIH 35 Ls46
Mrkopalj HR 35 Lp45
Mrohaung = Mrauk-U MYA 86 Pg35
Mrzeżyno PL 40 Lq36
M'Saken TN 126 Lf28
Msak Mallat LAR 133 Lf33
Msalalo EAT 146 Mh48
Mšanec' UA 43 Mc41
Msanga EAT 147 Mk49
Msanzi EAT 146 Mf50
Msata EAT 147 Mk49
Mscislav BY 48 Mf19
Msechela EAT 147 Mj51
Mšenélázně CZ 42 Lp40
Msesia EAT 146 Mg49
M'Sied MA 124 Ke31
M'Sila DZ 126 Lc28
Msimbati EAT 147 Na51
Msoro Z 146 Mf52
Msuna ZW 152 Md55
Mswebe Z 152 Md53
Mswega EAT 147 Mj50
Mszczonów PL 41 Ma39
Mt Aburassein RCA/SUD 141 Mc41
Mtakataka MW 153 Mh53
Mtakuja EAT 146 Mf49
Mtama EAT 147 Mk51
Mtamble EAT 147 Mk48
Mta Mepists'karo GE 57 Nb25
Mtan SYR 56 Mj29
Mtandawala EAT 147 Mk50
Mtandura EAT 147 Mk50
Mtanila EAT 146 Mg49
Mtarazi Falls ZW 152 Mg55
Mt Dangoura RCA/SUD 141 Md42
Mtembwe EAT 147 Mj50
Mtera Reservoir EAT 147 Mh49
Mt Gaoun RCA 140 Lh42
Mt.Greenough USA (AK) 165 Ck11
Mtito Andei EAK 144 Mk47
Mt. Kelly USA (AK) 165 Bj11
Mtondo EAT 147 Mk50
Mtongwe EAT 147 Mk48
Mto wa Mbu EAT 144 Mh47
Mts du Fazao TG 137 La41
Mts Karé RCA 140 Lj42
Mtskheta GE 57 Nc25
Mtubatuba ZA 155 Mg60
Mtuga Z 152 Me53
Mtukula EAT 147 Mj51
Mtwapa EAK 145 Mk47
Mtwara EAT 147 Na51
Mu F (NCL) 118 Td56
Muabanama MOC 153 Mj53
Muadiala RDC 149 Ma49
Muaguide MOC 147 Na52
Mualadzi MOC 152 Mg53
Mualama MOC 153 Mk54
Muaná BR (PA) 195 Hf46
Muanda RDC 148 Lg48
Muangai ANG 150 Lk52
Muang Beng LAO 87 Qa35
Muang Boran THA 88 Qa39
Muang Houn LAO 87 Qa35
Muang Huang LAO 87 Qb36
Muang Kham LAO 87 Qb36
Muang Khong LAO 89 Qc38
Muang Khua LAO 87 Qb35
Muang Khun LAO 87 Qb36
Muang Long LAO 87 Qa35
Muang Nan LAO 87 Qa36
Muang Ngoi LAO 87 Qb35
Muang Pa LAO 87 Qa36
Muang Pak-Cay LAO 87 Qa36
Muang Phin LAO 89 Qd37
Muang Phu Khoun LAO 87 Qb36
Muang Pon THA 87 Pj36
Muang Samsip THA 89 Qc38
Muang Sing LAO 87 Qa35
Muang Singh Historical Park THA 88 Pk38
Muang Sui LAO 87 Qb36
Muang Xai LAO 87 Qb35
Muanza MOC 153 Mh55
Muanzanza RDC 149 Ma49
Muapula MOC 153 Mj52
Muaquia MOC 147 Mj52
Muar MAL 93 Qb44
Muara BRU 94 Qh43
Muaraaman RI 93 Qb47
Muarabadak RI 95 Qj46
Muarabeliti RI 93 Qb47
Muara Binuangeun RI 93 Qc49
Muarabungo RI 93 Qb46
Muaradua RI 93 Qc48
Muaraenim RI 93 Qb47
Muara Hiu RI 95 Qh46
Muarainu RI 95 Qh46
Muaraklingi RI 93 Qb47
Muara Koman RI 95 Qh46
Muarakuwis RI 93 Qb47
Muaranayan RI 95 Qj46
Muarapangean RI 94 Qj44
Muarapantai RI 93 Qa46
Muararupit RI 93 Qb47
Muarasaibi RI 93 Pk46
Muarasaung RI 93 Qb48
Muarasiberut RI 93 Pk46
Muarasigep RI 93 Pk46
Muarasikabaluan RI 93 Pk46
Muarasimatalu RI 93 Pk46
Muarasoma RI 93 Pk45
Muaratalang RI 93 Qb47
Muaratebo RI 93 Qb46
Muaratembesi RI 93 Qb46
Muarateweh RI 95 Qh46
Muarawahau RI 94 Qj45
Muari RI 97 Rd46
Muatua MOC 153 Mk53
Mubambe RDC 146 Md51
Mubanzi EAU 144 Mf46
Mubayira ZW 152 Mf55
Mubende EAU 144 Mf45
Mubi WAN 139 Lg40
Mubo CHN (GSU) 72 Qd27
Muborak UZ 63 Oc26
Mubrani RI 114 Rg46
Mubur RI 92 Qd44
Mucajaí BR (RR) 193 Gk44
Mucajaí BR 193 Gk44
Mucambi Z 151 Mc52
Mucari ANG 148 Lj50
Muchaze MOC 152 Mg56
Muchea AUS (WA) 104 Qh61
Mucheve MOC 152 Mh56
Muchinga Mountains Z 146 Mf52
Muchinka Z 146 Mf52
Muchówka PL 41 Ma41
Muchuchu Ruins ZW 152 Mf55
Muck GB 20 Ko34
Muckadilla AUS (QLD) 109 Se59
Mučkapskij RUS 48 Nb20
Muckross IRL 19 Kl38
Mucojo MOC 147 Na52
Muconda ANG 151 Ma51
Mucondo ANG 148 Lh50
Mucope ANG 150 Lh54
Mucuali MOC 153 Mk54
Mucuaso ANG 151 Ma54
Mucubela MOC 153 Mj54
Mucuchies YV 192 Ge41
Mucugê BR (BA) 201 Hk52
Mucumbura MOC 152 Mf54
Mucumbura ZW 152 Mf54
Mucupia MOC 153 Mj55
Mucur TR 56 Mh26
Mucure YV 193 Gh41
Mucurí BR (BA) 203 Ja55
Mucurici BR (ES) 203 Hk55
Mucuripi BR (AM) 198 Gf47
Mucussueje ANG 151 Ma51
Mudabidri IND 84 Oh39
Mudanjiang CHN (HLG) 76 Re23
Mudanthurai Tiger Sanctuary IND 84 Oj41
Mudanya TR 45 Mj50
Mud Butte USA (SD) 169 Ej23
Muddanuru IND (APH) 85 Ok38
Muddebihal IND (KTK) 82 Oj37
Muddus n.p. S 16 Ma12
Muddy Gap USA (WY) 171 Eg24
Mudgal IND (KTK) 82 Oj37
Mudgee AUS (NSW) 111 Se62
Mudgod IND (KTK) 82 Oh38
Mudhai OM 61 Ng37
Mudhol IND (KTK) 82 Oh37
Mudigere IND (KTK) 84 Oh39
Mudigubba IND (APH) 84 Oj38
Mudon MYA 88 Pj37
Mudukulattur IND (TNU) 84 Ok41
Mudumalai Sanctuary IND 84 Oj40
Mudumu N.P. NAM 151 Mb55
Mudun SP 145 Nb45
Mudurnu TR 56 Mf25
Muecate MOC 153 Mk53
Mueda MOC 147 Mk51
Muel E 29 Kt49
Mueller Range AUS 103 Rd55
Muembe MOC 146 Mh52
Muende MOC 152 Mg53
Muftah SUD 135 Mg35
Mufulira Z 146 Me52
Mufu Shan CHN 75 Qg31
Mufu Shan CHN 75 Qh31
Mugambo = Lagosa EAT 146 Me48
Mugang CHN (YUN) 87 Qc34
Mugango EAT 144 Mg46
Muganskaja ravnina AZ 57 Ne26
Mugeba MOC 153 Mj54
Mugello I 34 Lm46
Mügeln D 32 Lo39
Muger ETH 142 Mk41
Muger ETH 142 Mk41
Muger Falls ETH 142 Mk41
Muggon AUS (WA) 104 Qh59
Mughal Sarai IND (UPH) 83 Pb33
Mughayra KSA 58 Mj31
Mughsayl OM 61 Ng37
Mugina BU 146 Me48
Muğla TR 47 Mj53
Mugling NEP 81 Pc32
Müglitztal D 32 Lo40
Mugota EAK 144 Mj45
Muguia MOC 147 Mk52
Mugumu EAT 144 Mh46
Muhagiria SUD 134 Mc40
Muhairiqah KSA 60 Nc34
Muhala RDC 146 Me48
Muhammad Qol SUD 135 Mj35
Muhavura EAU/RWA 141 Me46
Muhayil KSA 60 Nb36
Muhaywir IRQ 57 Na29
Muheza EAT 147 Mj48
Muheza EAT 147 Mk48
Muhinji Chini EAT 147 Mk50
Muhino RUS 71 Rd19
Mühlacker D 33 Lj42
Mühldorf D 33 Ln42
Mühlhausen D 32 Ll39
Mühlig-Hofmann-fjella 7 Lb33
Mühlviertel A 42 Lp42
Muhoi Kondui RUS 70 Qg19
Muhoršibir RUS (BUR) 70 Qd20
Muhovo BG 44 Md48
Muhu EST 38 Md32

Muhula = Namiroa ☒ MOC 153 Mk53
Muhulu ☒ RDC 141 Md46
Mui Ca Mau ☒ VN 89 Qc41
Mui Chan May Dong ☒ VN 89 Qe37
Muico ☒ MOC 147 Mk52
Mui Dôc ☒ VN 87 Qd37
Muié ☒ ANG 151 Ma53
Mui Ke Ga ☒ VN 89 Qe40
Mui Lai Gan ☒ VN 89 Qe40
Mui Lai Lai ☒ VN 87 Qd37
Mui Nai ☒ VN 89 Qc40
Mui Nam Tram ☒ VN 89 Qe38
Muine ☒ ANG 151 Ma54
Mui Ne ☒ VN 89 Qe40
Mui Ne Beach ☒ VN 89 Qe40
Mui Ron ☒ VN 87 Qd36
Mui Rong Quèn ☒ VN 87 Qc36
Muisné ☒ EC 196 Fk45
Mui Sot ☒ VN 87 Qc36
Muite ☒ MOC 153 Mk53
Muizenberg ☒ ZA 154 Lk63
Muju ☒ ROK 78 Rd27
Muju do Campos ☒ BR (PA) 199 Hc47
Muka ☒ Z 152 Md54
Mukačeve ☒ UA 43 Mc42
Mukah ☒ MAL 94 Qg44
Mukala ☒ RDC 149 Lj45
Mukana ☒ RDC 146 Md50
Mukandakunda ☒ Z 151 Mb52
Mukanga ☒ RDC 149 Ma49
Mukanya ☒ EAT 147 Mh50
Mukawwa Island ☒ ET 129 Mh34
Mukdaharn ☒ THA 89 Qc37
Mukdaharn N.P. ☒ THA 89 Qc37
Mukebo ☒ RDC 146 Me49
Muke Turi ☒ ETH 142 Mk41
Mukiteo ☒ USA (WA) 168 Dj22
Mukinbudin ☒ AUS (WA) 104 Qk51
Mukinge Hill ☒ Z 151 Mc52
Mu Ko Chang N.P. ☒ THA 89 Qb39
Mu Koh Angthong N.P. ☒ THA 88 Pk41
Mukomuko ☒ RI 93 Qa47
Mukono ☒ EAU 145 Mg47
Mu Ko Phetra N.P. ☒ THA 88 Pk42
Mukosa ☒ ZW 152 Mg54
Mu Ko Surin N.P. ☒ THA 88 Pj41
Mukokýn ☒ UA 41 Mf39
Mu Ko Tarutao N.P. ☒ THA 88 Pk42
Mukpalli ☒ IND (PJB) 80 Oh30
Mukrian ☒ IND (PJB) 80 Oh30
Mukry ☒ TM 63 Oc27
Muk Sukhteh ☒ IR 64 Ob31
Muktsar ☒ IND (PJB) 80 Oh30
Mukuku ☒ Z 146 Me52
Mukulaikwe ☒ Z 152 Md53
Mukunsa ☒ Z 146 Me50
Mukupa Kaoma ☒ Z 146 Me50
Mukutungu S.F. ☒ EAT 147 Mj50
Mul ☒ IND (MHT) 83 Ok35
Mula ☒ E 29 Kt52
Mulaku Atoll = Meemu Atoll ☒ MV 84 Qg44
Muldey ☒ AUS (NSW) 109 Se61
Muldza ☒ Z 152 Me53
Mulan ☒ CHN (HLG) 76 Re23
Mulanje ☒ MW 153 Mh54
Mulanje Mountains ☒ MW 153 Mh53
Mulaueur ☒ IND (TNU) 84 Oj40
Mulatos ☒ CO 192 Gb41
Mulaylah ☒ KSA 59 Ne32
Mulbagal ☒ IND (KTK) 85 Ok39
Mulchen ☒ RCH 208 Gd64
Mulde ☒ D 33 Lm41
Mule Creek Junction ☒ USA (WY) 169 Eh24
Mulegé ☒ MEX (BCS) 180 Ed32
Mulele ☒ Z 151 Mb54
Mulembe ☒ RDC 146 Me47
Mulende ☒ RDC 146 Me49
Muleshoe ☒ USA (TX) 174 Ej28
Muleta ☒ ETH 142 Na42
Mulevala ☒ MOC 153 Mk53
Mulga Park ☒ AUS (NT) 105 Rf58
Mulgathing ☒ AUS (SA) 108 Rg61
Muglidie ☒ AUS (QLD) 109 Sf58
Mulgrave ☒ CDN (NS) 176 Gk23
Mulgrave Hills ☒ USA (AK) 165 Bj12
Mulgul ☒ AUS (WA) 104 Qk58
Mulhacén ☒ E 27 Kr53
Mulhalli ☒ IND (KTK) 84 Oj39
Mülheim (Ruhr) ☒ D 32 Lg39
Mulhouse ☒ F 25 Lh43
Muli ☒ CHN (SCH) 87 Qa32
Muli ☒ MV 84 Qg44
Mulia ☒ RI 114 Rj47
Mulika Lodge ☒ EAK 144 Mk45
Mulilo ☒ Z 146 Me51
Muling ☒ CHN (HLG) 76 Rf23
Mulka ☒ AUS (SA) 108 Rk60
Mullaittivu ☒ CL 85 Pa41
Mullen ☒ USA (NE) 172 Ek24
Muller Range ☒ ANG 151 Sb48
Müller Range ☒ RI 94 Qg45
Mullet Peninsula ☒ IRL 19 Kk36
Mullewa ☒ AUS (WA) 104 Qh60
Mullingar ☒ IRL 19 Ko37
Mullins ☒ USA (SC) 178 Ga28
Mull of Galloway ☒ GB 20 Kq36
Mull of Kintyre ☒ GB 20 Kp35
Müllrose ☒ D 32 Lp38
Mullsjö ☒ S 31 Lo33
Mulobezi ☒ Z 151 Mc54
Mulondo ☒ ANG 150 Lh53
Mulonga Plain ☒ Z 151 Mb54
Mulongo ☒ RDC 146 Me49
Muloorina ☒ AUS (SA) 108 Rj60
Mulshi ☒ IND (MHT) 82 Og36
Multai ☒ IND (MHT) 82 Oj34
Mulu ☒ PK 65 Of30
Multan Fort ☒ PK 65 Of30
Multia ☒ FIN 38 Me28
Mulu ☒ ETH 142 Na41
Mulu ☒ MAL 94 Qh44
Muluala ☒ Z 151 Mb54
Mulu Caves ☒ MAL 94 Qh43
Mulundu ☒ Z 152 Me53
Mulu N.P., Gunung ☒ MAL 94 Qh43
Mulyungarie ☒ AUS (SA) 108 Sa61
Muma ☒ RDC 140 Mb44
Mumalla ☒ SUD 134 Mc40
Muman ☒ IR 64 Oa33
Mumbai ☒ IND (MHT) 82 Og36
Mumbei ☒ Z 151 Mb52
Mumbondo ☒ ANG 150 Lh51
Mumbué ☒ ANG 150 Lj52
Mumbwa ☒ Z 151 Mc53
Mumbwe ☒ RDC 146 Md51
Mumeng ☒ PNG 115 Sd49
Mumfor ☒ RI 114 Rh46
Mumias ☒ EAK 144 Mh45
Mummballup ☒ AUS (WA) 104 Qj62
Muna ☒ IND 81 Oj30
Muna ☒ MEX (YT) 183 Ff35
Muna ☒ RI 96 Rb48
Munaba ☒ IND (RJT) 82 Of33
Munaôernu ☒ IS 18 Jd24
Munamägi ☒ EST 39 Mh33
Munami ☒ RI 93 Qc48

Münchberg ☒ D 33 Lm40
Müncheberg ☒ D 32 Lp38
München ☒ D 33 Lm42
München-Riem ☒ D 33 Lm42
Münchique, P.N. ☒ CO 192 Gb44
Muncho Lake ☒ CDN (BC) 166 Dh16
Muncho Lake Prov. Park ☒ CDN 166 Dh16
Muncie ☒ USA (IN) 173 Fh25
Mundabullangana ☒ AUS (WA) 102 Qh56
Mundare ☒ CDN (AB) 169 Ed19
Munday ☒ USA (TX) 174 Fa29
Mundaú ☒ BR (CE) 201 Ja47
Mundaú ☒ BR 174 Fd28
Mundesley ☒ GB 21 Lb38
Mundford ☒ GB 21 La38
Mundi ☒ IND (MPH) 82 Oj34
Mundo Coelho ☒ BR (PA) 199 Hk49
Mundra ☒ IND (GUJ) 82 Oe34
Mundrabilla Motel ☒ AUS (WA) 105 Re61
Mundu ☒ SUD 144 Mf43
Mundubbera ☒ AUS (QLD) 109 Sf58
Mundul ☒ AFG 63 Of28
Mundwa ☒ IND (RJT) 80 Og32
Munenga ☒ ANG 148 Lh51
Munera ☒ E 29 Ks51
Mungallala ☒ AUS (QLD) 109 Sd59
Mungaoli ☒ IND (MPH) 80 Oj33
Mungeli ☒ IND (CGH) 83 Pa34
Mungeranie ☒ AUS (SA) 108 Rk60
Mungía ☒ E 28 Ks47
Mungindi ☒ AUS (NSW) 109 Se60
Mungjakarta A.L. ☒ AUS 106 Rh56
Munglinup ☒ AUS (WA) 104 Ra62
Mungo ☒ ANG 149 Lk49
Mungo ☒ AUS (NSW) 109 ...
Mungo N.P. ☒ AUS 111 Sb62
Mungo Park Memorial ☒ WAG 136 Kc39
Mungra Badshahpur ☒ IND (UPH) 83 Pb33
Munich ☒ D 33 Lm42
Muniesa ☒ E 29 Ku49
Munising ☒ USA (MI) 173 Fg22
Munkebo ☒ DK 30 Lt35
Munkfors ☒ S 31 Lo31
Munkumpu ☒ Z 151 Md52
Munmarlary ☒ AUS (NT) 106 Rg52
Munnar ☒ IND (KER) 84 Oj40
Munroe ☒ ROK 78 Rd27
Munshiganj ☒ BD 86 Pf34
Munshir Hat ☒ BD 86 Pf34
Münsingen ☒ D 33 Lk42
Münster ☒ CH 34 Lj44
Münster ☒ D 32 Lh39
Münster ☒ D 33 Lj38
Münster ☒ D 25 Lf42
Münster zu Ulm ☒ D 33 Ll42
Muntadgin ☒ AUS (WA) 104 Qk61
Muntele Mare ☒ RO 43 Md44
Munti Apuseni, P.N. ☒ RO 43 Md43
Munţii Călimani ☒ RO 43 Me43
Munţii Codru-Mona ☒ RO 43 Mc44
Munţii Fägäraşului ☒ RO 43 Me45
Munţii Gilău ☒ RO 43 Md44
Munţii Gurghiu ☒ RO 43 Me43
Munţii Lotrului ☒ RO 44 Md43
Munţii Măcinului, P.N. ☒ RO 45 Mj45
Munţii Maramureşului ☒ RO 43 Me43
Munţii Meseş ☒ RO 43 Md43
Munţii Metaliferi ☒ RO 43 Md44
Munţii Semenic ☒ RO 44 Mc45
Munţii Tarcului ☒ RO 44 Mc45
Munţii Vălcanului ☒ RO 44 Md44
Munţii Zarndului ☒ RO 43 Md44
Muntok ☒ RI 93 Qd47
Munţu ☒ RDC 149 Lk47
Munukata ☒ J 79 Rf29
Munyati ☒ ZW 152 Me53
Münzkirchen ☒ A 42 Lo42
Munzur Vadisi Milli Parkı ☒ TR 57 Mk28
Muocosimpolo ☒ S 16 Mb12
Muong Lan ☒ VN 87 Qc36
Muong Lay ☒ VN 87 Qb36
Muong Man ☒ VN 89 Qe40
Muong Tei ☒ VN 87 Qb34
Muonio ☒ FIN 16 Mb12
Mupa ☒ ANG 150 Lh54
Mupa, P.N.da ☒ ANG 150 Lh53
Muqakoori ☒ SP 145 Nd43
Muqaybirah ☒ YE 60 Nd39
Muqayhim ☒ KSA 60 Na34
Muqdisho ☒ SP 145 Nd44
Muqshin ☒ OM 61 Nh36
Muquém ☒ BR (ES) 203 Hk58
Muquém ☒ BR (BA) 199 Ha47
Muradiye ☒ TR 47 Mh52
Muradiye ☒ TR 57 Nb26
Muradiye Camii ☒ TR 47 Mh52
Murakami ☒ J 79 Rj26
Muralgarra ☒ AUS (WA) 104 Qj59
Muralla Romana de Lugo ☒ E 26 Kn48
Murallón, Cerro ☒ RA/RCH 210 Gd70
Muramgao ☒ IND (MHT) 83 Pa35
Muramvya ☒ BU 146 Me46
Murang'a ☒ EAK 144 Mj46
Murasan ☒ RI 96 Rc48
Murata ☒ SM 34 Ln47
Murato ☒ F 34 Lk48
Muravera ☒ I 36 Lk51
Murça ☒ P 26 Kn49
Murchison Range ☒ AUS 106 Rh55
Murchison Falls ☒ EAU 144 Mf44
Murchison Falls N.P. = Kabalega Falls N.P. ☒ EAU 144 Mf44
Murchison River ☒ AUS (WA) 104 Qh59

Murchison Roadhouse ☒ AUS (WA) 104 Qh59
Murcia ☒ E 29 Kt53
Murcia ☒ E 29 Kt53
Mur-de-Barrez ☒ F 25 Lc46
Mur-de-Bretagne ☒ F 22 Ks42
Murdochville ☒ CDN (QC) 176 Gh21
Murdock Point ☒ AUS 107 Sc53
Mureck ☒ A 35 Lo44
Mürefte ☒ TR 45 Mh50
Murehwa ☒ ZW 152 Mf53
Mureibit ☒ SYR 56 Mk27
Mureş ☒ RO 43 Ma44
Muret ☒ F 24 Lb47
Murfreesboro ☒ USA (AR) 174 Fd29
Murfreesboro ☒ USA (NC) 178 Gb27
Murfreesboro ☒ USA (TN) 175 Fg28
Murgan ☒ AUS (QLD) 109 Sf59
Murgap ☒ TM 62 Ob27
Murgap ☒ TJ 63 Oh26
Murgenella ☒ AUS (NT) 106 Rg51
Murgeşti ☒ RO 45 Mg45
Murgha Kibzai ☒ PK 65 Oe30
Murgia ☒ E 28 Ks48
Murgoo ☒ AUS (WA) 104 Qj59
Muri ☒ CHN (QHI) 72 Qa27
Muri ☒ BR (CE) 201 Ja48
Muricilândia ☒ BR (TO) 200 Hf49
Murieke ☒ PK 65 Oh30
Muriege ☒ ANG 149 Lk49
Murighiol ☒ RO 45 Mk45
Murin Bridge ☒ AUS (NSW) 111 Sb62
Muritiba ☒ CO 192 Gb42
Müritz ☒ D 32 Lo37
Müritz, N.P. ☒ D 32 Ln37
Murizidié Pass ☒ LAR 133 Lh34
Murliganj ☒ IND (BIH) 83 Pd32
Murmansk ☒ RUS 16 Mg11
Murmanskaya Rise ☒ 52 Md04
Murnaši ☒ RUS 16 Mg11
Murnau ☒ D 33 Lm43
Murnpeowie ☒ AUS (SA) 109 Se60
Muro del Alcoy ☒ E 29 Ku52
Muro Lucano ☒ I 37 Lq50
Murom ☒ RUS 48 Nb18
Muromgo ☒ EAT 144 Mf46
Muroran ☒ J 77 Sa24
Muros ☒ E 26 Kl47
Moroto ☒ J 79 Rh29
Muri ☒ IND (JKD) 168 Eb24
Murphysboro ☒ USA (IL) 175 Ff27
Murquishi ☒ 80 Od27
Murramarang National Park ☒ AUS (NSW) 111 Sh63
Murrat el Kubra ☒ ET 129 Mf30
Murray ☒ USA (KY) 175 Ff27
Murray ☒ USA (UT) 171 Ee25
Murray Bridge ☒ AUS (SA) 110 Rk63
Murray Downs ☒ AUS (NT) 106 Rh56
Murray Fracture Zone ☒ 11 Ca07
Murray Harbour ☒ CDN (PE) 176 Gj22
Murray Island ☒ AUS 107 Sb50
Murray River ☒ AUS 110 Qj62
Murray River ☒ AUS 111 Sc63
Murray River Basin ☒ AUS 110 Sa62
Murraysburg ☒ ZA 154 Mb61
Murray's Falls ☒ GUY 194 Ha44
Murray Sunset N.P. ☒ AUS 110 Sa63
Murrayville ☒ AUS (VIC) 110 Sa63
Murree ☒ PK 65 Og29
Murrhardt ☒ D 33 Lk42
Murrin ☒ MOC 153 Mj54
Murrin ☒ MOC 153 Mj54
Murrumbateman ☒ AUS (NSW) 111 Se63
Murrumburrah ☒ AUS (NSW) 109 Sf61
Murrupula ☒ MOC 153 Mk53
Murrurundi ☒ AUS (NSW) 109 Sf61
Murska Sobota ☒ SLO 42 Lr44
Mursko Središče ☒ HR 35 Lr44
Murtajapur ☒ IND (MHT) 82 Oj35
Murten ☒ CH 34 Lh44
Murter ☒ HR 35 Lq47
Murter ☒ HR 35 Lq47
Murua ☒ PNG 115 Se49
Muruasigar ☒ EAK 144 Mh45
Murud ☒ IND (MHT) 82 Og36
Murud Beach ☒ IND 82 Og36
Murudeshwar ☒ IND 84 Oh38
Murupara ☒ NZ 113 Tj65
Mururoa ☒ 11 Da12
Murwara ☒ IND (MPH) 83 Pa34
Murwillumbah ☒ AUS (NSW) 109 Sg60
Mürzzuschlag ☒ A 35 Lq43
Musa ☒ TR 57 Na26
Musa ☒ Z 151 Mc53
Musa Ali Terara ☒ DJI/ER/ETH 142 Nb40
Musaasaroole ☒ SP 145 Nc44
Musafirkhana ☒ IND (UPH) 83 Pa32
Musala ☒ WAL 136 Ke41
Musa Khel ☒ PK 65 Oe30
Musa Khel Bazar ☒ PK 65 Oe30
Musala ☒ BG 44 Md48
Musala ☒ RI 93 Pk45
Musale ☒ Z 152 Md53
Musallam ☒ IRQ 58 Nc29
Musandam Peninsula ☒ OM 64 Nj32
Musa Qal'eh ☒ AFG 65 Oc29
Musashi ☒ J 79 Rf29
Musawa ☒ WAN 138 Ld39
Muscat ☒ OM 61 Nk34
Muscatine ☒ USA (IA) 172 Fe25
Muschenheim ☒ E ...
Mu us Shamo ☒ CHN 72 Qd28
Muvattupuzha ☒ IND (KER) 84 Oj41
Muxi ☒ CHN (SCH) 74 Qb31
Muxia ☒ E 26 Kl47
Muxian ☒ CHN (YUN) 87 Qc34
Musale ☒ RI 93 Pk45
Muyinga ☒ BU 146 Mf47
Muy Muy ☒ NIC 184 Fh39
Muyuka ☒ CAM 138 Le42
Muyumba ☒ RDC 146 Md49
Muzaffarabad ☒ PK 65 Og29
Muzaffargarh ☒ PK 65 Of30
Muzaffarnagar ☒ IND (UPH) 81 Oj31
Muzaffarpur ☒ IND (BIH) 83 Pc32
Muzambinho ☒ BR (MG) 203 Hg56
Muzarabani ☒ ZW 152 Mf54
Muzen ☒ RDC 141 Md46
Muzeul Satului ☒ RO 45 Mf46
Müzejyê Hory ☒ CZ 42 Ln41
Muzillac ☒ F 22 Kr43
Muzo ☒ CO 192 Gc43
Muzquiz ☒ MEX (COH) 181 Ek32
Muztag ☒ CHN 68 Pg27
Muztagata ☒ CHN 66 Oh26
Mvagi ☒ CAM 139 Lg44
Mvengué ☒ CAM 139 Lg44
Mvomeozif ☒ EAT 147 Mj49
Mvomeoro ☒ RCB 148 Lg49
Mvoti ☒ ZA 155 Mf60
Mvuazi ☒ RDC 148 Lg48
Mvuma ☒ ZW 152 Mf54
Mvurwi ☒ ZW 152 Mf53
Mwanza Game Reserve ☒ MW 153 Mh54
Mwadui ☒ EAT 144 Mg47

Museuminsel in Berlin ☒ D 32 Lo38
Museumsmeile ☒ D 32 Lh40
Musgrave Harbour ☒ CDN (NF) 177 Hd21
Musgrave Range ☒ AUS 105 Rf59
Mushabani ☒ IND (JKD) 83 Pd34
Mushayfat ☒ SUD 135 Mf40
Mushenge ☒ RDC 149 Ma48
Mushima ☒ Z 151 Mc53
Mushima ☒ Z 151 Mc53
Mushipashi ☒ Z 146 Me51
Mushota ☒ Z 146 Me50
Mushrefah ☒ RO 48 Nb36
Mushu Island ☒ PNG 115 Sb47
Musin ☒ WAN 138 Le42
Musina ☒ ZA 152 Mf57
Muskauer Park ☒ D 32 Lp39
Muskegon ☒ USA (MI) 173 Fg24
Muskegon Heights ☒ USA (MI) 173 Fg24
Muslimabagh ☒ PK 65 Oe30
Muslim Pilgrimage site of Shek Husen ☒ ETH 142 Na42
Musofu ☒ Z 146 Me52
Musomeli ☒ EAT 144 Mg46
Musombe ☒ EAT 146 Mh49
Musoro ☒ Z 146 Mf52
Musoshi ☒ RDC 146 Me50
Musquodoboit Harbour ☒ CDN (NS) 176 Gj23
Musselburgh ☒ GB 20 Kr35
Mussende ☒ ANG 150 Lj52
Musserra ☒ ANG 148 Lg49
Mussian ☒ F 24 La45
Mussolo ☒ ANG 149 Lj51
Mussomeli ☒ I 36 Lo53
Mussoorie ☒ IND (UTT) 81 Ok30
Mussuma ☒ ANG 151 Ma53
Mussy-sur-Seine ☒ F 25 Le43
Mustafâbâd ☒ IND (UPH) 83 Pa33
Mustansar Kara Paşa Camii ☒ TR 56 Mh25
Mustafakemalpaşa ☒ TR 45 Mj50
Mustahil ☒ ETH 145 Nc43
Mustang ☒ NEP 81 Pb31
Mustang Island ☒ USA 181 Fb32
Mustér = Disentis ☒ CH 34 Lj44
Mustique ☒ WV 187 Gk39
Mustla ☒ EST 39 Mf32
Mustvee ☒ EST 38 Mg32
Muu Dan'ai PRK 76 Re25
Musungwa ☒ Z 151 Mc53
Muswellbrook ☒ AUS (NSW) 111 Sf62
Muszyna ☒ PL 41 Ma41
Mut ☒ ET 129 Me33
Mut ☒ TR 57 Mg27
Mutala ☒ MOC 153 Mj53
Mutambo dos Macombes ☒ MOC 147 Mk51
Mutambara ☒ BU 146 Me48
Mutambara ☒ ZW 152 Mg54
Mutampet ☒ IND (APH) 83 Ok36
Mutararam ☒ RI 93 Qc48
Mutare ☒ ZW 152 Mg54
Mutarnee ☒ AUS (QLD) 107 Sd55
Mutatá ☒ CO 192 Gb42
Mutavnligi N.P. (Mootwingee) ☒ AUS 108 Sb61
Mutengene ☒ CAM 138 Le42
Mutie ☒ N 30 Lf32
Mutiene ☒ RDC 148 Lh48
Mutinde ☒ EAT 146 Mf48
Muting ☒ RI 115 Sa49
Mutinhod ☒ MGA 49 Mg21
Mutis, Gunung ☒ RI 97 Rc50
Mutiweshiri ☒ ZW 152 Mf55
Mutoko ☒ ZW 152 Mg54
Mutomba Mukulu ☒ RDC 149 Me50
Mutooroo ☒ AUS (SA) 110 Sa62
Mutorashanga ☒ ZW 152 Mf54
Mutoto ☒ RDC 149 Mb48
Mutoto-saki ☒ J 79 Rf29
Mutrah ☒ OM 61 Nk34
Mutshatsha ☒ RDC 151 Mc51
Mutsu ☒ J 77 Sa25
Muttaburra ☒ AUS (QLD) 109 Sc57
Muttaparam ☒ IND (APH) ...
Muttonbird Island ☒ NZ 113 Td69
Muttukuru ☒ IND (APH) 85 Pa39
Mútuali ☒ MOC 153 Mj53
Mutuati ☒ EAK 144 Mk46
Mutukula ☒ EAU 144 Mf46
Mutum ☒ BR (AM) 199 Gk49
Mutum ☒ BR (MG) 203 Hj56
Mutum ☒ BR (MS) 202 Hd56
Mutumbi ☒ RDC 146 Me49
Mutum Biyu ☒ WAN 139 Lf41
Mutumparana ☒ RDC 146 Md49
Mutumbwe ☒ Z 151 Mc52
Mutum Daya ☒ WAN 139 Lf41
Mutum Paraná ☒ BR (RO) 198 Gh50
Mutungu-Tari ☒ RDC 148 Lj49
Mururame ☒ FIN 38 Mf28
Mvu ☒ CHN 72 Qc28
Muxi ☒ CHN (SCH) 74 Qb31
Muxima ☒ ANG 148 Lg50
Muyinga ☒ BU 146 Mf47
Muy Muy ☒ NIC 184 Fh39
Muyuka ☒ CAM 138 Le42
Muyumba ☒ RDC 146 Md49
Muzaffarabad ☒ PK 65 Og29
Muzaffargarh ☒ PK 65 Of30
Muzaffarnagar ☒ IND (UPH) 81 Oj31
Muzaffarpur ☒ IND (BIH) 83 Pc32
Muzambinho ☒ BR (MG) 203 Hg56
Muzarabani ☒ ZW 152 Mf54

Mwaga ☒ EAK 145 Mk47
Mwagné, P.N.de ☒ G 148 Lg45
Mwali = Mohéli ☒ COM 156 Nb52
Mwakibemba ☒ EAT 146 Mg49
Mwambo ☒ EAT 147 Na51
Mwana ☒ RDC 146 Mf48
Mwana-Ndeke ☒ RDC 146 Md48
Mwangala ☒ Z 151 Mb53
Mwangalala ☒ RDC 146 Md49
Mwango ☒ RDC 149 Ma49
Mwanza ☒ EAT 144 Mg47
Mwanza ☒ MW 153 Mh54
Mwanza ☒ RDC 146 Md49
Mwatate ☒ EAK 144 Mk47
Mwea National Reserve ☒ EAK 144 Mj46
Mweelrea ☒ IRL 19 Kl37
Mweka ☒ RDC 149 Ma48
Mwene-Biji ☒ RDC 149 Mb50
Mwene-Ditu ☒ RDC 146 Md49
Mwenezi ☒ ZW 152 Mf56
Mwenga ☒ RDC 146 Me47
Mwevelamabwe ☒ RDC 149 Mc50
Mwimbi ☒ EAT 146 Mf50
Mwinilunga ☒ Z 146 Mb51
Mwini Lunga ☒ Z 146 Mg51
Mwinilunga Petroglyphs ☒ Z 151 Mc51
Mwisi ☒ EAT 146 Mg48
Mwitika ☒ EAK 144 Mk46
Mwitikira ☒ EAT 147 Mh49
Myall Lakes N.P. ☒ AUS (NSW) 111 Sg62
Myalup ☒ AUS 104 Qh62
Mya, Mount ☒ CDN 166 Dj14
Myanaung ☒ MYA 86 Ph35
Myanmar ☒ MYA 58 Pb07
Myanganom ☒ MNG 70 Qa24
Myanganom ☒ MNG ...
Myaungmya ☒ MYA 86 Ph36
Mychla ☒ MYA 86 Pj36
Myczków ☒ PL 41 Mc41
Mye, Mount ☒ CDN 166 Dj14
Myingyan ☒ MYA 86 Ph35
Myinmu ☒ MYA 86 Ph35
Myitkyina ☒ MYA 86 Ph33
Myittha ☒ MYA 86 Ph35
Myjava ☒ SK 42 Ls42
Mykénai ☒ GR 46 Mc53
Mykélajiv ☒ UA 48 Mb41
Mykky'iv ☒ UA 49 Mf22
Mykolajivka ☒ UA 49 Mg23
Mykulyčí ☒ UA 41 Me40
Myla Kharai ☒ PK 65 Od33
Mynfontein ☒ ZA 155 Mb61
Myo ☒ MYA 86 Ph35
Myola ☒ AUS (QLD) 107 Sa55
Myōjin ☒ SUD 141 Me42
Myoshi ☒ J 79 Rg28
Myotha ☒ MYA 86 Ph35
Myra ☒ TR 56 Mf27
Myrdal ☒ N 30 Lf30
Myrdalsjökull ☒ IS 18 Ka27
Myre ☒ N 16 Lo11
Myres Castle ☒ GB 20 Kr34
Myrhorod ☒ UA 49 Mg21
Mýrnatangi ☒ IS 18 Ki23
Myrorna ☒ BR (AM) 198 Gj49
Myronivka ☒ UA 49 Mg21
Myra ☒ TR 56 Mf27
Myrtle Beach ☒ USA (SC) 178 Ga29
Myrtle Creek ☒ USA (OR) 168 Dj24
Myrtle Point ☒ USA (OR) 168 Dh24
Myrvicken ☒ S 16 Ln14
Mys Alevina ☒ RUS 55 Sc07
Mys Anva ☒ RUS 77 Sa22
Mys Buor-Haja ☒ RUS 55 Rc04
Mys Elizavety ☒ RUS 55 Sa06
Mysen ☒ N 30 Lm31
Mys Gamova ☒ RUS 76 Rf24
Mys Južnyj ☒ RUS 55 Ra08
Mys Kamčatskij ☒ RUS 55 Sa07
Mys Kanin Nos ☒ RUS 54 Na05
Mys Kolgompja ☒ RUS 38 Mj31
Mys Krii'on ☒ RUS 77 Sb23
Mys Kronockij ☒ RUS 55 Sa08
Mys Kurgolskij ☒ RUS 38 Mj31
Mys Lopatka ☒ RUS 55 Sa08
Mys Lovcova ☒ RUS 77 Sd23
Mys Navarin ☒ RUS 55 Tb06
Mys Neupokoeva ☒ RUS 54 Pd03
Mys Oljutorskij ☒ RUS 55 Tc07
Mysore ☒ IND (KTK) 84 Oj39
Mysore Palace ☒ IND 84 Oj39
Mysovka ☒ RUS 39 Mb35
Mys Ozernoj ☒ RUS 55 Ta07
Mys Rikorda ☒ RUS 77 Sd23
mys Smidta ☒ RUS 55 Ua05
Mys Tajgonos ☒ RUS 55 Sc08
Mys Terpenija ☒ RUS 55 Sb09
Mys Tolstoj ☒ RUS 55 Sa08
Myszków ☒ PL 41 Lu40
Myszyniec ☒ PL 41 Mb37
My Tho ☒ VN 89 Qd40
Mytilíni ☒ GR 47 Mg51
Myvatn ☒ IS 18 Kd25
Mze ☒ CZ 42 Ln39
Mzimba ☒ MW 146 Mh52
Mzuzu ☒ MW 146 Mh51

N

Naab ☒ D 33 Ln41
Naala ☒ TCH 139 Lh39
Naalehu ☒ USA (HI) 170 Cc36
Na'am ☒ SUD 141 Me43
Na'am ☒ SUD 141 Me43
Naantali = Nådendal ☒ FIN 38 Mb30
Nababeep ☒ ZA 154 Lj60
Nabadwip ☒ IND (WBG) 86 Pe34
Nabaji ☒ TCH 134 Ma38
Nabat ☒ TCH 134 Ma36
Nabatiyé ☒ RL 56 Mh29
Nabburg ☒ D 33 Ln41
Naberera ☒ EAT 147 Mj47
Nabeul ☒ TN 126 Lf27
Nabeina ☒ RI 97 Re47
Nabire ☒ RI 114 Rh47
Nabk Abu Qasr ☒ KSA 59 Ne32

Nabiganj ☒ BD 86 Pf33
Nabilatuk ☒ EAU 144 Mh44
Nabire ☒ RI 114 Rh47
Nabk Abu Qasr ☒ KSA 59 Ne32
Nabolgou ☒ TG 137 La40
Naboomspruit ☒ ZA 152 Me58
Nabon Reef ☒ AUS 105 Sd62
Nabq ☒ ET 129 Mh31
Nabq Reserve ☒ ET 129 Mh31
Nabua ☒ RP 90 Rb39
Nabua ☒ RP 90 Rb39
Naburn ☒ ...
Nabire ☒ ...
Nabouwalu ☒ FIJI 119 Tk54
Nabq ☒ ...
Naburi ☒ IND (MPH) 83 Pb33
Nacala ☒ MOC 153 Na53
Nacala Velha ☒ MOC 153 Na53
Nacavala ☒ MOC 153 Na53
Nacebe ☒ BOL 198 Gg51
Nachachi ☒ MEX (CHH) 180 Eg32
Nachindundo ☒ MOC 147 Na51
Nachingwea ☒ EAT 147 Na51
Nachna ☒ IND (RJT) 80 Og32
Náchod ☒ CZ 42 Lr40
Na Chuak ☒ THA 89 Qb38
Nachuge ☒ IND (AN) 88 Pg40
Nacimiento ☒ RCH 208 Gd64
Nacionalný park Pričbrus'e ☒ RUS 57 Nd24
Nackara ☒ AUS (SA) 110 Rk62
Naco ☒ MEX (SO) 180 Ef30
Naco ☒ USA (AZ) 171 Ef30
Nacogdoches ☒ USA (TX) 174 Fc30
Nacori Chico ☒ MEX (SO) 180 Ef30
Nacuñán ☒ RA (MD) 208 Gg63
Nad Al Sheba ☒ UAE 61 Nh33
Nachna Dahul ☒ CHN 71 Qh24
Nadarçye ☒ PL 40 Lr37
Nadawli ☒ GH 137 Kk40
Nadbużański Park Krajobrazowy ☒ PL 41 Mb38
Nádendal = Naantali ☒ FIN 38 Mc30
Naivasha ☒ EAK 144 Mj46
Naivasha, Lake ☒ EAK 144 Mj46
Nadi ☒ FJI 119 Tj54
Nadi ☒ SUD 135 Mf40
Nadiad ☒ IND (GUJ) 82 Og34
Nádlac ☒ RO 43 Ma44
Nadne ☒ ...
Nadbari ☒ IND (UTT) 81 Ok31
Nadbari ...
Nadi ☒ ...
Nadotki ☒ ...
Nadterečnyj ☒ RUS 57 Nd24
Nadur ☒ M 36 Lp54
Nadvirna ☒ UA 43 Me42
Nadym ☒ RUS 54 Ob06
Næbebud ☒ DK 30 Ll35
Naefferd ☒ AFG 63 Oc27
Nakagawa ☒ J 79 Sb23
Nakagusuku Castle ☒ J 79 Rd32
Nærbø ☒ N 30 Lf32
Nærøyfjorden ☒ N 17 Ld15
Næstved ☒ DK 30 Lm35
Nafada ☒ WAN 139 Lf40
Nafarete ☒ MEX (CHH) 181 Eh32
Náfpaktos ☒ GR 46 Mb52
Náfplio ☒ GR 46 Mc53
Naft Khaneh ☒ IRQ 57 Nc28
Nafud ad Dahi ☒ KSA 60 Nc35
Nafud al Uruq ☒ KSA 58 Nb33
Nafud as Sirr ☒ KSA 59 Nb32
Nafud ath Thuwayrat ☒ KSA 59 Nc32
Nag ☒ PK 65 Oc32
Naga ☒ DZ 125 Kg31
Naga ☒ RP 90 Rb39
Nagagami ☒ CDN 173 Fk21
Nagai Island ☒ USA 164 Bk18
Nagaland ☒ IND 86 Ph33
Nagambie ☒ AUS (VIC) 111 Sc64
Nagano ☒ J 79 Rk27
Nagaoka ☒ J 77 Rk27
Nagappattinam ☒ IND (TNU) 85 Ok40
Nagar ☒ IND (RJT) 80 Og33
Nagar ☒ IND (TNU) 85 Ok39
Nagarhole ☒ IND (KTK) 84 Oj39
Nagarhole N.P. ☒ IND 84 Oh40
Nagari ☒ IND (TNU) 85 Ok39
Nagarjunasagar-Srisailam ☒ IND (APH) 82 Ok37
Nagarote ☒ NIC 184 Fg39
Nagar Parkar ☒ PK 65 Of33
Nagarze ☒ CHN (TIB) 68 Pf31
Nagasaki ☒ J 79 Re29
Nagasamudram ☒ IND (APH) 84 Oj38
Nagasari ☒ IND (GUJ) 82 Of35
Nagash Mosque ☒ ETH 142 Mk39
Nagato ☒ J 79 Rf28
Nagatsugawa ☒ J 79 Rj28
Nagda ☒ IND (RJT) 80 Og32
Nagda ☒ IND (MHT) 83 Oh34
Nagel ☒ ...
Nagele ☒ NL 23 Lf38
Nagha Kalat ☒ PK 65 Od32
Naghan ☒ IR 59 Nf30
Nagina ☒ IND (UPH) 81 Ok31
Nagir ☒ PK 65 Oh27
Nago ☒ J 79 Rd32
Nagod ☒ IND (MPH) 83 Pa33
Nagod ☒ CL 85 Pa41
Nagoro ☒ ANG 151 Ma53
Nagorny ☒ RUS 55 Qo07
Nagoya ☒ J 79 Rj28
Nagpur ☒ IND (MHT) 83 Ok35
Nagqu ☒ CHN 68 Pg29
Nag's Head ☒ ...
Nagua ☒ DOM 186 Gf36
Nagua ☒ ...
Nagar ☒ ...
Nagykálló ☒ H 42 La43
Nagyatád ☒ H 42 Ls44
Nagybajom ☒ ...
Nagyhalász ☒ H 43 Mb43
Nagykanizsa ☒ H 42 Ls44
Nagykáta ☒ H 43 Lu43
Nagykörös ☒ H 43 Lu43
Nagyszénás ☒ H 43 Ma44
Naha ☒ J 79 Rd32
Nahach ☒ ...
Nahe ☒ D 33 Lh41
Nahanni Butte ☒ CDN (NWT) 167 Dh15
Nahanni Range ☒ CDN 167 Dj15

Nahavand ☒ IR 57 Ne28
Nahavand ☒ IR 57 Ne28
Nahe ☒ D 33 Lh41
Nahleg ☒ IR 114 Rh47
Nahodka ☒ RUS 77 Rg24
Nahodka ☒ RUS 54 Ob05
Nahoma Reef ☒ ZA 155 Md62
Nahoria ☒ IND (MPH) 83 Pb33
Nahoro ☒ EAT 147 Mj51
Nahr az Zab al Kabir ☒ IRQ 57 Nc28
Nahr az Zab as Saghir ☒ IRQ 57 Nc27
Nahuchita ☒ MEX (CHH) 181 Eh32
Nahuala ☒ MOC 153 Na53
Nahuelbuta, P.N. ☒ RCH 208 Gd64
Nahuel Huapi ☒ RA (RN) 208 Ge66
Nahuel Huapi, P.N. ☒ RA (RN) 208 Ge66
Nahuel Mapá ☒ RA (SL) 208 Gg63
Naicá ☒ USA (GA) 178 Fk30
Naiguata ☒ YV (GDG) 74 Qf35
Nai ☒ PNG 116 Se46
Naica ☒ MEX (CHH) 181 Eh32
Naicam ☒ CDN (SK) 169 Eh19
Naij Tal ☒ CHN (QHI) 69 Ph28
Naikliu ☒ RI 97 Rc50
Nailoon Prov. Park ☒ CDN ...
Naila ☒ D 33 Lm40
Naco ☒ ...
Nainital ☒ IND (UTT) 81 Ok31
Naipopo ☒ ...
Naiqiu ☒ CHN (SCH) 87 Qa31
Nairn ☒ GB 20 Kr33
Nairobi N.P. ☒ EAK 144 Mj46
Naissaar ☒ EST 38 Me31
Naivasha ☒ EAK 144 Mj46
Najaf ☒ IRQ 58 Nc30
Najafabad ☒ IR 59 Nf29
Najac ☒ F 24 Lc46
Najafabad ☒ IR 57 Ne28
Najibabad ☒ IND (UPH) 81 Ok31
Najin ☒ PRK 76 Rf24
Najitun ☒ GCA 183 Ff37
Najran ☒ KSA 60 Nb37
Naju ☒ ROK 78 Rd28
Naka ☒ ...
Nakachenje ☒ Z 152 Md53
Nakadori-jima ☒ J 79 Rd29
Nakagawa ☒ J 79 Sb23
Nakamura ☒ J 79 Rg29
Nakane ☒ RUS 55 Qb06
Nakanno ☒ RUS 55 Qb06
Nakano ☒ J 79 Rg27
Nakano-jima ☒ J 79 Rg27
Naka-Tane ☒ J 79 Rf30
Nakatsu ☒ J 79 Rf29
Nakawale ☒ EAT 146 Mh51
Nakerka-N.B.C.A. ☒ LAO 87 Qc36
Nakfa ☒ ER 135 Mk37
Nakfa Wildlife Reserve ☒ ER 135 Mk37
Nakhl ☒ OM 61 Nj34
Nakhl Shabbah ☒ KSA 60 Na35
Na Khoang ☒ VN 87 Qb35
Nakhola ☒ IND (ASS) 86 Pg32
Nakhon Nayok ☒ THA 88 Qa38
Nakhon Pathom ☒ THA 88 Qa38
Nakhon Phanom ☒ THA 87 Qc37
Nakhon Ratchasima ☒ THA 89 Qb38
Nakhon Sawan ☒ THA 88 Qa38
Nakhon Si Thammarat ☒ THA 88 Pk41
Nakhon Thai ☒ THA 87 Qa37
Nakhtarana ☒ IND (GUJ) 82 Oe34
Naki-East ☒ TG 137 La40
Nakifuma ☒ EAU 144 Mg45
Nakiloro ☒ EAU 144 Mh44
Nakina ☒ CDN (ON) 173 Fg20
Nakło nad Notecia ☒ PL 40 Ls37
Naklo ☒ SI 35 Lp44
Nako ☒ CDN (AK) 164 Cd16
Nakodar ☒ IND (PJB) 80 Oh30
Nakonde ☒ Z 146 Mg50
Nakuru ☒ EAK 144 Mj46
Nakrekal ☒ IND (APH) 83 Ok37
Naksoy ☒ DK 30 Lm35
Naku-Tombetsu ☒ J 77 Sb23
Nakur ☒ PK 65 Oc32
Nalalate Ruins ☒ ZW 152 Me55
Nalayh ☒ MNG 70 Qd22
Nalazi ☒ MOC 152 Mg58
Nalbant ☒ RO 45 Mj45
Nalbari ☒ IND (ASS) 86 Pf32
Naldurg ☒ IND (MHT) 82 Oj37
Nalerigu ☒ GH 137 La40
Nalgonda ☒ IND (APH) 83 Ok37
Nali ☒ IND (UPH) 83 Pb33
Nalikul ☒ IND (WBG) 86 Pe34
Nalivkino ☒ SK 43 Ma42
Nallamala Hills ☒ IND 82 Ok37
Nallhan ☒ TR 56 Mf26
Nalón ☒ E 26 Kp47
Nalong ☒ MYA 86 Pj36
Nalut ☒ LAR 126 Le29
Nalwangga ☒ EAT 147 Mk50
Namaacha ☒ MOC 155 Mg58
Namacurra ☒ MOC 153 Mk54
Namadgi N.P. ☒ AUS (ACT) 111 Se63
Namahadi ☒ ZA 155 Me60
Namak, Lake ☒ IR 57 Nf29
Namakzar-e Shadad ☒ IR 64 Nj30

Nandaime ☒ NIC 184 Fg40
Nandaly ☒ AUS (VIC) 111 Sb63
Nandankanan Biological Park ☒ IND 83 Pc35
Nandavaram ☒ IND (APH) 85 Ok38
Nanded ☒ IND (MHT) 82 Oj36
Nandewar Range ☒ AUS 109 Sf61
Nandewar Range ☒ IND (MHT) 82 Oj35
Nandgaon Kaji ☒ IND (MHT) 82 Oj35
Nandghat ☒ IND (CGH) 83 Pa35
Nandi ☒ ZW 152 Mf55
Nandian ☒ CHN (YUN) 87 Qb34
Nandikotkur ☒ IND (APH) 82 Ok38
Nandoman ☒ GH 137 Kj40
Nandowrie ☒ AUS (QLD) 109 Sd58
Nandu ☒ IND (MHT) 82 Oj35
Nandurbar ☒ IND (MHT) 82 Oh34
Nandyal ☒ IND (APH) 82 Ok38
Nanfeng ☒ CHN (JGX) 75 Qh33
Nanga ☒ MOC 147 Mk51
Nanga ☒ RI 95 Qf45
Nangade ☒ MOC 147 Mk51
Nangai Ketunga ☒ RI 95 Qf45
Nanga Mahap ☒ RI 95 Qf46
Nanga Mau ☒ RI 95 Qf46
Nangandu ☒ EAT 147 Mj49
Nanganga ☒ EAT 147 Mj49
Nanga Pinoh ☒ RI 95 Qf46
Nangaroro ☒ RI 96 Ra50
Nanga Sokan ☒ RI 95 Qf46
Nanga Suruk ☒ RI 94 Qg45
Nanga Tamin ☒ MAL 94 Qg44
Nangis ☒ F 23 Ld42
Nangola ☒ RMM 137 Kg39
Nangolet ☒ SUD 144 Mg43
Nangpakela ☒ RI 95 Qf45
Nangnan ☒ MYA 86 Pj35
Nang Rong ☒ THA 89 Qb38
Nanguruwe ☒ EAT 147 Na51
Nangwarry ☒ AUS (SA) 110 Sa64
Nangwashi ☒ Z 151 Mb54
Nang Xian ☒ CHN (TIB) 69 Pg31
Nan Hua ☒ CHN 75 Qg34
Nanhui ☒ CHN (SHG) 78 Ra30
Nanjangud ☒ IND (KTK) 84 Oj39
Nanjiang ☒ CHN (SCH) 72 Qd29
Nanjian Yizu Zizhixian ☒ CHN (YUN) 87 Qa34
Nanjing ☒ CHN (JGS) 78 Qk29
Nannup ☒ AUS (WA) 104 Qh63
Na No ☒ THA 87 Qa36
Nanoro ☒ BF 137 Kj39
Nanortalik ☒ ...
Nanpara ☒ IND (UPH) 81 Pa32
Nanpeng Liedao ☒ CHN 75 Qj34
Nanping ☒ CHN (FJN) 75 Qj33
Nanping ☒ CHN (HUB) 74 Qg31
Nanping ☒ CHN (SCH) 72 Qc29
Nanri Dao ☒ CHN 75 Qk33
Nanripo ☒ MOC 153 Mk53
Nansebo ☒ ETH 142 Mk42
Nansei Islands ☒ J 79 Rc33
Nansen, Mount ☒ CDN 163 Fa03
Nansen Sound ☒ CDN 163 Fa03
Nan Shan ☒ CHN 72 Qa27
Nantai ☒ EAT 144 Mg47
Nanterre ☒ F 23 Lc42
Nantes ☒ F 22 Ks43
Nanteuil-le-Haudouin ☒ F 23 Lc41
Nanti, Gunung ☒ RI 93 Qb47
Nantillanais ☒ ...
Nantlla ☒ CAM (NS) 139 Sb61
Nanton ☒ CDN (AB) 169 Ed20
Nanton ☒ GH 137 Kk41
Nantong ☒ CHN (JGS) 78 Ra29
Nantou ☒ RC 75 Ra34
Nantua ☒ F 25 Lf44
Nantucket ☒ USA (MA) 177 Ge25
Nantucket Island ☒ USA 177 Gf25
Nantucket Shoals ☒ USA 177 Gf25
Nantucket Sound ☒ USA 177 Gf25
Nantula ☒ MOC 147 Mk52
Nantuto ☒ MOC 153 Mj53
Nantwich ☒ GB 21 Kr37
Nanuque ☒ BR (MG) 203 Hk54
Nanutarra ☒ AUS (WA) 102 Qh57
Nanxi ☒ CHN (SCH) 74 Qc32
Nan Xian ☒ CHN (HUN) 74 Qg31
Nanxiong ☒ CHN (GDG) 75 Qh34
Nanxu ☒ CHN (GZG) 74 Qf34
Nanyang ☒ CHN (HNN) 73 Qg29
Nanyangdan Shan ☒ CHN 75 Ra32
Nan-yo ☒ J 77 Sa26
Nanyuki ☒ EAK 144 Mj46
Nanzamu ☒ CHN (LNG) 76 Rc25
Nanzhang ☒ CHN (HUB) 74 Qf30
Nanzhao ☒ CHN (HNN) 73 Qg29
Nanzheng ☒ CHN (SAA) 72 Qd29
Nanzhila Rest Camp ☒ Z 151 Mc54
Nao ☒ BD 86 Pe33
Naoklak ☒ USA (AK) 165 Ce11
Naolinco ☒ MEX (VC) 182 Fb36
Não-me-Toque ☒ BR (RS) 204 Hd60
Naora ☒ PNG 116 Sf51
Náoussa ☒ GR 46 Mc50
Napa, Cerro ☒ BR/RCH 206 Gf56
Napa ☒ USA (CA) 170 Dj26
Napabale Lake ☒ RI 96 Rb48
Na Pali Coast ☒ USA 170 Ca34
Napanwainam ☒ RI 114 Rh47
Napan-yaur ☒ RI 114 Rh47
Napata and Jebel Barkal Temples ☒ SUD 135 Mf37
Napatode ☒ EAK 144 Mj45
Napido ☒ RI 114 Rh46
Napier ☒ NZ 113 Tj65
Napier ☒ ZA 154 Lk63
Napier Mountains ☒ 7 Nc32
Naples ☒ I 37 Lp50
Naples ☒ USA (FL) 179 Fk32
Napo ☒ CHN (GZG) 87 Qd34
Napo ☒ PE 196 Gc46

Napoleon – Nikopol

Napoleon AUS (QLD) 109 Sc59
Napoleon USA (ND) 172 Fa22
Napoleon USA (OH) 173 Fh25
Nápoli I 37 Lp50
Nappamerrie AUS (QLD) 108 Sa59
Nappanee USA (IN) 173 Fh25
Napperby AUS (NT) 103 Rg57
Naqâda ET 129 Mg33
Naqb al-Hadjar YE 60 Nd38
Naqedeh IR 57 Nc27
Naqil al Farda YE 60 Nc38
Naqš-e-Šapur IR 64 Nh31
När S 31 Lt33
Nara J 79 Rh28
Nara RMM 131 Kg38
Narač BY 39 Mg36
Nara Canal PK 65 Oe32
Naracoorte AUS (SA) 110 Sa64
Naracoorte Caves Conservation Park AUS 110 Sa64
Naraha IND (BIH) 83 Pd32
Naraini IND (UPH) 83 Pa33
Narainpur IND (CGH) 83 Pa36
Narajiv UA 43 Me41
Naran PK 63 Og28
Narang AFG 63 Of28
Naranjal EC 196 Ga47
Naranjal PY 204 Hc58
Naranjito EC 196 Ga47
Naranjos BOL 206 Ha55
Naranjos MEX (VC) 182 Fb35
Narao J 79 Re29
Narasannapeta IND (APH) 83 Pc36
Narasapur IND (APH) 83 Pa37
Narasaraopet IND (APH) 83 Pa37
Narasimharajapura IND (KTK) 84 Oh39
Narasinghpur IND (ORS) 83 Pc35
Narathiwat THA 89 Qa42
Nara Visa USA (NM) 174 Ej28
Naravuka FJI 119 Tk54
Narayanganj BD 86 Pf34
Narayanganj IND (MPH) 83 Pa34
Narayangaon IND (MHT) 82 Og36
Narayanpet IND (APH) 82 Oj37
Narayan Sarovar IND 82 Oe34
Narberth GB 21 Kq39
Narbonne F 25 Lc47
Narborough = Isla Fernandina EC 197 Fe46
Narcondan Island IND 88 Ph39
Nardò I 37 Lt50
Nardoo AUS (NSW) 109 Sc60
Narečenski bani BG 45 Me49
Narellen AUS (NSW) 111 Sf63
Narembeen AUS (WA) 104 Qk62
Naréna RMM 136 Kf39
Nares Abyssal Plain 160 Gb07
Nares Strait 163 Gb03
Naretha AUS (WA) 105 Rc61
Narew PL 41 Md38
Narewka PL 41 Md38
Nargund IND (KTK) 82 Oh38
Na Rì VN 87 Qd34
Narib NAM 154 Lj58
Narin Nur CHN (NMZ) 72 Qe26
Narita J 79 Sa28
Nar'jan-Mar RUS 54 Nc05
Narlı TR 56 Mj27
Narmada IND 82 Oh35
Narman TR 57 Na25
Narnaul IND (HYA) 80 Oj31
Narni I 34 Ln48
Narochanski N.P. BY 39 Mg36
Naro-Fominsk RUS 48 Mj18
Naro Island RP 90 Rb40
Narok EAK 144 Mh46
Naro Moru EAK 144 Mj46
Narooma AUS (NSW) 111 Sf64
Naro Sura EAK 144 Mh46
Narovlja BY 48 Me20
Narowal PK 65 Oh29
Närpes = Närpiö FIN 38 Mb28
Narphung BHT 86 Pf32
Närpiö = Närpes FIN 38 Mb28
Narra RP 91 Qk41
Narrabri AUS (NSW) 109 Se61
Narrandera AUS (NSW) 111 Sd63
Narrawallee Beach AUS 111 Sf63
Narrogin AUS (WA) 104 Qj62
Narromine AUS (NSW) 111 Se62
Narrowsburg USA (NY) 177 Gc25
Narsampet IND (APH) 83 Ok37
Narsapur IND (APH) 82 Ok37
Narsarsuaq DK 163 Hc06
Narsi IND (MHT) 82 Oj36
Narsinghgarh IND (MPH) 82 Oj34
Narsinghpur IND (MPH) 83 Ok34
Narsipatnam IND (APH) 83 Pb37
Nart CHN (NMZ) 71 Qh24
Nart MNG 70 Qc21
Nartkala RUS (KBA) 57 Nb24
Naru-jima J 79 Re29
Narupa EC 196 Gb46
Naruto J 79 Rh28
Narva EST 38 Mj31
Narvacan RP 90 Ra37
Narva-Jõesuu EST 38 Mj31
Närvijoki FIN 38 Mb28
Narvik N 16 Lj11
Narwai IND (MPH) 83 Oj33
Narwana IND (HYA) 80 Oj31
Narwiański P.N. PL 41 Mc37
Narwinbi Aboriginal Reserve AUS 106 Rj53
Naryilco AUS (QLD) 108 Sa60
Naryn KS 66 Oh25
Naryn KS 66 Oj25
Naryn KZ 66 Oh23
Naryn RUS (TUV) 67 Ph20
Narynkol KZ 66 Pa24
Naryškino RUS 48 Mh19
Nås S 31 Lp30
Năsăud RO 43 Me43
Nasavrky CZ 42 Lq41
Nasbinals F 25 Ld46
Nascentes do Rio Parnaíba, P.N.das BR 200 Hh51
Nash Harbor USA (AK) 164 Bg15
Nashua USA (NH) 177 Ge24
Nashu Bum MYA 86 Pj33
Nashville USA (AR) 174 Fd29
Nashville USA (GA) 178 Fj30
Nashville USA (NC) 178 Ga28
Nashville USA (TN) 175 Fg27
Nashville Superspeedway USA (TN) 175 Fg27
Nashwaak Bridge CDN (NB) 176 Gg22
Nasia GH 137 Kk40
Nasibât Timâna ET 129 Mg34
Našice HR 35 Lt45
Nasielsk PL 41 Ma38
Nasik IND (MHT) 82 Og36
Nasik RI 95 Qd47
Nasik Road IND (MHT) 82 Og36
Nasi, Mount ETH 142 Mh41
Nasionale Addo Olifantpark ZA 155 Mc62
Nasionale Augrabieswatervalpark ZA 154 Ma60
Nasionale Krugerwildtuin = Kruger N.P. ZA 152 Mf57
Nasipit RP 91 Rc41
Nasir SUD 142 Mg41
Nasirabad IND (RJT) 80 Oh32
Nasirabad PK 65 Oe31
Nasiriyan IR 59 Nd29
Nasmah LAR 127 Lg30
Naso I 37 Lp52
Nasolot EAK 144 Mh45
Nasolot National Reserve EAK 144 Mh45
Nason SME 194 Hc43
Nasondoye RDC 149 Mc51
Naso Point RP 90 Ra40
Nasorolevu FJI 119 Tk54
Nasrapur IND (MHT) 82 Og36
Nasrullahganj IND (MPH) 82 Oj34
Nassarawa WAN 138 Ld41
Nassau BS 179 Gb33
Nassau D 33 Lh40
Nassau Island NZ 10 Bb11
Nass Basin CDN 166 Df17
Nassian CI 137 Kh41
Nassian CI 137 Kj41
Nässjö S 31 Lp33
Nassoukou DY 138 La40
Nassoumfou BF 131 Kk38
Nastola FIN 38 Mf30
Nasugbu RP 90 Ra38
Nasuraghena SOL 117 Tb51
Nata PA 185 Fk41
Nata RB 152 Md56
Nataja MW 153 Mh53
Natal BR (RN) 201 Jc48
Natal BR (TO) 200 Hf48
Natal RI 93 Pk45
Natal Downs AUS (QLD) 109 Sd56
Natal Felicidade, T.I. BR 199 Ha47
Natalinci SCG 44 Ma46
Natálio PY 204 Hc59
Natanz IR 59 Nf29
Nataraja Temple IND 85 Ok40
Nata Sanctuary RB 152 Md56
Natchez USA (MS) 175 Fe30
Natchez Trace Parkway (Mississippi) USA 175 Fe29
Natchez Trace Parkway (Tennessee) USA 175 Fg28
Natchez Trace Resort S.P. USA 175 Ff28
Natchitoches USA (LA) 174 Fd30
Nathahu MYA 88 Ph37
Nathan River AUS (NT) 106 Rh53
Na Thawi THA 88 Qa42
Nathdwara IND (RJT) 82 Og33
Nathenje MW 152 Mg53
Na Thon THA 88 Pk41
Nathorst Land N 16 Lh07
Nathrop USA (CO) 171 Eg26
Na-ti MYA 87 Pk34
Natiboani BF 137 La40
Natimuk AUS (VIC) 110 Sa64
Natinga = Garu GH 137 Kk40
Nation USA (AK) 165 Ck13
National Botanical Gardens (Pyin U Lwin) MYA 86 Ph35
National Chambal Wildlife Sanctuary IND 82 Oj33
National Hall of Fame for Famous A. Ind. USA 174 Fa28
National Hist. District (Bentonsport) USA 172 Fe25
Nationalpark CH 34 Ll44
National Park NZ 113 Th65
Nationalpark Eifel D 32 Lg40
National Radio Astronomy Observatory USA 177 Ga26
National Radio Astronomy Observatory VLA Telescope (Socorro NM) USA 171 Eg29
National Railroad Museum USA 178 Ga28
National West Coast Tourist Recreation Area NAM 150 Lg56
National Wool Museum AUS (VIC) 111 Sc65
Natitingou DY 137 La40
Natividade BR (TO) 200 Hg51
Nat ma taung N.P. MYA 86 Pg35
Natmauk MYA 86 Ph35
Natore BD 86 Pe33
Natrona USA (WY) 169 Eg24
Nattai N.P. AUS 111 Sf63
Nåttarö S 31 Lt32
Nattaung MYA 86 Pj36
Nättraby S 31 Lq34
Natuco MOC 153 Mj52
Natuna Besar RI 94 Qe43
Natuna Sea RI 92 Qd45
Natural Arch USA 175 Fh27
Natural Bridge USA (AL) 175 Fg28
Naturaliste Plateau 104 Qf62
Naturita USA (CO) 171 Ef26
Naturno = Naturns I 34 Ll44
Naturns = Naturno I 34 Ll44
Natuurpark Brownsberg SME 194 Hc43
Natuurreservaat Boven Coesewijne SME 194 Hc43
Natuurreservaat Brinckheuvel SME 194 Hc43
Natuurreservaat Centraal Suriname SME 194 Hb43
Natuurreservaat Copi SME 194 Hc43
Natuurreservaat Coppename Monding SME 194 Hc43
Natuurreservaat Galibi SME 194 Hc43
Natuurreservaat Hertenrits SME 194 Hb42
Natuurreservaat Peruvia SME 194 Hc43
Natuurreservaat Sipaliwini SME 194 Hb44
Natuurreservaat Wane Kreek SME 194 Hc43
Natuurreservaat Wia-Wia SME 194 Hc43
Nau TJ 63 Oe25
Nauabu PNG 116 Sf51
Nauari BR (PA) 194 Hc45
Naubise NEP 81 Pc32
Nauchas NAM 154 Lj57
Nauders A 34 Ll44
Nauela MOC 153 Mj53
Nauen D 32 Ln38
Naugachhia IND (BIH) 83 Pd33
Naujan RP 90 Ra39
Naujoji Akmenė LT 39 Mc34
Naukluft NAM 154 Lj58
Naukot PK 65 Oe33
Naulila ANG 150 Lh54
Naumatang RI 97 Rd49
Naumburg D 32 Lm39
Naumovskij RUS 49 Na22
Naungmo MYA 86 Ph33
Naung-Mon MYA 86 Pj32
Naupada IND (APH) 83 Pc36
Naupara IND (CGH) 83 Pb34
Nauroz Kalat PK 65 Oc31
Nauru 101 Ta10
Naushahro Firoz PK 65 Oe32
Nausori FJI 119 Tk55
Naustdal N 17 Lc15
Nauta PE 196 Gd48
Nautanwa IND (UPH) 83 Pb32
Naute Recreation Area NAM 154 Lk59
Nautla MEX (VC) 182 Fb35
Nautsi RUS 16 Me11
Nauvo = Nagu FIN 38 Mb30
Nauvo FIN 38 Mb30
Nava E 26 Kp47
Navacerrada E 27 Kr50
Navael'nja BY 41 Mf37
Navahermosa E 27 Kq51
Navahrudak BY 41 Mf37
Navahrudskae uzvyšša BY 41 Mf37
Navajo Ind. Res. USA 171 Ef27
Navajo Reservoir USA (NM) 171 Eg27
Naval RP 90 Rc40
Navalcarnero E 27 Kq50
Navalgund IND (KTK) 82 Oh38
Navalmanzano E 26 Kq49
Navalmoral de la Mata E 27 Kp51
Navalvillar de Pela E 27 Kp51
Navan IRL 19 Ko37
Navapolack BY 39 Mj35
Navapur IND (MHT) 82 Og35
Navarcles E 29 Lb49
Navarra E 28 Kt48
Navarre USA (FL) 175 Fg30
Navarrenx F 24 Ku47
Navarrés E 29 Ku51
Navarro RA (BA) 209 Ha63
Navarro USA (CA) 170 Dj26
Navascués E 28 Kt48
Navas del Madroño E 27 Ko51
Navasëlki BY 41 Mg38
Navasëlki BY 48 Me19
Navašino RUS 48 Nb18
Navasota USA (TX) 174 Fb30
Navassa Island C 186 Gc36
Navegantes BR (SC) 205 Hf59
Navegaon N.P. IND 83 Pa35
Nävekvarn S 31 Lr32
Navelgas E 26 Ko47
Naveslândia BR (GO) 202 He55
Navia E 26 Ko47
Navios MEX (DGO) 181 Eh34
Naviraí BR (MS) 202 Hc57
Naviti FJI 119 Tj54
Navlakhi IND (GUJ) 82 Of34
Navlja RUS 48 Mh19
Năvodari RO 45 Mj46
Navoiy UZ 63 Oc25
Navojoa MEX (SO) 180 Ef32
Navolato MEX (SL) 180 Eg33
Navoloki RUS 48 Na17
Navrongo GH 137 Kk40
Navsari IND (GUJ) 82 Og35
Navua FJI 119 Tk55
Nawa SYR 56 Mj29
Nawabganj BD 86 Pe33
Nawabshah PK 65 Oe32
Nawada IND (BIH) 83 Pc33
Nawagai PK 63 Of28
Nawah AFG 65 Od29
Na Wai THA 87 Pk36
Nawakshut RIM 130 Kb36
Nawani GH 137 Kk41
Nawapara BD 86 Pe34
Nawapara IND (ORS) 83 Pb35
Nawinda Kuta Z 151 Mc54
Nawng-awn MYA 87 Pk35
Nawnghkio MYA 86 Pj34
Nawngleng MYA 87 Pk34
Nawngpuawng MYA 86 Ph33
Na Wong THA 88 Pk42
Naxçivan AZ 57 Nc26
Naxçivan AZ 57 Nd26
Náxos GR 47 Mf53
Náxos GR 47 Mf53
Naxos I 37 Lq53
Nay F 24 Ku47
Naya Chor PK 65 Oe33
Nayagarh IND (ORS) 83 Pc35
Nayagram IND (WBG) 83 Pd34
Nayakanhatti IND (KTK) 84 Oj38
Nayarit MEX 182 Eh35
Nayau FJI 119 Ua54
Nayband IR 64 Nj29
Nayé SN 130 Kd38
Naylowr AFG 65 Od28
Nayoro J 77 Sb23
Nayouri BF 137 La39
Nayudupeta IND (APH) 85 Ok39
Nazaré BR (AP) 195 He44
Nazaré BR (BA) 201 Ja52
Nazare BR (PA) 195 Hf46
Nazaré BR (TO) 200 Hg49
Nazaré P 27 Kl51
Nazareth BOL 206 Gh53
Nazareth CO 192 Gc43
Nazareth IL 56 Mh29
Nazareth Speedway USA (PA) 177 Gc25
Nazas MEX (DGO) 181 Eh33
Nazca PE 197 Gc53
Nazca Ridge 190 Fb12
Naze J 79 Re31
Nazerat IL 56 Mh29
Nazilli TR 47 Mj53
Nazko CDN (BC) 168 Dj19
Nazomba MOC 147 Mk51
Nazran' RUS (ING) 57 Nc24
Nazret ETH 142 Mk41
Nbâk RIM 130 Kc37
Nbeïket Dlim RIM 131 Kg37
Ncanaha ZA 155 Mc62
Nchelenge Z 146 Me50
Ncue GQ 138 Lf44
Ndaba RWA 141 Me46
Ndaki RMM 131 Kk38
Ndala EAT 146 Mg48
N'Dalatando ANG 148 Lh50
Ndali DY 138 Lb41
Ndanda RCA 140 Mb43
Ndangane SN 130 Kb38
Ndarassa RCA 140 Mb42
Ndébougou RMM 131 Kh38
Ndeji WAN 138 Lc41
Ndékebalandji G 148 Lg46
Ndekesha RDC 149 Mb49
Ndélé RCA 140 Ma41
Ndélélé CAM 139 Lh43
Ndemba CAM 139 Lg43
Ndendé G 148 Lf47
Ndere EAK 144 Mh45
Ndere Island N.P. EAK 144 Mh46
N'dhala Gorge N.P. AUS 108 Rh57
Ndia SN 130 Kd38
Ndiago RIM 130 Kb37
Ndiguina CAM 139 Lh40
Ndigwa EAK 144 Mh46
Ndikiniméki CAM 138 Lf43
Ndikoko CAM 139 Lf43
Ndim RCA 140 Lh42
Ndindi G 148 Lf47
Ndindi SN 130 Kb38
Ndioum SN 130 Kc37
Ndioum Guènt SN 130 Kc38
Nditam CAM 139 Lf43
Ndiya WAN 138 Ld43
N'Djaména TCH 139 Lh39
Ndjolé CAM 139 Lf43
Ndjolé G 148 Lf46
Ndjoundou RCB 149 Lj46
Ndjounou G 148 Lg46
Ndoba Z 146 Me51
Ndofane SN 136 Kc39
Ndok CAM 139 Lh42
Ndokama CAM 138 Lf43
Ndokayo CAM 139 Lh43
Ndokouassikro CI 137 Kh42
Ndola Z 146 Me52
Ndole EAT 147 Mj49
Ndole Bay Z 146 Mf50
Ndolwane ZW 152 Md55
Ndom CAM 139 Lf43
Ndondo SOL 117 Ta50
Ndongolo G 148 Lf45
Ndop CAM 138 Lf43
Ndora Mountains WAN 139 Lf42
Ndorola BF 137 Kh40
Ndoto Mountains EAK 144 Mj45
Ndougou G 148 Le46
Ndoukou RCA 140 Ma43
Ndoumbou RCA 140 Lj42
Ndroq AL 44 Lu49
Ndu CAM 139 Lf42
Ndu RDC 140 Mb43
Nduli EAT 147 Mh49
Ndumo ZA 155 Mg59
Ndumo Game Reserve ZA 155 Mg59
Ndundu EAT 147 Mk50
Ndundu Rufiji EAT 147 Mk49
Nduye RDC 141 Me45
Ndzuani COM 156 Nc52
Néa Aghíalos GR 46 Mc51
Néa Artáki GR 45 Md52
Néa Epídavros GR 45 Md53
Néa Fókea GR 44 Md50
Neah Bay USA (WA) 168 Dh21
Néa Ionía GR 46 Mc51
Néa Kalikrátia GR 44 Md50
Neale Junction AUS (WA) 105 Rc60
Neale Junction Nature Reserve AUS 105 Rc60
Néa Mihanióna GR 46 Mc50
Néa Moni GR 47 Mg52
Néa Moudania GR 44 Md50
Néa Péramos GR 45 Me50
Neápoli GR 45 Md54
Neápoli GR 46 Mb50
Neápoli GR 47 Mf55
Neath GB 21 Kr39
Néa Triglia GR 44 Md50
Néa Zíhni GR 45 Md49
Nebbou BF 137 Kk40
Nebe RI 96 Rb50
Nebelat el Hagana SUD 134 Me39
Nebelhorn D 33 Ll43
Nebiler TR 47 Mg51
Neblina, Cerro de la EC 196 Fk46
Nebo AUS (QLD) 109 Se56
Nebolči RUS 48 Mg16
Nebo, Mount JOR 58 Mh30
Nebraska USA 172 Ek25
Nebraska City USA (NE) 174 Fc25
Nébrodi I 37 Lp53
Necaise USA (MS) 175 Ff30
Nece F (NCL) 118 Td56
Necedah USA (WI) 172 Fe24
Nechi CO 192 Gc41
Nechisar N.P. ETH 144 Mj43
Neckar D 33 Lj42
Neckargemünd D 33 Lj41
Neckarsulm D 33 Lk41
Necochea RA (BA) 209 Ha65
Necoclé CO 192 Gb41
Nécropoles de Bourzanga BF 137 Kk39
Necropoli Ánghelu Rúiu I 36 Lj50
Necropoli di Sulcis I 36 Lj51
Necropoli etrusca Cervéteri I 36 Ln48
Necropoli etrusca Tarquínia I 36 Lm48
Necropoli Sant'Andria Priu I 36 Lj50
Necropolis Deffufa SUD 135 Mf36
Necungas MOC 153 Mh54
Nédéley TCH 133 Lk38
Nedelišće HR 35 Lr44
Nederweert NL 23 Lf39
Nedrata ETH 142 Mk40
Neðribær IS 18 Jr25
Nedryhajliv UA 48 Mg20
Nedstrand N 30 Lf31
Nedumangad IND (KER) 84 Oj41
Needles CDN (BC) 168 Ea21
Needles USA (CA) 170 Ec28
Neepawa CDN (MB) 172 Fa20
Nefasit ER 142 Mk38
Nefas Mewch'a ETH 142 Mk40
Nefta TN 126 Ld29
Neftejugansk RUS 54 Oc06
Nefza TN 126 Le27
Negage ANG 148 Lh49
Négala RMM 136 Kf39
Nega Nega Z 152 Me53
Néganzi DY 138 Lb40
Negar IR 64 Nj31
Negara RI 95 Qh47
Negara RI 95 Qh50
Negaunee USA (MI) 173 Fg22
Negele ETH 145 Mk43
Negerilama RI 93 Qa44
Negev Desert IL 58 Mh30
Negginan CDN (MB) 172 Fb19
Neghele ETH 142 Mk42
Negola ANG 150 Lh53
Negomano MOC 147 Mk51
Negombo CL 85 Ok42
Negombo Beach CL 85 Ok42
Negotin SCG 44 Mc46
Negotino MK 44 Mc49
Negrași RO 45 Mf46
Nègrepelisse F 24 Lb46
Negrești-Oaș RO 43 Md43
Negrete RCH 208 Gd64
Negril JA 186 Ga36
Negril Beach JA 186 Ga36
Negril Point JA 186 Ga36
Negrine DZ 126 Ld28
Negro, Cerro RA 208 Ge65
Negro, Cerro RA 210 Gf68
Negros RP 91 Rb41
Negru Vodă RO 45 Mj47
Neguac CDN (NB) 176 Gh22
Nehaevskij RUS 48 Na20
Nehaj HR 35 Lp46
Nehalem USA (OR) 168 Dj23
Nehbandan IR 64 Oa30
Nehe CHN (HLG) 71 Rc21
Nehone ANG 150 Lj54
Neiba DOM 186 Ge36
Neifaru MV 84 Og43
Neihart USA (MT) 169 Ee22
Neijiang CHN (SCH) 74 Qc31
Neil Armstrong Air & Space Mus. USA 173 Fh25
Neilburg CDN (SK) 169 Ef19
Neilersdrif ZA 154 Ma60
Neill Island IND 88 Pg40
Neillsville USA (WI) 172 Fe23
Neilton USA (WA) 168 Dj22
Nei Mongol Gaoyuan CHN 72 Qa25
Neina NAM 150 Lj55
Neinsberg NAM 150 Lj56
Neišapur IR 62 Nk27
Neiva CO 192 Gc44
Neixiang CHN (HNN) 72 Qf29
Nejdek CZ 42 Ln40
Neji MEX (BC) 180 Eb29
Nejime J 79 Rf30
Nejo ETH 142 Mh41
Nejsvětější Trojice CZ 42 Ls41
Neka IR 62 Ng27
Nekemte ETH 142 Mj41
Nekla PL 40 Ls38
Nekmard BD 86 Pe33
Nekob MA 125 Kh30
Nekrasovskoe RUS 48 Na17
Nekró Manteíon GR 46 Ma51
Nelamangala IND (KTK) 84 Oj39
Nelaug N 30 Lj32
Nelia AUS (QLD) 107 Sb56
Nelidovo RUS 48 Mg17
Neligh USA (NE) 172 Fa24
Neligh Mill S.H.S USA 172 Fa24
Nellie, Mount AUS 103 Rc54
Nelligere IND (KTK) 84 Oj39
Nellore IND (APH) 85 Ok38
Nel'ma RUS 77 Rk22
Nelson CDN (BC) 168 Eb21
Nelson GB 21 Ks37
Nelson NZ 113 Tg66
Nelson RA (SF) 209 Gk61
Nelson Bay AUS (NSW) 111 Sg62
Nelson Forks CDN (BC) 166 Dh16
Nelson Island USA 164 Bh15
Nelson Lakes N.P. NZ 113 Tg67
Nelson River CDN 163 Fa07
Nelspoort ZA 154 Mb62
Nelspruit ZA 155 Mf58
Néma RIM 131 Kg37
Nemaiah Valley CDN (BC) 168 Dj20
Neman RUS 39 Mc35
Nemanva ZW 152 Mf56
Nembrala RI 97 Rb51
Nemenčinė LT 39 Mf36
Nemours F 23 Lc42
Nemrut Dağı TR 56 Mk26
Nemrut Dağı Milli Parkı TR 56 Mk27
Nemšová SK 42 Lt42
Nemunas 39 Mc35
Nemuro J 77 Sc24
Nemuro-hanto J 77 Sc24
Nemyriv UA 41 Md40
Nemyriv UA 49 Me21
Nenagh IRL 19 Km38
Nenana USA (AK) 165 Cf13
Nendo SOL 10 Ta11
Nenets Autonomous District RUS 54 Nd05
Nengone Village F (NCL) 118 Td56
Nenitoúria GR 47 Mf52
Nenjiang CHN (HLG) 71 Rc21
Neno MW 153 Mh53
Neo J 79 Rj28
Néo Erásmio GR 45 Me50
Neohóri GR 46 Mb51
Neola USA (UT) 171 Ee25
Néo Monastíri GR 46 Mc51
Néo Petrítsi GR 44 Md49
Neopolis BR (SE) 201 Jb51
Neosho USA (MO) 174 Fc27
Néos Marmarás GR 45 Md50
Néos Skopós GR 45 Md49
Nepal NEP 53 Pa07
Nepalganj NEP 81 Pa31
Nepara NAM 150 Lk54
Nepean CDN (ON) 177 Gc23
Nepeña PE 197 Ga50
Nephi USA (UT) 171 Ee26
Nephin IRL 19 Kl37
Nephin Beg Range IRL 19 Kl36
Nepolje SCG 44 Ma48
Nepomuk CZ 42 Lo41
Neptun RO 45 Mj47
Neptune Beach USA (FL) 178 Fk30
Neptune Islands AUS 110 Rj63
Nérac F 24 La46
Nerang AUS (QLD) 109 Sg59
Neratovice CZ 42 Lp40
Neravailu IND (APH) 85 Ok39
Nerčinsk RUS 71 Qj20
Nerehta RUS 48 Na17
Nereju RO 45 Mg45
Neresheim D 33 Ll42
Nereta LV 39 Mf34
Neringa-Nida LT 39 Ma35
Neriquinha ANG 151 Ma53
Nerja E 27 Kr54
Nerjungri RUS 55 Ra07
Nerl' RUS 48 Mj17
Nérondes F 25 Lc44
Nerópolis BR (GO) 202 Hf54
Nerpio E 27 Ks52
Nerren Nerren AUS (WA) 104 Qh59
Nerrima AUS (WA) 103 Rc55
Nerva E 27 Ko53
Nerva RUS 38 Mh30
Nervi I 34 Lk46
Nes N 30 Lk30
Nesbyen N 30 Lk30
Nesebăr BG 45 Mh48
Nesflaten N 30 Lg31
Nesgo PNG 116 Sf47
Nesjahverfi IS 18 Ke26
Neskaupstaður IS 18 Kg25
Neslandsvatn N 30 Lk32
Nesle F 23 Lc41
Nesna N 16 Lg12
Nesodden N 30 Ll31
Ness City USA (KS) 174 Fa26
Nessona MOC 153 Mh55
Nestáni GR 46 Mc53
Nesterov RUS 39 Mc36
Nesterovo RUS (BUR) 70 Qd19
Nestiary RUS 48 Nc17
Néstos GR 45 Me49
Néstos Délta GR 45 Me50
Nesttun N 30 Lf30
Nesvik N 30 Lg31
Netaar RI 115 Sa47
Netanya IL 56 Mh29
Netarhat IND (JKD) 83 Pc34
Nétéboulou SN 136 Kd39
Neterguent RIM 130 Kd36
Nethang-Temple CHN 68 Pf31
Netherlands NL 23 Ld38
Netherlands Antilles NL 187 Gf39
Netia MOC 153 Mk53
Netivot IL 58 Mh30
Netrakona BD 86 Pf33
Nettetal D 32 Lg39
Nettiling Lake CDN 163 Gb05
Nettuno I 36 Ln49
Neubrandenburg D 32 Lo37
Neubukow D 32 Lm36
Neuburg an der Donau D 33 Lm42
Neuchâtel CH 34 Lg44
Neuenhagen D 32 Lo38
Neuenhaus D 32 Lg38
Neuenkirchen D 32 Lk37
Neuf-Brisach F 25 Lh42
Neufchâteau B 23 Lf41
Neufchâteau F 23 Lf42
Neufchâtel-en-Bray F 23 Lb41
Neufchâtel-sur-Aisne F 23 Le41
Neufundland and Labrador CDN 163 Ha07
Neu-Halbstadt PY 207 Gk57
Neuhaus (Amt Neuhaus) D 32 Ll37
Neuhaus am Rennweg D 33 Lm40
Neuhof D 33 Lk40
Neuillé-Pont-Pierre F 24 La43
Neukirchen A 34 Ln43
Neukirchen D 32 Lk40
Neulengbach A 42 Lq42
Neum BIH 35 Ls48
Neumarkt A 35 Lo43
Neumarkt A 35 Lp43
Neumarkt in der Oberpfalz D 33 Lm41
Neumarkt-Sankt Veit D 33 Ln42
Neumünster D 32 Lk36
Neunburg D 33 Ln41
Neung-sur-Beuvron F 25 Lb43
Neunkirchen A 35 Lr43
Neunkirchen D 33 Lh41
Neuquén RA (NE) 208 Gf65
Neuquén RA 208 Ge65
Neuruppin D 32 Ln38
Neusiedl A 35 Lr43
Neusiedler See A 35 Lr43
Neusiedler See-Seewinkel, N.P. A 35 Lr43
Neuss D 32 Lg39
Neustadt bei Coburg D 33 Lm40
Neustadt (Aisch) D 33 Ll41
Neustadt am Rübenberge D 32 Lk38
Neustadt (Donau) D 33 Lm42
Neustadt/Dosse D 32 Ln38
Neustadt-Glewe D 32 Lm37
Neustadt (Holstein) D 32 Ll36
Neustadt (Orla) D 32 Lm40
Neustadt (Weinstraße) D 33 Lj41
Neustift A 34 Lm43
Neustrelitz D 32 Lo37
Neutral Junction AUS (NT) 108 Rg56
Neutraubling D 33 Ln42
Neu-Ulm D 33 Ll42
Neuvic F 25 Lc45
Neuville-aux-Bois F 23 Lc42
Neuville-de-Poitou F 24 La44
Neuville-sur-Saône F 25 Le45
Neuvy-sur-Barangeon F 25 Lc43
Neuwerk D 32 Lj37
Neuwied D 32 Lh40
Nevada USA (MO) 174 Fc27
Nevada USA 170 Ea26
Nevada City USA (CA) 170 Dk26
Nevado, Cerro el RA 208 Gf63
Nevado, Cerro RCH 210 Gd67
Nevado Ancohuma BOL 206 Gf53
Nevado Chorolque BOL 206 Gh56
Nevado Coropuna PE 197 Gd53
Nevado de Acay RA 207 Gg58
Nevado de Cachi RA 207 Gg58
Nevado de Chañi RA 207 Gh58
Nevado de Colima, P.N. MEX 182 Ej36
Nevado de Incahuasi RA/RCH 207 Gf59
Nevado del Candado RA 207 Gg59
Nevado del Huila CO 192 Gc44
Nevado del Huila, P.N. CO 192 Gc44
Nevado del Illimani BOL 206 Gg54
Nevado de Longavi RCH 208 Ge64
Nevado de Poquis RA/RCH 207 Gg57
Nevado de Ruiz CO 192 Gc43
Nevado de Tolima CO 192 Gc43
Nevado de Toluca, Volcan MEX (MEX) 182 Fa36
Nevado Huayna Potosi BOL 206 Gf54
Nevado Ojos del Salado RCH/RA 207 Gf59
Nevado Queva RA 207 Gg58
Nevado Sajama BOL 206 Gf55
Nevado Salcantay PE 197 Gd52
Nevado Tres Cruces RA/RCH 207 Gf59
Nevado Tres Cruces, P.N. RCH 207 Gf59
Nevaišiu LT 39 Mg35
Nevasa IND (MHT) 82 Oh36
Neveklov CZ 42 Lp41
Nevel' RUS 48 Me17
Nevel'sk RUS 77 Sa22
Nevers F 25 Ld44
Nevertire AUS (NSW) 109 Sd61
Nevesinje BIH 44 Lt47
Nevestino BG 44 Mc48
Neville CDN (SK) 169 Eg21
Nevlunghavn N 30 Lk32
Nevşehir TR 56 Mh26
Nevskoe RUS 39 Mc36
New Adubiase GH 137 Kk42
New Aiyansh CDN (BC) 166 Df18
Newala EAT 147 Mk51
New Albany USA (IN) 175 Fh26
New Albany USA (MS) 175 Ff28
New Alton Downs AUS (SA) 108 Rk59
New Amsterdam GUY 194 Hb42
Newark USA (DE) 177 Gc26
Newark USA (NJ) 177 Gc25
Newark USA (OH) 173 Fj25
Newark-on-Trent GB 21 Ku37
New Bataan RP 91 Rd42
New Bedford USA (MA) 177 Ge25
Newberg USA (OR) 168 Dj23
New Bern USA (NC) 178 Gb28
Newberry USA (SC) 178 Fk28
Newberry Nat. Vol. Mon. USA 168 Dk24
New Bight BS 186 Gc33
New Boston USA (TX) 174 Fc29
New Braunfels USA (TX) 181 Fa31
Newbridge IRL 19 Ko37
New Britain PNG 116 Se49
New Britain USA (CT) 177 Gd25
New Britain Trench PNG 116 Sf49
Newbrook CDN (AB) 167 Ed18
New Brunswick CDN 163 Gc09
New Brunswick USA (NJ) 177 Gc25
Newburgh USA (NY) 177 Gc25
Newbury GB 21 Kt39
Newburyport USA (MA) 177 Ge24
New Bussa WAN 138 Lc41
New Caledonia F 101 Ta12
New Caledonia 100 Ta12
New Caledonia Basin 100 Ta12
Newcastle AUS (NSW) 111 Sf62
Newcastle CDN (NB) 176 Gh22
Newcastle GB 19 Kp36
New Castle USA (IN) 175 Fh26
New Castle USA (PA) 173 Fk25
New Castle USA (VA) 178 Fk27
Newcastle USA (WY) 169 Eh24
Newcastle ZA 155 Me59
Newcastle Bay AUS 107 Sb51
Newcastle Range AUS (QLD) 107 Sb55
Newcastle-under-Lyme GB 21 Ks38
Newcastle upon Tyne GB 20 Kt36
Newcastle Waters AUS (NT) 106 Rg54
Newcastle West IRL 19 Kl38
New Corellla RP 91 Rc42
Newdale CDN (MB) 172 Ek20
New Debiso GH 137 Kj42
Newdegate AUS (WA) 104 Qk62
New Delhi IND (DEL) 80 Oh31
New Denver CDN (BC) 168 Eb21
New Dixie AUS (QLD) 107 Sb53
Newell USA (SD) 169 Ej23
Newell Highway AUS 109 Se61
Newellton USA (LA) 175 Fe29
New England USA (ND) 169 Ej22
New England N.P. AUS 109 Sg61
New England Plateau AUS (NSW) 109 Sg61
New England Seamounts 160 Gb06
Newe Zohar IL 58 Mh30
Newfolden USA (MN) 172 Fb21
New Forest AUS (WA) 104 Qh59
Newfound Gap USA 178 Fj28
Newfoundland CDN 163 Ha09
Newfoundland Basin 8 Hb05
Newfoundland Evaporation Basin USA 171 Ed25
New Georgia SOL 117 Sj50
New Georgia Group SOL 117 Sj50
New Georgia Sound SOL 117 Sj49
New Germany CDN (NS) 176 Gh23
New Glasgow CDN (NS) 176 Gj23
New Guinea RI/PNG 114 Rj47
New Guinea Trench 100 Rb09
Newhalem USA (WA) 168 Dk21
Newhalen USA (AK) 164 Cc16
New Halfa SUD 135 Mh38
New Hamilton USA (AK) 164 Bj14
New Hampshire USA 177 Ge24
New Hampton USA (IA) 172 Fd24
New Hanover PNG 116 Se47
New Hanover ZA 155 Mf60
Newhaven GB 21 La40
New Haven USA (CT) 177 Gd25
New Hazleton CDN (BC) 166 Dg18
New Hebrides 100 Ta11
New Hebrides Basin 100 Ta11
New Hebrides Trench 100 Ta11
New Iberia USA (LA) 175 Fe31
New Ireland PNG 116 Sf47
New Jersey USA 177 Gc25
New Kalala Z 151 Mc53
New Kapedmai LB 136 Kf41
Newkirk USA (NM) 171 Eh28
New Knockhock USA (AK) 164 Bh14
New Lanark GB 20 Kr35
New Leipzig USA (ND) 172 Ek22
New Lexington USA (OH) 173 Fj26
New Liskeard CDN (ON) 173 Ga22
New London USA (CT) 177 Gd25
New Longoro GH 137 Kj41
New Madrid USA (MO) 175 Ff27
Newman AUS (WA) 102 Qk57
Newmarket GB 21 La38
New Martinsville USA (WV) 173 Fk26
New Meadows USA (ID) 168 Eb23
New Mexico USA 171 Eg29
New Mirpur 65 Og29
Newnan USA (GA) 175 Fh29
New Norcia AUS (WA) 104 Qj61
New Norfolk AUS (TAS) 111 Sd67
New Orleans USA (LA) 175 Fe31
New Orleans USA 175 Fe31
New Paltz USA (NY) 177 Gc25
New Philadelphia USA (OH) 173 Fk25
New Pine Creek USA (OR) 168 Dk24
New Plymouth NZ 113 Th65
New Plymouth USA (ID) 168 Eb24
Newport CDN (NS) 176 Gh23
Newport GB 21 Ks38
Newport GB 21 Ks39
Newport GB 21 Kt40
Newport USA (AR) 175 Fe28
Newport USA (MA) 177 Gf23
Newport USA (NH) 177 Gd24
Newport USA (OR) 168 Dh23
Newport USA (RI) 177 Ge25
Newport USA (TN) 178 Fj28
Newport USA (VT) 177 Gd23
Newport USA (WA) 168 Eb21
Newport News USA (VA) 178 Gb27
Newport Pagnell GB 21 Ku38
New Port Richey USA (FL) 179 Fj31
New Providence Island BS 179 Gb33
Newquay GB 21 Kp40
New Richmond CDN (QC) 176 Gh21
New Richmond USA (WI) 172 Fd23
New Ringold USA (OK) 174 Fc28
New River Gorge Natl. River USA 178 Fk27
New Roads USA (LA) 175 Fe30
New Rochelle USA (NY) 177 Gd25
New Rockford USA (ND) 172 Fa22
New Romney GB 21 La40
New Ross IRL 19 Ko38
Newry AUS (NT) 103 Re54
Newry GB 19 Ko36
Newry USA (ME) 177 Ge23
New Schwabenland 7 Lb33
New Siberian Islands RUS 55 Sa03
New Smyrna Beach USA (FL) 178 Fk31
New South Wales AUS 101 Sa13
Newstead AUS (VIC) 111 Sc64
New Stuyahok USA (AK) 164 Cb16
Newton USA (IA) 172 Fd25
Newton USA (KS) 174 Fb26
Newton USA (MS) 175 Ff29
Newton USA (NJ) 177 Gc25
Newton USA (TX) 174 Fd30
Newton Abbot GB 21 Kr40
Newton Hills CDN (NS) 176 Gj23
Newtonmore GB 20 Kq33
Newton Peak NZ 113 Tf67
Newton Stewart GB 20 Kq36
Newtontoppen N 16 Lj06
Newtown GB 21 Kr38
New Town USA (ND) 169 Ej22
Newtownabbey GB 19 Kp36
Newtownards GB 19 Kp36
Newtown Saint Boswells GB 20 Ks35
Newtownstewart GB 19 Kn36
New Ulm USA (MN) 172 Fc23
New Waterford CDN (NS) 176 Gk22
New Westminster CDN (BC) 168 Dj21
New York PE 196 Gc48
New York USA (NY) 177 Gd25
New York USA 177 Gb24
New York USA 177 Gb24
New Zealand 101 Ta14
Nexø DK 31 Lq35
Neyestanek IR 64 Ng29
Neyriz IR 64 Nh31
Neyveli IND (TNU) 85 Ok40
Neyzar IR 57 Nf28
Nezam Abad IR 59 Nf29
Nezam-ol-Molk BakraviTomb IR 62 Nk27
Nez de Jobourg F 22 Kt41
Nez Perce Ind. Res. USA 168 Eb22
Nezvys'ko UA 43 Mf42
Ngaanyatjarra Land Council A.L. AUS 103 Rd57
Ngabang RI 95 Qe45
Ngabé RCB 148 Lj47
N'gabu MW 153 Mh54
Ngabwe Z 151 Md52
Ngadza RCA 140 Ma43
Ngai Giao VN 89 Qd40
Ngajira EAT 146 Mh49
Ngala WAN 139 Lh39
Ngalau Indah Caves RI 93 Qa46
Ngali RDC 149 Lk47
Ngali RI 96 Ra50
Ngaliwurru/Nungali A.L. AUS 106 Rf53
Ngalo RDC 140 Mb43
Ngalurrtja A.L. AUS 103 Rf57
Ngam CAM 139 Lh42
Ngam TCH 139 Lj40
Ngama TCH 139 Lj40
Ngamakwe ZA 155 Md62
Ngamba EAT 146 Mg50
Ngambé CAM 138 Lf43
Ngambé Tikar CAM 139 Lf43
Ngamdu WAN 139 Lg40
Ngamiland NAM 151 Ma55
Ngamo ZW 152 Md55
Ngamring CHN (TIB) 68 Pd31
Nganda MW 146 Mg51
Nganda SN 136 Kc39
Ngandane CI 137 Kh40
Ngangala SUD 144 Mf43
Ngangerabeli Plains EAK 145 Na46
Ngangganawili AUS (WA) 104 Ra59
Nganglong Kangri CHN 68 Pa29
Nganji RDC 146 Md47
Nganjuk RI 95 Qf49
Ngan So'n VN 87 Qd34
Nganzi ANG 148 Lg48
Ngao THA 87 Pk36
Ngaoundal CAM 139 Lg42
Ngaoundére CAM 139 Lg42
Ngapa MOC 147 Mk51
Ngapali MYA 86 Ph36
Ngara EAT 144 Mf47
Ngarangou TCH 133 Lh39
Ngarimbi EAT 147 Mk50
Ngarkat Conservation Park AUS 110 Sa63
Ngasamo EAT 144 Mg47
Ngaso Plain EAK 145 Mk44
Ngassao Noum CAM 139 Lh42
Ngathainggyaung MYA 88 Ph37
Ngato CAM 139 Lh44
Ngawi RI 95 Qf49
Ngawihi NZ 113 Th66
Ngaywa EAT 146 Mg48
Ngbala RCB 140 Lh44
N'Gelewa RDC 149 Mb46
Ngerengere EAT 147 Mk49
Nggatokae SOL 117 Sk50
Nggela Pile SOL 117 Ta50
Nggela Sule SOL 117 Ta50
Nghia Dan VN 87 Qc36
Nghia Hung VN 87 Qd35
Nghi Har VN 87 Qc36
Ngiapanda EAT 147 Mk49
Ngidinga RDC 148 Lh48
Nginyang EAK 144 Mh45
Ngo RCB 148 Lh47
Ngoasé CAM 139 Lg44
Ngoc Co Rinh VN 89 Qe38
Ngoc Hien VN 89 Qc41
Ngoc Linh VN 89 Qd38
Ngog Mapubi CAM 139 Lf44
Ngoïla CAM 139 Lh44
Ngoko RCB 148 Lh46
Ngola CAM 139 Lh44
Ngol Kedju WAN 138 Le42
Ngolo RDC 140 Lk45
Ngolo Z 146 Mf50
Ngoma EAU 144 Mf45
Ngoma NAM 151 Mc54
Ngoma Z 151 Mc53
Ngoma Bridge RB 151 Mc54
Ngoma Tsé-Tsé RCB 148 Lh48
Ngombé RCA 140 Mb43
Ngomedzap CAM 139 Lf44
Ngong CAM 139 Lg41
Ngong EAK 144 Mj46
Ngonga CAM 138 Lf43
Ngongo RCB 148 Lf47
Ngonye Falls Z 151 Mb54
Ngora EAU 144 Mg45
Ngorengore EAK 144 Mh46
Ngoring Hu CHN 69 Pj28
Ngorkou RMM 131 Kj38
Ngoro CAM 139 Lf43
Ngorongoro EAT 144 Mh47
Ngorongoro Conservation Area EAT 144 Mh47
Ngorongoro Crater EAT 144 Mh47
Ngoso RDC 149 Lk48
Ngote RDC 144 Mf44
Ngoto RCA 140 Lj43
Ngoulemakong CAM 139 Lf44
Ngoulonkila RCB 148 Lh47
Ngouma RMM 131 Kj38
Ngoumgbi G 148 Le46
Ngoura CAM 139 Lh43
Ngoura CAM 139 Lh43
Ngoura TCH 139 Lj39
Ngouri TCH 133 Lh39
Ngourti RN 133 Lg38
N'Goussa DZ 126 Lc29
Ngoutchèy TCH 133 Lj37
Ngouye Pété SN 130 Kd37
Ngouyo RCA 141 Mc43
Ngovayang CAM 138 Lf44
Ngoyeboma RCB 140 Lh45
Ngozi BU 146 Me47
Ngudu EAT 144 Mg47
Nguélémendouka CAM 139 Lg43
Nguema RDC 149 Mb49
Ngui RCA 140 Mb42
Nguia Bouar RCA 140 Lh43
Nguigmi RN 133 Lg38
Nguila CAM 139 Lf43
Nguiu AUS (NT) 106 Rf51
Ngukurr AUS (NT) 106 Rh53
Ngulakula EAT 147 Mk49
Nguna VU 118 Te54
Ngundu ZW 152 Mf56
Nguni EAK 145 Mk46
Ngunut RI 95 Qg50
Nguroje WAN 139 Lf42
Ngurore WAN 139 Lg41
Nguru WAN 138 Lf39
Nguruka EAT 146 Mf48
Ngurumanhija EAT 147 Mj51
Ngut CAM 138 Le43
Nguyakro CI 137 Kh42
Ngwaketse RB 155 Mc58
Ngwale EAT 147 Mj51
Ngwedaung MYA 86 Pj36
Ngwena ZW 152 Me55
Ngweze Pool Z 151 Mb54
Ngwo CAM 138 Le42
Nhachengue MOC 153 Mh57
Nhacoà GNB 136 Kc40
Nhacra GNB 136 Kc40
Nhamassonge MOC 152 Mg54
Nhamatanda MOC 152 Mh55
Nhamayabué MOC 153 Mh54
Nhamundá BR (PA) 199 Hb47
Nhamundá Mapuera, T.I. BR 194 Ha46
Nhandeara BR (SP) 202 He56
Nharêa ANG 150 Lj51
Nha Trang VN 89 Qe39
Nhemba MOC 152 Mg53
Nhill AUS (VIC) 110 Sa64
Nhlangano SD 155 Mf59
Nho Quan VN 87 Qc35
Nhulunbuy AUS (NT) 106 Rj52
Niablé CI 137 Kj42
Niada RCA 140 Ma43
Niafounké RMM 131 Kh38
Niagara USA (ND) 172 Fb22
Niagara Falls CDN (ON) 173 Ga24
Niagara Falls USA (NY) 173 Ga24
Niagara Falls USA/CDN 173 Ga24
Niagué CI 137 Kg43
Niah MAL 94 Qg44
Niah Caves MAL 94 Qg44
Niah N.P. MAL 94 Qg44
Niakaramandougou CI 137 Kh41
Niakhar SN 130 Kb38
Nialaha'u Point SOL 117 Ta50
Niambézaria CI 137 Kh43
Niamey RN 132 Lb39
Niamina RMM 137 Kg39
Niamtougou TG 137 La41
Niamvoudou CAM 139 Lg43
Niandankoro RG 136 Kf40
Nianfissa CI 137 Kg41
Niangara RDC 141 Md44
Niangara RDC 141 Me44
Niangoloko BF 137 Kh40
Niani CI 137 Kg43
Nia-Nia RDC 141 Md45
Nianing SN 130 Kb38
Niantanina RMM 136 Kf40
Nianyu IND (ARP) 86 Ph32
Nianzishan CHN (HLG) 71 Rb22
Niao Dao CHN 69 Pk27
Niaoshu Shan CHN 72 Qc28
Niapidou CI 137 Kg43
Niapu RDC 141 Md44
Niapu RDC 141 Me44
Niaro SUD 135 Mf40
Nias RI 93 Pj45
Niasar fire temple IR 57 Nf28
Nibe DK 30 Lk34
Nibong Tebal MAL 92 Qa43
Nicage MOC 147 Mk52
Nicaj-Shalë AL 44 Lu48
Nicaragua 184 Fg39
Nicasio PE 197 Ge53
Nice F 25 Lh47
Niceville USA (FL) 175 Fg30
Nīcgale LV 39 Mg34
Nichinan J 79 Rf30
Nichlaul IND (UPH) 83 Pb32
Nicholasville USA (KY) 175 Fh27
Nichole BD 86 Pe33
Nicholson AUS (WA) 103 Re55
Nicholson, Mount AUS (QLD) 109 Se58
Nicholson Range AUS 104 Qj59
Nicholson River AUS (QLD) 106 Rk54
Nichols Town BS 179 Ga33
Nicman CDN (QC) 176 Gg20
Nicobar Islands IND 88 Pg41
Nicola Mameet Ind. Res. CDN 168 Dk20
Nicolás Bruzzone RA (CD) 208 Gh63
Nicosia CY 56 Mg28
Nicosia I 37 Lp53
Nicótera I 37 Lq52
Nicoya CR 184 Fh40
Nictau CDN (NB) 176 Gg22
Nicuadala MOC 153 Mj54
Niculițel RO 45 Mj45
Nicupa MOC 153 Na53
Nidadavole IND (APH) 83 Pa37
Nidda D 33 Lk40
Nidderau D 33 Lj40
Nídri GR 46 Ma52
Nidzica PL 41 Ma37
Niéboré RG 136 Ke40
Niebüll D 32 Lj36
Niedalino PL 40 Lr36
Niederaula D 32 Lk40
Niederbronn-les-Bains F 23 Lh42
Niedere Tauern A 35 Lp43
Niederlausitz D 32 Lp39
Niedersachsen D 32 Lj38
Niedersächsisches Wattenmeer, N.P. D 32 Lh37
Niedrzwica Duża PL 41 Mc39
Niefang GQ 138 Lf45
Niéga BF 137 Kk39
Niégo BF 137 Kj40
Niekershoop ZA 154 Mb60
Nielisz PL 41 Md40
Niéllé CI 137 Kh40
Niellim TCH 140 Lj41
Niem RCA 140 Lh42
Niemba RDC 146 Me48
Niemce PL 41 Mc39
Niemelane RIM 130 Ke36
Niemisel S 16 Mb13
Niéna RMM 137 Kg40
Nienburg D 32 Lk38
Nierstein D 33 Lj41
Niesen CH 34 Lh44
Niesky D 32 Lp39
Nieu-Bethesda ZA 155 Mc61
Nieuw Amsterdam SME 194 Hc43
Nieuwegein NL 23 Lf38
Nieuw Nickerie SME 194 Hb43
Nieuwoudtville ZA 154 Lk61
Nieuwpoort B 23 Lc39
Nieuwpoort NL (NA) 193 Gf39
Niewęgłosz PL 41 Mc39
Niezabyszewo PL 40 Ls36
Nifi KSA 59 Nb33
Niğde TR 56 Mh27
Nigel ZA 155 Me59
Niger WAN 122 La08
Niger 123 La08
Niger Delta WAN 138 Lc43
Niger Fan 122 La09
Nigeria 123 La09
Nighasan IND (UPH) 81 Pa31
Nightmote USA (AK) 164 Bh15
Nigrangombe EAT 147 Mj50
Nigríta GR 44 Md50
Nigua 186 Ge36
Niha Caves RL 56 Mh29
Nihada OM 61 Nj34
Nihessiue MOC 153 Mk53
Nihing PK 65 Oc31
Nihoa USA 170 Bk34
Nihonmatsu J 77 Sa27
Niigata J 77 Rk27
Niihama J 79 Rg29
Niihau USA 170 Bk35
Niijima J 79 Rk28
Niimi J 79 Rg28
Niitsu J 77 Rk27
Níjar E 27 Ks54
Nijiao CHN (YUN) 87 Qb33
Nijkerk NL 23 Lf38
Nij Laluk IND (ASM) 86 Pg32
Nijmegen NL 23 Lf39
Nijverdal NL 23 Lg38
Níkea GR 46 Mc51
Nikel' RUS 16 Mf11
Nikifóros GR 45 Me49
Nikiniki RI 97 Rc50
Nikítas GR 45 Md50
Nikitskij monastyr RUS 48 Mk17
Nikkaluokta S 16 Lk12
Nikki DY 138 Lb41
Nikko J 77 Rk27
Nikko N.P. J 77 Rk27
Nikoemvon CAM 139 Lf44
Nikolaevo BG 45 Mf48
Nikolaevsk-na-Amure RUS 55 Sa08
Nikolo-L'vovskoe RUS 76 Rf24
Nikol'sk RUS 48 Nd19
Nikopol BG 45 Me47

Nikopol' – Nylstroom

Nikopol' ☐ UA 49 Mh22
Nikópoli ☐ GR 46 Ma51
Nikópoli ☐ GR 46 Ma51
Nikopos ad Istrum ☒ BG 45 Mf47
Nikshar ☐ IR 56 Mj25
Nikshar ☐ IR 64 Oa32
Niksić ☐ SCG 44 Lt48
Nikumaroro ☐ KIR 10 Ba10
Nilanga ☐ IND (MHT) 82 Oj36
Nilaveli Beach ☒ CL 85 Pa41
Nile ☐ ET 122 Mb07
Nile ☐ SUD 135 Mg36
Nile Delta ☒ ET 129 Mf30
Niles ☐ USA (MI) 173 Fg25
Nilgiri Mtn. Railway ☐ ☐ IND (KTK) 84 Oj40
Nili ☐ AFG 65 Od29
Nilka ☐ CHN (XUZ) 66 Pb24
Nillpass ☐ AFG 65 Od28
Nilphamari ☐ IND (MPH) 82 Oj33
Nimbahera ☐ IND (RJT) 82 Oh33
Nimbin ☐ AUS (NSW) 109 Sg60
Nimbotong ☐ RI 115 Sa47
Nimes ☐ F 25 Le47
Nimjat ☐ RIM 130 Kc37
Nim Ka Khera ☐ IND (RJT) 82 Oh33
Nimmitabel ☐ AUS (NSW) 111 Se64
Nimrud ☒ IRQ 57 Nb27
Nimule ☐ SUD 144 Mg44
Nimule N.P. ☒ SUD 144 Mg44
Nin ☐ HR 35 Lq46
Ninda ☐ ANG 151 Ma53
Nindigully ☐ AUS (QLD) 109 Se60
Nine Degree Channel ☒ IND 84 Og41
Ninette ☐ CAN (MB) 172 Fa21
Ninette ☐ NAM 150 La57
Ninetyeast Ridge ☒ 9 Pa12
Ninety Mile Beach ☒ AUS 111 Sd65
Ninety Mile Beach ☒ NZ
Ningaloo ☐ ☐ AUS (WA) 102 Qg57
Ningaloo Reef Marine Park ☒ AUS 102 Qg57
Ning'an ☐ CHN (HLG) 76 Re23
Ningari ☐ RMM 131 La33
Ningo Island ☐ PNG 116 Se48
Ningbo ☐ CHN (ZJG) 75 Ra31
Ningcheng ☐ CHN (NMZ) 73 Qk25
Ningdu ☐ CHN (FJN) 75 Qk32
Ningdu ☐ CHN (JGX) 75 Qk32
Ningeehah ☐ USA (AK) 164 Be14
Ningera ☐ PNG 115 Sa47
Ningerum ☐ PNG 116 Sa47
Ningguo ☐ CHN (AHU) 78 Qk30
Ninghai ☐ CHN (ZJG) 75 Ra31
Ninghe ☐ CHN (TJN) 73 Qj26
Ningi ☐ WAN 138 Le40
Ningjing Shan ☒ CHN 69 Pj30
Ningming ☐ CHN (GZG) 74 Qd34
Ningnan ☐ CHN (SCH) 87 Qb32
Ningqiang ☐ CHN (SAA) 72 Qd29
Ningshan ☐ CHN (SAA) 72 Qe26
Ningwu ☐ CHN (SAX) 72 Qg26
Ningxia Huizu Zizhiqu ☐ CHN 72 Qd27
Ning Xian ☐ CHN (GSU) 72 Qd28
Ningxiang ☐ CHN (HUN) 74 Qg31
Ningyuan ☐ CHN (HUN) 74 Qf33
Ninh Binh ☐ VN 87 Qe35
Ninh Hoa ☐ VN 89 Qe39
Ninh Son ☐ VN 89 Qe39
Ninia ☐ RI 114 Rk48
Niniigo Group ☒ PNG 115 Sa46
Ninilchik ☐ USA (AK) 164 Ce15
Ninive ☐ IRQ 57 Nb27
Ninjin ☐ CHN (SDG) 73 Qj27
Ninohe ☐ J 77 Sa25
Ninole ☐ USA (HI) 170 Cc36
Niño Héroes ☐ MEX (SL) 180 Ef32
Ninotminda ☐ GE 57 Nb25
Ninove ☐ B 23 Le40
Nioaque ☐ BR (MS) 202 Hc56
Nioaque, T.I. ☒ BR 202 Hc56
Niobrara ☐ USA (NE) 172 Fa24
Niobrara ☒ USA 172 Fa24
Niodior ☐ SN 136 Kb39
Niofoin ☐ CI 137 Kg41
Nioka ☐ RDC 144 Mf44
Nioka ☐ RDC 149 Mb49
Nioki ☐ RDC 149 Lj47
Nokolo-Koba ☒ SN 136 Kd39
Niokolo-Koba, P.N.du ☒ ☒ SN 136 Kd39
Niono ☐ RMM 131 Kh38
Nioro du Rip ☐ SN 136 Kc39
Nioro du Sahel ☐ RMM 130 Kf38
Niort ☐ F 24 Ku44
Niou ☐ BF 137 Kk39
Nioût ☐ RIM 131 La37
Nipa ☐ PNG 115 Sb49
Nipahpanjang ☐ RI 93 Qc46
Nipani ☐ IND (KTK) 82 Oh37
Nipawin ☐ CAN (SK) 165 Eh19
Nipawin Prov. Park ☒ CAN 169 Eh19
Nipepe ☐ MOC 153 Mj52
Niphad ☐ IND (MHT) 82 Oh35
Nipigon ☐ CAN (ON) 173 Ff21
Nipigon Bay ☒ CAN 173 Ff21
Nipipol ☐ MOC 153 Mj54
Nipomo ☐ USA (CA) 170 Dk28
Niquero ☐ C 179 Gb35
Nir ☐ IR 57 Nd26
Nira ☐ IND (MHT) 82 Oh36
Nioki ☐ RDC 149 Lj47
Nirgua ☐ YV 193 Gf40
Nirmal ☐ IND (APH) 82 Ok36
Nirwana Beach ☒ RI 96 Rh48
Niš ☐ SCG 44 Mb48
Nisa ☐ P 27 Kn51
Nisab ☐ YE 62 Nc37
Nisab ☐ KSA 59 Nc31
Nisab ☐ YE 60 Nd38
Nisai ☐ RI 96 Sb50
Niscemi ☐ I 37 Lp53
Niseko Shakotan Otaru-kaigan Q.N.P. ☒ J 77 Sa24
Nishi ☐ AFG 65 Oc35
Nishi ☐ CHN (HUN) 74 Qf31
Nishi-Chugokusanchi Q.N.P. ☒ J 79 Rg28
Nishino-jima ☒ J 79 Rk28
Nishi-no-Omote ☐ J 79 Re30
Nishi-Okoppe ☐ J 77 Sb23
Nishi-Sonogi-hanto ☒ J 79 Re29
Nishon ☐ UZ 63 Oc26
Nisía Petalíi ☒ GR 47 Me53
Nísio Strofádhes ☒ GR 46 Ma53
Niskis Banja ☐ SCG 44 Mc47
Nisko ☐ PL 41 Mc40
Nisporeni ☐ MD 49 Me42
Nissan Island ☒ PNG 117 Sh48
Nissedal ☐ N 30 Lj31
Nisséko ☐ BF 137 Kj40
Nissi ☐ EST 38 Me31
Nissi Ioan'inn ☐ GR 46 Lu53
Nissiros ☒ GR 47 Mh54
Nissum Fjord ☒ DK 32 Lj34
Nisut Plateau ☐ CDN 166 De15
Nita'a ☐ KSA 59 Nd34
Nita Downs ☐ AUS (WA) 102

320

Nylsvlei Nature Reserve ⬚ ZA 155 Me58
Nymagee ⬚ AUS (NSW) 111 Sd62
Nymboida ⬚ AUS (NSW) 109 Sg60
Nymboida N.P. ⬚ ⬚ AUS 109 Sg60
Nymburk ⬚ CZ 42 Lo40
Nymphe Bank ⬚ 19 Kn39
Nynäshamn ⬚ S 31 Ls32
Nyngan ⬚ AUS (NSW) 109 Sd61
Nyoka ⬚ Z 151 Md52
Nyoma Rap ⬚ 81 Ok29
Nyommalat ⬚ LAO 87 Qc37
Nyons ⬚ F 25 Lf46
Nyororo ⬚ EAT 146 Mh50
Nyřany ⬚ CZ 42 Lo41
Nyrud ⬚ N 16 Me11
Nysa ⬚ PL 40 Ls40
Nyssa ⬚ USA (OR) 168 Eb24
Nysted ⬚ DK 30 Lm36
Nyudo-saki ⬚ J 77 Rk25
Nyunzu ⬚ RDC 146 Md48
Nyuruamdanga ⬚ EAT 147 Mk49
Nyuta Archipelago ⬚ AUS 110 Rg42
Nyvycol ⬚ UA 41 Me40

O

Oahu ⬚ USA 170 Ca35
Oak Alley Plantation ⬚ USA 175 Fe31
Oakbank ⬚ AUS (SA) 110 Sa62
Oakburn ⬚ CDN (MB) 172 Fa28
Oakdale ⬚ USA (LA) 175 Fd30
Oakes ⬚ USA (ND) 172 Fa22
Oakey ⬚ AUS (QLD) 109 Sf59
Oak Grove ⬚ USA (LA) 175 Fe29
Oakham ⬚ GB 21 Ku38
Oak Harbour ⬚ USA (WA) 168 Dj21
Oak Hill ⬚ USA (AL) 175 Fg30
Oak Hill ⬚ USA (WV) 175 Fk28
Oak Lake ⬚ CDN (MB) 172 Ek21
Oakhurst ⬚ USA (CA) 170 Dg27
Oakland ⬚ USA (AL) 175 Fg30
Oakland ⬚ USA (CA) 170 Dg27
Oakland ⬚ USA (MD) 177 Ga26
Oakland ⬚ USA (NE) 172 Fb25
Oaklands ⬚ AUS (NSW) 111 Sd63
Oak Lawn ⬚ USA (IL) 173 Fg24
Oaklawn Park ⬚ USA (AR) 174 Fd28
Oakley ⬚ USA (ID) 168 Ed24
Oakley ⬚ USA (KS) 174 Ek25
Oakman ⬚ USA (AL) 175 Fg29
Oak Point ⬚ CDN (MB) 172 Fa24
Oakridge ⬚ USA (OR) 168 Dj24
Oak Ridge ⬚ USA (TN) 175 Fh27
Oakville ⬚ CDN (ON) 173 Ga24
Oakville ⬚ USA (WA) 168 Dj22
Oakwood ⬚ AUS (QLD) 109 Sd58
Oaky Creek ⬚ AUS (QLD) 109 Se57
Oamaru ⬚ NZ 113 Tf68
Oasis ⬚ USA (NV) 171 Ec25
Oasis II ⬚ ANT (RUS) 7 Qa32
Oates Land ⬚ 7 Sa32
Oatlands ⬚ AUS (TAS) 111 Sd67
Oaxaca ⬚ MEX (OAX) 182 Fb37
Oaxaca ⬚ MEX 182 Fb37
Oba ⬚ CDN (ON) 173 Fh21
Oba ⬚ WAN 138 Lc42
Obaa ⬚ RI 114 Rk49
Obaba ⬚ RCB 148 Lj46
Obaha ⬚ PNG 116 Se50
Obaidullaganj ⬚ IND (MPH) 82 Oj34
Obala ⬚ CAM 139 Lg43
Obalapuram ⬚ IND (APH) 84 Oj38
Obama ⬚ J 79 Rh28
Oban ⬚ AUS (QLD) 106 Rk56
Oban ⬚ CDN (SK) 169 Eg19
Oban ⬚ GB 20 Kq34
Oban ⬚ WAN 138 Lc43
Obanazawa ⬚ J 77 Sa26
Oban Hills ⬚ WAN 138 Lc43
O Barco ⬚ E 26 Ko48
Obbia = Hobyo ⬚ SP 143 Ne43
Obbnäs = Upinniemi ⬚ FIN 38 Me30
Obebie ⬚ WAN 138 Ld43
Obele ⬚ WAN 138 Ld43
Obelial ⬚ LT 39 Mf35
Obeliscs of Cascase ⬚ ER 142 Mk34
Oberammergau ⬚ D 33 Lk43
Oberes Donautal ⬚ D 33 Lk42
Ober-Donau ⬚ A 34 Lo43
Ober Gurgl ⬚ A 34 Lm44
Oberhausen ⬚ D 32 Lg39
Oberkirch ⬚ D 33 Lj42
Oberlausitz ⬚ D 32 Lp39
Oberlin ⬚ USA (LA) 175 Fd30
Obermai ⬚ F 23 Lh42
Obernburg ⬚ D 33 Lk41
Oberndorf ⬚ D 33 Lj43
Oberon ⬚ AUS (NSW) 111 Se62
Oberpfälzer Wald ⬚ D 33 Ln41
Oberstdorf ⬚ A 35 Lr43
Oberstdorf ⬚ D 33 Ll43
Obertyn ⬚ UA 43 Mf42
Oberwart ⬚ A 35 Lr43
Obi ⬚ RI 97 Rd46
Óbidos ⬚ BR (PA) 194 Hc46
Óbidos ⬚ P 27 Kl51
Obihiro ⬚ J 77 Sb24
Obilatu ⬚ RI 97 Rd46
Obispo Trejo ⬚ RA (CD) 207 Gj61
Ob Luang N.P. ⬚ THA 87 Pk36
Obluč'e ⬚ RUS (YAO) 76 Rf21
Obninsk ⬚ RUS 48 Mj18
Obo ⬚ CHN (QHI) 72 Qa27
Obo ⬚ RCA 141 Md44
Oboasi ⬚ GH 137 Kk42
Obobogorap ⬚ ZA 154 Ma59
Oboda ⬚ DJI 143 Nb39
Oboda ⬚ GH 137 Kk42
Obokote ⬚ RDC 141 Md46
Obolon ⬚ UA 49 Mg21

Osterburken D 33 Lk41
Österbybruk S 31 Ls30
Österbymo S 31 Lq33
Österforse S 16 Lj14
Östergarnsholm S 31 Lt33
Öster-Götland S 31 Lq32
Osterhofen D 33 Lo42
Osterholz-Scharmbeck D 32 Lj37
Øster Hurup DK 30 Ll34
Østerlars DK 31 Lp35
Osterode D 32 Ll39
Östersund S 16 Lh14
Østersundom = Itäsalmi FIN 38 Mf30
Östervåla S 31 Ls30
Ostfriesische Inseln D 32 Lh37
Ostfriesland D 32 Lh37
Osthammar S 31 Lt30
Ostia Antica I 36 Ln49
Östmark S 31 Lo30
Ostrava CZ 42 Lt41
Ostren i madhë AL 44 Ma49
Ostrec BG 45 Mh48
Ostritz D 32 Lp39
Ostróda PL 41 Lu37
Ostrogožsk RUS 48 Mk20
Ostroh UA 49 Md20
Ostrołęka PL 41 Mb37
Ostrov CZ 42 Ln40
Ostrov RO 45 Mh46
Ostrov RUS 39 Mj33
ostrov Ajon RUS 55 Tb04
ostrov Sergeja Kirova RUS 55 Ra04
ostrov Belyj RUS 54 Oc04
ostrov Bol'ševik RUS 55 Qa03
ostrov Bol'šoj Begičev RUS 55 Qd04
ostrov Bol'šoj Berezovyj RUS 38 Mj30
ostrov Bol'šoj Ljahovskij RUS 55 Sa04
ostrov Bol'šoj Tjuters RUS 38 Mh31
ostrov Čečen RUS 57 Nd23
ostrov Chortycja UA 49 Mh22
ostrov Gogland RUS 38 Mg30
ostrov Greem-Bell RUS 54 Oa02
Ostrov Iturup RUS 77 Sd23
ostrov Karaginskij RUS 55 Ta07
ostrov Kolgujev RUS 54 Nb05
ostrov Komsomolec RUS 54 Pc02
ostrov Kotel'nyj RUS 55 Rd03
ostrov Kotlin RUS 38 Mk30
ostrov Malyj Tjuters RUS 38 Mj30
Ostrov Moneron RUS 77 Sa22
ostrov Moščnyj RUS 38 Mh31
ostrov Novaja Sibir' RUS
ostrov Ogurchinskiy TM 62 Ng26
ostrov Oľhon RUS 70 Qd19
ostrov Onekotan RUS 55 Sc09
ostrov Paramušir RUS 55 Sc08
ostrov Rasšua RUS 55 Sc09
ostrov Rudoľfa RUS 54 Nd02
ostrov Seskar RUS 38 Mj30
ostrov Šiaškotan RUS 55 Sc09
ostrov Simušir RUS 55 Sc09
ostrov Tjulenij RUS 57 Nd23
ostrov Uľ RUS 55 Sc09
ostrov Vajgač RUS 54 Oa04
ostrov Vasiľevskij RUS 38 Mi31
ostrov Zapadnyj Berezovyj RUS 38 Mj30
Ostrowice PL 40 Lq37
Ostrowiec Świętokrzyski PL 41 Mb40
Ostrowiec PL 40 Lp38
Ostrowite PL 40 Lt38
Ostrów Lubelski PL 41 Mc39
Ostrów Mazowiecka PL 41 Mb38
Ostrów Wielkopolski PL 40 Ls39
Ostrožac BIH 35 Lq46
Ostrzeszów PL 40 Ls39
Ostuni I 37 Lq50
Ostuta MEX (OAX) 183 Fc37
Osumi-hanto J 79 Rf30
Osumi Islands J 79 Rf30
Osumi Strait J 79 Rf30
Osuna E 27 Kp53
Osun-Osogbo Sacred grove WAN Lc42
Oswego USA (KS) 174 Fc27
Oswego USA (NY) 177 Gb24
Oświęcim PL 41 Lu40
Osypenko UA 49 Mj22
Otacílio Costa BR (SC) 205 He59
Otago Peninsula NZ 113 Tf68
Otaki-Maori Racecourse NZ 113 Th66
Otakwa RI 114 Rj48
O'tamurot UZ 63 Oa24
Otar KZ 66 Oh24
Otaru J 77 Sa24
Otavalo EC 196 Ga45
Otavi NAM 150 Lj55
Otavi NAM 150 Lj55
Otchinjau ANG 150 Lg54
O.T.Downs AUS (NT) 106 Rh54
Otegen Batyr KZ 66 Oj24
Oteu Roşu RO 44 Mc46
Otepää EST 39 Mg32
Otepää kõrgustik EST 39 Mg32
Oterkpalu GH 137 Kk42
Oteşti de Jos RO 45 Me46
Otgon Tenger Uul MNG 67 Pj22
Otgon Tenger Uul Nature Reserve MNG 67 Pj22
Othello USA (WA) 168 Ea22
Othoni GR 46 Lu51
Oti GH 137 Lt41
Otijhungwa NAM 150 Lg54
Otijiandjasemo Hot Spring NAM 150 Lg54
Otjikondo NAM 150 Lh55
Otjimbingwe NAM 150 Lh57
Otjinene NAM 150 Lk56
Otjitanda NAM 150 Lg54
Otjitasu NAM 150 Lh56
Otjiwarongo NAM 150 Lj56
Otjosondu NAM 150 Lj56
Otjozondjupa NAM 150 Lj55
Otmek KS 66 Og24
Otnes N 17 Lf15
Otoca PE 197 Gd54
Otočac HR 35 Lq46
Otog Qi CHN (NMZ) 72 Qd26
Otok HR 35 Lr45
Otok HR 35 Ls46
Otongo MEX (HDG) 182 Fa35
Otong Qian Qi CHN (NMZ) 72 Qd26
Otpor RUS 72 Qd20
Otorowo PL 40 Lr38
Otoyo J 79 Rg29
Otra N 30 Lh31
Otranto I 37 Lt50
Otrokovice CZ 42 Ls41

Ötscher A 35 Lq43
Otsu J 79 Rh28
Otsuki J 79 Rk28
Otta N 17 Le15
Ottapalam IND (KER) 84 Oj40
Ottawa CDN (ON) 177 Gc23
Ottawa USA (IL) 173 Ff25
Ottawa USA (KS) 174 Fc26
Ottawa USA (OH) 173 Fh25
Ottawa Islands CDN 163 Fd07
Ottenby S 31 Lr34
Otter USA (CO) 171 Eg27
Otter USA (UT) 171 Ef25
Otter CDN (QC) 176 Gj21
Otter USA (MT) 169 Eg23
Otterbäcken S 31 Lp32
Otter Creek USA (FL) 178 Fj31
Otter Island USA 164 Be17
Otterndorf D 32 Lh37
Otter Pt. USA 164 Bj18
Otter Rapids CDN (ON) 173 Fk20
Ottertail USA (MN) 172 Fc22
Otterup DK 30 Ll35
Ottobrunn D 33 Lm42
Ottosdal ZA 155 Md59
Ottoshoop ZA 155 Md58
Ottumwa USA (IA) 172 Fd25
Otu CAM 138 Le43
Otukpa WAN 138 Ld42
Otumpa RA (SE) 207 Gj59
Otupe PE 196 Ga49
Oturkpo WAN 138 Le42
Otuzco PE 196 Ga49
Otway N.P. AUS 111 Sb65
Otwock PL 41 Mb38
Otynja UA 43 Me42
Ötztaler Alpen A 34 Ll44
Ouachita Mts. USA 174 Fd29
Ouaco F (NCL) 118 Tc56
Ouadâne RIM 130 Ke35
Ouadda RCA 140 Mb43
Ouagadougou BF 137 Kk39
Ouahabou BF 137 Kj40
Ouahigouya BF 137 Kj39
Ouahiré CI 137 Kg40
Ouaké DY 138 La41
Oualâta RIM 130 Kf36
Oualia RG 136 Ke40
Ouallam RN 132 Lc38
Ouanaréze DZ 132 Lg43
Ouananézh TCD 134 Ma37
Ouanda Djallé RCA 140 Mb42
Ouandago RCA 140 Mb41
Ouango RCA 140 Mc43
Ouango-Fitini CI 137 Kh41
Ouani RMM 131 Kh37
Ouaninou CI 136 Kg41
Ouanâne RIM 130 Ke36
Ouarâne RIM 130 Kb38
Ouarâne RIM 130 Kf35
Ouargaye BF 137 La40
Ouargla DZ 126 Lc30
Ouaritoufouloust RMM 132
Ouarkiy BF 137 Kj39
Ouarra CAM 139 Lh41
Ouarzazate MA 125 Kg30
Ouassa Bamvélé CAM 139 Lg43
Ouatagouna RMM 131 La38
Ouatara RN 132 Le39
Ouatir Galafondo RCA 140 La43
Oubangui RCB/RDC 140 Lj45
Ouch CHN (HUB) 74 Qg31
Oudaboumaa AUS (WA) 104 Qj60
Ouddorp NL 23 Ld39
Oudenaarde B 23 Ld40
Oude Pekela NL 23 Lh37
Oudna TN 126 Le27
Oudtshoorn ZA 154 Mb62
Oued Djaret DZ 126 Lb32
Oued Drâa MA 125 Kh30
Oued el Abiod RIM 130 Kd37
Oued el Hajar RIM 131 Kf43
Oued Guir DZ 125 Kj30
Oued Harket Besbes DZ 126 Lc28
Oued Mimoun DZ 125 Kk28
Oued Moulouya MA 125 Kj28
Oued Rhiou DZ 125 Kk28
Oued Saoura DZ 125 Kk31
Oued Tadant DZ 132 Ld34
Oued Tamanrasset DZ 132 Lc35
Oued Tamanrasset DZ 179 Fk33
Oued Tekouiat DZ 132 Lb34
Oued Tichkantine DZ 132 Lc35
Oued Tlelat DZ 125 Kk28
Oued Zem MA 125 Kg29
Oued Zenati DZ 126 Lc27
Ouéla RN 132 Lc39
Ouellé CI 137 Kg40
Ouéléssébougou RMM 137 Kg40
Ouémé DY 138 La42
Ouenkoro RMM 137 Kj39
Ouenza DZ 126 Lc28
Oué Oué DY 138 Lb41
Ouessa BF 137 Kj40
Ouessant F 22 Kq42
Ouésso DY 138 Lb41
Ouezzane MA 125 Kh28
Oufrane DZ 125 La31
Ougarou BF 137 La39
Ougarta DZ 125 Kj31
Oughterard IRL 19 Kl37
Ouidi RN 133 Lg38
Ouïdah DY 138 La42
Ouinardene RMM 131 Kk37
Ouinhi DY 138 La42
Ouistreham F 22 Ku41
Oujâf RIM 131 Kg37
Oujda MA 125 Kj28
Oujeft RIM 130 Kd36
Oulainen FIN 16 Mc13
Ould Lemmas Fair GB 19 Ko35
Ould -Djellal DZ 126 Lb29
Ouli CAM 139 Lh41
Oulins DZ 125 Kk29
Oulmès MA 125 Kg29
Oulu FIN 16 Md13
Oulujärvi FIN 16 Me13
Oulujoki FIN 16 Me13
Oulx I 34 Lg46
Oum Chalouba TCD 134 Ma38
Oum-Chegaag DARS 124 Kd32
Oum Dreïga DARS 124 Kc32
Oumé CI 137 Kh42
Oum el Achar DZ 124 Kf31
Oum el Assel DZ 125 Kg31
Oum el-Bouaghi DZ 126 Lc28
Oum-Hadjer TCD 134 Lk39
Oum el Khezz RIM 130 Kd37
Ounânrékaha CI 137 Kh41
Oundle GB 21 Ku38
Oungre CDN (SK) 169 Ej21

Ounianga Kébir TCH 134 Ma36
Ounianga Sérir TCH 134 Ma36
Ountivou TG 137 La42
Ouorra RCA 140 Lj42
Ouogo RCA 140 Lj42
Ourâfane RN 132 Le38
Ouragâhio CI 137 Kh42
Oura-Ndia RMM 131 Kh38
Ouranoúpoli GR 45 Me50
Ourâ USA (CO) 171 Eg27
Ouré-Kaba RG 136 Ke40
Ouré USA (UT) 171 Ef25
Ourém BR (PA) 195 Hg46
Ourense = Orense E 26 Kn48
Ouricuri BR (PE) 201 Hk49
Ourika Série RMM 137 Kh39
Ouriki RMM 137 Kh39
Ouro RCA 140 Lk43
Ouro Fino BR (MG) 203 Hg57
Ouro Branco BR (MG)
Ouro Preto BR (MG)
Ouro Preto d'Oeste BR (RO) 198 Gj51
Oursi BF 131 Kk38
Ourzarh MA 125 Kh28
Ourzazate MA 125 Kg30

[continued columns — Oxers Lookout to Ozurgeti]
Oxers Lookout AUS 102 Qk57
Oxford CDN (NS) 176 Gj23
Oxford GB 21 Kt39
Oxford NZ 113 Tg67
Oxford USA (MS) 175 Ff28
Oxford USA (NC) 178 Ga27
Oxia GR 46 Mb52
Oxkutzcab MEX (YT) 183 Ff35
Oxley Wild Rivers N.P. AUS 109 Sg61
Oxtotil MEX 182 Fa36
Oxtotitlán MEX 182 Fa37
Oxunboboyev UZ 63 Og25
Oya MAL 94 Qf44
Oyabi RCB 148 Lf45
Oyama J 79 Rk27
Oyama J 77 Rk27
Oyem G 148 Lf46
Oyé Yeeka TCH 133 Lk36
Oygon MNG 67 Pj21
Oyó SUD 129 Mf35
Oyo WAN 138 La42
Oyón PE 197 Gb51
Oyonnax F 25 Lf44
Oyqudqudug UZ 63 Oc25
Oyou Bezzé Denga RN 133 Lg37
Øyrlandsodden N 16 Lj07
Oysha RDC 141 Me45
Øysleba N 30 Lh32
Ouro Sawabé RN 132 La39
Ouro Sogui SN 130 Kd38
Oyster Island MYA 86 Pg36
Oysterville USA (WA) 168 Dh22
Oyten D 32 Lk37
Ozalj HR 35 Lq45
Ozalp TR 57 Nb26
Ozamiz RP 91 Rb40
Ozark USA (AL) 175 Fh30
Ozark USA (AL) 175 Fh30
Ozark USA (MO) 174 Fd27
Ozark Natl. Scenic Riverways USA 175 Fe27
Ozark Plateau USA 174 Fd27
Ozärow PL 41 Mb40
Özbaşı TR 47 Mh53
Öžd'any SK 43 Lu42
Özena PL 41 Mb41
Ozera Tunajča RUS 77 Sb22
Özerci UA 41 Mf39
Özerl'e RUS 48 Nk18
Özerna UA 43 Mf41
Özero Bol'šaja Itarga RUS 71 Qh20
ozero Bol'šoe Eravnoe RUS 70 Qf19
ozero Čany RUS 54 Od08
ozero Gusinoe RUS 70 Qd20
ozero Hanka RUS 49 Mk22
ozero Hindiktig-Hoľ RUS 67 Pe20
ozero Iľmen' RUS 48 Mf16
ozero Imandra RUS 16 Mg11
ozero Jalpuh UA 45 Mj45
ozero Kahul UA 45 Mj45
ozero Katlabuch UA 45 Mj45
ozero Kunašir RUS 77 Sd23
ozero Nero RUS 48 Mk17
ozero Šaksinskoe RUS 71 Qh20
ozero Samro RUS 38 Mj32
ozero Šikotan RUS 77 Sd24
ozero Svitjaz'ke UA 41 Md39
ozero Tajmyr RUS 54 Pa04
ozero Tere-Hoľ RUS 67 Ph20
ozero Tere-Hoľ RUS 67 Pf20
ozero Zelenyj RUS 77 Sd24
ozero Zeravšan AFG/TJ 63 Og27
ozero Zun-Torej RUS 71 Qh20
Ozersk RUS 39 Mc36
ozery RUS 48 Mk18
Ozhiski Lake CDN 172 Ff19
Ozi IND (TNU) 85 Ok39
Oziácevo RUS 77 Sb22
Ozieri I 36 Lk50
Ozimek PL 40 Lt40
Ozona USA (TX) 174 Ek30
Ozondati NAM 150 Lh56
Ozumba MEX (MEX) 182 Fa36
Ozurgeti GE 57 Nb25

P

Pacuária da Barra do Longa ANG 148 Lg51
Pacuativa CO 192 Ge45
Pacy-sur-Eure F 23 Ld41
Paczków PL 40 Ls40
Padaelo RI 96 Ra48
Pa Daet THA 87 Pk36
Padag PK 65 Oc31
Padako CI 137 Kh43
Padampur IND (ORS) 83 Pb35
Padang RI 93 Qa46
Padang RI 93 Qb48
Padangpanget RI 93 Qa48
Padang Besar MAL 92 Qa42
Padangguci RI 93 Qb48
Padangpanjang RI 93 Qa46
Padangsidempuan RI 93 Pk45
Padangtikar RI 93 Qd46
Padarosk BY 41 Me38
Padasjoki FIN 38 Mf29
Padawiya CL 85 Pa42
Padcaya BOL 207 Gh56
Padcoyo BOL 206 Gh56
Padé WAN (NSW) 111 Sc62
PadeaBesar RI 97 Rb47
Padej SCG 44 Ma45
Padeniya CL 85 Pa42
Paderborn D 32 Lj39
Paderu IND (APH) 83 Pb36
Padlankayudad RI 93 Qa46
Padibe EAU 144 Mg44
Padilla BOL 206 Gh55
Padina RO 45 Mh46
Padinska SCG 44 Ma45
Padjelanta N.p. S 16 Lj12
Padmanabhapuram IND 84 Oj41
Padnagarh IND (ORS) 83 Pb35
Pádova I 34 Lm45
Padrauna IND (UPH) 83 Pc32
Padre Bernardo BR (GO) 203 Hf53
Padre Burgos RP 90 Rd40
Padre Island USA 181 Fb32
Padre Island National Seashore USA 181 Fa32
Padre Vieira BR (CE) 201 Hk47
Padrón E 26 Km48
Padstow GB 21 Kq40
Padsville BY 39 Mh36
Padthaway AUS (SA) 110 Sa64
Paducah USA (KY) 175 Ff27
Paducah USA (TX) 174 Ek29
Padul E 27 Kr53
Padum 81 Oj29
Padwa IND (ORS) 83 Pb36
Paeroa NZ 112 Th64
Paestum I 37 Lp50
Pafos CY 56 Mg28
Pafuri ZA 152 Mf57
Pafuri Gate ZA 152 Mf57
Pag HR 35 Lq46
Pagadenbaru RI 95 Qd49
Pagadian RP 91 Rb42
Pagai Selatan RI 93 Qa47
Pagai Utara RI 93 Qa47
Pagancillo RA (LR) 207 Gf60
Paganzo RA (LR) 207 Gg61
Pagatan RI 95 Qh47
Pagayawan RP 91 Rb41
Page USA (AZ) 171 Ee27
Page USA (OK) 174 Fc29
Pageland USA (SC) 178 Fk28
Pagegžiai LT 39 Mc35
Pagerungan RI 93 Qc47
Paglat LT 39 Mb35
Pagny-sur-Mosur F 23 Lg42
Pagodas (Monywa) MYA 86 Ph34
Pago Pago USA 101 Ba11
Pagosa Springs USA (CO) 171 Eg27
Pagou BF 137 La39
Pagsanjan RP 90 Ra38
Paguiloa G 148 Le46
Paguyaman RI 91 Rb45
Pagwa River CDN (ON) 173 Fh20
Pagwi PNG 115 Sb48
Pahala USA (HI) 170 Cc36
Pahalgam 80 Oh28
Pahari IND (MPH) 83 Ok34
Paharikhera IND (MPH) 83 Pa33
Paharpur BD 86 Pe33
Paharpur PK 65 Of29
Pahaska Tepee USA (WY) 169 Ee23
Pahepa RI 91 Rc44
Pahiatua NZ 113 Th66
Pa Hin Ngam N.P. THA 87 Qa37
Pâhnes GR 47 Me55
Pahoa USA (HI) 170 Cc36
Pahokee USA (FL) 179 Fk32
Pahraničny BY 41 Md37
Pahrump USA (NV) 170 Ec27
Pahsien Cave RC 75 Ra44
Pahtavaara FIN 16 Me11
Pahute Mesa USA 170 Ea26
Pai THA 87 Pk36
Paiçandu BR (PR) 202 Hd57
Paide EST 38 Mf32
Paignton GB 21 Kr40
Paiko WAN 138 Ld41
Paila MYA 88 Ph39
Päijänne FIN 38 Mf29
Päijänteen kansallispuisto FIN 38 Mf29
Pailaco RCH 208 Gd66
Pailin K 89 Qb39
Paillaco RCH 208 Gd66
Pailolo Channel USA 170 Cb35
Paimbouf F 24 Ks43
Paimio FIN 38 Mc30
Paimpol F 22 Kr42
Paine RCH 208 Ge62
Paine Grande, Cerro RCH 208 Ge62
Painel BR (SC) 205 He59
Painesville USA (OH) 173 Fk25
Painted Churches CY 56 Mg28
Painted Desert USA 171 Ee28
Painted Desert USA 171 Ee28
Paint Rock USA (TX) 174 Fa30
Paintsville USA (KY) 178 Fj27
Paipa CO 192 Gd43
Paipote RCH 207 Gf59
Pai River Rafting THA 87 Pk36
Paisagem Cultural de Sintra P 27 Kl52
Paisha RC 75 Qa34
Paisley GB 20 Kq35
Paisley USA (OR) 168 Dk24
Paita F (NCL) 118 Td57
Paita PE 196 Fk48

Paiton RI 95 Qg49
Päiuşeni RO 43 Mc44
Pajaj GCA 184 Ff38
Pajala S 16 Mb12
Pajaro EC 196 Fk46
Pajapíta GCA 183 Fd38
Pajarito CO 192 Gd43
Paje EAT 147 Mk49
Pajé RB 152 Md57
Pajeczno PL 40 Lt39
Pajonal, Cerro RCH 207 Gf56
Pajule EAU 144 Mg44
Páka H 42 Lr44
Pakabong PNG 116 Sg47
Pakala IND (APH) 85 Ok39
Pakaraima Mountains GUY 194 Gk43
Pakashkan Lake CDN 172 Fe21
Pakaur IND (WBG) 83 Pd33
Pakbeng LAO 87 Qa36
Pak Charang THA 89 Qb38
Pak Chom THA 89 Qb37
Pak Chong THA 88 Qa38
Pa Kham THA 89 Qb38
Paki WAN 138 Le40
Pakima RDC 149 Mc47
Pakistan PK 65 Oc31
Pak Kading LAO 87 Qc36
Pakkat RI 93 Pk44
Pak Khat THA 87 Qb36
Paklenica N.P. HR 35 Lq46
Pak Mong LAO 87 Qb35
Pakokku MYA 86 Ph35
Pak Ou Caves LAO 87 Qb35
Pakowki Lake CDN 169 Ee21
Pakpattan PK 65 Og30
Pak Phayun THA 88 Qa42
Pakrac HR 35 Ls45
Pakruojis LT 39 Md35
Paksan LAO 87 Qc36
Pakse LAO 89 Qc38
Pak Tha LAO 87 Qa35
Pak Tho THA 88 Pk39
Pak Thong Chai THA 89 Qb38
Paku RI 93 Qa46
Pakuanaji RI 93 Qd46
Pakuli RI 96 Ra46
Pakwach EAU 144 Mf44
Pakwash Prov. Park CDN 172 Fd20
Pak Xeng LAO 87 Qb35
Pala TCH 140 Lh41
Palabek EAU 144 Mf44
Palabuan RI 95 Qc49
Palacagüina NIC 185 Fh39
Palace of Abbasi ET 129 Mf30
Palace on Wheels IND 80 Oh31
Palacio de Montechiaro I 36 Lo53
Palacio de la Granja de San Ildefonso E 27 Kq49
Palacios BOL 206 Gg52
Palacios HN 184 Fh38
Palacios RA (SF) 207 Gk61
Palacios USA (TX) 181 Fb31
Palafrugell E 29 Lc49
Palagruža HR 35 Lr47
Palaiochori GR 45 Md51
Palaiochóra GR 47 Mc55
Palais des Ducs F 25 Lf43
Palais des Papes F 25 Le47
Palais des Rois de Majorque F 25 Lc48
Palaiseau F 23 Lc42
Palaiyam IND (TNU) 84 Ok40
Palakkad IND (KER) 84 Oj40
Palakollu IND (APH) 83 Pb37
Palala ZA 136 Kf42
Palala ZA 152 Me58
Palamás GR 46 Mc51
Palamau N.P. IND 83 Pc34
Palamea RI 97 Rd46
Palana RUS (TAS) 111 Sd65
Palanan RP 90 Rb37
Palanan Point RP 90 Rb37
Palangān IR 62 Nj29
Palanga LT 39 Mb35
Palangkaraya RI 95 Qf47
Palani IND (TNU) 84 Oj40
Palani Hills IND 84 Oj40
Palanok UA 43 Mc42
Palanro RI 96 Qk46
Palantak PK 65 Ob31
Palapag RP 90 Rc39
Palapye RB 152 Md57
Palárikovo SK 42 Lt42
Palas de Rei E 26 Kn48
Palashbari IND (ASM) 86 Pf33
Palaspal IND (ORS) 83 Pb35
Palatka RUS 55 Sd07
Palatka USA (FL) 178 Fk31
Palatna SCG 44 Mb47
Palattsy KZ 72 Ph21
Palau I 36 Lk49
Palau PAL 101 Rd44
Palau de la Musica Catalana E 29 Lc49
Palau Güell E 29 Lc49
Palaui Island RP 90 Rb36
Palau Islands PAL 92 Rd42
Palauig RP 90 Ra38
Palau Palau RI 91 Rd45
Palawan RP 91 Qk41
Palawan Passage RP 94 Qj41
Palawan Trough 94 Qh42
Palayankottai IND (TNU)
Palazzina di Caccia di Stupinigi I 34 Lh46
Palazzo Ducale di Mántova I 34 Lm45
Palazzo Ducale d'Urbino I 34 Ln47
Palazzo Acréide I 37 Lp53
Palazzo Madama I 34 Lh45
Palazzo Reale di Caserta I 37 Lp49
Palca PE 197 Gc51
Palca PE 206 Gf54
Palca RCH 206 Gf55
Paldiski EST 38 Me31
Pale BIH 44 Lt47
Pale RCH 208 Gd66
Palé GQ 148 Le44
Palēkastro GR 47 Mg55
Paleleh RI 91 Rb45
Palembang RI 93 Qc47
Palencia E 27 Kq48
Paleneng RI 96 Ra48
Palenque MEX (CHP) 183 Fd37
Palenque MEX 183 Fd37
Palenque RA (BA) 185 Fj41
Paleohora GR 47 Me55
Paleóhori GR 45 Md50
Palermo I 36 Lo52
Palermo MEX (OAX) 183 Fc37

Palesse BY 41 Md39
Palesse BY 41 Mf38
Palestina CO 192 Gd43
Palestina USA (TX) 174 Fc30
Palestrina I 36 Ln49
Paletwa MYA 86 Pg35
Palghat → Palakkad IND (KER) 84 Oj40
Palgrave, Mount AUS 102 Qh57
Palho EC 196 Gb46
Palhoca BR (SC) 205 He59
Pali IND (CGH) 83 Pb34
Pali IND (MPH) 83 Pa34
Pali IND (RJT) 82 Og33
Palia IND (UPH) 81 Pa31
Pali-Aike, P.N. RCH 208 Gf72
Palian THA 88 Pk42
Palianawa IND (GUJ) 82 Of34
Paliat RI 95 Qd49
Palikir FSM 101 Sb09
Palin H 42 Lr44
Palwal IND (HYA) 81 Oj31
Palinuro I 37 Lq50
Paliouria GR 46 Mc54
Páliros GR 46 Mc54
Palisades Res. USA 169 Ee24
Palitana IND (GUJ) 82 Of35
Paliūniškis LT 39 Me35
Palizada MEX (CAM) 183 Fd36
Palk Bay CL 85 Ok41
Palkino RUS 39 Mg33
Palkohda IND (APH) 83 Pa34
Palk Strait IND/CY 85 Ok41
Palladam IND (TNU) 84 Oj40
Pallas-Ounastunturi kansallispuisto FIN 16 Mb11
Pallipatu IND (APH) 85 Ok39
Pallu IND (RJT) 80 Oh31
Palma MOC 147 Na51
Palma de Mallorca E 29 Lc51
Palmales EC 196 Fk47
Palma Sola MEX (VC) 182 Fb36
Palmarito de Cauto C 186 Gc35
Palmarito C 186 Gc35
Palmar Grande BOL 207 Gj56
Palmares BR (PE) 201 Jc50
Palmares do Sul BR (RS) 204 Hd61
Palmares de Cocalán, P.N. RCH 208 Ge63
Palmas de Monte Alto BR (BA) 203 Hj53
Palmas do Tocantins BR (TO) 200 Hf50
Palmas BR (PR) 205 He58
Palma Soriano C 179 Gb35
Palmas, T.I. BR 204 Hc58
Palmas Sur CR 185 Fj41
Palmas BR (TO) 200 Hg49
Palmática BR (AM) 196 Gh48
Palmdale USA (CA) 170 Ea28
Palmas USA (FL) 179 Fk32
Palmares BR (SP) 205 Hd55
Palmeira dos Índios BR (AL) 201 Jb50
Palmeirais BR (PI) 201 Hj49
Palmeirândia BR (MA) 195 Hh47
Palmeiras BR (TO) 200 Hg49
Palmeiras BR (BA) 201 Hk52
Palmeiras BR (MS) 202 Hc56
Palmeiras de Goiás BR (GO) 202 He54
Palmeirópolis BR (TO) 200 Hf52
Palmela P 27 Km52
Palmelampousses MS 157 Nj56
Palmer USA (AK) 165 Cf15
Palmer USA (MS) 175 Ff29
Palmer Land G 6 Gd33
Palmer Station ANT 6 Gd31
Palmerston AUS (QLD) 107 Sc54
Palmerston USA (FL) 179 Fk32
Palmerston North NZ 113 Th66
Palmerville AUS (QLD) 107 Sc54
Palm Harbor USA (FL) 179 Fj31
Palmilla MEX (TM) 182 Fa34
Palmira C 179 Ga34
Palmira EC (MD) 208 Gf62
Palmira CO 192 Gb44
Palmira RA (MD)
Palmra SYR 56 Mk29
Palmyra Atoll USA 11 Bb09
Palo Alto USA (CA) 170 Dj27
Palo Blanco RA (JU)
Palo Duro Canyon USA 174 Ek28
Palo Duro Canyon S.P. USA 174 Ek28
Paloh MAL 92 Qd44
Paloích SUD 135 Mg40
Palojärvi FIN 16 Mb11
Palojoensuu FIN 16 Mb11
Palomar RP 90 Ra40
Palomares MEX (OAX) 183 Fc37

Palomas E 27 Ko52
Palomas MEX (SLP) 182 Fa34
Palomas Viejo MEX (CHH) 180 Eg30
Palomas E 27 Kr51
Palombara BOL 206 Gj54
Palomino CO 192 Gd40
Palompon RP 90 Rc40
Paloncha IND (APH) 83 Pa37
Palopo RI 96 Ra47
Palos EC 196 Gb46
Palos, Cabo de E 29 La53
Palotina BR (PR) 204 Hd58
Palpa PE 197 Gc54
Palparara AUS (QLD) 108 Sa58
Palpetu RI 97 Rd47
Pålsboda S 31 Lq31
Palti RO 44 Md45
Palu RI 96 Ra50
Palu TR 57 Mk25
Pama RCA 140 Ma43
Pamalagan RI 94 Qe45
Pamandzi RA 156 Nd54
Pamangkat RI 94 Qe45
Pamarrá GR 45 Md50
Pamatacta RI 96 Rb46
Pamban Island IND 85 Ok41
Pambarra MOC 153 Mh58
Pambegua WAN 138 Le40
Pambuka ZW 152 Me56
Pambula Beach AUS 111 Sf64
Pamekasan RI 95 Qg49
Pameungpeuk RI 95 Qd49
Pamgarh IND (CGH) 83 Pb34
Pamiers F 24 Lb47
Pamir AFG/TJ 63 Og27
Pamlico Sd. USA 178 Gc28
Pampa USA (TX) 174 Ek28
Pampa Apeleg RA 210 Ge68
Pampa Aullagas BOL 206 Gg55
Pampachiri PE 197 Gd53
Pampa de Agnia RA (CB) 210 Gf67
Pampa de Chunchanga PE 197 Gc53
Pampa de Cortaderas PE 197 Gd53
Pampa de Huayuri PE 197 Gc53
Pampa del Agua Amarga RA 208 Gf65
Pampa de las 3 Hermanas RA 210 Gg69
Pampa de las Salinas RA 208 Gg61
Pampa de la Varita RA 208 Gf65
Pampa de la Yoya PE 197 Gd54
Pampa del Castillo RA (CB) 210 Gf68
Pampa del Castillo RA 210 Gf68
Pampa del Diamante RA 208 Gf63
Pampa del Indio RA (CH) 204 Ha59
Pampa del Infierno RA (CH) 207 Gk59
Pampa de los Guanacos RA (SE) 207 Gj59
Pampa del Salado RA 208 Gg62
Pampa del Setenta RA 208 Gh64
Pampa del Tamarugal RCH 206 Gf56
Pampa de Talagapa RA 208 Gf67
Pampa El Toro PE 196 Fk47
Pampa Hermosa PE 196 Gc49
Pampa Húmeda RA 209 Gk64
Pampa Pelada RA 210 Gg68
Pampas PE 197 Gb52
Pampa Salamanca RA 210 Gg68
Pampas PE 197 Gd53
Pampas de Sacramento PE 196 Gc49
Pampa Seca RA 208 Gh63
Pampa Verde RA (CH) 207 Gk59
Pampa Verdún RA 210 Ge69
Pampilhosa da Serra P 27 Km50
Pamplega E 28 Kr48
Pamplico CO 192 Gd42
Pamplona E 28 Kt48
Pamplona CO 192 Gd43
Pamporovo = Koloro, V. BG 45 Me49
Pamukada TR 47 Mh53
Pamukkale TR 47 Mk53
Pamunkek Atoll NZ 11 Bb11
Pamya WAL 136 Ke41
Pan MEX (YT) 183 Ff35
Panabo RP 91 Rc42
Panabá MEX (YT) 183 Ff35
Panache CDN 176 Fk23
Panaji IND (GOA) 84 Oh38
Panama PA 185 Ga41
Panama City USA (FL) 175 Fh30
Panama City USA (FL) 175 Fh30
Panama City Beach USA (FL) 175 Fh30
Panamá, Golfo de PA 185 Ga42
Panamaram IND (KER) 84 Oj40
Panamá, Istmo de PA 185 Ga41
Panamá Viejo PA 185 Gb41
Panamericana (British Columbia) CDN 169 Ea22
Panamericana (Coahuila) MEX 181 Ek33
Panamericana (El Salvador) ES 184 Ff39
Panamericana (Montana) USA 169 Ee22
Panamericana (Nicaragua) NIC 184 Fh39
Panamericana (Oaxaca) MEX 182 Fb37
Panamericana (Panamá) PA 185 Fk41
Panamericana (San Luis Potosi) MEX 182 Fa34

Panamericana (Sonora) MEX 180 Ef32
Panamint Range USA 170 Eb27
Panamint Springs USA (CA) 170 Eb27
Pan'an CHN (ZJG) 75 Ra31
Panao PE 197 Gc50
Panaon Island RP 90 Rc41
Panare THA 93 Qa42
Pareh-Chalai Beach THA 89 Qa42
Panarik RI 94 Qe44
Panatinane Island PNG 116 Sg51
Panawina Island PNG 116 Sg51
Panay RP 90 Rb40
Panban AUS (NSW) 111 Sb62
Pancake Rocks and Blowholes NZ 113 Tf67
Pancas BR (ES) 203 Hk55
Pancevo SCG 44 Ma46
Panchgani IND (MHT) 82 Og37
Panchgani Hill Resort IND 82 Og37
Pancho Villa MEX (CHH) 180 Ef30
Pâncota RO 43 Mb44
Pançudo BR (AP) 195 He46
Pancur RI 96 Ra46
Panda MOC 153 Mh58
Pandambili EAT 147 Mj49
Pandan RP 90 Rb38
Pandan RP 90 Rb40
Pandanan Island RP 94 Qj41
Pandan Beach RI 93 Pk45
Pandane MOC 153 Mh58
Pandanus AUS (QLD) 107 Sc55
Pande IND (CGH) 83 Pa34
Pandégelang RI 95 Qd49
Pandélys LT 39 Mf34
Pandhana IND (MPH) 82 Oj35
Pandharkawada IND (MHT) 82 Ok36
Pandharpur IND (MHT) 82 Oh37
Pandhurna IND (MPH) 83 Ok35
Pandi CO 192 Gc43
Pandie Pandie AUS (SA) 108 Rk59
Pandivere kõrgustik EST 38 Mg31
Pando ROU 209 Hc63
Pandora CR 185 Fj41
Pandrup DK 30 Ll33
Pandu RDC (ASM) 86 Pf32
Pandžikent TJ 63 Od26
Panelas BR (PE) 201 Jb50
Panes E 26 Kr47
Panetólio GR 46 Mb52
Panevėžys LT 39 Me35
Panga RDC 141 Md45
Pangandaran RI 95 Qd49
Pangani EAT 147 Mk48
Panganiban RP 90 Rc39
Panganuran RP 91 Rb42
Panga pank EST 39 Mc32
Pangeo RI 91 Rd44
Panggoe SOL 117 Sj49
Pangi RDC 146 Md47
Pangia PNG 115 Sc49
Pangkajene RI 96 Ra48
Pangkalan RI 96 Ra48
Pangkalanbrandan RI 92 Pk44
Pangkalanbun RI 95 Qf47
Pangkalandurian RI 93 Qb46
Pangkalanpinang RI 92 Qf45
Pangkalpinang RI 93 Qc46
Pangkalsusu RI 92 Pk44
Pangkor MAL 92 Qa43
Pangkyehtu MYA 86 Ph35
Pang La THA 87 Pk36
Panglao Island RP 90 Rb41
Panglong MYA 86 Pj35
Pangnirtung CDN 163 Gc05
Pango PNG 116 Sg47
Pango Aluquem ANG 148 Lh50
Pangody RUS 54 Ob06
Pangrango, Gunung RI 95 Qd49
Panguipulli RCH 208 Gd65
Panguitch USA (UT) 171 Ed27
Panguma WAL 136 Ke41
Pangutaran Group RP 91 Ra42
Pangutaran Island RP 91 Ra42
Panhala IND 82 Oh37
Panhandle USA (TX) 174 Ek28
Paničkovo BG 45 Mf48
Panié, Mont F (NCL) 118 Tc56
Panihar IND 82 Oj32
Panipat IND (HYA) 80 Oj31
Paniqui RP 90 Ra38
Panitan RP 90 Rb40
Panitian RP 91 Qk41
Panj AFG 63 Oe28
Panjang RI 93 Qc48
Panjgur PK 65 Ob31
Panji Poyon TJ 63 Oe27
Panjim → Panaji IND (GOA) 84 Oh38
Panjin CHN (LNG) 76 Rb25
Panjnad PK 65 Of31
Panjshir-Valley AFG 63 Oe28
Panka BHT 86 Pf32
Pankshin WAN 138 Le41
Panna IND (MPH) 83 Pa33
Panna N.P. IND (MPH) 83 Pa33
Pannawonica AUS (WA) 102 Qj57
Pannonhalma H 42 Ls43
Panopah RI 95 Qe47
Pánormos GR 47 Mf53
Panorama BR (SP) 202 Hd56
Pánormos GR 47 Mg53
Panshan, Mount CHN 73 Qj25
Panshan CHN (LNG) 76 Rb24
Panshi CHN (JLN) 76 Rd24
Panshui CHN (WBG) 83 Pd34
Pantai RI 96 Ra50
Pantal IND (WBG) 83 Pd34
Pantanaw MYA 86 Ph37
Pantal AFG 65 Od28
Pantar RI 97 Rb50
Panté Remio MAL 92 Qa43
Pantelleria I 36 Ln54
Pantin IND (KER) 84 Oj41
Pantalica I 37 Lq53

Pergamino ⌂ (BA) 209 Gk62
Pergamon Akropolis ⌂ TR 47 Mh51
Perge ⌂ TR 56 Mf27
Pérgine Valsugana ⌂ I 34 Lm44
Pérgola ⌂ I 35 Ln47
Perguica ⌂ CV 136 Jh37
Perhentian ⌂ MAL 92 Qb43
Gd21
Perico ⌂ RA (PJ) 207 Gh58
Pericos ⌂ MEX (SL) 180 Eg33
Périers ⌂ F 22 Kt41
Perigara, T.I. ⌂ BR 202 Hb54
Périgban ⌂ BF 137 Kj40
Perigi ⌂ RI 95 Qe45
Périgord ⌂ F 24 Lb44
Périgueux ⌂ F 24 La45
Perim + Barim ⌂ YE 60 Nb39
Periquer ⌂ YV 193 Gk43
Perişoru ⌂ RO 45 Mh46
Perista ⌂ GR 46 Mb52
Peristera ⌂ GR 45 Md51
Peristrema ⌂ TR 56 Mh26
Perithori ⌂ GR 46 Mb52
Perito Moreno ⌂ RA (SC) 210 Gd69
Perito Moreno Glacier ⌂ RA 210 Gd71
Perito Moreno, P.N. ⌂ RA 210 Gd69
Peritoró ⌂ BR (MA) 200 Hh48
Periyanagavillu ⌂ CL 85 Ok41
Periyar N.P. ⌂ IND 84 Oj41
Perleberg ⌂ D 32 Lm37
Perlmadulla ⌂ CL 85 Pa42
Perloja ⌂ LT 39 Me36
Perm' ⌂ RUS 54 Nd07
Perma ⌂ DY 137 La40
per Nazajtas ⌂ TJ 63 Og22
Pernambuco ⌂ BR 191 Ja10
Pernambuco Abyssal Plain ⌂ 190 Ja10
Pernampet ⌂ IND (APH) 85 Ok39
Pernik ⌂ BG 44 Md48
Pernió ⌂ FIN 38 Md30
Pernštejn ⌂ CZ 42 Lr41
Pérola ⌂ BR (PR) 202 Hd57
Pérola d'Oeste ⌂ BR (PR) 204 Hb58
Péronne ⌂ F 23 Lc41
Perote ⌂ MEX (VC) 182 Fb36
Peroto ⌂ BOL 206 Gg53
Perpendicular Cliffs ⌂ AUS 105 Rc62
Perpignan ⌂ F 25 Lc48
Perpyoyakou ⌂ DY 137 La40
Perre ⌂ TR 56 Mh27
Perrine ⌂ USA (FL) 179 Fk33
Perros-Guirec ⌂ F 22 Kr42
Perry ⌂ CDN (ON) 173 Fj22
Perry ⌂ USA (FL) 178 Fj31
Perry ⌂ USA (GA) 178 Fj29
Perry ⌂ USA (IA) 172 Fc25
Perry ⌂ USA (ME) 176 Gg23
Perry ⌂ USA (OK) 174 Fb27
Perryton ⌂ USA (TX) 174 Ek27
Perryville ⌂ USA (AK) 164 Ca18
Perryville ⌂ USA (MO) 175 Ff27
Persbo ⌂ S 31 Lq30
Persepolis ⌂ IR 64 Ng31
Perseverancia ⌂ BR (AM) 198 Gh46
Perseverancia ⌂ BOL 206 Gj53
Persian Gulf ⌂ 59 Ne31
Perstorp ⌂ S 31 Lo34
Perth ⌂ AUS 111 Sd66
Perth ⌂ AUS (WA) 104 Qd61
Perth ⌂ CDN (ON) 177 Gb23
Perth ⌂ GB 20 Kr34
PerthAndover ⌂ CDN (NB) 176 Gg22
Perth Basin ⌂ 100 Qb13
Pertoili ⌂ GR 46 Mb51
Perttéli ⌂ FIN 38 Md30
Pertuis ⌂ F 25 Lf47
Pertuis Breton ⌂ F 24 Kt44
Pertunmaa ⌂ FIN 38 Mg29
Peru ⌂ BOL 206 Gg52
Peru ⌂ USA (IN) 173 Fg25
Peru ⌂ 191 Ga10
Peru Basin ⌂ 190 Fb10
Peru-Chile Trench ⌂ 190 Fb10
Perúgia ⌂ I 34 Ln47
Perugorría ⌂ RA (CR) 204 Ha60
Peruíbe ⌂ BR (SP) 205 Hg58
Perulmar Par Island ⌂ IND 84 Og40
Perumpavur ⌂ IND (KER) 84 Oj41
Perunduroi ⌂ IND (TNU) 84 Oj40
Perušić ⌂ HR 35 Lq47
Pervari ⌂ TR 57 Nb27
Pervomaevka ⌂ RUS (BUR) 70 Qe19
Pervomajsk ⌂ RUS 48 Nb18
Pervomajsk ⌂ UA 49 Mf21
Pervomajskij ⌂ RUS 48 Na19
Pervomajskoje ⌂ UA 49 Mj21
Pervoural'sk ⌂ RUS 54 Nd07
Pésaro ⌂ I 35 Ln47
Pescadoor ⌂ BR (MG) 203 Hk55
Pescadores ⌂ RC 75 Qk34
Pescanopskoe ⌂ RUS 49 Na22
Pescara ⌂ I 35 Lp48
Pescasseroli ⌂ I 36 Lo49
Peščanicy monastyr' ⌂ RUS 48 Mk20
Peschiera del Garda ⌂ I 34 Ll45
Péscia ⌂ I 34 Ll47
Pescina ⌂ I 36 Lo48
Pescocostanzo ⌂ I 37 Lp49
Pesco Sannita ⌂ I 37 Lp49
Pesé ⌂ PA 185 Fk42
Peshawar ⌂ PK 65 Of29
Peshkopi ⌂ AL 44 Ma49
Pes-kó ⌂ H 43 Lt42
Pesmes ⌂ F 25 Lf43
Pescčani ⌂ MK 44 Ma49
Peso da Régua ⌂ P 26 Kr49
Pesqueira ⌂ BR (PE) 201 Jb50
Pessac ⌂ F 24 Ku46
Pesquanyi mũyis ⌂ KZ 62 Nf24
Pessinus ⌂ TR 56 Mf26
Pêster ⌂ SCG 44 Lu47
Pestişani ⌂ RO 44 Md45
Pestovo ⌂ RUS 48 Mh16
Petäjävesi ⌂ FIN 38 Mf28
Petalás ⌂ GR 46 Mb52
Pétalax = Petolahti ⌂ FIN 38 Mb28
Petalidi ⌂ GR 46 Mb54
Petaluma ⌂ USA (CA) 170 Dj26
Petare ⌂ YV 193 Gg40
Petatlán ⌂ MEX (GUR) 182 Ek37
Petauke ⌂ Z 152 Mf21
Petawanga Lake ⌂ CDN 176 Gg22
Petchaburi ⌂ THA 88 Pk39
Pété ⌂ CAM 139 Lh40
Petenwell Lake ⌂ USA 172 Fe23
Peterbell ⌂ CDN (ON) 173 Fj21
Peterborough ⌂ AUS (SA) 110 Rh62
Peterborough ⌂ CDN (ON) 173 Ga23
Peterborough ⌂ GB 21 Ku38
Peterborough ⌂ USA (NH) 177 Gd24
Petergof ⌂ RUS 38 Mk17
Peterhead ⌂ GB 20 Kt33
Peter I Island ⌂ 7
Peterlee ⌂ GB 21 Kt36
Petermann A.L. ⌂ AUS 103 Rf58

Petermann Gletscher ⌂ DK 163 Gd02
Petermann Ranges ⌂ AUS 103 Re58
Peteroa, Volcán ⌂ RCH/RA 208 Ge63
Peter Pond Lake ⌂ CDN 167 Ef17
Petersburg ⌂ D 32 Lm39
Petersburg ⌂ USA (AK) 166 Dd17
Petersburg ⌂ USA (OK) 174 Fb29
Petersburg ⌂ USA (VA) 178 Gb27
Petersburg ⌂ USA (WV) 177 Ga26
Petersburg Nat. Battlefield ⌂ USA (VA) 178 Gb27
Petersfield ⌂ GB 21 Ku39
Peter's Mine ⌂ GUY 194 Ha42
Peterson's Cay N.P. ⌂ BS 179 Ga32
Petersville ⌂ USA (AK) 165 Ce14
Peth ⌂ IND (MHT) 82 Oh37
Pethel Peninsula ⌂ CDN 167 Ee14
Petilia Policastro ⌂ I 37 Lr51
Petín ⌂ E 26 Kn48
Pétionville ⌂ RH 186 Gd36
Petite Kabylie ⌂ DZ 126 Lc27
Petite Rivière de l'Artibonite ⌂ RH 186 Gd36
Petit Goâve ⌂ RH 186 Gd36
Petit Lac Manicouagan ⌂ CDN 176 Gg20
Petit Lac Opinaca ⌂ CDN 176 Gd19
Petit Loango ⌂ G 148 Le47
Petit Miquelon ⌂ F 177 Hb22
Petit Mont Cameroun ⌂ CAM 138 Le43
Petit Point ⌂ AUS 104 Qb58
Petit-Rocher ⌂ CDN (NB) 176 Gh22
Petit Saguenay ⌂ CDN (QC) 176 Ge21
Petkeljärven kansallispuisto ⌂ FIN 38 Mm28
Pet'ki ⌂ BY 41 Me38
Petladi ⌂ IND (GUJ) 82 Og34
Peto ⌂ MEX (YT) 183 Ff35
Petolahti = Petalax ⌂ FIN 38 Mb28
Petoskey ⌂ USA (MI) 173 Fh23
Petra ⌂ GR 47 Mf53
Petra ⌂ JOR 58 Mh30
Petras, Mount ⌂ 6 Dc34
Petriç ⌂ BG 44 Md49
Petrified Dunes ⌂ NAM 154 Lh58
Petrified Forest ⌂ NAM 154 Lh58
Petrified Forest N.P. ⌂ USA 171 Ef28
Petrified Wood Park ⌂ USA 169 Ej23
Petrila ⌂ RO 44 Md45
Petrila ⌂ HR 35 Lr45
Petřkov ⌂ UA 48 Mf20
Petriks'ka fortec'a ⌂ UA 49 Mj42
Petro ⌂ PK 65 Of32
Petroglyphs Provincial Park ⌂ CDN 173 Ga23
Petrohanski Prohod ⌂ BG 44 Md47
Petrohué ⌂ RCH 208 Gd66
Petrolândia ⌂ BR (PE) 201 Ja50
Petrolia ⌂ USA (CA) 170 Dh25
Petrolina ⌂ BR (AM) 198 Gg47
Petrolina de Goiás ⌂ BR (GO) 202 Hf54
Petrona Towers ⌂ MAL 92 Qb43
Petropavl ⌂ KZ 54 Ob08
Petropavlivka ⌂ UA 49 Mj21
Petropavlovka ⌂ RUS (BUR) 70 Qe20
Petropavlovka ⌂ THA 88 Na20
Petropavlovsk ⌂ RUS 49 Mj21
Petropavlovsk-Kamčatskij ⌂ RUS 55 Sd08
Petrópolis ⌂ BR (RJ) 205 Hj57
Petroquímica ⌂ BR (BA) 210 Gg68
Petroşani ⌂ RO 44 Md45
Petrovac ⌂ SCG 44 Mb46
Petrovaradin ⌂ SCG 44 Lu45
Petrovce ⌂ K 63 Oj32
Petrovice ⌂ CZ 42 Lq41
Petrovske ⌂ UA 49 Mh23
Petrovskoe ⌂ RUS 38 Ni19
Petrovskoe ⌂ RUS 38 Ml30
Petrovsk-Zabajkal'skij ⌂ RUS 70 Qe20
Petrusburg ⌂ ZA 155 Mc60
Petrus Steyn ⌂ ZA 155 Me59
Petrusville ⌂ ZA 155 Mc61
Petrykav ⌂ BY 48 Me19
Pet Sirut ⌂ IND (KTK) 82 Oj37
Petsmo ⌂ FIN 38 Mb27
Petuški ⌂ RUS 48 Mk18
Peuetsagoe, Mount ⌂ RI 92 Pj43
Peulik, Gunung-Claise ⌂ F 24 La44
Peuk ⌂ K 89 Qc39
Peulik, Mount ⌂ USA 164 Cb17
Peumo ⌂ RCH 208 Ge63
Peuralak ⌂ RI 92 Pj43
Pevek ⌂ RUS 55 Td05
Peyrat-le-Château ⌂ F 24 Lb45
Peyrehorade ⌂ F 24 Kt47
Pézenas ⌂ F 25 Ld47
Pezinok ⌂ SK 42 Ls42
Pezu ⌂ PK 65 Of29
Pfaffenhofen ⌂ D 33 Lm42
Pfälzerwald ⌂ D 33 Lh41
Pfarrkirchen ⌂ D 33 Ln42
Pfeiffer Big Sur S.P. ⌂ USA 170 Dj27
Pfitzner, Mount ⌂ AUS 108 Rh57
Pforzheim ⌂ D 33 Lj42
Pfronten ⌂ D 33 Ll43
Pfullendorf ⌂ D 33 Lk43
Pfungstadt ⌂ D 33 Lj41
Phae Muang Phi ⌂ THA 87 Qa36
Phagwara ⌂ IND (PJB) 80 Oh30
Phalaborwa ⌂ ZA 152 Mf57
Phaistos ⌂ GR 47 Me55
Phalaborwa ⌂ ZA 152 Mf57
Phala Road = Dinokwe ⌂ RB 155 Md57

Phaselis ⌂ TR 56 Mf27
Pha Sua Waterfall ⌂ THA 86 Pj36
Pha Taem ⌂ THA 89 Qc38
Pha Taem N.P. ⌂ THA 89 Qc38
Phat Diem ⌂ VN 87 Qd35
Pha Thai Cave ⌂ THA 87 Pk36
Pha To ⌂ THA 88 Pk41
Phatthalung ⌂ THA 88 Qa42
Phayakhapun Phiasi ⌂ THA 89 Qb38
Phayao ⌂ THA 87 Pk36
Phayuha Khiri ⌂ THA 88 Qa37
Phenix City ⌂ USA (AL) 175 Fh29
Phetchabun ⌂ THA 88 Qa37
Phiang ⌂ LAO 87 Qa36
Phibun Mangsahan ⌂ THA 89 Qc38
Phichit ⌂ THA 88 Qa37
Philadelphia ⌂ USA (MS) 175 Ff29
Philadelphia ⌂ USA (PA) 177 Gc26
Phil Lieng ⌂ VN 89 Qe40
Philip ⌂ USA (SD) 172 Ek23
Philip Island ⌂ AUS (VIC) 111 Sc65
Philippeville ⌂ B 23 Le40
Philippi ⌂ GR 45 Me49
Philippi ⌂ USA (WV) 177 Ga26
Philippine Basin ⌂ 10 Ra08
Philippine Sea ⌂ 100 Rb08
Philippine Trench ⌂ 52 Ra08
Philippolis ⌂ ZA 155 Mc61
Philipsburg ⌂ NL (NA) 187 Gj37
Phillipsburg ⌂ USA 175 Mc61
Phillip Creek ⌂ AUS (NT) 106 Rh55
Phillips ⌂ USA (WI) 172 Fe23
Phillipsburg ⌂ USA (KS) 174 Fa26
Phmits Cave ⌂ NAM 150 Lh56
Phillips Range ⌂ AUS 103 Rc54
Phimai ⌂ THA 89 Qb38
Phimai Historical Park ⌂ THA 89 Qb38
Phinda Resource Reserve ⌂ ZA 155 Mg59
Phippseya ⌂ N 16 Ma05
Phitsanulok ⌂ THA 88 Qa37
Phtshane Molopo ⌂ RB 155 Mc58
Phnom Aural W.S. ⌂ K 89 Qc40
Phnom Bokor N.P. ⌂ K 89 Qc40
Phnom Kulen N.P. ⌂ K 89 Qc39
Phnom Penh ⌂ K 89 Qc40
Phnom Prich W.S. ⌂ K 89 Qd39
Phnom Somkos W.S. ⌂ K 89 Qc40
Pho Chai ⌂ THA 89 Qb37
Phoenix ⌂ USA (AZ) 171 Ed29
Phoenix ⌂ USA (MI) 173 Ff22
Phoenix International Raceway ⌂ USA (AZ) 171 Ed29
Phoenix Islands ⌂ 100 Ba10
Pho Minh Pagoda ⌂ VN 87 Qd35
Phon ⌂ THA 89 Qb38
Phon Charoen ⌂ THA 87 Qb36
Phonda ⌂ IND (GOA) 84 Oh38
Phong Nha Caves ⌂ VN 87 Qd37
Phong Nha-Ke Bang National Park ⌂ VN 87 Qd37
Phongsali ⌂ LAO 87 Qa35
Phon Thong ⌂ THA 89 Qb37
Phon Hong ⌂ LAO 87 Qb36
Phon Phisai ⌂ THA 87 Qb36
Phonsavan ⌂ LAO 87 Qb36
Phou Phanang N.B.C.A. ⌂ LAO 87 Qb36
Phou Xang He N.B.C.A. ⌂ LAO 89 Qc38
Phra Buddha Taksin Mingmongkol ⌂ THA 89 Qa42
Phrae ⌂ THA 87 Qa36
Phra Mahathat Chedi ⌂ THA 88 Qa37
Phra Nakhon Kiri Historical Park ⌂ THA 88 Qa39
Phran Kratai ⌂ THA 88 Pk37
Phra Pathom Chedi ⌂ THA 88 Pk39
Phrasa Romeas ⌂ K 89 Qd37
Phra Phutthachai N.P. ⌂ THA 88 Qa38
Phủ Bái ⌂ VN 89 Qd37
Phu Bia ⌂ LAO 87 Qb36
Phuc Yên ⌂ VN 87 Qd35
Phu Den Din N.B.C.A. ⌂ LAO 87 Qb35
Phuduhudu ⌂ RB 151 Mc56
Phu Hin Rongkla N.P. ⌂ THA 88 Qa37
Phu Hung ⌂ VN 89 Qd40
Phu Kao Phu Phan Kham N.P. ⌂ THA 89 Qb37
Phuket ⌂ THA 88 Pk42
Phu Khao Khoay N.B.C.A. ⌂ LAO 87 Qb36
Phu Khieo ⌂ THA 89 Qb38
Phu Kradung ⌂ THA 89 Qa38
Phulaut ⌂ IND (BIH) 83 Pd33
Phulbani ⌂ IND (ORS) 83 Pc35
Phulbari ⌂ BD 86 Pe33
Phu Leu ⌂ LAO 87 Qc36
Phu Loc N.B.C.A. ⌂ LAO 87 Qb36
Phu Miang ⌂ LAO 87 Qb36
Phumi Damnak ⌂ K 89 Qc40
Phumi Dei Lo ⌂ K 89 Qc40
Phu My ⌂ VN 89 Qe40
Phu Nampa ⌂ LAO 87 Qb35
Phung Hiep ⌂ VN 89 Qd41
Phu Nonh ⌂ VN 89 Qe40
Phunphin ⌂ THA 88 Pk41
Phuoc Long ⌂ VN 89 Qd40
Phuong Lam ⌂ VN 89 Qd40
Phu Phadeng ⌂ LAO 87 Qb36
Phu Rua ⌂ THA 89 Qa38
Phu Rua N.P. ⌂ THA 87 Qb37
Phu Sa Dok Bua N.P. ⌂ THA 89 Qc37
Phu Samun ⌂ LAO 87 Qb36
Phu Tho ⌂ VN 87 Qc35
Phuthaditjhaba ⌂ ZA 155 Me60
Phu Tuc ⌂ VN 89 Qe39
Phu Wieng N.P. ⌂ THA 89 Qb37
Phu Xua ⌂ LAO 87 Qb36
Phu Yen ⌂ VN 87 Qa37
Piaçabuçu ⌂ BR (AL) 201 Jb51
Piacenza ⌂ I 34 Lk46
Piamonte ⌂ RA (SF) 209 Gk62
Piana degli Albanesi ⌂ I 36 Lo53
Piana del Fúcino ⌂ I 36 Lo49
Piana-Mwanga ⌂ RDC 146 Me49
Pianella ⌂ I 35 Lp48
Pianella ⌂ I (SF) 201 Jh49
Pianguan ⌂ CHN (SAX) 72 Qf26
Piankan ⌂ RDC 149 La47
Piano Mutombo ⌂ RDC 149 Lc48
Pian Rang–Thap Cham ⌂ VN 89 Qe40
Pian-Upe Game Reserve ⌂ EAU 144 Mf45
Piantanida ⌂ RA 208 Gc65
Pian Thiet ⌂ VN 89 Qe40
Piao Phru To Daeng ⌂ THA 88 Qa42
Pharenda ⌂ IND (UPH) 83 Pb32
Pharr ⌂ USA (TX) 181 Fa32

Piaski ⌂ PL 41 Mc39
Piată ⌂ BR (BA) 201 Hk52
Piątek ⌂ PL 41 Lu38
Piatra ⌂ RO 45 Mf47
Piatra Craiului ⌂ RO 45 Mf45
Piatra Craiului, P.N. ⌂ RO 45 Mf45
Piatra-Neamţ ⌂ RO 49 Md22
Piatra-Olt ⌂ RO 45 Me46
Piatra Seciului ⌂ RO 43 Me43
Piauí ⌂ BR 191 Hj10
Piazza Armerina ⌂ I 37 Lp53
Piazzale delle Erbe di Verona ⌂ I 34 Lm45
Pibor Post ⌂ SUD 142 Mg42
Pica ⌂ RCH 206 Gf56
Picada ⌂ BR (MT) 202 Hc54
Pica d'Estats ⌂ E 28 Lb48
Pičaevo ⌂ RUS 48 Nb19
Picard ⌂ F (GF) 195 Hd40
Picardie ⌂ F 23 Lc41
Picardy ⌂ F 23 Lc41
Piçarrao ⌂ BR (PI) 201 Hk50
Picayune ⌂ USA (MS) 175 Ff30
Pic d'Anie ⌂ F 24 Ku48
Pic de Mauberme ⌂ F 24 La48
Pic de Tibé ⌂ RG 136 Kf41
Pic d'Orhy ⌂ F 28 Kt48
Pic du Canigou ⌂ F 25 Lc48
Pic du Midi ⌂ F 24 Ku48
Pic du Midi de Bigorre ⌂ F 24 La47
Pich ⌂ MEX (CAM) 183 Fd36
Pichaca ⌂ RA (SA) 207 Gh57
Pichanco ⌂ RCH (AS) 207 Gh57
Pichicuy ⌂ RCH 208 Ge62
Pichilemu ⌂ RCH 208 Ge63
Pichilinigue ⌂ MEX (BCS) 180 Ee33
Pichincha, Volcán Guagua ⌂ EC 196 Ga46
Pickens ⌂ USA (SC) 175 Ff29
Pickens ⌂ USA (SC) 178 Ff28
Pickering ⌂ GB 21 Ku36
Pico Almanzor ⌂ E 27 Kp50
Pico Alto ⌂ BR 201 Ja48
Pico Alto ⌂ PE 197 Gb52
Pico Alto ⌂ PE 197 Gb52
Pico Basile ⌂ GQ 138 La44
Pico Basile, P.N.de ⌂ GQ 138 Le44
Pico Bolívar ⌂ YV 192 Ge41
Pico Bonito, P.N. ⌂ HN 184 Fg38
Pico del Diablo ⌂ MEX 180 Ec30
Pico del Teide ⌂ E 124 Kb31
Pico de Orizaba, P.N. ⌂ MEX 182 Fb36
Pico de Pircas Negras ⌂ RA/RCH 207 Gf58
Pico de Salamanca ⌂ RA (CB) 210 Gg68
Pico de San Francisco ⌂ RA/RCH 207 Gf58
Pico Echeverría ⌂ MEX 180 Ed31
Pico Espejo ⌂ YV 192 Ge41
Pico Itapari ⌂ BR 205 Hf58
Pico Rondon ⌂ BR 193 Gj45
Pico São Tomé ⌂ E 26 Kq47
Picota ⌂ PE 196 Gb49
Pico Truncado ⌂ RA (SC) 210 Gg68
Pic Peric ⌂ F 24 Lb48
Picquigny ⌂ F 23 Lc41
Pic River (I. R.) ⌂ CDN (ON) 173 Fg21
Pic Tiska ⌂ DZ 132 Le34
Picton ⌂ AUS (NSW) 111 Sf63
Picton ⌂ NZ 113 Tf66
Picton ⌂ USA (NS) 176 Gj23
Pictou Island ⌂ CDN 176 Gj23
Pictured Rock Nat. Lakeshore ⌂ USA 173 Fg22
Picudo, Cerro ⌂ RA 210 Gf69
Picún Leufú, Cerro ⌂ RA 208 Gf65
Picún Leufú ⌂ RA (NE) 208 Gf65
Pic Zoumri ⌂ RN 133 Lg35
Pidarak ⌂ PK 65 Ob33
Pidhajci ⌂ UA 43 Mf41
Pidikalo ⌂ IND (CGH) 83 Pb34
Pidkamin' ⌂ UA 43 Mf41
Pidkolenu ⌂ IND (APH) 83 Ok37
Piduratalagala ⌂ CL 85 Pa42
Piebli ⌂ CI 137 Kg42
Piedade ⌂ BR (SP) 205 Hg57
Piede da Cuesta ⌂ CO 192 Gd42
Pie de la Cuesta ⌂ MEX (GUR) 182 Fa37
Piedmont ⌂ USA (AL) 175 Fh29
Piedmont = Piemonte ⌂ I 34 Lh46
Piedmont N.W.R. ⌂ USA 178 Fj29
Piedra, Cerro ⌂ RCH 208 Gd66
Piedra del Aguila ⌂ RA (NE) 208 Ge66
Piedra de la Virgen ⌂ YV 193 Gk43
Piedra Echada ⌂ RA (BA) 209 Gj64
Piedrahita ⌂ E 27 Kp50
Piedras Blancas ⌂ CR 185 Fj41
Piedras Negras ⌂ GCA 184 Fe37
Piedras Negras ⌂ MEX (COH) 181 Ek31
Piedras Negras ⌂ PE 197 Ge54
Piedra Sola ⌂ ROU 204 Hb62
Piekary Śląskie ⌂ PL 41 Lt40
Piekoszów ⌂ PL 41 Ma40
Piekszemün ⌂ FIN 38 Mg28
Piła ⌂ I 37 Mr51
Pielisen museo ⌂ FIN 38 Mm28
Pielejekijase n.p. ⌂ S 16 Lj12
Piemonte ⌂ I 34 Lh46
Pienaarsrivier ⌂ ZA 155 Me58
Pieniąndz ⌂ CO 192 Gb44
Pienżno ⌂ PL 41 Ma36
Pieńiński N.P., P.N. ⌂ SK 41 Ma41
Piacenza ⌂ I 34 Lk46
Pierce ⌂ USA (ID) 168 Ec22
Pierceland ⌂ CDN (SK) 169 Ef18
Pierre ⌂ USA (SD) 172 Fa23
Pierre-Buffière ⌂ F 24 Lb45
Pierrefonds ⌂ F 23 Lc41
Pierrefort ⌂ F 25 Lc46
Pierrelatte ⌂ F 25 Le46
Pierre Payen ⌂ RH 186 Gd36
Pierre Hoho ⌂ F (GF) 194 Hd44
Pierre-Ton ⌂ CDN (MB) 172 Ek21
Piešťany ⌂ SK 42 Ls42
Piesyce ⌂ PL 40 Ly40
Pietarsaari ⌂ FIN 16 Mb14

Pietermaritzburg ⌂ ZA 155 Mf60
Pietermaritzburg ⌂ ZA 152 Me57
Pinehouse Lake ⌂ CDN (SK) 167 Eg18
Pie Town ⌂ USA (NM) 171 Ef28
Piet Plessis ⌂ ZA 155 Mc59
Pietrasanta ⌂ I 34 Ll47
Piet Retief ⌂ ZA 155 Mf59
Pietritas ⌂ RA (BA) 209 Gj63
Pieve di Cadore ⌂ I 35 Ln44
Pieve San Stéfano ⌂ I 34 Lm47
Pilo ⌂ EC 196 Ga46
Pigeon Hole ⌂ AUS (NT) 106 Rf51
Pigeon Point ⌂ TT 187 Gk48
Piges ⌂ GR 46 Mb51
Piggs Peak ⌂ SD 155 Mf58
Pigü ⌂ RA (BA) 209 Gj64
Pigüé ⌂ RA (BA) 209 Gj64
Pihani ⌂ IND (UPH) 83 Pa32
Pihuamo ⌂ MEX (JLC) 182 Ej36
Pijijiapan ⌂ MEX (CHP) 183 Fd38
Pikalevo ⌂ RUS 48 Mh16
Pikangikum ⌂ CDN (ON) 172 Fc20
Pikas ⌂ I 35 Le42
Pikasilla ⌂ EST 39 Mg32
pik Dankova ⌂ KS/CHN 66 Oj25
pik Kalinina ⌂ TJ 63 Og24
pik Karasak ⌂ TJ/CHN 63 Og26
Pikou ⌂ CHN (LNG) 73 Ra26
pik Revoljuciju ⌂ TJ 63 Og24
pik Sedova ⌂ RUS 54 Nd04
Pila ⌂ RP 91 Ra40
Pila ⌂ E (CA) 209 Ha64
Pila Island ⌂ MYA 88 Pj40
Pilanesberg N.P. ⌂ ZA 155 Md58
Pilang ⌂ RI 95 Qh47
Pilani ⌂ IND (RJT) 80 Oh31
Pilão Arcado ⌂ BR (BA) 201 Hj50
Pilar ⌂ BR (AL) 201 Jb51
Pilar ⌂ E (C) 208 Gj61
Pilar ⌂ PY 204 Ha59
Pilar ⌂ RA (BA) 209 Ha63
Pilar ⌂ RP 90 Rd40
Pilar de Goiás ⌂ BR (GO) 202 Hf53
Pilas ⌂ E 27 Ko53
Pilas Group ⌂ RP 91 Ra42
Pilas Island ⌂ RP 91 Ra42
Pilatus ⌂ CH 34 Lj44
Pilawa ⌂ PL 41 Mb39
Picanciyu ⌂ CHN (HUN) 74 Qd32
Pilcomayo ⌂ BOL 207 Gk56
Pilcopata ⌂ PE 206 Gf53
Pile Bay Village ⌂ USA (AK) 164 Cd16
Pilgrim's Rest ⌂ ZA 155 Mf58
Pilgrimsard ⌂ S 16 Ln14
Pilibbhit ⌂ IND (UPH) 81 Ok31
Pilimpikou ⌂ BF 137 Kj39
Pilio ⌂ GR 44 Md51
Pilis ⌂ H 43 Lu42
Pilisvörösvár ⌂ H 43 Lt43
Pilkington ⌂ AUS (WA) 103 Rd56
Pillaro ⌂ EC 196 Gb46
Pilón ⌂ C 179 Ga36
Piloo ⌂ RA 209 Ha62
Pilot Peak ⌂ USA 170 Eb26
Pilot Station ⌂ USA (AK) 164 Cb17
Pilot Station ⌂ USA (AK) 164 Bj15
Pilsko ⌂ PL/SK 43 Lu41
Pilsrundāle ⌂ LV 39 Me34
Piltene ⌂ LV 39 Mb33
Pilzikova ⌂ CI LT 30 Md36
Pilzno ⌂ PL 41 Mb41
Pima and Space Museum ⌂ USA 171 Ee29
Pima ⌂ AUS (WA) 104 Qd61
Pimbee ⌂ AUS (WA) 104 Qb58
Pimenta Bueno ⌂ BR (RO) 198 Gk51
Pimenteiras ⌂ BR (PI) 201 Hk49
Pimenteiras ⌂ BR (RO) 206 Gk52
Pimentel Barbosa, T.I. ⌂ BR 202 Hd51
Pimlico Race Course ⌂ USA (MD) 177 Gb26
Pimpalner ⌂ IND (MHT) 82 Oh35
Pimpinela ⌂ YV 193 Gf41
Pina ⌂ GH 137 Kk40
Pinácalo, Cerro ⌂ RA 210 Gd71
Pinamalayan ⌂ RP 90 Ra40
Pinanga ⌂ RP 91 Rb45
Pinapan, Mount ⌂ RI 93 Pk44
Pinarbaşi ⌂ TR 56 Mg26
Pinarbaşi ⌂ TR 56 Mh27
Pinarcik ⌂ TR 47 Mh53
Pinar del Río ⌂ C 179 Fj34
Pinarello ⌂ F 36 Lk49
Pinarhisar ⌂ TR 45 Mh49
Pinar N.P. ⌂ RP 90 Rb39
Pincally ⌂ AUS (NSW) 108 Sa61
Pinchwehi ⌂ H 42 Lt44
Pincher ⌂ CDN (AB) 169 Ed21
Pinchney Island N.W.R. ⌂ USA 178 Fk29
Pinckneyville ⌂ USA (IL) 175 Ff27
Pinczów ⌂ PL 41 Ma40
Pin Valley N.P. ⌂ IND 81 Oj30
Pioche ⌂ USA (NV) 170 Ec27
Piodi ⌂ RDC 149 Me49
Pío IX ⌂ BR (PI) 201 Hj50
Pio Duran ⌂ RP 90 Rb39
Pio Lac ⌂ CO 192 Gc44
Pioche ⌂ USA (NV) 170 Ec27
Pioneer ⌂ USA (AS) 110 Sa63
Pion ⌂ F 34 Lk48
Piskemi ⌂ UZ 63 Of25
Pinon ⌂ USA (AZ) 171 Eh29
Pinon ⌂ MEX (ZCT) 182 Ek34
Pinoos ⌂ E 29 Kr53
Pinoon-Puente ⌂ E 27 Kt53
Pinnaroo ⌂ AUS (SA) 110 Sa63
Pinrang ⌂ RI 96 Qk47
Pinsk ⌂ BY 41 Mg38
Pintado Grande ⌂ ROU 204 Hb62
Pintura ⌂ RA 210 Gf67
Pinter ⌂ MEX (YT) 183 Ff35
Pioner Island ⌂ 51 Ga02
Pioneer Mountains ⌂ USA 169 Ed23
Pioneers Mountains ⌂ SD 51 Ga02
Pioneer Museum (Iroquois Falls) ⌂ CDN 173 Fk21
Pioneer Woman Mus. ⌂ USA 174 Fb27
Piossasco ⌂ I 34 Lh46
Pip ⌂ IR 64 Nj33
Pipalda ⌂ IND (RJT) 82 Oj32
Pipalyatjara ⌂ AUS 105 Rf59
Pipar ⌂ IND (RJT) 80 Og32
Piperi ⌂ GR 47 Md53
Pipestone ⌂ CDN (MB) 172 Ek21
Pipinas ⌂ RA (BA) 209 Hb63
Pipli ⌂ IND (ORS) 83 Pc35
Pippara ⌂ IND (APH) 83 Pa37
Pipar River ⌂ RI 114 Rk48
Pipriac ⌂ F 22 Kt43
Piprod ⌂ IND (MPH) 83 Pa34
Pique ⌂ CDN (ON) 173 Fh25
Pira ⌂ DY 138 La41
Pirabeiraba ⌂ BR (SC) 205 Hf59
Piracanjuba ⌂ BR (GO) 202 Hf54
Piracicaba ⌂ BR (SP) 205 Hg57
Piracuruca ⌂ BR (PI) 201 Hk47
Pirai do Sul ⌂ BR (PR) 205 Hf58
Piraju ⌂ BR (SP) 202 Hf57
Pirajuí ⌂ BR (SP) 202 Hf57
Pirakuna, T.I. ⌂ BR 202 Hf57
Pirambu ⌂ BR (SE) 201 Jb51
Piran ⌂ SLO 42 Lo45
Pirané ⌂ RA (FO) 204 Ha58
Pirapora ⌂ BR (MG) 203 Hj54
Piratini ⌂ BR (RS) 204 Hd61
Piray ⌂ RA 204 Hc60
Pirdop ⌂ BG 45 Me48
Pires do Rio ⌂ BR (GO) 202 Hf54
Piri ⌂ GNB 136 Kc39
Piriápolis ⌂ ROU 204 Hc63
Pira-Pora, Cerro ⌂ RCH 207 Gf56
Pirmasens ⌂ D 33 Lh41
Pirnesu ⌂ I 37 Lr50
Pirot ⌂ SCG 44 Mc47
Pirra ⌂ PE 196 Fk48
Pirtleville ⌂ USA (AZ) 171 Ef30
Piru ⌂ RI 97 Re47
Piryli ⌂ GR 46 Mb53
Pisa ⌂ I 34 Ll47
Pisagua ⌂ RCH 206 Ge55
Pisac ⌂ PE 197 Ge52
Pisana ⌂ RO 45 Me44
Pisagua ⌂ RCH 206 Ge55
Piscataquis ⌂ USA (ME) 176 Gf23
Pisco ⌂ PE 197 Gc53
Piscobamba ⌂ PE 197 Gb50
Pisek ⌂ CZ 42 Lp41
Pisgah Crater ⌂ USA 170 Eb28
Pishan ⌂ CHN (XUZ) 66 Oj27
Pishin ⌂ IR 64 Nj32
Pishin ⌂ PK 65 Od30
Pising ⌂ RI 96 Ra48
Pismo Beach ⌂ USA (CA) 170 Dk28
Piso Firme ⌂ BOL 206 Gk53
Pisogne ⌂ I 34 Ll45
Piso Livádi ⌂ GR 47 Mf53
Pissa ⌂ RCA 148 Lj44
Pissis, Cerro ⌂ RA 207 Gf59
Pissos ⌂ F 24 Ku46
Pista ⌂ MEX (YT) 183 Ff35
Pisticci ⌂ I 37 Lr50
Pistóia ⌂ I 34 Ll47
Pistol River ⌂ USA (OR) 168 Dh25
Pit ⌂ RDC 149 Lk48
Pita ⌂ RG 136 Kd40
Pitaga ⌂ CDN (NF) 176 Gh19
Pital ⌂ CO 192 Gb45
Pital ⌂ CR 185 Fh40
Pitanga ⌂ BR (PR) 204 He58
Pitangueiras ⌂ BR (SP) 202 Hf56
Pitanguí ⌂ BR (MG) 203 Hj55
Pitaya ⌂ PE 197 Gd51
Pitcairn Island ⌂ 11 Db12
Pitches ⌂ GNB 136 Kd39
Pithampur ⌂ IND (WBG) 86 Pe34
Pithapuram ⌂ IND (APH) 83 Pb37
Pithara ⌂ AUS (WA) 104 Qj61
Pithiviers ⌂ F 23 Lc42
Pithoragarh Ski area ⌂ IND 81 Pa31
Pithora ⌂ IND (RJT) 80 Og32
Pithoragarh Hill Resort ⌂ IND 81 Pa31
Pithoro ⌂ PK 65 Oe33

Pine Grove ⌂ AUS (WA) 104 Qh59
Pine Islands ⌂ USA (FL) 179 Fk33
Pineland ⌂ USA (TX) 174 Fd30
Pinerolo ⌂ I 34 Lh46
Pinetown ⌂ ZA 155 Mf59
Pinetown ⌂ USA (KY) 178 Fj27
Pineville ⌂ USA (LA) 175 Fd30
Pineville ⌂ USA (WV) 174 Fc27
Pinewood ⌂ USA 171 Ee28
Piney Buttes ⌂ USA 169 Eh23
Pingan ⌂ CHN (QHI) 72 Qb27
Pingba ⌂ CHN (GZH) 74 Qd32
Pingchang ⌂ CHN (SCH) 72 Qd30
Pingchao ⌂ CHN (JGS) 78 Ra29
Pingdingshan ⌂ CHN (HNN) 73 Qg29
Pingding shan ⌂ CHN 76 Re22
Pingelly ⌂ AUS (WA) 104 Qj62
Pingeyrar ⌂ IS 18 Ju25
Pinggu ⌂ CHN (GZG) 74 Qd31
Pinghe ⌂ CHN (FJN) 75 Qj33
Pinghu ⌂ CHN (ZJG) 78 Ra31
Pingjiang ⌂ CHN (HUN) 74 Qf31
Pingli ⌂ CHN (SAX) 72 Qe29
Pingli ⌂ CHN (MHT) 82 Oh37
Pingliang ⌂ CHN (GSU) 72 Qd28
Pinglu ⌂ CHN (SAX) 72 Qe26
Pingluo ⌂ CHN (NHZ) 72 Qc26
Pingmul ⌂ IS 18 Kf25
Pingnan ⌂ CHN (FJN) 75 Qj32
Pingnan ⌂ CHN (GZG) 74 Qf34
Pingquan ⌂ CHN (HBI) 73 Qj25
Pingree ⌂ USA (ND) 172 Fa22
Pingtan ⌂ CHN (FJN) 75 Qk33
Pingtang ⌂ CHN (GZH) 74 Qd32
Pingtung ⌂ RC 75 Ra34
Pinhal, N.P. ⌂ BG 44 Md49
Pinheiro ⌂ BR (MA) 200 Hh47
Pinheiro Machado ⌂ BR (RS) 204 Hd61
Pinheiros ⌂ BR (ES) 203 Hk55
Pinhõs ⌂ P 26 Kn49
Pinjarra ⌂ AUS (WA) 105 Rb61
Pinjin ⌂ AUS (WA) 105 Rb61
Pinkafeld ⌂ A 35 Lr43
Pinkawillinie Conservation Park ⌂ AUS (SA) 110 Rh61
Pinkowski ⌂ MYA 86 Pj36
Pinkhwun ⌂ MYA 86 Pj36
Pinkilla ⌂ AUS (QLD) 109 Sb59
Pink Mountain ⌂ CDN (BC) 166 Dj14
Pinlaung ⌂ MYA 86 Pj35
Pinlebu ⌂ MYA 86 Ph34
Pinnacle ⌂ AUS (NF) 177 Gc26
Pinnacles ⌂ AUS 104 Qh61
Pinnacles Nat. Mon. ⌂ USA 170 Dk27
Pinnaroo ⌂ AUS (SA) 110 Sa63
Pinner ⌂ GB 21 Ku39

Pipestone ⌂ USA (MN) 172 Fb24
Pipestone Nat. Mon. ⌂ USA 172 Fb23
Piplochorry ⌂ GB 20 Kr34
Pitka ⌂ USA (LA) 174 Fd30
Pitkovo ⌂ RUS 38 Mk30
Pitlam ⌂ IND (APH) 82 Ok36
Pitlochry ⌂ GB 20 Kr34
Pitoa ⌂ CAM 139 Lg41
Pitomača ⌂ HR 35 Ls45
Pitoru ⌂ BR (PA) 200 Hg47
Pitrufquén ⌂ RCH 208 Gd65
Pitsane ⌂ RB 155 Mc58
Pitt, P.N. H. ⌂ YV 193 Gg40
Pitt Island ⌂ CDN 166 Dg19
Pittsburg ⌂ USA (KS) 174 Fc27
Pittsburgh ⌂ USA (PA) 173 Ga25
Pittsfield ⌂ USA (IL) 172 Fe26
Pittsfield ⌂ USA (MA) 177 Gd23
Pittston ⌂ USA (PA) 177 Gc25
Pitts Town ⌂ BS 186 Gc34
Pittsworth ⌂ AUS (QLD) 109 Sf59
Pitu ⌂ RI 91 Rd44
Pituil ⌂ RA (LR) 207 Gg60
Pitvaros ⌂ H 43 Ma44
Piu ⌂ PNG 115 Sd49
Pium ⌂ BR (TO) 202 He51
Piumhi ⌂ BR (MG) 203 Hh56
Pium, T.I. ⌂ BR 193 Gk44
Piura ⌂ PE 196 Fk48
Pise ⌂ RA (LR) 207 Gg60
Piva ⌂ PE 196 Fk48
Piva ⌂ SCG 44 Lt47
Piz Bernina ⌂ CH 34 Lk44
Pizarras ⌂ PE 196 Ga48
Pizhi ⌂ WAN 138 La41
Pizzighettone ⌂ I 34 Lk45
Pizzo ⌂ I 37 Lr52
Pizzo di Coca ⌂ I 34 Ll44
Pjandž ⌂ TJ 63 Oe27
Pjaozero ⌂ RUS 54 Pb04
Pjasinskij zaliv ⌂ RUS 54 Pa04
Pjatigorsk ⌂ RUS 57 Nb23
Pjatychatky ⌂ UA 49 Mf22
Pjóðgarðurinn i Skaftafelli ⌂ IS 18 Kc26
Pjóðgarðurinn ⌂ IS 18 Ju26
Pjóðgarðurinn Snæfellsjökull ⌂ IS 18 Ju26
Pjórsa ⌂ IS 18 Ka26
Pjóðveldisbærinn ⌂ IS 18 Jk26
Pjóðsárdalur ⌂ IS 18 Jk26
Pkhet Fort ⌂ USA (CA) 170 Ea26
Playa Azul de Acapulco ⌂ MEX (MHC) 182 Ej37
Playa Azul de Acapulco ⌂ MEX (MHC) 182 Ej37
Playa Bávaro ⌂ DOM 186 Ge36
Playa Bengé ⌂ NL 193 Gf39
Playa Bibijagua ⌂ C 179 Fj35
Playa Blanca ⌂ C 186 Gc35
Playa Bonita ⌂ DOM 186 Gf36
Playa Costa del Sol ⌂ ES 184 Ff39
Playa Curbina ⌂ MEX (BC) 180 Ec30
Playa Dayaniguas ⌂ C 179 Fk34
Playa de Florida ⌂ C 179 Ga35
Playa del Carmen ⌂ MEX (QTR) 183 Fg35
Playa del Coco ⌂ CR 184 Fh40
Playa del Morro ⌂ DOM 186 Ge36
Playa Girón ⌂ C 179 Fk34
Playa Grande ⌂ BR (MT) 202 Hc53
Playa Grande ⌂ PE 197 Gb51
Playa Hermosa ⌂ MEX (BCS) 180 Ec30
Playa Kalki ⌂ NL 193 Gf39
Playa Laguna Grande ⌂ DOM 186 Ge36
Playa las Cañas ⌂ C 179 Ga34
Playa Las Corchos ⌂ MEX 182 Eh35
Playa Malarrimo ⌂ MEX 180 Ec31
Playa Minitas ⌂ DOM 186 Gf36
Playa Princess ⌂ MEX 182 Fa37
Playa Punta Gorda ⌂ DOM 186 Gf36
Playa Rosario ⌂ C 179 Fj34
Playa S. Esteban ⌂ EC 196 Fk47
Playas ⌂ EC 196 Fk47
Playa Uvero ⌂ C 179 Gb35
Playa Vicente ⌂ MEX (VC) 182 Fc36
Playa Huincul ⌂ RA (NE) 208 Gf65
Plaza Mayor de Almagro ⌂ E 27 Kr52
Plaza Mayor de Trujillo ⌂ E 27 Kp51
Pleasanton ⌂ USA (TX) 181 Fa31
Pleasant Valley ⌂ USA (CO) 171 Ef27
Pleasantville ⌂ USA (NJ) 177 Gc26
Pleasure Point ⌂ USA (CA)
Plébéinitemplom ⌂ H 42 Ls43
Plei Can ⌂ VN 89 Qd38
Pleiku ⌂ VN 89 Qd38
Pleiße ⌂ D 32 Ln40
Plélan-le-Grand ⌂ F 22 Ks43
Pléneuf-Val-André ⌂ F 22 Ks42
Plentywood ⌂ USA (MT) 169 Eh21
Plešanica ⌂ BY 39 Mh36
Plešivec ⌂ SK 43 Ma42
Pless ⌂ F 22 Kr42
Plestin-les-Grèves ⌂ F 22 Kr42
Pleszew ⌂ PL 40 Ls39
Pleternica ⌂ HR 35 Ls45
Plettenbergbaai ⌂ ZA 154 Mb63
Pleven ⌂ BG 45 Me47
Plevna Downs ⌂ AUS (QLD) 108 Sb59
Pleyben ⌂ F 22 Kr42
Pleystein ⌂ D 33 Ln41
Pliska ⌂ BG 45 Mh47
Plitvice Jezera ⌂ HR 35 Lq46
Plitvička jezera, N.P. ⌂ HR 35 Lq46
Pljussa ⌂ RUS 41 Mf40
Pljevlja ⌂ SCG 44 Lu47
Pljussa ⌂ RUS 38 Mj33
Ploče ⌂ HR 35 Ls48
Plochingen ⌂ D 33 Lk42
Plöckenpass ⌂ A 35 Ln44
Plöckenstein = D/A/CZ 33 Lo42
Plodovoe ⌂ RUS 38 Mj30
Ploemeur ⌂ F 22 Kr43
Ploërmel ⌂ F 22 Ks43
Ploieşti ⌂ RO 45 Mg46
Plomári ⌂ GR 47 Mg52
Plombières-du-Lac ⌂ F
Plombières-les-Bains ⌂ F 25 Lg43
Plön ⌂ D 32 Ll36
Plonéis ⌂ F 22 Kq42
Płońsk ⌂ PL 41 Ma38
Plopeni ⌂ RO 45 Mj47
Plopii-Slăviteşti ⌂ RO 45 Me46
Plopii-Slăviteşti ⌂ RO 44 Md46
Plopis ⌂ RO 44 Md44
Plopsk ⌂ RUS 48 Mf17
Ploty ⌂ PL 40 Lp37
Plouagat ⌂ F 22 Kr42
Plouay ⌂ F 22 Kr43
Ploudalmézeau ⌂ F 22 Kq42
Plouescat ⌂ F 22 Kq42
Plougasnou ⌂ F 22 Kr42

Plouguerneau – Preetz

Plouguerneau F 22 Kq42
Plouha F 22 Ks42
Plovdiv BG 45 Me48
Plover USA (WI) 172 Ff23
Plozévet F 22 Kq43
Pluak Daeng THA 88 Qa39
Plummer USA (ID) 168 Eb22
Plummer, Mount USA 164 Ca15
Plum Point CDN 177 Hb20
Plumpuddingeiland NAM 154 Lh59
Plumpudding Island NAM 154 Lh59
Plumridge Lakes Nature Reserve AUS 105 Rc60
Plumtree ZW 152 Md56
Plungė LT 39 Mb35
Plunkett CDN (SK) 169 Eh20
Pluvigner F 22 Kr43
Plužine SCG 44 Lt47
Płużnica PL 40 Lt37
Plymouth GB 21 Kq40
Plymouth USA (IN) 173 Fg25
Plymouth USA (NC) 178 Gb28
Plymouth USA (NH) 177 Ge24
Plymouth USA (WA) 168 Ea23
Plymouth USA (WI) 173 Fg24
Plynlimon GB 21 Kr38
Plzeň CZ 42 Lo41
Pmere Nyente A.L. AUS 108 Rh58
Pniewy PL 40 Lr38
Pô BF 137 Kk40
Po I 34 Ll46
Poa BF 137 Kj39
Poano GH 137 Kk42
Poarch Creek Res. USA 175 Fg30
Pobè DY 138 Lb42
Pobeda Ice Island 7 Pd31
Pobedino RUS 39 Mc36
Pobedy peak KS 66 Pa24
Pobé Mengao BF 137 Kk39
Poběžovice CZ 42 Ln41
Pobiedziska PL 40 Ls38
Pobierowo PL 40 Lp36
Pobitite kamani BG 45 Mh47
Población RCH 208 Ge63
Pocahontas CDN (AB) 168 Eb19
Pocahontas USA (AR) 175 Fe27
Pocahontas USA (IA) 172 Fc24
Pocahontas S.P. USA (VA) 177 Gb27
Pocajiv UA 41 Mf40
Počajiv UA 41 Mf40
Pocatello USA (ID) 169 Ed24
Počep RUS 48 Mg19
Pochomil NIC 184 Fg40
Počinok RUS 48 Mg18
Počitelj BIH 35 Ls47
Pocking D 33 Lo42
Pocklington Reef PNG 117 Sh51
Poço de Fora BR (BA) 201 Ja50
Poçoes BR (BA) 203 Hk53
Pocola RO 43 Mc44
Poconé BR (MT) 202 Hb54
Poço Redondo BR (SE) 201 Jb50
Poços BR (BA) 201 Hj50
Poços de Caldas BR (MG) 203 Hg56
Pocosin Lakes N.W.R. USA 178 Gb28
Poço Verde BR (SE) 201 Ja51
Pocrane BR (MG) 203 Hk55
Pocri PA 185 Fk42
Pocsaj H 43 Mb43
Podalakur IND (APH) 85 Ok38
Podari RO 44 Md46
Podberez'e RUS 39 Mj33
Podberez'e RUS 48 Mf16
Podberez'e RUS 48 Mf17
Podbořanský Rohozec CZ 42 Lo40
Podbořany CZ 42 Lo40
Podborov'e RUS 39 Mj33
Podbožur SCG 44 Lt48
Poddor'e RUS 48 Mf17
Poděbrady CZ 42 Lq40
Podgora HR 35 Ls47
Podgorac SCG 44 Mb47
Podgorenskij RUS 48 Mk20
Podgorica SCG 44 Lu48
Podi RI 96 Ra46
Podil UA 49 Mg21
Podile IND (APH) 85 Ok38
Podil's'ka vysočyna UA 43 Mf41
Podils'kyj Tovtry N.P. UA 49 Md21
Podkamennaja Tunguska RUS 54 Pd06
Podkova BG 45 Mf49
Podlasie PL 41 Mc38
Podocarpus, P.N. EC 196 Ga48
Podoleš'e RUS 38 Mj32
Podol'sk RUS 48 Mj18
Podor SN 130 Kc37
Podorožnje UA 43 Me41
Podrašnica BIH 35 Lr46
Podravina HR 35 Ls45
Podromanija BIH 44 Lt47
Podujevo SCG 44 Mb48
Podyjí, N.P. CZ 42 Lr42
Poe Bank 88 Pj41
Poechos PE 196 Fk48
Poel D 32 Lm36
Poeppel's Corner AUS 108 Rk58
Poesoegroenoe SME 194 Hc43
Pofadder ZA 154 Lk60
Poganovski manastir SCG 44 Mc48
Pogar RUS 48 Mg19
Poggibonsi I 34 Lm47
Póggio Mirteto I 36 Ln48
Pognoa BF 137 La40
Pogo CI 137 Kh40
Pogo RMM 137 Kh39
Pogoanele RO 45 Mg46
Pogradec AL 46 Ma50
Pograničnyj RUS 76 Rf23
Poh RI 96 Rb46
P'ohang ROK 79 Re27
Pohénegamook CDN (QC) 176 Gf22
Pohja = Pojo FIN 38 Md30
Pohja - Eesti klint EST 38 Mg31
Pohjanmaa FIN 16 Mb14
Pohokura NZ 113 Th65
Pohong CHN (GZG) 74 Qd34
Pohořelice CZ 42 Lr42
Pohoří na Šumavě CZ 42 Lp42
Pohorje SLO 42 Lq44
Pohrebyšče UA 49 Me21
Pohri IND (MPH) 82 Oj33
Pohutu Geysir NZ 112 Tj65
Poiana Lacului RO 45 Me46
Poiana Mare RO 44 Md47
Poiana Stampei RO 43 Mf43
Poiana Teiului RO 49 Md22
Poibrene BG 45 Md48
Pöide EST 39 Md32
Poie RDC 149 Mb47
Poienile de Sub Munte RO 43 Me43
Poigar RI 91 Rc45
Poindimié F (NCL) 118 Tc56
Point Adam USA (AK) 164 Cd16
Point Alexander AUS 106 Rj52
Point Amour Lighthouse Interpretation Center CDN 177 Hb20
Point Angeles USA (WA) 168 Dj21
Point Arena USA (CA) 170 Dj26
Point Arrowsmith AUS 106 Rj52
Point au Fer Island USA 175 Fe31
Point-au-Père Lighthouse CDN 176 Gf21
Point Baker USA (AK) 166 Dd17
Point Banks USA (AK) 164 Cd16
Point Barrow USA (AK) 165 Cb10
Point Bell AUS 110 Rg62
Point Berliet RN 132 Le35
Point Blaze AUS 106 Rf52
Point Bridget USA (AK) 166 Dc16
Point Brown AUS 110 Rg62
Point Bugui RP 90 Rb39
Point Calimere IND 85 Ok40
Point Cloates AUS 102 Qg57
Point Culver AUS 105 Rc62
Point d'Entrecasteaux AUS 104 Qh63
Point Dover AUS 105 Rc62
Point Drummond AUS 110 Rh63
Point Dume Beach USA 170 Ea28
Pointe a la Hache USA (LA) 175 Ff31
Pointe á Michel CDN 176 Gf21
Pointe-á-Pitre F (GL) 187 Gk37
Pointe Béhague F 195 He43
Pointe de Barfleur F 22 Kt41
Pointe-de-l'Est Nat. Wildlife Area CDN 176 Gk22
Pointe de l'Quest CDN 176 Gh21
Pointe de Penhir F 22 Kq42
Pointe de Saint- Mathieu F 22 Kq42
Pointe de Souellaba CAM 138 Le44
Pointe du Raz F 22 Kq42
Point Edward Casino USA 173 Fj24
Pointe Heath CDN 176 Gk21
Pointe Lefèvre F (NCL) 118 Td56
Pointe-Noire F (GL) 187 Gk37
Pointe-Noire RCB 148 Lf48
Pointe-Parent CDN (QC) 176 Gk20
Pointe Pongara G 148 Le45
Pointe Quest RH 186 Gd35
Point Escarpada RP 90 Rb36
Point Escuminac CDN 176 Gh22
Point Franklin USA (AK) 165 Ca10
Point Harbor USA (NC) 178 Gc27
Point Hibbs AUS 111 Sc67
Point Hicks AUS 111 Se64
Point Hillier AUS 104 Qj63
Point Hope USA (AK) 165 Bg11
Point Hope USA (AK) 165 Bg11
Point Isabel Lighthouse S.H.P. USA 181 Fb32
Point Jahleel AUS 106 Rf51
Point Lay USA (AK) 165 Bj11
Point Leith CDN 167 Ea13
Point Malcolm AUS 105 Rb62
Point Maud AUS 102 Qg57
Point McNeill CDN (BC) 168 Dg20
Point Mellon CDN (BC) 168 Dj21
Point Nuyts AUS 104 Qj63
Point of Ayre GB 21 Kq36
Point Pedro CL 85 Pa41
Point Pedro CL 85 Pa41
Point Pelee N.P. CDN 173 Fj25
Point Pleasant USA (NJ) 177 Gc25
Point Pleasant USA (WV) 175 Fj26
Point Renfrew CDN (BC) 168 Dh21
Point Reyes USA 170 Dj27
Point Reyes Nat. Seashore USA 170 Dj26
Point Riou USA 166 Ck16
Point Salvation AUS 105 Rb60
Point Salvation A.L. AUS 105 Rc60
Point Samson AUS (WA) 102 Qj56
Point Sir Issac AUS 110 Rh63
Point Spencer USA (AK) 164 Bg13
Point Stuart AUS (NT) 106 Rf52
Point Sur USA 170 Dk27
Point Torment AUS 102 Rb54
Point Townsend USA (WA) 168 Dj21
Point Westhall AUS 110 Rg62
Point Whidbey AUS 110 Rh63
Poissonnier Point AUS 102 Qk55
Poissy F 23 Lc42
Poitiers F 24 La44
Poitou F 24 Ku44
Poitou-Charente F 24 Ku44
Poivre SY 145 Ng48
Poix-de-Picardie F 23 Lb41
Pojarkovo RUS 71 Re21
Pojezierze Bytowskie PL 40 Ls36
Pojezierze Ełckie PL 41 Mc36
Pojezierze Iławskie PL 41 Lu37
Pojezierze Mrągowskie PL 41 Mb37
Pojezierze Pomerskie PL 40 Lr37
Pokaran IND (RJT) 80 Of32
Pokataroo AUS (NSW) 109 Se60
Pokemouche CDN (NB) 176 Gh22
Pokeno NZ 112 Th64
Pokenui NZ 112 Tg63
Pokhara NEP 81 Pc31
Pokigron SME 194 Hc43
Po-kil Do ROK 78 Rd28
Pokka FIN 16 Mc11
Poko RDC 141 Md44
Pokok Sena MAL 92 Qa42
Pokrov RUS 48 Mk18
Pokrovka KS 63 Of24
Pokrovka KZ 66 Oh24
Pokrovskaja Arčada RUS 48 Nc19
Pokrovs'ke UA 48 Mk21
Pokrovs'ke UA 49 Mj22
Pokuma Z 152 Md54
Pola RP 90 Ra39
Polacca USA (AZ) 171 Ee28
Polack BY 48 Me18
Pola de Laviana E 26 Kp47
Pola de Lena E 26 Kp47
Pola de Siero E 26 Kp47
Pola de Somiedo E 26 Ko47
Poladpur IND (MHT) 82 Og37
Polaia Kalan IND (MPH) 82 Oj34
Połajewo PL 40 Lr38
Poland USA (NY) 177 Gc24
Poland 15 Lb04
Połaniec PL 41 Mb40
Polanów PL 40 Lr36
Polar Bear Express CDN 173 Fk20
Polar Plateau ANT 6 Eb36
Polatlı TR 56 Mg26
Polavaram IND (APH) 83 Pa37
Połczyn-Zdrój PL 40 Lr37
Poldasht IR 57 Nc26
Pole Abyssal Plain 5 Lc01
Pol-e'Alam AFG 65 Oe28
Polebridge USA (MT) 168 Ec21
Polee RI 97 Rf47
Pol-e Fasa IR 64 Ng31
Pol-e Khomri AFG 63 Oe28
Pol-eSefid IR 62 Ng27
Polesella I 34 Lm46
Polésine I 34 Lm46
Poleski P.N. PL 41 Md39
Polessk RUS 39 Mb36
Polewali RI 96 Qk47
Pol-e Zal IR 59 Ne29
Polgár H 43 Mb43
Polgárdi H 42 Lt43
Poli CAM 139 Lg41
Poli RC 75 Ra33
Poliçan AL 46 Ma50
Police PL 40 Lp37
Policemans Point AUS (SA) 110 Rk63
Polička CZ 42 Lr41
Policoro I 37 Lr50
Polidámio GR 46 Mc51
Políegos GR 47 Me54
Polígiros GR 44 Md50
Polignano a Mare I 37 Ls49
Poligny F 25 Lf44
Polihnítos GR 47 Mg51
Polikastro GR 46 Mc50
Polillo Island RP 90 Ra38
Polillo Islands RP 90 Ra38
Polímilos GR 46 Mc50
Políochni GR 47 Mf51
Polis CY 56 Mg28
Polis'ke UA 48 Me20
Polístena I 37 Lr52
Poljana BG 45 Mg48
Poljany RUS 38 Mk30
Poljice BIH 44 Lt46
Polkowice PL 40 Lr39
Polla I 37 Lq50
Pollachi IND (TNU) 84 Oj40
Pollença E 29 Ld51
Pollilo RP 90 Ra38
Pollino, P.N.del I 37 Lr51
Pollo USA (TX) 174 Fc30
Pollock USA (LA) 175 Fd30
Polmak N 16 Me10
Polna RUS 38 Mj32
Polobaya Grande PE 197 Ge54
Pologi RO 45 Mf46
Polohy UA 49 Mj22
Polokwane = Pietersburg ZA 152 Me57
Polom SCG 44 Ma46
Polomolok RP 91 Rc42
Poloniny, Národný park SK 43 Mc41
Polonnaruwa CL 85 Pa42
Polonne UA 49 Md20
Pólo Norte BR (AM) 198 Gf49
Polonyna Runa UA 43 Mc42
Polonyns'kyj chrebet UA 43 Mc42
Polovragi RO 44 Md45
Polski Trămbeš BG 45 Mf47
Polson USA (MT) 168 Ec22
Poltava UA 49 Mh21
Põltsamaa EST 38 Mf32
Poluostrov Cheleken TM 62 Ng26
Poluostrov Jamal RUS 54 Ob04
Poluostrov Kanin RUS 54 Na05
poluostrov Kanin RUS 54 Na05
Poluostrov Rybačij RUS 16 Mf11
Poluostrov Svjatoi Nos RUS 70 Qe19
Polur IND (TNU) 85 Ok39
Pölva EST 39 Mh32
Polvijärvi FIN 38 Mk28
Polvora PE 196 Gb49
Polyantho GR 45 Mf49
Polynesia 10 Ba10
Polyuc MEX (QTR) 183 Ff36
Poma RDC 149 Mc46
Pomabamba PE 197 Gb50
Pomahuaca PE 196 Ga48
Pomán RA (CA) 207 Gg60
Pomarance I 34 Ll47
Pomarkku FIN 38 Mc29
Pomasi, Cerro de PE 197 Ge53
Pombal BR (PB) 201 Jb49
Pombal P 26 Km51
Pombas BR (AM) 198 Gj46
Pomene MOC 153 Mh57
Pomeranian Bay D 40 Lp36
Pomeroy USA (OH) 175 Fj26
Pomeroy USA (WA) 168 Eb22
Pomeroy ZA 155 Mf60
Pomézia I 36 Ln49
Pomfret ZA 154 Mb58
Pomio PNG 116 Sf48
Pomona AUS (QLD) 109 Sg59
Pomona RA (RN) 208 Gh65
Pomonaeiland NAM 154 Lh59
Pomona Island NAM 154 Lh59
Pomorie BG 45 Mh48
Pomorjany UA 43 Me41
Pomos CY 56 Mg28
Pompano Beach USA (FL) 179 Fk32
Pompei I 37 Lp50
Pompéia BR (SP) 202 He57
Pompeu BR (MG) 203 Hh55
Pompey F 23 Lg42
Pompeys Pillar USA (MT) 169 Eg23
Pompeys Pillar USA 169 Ef23
Pom Phra Chunlachomkiao THA 88 Qa39
Pomun Temple ROK 78 Rd27
Pomuq UZ 63 Oc26
Ponape Island FSM 100 Sb09
Ponca USA (NE) 172 Fb24
Ponca City USA (OK) 174 Fb27
Ponce USA (PR) 187 Gg36
Poncha Springs USA (CO) 171 Eg26
Ponchatoula USA (LA) 175 Fe30
Ponda EAT 147 Mk50
Pond Creek USA (OK) 174 Fb27
Pond Creek N.W.R. USA 174 Fc29
Pondicherry IND (PND) 85 Ok40
Pondicherry IND 85 Ok40
Pond Inlet CDN 163 Ga04
Pondosa USA (CA) 168 Dk25
Pondung Lamanggang RI 93 Qa47
Poneloya NIC 184 Fg39
Ponérihouen F (NCL) 118 Tc56
Ponferrada E 26 Ko48
Pong THA 87 Qa36
Pongaí BR (SP) 202 Hf56
Pongara, P.N.de G 148 Le45
Pong Chi THA 88 Qa37
Pong Gua Waterfalls VN 89 Qe40
Pong Nam Ron THA 89 Qb39
Pongola ZA 155 Mf59
Pongola Bush Nature Reserve ZA 155 Mf59
Pongore ZW 152 Md55
Poniatowa PL 41 Mc39
Ponikiew Mała PL 41 Mb38
Ponikovica SCG 44 Lu47
Ponio TG 137 La40
Ponley K 89 Qc39
Ponnampet IND (KTK) 84 Oh39
Ponnani IND (KER) 84 Oh40
Ponneri IND (TNU) 85 Pa39
Ponoarele RO 44 Mc46
Ponoj RUS 54 Md05
Ponoj RUS 54 Na05
Ponoka CDN (AB) 169 Ed19
Ponondougou CI 137 Kg41
Ponorogo RI 95 Qf49
Ponoševac SCG 44 Ma48
Ponot RP 91 Rb41
Pons F 24 Ku45
Ponson Island RP 90 Rc40
Ponta Albina ANG 150 Lf53
Ponta Barra MOC 153 Mh57
Pontacq F 24 Ku47
Ponta da Baleia BR 203 Ja54
Ponta da Juatinga BR 205 Hh57
Ponta da Mota BR (SE) 201 Jb51
Ponta da Piedade P 27 Km53
Ponta da Serra, T.I. BR 193 Gk44
Ponta das Palmeirinhas ANG 148 Lg50
Ponta de Corumbaú BR 203 Ja54
Ponta de Mucuripe BR 201 Ja47
Ponta de Pedras BR (PA) 195 Hf46
Ponta de Porto Belo BR 205 Hf59
Ponta de Sagres P 27 Km54
Ponta do Arpoador BR 205 Hg58
Ponta do Boi BR 205 Hh57
Ponta do Calcanhar BR 201 Jc48
Ponta do Mutá BR 201 Ja52
Ponta do Ouro MOC 155 Mg59
Ponta do Rapa BR 205 Hf59
Ponta do Seixas BR 201 Jc49
Ponta dos Indios BR 195 He43
Ponta dos Naufragados BR 205 Hf59
Ponta do Sol CV 136 Jh37
Ponta Freitas Morna ANG 148 Lg49
Ponta Grande CV 136 Jh37
Ponta Grossa BR (PR) 205 He58
Pontailler-sur-Saône F 25 Lf43
Ponta Jericoacoara BR 201 Hk47
Pontal BR (SP) 202 Hf56
Pontal do Manguinha BR 201 Jb51
Pontalina BR (GO) 202 Hf54
Ponta Lipobane MOC 153 Mk54
Ponta Macacos MOC 153 Mj55
Ponta Macovane MOC 153 Mh56
Ponta Malongane MOC 155 Mg59
Ponta Maunhane MOC 147 Na52
Ponta Moreia CV 136 Jj38
Pont-à-Mousson F 23 Lg42
Pontão P 27 Km51
Ponta Paza BR 201 Jb51
Ponta Pelindã GNB 136 Kb40
Ponta Porã BR (MS) 202 Hc57
Ponta Rebordelo BR 195 Hf45
Pontarion F 24 Lb45
Pontarlier F 25 Lg44
Ponta Santo António BR 203 Ja54
Ponta São Sebastião MOC 153 Mh57
Pontassieve I 34 Lm47
Ponta Tarafo CV 136 Jj38
Pont-Audemer F 22 La41
Pontaumur F 25 Lc45
Pontcharra F 25 Lg45
Pontchâteau F 22 Ks43
Pont-d'Ain F 25 Lf44
Pont de Normandie F 22 La41
Pont-de-Roide F 25 Lg43
Pont-de-Vaux F 25 Le44
Pont du Gard F 25 Le47
Ponte Alta do Bom Jesus BR (TO) 200 Hg52
Ponteareas E 26 Km48
Ponte Branca BR (GO) 202 Hd54
Pontecorvo I 36 Lo49
Ponte da Barca P 26 Km49
Ponte del Diavolo I 35 Lo44
Ponte de Lima P 26 Km49
Pontedera I 34 Ll47
Ponte de Sor P 27 Km51
Pontedeume E 26 Km47
Ponte do Rio Verde BR (MS) 202 Hd55
Ponte Firme BR (MG) 203 Hg55
Pontefract GB 21 Kt37
Ponte Leccia F 34 Lk48
Ponte Nova BR (MG) 203 Hj56
Pontenova Villaodriz E 26 Kn47
Pont-en-Royans F 25 Lf45
Pontes e Lacerda BR (MT) 206 Ha53
Ponte Serrada BR (SC) 204 He59
Ponte Tresa I 34 Lj45
Pontevedra E 26 Km48
Pontgibaud F 25 Lc45
Ponthieu F 23 Lb40
Pontiac USA (IL) 173 Ff25
Pontianak RI 95 Qe46
Pontian Kechil MAL 93 Qb45
Pontic Mountains TR 56 Mg25
Pontivy F 22 Ks42
Pont-l'Abbé F 22 Kq43
Pont-l'Evêque F 22 La41
Ponto Alta do Tocantins BR (TO) 200 Hg51
Pontoise F 23 Lc41
Pontokerasiá GR 44 Md49
Pontorson F 22 Kt42
Pontotoc USA (MS) 175 Ff28
Pontrémoli I 34 Lk46
Pontresina CH 34 Lk44
Ponts E 29 Lb49
Pont-Sainte-Maxence F 23 Lc41
Pont-Saint-Esprit F 25 Le46
Pont-Saint-Vincent F 23 Lg42
Pont-sur-Yonne F 23 Ld42
Pont Valentré F 24 Lb46
Pontypool GB 21 Kr39
Ponuga PA 185 Fk42
Pony Express Station USA 174 Fb26
Ponza I 36 Ln50
Poochera AUS (SA) 110 Rh62
Poole GB 21 Kt40
Pool Malebo RDC 148 Lh48
Pool's Cove CDN (NF) 177 Hc22
Pooncarie AUS (NSW) 111 Sb62
Poopó BOL 206 Gg55
Poor Knights Islands NZ 112 Th63
Poorman USA (AK) 165 Cc13
Poor Man Ind. Res. CDN 169 Eh20
Põõsaspea neem EST 38 Md31
Poowong AUS (VIC) 111 Sc65
Pop UZ 63 Of25
Popa G 148 Lg46
Popa Falls NAM 151 Ma55
Popagaon NEP 81 Pb31
Popa, Mount MYA 86 Ph35
Popa Mountain Park MYA 86 Ph35
Popayán CO 192 Gb44
Popčevo MK 44 Mc49
Pope LV 39 Mb33
Popenguine SN 130 Kb38
Poperinge B 23 Lc40
Popeşti RO 43 Mc43
Popielów PL 40 Ls40
Poplar Bluff USA (MO) 175 Fe27
Poplarfield CDN (MB) 172 Fb20
Poplar Point CDN 172 Fb19
Poplar River Power Station and Strip Mine CDN 169 Eh21
Poplarville USA (MS) 175 Ff30
Popocatépetl MEX 182 Fa36
Popodara RG 136 Kd40
Popof Island USA 164 Bk18
Popoh RI 95 Qf50
Popo-kabaka RDC 148 Lj48
Pópoli I 36 Lo48
Popomanaseu, Mount SOL 117 Ta50
Popondetta PNG 116 Se50
Popovača HR 35 Lr45
Popovići BIH 35 Ls46
Popovo BG 45 Mg47
Popovyči UA 43 Mc41
Popow PL 40 Lt39
Poppi I 34 Lm47
Poprad SK 43 Ma41
Popšica SCG 44 Mb47
Popsko BG 45 Mf49
Poptún GCA 183 Ff37
Popular Point CDN (MB) 172 Fb20
Populónia I 34 Ll48
Poquis, Nevado de RA/RCH 207 Gg57
Porangahau NZ 113 Tj66
Porangatu BR (GO) 200 Hf52
Porata IND (ORS) 83 Pb36
Porazava BY 41 Me38
Porbandar IND (GUJ) 82 Oe35
Porcher Island CDN 166 De19
Porcuna E 27 Kq53
Porcupine USA (AK) 166 Db16
Porcupine Abyssal Plain 122 Ka05
Porcupine Gorge N.P. AUS (QLD) 107 Sc56
Porcupine Hills CDN 169 Ek19
Porcupine Plain CDN (YT) 165 Da12
Porcupine Prov. Forest CDN 169 Ek19
Þórðarhyrna IS 18 Kc26
Pordenone I 35 Ln45
Pordim BG 45 Me47
Pore CO 192 Ge43
Porebada PNG 115 Sd50
Poreč HR 35 Lo45
Porecatu BR (PR) 202 He57
Poreč'e RUS 38 Mj31
Porédaka RG 136 Kd40
Porga DY 137 La40
Porgera PNG 115 Sb48
Porhov RUS 48 Me17
Pori FIN 38 Mb29
Pori PRK 76 Rd25
Pori Jazz FIN 38 Mb29
Porirua NZ 113 Th66
Porjus S 16 Lk12
Porkkala FIN 38 Me31
Þorlákshöfn IS 18 Jt27
Porlamar YV 193 Gj40
Pormpuraaw AUS (QLD) 107 Sa53
Pornic F 24 Ks43
Poro Island RP 90 Rc40
Poroma PNG 115 Sb49
Poronajsk RUS 55 Sa09
Porongurup AUS (WA) 104 Qj63
Póros GR 45 Md53
Póros GR 46 Ma52
Porozina HR 35 Lp45
Porplišča BY 39 Mh36
Porquinhos-Aldeia Chinela, T.I. BR 200 Hh49
Porquis Junction CDN (ON) 173 Fk21
Porras FIN 38 Md30
Porrentruy CH 34 Lh43
Porretta Terme I 34 Ll46
Porriño E 26 Km48
Porsangenfjorden N 16 Mc10
Porsea RI 93 Pk44
Porsgrunn N 30 Lk31
Þórshöfn IS 18 Ke24
Þórsmörk IS 18 Ka27
Portachuelo BOL 206 Gj54
Portadown GB 19 Ko36
Portaferry GB 19 Kp36
Portage USA (AK) 165 Cf15
Portage USA (WI) 173 Ff24
Portage Glacier USA 165 Cf15
Portage la Prairie CDN (MB) 172 Fa20
Port Alberni CDN (BC) 168 Dh21
Port Albert AUS (VIC) 111 Sd65
Portalegre P 27 Kn51
Portales USA (NM) 174 Ej28
Port Alexander USA (AK) 166 Dc17
Port Alfred ZA 155 Md62
Port Alice CDN (BC) 168 Dg20
Port Alma AUS (QLD) 109 Sf57
Porta Nigra D 33 Lg41
Port Antonio JA 186 Gb36
Portara GR 47 Mf53
Portarlington IRL 19 Kn37
Port Arthur AUS (TAS) 111 Sd67
Port Arthur = Lüshun CHN (LNG) 73 Ra26
Port Arthur USA (TX) 174 Fd31
Port Askaig GB 20 Ko35
Port au Choix N.H.S. CDN 177 Hb20
Port Augusta AUS (SA) 110 Rj62
Port au Port Bay CDN 177 Ha21
Port-au-Prince RH 186 Gd36
Port Austin USA (MI) 173 Fj23
Port aux Choix CDN (NF) 177 Hb20
Portavadie GB 20 Kp35
Port Aventura E 29 Lb49
Porta Westfalica D 32 Lj38
Port Barton RP 90 Qk40
Port Bickerton CDN (NS) 176 Gk23
Port Blair IND (AAN) 88 Pg40
Port Blandfort CDN (NF) 177 Hc21
Port Bradshaw AUS 106 Rj52
Port Broughton AUS (SA) 110 Rj62
Port Burwell Prov. Park CDN 173 Fk24
Port Campbell AUS (VIC) 111 Sb65
Port Campbell National Park AUS (VIC) 111 Sb65
Port -Cartier CDN (QC) 176 Gg20
Port Charlotte USA (FL) 179 Fj32
Port Chilkoot USA (AK) 166 Dc16
Port Clarence USA 164 Bg13
Port Clements CDN (BC) 166 Dd19
Port Clinton USA (OH) 173 Fj25
Port Colborne CDN (ON) 173 Ga24
Port Curtis AUS 109 Sf57
Port d'Addaia E 29 Le50
Port-Daniel CDN (QC) 176 Gh21
Port Davey AUS 111 Sc67
Port-de-Bouc F 25 Le47
Port-de-Paix RH 186 Gd36
Port de Pollença E 29 Ld51
Port d'es Torrent E 29 Lb52
Port Dickson MAL 92 Qa44
Port Douglas AUS (QLD) 107 Sc54
Port Edward CDN (BC) 166 De18
Port Edward ZA 155 Mf61
Porteira BR (PA) 194 Hb46
Porteirinha BR (MG) 203 Hj53
Portél BR (PA) 195 He46
Portel P 27 Kn52
Portelândia BR (GO) 202 Hd54
Port Elgin CDN (ON) 173 Fk23
Port Elizabeth ZA 155 Mc62
Port Ellen GB 20 Ko35
Port Elliot AUS (SA) 110 Rk63
Portena RA (CD) 207 Gj61
Port-en-Bessin F 22 Ku41
Port Erin GB 21 Kq36
Porters Corner USA (MT) 169 Ed22
Porterville USA (CA) 170 Ea27
Porterville ZA 154 Lk62
Portes d'Enfer RDC 146 Md48
Port Essington CDN (BC) 166 Df18
Port Fairy AUS (VIC) 110 Sb65
Port Fitzroy NZ 112 Th64
Port Fourchon USA (LA) 175 Fe31
Port Fuâd ET 129 Mg30
Port-Gentil G 148 Le46
Port Germein AUS (SA) 110 Rk62
Port Gibson USA (MS) 175 Fe30
Port Gregory AUS (WA) 104 Qh60
Port Grimaud F 25 Lg47
Port Grosvenor ZA 155 Me61
Port Hacking AUS 111 Sf63
Port Harcourt WAN 138 Ld43
Port Hardy CDN (BC) 168 Dg20
Port Harrison = Inukjuak CDN 163 Ga07
Port Hastings CDN (NS) 176 Gk23
Porthcawl GB 21 Kr39
Port Hedland AUS (WA) 102 Qk56
Port Heiden USA (AK) 164 Ca17
Port Heiden USA (AK) 164 Ca17
Porthill USA (ID) 168 Eb21
Port Hope CDN (ON) 173 Ga24
Port Hope Simpson CDN 163 Ha08
Port Howard GB (GBF) 210 Ha71
Port Howe BS 186 Gc33
Port Huron USA (MI) 173 Fj24
Porțile de Fier, P.N. RO 44 Mc46
Portillo RCH 208 Ge62
Portimão P 27 Km53
Portinatx E 29 Lb51
Port Jackson AUS 111 Sf62
Port Jackson NZ 112 Th64
Port Jervis USA (NJ) 177 Gc25
Port-Joinville F 24 Ks44
Port Kembla AUS (NSW) 111 Sf63
Port Kenny AUS (SA) 110 Rh62
Portland AUS (VIC) 110 Sa65
Portland USA (IN) 173 Fh25
Portland USA (ME) 177 Ge24
Portland USA (OR) 168 Dj23
Portland USA (TN) 175 Fg27
Portland USA (TX) 181 Fb32
Portland Bay AUS 110 Sa65
Portland Inlet CDN 166 De18
Portland Island NZ 113 Tj65
Portland Point JA 186 Gb37
Portland Roads AUS (QLD) 107 Sb52
Port Langdon AUS 106 Rj52
Port-la-Nouvelle F 25 Ld47
Port Laoise IRL 19 Kn37
Port Latta AUS (TAS) 111 Sc66
Port Lavaca USA (TX) 181 Fb31
Port Lincoln AUS (SA) 110 Rh63
Portlock USA (AK) 164 Ce16
Portlock Reefs PNG 115 Sc50
Port Loins USA (AK) 164 Cd17
Port Loko WAL 136 Kd41
Port Loring CDN (ON) 173 Fk23
Port-Louis F (GL) 187 Gk37
Port-Louis F 22 Kr43
Port Louis MS 157 Nj56
Port MacDonnell AUS (VIC) 110 Sa65
Port Macquarie AUS (NSW) 109 Sg61
Port Mansfield USA (TX) 181 Fb32
Port Maria JA 186 Gb36
Port Mayaca USA (FL) 179 Fk32
Port McArthur AUS 106 Rj53
Portmeirion GB 21 Kq38
Port-Menier CDN (QC) 176 Gh21
Port Moller USA (AK) 164 Bk18
Port Moller USA (AK) 164 Bk18
Portmore JA 186 Gb37
Port Moresby PNG 115 Sd50
Port Musgrave AUS 107 Sa51
Portnacroish GB 20 Kp34
Portnahaven GB 20 Ko35
Port-Navalo F 22 Ks43
Port Neill AUS (SA) 110 Rj63
Port Nelson BS 186 Gc34
Port Nelson CDN 163 Fb07
Port Neville CDN (BC) 168 Dg20
Port Noarlunga AUS (SA) 110 Rk63
Port Nolloth ZA 154 Lj60
Porto BR (PI) 201 Hj47
Porto F 34 Lj48
Porto P 26 Km49
Porto Acre BR (AC) 198 Gg50
Porto Alegre BR (PA) 199 Hb48
Porto Alegre BR (RS) 204 He61
Porto Alegre STP 138 Ld45
Porto Alegre do Norte BR (MT) 200 He51
Porto Alencastro BR (MG) 202 He55
Porto Alto P 27 Km52
Porto Amboim ANG 150 Lg51
Porto Amelia = Pemba MOC 147 Na52
Porto Antunes BR (AM) 198 Gg47
Porto Arari BR (AP) 195 He45
Porto Azzurro I 34 Ll48
Portobelo PA 185 Ga41
Portobelo, P.N. PA 185 Ga41
Porto Bicentenário BR (RO) 198 Gj51
Porto Braga BR (AM) 198 Gh47
Porto Braga BR (MS) 202 Hb56
Porto Caiuá BR (MS) 202 Hd57
Porto Calvo BR (AL) 201 Jc50
Porto Camargo BR (PR) 202 Hd57
Porto Cervo I 36 Lk49
Porto Cesáreo I 37 Ls50
Porto Chique BR (MG) 203 Hh54
Port O'Connor USA (TX) 181 Fb31
Portocristo E 29 Ld51
Porto da Balsa P 26 Kn50
Porto da Folha BR (SE) 201 Jb50
Porto de Galinhas BR (PE) 201 Jc50
Porto de Pedras BR (AL) 201 Jc50
Porto do Mangue BR (RN) 201 Jb48
Porto do Moz BR (PA) 199 Hd46
Porto dos Gaúchos BR (MT) 199 Hb51
Porto do Son E 26 Km48
Porto Empédocle I 36 Lo53
Porto Esperança BR (MS) 202 Hb55
Porto Esperidião BR (MT) 206 Ha53
Porto Estrella BR (MT) 202 Hb53
Portoferráio I 34 Ll48
Porto Ferreira BR (SP) 203 Hg56
Portofino I 34 Lk46
Port of Ness GB 20 Ko32
Porto Franco BR (MA) 200 Hg49
Port of Spain TT 187 Gk40
Porto Grande BR (AP) 195 He45
Portogruaro I 35 Ln45
Porto Henrique MOC 155 Mg59
Porto Jofre BR (MT) 202 Hb54
Pórto Koufós GR 45 Md51
Porto Lindo, T.I. BR 202 Hc57
Port-Olry VU 118 Td53
Pörtom = Pirttikylä FIN 38 Mb28
Portomaggiore I 34 Lm46
Porto Manga BR (MS) 202 Hb55
Porto Marie NL 193 Gf39
Portomarín E 26 Kn48
Porto Mauá BR (RS) 204 Hc59
Porto Moniz P 124 Kb29
Porto Morrinho BR (MS) 202 Hb55
Porto Murtinho BR (MS) 202 Hb56
Porto Nacional BR (TO) 200 Hf51
Porto Novo CV 136 Jh37
Porto-Novo DY 138 Lb42
Porto Novo IND (TNU) 85 Ok40
Porto Primavera BR (MS) 202 Hd57
Port Orange USA (FL) 178 Fk31
Porto Recanati I 35 Lo47
Porto Reis BR (AM) 198 Gh47
Port Orford USA (OR) 168 Dh24
Porto Rico BR (PR) 202 Hd57
Portorož SLO 42 Lo45
Porto San Giórgio I 35 Lo47
Porto Sant'Elípido I 35 Lo47
Porto São Domingos BR (MG) 202 He55
Porto São José BR (MS) 202 Hd57
Portoscuso I 36 Lj51
Porto Seguro BR (BA) 203 Ja54
Porto Silva BR (AM) 198 Gg48
Porto Tolle I 34 Ln46
Porto Tórres I 36 Lj50
Porto União BR (SC) 205 He59
Porto Vecchio F 36 Lk49
Porto Velho BR (RO) 198 Gj50
Portovénere I 34 Lk46
Portoviejo EC 196 Fk46
Porto Vinte e Dois BR (AM) 198 Gj47
Porto Viro I 34 Ln45
Porto Walter BR (AC) 196 Gd50
Porto Xavier BR (RS) 204 Hc59
Portpatrick GB 19 Kp36
Port Phillip Bay AUS (VIC) 111 Sc65
Port Pirie AUS (SA) 110 Rj62
Port Radium CDN 162 Ea05
Portree GB 20 Ko33
Portrush GB 19 Ko35
Port Saîd ET 129 Mg30
Port Said ET 129 Mg30
Port Saint Joe USA (FL) 175 Fh31
Port Saint Johns ZA 155 Me61
Port-Saint-Louis-du-Rhône F 25 Le47
Port Saint Lucie USA (FL) 179 Fk32
Port Salerno USA (FL) 179 Fk32
Portsalon IRL 19 Kn35
Port Sanilac USA (MI) 173 Fj24
Pörtschach A 35 Lp44
Port Shepstone ZA 155 Mf61
Port Simpson CDN (BC) 166 De18
Portsmouth GB 21 Kt40
Portsmouth USA (NH) 177 Ge24
Portsmouth USA (OH) 175 Fj26
Portsmouth USA (VA) 178 Gb27
Portsmouth WD 187 Gk38
Portsoy GB 20 Ks33
Port Stephens AUS 111 Sg62
Port Stephens GB (GBF) 210 Gk72
Port Steward = Moojeeba AUS (QLD) 107 Sb53
Port Sudan SUD 135 Mj36
Port Sulphur USA (LA) 175 Ff31
Port-sur-Saône F 25 Lg43
Port Talbot GB 21 Kr39
Portugal 15 Kb05
Portugalete E 28 Kr47
Portumna IRL 19 Km37
Port-Vato VU 118 Te54
Port-Vendres F 25 Ld48
Port Victoria AUS (SA) 110 Rj63
Port Victoria EAK 144 Mh45
Port Vila VU 118 Te54
Port Vita USA (AK) 164 Cd16
Port Wakefield AUS (SA) 110 Rk63
Port Warrender AUS (WA) 103 Rc53
Port Washington USA (WI) 173 Fg24
Port William USA (AK) 164 Cd16
Port Wing USA (WI) 172 Fe22
Porumamilla IND (APH) 85 Ok38
Porvenir BOL 198 Gf51
Porvenir PE 196 Gb47
Porvenir RCH 210 Ge72
Porvenir Cumuripa MEX (SO) 180 Ef31
Porvoo = Borga FIN 38 Mf30
Porzellanmanufaktur Meissen D 32 Lo39
Porzuna E 27 Kq51
Posadas E 27 Kp53
Posadas RA (MI) 204 Hc59
Posavina HR 35 Lr45
Poschiavo CH 34 Ll44
Posedarje HR 35 Lq46
Pošehon'e RUS 48 Mk16
Po Sha Nu Tower VN 89 Qe40
Posio FIN 16 Me12
Positano I 37 Lp50
Poso RI 96 Ra46
Posof TR 57 Nb25
Posong ROK 78 Rd28
Posoria EC 196 Fk47
Posse BR (GO) 203 Hg53
Possel RCA 140 Lk43
Possessioneiland NAM 154 Lh59
Possession Island NAM 154 Lh59
Pößneck D 32 Lm40
Post USA (OR) 168 Dk23
Post USA (TX) 174 Ek29
Poșta Câlnău RO 45 Mg45
Posta Cambio a Zalazar RA (FO) 207 Gk58
Post Arinda GUY 194 Ha43
Post Falls USA (ID) 168 Eb22
Posties AUS 110 Rj63
Postmasburg ZA 154 Mb60
Posto Ajuricaba BR (AM) 193 Gj45
Posto Cocraimore BR (PA) 199 Hd49
Posto Funa BR (AM) 199 Gk46
Posto Funai BR (AM) 194 Ha46
Posto Funai BR (AM) 196 Gd48
Posto Funai BR (AM) 198 Gk46
Posto Funai BR (AM) 198 Gk46
Posto Funai BR (AP) 195 He44
Postojna SLO 42 Lp45
Postojnska jama SLO 42 Lp45
Postomino PL 40 Lr36
Posto Uaça BR (AP) 195 He44
Postrer Valle BOL 206 Gj55
Posušje BIH 35 Ls47
Pota RI 96 Ra50
Potala CHN 69 Pf31
Pótam MEX (SO) 180 Ee32
Potamós GR 45 Md55
Potamoúla GR 46 Mb52
Potangi IND (ORS) 83 Pb36
Potash City JOR 58 Mh30
Potawatomi Ind. Res. USA 174 Fc26
Potchefstroom ZA 155 Md59
Potcoava RO 45 Me46
Poté BR (MG) 203 Hk54
Poteau USA (OK) 174 Fc28
Potenza I 37 Lq50
Potenza Picena I 35 Lo47
Poterillos RCH 207 Gf59
Potero Seco RCH 207 Ge59
Potes E 26 Kq47
Potfontein ZA 155 Mc61
Potgietersrus ZA 155 Me58
Potholes Reservoir USA 168 Ea22
Pothungoli IND (CGH) 83 Pa36
Poti GE 57 Na24
Potiguara, T.I. BR 201 Jc49
Potin IND (ARP) 86 Pg32
Potiraguá BR (BA) 203 Ja53
Potirendaba BR (SP) 202 Hf56
Potiskum WAN 139 Lf40
Pot Mountain USA 168 Ec22
Potoci BIH 35 Ls47
Potomac Highlands USA 175 Fk26
Potoru WAL 136 Ke42
Potosí BOL 206 Gh55
Potosi GUY 194 Ha42
Potosí NIC 184 Fg39
Potosi USA (MO) 175 Fe27
Potrero del Llano MEX (CHH) 181 Eh31
Potrero del Llano MEX (DGO) 181 Eh32
Potro, Cerro del RA/RCH 207 Gf60
Potsdam D 32 Lo38
Potsdam USA (NY) 177 Gc23
Pottsville USA (PA) 177 Gb25
Pottuvil CL 85 Pa42
Pötürge TR 57 Mk26
Potworów PL 41 Ma39
Pouancé F 22 Kt43
Pouch Cove CDN (NF) 177 Hd22
Pouéré RCB 148 Lh46
Poughkeepsie USA (NY) 177 Gd25
Pougol RCA 140 Lj42
Pouh K 89 Qc39
Poulnabrone Dolmen IRL 19 Kl37
Poum F (NCL) 118 Tc56
Pouma CAM 138 Lf44
Poumalé RCA 140 Lk43
Pound USA (WI) 173 Ff23
Pound Maker Ind. Res. CDN 169 Ef19
Poun Loung VN 87 Qc35
Poura BF 137 Kj40
Pourerere NZ 113 Tj66
Pouri IND (MPH) 83 Pa34
Pouso Alegre BR (AM) 198 Gj49
Pouso Alegre BR (MG) 203 Hh57
Pouso Grande BR (PA) 199 Hb48
Pouso Redondo BR (SC) 205 Hf59
Pouss CAM 139 Lh40
Pouto NZ 112 Th64
Pouytenga BF 137 Kk39
Pouzauges F 24 Ku44
Považská Bystrica SK 42 Lt41
Povča UA 41 Mg40
Poverty Beach USA 177 Gc26
Povoação BR (ES) 203 Ja55
Povoação Velha CV 136 Jj37
Póvoa de São Miguel P 27 Kn52
Póvoa de Varzim P 26 Km49
Povorot RUS (BUR) 70 Qd20
Povors'k UA 41 Mf39
Powari IND (HPH) 81 Ok30
Powderville USA (MT) 169 Eh23
Powell USA (WY) 169 Ef23
Powell Point AUS 104 Ra62
Powell Point BS 179 Gb33
Powell River CDN (BC) 168 Dh21
Power USA (MT) 169 Ee22
Powerview CDN (MB) 172 Fb20
Powis Castle GB 21 Kr38
Powlathanga AUS (QLD) 107 Sc56
Powooiliak Camp USA (AK) 164 Be14
Poxoréo BR (MT) 202 Hc53
Poxyaxum MEX (CAM) 183 Fe36
Poya F (NCL) 118 Tc56
Poyanghu Z.B. CHN 75 Qj31
Poyracık TR 47 Mh51
Poysdorf A 42 Lr42
Poytug UZ 63 Og25
Pozantı TR 56 Mh27
Pozao CHN (GZG) 74 Qd34
Požarevac SCG 44 Mb46
Poza Rica MEX (VC) 182 Fb35
Požarskoe RUS 77 Rh22
Pozedrze PL 41 Mb36
Požega HR 35 Ls45
Požega SCG 44 Ma47
Poznań PL 40 Lr38
Pozo Alcón E 27 Ks53
Pozo Almonte RCH 206 Gf56
Pozo Azul PY 204 Ha58
Pozoblanco E 27 Kq52
Pozo-Cañada E 29 Kt52
Pozo Colorado PY 207 Ha57
Pozo Coyote MEX (SO) 180 Ed31
Pozo de las Animas RA 208 Gf63
Pozo del Molle RA (CD) 209 Gj62
Pozo del Tigre BOL 206 Gj54
Pozo del Tigre RA (FO) 207 Gk58
Pozo del Toba RA (SE) 207 Gj59
Pozo de Maza RA (FO) 207 Gk57
Pozohondo E 29 Kt52
Pozo Hondo RA (SE) 207 Gh59
Pozón YV 193 Gg42
Pozuelo de Alarcón E 27 Kr50
Pozuzo PE 197 Gc51
Pozzallo I 37 Lp54
Pozzuoli I 37 Lp50
Prača BIH 44 Lt47
Prachatice CZ 42 Lo41
Prachinburi THA 88 Qa38
Prachovské skály CZ 42 Lq40
Prachuap Khirikhan THA 88 Pk40
Pradelles F 25 Ld46
Prades E 29 La49
Prades F 24 Lc48
Pradła PL 41 Lu40
Prado BR (BA) 203 Ja54
Prado E 27 Kr50
Prado del Rey E 27 Kp54
Pradoluengo E 28 Kr48
Pradópolis BR (SP) 202 Hf56
Præstø DK 30 Ln35
Prague CZ 42 Lp40
Prague USA (OK) 174 Fb28
Praha CZ 42 Lp40
Prahovo SCG 44 Mc46
Praia BR (PA) 199 Hc48
Praia CV 136 Jj38
Práia a Mare I 37 Lq51
Praia da Baleia BR (CE) 201 Ja47
Praia da Barata BR (AM) 198 Gg46
Praia da Barra P 26 Km50
Praia da Conceicão BR (PE) 201 Jc49
Praia das Chocas MOC 153 Na53
Praia da Vieira P 26 Km51
Praia de Chongoene MOC 152 Mh58
Praia de Macaneta MOC 155 Mg58
Praia de Mira P 26 Km50
Praia de Zalala MOC 153 Mj54
Praia de Zavala MOC 153 Mh58
Praia de Závora MOC 153 Mh58
Praia do Bilene MOC 155 Mg58
Praia do Forte BR (BA) 201 Ja52
Praia do Maçarico BR (AM) 198 Gg46
Praia do Tofo MOC 153 Mh57
Praia do Wimbe MOC 147 Na52
Praia do Xai-Xai MOC 155 Mg58
Praia Grande BR (SC) 205 Hf60
Praia Grande BR (SP) 205 Hg58
Praid RO 43 Mf44
Praikalogu RI 96 Qk50
Prainha BR (AM) 198 Gg49
Praínha BR (PA) 195 He47
Praínha BR (PA) 199 Hd46
Prainha Nova BR (AM) 199 Gk49
Prairie AUS (QLD) 107 Sc56
Prairie Dog Colony CDN 169 Eg21
Prairie Du Chien USA (WI) 172 Fe24
Prairie River CDN (SK) 169 Ej19
Prakham K 89 Qc39
Prakhon Chai THA 89 Qb38
Pralognan F 25 Lg45
Pra-Loup F 25 Lg46
Prámanda GR 46 Mb51
Prambanan RI 95 Qf49
Prampram GH 137 La43
Pran Buri THA 88 Pk39
Prang GH 137 Kk41
Prangli EST 38 Me31
Prapat RI 93 Pk44
Prarie Downs AUS (WA) 102 Qk57
Prasat THA 89 Qb38
Prasat Sadok Kok Thom THA 89 Qb39
Prasat Sikhoraphum THA 89 Qb38
Praserganj IND (WBG) 86 Pe35
Praslin SY 145 Nh48
Praszka PL 40 Lt39
Prata BR (MG) 202 Hf55
Pratabpur IND (CGH) 83 Pb34
Pratapgad Fort IND 82 Og37
Pratapgarh IND (RJT) 82 Oh33
Pratapur IND (ORS) 83 Pc36
Prat, C.A. ANT (RCH) 6 Ha31
Prategí BR (BA) 201 Ja52
Prathai THA 89 Qb38
Pra That Cave THA 88 Pk38
Prato I 34 Lm47
Prats de Lluçanès E 29 Lc49
Prats-de-Mollo F 24 Lc48
Pratt USA (KS) 174 Fa27
Prattenville AUS (NSW) 109 Sc61
Prattville USA (AL) 175 Fg29
Pravara Sangam IND (MHT) 82 Oh36
Pravasuni IND (ORS) 83 Pc35
Pravčická brána CZ 42 Lp41
Pravda UA 41 Me40
Pravdinsk RUS 39 Mb36
Pravec BG 45 Md48
Pravia E 26 Ko47
Praya RI 96 Qj50
Prazaroki BY 39 Mj35
Preacher's Cave BS 179 Gb33
Preah Sihanouk National Park = Ream N.P. K 89 Qb40
Prebble Island CDN 167 Ed15
Precipice N.P. AUS (QLD) 109 Sf58
Prečistoe RUS 48 Mg18
Prečistoe RUS 48 Na16
Predajane SCG 44 Mc48
Predazzo I 34 Lm44
Predbajkal'skaja vpadina RUS 70 Qc19
Predeal RO 45 Mf45
Pre Delta, P.N. RA 209 Gk62
Predești RO 45 Me46
Predjamski grad SLO 42 Lp45
Preeceville CDN (SK) 169 Ej19
Pré-en-Pail F 22 Ku42
Preetz D 32 Ll36

Qijiaojing CHN (XUZ) 67 Pf24
Qila Abdullah PK 65 Od30
Qila Ladgasht PK 64 Ob32
Qilaotu Shan CHN 73 Qk25
Qila Saifullah PK 65 Oe30
Qilian CHN (QHI) 72 Qa26
Qilian Shan CHN 69 Pk26
Qilwah KSA 60 Na36
Qimen CHN (AHU) 75 Qj31
Qin'an CHN (GSU) 72 Qc28
Qincheng Shan CHN 74 Qb30
Qing'an CHN (HLG) 76 Rd22
Qingchengzi CHN (LNG) 76 Rb25
Qingdao CHN 73 Ra27
Qingdong Ling CHN 74 Qk27
Qinghai CHN 53 Pb06
Qinghai Hu CHN 72 Qa27
Qinghai Nanshan CHN 69 Pk27
Qinghe CHN (HBI) 73 Qh27
Qinghe CHN (XUZ) 67 Pf22
Qingemen CHN (LNG) 76 Ra25
Qingjiang Mosque CHN 75 Qk33
Qinglong CHN (GZG) 74 Qe35
Qingpu CHN (SHG) 78 Ra30
Qingshan CHN (HLG) 71 Rd21
Qingshizui CHN (QHI) 72 Qc28
Qingshui CHN (GSU) 69 Pk26
Qingshuihe CHN (NMZ) 72 Qf26
Qingshuihe CHN (XJG) 69 Pf29
Qingshuihe CHN (GDG) 75 Qd33
Qingtian CHN (ZJG) 75 Ra31
Qingtongxia CHN (NHZ) 72 Qd27
Qing Xiling CHN (HBI) 73 Qh26
Qingyang CHN (AHU) 78 Qj30
Qingyang CHN (GDG) 75 Qg34
Qingyuan CHN (GDG) 75 Qg34
Qingyuan CHN (LNG) 76 Rc24
Qingyuan CHN (ZJG) 75 Qk32
Qingyuanshan CHN 75 Qk33
Qingyunshan CHN 75 Qh32
Qingzhang Gaoyuan CHN 68 Pb29
Qingzhen CHN (GZH) 74 Qd30
Qingzhen Dasi CHN 72 Qd27
Qingzhou CHN (SDG) 73 Qk27
Qinhuangdao CHN (HBI) 73 Qk26
Qin Ling CHN 72 Qd29
Qintang CHN (GZG) 74 Qe34
Qin Xian CHN (SAX) 73 Qg27
Qinyang CHN (HNN) 73 Qh28
Qinzhou CHN (GZG) 74 Qe35
Qionghai CHN (HAN) 75 Qf36
Qionglai CHN (SCH) 74 Qb30
Qionglai Shan CHN 74 Qb30
Qiongzhong CHN (HAN) 75 Qk36
Qiqihar CHN (NMZ) 71 Ra19
Qiqihar CHN (HLG) 71 Rb22
Qira IR 64 Ng31
Qira CHN (XUZ) 68 Pa27
Qirkan Nature Reserve AZ 57 Ne26
Qisha CHN (GZG) 74 Qe35
Qishn YE 61 Nf38
Qishran KSA 60 Mk35
Qishui CHN (CGQ) 72 Qe30
Qitai CHN (XUZ) 67 Pe24
Qitaihe CHN (HLG) 76 Rf23
Qitian Ling CHN 75 Qg33
Qiubei CHN (YUN) 67 Qc33
Qiu Cheng, Tomb = Imperial Tombs of the Ming and Qing Dynasties CHN (JGS) 78 Qk29
Qiuxian CHN (JGX) 75 Qh37
Qiuzhe CHN (SCH) 74 Qc31
Qixia CHN (SDG) 73 Ra27
Qi Xing Gong Yuan CHN 74 Qf33
Qi Xing Yan CHN 74 Qf33
Qiyang CHN (HUN) 74 Qf32
Qi Yun Ta CHN 73 Qg28
Qizhou CHN (HUB) 75 Qh30
Qizhou Liedao CHN 75 Qf35
Qizilcha UZ 63 Od25
Qiziltepa UZ 63 Oc25
Qiz Qalasi AZ 57 Ne25
Qobustan AZ 57 Nd27
Qoltag CHN 67 Pe24
Qom IR 57 Nf28
Qolaman IR 62 Nj26
Qo'mqo'rg'on UZ 63 Od27
Qong'irot UZ 62 Nk24
Qongkol CHN (XUZ) 67 Pd27
Qo'qon UZ 63 Oe25
Qorabovur Qirlari UZ 62 Nj24
Qorakata bot'ig'i UZ 63 Oc25
Qorako'l UZ 63 Od26
Qora'zak UZ 62 Of24
Qoraqalpog'iston UZ 62 Nj24
Qoratepa UZ 63 Od26
Qorovulbozor UZ 63 Od26
Qorveh IR 57 Nd28
Qoryooley SP 145 Nc45
Qosheh SP 62 Na28
Qo'shrabot UZ 62 Od26
Qosmeliyon AZ 57 Ne26
Qotb Abad IR 64 Ng31
Qotb Abad IR 64 Nj32
Qotur IR 57 Nc26
Qoubaiyat RL 56 Mj28
Qozoq Qultig'i AFG 65 Oc30
Qozogdaryo UZ 62 Nk24
Quacha Nek ZA 155 Me61
Quafmollë AL 44 Lc49
Quaid-e-Azam Residency PK 65 Od30
Quairading AUS 104
Quakenbrück D 32 Lh38
Qualia RMM 136 Kk39
Qualicum Beach CDN 168
Quamalung CHN (QHI) 69 Pk28
Quambatook AUS (VIC) 111 Sb63
Quambone AUS (NSW) 109 Sd61
Quamby AUS (QLD) 107 Sa56
Quanah USA (TX) 174 Fa28
Quanary F (GF) 195 He43
Quan Ba VN 87 Qc30
Quanbun AUS (WA) 103 Rc55
Quan Dao Nam Du VN 89 Qc41
Quang Ngai VN 89 Qe38
Quang Tri Citadel VN 89 Qd38
Quangxi CHN (LNG) 76 Rd24
Quanzhou CHN (FJN) 75 Qk33
Quanzhu CHN (GZG) 74 Qf32
Quanzhou CHN (NMZ) 72 Qf26
Qu'Appelle CDN (SK) 169 Ej20
Qu'Appelle River CDN 169 Ej20
Quaqtaq = Julianehåb DK 163 Hc06
Quaqtaq CDN 163 Gc06
Quaqual NIC 185 Fj34
Quarles Mountains RI 96 Qk47

Quarré-les-Tombes F 25 Le43
Quarteira P 27 Km53
Quartu Sant' Elena I 36 Lk51
Quartz Lake CDN 173 Fh20
Quartzsite USA (AZ) 170 Ec29
Quba AZ 57 Ne25
Qubadli AZ 57 Nd26
Quchan IR 62 Nk27
Quday SYR 56 Mk28
Qudong CHN (GZG) 74 Qe33
Queanbeyan AUS (NSW) 111 Se63
Québec CDN (QC) 176 Ge22
Québec CDN 163 Ha07
Quebo GNB 136 Kc40
Quebra-Canela BR (AM) 198 Gg49
Quebracho ROU 204 Hb61
Quebrada de Humahuaca RA 207 Gg50
Quebrada de Jaspe YV 193 Gk43
Quebrada de la Flecha RA 207 Gg58
Quebrada de las Conchas RA 207 Gh58
Quebrada del Condorito, P.N. RA 208 Gh61
Quebrada de los Cuervos ROU 204 Hd57
Quedas do Calandula ANG 148 Lj50
Quedas do Iguaçu BR (PR) 204 Hd58
Quedas do Monte Negro ANG 150 Lg54
Quedas do Ruacaná ANG 150 Lh54
Quedlinburg D 32 Lm39
Queen Alexandra Range 7 Bb35
Queen Bess, Mount CDN 168 Dh20
Queen Charlotte City CDN (BC) 166 Dd19
Queen Charlotte Islands CDN 162 Db08
Queen Charlotte Is. Mus. CDN 166 Dd19
Queen Charlotte Mts. CDN 166 Dd19
Queen Charlotte Sound CDN 166 Dd20
Queen Charlotte Strait CDN 168 Df20
Queen Elizabeth Islands CDN 162 Ec02
Queen Elizabeth N.P. EAU 141 Me46
Queen Elizabeth Range 7 Bb35
Queen Mary Land 7 Pc33
Queen Maud Gulf CDN 162 Ed05
Queen Maud Mountains 6 Cb36
Queenscliff AUS (VIC) 111 Sc65
Queensland AUS 101 Sa12
Queenstown ZA 155 Md61
Queenstown AUS (TAS) 111 Sc67
Queenstown NZ 113 Te68
Queen Victoria Rock AUS (WA) 104 Ra61
Queen Victoria Spring Nature Reserve AUS 105 Rb61
Que'ergou CHN (XUZ) 67 Pd24
Queets USA (WA) 168 Dh22
Quéhué RA (LP) 208 Gh64
Queilén RCH 210 Gd67
Queimada Nova BR (PI) 201 Hk50
Queimadas BR (BA) 201 Ja51
Queimadas BR (PB) 201 Jc49
Queimadas, T.I. BR 205 He58
Queimados BR (RJ) 205 Hj57
Quela ANG 148 Lj50
Quelele ANG 149 Lk50
Quelimane MOC 153 Mj54
Quellón RCH 210 Gd67
Quelluno PE 197 Gd52
Quelo ANG 148 Lg49
Quemado USA (NM) 171 Ef28
Quemchi RCH 208 Gd67
Quemú-Quemú RA (LP) 209 Gj64
Que Phong VN 87 Qc36
Quepos CR 185 Fh41
Quequén RA (BA) 209 Ha65
Querari CO 193 Gf45
Quercoto PE 196 Ga49
Querência do Norte BR (PR) 202 Hd57
Querétaro MEX (QRT) 182 Ek35
Querétaro MEX 182 Ek35
Querfurt D 32 Lm39
Querobabi MEX (SO) 180 Ee30
Querobamba PE 197 Gd52
Quesada E 27 Kr53
Queshan CHN (HNN) 73 Qh29
Quesnel CDN (BC) 168 Dj19
Quesnel Mus. CDN 168 Dj19
Que Son VN 89 Qe38
Quesobamba BOL 207 Gf54
Questembert F 22 Ks43
Quetena Grande BOL 207 Gg57
Quetico Prov. Park CDN 172 Fe21
Quetta PAK 65 Od30
Queulat, P.N. RCH 210 Ge68
Queva, Nevado RA 207 Gg58
Quevedo EC 196 Ga46
Quezaltenango GCA 184 Fe38
Quezon RP 90 Rb38
Quezon RP 91 Qk41
Quezon RP 91 Rc42
Quiabaya BOL 206 Gf53
Quiahuiztlán MEX 183 Fb36
Quiandeluz BR (PA) 195 Hg47
Quiapa AZ 155 Md61
Quibala ANG 148 Lh49
Quibala II ANG 150 Lh51
Quibaxe ANG 148 Lh50
Quibdó CO 192 Gb43
Quiberon F 22 Kr43
Quicabo BOL 206 Gf53
Quicabe ANG 148 Lg50
Quicacha PE 197 Gd53
Quiçama, P.N.da ANG 148 Lg50
Quichaura, Cerro RA 210 Gc67

Quilmes RA (BA) 209 Ha63
Quilmes RA 207 Gg59
Quilombo BR (SC) 204 Hd59
Quilon = Kollam IND (KER) 84 Oj41
Quilpie AUS (QLD) 109 Sc59
Quilua MOC 153 Mk54
Quimantag CHN 69 Pf27
Quimbala ANG 148 Lh48
Quimbele ANG 148 Lj48
Quimbonge ANG (NSW) 111 Sd63
Quimili RA 207 Gg59
Quimper F 22 Kq43
Quimperlé F 22 Kr43
Quinabucasan Point RP 90 Rb38
Quinalasag I 36 Lf33
Quinapondan RP 90 Rc40
Quinault Ind. Res. USA 168 Dk22
Quincemil PE 197 Ge52
Quincy USA (CA) 170 Dk26
Quincy USA (FL) 175 Fh30
Quincy USA (IL) 175 Fe26
Quincy USA (MA) 177 Ge24
Quincy Hills USA 175 Fe26
Quindanning AUS (WA) 104 Qj62
Quindío, Nev. del CO 192 Gb44
Quinengue ANG 150 Lh53
Quingey F 25 Lf43
Quinhagak USA (AK) 164 Bk16
Quinhámel GNB 136 Kc40
Qui Nhon VN 89 Qe39
Quinlubian Group RP 90 Ra40
Quinlubian Island RP 90 Ra40
Quinkan and Regional Cultural Centre (Laura) AUS 107 Sc53
Quinta BR (RS) 204 Hd62
Quintana de Castillo E 26 Ko48
Quintana del Puente E 26 Kq48
Quintana Roo MEX 183 Ff36
Quintanar de la Orden E 27 Kr51
Quintanar del Rey E 29 Kt51
Quintero RCH 208 Ge62
Quintin F 22 Ks42
Quinto E 29 Ku49
Quinzala ANG 148 Lh49
Quionga MOC 147 Na51
Quioniga ANG 148 Lh50
Quiotepec MEX 182 Fb37
Quipapá BR (PE) 201 Jb50
Quipungo ANG 150 Lh53
Quirauk USA 175 Ga26
Quiriguá GCA 184 Ff38
Quirihue RCH 208 Gd64
Quirima ANG 150 Lk51
Quirindi AUS (NSW) 109 Sf61
Quirinópolis BR (GO) 202 He55
Quiriquire YV 193 Gj41
Quiriza BOL 207 Gg54
Quiroga E 26 Kn48
Quiroga RA (CA) 207 Gh60
Quiróz YV 192 Ga40
Quiruvilca PE 196 Ga49
Quisiro YV 192 Gd40
Quissamã BR (RJ) 203 Hk57
Quissange MOC 153 Mh58
Quitandinha BR (PR) 205 Hf58
Quitapa ANG 149 Lk51
Quiteve ANG 148 Lh49
Quitman USA (MS) 175 Ff29
Quitman USA (TX) 174 Fc29
Quito EC 196 Ga46
Quitovac MEX 180 Ec30
Quivira N.W.R. USA 174 Fa26
Quivolgo RCH 208 Gd63
Quixabá BR (BA) 201 Hj51
Quixadá BR (CE) 201 Ja48
Quixaxe MOC 153 Na53
Quixeramobim BR (CE) 201 Ja48
Quixeré BR (CE) 201 Jb48
Quizenga ANG 148 Lj49
Qujing CHN (YUN) 87 Qb33
Quban Layyah CHN (QHI)
Qulai Kommunizm TJ 63 Oe26
Qumar Heyan CHN (QHI)
Qumarlêb CHN (QHI) 69 Pj31
Qummah KSA 60 Na36
Qundao CHN 73 Ra26
Quneitra SYR 56 Mh29
Qunfudh YE 60 Ne37
Qungqang CHN 69 Ph30
Qungtag CHN (TIB) 68 Pd31
Quobba AUS (WA) 104 Qg58
Quoin Island AUS 103 Rk62
Quorn AUS (SA) 108 Rk62
Qurayat OM 61 Nk34
Qurayd SUD 135 Me40
Qurdud SUD 135 Me40
Qureida SUD 135 Md40
Qurghonteppa TJ 63 Oe27
Qurrasa SUD 135 Mg38
Qus ET 129 Mg34
Qusar AZ 57 Ne25
Qusay'ir YE 61 Nf38
Quss Abu Sa'id ET 128 Md32
Qutang CHN 74 Qd30
Qutub Minar IND 80 Oj31
Quwo CHN (SAX) 73 Qg27
Quwu Shan CHN 72 Qc27
Qu Xian CHN (SCH) 74 Qd30
Quxu CHN (TIB) 68 Pf31
Quyang CHN (HBI) 73 Qh28
Quynh Luu VN 87 Qd36
Quzhou CHN (ZJG) 75 Qk31
Qyrqqyz-Qala UZ 62 Oa25

R

Raa Atoll MV 84 Og43
Raab A 35 Lq43
Raab A 35 Lq43
Raahe FIN 16 Mc13
Rääkkylä FIN 38 Mh28
Raanujärvi FIN 16 Mc12
Raas RI 95 Qh49
Raasay GB 20 Kn33
Raas Binna SP 143 Nf40
Raas Caluula SP 143 Nf40
Raas Caseyr SP 143 Nf40
Raas Gabbac SP 143 Nf41
Raas Iilig SP 143 Nf42
Raas Khansiir SP 143 Nd41
Raas Macbar SP 143 Nf41
Raas Surud SP 143 Nd40
Raas Xaafuun SP 143 Ng41
Raba HR 35 Lp46
Raba RI 96 Qk50
Rababe RP 143 Nd41
Rabac HR 35 Lp46
Rábade E 26 Kn47
Rábago E 27 Kr53
Rabak SUD 135 Mg39
Rabale WAN 132 Lc39
Rabastens-de-Bigorre F 27 Lb47

Rabaraba PNG 116 Se51
Rabat M 37 Lp55
Rabat MA 125 Kg29
Rabaul PNG 116 Se51
Rabbit Flat AUS (NT) 103 Rf56
Rabia RI 97 Rh45
Rabigh KSA 60 Md36
Rabka-Zdroj PL 41 Lu41
Rabnita MD 49 Me22
Rabodao RI 91 Rd46
Rabo da Onça BR (AM) 198 Gh46
Rabor IR 64 Nj31
Rabt Sbayta DARS 124 Kc33
Rabwah PK 65 Og30
Rabyanah LAR 128 Mb33
Raça SCG 44 Mb47
Racalmuto I 36 Lo53
Raccon Cay BS 179 Gb34
Racconigi I 34 Lh46
Raceland USA (LA) 175 Fe31
Rach Gia VN 89 Qc40
Rachid RN 138 Mb34
Rachgoba I 81 Oj29
Racici2 PL 41 Ma38
Racibórz PL 40 Lt40
Racine USA (WI) 173 Fg24
Rackla Range CDN 165 Dd13
Radan BG 44 Mc48
Radauti RO 43 Me43
Radcliff USA (KY) 175 Fh27
Radde RUS (YAO) 76 Rf21
Radebeul D 32 Lo39
Radeburg D 32 Lo39
Radechiv UA 41 Me40
Radeche UA 41 Me40
Radenci SLO 42 Lr44
Radenthein A 35 Lp44
Radeville UA 41 Mf40
Radford USA (VA) 178 Fk27
Radiovce MK 44 Ma49
Radilovo BG 45 Me48
Radin most RI MK 44 Ma48
Radium Hot Springs CDN (BC) 168 Ea20
Radkan IR 62 Nk27
Radlje ob Dravi SLO 42 Lq44
Radnevo BG 45 Mf48
Radno DK 30 Ll34
Radnor Forest GB 21 Kr38
Radolfzell D 33 Lk43
Radom PL 41 Mb39
Radom SUD 141 Mc41
Radomicko PL 40 Lp38
Radomir BG 44 Mc48
Radom Nat. Park SUD 141 Mc41
Radomsko PL 41 Lu39
Radomyśl nad Sanem PL 41 Mb40
Radomyśl Wielki PL 41 Ma40
Radovan BR 44 Md46
Radovec SCG 45 Md48
Radovljica S SLO 42 Lp44
Radstadt A 35 Lp43
Raducaneni RO 43 Mh43
Radun N 39 Mf36
Radviliškis LT 39 Md35
Radville CDN (SK) 169 Eh21
Radymno PL 41 Mc40
Radzanów PL 41 Ma38
Radziejów PL 40 Lt38
Radzionków PL 40 Lt40
Radzyń Chełmiński PL 41 Lt37
Radzyń Podlaski PL 41 Mc39
Rae-Bareli IND (UPH) 83 Ok35
Raeford USA (NC) 178 Ga28
Raesfeld D 32 Lg39
Raes Junction NZ 113 Te68
Raetihi NZ 113 Th65
Rafaela RA (SF) 209 Gk61
Rafael Freyre C 179 Gb35
Rafaï RCA 141 Md43
Rafaïwka UA 41 Mg39
Raffingora ZW 152 Mf55
Raffin Kada WAN 138 Le42
Rafha KSA 59 Nb31
Rafigani IND (BIH) 83 Pc33
Rafin Cabas WAN 138 Le40
Rafin Dinga WAN 138 Le41
Rafsanjan IR 64 Nj31
Raft Mountains USA 171 Ed25
Raftópoulou GR 46 Mb51
Ragada SUD 141 Mc41
Ragagelma LT 39 Md33
Raghopur IND (BIH) 83 Pd32
Raglan NZ 112 Th64
Raglan USA (LA) 174 Fd29
Ragley USA (LA) 174 Fd30
Rago n.p. N 16 Lh12
Ragueneau CDN (QC) 176 Gg21
Raha RI 96 Rb48
Rahad al-Bardi SUD 134 Mb40
Rahad Canal SUD 135 Mh38
Rahad Game Reserve SUD 135 Mh38
Rahama WAN 138 Le40
Rahatgarh IND (MPH) 83 Ok34
Raheste EST 39 Md32
Rahimabad IR 57 Ne27
Rahimatpur IND (WBG)
Rahimyar Khan PK 65 Of31
Rahole National Reserve EAK 145 Mk45
Rahovëc DZ 125 La28
Rahuri IND (MHT) 82 Oh36
Raidih IND (JKD) 83 Pc34
Raigarh IND (ORS) 83 Pb36
Raigarh IND (CGH) 83 Pb35
Raighalmarh SP 143 Nf42
Raikal IND (APH) 83 Ok36
Raikera IND (ORS) 83 Pb35
Raikova Pecina SCG 44 Mb48
Railway Mus. USA 170 Ec26
Raimundo, T.I. BR 193 Gg45
Raimundo BR (MS) 202 He55
Rahama USA 138 Le40
Raihatgarh IND (MPH) 83 Ok34

Rainbow Warrior Wreck Diving NZ 112 Th63
Rainier N.P., Mount USA 168 Dk22
Rainis RI 91 Rd43
Rainsville USA (AL) 175 Fh28
Rainy River CDN (ON) 172 Fc21
Raippaluoto FIN 38 Mb27
Raippo FIN 38 Mh30
Raipur IND (CGH) 83 Pa35
Raipur IND (RJT) 82 Oh33
Raipura IND (UTT) 81 Ok34
Rairangpur IND (ORS) 83 Pd37
Raisdorf D 32 Ll36
Raisen IND (MPH) 82 Oj34
Raisinghnagar IND (RJT) 80 Og31
Raisio FIN 38 Mb30
Raiskio Praskalo BG 45 Me48
Raith IND (UPH) 82 Of21
Raivala FIN 38 Mc29
Rai Valley NZ 113 Tg66
Raiz BR (MA) 195 Hj47
Rajada BR (PE) 201 Hk50
Rajagaon IND (CGH) 83 Pa36
Rajahmundry IND (APH) 83 Pa37
Rajaji N.P. IND 81 Oj30
Raja-Jooseppi FIN 16 Me11
Rajakhera IND (RJT) 81 Ok32
Rajampet IND (APH) 85 Ok38
Rajanpur PK 65 Of31
Rajapalayam IND (TNU) 84 Oj41
Rajapur IND (MHT) 82 Og37
Rajapur IND (UPH) 83 Pa32
Rajasthan IND 80 Oe32
Rajauli IND (BIH) 83 Pc33
Rajawada (Indore) IND 82 Oh34
Rajbari BD 86 Pe34
Rájec-Jestřebí CZ 42 Lr41
Rajec Poduchowny PL 41
Rajevo Selo HR 44 Lt45
Rajgangpur IND (ORS) 83 Pc35
Rajgarh IND (RJT) 80 Oh31
Rajgarh IND (MPH) 82 Oj34
Rajgir IND (BIH) 83 Pc33
Rajik RI 92 Qd47
Rajkot IND (GUJ) 82 Of34
Rajmahal IND (JKD) 83 Pd33
Rajmahal Hills IND 83 Pd33
Raj Nandgaon IND (CGH) 83 Pa35
Rajpipla IND (GUJ) 82 Og35
Rajpur IND (MPH) 82 Oh34
Rajpur IND (PJB) 80 Oj30
Rajsamand IND (RJT) 82 Og33
Rajshahi BD 86 Pe33
Raka CHN (TIB) 68 Pc31
Rakaca H 43 Ma42
Rakai EAU 141 Me46
Rakaia NZ 113 Tf67
Rakaunui NZ 113 Tj66
Rakaya BF 137 Kk40
Rakhine-Kainary IND (JKD)
Rakhyut OM 61 Ng37
Rakiraki FJI 119 Tk54
Rakit RI 95 Qe48
Rakitnoe RUS 77 Rh23
Rakkestad N 30 Lm31
Rakonsti J 77 Sa24
Rakops RB 151 Mc56
Rakovica HR 35 Lq46
Rakovník CZ 42 Lo40
Rakovski BG 45 Me48
Rakuchernyi mülys KZ 62 Nf24
Rakvere EST 38 Mg31
Rakvi RI 114 Rh47
Ralco RCH 208 Ge64
Raleigan IND (MHT) 83 Ok35
Raleigh USA (NC) 175 Fd30
Raleigh Bay USA 178 Ga28
Raleighvallen SME 194 Hb43
Ralik Chain USA 100 Ta09
Ralls USA (TX) 174 Fa29
Ralston USA (OK) 174 Fc27
Ralún RCH 210 Gd67
Rama BR 35 Ls47
Rama YE 60 Nd37
Ramabhadrapuram IND (APH) 83 Pb36
Ramah Navajo Ind. Res. USA 171 Ef28
Ramak AFG 65 Od30
Ramalaguen SUD 135 Mf40
Ramalingeswara Temple IND 85 Ok41
Ramallah IL 58 Mh30
Raman THA 88 Qa42
Ramanagaram IND (KTK) 84 Oj40
Ramanathapuram IND (TNU) 85 Ok41
Ramanathaswamy Temple (Rameswaram) IND (TNU) 84 Ok41
Ramanpura IND (CGH)
Ramanuj Ganj IND (CGH) 83 Pb34
Ramapuram IND (APH) 82 Oj36
Ramat Fort IND PK 65 Ok31
Rambervillers F 23 Lg42
Rambouillet F 23 Lb42
Rambre MYA 86 Pg36
Rambre Island = Rambrè MYA 86 Pg36
Rambutyo Islands PNG

Ramlat ar-Rabkha OM 61 Nh35
Ramlat Dahm YE 60 Nc37
Ramlat Ghafah 61 Nh35
Ramlat Umm al Arid OM 61 Ng36
Ramlat Zallaf LAR 127 Lg32
Ramlinville LAR / ETH 142 Na39
Ramnad IND 83 Pd33
Ramnagar IND (CGH) 83 Pa33
Ramnagar IND (UTT) 81 Ok31
Ramna S 31 Lr31
Ramnicu Sărăt RO 45 Mh45
Ramnicu Vâlcea RO 43 Me45
Rameth 142 Na42
Ramo RP 90 Ra37
Ramon USA (CA) 170 Eb29
Ramón Castilla PE 198 Gf48
Ramón Corona MEX (DGO)
Ramon 181 Ej33
Ramona USA (CA) 170 Eb29
Ramona RA 199 Ha47
Ramos Island RP 94 Qj41
Ramos Arizpe MEX (COH)
Ramotswa RB 155 Mc58
Rampart USA (AK) 165 Ce13
Rampart IND (GUJ) 82 Oe34
Rampur IND (HPH) 81 Oj30
Raon-l'Etape F 23 Lg42
Raoping CHN (GDG) 75 Qj34
Raoul Island NZ 112 Ua60
Rapale MOC 153 Mk53
Rapallo I 34 Lk46
Rapa Nui, P.N. RCH 197 Gc54
Rapar IND (GUJ) 82 Of34
Rapel je CHN (MI) 173 Fg23
Rapid Bay AUS (SA) 110 Rk63
Rapid City USA (SD) 169 Ej23
RapideBlancStation CDN (QC) 176 Gd22
Rapides de Gembele RDC 140 Md44
Rapides de Koudo DY 138 Lb40
Rapides de l'Éléphant RDC 140 LA43
Rapides de l'Ogooué G 148 Lf47
Rapides de Nyanga G 148 Lf47
Rapid River USA (MI) 173 Fg23
Rapina EST 38 Mg31
Rápla EST 39 Mf31
Rappang RI 96 Qk47
Rapperswil CH 34 Lj43
Rappottenstein A 42 Lq42
Raquette NZ
Rara N.P. NEP 81 Pa31
Raranga Island AUS 106 Rj51
Rarru RI 95 Qe44
Ranai, Mount RI 94 Qe43
Ranaka RB 155 Mc58
Ranakah, Gunung RI 96 Ra50
Ranahal BD 86 Pe34
Ranas y Toluquilla MEX 182 Fa35
Ranau MAL 94 Qj43
Ranau RCH 208 Gd65
Rancharia BR (SP) 202 He57
Ranchi IND (JKD) 83 Pc34
Ranchi Plateau IND 83 Pc34
Rancho Alegre MEX (BC) 180 Ec30
Rancho Cordova USA (CA) 170 Dk26
Rancho Grande MEX (ZCT) 182 Ej34
Rancho Nuevo MEX (CHH) 180 Eg30
Rancho Veláz C 179 Fk34
Randa DJI 143 Nd40
Randalstown GB 19 Ko36
Randangan Panua Reserve RI 91 Ra45
Randegg A 137 Lp53
Randegal CHN (MHT) 83 Ok35
Randers DK 30 Ll34
Randfontein ZA 155 Md59
Randle USA (WA) 168 Dk22
Randoway RI 114 Rk46
Randudongkal RI 95 Qe49
Raneru SN 130 Kd38
Ranfurly CDN (AB) 169 Ee19
Ranfurly NZ 113 Tf68
Rangae THA 89 Qa42
Rangamati BD 86 Pg34
Rangapet IND (APH)
Ranganathaswamy Temple IND 85 Ok40
Ranganathittu Sanctuary IND 84 Oj40
Rangaon IND (WBG) 86 Pe34
Rangeley USA (ME) 177 Ge23
Rangely USA (CO) 171 Ef25
Rangers Valley AUS (QLD) 109 Sc57
Ranger uranium mine AUS (NT) 106 Rg52
Rangoon = Yangon MYA 86 Ph36
Rangoon = Yangon MYA 86 Ph36
Rangoon IND (KTK) 82 Oj38
Rangpur BD 86 Pe33
Rangsang RI 93 Qb45
Rangsit NEP 81 Pa31
Ranibennur IND (KTK) 84 Oj39
Ranigani IND (BIH) 83 Pd32
Raniganj IND (UPH) 83 Pb32
Raniganj IND (WBG) 86 Pd34
Ranigani IND (ORS) 83 Pb36
Ranikhet IND (UTT) 81 Ok31
Ranipet IND (TNU) 85 Ok39
Ranir Bazar IND (TRP)
Ranipur IND (UPH)
Ranital IND (HPH) 80 Oj29
Ranital IND (RJT) 82 Oh33
Ranken Store AUS (NT)
Rankin IND 86 Pf34
Rankin's Springs AUS (NSW)

Réalmont F 24 Lc47
Ream N.P. = Preah Sihanouk National Park K 89 Qd41
Reao Atoll 11 Da11
Rebaa DZ 126 Lc30
Rebecca, Mount AUS (WA) 104 Qh59
Rebiana Sand Sea LAR 128 Mb33
Rebild Bakker, Nationalpark DK 30 Ll34
Rebirechioulet F 24 La47
Rebollera E 27 Kq52
Reboucas BR (PR) 205 He58
Rebun-to J 77 Sa23
Reburi J 77 Sa23
Recanati I 35 Lo47
Recaş RO 42 Mb45
Receca RO 43 Me45
Recea RO 43 Md44
Recey-sur-Ource F 25 Le43
Réčica IRL 19 Kl38
Recife BR (AM) 196 Ga49
Recife BR (PE) 201 Jc50
Recife da Silva BR 195 Hh46
Recife Manuel Luís BR 195 Hh46
Récif Petrie F (NCL) 118 Tc55
Récifs de l' Astrolabe F (NCL)
Récifs d'Entrecasteaux F (NCL) 118 Tb55
Récifs et Îlots Chesterfield F (PYF) 10 Sb12
Recklinghausen D 32 Lh39
Reclining Buddha CHN 87 Pk33
Recoaro Terme I 34 Lm45
Reconquista RA (SF) 204 Ha60
Recontre East (NF) 177 Hc22
Recreio São Felix, T.I. BR 199 Ha47
Recreo RA (SF) 209 Gk61
Recuay PE 197 Gb50
Rečycae J 49 Mf19
Reda PL 40 Lt37
Redang MAL 92 Qb43
Redange-sur-Attert L 23 Lf41
Redbank AUS (VIC) 111 Sb64
Red Bank D 32 Lh40
Red Basin CHN 74 Qc30
Red Bluff USA (CA) 170 Dj25
Red Bluff USA (AL) 175 Fg30
Red Bluff N.P. CDN 177 Hb20
Red Bays BS 179 Ga33
Redbird USA (WY) 169 Eh24
Red Cliff USA (CO) 171 Eg26
Redcliff CDN (AB) 169 Ee20
Redcliff ZW 152 Me55
Redcliffe AUS (QLD) 109 Sg59
Red Cliff Ind. Res. USA 172 Fe22
Red Cloud USA (NE) 174 Fa25
Red Deer CDN (AB) 169 Ed19
Red Deer Valley Badlands CDN 169 Ed20
Reddersburg ZA 155 Md60
Redding USA (CA) 170 Dj25
Redditch GB 21 Ks38
Redencão BR (CE) 201 Ja48
Redencão BR (PA) 200 He49
Redencão BR (PA) 200 He50
Redenção do Gurguéia BR (PI) 200 Hh50
Redentora BR (RS) 204 Hd59
Redesdale AUS (VIC) 111 Sc64
Redeyef TN 126 Le28
Redfield USA (SD) 172 Fa23
Redford USA (QLD) 109 Sd58
Red Fort (Delhi) IND 80 Oj31
Red Fort KWT 59 Nd31
Redhakhol IND (ORS) 83 Pb35
Red Hill USA (NM) 171 Ef28
Red Hill P. Henry Nat. Mem. USA 178 Ga27
Red Hills USA 174 Fa27
Red Hills S.P. USA 175 Ff26
Red Indian Lake CDN 177 Hb21
Redig USA (SD) 169 Ej23
Redkino RUS 201 Jc48
Red Lake CDN 172 Fd20
Red Lake Ind. Res. CDN 172 Fc21
Red Lake Road CDN (ON) 172 Fd20
Redlands USA (CA) 170 Eb28
Red Lion USA (PA) 177 Gb26
Red Lodge USA (MT) 169 Ef23
Red Mercury Island NZ 112 Th64
Redmond USA (OR) 168 Dk23
Red Mtn. USA 169 Ed22
Red Oak USA (IA) 174 Fc25
Redon F 22 Ks43
Redonda AK 187 Gj37
Redondo P 27 Kn52
Redoubt Vol. USA (AK) 164 Cd16
Redoute Flatters RN 132 Ld33
Red River IND 86 Pf34
Red River USA (TX) 174 Fb28
Reds, Gunung RI 93 Qg47
Red River Delta VN 87 Qd35
Red River Gorge USA 175 Fj27
Red Rock CDN (BC) 166 Dj19
Redruth GB 21 Kp40
Red Sea 142 Nd37
Redvers CDN (SK) 172 Ek21
Red Volta GH/BF 137 Kk40
Redwater CDN (AB) 169 Ed19
Red Wing USA (MN) 172 Fd23
Redwater USA (TX) 174 Fc28
Redwood City USA (CA) 170 Dj27
Redwood Falls USA (MN) 172 Fc23

Refugio ☐ USA (TX) 181 Fb31
Refugio Beach ☐ USA 170 Dk28
Refugio de Fauna Laguna Castillos ☐ ROU 209 Hc63
Regala ☐ MA 125 Kb28
Regalbuto ☐ I 37 Lp53
Regen ☐ D 33 Ln41
Regen ☐ D 33 Lo42
Regência ☐ BR (ES) 203 Ja55
Regencia ☐ BR 203 Ja55
Regeneração ☐ BR (PI) 201 Hj49
Regensburg ☐ D 33 Ln41
Regenstauf ☐ D 33 Ln41
Regente Feijó ☐ BR (SP) 202 He57
Regestan ☐ AFG 65 Oc30
Reggane ☐ DZ 125 La32
Réggio di Calábria ☐ I 37 Lq52
Réggio nell'Emília ☐ I 34 Ll46
Regöcz ☐ MA 44 Me44
Reghin ☐ RO 43 Me43
Regina ☐ F (GF) 195 Hd43
Regina ☐ CDN (SK) 169 Eh20
Regina Beach ☐ CDN (SK) 169 Eh20
Reginio ☐ GR 46 Mc52
Reginópolis ☐ BR (SP) 202 Hf56
Registro ☐ BR (SP) 205 Hg58
Regnitz ☐ D 33 Lm41
Reguengos de Monsaraz ☐ P 27 Kn52
Regway ☐ CDN (SK) 169 Eh21
Rehau ☐ D 33 Ln42
Rehburg-Loccum ☐ D 32 Lk38
Rehli ☐ IND (MPH) 83 Oe34
Rehoboth ☐ NAM 154 Lj57
Rehoboth Beach ☐ USA (DE) 177 Gd26
Rehoboth Station ☐ NAM 154 Lj57
Rehovot ☐ IL 58 Mh30
Reial Monestir de Poblet ☐ E 29 Lb49
Reichenau ☐☐ D 33 Lk43
Reichenbach ☐ D 33 Ln42
Reichshoffen ☐ F 23 Lh42
Reid ☐ AUS (WA) 105 Re61
Reid Reef ☐ FJI 119 Ua54
Reidsville ☐ USA (GA) 178 Fj29
Reidsville ☐ USA (NC) 178 Ga27
Reigate ☐ GB 21 Ku39
Re'im ☐ IL 58 Mh30
Reims ☐☐ F 23 Lf41
Reinach ☐ CH 34 Lj43
Reinbek ☐ D 32 Ll37
Reinberg ☐ D 32 Lo36
Reinbolt Hills ☐ 7 Oc32
Reindeer Lake ☐ CDN 172 Fa19
Reindeer Lake ☐ CDN 162 Ec07
Reindeer Station ☐ USA (AK) 165 Bk12
Reinheim ☐ D 33 Lj41
Reinosa ☐ E 26 Kq48
Reinhjolsfjäll ☐ IS 18 Jk25
Reisa n.p. ☐ N 16 Mb11
Reit im Winkl ☐ D 33 Ln43
Reitz ☐ ZA 155 Me59
Reivilo ☐ ZA 154 Mc59
Rejaf ☐ SUD 144 Mf43
Rejdovo ☐ RUS 77 Se23
Rejowiec ☐ PL 41 Md39
Rejštejn ☐ CZ 42 Lo41
Rekavice ☐ BIH 35 Ls46
Reken ☐ D 32 Lh39
Reliance ☐ CDN 167 Ef14
Reliance ☐ DZ 125 La28
Relleu ☐ E 29 Ku52
Remada ☐ TN 126 Lf29
Remagen ☐ D 32 Lh40
Remanso ☐ BR (AM) 198 Gf49
Remanso ☐ BR (PI) 201 Hj50
Remarkable, Mount ☐ AUS (QLD) 107 Rk56
Remarkable, Mount ☐ AUS 103 Rd54
Rembang ☐ RI 95 Qf49
Remda ☐ RUS 38 Mh32
Remedios ☐ C 174 Ga34
Remel el Abiod ☐ TN 126 Le30
Remhoogte Pass ☐ NAM 154 Lj58
Remígio ☐ BR (PB) 201 Jc49
Rémire ☐ SY 145 Ng48
Remiremont ☐ F 25 Lg42
Remón-Montjoly ☐ F (GF) 195 Hd43
Remolino ☐ CO 192 Gc40
Rempang ☐ RI 93 Qc45
Remparts d'Aigues-Mortes ☐ F 25 Le47
Rems ☐ D 33 Lk42
Remscheid ☐ D 32 Lh39
Remuzat ☐ F 25 Lf46
Rencén ☐ LV 39 Mf33
Renco ☐ ZW 152 Mf56
Renda ☐ LV 39 Mc33
Rendina ☐ GR 45 Md50
Rendova ☐ SOL 117 Sj50
Rendsburg ☐ D 32 Lk36
René Brunelle Prov. Park ☐ CDN 173 Fj21
Renfrew ☐ CDN (ON) 177 Gb23
Rengali ☐ IND (ORS) 83 Pc35
Rengat ☐ RI 93 Qc46
Rengma Hills ☐ IND 84 Pg32
Rengo ☐ RCH 208 Ge63
Renhe ☐ CHN (YUN) 87 Qa32
Renhua ☐ CHN (GDG) 75 Qg33
Renhuai ☐ CHN (GZH) 74 Qd32
Reni ☐ IND (RJT) 80 Oh31
Reni ☐ UA 45 Mj45
Renigunta ☐ IND (APH) 85 Ok39
Renington ☐ IND 148 Lq49
Renko ☐ FIN 38 Md30
Renlundin museo ☐ FIN 16 Mb14
Rennell Island ☐ SOL 117 Ta51
Rennell Rise ☐ 117 Sj51
Rennes ☐☐ F 22 Kt42
Rennesøy ☐ N 30 Lf31
Rennie ☐ CDN (MB) 172 Fc21
Renningen ☐ D 33 Lj42
Reno ☐ USA (NV) 170 Ea26
Renous ☐ CDN 176 Gh22
Renovo ☐ USA (PA) 177 Gb25
Renqiu ☐ CHN (HBI) 73 Qh27
Renshi ☐ CHN (SCH) 74 Qd30
Renshou ☐ CHN (SCH) 74 Qc31
Rensselaer ☐ USA (IN) 173 Fg25
Renton ☐ USA (WA) 168 Dj22
Renwick ☐ NZ 113 Tg66
Réo ☐ BF 137 La40
Reo ☐ RI 96 Ra50
Repalle ☐ IND (APH) 83 Pa37
Repartimento ☐ BR (AM)
Repartimento ☐ BR (AM) 199 Hb47
Repetek Desert Reserve ☐ TM 62 Oa26
Rep'evka ☐ RUS 48 Mb20
Repovden kansallispuisto ☐ FIN 38 Mb29
Repuponga ☐ a 16 Mc05
Represa Agua Vermelha ☐ BR 202 He55
Represa Barra Bonita ☐ BR 202 Hf57
Represa Camargos ☐ BR 203 Hh56
Represa Capivara ☐ BR 202 He57
Represa de Acaray ☐ PY 202 Hc58

Represa de Balbina ☐ BR 194 Ha46
Represa de Boa Esperança ☐ BR 200 Hj49
Represa de Chavantes ☐ BR 205 Hf57
Represa de Foz do Areia ☐ BR 205 He58
Represa de Furnas ☐ BR 203 Hg56
Represa de Itaipu ☐ BR/PY 205 Ja55
Represa del Río Negro ☐ ROU 204 Hb62
Represa de Paraibuna ☐ BR 204 Hb62
Represa de Salto Grande ☐ ROU/RA 204 Hb61
Represa de Samuel ☐ BR 198 Gj50
Represa de Tucuruí ☐ BR 200 H48
Represa Emborcação ☐ BR 203 Hg55
Represa Ilha Grande ☐ BR 202 Hd56
Represa Ilha Solteira ☐ BR 202 He56
Represa Jupiá ☐ BR 202 Hd56
Represa Jurumirim ☐ BR 202 Hf57
Represa Passo Real ☐ BR 204 Hd60
Represa Peixoto ☐ BR 203 Hg56
Represa Porto Primavera ☐ BR 202 Hd56
Represa Promissão ☐ BR 202 Hf56
Represa Salto Osório ☐ BR 204 Hd58
Represa Salto Santiago ☐ BR 204 Hd58
Represa Três Irmãos ☐ BR 202 He56
Represa Três Marias ☐ BR 203 Hh55
Reptilespore ☐ ZA 152 Me57
Reptile Footprints ☐ ZA 152 Me57
Republic ☐ USA (MO) 174 Fd27
Republic ☐ USA (WA) 168 Ea21
Repulse Bay ☐ CDN 163 Fc05
Requena ☐ E 29 Kt51
Requena ☐ PE 196 Gd48
Requena ☐ BR (AJ) 209 Gk64
Requena ☐ YV 193 Gh42
Réquista ☐ F 25 Lc44
Resa ☐ RP 91 Rb42
Resadiye ☐ TR 57 Mh54
Resadiye ☐ TR 56 Mj25
Resadiye Yarmadasi ☐ TR 47 Mh54
Resas ☐ CO 192 Gb44
Resavska Pecina ☐ SCG 44 Mb46
Reschenpass = Passo di Résia ☐☐ A 34 Ll44
Resen ☐ MK 44 Mb49
Resende ☐ BR (RJ) 205 Hh57
Reserva ☐ CO 196 Gd46
Reserva ☐ BR (PR) 205 Hf57
Reserva Biológica Atol das Rocas ☐ BR 201 Jd47
Reserva Biológica Augusto Ruschi ☐ BR 203 Hk55
Reserva Biológica Cordillera de Sama ☐ BOL 207 Gh56
Reserva Biológica de Pedra Talhada ☐ BR 201 Jb50
Reserva Biológica da Serra Negra ☐ BR 201 Ja54
Reserva Biológica de Córrego Grande ☐ BR 203 Ja55
Reserva Biológica de Saltinho ☐ BR 201 Jc50
Reserva Biológica de Santa Isabel ☐ BR 201 Jb51
Reserva Biológica de Sooretama ☐ BR 203 Ja55
Reserva Biológica de Una ☐ BR 203 Ja53
Reserva Biológica do Abufari ☐ BR 198 Gj48
Reserva Biológica do Combolos ☐ BR 203 Hk55
Reserva Biológica do Córrego do Veado ☐ BR 203 Hk55
Reserva Biológica do Guaporé ☐ BR 206 Gj52
Reserva Biológica do Gurupi ☐ BR 200 Hg47
Reserva Biológica do Jaru ☐ BR 198 Gh50
Reserva Biológica do Lago Piratuba ☐ BR 194 Hd45
Reserva Biológica do Poço das Antas ☐ BR 205 Hj57
Reserva Biológica do Rio Trombetas ☐ BR 194 Hb46
Reserva Biológica do Tapirapé ☐ BR 200 He48
Reserva Biológica do Tinguá ☐ BR 205 Hj57
Reserva Biológica do Uatumã ☐ BR 194 Ha46
Reserva Biológica Guaribas ☐ BR 201 Jc49
Reserva Biológica Marinha do Arvoredo ☐ BR 205 Hf59
Reserva Biológica Nacas ☐ RCH 208 Ge65
Reserva Biológica Río Blanco ☐ RCH 208 Ge62
Reserva Biológica Río Clarillo ☐ RCH 208 Ge62
Reserva Biósfera Isla San Pedro Martir ☐ MEX (BC) Ed31
Reserva Biósfera Sierra del Rosario ☐ C 179 Fj34
Reserva de Ambriz ☐ ANG 148 Lg49
Reserva de Biósfera Menorca ☐ E 29 Lc50
Reserva de Biósfera Calakmul ☐ MEX 183 Ff36
Reserva de la Biósfera de Río Platano ☐ HN 185 Fh38
Reserva de la Biósfera de S. de Las Minas ☐ GCA 184 Ff38
Reserva de la Biósfera el Pinacate y Gran Desierto de Altar ☐ MEX 180 Ed30
Reserva de la Biósfera el Vizcaíno ☐ MEX (BC) Ed32
Reserva de la Biósfera Estación Biológica del Beni ☐ BOL 206 Gg53
Reserva de la Biósfera Maya ☐ GCA 183 Ff37
Reserva de la Biósfera Montes Azules ☐ MEX 183 Fe37
Reserva de la Biósfera Pantanos de Centla ☐ MEX 183 Fe36
Reserva de la Biósfera Pilón Lajas ☐ BOL 206 Gg53
Reserva de la Biósfera Sian Ka'an ☐ MEX 183 Fg36
Reserva de las Biósfera Bosawas ☐ NIC 185 Fh38
Reserva de Maputo ☐ MOC 155 Mg59
Reserva de Marromeu ☐ MOC 153 Mh55
Reserva de Namibe ☐ ANG 150 Lg53
Reserva de Prod. Faunística Cuyabeno ☐ EC 196 Gb46
Reserva do Cabo Pomene ☐ MOC 153 Mh57
Reserva do Gilé ☐ MOC 153 Mk54
Reserva do Niassa ☐ MOC 147 Mj52

Reserva do Sanga ☐ MOC 146 Mh50
Reserva Ecológica El Angel ☐ EC 196 Gb45
Reserva Ecológica Juami-Japurá ☐ BR 198 Gg47
Reserva Ecológica Jutaí-Solimões ☐ BR 198 Gg47
Reserva Especial de la Biósfera Islas del Golfo de California ☐ MEX Ed31
Reserva Especial de la Biósfera Islas del Golfo de California ☐ MEX Ee33
Reserva Especial de la Biósfera IslaThurón ☐ MEX 180 Ed31
Reserva Especial do Milando ☐ ANG 148 Lj50
Reserva Forestal do Río Negro ☐ BR 199 Hb55
Reserva Forestal Mundurucânia ☐ BR 199 Ha49
Reserva Forestal Sipapo ☐ YV 193 Gg43
Reserva Marina Galápagos, P.N. y ☐ EC 188 Fe47
Reserva Nacional Alacalufes ☐ RCH 210 Gc72
Reserva Nacional Alto Bío Bío ☐ RCH 208 Ge65
Reserva Nacional Amazónica Manuripi Heath ☐ BOL 198 Gg51
Reserva Nacional Archipiélago de las Guaitecas ☐ RCH 210 Gc69
Reserva Nacional Calipuy ☐ PE 197 Ga50
Reserva Nacional Cerro Castillo ☐ RCH 210 Gd68
Reserva Nacional Coihaique ☐ RCH 210 Gd68
Reserva Nacional de Fauna Andina Eduardo Avaroa ☐ BOL 207 Gg56
Reserva Nacional de Muela ☐ E 29 Ku51
Reserva Nacional de Paracas ☐ PE 197 Gb53
Reserva Nacional Estricta Colonia Benítez ☐ RA 204 Ha59
Reserva Nacional Estricta El Leoncito ☐ RA 208 Gf62
Reserva Nacional Estricta San Antonio ☐ RA 204 Hd58
Reserva Nacional Federico Albert ☐ RCH 208 Gd63
Reserva Nacional Formosa ☐ RA 207 Gk56
Reserva Nacional Gil del Vilches ☐ RCH 208 Ge63
Reserva Nacional Hernando de Magallanes ☐ RCH 210 Gd72
Reserva Nacional Junín ☐ PE 197 Gc51
Reserva Nacional Kalatalixar ☐ RCH 210 Gc70
Reserva Nacional Lachay ☐ PE 197 Gb51
Reserva Nacional Lago Carlota ☐ RCH 210 Gd68
Reserva Nacional Lago Cochrane ☐ RCH 210 Gd69
Reserva Nacional Lago las Torres ☐ RCH 210 Gd68
Reserva Nacional Lago Palena ☐ RCH 210 Gd67
Reserva Nacional Lago Peñuelas ☐ RCH 208 Ge62
Reserva Nacional Lago Rosselot ☐ RCH 140 Ld42
Reserva Nacional Laguna Torca ☐ RCH 210 Gd72
Reserva Nacional Laguna Varillar ☐ RCH 210 Gd72
Reserva Nacional Las Chinchillas ☐ RCH 208 Ge61
Reserva Nacional Las Vicuñas ☐ RCH 206 Gf55
Reserva Nacional L.General Carrera ☐ RCH 210 Gd69
Reserva Nacional Los Flamencos ☐ RCH 207 Gg57
Reserva Nacional Los Ruiles ☐ RCH 208 Gd63
Reserva Nacional Malalcahuello ☐ RCH 208 Ge65
Reserva Nacional Malleco ☐ RCH 208 Ge65
Reserva Nacional Nalcas ☐ RCH 208 Ge65
Reserva Nacional Natural Nukak ☐ CO 192 Gd44
Reserva Nacional Natural Puinawai ☐ CO 192 Ge44
Reserva Nacional Nuble ☐ RCH 208 Ge64
Reserva Nacional Otamendi ☐ RA 209 Ha61
Reserva Nacional Pacaya-Samiria ☐ PE 196 Gd48
Reserva Nacional Pampa del Tamarugal ☐ RCH 206 Gf56
Reserva Nacional Pampa Galeras ☐ PE 197 Gc52
Reserva Nacional Paposo ☐ RCH 207 Ge58
Reserva Nacional Radal Siete Tazas ☐ RCH 208 Gd63
Reserva Nacional Ralco ☐ RCH 208 Ge64
Reserva Nacional Río Blanco ☐ RCH 208 Ge62
Reserva Nacional Río Clarillo ☐ RCH 208 Ge62
Reserva Nacional Río Los Cipreses ☐ RCH 208 Ge63
Reserva Nacional Salinas-Aguas Blanca ☐ PE 197 Ge54
Reserva Nacional Tariquia ☐ BOL 207 Gh56
Reserva Nacional Titicaca ☐ PE 206 Gf53
Reserva Nacional Valdivia ☐ RCH 208 Gd64

Réserve de Faune d'Arli ☐ BF 137 La40
Réserve de faune de Bahr Salamat ☐ TCH 139 Lk40
Reserve Island ☐ NZ 113 Td68
Réserve de faune de Binder-Léré ☐ TCH 140 Lh41
Réserve de Faune de Bontioli ☐ BF 137 Kj40
Réserve de faune de Dimonika ☐ RCB 148 Lg47
Réserve de faune de Fada Archei ☐ TCH 134 Ma37
Réserve de Faune de Kourtiagou ☐ BF 138 La40
Réserve de faune de Kpèssi ☐ TG 137 La41
Réserve de faune de la Ouandjia-Vakaga ☐ RCA 140 Md41
Réserve de faune de l'Aouk-Aoukale ☐ RCA 140 Ma41
Réserve de faune de la Yata-Ngaye ☐ RCA 140 Md41
Réserve de faune de l'Oti ☐ TG 137 La40
Réserve de faune de Mandélia ☐ TCH 139 Lh40
Réserve de faune de Mont Fouari ☐ RCB 148 Lf47
Réserve de faune de Nyanga-Nord ☐ RCB 148 Lg47
Réserve de faune de Pama ☐ BF 137 La40
Réserve de faune de Pangar et Djérem ☐ CAM 139 Lj43
Réserve de faune de Siniaka-Minia ☐ TCH 139 Lk40
Réserve de Faune de Tsoulou ☐ RCB 148 Lg47
Réserve de faune de Zemongo ☐ RCA 141 Mc42
Réserve de faune du Bas Chari ☐ TCH 139 Lh41
Réserve de faune du Dzanga-Sangha ☐ RCA 140 Lj44
Réserve de faune du Ferlo Nord ☐ SN 130 Kc38
Réserve de faune du Ferlo Sud ☐ SN 130 Kc39
Réserve de faune du Gribingui-Bamingui ☐ RCA 140 Lk42
Réserve de faune du Nana-Bamingui ☐ RCA 140 Ma42
Réserve de faune du N'Zo ☐ CI 137 Kg42
Réserve de faune du Sahel ☐ BF 137 Kk38
Réserve de faune du Singou ☐ BF 137 La40
Réserve de faune Hernando de Magallanes ☐ RCH 210 Gd72
Réserve de faune Ouadi Rimé-Ouadi Achim ☐ TCH 133 Lh36
Réserve de Fina ☐ RMM
Réserve de Gourma ☐ RMM 131 Kj38
Réserve de Kalfou ☐ CAM 139 Lh40
Réserve de Kéniébaoulé ☐ RMM 136 Kf39
Réserve de Kongassambougou ☐ RMM 136 Kf39
Réserve de la Faune de la Léfini ☐ RCB 148 Lh47
Réserve de la Montagne des Sources ☐ F (NCL) 118 Td57
Réserve de la Nana Barya ☐ RCA 140 Lj42
Réserve de Rabi-Ndogo ☐ G 148 Le47
Réserve de Wonga-Wongué ☐ G 148 Le46
Réserve de Badinko ☐ RMM 136 Kf39
Réserve du Bafing Makana ☐ RMM 136 Kc39
Réserve du Bassin inférieur de l'Ogooué ☐ G 148 Lf46
Réserve Duchénier ☐ CDN 176 Gf21
Réserve du Dja ☐ CAM 139 Lj44
Réserve Faunique Ashuapmushuan ☐ CDN 176 Gd21
Réserve faunique Assinica et des Lacs Albanel-Mistissini-et-Waconichi ☐ CDN 176 Gc20
Réserve Faunique de Matane et Dunière ☐ CDN 176 Gg21
Réserve faunique de Papineau-Labelle ☐ CDN 177 Gc22
Réserve faunique de Port-Cartier / Sept-Îles ☐ CDN 176 Gg20
Réserve Faunique de Rimouski ☐ CDN 176 Gf21
Réserve Faunique des Chic-Chocs ☐ CDN 176 Gh21
Réserve Faunique des Laurentides ☐ CDN 176 Ge21
Réserve Faunique La Vérendrye ☐ CDN 173 Gb22
Réserve Faunique Mastigouche ☐ CDN 176 Gd21
Réserve Faunique Portneuf ☐ CDN 176 Gd21
Réserve Faunique Rouge-Matawin ☐ CDN 176 Gc22
Réserve Faunique St-Maurice ☐ CDN 176 Gd22
Réserve floristique de Yangambi ☐ RDC 141 Mc45
Réserve forestière de Luki ☐ RDC 148 Lg48
Réserve (Hagar Nish Plateau) ☐ ER 135 Mj37
Réserve Manicouagan ☐ CDN 176 Gf20
Réserve Naturelle de Scandola ☐ F 34 Lj48
Réserve Naturelle Intégrale Dite Sanctuaire des Addax ☐ RN 132 Le36
Réserve naturelle intégrale du Mont Nimba ☐ CI/RG 136 Kf42
Réserve partiel du Bufalo ☐ ANG 150 Lg52
Réserve Marinas ☐ HN 184 Fg37
Réserve ☐ USA (SK) 169 Ef22
Réserve ☐ RMM 171 Er29
Réserve ☐ RCB 140 Lj45
Réserve de Biosphère ☐ RMM 137 Kj39
Réserve de Biosphère Arganeraie ☐ MA 124 Kf31
Réserve de Biosphère Oasis du Sud Marocain ☐ MA 125 Kh30
Réserve de Biosphère Mare aux Hippopotames ☐ BF 137 Kh40
Réserve de Campo ☐ CAM 138 Le44
Réserve de Douentza ☐ RMM 137 Kj38
Réserve de faune à Okapi ☐ RDC 141 Md44
Réserve de faune Bomu Occidentale ☐ RDC 141 Mc43
Réserve de faune Bomu Orientale ☐ RDC 141 Mc43
Réserve-de-Faune d'Abdoulaye ☐ TG 137 La41

Resistencia ☐ RA (CH) 204 Ha59
Resița ☐ RO 44 Mb45
Resko ☐ PL 40 Lq37
Resolution Island ☐ NZ 113 Fa04
Resplendor ☐ BR (MG) 203 Hk55
Restauração ☐ BR (RR) 194 Gk45
Restinga de Jurubatiba, P.N.do ☐ BR 203 Hk57
Restinga de Marambaia ☐ BR 205 Hh57
Restinga Seca ☐ BR (RS) 204 Hd60
Reszel ☐ PL 41 Mb36
Retalhuleu ☐ GCA 184 Fe38
Retém Atalaya ☐ RCH 208 Ge62
Retezat ☐ RO 44 Mc45
Retezat, P.N. ☐ RO 44 Mc45
Retford ☐ GB 21 Ku37
Rethel ☐ F 23 Lf41
Rethem ☐ D 32 Lk38
Réthimno ☐ GR 47 Me55
Reti ☐ PK 65 Oe31
Retie ☐ RDC 144 Mf44
Retiro ☐ BR (MT) 202 Hd52
Retreat ☐ AUS (QLD) 108 Sb58
Retretti ☐ FIN 38 Mk29
Retuerta del Bullaque ☐ E 27 Kq51
Return Islands ☐ USA (AK) 165 Cf10
Retz ☐ A 42 Lq42
Reungeut ☐ RI 92 Pj43
Réunion ☐ F 157 Nh56
Réunion ☐ 123 Nb12
Reus ☐ E 27 Lb49
Reuterstadt Stavenhagen ☐ D 32 Ln37
Reuthingen ☐ D 33 Lk42
Reutte ☐ A 34 Ll43
Reva ☐ USA (SD) 169 Ej23
Revda ☐ RUS 50 Nj16
Revdal ☐ N 16 Lk11
Revelganj ☐ IND (BIH) 83 Pc33
Revelstoke ☐ CDN 168 Ea20
Reventador, Volcán ☐ EC 196 Gb46
Revfülöp ☐ H 42 Ls44
Révia = Cassembe ☐ MOC 147 Mj52
Revigny-sur-Ornain ☐ F 23 Le42
Revillagigedo Channel ☐ USA 166 De18
Revillagigedo Island ☐ USA 166 De18
Revnice ☐ CZ 42 Lp41
Revúca ☐ SK 43 Ma42
Rewa ☐ IND (MPH) 83 Pa33
Rewa ☐ FIJI 119 Ua54
Rewa ☐ USA (SD) 169 Ee24
Rexburg ☐ USA (ID) 169 Ee24
Rey ☐ IR 62 Nf28
Rey Bouba ☐ CAM 139 Lh41
Reyes ☐ BOL 206 Gg52
Reyhanli ☐ TR 56 Mj27
Reykholt ☐ IS 18 Jt26
Reykholt ☐ IS 18 Jt26
Reykjadísur ☐ IS 18 Ka25
Reykjafjördur ☐ IS 18 Jj24
Reykjahlíð ☐ IS 18 Js27
Reykjanes Ridge ☐ 163 Jc06
Reykjanesta ☐ IS 18 Js27
Reynaga ☐ MEX (JLC) 182 Eh36
Reynoldsburg ☐ USA 173 Fj26
Reynolds Range ☐ AUS 103 Rg57
Rezé ☐ F 24 Kt43
Rézekne ☐ LV 39 Mh34
Rezekne ☐ LV 39 Mh34
Rezina ☐ MD 49 Mg22
Rezvan ☐ IR 62 Nf27
Rezvan Shahr ☐ IR 57 Ne27
Rgotina ☐ SCG 44 Mc46
Rhafsai ☐ MA 125 Kg28
Rhayader ☐ GB 21 Kr38
Rheda-Wiedenbrück ☐ D 32 Lj39
Rheinau ☐ D 33 Lh42
Rheine ☐ D 32 Lh38
Rheinfall ☐ CH 34 Lj43
Rheinfelden ☐ D 33 Lh43
Rheinland-Pfalz ☐ D 33 Lh42
Rheinstetten ☐ D 33 Lj42
Rhémiès ☐ DZ 126 Kq32
Rhinconich ☐ GB 20 Kq32
Rhin ☐ F 23 Lg43
Rhine ☐ 14 La05
Rhinelander ☐ USA (WI) 172 Ff23
Rhino Camp ☐ EAU 144 Mf44
Rhinow ☐ D 32 Ln38
Rho ☐ I 34 Lk45
Rhode Island ☐ USA 177 Ge25
Rhodes ☐ GR 47 Mj54
Rhodes ☐ ZA 155 Md60
Rhododendron ☐ USA (OR) 168 Dk23
Rhodope Mountains ☐ BG/GR 44 Md49
Rhön ☐ D 33 Lk40
Rhondda ☐ GB 21 Kr39
Rhône-Alpes ☐ F 25 Le45
Rhônegletscher ☐ CH 34 Lj44
Rhoufi ☐ DZ 126 Ld28
Rhourd-el-Baguel ☐ DZ 126 Ld30
Rhume ☐ D 32 Lh39
Rhyolite Ghost Town ☐ USA 170 Eb27

Ribarica ☐ BG 45 Me48
Ribat ☐ TN 126 Lf28
Ribatejo ☐ P 27 Km51
Ribat-el-Kheir ☐ MA 125 Kh29
Ribe ☐ DK 30 Lj35
Ribeauvillé ☐ F 25 Lg42
Ribeira + Santa Eugenia ☐ E 26 Km48
Ribeira da Cruz ☐ CV 136 Jh37
Ribeira Grande ☐ CV 136 Jh37
Ribeira Branco ☐ BR (SP) 205 Hf58
Ribeirão do Pinhal ☐ BR (PR) 207 Gf60
Ribeirão Preto ☐ BR (SP) 203 Hg56
Ribera ☐ I 36 Lo53
Ribérac ☐ F 24 La44
Ribera Cascalheira ☐ BR (MT) 200 Hb52
Ribera des Néves ☐ BR (MG) 203 Hh55
Riberalta ☐ BOL 198 Gg51
Ribeirão ☐ BR (PE) 201 Jc50
Ribera Escale ☐ BR (SP) 205 Hf58
Ribérica ☐ SLO 42 Lp44
Ribnica ☐ BIH 44 Ls46
Ribnitz-Damgarten ☐ D 32 Lm36
Ribnovo ☐ BG 130 Kc38
Řičany ☐ CZ 42 Lp41
Ricardo Flores Magón ☐ MEX (CHH) 180 Eg31
Ricaurte ☐ CO 192 Gc44
Riccarton Park ☐ NZ 113 Tg67
Riccia ☐ I 37 Lp49
Rice ☐ USA (CA) 170 Ee28
Rice Bowls ☐ USA (HI) 170 Cb35
Rice Lake ☐ USA (WI) 172 Fe23
Rice Lake N.W.R. ☐ USA 172 Fd22
Richan ☐ CDN (ON) 172 Fd21
Richards Bay ☐ ZA 155 Mg60
Richards Bay Nature Reserve ☐ ZA 155 Mg60
Richardsbaai ☐ ZA 155 Mg60
Richardson, Cerro ☐ RA/RCH 210 Gd69
Richardson Highway ☐ USA (AK) 165 Ch14
Richardson Mountains ☐ CDN 167 Ea13
Richdale ☐ CDN (AB) 169 Ee20
Richelieu ☐ F 24 La44
Richey ☐ USA (MT) 169 Ee22
Richfield ☐ USA (ID) 168 Ec24
Richfield ☐ USA (NC) 178 Fk28
Richfield ☐ USA (UT) 171 Ee26
Richibucto ☐ CDN (NB) 176 Gh22
Rich Lake ☐ CDN (AB) 169 Ee18
Richland ☐ USA (GA) 178 Fh29
Richland ☐ USA (OR) 168 Ea23
Richland ☐ USA (WA) 168 Ea22
Richland Center ☐ USA (WI) 172 Fe24
Richlands ☐ USA (VA) 178 Fk27
Richmond ☐ AUS (NSW) 111 Sf62
Richmond ☐ AUS (QLD) 107 Sb56
Richmond ☐ CDN (BC) 168 Dj21
Richmond ☐ GB 21 Kt36
Richmond ☐ GB 21 Ku39
Richmond ☐ USA (CA) 170 Dj27
Richmond ☐ USA (IN) 175 Fh26
Richmond ☐ USA (KY) 175 Fh27
Richmond ☐ USA (VA) 177 Gb27
Richmond Hill ☐ USA (QLD) 109 Sc57
Richmond Hill ☐ CDN (ON) 173 Ga24
Richmond Hill ☐ USA (VA) 178 Fk30
Richmond International Raceway ☐ USA 177 Gb27
Richmont ☐ USA (MS) 175 Ff30
Richterswald N.P. ☐ ZA 154 Lk60
Richton ☐ USA (MS) 175 Ff30
Richwood ☐ USA (WV) 175 Fk26
Ricobayo ☐ E 26 Kp49
Ricran ☐ PE 197 Gc51
Ridderkerk ☐ NL 23 Le39
Riddle ☐ USA (OR) 168 Dj24
Rideau Hills ☐ CDN 177 Gb23
Ridgecrest ☐ USA (CA) 170 Eb28
Ridgeland ☐ USA (SC) 178 Fk29
Ridgeway ☐ USA (SC) 178 Fk28
Riding Mountain ☐ CDN 172 Ek20
Riding Mountain N.P. ☐ CDN 172 Ek20
Riebeekkasteel ☐ ZA 154 Lk62
Riebeekkastaad ☐ ZA 155 Md59
Riebook Oos ☐ ZA 155 Md62
Riecito ☐ YV 193 Gf40
Ried ☐ A 33 Lo43
Ried im Innkreis ☐ A 42 Lo43
Riegersburg ☐ A 35 Lq43
Riesa ☐ D 32 Lo39
Riesi ☐ I 37 Lp53
Rietavas ☐ LT 39 Mb35
Rietbron ☐ ZA 154 Mb61
Rietfontein ☐ ZA 154 Ma59
Rietfontein ☐ NAM 151 Ma58
Rieti ☐ I 36 Ln48
Rietschen ☐ D 32 Lp39
Rietveld Schröderhuis ☐ NL 23 Lf38
Rietvlei ☐ ZA 155 Md61
Rieupeyroux ☐ F 24 Lc45
Rieux ☐ F 25 Lb47
Rift Valley ☐ EAT/EAK 144 Mj47
Riga ☐☐ LV 39 Me34
Rigacikun ☐ WAN 138 Ld40
Rigan ☐ IR 64 Nk31
Rigestan ☐ AFG 64 Ob30
Riggins ☐ USA (ID) 168 Eb23
Rig Rig ☐ TCH 133 Lh38
Riihimäki ☐ FIN 38 Me30
Riihimäki ☐ FIN 38 Me30
Riiitasuo ☐ FIN 38 Mc29
Riisitunturin kansallispuisto ☐ FIN 16 Mg12
Rijau ☐ WAN 138 Lc39
Rijeka ☐ HR 35 Lp45
Rijeka Crnojevića ☐ SCG 44 Lt48
Rijksmuseum ☐ NL 23 Le38
Rijssen ☐ NL 23 Lg38
Rikubetsu ☐ J 77 Sb24
Rikuchu-Kaigan ☐ J 77 Sb25
Rikuzen-to ☐ J 77 Sa25
Rila ☐ BG 44 Md48
Rila, N.P. ☐ BG 44 Md48
Riley ☐ USA (OR) 168 Ea24
Rima ☐ WAN 138 Lc38
Rimagne, S.R. ☐ USA 170 Eb27
Rimah, Wadi ar ☐ KSA 58 Na29
Rimatara ☐ F 10 Cb12
Rimava ☐ SK 43 Ma42
Rimavská Sobota ☐ SK 43 Ma42
Rimba Panti Nature Reserve ☐ RI 93 Pk45

Rimbey ☐ CDN (AB) 169 Ec19
Rimbo ☐ S 31 Lt31
Rimforsa ☐ S 31 Lq32
Rimini ☐☐ I 35 Ln46
Rimini ☐ 46 Mb50
Rimouski ☐ CDN (QC) 176 Gf21
Rinbung ☐ CHN (TIB) 68 Pe31
Rindal ☐ N 16 Le14
Rindani ☐ S 31 Lq34
Ringaskiddy ☐ IRL 19 Kn39
Ringe ☐ DK 30 Ll35
Ringgold ☐ USA (LA) 174 Fd29
Ringgold Isles ☐ FJI 119 Ub54
Ringim ☐ WAN 138 Le39
Ringkøbing ☐ DK 30 Lj35
Ringkøbing Fjord ☐ DK 30 Lj35
Ringling Museum of Art ☐ USA 179 Fj32
Ring of Kerry ☐ IRL 19 Kk39
Ringsted ☐ DK 30 Lm35
Ringvassøy ☐ N 16 Lk11
Ringwood ☐ GB 21 Kt40
Rinia ☐ GR 47 Mf53
Rinia ☐ GR 47 Mf53
Rinjani ☐ RI 96 Qj50
Rinjani, Gunung ☐ RI 96 Qj50
Rinquiari ☐ CO 192 Gd44
Rintala ☐ RUS 30 Mk31
Rinteln ☐ D 32 Lk38
Río Abiseo, P.N. ☐☐ PE 196 Gb49
Río Andirio-Bridge ☐ GR 46 Mb52
Río Aragón ☐ E 28 Kt48
Río Areia, T.I. ☐ BR 204 Hd58
Río Ariapo ☐ BR (AM) 193 Gh45
Río Azul ☐ GCA 183 Ff37
Riobamba ☐ EC 196 Ga46
Río Bananal ☐ BR (ES) 203 Hk55
Río Bec ☐ MEX 183 Ff36
Río Benito ☐ GQ 138 Le45
Río-Biá ☐ BR 198 Gg48
Río Blanco ☐ BOL 206 Gj52
Río Branco ☐ BR (AC) 198 Gg50
Río Branco ☐ BR (MT) 202 Ha53
Río Branco ☐ ROU 204 Hd61
Río Blanco ☐ CO 192 Gd44
Río Blanco ☐ NIC 185 Fh39
Río Blanco ☐ CO 171
Río Blanco ☐ RA 207 Gf60
Río Blanco ☐ PE 196 Gd48
Río Blanco ☐ RA 199 Ha51
Río Blanco ☐ RA 200 Hh51
Río Bonito ☐ BR (RJ) 205 Hj57
Río Branco ☐ BR (PE) 201 Jc50
Río Brazo del Norte ☐ MEX 181 Ej31
Río Bueno ☐ JA 186 Gb36
Río Caribe ☐ YV 193 Gj40
Río Cahncalá ☐ MEX (CHP) 183 Fe37
Río Cauto ☐ C 179 Gb35
Río Cebullos ☐ RA (CD) 208 Gh61
Río Chico ☐ YV 193 Gh40
Río Claro ☐ BR (SP) 203 Hf57
Río Claro ☐ CR 185 Fj41
Río Colorado ☐ RA (RN) 209 Gk64
Río Conchas ☐ BR (MT) 202 Hc53
Río Corrientes ☐ EC 196 Gb47
Río Cuarto ☐ RA (CD) 208 Gh62
Río das Cobras, T.I. ☐ BR 204 Hd58
Río das Ostras ☐ BR (RJ) 203 Hj56
Río das Pedras ☐ MOC 153 Mh57
Río de Janeiro ☐ BR (RJ) 205 Hj57
Río de Janeiro ☐ BR 191 Hd12
Río de la Plata ☐ RA/ROU 209 Hb63
Río de los Sauces ☐ RA (CD) 208 Gh62
Río de Oro ☐ CO 192 Gd41
Río do Antônio ☐ BR (BA) 203 Hk53
Río do Pires ☐ BR (BA) 201 Hj52
Río do Prado ☐ BR (MG) 203 Hk54
Río do Jacuípe ☐ BR (BA) 201 Ja52
Río do Sul ☐ BR (SC) 205 Hf59
Río Douro ☐ P 26 Kn49
Río Dulce, P.N. ☐ GCA 184 Ff38
Río Ebro ☐ E 28 Ks48
Río Frío ☐ RA (CB) 208 Gf62
Río Frío Cave ☐ BH 184 Ff37
Río Gallegos ☐ RA (SC) 210 Gf72
Río Grande ☐ BOL 206 Gj55
Río Grande ☐ BR 200 Hj51
Río Grande ☐ BR (SE) 201 Ja51
Río Grande ☐ MEX (OAX)
Río Grande ☐ MEX (ZCT) 182 Ej34
Río Grande ☐ NIC 184 Fg39
Río Grande ☐ RA (TF) 210 Gg72
Río Grande ☐ RA (SJ) 208 Gf62
Río Grande ☐ RA (SC) 208 Gf58
Río Grande ☐ USA (PR) 187
Río Grande ☐ YV 193 Gj42
Río Grande ☐ YV 193 Gk42
Río Grande ☐ RA (SA) 207 Gj58

Río Grande City ☐ USA (TX) 181 Fa32
Río Grande de Tarija ☐ BOL/RA 207 Gh57
Río Grande do Norte ☐ BR 191 Ja10
Río Grande do Piauí ☐ BR (PI) 201 Hj49
Río Grande do Sul ☐ BR 191 Hd13
Río Grande Gorge ☐ USA 171 Eh27
Río Gregorio, T.I. ☐ BR 196 Ge50
Río Guadalquivir ☐ E 27 Ko54
Río Guadiana ☐ P 27 Kn53
Río Guaporé, T.I. ☐ BR 206 Gh52
Río Hato ☐ PA 185 Fk41
Río Hondo ☐ GCA 184 Ff38
Río Ichilo ☐ BOL 206 Gh54
Rioja ☐ PE 196 Gb49
Río Jaramá ☐ E 27 Kr50
Río Jaú, P.N. do ☐ BR 198 Gj47
Río Júcar ☐ E 29 Ku51
Río Lagartos ☐ MEX (YT) 183 Ff35
Río Largo ☐ BR (AL) 201 Jc50
Río Lindo ☐ HN 184 Ff38
Riom ☐ F 25 Ld45
Río Maina ☐ BR (SC) 205 Hf60
Río Maior ☐ P 27 Km51
Río Mayo ☐ RA (CB) 210 Ge68
Río Mequens, T.I. ☐ BR 206 Gk52
Riom-ès-Montagnes ☐ F 25 Lc45
Río Miño ☐ E/P 26 Km48
Río Negrinho ☐ BR (SC) 205 Hf59
Río Negro ☐ BOL 198 Gh51
Río Negro ☐ BR (MS) 202 Hc55
Río Negro ☐ CO 192 Gc42
Río Negro ☐ CO 192 Gc44
Río Negro ☐ PY 204 Hb58
Río Negro ☐ RA 208 Hb59
Río Negro ☐ RCH 208 Gd66
Río Negro ☐ ROU 204 Hb62
Río Negro Ocáia, T.I. ☐ BR 198 Gh51
Río Nionego ☐ CO 192 Gc44
Río Nexpa ☐ MEX 182 Ej37
Río Novo ☐ BR (MG) 203 Hj56
Río Paranaíba ☐ BR 203 Hg55
Río Pardo ☐ BR (RS) 204 Hd60
Río Pardo das Minas ☐ BR 203 Hj53
Río Paru d'Este, T.I. ☐ BR 194 Hc45
Río Pico ☐ RA (CB) 210 Ge68
Río Pilcomayo, P.N. ☐ RA 204 Ha58
Río Pindaré, T.I. ☐ BR 200 Hh47
Río Platano ☐ HN 185 Fh38
Río Pomba ☐ BR (MG) 203 Hj56
Río Preto da Eva ☐ BR (AM) 198 Ha47
Ríobanco ☐ CO 192 Gd44
Río Primero ☐ RA (CD) 209 Gj61
Río Quente ☐ BR 202 Hf54
Río Rancho ☐ USA (NM) 171 Eg26
Río Seco ☐ YV 192 Ge40
Río Segundo ☐ RA (CD) 207 Gj61
Río Segura ☐ E 27 Ks52
Río Sereno ☐ PA 185 Fj41
Río Simpson, P.N. ☐ RCH 210 Gd68
Río South/Juan ☐ DOM 186 Ge36
Ríosucio ☐ CO 192 Gb42
Ríosucio ☐ CO 192 Gc44
Río Tajo ☐ E 27 Kr50
Río Teá, T.I. ☐ BR 198 Gg46
Río Tercero ☐ RA (CD) 208 Gh62
Río Tigre ☐ EC 196 Gb47
Río Tinto ☐ BR (PB) 201 Jc49
Río Tocuyo ☐ YV 193 Gf40
Río Tuba ☐ RP 94 Qj42
Riouw ☐ RI 93 Qc45
Río Verde ☐ BR (GO) 202 He54
Río Verde ☐ EC 196 Ga46
Río Verde ☐ MEX (QTR) 183 Ff36
Ríoverde ☐ MEX (SLP) 182 Ek35
Río Verde de Mato Grosso ☐ BR (MS) 202 Hc55
Río Vermelho ☐ BR (MG) 203 Hj55
Río Viejo, P.N. ☐ YV 192 Ge40
Río Villegas ☐ RA (RN) 208 Ge66
Río Víso ☐ CO 192 Gd44
Rípac ☐ BIH 35 Lq46
Ripanj ☐ SCG 44 Ma46
Ripky ☐ UA 48 Mf20
Ripley ☐ USA (MS) 175 Ff28
Ripley ☐ USA (TN) 175 Ff28
Ripley ☐ USA (WV) 175 Fk26
Ripoll ☐ E 29 Lc48
Ripon ☐ GB 21 Kt36
Riponpet ☐ IND (KTK) 84 Oh39
Rippinville ☐ USA 177 Gc23
Ripplebrook ☐ USA 168 Dj23
Riquewihr ☐☐ F 25 Lh42
Rireibo do Pinhal ☐ BR (BA) 201 Ja51
Risalpur ☐ PK 65 Og28
Risåsk ☐ S 16 Lh13
Riscal de California ☐ MEX 180 Ec31
Riscle ☐ F 24 Ku47
Rishikesh ☐ IND (UTT) 81 Ok30
Rishiri ☐ J 77 Sa23
Rishiri-Rebun-Sarobetsu N.P. ☐ J 77 Sa23
Rishiri-to ☐ J 77 Sa23
Rising Star ☐ USA (TX) 174 Fa29
Risin & Kellingin ☐ DK 18 Kn23
Risle ☐ F 22 La41
Rison ☐ USA (AR) 175 Fd29
Risør ☐ N 30 Lk32
Risoul 1850 ☐ F 25 Lg46
Rissa ☐ N 16 Lj14
Rissani ☐ MA 125 Kh30
Risti ☐ EST 38 Md32
Ristna ☐ EST 38 Mc32
Ristijärvi ☐ FIN 16 Mg13
Ristilä ☐ FIN 38 Mg28
Ristna range ☐ AUS 104 Qk57
Ristna River ☐ AUS (NT) 106 Rj54
Robe ☐ AUS (SA) 110 Rk64
Roebe ☐ ETH 142 Na42
Röbel ☐ D 32 Ln37
Robert Lee ☐ USA (TX) 174 Ek30
Robert's Arm ☐ CDN (NF) 177 Hd21
Roberts Creek Mtn. ☐ USA 170 Eb26
Robertsfors ☐ S 16 Ma13
Robertsganj ☐ IND (UPH) 83 Pb33
Robertson ☐ ZA 154 Lk62
Robertson ☐ LB 136 Ke42
Roberts Town ☐ USA 110 Nd62
Robertval ☐ CDN (QC) 176 Gd21
Robi ☐ ETH 142 Na42
Robinson ☐ AUS (QLD) 107 Sb55
Robinson Camp ☐ ZW 151 Me55
Robinson Crusoe, I. ☐ RCH 208 Gc63
Robinson, Mount ☐ AUS 102 Qk57
Robinson River ☐ AUS (NT) 106 Rj54
Robinson River ☐ PNG 116 Se51
Robledo ☐ E 27 Kr51
Robledo de Chavela ☐ E 27 Kq50
Roblin ☐ CDN (MB) 172 Ek20
Robore ☐ BOL 207 Ha54
Robrecht ☐ D 32 Lk39
Robowakatas ☐ RI 114 Rh46
Robore ☐ BOL 207 Ha54
Robsart ☐ CDN (SK) 169 Ef21
Robson, Mount ☐ USA 168 Ea19
Robstown ☐ USA (TX) 181 Fb32
Rocamadour ☐☐ F 24 Lb46

Rocanville ☐ CDN (SK) 172 Ek20
Roca Redonda ▲ EC 197 Fe45
Roça Tapirapé ◉ BR (PA) 200 He50
Roccadàspide ◉ I 37 Lq50
Roccaimperiale ◉ I 37 Lr50
Roccacamena ◉ I 36 Lo53
Roccastrada ◉ I 34 Lm47
Roccella Iònica ◉ I 37 Lr52
Rocha ◉ ROU 209 Hc63
Rochdale ◉ GB 21 Ks37
Roche Cabrit ☐ F (GF) 194 Hd43
Rochechouart ◉ F 24 La45
Rochedo ◉ BR (MS) 202 Hc55
Rochefort ◉ B 23 Lf40
Rochefort ◉ F 24 Ku45
Rochefort ◉ F 24 Ku45
Rochefort ◉ USA (IL) 173 Ff25
Rocher Ako'akas ☐ CAM 139 Lf44
Rocher Corneille ▲ F 25 Ld46
Rocher d'Ifandana ☐ RM 157 Nd56
Rocher du Mézessé ☐ CAM 139 Lg44
Rocher River ◉ CDN 167 Ed15
Rochesserivière ◉ F 25 Lc46
Rochester ◉ GB 21 La39
Rochester ◉ USA (MN) 173 Fg25
Rochester ◉ USA (MN) 172 Fd23
Rochester ◉ USA (NH) 177 Gd24
Rochester ◉ USA (NY) 177 Gb24
Roche Tado ☐ F (GF) 194 Hd43
Rochlitz ◉ D 32 Ln39
Rock Creek ◉ CDN (BC)
Rock Creek ◉ CDN (YT) 165 Da13
Rockdale ◉ USA (TN) 174 Fa28
Rockdale ◉ USA (TX) 174 Fb30
Rockefeller Plateau ☐ 14 Ka04
Rock Engravings ☐ NAM 154 Lt59
Rock Engravings ☐ NAM
Rock Falls ◉ USA (IL) 173 Ff25
Rockford ◉ USA (AL) 175 Fg28
Rockford ◉ USA (IL) 173 Ff24
Rock Fort Temple (Trichy) ☐ IND 84 Ok40
Rockglen ◉ CDN (SK) 169 Ej21
Rockhampton ◉ AUS (QLD) 109 Sf57
Rockhampton Downs ◉ AUS (NT) 106 Rh55
Rock Hill ◉ USA (SC) 178 Fk28
Rockingham ◉ AUS (WA) 104 Qh62
Rockingham ◉ USA (NC) 178 Ga28
Rockingham Bay ☐ AUS (QLD) 107 Sd55
Rockland ◉ USA (ND) 172 Fa21
Rockland ◉ CDN (ON) 177 Gc23
Rockland ◉ USA (MA) 177 Gf23
Rock 'n' Roll Hall of Fame (Cleveland) ☐ USA
Rock of Cashel ☐ IRL 19 Kn38
Rock Paintings ☐ LS 155 Me61
Rock Paintings ☐ RB 155 Mc58
Rock Paintings ☐ ZA 154 Ma61
Rock Port ◉ USA (MO) 174 Fc25
Rockport ◉ USA (TX) 181 Fb31
Rock Rapids ◉ USA (IA) 172 Fb24
Rock River ◉ USA (WY) 171 Eh25
Rock Sound ◉ BS 179 Gb33
Rock Springs ◉ USA (MT)
Rock Springs ◉ USA (TX)
Rock Springs ◉ USA (WY) 171 Ef25
Rockstone ◉ GUY 194 Ha42
Rockton ◉ AUS (NSW) 111 Se64
Rockville ◉ USA (IN) 175 Fg26
Rockville ◉ USA (ID) 171 Ed26
Rockwood ◉ USA (ME) 177 Gf23
Rockwood ◉ USA (TN) 175 Fh28
Rocky Boy ◉ USA (MT) 169 Ef21
Rocky Boy Ind. Res. ☐ USA 169 Ef21
Rocky Ford ◉ USA (CO) 174 Ej26
Rocky Gully ◉ AUS (WA) 104 Qj63
Rocky Island ◉ ET 129 Mj34
Rocky Mount ◉ USA (NC) 178 Gb28
Rocky Mount ◉ USA (VA) 178 Ga27
Rocky Mountain House ◉ CDN (AB) 169 Ec19
Rocky Mountain N.P. ☐ USA 171 Eh25
Rocky Mountains ☐ CDN/USA 160 Db04
Rocky Mtns. Forest Reserve ☐ CDN 169 Ec20
Rocky Mtns. House N.H.S. ☐ CDN 168 Eb19
Rocky Point ◉ USA (AK) 164 Bj13
Roda Velha ◉ BR (BA) 200 Hd52
Rocroi ◉ F 23 Le41
Roda Velha ◉ BR (BA) 200 Hd52
Roddickton ◉ CDN 177 Hb20
Rödeby ◉ S 31 Lq34
Redbyhavn ◉ DK 30 Lm36
Roddickton ◉ CDN 177 Hb20
Rodel ☐ GB 20 Kn33
Rodeo ◉ RA (SJ) 207 Gf61
Rodeo ◉ USA (NM) 171 Ef30
Rodez ◉ F 25 Lc46
Rodi Gargànico ◉ I 37 Lr49
Rodina Mat ☐ UA 49 Mf20
Roding ◉ D 33 Ln42
Rodna ◉ RO 43 Me43
Rodna, P.N. ☐ RO 43 Me43
Rodniki ◉ RUS 38 Na17
Rodolivos ◉ GR 45 Md56
Ródos ☐ GR 47 Mj54
Ródos ☐ GR 47 Mj54
Rodovia Perimetral Norte ☐ BR 194 Hb45
Redvig ◉ DK 30 Ln35
Roebourne ◉ AUS (WA) 102 Qj56
Roebuck Plains ◉ AUS (WA) 102 Rb54
Roedtan ◉ ZA 155 Me58
Roela ◉ EST 38 Mg31
Roermond ◉ NL 23 Lf39
Roeselare ◉ B 23 Ld40
Roesveltpiek ◉ SME 194 Hc44
Roesti ◉ RO 44 Me46
Roetgen ◉ D 32 Lg40
Rofia ☐ WAN 138 Le40
Rogaˇ ◉ HR 35 Lr47
Rogaˇčevka ◉ RUS 48 Mk20
Rogačica ◉ SCG 44 Lu46
Rogaguado ◉ BOL 206 Gh52
Rogalinski Park Krajobrazowy ☐ PL 40 Lr38
Rogatec ◉ SLO 42 Lq44
Rogatica ◉ BIH 44 Lu47
Rogers ◉ USA (AR) 174 Fc27
Rogers City ◉ USA (MI) 173 Fj23
Rogers Pass ◉ CDN (BC) 168 Eb20
Rogersville ◉ CDN (NB) 176 Gh22
Rogo ◉ WAN 138 Ld40

Rogone ☐ MOC 153 Mj53
Rogovo ◉ RUS 39 Mj33
Rogowo ◉ PL 40 Ls38
Rogoz ◉ RO 43 Md43
Rogoźnica ◉ PL 41 Mc38
Rogoźno ◉ PL 40 Lr38
Rogun ◉ WAN 138 Ld41
Rohan ◉ F 22 Ks42
Rohat ◉ IND (RJT) 82 Og33
Rohatyn ◉ UA 43 Me41
Rohoźník ◉ SK 42 Ls42
Rohrbach ◉ A 42 Lp42
Rohrbachs-Bitche ◉ F 23 Lh41
Rohri ◉ PK 65 Oe32
Rohtak ◉ IND (HYA) 80 Oj31
Rohtas ◉ IND 83 Pb33
Rohtas Fort ☐ PK 65 Og29
Rohukúla ◉ EST 38 Me31
Roiunerme ◉ EST 38 Me31
Roi Et ◉ THA 89 Qb37
Roismala ◉ FIN 38 Mc29
Roissy ◉ F 23 Lc42
Roja ☐ RA (BA) 209 Gk63
Rojhan ◉ PK 65 Oe31
Roka ◉ EAK 145 Mk47
Rokan ◉ RI 93 Qa45
Rokiciny ◉ PL 41 Lu39
Rokiškis ◉ LT 39 Mf35
Rokkasho ◉ J 77 Sb32
Rokokomoko ◉ RI 97 Rb48
Rokomoko ◉ RI 97 Rb48
Rokuan kansallispuisto ☐ FIN 16 Md13
Rokycany ◉ CZ 42 Lo41
Rokytne ◉ UA 48 Mf39
Roland ◉ CDN (MB) 172 Fb21
Roland in Bremen ☐ D 32 Lj38
Roldal ◉ N 30 Lg31
Roldan ◉ RA (SF) 209 Gk62
Rolette ◉ USA (ND) 172 Fa21
Rolim de Moura ☐ BR (RO) 198 Gk51
Rolla ◉ USA (OK) 174 Fa28
Rolla ◉ USA (MO) 174 Fe27
Rolla ◉ USA (ND) 172 Fa21
Rolleston ◉ AUS (QLD) 109 Se58
Rollet ◉ CDN (QC) 173 Ga22
Rolling Fork ◉ USA (MS)
Rollingstone ◉ AUS (QLD) 107 Sd55
Rolling Hills ◉ CDN (AB) 169 Ee20
Rolling R. Ind. Res. ☐ CDN
Rollo ◉ BF 137 Kk39
Roluos Group ☐ K 89 Qc39
Roma ◉ AUS (QLD) 109 Se59
Roma ◉ LS 155 Me61
Roma ☐ S 31 Lt33
Roma ◉ USA (TX) 181 Fa32
Romaine ◉ CDN (QC) 176 Gb20
Roman ◉ RO 43 Mf43
Roman ◉ BG 45 Md47
Roman Baths ☐ GB 21 Ks39
Romanche Gap ☐ 8 Ka09
Romang ◉ RA (SF) 204 Ha60
Romang ◉ RI 97 Rd49
Romània ◉ RO 15 Ma05
Romanovka ◉ RUS (BUR)
Romanshorn ◉ CH 34 Lk43
Romans-sur-Isère ◉ F 25 Lf45
Romanthische Straße ☐ D 33 Lk41
Romanzof Mountains ☐ USA (AK) 165 Ch11
Romària ◉ BR (MG) 203 Hg55
Romblon ◉ RP 90 Rb39
Romblon Island ☐ RP 90 Rb39
Romblon Strait ☐ RP 90 Rb39
Rome ◉ I 36 Ln49
Rome ◉ USA (GA) 175 Fh28
Romilly-sur-Seine ◉ F 23 Ld42
Romiton ◉ UZ 63 Oc26
Rommlott-vár ☐ H 42 Ls44
Rommani ◉ MA 125 Kh29
Romney ◉ USA (WV) 177 Ga26
Romny ◉ RUS 71 Ra20
Romny ◉ UA 48 Mg20
Rømø ☐ DK 30 Lj35
Rømo ◉ RI 94 Qe45
Romodan ◉ UA 49 Mg21
Romorantin-Lanthenay ◉ F 25 Lb43
Rømø Sommerland ☐ DK 30 Lj35
Romsdalen ☐ N 17 Ld14
Romsey ◉ GB 21 Kt40
Rondo Calzada ☐ MEX (TB) 183 Fd37
Ronan ◉ USA (MT) 168 Ec22
Roncador Reef ☐ SOL 117 Sk49
Roncesvalles ◉ E 28 Kt47
Ronchamp ☐ F 25 Lg43
Roncigione ◉ I 36 Ln48
Ronda ◉ E 27 Kp54
Ronda Alta ◉ BR (RS) 204 Hd59
Rondane N. ☐ N 17 Le15
Rønde ◉ DK 30 Ll34
Rønde ◉ WG (RS) 200 Hf48
Rondônia ◉ BR 191 Gb11
Rondonópolis ◉ BR (MT) 202 Hc54
Rond-Point de Gaulle ☐ TCH 133 Lj36
Ronehamn ◉ S 31 Lt30
Rongai ◉ EAK 144 Mh46
Rong'an ◉ CHN (GZG) 74 Qe33
Rongbuk Cave ☐ THA 89 Qa39
Rongbuk Monastery ☐ CHN (SDG) 73 Pb28
Rongenj'o ◉ IND (MGA) 86 Pf33
Rong Kat ◉ THA 89 Qb38
Rong Kwang ◉ THA 87 Qa38
Ronglang ◉ CHN 73 Qd27
Rong Xian ◉ CHN (GZG) 74 Qf34
Rong Xian ◉ CHN (SCH) 74 Qa31
Ronien Daun Sam ☐ K 89 Qb39
Ron Morel Mus. ☐ CDN 173 Fj21
Ronne Ice Shelf ☐ ANT 6 Gd34
Ronne Ice Shelf ☐ ANT 6 Gd34
Rønne ◉ DK 31 Lp35
Rønnebæk ◉ DK 30 Ll35
Rønnöfors ◉ S 16 Lg14
Ronse ◉ B 23 Ld40
Roobikkraal ◉ ZA 155 Mc61
Roodewal ◉ NAM 154 Lh57
Rooilands ◉ ZA 155 Md59
Rooiklaap ◉ ZA 155 Ma58
Rook Sea ☐ ANT 6 Bd33
Rooira ◉ NAM 154 Lj58
Roorand ◉ NAM 154 Lj58
Roorkee ◉ IND (UTT) 81 Oj31
Roosboom ◉ ZA 155 Mf60
Roosendaal ◉ NL 23 Le39
Roosevelt ◉ USA (UT)

Roosevelt ◉ USA (UT) 171 Ef25
Roosevelt Campobello Internat. Park ☐ CDN 176 Gg23
Roosevelt Island ☐ 6 Bc34
Roosevelt, Mount ▲ CDN 166 Dh16
Roosevelt N.P. Nth. Unit ☐ USA 169 Ej22
Roosevelt N.P. Sth. Unit ☐ USA 169 Ej22
Roosevelt, T.I. ☐ BR 199 Gk51
Roosville ◉ CDN (BC) 168 Ec21
Root Lake ◉ CDN (MB) 169 Ek18
Ropar ◉ IND (PJB) 80 Oj30
Ropczyce ◉ PL 41 Mb40
Roper Bar ◉ AUS (NT) 106 Rh53
Roper River ◉ AUS 106 Rh53
Roper Valley ◉ AUS (NT) 106 Rh53
Ropotovo ◉ MK 44 Mb49
Roquefort ◉ F 24 Ku46
Roque Gonzales ◉ BR (RS) 204 Hc60
Roque Pérez ◉ RA (BA) 209 Ha63
Roquesteron ◉ F 25 Lg46
Roquetaillade ☐ F 24 Ku46
Roquetas de Mar ◉ E 27 Ks54
Roquetes ◉ E 29 La50
Roraima ◉ BR 191 Gb09
Roraima, Mount ▲ GUY/YV 194 Gk43
Rore ◉ BIH 35 Lr46
Rori ◉ IND (PJB) 80 Oh31
Rori ◉ RI 114 Rj46
Røros ◉ N 17 Lf14
Rørøs ◉ DK 30 Ll34
Rørvig ◉ DK 30 Ll34
Rørvik ◉ N 16 Lf13
Ros' ◉ BY 41 Me37
Roşal ◉ RUS 48 Mk18
Rosal de la Frontera ◉ E 27 Kn53
Rosales ◉ RP 90 Ra38
Rosalia ◉ USA (WA) 168 Eb22
Rosalindbank ☐ 185 Fk37
Rosamorada ◉ MEX (NYT) 181 Eh34
Rosans ◉ F 25 Lf46
Rosário ◉ BR (MA) 195 Hh47
Rosário ◉ DOM 186 Ge36
Rosario ◉ MEX (SI) 180 Ef32
Rosario ◉ PE 207 Ge58
Rosario ◉ PY 204 Hb58
Rosario ◉ RA (SF) 209 Gk62
Rosario ◉ ROU 209 Hb63
Rosario ◉ RP 90 Ra37
Rosario ◉ YV 192 Gd40
Rosario de la Frontera ◉ RA (SA) 207 Gh58
Rosário del Tala ◉ RA (ER) 207 Gn58
Rosário do Sul ◉ BR (RS) 204 Hc61
Rosario Oeste ◉ BR (MT) 202 Hb53
Rosarito ◉ MEX (BC) 180 Ec31
Rosarito ◉ MEX (BCS) 180 Ee32
Rosa Seamount ☐ 160 Ee32
Rosa Zarate ◉ EC 196 Ga45
Roscales ◉ E 26 Kq48
Roscoff ◉ F 22 Kr42
Roscommon ◉ IRL 19 Km37
Roscrea ◉ IRL 19 Kn38
Rose ◉ SCG 44 Lt48
Roseau ◉ USA (MN) 172 Fb21
Roseau ☐ WD 187 Gk38
Rose BlancheHarbour Le Cou ◉ CDN (NF) 177 Ha22
Rosebud ◉ USA (TX) 174 Fb30
Rosebud Ind. Res. ☐ USA 172 Ek24
Roseburg ◉ USA (OR) 168 Dj24
Rosedale ◉ AUS (QLD) 109 Sd57
Rosedown Plantation ☐ USA 175 Fe30
Rose Harbour ◉ CDN (BC) 166 Dd19
Rose Hill = Beau-Bassin ◉ MS 157 Nj11
Rosehill Gardens ☐ AUS (NSW) 111 Sf62
Rosemont Plantation ☐ USA
Rosenberg ◉ USA (TX) 174 Fc31
Rosendal ◉ N 30 Lg31
Rosendal ◉ ZA 155 Md60
Rosengarten ☐ D 32 Lk37
Rosenheim ◉ D 33 Ln43
Rose Prairie ◉ CDN 166 De18
Roses ◉ E 28 Ld48
Rosetta degli Abruzzi ◉ I 35 Lp48
Roseton ◉ USA (SK) 169 Eg20
Rosewood ◉ AUS (NT) 103 Re54
Rosh Pinah ◉ NAM 154 Lj59
Roshtkhar ◉ IR 64 Nk28
Rosia de Secas ◉ RO 43 Md44
Rosia Nouă ◉ RO 43 Mc44
Rosica ◉ BG 45 Mf47
Rosice ◉ CZ 42 Lr41
Rosignano Marittimo ◉ I 34 Ll47
Rosignano Solvay ◉ I 34 Ll47
Rosignol ◉ GUY 194 Ha42
Rosiori ◉ RO 43 Mh43
Rosiori de Vede ◉ RO 45 Me46
Roskilde ☐ DK 30 Ln35
Roskilde Rockfestival ☐ DK 30 Ln35
Roslagen ☐ S 31 Lt30
Roslavl' ◉ RUS 48 Mg19
Roslavl' ☐ RUS 48 Mg19
Rossan Point ◉ IRL 19 Km36
Rossarden ◉ AUS (TAS) 111 Sd66
Ross Bay Jtn. ◉ CDN (NF)
Ross-Bethio ◉ SN 130 Kb37
Ross Ice Shelf ☐ ANT 6 Bd35
Rössing ◉ NAM 150 Lh57
Rössing Uranium Mine ☐ NAM 150 Lh57
Rosson ◉ RI 114 Rj47
Røst ◉ N 16 Lg12

Rost ◉ N 16 Lg12
Rostaq ◉ AFG 63 Oe27
Røstlandet ◉ N 16 Lg12
Rosthern ◉ CDN (SK) 169 Eg19
Rostkala ◉ TJ 63 Of27
Rostock ◉ D 32 Ln36
Rostov ◉ RUS 48 Mk17
Rostov-na-Donu ◉ RUS 48 Mk22
Rostrenen ◉ F 22 Kr42
Røsvik ◉ N 16 Lh12
Roswell ◉ USA (GA) 175 Fh28
Roswell ◉ USA (NM) 171 Eh29
Rota ☐ IR 64 Ng30
Rota ◉ E 27 Ko54
Rot am See ◉ D 33 Ll41
Rota ◉ RUS 48 Nb19
Rotenburg (Tauber) ◉ D 33 Ll41
Rotenburg (Wümme) ◉ D 32 Lk37
Roth ◉ D 33 Lm42
Rotherham ◉ GB 21 Kt38
Rothesay ◉ GB 20 Kp35
Rothschild ◉ USA (WI) 172 Ff23
Roti ☐ RI 97 Rb51
Roti ◉ RI 97 Rb51
Rotifunk ◉ WAL 136 Kd41
Rotorua ◉ NZ 112 Tj65
Rotoskilderye ◉ ZA 154 Ma61
Rotondella ◉ I 37 Lr50
Rotoskilderye ☐ RB 155 Mc58
Rott ◉ D 33 Ln42
Rottenbüren ◉ D 33 Ll42
Rottenburg ◉ D 33 Lj42
Rottenburg ◉ D 33 Lj42
Rotterdam ◉ NL 23 Le39
Rottne ◉ S 31 Lq33
Rottneros ◉ S 30 Lo31
Rottnest Island ☐ AUS 104 Qh61
Rottumeroog ☐ NL 23 Lg37
Rottumerplaat ☐ NL 23 Lg37
Rottweil ◉ D 33 Lj42
Rotuma ◉ FJI 119 Tj52
Rötz ◉ D 33 Ln41
Roualist Bank 89 Qc41
Roubaix ◉ F 23 Ld40
Roucinice nad Labe ◉ CZ 42 Lp40
Roudouroù, Cerro ▲ RA 208 Ge65
Rouen ◉ F 23 Lb41
Rough Rock ◉ USA (AZ) 171 Ef27
Rouhia ◉ TN 126 Le28
Rouillac ◉ F 24 Ku45
Roulans ◉ F 25 Lg43
Round Mountain ◉ USA 109 Sg61
Round Mountain ◉ USA (TX) 174 Fa30
Round Rock ◉ USA (AZ) 171 Ef27
Round Rock ◉ USA (TX) 174 Fb30
Roundup ◉ USA (MT) 169 Ef22
Round Valley Ind. Res. ☐ USA 170 Dj26
Roura ◉ F (GF) 195 Hd43
Rousay ☐ GB 20 Kr31
Roussillon ◉ F 25 Le45
Roussillon ☐ F 25 Lf47
Route 66 ☐ USA 174 Fa28
Route 66 Mus. ☐ USA 174 Fa28
Route 66 (Missouri) ☐ USA 174 Fd27
Route 66 (New Mexico) ☐ USA 171 Eh28
Route 66 (New Mexico) ☐ USA 171 Eh28
Route 66 S.P. ☐ USA 175 Fe26
Route des Crètes ☐ F 25 Lg43
Route des Grandes Alpes ☐ F 25 Lg45
Route des Kasbahs ☐ MA
Route Napoléon ☐ F 25 Lg47
Route transsaharienne ☐ DZ/RN 132 Lc35
Rouxville ◉ ZA 155 Md61
Rouyn-Noranda ◉ CDN (QC) 173 Ga21
Rovaniemi ◉ FIN 16 Mc12
Rovato ◉ I 34 Ll45
Roven'k ◉ SK 43 Mb41
Roven'ki ◉ RUS 48 Mk21
Roveredo ◉ CH 34 Lk44
Rovereto ◉ I 34 Lm45
Rovershagen ◉ D 32 Ln36
Roverud ◉ N 30 Ln30
Rovigo ◉ I 34 Lm45
Rovinari ◉ RO 44 Md46
Rovine di Roselle ☐ I 34 Lm48
Rowena ◉ AUS (NSW) 109 Se60
Rowley Shoals ☐ AUS 102 Qk54
Rowy ◉ PL 40 Ls36
Roxas ◉ RP 90 Ra39
Roxas ◉ RP 90 Ra38
Roxas ◉ RP 90 Rb40
Roxboro ◉ USA (NC) 178 Ga27
Roxborough Downs ◉ AUS (QLD) 108 Rk57
Roxby Downs ◉ AUS (SA) 108 Rj61
Roy ◉ USA (NM) 171 Eh28
Roy ◉ USA (UT) 171 Ed25
Royal Bardia N.P. ☐ NEP 81 Pa31
Royal Botanic Gardens ☐ AUS
Royal Canal ☐ IRL 19 Kn37
Royal Chitwan N.P. ☐ NEP 81 Pc32
Royal Citadel (Polonnaruwa) ☐ CL 85 Pa42
Royal Easton Richmond ◉ USA
Royal Exhibition Building and Carlton Gardens ☐ AUS (VIC) 111 Sc64
Royal Gorge ☐ USA 171 Eh26
Royal Manas N.P. ☐ BHT 86 Pf32
Royal N.P. ☐ AUS 111 Sf63
Royal Palace ◉ RN 86 Pg33
Royal Palm Beach ◉ USA (FL) 179 Fk32
Royal Pavilion ☐ GB 21 Ku40
Royal Sukla Phanta N.P. ☐ NEP 81 Pa31
Royal Tombs ☐ VN 89 Qd37
Royal Tunbridge Wells ☐ GB 21 La39
Royan ◉ F 24 Kt45
Roy Hill ◉ AUS (WA) 102 Qk56
Røyken ◉ N 30 Ll30
Røykkfossen ☐ N 16 Ma11
Røyrvik ◉ N 16 Lg13
Royston ◉ GB 21 Kt38
Royston ◉ USA (GA) 178 Fj28
Rozaj ◉ SCG 44 Ma48
Rozan ◉ PL 41 Mb38
Rozay-en-Brie ◉ F 23 Lc42
Rozdol'ne ◉ UA 49 Mg23
RozdiI'ne ☐ UA 49 Mg23
Rozivka ◉ UA 49 Mh22
Rozkišovice pod Třemšínem ◉ CZ 42 Lo41
Rožňava ◉ SK 43 Ma42

Rožnov pod Radhoštěm ◉ CZ 42 Lt41
Rozogi ◉ PL 41 Mb37
Rozoy ◉ F 23 Le41
Rożok ◉ RUS 48 Nb19
Rozprza ◉ PL 41 Lu39
Rozrozławski P.N. ☐ PL 41 Md40
Roztoky ◉ CZ 42 Lp40
Rozvadov ◉ CZ 42 Ln41
Rsavsk ◉ UA 41 Mi40
Rrogozhinë ◉ AL 44 Lu49
Rti Kamenjak ☐ HR 35 Lo46
Rt Ploča ☐ HR 35 Lq47
Rt Rat ☐ HR 35 Lo46
Ruacana ◉ NAM 150 Lh54
Ruacana Falls ☐ NAM 150 Lh54
Ruaha N.P. ☐ EAT 146 Mh49
Ruahine Range ☐ NZ 113 Tj66
Ruapehu, Mount ▲ NZ 113 Th65
Ruapuke Island ☐ NZ 113 Te69
Ruatoria ◉ NZ 112 Tk64
Rub al Khali ☐ KSA 61 Ng33
Rubah ◉ EAT 146 Mf46
Rubatscherd ☐ N 30 Lf31
Rubeho Mountains ☐ EAT 147 Mj49
Rubengera ◉ RWA 146 Me47
Rubéš ◉ F 25 Lg43
Ruoveai ◉ FIN 38 Mc29
Rubi ◉ RDC 141 Mc44
Rubiás ◉ E 26 Kn47
Rubino ◉ CI 137 Kh42
Rubio ◉ YV 192 Gd42
Rubondo Island N.P. ☐ EAT 144 Mf47
Rubtsovsk ◉ RUS 54 Pa08
Ruby ◉ USA (AK) 165 Cc13
Ruby ◉ USA (WA) 168 Eb21
Ruby Mts. ☐ USA 170 Eb25
Ruby Mts. Scenic Area ☐ USA 170 Ec25
Ruby Range ☐ CDN 166 Da15
Rubys Inn ◉ USA (UT) 171 Ed27
Rubyvale ◉ AUS (QLD) 109 Sd57
Ruby Valley ◉ USA (NV) 170 Eb25
Rucaporoi, Cerro ▲ RA 208 Ge65
Rucăr ◉ RO 45 Mf45
Rucava ◉ LV 39 Mb34
Rucheng ◉ CHN (HUN) 75 Qg33
Ruciane-Nida ◉ PL 41 Mb37
Rudi ◉ IR 64 Ng28
Rudall ◉ AUS (SA) 110 Rj62
Rudall River N.P. ☐ AUS 102 Rb57
Rudarpur ◉ IND (UPH) 83 Pb32
Rudawa Śląska ☐ PL 41 Lt40
Rudauli ◉ IND (UPH) 83 Pa32
Rudaybá ◉ SUD 135 Mf38
Rudbar ◉ AFG 64 Ob30
Rude ◉ HR 35 Lq45
Ruda-Cervyns'ka ☐ UA 41 Mf39
Rudkøbing ◉ DK 30 Ll36
Rudky ◉ UA 43 Md41
Rudna ◉ PL 40 Lr39
Rudnaja Pristan' ◉ RUS 77 Rh23
Rudnichnyi ◉ KZ 64 Oa24
Rudnik ◉ SCG 44 Ma46
Rudny ◉ KZ 54 Na08
Rüdersdorf ◉ D 32 Lo38
Rüdesheim ◉ D 33 Lj41
Rudhauli ◉ IND (UPH) 83 Pb32
Rudilla ◉ E 29 Kt50
Rüdnitz ◉ D 32 Lo38
Rudňany ◉ SK 43 Ma42
Rudnica ◉ SCG 44 Ma47
Rudka ◉ UA 41 Mf39
Rudo ◉ BIH 44 Lu47
Rudolstadt ◉ D 32 Lm40
Rudsar ◉ IR 57 Nf27
Rue ◉ F 23 Lb40
Rueda ◉ E 26 Kq49
Ruente Nacional ☐ CO 192 Gd43
Rufa'a ◉ SUD 135 Mg38
Ruffec ◉ F 24 La44
Ruffin ◉ EAT 147 Mk49
Rufino ◉ BR (PA) 194 Hb46
Rufino ◉ RA (SF) 209 Gj63
Rufisque ◉ SN 130 Kb38
Rufunsa ◉ Z 152 Me53
Rugaata ◉ EAT 147 Mj48
Rugaata ◉ EAT 147 Mj48
Rugao ◉ CHN (JGS) 78 Ra29
Rugby ◉ GB 21 Kt38
Rugby ◉ USA (ND) 172 Fa21
Rügen ☐ D 32 Ln36
Rügen ☐ D 32 La42
Rugombo ◉ BU 146 Me47
Ruhengeri ◉ RWA 146 Me47
Ruhland ◉ D 32 Lo39
Ruhner Berg ▲ D 32 Lm37
Ruhnu saar ☐ EST 39 Md33
Ruhr ☐ D 32 Lh39
Ruhuna N.P. ☐ CL 85 Pa42
Ruicheng ◉ CHN (JGX) 75 Qe31
Ruidera ◉ E 27 Ks52
Ruidoso ◉ USA (NM) 171 Eh30
Ruidoso Downs ◉ USA (NM) 171 Eh30
Ruili ◉ CHN (YUN) 86 Pj33
Ruines d'Assodé ☐ RN 132 Le36
Ruines de Loropéni ☐ BF 137 Kj40
Ruines d'Empúries ☐ E 29 Ld48
Ruines de Ouara ☐ TCH 134 Ma37
Ruiru ◉ EAK 144 Mj46
Ruisbroek ◉ B 23 Le40
Ruiz, Nevado de ▲ CO 192 Gc43
Rüjiena ◉ LV 39 Mf33
Rukubule ◉ EAT 144 Mf47
Rukumkot ◉ NEP 83 Pb31
Rukungiri ◉ EAU 144 Me46
Rukwa ☐ EAT 146 Mf50
Rum ◉ USA (MN) 172 Fd23
Rum ☐ GB 20 Ko34
Ruma ◉ SCG 44 Lu45
Ruma ◉ WAN 138 Ld39
Rumah Anyi ◉ MAL 94 Qf45
Rumah Kutai ◉ MAL 94 Qg45
Rumah Layang ◉ MAL 94 Qe44
Rumah Maya ◉ MAL 94 Qd44
Rumahtinggih ◉ RI 115 Sa49
Rumbek ◉ SUD 141 Me41
Rumburk ◉ CZ 40 Lp40
Rumcica ☐ RUS 48 Mj18
Rum Cay ☐ BS 186 Gc34

Rumeila ◉ SUD 135 Mj39
Rumia ◉ PL 40 Ls36
Rumilly ◉ F 25 Lf45
Rumoi ◉ J 77 Sa24
Rumpi Hills ☐ CAM 138 Le43
Rumšiškes ◉ LT 39 Me35
Rumuruti ◉ EAK 144 Mj46
Runan ◉ CHN (HNN) 73 Qh29
Runde ◉ ZW 152 Mf55
Rundu ◉ NAM 150 Lk54
Runduma ◉ RI 97 Rc48
Runestan ◉ DK 30 Ln35
Rungsted ◉ DK 30 Ln35
Rungu ◉ RDC 141 Md44
Rungwa ☐ EAT 146 Mf49
Rungwa ◉ EAT 146 Mf49
Rungwa Game Reserve ☐ EAT 146 Mf49
Rungwe, Mount ▲ EAT 146 Mh50
Runiz ◉ IR 64 Ng31
Runmarö ☐ S 31 Lt32
Runtina ◉ S 31 Ls32
Runzewe ◉ EAT 144 Mf47
Ruokolahti ◉ FIN 38 Mj29
Ruokoärvi ◉ FIN 16 Mc12
Ruoqiang ◉ CHN (XUZ) 69 Pa27
Ruovesi ◉ FIN 38 Me29
Rupanyup ◉ AUS (VIC) 111 Sb64
Rupat ☐ RI 93 Qa45
Rupea ◉ RO 43 Mf44
Rupert ◉ USA (ID) 168 Ed24
Rupert ◉ EAT 147 Mj50
Rzeczenica ☐ PL 40 Ls37
Rupia ◉ EAT 147 Mj50
Rupia ◉ USA (ID) 168 Ed24
Ruppert Coast ☐ 6 Cd34
Rura ◉ RN (UPH) 83 Oj32
Rurópolis Presidente Médici ◉ BR (PA) 199 He48
Rurrenabaque ◉ BOL 206 Gg53
Rurum ◉ WAN 138 Le40
Rusape ◉ ZW 152 Mg55
Ruse ◉ BG 45 Mf47
Rusera ☐ IND (BIH) 83 Pd33
Rushan ◉ CHN (SDG) 73 Ra27
Rushden ◉ GB 21 Kt38
Rushing ◉ ZW 152 Mf55
Rushungi ◉ EAT 147 Mk50
Rushville ◉ USA (IN) 172 Fj24
Ruşii, P.N.de ☐ RO 44 Mf47
Rusk ◉ USA (TX) 174 Fc30
Ruskeala ◉ RUS 38 Mk29
Rusné ◉ LT 39 Mb35
Ruso ◉ THA 89 Qa42
Russas ◉ BR (CE) 201 Jb48
Russell ◉ CDN (MB) 172 Fa20
Russell ◉ NZ 112 Th63
Russell ◉ USA (KS) 174 Fa26
Russell Islands ☐ SOL 117 Sk50
Russell, Mount ▲ USA (AK) 165 Cc14
Russell Springs ◉ USA (KS) 174 Fa26
Russel Range ☐ AUS 105 Rb62
Russelville ◉ USA (AL) 175 Fg28
Russia ◉ RUS 53 Oa03
Russkaja ◉ ANT (RUS) 6 Da33
Russlleville ◉ USA (AL) 175 Fg28
Rust de Winter Nature Reserve ☐ ZA 155 Me58
Rust de Winter Nature Reserve ☐ ZA 155 Me58
Rustavi ◉ GE 57 Nc25
Rust ◉ USA (SL) 180 Ej33
Rustenburg ◉ GUY 194 Ha43
Rustenburg ◉ ZA 155 Md58
Rustenburg Nature Reserve ☐ ZA 155 Md58
Rusterfjelbma ◉ N 16 Me10
Ruston ◉ USA (LA) 175 Fd29
Rusumo Falls ☐ EAT 144 Mf47
Ruszów ◉ PL 40 Lq39
Rutana ◉ BU 146 Me47
Rute ◉ E 27 Kq53
Rutenga ◉ ZW 152 Mf55
Rutete ◉ EAT 147 Mj50
Rüthen ◉ D 32 Lj39
Ruther ◉ RO 43 Mh43
Rutherford ◉ USA (NC) 178 Fj28
Ruthin ◉ GB 21 Kr37
Ruti ◉ CH 34 Lj43
Rutigliano ◉ I 37 Lr49
Rutka-Tartak ◉ PL 41 Mc36
Rutland ◉ GB 21 Kt38
Rutland ◉ USA (VT) 177 Gd24
Rutland Island ☐ IND 88 Pg40
Rutland Plains ◉ AUS (QLD) 107 Sb54
Rutledaden ◉ N 17 Lc15
Rutog ◉ CHN (TIB) 69 Ok30
Rutshuru ◉ RDC 141 Me46
Rutul ◉ RUS (DAG) 57 Nd25
Ruunanokoskt ☐ FIN 16 Mf14
Ruvu ◉ EAT 147 Mk48
Ruvubu, P.N.de la ☐ BU 146 Mf47
Ruvuma ☐ EAT/MOC 147 Mj51
Ruvuvel Coast ☐ EAT 147 Mk48
Ruwais ◉ UAE 61 Ng33
Ruwenzori Mountains N.P. ☐ EAU 141 Me45
Ruyang ◉ CHN (HNN) 73 Qg28
Ru-ye Sang ◉ AFG 63 Od28
Ruyigi ◉ BU 146 Mf47
Ruyuan ◉ CHN (GDG) 75 Qg33
Ruzaevka ◉ RUS 48 Nc18
Ružany ◉ BY 41 Me38
Ruzhou ◉ CHN (HNN) 73 Qg28
Ruzana ◉ KS 63 Ok25
Rvandea ◉ 12 Jk10
Rwindi ◉ RDC 141 Me46
Ry ☐ DK 30 Lk34
Ryan ◉ USA (OK) 174 Fb29
Ryan, Mount ▲ AUS 111 Se62
Rybachye ◉ KZ 54 Pa09
Rybczewicz ☐ PL 41 Mc39
Rybinsk ◉ RUS 48 Mk16
Rybinsk Reservoir ☐ RUS 48 Mk16

Rýmařov ◉ CZ 42 Ls41
Ryn ◉ PL 41 Mb37
Ryotakusanchi ☐ J 79 Rj27
Ryongthong Temple ☐ PRK
Ryota ◉ J 77 Rk26
Rypin ◉ PL 41 Lu37
Ryukyu Islands ☐ J 52 Ra07
Ryukyu Trench ☐ 52 Ra08
Rząśnik ◉ PL 41 Mb38
Rzepin ◉ PL 40 Lp38
Rzeszów ◉ PL 41 Mb40
Řžev ◉ RUS 48 Mh17
Řýšiv ◉ UA 49 Mf21

S

Sa ◉ PNG 115 Sc48
Sa ◉ RMM 131 Kh38
Saa ◉ CAM 139 Lf43
Saab ◉ S 31 Ls32
Saacow = Jilib ◉ SP 145 Nb45
Saadani National Park ☐ EAT 147 Mk48
Saaifontein ◉ ZA 154 Ma61
Sääksjärvi ◉ FIN 38 Mj29
Saalbach ◉ A 35 Ln43
Saalburg ◉ D 33 Lj41
Saale ☐ D 33 Lm40
Saalfeld ◉ D 32 Lm40
Saalfelden am Steinernen Meer ◉ A 35 Ln43
Saam ☐ SU 64 Oa31
Saan ◉ SYR 56 Mj28
Saanich ◉ CDN (BC) 168 Dj21
Saar ☐ D 33 Lg41
Saarbrücken ◉ D 33 Lg41
Saarburg ◉ D 33 Lg41
Saaremaa ☐ EST 39 Mc33
Saari ◉ FIN 38 Mh29
Saarijärvi ◉ FIN 38 Mf28
Saaristomeren kansallispuisto = Skärgårdshavets n.p. ☐ FIN 38 Mb31
Saarland ☐ D 33 Lg41
Saarlouis ◉ D 33 Lg41
Saarschleife ☐ D 33 Lg41
Saartuz ◉ TJ 63 Oe27
Saas ◉ CH 34 Lh44
Saatli ◉ AZ 57 Ne26
Sabadell ◉ E 29 Lc49
Sabah ☐ MAL 94 Qg43
Sabaiya ◉ SUD 141 Md42
Sabak ◉ MAL 92 Qa44
Saban ◉ RI 96 Qk49
Šabac ◉ SCG 44 Lu45
Šabanovac ◉ RO 49 Md22
Šabanovac ◉ RO 49 Md22
Sabará ◉ BR (MG) 203 Hj55
Sabarei ◉ EAK 144 Mj45
Sabáudia ◉ I 36 Ln49
Saba Yoi ◉ THA 89 Qa42
Sabbioneta ◉ I 34 Ll45
Sabderat ◉ ER 142 Mh41
Sabha ◉ LAR 127 Lh31
Sabi ☐ RI 92 Pk43
Sabie ◉ LV 39 Mc33
Sabile ◉ LV 39 Mc33
Sabina Grande ◉ YV 192 Ge41
Sabinal ◉ RI 96 Qd46
Sabaniago ☐ GCA 184 Fe38
Sabana Grande ◉ YV 192 Ge41
Sabanagrande ◉ HN 184 Fd38
Sabanagrande ◉ CO 192 Gc40
Sabanalarga ◉ CO 192 Gd41
Sabanalarga ◉ CO 192 Gd43
Sabaluka Game Reserve ☐ SUD 135 Mg37
Saban Marine Park ☐ NL (NA) 187 Gj37
Sabana ◉ I 36 Gc35
Sabana ◉ OM 61 Nj34
Sadad ◉ SYR 56 Mj28
Sadani ◉ EAT 147 Mk49
Sadao ◉ THA 88 Qa42
Sadasoepet ◉ IND (APH) 82 Oj37
Sadda ◉ PK 65 Of28
Sadd-e Eskandar ☐ IR 62 Ng27
Saddle L. Ind. Res. ☐ CDN
Saddle Mount ▲ USA 169 Ed24
Saddle-Peaks ▲ IND 88 Pg38
Saddle-Peaks ▲ VU 118 Te56
Sadd Malky ☐ KSA 60 Nb37
Sa Dec ◉ VN 89 Qc40
Saef ◉ S 31 Ls32
Sadi ◉ S 79 Rf29
Saiki ◉ J 79 Rf29
Sailolof ◉ RI 97 Rf46
Sailu ◉ IND (MHT) 83 Oj35
Saimaa ☐ FIN 38 Mj29
Saimenski kanal ☐ FIN/RUS 38 Mj29
Sain Alto ◉ MEX (ZCT) 182 Ej34
Saindak ◉ PK 64 Oa31
Sai Ngam ◉ THA 88 Pk37
Saînoootou ◉ SN 136 Kd39
Saint Abb's Head ▲ GB 20 Ks36
Saint Adolphe ◉ CDN 172 Fb21
Saint-Affrique ◉ F 25 Lc47
Saint-Agrève ◉ F 25 Le46
Saint-Aignan ◉ F 24 Lb43
Saint Alban's ◉ CDN (NF)
Saint Albans ◉ GB 21 Kt39
Saint Albans ◉ USA (VT) 177 Gd23
Saint Albans ◉ USA (WV)
Saint Albert ◉ CDN (AB)
Saint Albert ☐ CDN (AB)
SaintAlbans ◉ F 25 Le46
Saint Albert Dome ☐ PNG 115 Sb48
Saint-Alexandre ◉ CDN (QC) 176 Gf22
Saint-Amand-en-Puisaye ◉ F 25 Ld43
Saint-Amand-les-Eaux ◉ F 23 Ld40
Saint-Amand-Montrond ◉ F 25 Lc44
Saint-Ambroise ◉ CDN (QC) 176 Ge21
Saint-André ◉ F 25 Le46
Saint-André ☐ F (RE) 157 Nh56
Saint-André-de-Cubzac ◉ F 24 Ku45
Saint-André-de-l'Eure ◉ F 23 Lb42
Saint-André-les-Alpes ◉ F 25 Lg47
Saint Andrew ☐ CDN (NB)
Saint Andrew's ◉ CDN (NF) 177 Ha22
Saint Andrews ◉ GB 20 Ks34
Saint Andrews ◉ GB 20 Ks34
Saint Anne Marine N.P. ☐ SY
Saint Anthony ◉ USA (ID)
Saint-Antoine ◉ F 36 Lq48
Saint Arnaud ◉ AUS (VIC)
Saint Arnaud ◉ NZ 113 Tg66
Saint-Aubin-d'Aubigné ◉ F 22 Kt42
Saint-Aubin-du-Cormier ◉ F 22 Kt42
Saint-Augustin ◉ CDN (QC) 176 Ge21
Saint-Augustin ☐ USA (FL) 178 Fk31
Saint Augustine Beach ◉ USA (FL) 178 Fk31
Saint Austell ◉ GB 21 Kq40
Saint Barbe ◉ CDN 177 Hb20
Saint Barthélemy ☐ F (GL) 187 Gh36
Saint-Beat ◉ F 24 La48
Saint-Benoit ☐ F (RE) 157 Nh56

Saint-Benoît-du-Sault – San Felipe de Jesús

Santo Antonio – Segamat

Santo Antonio BR (RO) 198 Gg50
Santo António STP 138 Ld45
Santo Antônio da Barra BR (GO) 202 He54
Santo Antônio da Platina BR (PR) 202 He57
Santo Antonio de Leverger BR (MT) 202 Hb53
Santo Antônio do Içá BR (AM) 198 Gg47
Santo Antônio do Jacinto BR (MG) 203 Hk54
Santo Antônio do Sudoeste BR (PR) 204 Hd59
Santo Augusto BR (RS) 204 Hd59
Santo Corazón BOL 206 Ha54
Santo Cristo BR (RS) 204 Hc59
Santo Domingo C 179 Fk34
Santo Domingo DOM 186 Gf36
Santo Domingo MEX (BC) 180 Ec31
Santo Domingo MEX (BCS) 180 Ee33
Santo Domingo MEX (DGO) 181 Eh33
Santo Domingo MEX (SLP) 182 Ek34
Santo Domingo NIC 185 Fh39
Santo Domingo RA (SA) 207 Gj58
Santo Domingo YV 192 Gd42
Santo Domingo de Acobamba PE 197 Gc51
Santo Domingo de la Calzada E 28 Ks48
Santo Domingo de los Colorados EC 196 Ga46
Santo Domingo de Silos E 26 Kr49
Santo Domingo Pueblo USA (NM) 171 Eg28
Santo Domingo Tehuantepec MEX (OAX) 183 Fc37
Santo Estevão BR (BA) 201 Ja52
Santo Expedito BR (SP) 202 He56
Santo Inácio BR (BA) 201 Hj51
Santo Inácio BR (PR) 202 He57
San Tomé YV 193 Gh41
Santoña E 28 Kr47
Santonia F (GF) 194 Hc43
Santo Niño RP 91 Rc42
Santópolis do Aguapú BR (SP) 202 He56
Santos AUS (QLD) 108 Sa60
Santos BR (SP) 205 Hg57
Santos Dumont BR (MG) 203 Hj56
Santos Lugares RA (SE) 207 Gj59
Santos Mercado BOL 198 Gg50
Santos Reyes Nopala MEX (OAX) 182 Fb37
Santo Tirso P 26 Km49
Santo Tomás MEX (BC) 180 Eb30
Santo Tomás MEX (CHH) 180 Eg31
Santo Tomás NIC 185 Fh39
Santo Tomás PE 197 Gd53
Santo Tomas RP 91 Rc42
Santo Tomé RA (CR) 204 Hb60
Santo Tome RA (SF) 209 Gk61
Sant Pere de Rodes E 28 Ld48
Santpur IND (KTK) 82 Oj36
Santuari de Lluc E 29 Lc51
Santuari de Sant Salvador E 29 Ld51
Santuario de las Lajas CO 196 Gb45
Santuario delle Santa Casa I 35 Lo47
Santuario de Loyola E 28 Ks47
Santuario di San Michele I 37 Lq49
Santuário do Bom Jesus BR 203 Hj56
Santuario Laguna El Peral RCH 208 Ge62
Santuario Nacional Calipuy PE 197 Ga50
Santuario Nacional de Ampay PE 197 Gd52
Santuario Nacional Huayllay PE 197 Gb51
Santuario Nacional Lagunas de Mejía PE 197 Ge54
Santuario Nacional Manglares de Tumbes PE 196 Fk47
Santuario Nacional Tanaconas Namballes PE 196 Ga48
Santubong MAL 94 Qf45
Santu Lussúrgiu I 36 Lj50
Sant Vicenç E 29 Lb49
San Ubaldo NIC 185 Fh40
Sanup Plateau USA 171 Ed28
Sanur Beach RI 95 Qh50
San Valentín, Cerro RCH 210 Gd69
San Vicente BOL 207 Gg56
San Vicente CO 192 Gd42
San Vicente EC 196 Fk46
San Vicente ES 184 Ff39
San Vicente MEX (BC) 180 Eb30
San Vicente RA (BA) 209 Ha63
San Vicente RA (MI) 204 Hc59
San Vicénte YV 193 Gg43
San Vicente de Alcántara E 27 Kn51
San Vicente de Caguan CO 192 Gc44
San Vicente de Cañete PE 197 Gb52
San Vicente de la Barquera E 26 Kq47
San Vicente Tancuayalab MEX (SLP) 182 Fa35
San Victor GUY 194 Gk42
San Vincente MEX (SLP) 181 Ek33
San Vincenzo I 34 Ll47
San Vitale di Ravenna I 34 Ln46
San Vito CR 185 Fj41
San Vito I 36 Lk51
San Vito al Tagliamento I 35 Ln45
San Vito dei Normanni I 37 Ls50
San Vito lo Capo I 36 Ln52
Sanxenxo = Sangenjo E 26 Km48
Sanya CHN (HAN) 75 Qe36
Sanya Juu EAT 144 Mj47
Sanyang CHN (AHU) 78 Qk30
Sanyati ZW 152 Me54
Sanying CHN (NHZ) 72 Qd27
Sanying CHN (YUN) 87 Qa32
Sanyuan CHN (SAA) 72 Qe28
Sanza I 37 Lq50
Sanza Pombo ANG 148 Lh49
São Antônia BR (RR) 194 Gk44
São Antonio BR (AM) 198 Gk49
São Antonio BR (AP) 195 He45
São Antonio BR (PA) 199 Hc49
São António da Abunari BR (AM) 199 Gk46
São Antônio das Missões BR (RS) 204 Hc60
São Antonio de Jesus BR (BA) 201 Ja52
São Antônio de Padua BR (RJ) 203 Hj56
São Antônio do Amparo BR (MG) 203 Hh56
São Antônio do Monte BR (MG) 203 Hh56
São Antônio dos Lopes BR (MA) 200 Hh48
São Benedito BR (CE) 201 Hk48
São Benedito BR (MT) 202 Hb54
São Benedito do Rio Preto BR (MA) 201 Hj47
São Bento BR (MA) 195 Hh47
São Bento BR 201 Jc49
São Bento do Norte BR (RN) 201 Jb48
São Bento do Sul BR (SC) 205 Hf59
São Bernardo BR (AM) 198 Gg50
São Bernardo BR (MA) 201 Hj47
São Bernardo do Campo BR (SP) 205 Hg57
São Borja BR (RS) 204 Hc60
São Brás BR (AM) 198 Gf49
São Brás de Alportel P 27 Kn53
São Caetano BR (PE) 201 Jb50
São Caetano de Odivelas BR (PA) 195 Hf46
São Carlos BR (RO) 198 Gh51
São Carlos BR (SC) 204 Hd59
São Carlos BR (SP) 202 Hg57
São Cosme BR (PA) 195 He46
São Cristóão ANG 150 Lg52
São Cristóvão BR (SE) 201 Jb51
São Cristóvão do Sul BR (SC) 205 He59
São Desidério BR (BA) 200 Hh52
São Domingos BR (GO) 200 Hg52
São Domingos BR (GO) 202 Hf54
São Domingos BR (MA) 200 Hh49
São Domingos BR (MS) 202 Hb55
São Domingos GNB 136 Kb39
São Domingos do Capim BR (PA) 195 Hg46
São Domingos do Capim Novo BR (PA) 195 Hg47
São Domingos do Maranhão BR (MA) 200 Hh48
São Domingos do Prata BR (MG) 203 Hj55
São Domingos, T.I. BR 200 He51
São Felício BR (AP) 194 Hd45
São Felix do Araguaia BR (MT) 200 He51
São Felix do Coribe BR (BA) 200 Hh52
São Felix do Xingu BR (PA) 200 He49
São Fidelis BR (RJ) 203 Hk56
São Filipe CV 136 Jh38
São Francisco BR (MG) 203 Hh53
São Francisco BR 201 Jb50
São Francisco das Chagas BR (AM) 199 Hb47
São Francisco das Chagas BR (PI) 200 Hh50
São Francisco das Chagas BR 201 Ja48
São Francisco de Assis BR (RS) 204 Hc60
São Francisco de Paula BR (RS) 205 He60
São Francisco de Sales BR (MG) 202 Hf55
São Francisco do Maranhão BR (MA) 201 Hj49
São Francisco do Sul BR (SC) 205 Hf59
São Gabriel BR (RS) 204 Hc61
São Gabriel da Cachoeira BR (AM) 198 Gg46
São Gabriel da Palha BR (ES) 203 Hk55
São Gabriel de Goiás BR (GO) 203 Hg53
São Gabriel do Oeste BR (MS) 202 Hc55
São Geraldo do Araguaia BR (PA) 200 Hf49
São Gonçalo do Abaeté BR (MG) 203 Hh55
São Gonçalo do Amarante BR (CE) 201 Ja47
São Gonçalo dos Campos BR (BA) 201 Ja52
São Gotardo BR (MG) 203 Hg55
Sao Hill EAT 146 Mh50
São Ifigênia de Minas BR (MG) 203 Hj55
São Jerônimo BR (RS) 204 He60
São Jerônimo da Serra BR (PR) 202 He57
São Jerônimo, T.I. BR 202 He57
São João BR (AM) 199 Gk48
São João BR (PR) 204 Hd58
São João Batista BR (MA) 195 Hh47
São João Batista BR (SC) 205 Hf59
São João da Barra BR (RJ) 203 Hk56
São João da Boa Vista BR (SP) 203 Hg56
São João d'Aliança BR (GO) 203 Hg53
São João da Madeira P 26 Km50
São João da Ponte BR (MG) 203 Hh53
São João da Pracajuba BR (PA) 195 He46
São João da Serra BR (PI) 201 Hk48
São João del Rei BR (MG) 203 Hh56
São João de Pirbas BR (PA) 195 Hg46
São João de Rio Pardo BR (SP) 203 Hg56
São João do Araguaia BR (PA) 200 Hf48
São João do Caiuá BR (PR) 202 Hd57
São João do Paraiso BR (MG) 203 Hk53
São João do Paraná BR (PA) 199 Hb50
São João do Piauí BR (PI) 201 Hj50
São João dos Patos BR (MA) 200 Hj49
São João dos Poleiros BR (MA) 200 Hj48
São João do Tigre BR (PB) 201 Jb50
São João do Triunfo BR (PR) 205 He58
São João Evangelísta BR (MG) 203 Hj55
São Joaquim BR (AM) 198 Gg45
São Joaquim BR (SC) 205 Hf60
São Joaquim da Barra BR (SP) 203 Hg56
São Joaquim, P.N.de BR 205 Hf60
São José BR (AC) 198 Gf50
São José BR (PA) 195 Hf47
São José BR (RS) 204 Hd61
São José BR (SC) 205 Hf59
São José das Laranjeras BR (SP) 202 He57
São José da Tapera BR (AL) 201 Jb50
São José de Anaua BR (RR) 193 Gk45
São José de Belmonte BR (PE) 201 Ja49
São José de Mipibu BR (RN) 201 Jc49
São José de Piranhas BR (PB) 201 Ja49
São Jose de Ribamar BR (MA) 195 Hh47
São José do Caciporé BR (AP) 195 He44
São José do Cerrito BR (SC) 205 He59
São José do Egito BR (PE) 201 Jb49
São José do Norte BR (RS) 204 Hd61
São José do Peixe BR (PI) 201 Hj49
São José do Piria BR (PA) 195 Hg46
São José do Rio Claro BR (MT) 202 Hb52
São José do Rio Preto BR (SP) 202 Hf56
São José dos Ausentes BR (RS) 205 He60
São José dos Campos BR (SP) 205 Hh57
São José dos Martírios BR (TO) 200 Hf49
São José dos Pinhais BR (PR) 205 Hf58
São José do Xingu BR (MT) 199 Hd51
São Julia do Jurupari BR (PA) 195 He45
São Leopoldo BR (RS) 204 He60
São Leopoldo, T.I. BR 198 Gf48
São Lourenço BR (MG) 203 Hh57
São Lourenço do Oeste BR (SC) 204 Hd59
São Lourenço do Sul BR (RS) 204 He61
São Lucas ANG 150 Lj51
São Luís BR (AM) 198 Gh46
São Luís BR (AM) 198 Gk47
São Luís BR (MA) 195 Hh47
São Luís BR (RR) 194 Gk45
São Luís do Quitunde BR (AL) 201 Jc50
São Luís do Tapajós BR (PA) 199 Hb48
São Luis Gonzaga BR (MA) 200 Hh48
São Luís Gonzaga BR (RS) 204 Hc60
São Luiza do Oeste BR (RO) 198 Gk51
São Luzia do Pacui BR (AP) 195 He45
São Manuel BR (MT) 202 Hc53
São Manuel BR (SP) 202 Hf57
São Manuel ou Teles Pires BR 199 Hb50
São Marcos BR (RS) 204 He60
São Marcos da Serra P 27 Km53
São Marcos, T.I. BR 193 Gk44
São Marcos, T.I. BR 202 Hd53
São Martinho BR (RS) 204 Hd59
São Martinho de Angueira P 26 Ko49
São Mateus BR (ES) 203 Ja55
São Mateus do Maranhão BR (MA) 200 Hh48
São Mateus do Sul BR (PR) 205 He58
São Miguel BR (AP) 195 He45
São Miguel BR (MT) 202 Hd52
São Miguel BR (RN) 201 Ja49
São Miguel Arcanjo BR (SP) 205 Hg57
São Miguel das Missões BR (RS) 204 Hc60
São Miguel das Missões BR 204 Hc60
São Miguel d'Oeste BR (SC) 204 Hd59
São Miguel do Guamá BR (PA) 195 Hg46
São Miguel do Iguaçu BR (PR) 204 Hc58
São Miguel dos Campos BR (AL) 201 Jb50
São Miguel dos Macacos BR (PA) 195 He46
São Miguel do Tapuio BR (PI) 201 Hk48
Saoner IND (MHT) 83 Ok35
São Nicolau ANG 150 Lg53
Saonli IND (MPH) 83 Ok35
São Paulo BR (SP) 205 Hg57
São Paulo BR 191 Hb12
São Paulo do Potengi BR (RN) 201 Jc48
São Pedro BR (AM) 198 Gg46
São Pedro BR (AM) 198 Gg48
São Pedro BR (AM) 198 Gj47
São Pedro BR (PA) 195 He47
São Pedro BR (PR) 204 Hd59
São Pedro BR (SP) 202 Hg57
São Pedro CV 136 Jh37
São Pedro da Aldeia BR (RJ) 205 Hj57
Sao Pedro do Ico BR (AC) 198 Gf50
São Pedro do Piauí BR (PI) 201 Hj48
São Pedro dos Crentes BR (MA) 200 Hg49
São Pedro do Sepatini, T.I. BR 198 Gh49
São Pedro do Sul BR (RS) 204 Hc60
São Pedro, T.I. BR 199 Ha47
São Perdo da Quilemba ANG 148 Lh50
Sao Pualo de Olivença BR (AM) 198 Gf47
São Raimundo das Mangabeiras BR (MA) 200 Hh49
São Raimundo Nonato BR (PI) 201 Hj50
Saorge F 25 Lh47
São Romão BR (AM) 198 Gg48
São Romão BR (MG) 203 Hh54
São Roque BR (SP) 205 Hg57
São Roque de Minas BR (MG) 203 Hg56
São Sebastião BR (AL) 201 Jb50
São Sebastião BR (SP) 205 Hh57
São Sebastião da Amoreira BR (PR) 202 He57
São Sebastião da Boa Vista BR (PA) 195 Hf46
São Sebastião do Paraiso BR (MG) 203 Hg56
São Sebastião do Tocantins BR (TO) 200 Hf48
São Sebastião do Uatumã BR (AM) 199 Hb47
São Sepé BR (RS) 204 Hd61
São Simão BR (GO) 202 He55
São Simão BR (RS) 204 He61
São Simão BR (SP) 203 Hg56
São Teotónio P 27 Km53
São Tomé BR (AP) 195 He46
São Tomé STP 138 Ld45
São Tomé STP 138 Ld45
São Tomé and Príncipe 123 La09
Saourikro CI 137 Kh42
São Valentim BR (RS) 204 Hd59
São Vendelino BR (RS) 204 He60
São Vicente BR (AC) 196 Ge49
São Vicente BR (MT) 202 Hc53
São Vicente BR (PA) 195 He46
São Vicente BR (SP) 205 Hg57
São Vicente do Sul BR (RS) 204 Hc60
São Vicente Ferrer BR (MA) 195 Hh47
Sapa VN 87 Qb34
Sápai GR 45 Mf49
Sapajou F (GF) 194 Hd43
Sapanjang RI 95 Qh49
Saparua RI 97 Re47
Saparua RI 97 Re47
Sapat RI 93 Qb46
Sapé BR (PB) 201 Jc49
Sapele WAN 138 Lc43
Sapelo Island National Estuarine Research Reserve USA 178 Fk30
Sapernoe RUS 38 Mk30
Sapidan IR 59 Nf30
Sapiénza GR 46 Mb54
Sapinero USA (CO) 171 Eg26
Sapiranga BR (RS) 204 He60
Sapi Safari Area ZW 152 Me53
Sápmi N 16 Mc11
Sapoba WAN 138 Lc42
Sapodilla Cays BH 184 Ff37
Saponé BF 137 Kk39
Sapo N.P. LB 136 Kf43
Sapo Sapo RDC 149 Mb48
Saposoa PE 196 Gb49
Sapoui BF 137 Kk40
Sapožok RUS 48 Na19
Sapphir Mts. USA 168 Ed22
Sappho USA (WA) 168 Dh21
Sapporo J 77 Sa24
Sapri I 37 Lq50
Sapšal'skij hrebet RUS 67 Pe20
Sapt al Ulaya KSA 60 Na36
Sapucaia BR (AM) 199 Hb47
Sapucaia BR (RJ) 203 Hj57
Sapucaia do Sul BR (RS) 204 He60
Sapuka-Besar RI 96 Qk49
Sapulpa USA (OK) 174 Fb28
Sapulu RI 95 Qg49
Sapulut MAL 94 Qj43
Saqim YE 60 Nb37
Saqiyah IRQ 57 Nb28
Saqqez IR 57 Nd27
Saqr YE 61 Nf38
Saquisilí EC 196 Ga46
Sara BF 137 Kj40
Sara FIN 38 Mc28
Sara RI 114 Rg47
Sara RP 90 Rb40
Sarab IR 57 Nd27
Sarab Dowreh IR 57 Ne29
Sarab-e Jahangir IR 59 Nd29
Sarâbît el Khâdim ET 129 Mg31
Saraburi THA 88 Qa38
Sarad IND (MHT) 82 Og35
Sarafchegan IR 57 Nf28
Saraf Doungous TCH 139 Lk39
Saraféré RMM 131 Kj38
Saragt TM 62 Oa27
Saraguro EC 196 Ga47
Sara Hahan SP 143 Nd40
Sarai RUS 48 Na19
Saraidana IND (MPH) 83 Pa34
Sarai Gambila PK 65 Of29
Sar'ain IR 57 Nd26
Saraipali IND (CGH) 83 Pb35
Säräisniemi FIN 16 Md13
Saraiu RO 45 Mj46
Sarajevo BIH 44 Lt47
Sara-Kawa TG 137 La41
Sarakhs IR 62 Oa27
Sarakína GR 46 Mb50
Sarakína GR 46 Mb51
Sarakiní GR 46 Mb50
Sara Koyra RN 132 La38
Saramati MYA 86 Ph33
Sarameriza PE 196 Gb48
Saramon F 24 La47
Saran IR 62 Ng28
Saranac Lake USA (NY) 177 Gc23
Saranci BG 44 Md48
Saránd H 43 Mb43
Sarandë AL 46 Ma51
Sarandi BR (PR) 202 He57
Sarandi BR (PR) 204 Hd58
Sarandi BR (RS) 204 Hd59
Sarandí del Yí ROU 204 Hc62
Sarandí Grande ROU 204 Hb62
Sarangani Island RP 91 Rc43
Sarangarh IND (CGH) 83 Pb35
Sarangpur IND (MPH) 82 Oj34
Saran, Gunung RI 95 Qf46
Saransk RUS 48 Nc18
Sarantáporo GR 46 Mc50
Sarapali IND (ORS) 83 Pc35
Sarapul RUS 54 Nc07
Sarare, T.I. BR 206 Ha53
Saraskheri IND (MPH) 82 Oj33
Sarasota USA (FL) 179 Fj32
Šarašova BY 41 Me38
Sarat Abidah KSA 60 Nb36
Šara-Tagot RUS 70 Qd19
Sarath IND (JKD) 83 Pd33
Saratoga Hot Springs USA 171 Eg25
Saratoga N.H.P. USA 177 Gd24
Saratoga Racetrack USA (NY) 177 Gd24
Saratoga Springs USA (NY) 177 Gd24
Saravah IR 57 Ne27
Saravan IR 64 Ob32
Sarawak MAL 94 Qg44
Sarawak Cultural Village MAL 94 Qf45
Saray TR 45 Mh49
Saraya SN 136 Ke39
Sarayan IR 64 Nk29
Sarayköy TR 47 Mj53
Sarbaz IR 64 Oa32
Sarbaz IR 64 Oa32
Sarbinowo PL 40 Lq36
Sar Bisheh IR 64 Nk29
Sárbogrd H 43 Lt44
Sarbulak CHN (XUZ) 67 Pe22
Sarco RCH 207 Ge60
Sárdara I 36 Lj51
Sardarshahr IND (RJT) 80 Oh31
Sardasht IR 59 Nf30
Sardes TR 47 Mj52
Sardhana IND (UPH) 81 Oj31
Sardinas EC 196 Gb46
Sardinata CO 192 Gd41
Sardinia I 36 Lj50
Sardinia I 36 Lj50
Sardis USA (GA) 178 Fk29
Sardrud IR 57 Nd27
Sarege RI 96 Qk49
Sarékali RG 136 Kd40
Sareks n.p. S 16 Lj12
Sarektjåkka S 16 Lj12
S'Arenal E 29 Lc51
Saré Ndiaye SN 136 Kc39
Šarengrad HR 35 Lu45
Sar-e Pol AFG 63 Oc27
Sar-e-Pol-e-Sahab IR 57 Nc28
Sar-e Raqowl AFG 65 Od28
Saréyamou RMM 131 Kj37
Sarfayt OM 61 Ng37
Sargapur IND (KTK) 82 Oj37
Sargasso Sea 160 Ga06
Sargodha PK 65 Og29
Sargur IND (KTK) 84 Oj40
Sarh TCH 140 Lk41
Sarhad AFG 63 Og27
Sarhad IR 64 Oa31
Sarhala CI 137 Kg41
Šarhorod UA 49 Me21
Sari IR 62 Ng27
Saria GR 47 Mh55
Saria GR 47 Mh55
Saria 80 Oh29
Sariba Island PNG 116 Sf51
Saric MEX (SO) 180 Ee30
Sarie Marais Base ANT (SA) 6 Kd33
Sariet ez Zit TN 126 Lf28
Sarif YE 61 Nf37
Sarıgöl TR 47 Mj52
Sarigua, P.N. PA 185 Fk41
Sarika Falls THA 88 Qa38
Sarıkamış TR 57 Nb25
Sarıkaya TR 56 Mh26
Sarikei MAL 94 Qf44
Sariko'l UZ 63 Od26
Sarikorola RMM 137 Kg39
Sarıköy TR 45 Mh50
Sarimoy UZ 62 Oa25
Sarimoy UZ 62 Ob25
Sarina AUS (QLD) 109 Se56
Sariñena E 28 Ku49
Sar-i-Parom PK 65 Ob32
Sarıpınar TR 57 Mk26
Saripoi RI 95 Qh46
Sariq UZ 63 Od27
Sarir al Qattusah LAR 127 Lh32
Sariri PNG 116 Se50
Sarir Kalanshiyú LAR 127 Ma32
Sarir Tibesti LAR 133 Lj34
Sarir Umm 'Illah LAR 127 Lh32
Sariska Tiger Reserve IND 80 Oj32
Šarišský hrad SK 43 Mb41
Sarita USA (TX) 181 Fb32
Sariwon PRK 78 Rc26
Sariyer TR 45 Mk49
Šar'ja RUS 48 Mg16
Sark GB 22 Ks41
Sarkadkeresztúr H 43 Mb44
Sarkala IND 82 Of35
Sarkan KZ 66 Ok23
Šarkavščyna BY 39 Mh35
Sarkhej IND (GUJ) 82 Og34
Şarkikaraağaç TR 56 Mf26
Sarkin Kudin WAN 138 Le41
Şarkışla TR 56 Mj26
Şarköy TR 45 Mh50
Sarlat-la-Canéda F 24 Lb46
Sărmăşag RO 43 Mc43
Sarmette VU 118 Td54
Sarmi RI 114 Rk46
Sarmiento RA (CB) 210 Gf68
Sarmiento RA (CD) 208 Gh61
Sarmizegetusa Regia RO 44 Md45
Särna S 17 Lg15
Sarnaki PL 41 Mc38
Sarnano I 35 Lo47
Sarnath IND 83 Pb33
Sarnen CH 34 Lj44
Sarner See CH 34 Lj44
Sărnevo BG 45 Mf48
Sarnia CDN (ON) 173 Fj24
Sárnico I 34 Lk45
Sarno I 37 Lp50
Sarny UA 48 Md20
Särö S 30 Lm33
Saroako RI 96 Ra47
Sarolangun RI 93 Qb47
Saroma J 77 Sb23
Saromoana RM 156 Ne54
Saronída GR 45 Md53
Saronída GR 45 Md53
Saronikós Kólpos GR 45 Md53
Saronno I 34 Lj45
Sarore RI 115 Sa50
Sárosd H 43 Lt43
Saros Körfezi TR 45 Mg50
Sárospatak H 43 Mb42
Šarovce SK 43 Lt42
Sarowbi AFG 65 Oe28
Sarowbi AFG 65 Oe29
Šar Planina MK/SCG 44 Ma48
Šar Planina, N.P. SCG 44 Mb48
Sarpsborg N 30 Ll31
Sarralbe F 23 Lh42
Sarrapio YV 193 Gh42
Sarrebourg F 23 Lh42
Sarreguemines F 23 Lh41
Sarre-Union F 23 Lh42
Sarria E 26 Kn48
Sarro RMM 137 Kh39
Sarstoon N.P. BH 184 Ff38
Sartam IND (ARP) 86 Pg31
Sartell USA (MN) 172 Fc23
Sartène F 36 Lj49
Sarteneja BH 183 Ff36
Sarteneja BH 183 Ff36
Sárti GR 45 Md50
Sarubetsu J 77 Sb24
Sarufutsu J 77 Sb23
Saruhanlı TR 47 Mh52
Sarulla RI 93 Pk45
Sarumatinggi RI 93 Pk44
Sarumatinggi RI 93 Pk45
Sarungga RI 95 Qh47
Saru Pathar IND (ASM) 86 Pg32
Saruq IR 57 Ne28
Saruwaged Range PNG 115 Sd49
Sarvada IND (MHT) 82 Oh37
Sárvár H 42 Lr43
Sarvestan IR 64 Ng31
Sarwan IND (MPH) 82 Oh34
Saryaghash KZ 63 Oe25
Sary-Bulak KS 66 Oh25
Saryesik - Atyrau KZ 66 Oj23
Sarykemer KZ 63 Of24
Saryolen KZ 67 Pc22
Saryozek KZ 66 Oj23
Saryshaghan KZ 66 Og22
Sarysu KZ 63 Od23
Sary-Taš KS 63 Og26
Sarzana I 34 Lk46
Sarzeau F 22 Ks43
Sarzedas P 27 Kn51
Sasabe USA (AZ) 171 Ee30
Sasak RI 93 Pk46
Sasan caravanserai IR 57 Nf28
Sasan Gir N.P. IND 82 Of35
Sasaram IND (BIH) 83 Pc33
Sasari, Mount SOL 117 Sk50
Sa Savina E 29 Lb52
Sasbeneh ETH 143 Nb42
Sásd H 42 Lt44
Sasebo J 79 Re29
Sasino PL 40 Ls36
Saskal' RUS 71 Rd20
Saskatchewan CDN 162 Ec07
Saskatchewan Landing Prov. Park CDN 169 Ef20
Saskatchewan River CDN 169 Ej19
Saskatchewan River Crossing CDN (AB) 168 Eb19
Saskatoon CDN (SK) 169 Eg19
Saskylah RUS 55 Qc04
Sasolburg ZA 155 Md59
Sasoma 81 Oj28
Sason TR 57 Na26
Sasovo RUS 48 Na18
Sassandra CI 137 Kg43
Sássari I 36 Lj50
Sassélé RCA 140 Lj43
Sassie Island AUS 107 Sb51
Sassnitz D 32 Lo36
Sassoferrato I 35 Ln47
Sasso Lungo = Langkofel I 34 Lm44
Sasso Marconi I 34 Lm46
Sassoumbouroum RN 132 Le39
Sassuolo I 34 Ll46
Sástago E 29 Ku49
Šaštín-Stráže SK 42 Ls42
Sastown LB 136 Kf43
Sastre RA (SF) 209 Gk61
Sasu RI 91 Rd45
Sasvad IND (MHT) 82 Oh36
Sasykkul' TJ 63 Og27
Sasykol KZ 66 Pa22
Sata J 79 Rf30
Satadougou RMM 136 Ke39
Satama-Sokoro CI 137 Kh42
Satama-Sokoura CI 137 Kh42
Sata misaki J 79 Rf30
Satana IND (MHT) 82 Oh35
Satana USA (KS) 174 Ek27
Sataplia Nakrdzali GE 57 Nb24
Satara IND (MHT) 82 Og37
Satara ZA 155 Mf58
Satellite Beach USA (FL) 179 Fk31
Satéma RCA 140 Ma43
Såtenäs S 30 Ln32
Satengar RI 96 Qj49
Säter S 31 Lq30
Satevó MEX (CHH) 180 Eg32
Sathing Phra THA 88 Qa42
Šatili GE 57 Nc24
Sātiņi LV 39 Mc34
Satipo PE 197 Gc51
Satiri BF 137 Kh40
Satiwala PK 65 Og30
Satkania BD 86 Pg34
Satkhira BD 86 Pe34
Satna IND (MPH) 83 Pa33
Sato J 79 Re30
Šatoj RUS (CHE) 57 Nc24
Šator BIH 35 Lr46
Sátoraljaújhely H 43 Mb42
Šatorina HR 35 Lq46
Satovča BG 45 Md49
Satpura Range IND 82 Oh35
Şatra RO 43 Md43
Satrokala RM 157 Nc57
Satsuma USA (AL) 175 Ff30
Satsuma-hanto J 79 Rf30
Satsuma-Iwojima J 79 Rf30
Satsunan Islands J 79 Re32
Sattahip THA 88 Qa39
Satthwa MYA 86 Ph36
Satti 81 Oj28
Satui RI 95 Qh47
Satuk THA 89 Qb38
Satu Mare RO 43 Mc43
Satun THA 88 Qa42
Satur IND (TNU) 84 Oj41
Šatura RUS 48 Mk18
Saturnino María Laspiur RA (CD) 209 Gj61
Satwas IND (MPH) 82 Oj34
Saty KZ 66 Ok24
Satyamangalam IND (TNU) 84 Oj40
Satyjiv UA 41 Mf40
Saucats F 24 Ku46
Sauce RA (CR) 204 Ha61
Sauce Blanco RA (RN) 209 Gj66
Sauce de la Luna RA (ER) 204 Ha61
Saucillo MEX (CHH) 181 Eh31
Sauclières F 25 Ld47
Sauda N 30 Lg31
Saudade BR (AM) 198 Gh48
Saudainu RI 93 Pk46
Saudakent KZ 63 Oe24
Sauðanes IS 18 Ke24
Sauðárkrókur IS 18 Ka25
Saudável BR (BA) 201 Hj52
Saúde BR (AM) 196 Ge49
Saúde BR (BA) 201 Hk51
Saudi Arabia KSA 53 Na07
Saue EST 38 Me31
Sauer D 33 Lg41
Sauer ZA 154 Lk62
Sauerland D 32 Lh39
Saugues F 25 Ld46
Saujil RA (CA) 207 Gg60
Saujon F 24 Ku45
Sauk Centre USA (MN) 172 Fc23
Saukorem RI 114 Rg46
Sauk Rapids USA (MN) 172 Fc23
Saul F (GF) 194 Hd44
Saula BR (PA) 194 Hb46
Sauland N 30 Lj31
Săuleşti RO 44 Md46
Saulieu F 25 Le43
Saulkrasti LV 39 Me33
Sault F 25 Lf46
Sault Sainte Marie CDN (ON) 173 Fh22
Sault Sainte Marie USA (MI) 173 Fh22
Saum USA (MN) 172 Fc22
Saumarez Reefs AUS 109 Sg56
Saumlakki RI 97 Rf49
Saumur F 24 Ku43
Saundatti IND (KTK) 82 Oh38
Saunders, Mount 7 Tb36
Sauren PNG 116 Se48
Sauri Hill WAN 138 Ld40
Saurimo ANG 149 Ma50
Sauriwaunawa GUY 194 Ha44
Sausar IND (MPH) 83 Ok35
Sausu RI 96 Ra46
Sautar ANG 150 Lk51
Sautatá CO 192 Gb42
Saut de Doubs F 25 Lg43
Saut Sabbat F (GF) 194 Hd43
Sautso-canyon N 16 Mb11
Sauveterre-de-Béarn F 24 Ku47
Sauveterre-de-Guyenne F 24 Ku46
Sauvo FIN 38 Mc30
Sauxillanges F 25 Ld45
Sauzé-Vaussais F 24 Ku44
Sav IR 64 Ng29
Sava HN 184 Fg38
Sava HR/BIH 35 Ls45
Savage USA (MT) 169 Eh22
Savage River AUS (TAS) 111 Sc66
Savage River N.P. AUS (TAS) 111 Sc66
Savai'i Island WS 10 Ba11
Savalou DY 138 La42
Savalou Mts DY 138 La41
Savane MOC 153 Mh55
Savanna USA (OK) 174 Fc28
Savannah USA (GA) 178 Fk29
Savannah USA (MO) 174 Fc26
Savannah USA (TN) 175 Ff28
Savannah Downs AUS (QLD) 107 Sa55
Savannah Sound BS 179 Gb33
Savannakhét LAO 89 Qc37
Savanna-la-Mar JA 186 Ga36
Savant Lake CDN (ON) 172 Fe20
Savantvadi IND (MHT) 82 Og38
Savanur IND (KTK) 82 Oh38
Savarkundla IND (GUJ) 82 Of35
Săvârşin RO 43 Mc44
Savaştepe TR 47 Mh51
Savate ANG 150 Lj54
Savazy RM 157 Nc57
Savé DY 138 Lb41
Save F 24 Lb47
Save MOC 153 Mh56
Save ZW 152 Mf55
Saveh IR 57 Nf28
Savelugu GH 137 Kk41
Savenay F 22 Kt43
Săveni RO 49 Md22
Saverdun F 24 Lb47
Saverne F 23 Lh42
Savigliano I 34 Lh46
Savignano sul Rubicone I 34 Ln46
Savitaipale FIN 38 Mh29
Savitri Temple IND 80 Oh32
Šavnik SCG 44 Lu48
Savoie F 25 Lg45
Savo Island SOL 117 Sk50
Savona CDN (BC) 168 Dk20
Savona I 34 Lj46
Savonlinna FIN 38 Mj29
Savonranta FIN 38 Mk28
Savoonga USA (AK) 164 Be14
Sävsjö S 31 Lp33
Savu RI 96 Ra51
Savu RI 96 Ra51
Savusavu FJI 119 Tk54
Savu Sea RI 96 Ra50
Savute RB 151 Mc55
Saw MYA 86 Ph35
Sawabi PK 65 Og28
Sawahan RI 95 Qf49
Sawahlunto RI 93 Qa46
Sawai Madhopur IND (RJT) 82 Oj33
Sawaleke FJI 119 Tk54
Sawang Daen Din THA 87 Qb37
Sawankhalok THA 88 Pk37
Sawara J 79 Sa28
Sawarangan RI 95 Qh48
Sawatch Mts. USA 171 Eg26
Sawbill CDN (NF) 176 Gg19
Sawe LB 136 Kg43
Sawin PL 41 Md39
Sawinnu LAR 127 Ma30
Sawkanah LAR 127 Lh31
Sawla GH 137 Kj41
Sawmill Bay CDN 167 Ea13
Sawmills ZW 152 Me55
Sawt-Law MYA 87 Pk32
Sawtooth Mts. USA 168 Ec24
Saxby Downs AUS (QLD) 107 Sb56
Saxman USA (AK) 166 De18
Saxmundham GB 21 Lb38
Saxnäs S 16 Lh13
Say RMM 137 Kh39
Say RN 132 Lb39
Sayabec CDN (QC) 176 Gg21
Sayak KZ 66 Oj22
Sayalkudi IND (TNU) 84 Ok41
Sayán PE 197 Gb51
Sayang RI 97 Re45
Sayat TM 63 Ob26
Sayaxché GCA 183 Fe37
Saydnaya SYR 56 Mj29
Sayé CI 137 Kj41
Sayengga RI 114 Rg47
Sayhut YE 61 Nf38
Saylac SP 143 Nb40
Säyneinen FIN 16 Me14
Saynshand MNG 70 Qf23
Saynshand MNG 70 Qb24
Sayre USA (OK) 174 Fa28
Sayre USA (PA) 177 Gb25
Sayrob UZ 63 Od26
Say Tha Ni LAO 87 Qb36
Sayula MEX (JLC) 182 Ej36
Say'un YE 60 Ne38
Saza EAT 146 Mg50
Saza'i Kalan AFG 63 Od27
Sazan AL 46 Lu50
Sazin PK 63 Og28
Šazud TJ 63 Og27
Sbaa DZ 125 Kk31
Sbeïtla TN 126 Le28
Scaddan AUS (WA) 105 Ra62
Scaër F 22 Kr42
Scăeşti RO 44 Md46
Scafell Pike GB 21 Kr36
Scaife Mountains 6 Gc33
Scalasaig GB 20 Ko34
Scalea I 37 Lq51
Scalloway GB 20 Kt30
Scammon Bay USA (AK) 164 Bh15
Scandia CDN (AB) 169 Ed20
Scandinavia 14 Lb03
Scanno I 36 Lo49
Scansano I 34 Lm48
Scanzano Iónico I 37 Lr50
Scarborough AUS 104 Qh61
Scarborough GB 21 Ku36
Scarborough TT 187 Gk40
Scarborough Reef RP 90 Qj38
Scarborough Shoal 90 Qj38
Scarinish GB 20 Ko34
Scărisoara RO 43 Mc44
Scarp GB 20 Kn32
Scarriff IRL 19 Km38
Scawfell Bank 89 Qd42
Scawfell Island AUS 109 Se56
Ščedrohir UA 41 Me39
Ščekino RUS 48 Mj19
Scenic USA (SD) 169 Ej24
Schaalsee D 32 Ll37
Schaffhausen CH 34 Lj43
Schagen NL 23 Le38
Schakalskuppe NAM 154 Lj59
Scharbeutz D 32 Ll36
Schärding A 42 Lo42
Scharhörn D 32 Lj37
Scharmützelsee D 32 Lp38
Scheeßel D 32 Lk37
Schefferville CDN 163 Gc08
Scheibbs A 42 Lq42
Scheifling A 35 Lp43
Schell Creek Range USA 170 Ec26
Schenectady USA (NY) 177 Gc24
Schesaplana CH/A 34 Lk43
Scheßlitz D 33 Lm41
Scheveningen NL 23 Le38
Schiermonnikoog NL 23 Lg37
Schiermonnikoog NL 23 Lg37
Schiermonnikoog, N.P. NL 23 Lg37
Schiffdorf D 32 Lj37
Schifffahrtsmuseum D 32 Lj37
Schiffshebewerk Rothensee D 32 Lm38
Schiltach D 33 Lj42
Schio I 34 Lm45
Schirmeck F 23 Lh42
Schitu Goleşti RO 45 Mf45
Schkeuditz D 32 Ln39
Schladen D 32 Ll38
Schladming A 35 Lo43
Schlanders = Silandro I 34 Ll44
Schlei D 32 Lk36
Schleiden D 32 Lg40
Schleinitz Range PNG 116 Sf47
Schleiz D 33 Lm40
Schleswig D 32 Lk36
Schleswig-Holstein D 32 Lk36
Schleswig-Holsteinisches Wattenmeer, N.P. D 32 Lj36
Schleusingen D 33 Ll40
Schlieben D 32 Lo39
Schlitz D 32 Lk40
Schloss Altenburg D 32 Ln40
Schloss Aschaffenburg D 33 Lk41
Schloss Augustusburg D 32 Lg40
Schloss Clemenswerth D 32 Lh38
Schloss Duwisib NAM 154 Lj58
Schloss Dyck D 32 Lg39
Schloss Esterházy A 35 Lr43
Schlossgarten in Ludwigslust D 32 Lm37
Schloss Gottorf bei Schleswig D 32 Lk36
Schloss Güstrow D 32 Ln37
Schloss Hartenfels in Torgau D 32 Ln39
Schloss Jever D 32 Lh37
Schloss Linz A 42 Lp42
Schloss Ludwigsburg D 33 Lk42
Schloss Neuschwanstein D 33 Ll43
Schlosspark Neustrelitz D 32 Lo37
Schloss Porcia in Spittal an der Drau A 35 Lo44
Schloss Schwerin D 32 Lm37
Schloss und Park von Sanssouci D 32 Ln38
Schloss Wilhelmsburg Schmalkalden D 32 Ll40
Schloss Wilhelmshöhe D 32 Lk39
Schloss zu Gotha D 32 Ll40
Schlüchtern D 33 Lk40
Schlüsselfeld D 33 Ll41
Schmalkalden D 32 Ll40
Schmallenberg D 32 Lj39
Schmidt RCH 208 Gd65
Schmidtsdrift ZA 155 Mc60
Schmölln D 32 Ln40
Schmücke D 32 Lm39
Schneeberg D 33 Ln40
Schneverdingen D 32 Lk37
Schoberspitze A 35 Lp43
Schokland NL 23 Lf38
Schönberg D 32 Ll36
Schönberg D 32 Ll37
Schönbrunn A 42 Lr42
Schönebeck D 32 Lm38
Schongau D 33 Ll43
Schöningen D 32 Ll38
Schönsee D 33 Ln41
Schoombee ZA 155 Mc61
Schopfheim D 33 Lh43
Schörfling A 35 Lo43
Schorndorf D 33 Lk42
Schouten Islands PNG 115 Sc47
Schramberg D 33 Lj42
Schreiber CDN (ON) 173 Fg21
Schrobenhausen D 33 Lm42
Schruns A 34 Lk43
Schuckmansburg NAM 151 Mc54
Schurz USA (NV) 170 Ea26
Schuyler USA (NE) 172 Fb25
Schwaan D 32 Ln37
Schwabach D 33 Lm41
Schwäbische Alb D 33 Lk42
Schwäbisch Gmünd D 33 Lk42
Schwäbisch Hall D 33 Lk41
Schwabmünchen D 33 Ll42
Schwaigern D 33 Lj41
Schwalmstadt D 32 Lk40
Schwalmtal D 32 Lk40
Schwandorf D 33 Ln41
Schwaner Range RI 95 Qf46
Schwanewede D 32 Lj37
Schwarmstedt D 32 Lk38
Schwarze Elster D 32 Lo39
Schwarzenbek D 32 Ll37
Schwarzenberg D 33 Ln40
Schwarzrand NAM 154 Lj58
Schwatka Mts. USA (AK) 165 Cb12
Schwaz A 34 Lm43
Schwechat A 42 Lr42
Schwedt D 32 Lp37
Schweich D 33 Lg41
Schweinfurt D 33 Ll40
Schweizer Jura CH 34 Lg44
Schweizer Reneke ZA 155 Mc59
Schwerin D 32 Lm37
Schweriner See D 32 Lm37
Schwerin Mural AUS 103 Re58
Schwerte D 32 Lh39
Schwetzingen D 33 Lj41
Schwielochsee D 32 Lp38
Schwyz CH 34 Lj43
Sciacca I 36 Lo53
Scicli I 37 Lp54
Ščigry RUS 48 Mj20
Scilla I 37 Lq52
Ścinawa PL 40 Lr39
Scoarţa RO 44 Md45
Scobey USA (MT) 169 Eh21
Ščomyslica BY 39 Mh37
Scone AUS (NSW) 111 Sf62
Scooba USA (MS) 175 Ff29
Scoresby Land DK 163 Jd04
Scoresby Sound DK 163 Jd04
Scoresbysund = Ittoqqortoormiit DK 163 Jd04
Scorniceşti RO 45 Me46
Scorpion Bight AUS 105 Rd62
Ščors UA 48 Mf20
Ščorsy BY 41 Mg37
Scotia USA (CA) 168 Dh25
Scotia Bay CDN (BC) 166 Dd16
Scotia Ridge 190 Ha15
Scotia Sea 190 Ha15
Scotland GB 20 Kq34
Scotland Neck USA (NC) 178 Gb27
Scott Base ANT (NZ) 7 Tb34
Scott Canyon ANT 7 Td33
Scott City USA (KS) 174 Ek26
Scott Coast 7 Ta34
Scott Mountains 7 Nc32
Scott Reef AUS 102 Ra53
Scottsbluff USA (NE) 171 Ej25
Scotts Bluff Nat. Mon. USA 171 Ej25
Scottsboro USA (AL) 175 Fg28
Scottsburg USA (IN) 175 Fh26
Scottsburgh ZA 155 Mf61
Scottsdale AUS (TAS) 111 Sd66
Scottsdale USA (AZ) 171 Ee29
Scottsville USA (KY) 175 Fg27
Scottsville USA (VA) 177 Ga27
Scotty's Castle USA 170 Eb27
Scotty's Junction USA (NV) 170 Eb27
Scourie GB 20 Kp32
Scrabster GB 20 Kr32
Scranton USA (KS) 174 Fc26
Scranton USA (ND) 169 Ej22
Scranton USA (PA) 177 Gc25
Ščučyn BY 41 Me37
Scunthorpe GB 21 Ku37
Scuol CH 34 Ll44
Ščyrec' UA 43 Md41
Seabra BR (BA) 201 Hk52
Seabreeze Amusement Park USA 177 Gb24
Seaford USA (DE) 177 Gc26
Seaforth AUS (QLD) 109 Se56
Seagaia Ocean Dome J 79 Rf30
Sea Gardens RI 92 Ph43
Seahouses GB 20 Kt35
Sea Isle City USA (NJ) 177 Gc26
Sea Lake AUS (VIC) 111 Sb63
Seal C. USA 164 Ca18
Seal Cay BS 179 Gb34
Seal Cove CDN (NF) 177 Hb21
Sea Lion Island GB 210 Ha72
Seal Is. USA 164 Ca17
Seal Point ZA 155 Mc63
Sealy USA (TX) 181 Fb31
Seamer GB 21 Ku36
Sea of Azov UA/RUS 48 Mj22
Sea of Galilee IL 56 Mh29
Sea of Heat CHN 87 Pk33
Sea of Japan 77 Rh25
Sea of Marmara TR 45 Mj50
Sea of Okhotsk RUS 55 Sb07
Sea of the Hebrides GB 20 Ko34
Sea Park ZA 155 Mf61
Seara BR (SC) 204 Hd59
Searchlight USA (NV) 170 Ec28
Searchmont CDN (ON) 173 Fh22
Searcy USA (AR) 175 Fe28
Seaside USA (OR) 168 Dj23
Seaside Point USA (OR) 168 Dh23
Seaspray AUS (VIC) 111 Sd65
Sea Temple RI 95 Qh50
Seattle USA (WA) 168 Dj22
Seaview Range AUS (QLD) 107 Sc55
Seaward Kaikoura Range NZ 113 Tg67
Sea World AUS 109 Sg59
Sea World USA 179 Fk31
Sea World of San Antonio USA 181 Fa31
Seba RI 96 Ra51
Sébaco NIC 184 Fg39
Sebakung RI 95 Qj46
Se Bangfai LAO 89 Qc37
Sebangka RI 93 Qc45
Sebaring RP 94 Qj41
Sebastian USA (FL) 179 Fk32
Sebastian Inlet USA (FL) 179 Fk32
Sebastopol USA (CA) 170 Dj26
Sebastopol USA (MS) 175 Ff29
Sebatik RI 94 Qj43
Sebauh MAL 94 Qg44
Sebayan, Gunung RI 95 Qf46
Sebba BF 137 La39
Sebderat ER 142 Mj38
Sebdou DZ 125 Kk28
Šebekino RUS 48 Mj20
Sébékoro RMM 136 Kf39
Seberi BR (RS) 204 Hd59
Seberida RI 93 Qb46
Sebeş RO 44 Md45
Sebesi RI 93 Qc48
Sebeta ETH 142 Mk41
Sébété RMM 131 Kg38
Sebež RUS 39 Mj34
Sebežskij N.P. RUS 39 Mj34
Şebinkarahisar TR 57 Mk25
Sebiş RO 43 Mc44
Sebit EAK 144 Mh45
Sebkha Aïn Belbela DZ 125 Kh32
Sebkha Azzel-Matti DZ 125 La33
Sebkha de Timimoun DZ 125 La31
Sebkha de Tindouf DZ 125 Kg32
Sebkha el Mellah DZ 125 Kk31
Sebkha Mekerrhane DZ 125 La32
Sebkha Ndrhamcha RIM 130 Kc36
Sebkha Tah DARS 124 Kd32
Sebkhat El Kébira DZ 125 Kk28
Sebkhet Afouidich DARS 130 Kc35
Sebkhet Aghzoumal DARS 124 Kd33
Sebkhet Chemchâm RIM 130 Kd35
Sebkhet ei Jill RIM 130 Kd34
Sebkhet En Nou TN 126 Le28
Sebkhet Ghallamane RIM 131 Kf34
Sebkhet Grinnah DARS 130 Kc34
Sebkhet Iguetti RIM 124 Kf33
Sebkhet Oumm ed Droûs Guebli RIM 130 Ke34
Sebkhet Oumm ed Droûs Telli RIM 124 Ke33
Sebkhet Sidi El Hani TN 126 Lf28
Sebkhet Tanouzkka DARS 130 Kc34
Sebkhet Tidsit DARS 130 Kc34
Seblat, Gunung RI 93 Qb47
Sebnitz D 32 Lp40
Sebol GCA 184 Ff38
Sebonpopo RI 91 Re45
Sebring USA (FL) 179 Fk32
Sebta = Ceuta E 125 Kh28
Sebt-des-Gzoula MA 124 Kf29
Sebuku RI 93 Qc48
Sebuku RI 93 Qc48
Sebuku RI 95 Qj47
Šebunino RUS 77 Sa22
Secador BR (MS) 202 Hc57
Secemin PL 41 Lu40
Sečenovo RUS 48 Nc18
Sechín PE 197 Ga50
Sechura PE 196 Fk48
Seclin F 23 Ld40
Secondigny F 24 Ku44
Sečoveljske soline SLO 42 Lo45
Secretary Island NZ 113 Td68
Secuieni RO 49 Md22
Secunderabad IND (APH) 82 Ok37
Security USA (CO) 171 Eh26
Seda LT 39 Mc34
Sedalia USA (MO) 174 Fd26
Sedan AUS (QLD) 109 Sb58
Sedan F 23 Le41
Sedan USA (KS) 174 Fb27
Sedan USA (NM) 174 Ej27
Sedanau RI 94 Qd44
Seddon NZ 113 Th66
Sedeh IR 64 Ng30
Sedeh IR 64 Ng30
Sedeh IR 64 Nk29
Sedeinga Temple SUD 135 Mf35
Séderon F 25 Lf46
Sedgefield ZA 154 Mb63
Sédhiou SN 136 Kc39
Sédini I 36 Lj50
Sedjenane TN 126 Le27
Sedlčany CZ 42 Lp41
Sedlyšče UA 41 Me39
Sedoa RI 96 Ra46
Sedona USA (AZ) 171 Ee28
Sedrata DZ 126 Lc30
Sedrata DZ 126 Ld27
Sedro Wolley USA (WA) 168 Dj21
Šeduva LT 39 Md35
Sędziszów PL 41 Ma40
Seebe CDN (AB) 168 Ec20
Seeberg A/SLO 35 Lp44
Seefeld A 34 Lm43
Seehausen D 32 Lm38
Seeheim NAM 154 Lj59
Seeis NAM 150 Lj57
Seekoegat ZA 154 Mb62
Seekwa GH 137 Kj42
Seeley Lake USA (MT) 169 Ed22
Seelig, Mount 6 Ed35
Seelow D 32 Lp38
Seemore Downs AUS (WA) 105 Rc61
Seer MNG 67 Pg21
Sées F 22 La42
Şefaatli TR 56 Mh26
Sefar DZ 132 Le33
Seferihisar TR 47 Mg52
Séféto RMM 130 Kf38
Sefid Abeh IR 64 Oa30
Sefophe RB 152 Md57
Sefoula MA 125 Kj29
Sefrou MA 125 Kh29
Segag ETH 143 Nb42
Segala ER 142 Na38
Ségala RMM 130 Ke38
Segamat MAL 92 Qb44

Segangane ▲ MA 125 Kj28
Şegarcea ☐ RO 44 Md46
Ségbana ☐ DY 138 Lb40
Şegbwema ▲ WAL 136 Ke42
Segesta ▣ I 36 Ln53
Seget ☒ RI 97 Rf46
Seghe ☐ SOL 117 Sj50
Segorbe ☐ E 29 Ku51
Ségou ▲ CO 192 Gc42
Segovia ▣ USA ▣ E 26 Kp43
Segré ☐ F 22 Ku43
Segrun ☐ RI 93 Pj44
Séguéla ☐ RMM 137 Kj39
Seguédine ☐ TCH 138 Lg35
Séguéla ☐ CI 137 Kg42
Séguéla ☐ RMM 131 Kg38
Séguénéga ☐ BF 137 Kj39
Segunda ☐ USA (TX) 171 Fb31
Segunda (VI) 187 Qd36
Segura ☐ P 27 Kr51
Segura de la Sierra ☐ E 27 Ks52
Segurola ☐ RA (BA) 209 Hb64
Sehithwa ☐ RB 155 Mh53
Sehlabathebe N.P. ☐♦ LS 155 Me60
Seho ☒ RI 97 Rc47
Sehonghong ☐ LS 155 Me60
Sehulea ☐ IND (MPH) 82 Oj34
Sehwa ☐ PNG 116 Sf50
Sehwan ☐ PK 65 Od32
Seia ☐ P 26 Kn50
Seibert ☐ USA (CO) 174 Ej26
Seica Mare ☐ RO 43 Me44
Seikan Tunnel ▣ J 77 Sa25
Seilhac ☐ F 24 Lb44
Seiling ☐ USA (OK) 174 Fa27
Seinäjoki ☐ FIN 38 Md28
Seine ☐ F 23 Ld42
Seine Bank ☒ 124 Kc29
Seini ☐ RO 43 Md43
Seinma ☒ RI 114 Rk48
Seira ☒ RI 97 Rf49
Seirijai ☐ LT 39 Md36
Seitsemisen kansallispuisto ♠ FIN 38 Md29
Seixal ☐ EAT 147 Mj49
Sejera ☐ DK 30 Lm35
Sejmčan ☐ RUS 55 Sc06
Sejny ☐ PL 41 Md36
Sejorong ☒ RI 96 Qj50
Seka ☐ RA (CC) 207 Gj60
Şekean ☐ TR 47 Mk52
Seka Banza ☐ RDC 148 Lg48
Sekadau ☐ RI 95 Qf45
Sekak ☒ RI 114 Rg46
Sekayu ☒ RI 91 Qk45
Sekenke ☐ EAT 146 Mh48
Seki ☐ AZ 57 Nd25
Seki ☐ J 79 Rj28
Sekigahara-Oro Q.N.P. ☐♦ J 79 Rj28
Sekodi ☒ RI 93 Qb45
Sekondi ☐ GH 137 Kk43
Sekong ☐ LAO 89 Qd38
Sek'ot'a ☐ ETH 142 Mk39
Sekpiegu ☐ GH 137 Kk41
Sekuau ☒ MAL 94 Qg44
Sekulovo ☒ RI 95 Qf45
Sekupang ☒ RI 93 Qd45
Sela ☐ BF 137 Kk40
Se La ▲ IND 86 Pg32
Selalang ☒ MAL 94 Qf44
Selama ☒ MAL 94 Qg44
Selangan ☒ MAL 94 Qg44
Selaón ▲ S 31 Ls31
Selaphum ☐ THA 89 Qb37
Selárgius ▣ I 36 Lk51
Şelaru ☒ RI 97 Rf50
Selassi ☒ RI 114 Rg47
Selat ☐ USA 84 Ri96 Oj50
Selatan ☒ RI 97 Rd48
Selat Aruri ☒ RI 114 Rh46
Selatan ☒ RI 97 Rd48
Selat Bangka ☒ RI 93 Qc47
Selat Bengkalis ☒ RI 93 Qa45
Selat Berhala ☒ RI 93 Qa46
Selat Bungalaut ☒ RI 91 Pk46
Selat Dampier ☒ RI 97 Rf46
Selat Durian ☒ RI 93 Qb45
Selat Lombok ☒ RI 95 Qh50
Selat Nautilus ☒ RI 114 Rg48
Selat Ombai ☒ RI 97 Rc50
Selatpanjang ☒ RI 93 Qa45
Selat Rupat ☒ RI 93 Qa45
Selat Sanding ☒ RI 96 Qk50
Selat Siberut ☒ RI 91 Pk46
Selat Woinui ☒ RI 114 Rh46
Selat Yapen ☒ RI 114 Rj46
Selawik ☐ USA (AK) 165 Ca12
Selawik National Wildlife Refuge ☐♦ USA 165 Ca12
Selayar ☒ RI 96 Qk47
Selb ☐ D 33 Lm42
Selbitz ☐ D 33 Lm40
Selbjørnsfjorden ☒ N 30 Lf31
Selby ☐ USA (WV) 177 Ga26
Selby ☐ GB 21 Kt37
Selby ☐ USA (SD) 172 Ek23
Selço ☐ RUS 39 Mj32
Selçuk ☐ TR 47 Mh53
Seldovia ☐ USA (AK) 164 Ce16
Selebi-Phikwe ☐ RB 152 Md57
Selecuk ☒ RI 70 Qc19
Selemdža ☒ RUS 71 Re20
Selendi ☐ TR 47 Mj52
Selenga ☒ MNG 70 Qa21
Selenge ☐ MNG 70 Qa21
Selenge ☐ MNG 70 Qa21
Selenge ☐ RDC 149 Lk46
Selenge Gol ▲ MNG 70 Qa21
Selengei ☐ EAT 144 Mj47
Selenginsk ☐ RUS (BUR) 70 Qd20
Sélestat ▣ F 25 Lh42
Senica ▣ SK 42 Lq42
Senigállia ☐ I 35 Lo47
Seltos ☐ IS 18 Ju27
Silibabi ☐ RIM 130 Kd38
Seligenstadt ☐ D 33 Lk40
Sélim ☐ RCA 141 Md43
Selim Caravanserai ☐ ARM 57 Nc26

Selongey ▣ F 25 Lf43
Selopuginо ☐ RUS 71 Qj20
Selous ☐ ZW 152 Mf55
Selous Game Reserve ▣☐ EAT 147 Mj50
Selous, Mount ▲ CDN 166 Dd14
Selpel ☒ RI 97 Rf46
Selsele-ye Kuh-e Tirband-e Torkestan ▲ AFG 63 Oc28
Selsele-ye Safid Kuh ▲ AFG 64 Ob28
Selseleye Siyah Kuh ▲ AFG 65 Ob29
Selsey Bill ▲ GB 21 Ku40
Seltz ☐ F 23 Lj42
Selu ☐ IND (MHT) 82 Oj36
Seluan ☒ RI 94 Qd43
Selva ☐ RA (SE) 207 Gj60
Selva Alegre ☐ EC 196 Ga45
Selvas ☒ BR 190 Gb10
Selwyn Range ▲ AUS (QLD) 108 Sa56
Selwyn Mountains ▲ CDN 166 De14
Selwyn Mountains ▲ AUS (QLD) 107 Rk56
Sémacueza ☐ MOC 153 Mh55
Sémana ☐ RMM 137 Kg40
Semanu ☒ RI 94 Qj44
Semarang ☐ RI 95 Qf44
Semarwara ☒ IND (RJT) 82 Og34
Sematan ☒ MAL 94 Qe45
Sematang ☒ RI 91 Ra45
Semau ☒ RI 95 Qh50
Sembabule ☒ EAU 144 Mf46
Sembabeh ☒ IND (MHT) 82 Oj35
Semberang ☒ RI 91 Qk45
Sembehun ☒ WAL 136 Kd42
Semberong, Mount ▲ RI 92 Pj43
Şemdinli ☐ TR 57 Nc27
Semeles ☐ SUD 135 Mf39
Semenic-Cheile Caraşului, P.N. ☐♦ RO 44 Md45
Semenivka ☐ UA 48 Mj19
Semenov ☐ RUS 48 Nc17
Semënovka ☐ RUS 71 Rd20
Semera ☐ MAL 94 Qf45
Semeru, Gunung ▲ RI 95 Qg50
Semeteh ☒ RI 93 Qb47
Semen ☐ KZ 54 Pa08
Sémien ☒ CI 137 Kg42
Semikarakorsk ☐ RUS 49 Na22
Seral ☒ RI 91 Rc45
Seraing ☐ B 23 Lf40
Semiluki ☐ RUS 48 Mk20
Seminoe Reservoir ☒ USA 171 Eg24
Seminole ☐ USA (OK) 174 Fb28
Seminole ☐ USA (TX) 174 Ej29
Seminole Canyon S.P. ☐♦ USA 181 Ek31
Seminole Nation Mus. ☐ USA 174 Fb28
Semirara Islands ▲ RP 90 Ra39
Semirom ☐ IR 59 Nf30
Semitau ☒ RI 94 Qf44
Semliki Wildlife Reserve ☐♦ EAU 144 Mf45
Semmeringbahn ☐ A 35 Lq43
Semna ☐ SUD 129 Mf39
Semnan ☐ IR 62 Ng28
Semna West Temple ☐ SUD 129 Mf35
Semolale ☐ RB 152 Me56
Semox ☐ GCA 184 Ff38
Sempacher See ☒ CH 34 Lj43
Sempeter ☐ SLO 42 Lq44
Semporna ☒ MAL 91 Qk43
Semt ☐ IND (MPH) 83 Ok34
Semuliki ☒ EAU 144 Mf45
Semur-en-Auxois ▣ F 25 Le43
Sena ☐ BOL 198 Gj51
Senador Firmino ☐ BR (MG) 203 Hj56
Senador José Porfírio ☐ BR (PA) 195 Hd47
Senador Pompeu ☐ BR (CE) 201 Ja48
Senafe ☐ ER 142 Mk38
Senaki ☐ GE 57 Nb24
Señal Canoas ▲ PE 197 Gb51
Señal Huascaran ▲ PE 197 Gb50
Señal Mongon ▲ PE 197 Ga50
Sena Madureira ☐ BR (AC) 198 Gf50
Senanga ☐ Z 151 Mb54
Senatobia ☐ USA (MS) 175 Ff28
Senayang ☒ RI 93 Qc46
Senchi ☒ GH 137 La42
Sendafa ☐ ETH 142 Mk41
Sendai ☐ J 77 Rk30
Sendai ☐ J 79 Rf30
Sendangbiru ☒ RI 95 Qg50
Sendelingsfontein ☐ ZA 155 Md59
Senden ☐ D 33 Lj42
Sendhwa ☐ IND (MPH) 82 Oh35
Şendreni ☒ RO 44 Mh45
Senec ☐ SK 42 Lq42
Seneca ☐ USA (OR) 168 Ea23
Seneca ☐ USA (SC) 172 Fa23
Seneca Caverns ☐ USA 177 Ga26
Seneca Rocks ▲ USA (WV) 177 Ga26
Senegal ▣ RIM/SN 130 Kc37
Sénégal ☐ 123 Ka08
Senekal ☐ ZA 155 Md60
Seney ☐ USA (MI) 173 Fh22
Seney N.W.R. ▣ USA 173 Fg22
Senftenberg ☐ D 32 Lo39
Sengar ▣ IND 153 Mh52
Sengan ☐ WAN 138 Lc43
Sengata ☒ RI 94 Qj45
Sengati ☐ RI 93 Qb46
Sêngge Zangbo = Indus ☐ CN 68 Pa30
Senggigi Beach ☐ RI 96 Qj50
Senggigi ☐ RI 93 Qa45
Sengkang ☒ RI 96 Ra48
Senhor do Bonfim ☐ BR (BA) 201 Hk51
Senhora do Porto ☐ BR (MG) 203 Hj55
Senica ▣ SY 39 Mh37
Senica ☐ SK 42 Lq42
Senigállia ☐ I 35 Lo47
Senj ☐ HR 35 Lp46
Senja ▲ N 16 Lj11
Senji = Gingee ☐ IND (TNU) 85 Ok39
Senkobo ☐ Z 151 Mc54
Sénkérgni ☐ RMM 130 Ke38
Sélinunte ▣ I 36 Ln53
Seliu ☒ RI 95 Qd47
Selitárovo ☐ RUS 48 Mg17
Seljakloa ☐ EST 38 Md31
Seljatyn ☐ UA 43 Mf43
Seljord ☐ N 30 Lj31
Selkirk ☐ CDN (MB) 172 Fb20
Selkirk ☐ GB 20 Kr35
Selkirk Mountains ▲ CDN 168 Eb20
Selläuroich ☐ DARS 130 Kd34
Sellers ☐ USA (SC) 178 Ga28
Sellers-sur-Cher ▣ F 24 Lb43
Selinova ☐ USA (TX) 174 Fb33
Selma ☐ USA (AL) 175 Fg30
Selmer ☐ USA (TN) 175 Ff28
Selmice ☐ RUS 166 Mc58
Sélo Kouré ▲ RG 136 Kd42

Sentinela do Sul ☐ BR (RS) 204 He61
Sentinel Peak ▲ CDN 166 Dj18
Sento-Sé ☐ BR (BA) 201 Hk50
Sentrum ☐ ZA 155 Md58
Senu ☒ RI (NMP) 86 Pg33
Senyavin Islands ▲ FSM 10 Sb09
Senyo ☐ GQ 138 La45
Seokguram Grotto ☐♦ ROK 79 Re28
Seondha ☒ IND (MPH) 83 Ok32
Seoni ☒ IND (MPH) 83 Ok34
Seoni Chhapara ☒ IND (MPH) 83 Ok34
Seoni Malwa ☒ IND (MPH) 82 Oj34
Seorinarayan ☒ IND (CGH) 83 Pb35
Sepa ☒ RI 97 Re47
Sépaur ☒ RI 93 Qa45
Sepatan ☒ RI (NM) 171 Ej29
Sepang ☒ MAL 92 Qa44
Separ ☐ USA (NM) 171 Ef29
Separation Point ▲ NZ 113 Tg66
Separeva Banja ☐ BG 44 Md48
Sepasu ☒ RI 94 Qj45
Sepeteri ☐ WAN 138 Lb41
Šepetivka ☐ UA 49 Md20
Sepik River ☐♦ PNG 115 Sb48
Sepik River Cruises ▣ PNG 115 Sb48
Sepit Dasht ☐ IR 59 Ne29
Seppa ☒ IND (ARP) 86 Pg32
Seppai ☒ PL 41 Mb36
Sept-Îles ☐ CDN (QC) 176 Gg20
Sepúlveda ☐ E 26 Kr49
Sequeira ☒ RI 91 Qk45
Sequeiros ☐ BR 203 Hk56
Sequoia N.P. ☐♦ USA 170 Hd61
Sequoyah Caverns ☐♦ USA 175 Fh28
Sequoyah N.W.R. ☐♦ USA 174 Fc28
Serafetín Dağları ▲ TR 57 Na24
Serafina ☐ USA (NM) 171 Eh28
Serai ☒ RI 91 Rc45
Seram ☒ RI (KTK) 82 Oj37
Seram Laut ☒ RI 97 Rf47
Ser Monastery ▲ CHN 69 Pf31
Serampore ☒ IND (WBG) 86 Pe34
Serang ☒ RI 95 Qd49
Serano ☒ RA (CB) 209 Gj63
Serasan ☒ RI 94 Qe44
Serasan Strait ☒ RI/MAL 94 Qe44
Seraya ▲ RI 94 Qd44
Serbeulang Range ▲ RI 92 Pj44
Serbia and Montenegro ☐ 15 Lb05
Serca ☐ CHN (TIB) 69 Ph30
Serchip ☒ IND (MZR) 86 Pg34
Serdjilis ☐ SYR 56 Mj28
Serdobsk ☐ RUS 48 Nd18
Serdoba ☒ RUS 48 Nc19
Serébou ☐ CI 137 Kj42
Serebryansk ☐ KZ 67 Pc23
Sered ☐ SK 42 Lq42
Serédou ☒ RG 136 Kf41
Seredžius ☐ LT 39 Md35
Sereflikoçhisar ☐ TR 56 Mg28
Sereflikochisar ☐ TR 56 Mg28
Seregno ☐ I 34 Lk45
Seremban ☒ MAL 92 Qa44
Seremeño ▲ RCH 206 Ga56
Serengeti N.P. ▣♦ EAT 144 Mh47
Serengeti Plain ▲ 144 Mh47
Serenje ☐ Z 146 Mf52
Serere ☐ EAU 144 Mf45
Séres ☐ GR 44 Md49
Serfaus ☐ A 34 Ll43
Sergelen ☐ MNG 70 Qf22
Sergines ▣ F 23 Ld42
Sérgio ☐ BR 201 Jb51
Sérgipe ☐ BRU 34 Qk43
Serian ☒ MAL 94 Qf44
Seri Burat ☐ MAL 92 Qb44
Sérifos ☐ GR 47 Me53
Sérifos ☐ GR 47 Me53
Serikandi ☐ RI 97 Rd47
Serikambelo ☐ RI 97 Rd47
Serikure ☐ CHN (XUZ) 68 Oj26
Serikin ☒ MAL 94 Qf45
Seringal Jaboti ☒ RI (RO) 198 Gf50
Seringal Macatuba ☐ BR (AM) 198 Gf50
Seringal Novo Acordo ☐ BR (RO) 198 Gj51
Seringal Novo Andirá ☐ BR (AM) 198 Gf50
Seringal São Pedro ☐ BR (RO) 177 Gd24
Seringapatam Reef ▲ AUS 102 Rb52
Serinhisar ☐ TR 56 Mf27
Serinya Island ▲ EAU 144 Mg46
Serkin Yamma ▲ RN 132 Ld39
Serkout ☒ DZ 132 Lc34
Serkout ☒ DZ 132 Lc34
Sermaize-les-Bains ▣ F 23 Le42
Sermata ☒ RI 97 Rd49
Sermanche ▣ F 25 Lf43
Sernovodsk ☐ RUS 77 Sc24
Séron ☐ E 27 Ks53
Serón de Nágima ☐ E 28 Ks49
Seronera ☐ EAT 144 Mh47
Seronga ☐ RB 151 Mb55
Seros ☐ E 29 La49
Seroue ☐ RI 97 Rd47
Serouenout ☒ DZ 132 Ld33
Serov ☐ RUS 54 Oa07
Serowe ☐ RB 152 Md57
Serpa ☐ P 27 Kp53
Serpentine ☐ AUS (VIC) 111 Sc63
Serpentine Hot Springs ☐ USA 175 Fd29
Serpent's Mouth ☒ YV 193 Gk41
Serpuhov ☐ RUS 48 Mj18
Serra Acara ou Acari ▲ BR 194 Ha45
Serra Bodoquena, P.N. da ☐♦ BR 202 Hd52
Serra Bonita ☐ BR (MG) 203 Hj54
Serra Branca ☐ BR (PB) 201 Jb49
Serra Cafema ▲ RA 155 Lh54
Serraca capriola ▣ I 37 Lq49
Serra da Batista ☐ BR (PI) 201 Hk51
Serra da Bocaina, P.N. de ☐♦ BR 205 Hg57
Serra da Canastra ▲ BR 203 Hg55
Serra da Canastra, P.N.da ☐♦ BR 203 Hg55

Serra da Chela ▲ ANG 150 Lg54
Serra da Cutia, P.N. ☐♦ BR 198 Gh51
Serra da Estrela ▲ P 26 Kn50
Serra da Ibiapaba ▲ BR 201 Hk47
Serra da Mantiqueira ▲ BR 203 Hh57
Serra da Moca, T.I. ☐♦ BR 193 Gk44
Serra da Mocidade, P.N. da ☐♦ BR 200 Hh49
Serra das Alpercatas ▲ BR 200 Hh49
Serra das Araras ▲ BR (MG) 203 Hh53
Serra das Araras ▲ BR 202 Hb53
Serra das Confusões, P.N.da ☐♦ BR 200 Hh52
Serra das Cordilheiras ▲ BR 200 Hj49
Serra das Divisões ou da Santa Marta ▲ BR 202 Hd54
Serra das Margabeiras ▲ BR 200 Hh51
Serra das Marrecas ▲ BR 201 Hk50
Serra das Safiras ▲ BR 203 Hk55
Serra da Tabatinga ▲ BR 200 Hh51
Serra do Divisor ▲ BR/PE 196 Gd50
Serra do Itapicuru ▲ BR 200 Hh49
Serra de Itúba ▲ BR 201 Ja51
Serra de Llevant ▲ E 29 Ld51
Serra de Maracaju ▲ BR 202 Hd53
Serra de Monchique ▲ P 27 Km53
Serra de Neve ▲ ANG 150 Lg52
Serra de Outes ☐ E 26 Km48
Serra de Piauí ▲ BR 201 Hj50
Serra de Prades ▲ E 29 La49
Serra de Santa Bárbara ▲ BR 206 Ha53
Serra de Santa Maria ▲ BR 203 Hg53
Serra de São Felipe ▲ BR 202 Ho54
Serra de São Jerônimo ▲ BR 202 Hc54
Serra de Tramuntana ▲ E 29 Lc51
Serres ▣ F 25 Lf46
Serrières ▣ F 25 Le45
Serra de Uneiuxi ▲ EC 196 Fk47
Serradilla ☐ E 27 Ko51
Serra do Aguapeí ▲ BR 206 Ha53
Serra do Almeirim ▲ BR 199 Hd46
Serra do Bom Jesus da Gurgueia ▲ BR 201 Hj50
Serra do Boqueirão ▲ BR 200 Hj51
Serra do Cabral ▲ BR 203 Hh54
Serra do Cachimbo ▲ BR 199 Hb50
Serra do Caldeirão ▲ P 27 Kn53
Serra do Capauari ▲ BR 198 Gf46
Serra do Caramulo ▲ P 26 Kn50
Serra do Chaparaí ▲ BR 203 Hj56
Serra do Chifre ▲ BR 203 Hk54
Serra do Chilengue ▲ ANG 150 Lj52
Serra do Cipó, P.N.da ☐♦ BR 203 Hj55
Serra do Divisor, P.N.da ☐♦ BR 196 Gd50
Serra do Espinhaço ▲ BR 203 Hj54
Serra do Estreito ▲ BR 201 Hj51
Serra do Estrondo ▲ BR 200 Hg50
Serra do Periquito ▲ BR 201 Ja50
Serra do Ramalho ☐ BR (BA) 200 Hj52
Serra do Ramalho ▲ BR 200 Hh52
Serra do Rio Preto ▲ BR 203 Hg54
Serra do Roncador ▲ BR 200 Hc52
Serra dos Aimorés ▲ BR 203 Hk55
Serra do Salitre ☐ BR (MG) 203 Hg55
Serra dos Apiacás ▲ BR 199 Hb51
Serra dos Caiabis ▲ BR 199 Hb51
Serra dos Carajás ▲ BR 200 He48
Serra dos Cariris Novos ▲ BR 201 Hk49
Serra dos Cristais ▲ BR 203 Hg54
Serra dos Dois Irmãos ▲ BR 201 Hk50
Serra dos Gradaús ▲ BR 200 He50
Serra do Sincorá ▲ BR 201 Hk52
Serra dos Órgãos, P.N.da ☐♦ BR 205 Hj57
Serra dos Pacaás Novos ▲ BR 198 Gj51
Serra dos Pilões ▲ BR 203 Hg54
Serra dos Propeiros ▲ BR 203 Hh53
Serra dos Três Irmãos ▲ BR 198 Gh50
Serra dos Xavantes ▲ BR 200 Hf51
Serra do Tiracambu ▲ BR 200 Hg47
Serra do Tombador ▲ BR 199 Hb51
Serra do Tombador ▲ BR 200 Hf51
Serra do Traira ▲ BR 198 Gd46
Serra do Tumucumaque ▲ BR 194 Ha45
Serra Dourada ▲ BR (BA) 200 Hj52
Serra Dourada ▲ BR (MT) 202 Hd52
Serra Formosa ▲ BR 202 Hc52
Serra Geral ▲ BR 204 He60
Serra Geral de Goiás ▲ BR 200 Hh51
Serra Geral do Paraná ▲ BR 203 Hg53
Serra Hills ▲ PNG 115 Sa47
Serra Jurique ▲ BR 202 Hc54
Serra Linda ▲ BR 201 Hj50

Serra Lombarda ▲ BR 195 He44
Serra Mecula ▲ MOC 147 Mj51
Serra Morena, T.I. ☐♦ BR 199 Ha51
Serrana ☐ BR (SP) 203 Hg56
Serrana de Cuenca ▲ E 29 Ks50
Serra Negra ☐ BR (PR) 205 Hf58
Serra Negra ☐ BR (BA) 201 Hj55
Serranía Ayapel ▲ CO 192 Gc42
Serranía de Abibe ▲ CO 192 Gb43
Serranía de Baudó ▲ CO 192 Gb44
Serranía de Chiribiquete ▲ CO 192 Gd45
Serranía de Imataca ▲ YV 193 Gk42
Serranía de la Cerbatana ▲ YV 193 Gg42
Serranía de la Macarena ▲ CO 192 Gd44
Serranía de la Macarena, P.N. ☐♦ YV 193 Gg45
Serranía del Darién ▲ PA 185 Gb41
Serranía de Mapichi ▲ YV 193 Gf45
Serranía de Naquen ▲ BR/CO 192 Gc42
Serranía de San Lucas ▲ CO 192 Gc42
Serranía de Sicasica ▲ BOL 206 Gg54
Serranía San Luís, P.N. ☐♦ PY 202 Hb57
Serrania del Burro ▲ MEX 181 Ej31
Serranías Huapi ▲ NIC 185 Fh39
Serranópolis ☐ BR (GO) 202 Hd55
Serra Paranapicaba ▲ BR 205 Hf58
Serra Paranaquara ▲ BR 199 Hd46
Serra Parima ▲ BR 193 Gh44
Serrararia ▲ BR (MA) 200 Hg47
Serra San Bruno ▣ I 37 Lr52
Sêrra Talhada ☐ BR (PE) 201 Ja49
Sfaka ☐ GR 47 Mf55
Sfáka ☐ GR 47 Mf55
Serres ▣ F 25 Lf46
Serrinha ☐ BR (BA) 201 Ja51
Serrita ☐ BR (PE) 201 Ja49
Serrota ▲ E 27 Kp51
Sertã ▣ P 27 Km51
Sertânia ▲ BR (PE) 201 Ja49
Sertanópolis ☐ BR (PR) 202 He57
Sertãozinho ☐ BR (SP) 202 Hf56
Sêrtar ☐ CHN (SCH) 72 Qa31
Serua ☒ RI 97 Re49
Serui ☒ RI 114 Rj46
Serule ☐ RB 152 Me56
Serutu ☒ RI 95 Qe46
Seruwai ☒ RI 92 Pj43
Servia ☐ GR 46 Mc50
Serviceton ☐ AUS 110 Sa64
Serwaru ☒ RI 97 Rd50
Sérxu ☐ CHN (SCH) 69 Pg29
Séryševo ☐ RUS 71 Re20
Sesayng ☒ RI 94 Qf43
Sese ☐ RDC 144 Mc44
Sesegonago Lake ☒ CDN 172 Fe20
Sesfontein ☐ NAM 150 Lg55
Seshego ☒ ZA 152 Me57
Sesheke ☐ Z 151 Mb54
Seshkhaliu ☒ IND (ORS) 83 Pb36
Sesia ▣ I 27 Kf32
Sesriem ☐ NAM 154 Lh58
Sesriemafgrond ☒ NAM 154 Lh58
Sesriem Canyon ☒ NAM 154 Lh58
Sesser ▲ ANG 151 Ma52
Sessa Aurunca ☐ I 36 Lo49
Sesto Calende ☐ I 34 Lj45
Sesto Fiorentino ☐ I 34 Lm47
Sestriere ☐ I 34 Lg46
Sestri Levante ☐ I 34 Lk46
Sestroretsk ☐ RUS 38 Mk30
Sévete ☐ HR 35 Lr45
Seta ☐ LT 39 Md35
Setapak ☐ MAL 92 Qa44
Sète ☐ F 25 Ld47
Sete Barras ☐ BR (SP) 205 Hg58
Sete Cerros, T.I. ☐ BR 202 Hc57
Sete Cidades, P.N.de ☐♦ BR 201 Hk48
Sete de Setembro, T.I. ☐ BR 198 Gk51
Sete Lagoas ☐ BR (MG) 203 Hh55
Sete Quedas (MS) 202 Hb57
Sete Quedas (MS) 202 Hb51
Setesdal ▲ N 30 Lh32
Setermoen ☐ N 16 Lk11
Setesdal ▲ N 30 Lh32
Sethamuak ☐ LAO 89 Qc37
Seti ▣ NEP 81 Pa33
Setif ☐ DZ 126 Lc27
Seti River Rafting ▣ NEP 81 Pa31
Setiyya ☒ IND (TNU) 85 Ok40
Setlagole ☐ ZA 155 Mc59
Seto-Nakai N.P. ☐♦ J 79 Rf29
Setonia ▲ BR 203 Hk56
Setouchi ☐ J 79 Rf30
Setpaki ☐ RUS 48 Na21
Setraki ▲ RUS 48 Na21
Sets Cinematográficos (Durango) ☐ MEX 181 Eh33
Sette Cama ☐ G 148 Le47
Séttimo Torinese ☐ I 34 Lh45
Settle ☐ GB 21 Ks36
Settlers ☐ ZA 155 Me58
Setúbal ▣ P 27 Km52
Seui ☐ I 36 Lk51
Seulimeum ☒ RI 92 Ph43
Seurre ▣ F 25 Lf44
Seu Vella de Lleida ☐ E 29 La49
Sévaré ☐ RMM 131 Kh38
Sevastópol' ☐ UA 48 Mj23
Ševčenko ☐ UA 48 Mj21
Sevenoaks ☐ GB 21 La39
Seven Persons ☐ CDN (AB) 169 Ee21
Seven Sisters ☐ GB 21 La40
Seventy-Five Mile Beach ▲ AUS 109 Sg58

Severy ☐ USA (KS) 174 Fb27
Sevettijarvi ☐ FIN 16 Me11
Sevier ☐ USA (UT) 171 Ed26
Sevier Desert ▲ USA 171 Ed26
Sevierville ☐ USA (TN) 178 Fj28
Sevilla ☐ CO 192 Gc43
Sevilla ☐ ▣ E 27 Kp53
Sevilla ☐ USA (SN) 69 Ef21
Sevilleta N.W.R. ☐♦ USA 171 Eg28
Ševkatiye ☐ TR 45 Mh50
Ševlievo ☐ BG 45 Mf48
Sevluš ☐ UA 43 Md43
Sevnica ☐ SLO 42 Lq44
Sevöstári ☐ AFG 65 Oc27
Seward ☐ USA (AK) 164 Ce16
Sewakay ☐ ZA 45 Mg47
Seward ☐ USA (NE) 174 Fb25
Seward ☐ USA (KS) 174 Ek28
Seward Peninsula ▲ USA (AK) 164 Bh13
Sewell ☐ RCH 208 Ge63
Sexmith ☐ CDN (AB) 167 Ea18
Seyaru's ☐ EAT 147 Mj48
Seychelles ☐ 123 Nb10
Seychelles Bank ▲ 145 Nh48
Seychelles-Mauritius Plateau ☒ 52 Oa10
Seydişehir ☐ TR 56 Mf27
Seydişehir ☐ TR 56 Mf27
Seydoölşfjörður ☐ IS 18 Kd25
Seydvan ☐ IR 57 Ne28
Seymour ☐ AUS (VIC) 111 Sc64
Seymour ☐ IN 175 Fh26
Seymour ☐ USA (TX) 174 Fa29
Seymour ☐ ZA 155 Md62
Seyne ☐ F 25 Lg46
Seyni ☐ RUS 48 Na19
Şeytan Kalesi (Devils Castel) ▣ TR 57 Nb25
Şeytan Sofrası ▣ TR 47 Mg51
Seyyed Abad ☐ IR 62 Ng27
Seyyedi ☐ IR 57 Nd28
Sézanne ▣ F 23 Ld42
Sezana ☐ SLO 42 Lo45
Sezela ☐ ZA 155 Mf61
Sezie ☐ MYA 86 Pj33
Sezze ☐ I 36 Lo49
Sfântu Gheorghe ☐ RO 45 Mf45
Sfântu Gheorghe ☐ RO 45 Mk46
Sfax ☐ TN 126 Lf28
Sfinári ☐ GR 45 Md55
Sfissifa Bou Ghellaba ☐ DZ 125 Kk29
Sfizef ☐ DZ 125 Kk28
's-Gravenhage ☐ NL 23 Le38
Shaanxi ☐ CHN 72 Qd29
Shaba Carvings ☐ ETH 144 Mj43
Sha'bab ☐ KSA 58 Mj33
Shaba National Reserve ☐♦ EAK 144 Mj45
Shabala ☐ SUD 135 Mh39
Shabestar ☐ IR 57 Nc26
Shabqadar ☐ PK 65 Of28
Shabunda ☐ RDC 146 Md47
Shabwah ☐ YE 60 Nd38
Shache ☐ CHN 66 Oj26
Shackelton ☐ AUS ▲ 104 Qg35
Shackleton Glacier ☒ 6 Bc35
Shackleton Ice Shelf ☒ 7 Rg32
Shackleton Inlet ☒ 7 Tc35
Shackleton Range ▲ 6 Jc35
Shadao ☐ CHN (HUB) 74 Qe31
Shada Palace ▣ KSA 60 Nb36
Shadwān ☒ ET 129 Mg32
Shaftesbury ☐ GB 21 Ks39
Shagamu ☐ WAN 138 Lb42
Shagan ☐ EAT 147 Mk48
Shagap ▲ EAK 144 Ca14
Shaghah ☒ KZ 63 Oc23
Shagoujie ☐ CHN (SAA) 72 Qe29
Shagwa ☐ WAN 138 Lc40
Shahabad ☐ IND (HYA) 81 Oj30
Shahabad ☐ IND (MHT) 82 Oj36
Shahapur ☐ IND (MHT) 82 Og36
Shahar ☐ PK 65 Oc32
Shahbandar ☐ PK 65 Oc33
Shahbaz Kalat ☐ PK 65 Ob32
Shah Bodagh ▲ IR 59 Nd29
Shahdad ☐ IR 59 Nh30
Shahdadkot ☐ PK 65 Od32
Shahdadpur ☐ PK 65 Oe33
Shahdol ☐ IND (MPH) 83 Pb34
Shahe ☐ CHN (HBI) 73 Qh27
Shahe ☐ CHN (SDG) 73 Qj27
Shaheganj ☐ IND (UPH) 83 Pb32
Shah Ismaï'il ☐ IR 59 Nf29
Shahjahanpur ☐ IND (UPH) 81 Ok32
Shah Juy ☐ AFG 65 Od29
Shah Khalil Mausoleum ☒ IR 64 Nh30
Shah-Maqsud Range ▲ AFG 65 Oc29
Shah Maran ☐ IR 64 Ng31
Shaharbithat ☐ OM 61 Nj37
Shaharestan ☐ AFG 65 Oc29
Shara Daisey ▲ KZ 63 Oc24
Shar-e Babak ☐ IR 59 Ng30
Shargal ☐ MNG 70 Qb21
Shargalljuut Water Springs ▣ MNG 70 Qa22
Shargun ☐ UZ 63 Of26
Sharhad ▲ PK 65 Oh30
Shahnyabz ☐ UZ 63 Oe26
Shârk ☐ DY 138 La42
Shahrak ☐ AFG 65 Oc29
Shahr-e Khord ☐ IR 59 Nf29
Shahrestan ☐ AFG 65 Oc29
Sharg'un ☐ UZ 63 Of26
Sharga ☐ MNG 70 Qa22
Sharga Govi ▲ MNG 67 Ph22
Sharga ☐ MNG 70 Qa21
Sharga Nature Reserve ☐♦ MNG 70 Qa22
Shahrud ☐ IR 59 Ng28
Shahdadpur ☐ PK 65 Oe33
Shahristan ☐ AFG 65 Oc29
Shahsavar ☐ IR 59 Nf28
Shahumyab ☐ UZ 63 ▲
Shak'adori ☐ ETH 144 Mk42
Shakiso ☐ ETH 142 Mk42
Shaktoulik ☐ USA (AK) 164 Bk13
Shaktoolik ▣ SP 145 Nd45
Severo-Ossetinskij zapovednik ☐♦ RUS 57 Nb24
Severo-Sibirskaja nizmennost' ▲ RUS 54 Pa04
Shalatein ☒ ET 129 Mh34

Shalimar Gardens ☐ ▣ PK 65 Oh30
Shalkar ☐ RUS (UT) 171 Ed26
Shaluli Shan ▲ CHN 69 Pk30
Shamal ☐ AFG 65 Oc29
Shambe ☐ SUD 141 Mf42
Shambo, Mount ▲ USA 171 Ed24
Shamboyacu ☐ PE 196 Gb49
Shambu ☐ ETH 142 Mj41
Shamis ☐ UAE 61 Nj34
Shamlaji ☐ IND (GUJ) 82 Og34
Shamli ☐ IND (UPH) 81 Oj31
Shamman ☐ SUD 135 Mh39
Shamputa ▲ Z 152 Md53
Shamrock ☐ USA (SK) 169 Eg20
Shamrock ☐ USA (TX) 174 Ek28
Shamsabad ☐ IND (APH) 82 Ok37
Shamsabad ☐ IND (MPH) 82 Oj34
Shamva ☐ ZW 152 Mf54
Shanaghatty ☐ KZ 67 Pd21
Shanbabe ☐ CHN (HUB) 75 Qh30
Shandan ☐ CHN (GSU) 72 Qa26
Shandon Downs ☐ AUS (NT) 106 Rh54
Shandong ☐ CHN 73 Qj27
Shandong Peninsula ▲ CHN 73 Ra27
Shandrukh ☒ IR 57 Ne29
Shandarpas ▲ PK 63 Og27
Shangani ☐ ZW 152 Me55
Shangcai ☐ CHN (HNN) 73 Qh29
Shangcheng ☐ CHN (HNN) 73 Qh30
Shangchuan Dao ▲ CHN 75 Qg35
Shangdu ☐ CHN (NMZ) 73 Qg26
Shangey-Tiev ☐ WAN 138 Lc43
Shangfu ☐ CHN (JGX) 75 Qh31
Shanggao ☐ CHN (JGX) 75 Qh31
Shanghai ☐ CHN 78 Ra30
Shanghai ☐ CHN 78 Ra30
Shanghai International Circuit ▣ CHN 78 Ra30
Shanghai Shi ☐ CHN 78 Ra30
Shanghe ☐ CHN (SDG) 73 Qj27
Shangha ☐ CHN (HNN) 73 Qh29
Shangmombo ▲ Z 151 Mb54
Shangqiu ☐ CHN (HNN) 73 Qh28
Shangrao ☐ CHN (JGX) 75 Qj31
Shangshui ☐ CHN (HNN) 73 Qh29
Shangxi ☐ CHN (GZG) 74 Qd34
Shanglin ☐ CHN (GZG) 74 Qd34
Shangnan ☐ CHN (SAA) 72 Qf29
Shangombo ▲ Z 151 Mb54
Shangqiu ☐ CHN 73 Qh28
Shangxi ☐ CHN (JGX) 75 Qj31
Shangshui ☐ CHN (HNN) 73 Qh29
Shangyi ☐ CHN (HBI) 73 Qg26
Shangyou Yichang ☐ CHN (XUZ) 66 Pa25
Shangzhi ☐ CHN (HLG) 76 Re23
Shangzhou (SAA) 72 Qe29
Shanhaiguan ☐ CHN (HBI)
Shanhaiguan Start of the Great Wall ▣ CHN 73 Qj25
Shanhetun ☐ CHN (HLG) 76 Rd23
Shanh Gongma ☐ CHN (QHI) 69 Pk29
Shani ☐ WAN 139 Lg40
Shaniko ☐ USA (OR) 168 Dk23
Shanjuandong ☐ CHN 78 Qk30
Shankh Monastery ▲ MNG 70 Qb22
Shan ☐ CHN 72 Qf27
Shankou ☐ CHN (GZG) 74 Qd34
Shankou ☐ CHN (HUN) 74 Qf31
Shanlenggang ☐ CHN (SCH) 74 Qa31
Shanngaw Taungdan ▲ MYA
Shannon ☐ IRL 19 Km38
Shannon ▲ AUS 104 Qg33
Shannon R. ☐ MYA 87 Pk35
Shanshan (XUZ) 67 Ph24
Shantarskiye Ostrova ▲ RUS 55 Rd07
Shan Xian ☐ CHN (WBG) 86 Pa37
Shanxi ☐ CHN (SN) 69 Ef21
Shanxi ☐ PE 196 Gb49
Shanxi ☐ CHN 72 Qf27
Shan Xian ☐ CHN (SDG) 78 Qj28
Shanxian ☐ CHN (HBI) 73 Qh29
Shaoguan ☐ CHN (GDG) 75 Qg33
Shaolin Temple (Songshan) ☐ CHN 177 Fc25
Shanshan ☐ CHN (XUZ) 67 Ph24
Shaowu ☐ CHN (FJN) 75 Qj32
Shaoxing ☐ CHN (ZJG) 75 Ra31
Shaoyang ☐ CHN (HUN) 74 Qf31
Shahhat ☐ LAR 127 Ma29
Shaping ☐ CHN (GZH) 74 Qd34
Shapinsay ☐ GB 20 Kr31
Shaqlawa ☐ IRQ 57 Nc27
Shaqra' ☐ KSA 59 Nc33
Shaqra ☐ YE 60 Nd38
Shar ☐ KZ 66 Pa21
Shara Iwah ☐ Q 61 Ng33
Shahumyab ▲ ☐
Sheno ☐ ETH 142 Mk41
Shentang Shan ▲ CHN 74 Qf34
Shen Xian ☐ CHN (HBI) 73 Qh28
Sharbithat ☐ OM 61 Nj37
Shar Now ☐ AFG 63 Oc28
Sharbazer ☐ KZ 63 Od24
Sharga Morit Uul ▲ MNG 70 Qa22

Sha Tin ☐ CHN (GDG) 75 Qh34
Shatrana ☐ IND (PJB) 80 Oj31
Shatt-el-Arab ☒ IRQ 59 Nd30
Shaubak ☐ JOR 58 Mh30
Shaukat ☐ KZ 63 Oe24
Shaumari W.S. ☐ JOR 58 Mj30
Shawan ☐ CHN (XUZ) 67 Pc23
Shawano ☐ USA (WI) 173 Ff23
Shawinigan ☐ CDN ☐ 176 Gd22
Shawnee ☐ USA (OK) 174 Fb28
Shaweetown S.H.S. ☐ USA 175 Ff27
Shaykhabad ☐ AFG 65 Oe28
Sheykh Farid ar-Din Attar ☒ IR 62 Nk27
Shey Phoksundo N.P. ☐♦ NEP 81 Pb31
Shezongo ☒ 152 Md54
Shetland Islands ▲ GB 20 Ku30
Shetpe ☐ KZ 62 Ng23
Shetrawa ☐ IND (RJT) 80 Og32
Shetrunjaya Hill ▲ IND 82 Of35
Shëvasija ☐ AL 46 Lu51
Shewa ☐ CHN (XUZ) 67 Pc23
Shevgaon ☐ IND (MHT) 82 Oh36
She Xian ☐ CHN (HBI) 73 Qh28
Sheyang ☐ CHN (JGS) 78 Ra29
Sheyenne Grassland N.P. ▲ USA 172 Fa22
Shibam ☐ YE 60 Ne38
Shibam ☐ IR 57 Ne29
Shibaozhai ☐ CHN 74 Qc30
Shibata ☐ J 77 Sa24
Shibecha ☐ J 77 Sc24
Shibetsu ☐ J 77 Sb23
Shibetsu ☐ J 77 Sc24
Shibin el-Kôm ☐ ET 129 Mf30
Shib Yak ☐ AFG 64 Oa29
Shicheng ☐ CHN (JGX) 75 Qj32
Shiel Bridge ☐ GB 20 Kp33
Shieldaig ☐ GB 20 Kp33
Shields ☐ USA (ND) 172 Ek22
Shieli ☐ KZ 63 Oe24
Shigu ☐ CHN (YUN) 87 Qa32
Shihan ☐ YE 61 Ng37
Shihezi ☐ CHN (XUZ) 67 Pc23
Shihuajie ☐ CHN (HUB) 72 Qf29
Shijiazhuang ☐ CHN (HBI) 73 Qh26
Shikabe ☐ J 77 Sa24
Shikarpur ☐ IND (KTK) 84 Oh38
Shikarpur ☐ PK 65 Oe32
Shikarpur ☐ J 79 Rk28
Shikkodabad ☐ IND (UPH) 81 Ok32
Shikoku ▲ J 79 Rh29
Shikoku-sanchi ▲ J 79 Rh29
Shikongong ▲ J 79 Rh29
Shikotsu-Toya N.P. ☐♦ J 77 Sa24
Shilabo ☐ ETH 143 Nc42
Shilah ☐ UAE 61 Nf34
Shilk ☐ KZ 66 Ok24
Shilikti ☐ KZ 67 Pc22
Shilkhpura ☐ IND (RJT) 80 Oh32
Shillong ☐ IND (MGA) 86 Pf33
Shillong ☐ IR 57 Nf27
Shekela ☐ Z 151 Mb53
Shekhawati ☐ IND (RJT) 80 Oj33
Shimbiris ▲ SP 143 Nd40
Shimentou ☐ IL 56 Mh29
Shimonoseki ☐ PK 65 Qg30
Shimen ☐ CHN (HBI) 74 Qf31
Shimizu ☐ J 77 Sb24
Shimla ☐ IND (HPH) 81 Oj30
Shimoda ☐ J 79 Rk28
Shimkarpur ☐ IND (KTK) 84 Oh39
Shimokitamen ☐ J 79 Rk30
Shimokita Q.N.P. ☐ J 77 Sa25
Shimoda ☐ J 79 Re30
Shimo-koshiki-jima ▲ J 79 Re30
Shimoni Caves ▣ EAK 147 Mk48
Shimonoseki ☐ J 79 Re29
Shimoni ☐ USA (AK) 172 Fc24
Shimonenga ☒ Z 152 Md53
Shimwini Bushveld Camp ☐ ZA 152 Mf58
Shinak Pass ☒ IRQ 57 Nc27
Shelikof Strait ☒ USA (AK) 164 Ca16
Shelim ☐ OM 61 Nh36
Shelburne Museum ☐ USA 177 Gd23
Shim Xian ☐ CHN (WY) 169 Eg23
Shelbyville ☐ USA (IN) 175 Fh26
Shelbyville ☐ USA (TN) 175 Fg28
Shelbyville ☐ USA (KY) 175 Fh26
Sheldon ☐ USA (IA) 172 Fc24
Sheldon ☐ CDN (QC) 176 Gg20
Sheldon Nat. Wildlife Refuge ☐♦ USA 168 Ea23
Shingwedzi ☒ ZA 152 Mf57
Shinjo ☐ J 77 Sa25
Shinkafe ☐ WAN 132 Ld39
Shinko ☐ RDC 149 Mc47
Shinnston ☐ USA (WV) 177 Ga26
Shinyanga ☐ EAT 144 Mg47
Shiogama ☐ J 77 Sa25
Shiojiri ☐ J 79 Rj27
Shipasbamba ☐ PE 196 Gb48
Shir Dima ☐ CHN (YUN) 87 Qb34
Shippagan ☐ CDN (NB) 176 Gh21
Shippensburg ☐ USA (PA) 177 Gb25
Shipunu ☐ CHN (ZJG) 75 Ra31
Shipul Jabbar ☒ IRQ 57 Nd30
Shiquanhe ☐ CHN (TIB) 68 Ok29
Shiquan ☐ CHN (SAA) 72 Qe29
Shiquanhe ☐ CHN (TIB) 68 Ok29
Shira'ayn ☐ KSA 59 Nc35
Shirabad ▲ IR 57 Ne26
Shirahama ☐ J 79 Rj29
Shirakami-Sanchi ▲ J 77 Sa25
Shirakawa-go ▲ J 77 Rk27
Shirane-san ▲ J 79 Rk28
Shiranesan ▲ J 77 Sa24
Shirane ▲ J 79 Rk28
Shiraoi ☐ J 77 Sa24
Shiraz ☐ IR 59 Nf30
Shirdi ☐ IND (MHT) 82 Oh36
Shir Khan ☐ AFG 64 Oe27
Shireet ☐ MNG 70 Pg22
Shiretoko N.P. ☐♦ J 77 Sc23
Shiretoko-misaki ▲ J 77 Sc23
Shirin ☐ UZ 63 Oe26
Shirin Tagab ☐ AFG 64 Ob27
Shiriya-saki ▲ J 77 Sa25
Shirlay ☐ NAM 154 La58
Shirley ☐ USA (IN) 178 Ga29
Shirvan Mazin ☐ IRQ 57 Nc27
Shiryasaki ▲ J 77 Sa25
Shishalin Volcano ▲ USA 164 Bh18
Shivpuri N.P. ☐♦ IND (MPH) 81 Oj33
Shiwa Ngandu ☒ Z 146 Mf51
Shixing ☐ CHN (GDG) 75 Qh33
Shiza ▲ GR 46 Mb54
Shizawa ☐ J 79 Rk28
Shizunai ☐ J 77 Sb24
Shinak Pass ☒ IRQ 57 Nc27

Slieve Bloom Mountains – Steenvoorde

Slieve Bloom Mountains IRL 19 Kn37
Slieve League IRL 19 Km36
Sligachan GB 20 Ko33
Sligo IRL 19 Km36
Sligo Bay IRL 19 Km36
Slim DZ 126 Lb28
Slisenvaara RUS 38 Mk29
Slite S 31 Lt33
Slivata BG 44 Md47
Sliven BG 45 Mg48
Slivnica BG 44 Md48
Slivo Pole BG 45 Mg47
Sliwice PL 40 Lt37
Sljudjanka RUS 70 Qb20
Sloboda LV 39 Mh34
Slobozia RO 45 Mh46
Slobozia Mare MD 45 Mj45
Slocan CDN (BC) 168 Eb21
Słomniki PL 41 Ma40
Slonim BY 41 Mf37
Slough GB 21 Ku39
Slovakia SK 43 Lu42
Slovenia SLO 42 Lp45
Slovenj Gradec SLO 42 Lq44
Slovenska Bistrica SLO 42 Lq44
Slovenská L'upča SK 43 Lu42
Slovenský raj, N.P. SK 43 Ma42
Slov'jans'k UA 49 Mj21
Słowiński P.N. PL 40 Ls36
Słubice PL 40 Lp38
Sluck BY 48 Md19
Slunj HR 35 Lq45
Słupca PL 40 Ls38
Słupia PL 41 Mb40
Słupno PL 41 Lu38
Słupsk PL 40 Lr36
Slurry ZA 155 Mc58
Slussfors S 16 Lj13
Slyne Head IRL 19 Kk37
Småland S 31 Lp33
Smålandsstenar S 31 Lo33
Smalininkai LT 39 Mc35
Smaljanïca BY 41 Me38
Smaljavičy BY 48 Me18
Small Malaita = Maramasike SOL 117 Ta50
Smallwood Reservoir CDN 163 Gd08
Smara DARS 124 Ke32
Smârdioasa RO 45 Mf47
Smarhon' BY 39 Mg36
Smarje pri Jelšah SLO 42 Lq44
Smeaton CDN (SK) 169 Eh19
Smeberg S 30 Lm32
Smedby S 31 Lr34
Smederevo SCG 44 Ma46
Smedjebacken S 31 Lq30
Smethport USA (PA) 173 Ga25
Smidovič RUS (YAO) 76 Rg21
Smierdnica PL 40 Lp37
Smigiel PL 40 Lr38
Smila UA 49 Mf21
Smilec BG 45 Me48
Smiley CDN (SK) 169 Ef20
Smiltene LV 39 Mf33
Smith CDN (AB) 167 Ed18
Smith Bay CDN 163 Ga03
Smith Bay USA (AK) 165 Cc10
Smith Center USA (KS) 174 Fa26
Smithers CDN (BC) 166 Dg18
Smith Ferry USA (ID) 168 Eb23
Smithfield USA (NC) 178 Ga28
Smithfield ZA 155 Md61
Smith Group, Sir J. AUS 107 Se56
Smith Island IND 88 Pg39
Smith Island USA 178 Gb29
Smith Point AUS 106 Rg51
Smith River CDN (BC) 166 Dg16
Smith's Knoll 21 Lc38
Smithton AUS (TAS) 111 Sc66
Smithtown AUS (NSW) 109 Sg61
Smithville USA (TN) 175 Fh28
Smithville USA (WV) 175 Fk26
Smithville House AUS (NSW) 108 Sa61
Smjadovo BG 45 Mh47
Smjörfjöll IS 18 Kf25
Smogulec PL 40 Ls37
Smojlovo RUS 39 Mj33
Smoke Creek Desert USA 170 Ea25
Smoke Hole Caverns USA 177 Ga26
Smoky Falls CDN (ON) 173 Fj20
Smoky Falls CDN 173 Fk20
Smoky Hills USA 174 Fa26
Smoky Lake CDN (AB) 167 Ed18
Smoky River CDN 167 Ea18
Smøla N 16 Ld14
Smołdzino PL 40 Ls36
Smolenice SK 42 Ls42
Smolensk RUS 48 Mg18
Smolensko-Moskovskaja vozyšennost' RUS 48 Mg18
Smoljan BG 45 Me49
Smoljaninovo' RUS 76 Rg24
Smolnik PL 41 Mc41
Smolsko BG 45 Md48
Smooth Rock Falls CDN (ON) 173 Fk21
Smože UA 43 Md42
Smygehamn S 31 Lo35
Smygehuk S 31 Lo35
Smyha UA 41 Mf40
Smyley Island 6 Ga33
Smyrna USA (DE) 177 Gc26
Smyrna USA (GA) 175 Fh29
Snabai RI 114 Rh46
Snaefell GB 21 Kq36
Snæfell IS 18 Ke26
Snæfellsnes IS 18 Js26
Snækollur IS 18 Ka26
Snake and Manjang Caverns ROK 78 Rd29
Snake Indian River CDN 168 Ea19
Snake Island AUS 111 Sd65
Snake River CDN (YT) 165 Dd13
Snake River USA 168 Eb23
Snake River Canyon USA 168 Eb22
Snake River Plains USA 168 Ed24
Snaran Jogizai PK 65 Oe30
Snare Lakes CDN 167 Ec13
Snåsa N 16 Lg13
Snedsted DK 30 Lj34
Sneek NL 23 Lf37
Sneekermeer NL 23 Lf37
Sneem IRL 19 Kl39
Sneeuberg ZA 155 Mc61
Snežnaja RUS 70 Qc20
Sniebal IND (MZR) 86 Pg34
Śnieżka PL 40 Lq40
Śnieżnik Kłodzki PL 40 Lr40
Snihurivka UA 49 Mg22
Snina SK 43 Mc42
Snjatyn UA 43 Mf42
Snježna Marija HR 35 Lr45
Snøhetta N 17 Le16
Snøhuten N 30 Lg31
Snoqualmie Pass USA (WA) 168 Dk22
Snøtoppen N 16 Lk05
Snou BY 41 Mg37
Snoul K 89 Qd39
Snoul W.S. K 89 Qd39
Snowdon GB 21 Kq37
Snowdonia N.P. GB 21 Kr38
Snowdrift CDN 167 Ee14
Snowflake CDN (MB) 172 Fa21
Snowflake USA (AZ) 171 Ee28
Snow Hill USA (MD) 177 Gc26
Snow Lake CDN (MB) 169 Ek18
Snow Lake USA (AR) 175 Fe28
Snow Mount USA 170 Dj26
Snowshoe Peak USA 168 Ec21
Snowtown AUS (SA) 110 Rk62
Snowville USA (UT) 171 Ed25
Snowy Mountains AUS 111 Se64
Snowy River AUS 111 Se64
Snowy River N.P. AUS 111 Se64
Snug Corner BS 186 Gd34
Snyder USA (TX) 174 Ek29
So BF 131 Kk38
Soacha CO 192 Gc43
Soahany RM 157 Nc55
Soalala RM 156 Nc54
Soalara RM 157 Nb57
Soaloka RM 157 Nc55
Soamanonga RM 157 Nc57
Soanierana-Ivongo RM 157 Ne54
Soanindrarivy RM 157 Nd55
Soap Lake USA (WA) 168 Ea22
Soaserana RM 157 Nc56
Soata CO 192 Gd42
Soave I 34 Lm45
Soavina RM 157 Nd56
Soavina RM 157 Ne56
Soavinandriana RM 157 Nd55
Soba WAN 138 Le40
Sobaek Sanmaek ROK 78 Rd28
Sobaeksan N.P. ROK 78 Re27
Sobat SUD 141 Mg41
Soberania, P.N. PA 185 Ga41
Sobibór PL 41 Md39
Sobinka RUS 48 Na18
Sobo-Katamuki Q.N.P. J 79 Rf29
Sobolevo RUS 48 Na18
Sobótka PL 41 Mb40
Sobra HR 35 Ls48
Sobradinho BR (BA) 201 Hk50
Sobradinho BR (DF) 203 Hg53
Sobradinho BR (RS) 204 Hd60
Sobrado BR 200 Hg52
Sobral BR (AC) 197 Ge50
Sobral BR (CE) 201 Hk47
Sobrance SK 43 Mc42
Søby DK 30 Ll36
Socaire RCH 207 Gg57
Socastee USA (SC) 178 Ga29
Socavão BR (PR) 205 Hf58
Sochaczew PL 41 Ma38
Sochinsky nacional'nyj park RUS 49 Mk23
Soči RUS 49 Mk24
Society Hill USA (SC) 178 Ga28
Society Islands 11 Ca11
Socodor RO 43 Mb44
Socompa PE 207 Gf58
Socompa RA (SA) 207 Gf58
Socompa, Volcán RCH/RA 207 Gf58
Socorro BR (PR) 204 He58
Socorro BR (SP) 203 Hg57
Socorro CO 192 Gd42
Socorro RP 90 Rc41
Socorro USA (NM) 171 Eg28
Socorro USA (TX) 171 Eg30
Socota CO 192 Gd42
Socota PE 196 Ga49
Socotra YE 61 Nh39
Soc Trang VN 89 Qc41
Socuéllamos E 29 Ks51
Soda Creek CDN (BC) 168 Dj19
Sodakor IND (RJT) 80 Of32
Sodankylä FIN 16 Md12
Soda Springs USA (ID) 169 Ee24
Söderåkra S 31 Lr34
Söderarm S 31 Lu31
Söderåsens n.p. S 30 Lo35
Söderbärke S 31 Lq30
Söderfors S 31 Ls30
Söderhamn S 17 Lj15
Söderköping S 31 Lq32
Södermanland S 31 Lr31
Södertälje S 31 Ls31
Södertörn S 31 Ls31
Södervik S 31 Lt31
Sodi RI 96 Qk46
Sodiri SUD 134 Me38
Sodium ZA 154 Mb61
Sodo ETH 142 Mj42
Sodore ETH 142 Mk41
Södra Midsjöbanken 31 Ls35
Södra Ölands odlingslandskap S 31 Lr34
Södra Vi S 31 Lq33
Sodwana Bay N.P. ZA 155 Mg59
Soe RI 97 Rc50
Soekmekaar ZA 152 Me57
Soeng San THA 89 Qb38
Soesdyke GUY 194 Ha42
Soest D 32 Lj39
Soetdoring Nature Reserve ZA 155 Md60
Sofádes GR 46 Mc51
Sofara RMM 131 Kh38
Sofia BG 44 Md48
Sofija BG 44 Md48
Sofijivka UA 49 Mg21
Sofijskij sobor RUS 48 Mf16
Sofiysky sobor UA 48 Mf20
Sof Omar Caves ETH 142 Na42
Sofporog RUS 16 Mf13
Sogakofe GH 137 La42
Sogamoso CO 192 Gd43
Sögel D 32 Lh38
Sogeri PNG 115 Sd50
Sogndal N 17 Ld15
Sognefjorden N 17 Lc15
Sogod RP 90 Rc40
Sogolle TCH 133 Lh38
Sogoot MNG 70 Pk21
Sogossagasso BF 137 Kh40
Soguip'o ROK 78 Rd29
Soğukpınar TR 45 Mk50
Soğuksu Milli Parkı TR 56 Mg25
Söğüt TR 56 Me27
Söğütlü TR 57 Na26
Sog Xian CHN (TIB) 69 Pg30
Sohâg ET 129 Mf32
Sohagi IND (MPH) 83 Pa33
Sohar OM 61 Nj33
Sohela IND (ORS) 83 Pb35
Sohey IR 64 Ng29
Sohna IND (HYA) 80 Oj31
Sohós GR 44 Md50
Sohuksan Do ROK 78 Rc28
Soignies B 23 Le40
Soila IND (RJT) 80 Og32
Şoimi RO 43 Mc44
Soin BF 137 Kj39
Soini FIN 28 Me28
Sointula CDN (BC) 168 Dg20
Soissons F 23 Ld41
Soja J 79 Rg28
Sojat IND (RJT) 82 Og33
Sojol RI 91 Ra45
Sojoton Point RP 90 Rb41
Sojuz ANT (RUS) 6 Gc33
Sokal' UA 41 Me40
Sokch'o ROK 78 Re26
Söke TR 47 Mh53
Sokele RDC 149 Mc50
Sokhumi GE 57 Na24
Sokhumi GE 57 Na24
Sokna N 30 Lk30
Soko CI 137 Kj42
Soko Banja SCG 44 Mb47
Sokodé TG 137 La41
Sokoiyo RI 96 Ra47
Sokolac BIH 44 Lt47
Sokoliv UA 43 Mf41
Sokółka PL 41 Md37
Sokollu Camii TR 45 Mh49
Sokolo RMM 131 Kg38
Sokolov CZ 42 Ln40
Sokołów Małopolski PL 41 Mc40
Sokołów Podlaski PL 41 Mc38
Sokolski manastir BG 45 Mf48
Sokoły PL 41 Mc38
Sokorbey RN 132 Lb39
Sokoto WAN 132 Lc39
Sokoto WAN 138 Lc40
Sokoulama RG 136 Kf41
Sokoura RMM 137 Kj39
Soksok RN 132 Ld38
Sola C 179 Gb35
Sola N 30 Lf32
Sola VU 118 Td52
Sola de Vega MEX (OAX) 182 Fb37
Solahpet IND (KTK) 82 Oj37
Solan IND (HPH) 81 Oj30
Solana RP 90 Ra37
Solana USA (FL) 179 Fk32
Solana del Pino E 27 Kq52
Solander Island NZ 113 Td69
Solânea BR (PB) 201 Jc49
Solano RP 90 Ra37
Solano YV 193 Gg45
Solar de Mateus P 26 Kn49
Solares E 28 Kr47
Solat RI 91 Rd45
Solberg S 16 Lj14
Sol'cy RUS 48 Mf16
Soldado Monge EC 196 Gb47
Sol de Julio RA (SE) 207 Gj60
Sol de Mañana BOL 207 Gg57
Sölden A 34 Lm44
Soldotna USA (AK) 164 Ce15
Solé BF 131 Kj38
Soleb Temple SUD 135 Mf35
Solec Kujawski PL 40 Lt37
Soledad CO 192 Gc40
Soledad USA (CA) 170 Dk27
Soledad YV 193 Gj41
Soledad de Doblado MEX (VC) 182 Fb36
Soledad de G. Sánchez MEX (SLP) 182 Ek34
Soledade BR (PB) 201 Jb49
Soledade BR (RS) 204 Hd60
Solemar BR (SP) 205 Hg58
Solenzara F 36 Lk49
Solenzo BF 137 Kh39
Sole Pit 21 Lb37
Solh Abad IR 64 Nj28
Solhan TR 57 Na26
Soli RN 132 Ld38
Solihull GB 21 Kt38
Solikamsk RUS 54 Nd07
Soliman TN 126 Lf27
Solimões = Amazon BR 198 Gj47
Solingen D 32 Lh39
Solís de Mataojo ROU 209 Hc63
Solita CO 192 Gc45
Solitaire NAM 154 Lj57
Sölktäler A 35 Lo43
Sollebrunn S 30 Ln32
Sollefteå S 16 Lj14
Sollentuna S 31 Ls31
Sóller E 29 Lc51
Solliden S 31 Lr34
Sollihøgda N 30 Ll31
Solna BF 137 La39
Solncevo RUS 48 Mj20
Solnečnogorsk RUS 48 Mj17
Solnice CZ 42 Lr40
Solo RI 95 Qf49
Šolohovskij RUS 49 Na21
Solok RI 93 Qa46
Sololo EAK 145 Mk44
Soloma GCA 184 Fe38
Solomon Islands 101 Ta10
Solomon Islands 117 Sj48
Solomon Sea PNG 116 Sf49
Solomon's Wall RB 152 Me57
Solon CHN (NMZ) 71 Ra22
solonchakovyye vpadiny Unguz TM 62 Nk26
Solone UA 49 Mh21
Solongtyn davaa MNG 70 Pk21
Solonópole BR (CE) 201 Ja48
Solor RI 97 Rb50
Solothurn CH 34 Lh43
Solotvyn UA 43 Me42
Solotvyna UA 43 Md43
Solov'evsk RUS 71 Qh21
Solsona E 28 Lb49
Solsvik N 17 Lc15
Solt H 43 Lu44
Šolta HR 35 Lr47
Soltan Abad IR 62 Nj27
Soltan Bagh AFG 65 Oe29
Soltaniyeh IR 57 Ne27
Soltau D 32 Lk38
Solti-lapály H 43 Lu44
Soltvadkert H 43 Lu44
Solusi ZW 152 Me56
Solvang USA (CA) 170 Dk28
Solvarbo S 31 Lq30
Sölvesborg S 31 Lp34
Solway Firth GB 20 Kr36
Solwezi Z 151 Md52
Soly BY 39 Mg36
Solymar ROU 209 Hc63
Sol y Nieve E 27 Kr53
Som IND (RJT) 82 Og33
Soma J 77 Sa27
Soma TR 47 Mh51
Somabhula ZW 152 Me55
Somadougou RMM 131 Kh38
Somaén E 29 Ks49
Somain F 23 Ld40
Somalia 123 Na09
Somali Basin 9 Nb09
Somali Plateau ETH 142 Na41
Somalomo CAM 139 Lg44
Somavaram IND (APH) 83 Pb37
Somba RI 96 Qk47
Sómbak'e = Yellowknife CDN 167 Ec14
Sombo ANG 149 Ma50
Sombor SCG 44 Lu45
Sombrerete MEX (ZCT) 182 Ej34
Sombrero KNA 187 Gj36
Sombrero RCH 210 Gf72
Sombrero Channel IND 88 Pg42
Sombrero Negro RA (FO) 207 Gk57
Sombrio BR (SC) 205 Hf60
Şomcuta Mare RO 43 Md43
Somdet THA 89 Qb37
Somero FIN 38 Md30
Somers AUS (VIC) 111 Sc65
Somerset AUS (QLD) 107 Sb51
Somerset AUS (TAS) 111 Sc66
Somerset CDN (MB) 172 Fa21
Somerset USA (KY) 175 Fh27
Somerset USA (PA) 177 Ga26
Somerset-East ZA 155 Mc62
Somerset Island CDN 163 Fb04
Somerset Oos ZA 155 Mc62
Somerset West ZA 154 Lk63
Somerton AUS (NSW) 109 Sf61
Somianki PL 41 Mb38
Somil ANG 151 Ma53
Somina BIH 44 Lt48
Somina SCG 44 Lt48
Sömmerda D 32 Lm39
Sommerdown NAM 150 Lk56
Sommesous F 23 Le42
Sommières F 25 Le47
Somo RMM 137 Kh39
Somogyvár H 42 Ls44
Somonino PL 40 Lt36
Somosomo FJI 119 Ua54
Somotillo NIC 184 Fg39
Sompeta IND (APH) 83 Pc36
Som Poi THA 89 Qb38
Sompolno PL 40 Lt38
Somra MYA 86 Ph33
Soná PA 185 Fk41
Sonaco GNB 136 Kc39
Sonagiri IND 83 Ok33
Sonai-Rupa N.P. IND 86 Pg32
Sonamukhi BD 86 Pe33
Sonamukhi IND (WBG) 83 Pd34
Sonapur IND (ORS) 83 Pb35
Sonari IND (ASM) 86 Ph32
Sonarigaon IND (ASM) 86 Ph32
Sonbong PRK 76 Rf24
Sonch'on PRK 76 Rc26
Soncillo E 28 Kr48
Sonda PK 65 Oe33
Sóndalo I 34 Ll44
Søndeled N 30 Lk32
Sønderborg DK 30 Lk36
Sønder Nissum DK 30 Lj34
Sønder Omme DK 30 Lj35
Sondershausen D 32 Ll39
Søndersø DK 30 Ll35
Søndervig DK 30 Lj34
Sondi RI 93 Pk44
Sondo IND (MHT) 83 Ok36
Son Dong VN 87 Qd35
Søndrestrømfjord = Kangerlussuaq DK 163 Hb05
Sóndrio I 34 Lk44
Sondu EAK 144 Mh46
Son en Breugel NL 23 Lf39
Sonepat IND (HYA) 80 Oj31
Song MAL 94 Qg45
Song THA 87 Qa36
Song WAN 139 Lg41
Songa MOC 152 Mg53
Songa RDC 149 Mc50
Songa RI 97 Rd46
Songbu CHN (HUB) 75 Qh30
Song Cau VN 89 Qe39
Song Da VN 87 Qb35
Songea EAT 146 Mh51
Songgwangsa Temple ROK 78 Rd28
Song Hong VN 87 Qc34
Songhua Hu CHN 76 Rd24
Songijang CHN (SHG) 78 Ra30
Songir IND (GUJ) 82 Og34
Songir IND (MHT) 82 Oh35
Songjiang CHN (JLN) 76 Re24
Songjianghe CHN (JLN) 76 Rd24
Songkan CHN (GZH) 74 Qd31
Songkhla THA 89 Qa42
Songkhon LAO 89 Qc37
Song Khwae THA 87 Qa36
Song-Köl KS 66 Oh25
Songkou CHN (FJN) 75 Qk33
Songling CHN (NMZ) 71 Ra22
Song Ling CHN 73 Qk25
Song Luy VN 89 Qe40
Songmen CHN (ZJG) 75 Ra31
Songming CHN (YUN) 87 Qb33
Songnim PRK 78 Rc26
Songnisan N.P. ROK 78 Rd27
Songo ANG 148 Lh49
Songo SUD 141 Mc41
Songo-lolo RDC 148 Lh48
Songo Mnara EAT 147 Mk50
Songpan CHN (SCH) 72 Qb29
Song Phinong THA 88 Qa38
Songsha CHN (TIB) 68 Pa30
Songshan CHN 73 Qg28
Songshan Z.B. CHN 73 Qh25
Songtao CHN (GZH) 74 Qe31
Songxi CHN (FJN) 75 Qk32
Song Xian CHN (HNN) 72 Qg28
Songyang CHN (ZJG) 75 Qk31
Songyu ROK 79 Re27
Songyuan CHN (JLN) 76 Rc23
Songzi CHN (HUB) 74 Qf30
Sonhat IND (CGH) 83 Pb34
Son Hiep VN 89 Qe39
Son Hoa VN 89 Qe39
Sonid Youqi CHN (NMZ) 70 Qg24
Sonid Zuoqi CHN (NMZ) 71 Qg24
Sonjo EAT 144 Mh47
Sonkovo RUS 48 Mj17
Sonkwale Mountains WAN 138 Le42
Son La VN 87 Qb35
Son Mbong CAM 138 Lf44
Sonmiani PK 65 Od33
Sonneberg D 33 Lm40
Sonoita USA (AZ) 171 Ee30
Sonoma Range USA 170 Eb25
Sonora BR (MS) 202 Hc54
Sonora MEX 180 Ee31
Sonora USA (CA) 170 Dk27
Sonora USA (TX) 174 Ek30
Sonoran Desert USA 170 Ec29
Sonora Pass USA 170 Ea26
Sonoumom DY 138 Lb41
Sonoyta MEX (SO) 180 Ed30
Sonozo CI 137 Kg41
Sonpar Hills IND 83 Pb33
Sonpuri IND (GUJ) 82 Of35
Sonqor IR 57 Nd28
Sonseca E 27 Kr51
Sonsón CO 192 Gc43
Sonsonate ES 184 Ff39
Sonsorol Islands PAL 90 Rg43
Sonstraal ZA 154 Mb59
Sonta RDC 146 Me51
Sontang RI 93 Qa45
Son Tay VN 87 Qc35
Sonthofen D 33 Ll43
Sontra D 32 Lk39
Soomaa rahvuspark EST 39 Mf32
Sooya SP 145 Nb45
Sopachuy BOL 206 Gh55
Sopchoppy USA (FL) 175 Fh30
Soperton USA (GA) 178 Fj29
Sophie F (GF) 194 Hd43
Sop Huai THA 87 Pk36
Sopianae H 42 Lt44
Sopinusa RI 114 Rg47
Soplin PE 196 Gb47
Sop Moei THA 88 Pj37
Sopore 80 Oh28
Sopot PL 40 Lt36
Sopot SCG 44 Ma46
Sopotnica MK 44 Mb49
Sop Prap THA 87 Pk37
Sopron H 42 Lr43
Soprtrán CO 192 Gc42
Soputan RI 91 Rc45
Sora I 36 Lo49
Sorab IND (KTK) 84 Oh38
Sorada IND (ORS) 83 Pc36
Sorah PK 65 Oe32
Soraksan ROK 78 Re26
Soraksan N.P. ROK 78 Re26
Sora Mboum CAM 139 Lh42
Sorano I 34 Lm48
Sorapa PE 206 Gf54
sor Arys KZ 63 Od23
sor Ashchkol KZ 63 Od23
Sorata BOL 206 Gf53
Sorau WAN 139 Lg41
Søraust-Svalbard naturreservat N 16 Ma07
Sorbas E 27 Ks53
Sore F 24 Ku46
Sorel CDN (QC) 176 Gd22
Sorell AUS (TAS) 111 Sd67
Soresina I 34 Lk45
Sør-Flatanger N 16 Lf13
Sórgono I 36 Lk50
Sorgues-l'Ouvèze F 25 Le46
Sorgun TR 56 Mh26
Sør-Gutvika N 16 Lf13
Sori DY 138 Lb40
Soria E 28 Ks49
Soriano ROU 204 Ha62
sor Kajdak KZ 62 Ng23
Sørkappøya N 16 Lj07
Sorkh Ab AFG 64 Ob29
Sørland N 30 Lg32
Sor Laspur PK 63 Og27
Sørli N 16 Lg13
Sornac F 25 Lc45
Sorø DK 30 Lm35
Soro IND (ORS) 83 Pd35
Soro PK 65 Od30
Soro = Bahr el Ghazal TCH 133 Lj38
Sorobango CI 137 Kj41
Soroca MD 49 Me21
Sorocaba BR (SP) 205 Hg57
sor Oli Kultyk KZ 62 Ng23
Sorombéo CAM 139 Lh41
Sorondideri RI 114 Rh46
Sorong RI 97 Rf46
Sororó, T.I. BR 200 Hf48
Soroti EAU 144 Mg45
Sorrento CDN (BC) 168 Ea20
Sorrento I 37 Lp50
Sorriso BR (MT) 202 Hc52
Sorsakoski FIN 38 Mh28
Sorsan Grasslands IND 82 Oj33
Sorsele S 16 Lj13
Sorso I 36 Lj50
Sorsogon RP 90 Rc39
Sør-Spitsbergen n.p. N 16 Lj07
Sørstraumen N 16 Ma11
Sort E 28 Lb48
Sortavala RUS 38 Ml29
Sortland N 16 Lh11
Sørumsand N 30 Lm31
Sørvågen N 16 Lg12
Sørvágur DK 18 Kn28
Sosan ROK 78 Rd27
Sosan Haean N.P. ROK 78 Rd27
Sösdala S 31 Lo34
Sos del Rey Católico E 28 Kt48
Sosedka RUS 48 Nb19
Sosneado, Cerro RA 208 Gf63
Sosnenskij RUS 48 Mj19
Sosnicy RUS 38 Mk31
Sosnogorsk RUS 54 Nc06
Sosnove UA 49 Md20
Sosnovka RUS 48 Na19
Sosnovo RUS 38 Ml30
Sosnovo-Ozërskoe RUS (BUR) 70 Qf19
Sosnovyj Bor RUS 38 Mk31
Sosnowica PL 41 Md39
Sosnowiec PL 41 Lu40
Sosolo SOL 117 Sj49
Sosonpal IND (CGH) 83 Pa36
Sospel F 25 Lh47
Sosso RCA 140 Lh44
Sossobé RMM 131 Kh38
Sossusvlei NAM 154 Lh58
Sossusvlei Lodge NAM 154 Lh58
Sossusvlei Pan NAM 154 Lh58
Šoštanj SLO 42 Lq44
Šostka UA 48 Mg20
Sosúa DOM 186 Ge36
Sošyčne UA 41 Me39
Sotara, Volcán CO 192 Gb44
Soteapan MEX (VC) 183 Fc36
Sotian RMM 137 Kg40
Sotik EAK 144 Mh46
Sotillo de la Adrada E 27 Kq50
Soto RA (CD) 208 Gh61
Soto del Barco E 26 Ko47
Sotogrande E 27 Kp54
Sotok RI 95 Qf45
Soto La Marina MEX (TM) 182 Fa34
Sotomayor CO 192 Gb45
Sotouboua TG 137 La41
Sotra N 30 Lf30
Sottunga FIN 38 Ma30
Sottunga FIN 38 Ma30
Sotuta MEX (YT) 183 Ff35
Souanké RCB 139 Lh44
Souassi TN 126 Lf28
Soubakaniédougou BF 137 Kh40
Soubakpérou DY 138 La41
Soubané RG 136 Kc40
Soubéira BF 137 Kk39
Soubré CI 137 Kg43
Souchang CHN (ZJG) 75 Qk31
Soudan AUS (NT) 106 Rj56
Soudougui BF 137 La40
Souf DZ 126 Ld29
Soufflenheim F 23 Lh42
Soufli GR 45 Mg49
Soufrière WL 187 Gk39
Sougueur DZ 126 La28
Souhoulé RG 136 Kf42
Souillac F 24 Lb46
Souillac MS 157 Nj56
Souilly F 23 Lf41
Souk-Ahras DZ 126 Ld27
Souk-el-Arba-des-Beni-Hassan MA 125 Kh28
Souk-el-Arba-du-Rharb MA 125 Kg28
Souk-Jemâa-de-Oulad-Abbou MA 125 Kg29
Soukoukoutane RN 132 Lb38
Souk Tenadjeleline RMM 132 La36
Soul ROK 78 Rd27
Soul ROK 78 Rd27
Soulabali SN 136 Kc39
Soulac-sur-Mer F 24 Kt45
Soúli GR 46 Mc53
Soulíou GR 46 Ma51
Soulópoulo GR 46 Ma51
Sound of Barra IRL 20 Kn33
Sound of Harris GB 20 Kn33
Sound of Jura GB 20 Kp35
Sound of Monach GB 20 Kn33
Sound of Mull GB 20 Kp34
Sound of Sleat GB 20 Kp33
Sounds of Starlight Theatre AUS 108 Rg57
Soungrougrou SN 136 Kc39
Souq al-Milh YE 60 Nc38
Source Bleu de Meski MA 125 Kh30
Source chaude de Déssikou RCA 140 Lk42
Source chaude de Soborom TCH 133 Lj35
Source du Nil BU 146 Me47
Sour-el-Ghozlane DZ 126 Lb27
Souris CDN (MB) 172 Ek21
Souris CDN (PE) 176 Gj22
Souroukaha CI 137 Kh41
Sourountouna RMM 137 Kh39
Sourpi GR 46 Mc51
Sousa BR (PB) 201 Ja49
Sousceyrac F 24 Lc46
Sousel P 27 Kn52
Sous-Massa, P.N. MA 124 Kf30
Sousse TN 126 Lf28
Soustons F 24 Kt47
South Africa 123 Ma13
South-America 8 Gb11
Southampton GB 21 Kt40
Southampton USA (NY) 177 Gd25
Southampton Island CDN 163 Fd06
South Andaman IND 88 Pg39
South Australia AUS 101 Rb13
South Australian Basin 100 Ra14
Southaven USA (MS) 175 Ff28
South Banda Basin RI 97 Rd49
South Banggi Strait MAL 94 Qj42
Southbank CDN (BC) 166 Dh18
South Bay CDN (ON) 172 Fd20
South Bay USA (FL) 179 Fk32
South Baymouth CDN (ON) 173 Fj23
South Bend USA (IN) 173 Fg25
South Bimini BS 179 Ga33
South Boston USA (VA) 178 Ga27
South Brahmaputra Hills IND 86 Pg33
South Branch CDN (NF) 177 Ha22
Southbridge NZ 113 Tg67
South Brook CDN (NF) 177 Hb21
South Brookfield CDN (NS) 176 Gh23
South Bruny Island AUS 111 Sd67
South Bruny N.P. AUS 111 Sd67
South Carolina USA 178 Fk28
South Carolina USA 178 Fk28
South Cay CO 185 Fk38
South Channel RP 90 Ra38
South China Basin 10 Qb08
South China Sea 10 Qb08
South Coast Highway AUS 104 Ra62
South Dakota USA 172 Ek23
South Downs GB 21 Ku40
South East RB 155 Mc58
South East Aru Marine Reserve RI 114 Rh49
South East Cape AUS 111 Sd67
Southeast Cape USA 164 Bf14
Southeast Forests N.P. AUS 111 Se64
Southeast Indian Ridge 100 Qa14
South East Pacific Basin 190 Ea14
South East Point AUS 111 Sd65
Southeast Point BS 186 Gd35
Southend-on-Sea GB 21 La39
Southerland Falls NZ 113 Td68
Southern Alps NZ 113 Te68
Southern Altay Gobi Nature Reserve MNG 67 Pj24
Southern Central Reserve A.L. AUS 105 Rc59
Southern Cross AUS (WA) 104 Qk61
Southern Indian Lake CDN 163 Fa07
Southern Laos Cruise LAO/K 89 Qc38
Southern N.P. SUD 141 Me42
Southern Pines USA (NC) 178 Ga28
Southern Sporades GR 47 Mf52
Southern Uplands GB 20 Kq35
Southey CDN (SK) 169 Eh20
South Fiji Basin 100 Tb12
South Foreland GB 21 Lb39
South Fork USA (CO) 171 Eg27
SouthFrancisco de Macoris DOM 186 Ge36
South Galway AUS (QLD) 108 Sb58
South Georgia GB 190 Ja15
South Georgia GB 191 Ja15
South Goulburn Island AUS 106 Rg51
South Gut Saint Ann's CDN (NS) 176 Gk22
South Harbour CDN (NS) 176 Gk22
South Hatia Island BD 86 Pf34
South Haven USA (MI) 173 Fg24
South Hill USA (VA) 178 Ga27
South Honshu Ridge 10 Rb06
South Horr EAK 144 Mj45
South Island AUS 109 Sf56
South Island EAK 144 Mj44
South Island NZ 113 Te67
South Island N.P. EAK 144 Mj44
South Junction CDN (MB) 172 Fc21
South Kinangop EAK 144 Mj46
South Kitui National Reserve EAK 145 Mk46
South Korea ROK 53 Ra06
South Lake Tahoe USA (NV) 170 Ea26
South Luangwa N.P. Z 146 Mf52
South Luconia Shoals 94 Qg43
South Male Atoll MV 84 Og44
South Miladhunmadulu Atoll = Noonu Atoll MV 84 Og43
South Molton GB 21 Kr39
South Mtn. USA 168 Eb24
South Nahanni River CDN 166 Dh15
South Nilandhoo Atoll = Dhaalu Atoll MV 84 Og44
Southold USA (NY) 177 Gd25
South Orkney Islands GB 190 Hb14
South Orkney Islands GB 191 Hb15
South Ossetia GE 57 Nc24
South Padre Island USA (TX) 181 Fb32
South Padre Island USA (TX) 181 Fb32
South Pass City USA (WY) 171 Ef24
South Pole ANT 6 Ga36
South Porcupine CDN (ON) 173 Fk21
Southport AUS (QLD) 109 Sg59
Southport AUS (TAS) 111 Sd67
Southport CDN (NF) 177 Hd21
Southport GB 21 Kr37
Southport USA (NC) 178 Ga29
South Prince of Wales Wilderness USA 166 Dd18
South Pt. BS 186 Gc34
South Point = Ka Lae USA 170 Cc36
South Ronaldsay GB 20 Ks32
South Salmara IND (ASM) 86 Pf33
South Sandwich Islands GB 190 Jb15
South Sandwich Islands GB 191 Jb15
South Sandwich Trench 190 Jb15
South Saskatchewan River CDN 169 Ef20
South Scotia Ridge 6 Hb31
South Shetland Islands ANT 6 Ha31
South Shields GB 20 Kt36
South Sioux City USA (NE) 172 Fb24
South Solomon Trench 117 Ta51
South Stradbroke Island AUS 109 Sg59
South Taranaki Bight NZ 113 Th66
South Tasman Rise 100 Sa14
South Thiladhunmathee Atoll = Haa-Dhaalu Atoll MV 84 Og42
South Tucson USA (AZ) 171 Ee29
South Turkana National Reserve EAK 144 Mh45
South Uist GB 20 Kn33
South West Cape AUS 111 Sc67
Southwest Cape NZ 113 Td69
Southwest Indian Ridge 9 Na14
Southwest N.P. AUS 111 Sd67
Southwest Pacific Basin 11 Cb13
Southwest Point BS 179 Gb33
Southwest Point BS 186 Gc34
Southwest Point BS 186 Gd35
South West Rocks AUS (NSW) 109 Sg61
Southwold GB 21 Lb38
South Yandaminta AUS (NSW) 108 Sa60
Souto Soares BR (BA) 201 Hk52
Soutpan ZA 155 Md60
Soutpansberg ZA 152 Me57
Souvigny F 25 Ld44
Sovata RO 43 Mf44
Soverato I 37 Lr52
Sovereign Hill AUS (VIC) 111 Sb64
Sovetsk RUS 39 Mb35
Sovetskaja ANT (RUS) 7 Pb34
Sovetskaja RUS 48 Nb21
Sovetskij RUS 38 Mj30
Sovetskoe RUS (KBA) 57 Nb24
Sowa Pan RB 151 Mc56
Sowczyce PL 40 Lt40
Soweto ZA 155 Md59
Sowia Góra PL 40 Lq38
Sowma'eh Sara IR 57 Ne27
Soy EAK 144 Mh45
Soyaló MEX (CHP) 183 Fd37
Soya-misaki J 77 Sb23
Soyet IND (MPH) 82 Oj33
Soyo ANG 148 Lg49
Sozak KZ 63 Oe23
Sozopol BG 45 Mh48
Sozu J 77 Rj27
Spa B 23 Lf40
Spain 15 Kb06
Spalding AUS (SA) 110 Rk62
Spalding GB 21 Ku38
Spálené Poříčí CZ 42 Lo41
Spaniard's Bay CDN (NF) 177 Hd22
Spanish Fork USA (UT) 171 Ee25
Spanish Head GB 21 Kq36
Spanish Town JA 186 Gb37
Spanwerk ZA 155 Md58
Sparks USA (NV) 170 Ea26
Sparreholm S 31 Lr31
Sparta USA (GA) 178 Fj29
Sparta USA (NC) 178 Fk27
Sparta USA (TN) 175 Fh28
Sparta USA (WI) 172 Fe24
Spartanburg USA (SC) 178 Fk28
Spárti GR 46 Mc53
Sparwood CDN (BC) 168 Ec21
Spas-Klepiki RUS 48 Na18
Spaso Jakovlenskij monastyr RUS 48 Mk17
Spasovo BG 45 Mj47
Spassk-Dal'nij RUS 76 Rg23
Spassk-Rjazanskij RUS 48 Na18
Spatsizi Plateau CDN 166 Df17
Spatsizi Plateau Wilderness Prov. Park CDN 166 Df17
Spean Bridge GB 20 Kq34
Spearfish USA (SD) 169 Ej23
Spearman USA (TX) 174 Ek27
Speculator USA (NY) 177 Gc24
Speedwell Island GB 210 Ha72
Speightstown BDS 187 Ha39
Spello I 35 Ln47
Spencer USA (IA) 172 Fc24
Spencer USA (IN) 175 Fg26
Spencer USA (NE) 172 Fa24
Spencer USA (TN) 175 Fh28
Spencer USA (WV) 175 Fk26
Spencer Bay NAM 154 Lh58
Spencer Bridge CDN (BC) 168 Dk20
Spencer Gulf AUS 110 Rj63
Spentrup DK 30 Ll34
Speos of Horemheb ET 129 Mg33
Sperrin Mountains GB 19 Kn36
Spessart D 33 Lk41
Spétses GR 45 Md53
Spétses GR 45 Md53
Speyer D 33 Lj41
Speyside Beach TT 187 Gk40
Spezand PK 65 Od30
Spezzano Albanese I 37 Lr51
Spezzano della Sila I 37 Lr51
Spiddle IRL 19 Kl37
Spiekeroog D 32 Lh37
Spielcasino Baden-Baden D 33 Lj42
Spiez CH 34 Lh44
Spijkenisse NL 23 Le39
Špilberk CZ 42 Lr41
Spíleon Diroú GR 46 Mc54
Spíleo Stalaktíton GR 47 Mf53
Spilimbergo I 35 Ln44
Spiljani SCG 44 Ma48
Spilsby GB 21 La37
Spinazzola I 37 Lr50
Spin Buldak AFG 65 Od30
Špindlerův Mlýn CZ 42 Lq40
Spioenkop ZA 155 Me60
Spirit Lake USA (IA) 172 Fc24
Spirit Lake Ind. Res. USA 172 Fa22
Spirit River CDN (AB) 167 Ea18
Spiritwood CDN (SK) 169 Eg19
Spirovo RUS 48 Mh17
Spišská Belá SK 43 Ma41
Spišský hrad SK 43 Ma42
Spitak ARM 57 Nc25
Spitsbergen N 16 Lg06
Spitskopvlei ZA 155 Mc61
Spittal an der Drau A 35 Lo44
Spitz A 42 Lq42
Spitzkoppe NAM 150 Lh56
Spitzkoppe Rock Paintings NAM 150 Lh56
Spiveys Corner USA (NC) 178 Ga28
Split HR 35 Lr47
Splügen CH 34 Lk44
Splügenpass = Passo dello Spluga I/CH 34 Lk44
Spodsbjerg DK 30 Ll36
Spofford USA (TX) 181 Ek31
Spoggies AUS 110 Rg62
Špogi LV 39 Mg34
Spokane USA (WA) 168 Eb22
Spokane House USA 168 Eb22
Spokane Ind. Res. USA 168 Eb22
Špola UA 49 Mf21
Spoleto I 35 Ln48
Spook Cave USA 172 Fe24
Spookmyndorp NAM 154 Lh59
Spooner USA (WI) 172 Fe23
Spotorno I 34 Lj46
Spotted House USA (WY) 169 Eh23
Spøttrup DK 30 Lj34
Sprague USA (WA) 168 Eb22
Spratly Islands 94 Qh40
Spray USA (OR) 168 Ea23
Spree D 32 Lp39
Spreewald D 32 Lp39
Spremberg D 32 Lp39
Sprengisandur IS 18 Kb26
Spring RO 44 Md45
Springbok ZA 154 Lj60
Spring Creek AUS (QLD) 107 Sc55
Spring Creek USA (NV) 170 Ec25
Springdale CDN (NF) 177 Hb21
Springdale USA (AR) 174 Fc27
Springe D 32 Lk38
Springer USA (NM) 171 Eh27
Springerville USA (AZ) 171 Ef28
Springfield USA (CO) 174 Ej27
Springfield USA (GA) 178 Fk29
Springfield USA (IL) 175 Ff26
Springfield USA (KY) 175 Fh27
Springfield USA (MA) 177 Gd24
Springfield USA (MO) 174 Fd27
Springfield USA (OH) 173 Fj26
Springfield USA (OR) 168 Dj23
Springfield USA (TN) 175 Fg27
Springfield USA (VT) 177 Gd24
Springfield Plateau USA 174 Fd27
Springfontein ZA 155 Mc61
Spring Garden GUY 194 Ha42
Springhill CDN (NS) 176 Gh23
Spring Hill USA (FL) 179 Fj31
Springhill USA (LA) 174 Fd29
Springrale AUS (QLD) 108 Sa57
Spring Ridge AUS (NSW) 109 Sf61
Springs ZA 155 Me59
Springside CDN (SK) 169 Ej20
Springs Junction NZ 113 Tg67
Springsure AUS (QLD) 109 Se58
Springvale AUS (WA) 103 Rd54
Springvale USA (ME) 177 Ge24
Springvale Homestead AUS (NT) 106 Rg53
Spring Valley ZA 155 Md62
Springview USA (NE) 172 Fa24
Springville USA (NY) 173 Ga24
Springville USA (UT) 171 Ee25
Springwater CDN (SK) 169 Ef19
Sproge S 31 Lt33
Spruce Grove CDN (AB) 169 Ed19
Spruce Home CDN (SK) 169 Eh19
Spruce Island USA 164 Cd17
Spruce Meadows CDN (AB) 169 Ec20
Spruce Pine USA (NC) 178 Fj28
Spruce Woods Prov. Park CDN 172 Fa21
Spur USA (TX) 174 Ek29
Spurn Head GB 21 La37
Spuž SCG 44 Lu48
Squamish CDN (BC) 168 Dj21
Squaw Creek N.W.R. USA 174 Fc25
Squaw Lake USA (MN) 172 Fc22
Squaw Valley USA (CA) 170 Dk26
Squillace I 37 Lr52
Squinzano I 37 Lt50
Squires Mem. Prov. Park CDN 177 Hb21
Sragen RI 95 Qf49
Sravanabelgola IND 84 Oj39
Sravasti IND 83 Pb32
Srb HR 35 Lr46
Srbac BIH 35 Ls45
Srbica SCG 44 Ma48
Srbobran SCG 44 Lu45
Srbovac SCG 44 Ma48
Srdiečko SK 43 Lu42
Sre Ambel K 89 Qb40
Srebărna BG 45 Mh46
Srebărna Nature Reserve BG 45 Mg47
Srebrenica BIH 44 Lu46
Srebrenik BIH 44 Lt46
Sredec BG 45 Mf48
Sredec BG 45 Mh48
Sredinnyj hrebet RUS 55 Ta07
Sredna Gora BG 45 Me48
Srednebelaja RUS 71 Re20
Srednerusskaja vozvyšennost' RUS 48 Mj19
Sre Koki K 89 Qd39
Śrem PL 40 Ls38
Sremska Mitrovica SCG 44 Lu46
Sremski Karlovci SCG 44 Lu45
Sre Noy K 89 Qc39
Sre Peang K 89 Qb39
Sretensk RUS 71 Qj19
Sribawono RI 93 Qc48
Sribne UA 48 Mg20
Sri Dungargarh IND (RJT) 80 Oh31
Srigiripadu IND (APH) 83 Ok37
Sri Jayewardenepura CL 85 Ok42
Srikakulam IND (APH) 83 Pb36
Sri Kalahasti IND (APH) 85 Ok39
Sri Karanpur IND (RJT) 80 Og31
Sri Krishna Mutt (Udupi) IND 84 Oh39
Sri Lanka CL 53 Pa09
Srimangal BD 86 Pf33
Sri Mohangarh IND (RJT) 80 Of32
Srinagar IND (UTT) 81 Ok30
Srinagar 80 Oh28
Srinagarindra N.P. THA 88 Pk38
Srinakarin Reservoir THA 88 Pk38
Sringeri IND 84 Oh39
Srinivaspur IND (KTK) 84 Ok39
Srirangam IND (TNU) 85 Ok40
Srirangapatna IND (KTK) 84 Oj39
Srisailam IND (APH) 82 Ok37
Srivilliputtur IND (TNU) 84 Oj41
Środa Wielkopolska PL 40 Ls38
Srokowo PL 41 Mb36
Sr'reenshamali SYR 56 Mk27
Ssese Islands EAU 144 Mg46
Staaten River N.P. AUS (QLD) 107 Sb54
Stabbursdalen n.p. N 16 Mc10
Stachanov UA 49 Mk21
Stachy CZ 42 Lo41
Stack Skerry GB 20 Kq31
Stad N 17 Lc14
Staðarfell IS 18 Js25
Staðarhóll IS 18 Jt25
Staðarskáli IS 18 Jt25
Stade D 32 Lk37
Staderton ZA 155 Me59
Stadskanaal NL 23 Lh38
Stadthagen D 32 Lk38
Stadtlohn D 32 Lg38
Staffa GB 20 Ko34
Staffanstorp S 30 Lo35
Staffelberg D 33 Lm40
Stafford GB 21 Ks38
Stagira GR 45 Md50
Stahnsdorf D 32 Lo38
Staicele LV 39 Me33
Stajki BY 41 Mg37
Staked Plains = Llano Estacado USA 174 Ej29
Stakliškės LT 39 Me36
Stalbe LV 39 Mf33
Stalker Castle GB 20 Kp34
Ställdalen S 31 Lp31
Staller Sattel I/A 34 Ln44
Staloluokta S 16 Lj12
Staloluokta fjällstation S 16 Lj12
Stalowa Wola PL 41 Mc40
Stambolijski BG 45 Me48
Stamford AUS (QLD) 109 Sb56
Stamford GB 21 Ku38
Stamford USA (CT) 177 Gd25
Stamford USA (TX) 174 Fa29
Stamford Bridge GB 21 Ku37
Stampriet NAM 154 Lk58
Stamsund N 16 Lg11
Stânceni RO 43 Mf44
Standing Rock Ind. Res. USA 172 Ek23
Standing Stone S.P. USA 175 Fh27
Standish USA (MI) 173 Fj24
Stanford USA (KY) 175 Fh27
Stanford USA (MT) 169 Ee22
Stånga S 31 Lt33
Stanger ZA 155 Mf60
Stanhope AUS (VIC) 111 Sc64
Stanhope GB 21 Ks36
Staniard Creek BS 179 Gb33
Stanica Bagaevskaja RUS 49 Na22
Staniel Cay Beach BS 179 Gb33
Stanišić SCG 44 Lu45
Staňkov CZ 42 Lo41
Stanley AUS (TAS) 111 Sc66
Stanley GB (GBF) 210 Hb71
Stanley USA (ND) 169 Ej21
Stanley Mission CDN (SK) 167 Eh18
Stanley, Mount EAU/RDC 144 Mf45
Stanley Reservoir IND 84 Oj40
Stanmore ZW 152 Me56
Stanovoe RUS 48 Mk19
Stanovoye Nagor'ye RUS 55 Qc07
Stanovoy Khrebet RUS 55 Ra07
Stans CH 34 Lj44
Stansbury AUS (SA) 110 Rj63
Stansmore Range AUS 103 Rd56
Stanthorpe AUS (QLD) 109 Sf60
Stanton Bank GB 20 Kh34
Stanwell AUS (QLD) 109 Sf57
Stanwell Park AUS (NSW) 111 Sf63
Stanwood USA (WA) 168 Dj21
Stanyčno-Luhans'ke UA 48 Mk21
Staphorst NL 23 Lg38
Stapleford ZW 152 Mg55
Staples USA (MN) 172 Fc22
Stapleton USA (NE) 172 Ek25
Stąporków PL 41 Ma39
Stara PL 41 Lu39
Starachowice PL 41 Mb39
Staraja Russa RUS 48 Mf17
Stara Kiszewa PL 40 Lt36
Stara Moravica SCG 44 Lu45
Stara Novalja HR 35 Lp46
Stara Pazova SCG 44 Ma46
Stara Rečka BG 45 Mg47
Stara Reka BG 45 Mg48
Stara Vyživka UA 41 Me39
Stara Zagora BG 45 Mf48
Starbuck Island KIR 11 Ca10
Star City USA (AR) 175 Fe29
Stare Dolistowo PL 41 Mc37
Stare Jeżewo PL 41 Mc37
Stare Kiełbonki PL 41 Mb37
Stare Strącze PL 40 Lr39
Stargard Szczeciński PL 40 Lq37
Starica RUS 48 Mh17
Starica RUS 48 Mh19
Starigrad HR 35 Lr47
Stari grad Mostar BIH 35 Ls47
Stari grad Sarajevo BIH 44 Lt47
Stari Ras SCG 44 Ma47
Starke USA (FL) 178 Fj31
Starkville USA (MS) 175 Ff29
Starkweather USA (ND) 172 Fa21
Starnberg D 33 Lm42
Starnberger See D 33 Lm43
Starobil's'k UA 48 Mk21
Starobin BY 48 Md19
Starodub RUS 48 Mg19
Starogard PL 40 Lq37
Starogard Gdański PL 40 Lt37
Starojur'evo RUS 48 Na19
Starokostjantyniv UA 49 Md21
Starominskaja RUS 49 Mk22
Staro Nagoričane MK 44 Mb48
Staro Petrovo Selo HR 35 Ls45
Starosel BG 45 Me48
Staro Selo BG 45 Mg47
Starotitarovskaja RUS 49 Mj23
Starožilovo RUS 48 Mk18
Start Point GB 21 Kr40
Stary Dvor RUS 48 Na17
Stary Dzierzgoń PL 41 Lu37
Staryi Oskol RUS 48 Mj20
Staryja Darohi BY 48 Me19
Staryj Sambir UA 43 Mc41
Starý Smokovec SK 43 Ma41
Staßfurt D 32 Lm39
Staszów PL 41 Mb40
State College USA (PA) 177 Gb25
State Line USA (MS) 175 Ff30
State Mosque MAL 92 Qa44
Statenville USA (GA) 178 Fj30
Statesboro USA (GA) 178 Fk29
Statesville USA (NC) 178 Fk28
Stathelle N 30 Lk31
Station de capture d'Epulu RDC 141 Me45
Statue of Liberty USA 177 Gd25
Stăuceni MD 49 Me22
Staunton USA (VA) 177 Ga26
Staunton River S.P. USA 178 Ga27
Stavanger N 30 Lf32
Stave SCG 44 Lu46
Stavelot B 23 Lf40
Stavern N 30 Lk32
Stavky UA 41 Me39
Stavre S 16 Lh14
Stavrodrómi GR 46 Mb53
Stavrós GR 45 Md50
Stavroskiádi GR 46 Ma50
Stavroúpoli GR 45 Me49
Stawiski PL 41 Mc37
Stawiszyn PL 40 Lt39
St-CharlesGarnier CDN (QC) 176 Gf21
Steamboat USA (OR) 168 Dj24
Steamboat Springs USA (CO) 171 Eg25
Stebbins USA (AK) 164 Bj14
Stebnyk UA 43 Md41
Steele USA (MO) 175 Ff27
Steele USA (ND) 172 Fa22
Steele, Mount CDN 166 Ck15
Steelpoort ZA 155 Mf58
Steelville USA (MO) 175 Fe27
Steen CDN (AB) 167 Eb16
Steenbergen NL 23 Le39
Steens Mountain USA 168 Ea24
Steenvoorde B 23 Lc40

Tabon Caves ▣ RP 91 Qk41
Tabong ▣ MYA 86 Pj32
Tábor ▣ CZ 42 Lp41
Tabora ▣ EAT 146 Mg48
Tabora ▣ EAT 147 Mj51
Tabory ▣ RUS 38 Mi31
Taboúoù ▣ CI 137 Kg43
Tabrinkout ▣ RIM 130 Kc36
Tabriz ▣ IR 57 Nd26
Tabriz ▣ IR 57 Nd27
Tabuaeran ▣ KIR 11 Ca09
Tabuan ▣ RI 93 Qi48
Tabubil ▣ PNG 115 Sa48
Tabudarat ▣ RI 95 Qh47
Tabuenca ▣ E 28 Kt49
Tabuk ▣ RP 90 Ra37
Tabuk ▣ KSA 58 Mj31
Tabuk Fort ▣ KSA 58 Mj31
Tabuleiro do Norte ▣ BR (CE) 201 Ja48
Tabur ▣ SUD 134 Mb40
Tabwemasana ▲ VU 118 Td53
Täby ▣ S 31 Lt31
Taca ▣ CZ 42 Lp41
Tacabamba ▣ PE 196 Ga49
Tacajó ▣ BR 186 Gc35
Tacalaya ▣ PE 197 Ge54
Tacámbaro de Codallos ▣ MEX (MHC) 182 Ek36
Tacaná, Volcán ▲ GCA/MEX 183 Fd38
Tacaratu ▣ BR (PE) 201 Ja50
Tacarigua ▣ YV 193 Gg40
Tachakou ▣ CHN (XUZ) 67 Pc23
Tacharane ▣ RMM 131 La37
Tacheng ▣ CHN (XUZ) 66 Pb22
Tachie ▣ CDN 166 Dh18
Tachilek ▣ MYA 87 Pk35
Tachiumet ▣ LAR 126 Lt32
Tachov ▣ CZ 42 Ln41
Tach Thu ▣ VN 89 Qe38
Tacinskij ▣ RUS 49 Na21
Tacipi ▣ RI 96 Ra48
Tacloban ▣ RP 90 Rc40
Tacna ▣ PE 206 Ge55
Tacoma ▣ USA (WA) 168 Dj22
Taco Pozo ▣ RA (CP) 207 Gj58
Tacora ▣ RCH 206 Gf54
Tacora, Volcán ▲ RCH 206 Gf54
Taco Taco ▣ C 179 Fj34
Tacuarembó ▣ ROU 204 Hc61
Tacuati ▣ PY 202 Hb57
Tacugama Chimpanzee Sanctuary ▣ WAL 136 Kd41
Tacuru ▣ BR (MS) 202 Hc57
Tad ▣ PK 65 Oc33
Tada ▣ IND 85 Ok35
Tadahadi ▣ SOL 117 Ta51
Tadalt ▣ MA 124 Kf31
Tadânet Keyna ▣ RMM 131 Kj36
Tadarimana, T.I. ▣ BR 202 Hc54
Taddert ▣ MA 125 Kg30
Tadepallegudem ▣ IND (APH) 83 Pa37
Tadientourt ▣ DZ 126 Le32
Tadine ▣ F (NCL) 118 Td56
Tadjemout ▣ DZ 126 Lb29
Tadjoura ▣ DJI 143 Nb40
Tadjrouna ▣ DZ 126 Lb29
Tadmur ▣ SYR 56 Me28
Tado ▣ RMM (ARP) 86 Pg32
Tadoba-Andhari N.P. ▣ IND 83 Ok35
Tadoussac ▣ CDN (QC) 176 Gf21
Tadpatri ▣ IND 85 Ok38
Tadubil ▣ IND (MNP) 86 Ph33
Taduno ▣ RI 97 Rd44
Taech'ondong ▣ ROK 78 Rd27
Taech'ongdo ▣ PRK 78 Rc27
Taegu ▣ ROK 78 Rd28
Taejon ▣ ROK 78 Rd27
Taejong ▣ ROK 78 Rd27
Taevaskoja ▣ EST 39 Mg32
Tafahi ▣ TO 10 Ba11
Tafalla ▣ E 28 Kt48
Tafelberg ▣ SME 194 Hd44
Tafermaar ▣ RI 114 Rh49
Tafetan ▣ MEX (MHC) 182 Ek36
Tafia ▣ JOR 58 Mh30
Tafila al Mala ▣ MA 125 Kh33
Tafinkar ▣ RMM 132 Lb38
Tafiré ▣ CI 137 Kh41
Tafraoute ▣ MA 124 Kf33
Tafresh ▣ IR 57 Nf28
Taft ▣ IR 64 Nh30
Taft ▣ RP 90 Rc40
Taft ▣ USA (CA) 170 Ea28
Taga ▣ RMM 131 Kh38
Taga ▣ SUD 135 Mf36
Tagant ▣ RIM 130 Kd37
Tagarak ▣ IR 57 Ne29
Tagarane Gabout ▣ RMM 131 La38
Tagaung ▣ MYA 86 Pj34
Tagbalé ▣ RCA 140 Ma43
Tagbilaran ▣ RP 90 Rb41
Tagegalijabo ▣ CHN (TIB) 68 Pd29

Taibique ▣ E 124 Ka32
Taibus Qi ▣ CHN (NMZ) 73 Qh25
Taicang ▣ CHN (JGS) 78 Ra30
Taichung ▣ RC 75 Ra33
Taicy ▣ RUS 38 Mi31
Taigetos ▣ GR 46 Mc54
Taihang ▣ CHN (SAX) 73 Qg27
Taihape ▣ NZ 113 Th65
Taihe ▣ CHN (AHU) 73 Qh29
Taihe ▣ CHN (JGX) 75 Qg32
Taikang ▣ CHN (HNN) 73 Qh28
Tai Hu ▣ CHN 78 Ra30
Taikang ▣ CHN (HNN) 73 Qh28
Taikkyi ▣ MYA 88 Ph37
Tailai ▣ CHN (HLG) 71 Rb22
Tailem Bend ▣ AUS (SA) 110 Rh63
Taim ▣ BR (RS) 204 Hd62
Taimana ▣ RMM 131 La37
Taimati ▣ PA 185 Ga41
Tain ▣ GB 20 Kq33
Tainan ▣ RC 75 Ra34
Tainhas ▣ BR (RS) 205 He60
Taining ▣ CHN (FJN) 75 Qk32
Tai-Nui l'Hermitage ▣ F 23 Ng48
Taió ▣ BR (SC) 205 He59
Taioibeiras ▣ BR (MG) 203 Hj53
Taiof Island ▣ PNG 117 Sh48
Taioura Head ▣ NZ 113 Tf68
Taipa do Tocantins ▣ BR (TO) 200 Hg52
Taipei ▣ RC 75 Ra33
Taipei Financial Centre ▣ RC 75 Ra33
Taiping ▣ CHN (GZG) 74 Qd34
Taiping ▣ CHN (GZG) 74 Qf34
Taiping ▣ MAL 92 Qa43
Taipingchuan ▣ CHN (JLN) 71 Rb23
Tai Po ▣ CHN 74 Qg34
Tair ▣ YE 60 Nc39
Tairaz ▣ RC 75 Ra33
Tairaz ▣ YE 60 Nc39
Tajaé ▣ RI 201 Ja48
Taijen ▣ RC 75 Ra34
Tai Rom Yen N.P. ▣ THA 88 Pk41
Taishan ▣ CHN (SAX) 73 Qg27
Taishan ▣ CHN (GDG) 75 Qh34
Taishir ▣ RC 75 Ra34
Taishitaipogu ▣ RI 93 Qa47
Taitpu ▣ NZ 113 Tg67
Taitung ▣ RC 75 Ra34
Taivassalo ▣ FIN 38 Mb30
Taliparamba ▣ IND (KER) 84 Oh39
Taipaw ▣ RP 91 Ra43
Taisei ▣ J 79 Rf29
Taiwang ▣ RI 96 Qi50
Taiwan ▣ RC 75 Ra33
Taiyang Dao ▣ CHN 76 Rd23
Taiyuan ▣ CHN (SAX) 73 Qg27
Taizhou ▣ CHN (JGS) 78 Ra30
Tajumulco, Volcán ▲ GCA 184 Fd38
Takab ▣ IR 57 Nd27
Takabba ▣ EAK 145 Na44
Takachiho ▣ J 79 Rf29
Takahashi ▣ J 79 Rg28
Takalou ▣ TCH 139 Lk40
Takama ▣ GUY 194 Ha43
Takamaka ▣ SY 145 Nh48
Takamatsu ▣ J 79 Rf28
Takanabe ▣ J 79 Rf29
Takao, Gunung ▲ RI 96 Qj50
Takaoka ▣ J 77 Rg27
Takapuna ▣ NZ 112 Th64
Takara ▣ RCA 140 Ma41
Takara-jima ▲ J 79 Re32
Takatokaman ▣ RB 155 Mc57
Takatshwane ▣ RB 154 Ma57
Takatsuki ▣ J 79 Rf28
Takaungu ▣ EAK 145 Na47
Takayama ▣ J 77 Rg27
Take ▣ J 79 Rg28
Take-jima ▲ J 79 Rf30
Takengon ▣ RI 92 Pj43
Takeo ▣ J 79 Rf29
Takeo ▣ K 89 Qc40
Takestan ▣ IR 57 Ne27
Taketa ▣ J 79 Rf29
Tai Fa ▣ THA 88 Qa38
Takhadid ▣ IRQ 59 Nc31
Takhilt ▣ MNG 67 Pj23
Takhro ▣ BF 89 Qb38
Takht-e-Bahi ▣ PK 65 Of28
Takht-e Soleyman ▣ IR 57 Nd27
Takht-i-Sangin ▣ TJ 63 Oe27
Takht-i-Sulaiman ▣ PK 65 Oe30
Takiéta ▣ RN 132 Le39
Takiéta ▣ RN 132 Le39
Takikro ▣ CI 137 Kj42
Takingeun = Takengon ▣ RI 92 Pj43
Takinoue ▣ J 78 Sb23
Takis ▣ PNG 116 Sf48
Takisung ▣ RI 96 Qh49
Takla Landing ▣ CDN (BC) 166 Dh18
Takla Makan Desert ▣ CHN 52 Pa06
Takli Dhokeshwar ▣ IND (MHT) 82 Oh36
Takoban, Mount ▲ PNG 117 Sh49
Takobanda ▣ RCA 140 Ma42
Takokaju Mountains ▲ RI 96 Qk46
Takoradi ▣ GH 137 Kk43
Takorka ▣ RN 132 Ld39
Takoumbaïta ▣ CI 137 Kh42
Takoutala ▣ SN 130 Kd40
Takpama ▣ TG 137 La41
Takpoima ▣ LB 136 Kd42
Takro Falls ▣ THA 88 Qa38

Talanga ▣ HN 184 Fg38
Talangbatu ▣ RI 93 Qi48
Talangjatuh ▣ RI 93 Qc47
Talang Rimbo ▣ RI 93 Qc47
Talang Selengku ▣ RI 93 Qc47
Talang Sipucuk ▣ RI 93 Qc47
Talara ▣ PE 196 Fk48
Talaroo ▣ AUS (QLD) 107 Sb55
Talarrubias ▣ E 27 Kp51
Talas ▣ KS 66 Og24
Talas Ala Too ▲ KZ/KS 63 Of24
Talasea ▣ PNG 116 Sf48
Talata-Ampano ▣ RM 157 Nd56
Talatakoh ▣ RI 96 Rb46
Talata Mafara ▣ WAN 138 Ld39
Tal at Damya ▣ DARS 124 Kf32
Talavera de la Reina ▣ E 27 Kq51
Talawanta ▣ AUS (QLD) 107 Sa55
Talawdi ▣ SUD 135 Mf40
Talayap ▣ RI 93 Qd45
Talaya ▣ RUS (NSW) 111 Se63
Talbot Island ▣ AUS 107 Sb50
Talbotton ▣ USA (GA) 175 Fh29
Talbrak ▣ SYR 57 Na27
Talca ▣ RCH 208 Ge63
Talcahuano ▣ RCH 208 Gd64
Talcher ▣ IND (ORS) 83 Pc35
Tal Chhapar Wildlife Sanctuary ▣ IND 80 Oh32
Talcho ▣ RN 132 Lb38
Taldom ▣ RUS 48 Mj17
Taldy-Bulak ▣ KS 66 Og24
Taldykorgan ▣ KZ 66 Og23
Taldy-Kurgan ▣ KZ 66 Og23
Taleex ▣ SP 143 Ne41
Talegaon ▣ IND (MHT) 82 Ok35
Talera ▣ IND (MHT) 82 Og37
Talgarth ▣ GB 21 Kr39
Talguharal ▣ SUD 135 Mh36
Talhabpass ▣ AFG 65 Oc30
Talhah ▣ KSA 60 Na38
Talhar ▣ PK 65 Oe34
Taliabu ▣ RI 97 Rd40
Talikota ▣ IND (KTK) 82 Oj37
Tali Laki Reef ▣ PNG 116 Sf51
Talimã ▣ BR (PA) 194 Hc45
Taling Chan ▣ THA 88 Qa39
Taliouine ▣ MA 125 Kg30
Talipan ▣ RP 91 Ra43
Talisei ▣ RI 91 Rc41
Talisayan ▣ RP 91 Rc41
Talişş ▣ IR 57 Ne27
Talitsa ▣ RUS 70 Py19
Talkeetna ▣ USA (AK) 165 Ce14
Talkeetna Mountains ▲ USA (AK) 165 Cf14
Tall Afar ▣ IRQ 57 Nb27
Tallahassee ▣ USA (FL) 175 Fh30
Tallahatchie N.W.R. ▣ USA 174 Fe27
Tallangatta ▣ AUS (VIC) 111 Se64
Tallapalem ▣ IND (APH) 83 Pb37
Tallard ▣ F 25 Lf46
Tallaringa Conservation Park ▣ AUS 108 Rg60
Tallase ▣ USA (AL) 175 Fh29
Tallgrass Prairie N.P. ▣ USA 174 Fb26
Tallinn ▣ ☆ ● EST 38 Me31
Tall Kaia ▣ AFG 65 Ob30
Tall Kayf ▣ IRQ 57 Nb27
Tall Kujik ▣ IRQ 57 Nb27
Talloires ▣ F 25 Lg45
Tallsjö ▣ S 16 Lk13
Tall Trees Grove ▣ USA 168 Dj25
Tallulah ▣ USA (LA) 175 Fe29
Tallykalyla ▣ FIN 38 Mf37
Tall Uwaynat ▣ IRQ 57 Nb27
Talmaciu ▣ RO 44 Me45
Talmage ▣ USA (UT) 171 Ee25
Talmest ▣ MA 124 Kf30
Talmont-Saint-Hilaire ▣ F 24 Ks44
Talnah ▣ RUS 54 Pb05
Tal'ne ▣ UA 49 Mf21
Taloda ▣ IND (GUJ) 82 Og35
Taloga ▣ USA (OK) 174 Fa27
Talogan ▣ AFG 65 Oe27
Talodi Beach ▣ RI 96 Qk50
Talos Dome ▲ 7 Rc33
Talovala ▣ RUS 48 Na20
Taloyoak ▣ CDN 163 Fb05
Talpada ▣ IND (ORS) 83 Pd35
Talping Ling ▣ CHN 71 Ra22
Talrahah ▣ SYR 56 Mj28
Talsara ▣ IND (ORS) 83 Pd35
Talshand ▣ MNG 67 Pk23
Talsi ▣ LV 39 Mc33
Talsinnt ▣ MA 125 Kj29
Talu ▣ RI 93 Qb46
Taludaan ▣ RI 91 Rb45
Talukkuantan ▣ RI 93 Qc46
Talwood ▣ AUS (QLD) 109 Se60
Tama ▣ RN 132 Ld38
Tama ▣ USA (IA) 172 Fd24
Tamadanh ▣ RI 114 Rg48
Tamagaram-Takava ▣ RN 132 Le38
Tamala ▣ RUS 48 Nb19
Tamale ▣ GH 137 Kk41
Tamames ▣ E 26 Ko50
Tamaná, Cerro ▲ CO 192 Gb43
Tamanar ▣ MA 124 Kf30
Tamanco ▣ PE 196 Gc48
Tamanda ▣ Z 146 Mg52
Tamandourrit ▣ RMM 131 Kk36
Tamanhos ▣ P 26 Kn50
Tamanrasset ▣ DZ 132 Lc34
Tamanthi ▣ LAR 127 Lk35
Tamási ▣ H 42 Lt44
Tamana BF 137 Kk39

Tamazula de Gordiano ▣ MEX (JLC) 182 Ej36
Tamazunchale ▣ MEX (SLP) 182 Fa35
Tambacounda ▣ SN 136 Kd39
Tamba Urmar ▣ IND (PJB) 80 Oh30
Tambelan ▣ MAL 94 Qi42
Tambien ▣ RI 93 Qc47
Tambacsawah ▣ RI 93 Qc47
Tambaqui ▣ RI 95 Qg50
Tambaga ▣ RI 96 Ra47
Tambara ▣ MOC 153 Mh54
Tambaran ▣ PK 65 Oe33
Tambaran ▣ BF 137 La40
Tambawel ▣ WAN 138 Lc39
Tambea ▣ ANG 150 Lh52
Tambea ▣ RI 96 Ra48
Tambeul ▣ SOL 117 Sk50
Tambellup ▣ AUS (WA) 104 Qj63
Tambero ▣ Z 152 Md54
Tan Emeilel ▣ DZ 126 Le32
Tanelli ▣ RI 97 Rd46
Tanezrouft ▣ DZ/RMM 131 Kk34
Tanga ▣ EAT 147 Mk48
Tanga ▣ RUS 70 Qf20
Tangenberg ▣ RI 95 Qd46
Tangadee ▣ AUS (WA) 104 Qk58
Tangafoss ▣ IS 18 Ka26
Tangal ▣ RI 96 Qj50
Tangaram ▣ RI 97 Rd47
Tanggale ▣ TCH 133 Lk37
Tangela Peak ▲ WAN 139 Lf41
Tanggula ▲ CHN 68 Pe29
Tanggula Shan ▲ CHN 68 Pe29
Tanggula Shankou ▣ CHN 69 Pf29
Tanggi ▣ CHN (HNN) 73 Qh26
Tanghai ▣ CHN (HNN) 73 Qa26
Tangi Sorkheh ▣ IR 64 Nh32
Tangua ▣ CO 192 Ga45
Tanguelbai ▣ RI 95 Qf49
Tanguen-Dassouri ▣ BF 137 Kk39
Tanguiéta ▣ DY 137 La40
Tangyuan ▣ MYA 87 Pk34
Tangyuan ▣ CHN (HLG) 76 Re22
Tanhacu ▣ BR (BA) 203 Hk53
Tan Hiep ▣ VN 89 Qd40
Tani ▣ K 89 Qc40
Taninga ▣ MOC 155 Mk54
Taninthari ▣ MYA 88 Pk39
Tanintharyi ▣ CL 85 Pa41
Taniwel ▣ RI 97 Rd46
Tanjay ▣ RP 90 Rb41
Tanjona Angontsy ▣ RM 156 Nf53
Tanjona Ankaboa ▣ RM 156 Ne52
Tanjona Anorontany ▣ RM 156 Ne51
Tanjona Belao ▣ RM 156 Ne54
Tanjona Bobaomby ▣ RM 156 Nf51
Tanjona Larree ▣ RM 157 Ne54
Tanjona Masoala ▣ RM 156 Nf53
Tanjona Vilanandro ▣ RM 156 Nc54
Tanjona Vohimena ▣ RM 157 Nc58
Tanjore = Thanjavur ▣ IND (TNU) 85 Ok40
Tanjunanda ▣ RI 93 Qb46
Tana ▣ VU 118 Te55
Tanabe ▣ J 79 Rh29
Tanaga ▣ SP 202 Hf56
Tanagura ▣ J 79 Rj27
Tanah Merah ▣ MAL 92 Qa43
Tanahmasa ▣ RI 93 Qa47
Tanahgrogot ▣ RI 95 Qj46
Tanahjampea ▣ RI 96 Ra49
Tanahkuning ▣ RI 94 Qj44
Tanahmalalila ▣ RI 93 Qd46
Tanahmerah ▣ RI 93 Qd46
Tanah Merah Indah-Lempake ▣ RI 95 Qj46
Tanah Rata ▣ MAL 92 Qa43
Tanak ▣ RI 96 Qj50
Tan an ▣ N 16 Mk10
Tanaf ▣ SN 136 Kc39
Tanah Api ▣ RI 94 Qi47
Tana bru ▣ N 16 Me10
Tan-Ben ▣ RI 97 Rf50
Tana-Ahenet ▣ DZ 132 La34
Tanahgrogot ▣ RI 95 Qj46
Tanala ▣ RM 157 Nd57
Tanama ▣ BF 137 Kk39
Tanamalwila ▣ CL 85 Pa42
Tanami Desert ▣ AUS 103 Re55
Tan An ▣ VN 89 Qd40
Tanana ▣ USA (AK) 165 Cd13
Tanandava ▣ RM 157 Nd56
Tanangozi ▣ EAT 146 Mh49
Tanani ▣ RI 97 Rf49
Tanay ▣ RI 96 Qj50
Tanba-kochi ▣ J 79 Rf28
Tanauan ▣ RP 90 Ra38
Tanba-kochi ▣ J 79 Rh29
Tan Chau ▣ VN 89 Qc40
Tancheng ▣ CHN (SDG) 78 Qk28
Tanchon ▣ PRK 76 Re25
Tancoyol de Serra ▣ MEX (HDG) 182 Fa35
Tanda ▣ IND (APH) 82 Oj34
Tanda ▣ IND (UTT) 81 Pa31
Tanda ▣ RMM 131 La37

Tandaro ▣ EAK 144 Mj43
Tanda Urmar ▣ IND (PJB) 80 Oh30
Tandek ▣ MAL 94 Qj42
Tandil ▣ IND (HPH) 81 Oj29
Tandil ▣ RA (BA) 209 Ha64
Tando ▣ IN 86 Pg36
Tando Adam ▣ PK 65 Oe33
Tando Allahyar ▣ PK 65 Oe33
Tando Bago ▣ PK 65 Oe33
Tando Muhammad Khan ▣ PK 91 Qk45
Tando Zinze ▣ ANG 148 Lg48
Tandrano ▣ RM 157 Nd56
Tandur ▣ IND (APH) 82 Oj37
Taneichi ▣ J 77 Sa26
Taneka ▣ Z 146 Me52
Tanezrouft ▣ DZ/RMM 131 Kk34
Tanga ▣ EAT 147 Mk48
Tanga ▣ RUS 70 Qf20
Tangadee ▣ AUS (WA) 104 Qk58
Tangafoss ▣ IS 18 Ka26
Tangal ▣ RI 96 Qj50
Tangaram ▣ RI 97 Rd47
Tanggale ▣ TCH 133 Lk37
Tangel Peak ▲ WAN 139 Lf41
Tanggula ▲ CHN 68 Pe29
Tanggula Shan ▲ CHN 68 Pe29
Tanggula Shankou ▣ CHN 69 Pf29
Tanggi ▣ CHN (HNN) 73 Qh26
Tanghai ▣ CHN (HBI) 73 Qk26
Tangi Sorkheh ▣ IR 64 Nh32
Tangua ▣ CO 192 Ga45
Tanguelbai ▣ RI 95 Qf49
Tangerang ▣ RI 93 Qd49
Tangerhütte ▣ D 32 Lm38
Tangorin ▣ AUS (QLD) 109 Sc56
Tangra Yumco ▣ CHN 68 Pd30
Tang Rah ▣ IR 62 Nh27
Tangshan ▣ CHN (HBI) 73 Qk26
Tangudan Group ▲ RP 91 Ra42
Tangyuan ▣ CHN (HLG) 76 Re22
Tanhaçu ▣ BR (BA) 203 Hk53
Tanintharyi ▣ MYA 88 Pk39
Tanjay ▣ RP 90 Rb41
Tanjong Piai ▣ MAL 92 Qa44
Tanjung ▣ RI 95 Qd47
Tanjung Kait ▣ RI 95 Qd47
Tanjung Kamdara ▣ RI 115 Sa47
Tanjung Karang ▣ MAL 92 Qa43
Tanjung Karawong ▣ RI 95 Qd48
Tanjung Keling Beach ▣ MAL 93 Qb44
Tanjung Keluang ▣ RI 95 Qf46
Tanjung Keluang ▣ RI 95 Qf47
Tanjung Kenam ▣ RI 93 Qd44
Tanjung Kidurong ▣ MAL 94 Qg44
Tanjung Kolat ▣ RI 95 Qh49
Tanjung Labuanbini ▣ RI 91 Qk45
Tanjung Laru Mat ▣ RI 95 Rf49
Tanjung Layar ▣ RI 95 Qf48
Tanjung Leman ▣ MAL 92 Qc44
Tanjunglolo ▣ RI 93 Qa46
Tanjung Lumut ▣ RI 95 Qd47
Tanjung Malatayur ▣ RI 95 Qf46
Tanjung Mangkalihat ▲ RI 91 Qk45
Tanjung Manundi ▣ RI 114 Rh46
Tanjung Marsimang ▣ RI 97 Rf47
Tanjung Medang ▣ RI 93 Qa44
Tanjung Momfafa ▣ RI 97 Rf46
Tanjung Nasong ▣ MAL 94 Qh43
Tanjung Ngabordamalu ▣ RI 114 Rh49
Tanjung Pacinan ▣ RI 95 Qh49
Tanjung Panjang ▣ RI 95 Qd47
Tanjung Pasir ▣ MAL 94 Qf44
Tanjung Payong ▣ MAL 94 Qj44
Tanjung Pemarung ▣ RI 95 Qd47
Tanjung Perupuk ▣ RI 91 Qk45
Tanjung Peureulak ▣ RI 92 Pj43
Tanjung Piandang ▣ MAL 92 Qa43
Tanjung Pinang ▣ RI 93 Qc45
Tanjung Pisau ▣ MAL 94 Qj42
Tanjungpura ▣ RI 93 Qc45
Tanjung Purwo ▣ RI 95 Qh49
Tanjung Raya ▣ RI 93 Qc47
Tanjung qredeb ▣ RI 94 Qj44
Tanjung Sabra ▣ RI 114 Rg47
Tanjung Sadari ▣ RI 95 Qd48
Tanjung Sekopong ▣ RI 93 Qc48
Tanjung Selokan ▣ RI 93 Qd45
Tanjung Sempang Mangayau ▣ MAL 94 Qj42
Tanjung Senebui ▣ RI 93 Qa44
Tanjung Sepat ▣ MAL 92 Qa43
Tanjung Sianuk ▣ RI 95 Qd47
Tanjung Sigep ▣ MAL 94 Qj45
Tanjung South ▣ RI 95 Qh48
Tanjung Sugut ▣ MAL 94 Qj42
Tanjung Tongerai ▣ RI 114 Rg47
Tanjung Unggan ▣ RI 93 Qd44
Tanjung Vals ▣ RI 114 Rj50
Tanjung Wamonket ▣ RI 97 Rf46
Tanjung Warial ▣ RI 97 Rf46
Tanjung Watukebo ▣ RI 116 Rg48
Tanjung Weduar ▣ RI 114 Rg49
Tank ▣ PK 65 Of29
Tankara ▣ IND (GUJ) 82 Of34
Tankara ▣ KZ 62 Nf22
Tan Ky ▣ VN 87 Qc36
Tan Lac ▣ VN 87 Qc35
Tanlbung ▣ RI 95 Qd47
Tannay ▣ F 25 Ld43
Tännforsen ▣ S 16 Lg14
Tannin Bugt ▲ GRO 30 Li33
Tan-Nuhot ▣ CL 85 Pa41
Tannum Sands ▣ AUS (QLD) 109 Sf57
Tannumshede ▣ S 30 Lm32
Tanot ▣ IND (RJT) 80 Of32
Tanout ▣ RN 132 Le38
Tanout-ou-Fillali ▣ MA 125 Kh29
Tanque do Piaui ▣ BR (PI) 201 Hj49
Tanque Novo ▣ BR (BA) 201 Hj52
Tanque Nuevo ▣ MEX (COH) 181 Ej32
Tanquián de Escobedo ▣ MEX (SLP) 182 Fa35
Tanquinho ▣ BR (BA) 201 Hk52
Tansen ▣ NEP 81 Pb32
Tansilla ▣ BF 137 Kh39
Tansuluhh ▣ LAR 127 Ma29
Tantamayo ▣ PE 196 Gb50
Tantiy ▣ IRQ 59 Ne31
Tan-Tan ▣ MA 124 Kd32
Tanterada ▣ AUS (SA) 110 Sa64
Tantoyuca ▣ MEX (VC) 182 Fa35
Tantpur ▣ IND (UPH) 82 Oj32
Tanuki ▣ IND (APH) 83 Pa37
Tanum ▣ S 30 Lm32
Tanum Hällristningar ▣ S 30 Lm32
Tanuma ▣ J 79 Rj27
Tanumshede ▣ S 30 Lm32
Tanza ▣ RP 90 Ra38
Tanzania ▣ EAT 146 Mg49
Tanzhe & Jietai Temples ▣ CHN 73 Qh26
Taocun ▣ CHN (SDG) 73 Ra27
Taohuayuan ▣ CHN (HUN) 74 Qg31
Taoist and Buddhist Temples ▣ CHN 76 Rb25
Taojiang ▣ CHN (HUN) 74 Qg31
Taonan ▣ CHN (JLN) 71 Rb23
Taong Atoll ▣ MH 10 Ta08
Taoru ▣ SOL 117 Sj49
Taoudenni ▣ RMM 131 Kj34
Taoudrart ▣ RMM 131 Kh34
Taou Kowt ▣ RIM 130 Kd37
Taounate ▣ MA 125 Kh29
Taourirt ▣ MA 125 Kj29
Taos ▣ USA (NM) 171 Eh27
Taos Pueblo ▣ USA 171 Eh27
Taouz ▣ MA 125 Kh30
Taoyuan ▣ CHN (HUN) 74 Qf31
Taoyuan Dao ▣ CHN 75 Qj30
Tapa ▣ EST 38 Mf31
Tapachula ▣ MEX (CHP) 183 Fd38
Tapajós ▣ BR 199 Hb48
Tapak ▣ MAL 92 Qa43
Tapaktuan ▣ RI 92 Pj44
Tapalpa ▣ MEX (JLC) 182 Ej36
Tapalqué ▣ RA (BA) 209 Gk64
Tapan ▣ RI 93 Qc47
Tapauá ▣ BR (AM) 197 Gk49
Tapaua ▣ BR (AM) 198 Gk50
Tapejara ▣ BR (RS) 204 Hd60
Tapejara ▣ BR (RS) 205 He59
Tapera ▣ BR (PA) 195 He45
Taperas ▣ BR (PB) 201 Ja49
Taperinha ▣ BR (AM) 198 Gh48
Tapera do Oeste ▣ BR (BA) 203 Hj54
Tapes ▣ BR (RS) 204 Hd61
Taphan Hin ▣ THA 88 Qa38
Taphao Beach ▣ THA 89 Qb39
Taping ▣ CHN (YUN) 87 Pk34

Tarokehn ▣ LB 136 Kg43
Taroko ▣ RC 75 Ra33
Taroko N.P. ▣ RC 75 Ra33
Taroom ▣ AUS (QLD) 109 Se58
Taroudannt ▣ MA 124 Kf30
Taroom Group ▲ RP 91 Ra42
Tapira ▣ BR (MG) 203 Hg55
Tapirapéco, Serra ▲ YV 193 Gh45
Tapirapé ▣ BR (PA) 201 Hk52
Tapiramuta ▣ BR (BA) 201 Hk51
Tapirapé Karajá, T.I. ▣ BR 200 He51
Tapizé ▣ AL 44 Lu49
Tapjejung ▣ NEP 83 Pd32
Tárraco-Caparo, P.N. ▣ YV 192 Ge42
Taplejung ▣ NEP 83 Pd32
Tápol ▣ TCH 140 Lh41
Tapolca ▣ H 42 Ls44
Tapong ▣ IND (AAN) 88 Pg41
Tapon ▣ USA (VA) 177 Gb27
Tappahannock ▣ USA (VA) 177 Gb27
Tappalang ▣ RI 96 Qk47
Tappeh Hessar ▣ IR 62 Nn27
Tappeh N.P. ▣ IR 57 Nc27
Tappeh Taq ▣ IR 64 Nj28
Tappuguy ▣ RUS 71 Ra19
Tapul ▣ RP 91 Ra43
Tapul Group ▲ RP 91 Ra43
Tapul Island ▣ RP 91 Ra43
Taquara ▣ BR (RS) 205 He60
Taquarana ▣ BR (AL) 201 Ja50
Taquari ▣ BR 202 Hb55
Taquaritinga ▣ BR (SP) 202 Hf56
Taquarituba ▣ BR (SP) 205 Hf57
Tara ▣ AUS (QLD) 109 Sf59
Tara ▣ RUS 54 Oc07
Tara ▣ SCG 44 Lu47
Tarabuco ▣ BOL 206 Gh55
Tarabulus ▣ LAR 127 La29
Taracó ▣ PE 206 Gf53
Taradehi ▣ IND (MPH) 83 Ok34
Taragi ▣ J 79 Rf29
Tarago ▣ AUS (NSW) 111 Se63
Tarajim ▣ WAN 139 Lf40
Tarakan ▣ RI 94 Qj44
Tarakbits ▣ PNG 115 Sa48
Tarakeswar ▣ IND (WBG) 86 Pe34
Tarakom ▣ AFG 64 Oa30
Tarama Jima ▲ J 79 Rd33
Taramangalam ▣ IND (TNU) 84 Oj40
Taran ▣ IR 57 Ne27
Taranaki, Mount ▲ NZ 113 Th65
Taranaki N.P. ▣ NZ 113 Th65
Tarangar ▣ TM 62 Nh26
Tarangire N.P. ▣ EAT 147 Mj48
Tara, N.P. ▣ SCG 44 Lu47
Taransay ▲ GB 20 Kn33
Táranto ▣ I 37 La50
Tarapaca ▣ CO 198 Gf47
Tarapaco ▣ BR (AM) 198 Gi51
Tarapoto ▣ PE 196 Gb49
Taraq an Na'jah ▣ SYR 56 Mh28
Tarara ▣ BR (AM) 198 Gh48
Tarare ▣ F 25 Le45
Tararua Range ▲ NZ 113 Th66
Tarasa Dwip Island ▣ IND 88 Pg41
Tarat ▣ DZ 126 Le31
Tarata ▣ PE 197 Ge54
Tarauacá ▣ BR (AC) 197 Ge50
Tarazona de la Mancha ▣ E 29 Kt51
Tarbagataj Žotasy ▲ KZ 66 Pa22
Tarbat Ness ▲ GB 20 Kr33
Tarbela ▣ PK 65 Og28
Tarbela Reservoir ▣ PK 65 Og28
Tarbert ▣ GB 20 Kp35
Tarbert ▣ IRL 19 Kl38
Tarbes ▣ F 24 La47
Tarbrax ▣ AUS (QLD) 107 Sb56
Tarcento ▣ I 35 La44
Tarcoola ▣ AUS (SA) 108 Rh61
Tarczyn ▣ PL 41 Ma39
Tardets-Sorholus ▣ F 24 Ks47
Taree ▣ AUS (NSW) 109 Sg61
Taren Taran ▣ IND (PJB) 80 Oh30
Tarfa ▣ MA 124 Kd32
Targa ▣ RN 132 Lc37
Târgoviste ▣ BG 45 Mg47
Târgovişte ▣ RO 44 Mf46
Târgu Cărbunesti ▣ RO 44 Md46
Targu Jiu ▣ RO 44 Md45
Târgu Lăpus ▣ RO 43 Me43
Târgu Mures ▣ RO 43 Me44
Târgu-Neamt ▣ RO 43 Mf43
Târgu Ocna ▣ RO 49 Mg22
Târgu Secuiesc ▣ RO 44 Mf44
Tarhuna ▣ LAR 127 Lh30
Tari ▣ PNG 115 Sb48
Tarif ▣ UAE 61 Ng33
Tarifa ▣ E 27 Kp54
Tarija ▣ BOL 207 Gh56
Tarikere ▣ IND (KTK) 84 Oh39
Tarikhana Mosque ▣ IR 62 Nh27
Tarim ▣ YE 60 Nd38
Tarim He ▣ CHN 67 Pb24
Tarim Basin ▣ CHN 66 Pa24
Tarin Kowt ▣ AFG 65 Oc29
Tarka ▣ ZA 155 Md62
Tarkio ▣ USA (MT) 168 Ec22
Tarko-Sale ▣ RUS 54 Oc06
Tarkwa ▣ GH 137 Kk43
Tarlee ▣ AUS (SA) 110 Rk63
Tarlo N.P. ▣ AUS 111 Se63
Tarlton Downs ▣ AUS (NT) 108 Rj57

Taucha ▣ D 32 Ln39
Taufikhen ▣ SUD 141 Mf41
Taufkirchen ▣ D 33 Ln42
Taukum ▣ KZ 66 Oh23
Taulabé ▣ HN 184 Fg38
Taulov ▣ DK 30 Lk35
Taunay, T.I. ▣ BR 202 Hb56
Taung ▣ ZA 155 Mc59
Taung Skull Fossil Site ▣ ZA 155 Mc59
Taungdwin ▣ MYA 86 Ph34
Taungdwin ▣ MYA 86 Ph35
Taunggyi ▣ MYA 86 Pj35
Taungthar ▣ MYA 86 Ph35
Taungthonlon ▲ MYA 86 Ph33
Taunton ▣ GB 21 Kr39
Taunton ▣ USA (MA) 177 Ge25
Taunus ▲ D 33 Lk41
Taupo ▣ NZ 113 Tj65
Taupo, Lake ▣ NZ 113 Th65
Tauramena ▣ CO 192 Gd43
Taurianova ▣ I 37 Lr52
Taurisano ▣ I 37 Lt51
Tauroa Point ▲ NZ 112 Tg63
Tauron Caves ▣ TR 56 Mf27
Tausog ▣ RP 91 Ra43
Taustø ▣ E 28 Kt49
Tauta ▣ PNG 115 Sc48
Tauu Islands ▣ PNG 117 Sj48
Tauwharparae ▣ NZ 112 Tk65
Tavai ▣ PY 204 Hc59
Tavakli lekelesi ▣ TR 47 Mg51
Tavan Bogd ▲ MNG 67 Pd21
Tavani, Mount ▲ VU 118 Te54
Tavarua ▣ SOL 117 Sj50
Tavares ▣ BR (RS) 204 He61
Tavares ▣ USA (FL) 178 Fk31
Tavda ▣ RUS 54 Od07
Tavernes ▣ F 25 Lg47
Tavernes de la Valldigna ▣ E 29 Ku51
Taveta ▣ EAT 146 Mj47
Taveuni ▲ FIJ 119 Ua54
Tavildara ▣ TJ 63 Oe27
Tavira ▣ P 27 Kn53
Tavistock ▣ GB 21 Kq40
Ta Seng ▣ K 89 Qc39
Tavoy ▣ MYA 88 Pk38
Tavsanli ▣ TR 47 Mf26
Tavsanlı ▣ TR 47 Mk51
Tavui ▣ FIJ 119 Tj54
Tavurvur ▲ PNG 116 Sg48
Tawali ▣ RI 96 Qk46
Tawallah ▣ AUS (NT) 106 Rh54
Tawang ▣ IND (ARP) 86 Pf32
Tawangmangu ▣ RI 95 Qe49
Tawa Reservoir ▣ IND 83 Oh34
Tawargin ▣ IND (KTK) 82 Oj38
Tawas City ▣ USA (MI) 173 Fj23
Tawau ▣ MAL 94 Qj43
Tawau Hills N.P. ▣ MAL 94 Qj43
Tawila ▣ S 134 Md39
Tawilah ▣ SUD 134 Mc39
Tawi-Tawi Island ▣ RP 91 Qk43
Tawma ▣ MYA 86 Ph34
Tawu ▣ RC 75 Ra34
Tawum Bum ▲ MYA 86 Pj32
Taxco ▣ MEX (GUR) 182 Fa36
Taxi ▣ CHN (HLG) 71 Rd22
Taxiatosh ▣ UZ 62 Nk24
Taxila ▣ PK 65 Og29
Taxisco ▣ GCA 184 Fe38
Taxkorgan ▣ CHN (XUZ) 63 Og27
Tayabamba ▣ PE 197 Gb50
Tayabas Bay ▣ RP 90 Ra39
Tayandu ▣ RI 114 Rg49
Tayan ▣ RI 95 Qf46
Tayan Qi al Meraj ▣ IR 57 Nf23
Tayassir ▣ IL 58 Mh29
Tayeeglow ▣ SP 145 Nc43
Tayfur ▣ TR 45 Mg50
Tayinloan ▣ GB 20 Kp35
Taylor ▣ USA (LAR 127 Ma30
Taylor ▣ CDN (BC) 167 Dk17
Taylor ▣ USA (AZ) 171 Ee28
Taylor ▣ USA (NE) 172 Fa25
Taylor ▣ USA (TX) 174 Fb30
Taylor Canyon ▣ USA (NV) 170 Eb25
Taylor Highway ▣ USA (AK) 165 Cj14
Taylor Mts. ▲ USA (AK) 164 Cb15
Taylorville ▣ USA (IL) 175 Ff26
Taymā ▣ KSA 58 Mj32
Taymouth ▣ CDN 177 Gh22
Taymura, P.N. ▣ TLS 97 Rc50
Tayna, P.N. ▣ CO 192 Gc40
Taymyr (Dolgan-Nenets) Autonomous District ▣ RUS 54 Pb04
Taymyr Peninsula ▣ RUS 54 Pb03
Tay Ninh ▣ VN 89 Qd40
Tayoltita ▣ MEX (DGO) 180 Eh33
Tay Phuong Pagoda ▣ VN 87 Qc35
Tayrona, P.N. ▣ CO 192 Gc40
Taytay ▣ RP 90 Qk40
Taytay Bay ▣ RC 75 Qk34
Tayuan Si ▣ CHN 73 Qg26
Tayuling ▣ RC 75 Ra33
Taza ▣ IR 62 Nh27
Taza, Pte du ▲ DZ 126 Le32
Tazah ▣ IRQ 57 Nc28
Tazenakht ▣ MA 124 Kg30
Tazewell ▣ USA (TN) 178 Fj27
Tazewell ▣ USA (VA) 178 Fk27
Tazgzourt ▣ DZ 126 La31
Tazirbu ▣ LAR 128 Ma33
Tazirbu Oasis ▣ LAR 128 Ma33
Tazna, Cerro ▲ BOL 206 Gg56
Tazovskaja guba ▣ RUS 54 Od05
Tazovskij ▣ RUS 54 Od05
Tazzarine ▣ MA 124 Kg31
Tazzarine ▣ ES 124 Kf29
T'bilisi ▣ GE 57 Nc25
T'boli ▣ RP 91 Rc42
Tchabal Gangdaba ▲ CAM 139 Lg42
Tchabal Mbabo ▲ CAM 139 Lg42
Tchadoua ▣ RN 132 Ld39
Tchamba ▣ TG 137 La41
Tchamgisso ▣ TCH 140 Lh41
Tchamgisso ▣ TCH 140 Lh41
Tchangou ▣ J 79 Rf29
Tchentlo Lake ▣ CDN (BC) 166 Dh18
Tchibanga ▣ G 148 Lf47
Tchichi ▣ CI 137 Kj42
Tchie ▣ TCH 133 Lk37
Tchikapika ▣ RCB 148 Lj46
Tchilonge ▣ ANG 150 Lg51
Tchin-Tabaradene ▣ RN 132 Lc38
Tchissakata ▣ RCB 148 Lg48

339

Column 1

Ures ☐ MEX (SO) 180 Ee31
Urewera N.P. ☐ NZ 113 Tj65
Urganch ☐ UZ 62 Oa25
Urganli ☐ TR 47 Mh52
Urganch = Urganch ☐ UZ 62 Oa25
Ürgüp ☐ TR 56 Mh26
Urgut ☐ UZ 63 Od26
Urho ☐ CHN (XUZ) 67 Pc22
Urho Kekkosen kansallispuisto ☐ FIN 16 Me11
Uri ☐ TCH 133 Lk35
Uria ☐ RO 43 Me43
Uriah ☐ USA (AL) 175 Fg30
Uribe ☐ CO 192 Gb44
Uribia ☐ CO 192 Gd40
Uribica ☐ BOL 206 Gj53
Urica ☐ YV 193 Gh41
Uri Hauchab Mountains ▲ NAM 154 Lh58
Uriman ☐ YV 193 Gj43
Urique ☐ MEX (CHH) 180 Eg32
Urisirima ☐ GUY 194 Ha42
Uruk ☐ RUS 70 Oa20
Uriz ☐ UA 48 Md41
Urjala ☐ FIN 38 Md29
Urjumkanskij hrebet ▲ RUS 71 Qk24
Urjupino ☐ RUS 71 Qk19
Urjupinsk ☐ RUS 48 Na20
Urk ☐ NL 23 Lf38
Urla ☐ TR 47 Mg52
Urnes ☐ N 17 Lc15
Uromi ☐ WAN 138 Le42
Uroševac ☐ SCG 44 Mb48
Uroteppa ☐ TJ 63 Oe26
Urrampinyu Jiljiltjarri A.L. ▲ AUS 103 Rg58
Urrao ☐ CO 192 Gb42
Urszulewo ☐ PL 41 Lu38
Urt ☐ MNG 70 Qa24
Urt Moron ☐ CHN (QHI) 69 Pg27
Uruachic ☐ MEX (CHH) 180 Ef32
Uruaçu ☐ BR (GO) 202 Hf53
Uruçuca ☐ BR (BA) 203 Ja53
Uruapan ☐ MEX (MHC) 182 Ej36
Uruapan del Progreso ☐ MEX (MHC) 182 Ej36
Urubamba ☐ PE 197 Gd52
Urubamba ☐ PE 197 Gd52
Urubici ☐ BR (SC) 205 Hf60
Urubu Branco, T.I. ☐ BR 200 Hd50
Urucara ☐ BR (AM) 199 Hd47
Uruçuca ☐ BR (BA) 203 Ja53
Uruçuí ☐ BR (PI) 200 Hh49
Urucuia ☐ BR (MG) 203 Hh54
Uru Juruá, T.I. ☐ BR 200 Hh48
Uru-Eu-Wau-Wau, T.I. ☐ BR 198 Gj51
Uruguai ☐ EAT 146 Mh48
Uruguai ☐ BR 204 Hd59
Uruguaiana ☐ BR (RS) 204 Hb60
Uruguay ☐ BR/RA 204 Hd60
Uruguay ☐ YY 191 Ha13
Uruguinha ☐ BR (AP) 195 He45
Uruk = Erech ☐ IRQ 57 Nc29
Urukthapel ▲ PAL 90 Rh42
Urumaco ☐ YV 192 Ge41
Ürümqi ☐ CHN 67 Pd24
Urup ☐ RUS 49 Na22
Uruoca ☐ BR (CE) 201 Hh47
Urupês ☐ BR (SP) 202 Hf56
Uruq al Awarik ▲ KSA 60 Ne36
'Uruq al Mawarid ▲ KSA 60 Ne36
'Uruq Subay ▲ KSA 60 Nb34
Urussanga ☐ BR (SC) 205 Hf60
Uruwira ☐ EAT 146 Mf49
Uryzhar ☐ KZ 66 Pa22
Urzicen ☐ PL 41 Mc39
Urziceni ☐ RO 45 Mg46
Usa ☐ J 79 Ri29
Usácy ☐ BY 39 Mj35
Usagari ☐ EAT 146 Mg48
Usagre ☐ E 27 Ko52
Usak ☐ TR 56 Me26
Usakos ☐ NAM 150 Lh56
Usakovskoe ☐ RUS 55 Ua04
Usambara Mountains ▲ EAT 147 Mk48
U.S. Army Aviation Mus. ☐ USA 175 Fh30
Usayge Mountains ▲ 7 Ta33
Usaylay ☐ KSA 59 Nc33
Us-Bel'dir ☐ RUS (TUV) 70 Pk20
Uschodni ☐ BY 39 Mh37
Usedom ☐ D 32 Lo37
Usedom ☐ D 32 Lo36
Useless Loop ☐ AUS (WA) 104 Qg59
Usengi ☐ EAK 144 Mh46
Usfan ☐ KSA 58 Mk35
Ushaa ☐ Z 151 Mb53
Usharal ☐ KZ 63 Of24
Usharal ☐ KZ 66 Pa22
Ushayrah ☐ KSA 59 Nc33
Ushetu ☐ EAT 146 Mg48
Ushibuka ☐ J 79 Ri29
Ushirombo ☐ EAT 144 Mf47
Ushtobe ☐ KZ 66 Oe23
Ushuaia ☐ RA (TF) 210 Gf79
Usilampatti ☐ IND (TNU) 84 Oj41
Usim ☐ RI 114 Rjp46
Usina Apiacás ☐ BR (MT) 199 Hb51
Usina São Francisco ☐ BR (AM) 199 Ha48
Usingen ☐ D 33 Lj40
Usk = ☐ PNG 115 So48
Usk ☐ CDN (BC) 166 Df18
Usk ☐ GB 21 Ks39
Uska ☐ IND (UPH) 83 Pb32
Uskopije ☐ BIH 35 Ls47
Uslar ☐ D 32 Lk39
Usman' ☐ RUS 48 Mk19
Usoke ☐ EAT 146 Mg48
Usol'e-Sibirskoe ☐ RUS 70 Qb19
Uson ☐ RP 90 Rb39
Usovo ☐ RUS 48 Nb19
Uspallata ☐ RA (MD) 208 Gf62
Uspenie materiali ▲ BG 44 Mc47
Uspenskij sobor ☐ RUS 48 Mf18
Uspenskij sobor Rjazan' ☐ RUS 48 Mk18
Uspenskij sobor Tver' ☐ RUS 48 Mh17
Usquil ☐ PE 196 Ga49
Ussac ☐ F 25 Lc44
Ussat ☐ RCB ...
U.S. Space & Rocket Center ☐ USA 175 Fg28
Ussuri ☐ RUS 76 Rf24
Ussurijsk ☐ RUS 76 Rf24
Ust ... ☐ IND ...
Ust Muhammad ☐ PK 65 Oe31
Ust'-Barguzin ☐ RUS 70 Qe19
Ust'-Cil'ma ☐ RUS 54 Nc05
Ust'-Džeguta ☐ RUS (KCH) 57 Na23
Ust'-Džilinda ☐ RUS (BUR) 70 Qj19
Uster ☐ CH 34 Lj43
Ustibar ☐ BIH 44 Lu47
Ustikolina ☐ BIH 44 Lt47
Ust'-Ilimsk ☐ RUS 54 Qb18
Usť-Isborsk ☐ RUS ...
Ust' ned Orlici ☐ CZ 42 Lp41
Ustjarca ☐ BIH 44 Lt47
Ustjurt Plateau ▲ KZ/UZ 62 Nj24
Ust'-Kamčatsk ☐ RUS 55 Ta07

Column 2

Ust'-Karsk ☐ RUS 71 Qk19
Ust'-Koksa ☐ RUS (ALT) 67 Pc20
Ust'-Kujga ☐ RUS 55 Rd04
Ust'-Kut ☐ RUS 55 Qb07
Ust'-Labinsk ☐ RUS 49 Mk23
Ust'-Luga ☐ RUS 38 Mj31
Ust'-Maja ☐ RUS 55 Ro06
Ust'-Nera ☐ RUS 55 Sa06
Ust'-Omčug ☐ RUS 55 Sb06
Ust'-Ordynsk Buryat Autonomous District ☐ RUS 55 Qa08
Ust'-Ordynskij ☐ RUS (UOB) 70 Qc19
Ustovo ☐ BG 45 Me49
Ustrem ☐ BG 45 Mg48
Ustroń ☐ PL 41 Lt41
Ustronie Morskie ☐ PL 41 Lq38
Ustrzyki Dolne ☐ PL 41 Mc41
Ust'-Sobolevko ☐ RUS 77 Rk22
Ust'-Ulagan ☐ RUS (ALT) 67 Pe20
Ust'-Varga ☐ RUS 54 Na06
Ustyluh ☐ PL 41 Me40
Usu ☐ CHN (XUZ) 66 Pc23
Usuki ☐ J 79 Ri29
Usulutan ☐ ES 184 Ff39
Usumacinta ☐ GCA/MEX 183 Fe37
Usur ☐ IND (CGH) 83 Pa36
Usu-zan ☐ J 77 Sa24
Usvjaty ☐ RUS 48 Mf18
Uta ☐ RI 114 Rj47
Utah ☐ USA 171 Ed26
Utah Lake ☐ USA 171 Ed25
Utajärvi ☐ FIN 16 Md13
Utah ☐ N 30 Lf31
Utambalila ☐ EAT 146 Mg50
Utangala ▲ RI 91 Rh45
Utar ☐ RI 96 Qj50
Utegi ☐ EAT 144 Mg47
Ute Mountain Ind. Res. ▲ USA 171 Ee27
Utena ☐ LT 39 Mf35
Utete ☐ EAT 147 Mk50
U Thai ☐ LAO 87 Qa34
Uthai Thani ☐ THA 88 Qa38
Uthal ☐ PK 65 Od33
Uthomphon ☐ LAO 89 Qc37
U Thong ☐ THA 88 Pk38
Uthumph on Phisai ☐ THA 89 Qc38
Utiariti ☐ BR (MT) 206 Ha52
Utiariti, T.I. ☐ BR 206 Ha52
Utica ☐ CO 192 Gc43
Utica ☐ USA (MS) 175 Fe29
Utica ☐ USA (NY) 177 Gc24
Utica ☐ USA (OH) 173 Fj25
Utiel ☐ E 29 Kt51
Utikuma Lake ▲ CDN 167 Ec18
Utikuma River ☐ CDN 167 Ec17
Utila ☐ HN 184 Fg37
Utinga ☐ BR (BA) 201 Hk52
Utlängan ▲ S 31 Lq34
Utne ☐ N 30 Lg30
Uto ☐ IND (APH) 83 Ok36
Utö ▲ S 31 Ls32
Utö ☐ FIN 38 Mb30
Utraula ☐ IND (UPH) 83 Pb32
Utrecht ☐ NL 23 Lf38
Utrecht ☐ ZA 155 Mf59
Utrera ☐ E 27 Kp53
Utria, P.N. ☐ CO 192 Ga43
Utsira ▲ N 30 Lc31
Utsjoki ☐ FIN 16 Md11
Utstein Kloster ▲ N 30 Lf31
Utsunomiya ☐ J 77 Rk27
Uttamapalaiyam ☐ IND (TNU) 84 Oj41
Uttangarai ☐ IND (TNU) 85 Ok39
Uttaradit ☐ THA 88 Qa37
Uttaranchal ☐ IND 81 Ok30
Uttarkashi ☐ IND (UTT) 81 Ok30
Uttarkashi Ski area ☐ IND 81 Ok30
Uttar Pradesh State ☐ IND 83 Ok32
Uttoxeter ☐ GB 21 Kt38
Uttukkotta ☐ IND (APH) 85 Ok39
Utuado ☐ USA (PR) 187 Gg36
Utuana ☐ EC 196 Ga48
Utubulak ☐ CHN (XUZ) 67 Pd22
Utupua ▲ SOL 118 Td51
Uturuncu, Cerro ▲ BOL 207 Gg57
Utva ☐ IND 81 Oa34
Uukwi ☐ IND ...
Uukuniemi ☐ FIN 38 Mk29
Uummannaq = Dundas ☐ DK 163 Gc03
Uummannarsuaq = Kap Farvel ▲ DK 163 Hd07
Uusikaupunki = Nystadt ☐ FIN 38 Mb30
Uutapi ☐ NAM 150 Lh54
Uvalde ☐ USA (TX) 181 Fa31
Uvaly ☐ CZ 42 Lp40
Uvarovo ☐ RUS 48 Nb20
Uvdal ☐ N 30 Lj32
Uvdai stavkirke ▲ N 30 Lj30
Uvinza ☐ EAT 146 Mf49
Uvira ☐ RDC 146 Me47
Uvs nuur ☐ MNG 67 Pg20
Uvs Nuur Nature Reserve ▲ ☐ MNG 67 Pg20
Uvuvung ☐ RDC 149 Mc47
Uwajima ☐ J 79 Ri29
Uwakela ☐ RI 97 Rd49
Uwanda Game Reserve ▲ EAT 146 Mg49
Uwapa ☐ EAT 146 Mh48
Uwapa ☐ RI 114 Rh47
Uwaynat Wannin ☐ LAR 127 Lg31
Uwekuli ☐ RI 96 Qd45
Uxbridge ☐ GB ...
Uxel ☐ MEX 183 Ff37
Uxin Ju ☐ CHN (NMZ) 72 Qe26
Uxin Qi ☐ CHN (NMZ) 72 Qe26
Uxmal ▲ ☐ MEX 183 Ff35
Uyak Bay ☐ AK (AK) 164 Cc17
Uyo ☐ WAN 138 Le42
Uyowa ☐ EAT 146 Mf48
Uyuni ☐ MOC 153 Mj53
Uyugan ☐ RP 75 Ra35
Uyuni ☐ BOL 206 Gg56
Uyuni ☐ BOL 206 Gg56
Uzbekistan ☐ UZ 53 Oa05
Uzdowo ☐ PL 41 Ma37
Uzerche ☐ F 25 Lc44
Uzés ☐ F 25 Le46
Uzgen ☐ KS 63 Og25
Uzhhorod ☐ UA 43 Md41
Uzi ☐ J 79 Rj28
Uzlovaja ☐ RUS 48 Mk19
Üzümlü ☐ TR 57 Mk26
Uzunköprü ☐ TR 45 Mg49
Uzuni ☐ RUS 48 Mk19
Uzunkum ▲ KZ 66 Oj24
Uzwil ☐ CH 34 Lk43

Column 3 (V)

V

Vaalbos N.P. ▲ ZA 155 Mc60
Vaaldam Nature Reserve ▲ ZA 155 Me59
Vaalimaa ☐ FIN 38 Mh30
Vaalwater ☐ ZA 155 Me58
Vaasa ☐ FIN 38 Mb27
Vaavu Atoll = Felidhoo Atoll ▲ MV 84 Og44
Vabalninkas ☐ LT 39 Me35
Vabre ☐ F 24 Lc47
Vaca Guzmán ☐ BOL 206 Gj55
Vacaria ☐ BR (RS) 204 He60
Vacaville ☐ USA (CA) 170 Dj26
Vache ☐ J 32 Ll40
Vückelsäng ▲ S 31 Lj34
Vádakkevila ☐ IND (KER) 84 Oj41
Väddö ▲ S 31 Lt30
Vadehavet ☐ DK 30 Lj35
Vader ☐ USA (WA) 168 Dj22
Vadheim ☐ N 17 Lc15
Vadodara ☐ IND (GUJ) 82 Og34
Vadsø ☐ N 16 Md10
Vadstena ▲ S 31 Lp32
Valu Crişului ☐ RO 43 Md43
Vaduz ● FL 34 Lk43
Vadvetjåkka n.p. ▲ S 16 Lk11
Værøy ▲ N 16 Lg17
Vaga ☐ RCB 148 Lh46
Vágahólmen ▲ N 16 Lg12
Vágámo ☐ N 17 Le15
Vagaj ☐ DK 18 Kn28
Vaginka ☐ RUS ...
Vagar ▲ DK 18 Kn28
Vagney ☐ F 25 Lg43
Vaghara ▲ SOL 117 Sj49
Vagnhärad ☐ S 31 Lr32
Vágsele ▲ S 16 Lk13
Vágur ☐ DK 18 Kn29
Váh ☐ SK 43 Lu41
Vaiden ☐ USA (MS) 175 Ff29
Vaiaku ● TUV 101 Tb10
Vaihingen (Enz) ☐ D 33 Lj42
Vaikuntha Perumal Temple ☐ IND 85 Ok39
Vailly-sur-Sauldre ☐ F 25 Lc43
Vaïninikkala ☐ FIN 38 Mj30
Vainode ☐ LV 39 Mb34
Vaishali ☐ IND (BIH) 83 Pc33
Vaison-la-Romaine ☐ F 25 Lf46
Vaïtäkebir ☐ TR 57 Mk25
Vakf1 ☐ TR 45 Mg50
Vaïl Abad ☐ IR 64 Nk31
Vaïkuta ☐ THA 88 Qa38
Vakuta Island ▲ PNG 116 Sf50
Válamo monastyr' ▲ RUS 38 Mf29
Valadim ☐ MOC 147 Mj52
Valamon luostari ▲ RUS 38 Mj28
Valappadi ☐ IND (TNU) 84 Ok40
Valaská Belá ☐ SK 42 Lt42
Valaská Polanka ☐ CZ 42 Ls41
Valaské Meziříčí ☐ CZ 42 Ls41
Valavanni ☐ IND (PND) 85 Ok40
Valayat ☐ IR 59 Nf31
Valberg ☐ S 30 Lo31
Valbo ☐ S 31 Lr30
Valbone ☐ AL 44 Lu48
Válcdram ☐ BG 44 Mb47
Valčedol ☐ BG 45 Mh47
Valdagno ☐ I 34 Lm46
Val d'Agri e Lagonegrese, P.N. ☐ I 37 Lr50
Valdahon ☐ F 25 Lg43
Valdaisky N.P. ☐ RUS 48 Mg17
Valdaj ☐ RUS 48 Mg17
Valdefuentes ☐ E 27 Ko51
Valdelagua ☐ E 27 Kr51
Valdeltormo ☐ E 29 La50
Valdemärpils ☐ LV 39 Mc33
Valdemaro Slot ▲ DK 30 Ll35
Valdemärsvik ☐ S 31 Lr32
Valdemeca ☐ E 29 Kt50
Valdemoro ☐ E 27 Kr50
Valdeneocada ☐ E 28 Kr48
Valdepeñas ☐ E 27 Kr52
Valdepeñas de Jaén ☐ E 27 Kr53
Valderas ☐ E 26 Kp48
Valderrobres ☐ E 29 La50
Valdez ☐ EC 192 Ga45
Valdez ☐ RA (SA) 209 Gk63
Valdez ☐ RP 94 Qj41
Valdivia ☐ USA (AK) 165 Cg15
Val d'Isère ☐ F 25 Lg45
Valdobbíadene ☐ I 34 Lm45
Val-d'Or ☐ CDN 173 Gb21
Val d'Orcia ☐ I 34 Lm48
Valdosta ☐ USA (GA) 178 Fj30
Valdres ☐ N 30 Lj30
Valença ☐ BR (BA) 203 Ja53
Valença ☐ BR (RJ) ...
Valea Argovei ☐ RO 45 Mg46
Valea lui Mihai ☐ RO 43 Md43
Valea Mare-Pravăţ ☐ RO 45 Mf45
Valea Víilor ☐ RO 45 Me44
Vale do Guaporé, T.I. ☐ BR 206 Gk52
Valejkidki ☐ BY 39 Mh36
Valença ☐ CDN (BC) 168 Ea19
Valença ☐ BR (BA) 203 Ja53
Valença do Minho ☐ P 26 Km48
Valença do Piauí ☐ BR (PI) 201 Hk49
Valençay ☐ F 24 Lb43
Valence ☐ F 25 Le46
Valence-sur-Baïse ☐ F 24 La47
València ☐ RP 91 Rc42
València ☐ E 29 Ku51
Valencia ☐ YY 193 Gg40
Valencia de Alcántara ☐ E 27 Kn51
Valencia de Don Juan ☐ E 26 Kp48
Vălenii de Munte ☐ RO 45 Mg45
Valentigney ☐ F 25 Lg43
Valentia ☐ ...
Valentin ☐ BR (BA) 200 Ja51
Valentin Gentil ☐ BR (SP) 202 He56
Valentin ☐ ROU 204 Hb61
Valentines ☐ ROU 77 Rh24
Valentine N.W.R. ☐ USA 172 Ek24
Valenza ☐ I 34 Lj45
Valera ☐ YV 192 Ge41
Valevåg ☐ N 30 Lf31
Valga ▲ EST 39 Mf33
Valjala ☐ EST 39 Mc32
Valjevo ☐ SCG 44 Lu46

Column 4

Valka ☐ LV 39 Mf33
Valkeakoski ☐ FIN 38 Me29
Valkeala ☐ FIN 38 Mg30
Valkenswaard ☐ NL 23 Lf39
Valko = Valkom ☐ FIN 38 Mg30
Valkom = Valko ☐ FIN 38 Mg30
Valky ☐ UA 48 Mh21
Valkyrjedomen ▲ 7 Md33
Valla ☐ S 31 Lp34
Valladolid ☐ E 26 Kq49
Valladolid ☐ EC 196 Ga48
Valladolid ☐ MEX (YT) 183 Ff35
Vallargärdet ☐ S 31 Lo31
Valle de Boi ☐ E 28 La48
Vall del Madriu-Perafita-Claror ☐ AND 28 La48
Valledano ☐ E 29 Lc51
Valle Altares ☐ RA 210 Gf67
Valle Castor ☐ RCH 210 Ge70
Valle d'Aosta ☐ I 34 Lh45
Valle de Allende ☐ MEX (CHH) 181 Eh32
Valle de Bravo ☐ MEX (MEX) 182 Ek36
Valle de Cabuérniga ☐ E 26 Kq47
Valle de Calingasta ▲ RA 208 Gf61
Valle de Chapalcó ▲ RA 208 Gh64
Valle de Guanape ☐ YV 193 Gh41
Valle del templi ☐ I 36 Lo53
Valle de la Luna ▲ BOL 206 Gf54
Valle de la Luna = Parque Provincial Ischigualasto ▲ RA 207 Gg61
Valle de la Luna ▲ RCH 207 Gf57
Valle de la Pascua ☐ YV 193 Gh41
Valle del Rio Deseado ☐ RA 210 Gf69
Valle del Rio Elqui ☐ RCH 207 Ge60
Valle de Santiago ☐ MEX (GJT) 182 Ek35
Valle de Viñales ☐ C 179 Fj34
Valle de Zaragoza ☐ MEX (CHH) 180 Eh32
Valle do Douro ☐ BR 26 Kn49
Valleduper ☐ CO 192 Gd40
Vallée de la Lufira ☐ RDC 146 Md51
Vallée de l'Azaouagh ☐ RMM/RN 132 Lc37
Vallée de l'Azar ☐ RMM 132 Lb38
Vallée de l'Ourika ☐ MA 125 Kg30
Vallée de Mai N.P. ☐ SY 145 Nh48
Vallée du Dadès ☐ MA 125 Kg30
Vallée du Ferlo ☐ SN 130 Kd38
Vallée du M'Zab ☐ DZ 126 Lb29
Vallée du Serpent ☐ RMM 131 Kf38
Vallée du Tilemsi ☐ RMM 131 La36
Vallée du Ziz ☐ MA 125 Kh30
Valle Encantado ☐ RA 208 Gg66
Valle Fertil ▲ RA 208 Gg61
Valle General Racedo ☐ RA 210 Gf67
Valleggrande ☐ BOL 206 Gh55
Valle Gran Rey ☐ E 124 Kb31
Vallehermoso ☐ E 124 Kb31
Vallehermoso ☐ MEX (QTR) 183 Ff36
Valle Hermoso ☐ MEX (TM) 181 Fb33
Valle Maraco Grande ▲ RA 208 Gh64
Valle-mi ☐ PY 202 Hb57
Valle Nacional ☐ MEX (OAX) 183 Fc37
Vallenar ☐ RCH 207 Ge60
Valle Nereco ▲ RA 208 Gh64
Valle Nevado ☐ RCH 208 Ge62
Vallentuna ☐ S 31 Lt31
Valletta ● M 37 Lp55
Valley ☐ USA (AL) 175 Fh29
Valley ☐ USA (WI) 169 Ff23
Valley City ☐ USA (ND) 172 Fa22
Valley Falls ☐ USA (OR) 168 Dk24
Valley Mills ☐ USA (TX) 174 Fb30
Valley of Desolation ☐ ZA 154 Mc60
Valley of Fire S.P. ☐ USA 171 Ec28
Valley of Flowers N.P. ☐ IND 81 Ok30
Valley of Kings ☐ ET 129 Mg33
Valley of wild elephants = Yexiangguu ☐ CHN 87 Qa34
Valley of Willow ☐ USA 165 Ck11
Vally R. Ind. Res. ▲ CDN 172 Ea20
Valley Station ☐ USA (KY) 175 Fh26
Valleyview ☐ CDN (AB) 167 Eb18
Vallgrund ☐ FIN 38 Ma30
Valli di Comacchio ☐ I 34 Lm46
Vallières ☐ RH 186 Ge36
Vallon-Pont-d'Arc ☐ F 25 Le46
Vallorbe ☐ CH 34 Lg44
Valls ☐ E 29 La49
Vallsta ☐ S 17 Lr15
Val Maira ☐ I 34 Lh47
Val Mesik ☐ CHN (SK) 169 Eg21
Valmiera ☐ LV 39 Me33
Valognes ☐ F 22 Kt41
Valoy ▲ N 16 Lh13
Valožyn ☐ BY 39 Mg36
Valpacos ☐ P 26 Kn49
Val-Paradis ☐ CDN 173 Ga21
Valparai ☐ IND (TNU) 84 Oj40
Valparaíso ☐ BR (AC) 198 Gd49
Valparaíso ☐ BR (SP) 202 He56
Valparaíso ☐ CO 192 Gc45
Valparaíso ☐ MEX (ZCT) 182 Ej34
Valparaíso ☐ RCH 208 Ge62
Valpovo ☐ HR 35 Lt45
Valréas ☐ F 25 Le46
Valsäd ☐ IND (GUJ) 82 Og35
Valse ☐ RI 114 Rk47
Valsjöbyn ▲ S 16 Lh13
Valsoyfjord ☐ N 30 Lg29
Valtellina ▲ I 34 Lk44
Valternlándia ☐ BR (AM) 198 Gh49
Valthermond ☐ NL 23 Lg38
Valtimo ☐ FIN 16 Mg14
Valuyki ☐ RUS 48 Mk20
Valul lui Traian ☐ MD 49 Me22
Valverde ☐ E 124 Kb31
Valverde de Júcar ☐ E 29 Ks51
Valverde del Camino ☐ E 27 Kn53

Column 5

Valverde de Leganés ☐ E 27 Ko52
Valverde del Fresno ☐ E 27 Ko50
Vamberk ☐ CZ 42 Lr40
Vamdrup ☐ DK 30 Lk35
Vämhus ▲ S 17 Ln15
Vamlingbo ☐ S 31 Lt33
Vammala ☐ FIN 38 Mc29
Vampula ☐ FIN 38 Mc29
Van ☐ TR 57 Nb26
Vanadzor ☐ ARM 57 Nc25
Vanavara ☐ RUS 55 Qa06
Van Asch van Wijckgebergte ▲ SME 194 Hc44
Van Buren ☐ USA (AR) 174 Fc28
Van Buren ☐ USA (ME) 176 Gg22
Van Canh ☐ VN 89 Qe36
Van Canh ☐ VN 89 Qe36
Vanceburg ☐ USA (KY) 175 Fj26
Vancouver ☐ CDN 168 Dj21
Vancouver ☐ USA (OR) 168 Dj23
Vancouver Island ☐ CDN 168 Dh21
Vancouver Island Range ☐ CDN 168 Dh21
Vanda = Vantaa ☐ FIN 38 Me30
Vandalur ☐ IND (TNU) 85 Ok39
Vanderbijlpark ☐ ZA 155 Md59
Vandergrift ☐ USA (PA) 173 Ga25
Vanderhoof ☐ CDN (BC) 168 Dj19
Vanderkloof ☐ ZA 155 Mc61
Vanderlin Island ▲ AUS 107 Rj53
Van Diemen Gulf ☐ AUS 106 Rf51
Vänern ☐ S 31 Ln32
Vänersborg ☐ S 30 Ln32
Vangaindrano ☐ RM 157 Nd57
Vangazi ☐ LV 39 Me33
Vang Ninh ☐ VN 89 Qe36
Vangunu, Mount ▲ SOL 117 Sj50
Vang Vieng ☐ LAO 87 Qb36
Vani ☐ GE 57 Nb24
Vanimo ☐ PNG 115 Sa47
Vanino ☐ RUS 55 Sa09
Vaniyambadi ☐ IND (TNU) 85 Ok39
Vänju Mare ☐ RO 44 Mc46
Vankarem ☐ RUS 55 Ua04
Vannes ☐ F 22 Ks43
Vanoise, P.N.de la ☐ F 25 Lg45
Vanoua ☐ SOL 117 Sj50
Van Reenen ☐ ZA 155 Me60
Vanrhynsdorp ☐ ZA 154 Lk61
Vanrook ☐ AUS (QLD) 107 Sa54
Vansbro ☐ S 31 Ln30
Vanstadensrus ☐ ZA 155 Md60
Vantaa = Vanda ☐ FIN 38 Me30
Vantage ☐ USA (WA) 168 Dk22
Van Tassell ☐ USA (WY) 171 Eh24
Vanthli ☐ IND (GUJ) 82 Of35
Vant's Drift ☐ ZA 155 Mf60
Vanttauskoski ☐ FIN 16 Md12
Vanua Balavu ▲ FJI 119 Ua54
Vanua Lava ▲ VU 118 Td52
Vanua Levu ▲ FJI 119 Tk54
Vanuatu ☐ VU 101 Ta11
Vanuire, T.I. ☐ BR 202 He56
Vanvikan ☐ N 16 Lf14
Van Wert ☐ USA (OH) 173 Fh25
Van Wyksdorp ☐ ZA 154 Ma61
Van Wyksvlei ☐ ZA 154 Mb61
Van Zylsrus ☐ ZA 154 Mb59
Vao ☐ EST 39 Mf32
Vaqueria ☐ RA (NE) 181 Fa33
Varades ☐ F 22 Kt43
Varadero ☐ C 179 Fk34
Varakallu ☐ IND (APH) 82 Ok38
Varallo ☐ I 34 Lj45
Varaiuo ☐ IR 57 Nf28
Varanasi ☐ IND (UPH) 83 Pb33
Varangerbotn ☐ N 16 Me10
Varangerfjorden ☐ N 16 Me10
Varangerhalvøya ☐ N 16 Me10
Varano ☐ I 37 Lr49
Várar ☐ IND 82 Oe34
Värätec ☐ RO 45 Mf43
Varaždin ☐ HR 35 Lr44
Varaždinske Toplice ☐ HR 35 Lr44
Varazze ☐ I 34 Lj46
Varberg ☐ S 30 Ln34
Várbica ☐ BG 45 Mg48
Várda ☐ GR 46 Mb52
Vardannapet ☐ IND (APH)
Vardar Kisura ☐ MK 44 Mc49
Vardarski Rid ☐ MK 44 Mc49
Varde ☐ DK 30 Lj35
Vardin ☐ IR 57 Nd26
Vardo ☐ BR (RR) ...
Vardø ☐ N 16 Me10
Várdö ▲ FIN 38 Ma30
Vardzia ☐ GE 57 Nb25
Varekil ☐ S 30 Lm32
Varel ☐ D 32 Lj37
Varela ☐ RA (SL) 208 Gh63
Varena ☐ LT 39 Me36
Varennes-sur-Allier ☐ F 25 Ld44
Varennes-en-Argonne ☐ F 23 Lf41
Varennes-sur-Allier ☐ F 25 Ld44
Vareš ☐ BIH 44 Lt46
Varese ☐ I 34 Lj45
Varese Ligure ☐ I 34 Lk46
Várgarda ☐ S 30 Ln32
Várgarde Grande ☐ BR (MA) 201 Hj47
Vargem ☐ BR (MG) 203 Hh56
Vargem Grande ☐ BR (MA) 201 Hj47
Vargem Grande do Sul ☐ BR (SP) ...
Vargön ☐ S 30 Ln32
Varilhes ☐ F 24 Lb47
Varina ☐ PE 207 Gc58
Varjota ☐ BR (CE) 201 Hk48
Varkallu ☐ IND (KER) 84 Oj41
Varkaus ☐ FIN 38 Mg28
Varklani ☐ LV 39 Mf34

Column 6

Varnjany ☐ BY 39 Mg36
Varnsdorf ☐ CZ 42 Lp40
Varoška Rijeka ☐ BIH 35 Lr45
Várpalota ☐ H 42 Lt43
Vársag ☐ RO 43 Mf44
Vársinec ☐ RO 44 Md47
Várslo ☐ BG 45 Mh47
Varto ☐ TR 57 Na26
Vartsilä ☐ FIN 38 Mk28
Vara-Kuaste ☐ EST 39 Mg32
Varva ☐ UA 48 Mg20
Varvara ☐ BG 45 Me48
Varzaneh ☐ IR 64 Ng29
Várzea ☐ BR (CE) ...
Várzea Alegre ☐ BR (CE) 201 Ja49
Várzea da Palma ☐ BR (MG) ...
Várzea do Poço ☐ BR (BA) 201 Hk51
Várzea Grande ☐ BR (PI) 202 Hb53
Várzea Grande ☐ BR (BA) 200 Hh52
Várzelándia ☐ BR (MG) 203 Hh53
Varzo ☐ I 34 Lj44
Varzy ☐ F 25 Ld43
Várciste ☐ EST 38 Me31
Varzob ☐ TJ 63 Oe26
Vasálcisnamény ☐ H 43 Mc42
Vasálvo da Gama ☐ BR (GOA) 82 Og38
Vasconcelos ☐ MEX (VC) 183 Fc37
Vashevka ☐ RUS 76 Rh22
Vasili ☐ GR 46 Ma52
Vasjuganskaja ravnina ▲ RUS 54 Od07
Vaskelovo ☐ RUS 38 Mf30
Vaskivesi ☐ FIN 38 Md28
Vaslui ☐ RO 45 Mh43
Vassar ☐ USA (MI) 173 Fj24
Vassiliá ☐ GR 44 Md50
Vassilikó = GR 46 Ma53
Vassilis ☐ S 16 Lh13
Västerås ☐ S 31 Lr31
Väster-Götland ▲ S 30 Ln32
Västerfjäll ▲ S 16 Lh12
Väster-Haninge ☐ S 31 Lt31
Västervik ☐ S 31 Lr33
Vásthi ☐ GR 44 Ma49
Vastenjaure ☐ S 16 Lh12
Vasto ☐ I 37 Lq48
Västra Ämterik ☐ S 30 Lo31
Västra-Götland ▲ S 30 Ln32
Vasvár ☐ H 42 Lr43
Vasy'kiv ☐ UA 49 Mf20
Vasyl'kivka ☐ UA 49 Mj21
Vasyšcevo ☐ UA 48 Mj21
Vaté = Éfaté ▲ VU 118 Td53
Vatan ☐ F 25 Lc43
Vatersay ▲ GB 20 Kn34
Váthi ☐ GR 47 Mg54
Vathia ☐ GR 47 Mg54
Vatican City ● 37 Lm49
Vatnajökull ☐ IS 18 Kd26
Vatnesuobss ☐ IS 18 Jz26
Vatolatsara ☐ RM 157 Nc57
Vatomandry ☐ RM 157 Nd56
Vatra Dornei ☐ RO 43 Mf43
Vatra Moldovitei ☐ RO 43 Mf43
Vattaam ☐ IND (TNU) 85 Ok41
Vattaakundu ☐ IND (TNU) ...
Vättis ☐ CH 34 Lk43
Vatulele ▲ FJI 119 Tj55
Vatutine ☐ UA 49 Mf21
Vaucouleurs ☐ F 23 Lf42
Vaudreuil ☐ F 22 Lb41
Vaughan ☐ USA (NM) 171 Eh28
Vaughn ☐ USA (MT) 169 Ed22
Vaui ☐ BR (AL) ...
Vaukavysk ☐ BY 41 Me37
Vaukavyskaje vzvyšša ▲ BY 41 Me37
Vauvert ☐ F 25 Le46
Vauxhall ☐ CDN (AB) 169 Ed20
Vava'u ▲ TO 119 Tk53
Vavoua ☐ CI 137 Kg42
Vavuniya ☐ CL 85 Pa41
Vaxholm ☐ S 31 Lt31
Växjö ☐ S 31 Lp34
Växtorp ☐ S 30 Ln34
Vayalpad ☐ IND (APH) 85 Ok39
Vayk ☐ ARM 57 Nc25
Vazante ☐ BR (MG) 203 Hg54
Vazobe ▲ RM 157 Nd55
Vazquez ☐ ROU 204 Hc61
Veadeiros ☐ BR (GO) ...
Veal Rinh ☐ K 89 Qd40
Vechelde ☐ D 32 Lk38
Vechta ☐ D 32 Lj38
Vecpiebalga ☐ LV 39 Mf33
Vecses ☐ H 43 Lu43
Vecumnieki ☐ LV 39 Me34
Vedaranyam ☐ IND (TNU) 85 Pa40
Vedde ☐ S 30 Ln33
Veddige ☐ S 30 Ln33
Vedea ☐ RO 45 Mf47
Vedelago ☐ I 34 Lm45
Vedia ☐ EC 192 Ga43
Vedno ☐ RUS 48 Oh36
Vediai ☐ NL 23 Lg37
Vedrano ☐ IND (APH)
Vega ☐ N 16 Lf13
Vega ☐ USA (TX) 174 Ej28
Vega Baja ☐ USA (PR) 187 Gg36
Vega de Alatorre ☐ MEX (VC) 182 Fb35
Vegadeo ☐ E 26 Kn47
Vegamót ☐ IS 18 Jz26
Vegárshei ☐ N 30 Lh32
Vegesack ☐ D 32 Lj37
Veguetas ☐ PE 197 Gb51
Vegusdal ☐ N 30 Lh32
Vehkalahti ☐ FIN 38 Mg30
Vehu ☐ FIN 38 Md28
Veinticinco de Mayo ☐ RA (BA) 209 Gk63
Veinticinco de Mayo ☐ RA (SF) 204 Ha60
Veinte de Noviembre ☐ MEX 183 Ff37
Vejen ☐ DK 30 Lk35
Vejer de la Frontera ☐ E 27 Kp54
Vejle ☐ DK 30 Lk35
Vekilbazar ☐ TM 62 Nk27
Vela ☐ RA (BA) ...
Velacrik ☐ EC 196 Ga48
Vela Luka ☐ HR 35 Lr48
Velanai Island ▲ CL 85 Ok40
Velappur ☐ IND (APH) ...
Velasco Ibarra = Empalme ☐ EC 196 Ga46

Column 7

Velenje ☐ SLO 42 Lq44
Veles ☐ MK 44 Mb49
Velestíno ☐ GR 46 Mc51
Velez ☐ BIH 35 Ls47
Vélez ☐ CO 192 Gd42
Vélez Blanco ☐ E 27 Ks53
Vélez-Málaga ☐ E 27 Kq54
Vélez Rubio ☐ E 27 Ks53
Vélia ☐ I 37 Lq50
Velika ☐ HR 35 Ls45
Velika Gorica ☐ HR 35 Lr45
Velikaja Kema ☐ RUS 77 Rj23
Velika Kladuša ☐ BIH 35 Lr45
Velika Plana ☐ SCG 44 Mb47
Velika Planina ▲ SLO 42 Lq44
Velika Slatina ☐ SCG 44 Ma48
Velika Lukis ☐ RUS 48 Mf17
Veliki Gradište ☐ SCG 44 Mb46
Veliki Grđevac ☐ HR 35 Ls45
Veliko Tărnovo ☐ BG 45 Mf47
Veliki Preslav ☐ BG 45 Mg47
Veliki Radinci ☐ SCG 44 Lu45
Veliki Šiljegovac ☐ SCG 44 Mb47
Velikovisočnoe ☐ RUS 54 Nc04
Velingara ☐ SN 130 Kc38
Velingara ☐ SN 136 Kc39
Velingrad ☐ BG 45 Me48
Veliž ☐ RUS 48 Mf18
Veljun ☐ HR 35 Lr45
Vel'ká Lomnica ☐ SK 43 Ma41
Vel'ke Losiny ☐ CZ 42 Ls41
Vel'ke Kapušany ☐ SK 43 Mc42
Velké Losiny ☐ CZ 42 Ls41
Velké Meziříčí ☐ CZ 42 Lr41
Velké Dederkaly ☐ UA 41 Me40
Velké Mezty ☐ UA 41 Me40
Vel'kyj Berezmyj ☐ UA 43 Mc42
Velikyj Burluk ☐ UA 48 Mk20
Vella Lavella ▲ SOL 117 Sj49
Velletri ☐ I 36 Ln49
Vellinge ☐ S 30 Ln35
Vellmar ☐ D 32 Lk39
Velloso ☐ IND (TNU) 85 Ok39
Velluru ☐ IND (APH)
Velmerstot ▲ D 32 Lj39
Velneshwar Beach ☐ IND 82 Og37
Velo-Kelys 54 Na06
Velsen ☐ NL 23 Le38
Velsk ☐ RUS 48 Na06
Velten ☐ D 32 Lo38
Velva ☐ USA (ND) 172 Ek21
Vemb ☐ DK 30 Lj34
Vemdalen ☐ S 17 Ln14
Vemork ☐ N 30 Lj31
Vempalle ☐ IND (APH) 85 Ok38
Vemula ☐ IND (APH)
Vemulavada ☐ IND 83 Ok36
Veli nad Lužnicí ☐ CZ 42 Lp41
Veli nad Moravou ☐ CZ 42 Ls42
Veseloe ☐ RUS 39 Lu36
Veselovskoe Vodohranilišče ☐ RUS 49 Na22
Veselynove ☐ UA 49 Mf22
Vesoul ☐ F 25 Lg43
Vespasiano ☐ BR (MG) 203 Hj55
Vessigebro ☐ S 30 Ln34
Vesterø Havn ☐ DK 30 Ll33
Vesterø ☐ N 30 Li31
Vestfjorden ☐ N 16 Lg12
Vestmanna ☐ DK 18 Kn28
Vestmannaeyjar ▲ IS 18 Jz27
Vestnes ☐ N 17 Lc14
Vestre Jakobselv ☐ N 16 Me10
Vestvågøy ▲ N 16 Lg11
Vesuvio, Vulcano ▲ I 37 Lp50
Veszprém ☐ H 42 Ls43
Vetapalem ☐ IND (APH) 85 Pa38
Vetlanda ☐ S 31 Lp33
Vetluga ☐ RUS 48 Nc17
Vettweiss ☐ D 32 Lg40
Vevay ☐ USA (IN) 173 Fh26
Vevelstad = Forvika ☐ N 16 Lg13
Vevey ☐ CH 34 Lg44
Vévi ☐ GR 46 Mb50
Veymandhoo ▲ MV 84 Og44
Veynes ☐ F 25 Lf46
Veyrier ☐ IR 59 Ne30
Vezelay ☐ F 25 Ld43
Vezirköprü ☐ TR 56 Mf25
Vezza d'Oglio ☐ I 34 Ll44
V. Guerrero ☐ MEX (BC) 180 Ec29
V. Guerrero ☐ MEX (DGO) 182 Ej34
Viacha ☐ BOL 206 Gf54
Viadana ☐ I 34 Ll46
Viaduc-de-Garabit ☐ F 25 Ld45
Viaducto la Polvorilla ☐ RA 207 Gg58
Viamao ☐ BR (RS) 204 Hd59
Viamonte ☐ RA (CD) 209 Gj62
Viana ☐ BR ...
Viana ☐ ANG 148 Lg50
Viana ☐ BR (MA) 200 Hh47
Viana do Alentejo ☐ P 27 Km52
Viana do Bolo ☐ E 26 Kn48
Viana do Castelo ☐ P 26 Km49
Vianden ☐ L 23 Lg41
Viangchan ☐ LAO 88 Qb36
Vianópolis ☐ BR (GO) 202 Hf54
Viar ☐ E 27 Kp53
Viasco ☐ F 24 Lc48
Viborg ☐ DK 30 Lk34
Vibo Valentia ☐ I 37 Lr52
Viborg ☐ USA (SD) 172 Fa24
Vic ☐ E 29 Lc49
Vicam ☐ MEX (SO) 180 Ee32
Vicecconsa ☐ E 26 Kq47
Vic-en-Bigorre ☐ F 24 La47
Vicente Guerrero ☐ MEX (BC) ...
Vicente Guerrero ☐ MEX (DGO) 182 Ej34
Vicente Guerrero ☐ MEX (DGO) 182 Ej34

Column 8

Vergeleë ☐ ZA 155 Mc58
Vergina ☐ GR 46 Mc50
Vergt ☐ F 24 La45
Verhnebatsk ☐ RUS 54 Pb06
Verhnetulomskij ☐ RUS 16 Mg11
Verhnetulomskoe Vodohranilišče ☐ RUS 16 Mf11
Verhnezejskaja ravnina ▲ RUS 55 Rb08
Vernhie Oser'ki ☐ RUS 38 Mf30
Vernhie Usugh ☐ RUS 71 Qh19
Verila ▲ BG 45 Me50
Verila ▲ BG 44 Md48
Verin ☐ E 26 Kn49
Verinsko ☐ BG 44 Md48
Verkhoyanskiy Mountains ▲ RUS 55 Rb05
Verl ☐ D 32 Lj39
Vermand ☐ F 23 Ld41
Vermegliano ☐ N 16 Lj05
Vermenton ☐ F 25 Ld43
Vermilion ☐ CDN 169 Ee19
Vermilion ☐ USA (SD) 172 Fb24
Vermont ☐ USA 177 Gd23
Vernadsky ☐ ANT (UA) 6 Gc32
Vernal ☐ USA (UT) 171 Ef25
Vernazza ☐ I 34 Lk46
Verne ☐ IR 57 Nd26
Verneuil-sur-Avre ☐ F 22 La42
Vernon ☐ CDN (BC) 168 Ea20
Vernon ☐ F 23 Lb41
Vernon ☐ USA (TX) 174 Fa28
Vernon ☐ USA (UT) 171 Ed25
Vernon Crossing, A.L. ▲ AUS 106 Rf52
Vero Beach ☐ USA (FL) 179 Fk32
Véronica ☐ RA (BA) 209 Ha63
Verona ☐ I 34 Ll45
Verona ☐ USA (MO) 174 Fd27
Versailles ☐ USA (IN) 175 Fh26
Versailles ☐ USA (KY) 175 Fh26
Versino-Darasunskij ☐ RUS 71 Qh19
Versmold ☐ D 32 Lj38
Verteilen ☐ RUS 86 Nc18
Vertentes ☐ BR (PE) 201 Jc49
Vertiskos ▲ GR 44 Md50
Vertou ☐ F 22 Kt43
Verulam ☐ ZA 155 Mf60
Verviers ☐ B 23 Lf40
Vesanka ☐ FIN 38 Mf28
Vescovato ☐ F 36 Lk48
Vesele ☐ UA 49 Mh22
Veseli nad Lužnicí ☐ CZ 42 Lp41
Veseli nad Moravou ☐ CZ 42 Ls42
Veselovskoe ☐ RUS (SF) ...
Vesoul ☐ F 25 Lg43
(continued below in reading order)
Vestre Coburg ☐ D 33 Ll42
Vianna ☐ BR (RS) ...

Column 9

Vico ☐ F 34 Lj48
Viçosa ☐ BR (AL) 201 Jb50
Viçosa do Ceará ☐ BR (CE) 201 Hk47
Vic-sur-Cère ☐ F 25 Ld46
Victor Harbour ☐ AUS (SA) 110 Rk63
Victoria ☐ USA 101 Sa13
Victoria = Limbé ☐ CAM 138 Le43
Victoria ☐ CDN (BC) 168 Dj21
Victoria ☐ CO 192 Gd42
Victoria ☐ RA (ER) 209 Gk62
Victoria ☐ RCH 208 Gd65
Victoria ☐ RA (TF) ...
Victoria ☐ RP 90 Ra39
Victoria ☐ SY 145 Nh48
Victoria Beach ☐ CDN (MB) 172 Fb20
Victoria Falls ☐ Z/ZW 151 Md54
Victoria Falls ☐ ZW 151 Mc54
Victoria Highway ▲ AUS 103 Re53
Victoria Island ▲ CDN 162 Eb04
Victoria Lake ☐ CDN 177 Hb21
Victoria Memorial ☐ IND 86 Pe34
Victoria, Mount ▲ MYA 86 Pg35
Victoria, Mount ▲ NZ 113 Tg67
Victoria Nile ☐ EAU 144 Mf44
Victoria Park Racecourse ▲ AUS (SA) 110 Rk63
Victoria River ☐ AUS (NT) 106 Rf53
Victoria River Downs ☐ AUS (NT) 106 Rf54
Victorias ☐ RP 90 Rb40
Victoria Strait ☐ CDN 162 Fa04
Victoriaville ☐ CDN (QC) 176 Ge22
Victoria West ☐ ZA 154 Mb61
Victor, Mount ▲ 7 Mc33
Victor Rosales ☐ MEX (ZCT) 182 Ej34
Victorville ☐ USA (CA) 170 Eb28
Victory, Mount ▲ PNG 116 Se50
Vicuña ☐ RCH 207 Ge60
Vicuña Mackenna ☐ RA (CD) 208 Gh62
Vicus ▲ PE 196 Fk48
Vida ☐ USA (MT) 169 Eh22
Vidal ☐ USA (CA) 170 Ec28
Vidal Ramos ☐ BR (SC) ...
Vidal Junction ☐ USA (CA) 170 Ec28
Vidamlja ☐ BY 41 Md38
Vidareidi ▲ DK 18 Ko28
Vidauban ☐ F 25 Lg47
Videbæk ☐ DK 30 Lj34
Videira ☐ BR (SC) 204 He59
Videle ☐ RO 45 Mf46
Viganella ☐ I 34 Lj44
Vidhenda ☐ IND ...
Vidin ☐ BG 44 Mc47
Vidisha ☐ IND (MPH) 83 Oj33
Vidlitsa ☐ RUS 38 Mf29
Vidzemes augstiene ▲ LV 39 Mf33
Vidzy ☐ BY 39 Mg36
Viechtach ☐ D 33 Ln42
Viedma ☐ RA 209 Gk66
Viedma ☐ RA (RN) 209 Gj66
Vielha ☐ E 28 La48
Vielmur-sur-Agout ☐ F 24 Lc47
Vielsalm ☐ B 23 Lf40
Viena ☐ BR (PA) 195 Hf46
Vierema ☐ FIN 16 Mf13
Viernheim ☐ D 33 Lj41
Viersen ☐ D 32 Lg39
Vierwaldstätter See ☐ CH 34 Lj44
Vierzehnheiligen ☐ D 33 Lm40
Vierzon ☐ F 25 Lc43
Viesite ☐ LV 39 Mf34
Vieste ☐ I 37 Lr49
Vietas ▲ S 16 Lj12
Viet Tri ☐ VN 87 Qd35
Vieux Bordeaux ☐ F 24 Ku46
Vieux-Fort ☐ CDN 177 Hb20
View Point (Fish River Canyon) ☐ NAM 154 Lj59
Vif ☐ F 25 Lf45
Vig ☐ DK 30 Ll35
Vigan ☐ RP 90 Ra37
Vigevano ☐ I 34 Lj45
Vigia ☐ BR (PA) 195 Hf46
Vigia Chico ☐ MEX (QTR) 183 Ff36
Vignola ☐ I 34 Ll46
Vigo ☐ E 26 Km48
Vigrestad ☐ N 30 Lf32
Vihanti ☐ FIN 16 Me13
Vihari ☐ PK 65 Og30
Vihiers ☐ F 24 Ku43
Vihorlat ▲ SK 43 Mc42
Vihti ☐ FIN 38 Me30
Viitasaari ☐ FIN 38 Mf28
Vijainagar ☐ IND (APH) 83 Pa37
Vijayadurg ☐ IND (MHT) 82 Og37
Vijaynagar ☐ IND (RJT) 82 Oe33
Vijayawada ☐ IND (APH) 83 Pa37
Vijes ☐ CO 192 Gb43
Vik ☐ N 30 Lf30
Vik ☐ S 31 Lp35
Vikajärvi ☐ FIN 16 Md12
Vikarbyn ☐ S 17 Ln15
Vikedal ☐ N 30 Lf31
Vikekhori ☐ RM 157 Sk50
Vikersund ☐ N 30 Lk31
Vikfjord ☐ N 16 Lh11
Vikindu ☐ EAT 147 Mk49
Viking ☐ CDN (AB) 169 Ee19
Vikna ☐ N 16 Lf13
Viksjöfors ☐ S 17 Lq15
Vikos-Aoos ☐ GR 46 Ma51

Vikran ◻ N 16 Lk11
Viksøyri ◻ N 17 Ld15
Vila Aurora ◻ BR (AP) 195 Hg47
Vila Bela da São Trinidade ◻ BR (MT) 206 Ha53
Vila Capixabas ◻ BR (AC) 206 Ke48
Vila Conceição ◻ BR (PA) 200 Hg47
Vila de Manica ◻ MOC 152 Mg54
Vila de Rei ◻ P 27 Km51
Vila de Sena ◻ MOC 153 Mh54
Vila do Bispo ◻ P 27 Km53
Vila do Maio ◻ CV 136 Jj38
Vila dos Remédios ◻ BR (RN) 201 Jd47
Vila Flor ◻ ANG 150 Lh52
Vila Flor ◻ P 26 Kn49
Vilafranca del Maestrat ◻ E 29 Ku50
Vilafranca del Penedès ◻ E 29 Lb49
Vila Franca de Xira ◻ P 27 Km52
Vilagarcia de Arousa ◻ E 26 Km48
Vila Gesell ◻ RA (BA) 209 Hb64
Vila Gobernador Gálvez ◻ RA (SF) 209 Gi62
Vilakalaka ◻ VU 118 Td53
Vilaine = Villalba ◻ E 26 Kn47
Vila Martins ◻ BR (AM) 198 Gj49
Vila Meriti ◻ BR (AM) 199 Ha48
Vila Mouzinho ◻ MOC 153 Mh53
Vila Nazaré ◻ BR (AM) 198 Gj47
Vijäni ◻ LV 39 Mg34
Vilankulo ◻ MOC 153 Mh57
Vilano Beach ◻ USA (FL) 178 Fk31
Vila Nova ◻ ANG 150 Lj52
Vila Nova da Fronteira ◻ MOC 153 Mh54
Vila Nova de Famalicão ◻ P 26 Km49
Vila Nova de Foz Côa ◻ P 26 Kn49
Vila Nova de Milfontes ◻ P 27 Km53
Vila Nova de Paiva ◻ P 26 Kn50
Vila Nova do Piaul ◻ BR (PI) 201 Hk49
Vila Nova do Seles ◻ ANG 150 Lh51
Vila Nova ◻ ANG 150 Lj52
Vila Nova Sintra ◻ CV 136 Jh38
Vila Palestina ◻ BR (PA) 200 Hg48
Vila Porto Franco ◻ BR (AM) 199 Ha49
Vila Pouca de Aguiar ◻ P 26 Kn49
Vilar ◻ P 26 Kn50
Vila-real ◻ E 29 Ku51
Vila Real ◻ P 26 Kn49
Vila Real de Santo Antonio ◻ P 27 Kn53
Vilar Formoso ◻ P 26 Kn50
Vila Rica ◻ BR (MS) 202 Hc57
Vila Rica ◻ BR (MT) 200 He51
Vilarinho do Monte ◻ BR (PA) 199 Hd46
Vila Sagrado Coração de Jesus ◻ BR (AM) 199 Ha48
Vila Tambaqui ◻ BR (AM) 198 Gh47
Vila Tepequem ◻ BR (RR) 193 Gk44
Vilattikulam ◻ IND (TNU) 84 Ok41
Vila Tugendhat ▣ CZ 42 Lr41
Vila Valério ◻ BR (ES) 203 Hk55
Vila Velha ◻ BR (AP) 195 He44
Vila Velha ◻ BR (ES) 203 Hk56
Vila Velha de Ródão ◻ P 27 Kn51
Vila Verde de Ficalho ◻ P 27 Kn53
Vila Viçosa ◻ P 27 Kn52
Vilcabamba ◻ EC 196 Ga48
Vilcabamba Viejo ◻ PE 197 Gd52
Vilches ◻ E 27 Kr52
Vildbjerg ◻ DK 30 Lj34
Vilejka ◻ BY 39 Mg36
Vileišas ◻ RA (SE) 207 Gj59
Vilhelmina ◻ S 16 Lj13
Vilhena ◻ BR (RO) 206 Gk52
Viljandi ◻ EST 39 Mf32
Viljoenskroen ◻ ZA 155 Md59
Viljuj ◻ RUS 55 Rd06
Viljujsk ◻ RUS 55 Sc06
Viljuskoje plato ▲ RUS 55 Qc05
Viljujskoje vodohranilisce ◻ RUS 55 Qc06
Vikaviskis ◻ LT 39 Md36
Vilkija ◻ LT 39 Md35
Villa Abecia ◻ BOL 206 Gh56
Villa Adriana □ I 36 Lo49
Villa Ahumada ◻ MEX (CHH) 180 Eg30
Villa Alegre ◻ RCH 208 Ge62
Villa Alemana ◻ RCH 208 Ge63
Villa Alhué ◻ RCH 208 Ge63
Villa Amengual ◻ RCH 210 Gd68
Villa Ana ◻ RA (SF) 204 Ha60
Villa Angela ◻ RA (CH) 207 Gk59
Villa Atamisqui ◻ RA (SE) 207 Gj60
Villa Atuel ◻ RA (MD) 208 Gg63
Villa Azueta ◻ MEX (VC) 183 Fd36
Villaba ◻ RP 90 Rc40
Villa Berthet ◻ RA (CH) 207 Gk59
Villablino ◻ E 26 Ko48
Villa Bruzual ◻ YV 193 Gf41
Villa Bustos ◻ RA (LR) 207 Gj60
Villacañas ◻ E 27 Kr51
Villa Cañas ◻ RA (SF) 209 Gk63
Villacarrilo ◻ E 27 Kr52
Villa Carlos Paz ◻ RA (CD) 208 Gh61
Villacarriedo ◻ E 28 Kr47
Villacastin ◻ E 27 Kq50
Villach ▲ A 35 Lo44
Villacidro ◻ I 36 Lj51
Villa Constitución ◻ RA (SF) 209 Gk62
Villada ◻ E 26 Kq48
Villadama ◻ MEX (NL) 181 Ek32
Villa de Arista ◻ MEX (SLP) 182 Ek34
Villa de Cura ◻ YV 193 Gg40
Villa de Guadelupe ◻ MEX (CAM) 183 Fe36
Villa del Carmen ◻ ROU 204 Hb62
Villa de Leyva ◻ CO 192 Gd43
Villa del Rio ◻ E 27 Kq53
Villa del-Lares ◻ E 27 Ks45
Villa del Rosario ◻ E 209 Gj61
Villa del Totoral ◻ RA (CD) 207 Gh61
Villa de María ◻ RA (CD) 207 Gj60
Villa de Reyes ◻ MEX (SLP) 182 Ek35
Villa d'Este □ I 36 Ln49
Villa de Zaachila ◻ MEX (OAX) 182 Fb37
Villa Figueroa ◻ RA (SE) 207 Gj59

Villaflores ◻ MEX (CHP) 183 Fd37
Villa Florida ◻ PY 204 Hb59
Villa Foscari □ I 34 Ln45
Villafranca del Bierzo ◻ E 26 Ko48
Villafranca de los Barros ◻ E 27 Ko52
Villafranca de los Caballeros ◻ E 27 Kr51
Villafranca di Verona □ I 34 Ll45
Villafranco del Guadalquivir ◻ E 27 Ko53
Villa General Belgrano ◻ RA (CD) 208 Gh62
Villa General Güemes ◻ RA (FO) 204 Ha58
Villa General M.Belgrano ◻ RA (FO) 204 Ha58
Villa General Roca ◻ RA (SL) 208 Gg62
Villages de Pygmés ▣ RDC 141 Me54
Vila Gesell ◻ RA (BA) 209 Hb64
Villa Gobernador Gálvez ◻ RA (ZCT) 182 Ek34
Villa González Ortega ◻ MEX (ZCT) 182 Ek34
Villa Guadelupe ◻ MEX (SO) 180 Ed30
Villaguay ◻ RA (ER) 204 Ha61
Villa Guillermina ◻ RA (SF) 204 Ha60
Villaharta ◻ E 27 Kq52
Villahermosa ◻ E 27 Ks52
Villahermosa ▣ MEX (CAM) 183 Ff37
Villa Hermosa ◻ MEX (SO) 180 Ed30
Villahermosa ▣ MEX (TB) 183 Fd36
Villa Hidalgo ◻ MEX (JLC) 182 Ej35
Villahoz ◻ E 28 Kr48
Villa Huidobro ◻ RA (CD) 208 Gh63
Villa Iris ◻ RA (BA) 208 Gh64
Villa Jesús María ◻ MEX (BC) 180 Ed31
Villajoyosa = La Vila Joiosa ◻ E 29 Ku52
Villa Juárez ◻ MEX (AGS) 182 Ej34
Villa Juárez ◻ MEX (SO) 180 Ef32
Villa Junqueiro ◻ MOC 153 Mj53
Villa Krause ◻ RA (SJ) 208 Gf61
Villa La Angostura ◻ RA (NE)
Villa Larca ◻ RA (SL) 208 Gg62
Villalba = Villalba ◻ E 26 Kn47
Villa Lola ◻ YV 193 Gj42
Villalón de Campos ◻ E 26 Kp48
Villalonga ◻ RA (BA) 209 Gj65
Villa López ◻ MEX (CHH)
Villa Madero ◻ MEX (CAM) 183 Fe36
Villa Mainero ◻ MEX (TM) 181 Fa33
Villamalea ◻ E 29 Kt51
Villamanrique ◻ E 27 Kr52
Villa Martín ◻ BOL 206 Gg56
Villamartin ◻ E 27 Kp53
Villa Mascardi ◻ RA (RN) 208 Ge66
Villa Matamoros ◻ MEX (CHH) 181 Eh32
Villamayor ◻ E 28 Ku49
Villamayor de Santiago ◻ E 29 Ks51
Villa Mazán ◻ RA (LR) 207 Gg60
Villa Media Agua ◻ RA (SJ) 208 Gf61
Villa Mercedes ◻ RA (SL) 208 Gg62
Villa Minetti ◻ RA (SF) 204 Ha60
Villa M.Moreno ◻ RA (TU)
Villa Montes ◻ BOL 206 Gj56
Villandraut ◻ F 24 Ku46
Villandry □ F 24 La43
Villa Nova de Cerveira ◻ P 26 Km49
Villanubla ◻ E 26 Kq49
Villanueva ◻ BOL 198 Gh51
Villanueva ◻ MEX (ZCT) 182 Ej34
Villanueva ◻ NIC 184 Fg39
Villanueva ◻ YV 193 Gf42
Villanueva de Alcorón ◻ E 29 Ks50
Villanueva de Argaño ◻ E 28 Kr48
Villanueva de Córdoba ◻ E 27 Kq52
Villanueva de Gállego ◻ E 28 Ku49
Villanueva de la Fuente ◻ E 27 Ks52
Villanueva de la Jura ◻ E 29 Kt51
Villanueva de la Serena ◻ E 27 Kp52
Villanueva de la Sierra ◻ E 27 Ko50
Villanueva del Campo ◻ E 26 Kp49
Villanueva del Fresno ◻ E 27 Kn52
Villanueva del Huerva ◻ E 29 Kt49
Villanueva de los Castillejos ◻ E 27 Kn53
Villanueva de los Infantes ◻ E 27 Ks52
Villanueva del Río y Minas ◻ E 27 Ko53
Villa O'Higgins ◻ RCH 210 Gd70
Villa Ojo de Agua ◻ RA (SE) 207 Gj60
Villa Ortega ◻ RCH 210 Gd68
Villa Paranacito ◻ RA (ER) 204 Ha62
Villapinzon ◻ CO 192 Gd43
Villaputzu □ I 36 Lk51
Villa Regina ◻ RA (RN) 208 Mg51
Villa Regina ◻ RA (RN) 208 Gg64
Vila Rica ◻ RA (CD) 208 Gj61
Villarente ◻ E 26 Kp48
Villaralto ◻ E 27 Kq52
Villarejo de Salvanés ◻ E 27 Kr50
Villa Rica ◻ E 26 Kn49
Villa Romana del Casale ▣ I 37 Lp53
Villaroya ◻ DOM 186 Ge38
Villarrica ◻ PY 204 Hb59
Villarrica ◻ RCH 208 Gd65

Villarrica, P.N. ▣ RCH 208 Ge65
Villarrica, Volcán ▲ RCH 208 Gd65
Villarrin de Campos ◻ E 26 Kp49
Villarrobledo ◻ E 29 Ks51
Villarroya de la Sierra ◻ E 28 Kt49
Villarrubia de los Ojos ◻ E 27 Kr51
Villarta de los Montes ◻ E 27 Kg51
Villa Sánchez Magallanes ◻ MEX (TB) 183 Fd36
Villa San Giovanni □ I 37 Lq52
Villa San José de Vinchina ◻ RA (LR) 207 Gf60
Villa Santa Maria □ I 37 Lp49
Villa Serano ◻ BOL 206 Gh55
Villasimius □ I 36 Lk51
Villa Trinidad ◻ RA (SF) 207 Gk61
Villa Unión ◻ BOL 206 Gh54
Villa Unión ◻ MEX (DGO) 180 Eh34
Villa Unión ◻ MEX (SL) 180 Eg34
Villa Unión ◻ MEX (LR) 207 Gf60
Villa Valeria ◻ RA (CD) 208 Gh63
Villa Vásquez ◻ DOM 186 Ge36
Villavicencio ◻ CO 192 Gd43
Villaviciosa ◻ E 26 Kp47
Villaviciosa de Córdoba ◻ E 27 Kq52
Villa Viscarra ◻ BOL 206 Gh54
Villa Ygatimí ◻ PY 204 Hc58
Villazón ◻ BOL 207 Gh57
Villedieu-les-Poêles ◻ F 22 Kt42
Villefagnan ◻ F 24 La44
Villefort ◻ F 25 Ld46
Villefranche-de-Conflent □ F 24 Lc48
Villefranche-de-Lauragais ◻ F 24 Lb47
Villefranche-de-Rouergue ◻ F 25 Lc46
Villefranche-du-Périgord ◻ F 24 Lb46
Villefranche-sur-Cher ◻ F 25 Lb43
Villefranche-sur-Mer □ F 25 Lh47
Villefranche-sur-Saône ◻ F 25 Le45
Villena ◻ E 29 Ku52
Villeneuve □ I 35 Lh45
Villeneuve-lès-Avignon ◻ F 25 Le47
Villeneuve-sur-Lot ◻ F 24 La46
Villeneuve-sur-Yonne ◻ F 23 Ld42
Ville Platte ◻ USA (LA) 175 Fd30
Villerupt ◻ F 23 Lf41
Villeréal ◻ F 24 La46
Villeroy ◻ CDN (QC) 176 Ge22
Villers-Bocage ◻ F 22 Ku41
Villers-Bocage ◻ F 23 Lc41
Villers-Bretonneux ◻ F 23 Lc41
Villers-Cotterêts ◻ F 23 Ld41
Villerexel ◻ F 25 Lg43
Villeurbanne ◻ F 25 Le45
Villiers ◻ ZA 155 Me59
Villiers-Saint-Georges ◻ F 23 Ld42
Villingen-Schwenningen ◻ D 33 L42
Villupuram ◻ IND (TNU) 85 Ok40
Vilnius ▣ LT 39 Mf36
Vil'njans'k ◻ UA 49 Mh21
Vil'nohirs'k ◻ UA 49 Mh21
Vilppula ◻ FIN 38 Me28
Vils ◻ D 33 Ln41
Vils □ D 33 Lm41
Vilsandi rahvuspark ▣ EST 39 Mb32
Vil'šany ◻ UA 48 Mh20
Vilsbiburg ◻ D 33 Lm42
Vilshofen ◻ D 33 Lo42
Viluco ◻ RCH 208 Ge62
Vilyui □ BR (RS) 204 He61
Vimianzo ◻ E 26 Km47
Vimieiro ◻ P 27 Kn52
Vimioso ◻ P 26 Ko49
Vimmerby ◻ S 31 Lq33
Vimoutiers ◻ F 22 La42
Vimperli ◻ CZ 42 Lo41
Vinac ◻ BIH 35 Ls46
Viña del Mar ◻ RCH 208 Ge62
Vinaninkazo ◻ RM 156 Nf53
Vinaròs ◻ E 29 La50
Vinay ◻ F 25 Lf45
Vincennes ◻ USA (IL) 175 Fg26
Vincennes Bay ≋ 7 Oc32
Vincent ◻ USA (TX) 174 Ek29
Vincente Noble ◻ DOM 186 Ge36
Vinchiaturo □ I 37 Lp49
Vinchina ◻ RA (LR) 207 Gf60
Vindafjord ≋ N 30 Lf31
Vindelälven □ S 16 Lk13
Vinderup ◻ DK 30 Lj34
Vindex ◻ AUS (QLD) 108 Sb57
Vindhya Range ▲ IND 82 Oj34
Vindö ◻ S 31 Ls31
Vinegar Hill ▲ USA 168 Dk23
Vineland ◻ USA (CO) 171 En26
Vineland ◻ USA (NJ) 177 Gc26
Vinga ◻ RO 43 Mb44
Vingåker ◻ S 31 Lq32
Vinh ◻ VN 87 Qc36
Vinhais ◻ P 26 Ko49
Vinh Cam Ranh ◻ VN 89 Qe40
Vinh Chao ◻ VN 89 Qe37
Vinh Da Nang ◻ VN 89 Qe37
Vinh Duang Quat ◻ VN 89 Qe37
Vinh Hy ◻ VN 89 Qe40
Vinh Loc ◻ VN 87 Qe37
Vinh Long ◻ VN 89 Qd40
Vinh Moc Tunnel ▣ VN 87 Qd37
Vinh Padaran ◻ VN 89 Qe40
Vinh Phan Ri ◻ VN 89 Qe40
Vinh Phan Thiet ◻ VN 89 Qe40
Vinh Rach Gia ◻ VN 89 Qd40
Vinh Son ◻ VN 89 Qe39
Vinh Trang Pagoda ▣ VN 89 Qd40
Vinh Van Phong ◻ VN 89 Qe39
Vinica ◻ MK 44 Mc49
Viniste ◻ BG 44 Me47
Vinkovci ◻ HR 35 Lt45
Vinnicja ◻ UA 49 Me21
Vinnjytsja ◻ UA 49 Me21
Vinograd ◻ BG 45 Mf47
Vinon-sur-Verdon ◻ F 25 Lf47
Vinstumbui ◻ RDC 141 Me46
Vinstra ◻ N 30 Ll29
Vintar ◻ RP 90 Ra36
Vintermarknad ◻ S 16 Lk12
Vinukonda ◻ IND (APH) 83 Ok37
Vinza ◻ RCB 148 Lh47
Violet Town ◻ AUS (VIC) 111 Sd64
Violet Valley A.L. ◻ AUS 103 Mg51
Viphya Mountains ▲ MW 146 Mg51
Vipiteno = Sterzing □ I 35 Lm44
Vir □ HR 35 Lp46
Vira ◻ CH 35 Lk44
Vircova ◻ F 25 Lf47
Viramgam ◻ IND (GUJ) 82 Og35
Viranşehir ◻ TR 56 Mk27
Virac ◻ RP 90 Rc39
Virachey N.P. ▣ K 89 Qd38
Virandozero ◻ RUS 38 Mk14
Viramalai ◻ IND (TNU) 84 Ok41
Viranqala ◻ IND (APH) 83 Pa36
Vizille ◻ F 25 Lf45
Vizinga ◻ RUS 48 Nd04
Vizovice ◻ CZ 42 Ls41
Vizzini □ I 37 Lp53

Virarajendrapet ◻ IND (KTK) 84 Oh39
Virawah ◻ PK 65 Of33
Virazon ◻ RA 209 Ha65
Virazon ◻ RA 209 Ha65
Virbalis ◻ LT 39 Mc36
Vire ◻ F 22 Ku42
Virei ◻ ANG 150 Lg53
Virei ◻ LV 39 Mg33
Virf Cindrel ▲ RO 44 Md45
Virf Fâncelul ▲ RO 43 Md44
Virf Svinecea ▲ RO 44 Mc46
Virgem da Lapa ◻ BR (MG) 203 Hj54
Virgin Gorda ◻ GB 187 Gh36
Virginia ◻ AUS (SA) 110 Rk63
Virginia ◻ IRL 19 Kn37
Virginia ◻ USA (MN) 172 Fd22
Virginia ◻ USA (NV) 170 Ea26
Virginia ◻ ZA 155 Md60
Virginia Beach ◻ USA (VA) 178 Gb27
Virginia City ◻ USA (MT) 169 Ee23
Virginia City ◻ USA (NV) 170 Ea26
Virgin Islands ◻ GB 187 Gh36
Virgin Islands ◻ US 187 Gh36
Virgin Islands N.P. ▣ USA 187 Gh36
Virginópolis ◻ BR (MG) 203 Hj55
Virgin Passage ≋ USA 187 Gh36
Viriñaure ◻ S 16 Lj12
Virkby = Virkkala ◻ FIN 38 Md30
Virkkala = Virkby ◻ FIN 38 Md30
Virklund ◻ DK 30 Lk34
Virojoki ◻ FIN 38 Mf30
Virolahden ◻ FIN 38 Mf30
Viroqua ◻ USA (WI) 172 Fe24
Virovitica ◻ HR 35 Ls45
Virpazar ◻ SCG 44 Lu48
Virrat ◻ FIN 38 Md28
Virsbo ◻ S 31 Lq31
Virserum ◻ S 31 Lq33
Virtasalmi ◻ FIN 38 Mh28
Virton ◻ B 23 Lf41
Virttaa ◻ FIN 38 Mc30
Virú ◻ PE 197 Ga50
Viruá, P.N. do ▣ BR 194 Gk45
Virudó ◻ CO 192 Gb43
Virudunagar ◻ IND (TNU) 84 Oj41
Vis ◻ HR 35 Lr47
Vis □ HR 35 Lr48
Visaginas ◻ LT 39 Mg35
Visalaukat ◻ LT 39 Mh35
Visalia ◻ USA (CA) 170 Ea27
Visarwari ◻ IND (MHT) 82 Oj36
Vischering □ D 32 Lh39
Visconde do Rio Branco ◻ BR (MG) 203 Hj56
Viscount Melville Sound ≋ CDN 167 Ec04
Viseirey ◻ CDN (QC) 176 Ge22
Viscri □ RO 43 Mf44
Višegrad ◻ BIH 44 Lu47
Višegrad ▣ BR (PA) 195 Hg46
Viseu ◻ P 26 Kn50
Viseu de Sus ◻ RO 43 Md43
Višgorodok ◻ RUS 39 Mj33
Vishakhapatnam ◻ IND (APH) 83 Pb37
Vishalla Village ▣ IND 82 Og34
Vishnupur ◻ IND (WBG) 83 Pd34
Vishwa Shanti Stupa ▣ IND 83 Pc33
Višnja ◻ RO 43 Mf44
Visingsö □ S 31 Lp33
Visita ◻ USA (MT) 199 Ha49
Viskafors ◻ S 30 Lo33
Vislanda ◻ S 31 Lp34
Visočica ◻ HR 35 Lq46
Viso del Marqués ◻ E 27 Kr52
Visoki Dečani ◻ SCG 44 Ma48
Visoko ◻ BIH 44 Lt47
Visp ◻ CH 34 Lh44
Vissahna ◻ USA (SC) 178 Mc61
Vissanapeta ◻ IND (APH) 83 Pa37
Vissefjärda ◻ S 31 Lq34
Visselhövede ◻ D 32 Lk38
Vista Alegre ◻ BR (AM) 198 Gg56
Vista Alegre ◻ ANG 148 Lh50
Vistula ◻ PL 41 Lu38
Vistula Lagoon ≋ PL/RUS 41 Lu36
Výstytis ◻ LT 39 Mc36
Visuel ◻ FIN 33 Mc64
Visuvisu Point ≋ SOL 117 Sj49
Vitaaa ◻ IND (MHT) 82 Oj37
Vitale ◻ F (GF) 194 Hd44
Vitebsk ◻ BY 48 Mf18
Viterbo □ I 34 Ln48
Vitez ◻ BIH 35 Ls46
Vi'Thanh ◻ VN 89 Qd40
Vithkuq ◻ AL 46 Ma50
Vitiaz I Deep ≋ 10 Ta12
Vitiaz II Deep ≋ 10 Tb13
Vitiaz Strait ≋ PNG 115 Sd48
Vitiaz Trench ≋ 10 Ta10
Vitigudino ◻ E 26 Ko50
Viti Levu □ FJI 119 Tj55
Vitim ◻ RUS 70 Qg19
Vitina ◻ SCG 44 Mb48
Vitolişte ◻ MK 44 Mb49
Vitor ◻ PE 197 Ge54
Vitória ▣ BR (ES) 203 Hk56
Vitória ◻ BR (PA) 199 Hd47
Vitória da Conquista ◻ BR (BA) 203 Hk53
Vitória de Santo Antão ◻ BR (PE) 201 Jc50
Vitória do Mearim ◻ BR (MA) 200 Hh47
Vitória-Seamount ≋ 190 Ja12
Vitória Seamount ≋ 190 Ja12
Vitorino Freire ◻ BR (MA) 200 Hh48
Vitória, N.P. ▣ BG 44 Md48
Vitré ◻ F 22 Kt42
Vitrolles ◻ F 25 Lf47
Vitry-le-François ◻ F 23 Le42
Vitsyumbi ◻ RDC 141 Me46
Vittangi ◻ S 16 Ma12
Vittel ◻ F 23 Lf42
Vittoria □ I 37 Lp54
Vittória □ I 37 Lp54
Vittorio Véneto □ I 34 Ln45
Vittsjö ◻ S 31 Lp34
Vitú □ I 35 Lk48
Viveiro ◻ E 26 Kn47
Viver ◻ E 29 Ku51
Vivero □ CDN (MB) 172 Fb21
Viviers ◻ F 25 Le46
Vivo ◻ ZA 152 Me57
Vivonne ◻ F 24 La44
Vizcaíno ◻ MEX (BCS) 180 Ed32
Vize ◻ TR 45 Mh49
Vizianagram ◻ IND (APH) 83 Pb36

Vjal.Čučavičy ◻ BY 41 Mg38
Vjalikija Matykaly ◻ BY 41 Md38
Vjartsilja ◻ RUS 38 Mj24
Vjatskoe ◻ RUS 48 Na17
Vjazemskij ◻ RUS 77 Rh22
Vjaz'ma ◻ RUS 48 Mh18
Vjazniki ◻ RUS 48 Na17
Vladikavkaz ▣ RUS (SOA) 57 Nc24
Vladimir ◻ RUS 48 Na17
Vladimir ◻ SCG 44 Lu48
Vladimirovo ◻ BG 44 Md47
Vladivostok ▣ RUS 76 Rf24
Vlachi ◻ GR 46 Mb52
Vlahita ◻ RO 43 Mf44
Vlahiá ◻ GR 45 Md52
Vlaming Head Lighthouse ▣ AUS 102 Qh56
Vlasenica ◻ BIH 44 Lt46
Vlasotince ◻ SCG 44 Mc48
Vlorë ◻ AL 46 Lu50
Vlotho ◻ D 32 Lj38
Vlttava □ CZ 42 Lp41
Vöbbenet ◻ CZ 42 Lp41
Vodil □ UZ 63 Of25
Vodňany ◻ CZ 42 Lp41
vodní nádrž Hracholusky □ CZ 42 Lo41
Vodnjan ◻ HR 35 Lo46
Voeskovo ◻ DK 30 Li33
Voerde ◻ D 32 Lg39
Vogan ◻ TG 137 La42
Vogar ◻ CDN (MB) 172 Fb20
Vogelkop ▲ RI 97 Rf46
Vogelkop ▲ RI 97 Rf46
Vogelsberg ▲ D 33 Lk40
Vogelweide ◻ NAM 154 La59
Voghera □ I 34 Lk46
Voh ◻ F (NCL) 118 Tc56
Vohburg ◻ D 33 Lm42
Vohemar = Iharana ◻ RM 156 Ne52
Vohenstrauß ◻ D 33 Ln41
Vohidiala ◻ RM 157 Ne54
Vohilengo ◻ RM 157 Ne54
Vohimasina ◻ RM 157 Ne54
Vohipeno ◻ RM 157 Nd57
Vohitrambo ◻ RM 157 Ne54
Vohma ◻ EST 39 Mc32
Voi ◻ EAK 145 Mk47
Voinama ◻ RI 97 Rf36
Voikoski ◻ FIN 38 Mg29
Voineasa ◻ RO 44 Md45
Voineasa ◻ RO 44 Me45
Voinjama ◻ LB 136 Kf41
Voiron ◻ F 25 Lf45
Voitberg ◻ A 35 Lq44
Voiteg ◻ RO 44 Mb45
Voitsberg ▲ A 35 Lq44
Vojens ◻ DK 30 Lk35
Vojnica ◻ RUS 16 Mf13
Vojnik ◻ SLO 35 Lq44
Vojnojo ◻ BG 45 Mh47
Vojvodina ◻ SCG 44 Lu45
Vokeo Island ◻ PNG 115 Sc47
Vokhma ◻ RUS 48 Nc16
Volary ◻ CZ 42 Lo42
Volca ◻ USA (MT) 169 Eh23
Volcán ◻ PA 185 Fj41
Volcán ◻ RA (PJ) 207 Gh57
Volcán Alcedo ▲ EC 197 Fe46
Volcán Altar ▲ EC 196 Ga46
Volcán Antisana ▲ EC 196 Ga46
Volcán Antofalla ▲ RA 207 Gg58
Volcán Aracar ▲ RA/RCH 208 Gg58
Volcán Aracar ▲ RA 207 Gg58
Volcán Arenal, P.N. ▣ CR 185 Fh40
Volcán Atitlan ▲ GCA 184 Fe38
Volcán Barú, P.N. ▣ PA 185 Fj41
Volcán Calbuco ▲ RCH 208 Gd66
Volcán Callaqui ▲ RCH 208 Ge64
Volcán Cayambe ▲ EC 196 Ga46
Volcán Chachani ▲ PE 197 Ge54
Volcán Chiguana ▲ BOL 206 Gg56
Volcán Chillán ▲ RCH 208 Ge64
Volcán Chimborazo ▲ EC 196 Ga46
Volcán Choshuenco ▲ RCH 208 Gd66
Volcán Concepción ▲ NIC 184 Fh40
Volcán Copahue ▲ RA/RCH 208 Ge64
Volcán Copiapó ▲ RCH 207 Gf59
Volcán Corcovado ▲ RCH 210 Gd67
Volcán Cotopaxi ▲ EC 196 Ga46
Volcán Cumbal ▲ CO 192 Gb45
Volcán Darwin ▲ EC 197 Fe46
Volcán de Colima ▲ MEX 182 Ej36
Volcán de Fuego ▲ GCA 184 Fe38
Volcán Domuyo ▲ RA 208 Ge64
Volcán Doña Juana ▲ CO 192 Gb45
Volcán Fernandina ▲ EC 197 Fe46
Volcán Galeras ▲ CO 192 Gb45
Volcán Guagua Pichincha ▲ EC 196 Ga46
Volcán Gualtatiri ▲ RCH 206 Gf55
Volcán Huequi ▲ RCH 208 Gd67
Volcán Illiniza ▲ EC 196 Ga46
Volcán Ipala ▲ GCA 184 Fe38
Volcán Isluga ▲ RCH 206 Gf55
Volcán Isluga, P.N. ▣ RCH 206 Gf55
Volcán Lanin ▲ RCH 208 Gd65
Volcán Lascar ▲ RCH 207 Gg57
Volcán Las Virgenes ▲ MEX 180 Ed32
Volcán Licancábur ▲ RCH 207 Gg57
Volcán Llaima ▲ RCH 208 Gd65
Volcán Llullaillaco ▲ RCH/RA 207 Gg57
Volcán Lonquimay ▲ RCH 208 Gd65
Volcán Maipo ▲ RCH/RA 208 Gf63
Volcán Masaya, P.N. ▣ NIC 184 Fg39
Volcán Michimahuida ▲ RCH 210 Gd67
Volcán Misti ▲ PE 197 Ge54
Volcán Momotombo ▲ NIC 184 Fg39
Volcán Mayon ▲ RP 90 Rb39
Volcán Osorno ▲ RCH 208 Gd66
Volcán Parinacota ▲ RCH 206 Gf55
Volcán Peteroa ▲ RCH/RA 208 Ge63
Volcán Pico de Orizaba ▲ MEX 182 Fb36

Volcán Poás, P.N. ▣ CR 185 Fh40
Volcán Puracé ▲ CO 192 Gb44
Volcán Puyehué ▲ RCH 208 Gd66
Volcán Reventador ▲ EC 196 Gb46
Volcán Sabancaya ▲ PE 197 Ge53
Volcán San José ▲ RA/RCH 208 Gf62
Volcán San Pedro ▲ RCH 207 Gg56
Volcán Socompa ▲ RCH/RA 207 Gg58
Volcán Sotara ▲ CO 192 Gb44
Volcán Sumaco ▲ EC 196 Gb46
Volcán Tacaná ▲ GCA/MEX 183 Fe38
Volcán Tacora ▲ RCH 206 Gf54
Volcán Tajumulco ▲ GCA 184 Fe38
Volcán Tenorio, P.N. ▣ CR 185 Fh40
Volcán Ticsani ▲ PE 197 Ge54
Volcán Tinguiririca ▲ RCH 208 Ge63
Volcán Tremen ▲ RA 208 Ge64
Volcán Tungurahua ▲ EC 196 Ga46
Volcán Tupungato ▲ RA/RCH 208 Gf62
Volcán Viedma ▲ RA 210 Gd70
Volcán Villarrica ▲ RCH 208 Gd65
Volcán Wolf ▲ EC 197 Fe45
Volcano ◻ USA 88 Na19
Volga ▣ RUS 48 Na19
Volga □ RUS 48 Na19
Volgograd ◻ RUS 48 Na17
Volgorečensk ◻ RUS 48 Na17
Volíssos ◻ GR 47 Mf52
Volkach ◻ D 33 Ll41
Völkermarkt ▲ A 35 Lp44
Vogelweide □ NAM 154 La59
Völklingen ◻ D 33 Lg41
Volkovo ◻ RUS 39 Mh33
Volkspelemonument ▣ ZA 155 Me59
Volksrust ◻ ZA 155 Me59
Vollsjö ◻ S 31 Lp34
Volnovacha ◻ UA 49 Mj22
Volo ◻ USA 117 Sk50
Voločsk ◻ UA 49 Md21
Voločanka ◻ RUS 54 Pc04
Volodarsk ◻ RUS 48 Nb17
Volodymerc' ◻ UA 41 Mg39
Volodymyr-Volyns'kyj ◻ UA 41 Me40
Vologda ◻ RUS 48 Mj20
Volokolamsk ◻ RUS 48 Mh17
volcán Korjakskaja Sopka ▲ RUS 55 Sd08
vulkan Tjatja ▲ RUS 77 Sd23
Vulkulen ◻ RO 45 Mg46
Vulturu ◻ RO 45 Mh45
Vumba Mountains ▲ ZW 152 Mf56
Vumba Rock Paintings ▣ MOC 152 Mg55
Vumbwe ◻ MW 146 Mg52
Vung Tau ◻ VN 89 Qd40
Vunisea ◻ FJI 119 Tk55
Vuntut National Park ▣ CDN (YT) 165 Ck11
Vuollerim ◻ S 16 Ma12
Vuottas ◻ S 16 Ma12
Vuoksi ▣ RUS 48 Nd18
Vuoksi □ RUS 48 Nd18
Vuoyyuru ◻ IND (APH) 83 Pa37
Vuran ◻ WAN 138 La41
Vyperla ◻ IND (GUJ) 82 Oj35
Vyara ◻ IND (GUJ) 82 Og35
Vyborg ◻ RUS 38 Mj30
Vyborgskii zamok ▣ RUS 38 Mh30
Vyčegda ▣ RUS 54 Nb06
Vydrino ◻ RUS (BUR) 70 Qc20
Vydryći ◻ UA 41 Me39
Vygoniči ◻ RUS 48 Mh19
Vyksa ◻ RUS 48 Nb18
Vykove ◻ UA 45 Mk45
Vynnyky ◻ UA 43 Md41
Vynohradiv ◻ UA 43 Mc42
Vypolzovo ◻ RUS 48 Mh17
Vyrica ◻ RUS 39 Mh33
Vyšgorodok ◻ RUS 39 Mj33
Vyšhorod ◻ UA 48 Mf20
Vyska □ CZ 43 Mc42
Vyskov ◻ CZ 42 Lr41
Vyšné Nemecké ◻ SK 43 Mc42
Vyšné Ružbachy ◻ SK 43 Ma41
Vyšnij Voloček ◻ RUS 48 Mh17
Vysock ◻ RUS 38 Mj30
Vysoké Mýto ◻ CZ 42 Lr41
Vysokovsk ◻ RUS 48 Mj17
Vyšší Brod ◻ CZ 42 Lp42
Vythiri ◻ IND (KER) 84 Oj40
Vyžnycja ◻ UA 43 Md42
Vyžnyc'k N.P. ▣ UA 43 Md42

Wa ◻ CI 136 Kf42
Wa ◻ GH 137 Kj40
Waaciye ◻ SP 143 Ne40
Waajid ◻ SP 145 Nb44
Waal □ NL 23 Lf39
Waala ◻ F (NCL) 118 Tb55
Waalre ◻ NL 23 Lf39
Waalwijk ◻ NL 23 Lf39
Waanyi Garawa A.L. ◻ AUS 106 Rj55
Waar ◻ RI 114 Rh47
Waat ◻ SUD 141 Mg41
Wabag ◻ PNG 115 Sb48
Wabakimi Prov. Park ▣ CDN 172 Ff20
Wabasca-Desmarais ◻ CDN (AB) 167 Ed18
Wabasca Ind. Res. ◻ CDN 167 Ed18
Wabash ◻ USA (IN) 173 Fh25
Wabasha ◻ USA (MN) 172 Fd23
Wabe Gestro □ ETH 142 Na42
Wabe Shebele Wenz □ ETH 145 Nb43
Wabo ◻ PNG 115 Sc49
Wabrzezno ◻ PL 40 Lt37
Wabu Hu ≋ CHN 72 Qj29
Wabush ◻ CDN (NF) 176 Gh20
Wabuska ◻ USA (NV) 170 Ea26
Wachau ▣ A 42 Lq42
Wache ◻ ETH 145 Mk43
Wachtebeke ◻ B 23 Ld39
Waco ◻ CDN (QC) 176 Gh20
Waco ◻ USA (TX) 174 Fb30
Wad ◻ PK 65 Od31
Wad az-Zarga ◻ SUD 135 Mg39
Wadbilliga N.P. ▣ AUS 111 Se64
Wadbristoo ◻ SUD 135 Mg37
Waddan ◻ LAR 127 Lj31
Waddenzee ≋ NL 23 Lf37
Waddikee ◻ AUS (SA) 110 Rh62
Waddington, Mount ▲ CDN 168 Dh20

Waddy Point ◻ AUS 109 Sg58
Wadebridge ◻ GB 21 Kq40
Wad al Haddad ◻ SUD 135 Mg39
Wad en Nail ◻ SUD 135 Mg40
Wädenswil ◻ CH 34 Lj43
Wadesboro ◻ USA (NC) 178 Fk28
Wadeye ◻ AUS (NT) 103 Re53
Wad Hassib ◻ SUD 134 Mf39
Wadhwan ◻ IND (GUJ) 82 Of34
Wadi ◻ IND (KTK) 82 Oj37
Wadi al-Hayat ▣ LAR 127 Lg32
Wadi Al-Hitan (Whale Valley) ▣ ▣ ET 129 Mf32
Wadi al-Milk □ SUD 135 Mf37
Wadi al-Warriya ▣ UAE 61 Nj33
Wadi ar Ru'ays □ LAR 127 Lk32
Wadi as Sulaymaniyah ▣ KSA 58 Na30
Wadi Dhayqah ▣ OM 61 Nk34
Wadi Hadramaut ▣ YE 60 Ne37
Wadi Halfa ◻ SUD 129 Mf35
Wadi Howar □ SUD 134 Ma37
Wadi Huwar □ SUD 134 Mg37
Wadi Mathendous ▣ LAR 126 L33
Wadi Mujib ▣ JOR 58 Mh30
Wadi Muqaddam □ SUD 135 Mf38
Wadi Musa ◻ JOR 58 Mh30
Wadi Nahr ▣ LM 61 Nj34
Wadi Rum ▣ JOR 58 Mh31
Wadi Tanezzruft ▣ LAR 126 La33
Wadi Tathlith ▣ KSA 60 Nb35
Wadi Zabid ▣ YE 60 Nb38
Wadi Zazamt ▣ LAR 127 Lk30
Wadley ◻ USA (GA) 178 Fj29
Wad Madani ◻ SUD 135 Mg39
Wadomari ◻ J 79 Re32
Wadowice ◻ PL 41 Lu41
Wad Rawa ◻ SUD 135 Mg39
Wadwani ◻ IND (MHT) 82 Oj36
Wadzar Shan ▣ WAG 136
W-shaped Stone ▣ WAG 136
Vube ◻ FJI 119 Ua55
Vube ◻ RDC 141 Me44
Vubu ◻ ZA 155 Me59
Wager Bay ≋ CDN 163 Fd05
Waghäi ◻ IND (GUJ) 82 Og35
Wagin ◻ AUS (WA) 104 Qj62
Wagnitz ◻ D 33 Lk42
Wagram ◻ A 42 Lq42
Wagyagira ◻ RI 97 Rf36
Wagontire ◻ USA (OR) 168 Ea24
Waha ◻ RI 97 Re44
Wahai ◻ RI 114 Rj48
Wahat al Jufra ▣ LAR 127 Lj31
Wahat Salima ▣ SUD 129 Md35
Wahat Cantonment □ PK 65 Og29
Wahiawa ◻ USA (HI) 170 Cb35
Wahibah Sands ▣ OM 61 Nk35
Wahoo ◻ USA (NE) 174 Fb25
Wahpeton ◻ USA (ND) 172 Fb22
Wahran ▣ DZ 125 Kg28
Wahroonga ◻ AUS (NSW) 109 Sf56

Wakefield ◻ USA (MA) 177 Ge24
Wake Forest ◻ USA (NC) 178 Ga28
Wakeham ◻ CDN (QC) 178 Sa23
Wakinosawa ◻ J 77 Sa25
Wakkanai ◻ J 77 Sa23
Wakkerstrom ◻ ZA 155 Mf59
Waklarok ◻ USA (AK) 164 Bh14
Wakol ◻ T PNG 116 Se49
Wakomata Lake ≋ CDN 173 Fj22
Wakooka ◻ AUS (QLD) 107 Sc55
Wakool ◻ AUS (NSW) 111 Sc63
Wakulla Sprs. S.P. ▣ USA
Walamba ◻ Z 146 Me52
Walamai ◻ IND (MHT) 82 Oj36
Wal Athiang ◻ SUD 141 Mg42
Walbrzych ◻ PL 40 Lr40
Walbundrie ◻ AUS (NSW) 111 Sd63
Walburton River ▣ AUS 108 Rk59
Walcha ◻ AUS (NSW) 109 Sf61
Walcheren ▲ NL 23 Ld39
Walcott ◻ USA (WY) 171 Eg25
Watez ◻ PL 40 Lt37
Waldbröl ◻ D 32 Lh40
Waldburg ◻ AUS (WA) 104 Qj58
Waldburg Range ▲ AUS
Walden ◻ USA (CO) 171 Eg25
Walden ◻ D 32 Lk39
Waldegrave Island ▲ AUS 110 Rh62
Walden ◻ USA (AR)
Waldkirch ◻ D 33 Lh42
Waldkirchen ◻ D 33 Lo42
Waldkraiburg ◻ D 33 Ln42
Waldport ◻ USA (OR) 168 Dh23
Waldquell ◻ USA (AR) 174 Fc28
Waldshut-Tiengen ◻ D 33 Lj43
Waldstatt ◻ USA (CO) 171 Eg25
Wales ◻ GB 21 Kq38
Waleska ◻ USA (NC) 164 Bf13
Walewale ◻ GH 137 Kk40
Walfish Ridge ≋ (ASW) 109 Se61
Walgett ◻ AUS (NSW) 109 Se61
Walgoolan ◻ AUS (WA) 104 Qk61
Walgra ◻ AUS (QLD) 108 Rk56
Walgreen Coast ▣ 6 Ec33
Walhalla ◻ D 33 Ln41
Walhalla ◻ USA (ND) 172 Fb21
Walhalla ◻ USA (SC) 178 Fj28
Walikale ◻ RDC 141 Me46
Walindi Plantation Resort ◻ PNG 116 Sf48
Walis Island ▲ PNG 115 Sb47
Wall ◻ USA (SD) 169 Ek24
Walla Walla ◻ USA (WA) 168 Ea22
Wallace ◻ USA (ID) 168 Eb22
Wallace ◻ USA (NC) 178 Ga28
Wallace ◻ USA (NE) 174 Ek25
Wallaceburg ◻ CDN (ON) 173 Fj24
Walloon Downs ◻ AUS (WA)
Wallal Downs ◻ AUS (WA) 102 Ra55
Wallan ◻ AUS (VIC) 111 Sc64
Wallangarra ◻ AUS (NSW) 109 Sf60
Wallanthery ◻ AUS (NSW) 111 Sc62
Wallara Ranch Roadhouse ◻ AUS (NT) 103 Rg58
Wallaroo ◻ AUS (SA) 110 Rg62
Wallasey ◻ GB 21 Kr37
Walla Walla ◻ USA (WA) 168 Ea22
Walldürn ◻ D 33 Lk41
Walled City of Ma'in ▣ YE 60 Nc37
Wallerawang ◻ AUS (NSW) 109 Se62
Wallingford ◻ GB 21 Kt39
Walling Rock ◻ USA (WA) 104 Ra60
Wallis and Futuna ◻ F 101 Tb11
Wall of Gengis Khan ▣ MNG 71 Qg21
Wallowa ◻ USA (OR) 168 Eb23
Wallowa Mountains ▲ USA 168 Eb23
Walls ◻ GB 20 Ks31
Walls of China ▣ ▣ AUS 111 Sb63
Wallumbilla ◻ AUS (QLD) 109 Se59
Walney, Island of ▲ GB 21 Kr36
Walnut ◻ USA (CA) 170 Ec27
Walnut ◻ USA (MS) 175 Ff28
Walnut Canyon Nat. Mon. ▣ USA 171 Ee28
Walnut Grove ◻ USA (CA) 172 Fc23
Walnut Ridge ◻ USA (AR) 175 Fe27
Walong ◻ IND (ARP) 86 Pj31
Walosi ◻ RI 96 Rb48
Walpole ◻ AUS (WA) 104 Qj63
Walpole-Nonalup N.P. ▣ AUS 104 Qj63
Walrus Island ▲ USA 164 Bk16
Walrus Island ▲ USA 164 Bh17
Walsall ◻ GB 21 Ks38
Walsenburg ◻ USA (CO) 171 Eh27
Walsh ◻ USA (CO) 174 Ej27
Walterboro ◻ USA (SC) 178 Fk29
Waltham ◻ CDN (QC) 178 Gb23
Waltham ◻ USA (WY) 169 Eg24
Walton ◻ CDN (NS) 176 Gj23
Walton, Mount ▲ AUS
Walton-on-the-Naze ◻ GB 21 Lb39
Waltzing Matilda Center ▣ AUS (QLD) 108 Sb57
Walu Besa ◻ RI 97 Re47
Walwa ◻ AUS (VIC) 111 Sd63
Walungurru ◻ AUS (NT) 103 Rf57
Walvis Bay ◻ ▣ NAM 154 Lh57
Walvis Bay Nature Reserve ▣ NAM 154 Lh57
Walvis Ridge ≋ 12 Ka12
Waly Chrobrego ▣ PL 40 Lp37
Wamal ◻ RI 114 Rk50
Wamar ▲ RI 114 Rh48
Wamar ▲ RI 114 Rj48
Wamba ◻ RDC 148 Mj45
Wamba ◻ RDC 148 Ll48
Wamba Luadi ◻ RDC 149 Lj49

Wamba Mountains ▲ **WAN** 139 Lf42
Wambiana ◻ **AUS** (QLD) 107 Sd56
Wamboin ◻ **AUS** (NSW) 109 Sd61
Wamdé Tabal ▲ **BF** 131 Kk38
Wamego ◻ **USA** (KS) 174 Fb26
Wamena ◻ **RI** 114 Rk48
Wamis ◻ **LAR** 127 Lg30
Wampana-Karlantijpa A.L. ◰ **AUS** 106 Rf54
Wampaya Aboriginal Reserve ◰ **AUS** 106 Rh54
Wamsutter ◻ **USA** (WY) 171 Eg25
Wana ◻ **PK** 65 Oe29
Wanaaring ◻ **AUS** (NSW) 109 Sc60
Wanadou ◻ **RG** 136 Kf41
Wanaka ◻ **NZ** 113 Te68
Wanasabari ◻ **RI** 96 Rb48
Wanau ◻ **RI** 114 Rg46
Wanblee ◻ **USA** (SD) 172 Ek24
Wanda ◻ **RA** (MI) 204 Hc58
Wandai ◻ **RI** 114 Rj47
Wandammen Peninsula ▲ **RI** 114 Rh47
Wandammen / Wondiwoi Mountains Reserve ✪ **RI** 114 Rh47
Wanda Shan ▲ **CHN** 76 Rf23
Wandering ◻ **AUS** (WA) 104 Qj62
Wanderlândia ◻ **BR** (TO) 200 Hg49
Wando ◻ **PNG** 115 Sa50
Wando ◻ **ROK** 78 Rd28
Wandoan ◻ **AUS** (QLD) 109 Se59
Waneroo ◻ **AUS** (WA) 104 Qh61
Wanesabe ◻ **RI** 96 Qj50
Wang ▲ **PL** 40 Lq40
Wang ◻ **PNG** 116 Sg47
Wangamana ◻ **AUS** (NSW) 109 Sc60
Wanga Mountains ▲ **WAN** 138 Lf42
Wanganui ◻ **NZ** 113 Th65
Wangaratta ◻ **AUS** (VIC) 111 Sd64
Wangary ◻ **AUS** (SA) 110 Rh63
Wangasi-Turu ◻ **GH** 137 Kk41
Wangben ◻ **CHN** (JLN) 76 Rb24
Wangcang ◻ **CHN** (SCH) 72 Qd29
Wang Chan ◻ **THA** 89 Qa39
Wangcheng ◻ **CHN** (HUN) 74 Qg31
Wang Chin ◻ **THA** 87 Pk37
Wang Chomphu ◻ **THA** 88 Qa37
Wangdue Phodrang ◻ **BHT** 86 Pe32
Wangen ◻ **D** 33 Lk43
Wangerooge ◫ **D** 32 Lh37
Wanggamet, Gunung ▲ **RI** 96 Ra51
Wanggao ◻ **CHN** (GZG) 74 Qf33
Wanggar ◻ **RI** 114 Rh47
Wang Hin ◻ **THA** 88 Qa37
Wangi Falls ≋ **AUS** 106 Rf52
Wangiwangi ▲ **RI** 97 Rb48
Wangjiang ◻ **CHN** (AHU) 78 Qj30
Wangkui ◻ **CHN** (HLG) 76 Rd22
Wangmo ◻ **CHN** (GZH) 74 Qd33
Wang Nam Yen ◻ **THA** 89 Qb39
Wang Noi ◻ **THA** 88 Qa38
Wang Nua ◻ **THA** 87 Pk36
Wangon ◻ **RI** 95 Qe49
Wangqing ◻ **CHN** (JLN) 76 Re24
Wang Sam Mo ◻ **THA** 89 Qb37
Wang Saphung ◻ **THA** 88 Qa37
Wang Thong ◻ **THA** 88 Qa37
Wang Wiset ◻ **THA** 88 Pk42
Wang Zhaojun ⌂ **CHN** 72 Qf25
Wangziguan ◻ **CHN** (GSU) 72 Qc29
Wanham ◻ **CDN** (AB) 167 Ea18
Wan Hsa-la ◻ **MYA** 87 Pk35
Wanhuayan ▲ **CHN** 75 Qg33
Wani ◻ **IND** (MHT) 83 Ok35
Wanie-Rukula ◻ **RDC** 141 Mc45
Wanigela ◻ **PNG** 116 Se50
Wanimiyn A.L. ◰ **AUS** 106 Rf53
Wanjarri Nature Reserve ✪ **AUS** 104 Ra59
Wanjiabu ◻ **CHN** (JGX) 75 Qh31
Wankaner ◻ **IND** (GUJ) 82 Of34
Wankawayn ◻ **SP** 145 Nc44
Wan Kongmöng ◻ **MYA** 87 Pk35
Wan Long ◻ **MYA** 87 Pk34
Wanna ◻ **AUS** (WA) 104 Qj57
Wannaska ◻ **USA** (MN) 172 Fc21
Wannian ◻ **CHN** (JGX) 75 Qj31
Wanning ◻ **CHN** (HAN) 75 Qf36
Wanparti ◻ **IND** (APH) 82 Ok37
Wan Pong ◻ **MYA** 87 Pk35
Wanquan ◻ **CHN** (HBI) 73 Qh25
Wanshan Qundao ▲ **CHN** 75 Qh35
Wansheng ◻ **CHN** (CGQ) 74 Qd31
Wansra ◻ **RI** 114 Rh46
Wantage ◻ **GB** 21 Kt39
Wantoat ◻ **PNG** 115 Sd49
Wanuskewin Heritage P. ⌂ **CDN** 169 Eg19
Wan Xian ◻ **CHN** (CGQ) 74 Qe30
Wanyuan ◻ **CHN** (SCH) 72 Qe29
Wanzai ◻ **CHN** (JGX) 75 Qh31
Wapakoneta ◻ **USA** (OH) 173 Fh25
Wapato ◻ **USA** (WA) 168 Dk22
Wapawekka Hills ▲ **CDN** 169 Eh18
Wapella ◻ **CDN** (SK) 172 Ek20
Wapenamanda ◻ **PNG** 115 Sb48
Wapi ◻ **IND** (GUJ) 82 Og35
Wapi Pathum ◻ **THA** 89 Qb38
Waplewo ◻ **PL** 41 Ma37
Wapotih ◻ **RI** 97 Rd47
Waprak ◻ **RI** 114 Rh47
Wapsa Khani ◻ **NEP** 81 Pd32
Wapuli ◻ **GH** 137 La41
Wapumba Island ▲ **PNG** 115 Sb50
Wapweelah ◻ **AUS** (NSW) 109 Sc60
Waqên ◻ **CHN** (SCH) 72 Qb29
Wara ◻ **WAN** 138 Lc40
Warakurna ◻ **AUS** (WA) 103 Re58
Warambif ◻ **PNG** 116 Sg48
Warandab ◻ **ETH** 143 Nc42
Warandji ◻ **DY** 138 Lb40
Warangal ◻ **IND** (APH) 83 Ok36
Warao Indians ☺ **YV** 193 Gk44
Waraseoni ◻ **IND** (MPH) 83 Pa35
Waratah ◻ **AUS** (TAS) 111 Sc66
Wara Wara Mountains ▲ **WAL** 136 Ke41
Warbreccan ◻ **AUS** (QLD) 108 Sb58
Warburg ◻ **D** 32 Lk39
Warburton ◻ **AUS** (WA) 105 Rd59
Warburton A.L. ◰ **AUS** 105 Rd59
Warburton Range ▲ **AUS** 105 Rd59
Ward ◻ **NZ** 113 Th66
Wardang Islands ✪ **AUS** 110 Rj63
Wardé ◻ **RMM** 131 Kg38
Warden ◻ **ZA** 155 Me59
Wardenburg ◻ **D** 32 Lj37
Warder ◻ **ETH** 143 Nc42
Wardha ◻ **IND** (MHT) 83 Ok35
Wardo ◻ **RI** 114 Rh46
Ware ◻ **CDN** (BC) 166 Dh17
Ware ◻ **USA** (MA) 177 Gd24
Waregem ◻ **B** 23 Ld40
Warego Mine ◻ **AUS** (NT) 106 Rh55
Wareham ◻ **GB** 21 Ks40
Waremme ◻ **B** 23 Lf40
Waren ◻ **D** 32 Ln37
Waren ◻ **RI** 114 Rj47
Warenbayne ◻ **AUS** (QLD) 109 Sf59
Warenda ◻ **AUS** (QLD) 108 Sa57
Warendorf ◻ **D** 32 Lj39
Wargaadhi ◻ **SP** 145 Nd44
War Galon ◻ **SP** 143 Nd42
Warialda ◻ **AUS** (NSW) 109 Sf60
Wari Godri ◻ **IND** (MHT) 82 Oh36
Warilau ▲ **RI** 114 Rh48
Warin Chamrap ◻ **THA** 89 Qc38
Waring Mountains ▲ **USA** (AK) 165 Ca12
Waritchaphum ◻ **THA** 89 Qb37
Warka ◻ **PL** 41 Mb39
Warkopi ◻ **RI** 114 Rh46
Warkworth ◻ **NZ** 112 Th64
Warlubie ◻ **PL** 40 Lt37
Warman ◻ **CDN** (SK) 169 Eg19
Warmandi ◻ **RI** 114 Rg46
Warmbad ◻ ⌂ ✉ **NAM** 154 Lk60
Warmbad Hot Springs ✪ **NAM** 154 Lk60
Warmbad Warmwaterbronne ✪ **NAM** 154 Lk60
Warm Baths ◻ ▲ ✪ **ZA** 155 Me58
War Memorial ⌂ **NAM** 150 Lj55
Warmfontein ◻ **NAM** 154 Lk59
Warminster ◻ **GB** 21 Ks39
Warmquelle ◻ **NAM** 150 Lg55
Warmquelle Hot Springs ✪ **NAM** 150 Lg55
Warm Springs ◻ **USA** (NV) 170 Eb26
Warm Springs ◻ **USA** (OR) 168 Dk23
Warm Springs ◻ **USA** (VA) 177 Ga26
Warm Springs Ind. Res. ◰ **USA** 168 Dk23
Warnemünde ◻ ≈ **D** 32 Ln36
Warner ◻ **CDN** (AB) 169 Ed21
Warner Bros.Park ✪ **E** 27 Kr50
Warner Range ▲ **USA** 170 Ea25
Warner Robins ◻ **USA** (GA) 178 Fj29
Warnes ◻ **BOL** 206 Gj54
Warnes ◻ **RA** (BA) 209 Gk63
Warnice ◻ **PL** 40 Lp38
Warning, Mount ▲ **AUS** 109 Sg60
Warooka ◻ **AUS** (SA) 110 Rj63
Waroona ◻ **AUS** (WA) 104 Qh62
Waropko ◻ **RI** 115 Sa48
Warora ◻ **IND** (MHT) 83 Ok35
Warra ◻ **AUS** (QLD) 109 Sf59
Warracknabeal ◻ **AUS** (VIC) 110 Sb64
Warragul ◻ **AUS** (VIC) 111 Sc65
Warramboo ◻ **AUS** (SA) 110 Rh62
Warrego Highway ⊟ **AUS** 109 Se59
Warrego River ≈ **AUS** 109 Sc59
Warren ◻ **AUS** (NSW) 109 Sd61
Warren ◻ **CDN** (MB) 172 Fb20
Warren ◻ **USA** (AR) 175 Fd29
Warren ◻ **USA** (MI) 173 Fj24
Warren ◻ **USA** (MN) 172 Fb21
Warren ◻ **USA** (MT) 169 Ef23
Warren ◻ **USA** (OH) 173 Fk25
Warren ◻ **USA** (PA) 173 Ga25
Warrensburg ◻ **USA** (MO) 174 Fd26
Warrensburg ◻ **USA** (NY) 177 Gd24
Warrenton ◻ **USA** (GA) 178 Fj29
Warrenton ◻ **USA** (NC) 178 Ga27
Warrenton ◻ **USA** (VA) 177 Gb26
Warrenton ◻ **USA** (WA) 168 Dj22
Warrenton ◻ **ZA** 155 Mc60
Warren Vale ◻ **AUS** (QLD) 107 Sa55
Warri ◻ **WAN** 138 Lc43
Warriedar ◻ **AUS** (WA) 104 Qj60
Warriedar Hill ▲ **AUS** 104 Qj60
Warrington ◻ **GB** 21 Ks37
Warrinilla ◻ **AUS** (QLD) 109 Se58
Warrior ◻ **USA** (AL) 175 Fg29
Warrior Reefs ▲ **AUS** 107 Sb50
Warrnambool ◻ ▲ **AUS** (VIC) 110 Sb65
Warroad ◻ **USA** (MN) 172 Fc21
Warroora ◻ **AUS** (WA) 104 Qg57
Warrumbungle N.P. ✪ ▲ **AUS** 109 Se61
Warsa ◻ **RI** 114 Rh46
Warsaj ◻ **AFG** 63 Oe27
Warsaw ● ☐ ▲ **PL** 41 Ma38
Warsaw ◻ **USA** (IN) 173 Fh25
Warsaw ◻ **USA** (NY) 173 Ga24
Warsaw ◻ **USA** (VA) 177 Gb27
Warshi ◻ **IND** (MHT) 82 Oj36
Warshiikh ◻ **SP** 145 Nc44
Warstein ◻ **D** 32 Lj39
Warszawa ● ☐ ▲ **PL** 41 Ma38
Warszkowo ◻ **PL** 40 Lr36
Wart ◻ **LB** 136 Ke42
Warta ◻ **PL** 41 Lt39
Wartan ◻ **AUS** (QLD) 107 Sb55
Wartburg ☐ ⌂ **D** 32 Ll40
Wartburg ◻ **USA** (TN) 175 Fh27
Wartburton ◻ **ZA** 155 Mf59
Wartkowice ◻ **PL** 41 Lu39
Waru ◻ **RI** 95 Qj46
Waru ◻ **RI** 97 Rf47
Waru ▲ **RI** 97 Rf49
Warud ◻ **IND** (MHT) 83 Ok35
Waruga Stone Graves ⌂ **RI** 91 Rc45
Warumungu A.L. ◰ **AUS** 106 Rh55
Warwick ◻ **AUS** (QLD) 109 Sg60
Warwick ◻ ⌂ **GB** 21 Kt38
Warwick Channel ≈ **AUS** 106 Rj52
Warwick Downs ◻ **AUS** (QLD) 108 Rk56
Wasa ◻ **ANT** (S) 6 Kb33
Wasaga Beach ◻ **CDN** (ON) 173 Fk23
Wasagaming ◻ **CDN** (MB) 172 Fa20
Wasagu ◻ **WAN** 138 Lc40
Wasalandia ✪ **FIN** 38 Mb27
Wasatch Range ▲ **USA** 171 Ee25
Wasco ◻ **USA** (CA) 170 Ea28
Wasco ◻ **USA** (OR) 168 Dk23
Wase ◻ **WAN** 138 Le41
Waseca ◻ **USA** (MN) 172 Fd23
Washakie Needles ▲ **USA** 169 Ef24
Washap ◻ **PK** 65 Ob32
Washaung ◻ **MYA** 86 Pj33
Washburn ◻ **USA** (ND) 172 Ek22
Washim ◻ **IND** (MHT) 82 Oj35
Washington ◻ **GB** 21 Kt36
Washington ◻ **USA** (AR) 174 Fd29
Washington ◻ **USA** (GA) 178 Fj29
Washington ◻ **USA** (IL) 175 Ff25
Washington ◻ **USA** (IN) 175 Fg26
Washington ◻ **USA** (KS) 174 Fb26
Washington ◻ **USA** (MO) 172 Fe25
Washington ◻ **USA** (MO) 175 Fe26
Washington ◻ **USA** (NC) 178 Gb28
Washington ◻ **USA** (NJ) 177 Gc25
Washington ◻ **USA** (PA) 173 Fk25
Washington ◻ **USA** (UT) 171 Ed27
Washington ◻ **USA** (VA) 177 Ga26
Washington ▣ **USA** 168 Dk22
Washington Court House ◻ **USA** (OH) 175 Fj26
Washington D.C. ● ⌂ ⌂ **USA** (DC) 177 Gb26
Washington-Slagbaai N.P. ✪ ✪ **NL** 193 Gf39
Washita N.W.R. ✪ **USA** 174 Fa28
Washpool N.P. ☐ ✪ **AUS** 109 Sg60
Washpool Ranges ☐ ✪ **AUS** 109 Sg60
Washtucna ◻ **USA** (WA) 168 Ea22
Washuk ◻ **PK** 65 Oc32
Wasian ◻ **RI** 114 Rg46
Wasi Falls ≋ **PNG** 115 Sb49
Wasile ◻ **RI** 91 Rd45
Wasilków ◻ **PL** 41 Md37
Wasilla ◻ **USA** (AK) 165 Cf15
Wasimi ◻ **WAN** 138 Lb42
Wasir ▲ **RI** 114 Rh48
Wasit ⌂ **IRQ** 59 Nd29
Wasit ◻ **KSA** 60 Nd34
Wasjabo ◻ **SME** 194 Hb43
Waskaganish = Fort Rupert ◻ **CDN** (QC) 173 Ga20
Waskesiu Lake ◻ **CDN** (SK) 169 Eg19
Wasletan ◻ **RI** 97 Rf49
Wąsosz ◻ **PL** 40 Lr39
Wąsosz ◻ **PL** 40 Ls38
Waspan ◻ **HN** 185 Fh38
Wassadou ◻ **SN** 136 Kc39
Wassamu ◻ **J** 77 Sb23
Wassatch Plateau ▲ **USA** 171 Ee26
Wassaw N.W.R. ✪ **USA** 178 Fk30
Wassenaar ◻ **NL** 23 Le38
Wasser ◻ **NAM** 154 Lk59
Wasserburg ◻ ▲ **D** 33 Ln42
Wasserkuppe ▲ **D** 33 Lk40
Wasserschloss Glücksburg ⌂ **D** 32 Lk36
Wassou ◻ **RG** 136 Kd40
Wassu ◻ **WAG** 136 Kc39
Wassu-Cocal, T.I. ☺ **BR** 201 Jc50
Wassy ◻ **F** 23 Le42
Wasu ◻ **PNG** 115 Sd49
Wasua ◻ **PNG** 115 Sb50
Wasur N.P. ✪ ✪ **RI** 115 Sa50
Waswanipi Ind. Res. ◰ **CDN** 176 Gc21
Watalgan ◻ **AUS** (QLD) 109 Sg58
Watam ◻ **PNG** 115 Sc49
Watam ◻ **RI** 91 Re45
Watambayoli ◻ **RI** 96 Ra46
Watampone ◻ **RI** 96 Ra48
Watamu Marine N.P. ✪ ≈ **EAK** 145 Na47
Wat Analayo ▲ **THA** 87 Qa36
Watarais ◻ **PNG** 115 Sd49
Watarrka N.P. ✪ **AUS** 103 Rf58
Watawa ◻ **RI** 97 Rd47
Wat Chang Hai ▲ **THA** 89 Qa42
Watee ◻ **SOL** 117 Tb51
Waterberg ▲ **ZA** 155 Md58
Waterbergplateau ✪ ⌂ **NAM** 150 Lj56
Waterberg Plateau Park ✪ ✪ **NAM** 150 Lj56
Waterbury ◻ **USA** (CT) 177 Gd25
Waterbury ◻ **USA** (VT) 177 Gd23
Water Cay ◻ **BS** 179 Ga32
Water Cay ▲ **BS** 186 Gc34
Waterfall (Changbai Shan) ≋ **CHN/PRK** 76 Rd25
Waterford ◻ **AUS** (QLD) 108 Rk57
Waterford ◻ **IRL** 19 Kn38
Waterford ◻ **ZA** 155 Mc62
Waterford Harbour ≈ **IRL** 19 Ko38
Waterhen ◻ **CDN** (MB) 172 Fa20
Waterhen Ind. Res. ◰ **CDN** 172 Fa20
Waterloo ◻ ✉ **B** 23 Le40
Waterloo ◻ **SME** 194 Hb43
Waterloo ◻ **USA** (IA) 172 Fd24
Waterloo ◻ **USA** (IL) 175 Fe26
Waterloo ◻ **WAL** 136 Kd41
Watermeule ⌂ **ZA** 154 Mb62
Water Mill ⌂ **ZA** 154 Mb62
Waterpoort ◻ **ZA** 152 Me57
Watersmeet ◻ **USA** (MI) 172 Ff22
Waterton Lakes N.P. ✪ **CDN** 168 Ec21
Waterton Park ◻ **CDN** (AB) 169 Ed21
Watertown ◻ **USA** (NY) 177 Gc24
Watertown ◻ **USA** (SD) 172 Fb23
Watertown ◻ **USA** (WI) 173 Ff24
Waterval-Boven ◻ **ZA** 155 Mf58
Water Valley ◻ **USA** (MS) 175 Ff28
Waterville ◻ **IRL** 19 Kk39
Waterville ◻ **USA** (MA) 177 Gf23
Wates ◻ **RI** 95 Qf49
Watford ◻ **GB** 21 Ku39
Watford City ◻ **USA** (ND) 169 Ej22
Watheroo ◻ **AUS** (WA) 104 Qj61
Watheroo N.P. ✪ **AUS** 104 Qh61
Watino ◻ **CDN** (AB) 167 Eb18
Wat Khuhaphimuk ▲ **THA** 89 Qa42
Watkins Glen ◻ **USA** (NY) 177 Gb24
Wat Luang Temple ▲ **LAO** 89 Qc38
Watmuri ◻ **RI** 97 Rf49
Watom Island ✪ ✪ **PNG** 116 Sg48
Watonga ◻ **USA** (OK) 174 Fa28
Wat Photivihan ▲ **MAL** 92 Qb42
Wat Phra Borom That ▲ **THA** 88 Pk37
Wat Phra Si Rattana Mahathat ▲ **THA** 88 Qa37
Wat Phra Sri Rattana Mahathat (Lop Buri) ▲ **THA** 88 Qa38
Wat Phrathat Chohae ▲ **THA** 87 Qa36
Wat Phra That Phanom ⌂ **THA** 89 Qc37
Wat Phra Thra That Sop Waen ▲ **THA** 87 Qa36
Wat Phrayuen Buddhabahtyukol ▲ **THA** 88 Qa37
Wat Phu Dan Tae ▲ **THA** 89 Qc37
Wat Phu Temple ☐ ▲ **LAO** 89 Qc38
Watpi ◻ **PNG** 116 Sg48
Wat Pra That Lampang Luang ▲ **THA** 87 Pk36
Watrous ◻ **CDN** (SK) 169 Eh20
Wat Sa Kamphaeng ▲ **THA** 89 Qc38
Watseka ◻ **USA** (IL) 173 Fg25
Watsi ◻ **RDC** 149 Ma46
Watsi Kengo ◻ **RDC** 149 Ma46
Watsomba ◻ **ZW** 152 Mg55
Watson ◻ **AUS** (SA) 105 Rf61
Watson ◻ **CDN** (SK) 169 Eh19
Watson ◻ **USA** (AR) 175 Fe29
Watson Lake ◻ **CDN** (YT) 166 Df15
Watsonville ◻ **USA** (CA) 170 Dk27
Wat Sothon Wararam Woravihan ▲ **THA** 88 Qa39
Wat Suwan Khuha ▲ **THA** 88 Pk41
Wattangsoppeng ◻ **RI** 96 Ra48
Wattegama ◻ **CL** 85 Pa42
Wattens ◻ **A** 34 Lm43
Wat Tham Mankhon ▲ **THA** 88 Pk39
Watthana Nakhon ◻ **THA** 89 Qb39
Wattwil ◻ **CH** 34 Lk43
Wat Udom ✪ **THA** 89 Qb37
Watutau ◻ **RI** 96 Ra46
Wat Xieng Thong ▲ **LAO** 87 Qb36
Wat Yan Sangwararam ▲ **THA** 88 Qa39
Watzmann ▲ **D** 33 Ln43
Watzmann ▲ **I** 34 Ln44
Wau ◻ **PNG** 115 Sd49
Wau ◻ **RI** 114 Rg46
Wau ◻ **SUD** 141 Md42
Waubay N.W.R. ✪ **USA** 172 Fb23
Wauchope ◻ **AUS** (NSW) 109 Sg61
Wauchope ◻ **AUS** (NT) 106 Rh56
Wauchula ◻ **USA** (FL) 179 Fk32
Waukaringa ◻ **AUS** (SA) 110 Rk62
Waukegan ◻ **USA** (IL) 173 Ff24
Waukegan ◻ ✪ **USA** (IL) 173 Fg24
Waukesha ◻ **USA** (WI) 173 Ff24
Waupaca ◻ **USA** (WI) 173 Ff23
Waupun ◻ **USA** (WI) 173 Ff24
Waurika ◻ **USA** (OK) 174 Fb28
Wausau ◻ **USA** (WI) 172 Ff23
Wausaukee ◻ **USA** (WI) 173 Ff23
Wautoma ◻ **USA** (WI) 173 Ff23
Wauwatosa ◻ **USA** (WI) 173 Ff24
Waveland ◻ **USA** (MS) 175 Ff30
Waverly ◻ **USA** (IA) 172 Fd24
Waverly ◻ **USA** (NE) 174 Fb25
Waverly ◻ **USA** (TN) 175 Fg27
Waverly Downs ◻ **AUS** (NSW) 109 Sb60
Waverly Plantation ⌂ **USA** 175 Ff29
Wave Rock ▲ **AUS** 104 Qk62
Waves ◻ **USA** (NC) 178 Gc28
Waves ◻ ▲ ✪ **USA** 178 Gc28
Wavre ◻ **B** 23 Le40
Wawa ◻ **CDN** (ON) 173 Fh22
Wawa ◻ **SUD** 135 Mf35
Wawa ◻ **WAN** 138 Lc41
Waw al Kabir ◻ **LAR** 127 Lj33
Waw al Namus ▲ **LAR** 133 Lj33
Wawanesa ◻ **CDN** (MB) 172 Fa21
Wawel ⌂ **PL** 41 Lu40
Wawiawga = Kudoni ◻ **GH** 137 La40
Wawi, T.I. ☺ **BR** 199 Hd51
Wawo ◻ **RI** 96 Ra47
Wawotobi ◻ **RI** 96 Rb47
Waxahachie ◻ **USA** (TX) 174 Fb29
Waxxari ◻ **CHN** (XUZ) 68 Pd26
Waya ▲ **FJI** 119 Tj54
Wayam ▲ **RI** 97 Rf45
Wayao ◻ **CHN** (YUN) 87 Pk33
Waycross ◻ **USA** (GA) 178 Fj30
Wayerton ◻ **CDN** (NB) 176 Gh22
Waykadai ◻ **RI** 97 Rc46
Way Kambas National Park ✪ **RI** 93 Qc48
Waykilo ◻ **RI** 97 Rc46
Wayne ◻ **USA** (NE) 172 Fb24
Wayne ◻ **USA** (WV) 175 Fj26
Waynesboro ◻ **USA** (GA) 178 Fk29
Waynesboro ◻ **USA** (MS) 175 Ff30
Waynesboro ◻ **USA** (PA) 177 Gb26
Waynesboro ◻ **USA** (TN) 175 Fg28
Waynesboro ◻ **USA** (VA) 177 Ga26
Waynesburg ◻ **USA** (PA) 173 Fk26
Waynesville ◻ **USA** (MO) 174 Fd27
Waynesville ◻ **USA** (NC) 178 Fj28
Waynoka ◻ **USA** (OK) 174 Fa27
Wayongon ◻ **MYA** 86 Ph34
Wayu ◻ **EAK** 145 Mk46
Waza ◻ **CAM** 139 Lh40
Wazah ◻ **AFG** 65 Oe29
Waza, P.N.de ✪ ✪ **CAM** 139 Lh40
Wazin ◻ **LAR** 126 Lf30
Wazirabad ◻ **PK** 65 Oh29
W du Niger, P.N.du ■ ✪ **DY** 138 Lb39
We ◻ **CAM** 138 Lf42
Wé ◻ **F** (NCL) 118 Td56
Weam ◻ **PNG** 115 Sa50
Weano Gorge ▲ **AUS** 102 Qk57
Wearhead ◻ **GB** 21 Ks36
Weatherford ◻ **USA** (OK) 174 Fa28
Weatherford ◻ **USA** (TX) 174 Fb29
Weaverville ◻ **USA** (CA) 170 Dj25
Weber ◻ **NZ** 113 Tj66
Weber Basin ≈ **RI** 97 Re49
Webi Shebele ≈ **SP** 145 Nb45
Webster ◻ **USA** (SD) 172 Fb23
Webster ◻ **USA** (WV) 175 Fk26
Webster City ◻ **USA** (IA) 172 Fd24
Webuye ◻ **EAK** 144 Mh45
Wechadłów ◻ **PL** 41 Ma40
Wechecha, Mount ▲ **ETH** 142 Mk41
Wechselburg ⌂ **D** 32 Ln40
Weddell Island ▲ **GB** 210 Gk71
Weddell Sea ≈ **ANT** 6 Hb33
Wedderburn ◻ **AUS** (VIC) 111 Sb64
Wedel ◻ **D** 32 Lk37
Wedel-Jarisberg-Land ▲ **N** 16 Lh07
Wednesday Island ▲ **AUS** 107 Sb51
Wedowee ◻ **USA** (AL) 175 Fh29
Wedweil ◻ **SUD** 141 Md41
Weebo ◻ **AUS** (WA) 104 Ra60
Weed ◻ **USA** (CA) 168 Dj25
Weedarrah ◻ **AUS** (WA) 104 Qh58
Weeim ▲ **RI** 97 Rf46
Weeki Wachee ✪ **USA** 179 Fj31
Weemelah ◻ **AUS** (NSW) 109 Se60
Weenen ◻ **ZA** 155 Mf60
Weenen Nature Reserve ✪ **ZA** 155 Mf60
Weener ◻ **D** 32 Lh37
Weert ◻ **NL** 23 Lf39
Weethalle ◻ **AUS** (NSW) 111 Sd62
Wee Waa ◻ **AUS** (NSW) 109 Se61
Wegdraai ◻ **ZA** 154 Ma60
Węgliniec ◻ **PL** 40 Lq39
Węgorzewo ◻ ⌂ **PL** 41 Mb36
Węgorzyno ◻ **PL** 40 Lq37
Węgrów ◻ **PL** 41 Mc38
Weh ▲ **RI** 92 Ph43
Wehni ◻ **ETH** 142 Mj39
Weichang ◻ **CHN** (HBI) 73 Qj25
Weida ◻ **D** 33 Ln40
Weiden ◻ **D** 33 Ln41
Weifang ◻ **CHN** (SDG) 73 Qk27
Weihai ◻ **CHN** (SDG) 73 Rb27
Weihe ◻ **CHN** (HLG) 76 Re23
Weihui ◻ **CHN** (HNN) 73 Qh28
Weikersheim ◻ **D** 33 Lk41
Weil am Rhein ◻ **D** 33 Lh43
Weilburg ◻ **D** 33 Lj40
Weilheim ◻ **D** 33 Lm43
Weilmoringle ◻ **AUS** (NSW) 109 Sd60
Weimar ◻ **D** 32 Lm40
Weinan ◻ **CHN** (SAA) 72 Qe28
Weingarten ◻ **D** 33 Lk43
Weinheim ◻ **D** 33 Lj41
Weining ◻ **CHN** (GZH) 87 Qc32
Weinviertel ▲ **A** 42 Lr42
Weipa ◻ **AUS** (QLD) 107 Sa52
Weipa South ◻ **AUS** (QLD) 107 Sa52
Weirton ◻ **USA** (WV) 173 Fk25
Weiser ◻ **USA** (ID) 168 Eb23
Weishan ◻ **CHN** (SDG) 78 Qj28
Weishan Yizu ◻ **CHN** (YUN) 87 Qa33
Weishi ◻ **CHN** (HNN) 73 Qh28
Weiße Elster ≈ **D** 32 Ln39
Weißenburg ◻ **D** 33 Ll41
Weißenfels ◻ **D** 32 Lm39
Weißenhorn ◻ **D** 33 Ll42
Weißensee ≈ **A** 35 Lo44
Weißwasser ◻ **D** 32 Lp39
Weitchpec ◻ **USA** (CA) 168 Dj25
Weitou ◻ **CHN** (FJN) 75 Qk33
Weitra ◻ **A** 42 Lp42
Weixi ◻ **CHN** (YUN) 87 Pk32
Wei Xian ◻ **CHN** (HBI) 73 Qh27
Weixin ◻ **CHN** (YUN) 87 Qc32
Weiya ◻ **CHN** (XUZ) 67 Ph25
Weiyuan ◻ **CHN** (GSU) 72 Qc28
Weiyuan ◻ **CHN** (SCH) 74 Qc31
Weiz ◻ **A** 35 Lq43
Weizhou Dao ▲ **CHN** 74 Qe35
Wejherowo ◻ **PL** 40 Lt36
Weko ◻ **RDC** 141 Mc45
Wekusko ◻ **CDN** (MB) 169 Fa18
Wekweti = Snare Lakes ◻ **CDN** 167 Ec13
Welab ◻ **RI** 114 Rk50
Welatam ◻ **MYA** 87 Pk32
Welbourn Hill ◻ **AUS** (SA) 108 Rh59
Welch ◻ **USA** (TX) 174 Ej29
Welch ◻ **USA** (WV) 178 Fk27
Weldiya ◻ **ETH** 142 Mk40
Weld Range ▲ **AUS** 104 Qj59
Welenchiti ◻ **ETH** 142 Mk41
Weleri ◻ **RI** 95 Qf49
Welford N.P. ✪ ✪ **AUS** 108 Sb58
Weligama ◻ **CL** 85 Pa43
Welirang, Gunung ▲ **RI** 95 Qg49
Wel Jara ◻ **EAK** 145 Na46
Welkite ◻ **ETH** 142 Mj41
Welkom ◻ ✪ **ZA** 155 Md59
Wellawaya ◻ **CL** 85 Pa42
Wellesley Basin ▲ **CDN** 165 Da14
Wellesley Islands ▲ **AUS** (QLD) 107 Rk54
Wellingborough ◻ **GB** 21 Ku38
Wellington ◻ **AUS** (NSW) 111 Se62
Wellington ◻ **GB** 21 Kr40
Wellington ● ✪ ✪ **NZ** 113 Th66
Wellington ◻ **USA** (CO) 171 Eh25
Wellington ◻ **USA** (KS) 174 Fb27
Wellington ◻ **USA** (TX) 174 Ek28
Wellington ◻ **USA** (UT) 171 Ee26
Wellington ◻ **WAL** 136 Kd41
Wellington ◻ **ZA** 154 Lk62
Wellington Caves ▲ **AUS** 111 Se62
Wellington Channel ≈ **CDN** 163 Fb03
Wells ◻ ⌂ **GB** 21 Ks39
Wells ◻ **USA** (NV) 171 Ec25
Wellsboro ◻ **USA** (PA) 177 Gb25
Wellsford ◻ **NZ** 112 Th64
Wells Gray Prov. Park ✪ ≋ ✪ **CDN** 168 Dk19
Wells, Mount ▲ **AUS** 103 Rd54
Wells-next-the-Sea ◻ **GB** 21 La38
Wellsville ◻ **USA** (NY) 177 Gb24
Wels ◻ ▲ **A** 42 Lp42
Welsford ◻ **CDN** (NB) 176 Gg23
Welshpool ◻ **GB** 21 Kr38
Welski Park Krajobrazowy ✪ **PL** 41 Lu37
Welton ◻ **USA** (AZ) 171 Ed29
Welutu ◻ **RI** 97 Rf49
Welver ◻ **D** 32 Lh39
Welwel ◻ **ETH** 143 Nc42
Welwitschia Plain ✪ **NAM** 150 Lh57
Welzheim ◻ **D** 33 Lk42
Wema ◻ **RDC** 149 Ma46
Wemyss Bay ◻ **GB** 20 Kq35
Wen ◻ **SUD** 141 Md41
Wenago ◻ **ETH** 142 Mk42
Wenatchee ◻ **USA** (WA) 168 Dk22
Wenatchee Mtns. ▲ **USA** 168 Dk22
Wenceslau Bráz ◻ **BR** (PR) 205 Hf57
Wenchang ◻ **CHN** (HAN) 75 Qf36
Wenchang ◻ **CHN** (SCH) 72 Qd30
Wencheng ◻ **CHN** (ZJG) 75 Ra32
Wenchi ◻ **GH** 137 Kj42
Wenchuan ◻ **CHN** (SCH) 72 Qb30
Wenden ◻ **USA** (AZ) 171 Ed29
Wendeng ◻ **CHN** (SDG) 73 Rb27
Wendo ◻ **ETH** 142 Mk42
Wendo Genet Hot Springs ✪ **ETH** 142 Mk42
Wéndou-Mbôrou ◻ **RG** 136 Kd40
Wendover ◻ **GB** 21 Ku39
Wendover ◻ **USA** (UT) 171 Ed25
Wenfang ▲ **CHN** 73 Qh27
Wenga ◻ **RDC** 140 Lk45
Weng'an ◻ **CHN** (GZH) 74 Qd32
Wenge ◻ **RDC** 141 Mc45
Wengen ◻ ✪ **CH** 34 Lh44
Wenje ◻ **EAK** 145 Na46
Wenling ◻ **CHN** (ZJG) 75 Ra31
Wenlock ◻ **AUS** (QLD) 107 Sb52
Wen Miao ⌂ **CHN** 74 Qf33
Wenou ◻ **DY** 138 Lb41
Wenquan ◻ **CHN** (QHI) 69 Pk28
Wenquan ◻ **CHN** (XUZ) 66 Pa23
Wenquanzhen ◻ **CHN** (HUB) 75 Qh31
Wenshan ◻ **CHN** (YUN) 87 Qc34
Wen Shang ◻ **CHN** (SDG) 78 Qj28
Wenshui ◻ **CHN** (SAX) 72 Qg27
Wentworth ◻ **AUS** (NSW) 110 Sa63
Wentworth ◻ **CDN** (NS) 176 Gj23
Wentworth Falls ◻ ≋ **AUS** (NSW) 111 Sf62
Wenxi ◻ **CHN** (SAX) 72 Qf28
Wen Xian ◻ **CHN** (GSU) 72 Qc29
Wenzhen ◻ **CHN** (JGX) 75 Qj31
Wenzhou ◻ **CHN** (ZJG) 75 Ra32
Weott ◻ **USA** (CA) 170 Dj25
Wepener ◻ **ZA** 155 Md60
Wequan ◻ **CHN** (QHI) 69 Pf29
Wera ◻ **EAU** 144 Mg45
Weragantota ◻ **CL** 85 Pa42
Werda ◻ **RB** 154 Mb58
Werdau ◻ **D** 32 Ln40
Werdohl ◻ **D** 32 Lh39
Were Ilu ◻ **ETH** 142 Mk40
Wêreldend ◻ **ZA** 154 Ma58
Werinama ◻ **RI** 97 Re47
Weringa Downs ◻ **AUS** (QLD) 109 Se59
Werl ◻ **D** 32 Lh39
Werneck ◻ **D** 33 Ll41
Werner Lake ◻ **CDN** (ON) 172 Fc20
Wernigerode ◻ ▲ **D** 32 Ll39
Wer Ping ◻ **SUD** 141 Me41
Werra ≈ **D** 32 Lk39
Werribee ◻ **AUS** (VIC) 111 Sc64
Werri Creek ◻ **AUS** (NSW) 109 Sf61
Werrikimbe N.P. ☐ ✪ **AUS** (NSW) 109 Sg61
Wertheim ◻ **D** 33 Lk41
Werther ◻ **D** 32 Lj39
Werwaru ◻ **RI** 97 Re50
Wesel ◻ **D** 32 Lg39
Weser ≈ **D** 32 Lk39
Weserbergland ▲ **D** 32 Lk39
Weskus N.P. ✪ ✪ **ZA** 154 Lk62
Wesley ◻ **USA** (ME) 176 Gg23
Wesleyville ◻ **CDN** (NF) 177 Hd21
Wesoła ◻ **PL** 41 Mb38
Wessel Islands ▲ **AUS** 106 Rj51
Wesselsbron ◻ **ZA** 155 Md59
Wessington Springs ◻ **USA** (SD) 172 Fa23
West Antarctica ▲ **ANT** 6 Ec34
West Bank ▣ **IL** 58 Mh30
West Bay ◻ **GB** (CI) 179 Fk36
West Bend ◻ **CDN** (SK) 169 Ej20
West Bend ◻ **USA** (WI) 173 Ff24
West Bengal ▣ **IND** 83 Pd34
Westbourne ◻ **CDN** (MB) 172 Fa20
West Branch ◻ **USA** (MI) 173 Fh23
West Breaker ▲ **CO** 185 Ga38
Westbrook ◻ **USA** (ME) 177 Ge24
West Burra ▲ **GB** 20 Kt30
Westbury ◻ **AUS** (QLD) 109 Sc57
Westbury ◻ **GB** 21 Ks39
Westby ◻ **USA** (MT) 169 Eh21
West Caicos ▲ **GB** 186 Gd35
West Caroline Basin ≈ 100 Rb09
Westcliffe ◻ **USA** (CO) 171 Eh26
West Coast N.P. ✪ ✪ **ZA** 154 Lk62
West Des Moines ◻ **USA** (IA) 172 Fd25
West End ◻ **BS** 179 Ga32
West End ◻ **GB** (CI) 179 Ga36
West End ◻ **HN** 184 Fg37
Westerberg ◻ **ZA** 154 Mb60
Westerhever Leuchtturm ⌂ **D** 32 Lj36
Westerland ◻ ✪ ✪ **D** 32 Lj36
Westerly ◻ **USA** (RI) 177 Ge25
Western Australia ▣ **AUS** 101 Qb12
Western Cape ▣ **ZA** 154 Ma62
Western Caucasus ■ ▲ **RUS** 49 Mk23
Western Desert ✪ **ET** 128 Md31
Western Desert A.L. ◰ **AUS** 103 Re55
Western Dev. Mus. (Denholm) ⌂ **CDN** 169 Eg19
Western Dev. Mus. (Moose Jaw) ⌂ **CDN** 169 Eh20
Western Dev. Mus. (Saskatoon) ⌂ **CDN** 169 Eg19
Western Entrance ≈ **PNG/SOL** 117 Sh49
Western Ghats ▲ **IND** 52 Ob08
Western Hajar ▲ **OM** 61 Nj33
Western Highway ⊟ **AUS** 111 Sb64
Western Island ▲ **PNG** 115 Sc47
Western Port ≈ **AUS** (VIC) 111 Sc65
Western Qing Tombs = Qing Xiling ⌂ **CHN** (HBI) 73 Qh26
Western Sahara ▣ **MA/DARS** 124 Kd33
Western Sayan Mountains ▲ **RUS** 54 Pc08
Western Tannu-Ola Range ▲ **RUS** 67 Pf20
Western Thebes ☐ ✪ **ET** 129 Mg33
Westerschelde ≈ **NL** 23 Ld39
Westerstede ◻ **D** 32 Lh37
Westerville ◻ **USA** (OH) 173 Fj25
Westerwald ▲ **D** 32 Lh40
West European Basin ≈ 8 Ka05
West Falkland ▲ **GB** 210 Gk71
West Fargo ◻ **USA** (ND) 172 Fb22
Westfield ◻ **USA** (IN) 175 Fg25
Westfield ◻ **USA** (NY) 173 Ga24
Westfriesland ▲ **NL** 23 Le38
West Frisian Islands ≈ **NL** 23 Le37
Westgate ◻ **AUS** (QLD) 109 Sd59
Westgate ◻ **CDN** (MB) 169 Ek19
West Glacier ◻ **USA** (MT) 168 Ec21
West Group ▲ **AUS** 105 Ra63
West Ice Shelf ≈ 7 Pa32
West Island ▲ **AUS** 106 Rj53
Westland N.P. ☐ ✪ ✪ **NZ** 113 Te67
Westlea ◻ **AUS** (QLD) 109 Sc60
West Liberty ◻ **USA** (KY) 178 Fj27
Westlock ◻ **CDN** (AB) 167 Ed18
West Lunga N.P. ✪ ✪ **Z** 151 Mc52
West Macdonnell N.P. ✪ ✪ ✪ **AUS** 103 Rg57
Westmar ◻ **AUS** (QLD) 109 Se59
West Mariana Basin ≈ 100 Rb08
West Memphis ◻ **USA** (AR) 175 Fe28
Westminster ☐ ⌂ **GB** 21 Ku39
Westminster ◻ **USA** (MD) 177 Gb26
Westmoreland ◻ **AUS** (QLD) 106 Rk54
West Nicholson ◻ **ZW** 152 Me56
Weston ◻ **USA** (ID) 169 Ee24
Weston ◻ **USA** (WV) 175 Fk26
Weston ◻ **USA** (WY) 169 Eh23
Weston-super-Mare ◻ **GB** 21 Ks39
West Palm Beach ◻ ✪ **USA** (FL) 179 Fk32
West Plains ◻ **USA** (MO) 175 Fe27
West Point ▲ **AUS** 110 Rh63
West Point ◻ **CDN** (PE) 176 Gh22
Westpoint ◻ **GB** (GBF) 210 Gk71
West Point ◻ **USA** (MS) 175 Ff29
West Point ◻ **USA** (NE) 172 Fb25
West Point ◻ **USA** (VA) 177 Gb27
West Point ▲ **WAN** 138 Le43
West Poplar River ◻ **CDN** (SK) 169 Eg21
Westport ◻ **CDN** (NF) 177 Hb21
Westport ◻ ▲ **IRL** 19 Kl37
Westport ◻ **NZ** 113 Tf66
Westport ◻ **USA** (CA) 170 Dj26
Westport ▲ **USA** (WA) 168 Dh22
Westpunt ◻ **NL** (NA) 193 Gf39
Westray ◻ **CDN** (MB) 169 Ek19
Westray ▲ **GB** 20 Kr31
West Siberian Plain ▲ **RUS** 54 Ob06
West-Terschelling ◻ ✪ **NL** 23 Lf37
West Thumb ◻ **USA** (WY) 169 Ee23
West Travaputs Plateau ▲ **USA** 171 Ee26
West Union ◻ **USA** (IA) 172 Fe24
West Union ◻ **USA** (WV) 175 Fk26
West Valley City ◻ **USA** (UT) 171 Ed25
West Virginia ▣ **USA** 175 Fk26
West Wendover ◻ **USA** (NV) 171 Ec25
Westwood ◻ **AUS** (QLD) 109 Sf57
Westwood ◻ **USA** (CA) 170 Dk25
West Wyalong ◻ **AUS** (NSW) 111 Sd62
West Yellowstone ◻ **USA** (MT) 169 Ee23
Wetan ▲ **RI** 97 Re49
Wetar ▲ **RI** 97 Rd49
Wetaskiwin ◻ **CDN** (AB) 169 Ed19
Wete ◻ **EAT** 147 Mk48
Wete ◻ **RDC** 149 Mc48
Wetherby ◻ **GB** 21 Kt37
Wetlina ◻ **PL** 43 Mc41
Weto ◻ **WAN** 138 Ld42
Wetora ◻ **ETH** 142 Mj40
Wetteren ◻ **B** 23 Ld40
Wettersteingebirge ▲ **A** 34 Lm43
Wet Tropics National Park ■ ✪ **AUS** (QLD) 107 Sc55
Wet Tropics of Queensland ■ ✪ **AUS** (QLD) 107 Sc55
Wetumka ◻ **USA** (OK) 174 Fb28
Wetumpka ◻ **USA** (AL) 175 Fg29
Wetzikon ◻ **CH** 34 Lj43
Wetzlar ◻ **D** 32 Lj40
Wevok ◻ **USA** (AK) 165 Bg11
Wewahitchka ◻ **USA** (FL) 175 Fh30
Wewak ◻ ✪ ✪ **PNG** 115 Sb49
Wewoka ◻ **USA** (OK) 174 Fb28
Wexford ◻ ♫ **IRL** 19 Ko38
Wexford Harbour ≈ **IRL** 19 Ko38
Weyakwin ◻ **CDN** (SK) 169 Eh18
Weybridge ◻ **GB** 21 Ku39
Weyburn ◻ **CDN** (SK) 169 Ej21
Weyer Markt ◻ **A** 35 Lp43
Weyla ◻ **SP** 143 Ne41
Weymouth ◻ **CDN** (NS) 176 Gh23
Weymouth ◻ **GB** 21 Ks40
Whakamaru ◻ **NZ** 113 Th65
Whakapara ◻ **NZ** 112 Th63
Whakatane ◻ **NZ** 112 Tj64
Whale Bay ≈ **MYA** 88 Pk40
Whalebone ◻ **USA** (NC) 178 Gc28
Whale Cay ▲ **BS** 179 Gb33
Whale Sanctuary ■ ≈ ✉ **MEX** 180 Ec31
Whale Valley = Wadi Al-Hitan ■ ✪ **ET** Me30
Whale Watching (Fraser Island) ✉ **AUS** 109 Sg58
Whaley Bridge ◻ **GB** 21 Kt37
Whalsay ▲ **GB** 20 Ku30
Whananaki ▲ **NZ** 112 Th63
Whangamata ◻ ▲ **NZ** 112 Th64
Whanganui N.P. ✪ **NZ** 113 Th65
Whangara ◻ **NZ** 113 Tk65
Whangarei ◻ **NZ** 112 Th63
Wharton ◻ **USA** (TX) 181 Fb31
Wharton, Mount ▲ 7 Ta35
Wha Ti = Lac la Matre ◻ **CDN** 167 Eb14
Wheatland ◻ **USA** (WY) 171 Eh24
Wheaton ◻ **USA** (MN) 172 Fb23
Wheeler ◻ **USA** (TX) 174 Ek28
Wheeler Peak ▲ **USA** 171 Ec26
Wheeling ◻ **USA** (WV) 173 Fk25
Whim Creek ◻ **AUS** (WA) 102 Qj56
Whiskey Trail ⊟ **GB** 20 Ks33
Whitby ◻ **GB** 21 Ku36
Whitchurch ◻ **GB** 21 Ks38
White Bay ≈ **CDN** 177 Hb20
White Bird ◻ **USA** (ID) 168 Eb23
Whitebourne ◻ **CDN** (NF) 177 Hd22
White Cape Mount ▲ **USA** 176 Gf23
White City ◻ **USA** (OR) 168 Dj24
White City (Tel Aviv) ☐ ▲ **IL** 56 Mh29
White Cliff ▲ **BS** 186 Gd34
White Cliffs ◻ **AUS** (NSW) 108 Sb61
White Cliffs ◻ **AUS** (WA) 105 Rb60
White Cloud ◻ **USA** (MI) 173 Fh24
Whitecourt ◻ **CDN** (AB) 167 Ec18
White crowned pigeons ✪ **BS** 179 Gb33
White Desert ✪ ▲ **ET** 129 Me32
Whitedog ◻ **CDN** (ON) 172 Fc20
White Earth Ind. Res. ◰ **USA** 172 Fc22
Whitefish ◻ **USA** (MT) 168 Ec21
Whitefish Bay ≈ **CDN/USA** 173 Fh22
White Hall ◻ **USA** (IL) 175 Fe26
Whitehall ◻ **USA** (MT) 169 Ed23
Whitehall ◻ **USA** (NY) 177 Gd24
Whitehall ◻ **USA** (WI) 172 Fe23
White Hall S.H.S. ⌂ **USA** 175 Fh27
Whitehaven ◻ **GB** 21 Kr36
Whitehorse ◉ **CDN** (YT) 166 Dc15
White Horse ◻ **USA** (NM) 171 Eg28
White Island ▲ **NZ** 112 Tj64
White Lady Painting ✪ **NAM** 150 Lh56
White Lake ◻ **USA** (NC) 178 Ga28
Whitelaw ◻ **CDN** (AB) 167 Ea17
Whiteman Range ▲ **PNG** 116 Se48
Whitemark ◻ **AUS** (TAS) 111 Se66
White Mesa Natural Bridge ▲ **USA** 171 Ee27
White Mountain ◻ **USA** (AK) 164 Bj13
White Mountains ▲ **CDN** 177 Ge23
White Mountains ▲ **USA** (AK) 165 Cg13
White Mountains ▲ **USA** (AZ) 171 Ef29
White Mountains N.P. ✪ **AUS** (QLD) 107 Sc56
Whitemouth ◻ **CDN** (MB) 172 Fb21
White Mts. ▲ **USA** 170 Ea27
White Nile ≈ **SUD** 122 Mb08
White Nile ≈ **SUD** 135 Mg40
White Owl ◻ **USA** (SD) 169 Ej23
White Pass ≈ **CDN/USA** 166 Dc16
White River ◻ **CDN** (ON) 173 Fh21
White River ◻ **USA** (SD) 172 Ek24
White River Junction ◻ **USA** (VT) 177 Gd24
White River N.W.R. ✪ **USA** 175 Fe28
White Rock ▲ **NZ** 113 Th66
White Salmon ◻ **USA** (WA) 168 Dk23
White Sands ◻ **USA** (NM) 171 Eg29
White Sands Missile Range Museum ⌂ **USA** 171 Eg29
White Sands National Monument ✪ **USA** 171 Eg29
White Sands Space Harbor ✪ **USA** 171 Eg29
Whitesburg ◻ **USA** (KY) 178 Fj27
White Sea ≈ **RUS** 14 Mb03
Whiteshell Prov. Park ✪ ✪ **CDN** 172 Fc20
Whitestone Hill Battlefield S.H.S. ⌂ **USA** 172 Fa22
White Sulphur Springs ◻ **USA** (MT) 169 Ee22
Whiteville ◻ **USA** (NC) 178 Ga28
Whiteville ◻ **USA** (TN) 175 Ff28
White Volta ≈ **GH** 137 Kk41
Whitewater ◻ **USA** (MT) 169 Eg21
Whitewater ◻ **USA** (WI) 173 Ff24
White Wells ◻ **AUS** (WA) 104 Qj60
Whitewood ◻ **AUS** (QLD) 109 Sb56
Whitewood ◻ **CDN** (SK) 169 Ej20
Whitfield ◻ **AUS** (VIC) 111 Sd64
Whithorn ◻ **GB** 20 Kq36
Whitianga ◻ **NZ** 112 Th64
Whitlash ◻ **USA** (MT) 169 Ee21
Whitman Mission N.H.S. ⌂ **USA** 168 Ea23
Whitmire ◻ **USA** (SC) 178 Fk28
Whitmore Mountains ▲ 6 Ec35
Whitney ◻ **CDN** (ON) 173 Ga23
Whitney, Mount ▲ **USA** 170 Ea27
Whitsunday Group ▲ **AUS** 107 Se56
Whitsunday Island ▲ **AUS** 107 Se56
Whitsunday Islands N.P. ✪ ✪ ✪ **AUS** 107 Se56
Whitsunday Passage ≈ **AUS** 107 Se56
Whittier ◻ **USA** (AK) 165 Cf15
Whittlesea ◻ **AUS** (VIC) 111 Sc64
Whittlesea ◻ **ZA** 155 Md62
Why ◻ **USA** (AZ) 171 Ed29
Whyalla ◻ **AUS** (SA) 110 Rj62
Whyalla Maritime Museum ⌂ **AUS** 110 Rj62
Whycocomagh ◻ **CDN** (NS) 176 Gk23
Whycocomagh Ind. Res. ◰ **CDN** 176 Gk22
Wialki ◻ **AUS** (WA) 104 Qk61
Wiang Chai ◻ **THA** 87 Pk36
Wiang Ko Sai N.P. ✪ **THA** 87 Pk37
Wiang Sa ◻ **THA** 87 Qa36
Wiawer ◻ **EAU** 144 Mg44
Wiawso ◻ **GH** 137 Kj42
Wiay ▲ **GB** 20 Kn33
Wiązów ◻ **PL** 40 Ls40
Wibaux ◻ **USA** (MT) 169 Eh22
Wich'ale ◻ **ETH** 142 Mk40
Wichita ◻ **USA** (KS) 174 Fb27
Wichita Falls ◻ **USA** (TX) 174 Fa29
Wichita Mts. ▲ **USA** 174 Fa28
Wichita Mts. N.W.R. ✪ **USA** 174 Fa28
Wick ◻ **GB** 20 Kr32
Wickede ◻ **D** 32 Lh39
Wickenburg ◻ **USA** (AZ) 171 Ed29
Wickepin ◻ **AUS** (WA) 104 Qj62
Wickersham Dom ▲ **USA** (AK) 165 Cf13
Wickham ◻ **AUS** (WA) 102 Qj56
Wicklow ◻ **IRL** 19 Ko38
Wicklow Head ≈ **IRL** 19 Ko38
Wicklow Mountains ▲ **IRL** 19 Ko38
Wicklow Mountains N.P. ✪ ✪ **IRL** 19 Ko37
Wicko ◻ **PL** 40 Ls36
Widgee Mountain ▲ **AUS** 109 Sg59
Widgiemooltha ◻ **AUS** (WA) 104 Ra61
Widminy ◻ **PL** 41 Mc37
Wi Do ▲ **ROK** 78 Rd28
Widuchowa ◻ **PL** 40 Lp37
Więcbork ◻ **PL** 40 Ls37
Wiedenbrück, Rheda- ◻ **D** 32 Lj39
Wiehengebirge ▲ **D** 32 Lj38
Wiehl ◻ **D** 32 Lh40
Wielbark ◻ **PL** 41 Ma37
Wieleń ◻ **PL** 40 Lr38
Wieliczka ◻ **PL** 41 Ma41
Wielkopolski P.N. ✪ **PL** 40 Lr38
Wieluń ◻ **PL** 40 Lt39
Wien ● ☐ ▲ **A** 42 Lr42
Wiener Neustadt ◻ **A** 35 Lr43
Wienerwald ▲ **A** 42 Lq42
Wieniawa ◻ **PL** 41 Ma39
Wierden ◻ **NL** 23 Lg38
Wieruszów ◻ **PL** 40 Lt39
Wierzbica ◻ **PL** 41 Mb39
Wierzchowo ◻ **PL** 40 Lr37
Wierzchucino ◻ **PL** 40 Ls36
Wierzchy ◻ **PL** 40 Lt39
Wiesbaden ◉ ✪ **D** 33 Lj40
Wieselburg ◻ **A** 42 Lq42
Wiesenburg ◻ **D** 32 Ln38
Wiesentheid ◻ **D** 33 Ll41
Wiesloch ◻ **D** 33 Lj41
Wiesmoor ◻ **D** 32 Lh37
Wiesua ◻ **LB** 136 Ke42
Wietzer Berg ▲ **D** 32 Ll38
Wiga Hill ▲ **WAN** 139 Lg40
Wigan ◻ **GB** 21 Ks37
Wiggins ◻ **USA** (MS) 175 Ff30
Wigierski P.N. ✪ **PL** 41 Md36
Wigston ◻ **GB** 21 Kt38
Wigton ◻ **GB** 20 Kr36
Wijchen ◻ **NL** 23 Lf39
Wikki Warm Springs ✪ ✪ **WAN** 138 Lf41
Wik'ro ◻ **ETH** 142 Mk39
Wikrowo ◻ **PL** 41 Mb36
Wikwemikong Ind. Res. ◰ **CDN** 173 Fk23
Wil ◻ **CH** 34 Lk43
Wilanow ⌂ **PL** 41 Mb38
Wilberforce ◻ **AUS** (NSW) 111 Sf62
Wilbert ◻ **CDN** (SK) 169 Ef19
Wilbrunga Range ▲ **AUS** 103 Re56
Wilbur ◻ **USA** (WA) 168 Ea22
Wilburton ◻ **USA** (OK) 174 Fc28
Wilcannia ◻ **AUS** (NSW) 108 Sb61
Wilchta ◻ **PL** 41 Mb39
Wilczęta ◻ **PL** 41 Lu36
Wildalpen ◻ **A** 35 Lp43
Wildcat Hill ▲ **CDN** 169 Ej19
Wildcat Hill Prov. Park ✪ **CDN** 169 Ej19
Wilderness ▲ **USA** 187 Gg36
Wilderness N.P. ✪ ◰ **ZA** 154 Mb63
Wildeshausen ◻ **D** 32 Lj38
Wild Horse ◻ **CDN** (AB) 169 Ee21
Wild Horse ◻ **USA** (NV) 170 Ec25
Wildlife Sanctuary (Western Australia) ✪ **AUS** 105 Rc62
Wildspitze ▲ **A** 34 Ll44
Wildwood ◻ **USA** (NJ) 177 Gc26
Wilga ◻ **PL** 41 Mb39
Wilga Mia Ochre Mine ⌂ **AUS** 104 Qj59
Wilgena ◻ **AUS** (SA) 108 Rh61
Wilhelma ✪ **D** 33 Lk42
Wilhelm II Land ▲ 7 Pb33
Wilhelminagebergte ▲ **SME** 194 Hb44
Wilhelm, Mount ▲ **PNG** 115 Sc48
Wilhelmøya ▲ **N** 16 Ma06
Wilhelmsburg ◻ **A** 42 Lq42
Wilhelmshaven ◻ ⚓ **D** 32 Lj37
Wilhelmstal ◻ **NAM** 150 Lj56
Wilkes-Barre ◻ **USA** (PA) 177 Gc25
Wilkesboro ◻ **USA** (NC) 178 Fk27
Wilkes Land ▲ **ANT** 7 Rc32
Wilkie ◻ **CDN** (SK) 169 Ef19
Wilkins ◻ **USA** (NV) 171 Ec25
Wilkins Ice Shelf ≈ 6 Gb33
Wilków ◻ **PL** 41 Ma39
Willandra Lakes World Heritage ☐ ✪ **AUS** 111 Sb62
Willapa Hills ▲ **USA** 168 Dj22
Willard ◻ **USA** (NM) 171 Eg28
Willare Bridge ◻ **AUS** (WA) 102 Rb54
Willcox ◻ **USA** (AZ) 171 Ef29
Willem Pretorius Nature Reserve ✪ **ZA** 155 Md60
Willemstad ◉ ☐ ▲ **NL** (NA) 193 Gf39
Willen ◻ **CDN** (MB) 172 Ek20
Willeroo ◻ **AUS** (NT) 106 Rf53
Williambury ◻ **AUS** (WA) 104 Qh57
William Creek ◻ **AUS** (SA) 108 Rj60
Williamez Peninsula ▲ **PNG** 116 Se48
William, Mount ▲ **AUS** 111 Sb64
William Pt. ▲ **CDN** (SK) 167 Ef16
Williams ◻ **AUS** (WA) 104 Qj62
Williams ◻ **USA** (CA) 170 Dj26
Williamsburg ◻ **USA** (KY) 175 Fh27
Williamsburg ◻ **USA** (VA) 177 Gb27
Williams Lake ◻ **CDN** (BC) 168 Dj19
Williamson ◻ **USA** (WV) 178 Fj27
Williamson Glacier ≈ 7 Qd32
Williamsport ◻ **USA** (AK) 164 Cd16
Williamsport ◻ **USA** (PA) 177 Gb25
Williamston ◻ **USA** (NC) 178 Gb28
William's Town ◻ **BS** 186 Gc34
Williamstown ◻ **USA** (KY) 175 Fh26
Willians Island ▲ **BS** 179 Ga33
Williston ◻ **USA** (FL) 178 Fj31
Williston ◻ **ZA** 154 Ma61
Williston Lake ≈ **CDN** 166 Dj18
Williton ◻ **GB** 21 Kr39
Willits ◻ **USA** (CA) 170 Dj26
Willmar ◻ **CDN** (SK) 169 Ej21
Willmar ◻ **USA** (MN) 172 Fc23
Willmore Wilderness Prov. Park ▲ **CDN** 167 Ea19
Will, Mount ▲ **CDN** 166 Df17
Willow ◻ **USA** (AK) 165 Cf15
Willow Bunch ◻ **CDN** (SK) 169 Eh21
Willow Creek ◻ **CDN** (SK) 169 Ef21
Willowmore ◻ **ZA** 154 Mb62
Willowra ◻ **AUS** (NT) 103 Rg56
Willow Ranch ◻ **USA** (CA) 168 Dk25
Willow River ◻ **CDN** (BC) 166 Dj18
Willows ◻ **USA** (CA) 170 Dj26
Willow Tree ◻ **AUS** (NSW) 109 Sf61
Willowvale ◻ **ZA** 155 Me62
Will Rogers Mem. ⌂ **USA** 174 Fc27
Willston ◻ **USA** (ND) 169 Ej21
Wilma ◻ **USA** (FL) 175 Fh30
Wilmington ◻ **AUS** (SA) 110 Rk62
Wilmington ◻ **USA** (DE) 177 Gc26
Wilmington ◻ **USA** (IL) 173 Ff25
Wilmington ◻ **USA** (NC) 178 Gb28
Wilmington ◻ **USA** (OH) 175 Fj26
Wilpattu N.P. ✪ **CL** 85 Ok41
Wilpena-Pound ▲ **AUS** (SA) 108 Rk61
Wilpoorinna ◻ **AUS** (SA) 108 Rk60
Wilsall ◻ **USA** (MT) 169 Ee23
Wilseder Berg ▲ **D** 32 Lk37
Wilson ◻ **USA** (NC) 178 Gb28
Wilson Bluff ▲ **AUS** 105 Re61
Wilson Creek ◻ **USA** (WA) 168 Ea22
Wilson Hills ▲ 7 Sd32
Wilson Inlet ≈ **AUS** 104 Qj63
Wilson Island ▲ **CDN** 167 Ed15
Wilson Island ▲ **IND** 88 Pg39
Wilson, Mount ▲ **CDN** 166 Df14
Wilsons Promontory ▲ **AUS** 111 Sd65
Wilsons Promontory N.P. ✪ **AUS** 111 Sd65
Wilsonville ◻ **USA** (AL) 175 Fg29
Wilster ◻ **D** 32 Lk37
Wilton ◻ **GB** 21 Kt39
Wilton ◻ **USA** (ND) 172 Ek22
Wiltondale ◻ **CDN** (NF) 177 Hb21
Wiltz ◻ **L** 23 Lf41
Wiluna ◻ **AUS** (WA) 104 Ra59
Wimborne ◻ **CDN** (AB) 169 Ed20
Wimereux ◻ **F** 23 Lb40
Winburg ◻ **ZA** 155 Md60
Wincanton ◻ **GB** 21 Ks39
Winchelsea Islands ▲ **AUS** 106 Rj52
Wincherster ◻ **USA** (VA) 177 Ga26
Winchester ◻ ⌂ **GB** 21 Kt39
Winchester ◻ **USA** (IN) 173 Fh25
Winchester ◻ **USA** (TN) 175 Fg28
Winchester ◻ **USA** (WY) 169 Ef24
Wind Cave N.P. ✪ ▲ **USA** 169 Ej24
Winder ◻ **USA** (GA) 178 Fj29
Winderie ◻ **AUS** (WA) 104 Qh58
Windermere ◻ **GB** 21 Ks36
Windermere Valley Mus. ⌂ **CDN** 168 Eb20
Windham ◻ **USA** (AK) 166 Dd17
Windhoek ● ▲ ⌂ **NAM** 150 Lj57
Windidda ◻ **AUS** (WA) 104 Rb59
Windigo Lake ≈ **CDN** 172 Fe19
Windigo River ≈ **CDN** 172 Fe19
Windischgarsten ◻ **A** 35 Lp43
Windjana Gorge N.P. ✪ ▲ ✪ **AUS** 103 Rc54
Windom ◻ **USA** (MN) 172 Fc24
Windom Peak ▲ **USA** 171 Eg27
Windorah ◻ **AUS** (QLD) 108 Sb58
Window on China ⌂ **RC** 75 Ra33
Window Rock ◻ **USA** (AZ) 171 Ef28
Wind River Ind. Res. ◰ **USA** 169 Ef24
Wind River Range ▲ **USA** 169 Ef24
Windsbach ◻ **D** 33 Ll41
Windsor ◻ **AUS** (NSW) 111 Sf62
Windsor ◻ **AUS** (WA) 104 Qk60
Windsor ◻ **CDN** (NF) 177 Hc21
Windsor ◻ **CDN** (NS) 176 Gh23
Windsor ◻ **CDN** (ON) 173 Fj24
Windsor ⌂ **GB** 21 Ku39
Windsor ◻ **USA** (MO) 174 Fd26
Windsor ◻ **USA** (NC) 178 Gb28
Windsor ◻ **USA** (VT) 177 Gd24
Windsorton ◻ **ZA** 155 Mc60
Windsorton Road ◻ **ZA** 155 Mc60
Windward Islands ≈ **F** 11 Ca11
Windward Islands ▲ 187 Gf40
Windy Harbour ◻ **AUS** (WA) 104 Qj63
Wineglass Bay ≈ ✪ **AUS** 111 Se67
Winejok ◻ **SUD** 141 Md41
Wineperu ◻ **GUY** 194 Ha42
Winfield ◻ **CDN** (AB) 169 Ec19
Winfield ◻ **USA** (AL) 175 Fg29
Winfield ◻ **USA** (KS) 174 Fb27
Wing ◻ **USA** (ND) 172 Ek22
Wingdam ◻ **CDN** (BC) 168 Dj19
Wingham ◻ **AUS** (NSW) 109 Sg61
Wingon ◻ **MYA** 86 Ph34
Wingst ▲ **D** 32 Lk37
Winifred ◻ **USA** (MT) 169 Ef22
Winkipop ▲ **AUS** 111 Sf62
Winkler ◻ **CDN** (MB) 172 Fb21
Winklern ◻ **A** 35 Ln44
Winnathee ◻ **AUS** (NSW) 108 Sa60
Winneba ◻ ✪ ✪ **GH** 137 Kk43
Winnebago ◻ **USA** (NE) 172 Fb24
Winnebago Ind. Res. ◰ **USA** 172 Fb24
Winnemucca ◻ **USA** (NV) 170 Eb25
Winnemucca Lake ≈ **USA** 170 Ea25
Winner ◻ **USA** (SD) 172 Fa24
Winnett ◻ **USA** (MT) 169 Ef22
Winnfield ◻ **USA** (LA) 175 Fd30
Winnie Stowell ◻ **USA** (TX) 174 Fc31
Winning ◻ **AUS** (WA) 102 Qh57
Winnipeg ◉ **CDN** (MB) 172 Fb21
Winnipeg Art Gallery ⌂ **CDN** (MB) 172 Fb21
Winnipeg Beach ◻ **CDN** (MB) 172 Fb20
Winnipegosis ◻ **CDN** (MB) 172 Fa20
Winnsboro ◻ **USA** (LA) 175 Fe29
Winnsboro ◻ **USA** (SC) 178 Fk28
Winnsboro ◻ **USA** (TX) 174 Fc29
Winnweiler ◻ **D** 33 Lh41
Winona ◻ **USA** (MN) 172 Fe23
Winona ◻ **USA** (MS) 175 Ff29
Winschoten ◻ **NL** 23 Lh37
Winsen ◻ **D** 32 Lk38
Winsen (Luhe) ◻ **D** 32 Ll37
Winsford ◻ **GB** 21 Ks37

Wińsko ☐ PL 40 Lr39
Winslow ☐ USA (AZ) 171 Ee28
Winston ☐ USA (NM) 171 Ge29
Winston ☐ USA (OR) 168 Dj24
Winston-Salem ☐ USA (NC) 178 Fk27
Winsum ☐ NL 23 Lg37
Winterberg ☐ ZA 155 Md62
Winter Harbour ☐ CDN (BC) 168 Df20
Winters ☐ USA (TX) 174 Fa30
Winterset ☐ USA (IA) 172 Fc25
Winter Springs ☐ USA (FL) 178 Fk31
Winterswijk ☐ NL 23 Lg39
Winterthur ☐ CH 34 Lj43
Winterton ☐ ZA 155 Me60
Winthrop ☐ USA (ME) 177 Ge23
Winthrop ☐ USA (WA) 168 Rj59
Wintinna ☐ AUS (SA) 108 Rj59
Winton ☐ USA (MN) 172 Fe22
Winton ☐ NZ 113 Tg69
Winyan ☐ MYA 88 Pj38
Wipim ☐ PNG 115 Sb50
Wipperfürth ☐ D 32 Lh39
Wirawa ☐ RI 97 Rf48
Wirges ☐ D 32 Lh40
Wirliyajarrayi A.L. ☐ AUS
  178 Rf27
Wirmaf ☐ RI 97 Rf48
Wirrabara ☐ AUS (SA) 110 Rk62
Wirreaplaca ☐ AUS (SA) 108 Rk61
Wirrulla ☐ AUS (SA) 110 Rh62
Wirth Peninsula ☐ AUS
Wisbech ☐ GB 21 La38
Wiscasset ☐ USA (MA) 177 Gf24
Wisconsin ☐ USA 172 Fe23
Wisconsin Range ☐ 6 Dd36
Wisconsin Rapids ☐ USA (WI)
  172 Ff23
Wisdom ☐ USA (MT) 168 Ed23
Wiseman ☐ USA (AK) 165 Cf12
Wiseman's Ferry ☐ AUS (NSW)
  111 Sf62
Wishart ☐ CDN (SK) 169 Eh20
Wishek ☐ USA (ND) 172 Fa22
Wisil ☐ SP 143 Ne43
Wisła ☐ PL 41 Lu39
Wiślica ☐ PL 41 Ma40
Wismar ☐ D 32 Lm37
Wiśnice ☐ PL 41 Mb39
Wiśniowa ☐ PL 41 Mb41
Wissembourg ☐ F 23 Lh41
Wissen ☐ D 32 Lh40
Wistari Reef ☐ AUS (QLD)
  109 Sf57
Wisznia Mała ☐ PL 40 Ls39
Witagron ☐ SME 194 Hb43
Witaitonga ☐ RI 97 Rb48
Witbank ☐ ZA 155 Me58
Witbooisvlei ☐ NAM 154 Lk58
Wittonteinrand ☐ ZA 155 Md58
Witham ☐ GB 21 La37
Withernsea ☐ GB 21 La37
Witjira N.P. ☐ AUS (SA) 108 Rh59
Witkowo ☐ PL 40 Ls38
Witknarsweka ☐ ZA 155 Mc61
Witness Bay Ecological Res. ☐
  CDN 177 Hd23
Witney ☐ GB 21 Kt39
Witnica ☐ PL 40 Lp38
Witoszyce ☐ PL 40 Lr39
Witpütz ☐ NAM 154 Lj59
Witrivier ☐ ZA 155 Me59
Wittand ☐ ZA 154 Ma62
Wittelsberg ☐ ZA 155 Md60
Witteberge ☐ ZA 154 Ma62
Witteberg ☐ ZA 155 Mb62
Witteberge ☐ ZA 155 Md60
Witteklip ☐ ZA 155 Md58
Witten ☐ D 32 Lh39
Wittenberg ☐ USA (WI) 173 Ff23
Wittenberge ☐ D 32 Lm37
Wittenburra ☐ AUS (QLD)
  109 Sc60
Wittenoom ☐ AUS (WA) 102
  Qk57
Wittingen ☐ D 32 Ll38
Wittlich ☐ D 33 Lg41
Wittmund ☐ D 32 Lh37
Wittstock ☐ D 32 Lm37
Witu ☐ EAK 147 Na47
Witu ☐ PNG 116 Se48
Witu Islands ☐ PNG 116 Se48
Witviei ☐ NAM 150 Lk57
Witwater ☐ ZA 154 Lk61
Witzenhausen ☐ D 32 Lk39
Wizajny ☐ PL 41 Mc36
Wizna ☐ PL 41 Mc38
Władysławowo ☐ PL 40 Lt36
Wil Falls ☐ GH 137 La42
Wlingi ☐ RI 95 Qg50
Włocławek ☐ PL 40 Lt38
Włodawa ☐ PL 41 Md39
Włodzimierzów ☐ PL 41 Lu39
Włoszakowice ☐ PL 41 Lu40
Włoszczowa ☐ PL 41 Lu40
Wlotzkasbaken ☐ NAM 150 Lh57
Wobulenzi ☐ EAU 144 Mg45
Woburn ☐ CDN (QC) 176 Ge23
Woburn Abbey ☐ GB 21 Ku39
Woddy Point ☐ CDN (NF)
  177 Ha21
Wodonga ☐ AUS (VIC) 111 Sd64
Wodzisław Śląski ☐ PL 40 Lt40
Woe ☐ GH 137 La43
Wogakini ☐ PNG 116 Sf48
Wohlen ☐ CH 34 Lj43
Woippe ☐ PNG 115 Sd50
Woito ☐ ETH 144 Mj43
Wokam ☐ RI 114 Rf48
Wokha ☐ IND (NGL) 86 Ph32
Woking ☐ GB 21 Ku39
Wokole ☐ RI 97 Rh48
Wola Uhruska ☐ PL 41 Md39
Wolbrom ☐ PL 41 Lu40
Wotczyn ☐ PL 40 Lr37
Woldegk ☐ D 32 Lo37
Oleai Atoll ☐ FSM 10 Sa09
Wolf Bayou ☐ USA (AR) 175
  Fe28
Wolf Creek ☐ USA (MT) 169
  Ed22
Wolf Creek ☐ USA (OR) 168 Dj24
Wolfe Creek Meteorite Crater ☐
  AUS 103 Rd55
Wolfe Creek Meteorite National
  Park ☐ AUS 103 Rd55
Wolfenbüttel ☐ D 32 Ll38
Wolfgangsee ☐ A 35 Lo43
Wolfgangsee ☐ A 35 Lo43
Wolf Point ☐ USA (MT) 169 Eh21
Wolfratshausen ☐ D 33 Lm43
Wolfsberg ☐ A 35 Lp44
Wolfsburg ☐ D 32 Ll38
Wolf, Volcán ☐ EC 197 Fe45
Wolfville ☐ CDN 177 Gh23
Wolgast ☐ D 32 Lo36
Wolhusen ☐ CH 34 Lj43
Wollaston Lake ☐ CDN 162 Ed07
Wollaston Lake ☐ CDN 162 Ed07
Wollaston Peninsula ☐ CDN
  162 Eb05
Wollemi N.P. ☐ AUS 111 Sf62
Wollogorang ☐ AUS (NT)
  106 Rj54
Wolmaransstad ☐ ZA 155 Md59
Wolmirstedt ☐ D 32 Lm38
Wolo ☐ RI 114 Rf47
Wologizi Range ☐ LB 136 Kf41
Wolomin ☐ PL 41 Mb38
Wolong Giant Panda Reserve ☐
  CHN 74 Qb30
Wolsotate ☐ PL 43 Mc41
Wotów ☐ PL 40 Lr39

Wolseley ☐ CDN (SK) 169 Ej20
Wolseley ☐ ZA 154 Lk62
Wolseley ☐ USA (SD) 172 Fa23
Wolverhampton ☐☐ GB
  21 Ks38
Wolwefontein ☐ ZA 155 Mc62
Wombil Downs ☐ AUS (QLD)
  109 Sd60
Wombelbank ☐ AUS (QLD)
  109 Se58
Wonarah ☐ AUS (NT) 106 Rh55
Wonder Gorge ☐ Z 152 Me53
Wonder Mountains ☐ ☐ AUS
  165 Cj15
Wondai ☐ AUS (QLD) 109 Sf59
Wondinong ☐ AUS (WA)
  104 Qj59
Wonegizi Mountain ☐ LB
  136 Kf42
Wonegizi N.P. ☐ LB 136 Kf41
Wongan Hills ☐ AUS (WA)
  104 Qj61
Wonga Wongué ☐ G 148 Le46
Wongawol ☐ AUS (WA) 104
  Ra59
Wonju ☐ ROK 78 Rd27
Wono ☐ RI 96 Qk47
Wonogiri ☐ RI 95 Qf49
Wonoka ☐ AUS (SA) 108 Rk61
Wonosari ☐ RI 95 Qf49
Wonosobo ☐ RI 95 Qe49
Wonreli ☐ RI 97 Rc49
Wonsan ☐ PRK 76 Rd26
Wonto Koto ☐ RI 97 Rd46
Wonyulgunna Hill ☐ AUS
  104 Qk58
Woodanilling ☐ AUS (WA)
Woodbine Race Track ☐ CDN
  (ON) 173 Ga24
Woodborne ☐ USA (NY)
  177 Gc25
Woodbridge ☐ GB 21 Lb38
Wood Buffalo National Park ☐ ☐
  CDN (AB) 167 Ed16
Woodburn ☐ AUS (NSW)
  109 Sg60
Woodburn ☐ USA (OR) 168 Dj23
Woodenbong ☐ AUS (QLD)
  109 Sg60
Woodford ☐ AUS (QLD) 109
  Sg58
Woodgate ☐ AUS (QLD) 109
  Sg58
Woodgreen ☐ AUS (NT) 108
  Rh57
Woodhall Spa ☐ GB 21 Ku37
Wood Island ☐ CDN (PE)
  176 Gg29
Woodland ☐ USA (CA) 170 Dk26
Woodland ☐ USA (ME) 168 Dj23
Woodland Caribou Prov. Park ☐
  CDN 172 Fe19
Woodland Park ☐ USA (CO)
  171 Eh26
Woodlands ☐ AUS (WA) 104
  Qk58
Woodlands ☐ USA (TX) 174 Fc30
Woodiak Island ☐ PNG 116
  Sg50
Wood, Mount ☐ USA 169 Ee23
Wood Mountain ☐ CDN (SK)
Woodridge ☐ CDN (MB) 172
  Fb21
Woodroffe, Mount ☐ AUS
  105 Rf59
Woodrow ☐ USA (CO) 174 Ej26
Woodruff ☐ USA (UT) 171 Ee25
Woodruff ☐ USA (WI) 172 Ff23
Woodsfield ☐ USA (OH)
  Fk26
Woodside ☐ AUS (VIC) 111 Sd65
Woodside Beach ☐ AUS
  111 Sd65
Woodson ☐ USA (TX) 174 Fa29
Woods Point ☐ AUS (VIC)
  111 Sd64
Woodstock ☐ USA (VT)
  107 Sd55
Woodstock ☐ CDN (ON)
  108 Sa57
Woodstock ☐ AUS (WA) 102
  Qk56
Woodstock ☐ AUS 102 Qa57
Woodstock ☐ CDN (NB) 176
  Gg22
Woodstock ☐ CDN (ON)
  173 Fk24
Woodstock ☐ GB 21 Kt39
Woodstock ☐ USA (AL) 175 Fg29
Woodstock ☐ USA (IL) 173 Ff24
Woodsville ☐ USA (NH)
  Gd23
Woodvale ☐ AUS (QLD) 109
  Sd59
Woodville ☐ NZ 113 Th66
Woodville ☐ USA (MS) 175 Fe30
Woodville ☐ USA (TX) 174 Fd30
Woodward ☐ USA (OK) 174 Fa27
Woodworth ☐ USA (ND) 172
  Fa22
Wool ☐ RI 114 Rh46
Wooler ☐ GB 20 Ks35
Woolfield ☐ AUS (QLD) 109 Sb56
Woolgar ☐ AUS (NSW)
  109 Sg61
Woolgoolga ☐ AUS (WA)
  104 Qh59
Wooli ☐ AUS (NSW) 109 Sg60
Woolomombi ☐ AUS (NSW)
Woomera ☐ AUS (SA) 108 Rj61
Woomerangee Hill ☐ AUS
  104 Qh59
Woonsocket ☐ USA (SD)
Wooramel ☐ AUS (WA) 104 Qh58
Wooster ☐ USA (OH) 173 Fk25
Woraksan N.P. ☐ ROK 78 Rd27
Worb ☐ CH 34 Lh44
Worbis ☐ D 32 Ll39
Wuse ☐ WAN 138 Le41
Wusterhausen ☐ D 32 Ln38
Wustenhausen ☐ D 32 Ln38

Woumbou ☐ CAM 139 Lh43
Wounaplu ☐ CHN (HLG) 76 Re21
Wounded Knee Battlefield ☐
  USA 169 Ej24
Wour ☐ TCH 133 Lh35
Wowan ☐ AUS (QLD) 109 Sf57
Wowoni ☐ RI 97 Rb48
Woziwoda ☐ PL 40 Ls37
W, P.N.du- ☐ BF 131 La39
«W», P.N.du- ☐ RN 138 Ld39
Wrabanay ☐ AFG 65 Oe29
Wrangel Island ☐ RUS 55 Ua04
Wrangell ☐ USA (AK) 166 Dd17
Wrangell Island ☐ USA 166 Dd17
Wrangell Mountains ☐ ☐ USA
  165 Cj15
Wrangell - Saint Elias National
  Park and Preserve ☐ ☐ ☐
  USA 165 Cj15
Wray ☐ USA (CO) 174 Ej25
Wreck Bay ☐ AUS 111 Sf63
Wreck diving (Anegada) ☐ GB
  187 Gh36
Wreck diving (Anguilla) ☐ GB
  187 Gj36
Wreck diving (Antigua) ☐ AG
  187 Gj37
Wreckproof ☐ AUS (VIC)
  111 Sb64
Wreck diving (Barbuda) ☐ AG
  187 Gj37
Wrens ☐ USA (GA) 178 Fj29
Wrentham ☐ CDN (AB) 169 Ed21
Wrexham ☐ GB 21 Ks38
Wreys Bush ☐ NZ 113 Te68
Wriezen ☐ D 32 Lo38
Wright ☐ RP 90 Rc40
Wright ☐ USA (WY) 169 Eh24
Wright Brothers Nat. Mem. ☐
  USA 178 Gb28
Wrightsville ☐ USA 178 Fj29
Wrightsville Beach ☐ USA (NC)
  178 Gb28
Wrigley ☐ CDN 167 Dj14
Writing Rock ☐ USA 169 Ej21
Wrocki ☐ PL 41 Lt38
Wrocław ☐ ☐ PL 41 Ls39
Wronki ☐ PL 40 Lr38
Wroxham ☐ GB 21 Lb38
Wroxton ☐ CDN (SK) 172 Ek20
Września ☐ PL 40 Ls38
Wschowa ☐ PL 40 Lr39
Wschowa ☐ PL 41 Mb39
Wubin ☐ AUS (WA) 104 Qj61
Wuchang ☐ CHN (HLG) 76 Rd23
Wuchuan ☐ CHN (GDG) 74 Qf35
Wuchuan ☐ CHN (NMZ) 72 Qf25
Wuda ☐ CHN (NMZ) 71 Qd24
Wudalianchi ☐ CHN (HLG)
  71 Rd21
Wudalianchi Lake Excursion
  Area ☐ CHN 71 Rd21
Wudang Shan ☐ CHN 72 Qf29
Wudangshan ☐ CHN (HBI)
  72 Qf29
Wuding Zhao ☐ CHN 72 Qf25
Wuding He ☐ CHN (SAX) 72 Qf26
Wudinna ☐ AUS (SA) 110 Rh62
Wudong Shan ☐ CHN 75 Qh33
Wufeng ☐ CHN (HUB) 74 Qf30
Wugang ☐ CHN (HUN) 74 Qf32
Wugong ☐ CHN (SAA) 72 Qe28
Wuhai ☐ CHN (NMZ) 72 Qd26
Wuhe ☐ CHN (HUB) 75 Qh29
Wuhou Shrine ☐ CHN 75 Qa31
Wuhu ☐ CHN (AHU) 78 Qk30
Wüjang ☐ CHN (TIB) 68 Oe29
Wü-Muteba ☐ ANG 148 Lh49
Wujiang ☐ CHN (GZH) 74 Qd32
Wujiang ☐ CHN (JGS) 78 Ra30
Wujiangdu ☐ CHN (GZH)
  74 Qd32
Wukari ☐ WAN 138 Le42
Wulan ☐ CHN (QHI) 69 Pj28
Wulgo ☐ WAN 139 Lh39
Wulian ☐ CHN (QHI) 69 Pg28
Wulian ☐ CHN (SDG) 78 Qk28
Wuliang Shan ☐ CHN 87 Qa34
Wu Liang, Tomb of the Ming and
  Tombs of the Ming and Qing
  Dynasties ☐ ☐ CHN (JGS)
  78 Qk29
Wuliaru ☐ RI 97 Rf49
Wulichuan ☐ CHN (HBI)
  72 Qf29
Wuling Shan ☐ CHN 74 Qe32
Wuling Shan Z.B. ☐ CHN 73 Qj25
Wulingyuan Z.B. ☐ CHN 74 Qf31
Wulong ☐ CHN (CGQ) 74 Qd32
Wulumei Shan ☐ CHN 75 Qh31
Wuming ☐ CHN (GZG) 74 Qe33
Wümme ☐ D 32 Lk37
Wunaga ☐ SUD 141 Mf41
Wunarual ☐ SUD 141 Mf41
Wundanyi ☐ EAK 145 Mk47
Wun-dwin ☐ MYA 86 Ph35
Wuning ☐ CHN (JGX) 75 Qh31
Wun Rog ☐ SUD 141 Me41
Wun Shwai ☐ SUD 141 Me42
Wupatki Nat. Mon. ☐ USA
  171 Ee28
Wuping ☐ CHN (FJN) 75 Qj33
Wuqia ☐ CHN (SCH) 74 Qb31
Wuqia ☐ CHN (XUZ) 66 Oh26
Wuqiang ☐ CHN 74 Qb30
Wuqing ☐ CHN (HAN) 74 Qg30
Wuraga ☐ AUS (WA) 104 Qj60
Wuriyanga Mosque ☐ GH
  137 La40
Wuro ☐ WAN 132 Lc39
Würrallbil A.L. ☐ AUS 106 Rj53
Würzburg ☐ D 33 Lk41
Wurzen ☐ D 32 Ln39
Wusa ☐ WAN 138 Le41
Wushan ☐ CHN (SCH)
  69 Pk31
Wushengfan ☐ CHN 74 Qd30
Wushi ☐ CHN (XUZ) 66 Ok25
Wushishi ☐ WAN 138 Ld41
Wushulin ☐ CHN (GZG) 74 Qe35
Wutai ☐ CHN (SAX) 72 Qf26
Wutaishan ☐ CHN 72 Qf26
Wuta ☐ CHN (AHU) 78 Qj29
Wutongqiao ☐ CHN (SCH)
  74 Qa31
Wutut ☐ CHN (XUZ) 66 Ok25
Wutung ☐ PNG 115 Sa47
Wuvulu Island ☐ PNG 115 Sb46
Wuwei ☐ CHN (GSU) 72 Qb27
Wuwei ☐ CHN (CGQ) 74 Qd32
Wuxi ☐ CHN (JGS) 78 Ra30
Wu Xia ☐ CHN 74 Qe30
Wuxiang ☐ CHN (SAX) 72 Qf27
Wuxue ☐ CHN (HUB) 75 Qh30
Wuyang ☐ CHN (HNN) 73 Qg29

Woumbou ☐ CHN (ZJG) 75 Qk31
Wuyiling ☐ CHN (HLG) 76 Re21
Wuyishan ☐ CHN (FJN) 75 Qk32
Wuyi Shan ☐ CHN 75 Qj32
Wuyishan Z.B. ☐ ☐ CHN
  75 Qj32
Wuyuan ☐ CHN (JGX) 75 Qj31
Wuyuan ☐ CHN (NMZ) 72 Qe25
Wuzhai ☐ CHN (SAX) 72 Qf26
Wu Zhen, Tomb of = Imperial
  Tombs of the Ming and Qing
  Dynasties ☐ ☐ CHN (JGS)
  78 Qk29
Wuzhi Shan ☐ CHN (HNN) 73 Qg28
Wuzhi Shan ☐ CHN 75 Qe36
Wuzhong ☐ CHN (NHZ) 72 Qd27
Wuzhou ☐ CHN (GZG) 74 Qf34
Wyalkatchem ☐ AUS (WA)
Wyandemere Plain ☐ EAK 145
  Mk45
Wyandotte Cave ☐ USA 175 Fg26
Wyandra ☐ AUS (QLD) 109 Sc59
Wycheproof ☐ AUS (VIC)
  111 Sb64
Wydgee ☐ AUS (WA) 104 Qj60
Wygoda ☐ PL 41 Lu40
Wyk ☐ D 32 Lk36
Wylatowo ☐ PL 40 Ls38
Wyllie's Port ☐ ZA 142 Ne57
Wyloo ☐ AUS (WA) 102 Qj57
Wymondham ☐ GB 21 Lb38
Wynne ☐ USA (AR) 175 Fe28
Wynyard ☐ AUS (TAS) 111 Sc66
Wynyard ☐ CDN (SK) 169 Eh20
Wyoming ☐ USA (MI) 173 Fh24
Wyoming ☐ USA 171 Ef24
Wyoming Range ☐ USA 169
  Ed24
Wyperfeld N.P. ☐ ☐ AUS
  110 Sa63
Wyralinu Hill ☐ AUS 105 Rb62
Wyrzysk ☐ PL 40 Ls37
Wyseby ☐ AUS (QLD) 109 Se58
Wysoka ☐ PL 40 Lg38
Wysokie ☐ PL 41 Mb39
Wysokie Mazowieckie ☐ PL
  41 Mc38
Wyszków ☐ PL 41 Mb38
Wythenville ☐ USA (VA) 178 Fk27
Wyżyna Lubelska ☐ PL 41 Mc39

X

Xaafuun ☐ SP 143 Nf40
Xàbia ☐ E 29 La52
Xaçmaz ☐ AZ 57 Ne25
Xagdomba ☐ CHN (SCH)
  72 Qa28
Xaggxaka ☐ CHN (TIB) 69 Pg30
Xaidulla ☐ CHN (XUZ) 68 Oj27
Xainza ☐ CHN (TIB) 69 Pf30
Xaitongmoin ☐ CHN (TIB)
  68 Pe31
Xai-Xai ☐ MOC 155 Mg58
Xakriabá, T.I. ☐ BR 203 Hh53
Xalapa - Jalapa ☐ MEX (VC)
  182 Fb36
Xalin ☐ SP 143 Ne41
Xa Lon Pagoda ☐ VN 89 Qc41
Xalqobozot ☐ UZ 62 Nk24
Xam Neua ☐ LAO 87 Qc35
Xambioá ☐ BR (TO) 200 Hf49
Xamindele ☐ ANG 148 Lg49
Xam Nua ☐ LAO 87 Qc35
Xam Tay ☐ LAO 87 Qc35
Xanadu Beach ☐ BS 179 Ga32
Xandel ☐ ANG 148 Lj50
Xangongo ☐ ANG 150 Lh54
Xankändi ☐ AZ 57 Nd25
Xan Saray ☐ AZ 57 Nd25
Xanten ☐ D 32 Lg39
Xanthi ☐ GR 45 Me49
Xanthos ☐ TR 56 Mh52
Xanxerê ☐ BR (SC) 204 Hd59
Xapetuba ☐ BR (MG) 202 Hf55
Xapuri ☐ BR (AC) 198 Gf51
Xarardheere ☐ SP 143 Ne43
Xar Hure ☐ CHN (NMZ) 71 Qa24
Xarlag ☐ CHN (NMZ) 72 Qa26
Xassengue ☐ ANG 149 Lk51
Xàtiva ☐ E 29 Ku52
Xavantes ☐ UZ 62 Qa25
Xayar ☐ CHN (XUZ) 66 Pb25
Xcalak ☐ MEX (QTR)
  183 Fg36
Xcalak, Parque Nacional
  Arrecifes de ☐ MEX (QTR)
  183 Fg36
X-Can ☐ MEX (YT) 183 Fg35
Xé Bang Nouan N.B.C.A. ☐ LAO
  89 Qc38
Xebert ☐ CHN (NMZ) 71 Rb23
Xel-Ha ☐ MEX (QTR) 183 Fg35
Xenia ☐ USA (OH) 175 Fj26
Xe Pian N.B.C.A. ☐ LAO 89
  Qc38
Xerente, T.I. ☐ BR 200 Hf50
Xert ☐ E 29 La50
Xerta ☐ E 29 La50
Xertigny ☐ F 25 Lg42
Xe Sap N.B.C.A. ☐ LAO 89 Qd37
Xhami Ethem-Bey ☐ AL 44 Lu49
Xhorodomo ☐ RB 151 Mc56
Xhumaga ☐ RB 151 Mc56
Xhumbo ☐ RB 151 Mc56
Xiachuan Dao ☐ CHN 75 Qg34
Xiaguan ☐ CHN (GZG) 74 Qe34
Xiaguan ☐ CHN (HNN) 72 Qf29
Xiahe ☐ CHN (GSU) 72 Qb28
Xiajin ☐ CHN (FJN) 75 Qk33
Xi'an ☐ CHN (SAA) 72 Qe28
Xianfeng ☐ CHN (HUB) 74 Qe31
Xi'anfeng ☐ CHN 74 Qe31
Xiang ☐ CHN (AHU) 78 Qj30
Xianing ☐ CHN (HUN) 74 Qf32
Xianju ☐ CHN (ZJG) 75 Qk32
Xiangcheng ☐ CHN (HNN)
  73 Qg29
Xiangcheng ☐ CHN (SCH)
  69 Pk31
Xiangfan ☐ CHN (HUB) 74 Qf30
Xianggang Qi ☐ CHN (NMZ)
  73 Qg29
Xianghuang Qi ☐ CHN (NMZ)
Xiangji Temple ☐ CHN 72 Qe28
Xiangning ☐ CHN (SAX) 72 Qf27
Xiangride ☐ CHN (QHI) 69 Pj28
Xiangshan ☐ CHN (ZJG) 75 Ra31
Xiangsha Wan ☐ CHN 72 Qf25
Xiangshui ☐ CHN (JGS) 78 Qk28
Xiangtang Shiku ☐ CHN (HUN)
Xiangxi ☐ CHN (XUZ) 66 Ph24
Xianju ☐ CHN (ZJG) 75 Qk32
Xiangtan ☐ CHN (HUN) 74 Qf32
Xiangyuan ☐ CHN (SAX) 72 Qf27
Xiangzhou ☐ CHN (GZG)
  74 Qe34

Xiaochang ☐ CHN (HUB) 72 Qf29
  75 Qh30
Xiaodianzi ☐ AZ 57 Ne25
Xiaogan ☐ CHN (HUB) 75 Qg30
Xiaoguanxi ☐ CHN (YUN)
Xiaohe ☐ CHN (SAA) 72 Qe29
Xiaojiahe ☐ CHN (HLG) 76 Rg22
Xiaojin ☐ CHN (SCH) 74 Qb30
Xiaoling Tomb = Imperial
  Tombs of the Ming and Qing
  Dynasties ☐ ☐ CHN (JGS)
  78 Qk29
Xiaomei Guan ☐ CHN 75 Qh33
Xiaonanchuan ☐ CHN (QHI)
  69 Ph28
Xia San Xia ☐ CHN 74 Qe30
Xiaoshan ☐ CHN (ZJG) 78 Ra30
Xiaotian ☐ CHN (AHU) 78 Qj30
Xiaowutai Shan ☐ CHN 73 Qh25
Xiao Xian ☐ CHN (AHU) 78 Qj28
Xiaoxita ☐ CHN (HUB) 74 Qf30
Xiaoyangjie ☐ CHN (YUN)
  87 Qa33
Xicheng ☐ CHN (FJN) 75 Qk32
Xichong ☐ CHN (SCH) 74 Qc30
Xichou ☐ CHN (YUN) 87 Qa34
Xichuan ☐ CHN (GUT) 182 Ek35
Xichuan ☐ CHN (HNN) 73 Qg29
Xicotepec de Juarez ☐ MEX
  (PUE) 182 Fb35
Xidi ☐ CHN 78 Qk31
Xieng Ngeun ☐ LAO 87 Qb36
Xien Hon ☐ LAO 87 Qa36
Xiezhou Guandimiao ☐ CHN
Xifeng ☐ CHN (GSU) 72 Qd28
Xifeng ☐ CHN (GZH) 74 Qd32
Xifeng ☐ CHN (LNG) 76 Rc24
Xigangzi ☐ CHN (HLG) 76 Rg22
Xigaze ☐ CHN (TIB) 68 Pe31
Xiheying ☐ CHN (HBI) 73 Qh25
Xi Hu ☐ CHN 78 Ra30
Xihua ☐ CHN (HNN) 73 Qh29
Xiji ☐ CHN (NHZ) 72 Qc28
Xi Jiang ☐ CHN 74 Qf34
Xijiang ☐ CHN 74 Qf34
Xijin Reservoir ☐ CHN
Xikouzi ☐ CHN (NMZ) 71 Qa23
Xikrin do Rio Cateté, T.I. ☐ BR
  200 Hd49
Xilin ☐ CHN (GZG) 87 Qa33
Xi Ling Xia ☐ CHN 74 Qf30
Xiling = Works ☐ CHN (HLG)
Xilin Gol ☐ CHN (NMZ) 73 Qh24
Xilinhot ☐ CHN (NMZ) 73 Qh24
Xilingji ☐ CHN (SDG) 78 Ra28
Xilokastro ☐ GR 46 Mc52
Xilong-Shan Z.B. ☐ CHN 72
  Qb28
Xima ☐ GNB 136 Kc40
Xima ☐ MYA 86 Ph34
Ximeng ☐ CHN (YUN) 87 Pk34
Xin ☐ CHN (LNG)
  76 Rb25
Xingjiang Sk. ☐ CHN 75 Qk31
Xin'ansuo ☐ CHN (YUN) 87 Qa34
Xinavane ☐ MOC 155 Mg58
Xin Barag Youqi ☐ CHN (NMZ)
  71 Qj21
Xin Barag Zuoqi ☐ CHN (NMZ)
  71 Qk21
Xinbin ☐ CHN (LNG) 76 Rd24
Xincai ☐ CHN (HNN) 73 Qh29
Xinchang ☐ CHN (GZH) 74 Qd33
Xinchang ☐ CHN (ZJG) 75 Ra31
Xincheng ☐ CHN (GZG) 74 Qe34
Xincheng Weijin Mu ☐ CHN
  69 Pk26
Xindian ☐ CHN (HLG) 76 Rc23
Xindian ☐ CHN (SCH) 74 Qc30
Xindu ☐ CHN (SCH) 74 Qc30
Xinduqiao ☐ CHN (SCH) 69 Qa30
Xinfeng ☐ CHN (GDG) 75 Qh33
Xinfeng ☐ CHN (JGX) 75 Qj33
Xing'an ☐ CHN (GZG) 74 Qf33
Xing'an ☐ CHN (JGX) 75 Qj32
Xingcheng ☐ CHN (LNG)
  76 Ra25
Xinge ☐ ANG 149 Lk50
Xingguo ☐ CHN (JGX) 75 Qh33
Xinghai ☐ CHN (NMZ) 73 Qg25
Xinghua ☐ CHN (JGS) 78 Qk29
Xingning ☐ CHN (GDG) 75 Qh34
Xingping ☐ CHN (SAA) 72 Qe28
Xinguara ☐ BR (PA) 200 Hd49
Xingu, Río ☐ BR 200 Hd49
Xing Xian ☐ CHN (SAX) 72 Qf26
Xingxingxia ☐ CHN (XUZ)
  67 Ph25
Xingyang ☐ CHN (HNN) 73 Qg28
Xingyi ☐ CHN (GZH) 74 Qd33
Xinhua ☐ CHN (HUN) 74 Qf32
Xinhua ☐ CHN (XUZ) 66 Pb25
Xinhuang ☐ CHN (HUN) 74 Qe32
Xining ☐ CHN (QHI) 72 Qa27
Xinjiang ☐ CHN (SAX) 72 Qf27
Xinji ☐ CHN (HBI) 73 Qh27
Xinjie ☐ CHN (YUN) 87 Qa34
Xinjin ☐ CHN (SCH) 74 Qb30
Xinlong ☐ CHN (SCH) 69 Qa30
Xinmian ☐ CHN (SCH) 69 Qa30
Xinmin ☐ CHN (LNG) 76 Rb25
Xinning ☐ CHN (HUN) 74 Qf32
Xinqing ☐ CHN (HLG) 76 Re21
Xinshao ☐ CHN (HUN)
  74 Qf32
Xintai ☐ CHN (SDG) 78 Qk28
Xintian ☐ CHN (HUN) 74 Qg33
Xinxian ☐ CHN (SCH) 87 Qa32
Xinxiang ☐ CHN (HNN) 73 Qg28
Xinxing ☐ CHN (GDG) 74 Qg34
Xinyang ☐ CHN (HNN) 73 Qh29
Xinye ☐ CHN (HNN) 73 Qg29
Xinyi ☐ CHN (GDG) 74 Qf34
Xinyi ☐ CHN (JGS) 78 Qk28
Xinzhou ☐ CHN (SAX) 72 Qf26
Xinzo de Limia ☐ E 26 Kn49
Xiongyuecheng ☐ CHN (LNG)
  76 Rb25
Xiping ☐ CHN (HNN) 73 Qg29
Xiping ☐ CHN (SCH) 87 Qa32
Xiqu ☐ CHN (SCH) 87 Qa32

Xique-Xique ☐ BR (BA) 201 Hj51
Xirdalan ☐ AZ 57 Ne25
Xishui ☐ CHN (GZH) 74 Qd32
Xishui ☐ CHN (HUB) 75 Qh30
Xitole ☐ GNB 136 Kc40
Xi Ujimqin ☐ CHN (NMZ)
  71 Qj23
Xiushui ☐ CHN (JGX) 75 Qh31
Xiuwen ☐ CHN (GZH) 74 Qd32
Xiuwu ☐ CHN (HNN) 73 Qg28
Xiuyan ☐ CHN (LNG) 76 Rb25
Xiuying ☐ CHN (HAN) 75 Qf36
Xiwu ☐ CHN (QHI) 69 Pj29
Xixabangma Feng ☐ CHN
  68 Pc31
Xixia ☐ CHN (HNN) 73 Qg29
Xi Xian ☐ CHN (SAX) 72 Qf27
Xiadian ☐ CHN (AHU) 78 Qj30
Xixia Wangling ☐ CHN 72 Qd26
Xixona ☐ E 29 Ku52
Xiyang ☐ CHN (SAX) 72 Qf27
Xizang Zizhiqu ☐ CHN 53 Pa07
Xmaben ☐ MEX (CPH) 183 Ff37
Xocavand ☐ AZ 57 Nd26
Xochiapa ☐ MEX (VC) 183 Fc37
Xochicalco ☐ MEX (MEX) 182 Fa36
Xochimilco ☐ MEX (MEX)
  182 Fa36
Xochob ☐ MEX 183 Ff36
Xo'jayli ☐ UZ 62 Nh24
Xovos ☐ UZ 63 Oe25
Xpujil ☐ MEX 183 Ff36
Xuan'en ☐ CHN (HUB) 74 Qe31
Xuanhan ☐ CHN (SCH) 74 Qd30
Xuanwei ☐ CHN (YUN) 87 Qb33
Xuchang ☐ CHN (HNN) 73 Qg28
Xucheng ☐ CHN (GDG) 74 Qf35
Xudat ☐ AZ 57 Ne25
Xuddur ☐ SP 143 Nd41
Xuebao Ding ☐ CHN 72 Qb29
Xuefeng Shan ☐ CHN 74 Qf32
Xuejiadao ☐ CHN (SDG) 78 Ra28
Xuemendena ☐ CHN 87 Pk34
Xuemotin ☐ CHN (UTI) 81 Qk30
Xunqi ☐ CHN (GCA) 183 Ff37
Xunhua ☐ CHN (QHI) 72 Qa27
Xunhua ☐ CHN 69 Pj29
Xunke ☐ CHN (HLG) 76 Re21
Xunqian ☐ CHN (YUN) 87 Qa32
Xunwu ☐ CHN (JGX) 75 Qj33
Xuwen ☐ CHN (GDG) 74 Qf35
Xuyi ☐ CHN (JGS) 78 Qk29
Xuyong ☐ CHN (SCH) 74 Qc31
Xylóskalo ☐ GR 45 Md55

Y

Yaak ☐ USA (MT) 168 Ec21
Yaamba ☐ AUS (QLD) 109 Sf57
Ya'an ☐ CHN (SCH) 74 Qb31
Yaaq Braaway ☐ SP 145 Nb45
Yaba ☐ RI 97 Rd46
Yaba-Hita-Hikosan N.P. ☐ J
  79 Rf29
Yabanabat ☐ CAM 138 Le43
Yabayo ☐ CI 137 Kg43
Yabebyry ☐ PY 204 Hb59
Yabello ☐ ETH 144 Mk43
Yabia ☐ RDC 140 Mb44
Yablonovyy Range ☐ RUS
  55 Qc08
Yabrai Yanchang ☐ CHN 72 Qc26
Yabrin ☐ KSA 61 Nf34
Yabucoa ☐ USA (PR) 187 Gh36
Yabuli ☐ CHN (HLG) 76 Re23
Yabyonos ☐ CI 137 Kg42
Yacamba, P.N. ☐ YV 193 Gf41
Yacaré Norte ☐ PY 207 Ha57
Yacata ☐ FJI 119 Ua54
Yachats ☐ USA (OR) 168 Dh23
Yacheng ☐ CHN (HAN) 75 Qe36
Yacimiento Rio Turbio ☐ RA
  (SC) 210 Gd71
Yacuiba ☐ BOL 207 Gj56
Yadagiri Gutta ☐ IND 83 Ok37
Yadavindra Gardens ☐ IND
  81 Oj30
Yadgir ☐ IND (KTK) 82 Oj37
Yadikuo ☐ CI 137 Kh42
Yadkinville ☐ USA (NC) 178 Fk27
Yadmah ☐ KSA 60 Nc36
Yafran ☐ LAR 127 Lg29
Yagaba ☐ GH 137 Kk40
Yagasa Cluster ☐ FJI 119 Ua55
Yago ☐ CAM 139 Lh40
Yagradagzê Shan ☐ CHN
  69 Ph28
Yaguachi Nuevo ☐ EC 196 Ga46
Yaguajay ☐ C 179 Ga34
Yaguarón ☐ PY 204 Hb58
Yaguas ☐ CO 196 Gd47
Yaha ☐ THA 89 Qa42
Yahekou ☐ CHN (HNN) 73 Qg29
Yahualica de González Gallo ☐
  MEX (JLC) 182 Ej35
Yahuma ☐ RDC 140 Mb45
Yahyali ☐ TR 56 Mh26
Yaibai ☐ CHN (NMZ) 72 Qb26
Yajiang ☐ CHN (SCH) 69 Qa30
Yaka ☐ RCA 140 Lk43
Yakabindie ☐ AUS (WA) 104 Ra59
Yaka N.P. ☐ CI 137 Kh42
Yakeshi ☐ CHN (NMZ) 71 Ra22
Yakima ☐ USA (WA) 168 Dk22
Yakima Ind. Res. ☐ USA 168
  Dk22
Yakkabog ☐ UZ 63 Od26
Yakmach ☐ PK 65 Ob31
Yako ☐ BF 137 Kk39
Yakoma ☐ RDC 140 Mb44
Yakoto ☐ J 77 Sa26
Yaku-jima ☐ J 79 Rf30
Yakumo ☐ J 77 Sa26
Yakushima N.P. ☐ J 79 Rf30
Yakutat ☐ USA (AK) 166 Da16
Yala ☐ GH 137 Kk40
Yala ☐ THA 89 Qa42
Yalagüina ☐ NIC 184 Fh39
Yalata ☐ AUS (SA) 105 Rf61
Yalbaç ☐ TR 56 Mf26
Yalbalgo ☐ AUS (WA) 104 Qg58

Yeha ☐ ETH 142 Mk38
Yei ☐ SUD 144 Mf43
Yeji ☐ GH 137 Kk41
Yekaterinburg ☐ RUS 54 Oa07
Yekepa ☐ LB 136 Ke42
Yekö ☐ TCH 133 Lj37
Ye Kyun ☐ MYA 86 Pg36
Ye Shaba ☐ IR 57 Nd27
Yela Island ☐ PNG 117 Sh51
Yelahanka ☐ IND (KTK) 84 Oj39
Yelandur ☐ IND (APH) 83 Pa37
Yelantsi ☐ ☐ RCA 140 Lk43
Yelarbon ☐ AUS (QLD) 109 Sf60
Yelbarsli ☐ TM 62 Oa27
Yelcho ☐ ANT (RCH) 6 Gd31
Yelkenia ☐ TR 45 Mj49
Yell ☐ GB 20 Kt30
Yeldurthi ☐ IND (APH) 83 Pa37
Yélimané ☐ RMM 130 Ke38
Yellandu ☐ IND (APH) 83 Pa37
Yellapur ☐ IND (KTK) 82 Oh38
Yelladed ☐ IND (APH) 83 Ok36
  Qk61
Yellow Gras ☐ CDN (SK)
  169 Ej21
Yellowhead Pass ☐ CDN
  168 Ea19
Yellowknife ☐ CDN 167 Ec14
Yellandu ☐ IND (KTK) 84 Oj39
Yaralıgöz Dağı ☐ TR 56 Mh25
Yarrawin ☐ AUS (NSW) 109 Sd61
Yarbasan ☐ TR 47 Mj52
Yelwa ☐ WAN 138 Lc40
Yelwa ☐ WAN 138 Le41
Yelwa ☐ RDC 148 Lg48
Yelwa ☐ WAN 138 Le41
Yema ☐ RDC 148 Lg48
Yena Nanshan ☐ CHN 69 Pj26
Yema Shan ☐ CHN 69 Ph26
Yemassee ☐ USA (SC) 178 Fk29
Yembo ☐ ETH 142 Mh41
Yemen ☐ YE 53 Na08
Yemişli ☐ TR 56 Mj27
Yen Bai ☐ VN 87 Qc35
Yenchang ☐ CHN (TIB) 68 Pe30
Yen Chau ☐ VN 87 Qc35
Yendé Millimou ☐ RG 136 Ke41
Yendéré ☐ BF 137 Kh40
Yendi ☐ GH 137 Kk41
Yénéganou ☐ RCB 148 Lg47
Yengi Kand ☐ IR 57 Nc27
Yengişehir ☐ TR 56 Mf25
Yengo N.P. ☐ AUS 111 Sf62
Yenibaşak ☐ TR 57 Na26
Yenice ☐ TR 47 Mj51
Yeniceoba ☐ TR 56 Mj26
Yenicubuk ☐ TR 56 Mj26
Yeniköy ☐ TR 47 Mj51
Yeniköy ☐ TR 47 Mj53
Yenipazar ☐ TR 47 Mj53
Yenişehir ☐ TR 47 Mk52
Yeno ☐ G 148 Le46
Yeno ☐ G 148 Lf46
Yeola ☐ IND (MHT) 82 Oh35
Yeo Lake ☐ AUS 105 Rc59
Yeo Lake Nature Reserve ☐ AUS
  105 Rd60
Yeoval ☐ AUS (NSW) 111 Se62
Yeovil ☐ GB 21 Ks40
Yepachic ☐ MEX (CHH) 180 Ef31
Yepes ☐ E 27 Kr51
Yeppoon ☐ AUS (QLD) 109 Sf57
Yeraltı şehri (Derinkuyu) ☐ TR
  56 Mh26
Yerbas Loca ☐ RCH 208 Ge62
Yercaud ☐ IND (TNU) 84 Ok40
Yeremarou ☐ DY 138 Lc40
Yeretel Nature Reserve ☐ AUS
  111 Sc62
Yerevan ☐ ARM 57 Nc25
Yergara ☐ IND (KTK) 82 Oj37
Yeriho ☐ IL 58 Mh30
Yerilla ☐ AUS (WA) 104 Ra60
Yeriköprü ☐ TR 56 Mf26
Yermakovka ☐ RUS 54 Od07
Yermala ☐ IND (MHT) 82 Oj36
Yermo ☐ USA (CA) 170 Eb28
Yerrupalli ☐ IND (APH) 83 Ok36
Yérupajá, Cerro la ☐ PE 197 Gb51
Yerville ☐ F 22 La41
Yesagyo ☐ MYA 86 Ph35
Yesan ☐ ROK 78 Rd27
Yeshin ☐ MYA 86 Ph34
Yeşil Camii (İznik) ☐ TR
  45 Mj50
Yeşil Camii (Bursa) ☐ TR
  45 Mj50
Yeşilhisar ☐ TR 56 Mh26
Yeşilırmak ☐ TR 56 Mh25
Yeşilköy ☐ TR 45 Mj49
Yeste ☐ E 27 Ks52
Yet ☐ ETH 145 Nd43
Yetla de Juárez ☐ MEX (OAX)
  182 Fb37
Yetman ☐ AUS 111 Sf60
Ye-U ☐ MYA 86 Ph34
Yevlax ☐ AZ 57 Nd25
Ye Xian ☐ CHN (HNN) 73 Qg29
Yexiangqu ☐ CHN 87 Qa34
Yeyungou ☐ CHN (XUZ) 66 Pc25
Yhú ☐ PY 204 Hc58
Yi ☐ ROU 204 Hc62
Yian ☐ CHN (HLG) 76 Rc22
Yianade ☐ CHN (XUZ) 66 Ok26
Yibin ☐ CHN (SCH) 74 Qc31
Yichang ☐ CHN (HUB) 74 Qf30
Yicheng ☐ CHN (HUB) 74 Qf30
Yicheng ☐ CHN (SAX) 72 Qf27
Yichuan ☐ CHN (HNN) 73 Qg28
Yichun ☐ CHN (HLG) 76 Re22
Yichun ☐ CHN (JGX) 75 Qh32
Yifag ☐ ETH 142 Mk40
Yifeng ☐ CHN (JGX) 75 Qh31
Yiğityolu ☐ TR 56 Mf26
Yijun ☐ CHN (SAA) 72 Qe28
Yilan ☐ CHN (HLG) 76 Re22
Yildirim Camii ☐ TR 47 Mh51
Yıldızeli ☐ TR 56 Mh26
Yilehuli Shan ☐ CHN 71 Rb21
Yiliang ☐ CHN (YUN) 87 Qb33
Yiliang ☐ CHN (YUN) 87 Qb33
Yilong ☐ CHN (SCH) 74 Qd30
Yimen ☐ CHN (YUN) 87 Qa33
Yimin ☐ CHN (NMZ) 71 Qk21
Yinan ☐ CHN (SDG) 78 Qk28
Yinchuan ☐ CHN (NHZ) 72 Qd26
Yinan ☐ AUS (WA) 105 Rb61
Yingcheng ☐ CHN (HUB) 75 Qg30
Yingchengzi Tomb ☐ CHN
  73 Ra26
Yingde ☐ CHN (GDG) 75 Qg33

Photo Index, Credits/Contributers

Abbreviations:
G = Getty
Bav = Bavaria
Mau = Mauritius
P = Premium
Hub = Huber
Pic = Pictor
Lo = Look

Cover: globe image © NASA
p. I: Spacecapes; PhotoDisc Vol. 34
p. II–III: World Landmarks and Travel, PhotoDisc Vol. 60
p. IV: both P
p. V – l.: P, r.: Hub/Damm
p. VI – l.: Monheim, r.: P
p. VII – l.: P, r.: ifa/Jacobs
p. VIII – l.: G/Tomlinson, r.: G/Waite
p. IX – l.: P/Petsch, r.: G/Layda
p. X – l.: DasFotoarchiv, r.: Hub/Damm
p. XI: both P
p. XII – l.: P/p.Bunka, r.: ifa
p. XIII – l.: P/NGS, r.: P/Schwabel
p. XIV – t.: P, big pict.: P/Raymer/NGS
p. 1 – b.: P/Marka
p. 12 – t.: P, big pict.: ifa/PictureFinders
p. 13 – b.: M.Schneiders
p. 50 – t.: P, big pict.: Mau/Krinninger
p. 51 – b.: G/Ehlers
p. 98 – t.: ifa/Hunter, big pict.: P
p. 99 – b.: Alamy/R.Harding
p. 120 – t.: P, big pict.: P/Marka
p. 121 – b.: Cristofori
p. 158 – t.: P/Nawrocki, big pict.: P
p. 159 – b.: Essick/Aurora
p. 188 – t.: P, big pict.: G
p. 189 – b.: G/G. Pile
p. 211: Spacecapes; PhotoDisc Vol. 34, f.l.t.r.: G, G/R. Passmore, G/A. Wolfe
p. 216 – l.t.: G/W. Eastep, l.b.: G/N. Turner
p. 217 – r.t.: G/Del Vecchio, 1: G/R. Stahl,
2: G/D. Armand, 3: G/R. Everts, 4: G/J. Willis
p. 218 – l.t.: G/R. v. d. Hils, l.b.: G/J. Warden
p. 219 – r.t.: G, 1: G/M. Rogers, 2: G/D. Armand, 3: G/R. Klevansky,
4: G/Y. Layama
p. 220 – l.t.: G/N. DeVore, l.b.: G/H. Schmitz
p. 221 – r.t.: G/A. Cassidy, 1: G/p. Chelsey, 2: P/R. Eastwood, 3: Bav
p. 222 – l.t.: G/R. v. d. Hils, l.b.: G/Viennaslide-Jahn
p. 223 – r.t.: G/p. Chelsey, 1: G/C. Harvey, 2:G/E. Lansner, 3: G/G. Pile,
4: G/p. Chelsey
p. 224 – l.t.: G/A. Diesendruck, l.b.: G/A. Diesendruck
p. 225 – r.t.: G/p. Chelsey, 1: G/B. De Hogues, 2: G/J. Lamb, 3: G/B. Rieger,
4: G/R. Evans
p. 226 – l.t.: Pic, l.b.:G/J. Cornish
p. 227 – r.t.: G/D. Hiser, 1: BAV, 2: G/J. Horner, 3: G/T. Craddock
p. 228 – l.t.: G/C. Simpson, l.b.: Mau/Coll
p. 229 – r.t.: G/C. Burki, 1: G/J.Willis, 2: G/R. Ziak, 4: G/D. Waugh, 3: G/K.Morris,
2: G/R. Ziak, 4: G/D. Waugh
p. 230 – r.t.: G/p. Chelsey, l.b.: G/p. G.
p. 231 – r.t.: G/p. Harris, 1: G/p. Harris, 2: G/ A. Latham, 3: G/J. Horner,
4: G/M. Busselle
p. 232 – l.t.: A. Cassidy, l.b.: G/G. Grigoriou
p. 233 – r.t.: G/D. Hiser, 1: G/G. Grigoriou, 2: G/R. Frerck, 3: G/J. Cornish,
4: J. Strachan
p. 234 – l.t.: G/J. M. Truchet, l.b.: G/B. de Hogues
p. 235 – r.t.: G/H Kavanch, 1: PSP/Segal, 2: G/D. Hiser, 3: G/D. Nausbaum,
4: G/p. Weinberg
p. 236 – l.t.: G/A. Cassidy, l.b.: G/H. Kavanagh
p. 237 – r.t.: Pic, 1: G/D. Sutherland, 2: G/ p. Poulides, 3: Mau/T. Müller,
4: G/C. Haigh
p. 238 – l.t.: G/p. Chelsey, l.b.: G/H. Kavanagh
p. 239 – r.t.: G/A. Wolfe, 1: BAV/K. Yamashita, 2: G/N. Giambi, 3: G/G. Jecan, 4:
G/W. Krecichwost
p. 240 – l.t.: G/G. Chan, l.b.: G/M. Rees
p. 241 – r.t.: G/M. Busselle, 1: G/G. Allison, 2: Mau/Torino, 3: Pic., 4: G/A. Wolfe
p. 242 – l.t.: Mau/b. Kerth, l.b.: G/J. Strachan
p. 243 – r.t.: Mau/R. Mayer, 1: G/H. Molenkanp, 2: G/C. Coleman,
3: G/N. DeVore, 4: Mau
p. 244 – l.t.: G/H. Sitton, l.b.: G/H. Sitton
p. 245 – r.t.: Mau, 1: G/G. Hellier, 2: p. Seaward, 3: G/p. Tweedie, 4: G
p. 246 – l.t.: G/J. Running, l.b.: G/R. Frerck
p. 247 – r.t.: G/R. Giles, 1: Bav, 2: G/J. Beatty, 3: G/p. Rothfeld, 4: G/H. Kurihara
p. 248 – l.t.: G/p. Harris, l.b.: G
p. 249 – r.t.: G/J. Strachan, 1: G/p. Chelsey, 2: G/H. Kavanagh, 4: G/p. Harris
p. 250 – l.t.: G/K. Graham, l.b.: G/M. Mehlig
p. 251 – r.t.: G/T. Wood, 1: G, 2: P/Z. Williams, 3: G/J. Chard, 4: G/L. Ulrich
p. 252 – l.t.: G/N. DeVore, l.b.: G
p. 253 – r.t.: Pic, 1: G/p. Grandadam, 2: G, 3: G/J. Strachan, 4: Bav
p. 254 – l.t.: G/D. Levy, l.b.: G/A. Cassidy
p. 255 – r.t.: G/D. Tarckler, 1: P, 2: G/p. Huber, 3: G/p. Chelsey, 4: G/p. Tansey
p. 256 – l.t.: G/B. Krist, l.b.: Pic
p. 257 – r.t.: p. Harris, 1: G/D. Carrasco, 2: P/R. Klein, 3.: Bav/Picture Finders
p. 258 – l.t.: G/A. Booher, l.b.: G/R. Everts
p. 259 – r.t.: G/D. Hiser, 1: G/p. Egan, 2: Bav/Kanus, 3: G/A. Puzey, 4: G/A. Drake
p. 260 – l.t.: Mau/SDP, l.b.: G/p. Dietrich
p. 261 – r.t.: Pic, 1: G/p. Bauduin, 2: P/A. Mackillop, 3: G/B. Baunton
p. 262 – l.t.: G/A. Cassidy, l.b.: G/J. Strachan
p. 263 – r.t.: G/A. Booher, 1: Bav/Images, 2: G/J. Lamb, 4: G/C. Ehlers
p. 264 – l.t.: G/H. Schmitz, l.b.: G
p. 265 – r.t.: Pic, 1: P/B. Hedberg, 2: G/A. Mackillop, 3: G/R. Evans, 4: G/N.
Parfitt
p. 266 – l.t.: G/L. Resnick, l.b. G/L.Dutton
p. 267 – r.t.: G/D. Armand, 1: G/p. Seaward, 2: p. Seaward, 3: G/J.Jangoux,
4: G/R. Frerck
p. 268 – l.t.: G/A. Milliken, l.b.: G/J. Cornish
p. 269 – r.t.: G/Nick, 1: P/M. Segal, 2: P/T. Jelen, 3: G/D. Reese
p. 270 – l.t.: G/t. Benn, l.b.: G/p. Stone
p. 271 – r.t.: G/G. Pile, 1: G/t. Franken, 2: D. Paterson, 3: G/J. Strachan,
4: Hub/Schmid
p. 272 – r.t.: G/p. Mayman, 1: PSP/p. Petsch, 2: P/Mackillop
p. 273 – top: all dpa, b.: Mau/O'Brien
p. 274 – top: all dpa, b.l.: G/Rudolf, b.r.: both dpa

© 2006 Verlag Wolfgang Kunth GmbH & Co. KG, Munich
© GeoGraphic Publishers GmbH & Co. KG, Munich
Innere Wiener Straße 13
81667 Munich
Tel.: (49) 89 45 80 20-0
Fax: (49) 89 45 80 20-21
info@geographicmedia.de
www.geographicmedia.de

© Cartography: GeoGraphic Publishers GmbH & Co. KG, Munich
Map relief: 1 : 2,25 Mio./1 : 4,5 Mio./1 : 15 Mio./1 : 36 Mio./1 : 44 Mio./1 : 50 Mio./ 1 : 80 Mio. MHM ® Copyright © Digital Wisdom, Inc.

© English translation: Verlag Wolfgang Kunth GmbH & Co. KG, Munich

English language distribution:
GeoCenter International Ltd
Meridian House, Churchill Way West
Basingstoke Hampshire, RG21 6YR
United Kingdom
Tel.: (44) 1256 817 987
Fax: (44) 1256 817 988
sales@geocenter.co.uk
www.insightguides.com

Editing: Calina Kunth, Wolfgang Kunth, Norbert Pautner
Texts: Heike Barnitzke, Gesa Bock, Dirk Brietzke, Michael Kaiser, Wolfgang Kunth, Michael Elser, Ursula Klocker, Norbert Pautner
Picture research: Calina Kunth, Wolfgang Kunth, Micaëla Verfürth

Coordination and editing English version: Katja Baldewein, Demetri Lowe
Proofreading English version: Alison Moffat-McLynn, Penny Phenix

Design, Layout: Um|bruch, München
Graphic: Alexandra Matheis, Dorothea Happ, Christopher Kunth, Monika Preißl, Verena Ribbentrop
Reproduction: Fotolito Varesco, Auer (Italy)

Printed in the Slovak Republic

346